THE
GUINNESS
BOOK
OF

ANSWERS

THE
GUINNESS
BOOK
OF

ANSWERS

THE
COMPLETE
REFERENCE
HANDBOOK

GUINNESS BOOKS

Copyright © 1989 Guinness Publishing Ltd

First published in 1989. Reprinted 1989.

Editors: Beatrice Frei and Honor Head
Editorial Assistant: Barbara Edwards
Picture Editor: Alex Goldberg
Design and Layout: Christie Archer
Artwork: AdVantage Studios
                     Rob and Rhoda Burns
                     Pat Gibbon
                     Peter Harper

Published in Great Britain by Guinness Publishing Ltd,
33 London Road, Enfield, Middlesex.

'Guinness' is a registered trademark of Guinness
Superlatives Ltd

Phototypeset by Ace Filmsetting Ltd, Frome, Somerset
Printed and bound in Great Britain by BPCC Hazell Books
Ltd, Aylesbury, Bucks.

British Library Cataloguing in Publication Data

The book of answers—7th ed.
  1. Miscellaneous facts. Collections
  032'.02

ISBN 0-85112-334-1

ACKNOWLEDGEMENTS

Contributors

Brian Adams
Dr Robin Adams
John Arblaster
Clive Carpenter
The Rev Colin Davey
The Rev Clinton Bennett
Tim Furniss
Michael Heatley
Howard Loxton
Anne Marshall
Peter Matthews
Norris McWhirter
Jane McWhirter
Barbara Peterson
Dr John Pimlott
Patrick Robertson
Dr J. M. Sommerville, MRCP,
  MRCGP

Grateful thanks for additional help is
made to:

British Acupuncture Association
William R. Broom, National Council
  of Psychotherapists & Hypnotherapy
  Register
Esperanto Asocio de Britujo
Esperanto Translating Service
Ingrid Holford
Kodak Limited
M. R. Lee, Phobias Confidential
London Zoo
A. Patch, Forest Research Station,
  Wrecclesham
Moira Stowe
The Fresh Fruit & Vegetable
  Information Bureau
The Society of Metaphysicians

CONTENTS

Music & Dance 191-201

The Cinema 202-207

The Theatre 208-217

Sport 218-239

Metrology 240-245

Mathematics 246-262

Computers 263-269

Inventions 270-275

Chemistry 276-288

Physics 289-302

I keep six honest serving men
(They taught me all I knew);
Their names are What & Why & When
And How & Where & Who.

Just So Stories (1902)
'The Elephant's Child'
Rudyard Kipling

THE EARTH

Introduction

Dimensions

The equatorial diameter of the Earth is 12 756·274 km (*7 926·381 miles*) and the polar diameter is 12 713·505 km (*7 899·806 miles*) so the Earth is not a true sphere but an ellipsoid with an equatorial circumference of 40 075·02 km (*24 901·46 miles*), a polar of meridianal circumference of 40 007·86 km (*24 859·73 miles*), and a volume of 1 083 207 000 000 km³ (*259 875 300 000 cu. miles*). The Earth has a pear-shaped asymmetry with the north polar radius being 45 m (*148 ft*) longer than the south polar radius and there is also a slight ellipticity of the equator since its long axis (about longitude 37°W) is 159 m (*522 ft*) greater than the short axis. The greatest departures from the reference ellipsoid are a protuberance of 73 m (*240 ft*) in the area of Papua New Guinea and a depression of 105 m (*344 ft*) south of Sri Lanka in the Indian Ocean.

Mass and density

The Earth, including its atmosphere, has a mass of 5·974 × 10²¹ tonnes (*5 879 000 000 000 000 000 000 tons*) and the average density is 5·515 times that of water. The atmosphere weighs 5·24 × 10¹⁵ tonnes (*5 160 000 000 000 000 tons*) or 0·000088 per cent of the total mass. The Earth picks up cosmic dust but estimates vary widely with 30 000 tonnes/tons a year being the upper limit.

Structure

Modern theory suggests that the Earth has an outer shell or lithosphere 80 km (*50 miles*) thick, then an outer and inner rock layer or mantle extending 2809 km (*1745 miles*) deep, beneath which there is an iron-rich core consisting of a liquid outer core of radius 3482 km (*2164 miles*) and a solid inner core of radius 1222 km (*759 miles*). At the centre the core density is estimated to be 13·09 g/cm³, the temperature 4500°C, and the pressure 364 GPa 23 600 tonsf/in². If the iron-rich theory is correct then iron must be the most abundant element in the Earth.

Land and sea surfaces

The surface area of the Earth is 510 065 600 km² (*196 937 400 sq. miles*) of which 41·25 per cent or 210 400 000 km² (*81 200 000 sq. miles*) is covered by continental masses. However, only about two-thirds of the continental area or 29·08 per cent of the total Earth surface (148 330 000 km² (*57 270 000 sq. miles*)) is land above water with the remaining 70·92 per cent or 361 740 000 km² (*139 670 000 sq. miles*) being covered by sea or hydrosphere. The mean depth of the hydrosphere is 3554 m (*11 660 ft*) so the volume of the oceans is about 1 285 600 000 km³ (*308 400 000 cu. miles*) or 0·022 per cent by weight of the Earth, viz. 1·3 × 10¹⁸ tonnes/tons.

The oceans and seas

The strictest interpretations permit only three oceans – the Pacific, Atlantic and Indian. The so-called Seven Seas would require the three undisputed oceans to be divided by the equator into North and South and the addition of the Arctic Sea. The term Antarctic Ocean is not recognized by the International Hydrographic Bureau.

The continents

There is ever-increasing evidence that the Earth's land surface once comprised a single primaeval land mass, now called Pangaea, and that this split during the Upper Cretaceous period (65 000 000 to 100 000 000 years ago) into two super-continents, called Laurasia in the north and Gondwanaland in the south. The Earth's land surface embraces seven continents, each with their attendant islands. Europe, Africa and Asia, though politically distinct, physically form one land mass known as Afro-Eurasia. Central America is often included in North America (Canada, the USA and Greenland). Europe includes all the USSR territory west of the Ural Mountains. Oceania embraces Australasia (Australia and New Zealand) and the non-Asian Pacific islands.

Glossary

abyssal Pertaining to the depths of the oceans.
affluent A tributary stream flowing into a larger stream or river.
aiguille sharp point or pinnacle or rock.
alluvial fan Fan-shaped area of sediment deposited as a river ents a plain and slows down.
alluvium Sand, mud, silt, etc., carried by a river and deposited as the river slows down.
altitude Height above sea level.
archipelago A group of islands.
arête A sharp ridge between two *cirques*.
artesian well Well that taps water held in a permeable layer of rock, sandwiched between two impermeable layers of rock in a basin. The rim of the permeable section of the basin is higher than the level of the well, so the water contained in the permeable layer pushes the water up out of the well.
atoll A ring of coral islands or coral reefs.
avalanche A mass of snow and ice that slides down a mountainside because of its own weight.

bar Shingle and sand deposited in a line or ridge across a bay or mouth of a river.
barchan Crescent-shaped sand dune, the shape being due to the constant effect of the wind.
bayou Swampy creek leading off a river, found in flat land.
bergschrund Gap between the upper edge of a glacier and the rock wall in a *cirque*.
bight A large bay.
bill A small peninsula.
bluff A vertical cliff, standing out prominently from the surrounding countryside.
bog Area of wet spongy ground consisting of waterlogged and decaying moss and other plants.
bore A tidal wave running up a river estuary.

boulder clay Rocks and gravel dragged along by the base of a glacier and deposited when the glacier recedes.

bourne A stream that only flows intermittently.

bund A term used in the Indian subcontinent for an artificial embankment.

bush Scrubland not cleared for cultivation.

butte A flat-topped hill, often with steep sides.

cairn A man-made heap of stones.

caldera A crater flanked by steep cliffs. It is usually formed by the top of a volcano that has subsided.

canal A man-made waterway, either for transport or irrigation.

canyon A river-cut gorge, often of great depth, with steep sides.

cape A piece of land projecting into the sea.

cascade Small waterfall.

cataract Large waterfall.

cave Underground opening reached from the surface or from the sea.

cavern A cave.

chaparral Dry scrubland, particularly in the south-eastern US.

chimney A vertical crack in a rock face.

cirque A rounded basin in a mountainside, formed by the action of a glacier.

cliff Steep face of rock.

col A high valley across a mountain range or line of hills.

coombe A short valley into the side of a hill.

concordant coastline A submerged coastline consisting of drowned valleys and lines of islands, all running parallel with an inland range of mountains or hills.

confluence Point at which two rivers converge.

continent A single large landmass.

continental drift The movement of landmasses on the molten rock that makes up the Earth's interior.

continental shelf The offshore seabed, down to a depth of 200 m (*600 ft*).

contour Line joining all points at the same height.

coral The exoskeleton of a small marine animal. They live in colonies, and when each animal dies the calcium-rich exoskeleton remains. As generation succeeds generation, masses of coral build up into reefs, atolls, etc.

coral reef A line of coral rocks at or just below the surface of the sea.

cordillera Parallel lines of mountains.

corrasion Mechanical erosion of rocks by the action of other rocks, gravel, etc., in a river or by wind-borne sand.

corrosion Chemical erosion of rocks.

cove A small bay.

crater Hollow at the top of a volcanic cone, or the depression caused by the impact of a meteorite.

crevasse A vertical crack in a glacier or ice sheet.

cuesta A ridge or hill formed by sloping rock strata.

cwm A *cirque*.

dale An open valley.

deep A marine valley or trench, considerably deeper than the surrounding seabed.

delta Deposits of alluvium in a fan shape, formed where a river flows into the sea or a lake.

desert Area with very low rainfall in which little if any vegetation grows.

discordant coastline An irregular coastline in which the mountains, valleys and inlets are at right-angles to the coast.

drowned valley Valley that has been submerged by a rise in the sea level or by the land sinking.

drumlin Small hump-backed hill formed by the action of a glacier. Swarms of drumlins are exposed as ice-sheets recede.

dune A wind-formed accumulation of sand.

dust bowl Dry region that has been badly managed agriculturally, such that the topsoil has been removed by wind erosion.

dyke Vertical sheet of rock which cuts across the bedding or structural planes of the host rock.

earthquake Series of shock waves generated from a single point within the Earth's mantle or crust.

epicentre Point on the Earth's surface above the point at which the shock waves of an earthquake are generated.

equator Imaginary circle around the Earth's surface, midway between the poles.

equinox Time when the Sun appears vertically overhead at noon at the equator; about 21 March and 21 September.

erg Part of the Sahara Desert covered with sand.

erosion Removal or wearing away of the land surface by natural means.

estuary The mouth of a river, and the stretch immediately up-river of the mouth, that is tidal.

étang A shallow lake among coastal sand-dunes.

fall line The line showing where a number of rivers leave an upland area for a lowland area, in each case passing over a waterfall or series of waterfalls.

fathom Unit of depth at sea: 1·83 m (*6 ft*).

fell Bare hill.

fen Marshy land in which peat is formed.

fiord Glaciated steep-sided valley that runs into the sea and is subsequently flooded. They are typified by a great depth of water in the main body of the fiord, with a shallower bar across the mouth.

firth A narrow inlet in the sea coast in Scotland; either an estuary or a fiord.

flood plain Plain on either side of a river formed by alluvial deposits left when the river floods and then recedes again.

fold A vertical bend in the rock strata, formed by compression within the Earth's crust.

forest Large area of land, extensively covered with trees.

frost hollow Hollow into which cold air sinks from the surrounding slopes. The hollow is therefore more liable to suffer frost than the surrounding land.

garrigue Form of scrub found in dry limestone areas around the Mediterranean.

geyser A hot spring of such depth that steam periodically forms, erupting from the mouth of the spring in a fountain of steam and hot water.

glacier Mass of ice, formed due to great weight of snow, that slowly moves down a valley towards the sea.

glen Long narrow steep-sided valley in Scotland.

gorge A deep narrow rugged valley with near vertical walls.

grassland Large area where the rainfall is greater than that of a desert but not enough to support a forest.

great circle A circle on the Earth's surface whose centre is the Earth's centre.

gulf A large bay.

gully A narrow steep-sided channel formed by water erosion.

hammada Bare rocky desert found in the Sahara.
hanging valley Glaciated valley entering a main valley part-way up the valley side.
headland Isolated cliff projecting into the sea.
hot spring Spring whose water is heated by hot volcanic rocks.

iceberg Massive lump of ice which has broken off the end of a glacier or ice sheet and floats in the sea.
ice floe Floating sheet of ice that has detached from an ice shelf.
ice sheet Mass of ice and snow covering a land mass.
ice shelf Mass of ice and snow floating on the sea.
inlet Opening into the sea or lake coast.
inselberg An isolated hill in a relatively flat area.
irrigation Artificial supply of water to a crop-producing area.
island Mass of land surrounded by water. It may occur in a river, a lake, a sea or an ocean.
islet A small island.
isthmus A narrow neck of land connecting two land masses.

jebel A mountain range.
jungle A misnomer for tropical monsoon forest.

karst Type of limestone scenery produced by water erosion of limestone and dolomite rock. It is characterized by sinks, underground rivers and caves, and other erosion features.
kettle hole A hollow in the outwash plain of a glacier, formed where an ice block melts.
key (or cay) Small island or sandbank in the Caribbean.
knick point Point at which the slope of a river changes.
knoll Small rounded hill.
kyle A channel of water or strait in Scotland.

lagoon Expanse of water that has been separated from the sea by a narrow strip of land.
lake Expanse of water entirely surrounded by land.
landslide A mass of soil, mud and rock that slides down a mountainside or cliff-slope because of its own weight.
latitude A degree of latitude (°) is the angular distance of a point on the surface of the Earth, north or south of the equator, taken from the centre of the Earth. A line of latitude is the line joining all points with the same degree of latitude, i.e. it is a circle with the axis of the Earth between the two poles at its centre.
lava fountain Fountain of molten lava ejected from a volcano.
lava plateau Plateau formed from a flat sheet of volcanic rock.
levee River-bank formed during flooding of the river. As the river water spreads out, alluvium is deposited, the greatest quantity being along the line of the river-bank.
littoral That part of the seashore between high and low tide.
load Solid material carried by a river, ranging from boulders to fine silt.
loch An inlet of the sea, a fiord or a lake in Scotland.
longitude The angular distance between one of the Earth's meridians and the standard or Greenwich meridian.
longshore drift Movement of sand and shingle along the shore due to the action of the waves as they advance and retreat obliquely along the shore.
lough An inlet of the sea, a fiord or a lake in Ireland.
lunar day Time between successive crossings of a meridian by the Moon; about 24 hours 50 minutes.
lunar month Time between two successive new Moons, i.e. the time the Moon takes to travel around the Earth once; 29½ days.

maelstrom A large whirlpool.
magnetic pole Point at which the Earth's magnetic flux is strongest. The magnetic poles do not coincide with the true poles; furthermore they move slightly with time.
mangrove swamp A tropical coastal swamp typified by the extensive growth of mangroves, whose long tangled roots drop from the trunks and branches of the mangroves.
maquis Low scrub growing on rocky soil in the mediterranean area.
marsh Low-lying soft wet land.
massif A block of mountains which only breaks up into separate peaks towards the various summits.
meander A wide curve or loop in a river. These often link up in a series of meanders.
meridian Half a great circle on the Earth's surface, finishing at each pole and cutting the equator at right-angles, i.e. a line of longitude.
mesa A table-land with steep sides.
meteorite A solid lump of rock which enters the atmosphere from space and is large enough not to burn up in the atmosphere but to reach the Earth's surface.
midnight Sun Appearance of the Sun throughout the day and night. This occurs in latitudes close to the poles at times around the solstices.
monadnock An isolated hill or rock, left when the surrounding rock has been eroded more rapidly.
monsoon forest Tropical forest found where the monsoon climate is prevalent. Because of the dry season between monsoons, it is not so dense as tropical equatorial forest.
moor Area of high rolling land covered in grass, heather and bracken, often with marshy areas.
moraine Rock and other debris transported by a glacier. Terminal moraines are formed at the ends of glaciers; lateral moraines are formed at the sides of glaciers; median moraines are formed in the middle of glaciers where two glaciers meet and unite.
mountain Mass of high land projecting well above the level of the surrounding land.
muskeg A mossy swamp in northern Canada.

neap tide Small tidal difference between high and low tide, caused when the Sun and Moon are out of phase.
névé Granular snow, formed as snow is gradually impacted. Eventually *névé* forms the ice of a glacier.
nunatak Mountain peak projecting through an ice sheet.

oasis Area in a desert in which water occurs, giving rise to fertile land and allowing cultivation.
ocean A very large area of seawater, divided off by or surrounding the continents.
outwash Alluvium carried from the end of a glacier by the melting ice.
outwash plain Plain formed by the outwash of a glacier.
oxbow lake A lake formed when a river cuts off one

of its meanders, leaving a crescent-shaped or horse-shoe-shaped lake.

pack ice Ice floes that have been forced together to form an almost continuous sheet.

pampas Grasslands between the Andes and the Atlantic in South America.

pass A gap through a mountain range that is relatively easily traversable.

pediment Sloping plain that leads up to a mountain range.

percolation Descent of water through porous rock.

permafrost Ground that is always frozen solid.

piedmont Pertaining to the foot of a mountain or mountain range.

plain Extensive area of flat or gently rolling land.

plateau Extensive area of flat or gently rolling land that is raised above the level of the surrounding land.

plug Vertical core of solidified lava at the centre of a volcanic cone.

polder Area in the Netherlands that has been reclaimed from the sea.

pole One end of the Earth's axis; it remains stationary while all other points on Earth rotate round the axis.

pot-hole A hole worn down through solid rock by the swirling action of water or water and accompanying debris.

prairie Flat or rolling plains, largely grasslands, that occupy the central areas of North America east of the Rockies.

profile The profile of a river is a cross-section of its total length, showing the various slopes and changes of slope.

promontory A headland.

puy A French term for an isolated cone of a long-extinct volcano.

quagmire Soft wet ground which shakes when walked on.

quicksand Loose sand in a dense suspension in water. Although it may look solid, its properties are those of a liquid.

race A rapid marine current caused by the tides.

rainbow An arc formed of the colours of the spectrum. It is caused by raindrops refracting the sunlight.

ravine Small steep-sided valley, usually caused by water erosion.

reef Line of rocks just below the surface of the sea.

reg Area of the Sahara Desert consisting of gravel and small rocks, but no sand.

ria An inlet of the sea, formed from a drowned, i.e. submerged, river valley.

rift Valley formed by the sinking of a section of land between two parallel faults.

river capture Process by which one river erodes a larger and larger valley, eventually cutting into the valley of another river and 'capturing' its waters.

river terrace Flat land on either side of a river, left when a river erodes a channel well below the level of its flood plain.

roads (roadstead) Large area of deepwater anchorage for ships, usually well protected from bad weather.

run-off Rainfall which pours over the ground surface and into streams and rivers.

salt dome Mass of salt that has been forced up through layers of rock until it lies relatively close to the Earth's surface.

salt lake A lake in a hot dry climate that has only a limited outlet or no outlet at all. As water evaporates, the concentration of salt in the water increases.

salt marsh Area of marsh that is flooded by seawater at high tides.

salt pan An area of salt water that has evaporated completely, leaving behind a deposit of salt.

sandbank Line or bank of sand just below the surface of the sea or of a river.

savanna Area of grassland with few trees, found to the north and south of the equatorial areas. There is a wet and a dry season each year, limiting the growth of trees.

scarp (escarpment) A steep slope, often forming the steeper slope of a cuesta.

scree Broken rocks at the foot of a rocky slope. They are broken off by the action of weathering and tumble down the slope.

sea level Mean level between high and low tides.

shoal Area of sandbanks.

sidereal day The interval of time for a star to describe a circle around the pole star.

sierra Long mountain range, usually very jagged.

sill A slab of igneous rock, forced when molten between two layers of sedimentary rock and subsequently exposed by erosion.

snowdrift Bank or mass of snow that has been deposited in one place by the wind.

snowfield Permanent mass of snow.

snowline On a high land, the level above which snow is permanently present.

solar day The interval of time between the Sun appearing in the meridian of any one place.

solstice The time when the Sun appears vertically overhead at its most northerly or southerly point; about 21 June and 22 December.

sound A narrow inlet of the sea.

source The point at which a river begins – a spring, lake, etc.

spit A long narrow strip of shingle or sand, attached at one end to a land mass, projecting into the sea or across an estuary.

spring A flow of water up through the ground and out at a particular point. It can be permanent or intermittent.

spring tide Great tidal difference between high and low tide, caused when the Sun and Moon are in phase.

stack An isolated pillar of rock off the coast, caused by erosion.

steppes Flat grasslands, from central Europe to eastern Russia and on into south-west Siberia.

strait A narrow stretch of sea connecting two large expanses of sea or ocean.

subtropical The region between the tropics and temperate regions.

swamp Low marshland that is permanently wet.

swash Flow of water up a beach after a wave has broken.

taiga Vast belt of coniferous forests in the northern hemisphere, particularly Siberia.

tarn A mountain lake, often occupying a *cirque*.

temperate The region between subtropical regions and polar circles, excluding the continental and eastern coastal regions of the northern hemisphere.

tide Rise and fall of the surface of the sea, caused by the gravitational pull of the Sun. The gravitational pull of the Sun also influences the tides.

tombolo A bar joining an island to the mainland.

trench A long deep submarine valley.

tributary A river which flows into another river rather than into a lake or the sea.

Tropic of Cancer Latitude 23°N. The position at which the Sun appears vertically overhead at midday on the 21 June solstice.

Tropic of Capricorn Latitude 23°S. The position at which the Sun appears vertically overhead at midday on the 22 December solstice.

tropics Region between the Tropics of Cancer and Capricorn.

truncated spur A spur that has at some time been foreshortened by the action of a glacier.

tsunami A tidal wave caused by an earthquake under the sea's surface.

tundra Area in the northern hemisphere, north of the coniferous forest belt, typified by the absence of trees. The ground is covered by mosses, lichens and a few other plants that can survive the long harsh winters and short cool summers.

undertow The undercurrent after a wave has broken on a beach.

volcanic ash Particles of lava ejected by a volcano and often falling over a wide area.

volcano Vent or fissure in the Earth's crust through which molten magma can force its way to the surface.

wadi A watercourse in the desert. It is usually dry but can contain water after the occasional rainstorms.

waterfall Abrupt fall of water in the course of a river.

water gap Gap in a ridge or line of hills, cut by a river.

watershed The dividing line, running along high land, between the tributaries feeding into two separate river systems.

water table The surface of a water-saturated part of the ground.

well A hole dug from ground level to below the surface of the water table.

whirlpool A circular eddy of water, formed by the interaction of two or more currents.

year Time taken for the Earth to complete one revolution about the Sun.

zenith Point vertically above the ground.

Oceans

Ocean with adjacent seas	Area in millions (km²)	Area in millions (miles²)	Percentage of world area	Greatest depth (m)	Greatest depth (ft)	Greatest depth location	Average depth (m)	Average depth (ft)
Pacific	181·20	69·96	35·52	10 924	35 840	Mariana Trench	4188	13 740
Atlantic	106·48	41·11	20·88	9 460	31 037	Puerto Rico Trench	3736	12 257
Indian	74·06	28·59	14·52	7 542	24 744	Java Trench	3872	12 703
Total	361·74	139·66	70·92					

If the adjacent seas are detached and the Arctic Sea regarded as an ocean, the oceanic areas may be listed thus:

	Area (km²)	Area (miles²)	Percentage of sea area
Pacific	166 240 000	64 190 000	46·0
Atlantic	86 560 000	33 420 000	23·9
Indian	73 430 000	28 350 000	20·3
Arctic	13 230 000	5 110 000	3·7
Other Seas	22 280 000	8 600 000	6·1

Ocean depths are zoned by oceanographers as bathyl (down to 2000 m or 6560 ft); abyssal (between 2000 m and 6000 m (6560 ft and 19 685 ft)) and hadal (below 6000 m (19 685 ft)).

Seas

Principal seas	Area (km²)	Area (miles²)	Average depth (m)	Average depth (ft)
1. South China*	2 974 600	1 148 500	1200	4000
2. Caribbean Sea	2 753 000	1 063 000	2400	8000
3. Mediterranean Sea	2 503 000	966 750	1485	4875
4. Bering Sea	2 268 180	875 750	1400	4700
5. Gulf of Mexico	1 542 985	595 750	1500	5000
6. Sea of Okhotsk	1 527 570	589 800	840	2750
7. East China Sea	1 249 150	482 300	180	600
8. Hudson Bay	1 232 300	475 800	120	400
9. Sea of Japan	1 007 500	389 000	1370	4500
10. Andaman Sea	797 700	308 000	865	2850

Seas continued

Principal seas	Area (km²)	Area (miles²)	Average depth (m)	Average depth (ft)
11. North Sea	575 300	222 125	90	300
12. Black Sea	461 980	178 375	1100	3600
13. Red Sea	437 700	169 000	490	1610
14. Baltic Sea	422 160	163 000	55	190
15. Persian Gulf†	238 790	92 200	24	80
16. Gulf of St Lawrence	237 760	91 800	120	400
17. Gulf of California	162 000	62 530	810	2660
18. English Channel	89 900	34 700	54	177
19. Irish Sea	88 550	34 200	60	197
20. Bass Strait	75 000	28 950	70	230

* The Malayan Sea, which embraces the South China Sea and the Straits of Malacca (8 142 000 km² (*3 144 000 miles²*)), is not now an entity accepted by the International Hydrographic Bureau.
† Also referred to as the Arabian Gulf.

Deep-sea trenches

Length (km)	Length (miles)	Name	Deepest point	Depth (m)	Depth (ft)
2250	1400	Mariana Trench,* W Pacific	Challenger Deep †	10 924	35 840
2575	1600	Tonga-Kermadec Trench,‡ S Pacific	Vityaz 11 (Tonga)	10 850	35 598
2250	1400	Kuril-Kamchatka Trench,* W Pacific		10 542	34 587
1325	825	Philippine Trench, W Pacific	Galathea Deep	10 539	34 578
		Idzu-Bonin Trench (sometimes included in the Japan Trench, see below)		9 810	32 196
320+	200+	New Hebrides Trench, S Pacific	North Trench	9 165	30 080
640	400	Solomon or New Britain Trench, S Pacific		9 140	29 988
800	500	Puerto Rico Trench, W Atlantic	Milwaukee Deep	8 648	28 374
560	350	Yap Trench,* W Pacific		8 527	27 976
1600	1000	Japan Trench,* W Pacific		8 412	27 591
965	600	South Sandwich Trench, S Atlantic	Meteor Deep	8 263	27 112
3200	2000	Aleutian Trench, N Pacific		8 100	26 574
3540	2200	Peru-Chile (Atacama) Trench E Pacific	Bartholomew Deep	8 064	26 454
		Palau Trench (sometimes included in the Yap Trench)		8 050	26 420
965	600	Romanche Trench, N-S Atlantic		7 864	25 800
2250	1400	Java (Sunda) Trench, Indian Ocean	Planet Deep	7 725	25 344
965	600	Cayman Trench, Caribbean		7 535	24 720
1040	650	Nansei Shotó (Ryukyu) Trench, W Pacific		7 505	24 630
240	150	Banda Trench, Banda Sea		7 360	24 155

* These four trenches are sometimes regarded as a single 7400 km *4600 mile* long system.
† Subsequent visits to the Challenger Deep since 1951 have produced claims for greater depths in this same longitude and latitude. In March 1959 the USSR research ship Vityaz claimed 11 033 m (*36 198 ft*), using echo-sounding only.
‡ Kermadec Trench is sometimes considered to be a separate feature. Depth 10 047 m (*32 974 ft*).

The continents

Continent	Area in km²	Area in miles²	North to South (km)	Greatest distance between extremities of land masses North to South (miles)	East to West (km)	East to West (miles)
Asia	43 998 000	16 988 000	6435	4000	7560	4700
America	41 918 000	16 185 000				
North America	21 510 000	8 305 000	6565	4080	6035	3750
Central America	2 745 000	1 060 000	1320	820	1530	950
South America	17 598 000	6 795 000	7240	4500	5150	3200

The continents *continued*

Continent	Area in km²	Area in miles²	North to South (km)	Greatest distance between extremities of land masses North to South (miles)	East to West (km)	East to West (miles)
Africa	29 800 000	*11 506 000*	7080	*4400*	6035	*3750*
Antarctica	c. 13 600 000	*c. 5 500 000*	—	—	4340	*2700**
Europe†	9 699 000	*3 745 000*	2900	*1800*	4000	*2500*
Australia	7 618 493	*2 941 526*	3000	*1870*	3700	*2300*

* Greatest transit from coast to coast.
† Includes 5 571 000 km² (*2 151 000 miles²*) of USSR territory west of the Urals.

Peninsulas

	Area in km²	Area in miles²		Area in km²	Area in miles²
Arabia	3 250 000	*1 250 000*	Labrador	1 300 000	*500 000*
Southern India	2 072 000	*800 000*	Scandinavia	800 300	*309 000*
Alaska	1 500 000	*580 000*	Iberian Peninsula	584 000	*225 500*

Deserts

Name	Approx. area in km²	Approx. area in miles²	Territories
The Sahara	8 400 000	*3 250 000*	Algeria, Chad, Libya, Mali, Mauritania, Niger, Sudan, Tunisia, Egypt, Morocco. Embraces the Libyan Desert (1 550 000 km² (*600 000 miles²*)) and the Nubian Desert (260 000 km² (*100 000 miles²*))
Australian Desert	1 550 000	*600 000*	Australia. Embraces the Great Sandy (or Warburton) (420 000 km² (*160 000 miles²*)), Great Victoria (325 000 km² (*125 000 miles²*)), Simpson (Arunta) (310 000 km² (*120 000 miles²*)), Gibson (220 000 km² (*85 000 miles²*)) and Stuart Deserts
Arabian Desert	1 300 000	*500 000*	Southern Arabia, Saudi Arabia, Yemen. Includes the Ar Rab'al Khali or Empty Quarter (647 500 km² (*250 000 miles²*)), Syrian (325 000 km² (*125 000 miles²*)) and An Nafud (129 500 km² (*50 000 miles²*)) Deserts
The Gobi	1 040 000	*400 000*	Mongolia and China (Inner Mongolia)
Kalahari Desert	520 000	*200 000*	Botswana
Takla Makan	320 000	*125 000*	Sinkiang, China
Sonoran Desert	310 000	*120 000*	Arizona and California, USA and Mexico
Namib Desert	310 000	*120 000*	In SW Africa (Namibia)
Kara Kum*	270 000	*105 000*	Turkmenistan, USSR
Thar Desert	260 000	*100 000*	North-western India and Pakistan
Somali Desert	260 000	*100 000*	Somalia
Atacama Desert	180 000	*70 000*	Northern Chile
Kyzyl Kum*	180 000	*70 000*	Uzbekistan-Kazakhstan, USSR
Dasht-e Lut	52 000	*20 000*	Eastern Iran (sometimes called Iranian Desert)
Mojave Desert	35 000	*13 500*	Southern California, USA
Desierto de Sechura	26 000	*10 000*	North-west Peru

* Together known as the Turkestan Desert.

Mountains

Key to Ranges: H = Himalaya K = Karakoram KS = Kunlun Shan HK = Hindu Kush P = Pamir
S = Sinkiang, China.
Subsidiary peaks or tops in the same mountain massif are italicized.

Mountain	Height (m)	Height (ft)	Range	Date of First Ascent (if any)
Mount Everest	8848	*29 028*	H	29 May 1953
[Qomolangma-feng (Chinese); Sagarmatha (Nepalese); Mi-ti gu-ti cha-pu long-na (Tibetan)] *Everest South Summit*	8750	28 707	H	*26 May 1953*
K2 (Chogori)	8610	*28 250*	K	31 July 1954

Mountains

Mountain	Height (m)	Height (ft)	Range	Date of First Ascent (if any)
Kangchenjunga	8597	28 208	H	25 May 1955
Lhotse	8511	27 923	H	18 May 1956
Subsidiary Peak	*8410*	27 591	*H*	*unclimbed*
Yalung Kang Kangchenjunga West	8502	27 894	H	14 May 1973
Kangchenjunga South Peak	8488	27 848	H	19 May 1978
Makalu I	8481	27 824	H	15 May 1955
Kangchenjunga Middle Peak	8475	27 806	H	22 May 1978
Lhotse Shar	8383	27 504	H	12 May 1970
Dhaulagiri I	8167	26 795	H	13 May 1960
Manaslu I (Kutang I)	8156	26 760	H	9 May 1956
Cho Oyu	8153	26 750	H	19 Oct 1954
Nanga Parbat (Diamir)	8124	26 660	H	3 July 1953
Annapurna I	8091	26 546	H	3 June 1950
Gasherbrum I (Hidden Peak)	8068	26 470	K	5 July 1958
Broad Peak I	8047	26 400	K	9 June 1957
Shisham Pangma (Gosainthan)	8046	26 398	H	2 May 1964
Gasherbrum II	8034	26 360	K	7 July 1956
Broad Peak Middle	*8016*	26 300	*K*	*28 July 1975*
Annapurna East	8010	26 280	H	29 Apr 1974
Makalu South-East	8010	26 280	H	Unclimbed
Broad Peak Central	8000	26 246	K	28 July 1975
Gasherbrum III	7952	26 090	K	11 Aug 1975
Annapurna II	7937	26 041	H	17 May 1960
Gasherbrum IV	7923	26 000	K	6 Aug 1958
Gyachung Kang	7921	25 990	H	10 Apr 1964
Nanga Parbat Vorgipfel	7910	25 951	H	11 July 1971
Kangbachen	7902	25 925	H	26 May 1974
Disteghil Sar	7884	25 868	K	9 June 1960
Nuptse	7879	25 850	H	16 May 1961
Himalchuli	7864	25 801	H	24 May 1960
Khinyang Chchish	7852	25 762	K	26 Aug 1971
Manaslu II (Peak 29) Dakuro, Dunapurna	7835	25 705	H	Oct 1970
Masherbrum East	7821	25 660	K	6 July 1960
Nanda Devi West	7816	25 643	H	29 Aug 1936
Nanga Parbat North	7816	25 643	H	Unclimbed
Chomo Lönzo	7815	25 640	H	30 Oct 1954
Ngojumba Ri I (Cho Oyu II)	7805	25 610	H	5 May 1965
Masherbrum West	*7805*	25 610	*K*	*unclimbed*
Rakaposhi	7788	25 550	K	25 June 1958
Batura Muztagh I	7785	25 542	K	30 July 1976
Zemu Gap Peak	7780	25 526	H	Unclimbed
Gasherbrum II East	*7772*	25 500	*K*	*unclimbed*
Kanjut Sar	7760	25 460	K	19 July 1959
Kamet	7756	25 447	H	21 June 1931
Namcha Barwa	7756	25 445	H	Unclimbed
Dhaulagiri II	7751	25 429	H	18 May 1971
Saltoro Kangri I	7741	25 400	K	24 July 1962
Batura Muztagh II	7730	25 361	K	1978
Gurla Mandhata	7728	25 355	H	Unclimbed
Ulugh Muztagh	7725	25 340	KS	Unclimbed
Qungur II (Kongur)	7719	25 326	P	12 July 1981
Dhaulagiri III	7715	25 318	H	23 Oct 1973
Jannu	7709	25 294	H	27 Apr 1962
Tirich Mir	7706	25 282	HK	21 July 1950
Saltoro Kangri II	7705	25 280	K	Unclimbed
Molamenqing	7703	25 272	H	Unclimbed
Disteghil Sar E	7700	25 262	K	Unclimbed
Trich Mir, East Peak	*7691*	25 236	*HK*	*25 July 1963*
Saser Kangri I	7672	25 170	K	5 June 1973
Chogolisa South West	7665	25 148	K	2 Aug 1975
Phola Gangchhen	7661	25 135	H	Unclimbed
Dhaulagiri IV	7661	25 134	H	9 May 1975
Shahkang Sham	7660	25 131		Unclimbed
Chogolisa North-East ('Bride Peak')	7653	25 110	K	4 Aug 1958
Trivor	7650	25 098	K	17 Aug 1960
Fang	7647	25 088	H	17 May 1980

Mountain	Height (m)	Height (ft)	Range	Date of First Ascent (if any)
Ngojumba Ri II	7646	25 085		24 Apr 1965
Makalu II (Kangshungtse)	7640	25 066	H	22 Oct 1954
Khinyang Chchish South	7620	25 000	K	Unclimbed
Shisparé	7619	24 997	K	21 July 1974
Dhaulagiri V	7618	24 993	H	1 May 1975
Broad Peak North	*7600*	24 935	*K*	*unclimbed*
Amne Machin	7612	24 974	S	2 June 1960
Qungur I (Kongur Tiubie)	7595	24 918	P	16 Aug 1956
Peak 38 (Lhotse II)	7589	24 898	H	Unclimbed
Minya Konka	7587	24 891	S	28 Oct 1932
Annapurna III	7555	24 787	H	6 May 1961
Khula Kangri I	7554	24 784	H	Unclimbed
Changtse (North Peak)	7552	24 780	H	Unclimbed
Muztagh Ata	7546	24 757	P	Unclimbed
Skyang Kangri	7544	24 751	K	11 Aug 1976
Khula Kangri II	7541	24 740	H	Unclimbed
Khula Kangri III	7532	24 710	H	Unclimbed
Yalung Peak	7532	24 710	H	Unclimbed
Yukshin Gardas Sar	7530	24 705	K	Unclimbed
Mamostong Kangri	7526	24 692	K	Unclimbed
Annapurna IV	7525	24 688	H	30 May 1955
Khula Kangri IV	7516	24 659	H	Unclimbed
Saser Kangri II (K24)	7513	24 649	K	Unclimbed
Shartse	7502	24 612	H	23 May 1974

SOUTH AMERICA

The mountains of the Cordillera de los Andes are headed by Aconcagua at 6960 m (*22 834 ft*) (first climbed on 14 Jan 1897), which has the distinction of being the highest mountain in the world outside the great ranges of Central Asia.

Name	Height (m)	Height (ft)	Country
1. Cerro Aconcagua	6960	22 834	Argentina
2. Ojos de Salado	6885	22 588	Argentina–Chile
3. Nevado de Pissis	6780	22 244	Argentina–Chile
4. Huascarán, Sur	6768	22 205	Peru
5. Llullaillaco	6723	22 057	Argentina–Chile
6. Mercadario	6670	21 884	Argentina–Chile
7. Huascarán Norte	6655	21 834	Peru
8. Yerupajá	6634	21 765	Peru
9. Nevados de Tres Crucés	6620	21 720	Argentina–Chile
10. Coropuna	6613	21 696	Peru
11. Nevado Incahuasi	6601	21 657	Argentina–Chile
12. Tupungato	6550	21 490	Argentina–Chile
13. Sajama	6542	21 463	Bolivia
14. Nevado Gonzalez	6500	21 326	Argentina
15. Cerro del Nacimiento	6493	21 302	Argentina
16. El Muerto	6476	21 246	Argentina–Chile
17. Illimani	6462	21 200	Bolivia
18. Ancohuma (Sorata N)	6427	21 086	Bolivia
19. Nevado Bonete	6410	21 031	Argentina
20. Cerro de Ramada	6410	21 031	Argentina

NORTH AND CENTRAL AMERICA

Mt McKinley (first ascent 1913) is the only peak in excess of 6100 m (*20 000 ft*) in the entire North American continent. It was first climbed on 7 June 1913. The native name is Denali.

Name	Height (m)	Height (ft)	Country
1. McKinley, South Peak	6194	20 320	Alaska
2. Logan	6050	19 850	Canada
3. Citlaltépetl (Orizaba)	5699	18 700	Mexico
4. St Elias	5489	18 008	Alaska–Canada
5. Popocatépetl	5452	17 887	Mexico
6. Foraker	5304	17 400	Alaska
7. Ixtaccihuatl	5286	17 342	Mexico

NORTH AND CENTRAL AMERICA *continued*

Name	Height (m)	Height (ft)	Country
8. Lucania	5227	*17150*	Alaska
9. King Peak	5221	*17130*	Alaska
10. Blackburn	5036	*16522*	Alaska
11. Steele	5011	*16440*	Alaska
12. Bona	5005	*16420*	Alaska
13. Sanford	4940	*16207*	Alaska
14. Wood	4840	*15879*	Canada

Note: Mt McKinley, North Peak, is 5934 m (*19470 ft*).

AFRICA

All the peaks listed in Zaïre and Uganda are in the Ruwenzori group.

Name	Height (m)	Height (ft)	Location
1. Kilimanjaro (Uhuru Point,* Kibo)	5894	*19340*	Tanzania
Hans Meyer Peak, Mawenzi	*5148*	16890	
Shira Peak	*4005*	13139	
2. Mount Kenya (Batian)	5199	*17058*	Kenya
3. Ngaliema (Mount Stanley) (Margherita Peak)	5109	*16763*	Zaïre–Uganda
4. Duwoni or Mt Speke (Vittorio Emanuele Peak)	4896	*16062*	Uganda
5. Mount Baker (Edward Peak)	4843	*15889*	Uganda
6. Mount Emin (Umberto Peak)	4798	*15741*	Zaïre
7. Mount Gessi (Iolanda Peak)	4715	*15470*	Uganda
8. Mount Luigi di Savoia (Sella Peak)	4626	*15179*	Uganda
9. Ras Dashan (Rasdajan)	4620	*15158*	Semien Mts, Ethiopia
10. Humphreys Peak	4578	*15021*	Uganda

* Formerly called Kaiser Wilhelm Spitze.

HIGHEST EUROPEAN ALPS

The highest point in Italian territory is a shoulder of the main summit of Mont Blanc (Monte Bianco) through which a 4760 m (*15616 ft*) contour passes. The highest top exclusively in Italian territory is Picco Luigi Amedeo (4460 m (*14632 ft*)) to the south of the main Mont Blanc peak, which is itself exclusively in French territory.

Subsidiary peaks or tops on the same massif have been omitted except in the case of Mont Blanc and Monte Rosa, where they have been indented in italic type.

Name	Height (m)	Height (ft)	Country	First Ascent
1. Mont Blanc	4807	*15771*	France	1786
Monte Bianco di Courmayeur	*4748*	*15577*	France	1877
2. Monte Rosa				
Dufourspitze	*4634·0*	*15203*	Switzerland	1855
Nordend	*4609*	*15121*	Swiss–Italian border	1861
Ostspitze	*4596*	*15078*	Swiss–Italian border	1854
Zumstein Spitze	*4563*	*14970*	Swiss–Italian border	1820
Signal Kuppe	*4556*	*14947*	Swiss–Italian border	1842
3. Dom	4545·4	*14911*	Switzerland	1858
4. Lyskamm (Liskamm)	4527·2	*14853*	Swiss–Italian border	1861
5. Weisshorn	4505·5	*14780*	Switzerland	1861
6. Täschhorn	4490·7	*14733*	Switzerland	1862
7. Matterhorn	4475·5	*14683*	Swiss–Italian border	1865
Le Mont Maudit (Mont Blanc)	*4465*	*14649*	Italy–France	1878
Picco Luigi Amedeo (Mont Blanc)	*4460*	*14632*	Italy	
8. La Dent Blanche	4356·6	*14293*	Switzerland	1862
9. Nadelhorn	4327·0	*14196*	Switzerland	1858
10. Le Grand Combin de Grafaneire	4314	*14153*	Switzerland	1859
Dôme du Goûter (Mont Blanc)	*4304*	*14120*	France	1784
11. Lenzspitze	4294	*14087*	Switzerland	1870
12. Finsteraarhorn	4273·8	*14021*	Switzerland	1829*

* Also reported climbed in 1812 but evidence lacking.
Note: In the *Dunlop Book* (1st edition) this list was extended to include the 24 additional Alps over 4000 m (*13123 ft*).

EUROPE

The Caucasus range, along the spine of which runs the traditional geographical boundary between Asia and Europe, includes the following peaks which are higher than Mont Blanc (4807 m (*15 771 ft*)).

Name	Height (m)	Height (ft)
1. El'brus, West Peak	5663	18 481
El'brus, East Peak	5595	18 356
2. Dykh Tau	5203	17 070
3. Shkhara	5201	17 063
4. Pik Shota Rustaveli	5190	17 028
5. Koshtantau	5144	16 876
6. Pik Pushkin	5100	16 732
7. Jangi Tau, West Peak	5051	16 572
Janga, East Peak	5038	16 529
8. Dzhangi Tau	5049	16 565
9. Kazbek	5047	16 558
10. Katyn Tau (Adish)	4985	16 355
11. Pik Rustaveli	4960	16 272
12. Mishirgi, West Peak	4922	16 148
Mishirgitau, East Peak	4917	16 135
13. Kunjum Mishirgi	4880	16 011
14. Gestola	4860	15 944
15. Tetnuld	4853	15 921

ANTARCTICA

Areas of Eastern Antarctica remain unsurveyed. Immense areas of the ice cap around the Pole of Inaccessibility lie over 3650 m (*12 000 ft*) above sea-level rising to 4265 m (*14 000 ft*) in 82° 25′ S 65° 30′ E.

Name	Height (m)	Height (ft)
1. Vinson Massif	5140	16 863
2. Mt Tyree	4965	16 289
3. Mt Shinn	4800*	15 750*
4. Mt Gardner	4690	15 387
5. Mt Epperley	4602	15 098
6. Mt Kirkpatrick	4511	14 799
7. Mt Elizabeth	4480	14 698
8. Mt Markham	4350	14 271
9. Mt MacKellar	4290	14 074
10. Mt Kaplan	4250	13 943
11. Mt Sidley	4221*	13 850*
12. Mt Ostenso	4180	13 713
13. Mt Minto	4160	13 648
14. Mt Long Gables	4150	13 615
15. Mt Miller	4145	13 600
16. Mt Falla	4115	13 500
17. Mt Giovinetto	4087	13 408
18. Mt Lister	4070	13 353
19. Mt Fisher	4066	13 340
20. Mt Wade	4063	13 330
21. Mt Fridtjof Nansen	4010	13 156

* Volcanic as is Erebus 3794 m (*12 447 ft*).

OCEANIA

The nomenclature of New Guinean mountains remains extremely confused.

Name	Height (m)	Height (ft)	Location
1. Puncak Jayakusumu (formerly Peak Sukarno, Carstensz Pyramid)	4884	16 023	West Irian
Ngga Pulu	4861	15 950	West Irian
Sunday Peak	4860	15 945	West Irian
2. Oost Carstensz top	4840	15 879	West Irian
3. Peak Trikora (formerly Sukarno, formerly Wilhelmina)	4730	15 518	West Irian
4. Enggea (Idenburg top)	4717	15 475	West Irian
5. Peak Mandala (formerly Juliana)	4640	15 223	West Irian
6. Mt Wilhelm	4600	15 091	New Guinea
7. Peak Wisnumurti	4595	15 075	New Guinea
8. Point (unnamed)	4350	14 271	New Guinea
9. Mt Kubor	4300	14 107	New Guinea
10. Mt Leonard Darwin	4234	13 891	New Guinea
11. Mt Herbert	4267	13 999	New Guinea
12. *Mauna Kea	4205	13 796	Hawaii*
13. *Mauna Loa	4170	13 680	Hawaii*
14. Mt Bangeta	4107	13 474	New Guinea
15. Mt Kinabalu	4101	13 454	Sabah (Borneo)
16. Mt Sarawaket	4100	13 451	New Guinea
17. Mt Giluwe	4088	13 385	New Guinea
18. Mt Victoria	4073	13 362	Owen Stanley Range
19. Mt Hogan	4000	13 123	New Guinea

* Politically part of the USA since 21 Aug 1959.
Note: The highest mountain in North Island, New Zealand is the volcano Ruapehu (2797 m (*9176 ft*)). Mt Cook (3764 m (*12 349 ft*)) in South Island is the highest in New Zealand and is called Aorangi by the Maoris.
Australia's highest point is Mt Kosciusko (2230 m (*7316 ft*)) in the Snowy Mtns, New South Wales.

World's greatest mountain ranges

The greatest mountain system is the Himalaya–Karakoram–Hindu Kush–Pamir range with 104 peaks over 7315 m (24 000 ft). The second greatest range is the Andes with 54 peaks over 6096 m (20 000 ft).

Length (km)	Name	Length (miles)	Location	Culminating Peak	Height (m)	Height (ft)
7200	Cordillera de Los Andes	4500	W South America	Aconcagua	6960	22 834
4800	Rocky Mountains	3000	W North America	Mt Elbert (Colorado)‡	4400	14 433
3800	Himalaya–Karakoram–Hindu Kush	2400	S Central Asia	Mt Everest	8848	29 028
3600	Great Dividing Range	2250	E Australia	Kosciusko	2228	7310
3500	Trans-Antarctic Mts	2200	Antarctica	Mt Kirkpatrick	4529	14 860
3000	Brazilian Atlantic Coast Range	1900	E Brazil	Pico de Bandeira	2890	9482
2900	West Sumatran–Javan Range	1800	W Sumatra and Java	Kerintji	3805	12 484
2650	Aleutian Range	1650*	Alaska and NW Pacific	Shishaldin	2861	9387
2250	Tien Shan	1400	S Central Asia	Pik Pobeda	7439	24 406
2000	Central New Guinea Range	1250	Irian Jaya–Papua/N Guinea	Jayakusumu†	4883	16 020
2000	Altai Mountains	1250	Central Asia	Gora Belukha	4505	14 783
2010	Uralskiy Khrebet	1250	Russian SFSR	Gora Narodnaya	1894	6214
1930	Range in Kamchatka §	1200	E Russian SFSR	Klyuchevskaya Sopka	4850	15 910
1930	Atlas Mountains	1200	NW Africa	Jebel Toubkal	4165	13 665
1610	Verkhoyanskiy Khrebet	1000	E Russian SFSR	Gora Mas Khaya	2959	9708
1610	Western Ghats	1000	W India	Anai Madi	2694	8841
1530	Sierra Madre Oriental	950	Mexico	Citlaltépetl (Orizaba)	5699	18 700
1530	Kühhā-ye-Zāgros	950	Iran	Zard Kūh	4547	14 921
1530	Scandinavian Range	950	W Norway	Galdhopiggen	2470	8104
1450	Ethiopian Highlands	900	Ethiopia	Ras Dashan	c. 4600	c. 15 100
1450	Sierra Madre Occidental	900	Mexico	Nevado de Colima	4265	13 993
1370	Malagasy Range	850	Madagascar	Maromokotro	2876	9436
1290	Drakensberg (edge of plateau)	800	SE Africa	Thabana Ntlenyana	3482	11 425
1290	Khrebet Cherskogo	800	E Russian SFSR	Gora Pobeda	3147	10 325
1200	Caucasus	750	Georgia, USSR	El'brus, West Peak	5633	18 481
1130	Alaska Range	700	Alaska, USA	Mt McKinley, South Peak	6193	20 320
1130	Assam–Burma Range	700	Assam–W Burma	Hkakabo Razi	5881	19 296
1130	Cascade Range	700	Northwest USA–Canada	Mt Rainier	4392	14 410
1130	Central Borneo Range	700	Central Borneo	Kinabalu	4101	13 455
1130	Tihāmat ash Shām	700	SW Arabia	Jebel Hadhar	3760	12 336
1130	Appennini	700	Italy	Corno Grande	2931	9617
1130	Appalachians	700	Eastern USA–Canada	Mt Mitchell	2037	6684
1050	Alps	650	Central Europe	Mt Blanc	4807	15 771
965	Sierra Madre del Sur	600	Mexico	Teotepec	3703	12 149
965	Khrebet Kolymskiy (Gydan)	600	E Russian SFSR	—	2221	7290

* Continuous mainland length (excluding islands) 720 km (450 miles).
§ Comprises the Sredinnyy and Koryakskiy Krebets.
† Also known (before 1970) as Ngga Pulu, Mount Sukarno and Cartensz Pyramide.
‡ Mt Robson 3954 m (12 872 ft) is the highest mountain in the Canadian Rockies.

Volcanoes

It is estimated that there are about 850 active volcanoes of which 80 are submarine. Vulcanologists classify volcanoes as extinct, dormant or active (which includes rumbling, steaming or erupting). Areas of volcanoes and seismic activity are well defined, notably around the shores of the N Pacific and the eastern shores of the S Pacific, down the Mid-Atlantic range, the Africa Rift Valley and across from Greece and Turkey into Central Asia, the Himalayas and Meghalaya (Assam).

Cerro Aconcagua (6960 m (22 834 ft)), the highest Andean peak, is an extinct volcano, while Kilimanjaro (5895 m (19 340 ft)) in Africa, and Volcán Llullaillaco in Chile (6723 m (22 057 ft)) are classified as dormant. The highest point on the Equator lies on the shoulder of the dormant Cayambe (5786 m (18 982 ft)) in Ecuador on the 4875 m (15 995 ft) contour. Among the principal volcanoes active in recent times are:

Name	Height (m)	Height (ft)	Range or Location	Country	Date of Last Notified Eruption
Ojos del Salado	6885	22 588	Andes	Argentina–Chile	1981–Steams
Guallatiri	6060	19 882	Andes	Chile	1960
Cotopaxi	5897	19 347	Andes	Ecuador	1975
Lascar	5641	18 507	Andes	Chile	1968
Tupungatito	5640	18 504	Andes	Chile	1964
Popocatépetl	5451	17 887	Altiplano de Mexico	Mexico	1920–Steams
Sangay	5230	17 159	Andes	Ecuador	1976
Klyuchevskaya sopka	4850	15 913	Sredinnyy Khrebet (Kamchatka Peninsula)	USSR	1974
Purace	4590	15 059	Andes	Colombia	1977
Tajumulco	4220	13 881		Guatemala	Rumbles
Mauna Loa	4170	13 680	Hawaii	USA	1978
Tacaná	4078	13 379	Sierra Madre	Guatemala	Rumbles
Cameroon Mt	4070	13 350	(monarch)	Cameroon	1959
Erebus	3795	12 450	Ross I	Antarctica	1975
Rindjani	3726	12 224	Lombok	Indonesia	1966
Pico de Teide	3718	12 198	Tenerife, Canary Is	Spain	1909
Semeru	3676	12 060	Java	Indonesia	1976

Halemaumau (House of Everlasting Fire) firepit of Kilauea Volcano on Hawaii Island. (Popperfoto)

Volcanoes continued

Name	Height (m)	Height (ft)	Range or Location	Country	Date of Last Notified Eruption
Nyiragongo	3470	11385	Virunga	Zaïre	1977
Koryakskaya	3456	11339	Kamchatka Peninsula	USSR	1957
Irazu	3452	11325	Cordillera Central	Costa Rica	1967
Slamat	3428	11247	Java	Indonesia	1967
Mt Spurr	3374	11070	Alaska Range	USA	1953
Mt Etna	3308	10853	Sicily	Italy	1979

Other Notable Active Volcanoes

Name	Height (m)	Height (ft)	Range or Location	Country	Date of Last Notified Eruption
Lassen Peak	3186	10453	Cascade Range, California	USA	1915
Mt St Helens	2949	9677	Cascade Range, Washington	USA	1980
Tambora	2850	9351	Sumbawa	Indonesia	1913
The Peak	2060	6760	Tristan da Cunha	S Atlantic	1962
Mt Lamington	1687	5535		Papua New Guinea	1951
Mt Pelée	1463	4800		Martinique	1929–32
Hekla	1447	4747		Iceland	1980
La Soufrière	1280	c. 4200	St Vincent Island	Atlantic	1979
Vesuvius	1280	4198	Bay of Naples	Italy	1944
Kilauea	1240	4077	Hawaii	USA	1977
Faial	1043	3421	Azores	Azores	1968
Stromboli	926	3038	Island	Mediterranean	1975
Santorini	584	1960	Thera	Greece	1956
Vulcano	499	1637	Lipari Islands	Mediterranean	1888–90
Paricutin	370	1213		Mexico	1943
Surtsey	173	568	off SW Iceland	Iceland	1963–65
Anak Krakatau	155	510	Island	Indonesia	1960

Depressions and glaciers

World's deepest depressions	Maximum depth below sea level (m)	(ft)
Dead Sea, Jordan–Israel	395	1296
Turfan Depression, Sinkiang, China	153	505
Munkhafad el Qattâra (Qattâra Depression), Egypt	132	436
Poluostrov Mangyshlak, Kazakh SSR, USSR	131	433
Danakil Depression, Ethiopia	116	383
Death Valley, California, USA	86	282
Salton Sink, California, USA	71	235
Zapadnyy Chink Ustyurta, Kazakh SSR	70	230
Prikaspiyskaya Nizmennost', Russian SFSR and Kazakh SSR	67	220
Ozera Sarykamysh, Uzbek and Turkmen SSR	45	148
El Faiyûm, Egypt	44	147
Peninsula Valdiés Lago Enriquillo, Dominican Republic	40	131

Note: Immense areas of West Antarctica would be below sea level if stripped of their ice sheet. The deepest estimated crypto-depression is the bed rock on the Hollick–Kenyon plateau beneath the Marie Byrd Land ice cap (84° 37′ S 110° W) at – 2468 m (8100 ft). The bed of Lake Baykal (USSR) is 1484 m (4872 ft) below sea-level and the bed of the Dead Sea is 792 m (2600 ft) below sea-level. The ground surface of large areas of Central Greenland under the overburden of ice up to 341 m (11 190 ft) thick are depressed to 365 m (1200 ft) below sea-level. The world's largest exposed depression is the Prikaspiyskaya Nizmennost' stretching the whole northern third of the Caspian Sea (which is itself 28 m (92 ft) below sea-level) up to 400 km (250 miles) inland. The Qattâra Depression extends for 547 km (340 miles) and is up to 128 km (80 miles) wide.

WORLD'S LONGEST GLACIERS

km	miles	
515	c. 320	Lambert-Fisher Ice Passage, Antarctica (disc. 1956–7)
418	260	Novaya Zemlya, North Island, USSR 3004 km² (1160 miles²)
362	225	Arctic Institute Ice Passage, Victoria Land, E Antarctica
289	180	Nimrod-Lennox–King Ice Passage, E Antarctica
241	150	Denman glacier, E Antarctica
225	140	Beardmore Glacier, E Antarctica (disc. 1908)
225	140	Recovery Glacier, W Antarctica
200	124	*Petermanns Gletscher, Knud Rasmussen Land, Greenland
193	120	Unnamed Glacier, SW Ross Ice Shelf, W Antarctica
185	115	Slessor Glacier, W Antarctica

* Petermanns Gletscher is the largest in the Northern hemisphere: it extends 40 km (24.8 miles) out to sea.

GLACIATED AREAS OF THE WORLD

It is estimated that 15 600 000 km² (6 020 000 miles²) or about 10·4 per cent of the world's land surface is permanently covered with ice, thus:

	km²	miles²
South Polar Regions	13 597 000	5 250 000
North Polar Regions (inc. Greenland with 695 500)	1 965 000	758 500
Alaska–Canada	58 800	22 700
Asia	37 800	14 600
South America	11 900	4 600
Europe	10 700	4 128
New Zealand	984	380
Africa	238	92

The Dead Sea, renowned for its density which is five times that of normal sea water, is also the world's deepest depression. (Popperfoto)

OTHER NOTABLE GLACIERS

Name	Location	Length (km)	Length (miles)	Area (km²)	Area (miles²)
Vatnajökull	Iceland	141	88	8 800	3 400
Malaspina Glacier	Alaska	41	26	3 830	1 480
Nabesna Glacier	Alaska	70	43·5	1 990	770
Fedtschenko	Pamirs	75	47	1 346	520
Siachen Glacier	Karakoram	75	47	1 150	444
Jostedalsbre	Norway	100	62	1 075	415
Hispar-Biafo Ice Passage	Karakoram	122	76	323 620	125 240
Kangchenjunga	Himalaya	19	12	458	177
Tasman Glacier	New Zealand	29	18	137	53
Aletschgletscher	Alps	26·5	16·5	114	44

Quarayaq Glacier, Greenland, flows at a velocity of 20 to 24 m (*65 to 80 ft*) a day – this is the fastest major glacier.
Hassanabad Glacier, Karakoram advanced 9·5 km (*15·3 miles*) in 'several months' *c.* 1900.

World's deepest caves

Depth			
m	ft		
1455	4773	Reseau du Foillis, Haute Savoie	France
1321	4334	Reseau de la Pierre St Martin, Haute Savoie	France
1280	4200	Snezhnaya, Caucasus	USSR
1220	4002	Sistema Huautla	Mexico
1198	3930	Gouffre Berger	France
1185	3887	Sima de Ukendi	Spain
1150	3772	Avenc B15, Pyrenees	Spain
1111	3645	Schneeloch, Salzburg	Austria
1098	3602	Sima G.E.S. Malaga	Spain
1024	3359	Lamprechtsofen	Austria
1018	3339	Reseau Felix Trombe	France
308	1010	Ogof Ffynnon Ddu, Powys	Wales
214	702	Giant's Hole – Oxlow Caverns, Derbyshire	England
179	587	Reyfad Pot, Fermanagh	Ireland, N
140	459	Carrowmore Cavern	Ireland, Republic

Note: The most extensive cave system is the Mammoth Cave system in Kentucky, USA, discovered in 1799 and in 1972 linked with the Flint Ridge system so making a combined mapped length of 345 km (*213·3 miles*). The largest known cavern is the Sarawak Chamber, Lobang Nasip Bagus, Sarawak, surveyed in 1980, which has measurements of 700 m (*2300 ft*) in length, 300 m (*980 ft*) in average width and with a minimum height of 70 m (*230 ft*).

World's greatest rivers

The importance of rivers still tends to be judged on their length rather than by the more significant factors – their basic areas and volume of flow. In this compilation all the world's river systems with a watercourse of a length of 2400 km (*1500 miles*) or more are listed with all three criteria where ascertainable.

Length (km)	(miles)	Name of Watercourse	Source	Course and Outflow	Basin Area (km²)	(miles²)	Mean Discharge Rate (m³/s)	(ft³/s)	Notes
1 6670	4145	Nile (Bahr-el-Nil)–White Nile (Bahr el Jabel)–Albert Nile–Victoria Nile–Victoria Nyanza–Kagera–Luvironza	Burundi: Luvironza branch of the Kagera, a feeder of the Victoria Nyanza	Through Tanzania (Kagera), Uganda (Victoria Nile and Albert Nile), Sudan (White Nile), Egypt to eastern Mediterranean	3 350 000	1 293 000	3 120	110 000	Navigable length to first cataract (Aswan 1545 km (*960 miles*). UAR Irrigation Dept. states length as 6700 km (*4164 miles*). Discharge 2600 m³/s (*93 200 ft³/s*) near Aswan. Delta is 23 960 km² (*9250 miles²*)
2 6448	4007	Amazon (Amazonas)	Peru: Lago Villafro, head of the Apurimac branch of the Ucayali, which joins the Marañon to form the Amazonas	Through Colombia to Equatorial Brazil (Solimões) to South Atlantic (Canal do Sul)	7 050 000	2 722 000	180 000	6 350 000	Total of 15 000 tributaries, ten over 1600 km (*1000 miles*) including Madeira (3380 km (*2100 miles*)). Navigable 3700 km (*2300 miles*) up stream. Delta extends 400 km (*250 miles*) inland
3 5970	3710	Mississippi-Missouri-Jefferson-Beaverhead–Red Rock	Beaverhead County, southern Montana, USA	Through N. Dakota, S. Dakota, Nebraska–Iowa, Missouri–Kansas Illinois, Kentucky, Tennessee, Arkansas, Mississippi, Louisiana, South West Pass into Gulf of Mexico	3 224 000	1 245 000	18 400	650 000	Missouri is 3725 km (*2315 miles*) the Jefferson–Beaverhead–Red Rock is 349 km (*217 miles*). Lower Mississippi is 1884 km (*1171 miles*). Total Mississippi from Lake Itasca, Minn. is 3778 km (*2348 miles*). Longest river in one country. Delta is 36 000 km² (*13 900 miles²*)
4 5540	3442	Yenisey-Angara-Selenga	Mongolia: Iderlin branch of Selenga (Selenge)	Through Buryat ASSR (Selenga feeder) into Ozero Baykal, thence via Angara to Yenisey confluence at Strelka to Kara Sea, northern USSR	2 580 000	996 000	19 000	670 000	Estuary 386 km (*240 miles*) long. Yenisey is 3540 km (*2200 miles*) long and has a basin of 2 050 000 km² (*792 000 miles²*). The length of the Angara is 1850 km (*1150 miles*)
5 5530	3436	Yangtze Kiang (Chang' Chiang)	Western China, Kunlun Shan Mts (as Dre Che and T'ungt'ien)	Begins at T'ungt'ien, then Chinsha, through Yünnan Szechwan, Hupeh, Anhwei, Kiangsu, to Yellow Sea	1 960 000	756 000	21 800	770 000	Flood rate (1931) of 85 000 m³/s (*3 000 000 ft³/s*). Estuary 190 km (*120 miles*) long
6 5410	3362	Ob'-Irtysh	Mongolia: Kara (Black) Irtysh via northern China (Sin Kiang) feeder of Ozero Zaysan	Through Kazakhstan into Russia Russian SFSR to Ob' confluence at Khanty Mansiysk, thence Ob' to Kara Sea, northern USSR	2 978 000	1 150 000	15 600	550 000	Estuary (Obskaya Guba) is 725 km (*450 miles*) long. Ob' is 3679 km (*2286 miles*) long, Irtysh 2960 km (*1840 miles*) long

Length (km)	(miles)	Name of Watercourse	Source	Course and Outflow	Basin Area (km²)	(miles²)	Mean Discharge Rate (m³/s)	(ft³/s)	Notes
7 4830	3000	Hwang Ho (Yellow River)	China: Tsaring-nor, Tsinghai Province	Through Kansu, Inner Mongolia, Honan, Shantung to Po Hai (Gulf of Chili), Yellow Sea, North Pacific	979 000	378 000	2800 to 22 650	100 000 to 800 000	Changed mouth by 400 km (250 miles) in 1852. Only last 40 km (25 miles) navigable. Longest river in one country in Asia
8 4700	2920	Zaïre (Congo)	Zambia–Zaïre border, as Lualaba	Through Zaïre as Lualaba along to Zaïre (Congo) border to N.W. Angola mouth into the South Atlantic	3 400 000	1 314 000	41 000	1 450 000	Navigable for 1730 km (1075 miles) from Kisangani to Kinshasa (formerly Léopoldville). Estuary 96 km (60 miles) long
9 4400	2734	Lena-Kirenga	USSR Hinterland of west central shores of Ozero Baykal as Kirenga	Northwards through Eastern Russia to Lapter Sea, Arctic Ocean	2 490 000	960 000	16 300	575 000	Lena Delta (45 000 km² (17 375 miles²)) extends 177 km (110 miles) inland, frozen 15 Oct to 10 July. Second longest solely Russian river
10 4345	2700	Amur-Argun' (He lung Chiang)	Northern China in Khingan Ranges (as Argun')	North along Inner Mongolian–USSR and Manchuria–USSR border for 3743 km (2326 miles) to Tartar Strait, Sea of Okhotsk, North Pacific	2 038 000	787 000	12 400	438 000	Amur is 2850 km (1771 miles) long (711 600 basin and 388 000 flow); China Handbook claims total length to be 4670 km (2903 miles) of which only 925 km (575 miles) is exclusively in USSR territory
11 4240	2635	Mackenzie-Peace	Tatlatui Lake, Skeena Mts, Rockies, British Columbia, Canada (as River Finlay)	Flows as Finlay for 400 km (250 miles) to confluence with Peace. Thence 1690 km (1050 miles) to join Slave (415 km (258 miles) which feeds Great Slave Lake whence flows Mackenzie (1733 km (1077 miles)) to Beaufort Sea	1 841 000	711 000	11 300	400 000	Peace 1923 km (1195 miles)
12 4180	2600	Mekong (Me Nam Kong)	Central Tibet (as Lants'ang), slopes of Dza-Nag-Lung-Mong, 5000 m (16 700 ft)	Flows into China, thence south to form Burma–Laotian and most of Thai–Laotian frontiers, thence through Cambodia to Vietnam into South China Sea	987 000	381 000	11 000	388 000	Max flood discharge 48 000 m³/s (1 700 000 ft³/s)
13 4184	2600	Niger	Guinea: Loma Mts near Sierra Leone border	Flows through Mali, Niger and along Benin border into Nigeria and Atlantic	1 890 000	730 000	11 750	415 000	Delta extends 128 km (80 miles) inland and 200 km (130 miles) in coastal length
14 4000	2485	Rio de la Plata-Paraná	Brazil: as Paranaíba. Flows south to eastern Paraguay border and into eastern Argentina	Emerges into confluence with River Uruguay to form Rio de la Plata, South Atlantic	4 145 000	1 600 000	27 500	970 000	After the 120 km (75 mile) long Delta estuary, the river shares the 340 km (210 mile) long estuary of the Uruguay called Rio de la Plata (River Plate)

Length (km)	(miles)	Name of Watercourse	Source	Course and Outflow	Basin Area (km²)	(miles²)	Mean Discharge Rate (m³/s)	(ft³/s)	Notes
15 3750	2330	Murray-Darling	Queensland, Australia: as the Culgoa continuation of the Condamine, which is an extension of the Balonne-branch of the Darling	Balonne (intermittent flow) crosses into New South Wales to join Darling, which itself joins the Murray on the New South Wales–Victoria border and flows west into Lake Alexandrina, in South Australia	1 059 000	408 000	400	14 000	Darling c. 2740 km (1700 miles) Murray 2590 km (1609 miles) or 1870 km (1160 miles)
16 3690	2293	Volga	USSR	Flows south and east in a great curve and empties in a delta into the north of the Caspian Sea	1 360 000	525 000	8 200	287 000	Delta exceeds 280 km (175 miles) inland and arguably 450 km (280 miles)
17 3540	2200	Zambezi (Zambeze)	Zambia: north-west extremity, as Zambezi	Flows after 72 km (45 miles) across eastern Angola for 354 km (220 miles) and back into Zimbabwe (as Zambezi), later forming border with eastern end of Caprivi strip of Namibia, thence over Victoria Falls (Mosi-Oatunya) into Kariba Lake. Thereafter into Mozambique and out into southern Indian Ocean	1 330 000	514 000	7 000	250 000	Navigable 610 km (380 miles) up to Quebrabasa Rapids and thereafter in stretches totalling another 1930 km (1200 miles)
3380	2100	Madeira-Mamoré-Grande (Guapay)	Bolivia: rises on the Beni near Illimani	Flows north and east into Brazil to join Amazon at the Ilha Tupinambaram	Tributary of No. 2		15 000	530 000	World's longest tributary, navigable for 1070 km (663 miles)
3200	2000	Purus (formerly Coxiuara)	Peru: as the Alto Purus	Flows north and east into Brazil to join Amazon below Beruri	Tributary of No. 2		—	—	World's second longest tributary. Navigable for 2575 km (1600 miles). Pronounced meanders
18 3185	1979	Yukon-Teslin	North-west British Columbia, Canada, as the Teslin	Flows north into Yukon Territory and into Alaska, USA, and thence into Bering Sea	855 000	330 000	—	—	Delta 136 km (85 miles) inland, navigable (shallow draft) for 2855 km (1775 miles)
19 3130	1945	St Lawrence	Head of St Louis River, Minn. USA	Flows into Lake Superior, thence Lakes Huron, Erie, Ontario to Gulf of St Lawrence and North Atlantic	1 378 000	532 000	10 200	360 000	Estuary 407 km (253 miles) long or 616 km (383 miles) to Anticosti Island. Discovered 1535 by Jacques Cartier
20 3033	1885	Rio Grande (Rio Bravo del Norte)	South-western Colorado, USA: San Juan Mts	Flows south through New Mexico, USA, and along Texas–Mexico border into Gulf of Mexico, Atlantic Ocean	445 000	172 000	85	3 000	

Length (km)	(miles)	Name of Watercourse	Source	Course and Outflow	Basin Area (km²)	(miles²)	Mean Discharge Rate (m³/s)	(ft³/s)	Notes
21 2900	1800	Ganges–Brahmaputra	South-western Tibet as Matsang (Tsangpo)	Flows east 1240 km (770 miles) south, then west through Assam, north-eastern India, joins Ganges (as Jamuna) to flow into Bay of Bengal, Indian Ocean	1 620 000	626 000	38 500	1 360 000	Joint delta with Ganges extends 360 km (225 miles) across and 330 km (205 miles) inland. Area 80 000 km² (30 800 mile²) the world's largest. Navigable 1290 km (800 miles)
22 2900	1800	São Francisco	Brazil: Serra da Canastra	Flows north and east into South Atlantic	700 000	270 000	—	—	Navigable 238 km (148 miles)
23 2880	1790	Indus	Tibet: as Sengge	Flows west through Kashmir, into Pakistan and out into northern Arabian Sea	1 166 000	450 000	5 500	195 000	Delta (area 8000 km² (3100 miles²)) extends 120 km (75 miles) inland
24 2850	1770	Danube	South-western Germany: Black Forest as Breg and Brigach	Flows (as Donau) east into Austria, along Czech–Hungarian border as Dunaj into Hungary (440 km (273 miles)) as Duna, to Yugoslavia as Dunav along Romania–Bulgaria border and through Romania as Dunarea to Romania–USSR border as Dunay, into the Black Sea	815 000	315 000	7 000	250 000	Delta extends 96 km (60 miles) inland. Flows into territory of 8 countries.
25 2810	1750	Salween (Nu Chiang)	Tibet in Tanglha range	Flows (as Nu) east and south into western China, into eastern Burma and along Thailand border and out into Gulf of Martaban, Andaman Sea	325 000	125 000	—	—	
26= 2740	1700	Tigris–Euphrates (Shatt al-Arab)	Eastern Turkey as Murat	Flows west joining the Firat, thence into Syria as Al Furāt and south and east into Iraq joining Tigris flowing into Persian Gulf at Iran–Iraq border as Shatt al-Arab	1 115 000	430 000	400 low 2 700 high	50 000	
26= 2740	1700	Tocantins	Brazil: near Brazilia as Paraná	Flows north to join Pará in the Estuary Baía de Marajó and the South Atlantic	905 000	350 000	10 000	360 000	Not properly regarded as an Amazon tributary. Estuary 440 km (275 miles) in length

Length (km)	(miles)	Name of Watercourse	Source	Course and Outflow	Basin Area (km²)	(miles²)	Mean Discharge Rate (m³/s)	(ft³/s)	Notes
26= 2740	1700	Orinoco	South-eastern Venezuela	Flows north and west to Colombia border, thence north and east to north-eastern Venezuela and the Atlantic	1036000	400000	—	—	
29 2650	1650	Si Kiang (Hsi-Chiang)	China: in Yünnan plateau as Nanp'an	Flows east as the Hungshui and later as the Hsün to emerge as the Hsi in the South China Sea. west of Hong Kong	602000	232300	—	—	Delta exceeds 145 km (90 miles) inland and includes the Pearl River or Chu
30 2600	1616	Kolyma	USSR: in Khrebet Suntarkhayata (as Kulu)	Flows north across Arctic Circle into eastern Siberian Sea	534000	206000	3800	134000	
31= 2575	1600	Amu-Dar'ya (Oxus)	Wakhan. Afghanistan, on the border with Sinkiang China	Flows west to form Tadzhik SSR–Afghan border as Pyandzh for 680 km (420 miles) and into Turkmen SSR as Amu-Dar'ya. Flows north and west into Aral'skoye More (Aral Sea)	465000	179500	—	—	
31= 2575	1600	Nelson–Saskatchewan	Canada: Bow Lake. British Colombia	Flows north and east through Saskatchewan and into Manitoba through Cedar Lake into Lake Winnipeg and out through northern feeder as Nelson to Hudson Bay	1072000	414000	2250	80000	Saskatchewan 1940 km (1205 miles) in length
33 2540	1575	Ural	USSR: South-central Urals	Flows south and west into the Caspian Sea	220000	84900	—	—	
2410	1500	Japurá	South-west Colombia in Cordillera Oriental as the Caquetá	Flows east into Brazil as Japurá, thence forms a left bank tributary of the Amazon opposite Tefé	Tributary of No. 2		—	—	
34 2410	1500	Paraguay	Brazil: in the Mato Grosso as Paraguai	Flows south to touch first Bolivian then Paraguayan border, then across Paraguay and then on to form border with Argentina. Joins the Paraná south of Humaitá	1150000 Tributary of No. 14	440000	—	—	

OTHER RIVERS OF 1600 km (*1000 miles*) OR LONGER

			Area of Basin	
km	miles	Name and Location	(km²)	(miles²)
2335	*1450*	Arkansas, USA	Tributary of No. 3	
2335	*1450*	Colorado, USA	590 000	*228 000*
2285	*1420*	Dnepr (Dnieper), USSR	503 000	*194 200*
2255	*1400*	Rio Negro, Colombia–Brazil	Tributary of No. 2	
2188	*1360*	Orange (Oranje), South Africa	1 020 000	*394 000*
2160	*1343*	Olenek, USSR	246 000	*95 000*
2140	*1330*	Syr-Dar'ya, USSR	453 000	*175 000*
2100	*1306*	Ohio–Allegheny, USA	Tributary of No. 3	
2010	*1250*	Irrawaddy, China–Burma	430 000	*166 000*
1969	*1224*	Don, USSR	422 000	*163 000*
1950	*1210*	Columbia-Snake, Canada–USA	668 000	*258 000*
1900	*1180*	Indigirka–Khastakh, USSR	360 000	*139 000*
1850	*1150*	Sungari (or Sunghua), China	Tributary of No. 10	
1850	*1150*	Tigris, Turkey–Iraq	Included in No. 26	
1790	*1112*	Pechora, USSR	326 000	*126 000*
1638	*1018*	Red River, USA	Tributary of No. 3	
1600	*1000*	Churchill, Canada	390 000	*150 000*
1600	*1000*	Uruguay, Brazil–Uruguay–Argentina	Included in No. 14	
1600	*1000*	Pilcomayao, Bolivia–Argentina–Paraguay	Tributary of Paraguay and sub-tributary of Paraná	

Note: Some sources state that the Amazon tributary the Juruá is over 1823 km (*1133 miles*) long and the Lena tributary, the Vitim, is 1931 km (*1200 miles*) long.

Waterfalls

WORLD'S GREATEST WATERFALLS – BY HEIGHT

	Total Drop			
Name	(m)	(ft)	River	Location
1. Angel (highest fall – 807* m/*2648 ft*)	979	*3212*	Carrao, an upper tributary of the Caroni	Venezuela
2. Tugela (5 falls) (highest fall – 410 m/*1350 ft*)	947	*3110*	Tugela	Natal, S. Africa
3. Utigård (highest fall – 600 m/*1970 ft*)	800	*2625*	Jostedal Glacier	Nesdale, Norway
4. Mongefossen	774	*2540*	Monge	Mongebekk, Norway
5. Yosemite (Upper Yosemite – 435 m/*1430 ft*; Cascades in middle section – 205 m/*675 ft*; Lower Yosemite – 97 m/*320 ft*)	739	*2425*	Yosemite Creek, a tributary of the Merced	Yosemite Valley, Yosemite National Park, Cal., USA
6. Østre Mardøla Foss (highest fall – 296 m/*974 ft*)	656	*2154*	Mardals	Eikisdal, W. Norway
7. Tyssestrengane (highest fall – 289 m/*948 ft*)	646	*2120*	Tysso	Hardanger, Norway
8. Kukenaam (or Cuquenán)	610	*2000*	Arabopó, upper tributary of the Caroni	Venezuela
9. Sutherland (highest fall – 248 m/*815 ft*)	580	*1904*	Arthur	nr. Milford Sound, Otago, S. Island, New Zealand
10. Kile (or Kjellfossen) (highest fall – 149 m/*490 ft*)†	561	*1841*	Naerö fjord feeder	nr. Gudvangen, Norway
11. Takkakaw (highest fall – 365 m/*1200 ft*)	502	*1650*	A tributary of the Yoho	Daly Glacier, British Columbia, Canada
12. Ribbon	491	*1612*	Ribbon Fall Stream	4·9 km (*3 miles*) west of Yosemite Falls, Yosemite National Park, Cal., USA
13. King George VI	487	*1600*	Utshi, upper tributary of the Mazaruni	Guyana
14. Roraima	457	*1500*	An upper tributary of the Mazaruni	Guyana
15. Cleve-Garth	449	*1476*	—	New Zealand
16. Kalambo	426	*1400*	S.E. feeder of Lake Tanganyika	Tanzania–Zambia
17. Gavarnie	421	*1384*	Gave de Pau	Pyrénées Glaciers, France
18. Glass	403	*1325*	Iguazú	Brazil

WORLD'S GREATEST WATERFALLS – BY HEIGHT

Name	Total Drop (m)	(ft)	River	Location
19. Krimmler fälle (4 falls, upper fall 140 m/*460 ft*)	390	*1280*	Krimml Glacier	Salzburg, Austria
20. Lofoi	383	*1259*	—	Zaïre
21. Silver Strand (Widow's Tears)	356	*1170*	Merced tributary	Yosemite National Park, Cal., USA

* There are other very high but seemingly unnamed waterfalls in this area.
† Some authorities would regard this as no more than a 'Bridal Veil' waterfall, *i.e.*, of such low volume that the fall atomizes.

WORLD'S GREATEST WATERFALLS – BY VOLUME OF WATER

Name	Maximum Height (m)	(ft)	Width (m)	(ft)	Mean Annual Flow (m³/s)	(ft³/s)	Location
Boyoma (formerly Stanley) (7 cataracts)	60	200 (total)	730	2400 (7th)	17 000	c. 600 000	Zaïre River nr. Kisangani
Guaíra (or Salto dos Sete Quedas) ('Seven Falls')	114	374	4846	15 900	13 000	470 000*	Alto Paraná River, Brazil–Paraguay
Khône	21	70	10 670	35 000	11 000 to 12 000	400 000 to 420 000	Mekong River, Laos
Niagara:							
Horseshoe (Canadian)	48	160	760	2500	6000	212 000	Niagara River, Lake Erie to Lake Ontario
American	50	167	300	1000	(Horseshoe – 94%)		Niagara River, Lake Erie to Lake Ontario
Paulo Afonso	58	192	—	—	2800	100 000	São Francisco River, Brazil
Urubu-punga	12	40	—	—	2700	97 000	Alto Paraná River, Brazil
Cataratas del Iguazú (Quedas do Iguaçu)	93	308	c. 4000	c. 13 000	1700	61 660	Iguazú (or Iguaçu) River, Brazil–Argentina
Patos-Maribondo	35	115	—	—	1500	53 000	Rio Grande, Brazil
Victoria (Mosi-oa-tunya):							
Leaping Water	108 (maximum)	355	33	108	1100	38 430	Zambezi River, Zambia
Main Fall			821	2694			Zimbabwe
Rainbow Falls			550	1800			
Churchill (formerly Grand)	75	245	—	—	850 to 1100	30 000 to 40 000	Churchill (formerly Hamilton) River, Canada
Kaieteur (Köituök)	225	741	90 to 105	300 to 350	660	23 400	Potaro River, Guyana

* The peak flow has reached 50 000 m³/s (1 750 000 ft³/s).

Yosemite Falls, from the meadow. It first drops 436 m (1430 ft) and goes from rock to rock for about 200 m (700 ft) and then to another fall of 98m (320 ft) – twice the height of Niagara. (Popperfoto)

Lakes of the world

Name	Country	Area (km²)	Area (miles²)	Length (km)	Length (miles)	Maximum Depth (m)	Maximum Depth (ft)	Average Depth (m)	Average Depth (ft)	Height of Surface above Sea-level (m)	Height of Surface above Sea-level (ft)
1. Caspian Sea	USSR and Iran	371 800	143 550	1225	760	980	3215	205	675	−28	−92
2. Superior	Canada and USA	82 350	31 800	560	350	406	1333	147	485	183	600·4
3. Victoria Nyanza	Uganda, Tanzania, and Kenya	69 500	26 828	360	225	80	265	39	130	1134	3720
4. Aral'skoye More (Aral Sea)	USSR	65 500	25 300	450	280	68	223	15·8	52	53	174
5. Huron	Canada and USA	59 600	23 010	330	206	228	750	59	196	176	579
6. Michigan	USA	58 000	22 400	494	307	281	923	83	275	176	579
7. Tanganyika	Zaire, Tanzania, Zambia and Burundi	32 900	12 700	725	450	1435	4708	—	—	772	2534
8. Great Bear	Canada	31 800	12 275	373	232	82	270	73	240	118	390
9. Ozero Baykal	USSR	30 500	11 780	620	385	1940	6365	700	2300	455	1493
10. Malawi (formerly Nyasa)	Tanzania, Malawi, and Mozambique	29 600	11 430	580	360	678	2226	272	895	472	1550
11. Great Slave	Canada	28 500	10 980	480	298	163	535	73	240	156	512
12. Erie	Canada and USA	25 700	9930	387	241	64	210	18·2	60	174	572
13. Winnipeg	Canada	24 500	9464	428	266	36	120	15	50	217	713
14. Ontario	Canada and USA	19 500	7520	310	193	237	780	79	260	75	246
15. Ozero Ladozhskoye (Lake Ladoga)	USSR	17 700	6835	193	120	225	738	51	170	3·9	13
16. Ozero Balkhash	USSR	17 400	6720	482	300	26	85	—	—	339	1112
17. Lac Tchad (Chad)	Niger, Nigeria, Chad, and Cameroon	16 300	6300*	209	130	3·9–7·3	13–24	1·5	5	240	787
18. Ozero Onezhskoye (Onega)	USSR	9600	3710	233	145	110	361	32	105	33	108
19. Eyre	Australia	9580	3700†	185	115	19·8	65	—	—	−11·8	−39
20. Lago Titicaca	Peru and Bolivia	8300	3200	209	130	278	913	100	328	3811	12 506
21. Athabasca	Canada	8100	3120	334	208	124	407	—	—	213	699
22. Saimaa complex‡	Finland	c. 8030	c. 3100	326	203	—	—	—	—	75	249
23. Lago de Nicaragua	Nicaragua	8000	3089	160	100	60	200	—	—	33	110

* Highly variable area between 11 000 and 22 000 km² (4250 and 8500 miles²).
† Highly variable area between 8030 and 15 000 km² (3100 and 5800 miles²).
‡ The Saimaa proper (The Lake of a Thousand Isles) is, excluding the islands, 1300 km² (c. 500 miles²).

LAKES UNDER 770 km² (*3000 miles²*) BUT OVER 5180 km² (*2000 miles²*)

Area (km²)	(miles²)	Name	Country
6400	2473	Turkana (formerly Rudolf)	Kenya and Ethiopia
6380	2465	Reindeer	Canada
6100	2355	*Issyk Kul'	USSR
5775	2230	Torrens	Australia
5565	2149	Vänern	Sweden
5450	2105	Winnipegosis	Canada
5375	2075	Mobutu Sese Seko (formerly Albert)	Uganda and Zaire
5300	2050	Kariba (dammed)	Zimbabwe and Zambia

* Has a maximum depth of 700 m (*2303 ft*) and an average depth of 320 m (*1050 ft*). The height of the surface above sea-level is 1600 m (*5279 ft*).

Forests

What is a forest?
Put very simply, a forest is a large area of land covered by trees. It is the type of vegetation most likely to result from the process of ecological succession, assuming that soil and weather conditions permit it. This is because trees grow taller and live considerably longer than other plants and so become the dominant members of the plant community.

Forests can be classified on various principles, but they are commonly recognized as tropical rain forests, temperate deciduous forests and the coniferous forests of the northern hemisphere.

Tropical rain forests
Tropical rain forests can be subdivided into two distinct types, the equatorial rain forest and the monsoon forest.

Equatorial rain forests
Equatorial rain forests are found in the low-altitude areas of the equatorial regions, where rainfall is heavy, usually occurring every day, and there is no dry season. The forests are thus hot and wet, typified by a wide range of broad-leaved evergreen trees. However, because of the competition for survival, individual species of trees tend to be scattered.

Because of the luxuriant and rapid growth, many trees tend to grow to enormous heights in their attempts to get clear of the other vegetation and obtain enough light. Beneath this high canopy of leaves can be found many epiphytes – plants which grow on the branches and trunks of the trees and obtain their nourishment from the air, rotting bark and leaves and suchlike. Lianas are also common, climbing up other trees in their attempts to obtain enough light. Closer to the ground can be found a wide variety and profuse growth of shrubs and plants, while an equally wide range of mammals, snakes and insects can be found both on the ground and amongst the trees.

A huge amount of organic material is locked up in such a forest. However, the soils that support the trees and plants tend to be very poor. If the forest cover is removed, the few nutrients tend to be leached out of the soil and an unproductive infertile area results.

Typical trees found in equatorial rain forests are the tropical hardwoods such as mahogany, as well as the rubber tree.

Such forests are found in the Amazon basin, the basin of the River Zaïre, and the East Indies.

Monsoon forests
Monsoon forests differ from equatorial rain forests in that there is a distinct dry season between the monsoonal wet seasons. Enough rain falls during the monsoons to support the broad-leaved forests, but leaves are shed during the dry seasons. The forests are not as dense as the equatorial rain forests, and there is not such a wide variety of species, teak being one of the best-known species.

The major monsoon forests are found in south-east Asia in such countries as India, Burma, Malaysia, Thailand, etc.

Temperate deciduous forests
This is the natural type of vegetation of the temperate regions, typified by trees that shed their leaves during the winter.

The canopy of leaves is not nearly as dense as with the tropical forests, so trees are shorter and the light filtering through allows shrubs and plants to grow at ground level. Because of the annual fall of leaves, which subsequently rot down, the soil tends to be nutrient-rich.

The major areas of temperate deciduous forest are North America, Europe and eastern Asia. However, because these are also areas of population concentration, much of these forests have been modified by human intervention, and many areas have been cleared.

Typical species found in temperate deciduous forests are oak, ash, beech, chestnut and maple.

Northern coniferous forests
In terms of area, the coniferous forests of the northern hemisphere are the largest. They cover a huge swathe of North America, and an even larger area of northern Europe, Scandinavia and northern Asia. Fingers of forest also reach down into more southerly latitudes along the lines of mountains, e.g. the Rockies, and occur on other 'islands' of mountains such as the Alps.

The trees do not shed their leaves at any one season but do so continuously. Growth, however, occurs only during the limited warm season of three or four months. The leaves have a number of adaptations to the climate, including a thick waxy skin and a small surface area, both designed to reduce water loss. The canopy of these forests is very dense, and the leaves that fall to the ground do not decompose readily. The soil therefore tends to be nutritionally very poor, there is little or no undergrowth, and wildlife is scarce.

There is little variety in the species of tree found in these forests, spruce, pine and fir being the most common types, providing the world with its supply of softwood timber and woodpulp.

Thorn forests
Thorn forest is a particular type of forest, not as extensive as the types mentioned already, but covering large enough areas to warrant a mention. It occurs in tropical and subtropical areas which have low rainfall, and therefore consists of trees that can shed their leaves during the dry periods, e.g. acacia.

Perhaps the largest area of thorn forest is the *caatinga* of north-eastern Brazil which, in addition to thorn trees, contains a wide variety of cacti.

The importance of forests

Forests constitute an enormous reserve of organic material, with the added attraction that they are self-replenishing. However, trees take a long time to grow; commercial softwoods take a minimum of 25 years to reach a marketable size, while the time it takes a hardwood to reach maturity may well exceed 100 years. It is easy to see that rapid deforestation will remove areas of forest faster then they can be replaced. Furthermore, if some areas of forest, such as tropical rain forests, are completely destroyed rather than selectively cropped, then the poor soil remaining will never again support a mature forest.

The economic implications of deforestation are obvious. What is perhaps less well understood are the ecological implications. For example, photosynthesis converts carbon dioxide to oxygen. Industrial man produces more and more carbon dioxide each year as a result of factory emissions, car exhausts, etc. If we destroy forests at the same time, what effect will this have on the balance of oxygen and carbon dioxide in the air? (See The Greenhouse Effect.)

Forests are also an important part of the water cycle, preventing rapid run-off and erosion of the soil, and returning water to the air as water vapour from their leaves.

The greenhouse effect

A number of trace gases present in the atmosphere reflect back to the Earth part of the infra-red radiation that would otherwise escape into space. This has not been a problem in the past since the equilibrium surface temperature established was a natural stabilizing force in the environment. However, the expansion in human activity over the last few hundred years has led to an increase in the abundance of these gases and hence to a general global warming. Up till the present the increase in temperature has been very gradual but now it may be accelerating.

The most familiar greenhouse effect gas is carbon dioxide, the increase in which is due almost entirely to fossil fuel burning. Carbon dioxide has an abundance in the atmosphere of about 0·3 per cent by volume and has increased by about one quarter since the start of the Industrial Revolution. It is likely to double in the next 100 years if left unchecked and this would lead to a disastrous 3°C increase in the average global temperature.

However, this temperature rise may be matched by a combination of a number of other gases which are also increasing in abundance, for example methane, which is produced either as a by-product of intensive animal and plant farming or by escaping from oil and gas developments, and nitrogen oxides which may be produced either naturally or from industrial and farming sources. The nitrogen oxides also lead to an increase in the troposphere of another greenhouse effect gas, ozone, the increase from this source more than compensating for the decrease resulting from a depletion in stratospheric ozone due to CFCs.

Chlorofluorocarbons (CFCs), used as aerosol spray propellants and refrigerants, could have contributed devastatingly to global warming if major attempts had not been made to curb their use. The abundance of CFCs is increasing alarmingly in the troposphere, where they can reside for many years, but their main effect is the depletion of the ozone layer in the stratosphere with the subsequent possibility of intense ultra-violet radiation reaching ground level. (See The Ozone Layer.)

Improvements in technology as well as legislation banning the manufacture of deleterious products may well lead to a reversal in the increase in these harmful gases, but if left unchecked then the marked global warming would lead to major changes in currently existing weather patterns which could lead to a destruction of the most fertile centres of agriculture. There is also the possibility of a partial melting of the polar ice caps and the consequent flooding of coastal areas, which are often heavily populated.

The ozone layer

Ozone resides mainly in the upper atmosphere (in the stratosphere) and is formed when ultra-violet radiation from the Sun breaks up oxygen molecules into highly reactive oxygen atoms. These immediately react with other oxygen molecules to form ozone (O_3). This gas also absorbs ultra-violet radiation and splits back into oxygen molecules and oxygen atoms, the latter again reacting with other oxygen molecules to form more ozone. This process occurs over and over again until the ozone molecules eventually react with oxygen atoms to form stable oxygen molecules. Thus an equilibrium is established and ozone absorbs most of the intense ultra-violet radiation that would otherwise reach the Earth's surface.

However, in the last few decades, much use has been made of chlorofluorocarbons (CFCs) such as F_{11} (CFCl$_3$) and F_{12} (CF$_2$Cl$_2$) as aerosol spray propellants and refrigerants. Their worldwide use has led to their discharge into the atmosphere in high abundance and after spending a few years in the troposphere they eventually migrate to the stratosphere where ultra-violet radiation dissociates them into chlorine atoms and other molecular fragments. These chlorine atoms catalyse the dissociation of ozone back into oxygen molecules and each such atom could destroy about 100 000 ozone molecules before being contained in stable molecules such as hydrogen chloride (HCl) and chlorine nitrate ClONO$_2$).

By this process the total ozone in the stratosphere has dropped a few per cent in the last decade but in specific areas such as Antarctica it has dropped an alarming 50 per cent overall and in the layer from 15–20 km (*9–13 miles*) above Antarctica it does at times drop by 95 per cent of its value a decade ago and is hence so thinly distributed as to be considered an ozone 'hole' in the atmosphere. The Antarctic atmosphere also suffers particularly from a marked decrease in ozone content during the spring period and these regional and seasonal effects appear to have a common origin which is associated with the weather pattern which exists in this area during winter. The winds sweep in a circular pattern around the pole and isolate the stratosphere inside the vortex. The resulting very low temperatures at high altitude stabilize ice particles in the clouds and these act as sites for a chemical reaction between the previously produced hydro-

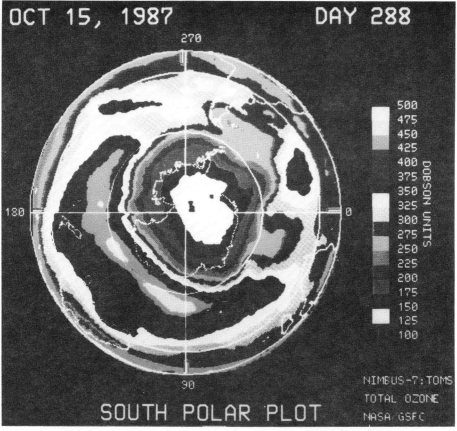

OCT 15, 1987   DAY 288

270

500
475
450
425
400
375
350
325
300
275
250
225
200
175
150
125
100

DOBSON UNITS

180   0

90

NIMBUS-7:TOMS

TOTAL OZONE

SOUTH POLAR PLOT   NASA/GSFC

Satellite map showing the 'hole' in the ozone layer over Antarctica on 15 October 1987. (Science Photo Library)

gen chloride and chlorine nitrate molecules. One of the reaction products is chlorine molecules which accumulate during the winter and then dissociate in the spring sunlight to produce an abundant new source of chlorine atoms in the Antarctic stratosphere and hence to a marked decrease in ozone which persists throughout the year.

Fortunately the Arctic area has a much weaker polar vortex and also has a higher average temperature than Antarctica during winter so that the ozone depletion effect is much less. However, even a mild decrease in the ozone layer in the densely populated northern hemisphere could ultimately have severe consequences, the increase in the more intense forms of ultra-violet radiation leading to health problems such as skin cancer and immune deficiencies as well as being a danger to crop and aquatic farming systems.

Although there may be underlying periodic decreases and increases in the stratospheric ozone density due to natural causes, the marked depletion in the last decade, which has been blamed on chlorofluorocarbons, has led to an attempt to introduce a worldwide ban on these chemicals and to replace them with less harmful products. However, there is now a large reservoir of CFCs in the troposphere and it may take a considerable period of time before their deleterious effect diminishes.

World's largest islands

All illustrations are to scale

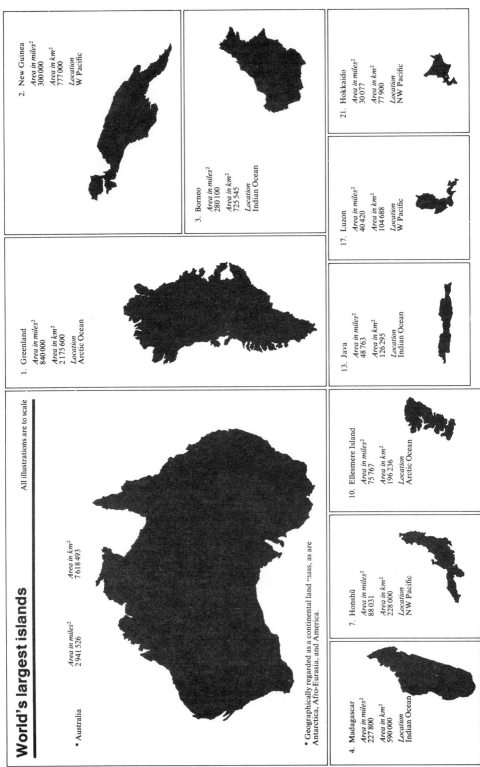

* Australia

Area in miles²
2 941 526

Area in km²
7 618 493

* Geographically regarded as a continental land mass, as are Antarctica, Afro-Eurasia, and America.

1. Greenland

Area in miles²
840 000

Area in km²
2 175 600

Location
Arctic Ocean

2. New Guinea

Area in miles²
300 000

Area in km²
777 000

Location
W Pacific

3. Borneo

Area in miles²
280 100

Area in km²
725 545

Location
Indian Ocean

4. Madagascar

Area in miles²
227 800

Area in km²
590 000

Location
Indian Ocean

7. Honshū

Area in miles²
88 031

Area in km²
228 000

Location
NW Pacific

10. Ellesmere Island

Area in miles²
75 767

Area in km²
196 236

Location
Arctic Ocean

13. Java

Area in miles²
48 763

Area in km²
126 295

Location
Indian Ocean

17. Luzon

Area in miles²
40 420

Area in km²
104 688

Location
W Pacific

21. Hokkaido

Area in miles²
30 077

Area in km²
77 900

Location
NW Pacific

5. **Baffin Island**
Area in miles²
183 810
Area in km²
476 065
Location
Arctic Ocean

6. **Sumatra**
Area in miles²
182 860
Area in km²
473 600
Location
Indian Ocean

8. Great Britain
Area in miles²
84 186
Area in km²
218 041
Location
North Atlantic

9. Victoria Island
Area in miles²
81 930
Area in km²
212 197
Location
Arctic Ocean

11. Celebes (Sulawesi)
Area in miles²
72 987
Area in km²
189 035
Location
Indian Ocean

12. South Island, New Zealand
Area in miles²
58 093
Area in km²
150 460
Location
SW Pacific

14. North Island, New Zealand
Area in miles²
44 281
Area in km²
114 687
Location
SW Pacific

15. Cuba
Area in miles²
44 217
Area in km²
114 522
Location
Caribbean Sea

16. Newfoundland
Area in miles²
43 359
Area in km²
112 300
Location
North-West Atlantic

18. Iceland
Area in miles²
39 769
Area in km²
103 000
Location
North Atlantic

19. Mindanao
Area in miles²
36 381
Area in km²
94 226
Location
W Pacific

20. Ireland (Northern Ireland and the Republic of Ireland)
Area in miles²
31 839
Area in km²
82 460
Location
North Atlantic

22. Hispaniola (Dominican Republic and Haiti)
Area in miles²
29 418
Area in km²
76 192
Location
Caribbean Sea

23. Sakhalin
Area in miles²
28 597
Area in km²
74 060
Location
NW Pacific

24. Tasmania
Area in miles²
26 215
Area in km²
67 900
Location
SW Pacific

25. Sri Lanka
Area in miles²
25 332
Area in km²
65 600
Location
Indian Ocean

GEOLOGY

Introduction

ROCKS OF THE EARTH'S CRUST

These are grouped in three principal classes:

(1) **Igneous rocks** have been solidified from molten *Magma*. These are divided into extrusive rock, viz. lava and pumice, or intrusive rock, such as some granites or gabbro which is high in calcium and magnesium and low in silicon. It should be noted that extreme metamorphism can also produce granitic rocks from sediment.

(2) **Sedimentary rocks** are classically formed by the deposition of sediment in water, viz. conglomerates (e.g. gravel, shingle, pebbles), sandstones and shales (layered clay and claystone). Peat, lignite, bituminous coal and anthracite are the result of the deposition of organic matter. Gypsum, chalk and limestone are examples of chemical sedimentation.

(3) **Metamorphic rocks** were originally igneous or sedimentary but have been metamorphosed (transformed) by the agency of intense heat, pressure or the action of water. Gneiss is metamorphosed granite; marble is metamorphosed limestone; and slate is highly pressurized shale. Metamorphic rocks made cleavable by intense heat and pressure are known generically as schist. Their foliate characteristics are shared by both gneiss and slate.

GEOCHEMICAL ABUNDANCES OF THE ELEMENTS

Element	Lithosphere* (per cent)	Hydrosphere† (per cent)
Oxygen	46·60	85·70
Silicon	27·72	0·000 35
Aluminium	8·13	0·000 000 1
Iron	5·00	0·000 000 004
Calcium	3·63	0·042
Sodium	2·83	1·078
Potassium	2·59	0·040
Magnesium	2·09	0·128
Titanium	0·44	0·000 000 000 1
Hydrogen	0·14	10·80
Manganese	0·095	0·000 000 001
Phosphorus	0·070	0·000 006
Fluorine	0·065	0·000 13
Sulfur	0·026	0·090
Carbon	0·025	0·002 6
Zirconium	0·017	0·000 000 000 1
Chlorine	0·013	1·935
Rubidium	0·009	0·000 012
Nitrogen	0·002	0·001 7
Chromium	0·001	0·000 000 033

* Assessment based on igneous rocks.
†Mean ocean concentrations based on a salinity of 3·5%.

GEO-CHRONOLOGY

Christian teaching as enunciated by Archbishop Ussher in the 17th century dated the creation of the Earth as occurring in the year 4004 BC. Lord Kelvin (1824–1907) calcaulated in 1899 that the Earth was of the order of possibly some hundreds of millions of years old. In 1905 Lord Rutherford suggested radioactive decay could be used as a measurement and in 1907 Boltwood showed that a sample of pre-Cambrian rock dated from 1640 million years before the present (BP) measured by the uranium-lead method.

Modern dating methods, using the duration of radioisotopic half-lives, include also the contrasts obtained from thorium-lead, potassium-argon, rubidium-strontium, rhenium-osmium, helium-uranium and in the recent range of up to 40 000 years BP carbon-14. Other methods include thermoluminescence since 1968 and racemization of amino acids since 1972 – the latter is dependent upon the change from optically active to inactive forms the decline of which varies with the elapse of time.

Glossary

ablation Removal of rock debris by wind action.

abrasion Wearing away of rock particles so that they get smaller; usually the action of particles rubbing together.

abstraction The absorption of one river by another.

acid rock Igneous rock with over 10% free quartz.

adobe A type of clay.

aeolian deposits Particles carried and deposited by the wind.

alluvial fan Sediment deposited by a river when there is a decrease in gradient.

alluvium Sands and gravels carried by rivers and deposited along the course of the river.

amber A type of resin.

amorphous Material having no regular arrangement.

anhedral Having no crystalline structure.

anticline Fold system in the form of an arch.

aquifer A stratum of rock containing water.

arenacious rocks Sedimentary sandstones, deposited by wind or water.

argillaceous rocks Sedimentary rocks deposited by water; usually marls, silts, shales, muds and clays.

artesian Aquifer between two impermeable strata, forming a basin such that a pressure head is generated.

ash Fine material formed by volcanic explosions.

asphalt Hydrocarbon, either solid or just fluid at normal temperatures.

asthenosphere The lowest part of the Earth's crust.

automorphic Grains having a crystal structure.

ball clay Reworked china clay.

banket A conglomerate of quartz.

basalt Fine-grained basic igneous rock, sometimes with a glassy characteristic.

basic rock Igneous rock containing little or no quartz.

basin Large depression.

batholith An intrusive mass of igneous rock.

bauxite An aluminium ore of aluminium oxide,

out of which the easily leached ions have been removed.

bedding plane Surface parallel to the surface of deposition. Some rocks split along bedding planes; others have less obvious physical characteristics such as changes of particle size.

biolith Rock of organic material, formed by organic processes.

bitumen Hydrocarbon mineral with a tarry texture, ranging from a viscous liquid to a solid.

black-band ironstone A sedimentary rock, formed principally from a form of coal and iron carbonate (siderite).

boghead coal Coal formed from algal and fungal material.

bort Anhedral diamonds in a granular mass.

boss Mass of igneous rock with steep contact surfaces with the surrounding rock.

boudinage Stretching of a rock layer to give a sausage-shaped structure.

boulder bed Sedimentary rock consisting of boulders together with fine-grained material.

breccia Sedimentary rock consisting of angular material of more than 2 mm (*0·08 in*) diameter.

brown coal Another name for lignite; a coal containing a low carbon content.

carbonate A large group of minerals, all having the carbonate group bond —CO_3 in common. They can be divided into sedimentary and non-sedimentary carbonates, limestone being the most common form of sedimentary carbonate.

carbonatite Magmatic rock consisting of calcium carbonate and occasionally other carbonates.

carstone A form of sandstone with a high proportion of limonite.

cassiterite Tin oxide ore.

cataclasis Mechanical break-up of rock.

caulk Barytes (barium sulphate).

celestite A strontium mineral found mainly in sedimentary rock.

ceylonite A spinel mineral.

chalcedony A silica-based mineral, found in many forms, some of which are semi-precious stone, e.g. agate, onyx, carnelian, jasper.

chalcocite Copper sulphide ore.

chalcopyrite One of the principal copper ores.

chalk Fine-grained white limestone, calcium carbonate.

charnockite Granular rock, mainly consisting of quartz, feldspar and hypersthene.

chernozem Black earth, with a high proportion of humus but a leached surface layer.

chert A form of silica, found as bands and nodules in sedimentary rocks.

chiastolite A form of aluminium silicate.

china clay Kaolin, formed by decomposition of feldspar in granite.

chlorite Green mineral consisting of talc units.

chondrites Stony meteorites.

chromite A chromium ore, containing iron.

chrysocolla A copper ore mineral, copper silicate.

chrysoprase A green chalcedony.

chrysotile A form of asbestos.

cinnabar Mercury sulphide, associated with volcanic activity.

citrine A yellow quartz.

clastic rock Fragments of rock, transported to a site of deposition and built up into a conglomerate.

clay A sedimentary rock with a fine particle structure and a soft plastic texture when wet.

cleat Jointing found in coal.

cleavage A flat plane of breakage, perhaps parallel to a crystal face.

cleavage plane Plane of fracture in a rock.

clint Ridge in limestone rock surface.

coal Stratified deposites of carbonaceous material, originally derived from vegetation, i.e. decayed vegetable matter.

cobble A rock particle, between 125 mm (*5 in*) and 250 mm (*10 in*) in diameter.

columnar structure Vertical columns or prisms, formed for example in lava and basalt, caused by the cooling of the rock.

competent Flow or flexion of a rock layer, in which it is not broken.

composite Igneous bodies which have more than one material in them, e.g. due to intrusion.

concretion Accumulations of sedimentary constituents in certain defined areas of rock, often around a nucleus.

conglomerate Rounded pebbles cemented together in one mass.

convergence Metamorphosis of two dissimilar rocks so that they become similar.

coral Organic skeletal material of dead aquatic animals.

corrasion Vertical erosion of a river bed by the river.

corundum Aluminium oxide, used as an abrasive and also found as gemstones, e.g. sapphire, ruby.

country rock Body of rock which encloses an intrusion by another rock, e.g. an igneous rock.

creep Gradual deformation of a rock by stress applied over a long time.

crystal Three-dimensional structure arising from the atomic structure of the substance. The symmetrical arrangement for a given substance means that the angles within the structure are constant for that substance.

culm Carboniferous rocks found in Devon and Cornwall.

cuprite Copper oxide, an important copper ore.

deflation Surface debris transported by the wind.

deformation Any change in a bed or stratum after it has been formed.

dendritic Branching into a many-fingered appearance.

denudation Any process that results in a lowering of the land surface.

detritus Particles of minerals and rocks formed by weathering and corrosion.

diamond A crystalline form of carbon. It has a cubic structure, distinguishing it from graphite.

diatomite The remains of unicellular plants called diatoms. It is a highly-absorbent powdery siliceous material.

diorite A coarse-grained igneous rock consisting of feldspar plus ferromagnesium minerals.

dog-tooth spar Calcite, crystallized into tooth-like forms.

dolerite An igneous rock similar to basalt.

dolomite Calcium magnesium carbonate, or limestone with a substantial proportion of magnesium carbonate.

dyke A sheet of igneous rock which cuts across the bedding or structural planes of the host rock.

earthquake Series of shock waves generated from a single point within the Earth's mantle or crust.

An unidentified microfossil found at Dogs Bay, Ireland. Microfossils include bacteria, diatoms, protozoa, some crustacea, larvae of some organisms and the skeletal fragments of others. They are important clues to the age of a rock where the sample available is small. (Science Photo Library)

elaterite An elastic or rubbery form of bitumen.
elvan A dyke of granite.
emerald A green form of beryl.
emery Fine granules of corundum and magnetite.
epicentre Point above the focus of an earthquake, on the Earth's surface.
epidiorite A metamorphic granular rock derived from igneous rock and containing the minerals of diorite.
epidotes Group of rock-forming silicate minerals.
erratic A stone or boulder carried by a glacier some distance from its source.
evaporite Sediment left by the evaporation of salt water.
extrusive Igneous rock that has flowed out at the Earth's surface.

fault A fracture plane in rock, along which displacement occurs.
feldspar Silicate minerals, in which the silicon ions are in part replaced with aluminium ions. Calcium, sodium and potassium feldspars exist, as do the rare barium feldspars.
feldspathoid Rock-forming silicates with sodium and/or potassium in the lattice structure. They never occur with quartz.
festoon bedding A type of cross-bedding.
fire clay Argillaceous fossil soil found with some coal seams.
flint A type of chert.
flowage Irreversible deformation, i.e. deforming a material beyond its elastic limit.
fluorite Calcium fluoride, found as veins in rocks.
fold A flexing of a rock stratum.
fool's gold Iron pyrites.

fossil Impression of an animal or plant, or its skeletal remains, buried by natural processes and then preserved.
fracture A break in a direction that is not a cleavage plane.
fuchsite Mica mineral containing chromium.
fulgurite A branching tube of fused silica, caused by lightning striking sandy soil.

gabbro Coarse-grained igneous rock, equivalent to basalt and dolerite. It contains feldspar, pyroxene and olivine as the major constituents.
galena Lead sulphide, the most important lead ore.
gangue The material in which an ore deposit from the metal is not extracted.
gannister Arenaceous stratum found beneath coal seams.
gas cap Collection of gas above an oil deposit.
gems Hard minerals, free from cleavages. Fragments are artificially cut and polished for decorative use.
garnet Semi-precious mineral with a wide range of colours, although red is the most commonly found.
geode A rock cavity containing crystals pointing inwards.
geosyncline Elongated basin, filled with sedimentary deposits. These deposits can then be deformed by orogenic forces.
glassy Non-crystalline rocks, caused for example by rapid cooling of molten material.
gneiss Banded rocks formed during metamorphosis. They are coarse-grained rocks.
granite Coarse-grained igneous rock, consisting essentially of quartz and feldspar and occurring as intrusive bodies in a variety of forms.
granule Rock particle of about 2–4 mm (0·08–0·16 in).
graphite Soft black form of carbon.
gravel The same size particles as granules.
grike A cleft in a limestone pavement.
grit Arenaceous rock in which the particle shape is angular.
gull A fissure caused by cambering, which tapers downwards and is then filled with material from above.
gumbo A soil which, when wet, gives a sticky mud.
gypsum An evaporite calcium sulphate mineral found in clays and limestone.

hade A fault plane's angle to the vertical.
haematite An iron-oxide iron ore.
halite Common salt, left as an evaporite.
hardness Mineral property propounded by Mohs. It measures the ability to scratch, as follows:

10	Diamond	5	Apatite
9	Corundum	4	Fluorite
8	Topaz	3	Calcite
7	Quartz	2	Gypsum
6	Orthoclase	1	Talc

hard-pan Strongly cemented material occurring below the surface of some sediments as a result of groundwater action.
hemicrystalline Rocks containing both crystalline and glassy material.
hornfels Fine-grained granular rock formed by thermal metamorphosis.
hornstone Fine-grained volcanic ash.
horst Area thrown up between two parallel faults.
humus Organic material in soil.

Iceland spar Variety of calcite.
igneous One of the three major divisions of rocks. Generally they are crystalline, although glassy forms can be found. They are either extrusive, i.e. produced on the Earth's surface as a result of volcanic action, or intrusive into other rocks, in which case they only appear on the Earth's surface if the surrounding rock is eroded.
impervious Does not allow the passage of water.
impregnation In-filling of pores by mineral material, e.g. oil.
inclusion A portion of one material totally enclosed within another.
incretion A cylindrical hollow concretion.
inlier Area of older rock surrounded by younger rock.
interbedded A layer of rock between two other layers.
intermediate rock Rock containing no more than 10% quartz plus a feldspar.
intrusion Igneous rock structure that has forced its way into pre-existing rock.

jade Gem stone of a hard compact aggregate.
jasper Red chert-like variety of chalcedony.
jet Homogeneous form of cannel coal or black lignite.
joint Fracture in a rock structure along which no movement can be observed.

kaolin The main constituent of china clay.
karst Type of limestone scenery produced by water erosion of limestone and dolomite rock. It is characterized by sinks, underground rivers and caves, and other erosion features, together with a red soil on the surface. If the soil is not present, then clints and grykes will be observed.
kieselguhr Diatomite.
kimberlite A brecciated peridotite containing mica and other minerals.
kyanite An aluminium silicate.

labradorite A type of feldspar.
lamination Thin layers of rock, each of them distinct.
landscape marble A type of limestone that, when sliced at right angles to the bedding plane, reveals patterns reminiscent of a landscape scene.
lapis lazuli A type of lazulite.
laterite An iron-oxide ore, out of which the easily-leached ions have been removed.
lava The mineral that flows out of volcanoes. It consists of molten silicates. In general they are basic, although acidic lava is known. Acidic lavas flow readily and tend to cover much larger areas, while basic lavas are more viscous.
leaching The removal of ions from a soil or rock by the through-flow of water.
lepidolite A type of mica.
lignite Brown coal, low in carbon content.
limestone A group of sedimentary rocks consisting of carbonates. Calcite and dolomite are the most important limestone rocks.
limonite A group of iron oxides and hydroxides.
lithifaction Formation of a large rock from small fragments.
loam Sand, silt and clay in equal proportions in a soil.
loess Deposits of wind-blown fine particles.
lustre The ability of minerals to reflect light.

magma The molten fluid within the Earth's crust. Igneous rocks are formed from the magma, although various constituents of the magma will be lost during this process of consolidation.
magnesite Magnesium carbonate.
magnetite An iron ore consisting of ferric oxide.
malachite A carbonate ore of copper.
marble Metamorphosed limestone, usually with other compounds giving marble its recognizable appearance.
marl A mudstone with a high calcium content.
metamorphism The process of heating, pressure and chemical action which cause rocks to change from one form to another in the Earth's crust.
mica A large group of silica-based minerals, characterized by the fact that the crystal structure gives cleavage into flat flexible sheets.
migmatite A form of gneiss.
mineral A chemical, formed naturally, with a constant composition and structure.
mobile belt A part of the Earth's crust in which metamorphosis, igneous activity and deformation occur.
monzonite Coarse igneous rock with a high feldspar content.
mud Wet clay soil in a near-liquid state.
mudstone A type of argillaceous rock, similar to shale, but without the property of splitting along bedding planes.
muscovite A type of mica.

natural gas Gaseous hydrocarbons found together with oil deposits.
neck A volcanic plug.
nodule A rounded concretion.

obsidian A type of rhyolite with a black glassy sheen to it.
oceanite A type of basalt.
oil Often called petroleum, oil is naturally occurring liquid hydrocarbon. It is invariably found in association with saline water and natural gas, and often with solid hydrocarbons.
oil shale A dark argillaceous rock. It does not contain liquid oil, but a solid organic material kerogen which gives oil on distillation.
olivine A group of silicates, containing ferrous iron and magnesium. They largely occur in igneous rocks.
onyx A type of banded chalcedony.
oolith A rounded lump of rock formed by accretion round a nucleus. Ooliths usually contain calcium minerals.
opal An amorphous type of silica, believed to have been derived from silica gel.
ore Mixture of the wanted mineral, the useless minerals and the surrounding rock.
orogeny The process or period of mountain building.
outlier A relatively small area of young rock, surrounded by older rock.
overburden Useless soil, etc., found on top of a bed of useful mineral.

peat An early form of coal. It is a dark-brown to black mass of partially decomposed vegetation.
pebble Rock fragment of 5–60 mm (*0·2-2·3 in*) diameter.
pedalfer Leached soil in a region with high rainfall.
pegmatite Coarse-grained igneous rock, usually granitic. Very long crystals may be apparent.

Sand particles from a beach near Coles House, Barbados. Sand is formed from arenaceous rock, a type of detrital sedimentary rock, usually sandstone. Particle size ranges from 1/16 mm to 2 mm. (Science Photo Library)

peridot Gem-quality olivine.
permeability Ability of water to percolate through a rock.
pervious Water passes through a pervious rock via cracks, fissures, etc.
pitchblende Uranium oxide ore.
plug The solidified lava and other material left in the neck of a volcano. Often the surrounding material is subsequently eroded away.
plutonic Igneous material of a deep-seated origin, i.e. originating from the magma.
podsol Soil found in cool temperate humid zones, in which substantial leaching has occurred.
porous Water is held in or passes through a rock in cavities between the mineral grains.
pudding stone A conglomerate.
pumice One of the pyroclastic rocks thrown out of a volcano. It contains a high proportion of air space.
pyrite Iron sulphide.
pyroclastic rock This can either by liquid lava thrown out of the volcano, or solid lumps of surrounding rock broken up by the volcanic action.

quartz A silica mineral with three different forms. Sand is the most common. Low quartz is a crystalline form, occurring in a variety of colours. At 573°C (*1063°F*) low quartz gives rise to high quartz, but its natural occurrence is rare.

red bed Sedimentary rocks containing a high proportion of ferric minerals, giving them a reddish colour.
residual deposit Minerals left when part of a rock is dissolved or leached away.
rhyolite Fine-grained or glassy volcanic rock, rich in quartz.
rock A mass of mineral material, usually consisting of more than one mineral type.
rock crystal Clear form of quartz.
ruby A red transparent form of corundum.
rudaceous rock Sedimentary rocks deposited as detritus by water or air, and divided into conglomerates and breccias.
rutile Titanium oxide ore.

salt dome Under pressure salt behaves like a magma, and can be forced up through an overlying sediment as a salt dome.
sand A type of quartz, formed of fine particles. It can also be taken to mean any fine particles of 0·0625–2 mm (*0·0025–0·08 in*).
sandstone Arenaceous rocks, consisting of fine grains cemented together by a variety of minerals.
sapphire A blue transparent form of corundum.
schist Metamorphosed rocks with the constituent minerals arranged in parallel.
scree Fragments formed by the weathering of rocks.
sedimentary rock Rock formed out of the material resulting from erosion and weathering, along with organic material. The principal sedimentary rocks are sandstone, limestone and shale.
shale A sedimentary rock composed of clay particles. The particles are orientated parallel to the bedding plane, giving the rock its characteristic fissility.
shingle Gravel or pebbles found on beaches.
silica Silicon dioxide, which can take a variety of forms, e.g. quartz, chalcedony, opal.
silicates The most prolific mineral group in the Earth's crust. They are based on a silicon oxide

structure, but a variety of other elements and ions can be substituted in this structure, particularly aluminium. The group includes the clays, the feldspars, the garnets, the micas, the silicas.
sill A sheet of igneous rock, lying along a bedding plane.
silt A type of argillaceous rock.
slate Argillaceous rock that has been metamorphosed. The slates all show cleavage, and may have new minerals showing up as marks or even crystals.
soapstone Any greasy rock, although usually applied to talc rocks.
soil The loose weathered material covering most of the Earth's land surface.
spinel A group of minerals, including magnetite and chromite.
stalactite Calcium carbonate formed as a spike hanging down from the ceiling in a limestone cave.
stalagmite Calcium carbonate formed as a spike standing up from the floor in a limestone cave.
stock An intrusive mass of igneous rock, smaller than a batholith.
streak A mineral's colour when in a powdered state, e.g. formed by scratching it.
subsoil Partly weathered rock lying between the soil and the bedrock.
syenite A group of coarse-grained igneous rocks containing feldspars and feldspathoids.

talc Magnesium silicate, the softest common mineral.
tar pit Areas where asphalt or bitumen rises to the surface from an underground hydrocarbon source.
terra rossa Red clayey soil formed as a result of carbonates being leached out of limestone.
topaz A clear semi-precious form of aluminium silicate.
tor Piles of un-kaolinized granite blocks, left by differential weathering of the rock around them.
touchstone A very hard fine-grained black form of basalt or chert.
tripoli A type of diatomite.
tufa A calc tufa is a chalky deposit of calcium carbonate, found mainly in limestone.
tundra Soils produced under extremely cold conditions.

ultrabasic rock Igneous ferromagnesium rock, with little or no feldspar, quartz or feldspathoid in it.
ultramarine A type of feldspathoid.

valley fill Loose material filling or partly filling a valley.
vein A sheet of mineral which has intruded into a fissure or joint of a rock.

water table The upper limit of the groundwater saturation.
weathering The breaking down of stationary rocks by mechanical means, e.g. action of ice and the Sun, and chemical means.
wind erosion Abrasive action of wind-driven particles of sand against stationary rocks.
wolframite A tungsten ore.

xenolith An inclusion of pre-existing rock in an igneous rock.

zeolite Group of silicates containing water of crystallization, and capable of reversible dehydration. They can act as powerful base exchangers.
zircon Zirconium silicate.

Geo-chronology

For early phases of the Earth's history, radiometric dating is the main method of dating events. Before a thousand million years ago dates may err as much as 10 per cent. When fossils became abundant at the start of the Palaeozoic era, the sequence is best defined by those fossils in stratigraphic sequence and assigning radiometric dates to these. Then, by interpolation, a date can be put forward for a geological event, or for the bed in which a fossil has been found. The table below is based on revisions up to 1982 of the timescale put forward by the US Geological Survey of 1980. Myr = one million years ago.

The four main geological divisions, going backwards in time, are: The Cenozoic (Gk *kainos*, new or recent, *zo-os*, living), the Mesozoic (Gk *mesos*, middle), the Palaeozoic (Gk *palaios*, ancient) and the Proterozoic (Gk *protos*, first). The earliest known life forms, spherical microfossils, date back to 3400 Myr.

DATES OF STARTS OF PHASES IN THE GEOLOGICAL TIMESCALE
(Myr = 1 million years ago)

	Myr
Hadean era	est. 4450
Archean era	3800
Proterozoic era	
Early Proterozoic	2500
Middle Proterozoic	1600
Late Proterozoic	900
Paleozoic era	
Early Cambrian	
Georgian	570
Middle Cambrian	
Acadian	550
Late Cambrian	
Potsdamian	530
Early Ordovician	
Tremadocian	520
Arenigian	507
Llanvirnian	493
Llandeilian	476
Late Ordovician	
Caradocian	458
Ashgillian	447
Silurian	
Llandoverian	435
Wenlockian	430
Ludlovian	423
Downtonian	417
Early Devonian	
Gedinnian	410
Siegenian	399
Emsian	394
Middle Devonian	
Eifelian/Couvinian	389
Givetian	383
Late Devonian	
Frasnian	378
Famennian	370
Early Carboniferous	
Tournaisian	360
Visean	348
Late Carboniferous	
Namurian	335
Westphalian	316
Stephanian	306

Early Permian	
Sakmarian	290
Artinskian	278
Kungurian	268
Late Permian	
Kazanian	256
Tatarian	249
Mesozoic era	
Early Triassic	
Scythian	245
Middle Triassic	
Anisian	240
Ladinian	235
Late Triassic	
Karnian	230
Norian	225
Rhaetian	216
Early Jurassic	
Hettangian	208
Sinemurian	205
Pliensbachian	197
Toarcian	188
Aalenian	182
Middle Jurassic	
Bajocian	177
Bathonian	170
Late Jurassic	
Callovian	164
Oxfordian	159
Kimmeridgian	154
Tithonian	145
Early Cretaceous	
Berriasian	138
Valanginian	133
Hauterivian	126
Barremian	123
Aptian	120
Albian	114
Late Cretaceous	
Cenomanian	96
Turonian	92
Coniacian	89
Santonian	88
Campanian	84
Maastrichtian	72
Cenozoic era	
Tertiary period	
Early Paleocene	
Danian	67
Late Paleocene	
Thanetian	61
Early Eocene	
Ypresian	55
Middle Eocene	
Lutetian	50
Bartonian	45
Late Eocene	
Priabonian	41
Early Oligocene	
Rupelian	37
Late Oligocene	
Chattian	33
Early Miocene	
Aquitanian	25
Burdigalian	19·5
Middle Miocene	
Langhian	14·7
Serravallian	13·3
Late Miocene	
Tortonian	11·5
Messinian	6.7

Early Pliocene	
Zanclean, etc.	5·3
Late Pliocene	
Piacenzian	3·25
Quaternary period	
Early Pleistocene	1·8
Late Pleistocene	730 000yr
Holocene	10 300yr

Late Mammal Stages (Europe)

Late Pliocene	
Early Villafranchian	3·25 Myr
Late Villafranchian	2·60 Myr
Pleistocene	
Early Biharian	1·90 Myr (?1·80 Myr)
Middle Biharian	c. 1·5 Myr
Late Biharian	730 000 yr
Toringian	480 000 yr

Gemstones

Gemstones are minerals possessing a rarity and usually a hardness, colour or translucency which gives them strong aesthetic appeal. Diamond, emerald, ruby and sapphire used to be classed as 'precious stones' and all others as 'semi-precious'. This distinction is no longer generally applied. The principal gemstones in order of hardness are listed below with data in the following order: name; birthstone (if any); chemical formula; classic colour; degree of ahrdness on Mohs scale 1–10; principal localities where found and brief notes on outstanding specimens. A metric carat is one-fifth of a gram.

Diamond (birthstone for April): C (pure crystalline isotope); fiery bluish-white; Mohs 10·0; S., S.W. and E. Africa and India with alluvial deposits in Australia, Brazil, Congo, India, Indonesia, Liberia, Sierra Leone and USSR (Urals). Largest uncut: *Cullinan* 3106 carats (over 20 oz) by Capt. M. F. Wells, Premier Mine, Pretoria, S. Africa, on 26 Jan 1905. Cut by Jacob Asscher of Amsterdam 1909. Largest cut: *Cullinan I* or *Star of Africa* from the above in British Royal Sceptre at 530·2 carats. *Koh-i-nor* originally 186 now re-cut to 106 carats; also in British Crown Jewels. The largest blue diamond is the 44·4 carat vivid blue *Hope Diamond* from Killur, Golconda, India, *ante* 1642 in the Smithsonian Institution, Washington DC, since November 1958. The rarest colour is blood red.

Diamonds can be produced by 1400°C (2500°F) and 600 000 atmospheres. About 55 000 000 carats are mined annually with Antwerp the world's largest market with an annual turnover of £1000 million.

It takes an average 280 tons of diamond-bearing ore to yield a 1 carat stone. The average diamond mined is 0·8 of a carat and less than 15% are used for jewellery (1 carat = 0·2 g).

Ruby (birthstone for July): Al_2O_3 (red corundum with trace of chromic oxide); 9·0; Brazil, Burma, Sri Lanka, Thailand. Largest recorded gem ruby from Burma *ante* 1886 weighed 400 carats. Most valuable of all gems per carat.

Sapphire (birthstone for September): Al_2O_3 (corundum); any colour but red, classically dark blue; 9·0; Australia, Burma, Sri Lanka, Kashmir, USA (Montana). Largest cut blue star: *Star of India*, 563·5 carats from Sri Lanka now in American Museum of Natural History, New York City. Largest star sapphire: 733 carat *Black Star of Queensland* from 1165 carat rough, found in 1934, owned by Kazanjian Foundation, Los Angeles.

Alexandrite (birthstone for June, alternative to pearl): $Al_2[BeO_4]$ (chrysoberyl with chromium traces); green (daylight) but red (artificial light); 8·5; Brazil, Moravia, Sri Lanka, USSR (Urals), Zimbabwe.

Cat's Eye: $Al_2[BeO_4]$ (chrysoberyl); yellowish to brownish-green with narrow silken ray; 8·5.

Topaz (birthstone for November): $Al_2SiO_4F_2$; tea-coloured; 8·0; Australia, Brazil, Sri Lanka, Germany, Namibia, USSR. The largest recorded is one of 270 kg (596 lb) from Brazil.

Spinel: $MgAl_2O_4$ with trace of Fe_2O_3; red; 8·0; mainly Burma, Sri Lanka, India and Thailand.

Emerald (birthstone for May): $Al_2Be_3Si_6O_{18}$ (beryl); vivid green; 7·5–8·0; Austria, Colombia, Norway, USA (N. Carolina), USSR (Urals), Zambia; largest recorded beryl prism (non-gem quality) 61·2 kg (135 lb) from Urals; largest beryl crystal 16 200 carats, Musó, Columbia. Devonshire stone of 1383·95 carats presented in 1831 is from the same area.

Aquamarine (birthstone for March): $Al_2Be_3Si_6O_{18}$ (beryl); pale limpid blue; 7·5–8·0; found in Brazil, Malagasy and USSR and elsewhere, including N. Ireland; largest recorded 110 kg (243 lb) near Marambaia, Brazil, 1910.

Garnet (birthstone for January): silicates of Al, Ca, Cr, Fe, Mg, Ti, V, Zr; purplish-red (Almandine, $Fe_3Al_2[SiO_4]_3$), 7·5–8·0; India, Sri Lanka, USA (Arizona), green (Demantoid, $Ca_3Fe_2[SiO_4]_3$), 6·5–7·0; USSR (Siberia and Urals), black (Malanite, $TiCa_3$ (Fe, Ti, Al)$_2$ [SiO_4]$_3$), 6·5.

Zircon: $Zr (SiO_4)$; colourless but also blue and red-brown (hyacinth); 7·0–8·5; Australia (N.S.W.), Burma, France, Norway, Sri Lanka, India, North America, Thailand, USSR (Siberia).

Tourmaline (birthstone for October, alternative to opal): complex boro-silicate of Al, Mg alkalis; notably deep green, bluish green, deep red; 7·0–7·25; Brazil, Sri Lanka, USA, USSR (Siberia).

Rock Crystal (birthstone for April, alternative to diamond): SiO_2; colourless; 7·0; Brazil, Burma, France, Madagascar, Switzerland, USA (Arkansas). The largest recorded crystal ball is one of 48 kg (106 lb) from Burma now in the US National Museum, Washington DC.

Rose Quartz: SiO_2; coarsely granular pale pink; 7·0; Bavaria, Brazil, Finland, Namibia, USA (Maine), USSR (Urals).

Cairngorm (Smoky Quartz): SiO_2; smoky yellow to brownish; 7·0; Brazil, Madagascar, Manchuria, Scotland (Cairngorm Mountains), Switzerland, USA (Colorado), USSR (Urals).

Amethyst (birthstone for February): SiO_2; purple; 7·0; Brazil, Sri Lanka, Germany, Madagascar, Uruguay, USSR (Urals).

Chrysoprase (chalcedony form) (birthstone for May, alternative to emerald): SiO_2 with nickel hydroxide impurity; apple green (opaque); 6·5–7·0; Germany, USA.

Jade: Jadeite $Na(Al,Fe^{+3})Si_2O_6$; dark to leek green; 6·5–7·0; Burma, China, Tibet (pale green and less valuable form is nephrite, $Ca_2(Mg,/Fe^{+3})_5Si_8O_{22}(OH)_2)$, China, Canada, New Zealand, USA.

Cornelian (chalcedony form), often (wrongly) spelt carnelian (birthstone for July, alternative to ruby): SiO_2 with ferric oxide impurity; blood red to yellowish-brown; 6·5–7·0; widespread, including Great Britain.

Agate (striped chalcedony): SiO_2; opaque white to pale grey, blue; 6·6–7·0; variety is moss agate (milky white with moss-like inclusions, often green); Brazil, Germany, India, Madagascar, Scotland.

Onyx: a black and white banded agate (see Agate).

Sardonyx (birthstone for August, alternative to peridot): a reddish-brown and white-banded agate (see Agate).

Jasper (chalcedony): SiO_2 with impurities; brown (manganese oxide), red (ferric oxide), yellow (hydrated ferric oxide), opaque; 6·5–7·0; Egypt, India.

Peridot (green olivine) (birthstone for August): $(Mg,Fe)_2[SiO_4]$; green; 6·5–7·0; Australia (Queensland), Brazil, Burma, Norway, St John's Island (Red Sea) now Zabargad Island, USA (Arizona).

Bloodstone or Blood Jasper (chalcedony) (birthstone for March, alternative to aquamarine): SiO_2; dark green with red spots (oxide of iron); 6·0–7·0.

Moonstone (feldspar) (birthstone for June, alternative to pearl): $K[AlSi_3O_8]$; white to bluish, iridescent; 6·0–6·5; Brazil, Burma, Sri Lanka.

Opal (birthstone for October): $SiO_2.nH_2O$; rainbow colours on white background; other varieties include fire opal, water opal, black opal; 5·0–6·5; Australia, Mexico and formerly Hungary, USA. The largest recorded is one of 34 215 carats named *Desert Flame of Andamooka* found in Australia in 1969.

Turquoise (birthstone for December); $CuAl_6[(OH)_8(PO_4)_4]5H_2O$; sky blue; 5·5–6·0; Egypt (Sinai Peninsula), Iran, Turkey, USA (California, Nevada, New Mexico, Texas).

Lapis Lazuli (birthstone for September, alternative to sapphire): $(Na,Ca)_8[(S,Cl,SO_4)_2(AlSiO_4)_6]$; deep azure blue, opaque; 5·5–5·75; Afghanistan, Chile, Tibet, USSR (Lake Baykal area).

Osidian (glassy lava): green or yellowish-brown; 5·0–5·5; volcanic areas.

Non-mineral gem material

Amber (organic): about $C_{40}H_{64}O_4$; honey yellow, clear, or paler yellow, cloudy; 2·0–2·5; mainly Baltic and Sicily coasts. A variety is fly amber in which the body of an insect is encased.

Coral (polyps of *Coelenterata*): varied colourations including Blood or Red Coral; Australasia, Pacific and Indian Oceans.

Pearl (birthstone for June): secretions of molluscs, notably of the sea-water mussel genus *Pinctada* and the fresh-water mussel *Quadrula*; western Pacific and Indian Oceans; largest recorded is the *Hope Pearl* weighing nearly 85 g (*3 oz*), circumference 114 mm (*4·5 in*). A nacreous mass of 6·4 kg (*14 lb 2 oz*) from a giant clam (*Tridacna gigas*) was recovered in the Philippines in 1934 and is known as the *Pearl of Allah*.

Earthquakes

It is estimated that each year there are some 500 000 detectable seismic or micro-seismic disturbances of which 100 000 can be felt and 1000 cause damage.

It was not until as recently as 1874 that subterranean slippage along overstressed faults became generally accepted as the cause of tectonic earthquakes. The collapse of caverns, or mine-workings, volcanic action, and also possibly the very rare event of a major meteoric impact can cause tremors. The study of earthquakes is called seismology.

The two great seismic systems are the Alps–Himalaya great circle and the circum-Pacific belt. The foci below the epicentres are classified as shallow (<50 km deep), intermediate (50–200 km) and deep (200–700 km).

In 1954 the Gutenberg-Richter scale was introduced to compare the strengths of seismic shocks. The scale measures the magnitude M_s. $M_s = \frac{2}{3}(\log_{10}E - 11·8)$ where E is the energy released in dyne/cm. In 1977 the more satisfactory Kanamori scale, using the concept of seismic moment, devised by K. Aki (Japan) in 1966, was adopted. It measures the magnitude Mw. $Mw = \frac{2}{3}[\log_{10}(2E \times 10^4) - 10·7]$. The Lebu shock, south of Concepción, Chile, on 22 May 1960 uniquely registered 9·5 on the Kanamori scale indicating an estimated energy of 10^{26} ergs. No earthquake has ever reached 9 on the Gutenberg-Richter scale. It has been estimated, however, that the great Lisbon earthquake of 1 Nov 1755, 98 years before the invention of seismographs, would have rated between 8¾ and 9. The death toll was 60 000.

Historic earthquakes

The five earthquakes in which the known loss of life has exceeded 100 000 have been:

c. 1·1 m	E. Mediterranean	*c.* July 1201
830 000	Shensi Province, China	2 Feb 1556
300 000	Calcutta, India	11 Oct 1737
242 000*	Tangshan, China (8.2R)	27 July 1976
180 000	Kansu Province, China (landslides) (8·6R)	16 Dec 1920
142 807	Kwanto Plain, Honshu, Japan (8·3R)	1 Sept 1923

The material damage done in the Kwanto Plain, which includes Tokyo, was estimated at £1 000 000 000.

Other notable earthquakes during this century with loss of life have been:

1906 Colombian coast (31 Jan) (8·6R; 8·8K)
1906 San Francisco, USA (18 Apr) (452) (8·3R)

* Unaccountably reduced to this figure on 22 Nov 1979 from 655 237 unannounced on 4 Jan 1977.

1908	Messina, Italy (28 Dec) (80 000) (7·5R)
1915	Avezzano, Italy (13 Jan) (29 970)
1932	Gansu Province, China (26 Dec) (70 000) (7·6R)
1935	Quetta, India (31 May) (600 000) (7·5R)
1939	Erzincan, Turkey (27 Dec) (30 000) (7·9R)
1950	Assam, India (15 Aug) (1500) (8·6R; 8·6K)
1952	Kamchatka, USSR (4 Nov) (8·5R; 9·0K)
1957	Andreanol, Aleutian Is., USA (9 Mar) (8·3R; 9·1K)
1960	Agadir, Morocco (29 Feb) (12 000) (5·8R)
1960	Lebu, Chile (22 May) (8·3R; 9·5K)
1964	Anchorage, Alaska (28 Mar) (131) (8·5R)
1970	Northern Peru (31 May) (66 800) (7·7R)
1971	Los Angeles (9 Feb) (64) (6·5R)
1972	Nicaragua (23 Dec) (5000) (6·2R)
1976	Guatemala (4 Feb) (22 700) (7·5R)
1976	Tangshan, China (27 July) (see above) (8·2R)
1977	Bucharest, Romania (4 Mar) (1541) (7·5R)
1978	Tabas, N.E. Iran (16 Sept) (25 000) (7·7R)
1980	El Asnam, Algeria (10 Oct) (2327) (7·5R)
1980	Potenza, Italy (23 Nov) (c. 3000) (6·8R)
1982	North Yemen (13 Dec) (2800) (6·0R)
1983	Eastern Turkey (30 Oct) (1233) (7·1R)
1985	Mexico (19 Sept) (9500) (8·1R)
1988	Armenia (7 Dec) (25 000) (6·8R)

R = Gutenberg-Richter scale. K = Kanamori scale.

Beno Gutenberg with the Gutenberg-Richter scale, introduced to compare the strengths of seismic shocks in 1954.

Attendant phenomena include:
(i) *Tsunami* (wrongly called tidal waves) or gravity waves which radiate in long, low oscillations from submarine disturbances at speeds of 725–790 kph (*450–490 mph*). The 1883 Krakatoa *tsunami* reached a height of 41 m (*135 ft*) and that off Valdez, Alaska, in 1964 attained a height of 67 m (*220 ft*). The word *tsu* (wild) *nami* (wave) is Japanese.
(ii) *Seiches* (a Swiss-French term of doubtful origin, pronounced sash). Seismic oscillations in landlocked water. Loch Lomond had a 60 cm (*2 ft*) seiche for 1 hr from the 1755 Lisbon 'quake.
(iii) *Fore and After Shocks.* These often occur before major 'quakes and may persist after these for months or years.

British earthquakes

The earliest British earthquake of which there is indisputable evidence was that of AD 974 felt all over England. The earliest precisely recorded was that of 1 May 1048, in Worcester. British earthquakes of an intensity sufficient to have raised or moved the chair of the observer (scale 8 on the locally used Davison's scale) have been recorded thus:

25 Apr	1180	Nottinghamshire
15 Apr	1185	Lincoln
1 June	1246	Canterbury, Kent
21 Dec	1246	Wells
19 Feb	1249	South Wales
11 Sept	1275	Somerset
21 May	1382	Canterbury, Kent
28 Dec	1480	Norfolk
26 Feb	1575	York to Bristol
6 Apr	1580*	London
30 Apr	1736	Menstrie, Clackmannan
1 May	1736	Menstrie, Clackmannan
14 Nov	1769†	Inverness
18 Nov	1795	Derbyshire
13 Aug	1816‡	Inverness
23 Oct	1839	Comrie, Perth
30 July	1841	Comrie, Perth
6 Oct	1863	Hereford
22 Apr	1884§	Colchester
17 Dec	1896	Hereford
18 Sept	1901	Inverness
27 June	1906‖	Swansea
30 July	1926	Jersey
15 Aug	1926	Hereford
7 June	1931	Dogger Bank (5·6R)
11 Feb	1957	Midlands
26 Dec	1979	Longtown, Cumbria
19 July	1984	W. Areas & Ireland (5·5R)

* About 6 p.m. First recorded fatality – an apprentice killed by masonry falling from Christ Church.
† 'Several people' reported killed. Parish register indicates not more than one. Date believed to be 14th.
‡ At 10.45 p.m. Heard in Aberdeen (133 km, *83 miles*), felt in Glasgow (185 km, *115 miles*). Strongest ever in Scotland.
§ At 9.18 a.m. Heard in Oxford (174 km, *95 miles*), felt in Exeter and Ostend, Belgium (152 km, *95 miles*). At least three, possibly five, killed. Strongest ever in British Isles at 6 on the Richter scale.
‖ At 9.45 a.m. Strongest in Wales. Felt over 98 000 km^2 (*37 800 miles^2*).

Other major natural disasters

Landslides caused by earthquakes in the Kansu Province of China on 16 Dec 1920 killed 180 000 people.

The Peruvian snow avalanches at Huarás (13 Dec 1941) and from Huascarán (10 Jan 1962) killed 5000 and 3000 people respectively. The Huascarán alluvion flood triggered by the earthquake of 31 May 1970 wiped out 25 000.

Both floods and famines have wreaked a greater toll of human life than have earthquakes. The greatest river floods on record are those of the Hwang-ho, China. From September into October 1887 some 900 000 people were drowned. The flood of August 1931 was reputed to have drowned or killed 3 700 000. A typhoon flood at Haiphong in Viet Nam (formerly Indo-China) on 8 Oct 1881 killed an estimated 300 000 people. The cyclone of 12–13 Nov 1970 which struck the Ganges Delta Islands, Bangladesh, drowned an estimated 1 000 000.

History's worst famines have occurred in Asia. In 1770 nearly one-third of India's total population died with 10 million dead in Bengal alone. It was revealed in May 1981 that the death toll from the northern Chinese famines of 1969–71 totalled some 20 000 000.

The Krakatoa eruptions of 26–8 Aug 1883 killed 36 000, mostly due to a *tsunami*. The Mont Pelée volcanic eruption in Martinique on 8 May 1902 killed over 30 000.

Measuring earthquakes

The scales on which earthquakes are measured are logarithmic scales – a fact which is frequently forgotten by journalists and members of the public. It means that an earthquake of, say, magnitude 8 on the Richter scale is 10 times as powerful as an earthquake of magnitude 7. Similarly, an earthquake of magnitude 8 is not twice as powerful as one of magnitude 4; it is $10 \times 10 \times 10 \times 10$ as powerful.

RICHTER SCALE

The Richter scale is the scale of measurement that most members of the public are used to hearing about. It is in fact a measurement of an earthquake's magnitude, and as such would mean little to the layman. However, it is possible to convert these readings of magnitude to a scale of intensity, i.e. an indication of the probable effects of an earthquake of a certain magnitude.

Magnitude	Probable effects
1	Detectable only by instruments.
2	Barely detectable, even near the epicentre.
4·5	Detectable within 32 km (*20 miles*) of the epicentre; possible slight damage within a small area.
6	Moderately destructive.
7	A major earthquake.
8	A great earthquake.

MERCALLI SCALE

The Modified Mercalli scale is an alternative, and more sophisticated, indication of the intensity of an earthquake.

Magnitude	Probable effects
1	Not felt by people. Doors may swing slightly.
2	Detected indoors by a few people. Hanging objects may swing.
3	Vibrations similar to those produced by a passing vehicle. Detected indoors by several people. A standing car may rock slightly.
4	Detected indoors by many people and outdoors by a few people. Crockery may clink. Parked cars may rock noticeably.
5	Detected indoors and outdoors by most people. Buildings tremble throughout. Trees and bushes shake slightly.
6	Detected indoors and outdoors by everyone. Many people frightened. Plaster cracks and some may fall.
7	General alarm. People find it difficult to stand. Bricks and stones are dislodged.
8	General fright. Considerable damage in buildings.
9	General panic. Ground cracks conspicuously. Some buildings collapse.
10	General panic. Ground cracks up to several inches. Landslides occur. Many buildings are destroyed.
11	General panic. Ground disturbances are many and widespread. Large sea waves develop. Few buildings remain standing.
12	General panic. Damage is total. Rivers are deflected. Surface waves are seen on the ground surface.

METEOROLOGY

Glossary of terms

absolute humidity The amount of water vapour in a unit volume of air, usually given in g/m³.

advection fog A fog formed when damp air moves over a cool surface, such as the sea, and the air temperature falls below the dew point. Water vapour in the air condenses as a fog.

altocumulus cloud A mass of small rounded medium clouds, close together and sometimes joined.

altostratus cloud High sheet of cloud, sometimes thick enough to cover the Sun or Moon.

anabatic wind A type of wind found in mountainous and hilly areas. The Sun warms the valley slopes, the air above the slopes is warmed and rises, and an anabatic wind blows as cooler air moves in under the rising air.

anemometer An instrument for recording wind speed.

anticyclone An area of high atmospheric pressure. Winds around an anticyclone in the northern hemisphere circulate in a clockwise direction, in the southern hemisphere the opposite.

arid Dry; rainfall so slight as to support little or no vegetation.

atmospheric pressure Pressure due to the weight of the atmosphere.

backing A change of wind direction in an anticlockwise direction, i.e. back around the compass. (See also veering.)

ball lightning A spherical glowing mass of energized air, usually about 30 cm (*1 ft*) in diameter. When it strikes an object it is immediately earthed, and so seems to disappear.

banner cloud Cloud formed on the leeward side of a hill or mountain, due to air rising up over the mountain and water vapour condensing in the reduced pressure found at that altitude.

bar A unit of pressure, equal to 750 mm of mercury at 0°C, or 10⁵ pascals.

barometer A device for measuring atmospheric pressure.

Beaufort scale Series of numbers, internationally agreed, indicating approximate scales of wind strength. (See associated article.)

Berg wind Hot and dry wind coming from the interior of South Africa and blowing down the mountains and off-shore.

blizzard A storm of powdery snow or ice accompanied by a very high wind. Visibility is very poor and much drifting occurs in the wind.

blood rain Rain coloured with dust particles, giving it a reddish-brown tinge.

blue Moon A change in colour to green or blue of the Moon, caused by dust (from a volcanic eruption, for example) in the upper atmosphere diffracting its light.

Bora Cold, usually dry NE wind blowing from the mountains in Yugoslavia and north-east Italy.

Brickfielder Very hot NE wind in south-east Australia, blowing during the summer months and carrying dust and sand.

Brocken spectre Magnified shadow of an observer in a mountainous area, cast on a cloud or bank of fog.

Buran Strong NE wind in USSR and central Asia. Most frequent in winter when it often carries snow and may then also be known as 'purga'.

calm No perceptible movement of air.

Chinook Warm dry and often turbulent W wind that blows on eastern side of Rocky Mountains, North America.

cirrocumulus cloud High cloud in lines of small rounded masses, often so close together as to form a sheet.

cirrostratus cloud High veil of cloud that often forms a halo round the Sun or Moon.

cirrus cloud High cloud consisting of broken feathery patches.

climate Distinct pattern of weather found in one or a number of geographical zones, where the essential governing factors are the same.

cloud Mass of condensed water vapour, consisting either of minute droplets of water or particles of ice.

cloudburst Very heavy, and usually short-lived, rainstorm.

cold front The boundary between an advancing mass of cold air and a receding mass of warm air, the boundary being angled back over the advancing cold air. Heavy showers often accompany a cold front.

condensation The change of matter, from vapour to liquid.

continental climate A temperate climate in which warm dry summers alternate with cool or cold winters. The precipitation in winter often falls as snow.

convection Transmission of heat by movement of particles of the substance. As regards meteorology, it refers to the upward movement of warm air which has been heated by contact with the Earth's surface.

convectional rain Rain resulting from damp air rising in a convection current. It passes the dew point, the water vapour condenses to cloud and rain results.

corona When the light from the Sun or Moon passes through a water droplet cloud, a ring of the colours of the rainbow (sometimes two rings) appears round the light source. The colour sequence is violet on the inside and red on the outside, and is due to diffraction.

cumulonimbus cloud A very large, tall, dark cloud with a low base, often wider at the apex than at the base. Typically, it produces thunderstorms.

cumulus cloud A tall cloud with a low base, not as large or dark as a cumulonimbus. It is often wider at its apex than its base.

cyclone An area of low pressure. In the tropics a cyclone can give rise to a violent storm with very strong winds and torrential rain.

deepening Increasing atmospheric pressure in a depression.

depression An area of low pressure, often referred to as a cyclone, it gives rise to unsettled wet weather, with winds radiating in an anticlockwise direction from the centre of the area of low pressure in the northern hemisphere, and in a clockwise direction in the southern hemisphere.

dew Drops of water deposited on the Earth's surface, plants, objects, etc., when air close to the Earth's surface cools down at night to below its dew point.

dew point Temperature to which air has to be cooled before it becomes saturated with water vapour. The water vapour then condenses out as water droplets, forming dew or cloud.

doldrums Belt of low atmospheric pressure in the equatorial region, where the trade winds converge. The weather here is turbulent, the surface winds light and variable, the movement of air largely being upwards.

drizzle Rain consisting of very small droplets of less than 0·5 mm (*0·02 in*) diameter.

drought A long period of dry weather.

equatorial climate High temperatures (over 30°C *86°F*), high humidity and a daily pattern of weather change rather than an annual pattern.

false cirrus cloud Sections of cloud that break away from the top of a cumulonimbus cloud.

Fata morgana A complicated superior mirage caused by distortion of light, both vertically and horizontally, when passing through several layers of air of different densities. The resulting mirage bears little resemblance to the viewed object and is more like a fairy landscape. Fata morgana usually occurs over water, and the name originated in Italy where the mirage is often seen over the Strait of Messina.

filling Increasing atmospheric pressure in the centre of a low pressure area.

Flachenblitz Unusual form of lightning which strikes upwards from the top of a cumulonimbus cloud into clear air.

fog Mass of air close to the ground that is cooled to below its dew point, forming tiny water droplets. Visibility is below 1 km (*0·6 mile*).

fogbow Rainbow in which the colours overlap, forming a white bow, due to the small size of the water droplets.

Föhn **wind** Dry, warm wind that blows down a hill or mountain. Any moisture in the air is deposited as the air rises up the mountain. The air is then warmed as it descends to lower altitudes.

front A line or plane separating masses of warm and cold air and produced by movement of the two air masses across the Earth's surface.

frost An air temperature at or below 0°C (*32°F*). Any dew formed at such temperature will be deposited as particles of ice.

gale A very high wind, strictly speaking in excess of force 7 on the Beaufort scale.

glazed frost Covering of ice formed when rain falls in air temperature at or below 0°C (*32°F*), or falls on to objects that are at or below 0°C (*32°F*).

glory Halo seen around a Brocken spectre.

Gregale Strong NE wind blowing in the southern Mediterranean mainly in the cooler months of the year.

Haboob Any wind of a strength to raise sand into a sand storm, particularly in Sudan.

hail Ice particles, of about 5 mm (*0·5 in*) diameter but sometimes considerably in excess of this size, which fall when moist air rises rapidly in cumulonimbus clouds and freezes.

halo Ring of light around the Sun or Moon, caused by refraction of the light through ice crystals in high cloud. It is usually white, but can be red on the inside and bluish on the outside.

Harmattan A dry and relatively cool NE or E wind which blows in north west Africa, average southern limit 5°N latitude in January and 18°N latitude in July. It is often dust laden and so dry as to wither vegetation and cause human skin to peel off. It nevertheless gives welcome relief from the usual humid heat of the tropics.

Helm Strong and often violent cold NE wind blowing down western slopes of Cross Fell range, Cumbria, mainly in late winter and spring. Very gusty.

high An area of high atmospheric pressure, i.e. an anticyclone. Highs usually bring sunny dry, weather.

high cloud Clouds occurring in the range 6000–12 000 m (*19700–39 400 ft*), or higher.

hill fog Low cloud covering high ground.

hoar frost Ice crystals deposited on the Earth's surface and objects on or close to the Earth's surface. It is formed when the dew point is at or below 0°C (*32°F*).

hot desert climate Very high daily temperatures, up to 50°C (*122°F*), with much cooler nights and very little rain at all.

humidity The amount of water vapour contained in the atmosphere.

hurricane A wind in excess of force 12 on the Beaufort scale. It can also refer to a tropical cyclone in the Caribbean and western North Atlantic. Hurricanes were first given names in Australia from 1887 to 1902 by Clement L. Wragge.

isobar A line on a map joining all the points having equal atmospheric pressure.

isohyet A line on a map joining all those points that have equal amounts of rainfall over a given time.

isotherm A line on a map joining all the points having the same temperature at a given time.

jet stream A strong and persistent wind found at high altitudes, blowing from west to east.

Karaburan Hot dusty NE wind in central Asia.

Khamsin Oppressive, hot, dry S wind over Egypt, most frequent between April and June, often laden with sand from the desert.

land breeze A wind blows, usually during the night in coastal regions, from land out to sea. The land cools more rapidly than the sea at night, the air over the land also cools and flows seawards.

lenticular cloud An isolated cloud shaped like a convex lens, found over a hill or mountain.

Levanter Moist E wind in region of Straits of Gibraltar, often strong and most frequent June-October.

lightning Development of static electricity due to the uprushing of air in a cumulonimbus thundercloud. Discharge of this static electricity causes the lightning flash.

low An area where the atmospheric pressure is markedly lower than the surrounding areas: a depression. Lows usually bring cloudy, wet weather.

low cloud Clouds occurring below about 2000 m (*6600 ft*).

mackerel sky A sky filled with high cirrocumulus or cirrostratus clouds. These small round separate cloud masses are supposed to resemble the markings on a mackerel.

mare's tail clouds Thin wispy high cirrus clouds.

maritime climate A climate that is influenced by the seas, i.e. with cool summers and mild winters.

Mediterranean climate A hot dry summer alternates with a mild wet winter.

medium cloud Clouds occurring between about 2000 and 6000 m (*6600 and 19 700 ft*).

microclimate Climate found in a limited area such as garden, room or refrigerator. It is dependent on very local factors.

millibar The unit of pressure most used to measure atmospheric pressure. It is 1/1000 of a bar, i.e. 10^2 pascals.

mirage The refraction of light when layers of the atmosphere have sharply differing densities due to contrasting temperatures. An inferior mirage (the more common type) is when an object seems to be floating in a pool of water. A superior mirage is when an object near the horizon seems to float above its true position.

mist Mass of air close to the ground that is cooled to below its dew point, forming tiny water droplets. Visibility is between 1000 and 2000 m (*3300 and 6600 ft*).

Mistral Dry cold NW or N wind blowing off-shore along the Mediterranean coasts of France and Spain. Particularly violent on the coast of Languedoc and Provence when it funnels down the Rhône Valley.

monsoon The wet stormy weather brought by south-easterly winds in south-east Asia between April and December. It is caused by warm wet south-easterly trade winds filling the low pressure created over the hot land mass. A second monsoon may occur later in the year if the reversing winds have to pass over any seas, e.g. south-east India and Sri Lanka.

monsoon climate This climate is characterized by a hot dry season and a cooler wet season when the monsoon rains arrive.

mountain climate Climate found in mountainous areas that differs from the climate of the surrounding lowland, approximating more to the climate found nearer the poles.

nacreous clouds Mother-of-pearl clouds occurring at very high altitudes over mountainous areas after sunset. They are lit by sunlight from below and can be visible from great distances.

nimbostratus cloud A low dark grey cloud with a flat base. It invariably brings persistent precipitation.

noctilucent cloud Bluish clouds that appear at very great altitudes – up to 100 km (*600 miles*). They are not true clouds at all, but probably formed by cosmic dust.

occlusion The advance of a cold front of air on to a warm front of air, or vice versa, the warm air being lifted up by the cold air.

orographic rain Rain caused when advancing damp air is forced upward over hills, mountains or other high land. As it cools, its temperature falls below its dew point and rain falls.

Pampero Piercing cold SW wind which blows from the Andes across the S. American pampas in Argentina and across Uruguay to the Atlantic.

parhelion A mock Sun, or image of the Sun, appearing to either side of the Sun. It is equivalent to the halo, and is caused by light being refracted in ice crystals.

planetary winds System of winds and areas of stiller air that occur on the Earth's surface due to the heating effect of the Sun and the rotation of the Earth on its axis. The system moves north and south each year with the movement of the equatorial belt of low pressure.

polar climate Strictly speaking, a cold desert climate. Summer temperatures rarely rise above freezing point, while the winters are intensely cold. There is little precipitation; what does occur falls as snow.

precipitation Water which falls from the atmosphere on to the Earth's surface. Depending on the circumstances, it can either occur as rain, hail, sleet, slush, snow, dew or frost.

prevailing wind The direction of the wind that tends to blow most frequently over a given area.

Purga Strong NE winter wind in USSR and central Asia, often raising snow from the ground to cause blizzards.

radiation fog On clear nights when there is little wind, warmth will be lost from the Earth's surface by radiation. The air immediately above the Earth's surface will be cooled and, if its temperature falls below its dew point, radiation fog will be formed.

rain Precipitation that falls as separate drops of water greater than 0·5 mm (*0·02 in*).

rainbow An arc of colours seen when light falls on a belt of rain. It is caused by refraction and reflection of the light, so the Sun must be behind the observer. A primary rainbow has violet on the inside and red on the outside. Occasionally a secondary rainbow is seen outside the primary rainbow; the colours are then reversed.

rainfall The total depth of precipitation of all kinds falling on a given place·or area in a given time.

rain gauge An instrument used to measure rainfall. This consists of a cylinder, covered by a funnel 125 or 200 mm (*5 or 8 in*) in diameter.

rain shadow An area that receives little rainfall due to the fact that it is in the lee of an area of high ground. Water in the air therefore falls as orographic rain over the high ground, and relatively dry winds pass over the rain shadow.

relative humidity The ratio between the amount of water vapour in a volume of air at a fixed temperature, and the amount of water vapour the same volume of air would hold at that temperature if it was saturated. It is expressed as a percentage.

ridge of high pressure An extended area of high pressure.

rime Layer of ice deposited on objects when the temperature is below freezing point and supercooled water droplets fall to earth.

Roaring Forties Region between latitudes 40° and 50°S where strong W winds, known as 'Brave West Winds', blow steadily. So named by sailors who first entered these latitudes.

Saint Elmo's fire Discharge of static electricity, seen as a luminous cloud, around the tips of tall objects sometimes during stormy weather.

Scirocco or *Sirocco* An oppressive hot dry S wind on the north coast of Africa blowing from the

Sahara. By the time this wind crosses the Mediterranean to Europe it has become slightly cooler but very moist. It produces languor and mental debility.

scud Shreds of low cloud, often below the level of the main cloud mass, driven along relatively quickly by a strong wind.

sea breeze A wind that blows, usually during the day in coastal regions, from sea on to the land. The land heats up more rapidly during the day than the sea, and the air above it rises. Cooler air then moves in from off the sea to take its place.

Seistan Strong N wind in summer in the Seistan region of eastern Iran and Afghanistan. It can attain velocities of over 160 kph (*100 mph*) and carries dust and sand.

Shamal Hot dry and dusty NW wind, persistent in summer in Iraq and the Persian Gulf.

sleet Precipitation consisting of a cold mixture of rain and snow.

smog An unpleasant mixture of fog and smoke or other industrial air-borne pollution.

snow Precipitation consisting of feathery crystals of water. It is formed at temperatures below freezing point.

Southerly buster Sudden cold S wind, usually strong in south eastern Australia. Temperature can fall 20C (*36F*) degrees or more in a very short time with the arrival of this wind.

squall A short-lived strong wind, lasting only for a minute or two and often coming from a different direction to the prevailing wind at the time. A short fierce rain shower may be associated with the squall.

stratocumulus cloud Rounded masses of medium or low cloud in a distinct and extensive layer.

stratus cloud Low cloud consisting of an unbroken uniform layer.

subpolar climate A short warm summer, but a bitterly cold windy winter. Permafrost is usual. Precipitation occurs in the winter as snow.

sun pillar A column of light above or below the Sun when it is low on the horizon. It is caused by the reflection of light in ice crystals.

sunshine The visible light received from the Sun. An indication of how sunny a place is is given by the number of hours of direct sunshine it receives in a day.

temperate maritime climate A warm damp summer alternates with a mild wet winter.

temperature inversion An increase of temperature with height (normally temperature decreases with height). It may be due to warm air rising in still conditions over relatively flat land, or due to cool air sinking down into valleys.

thaw The opposite of a freeze; the period when temperatures rise above freezing point and ice and snow melt to water.

thermal A rising current of warm air.

thermometer An instrument for measuring temperature.

thunderbolt A misnomer for the effect of a flash of lightning producing intense heat. Such a strike may fuse materials, boil water instantaneously, blow masonry apart, etc.

thunderstorm A fierce storm typified by very strong upward currents of air. This produces very heavy

High winds over South-East England brought down trees and caused extensive damage to property during the storms of 16 October 1987. (Popperfoto)

Hurricane 'Frederic' in the Gulf of Mexico, approaching the US coast at 1800 GMT on 12 September 1979. This photograph was taken on visible wave length from a satellite, stationary relative to the Earth, at an altitude of 35 880 km (*22 300 miles*) above the Equator. Note the curve of the Earth in the top left corner. (National Oceanic & Atmospheric Administration/National Environmental Satellite Service/Science Photo Library)

showers of rain, sometimes with hail, due to the very rapid cooling of the air as it rises. The static electricity caused by these rapidly moving masses of air produces lightning, which in turn gives rise to thunder, due to the explosive effects of the electrical discharge.

tornado A whirlwind produced by intensely strong upward currents of air. The diameter of the whirlwind is usually less than 500 m (*1600 ft*) and it travels in a straight line at speeds of about 20–60 kph (*10–40 mph*), causing great damage.

trade winds Winds of great regularity which blow from the subtropical belts of high pressure to the equatorial belt of low pressure. Due to the rotation of the Earth they blow from the north-east in the northern hemisphere and from the south-east in the southern hemisphere.

Tramontana Cool dry N wind blowing across the Spanish Mediterranean coast.

tropical cyclone A small intense depression, occurring in the tropics, and producing very fierce storms.

trough of low pressure An extended area of low pressure.

turbulence At low altitudes this describes the irregular movement of air, with gusty winds and frequent changes of wind direction. At higher altitudes it describes ascending and descending movements of air, due to unequal heating by the Earth's surface.

typhoon A tropical cyclone, particularly such a storm occurring in the China Sea.

veering A change of wind direction in a clockwise direction. (See also backing.)

visibility The greatest distance at which an object can be seen with the naked eye.

warm front The boundary between an advancing mass of warm air and the mass of cooler air over which it rises, the boundary being angled forward over the cold air. Rain usually precedes a warm front.

waterspout A tornado that occurs over water. Water and spray are sucked up by the rapidly spiralling winds, the spout often reaching a height of over 1 km (*3300 ft*).

westerlies Westerly winds that blow in the region between the subtropical high pressure belts and the polar circles. In fact they blow from the south-west in the northern hemisphere and from the north-west in the southern hemisphere.

wet bulb thermometer A type of hygrometer which gives an indication of atmospheric humidity.

whirlwind A small local vertical column of rapidly rotating air, with an area of low pressure at the centre.

whiteout Conditions of dense falling snow in which physical features are totally obscured to sight.

Williwaw Strong downslope wind in Alaska.

wind A movement of air, usually parallel to the Earth's surface.

Beaufort scale

A scale of numbers, designated Force 0 to Force 12, was originally devised by Commander Francis Beaufort (1774–1857) (later Rear-Admiral Sir Francis Beaufort, KCB, FRS) in 1805. (Force numbers 13 to 17 were added in 1955 by the US Weather Bureau but are not in international use since they are regarded as impracticably precise.)

Force No.	Descriptive term	Wind speed km/h	mph	knots
0	Calm	0–1	0–1	0–1
1	Light air	1–5	1–3	1–3
2	Light breeze	6–11	4–7	4–6
3	Gentle breeze	12–19	8–12	7–10
4	Moderate breeze	20–29	13–18	11–16
5	Fresh breeze	30–39	19–24	17–21
6	Strong breeze	40–50	25–31	22–27
7	Near gale	51–61	32–38	28–33
8	Gale	62–74	39–46	34–40
9	Strong gale	75–87	47–54	41–47
10	Storm	88–101	55–63	48–55
11	Violent storm	102–117	64–73	56–63
12	Hurricane	≥119	≥74	≥64

Constituents of air

Gas	Formula	% by volume
Invariable component gases of dry carbon dioxide-free air		
Nitrogen	N_2	78·110
Oxygen	O_2	20·953
Argon	A	0·934
Neon	Ne	0·001818
Helium	He	0·000524
Methane	CH_4	0·0002
Krypton	Kr	0·000114
Hydrogen	H_2	0·00005
Nitrous Oxide	N_2O	0·00005
Xenon	Xe	0·0000087
		99·9997647%
Variable components		
Water vapour	H_2O	0 to 7·0*
Carbon dioxide	CO_2	0·01 to 0·10 average 0·034
Ozone	O_3	0 to 0·000007
Contaminants		
Sulphur dioxide	SO_2	up to 0·0001
Nitrogen dioxide	NO_2	up to 0·000002
Ammonia	NH_3	trace
Carbon monoxide	CO	trace

* This percentage can be reached at a relative humidity of 100 per cent at a shade temperature of 40°C (*104°F*)

Cloud classification

Genus (with abbreviation)	Ht of base m	ft	Temp base level °C	Official description
Cirrus (Ci)	5000 to 13700	*16 500 to 45 000*	−20 to −60	Detached clouds in the form of white delicate filaments, or white or mostly white patches or narrow bands. They have a fibrous (hair-like) appearance or a silky sheen, or both. They are the highest of the standard forms averaging 8250 m (*27 000 ft*).
Cirrocumulus (Cc)	5000 to 13700	*16 500 to 45 000*	−20 to −60	Thin, white sheet or layer of cloud without shading, composed of very small elements in the form of grains, ripples, etc., merged or separate, and more or less regularly arranged.
Cirrostratus (Cs)	5000 to 13700	*16 500 to 45 000*	−20 to −60	Transparent, whitish cloud veil of fibrous or smooth appearance, totally or partly covering the sky, and generally producing halo phenomena.
Altocumulus (Ac)	2000 to 7000	*6500 to 23 000*	+10 to −30	White or grey, or both white and grey, patch, sheet or layer of cloud, generally with shading, composed of laminae, rounded masses, rolls, etc. which are sometimes partly fibrous or diffuse, and which may or may not be merged.
Altostratus (Ac)	2000 to 7000	*6500 to 23 000*	+10 to −30	Greyish or bluish cloud sheet or layer of striated, fibrous or uniform appearance, totally or partly covering the sky, and having parts thin enough to reveal the sun at least vaguely.
Nimbostratus (Ns)	900 to 3000	*3000 to 10 000*	+10 to −15	Grey cloud layer, often dark; its appearance is rendered diffuse by more or less continually falling rain or snow which in most cases reaches the ground. It is thick enough throughout to blot out the sun. Low, ragged clouds frequently occur below the layer with which they may merge.

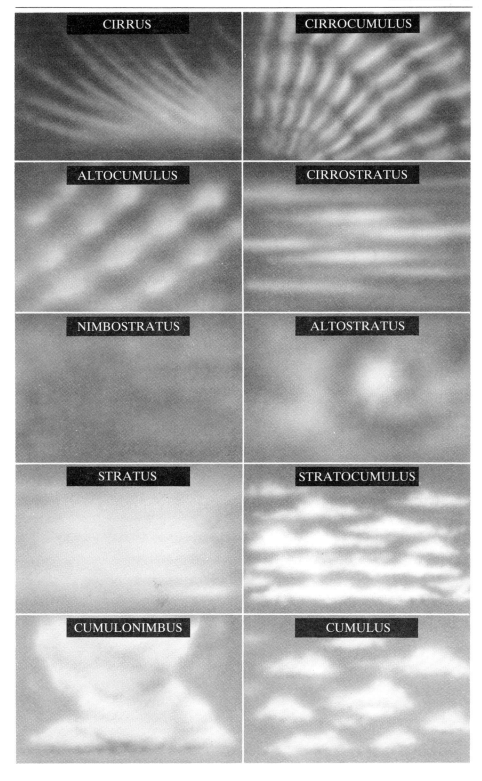

Genus (with abbreviation)	Ht of base		Temp base level	Official description
	m	ft	°C	
Stratocumulus (Sc)	460 to 2000	1500 to 6500	+15 to −5	Grey or whitish, or both grey and whitish, patch, sheet or layer of cloud which almost always has dark parts, composed of tessellations, rounded masses, rolls, etc., which are non-fibrous (except for virga) and which may or may not be merged.
Stratus (St)	surface to 460	surface to 1500	+20 to −5	Generally grey cloud layer with a fairly low uniform base below 1050 m (3500 ft), which may give drizzle, ice prisms or snow grains. When the sun is visible through the cloud its outline is clearly discernible. Stratus does not produce halo phenomena (except possibly at very low temperatures). Sometimes stratus appears in the form of ragged patches.
Cumulus (Cu)	460 to 2000	1500 to 6500	+15 to −5	Detached clouds, generally dense and with sharp outlines, developing vertically in the form of rising mounds, domes or towers, of which the bulging upper part often resembles a cauliflower. The sunlit parts of these clouds are mostly brilliant white; their bases are relatively dark and nearly horizontal.
Cumulonimbus (Cb)	460 to 2000	1500 to 6500	+15 to −5	Heavy and dense cloud, with a considerable vertical extent, in the form of a mountain or huge towers up to 20 000 m (68 000 ft) in the tropic. At least part of its upper portion is usually smooth, or fibrous or striated, and nearly always flattened; this part often spreads out in the shape of an anvil or vast plume. Under the base of this cloud, which is often very dark, there are frequently low ragged clouds either merged with it or not, and precipitation, sometimes in the form of virga – (fallstreaks or trails or precipitation attached to the underside of clouds).

Note: The rare nacreous or mother-of-pearl formation sometimes attains an extreme height of 24 000 m (80 000 ft).

Northern and Southern Lights

Polar lights are known as Aurora Borealis in the northern hemisphere and Aurora Australis in the southern hemisphere. These luminous phenomena are caused by electrical solar discharges between altitudes of 100–73 km (620–45 miles) and are usually visible only in the higher latitudes.

It is believed that in an auroral display some 100 million protons (hydrogen nuclei) strike each square centimetre of space in the exosphere or of atmosphere in the meso or thermospheres each second. Colours vary from yellow-green (attenuated oxygen), reddish (very low pressure oxygen), red below green (molecular nitrogen below ionized oxygen) or bluish (ionized nitrogen). Displays, which occur on every dark night in the year above 70°N or below 70°S (e.g. Northern Canada or Antarctica), vary in frequency with the 11-year sunspot cycle. Edinburgh may expect perhaps 25 displays a year against 7 in London, and Malta once a decade.

The most striking recent displays over Britain occurred on 25 Jan 1938 and 4–5 Sept 1958. On 1 Sept 1909, a display was reported from just above the equator at Singapore (1° 12′N) but is not uncritically accepted. In 1957, 203 displays were recorded in the Shetland Islands (geometric Lat. 63°N).

Ice Ages

A new method of dating events over the past million years has been established and relies on the precision with which ice-age cycles follow variations in the Earth's position in space and the shape of its orbit. These are calculated by established astronomical methods, and are observed in the Milankovitch theory as climatic rhythms. These rhythms correspond with cycles of about 90 000 years (changes in orbital configuration), 41 000 years (axis tilt) and 23 000 and 19 000 years (axis wobble or precession of the equinoxes). Ocean bed cores provide evidence of the last magnetic reversal 730 000 years ago, and give an important dating monitor. From these one can correlate the climatic phases or 'core stages', evident from marine fossils, with the orbital variations, and arrive at a timescale.

Although the 90 000 year cycle became regular only 800 000 years ago a count of 28 ice ages between 3 250 000 years and the start of an ice age 649 000 years ago gives a mean average between each ice age of 92 900 years. Seven more ice ages can thus be computed to the present day.

Ice age number	Start (rounded)
29	650 000 yr
30	550 000 yr
31	475 000 yr
32	350 000 yr
33	280 000 yr
34	188 000 yr
35	72 000 yr
36	due soon

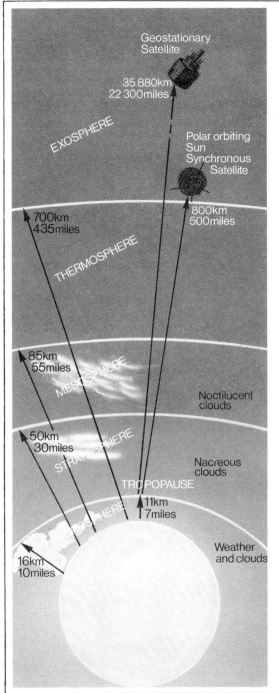

Geostationary Satellite

35 880km
22 300miles

Polar orbiting Sun Synchronous Satellite

700km
435miles

800km
500miles

EXOSPHERE

THERMOSPHERE

85km
55miles

Noctilucent clouds

50km
30miles

MESOSPHERE

Nacreous clouds

STRATOSPHERE

TROPOPAUSE

11km
7miles

16km
10miles

Weather and clouds

The Earth's Atmospheric Layers

TROPOSPHERE
The realm of clouds, rain and snow in contact with the lithosphere (land) and hydrosphere (sea). The upper limit, known as the tropopause, is 17 km *11 miles* (*58 000 ft*) at the equator or 6–8 km (*19 700–25 000 ft*) at the Poles. In middle latitudes in high pressure conditions the limits may be extended between 13 km (*8 miles*) to 7 km (*4 miles*) in low pressure conditions. Aviation in the troposphere is affected by jet streams, strong, narrow air currents with velocities above 60 knots and by CAT (Clear Air Turbulence) which if violent can endanger aircraft.

STRATOSPHERE
The second region of the atmosphere marked by a constant increase in temperature with altitude up to a maximum of $-3°C$ at about 50 km (*160 000 ft*).

MESOSPHERE
The third region of the atmosphere about 50 km (*160 000 ft*) marked by a rapid decrease in temperature with altitude to a minimum value even below $-113°C$ at about 85 km (*290 000 ft*) known as the mesopause.

THERMOSPHERE
The fourth region of the atmosphere above the mesophere characterized by an unremitting rise in temperature up to a night maximum during minimum solar activity of 225°C at about 230 km (*140 miles*) to above 1480°C in a day of maximum solar activity at 500 km (*310 miles*). This region is sometimes termed the heterosphere because of the widely differing conditions in night and day and during solar calm and solar flare.

EXOSPHERE
This is the fifth and final stage at 500 km (*310 miles*) in which the upper atmosphere becomes space and in which temperature no longer has the customary terrestrial meaning.

NOTE
The Appleton layer in the ionosphere at some 300 km is now referred to as the F_2 layer. The Heaviside layer at *c.* 100 km is now termed the E layer. They were named after the physicists Oliver Heaviside (1850–1925) and Sir Edward Appleton (1892–1965) and have importance in the reflection of radio waves.

Fog

The international meteorological definition of fog is a 'cloud touching the ground and reducing visibility to less than one kilometre (*1100 yd*).' For road traffic reports visibility below 180 m (*600 ft*) is described as 'fog'.

Fog requires the coincidence of three conditions:
(i) Minute hygroscopic particles to act as nuclei. The most usual source over land is from factory or domestic chimneys, whereas at sea, salt particles serve the same purpose. Such particles exist everywhere, but where they are plentiful the fog is thickest.
(ii) Condensation of water vapour by saturation.
(iii) The temperature at or below dew point. This may arise in two ways. The air temperature may simply drop to dew point, or the dew point may rise because of increased amounts of water vapour.

Sea fog persists for up to 120 days in a year on the Grand Banks, off Newfoundland. London has twice been beset by 114 hours continuous fog.

Thunder and Lightning

At any given moment there are some 2200 thunderstorms on the Earth's surface which are audible at ranges of up to 29 km (*18 miles*). The world's most thundery location is Bogor (formerly Buitenzorg), Java, Indonesia, which in 1916–19 averaged 322 days per year with thunder heard. The extreme in the United Kingdom is 38 days at Stonyhurst, Lancashire in 1912, and in Huddersfield, West Yorkshire in 1967.

Thunder arises after the separation of electrical changes in Cumulonimbus (q.v.) clouds. In the bipolar thundercloud the positive charge is in the upper layer. Thunder is an audible compression wave, the source of which is the rapid heating of the air by a return lightning stroke.

Lightning: The speed of lightning varies greatly. The downward leader strokes vary between 150 and 1500 km/s (*100 to 1000 miles per second*). In the case of the powerful return stroke a speed of 140 000 km/s (*87 000 miles per second*), nearly half the speed of light, is attained. The length of stroke varies with cloud height and thus between 90 m (*300 ft*) and 6 km (*4 miles*) lateral strokes as long as 32 km (*20 miles*) have been recorded. The central core of a lightning channel is extremely narrow – perhaps as little as 12 mm (*0·5 in*). In the case of the more 'positive giant' stroke the temperature reaches *c.* 30 000°C (*54 000°F*) or over five times that of the Sun's surface. In Britain the frequency of strikes is only 2.3 per km² (*6 per mile²*) per annum. British fatalities have averaged 11·8 per annum this century with 31 in 1914 but nil in 1937.

Multi-tongued lightning forks in the southern sky over Denver, Colorado. (Popperfoto)

ASTRONOMY

A guide to the scale of the solar system and the universe

The scale of the solar system is defined in terms of the 'astronomical unit' (A.U.) which is the average distance from the Earth to the Sun. A formal definition of this unit was adopted by the International Astronomical Union in 1938 and the currently accepted value is 149 597 870 km (*92 955 807 miles*). If the solar system is reduced to a scale such that the diameter of the Sun is diminished to the size of a beach ball 30·5 cm (*1 ft*) in diameter, then the largest planet Jupiter would only be a reddish-yellow plum 3·1 cm (*1·2 in*) in diameter whilst the Earth would be a very small blue-green pea only 0·28 cm (*0·1 in*) in diameter and the Sun would be at a distance of 32·7 m (*107 ft*). The edge of the solar system, defined as the farthest distance of Pluto from the Sun, would be 1·6 km (*1 mile*) away, whilst the remoteness of the solar system from all other heavenly bodies is stressed by the fact that the nearest star, Proxima Centauri, would be 8760 km (*5440 miles*) distant on this scale or approximately the distance from London to the west coast of North America. Beyond this, distance again becomes 'astronomical' in size and in order to visualize the vastness of space use is made of two extremely large units, both of which are related to properties of the Earth's orbit.

The first is the 'light year', so called since March 1888. Since light travels at 299 792·458 km/s (*186 282·397 miles/sec*) in vacuo, then in the course of a tropical year (i.e. 365·24219878 mean solar days at 1 January 12 hours Ephemeris time in AD 1900) light will travel 9 460 528 405 000 km (*5 878 499 814 000 miles*). However, the 'light year' is basically only of conceptual importance and stellar distances are actually measured in terms of the second unit, the 'parsec' (i.e. *parallax* in *seconds* of arc). If the position of a nearby star is viewed at a point on the Earth's orbit and then again six months later then it will appear to have moved against the background of more remote or 'fixed' stars (parallactic displacement). Measurement of the position of the star on both sides of the orbit allows the distance to be fixed since half of the angle subtended by the distant object across the orbit baseline is the parallax angle of the object (π) in seconds of arc (see diagram). The reciprocal of this value is the distance in parsecs and the size of this unit is therefore 206 264·806 A.U. or 30 856 776 000 000 km (*19 173 511 000 000 miles*) or 3·2616 light years.

An indication of distance is that light will travel to the Earth from the following heavenly bodies (surface to surface in the case of nearby objects) in the following times:

From the Moon (at mean distance)	1·26 sec
From the Sun (at mean distance)	8 min 17 sec
From Pluto (at mean distance)	5 h 20 min
From the nearest star Proxima Centauri	4·22 years
From the centre of the Galaxy (present distance)	27 700 years
From the most distant star in our Galaxy (present distance)	62 700 years
From the nearest extra-galactic body (the Large Magellanic Cloud)	174 000 years
From the Andromeda Nebula (limit of naked eye vision)	2 309 000 years
From the most distant quasar known (QSO 0051-279)	13 100 000 000 years
From the edge of the observable Universe	14 000 000 000 years

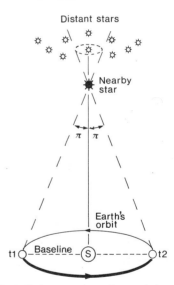

Parallactic Displacement of a nearby star relative to the background stars (π = parallax and t1 and t2 are the positions of the Earth at six monthly intervals, s = the sun).

The solar system

1. The age, formation, and death of the solar system

Meteoric evidence suggests that the solar system is 4530 ± 20 million years old with a formation time of less than 25 million years. This is only about one third of the age of the Universe and the presence of very heavy elements in both the Earth's crust and the Sun's photosphere is a result of debris from supernovae which had exploded at earlier times.

The Andromeda Galaxy which is over 2 million light years away and just about visible to the naked eye.

The solar system is believed to have been formed from a globe of gas and dust which consisted mainly of hydrogen but which also contained about 25% of helium and about 2% of other elements. During coalescence the globe started to rotate and flatten with the central core rotating faster, and therefore becoming denser, than the outer regions. In the latter, grains of both dust and ices of water, methane, and ammonia began to collide and coagulate in to larger and larger units, at first meteroids, then planetesimals, and then protoplanets which also acquired large atmospheres from the reservoir of hydrogen and helium. At the same time the core became much denser and eventually hot enough to trigger the fusion of hydrogen in to helium and the resulting protostar emitted large quantities of both matter and radiant energy in an attempt to achieve an equilibrium state. This resulted in a blowing away not only of the remnants of the original globe of gas and dust but also removed the primordial atmospheres of the inner planets, only the outer planets retaining (most) of their large atmospheres.

Once equilibrium is established, a star such as the Sun can continue to create energy through fusion for about 10 000 million years (i.e. for about a further 5000 million years from the present) but after that time a critical amount of hydrogen will have been used up and the core will consist almost entirely of helium and will be unable to sustain fusion. However, energy is still being radiated from the surface and drained from the star and in an attempt to re-establish equilibrium the core contracts and releases gravitational energy. This results in the onset of fusion reactions in the hydrogen envelope immediately surrounding the core and a consequent swelling up of the outer shell which, because of the reduced temperature, glows red and not white. The Sun will then be a 'red giant' about 40 million km (*25 million miles*) in diameter and the luminosity will be so high that the inner planets will be roasted. Over the next 100 million years the central core will become denser and hotter and then suddenly trigger the fusion of helium in to carbon and the energy release will blow away the outer atmosphere and probably destroy the rest of the solar system in the process. This will leave the naked core which is known as a 'white dwarf' star and which, whilst retaining about half the mass of the original Sun, will only be about one and a half times the diameter of the now defunct Earth, so the density will be about 50 000 times greater than that of the Earth. Such a white dwarf star is still capable of continuing to shine for several thousand million years more simply by using up the thermal energy which was stored up after the core collapse, but eventually it will become a burnt out cinder.

2. The Titius–Bode rule

A suggestion by Titius of Wittenberg in 1766 which was publicized by Johan Bode in 1772 suggested that the orbital distances adopted by the planets may not be arbitrary. They noted that the simple series 4, 4 + (3 × 2⁰), 4 + (3 × 2¹), 4 + (3 × 2²) etc, when divided by ten, reproduced the orbital distances in astronomical units of the six known planets, whilst the discovery of Uranus in 1781 also led to a satisfactory agreement:

The gap at 2·8 astronomical units (A.U.) was solved by the discovery of the asteroid Ceres in 1801 and the subsequent discovery of several thousand more asteroids orbiting between 2·3 and 3·3 A.U. However, the total mass of the asteroids is only a two-thousands of the Earth mass and therefore hardly planet size but attempts to form a coherent planet may have been disrupted by the nearby Jupiter when it may have been an even more massive proto-planet. Beyond Uranus the prediction is that the next two planets would be at 38·8 and 77·2 A.U. respectively, but giant Neptune is actually at 30·1 A.U. and small Pluto at 39·5 A.U. Whilst Pluto's orbit would appear to approximate to the Rule, it is actually very eccentric and highly inclined and therefore the agreement is almost coincidental. However, the fact that the two planets do not obey the Rule may actually be an indication of a catastrophe that may have befallen them during the early history of the solar system.

3. The Sun

Our nearest star, the Sun, is at a true distance of 1·00000102 astronomical units or 149 598 020 km (*92 955 900 miles*), with minimum (perihelion) and maximum (aphelion) distances of 147 097 800 km (*91 402 300 miles*) and 152 098 200 km (*94 509 400 miles*) respectively. Although the Sun has a diameter of 1 392 140 km (*865 040 miles*), which is 109·13 times greater than that of the Earth, and a mass of 1·9889 × 10²⁷ tonnes (*1·9575 × 10²⁷ tons*) or equal to 332 946·04 Earth masses, it is actually classified as a 'yellow dwarf' star of spectral type G2. The low density of the Sun, 1·408 g/cm³, is consistent with its overall composition by mass of 73% hydrogen, 25% helium, and 2% of other elements. The internal structure consists of a helium-rich core with a central temperature of 15 400 000°C and a pressure of 1 650 000 000 tons/in² 25·4 PPa, surrounded by a radiative layer several hundred thousand km/*miles* thick, a convective layer several tens of thousands km/*miles* thick in which heat is transported by convection in the form of cells, and a 300 km (*200 miles*) outer layer or photosphere which represents the maximum depth of visibility within the Sun and reveals the convective layer cells as a patchwork of granules. The observed overall temperature of the photosphere is 5507°C and it rotates at a rate of 25·38 days (27·28 days as viewed from Earth), this value being determined from observations of 'sunspots' which occur in this layer, their production being due to magnetic anomalies. The darkness of the sunspots is actually a contrast effect since they are still very bright but at a temperature about 2000°C less than the overall photosphere temperature.

The Sun's atmosphere consists of a 'chromosphere' extending about 10 000 km (*6000 miles*) above the photosphere. It has a low density but a sufficiently high temperature that all elements are in an ionized state and its pinkish hue is due to the presence of ionized hydrogen. The outer atmos-

	Mercury	Venus	Earth	Mars	—	Jupiter	Saturn	Uranus
Sequence	0·40	0·70	1·00	1·60	2·80	5·20	10·00	19·60
Actual distance	0·39	0·72	1·00	1·52	—	5·20	9·55	19·22

phere or 'corona' appears as a white halo and is an extremely thin gas at very high temperature (1 000 000°C). The most spectacular features extending from the top of the chromosphere and in to the corona are also prominences – huge jets of gas flung many thousands of km/*miles* into space and then looped back into the chromosphere by intense magnetic fields. The extremely high temperature of the corona results in a continuous blowing away of the outer atmosphere into space in the form of a plasma of protons and electrons (the solar wind) which permeates throughout the whole of the Solar System.

At the centre of the Sun hydrogen undergoes nuclear fusion and for a star of the Sun's size this occurs mainly by direct proton–proton reaction, i.e. two protons react together to form a deuteron, a positron, and a neutrino, then the deuteron reacts with another proton to form helium 3 and a photon, and the cycle is complete when two helium 3 nuclei react together to form helium 4 and two protons. The net result is that an extremely small amount of matter is converted to energy per cycle but the overall result for the Sun is that 4 million tonnes/*tons* of matter is lost per second. However, the high temperature and luminosity of the Sun are not due directly to the nuclear reaction but to the energy generated by the extremely high internal gas pressures required to counteract the intense gravitational contraction pressure which acts on such a large mass. Acting alone, this source of energy could only supply the Sun's needs for several tens of millions of years but this effect is extended to 10 000 million years since the nuclear fusion reaction replaces the energy lost through radiation.

4. The Moon

The Earth's only satellite has an average diameter of 3475·1 km (*2159·3 miles*) and a mass of 7·343 × 10¹⁹ tonnes (*7·232 × 10¹⁹ tons*) or 0·0123 Earth masses. The mean orbital distance is 384 399·1 km (*238 854·5 miles*), although the centre of gravity is displaced from the centre of figure by 1·8 km (*1·1 miles*) towards the Earth. The average minimum (perigee) and maximum (apogee) orbital distances are 363 295 km (*225 741 miles*) and 405 503 km (*251 968 miles*) respectively but because of the perturbing effects of the Sun and nearby planets the closest and farthest approaches in this century were 356 375 km (*221 441 miles*) on 4 January 1912 and 406 711 km (*252 718 miles*) on 2 March 1984 respectively. Although only 59% of the Moon's surface is visible from Earth since it is in 'captured rotation', extensive space probe photography has now recorded the whole of the lunar surface. The frozen lava 'seas' or 'maria', craters, and mountain ranges are all very familiar but theories concerning the actual origin of the craters remains controversial, although it is believed that whilst a certain number may be of volcanic origin, most may have resulted from multiple impacts by planetesimals during the violent early epochs in the solar system, the lack of an atmosphere or plate tectonics preserving a record of these periods in the lunar surface.

THE ORIGINS OF THE MOON

Whilst a number of theories have been put forward to explain the origin of the Moon, the only fact that is certain is that lunar surface rocks are about the same age as the Earth (4500 million years). Three

theories that gained popularity between 1950 and 1970 all have major objections, i.e. (*a*) the 'fission theory' which suggested that the Earth and Moon resulted from the fission of a single molten protoplanet – recent calculations suggest that even such a body would be too viscous to split apart in this manner; (*b*) the 'co-accretion theory' which suggested that the Earth and Moon were formed in a common orbit – the major objection to this theory is that there are major differences in the overall chemical composition of the two bodies (i.e. a large depletion of iron in the Moon compared to the Earth); and (*c*) the 'capture theory' which attempted to overcome the compositional differences by suggesting that the Moon was formed in a different place in the inner solar system and then captured in to Earth orbit – the major objection to this theory is that the Moon's orbit would have been highly elliptical and would not have decayed into its present circular orbit during the lifetime of the Solar System. The current theory which is gaining acceptance is the 'giant impact hypothesis' which suggests that during the violent early history of the Solar System the just-formed Earth was struck by a Mars-size planetesimal which disrupted both the mantle (surface layer) of the Earth and the planetesimal with such energy that the debris was volatilized and flung into space by gas pressure. The gas remained in the vicinity of the Earth just beyond the limit of instability (the Roche limit) and within 100 years began to coalesce into a partly or fully molten Moon. Minor modifications to the theory involve whether there were several planetesimals rather than one and how much of the planetesimal(s) was actually involved in forming the lunar body. Whilst this theory is not yet universally accepted it is the most plausible explanation of the Moon's origin offered so far.

5. The inner planets

MERCURY

Although looking remarkably like the Moon with similar craters and highlands, Mercury lacks the large frozen lava 'seas' or 'maria'. The most notable surface feature is the 'Caloris Basin' which is 1300 km (*800 miles*) in diameter and is surrounded by a ring of mountains rising up to 2000 m (*6500 feet*) above the surrounding surface. The planet has virtually no atmosphere which explains the large temperature variations between day and night (420°C dropping to −180°C). The latter value could not be understood until it was realized that Mercury rotated on its axis with a period equal to exactly two-thirds of its orbital period (see table). The result is that the Sun appears to dance about in the Mercurian sky and an actual 'day' on Mercury (sunrise-to-sunrise) is equivalent to two mercurian years or 176 Earth days. The extraordinary high density of the planet compared to its size is due to the fact that the iron-rich core is 3600 km (*2200 miles*) in diameter and contains 80% of the planet's mass. The relatively thin mantle or surface layer has recently been associated with the same type of 'giant impact' theory which led to the formation of the Moon (q.v.) but in Mercury's case the debris could not be retained to form a new moon.

VENUS

Although similar in size to the Earth, Venus is an intensely hostile planet with an atmosphere consisting almost entirely of carbon dioxide at a pressure 94 times that of the Earth and an average temperature of 464°C with little difference between the equator and the poles, this temperature being maintained by a 'runaway greenhouse effect' in which heat received from the Sun is trapped within the atmosphere. A thick cloud cover between 50 and 75 km (*30* and *45 miles*) above the surface contains a high concentration of aerosol droplets of sulfuric acid, the source of the sulfur possibly being due to emanations from active volcanoes. Although the surface is not visible from space it has been mapped by radar which has shown that 60% is a rolling plain whilst there are a number of notable highland regions, particular 'Ishtar Terra' in the north which is 2900 km (*1800 miles*) in diameter and contains the 'Maxwell Montes' mountain chain which rises up to 8 km (*5 miles*) above the surrounding plateau. Although Venus' rotation period is longer than its year (see tables) the actual 'day' (or sunrise-to-sunrise if it can be seen from the surface) is equivalent to 116 Earth days.

MARS
Although, like Venus, the atmosphere is almost entirely carbon dioxide the atmospheric pressure is only about one-hundredth of that of the Earth and the average temperature about 68°C lower. The surface is very complex and consists of a mixture of flat deserts, craters, volcanoes, mountains, and pole caps. A number of volcanoes are of an immense size such as 'Olympus Mons' in the Tharsis region which is up to 600 km (*370 miles*) in diameter and rises 26 km (*16 miles*) above the surrounding plain. There are also a number of large channels such as 'Valles Marineris' which is 4000 km (*2500 miles*) long, up to 200 km (*125 miles*) wide, and 6 km (*4 miles*) deep. Although there is now no direct evidence of the water that may have created these channels, it is possible that some water ice may be present at the poles under the frozen carbon dioxide caps. The two extremely small irregularly-shaped satellites of Mars, Phobos and Deimos, were discovered by Asaph Hall in August 1877.

6. The Asteroids
There are estimated to be about 40 000 asteroids of which only about 4000 have had their orbits determined. Most are extremely small, only a few metres/*yards* in diameter and orbit mainly between Mars and Jupiter, but one group, the Aten asteroids, discovered by E. F. Helin and I. M. Shoemaker (US) in January 1976, has orbits smaller than that of the Earth, whilst a single asteroid, Chiron, discovered by C. T. Kowal (US) in October 1977, has been found to orbit between Saturn and Uranus. The first and largest asteroid, Ceres, was discovered by G. Piazzi (Italy) on 1 January 1801 and only five asteroids are now considered to have diameters in excess of 322 km (*200 miles*):

Number	Name	Diameter km	miles	Year of Discovery
1	Ceres	936	*582*	1801
2	Pallas	532	*331*	1802
4	Vesta	519	*322*	1807
10	Hygeia	414	*257*	1849
511	Davida	361	*224*	1903

The three largest asteroids account for over half of the total mass of the asteroids, the latter being equivalent to only one twenty-fifth of the mass of our Moon.

7. The outer planets

JUPITER
The low density of the largest planet implies a composition consisting mainly of the primordial elements hydrogen and helium. A recent model suggests a structure consisting of a rock–iron–ice core about 15 000 km (*9000 miles*) in diameter and weighing about 15 Earth masses, surrounded by a shell of metallic hydrogen (and a minor amount of helium) which extends up to 55 000 km (*34 000 miles*) from the planet centre. The outer envelope consists mainly of liquid molecular hydrogen which eventually gives way to a gaseous atmosphere which contains 18% of helium by mass and small quantities of compounds such as water and ammonia ices and ammonium hydrosulfide; it is these compounds which impart the light and dark bands to the planet's atmosphere. The 'Great Red Spot' which has been observed for several centuries appears to be a swirling column rising up to 8 km (*5 miles*) above the surrounding clouds and the red colour may be due to the presence of phosphorus from the decomposition of a minor atmospheric constituent, phosphine. The planet radiates 69% more heat than it receives from the Sun but this can be entirely explained by dissipation of the primordial heat available in the planet.

The ring system of Jupiter was discovered in March 1979 and it consists of a bright central ring 7000 km (*4300 miles*) in width and less than 30 km (*20 miles*) in thickness, with an abrupt outer boundary at 129 130 km (*80 240 miles*) from the planet centre, a faint inner ring that may extend to the top of the planet's atmosphere, and a ghost-like halo which surrounds the inner ring. A small satellite, Metis, is embedded in the bright ring, whilst another small satellite Adrastea, lies at the edge of the ring.

Jupiter has 16 moons of which the four largest, the Galilean satellites (named after the co-discoverer Galileo Galilei), are worlds in their own right. The nearest to the planet, Io, is continuously subject to volcanic eruptions due to gravitational interactions with Jupiter and the second large satellite, Europa, which has a billiard ball smooth appearance, possibly due to remelting of the icy surface. The third moon, Ganymede, is the largest and heaviest satellite in the solar system with a diameter of 5262 km (*3270 miles*) and a mass 2·017 times greater than our own Moon. The outermost Galilean satellite, Callisto, is heavily cratered and may be showing evidence of the violent nature of the early solar system. Jupiter's other 12 moons are all very small and are grouped in to three distinct orbit bands, with four moons close to the planet, four at about 163 Jupiter radii, and four at about 314 Jupiter radii, the latter two groups probably being captured asteroids.

SATURN
The planet is generally considered to be like Jupiter but on a smaller scale. However, it radiates 76% more heat than it receives from the Sun and the outer atmosphere is also depleted in helium (down to 6%). It is suggested that whilst the rock–iron–ice

core is similar in size to that of Jupiter, the metallic hydrogen layer is much smaller, extending only 26 000 km (*16 000 miles*) from the planet centre. It is also rich in helium whilst the outer molecular hydrogen envelope is depleted and this is because of the presence of an intermediate zone 3000 km (*1900 miles*) thick in which helium is precipitating out and falling in to the metallic zone. It is the energy from this precipitation that creates the extra heat within the planet.

The distinct ring system which surrounds Saturn's equator is composed of water ice or ice-covered material and although the main ring system is 273 200 km (*169 800 miles*) in diameter, the overall thickness is only 10 m (*11 yds*). Although Voyager spacecraft images initially suggested that the main A, B, and C rings consisted of many thousands of separate ringlets, it now appears that this may mainly be an optical effect due to variations in reflectivity. Two extensive dusty rings (designated D and E) are present on the inside and the outside of the main rings respectively, whilst two very narrow rings (designated F and G) are present just outside of the main rings. The F ring is of particular interest since its narrowness appears to be controlled by two small 'shepherding' satellites named Prometheus and Pandora which orbit either side of the ring, whilst another small moon, Atlas, appears to control the outer edge of the main ring system.

Saturn has 17 known satellites but the existence of at least three more satellites in the Cassini and Encke ring gaps is inferred from ring perturbations. The largest satellite in the Saturn system, Titan, which has a diameter of 5150 km (*3200 miles*), is the only satellite with an extensive atmosphere which consists mainly of nitrogen with smaller amounts of methane and argon, and has a surface pressure about one and a half times greater than that of Earth. The surface is obscured by an orange haze which is due to the formation of complex organic molecules in the upper atmosphere. The remaining satellites are only small or medium in size and appear to be composed mainly of water ice, except perhaps for the outermost moon, Phoebe, which may be a captured asteroid.

URANUS
Just visible from Earth, the planet was discovered by William Herschel on 13 March 1781. Because of its smaller size, higher density, and the fact that it does not appear to radiate more heat than it receives from the Sun, then the internal structure is expected to be different from that of Jupiter and Saturn. A recent model suggests a rocky core 15 000 km (*9000 miles*) in diameter surrounded by a 'sea' of water, methane, and ammonia 10 000 km (*6000 miles*) thick, and an outer hydrogen-rich atmosphere containing about 26% of helium by mass and a small amount of methane. It is the latter which gives the planet its bland, bluish appearance (methane absorbs in the red). The large tilt of the axis (98° compared to earth's 23°) means that day and night can last up to 21 years on some parts of the planet, although the present sunlit south pole and dark north pole show surprisingly little difference in temperature. Occultations of stars in 1977 and 1978 revealed that Uranus had nine narrow rings in the orbital plane, and two further rings were discovered by the Voyager 2 spacecraft in January 1986. The rings are very dark and probably rich in carbon but the ring system has been photographed from Earth. The five satellites identified from Earth are all

medium sized and show the presence of water ice on the surface, but the smallest, Miranda, has a most extraordinary appearance and may have been totally disrupted and re-assembled at least once in its history. Ten small satellites were discovered by the Voyager Imaging Team during December 1985 and January 1986 and two of these, Cordelia and Ophelia, act as shepherding satellites for the major ring (epsilon).

NEPTUNE
The planet was discovered on 23 September 1846 by Johann Galle, assisted by Heinrich D'Arrest, based on mathematical predictions by Urban Leverrier and John Adams. Because of the similar size to Uranus, it may have a similar internal structure but it is much denser and radiates 85% more heat than it receives from the Sun (whereas the extra heat radiation from Uranus is negligible). The hydrogen-rich atmosphere definitely contains methane (which in this case gives the planet a green colour) but the amount of helium in the atmosphere is unknown. Ring arcs (incomplete rings) have been observed from stellar occultations to exist at about 65 000 to 70 000 km (*40 000 to 43 500 miles*) from the centre of the planet and it is suspected that such rings could be stabilized by the presence of as yet undiscovered small satellites. Neptune's main moon, Triton, is now considered to be much smaller than was previously estimated (diameter 2070 to 2500 km (*1300 to 1550 miles*)) but it has a definite atmosphere, consisting mainly of nitrogen and methane and the surface may be covered with lakes of impure nitrogen on which float icebergs composed of water, methane, and nitrogen. Little is known of the other moon, the remote Nereid, but many of the present outstanding questions relating to the Neptune system may be solved after processing of the data obtained from the encounter with the Voyager 2 spacecraft during August 1989.

PLUTO
The discovery of the outermost planet by Clyde Tombaugh was announced on 13 March 1930 but little was known about the planet until after the discovery of its moon Chiron by James Christy on 22 June 1978. The planet is now known to be quite small and has a low mass (see table) but it has a thin atmosphere containing methane, and methane ice may be present on the surface. The relatively high density of the planet has led to a new model of its interior which suggests that it has a core consisting of partially hydrated rock surrounded by a water ice layer up to 320 km (*200 miles*) thick, and an outer layer 10 km (*6 miles*) thick which consists mainly of methane.

The orbit of Pluto is so eccentric that at perihelion it is closer to the Sun than is Neptune, as it will be between 23 January 1979 and 15 March 1999, but the two planets are locked in a resonance which prevents them from coming together.

8. Comets
Comets have long been known to Man as apparitions in the sky but their actual structure is more mundane and they consist mainly of a central nucleus which can be regarded as a dirty snowball. On approaching the Sun, the ice starts to evaporate producing a coma around the nucleus and a tail or

Comet Bennett, photographed in 1970, shows clearly that the tail of the comet is two distinct streamers. (NASA)

tails which is a streaming away of ions and dust from the coma, the ions being repelled by sunlight and the dust by the solar wind, so that when moving away from the Sun the comet tails lead. Comets either orbit within the Solar System or adopt parabolic orbits which sweep them out of the System but the source of comets is actually unknown, although Jan Oort suggested that there is a reservoir or 'cloud' of comets in the outer solar system as a residue from the original accretion disc from which the Solar System was formed. A recent study suggests that there is an outer 'Oort Cloud' which is a halo of comets orbiting between 20 000 and 50 000 astronomical units and weighing 100 Earth masses, and a denser inner concentration of comets between

3000 and 20 000 astronomical units which weighs approximately 10 000 Earth masses and contains about a million million (10^{12}) comets. It is suggested that periodic perturbations by interstellar giant molecular clouds, or close encounters with other stars, triggers release of the comets into the inner solar system.

Halley's comet is the most famous and was named after Edmond Halley who correctly predicted its return in 1758, 16 years after his death. In March 1986 this comet was visited by five spacecraft and one of them, Giotto, photographed the nucleus and showed it to be an elongated, very blackened iceball about 15 km (9 miles) long and 8 km (5 miles) in cross-section.

9. Mean elements of the planetary orbits

Planet	Mean distance from Sun km	miles	Orbital eccentricity	Orbital inclination	Sidereal period days	Mean orbital velocity km/s	mps
Mercury	57 909 100	35 983 000	0·205630	7° 00′ 17″	87·9693	47·87	29·75
Venus	108 208 600	67 237 700	0·006777	3° 23′ 40″	224·7008	35·02	21·76
Earth	149 598 000	92 955 900	0·016713	— — —	365·2564	29·78	18·51
Mars	227 939 200	141 634 800	0·093392	1° 50′ 59″	686·9799	24·13	14·99
Jupiter	778 298 400	483 612 200	0·048479	1° 18′ 14″	4 332·59	13·06	8·12
Saturn	1 429 394 000	888 184 000	0·055543	2° 29′ 21″	10 759·2	9·66	6·00
Uranus	2 875 039 000	1 786 466 000	0·046299	0° 46′ 23″	30 688·5	6·81	4·23
Neptune	4 504 450 000	2 798 935 000	0·008987	1° 46′ 15″	60 182·3	5·44	3·38
Pluto	5 913 490 000	3 674 490 000	0·248537	17° 09′ 00″	90 777·6	4·74	2·94

The minimum (perihelion) and maximum (aphelion) distances from the Sun can be calculated from the the mean distance (a) and eccentricity (e) through the formulae: Perihelion $= a(1 - e)$ and Aphelion $= a(1 + e)$.

10. Physical parameters of the planets

Planet		Diameter km	Diameter miles	Equatorial sidereal rotation period d	h	m	s	Equatorial inclination	Mass* kg	Mass* tons	Density g/cm³	Escape velocity km/s	Escape velocity mps	Mean surface temperature °C	Apparent magnitude†
Mercury	Equ.	4 880	3 032	58	15	30	33·9	0°	$3·302 \times 10^{23}$	$3·250 \times 10^{20}$	5·428	4·25	2·64	+172	−0·42
Venus		12 103	7 520	R 243	00	32		177° 20'	$4·869 \times 10^{24}$	$4·792 \times 10^{21}$	5·245	10·36	6·44	+464	−4·40
Earth	Equ.	12 756	7 926		23	56	04·1	23° 26'	$5·974 \times 10^{24}$	$5·879 \times 10^{21}$	5·515	11·19	6·95	+15	—
	Polar	12 714	7 900												
Mars	Equ.	6 794	4 221	1	00	37	22·7	25° 11'	$6·419 \times 10^{23}$	$6·317 \times 10^{20}$	3·934	5·03	3·12	−53	−2·01
	Polar	6 752	4 196												
Jupiter	Equ.	142 984	88 846		9	50	30·0	3° 08'	$1·899 \times 10^{27}$	$1·869 \times 10^{24}$	1·325	60·19	37·40	−108	−2·70
	Polar	133 708	83 082												
Saturn	Equ.	120 536	74 898		10	39	22·4	26° 43'	$5·685 \times 10^{26}$	$5·595 \times 10^{23}$	0·685	36·07	22·41	−139	+0·67
	Polar	108 718	67 560												
Uranus	Equ.	51 118	31 763	R17		14	24·0	97° 52'	$8·683 \times 10^{25}$	$8·546 \times 10^{22}$	1·271	21·38	13·28	−197	+5·52
	Polar	49 946	31 035												
Neptune	Equ.	49 600	30 820		18	12		29° 34'	$1·023 \times 10^{26}$	$1·007 \times 10^{23}$	1·635	23·55	14·63	−193	+7·84
	Polar	48 600	30 200												
Pluto		2 284	1 419	R 6	09	18		117° 34'	$1·29 \times 10^{22}$	$1·27 \times 10^{19}$	2·1	1·23	0·76	−220	+15·12

R = Retrograde motion.
* Mass excluding satellites.
† The magnitudes are those at mean opposition except for Mercury and Venus where the values have been reduced to a distance of one astronomical unit (on this scale the magnitude of the Earth is −3·86).

(Far right) A picture of
Jupiter taken by Voyager 1 on 1 Feb 1979.

11. Physical parameters of the planets on scale Earth = 1

Planet	Equatorial diameter	Volume	Mass excluding satellites	Surface gravity
Mercury	0·3825	0·0562	0·055 27	0·3769
Venus	0·9488	0·8569	0·815 00	0·9033
Earth	1·0000	1·0000	1·000 00*	1·0000
Mars	0·5326	0·1506	0·107 45	0·3795
Jupiter	11·209	1323·3	317·828	2·637
Saturn	9·449	766·3	95·161	1·136
Uranus	4·007	63·1	14·536	0·917
Neptune	3·888	57·8	17·132	1·146
Pluto	0·179	0·0058	0·0022	0·067

* The Earth–Moon system weights 1·0123 Earth masses.

12. The rings and satellites of the solar system

THE RINGS OF SATURN

Feature	Distance from centre km	miles	Comments
Saturn radius	60 367	37 510	Radius at the 100 millibar level (all values in the other tables refer to the 1000 millibar level)
D Ring inner edge	67 000	41 600	This ring may actually extend down to the planet surface
C ring inner edge	74 400	46 200	A narrow gap, the Huygens Gap, is located at
outer edge	91 900	57 100	87 500 km (54 400 miles)
B Ring inner edge	91 900	57 100	A narrow gap, the Maxwell Gap, is located at the
outer edge	117 400	72 900	outer edge of the ring
Cassini Division centre	119 000	73 900	The existence of two undiscovered moons in this 4500 km (2600 miles) wide gap (at 118 210 km (73 450 miles) and 118 270 km (73 490 miles) respectively) is inferred from ring perturbations
A Ring inner edge	121 900	75 700	
Encke Division centre	133 590	83 010	The existence of an undiscovered moon in this 322 km (200 miles) wide gap at 133 600 km (83 020 miles) is inferred from ring perturbations
A Ring outer edge	136 600	84 900	A narrow gap, the Keeler Gap, is located at the outer edge of this ring
F Ring centre	140 300	87 200	Multiple stranded narrow eccentric ring 'shepherded' by two moons
G Ring centre	170 000	105 600	Fairly narrow optically thin ring
E Ring inner edge	180 000	112 000	Diffuse ring with maximum brightness near the orbit
outer edge	480 000	298 000	of Enceladus

THE RINGS OF URANUS

Feature	Distance from centre km	miles
Uranus radius	25 559	15 882
1986 U2R inner edge	37 000	23 000
1986 U2R outer edge	39 500	24 500
6 centre	41 850	26 000
5 centre	42 240	26 250
4 centre	42 580	26 460
Alpha centre	44 730	27 790
Beta centre	45 670	28 380
Eta centre	47 180	29 320
Gamma centre	47 630	29 600
Delta centre	48 310	30 020
1986 U1R centre	50 040	31 090
Epsilon centre	51 160	31 790

With the exceptions of the very diffuse 1986 U2R ring and the dominant Epsilon ring all the other rings are very narrow (widths less than 12 km (7 miles) – the Epsilon ring width varies between 22 to 93 km (14 and 58 miles) and the orbit also has the highest eccentricity (0·0079).

THE SATELLITES OF THE SOLAR SYSTEM

Planet	No.	Satellite Name	Distance from primary km	miles	Diameter km	miles
Earth	I	Moon	384 399	238 855	3475	2159
Mars	I	Phobos	9 378	5 827	22*	14*
	II	Deimos	23 459	14 577	13*	8*
Jupiter	XVI	Metis	127 960	79 510	40	25
	XV	Adrastea	128 980	80 140	20*	12*
	V	Amalthea	181 370	112 700	166*	103*
	XIV	Thebe	221 900	137 880	100*	62*
	I	Io	421 800	262 100	3642	2263
	II	Europa	671 000	417 000	3138	1950
	III	Ganymede	1 070 400	665 100	5262	3270
	IV	Callisto	1 882 600	1 169 800	4800	2983
	XIII	Leda	11 094 000	6 893 000	15	9
	VI	Himalia	11 480 000	7 133 000	170	106
	X	Lysithea	11 720 000	7 282 000	35	22
	VII	Elara	11 737 000	7 293 000	70	43
	XII	Ananke	21 200 000	13 200 000	25	16
	XI	Carme	22 600 000	14 000 000	40	25
	VIII	Pasiphae	23 500 000	14 600 000	60	37
	IX	Sinope	23 700 000	14 700 000	40	25
Saturn	XV	Atlas	137 670	85 540	31*	19*
	XVI	Prometheus	139 350	86 590	102*	63*
	XVII	Pandora	141 700	88 050	85*	53*
	XI	Epimetheus	151 420	94 090	117*	73*
	X	Janus	151 470	94 120	188*	117*
	I	Mimas	185 530	115 280	397	247
	II	Enceladus	238 030	147 900	498	310
	III	Tethys	294 670	183 100	1028	639
	XIII	Telesto	294 670	183 100	22*	12*
	XIV	Calypso	294 670	183 100	24*	15*
	IV	Dione	377 410	234 510	1118	695
	XII	Helene	377 410	234 510	32*	20*
	V	Rhea	527 070	327 510	1528	949
	VI	Titan	1 221 860	759 230	5150	3200
	VII	Hyperion	1 481 090	920 310	286*	178*
	VIII	Iapetus	3 561 670	2 213 120	1436	892
	IX	Phoebe	12 954 000	8 049 000	220	137
Uranus	VI	Cordelia	49 750	30 910	26	16
	VII	Ophelia	53 760	33 410	32	20
	VIII	Bianca	59 170	36 760	44	27
	IX	Cressida	61 770	38 380	66	41
	X	Desdemona	62 660	38 930	58	36
	XI	Juliet	64 360	39 990	84	52
	XII	Portia	66 100	41 070	110	68
	XIII	Rosalind	69 930	43 450	58	36
	XIV	Belinda	75 260	46 760	68	42
	XV	Puck	86 000	53 440	154	96
	V	Miranda	129 780	80 640	472	293
	I	Ariel	191 240	118 830	1158	719
	II	Umbriel	265 970	165 270	1169	727
	III	Titania	435 840	270 820	1578	980
	IV	Oberon	582 600	362 010	1523	946
Neptune	I	Triton	354 300	220 100	2300	1430
	II	Nereid	5 519 000	3 429 000	300	190
Pluto	I	Charon	19 640	12 200	1192	741

* Average diameter for highly irregularly shaped satellite.

The Galaxy

Only 5776 of the 100 000 million stars in the Galaxy are visible to the naked eye. The Sun is located in the outer regions of the Galaxy orbiting at an average distance of 29 700 light years and the orbital eccentricity is 0·07, but the present distance from the centre is 27 700 light years and it will reach the minimum distance of 27 600 light years (perigalacticon) in 15 million years time. The Galaxy has a diameter of about 70 000 light years so the most distant star in the Galaxy would be at 66 700 light years when the Sun is at apogalacticon (furthest distance from the centre). The orbital velocity of the Sun and a large number of nearby stars have been averaged to obtain the 'Local Standard of Rest' which is 220 km/sec (*137 miles/sec*) at the Sun's present distance so the orbital period is 237 million years. However, the Sun's actual motion is 27 km/sec (*17 miles/sec*) faster than the Local Standard of Rest.

1. The magnitude scale

Magnitude is a measure of stellar brightness such that the light of a star of any magnitude has a ratio of 2·511 886 to that of the next magnitude. This ratio arises from the fact that a first magnitude star is then exactly hundred (or 2·511 886⁵) times brighter than a sixth magnitude star. In the case of excep-

tionally bright bodies this value is expressed as a negative quantity, i.e. for the Sun the magnitude is −26·70, but this is the 'apparent magnitude' (m_V) as viewed from Earth and for comparison purposes the intrinsic brightness needs to be known and this is defined as the 'absolute magnitude' (M_V) which is the magnitude which the Sun or a star would have if viewed at a distance of ten parsecs. On this basis the Sun's magnitude would be reduced to +4·87 or a four billionfold reduction in brightness. The absolute magnitude is related to the apparent magnitude and the distance in parsecs (*d*) by means of the equation:

$$M_V = m_V + 5 - 5 \times \log(d)$$

2. The brightest stars

Rank	Name	Bayer designation	Visual magnitude		Brightness on scale Sun = 1	Distance in light years
			Apparent	Absolute		
1	Sirius	α Canis Majoris	−1·46*	+1·4	24	8·7
2	Canopus†	α Carinae	−0·72	−8·5	220 000	1200
3	Rigel Kentaurus†	α Centauri	−0·27‡	+4·1‡	A 1·6 B 0·5	4·3
4	Arcturus	α Bootis	−0·04	−0·1	98	34
5	Vega	α Lyrae	+0·03	+0·5	56	26
6	Capella	α Aurigae	+0·08‡	−0·6‡	A 87 B 69	45
7	Rigel	β Orionis	+0·12	−7·1	60 000	900
8	Procyon	α Canis Minoris	+0·38	+2·7	7·7	11·4
9	Archenar†	α Eridani	+0·46	−1·6	390	85
10	Betelgeuse	α Orionis	+0·50 v	−5·6 v, s	15 000	310
11	Hadar (Agena)†	β Centauri	+0·61	−5·1	9900	460
12	Altair	α Aquilae	+0·77	+2·3	11	16
13	Aldebaran	α Tauri	+0·85 v	−0·8 v	180	68
14	Acrux	α Crucis	+0·87‡	−4·3‡	A 2900 B 1900	360
15	Antares	α Scorpii	+0·96 v	−4·7 v, s	6700	330
16	Spica	α Virginis	+0·98	−3·5	2200	260
17	Pollux	β Geminorum	+1·14	+1·0	35	35
18	Fomalhaut	α Piscis Austrini	+1·16	+2·0	14	22
19	Deneb	α Cygni	+1·25	−7·5	88 000	1800
20	Mimosa	β Crucis	+1·25	−5·0 s	8900	425
21	Regulus	α Leonis	+1·35	−0·7	170	85
22	Adhara	ε Canaris Majoris	+1·50	−4·4	5000	490

* The apparent visual magnitude of Sirius will reach a maximum of −1·67 by AD 61000.
† Not visible from the British Isles.
‡ Combined magnitude for a double star system.
v Average value for very variable magnitude.
s Absolute magnitude estimated from spectroscopic data alone.

3. The nearest stars

Over the next 100 000 years the nearest approach to the Sun by any stars will be to within 2·84 light years by the binary system Alpha Centauri in AD 29 700 (N.B. present distance 4·35 light years).

Name	Distance in light years	Visual magnitude		Brightness on scale Sun = 1
		Apparent	Absolute	
Proxima Centauri	4·22	11·05	15·49	0·000 056
Alpha Centauri	4·35	A −0·01 B 1·33	A 4·37 B 5·71	A 1·58 B 0·46
Barnard's Star	5·98	9·54	13·22	0·000 46
Wolf 359	7·75	13·53	16·65	0·000 019
Lalande 21185	8·22	7·50	10·49	0·0056
Luyten 726-8*	8·43	A 12·52 B 13·02	A 15·46 B 15·96	A 0·000 058 B 0·000 037
Sirius	8·65	A −1·46 B 8·68	A 1·42 B 11·56	A 24·0 B 0·0021
Ross 154	9·45	10·6	13·3	0·000 42
Ross 248	10·4	12·29	14·77	0·000 11
Epsilon Eridani	10·8	3·73	6·13	0·31
Ross 128	10·9	11·10	13·47	0·000 36
61 Cygni	11·1	A 5·22 B 6·03	A 7·56 B 8·37	A 0·084 B 0·040
Epsilon Indi	11·2	4·68	7·00	0·14

3. The nearest stars continued

Name	Distance in light years	Visual magnitude Apparent	Visual magnitude Absolute	Brightness on scale Sun = 1
Luyten 789-6	11·2	A 12·7 B 13·4	A 15·0 B 15·7	A 0·000 089 B 0·000 047
Groombridge 34	11·2	A 8·08 B 11·06	A 10·39 B 13·37	A 0·0062 B 0·000 40
Procyon	11·4	A 0·38 B 10·7	A 2·65 B 13·0	A 7·7 B 0·000 56
Sigma 2398	11·6	A 8·90 B 9·69	A 11·15 B 11·94	A 0·0031 B 0·0015
Lacaille 9352	11·7	7·36	9·59	0·013
Giglas 51–15	11·7	14·81	17·03	0·000 014
Tau Ceti	11·8	3·50	5·71	0·46
Luyten's Star	12·3	9·82	11·94	0·0015
Luyten 725–32	12·5	12·04	14·12	0·000 20
Lacaille 8760	12·5	6·67	8·74	0·028
Kapteyn's Star	12·7	8·81	10·85	0·0041
Kruger 60	12·9	A 9·85 B 11·3	A 11·87 B 13·3	A 0·0016 B 0·000 42

* The B star companion is known as UV Ceti.

The Universe

1. Our Galaxy in the Universe

The number of galaxies in the Universe is estimated to be between 100 000 million and a million-million, indicating a total of between 10^{22} and 10^{23} stars. Our own Galaxy is part of a concentration of galaxies known as the 'Local Supercluster' whose centre of gravity is close to the most prominent member of the group, the Virgo Cluster. Our Galaxy has an infall velocity of about 220 km/s (*140 mps*) towards the centre of gravity but the whole Supercluster appears to be being drawn at a velocity of 500 km/s (*300 mps*) towards the even larger Hydra-Centaurus Supercluster. However both superclusters (and probably many more) appear to be attracted to a point in the sky which is within our galactic plane and therefore obscured by dust. However, this 'Great Attractor' would need to be so immense that it may not be a conventional concentration of mass but a loop in a 'cosmic string' – a remnant of the early history of the Universe.

2. Neutron stars and pulsars

On completion of its equilibrium cycle a star with the mass of our Sun will collapse to a 'white dwarf' in which the nuclei of the atoms are unaffected but the surrounding electron fields have been compressed and the density may be up to 100 000 times that of our Earth. However, for stars between 8 and 50 solar masses the contraction of the core leads to temperatures in excess of 1000 million °C and carbon and other elements undergo fusion reactions until iron is reached. When the core collapses the outer layers also collapse and after reaching the temperature of the core they undergo extremely rapid reactions to produce very heavy elements. The energies involved are so tremendous that the outer layers are then blown into space and the ejection of material is accompanied by such intense radiation that the 'supernova' so formed briefly outshines a whole galaxy. The remaining core which now weighs one to three solar masses collapses to a diameter of only 10 to 30 km (*6 to 20 miles*) so the density is 10^{14} times that of Earth. In these extremely dense conditions the electrons in the atoms collapse on to the nuclei and react with the protons to form neutrons so that the whole star can be considered as being one gigantic nucleus. The neutron star so formed appears to spin at up to 30 times per second and this rotation can be detected as a pulse by the interaction between the star's emission of radiation and its magnetic field. The first such 'pulsar' CP 1919 (now PSR 1919 + 21) was detected as a radio source by Dr Jocelyn Burnell (née Bell) on 28 November 1967 and several hundred such pulsars are now known, including the visual detection of pulsars by photography. However, in November 1982 a group led by D. Backer detected a new type known as 'millisecond pulsars' which had rotation rates up to 642 times per second in the case of PSR 1937 + 214, which is close to a theoretical limit of 2000 times per second when such a star would fly apart. The pulse beat of such pulsars is so constant that they are described as being the most accurate 'stellar clocks'. Such fast pulsars are believed to be formed either by normal neutron stars accreting material from a binary companion so that the spin rate goes up or a white dwarf star accreting sufficient matter from a companion star that it collapses to a rapidly rotating neutron star. The millisecond pulsars are expected to be stable for several 1000 million years compared to only 100 million years for the slower type.

3. Black holes

Stars in excess of 50 solar masses in weight have relatively short lifetimes and the core collapse is so extreme that it goes beyond the neutron stage into an apparent almost infinite density so that the diameter will only be about 3 km (*2 miles*) and the spin rate 10 000 revolutions per second. The gravitational force within the star is so intense that space becomes curved and radiation (photons) cannot escape and hence the term 'black hole'. In spite of their minute size, black holes can be detected if they are part of a binary system by observations of X-rays given off when matter from the companion star is dragged in to the black hole. One such binary system may be the unseen Cygnus X-1 and its supergiant companion HDE 226868. The black hole concept has not been decisively proven and as presently envisaged does not appear to take into account the sub-nuclear quantum barriers that the core collapse must overcome before an infinite density state can be reached.

4. Red shift and quasars

In 1912 Vesto Slipher discovered that the spectra of

most of the galaxies were displaced towards the red end of the spectrum (red-shifted) and only a few (such as the nearby Andromeda galaxy) were blue-shifted. If the galaxy emits its spectrum at wavelength λ and this is detected at wavelength λ_0 then the red shift or blue shift is defined as:

$$z = \frac{\lambda_0 - \lambda}{\lambda}.$$

If this change in wavelength is interpreted as a velocity Doppler shift then the speed of recession of the galaxy would be $v = z.c$ where 'c' is the velocity of light. Further, measurement of the actual distances of galaxies by Edwin Hubble led, in 1929, to the suggestion that the distance of a galaxy (r) and its red shift could be related through $z.c = H.r$ where 'H' is a constant known as the 'Hubble Constant' and also it follows that $v = H.r$. These formula are obviously flawed when z is greater than one since v would have to exceed c, but this problem was solved by modifying the formulae to take in to account Einstein's Theory of Relativity in the Special Relativity Doppler formula:

$$z = \left(\frac{c+v}{c-v}\right)^{1/2} - 1$$

so that v can never exceed c.

Red shifts became more meaningful after the discovery in 1963 by Maarten Schmidt that the quasi-stellar radio source or 'quasar' 3C 273, which was a star-like object, actually had a high red shift ($z =$ 0·158) indicating a large distance and a high luminosity. Many highly red-shifted quasars have now been discovered either as radio sources or optically and the current record holder is $z = 4.43$ for quasar 0051−279 discovered by Stephen Warren and others in November 1987. The nature of quasars and the interpretation of their high red shifts in terms of cosmological distances remains controversial, but the recent discovery of an ordinary galaxy 4C 41.17 with a red shift of 3·8 suggests that the cosmological interpretation may be true for most quasars. The red shift of quasar 0051−279 at $z = 4.43$ is popularly interpreted as indicating that it is at a distance of 93·4% of the 'edge of the observable Universe' but this is an incorrect assumption since the latter is in fact only the 'scale factor' of the Universe and when the reality of the Universe is taken into account, i.e. whether it is accelerating or decelerating, whether space is 'flat' or 'curved', and the fact that the Universe actually contains matter, then it is easy to produce any number of models which would suggest that the true distance of the above quasar is well beyond the 'edge of the observable Universe'. However the interpretation of the recession velocities of quasars as being due to a Doppler shift is also open to question and a more likely explanation is that inter-galactic redshifts are actually due to the expansion of space in an expanding Universe and galaxies are actually 'comoving' – stationary in expanding space. The interpretation of red shifts is then in terms of $z = (R^0/R) - 1$ where 'R' is the scale factor at the time of emission and 'R^0' is the present scale factor. Thus a red shift of $z = 4.43$ simply means that the Universe has expanded 5·43 times or 443% since the light left quasar 0051−279.

5. The history of the Universe

Nucleocosmochronology, which is a measure of the relative abundances of radioactive nuclei in order to determine the time scale for the nucleosynthesis

of these nuclei, together with estimates of the ages of globular clusters, can be combined with an estimate of the reciprocal of the Hubble Constant (which is known as the 'Hubble Time') to estimate the age of the Universe, and a current value is 14 ± 3 aeons (an aeon or gigayear being 1000 million years). The acceptance that the Universe has a definite age and the direct observations that it is also expanding, led to the suggestion that it may have initially existed as a point-like source or 'singularity'. Initial developments of the theory of the expansion of the Universe from a 'Big Bang' were carried out by Alexander Friedmann and Abbé Georges Lemaître but the so-called 'Standard Model' thus developed could not explain either the present large scale uniformity of the Universe or the smaller scale non-uniformity (i.e. the clumping of matter into galaxies). These problems were to a large extent overcome by the introduction of the 'Inflationary Universe' model by Alan Guth in 1979 and its subsequent revisions which suggested that all parts of the Universe were within contact with each other during the critical initial period, but when the Universe was between 10^{-35} seconds and 10^{-32} seconds old it underwent a transition which led to a 10^{50} times expansion to a diameter of 10 cm (*4 in*), with the subsequent expansion proceeding fairly linearly until the Universe has reached its present size. The concept that the whole mass and energy of the Universe began from nothing is difficult to accept but it is considered to have resulted from a quantum fluctuation, but from what remains uncertain although it may be explained with the development of a quantum theory for gravity. Although actual details of the development of the Universe remain sketchy, it appears to have occurred in a number of steps:

i. The initial period, which is usually known as the 'Planck Era' lasted from 10^{-45} to 10^{-43} seconds when the Universe temperature was 10^{32} K and the radius 10^{-54} in/cm and all the forces of Nature were equal. However, at the end of this time gravity assumed unique characteristics different from the other forces.

ii. After 10^{-35} seconds, when the temperature had dropped to 10^{27} K and the radius had expanded to 10^{-49} cm/in, then one suggestion is that the strong force separated from the electroweak force and triggered a 10^{50} expansion in the Universe to a diameter of 10 cm (*4 in*).

iii. The expansion period lasted until 10^{-32} seconds and matter (quarks and leptons) were formed by nucleation after the Universe had supercooled to 10^{22} K before returning to 10^{27} K. Quarks and leptons were initially formed in equal amounts to their anti-particles, and particles and anti-particles began to annihilate each other to form photons which at the beginning of the period were of sufficient energies to combine to reform matter/anti-matter pairs. However, at the end of this period only one particle of matter per 1000 million present at the beginning of this period was left and all of the anti-matter had been destroyed (the predominance of matter over anti-matter remains to be explained).

iv. Between 10^{-9} seconds and 0·1 seconds when the temperature fell from 10^{14} K to 10^{10} K quarks combined to form protons and neutrons with the slightly lower mass of the proton favouring its production.

v. In the next 1000 seconds surviving neutrons combined with protons to form nuclei of the light elements deuterium, helium, and lithium but beyond this time free neutrons would spontaneously decay.

vi. After 10^{13} seconds (about 100 000 years), when the temperature had fallen to 4000 K, the Universe became transparent to electromagnetic radiation and protons and electrons began to combine together to form atoms.

vii. Proto-galaxies began to form when the temperature had fallen to 400 K and the actual formation of coherent galaxies is placed at 1000 million years. However, in these early galaxies large stars were formed and these had relatively short lifetimes and exploded as supernovae to form the medium and heavy elements. Our own solar system was formed after about 9500 million years from the start (4500 million years from the present).

viii. The overall temperature of the Universe has now fallen to about 3 K ($-270°$C) as indicated by the detection of the microwave background radiation in space.

ix. The ultimate fate of the Universe is at present unknown, i.e. whether it will continue to expand outwards with all of the hydrogen eventually becoming exhausted so that the Universe will eventually be 'dead', or whether there is sufficient matter in the Universe to overcome the expansion and the Universe will collapse back on to itself to again become a singularity which will presumably undergo a 'Big Bang' and the cycle will repeat again. Whatever its fate, the quantum fluctuation mechanism which produced our Universe may well produce other universes so that the infinite vastness of space may very well be filled with many island universes.

Milestones in astronomy

1543
Modern astronomy is usually considered to have begun with Copernicus' establishment that the solar system is Sun-centred and not Earth-centred which contradicted the long held view (since the time of Ptolemy in AD 180) that the Universe was Earth-centred.

1596
After 20 years of work Tycho Brahe published the best pre-telescope star catalogue.

1608
Invention of the telescope by Hans Lippershey in Holland.

1609
Johannes Kepler published his first two laws of planetary motion (and the third ten years later).

1601
Galileo Galilei and Simon Marius independently discovered the major moons of Jupiter using the newly invented telescope.

1631
First observation of a transit of Mercury across the Sun by Gassendi (the first observation of a transit of Venus was eight years later by Horrocks and Crabtree).

1638
First identification of a variable star (Mira Ceti) by P. Holwarda.

1655
C. Huygens discovered the major moon of Saturn, Titan, and also correctly described the ring system.

1668
First reflector telescope built by Isaac Newton (the principles of reflecting telescopes had been published five years earlier by J. Gregory).

1675
By observations of the Jupiter moon, Io, O. Rømer proves that light must have a definite velocity.

1687
Publication of Newton's mathematical theories of celestial mechanics which explains the orbital motions of the planets and why the solar system is Sun-centred.

1705
Edmond Halley accurately predicts the return of Halley's comet in 1758.

1728
Discovery of the aberration of light by James Bradley.

1781
William Herschel discovered the planet Uranus and discovered its moon system six years later.

1801
G. Piazzi discovered the first and largest asteroid, Ceres.

1838
First measurement of the distance of a star (61 Cygni) by F. Bessel.

1846
J. Galle discovered Neptune based on mathematical predictions by U. Leverrer (and J. Adams). The major Neptune moon, Triton, was discovered in the same year by W. Lassel.

1862
Construction of the first great refractor telescopes.

1868
Discovery in the Sun's spectra independently by N. Lockyer and P. Janssen of an element that had not been previously identified on Earth (helium).

1872
H. Draper took the first photograph of the spectrum of a star (Vega).

1877
Asaph Hall discovered the two moons of Mars.

1897
The world's largest refracting telescope, 102 cm (*40 in*) in diameter, was built at the Yerkes Observatory, Wisconsin, USA.

1915
W. S. Adams' study of the binary companion to Sirius, Sirius B, lead to the identification of white dwarf stars.

1919
J. Perrin was the first to suggest that the Sun's energy could arise from the conversion of hydrogen in to helium.

This montage of Saturn and its 'shepherding' satellites combines photographs taken by Voyagers 1 and 2 in 1981. (NASA)

1923
Eleven years after his initial discovery, V. Slipher published his findings that most galaxies have their spectra shifted towards the red end of the spectrum (red-shifted) and this confirmed the prediction of W. de Sitter that this would be a requirement if the Universe was expanding.

1927
Abbé G. Lemaître (and independently A. Friedmann) introduced the 'Big Bang' concept to try and explain the beginning of the Universe.

1929
E. Hubble's measurement of the distances of nearby galaxies lead to the establishment of a relationship between distance and red shift.

1930
Clyde Tombaugh discovered the outermost planet Pluto by systematic photography.

1932
First detection of extra-terrestrial radio signals (from the Sagittarius constellation) by K. G. Jansky.

1937
First radio telescope built by G. Reber in the USA.

1948
Completion of the 508 cm (*200 in*) Hale reflecting telescope at the Mount Palomar Observatory, California, USA.

1957
E. M. and G. R. Burbidge, W. A. Fowler, and F. Hoyle introduced nucleocosmochronology as an independent method of estimating the age of the Universe.

1961
By using radar, a number of separate research teams accurately determined the value of the astronomical unit.

1962
The existence of quasi-stellar radio sources or 'quasars' was established by Maarten Schmidt.

1964
Several different groups established by radar that the rotation period of Venus is very long (243 days) and retrograde.

1965
G. H. Pettengill and R. B. Dyce established by radar that the rotation period of Mercury is exactly equal to two-thirds of its orbital period. Detection of the 3 K background radiation by A. Penzias and R. Wilson is considered as proof that the Universe was once very hot.

1967
Detection of the pulsating radio source or 'pulsar' CP 1919 by Miss J. Bell is considered as proof of the existence of neutron stars.

1973
First close-up views of Jupiter obtained with the fly-by of the Pioneer 10 spacecraft.

1974
First details of the surface featured of Mercury were obtained from Mariner 10 photographs.

1976
The world's largest reflecting telescope, 600 cm (*236 in*) in diameter, was completed at Mount Semirodriki, Caucasus, USSR.

1977
Discovery of the rings of Uranus from observations of the occulting of stars. C. Kowal discovered the most distant asteroid, Chiron, orbiting between Saturn and Uranus.

1978
J. W. Christy discovered Pluto's moon, Charon.

1979
Alan Guth proposes the 'Inflationary" theory to explain the initial formation of the Universe. First visit to Saturn by a spacecraft, Pioneer 11.

1981
The Voyager 1 and 2 observations of Saturn leads to the discovery of 'shepherding' satellites which control the width of the F ring.

1983
Launch of IRAS – Infrared Astronomical Satellite, which gathers enormous amounts of data on the Solar System and the Universe as a whole.

1986
The Voyager 2 fly-by of Uranus resulted in the discovery of ten new moons. Five space probes investigated Halley's comet at close quarters.

1989
Voyager 2 encountered the Neptunian system and there is the projected launch of the Space Telescope.

THE CALENDAR

Old Style (Julian) and new style (Gregorian) dates

The Roman Era began in 753 BC, but the Roman Calendar progressively became confused and needed reforming. The Julian Calendar was therefore introduced by Julius Caesar in 46 BC on the advice of the Egyptian astronomer Sosigenes. The year 46 BC was made to consist of 445 days – it is known as the 'Year of Confusion'. After this, each year consisted of 365 days, except for every fourth year which became a leap year – February contained 29 days instead of 28 – and the year thus contained 366 days. The Julian Calendar was in use throughout Europe until 1582. By then there was a 10-day difference between the Julian and the tropical year. Pope Gregory XIII therefore ordered that 5 Oct should become 15 Oct and only every fourth centennial year from 1600 should be a leap year.

The Gregorian Calendar is still in use, and other countries changed to this system as follows:

1582	Italy, France, Portugal, Spain
1583	Flanders, Holland, Prussia, Switzerland, and the Roman Catholic states in Germany
1586	Poland
1587	Hungary
1600	Scotland (except St Kilda till 1912)
1700	Denmark and the Protestant states in Germany
1700–40	Sweden (by gradual process)
1752	England and Wales, Ireland and the Colonies, including North America (11-day lag)
1872	Japan (12-day lag)
1912	China (13-day lag)
1915	Bulgaria (13-day lag)
1917	Turkey and the USSR (13-day lag)
1919	Romania and Yugoslavia (13-day lag)
1923	Greece (13-day lag)

In Britain, until 1752, the year started on 25 Mar (the date of the vernal equinox when the Julian Calendar was introduced). After this date the year's start was moved to 1 Jan.

The seasons

The four seasons in the northern hemisphere are astronomically speaking:

Spring	from the vernal equinox (20 Mar) to summer solstice (21 June till AD 2000).
Summer	from the summer solstice (21 June) to the autumnal equinox (23 Sept in 1989).
Autumn	(or Fall in USA) from the autumnal equinox (23 Sept) to the winter solstice (21 Dec or 22 Dec).
Winter	from the winter solstice (21 Dec) to the vernal equinox (20 Mar in 1989).

In the southern hemisphere, of course, autumn corresponds to spring, winter to summer, spring to autumn and summer to winter.

The solstices (from Latin *sol*, sun; *stitium*, standing) are the two times in the year when the sun is farthest from the equator and appears to be still. The equinoxes (from Latin *aequus*, equal; *nox*, night) are the two times in the year when day and night are of equal length when the sun crosses the equator.

The longest day (day with the longest interval between sunrise and sunset) is the day on which the *solstice* falls and in the northern hemisphere occurs on 21 June, or more rarely on 22 June.

Days of the week

ENGLISH	LATIN	SAXON
Sunday	Dies Solis	Sun's Day
Monday	Dies Lunae	Moon's Day
Tuesday	Dies Martis	Tiu's Day
Wednesday	Dies Mercurii	Woden's Day
Thursday	Dies Jovis	Thor's Day
Friday	Dies Veneris	Frigg's Day
Saturday	Dies Saturni	Saeternes' Day

Tiu was the Anglo-Saxon counterpart of the Nordic Tyr, son of Odin, God of War, who came closest to Mars (Greek, Ares) son of the Roman God Jupiter (Greek, Zeus). Woden was the Anglo-Saxon counterpart of Odin, Nordic dispenser of victory, who came closest to Mercury (Greek, Hermes), the Roman messenger of victory. Thor was the Nordic God of Thunder, eldest son of Odin and nearest to the Roman Jupiter (Greek, Zeus), who was armed with thunder and lightning. Frigg (or Freyja), wife of Odin, was the Nordic Goddess of Love, and equivalent to Venus (Greek, Aphrodite), Goddess of Love in Roman mythology. Thus four of the middle days of the week are named after a mythological husband and wife and their two sons.

Public and bank holidays

The days that mark the birth and death of Christ (Christmas Day and Good Friday) by English Common Law are public holidays.

At the beginning of the 19th century, by custom, the Bank of England was closed on at least 40 saints' days and anniversaries. In 1830 such bank holidays were cut to 18 and in 1834 to four.

On 25 May 1871 Parliament passed the Bank Holidays Act, introduced by Sir John Lubbock (later Lord Avebury) and this statute regulated bank holidays.

At present there are six bank holidays in England and Wales (New Year's Day, Easter Monday, May Day, Spring and Late Summer Holidays at the end of May and August respectively, and Boxing Day) and two Common Law holidays (Good Friday and Christmas Day). In Scotland there are seven bank holidays (New Year's Day, 2 January, Good Friday, May Day, Spring and Late Summer Holidays at the beginning of May and August respectively, and Christmas Day). In Northern Ireland there are nine bank holidays (New Year's Day, St Patrick's Day, Good Friday, Easter Monday, May Day, Spring and Late Summer Holidays at the end of May and August respectively, Christmas Day and Boxing Day) plus two other public holidays (Easter Tuesday and the anniversary of the Battle of the Boyne).

Christmas Day

The word 'Christmas' means the mass of Christ from the old England *Cristes maesse* which is celebrated by the Western church on 25 Dec. The actual day Christ was born is not known and 25 Dec as the day of Nativity was not generally observed until the 5th century AD.

New Year's Day

1 January. The first recorded New Year's festival is that constituted by Numa in 713 BC and dedicated to Janus.

Easter Day

Easter, the Sunday on which the resurrection of Christ is celebrated in the Christian world is, unlike Christmas which is fixed, a 'moveable feast'.

The celebration of Easter is believed to have begun in about AD 68. The English word Easter probably derives from *Eostre*, a Saxon goddess whose festival was celebrated about the time of the vernal equinox.

Easter Days and Leap Years 1980–2000

(Years in bold type are leap years)

1980	6 Apr	1987	19 Apr	1994	3 Apr
1981	19 Apr	**1988**	3 Apr	1995	16 Apr
1982	11 Apr	1989	26 Mar	**1996**	7 Apr
1983	3 Apr	1990	15 Apr	1997	30 Mar
1984	22 Apr	1991	31 Mar	1998	12 Apr
1985	7 Apr	**1992**	19 Apr	1999	4 Apr
1986	30 Mar	1993	11 Apr	**2000**	23 Apr

The date of Easter has been a matter of constant dispute between the eastern and western Christian churches. Much of the calendar of the Christian religion revolves around the date upon which, in any given year, Easter falls and repercussions extend in Christian countries into civil life.

The United Nations in 1949 considered the establishment of a perpetual world calendar, which would automatically and incidentally have fixed Easter, but the proposals were shelved indefinitely in 1956.

The Vatican Council in Rome in October 1963 approved the resolution to fix the date of Easter, subject to the agreement of other Christian churches, by 2058 votes to nine against.

The boldest scheme for calendar reform, which is winning increasing support, is that the year should be divided into four quarters of thirteen weeks, with each day of the year being assigned a fixed day of the week. By this scheme it is thought likely that Easter would always fall on Sunday, 8 Apr. For this calendar to conform with the mean solar year, a 'blank day' would be required each year in addition to the intercalary day in a leap year.

Leap Year

Leap years occur in every year the number of which is divisible by four, e.g. 1980, except centennial years, e.g. 1700, 1800, or 1900, which are treated as common or non-leap years *unless* the number of the *century* is divisible by four, e.g. 1600 was a leap year and 2000 will be a leap year.

The whole process is one of compensation for over-retrenchment of the discrepancy between the calendar year of 365 days and the mean solar year of 365·24219878 days. The date when it will be necessary to suppress a further leap year, sometimes assumed to be AD 4000, AD 8000, etc., is not in fact yet clearly specifiable, owing to minute variations in the earth-sun relationship.

The word 'leap' derives from the Old Norse *hlaupár*, indicating a leap in the sense of a jump. The origin probably derives from the observation that in a bissextile (i.e. leap) year any fixed day festival falls on the next day of the week but one to that on which it fell in the preceding year, and not on the next day of the week as happens in common years.

The term bissextile derives literally from a double (bis) day inserted after the sixth (sextile) day before the calends of March. Thus the Julian calendar compensated (albeit inaccurately) for the discrepancy between its year and the mean solar year.

Jewish Calendar

It is said that the Jewish Calendar, as used today, was formed in AD 358 by Rabbi Hillel II, though some say it was not formed until later. The complicated rules of the Jewish Calendar with regard to festivals and fasts have been studied and a calendar scheme has been formulated in which a Jewish year is one of the following six types: Minimal Common (353 days), Regular Common (354 days), Full Common (355 days), Minimal Leap (383 days), Regular Leap (384 days), or Full Leap (385 days).

In the following Calendar AM 5747 is a Full Common Year of 12 months, 51 Sabbaths and 355 days. AM 5748 is a Regular Common Year of 12 months, 51 Sabbaths and 354 days.

JEWISH CALENDAR 5747–48

Jewish month		AM	5747	AM	5748
Tishri	1st	1986	Oct 4	1987	Sept 24
Marcheshvan	1st		Nov 3		Oct 24
Kislev	1st		Dec 3		Nov 22
Tebet	1st	1987	Jan 2		Dec 22
Shebat	1st		Jan 31	1988	Jan 20
Adar	1st		Mar 2		Feb 19
Ve-Adar	1st				
Nisan	1st		Mar 31		Mar 19
Iyar	1st		Apr 30		Apr 18
Sivan	1st		May 29		May 17
Tammuz	1st		June 28		June 16
Ab	1st		July 27		July 15
Elul	1st		Aug 26		Aug 14

(AM – *anno mundi*, in the year of the world)

Islamic Calendar

Hijrah year	Muslim New Year	First day of Ramadan	Festival of Breaking the Fast	Festival Sacrifice
1405 AH	26 Sept 1984	20 May 1985	19 June 1985	26 Aug 1985
1406 AH	15 Sept 1985	9 May 1986	8 June 1986	15 Aug 1986
1407 AH	5 Sept 1986	29 Apr 1987	29 May 1987	5 Aug 1987
1408 AH	25 Aug 1987	17 Apr 1988	17 May 1988	24 July 1988
1409 AH	13 Aug 1988	6 Apr 1989	6 May 1989	13 July 1989
1410 AH	3 Aug 1989	27 Mar 1990	26 Apr 1990	3 July 1990
1411 AH	23 July 1990	16 Mar 1991	15 Apr 1991	22 June 1991
1412 AH	12 July 1991	4 Mar 1992	3 Apr 1992	10 June 1992
1413 AH	1 July 1992	22 Feb 1993	24 Mar 1993	31 May 1993
1414 AH	20 June 1993	11 Feb 1994	13 Mar 1994	20 May 1994
1415 AH	9 June 1994	31 Jan 1995	2 Mar 1995	9 May 1995
1416 AH	30 May 1995	21 Jan 1996	20 Feb 1996	28 Apr 1996
1417 AH	18 May 1996	9 Jan 1997	8 Feb 1997	17 Apr 1997
1418 AH	8 May 1997	30 Dec 1997	29 Jan 1998	7 Apr 1998
1419 AH	27 Apr 1998	19 Dec 1998	18 Jan 1999	27 Mar 1999
1420 AH	16 Apr 1999	8 Dec 1999	7 Jan 2000	15 Mar 2000

(AH – *anno Hegirae*, the Muslim era)

The Islamic Calendar is a lunar reckoning from the year of the *hijrah*, AD 622, when Mohammed travelled from Mecca to Medina. It runs in cycles of 30 years, of which the 2nd, 5th, 7th, 10th, 13th, 16th, 18th, 21st, 24th, 26th, and 29th are leap years; 1406 is the 26th year of the cycle. Common years have 354 days, leap years 355, the extra day being added to the last month, Zu'lhijjah. Except for this case, the 12 months beginning with Muharram have alternately 30 and 29 days.

Hijrah years are used principally in Iran, Turkey, Arabia, Egypt, in certain parts of India and in Malaya.

NAME (AND LENGTH) OF ISLAMIC MONTHS

1 Muharram (New Year) (30)	7 Rajab (30)
2 Safar (29)	8 Shaaban (29)
3 Rabia I (30)	9 Ramadan* (30)
4 Rabia II (29)	10 Shawwal (29)
5 Jumada I (29)	11 Zu'lkadah (30)
6 Jumada II (29)	12 Zu'lhijjah (29 or 30)

* The date on which Ramadan begins may vary from the calendar date. It actually starts only after the New Moon is sighted from the Naval Observatory in Cairo.

Chinese Calendar

The Chinese New Year begins at the first New Moon after the Sun enters Aquarius, meaning that the day will fall between 21 Jan and 19 Feb of the modern (Gregorian) calendar.

The zodiac

The zodiac (from the Greek *zōdiakos kyklos*, circle of animals) is an unscientific and astrological system devised in Mesopotamia *c.* 3000 BC.

The zodiac is an imaginary belt of pictorial constellations which lie as a backdrop quite arbitrarily 8 degrees on either side of the annual path or ecliptic of the Sun. It is divided into 12 sections each of 30 degrees. Each has been allocated a name from the constellation which at one time coincided with that sector. The present lack of coincidence of the zodiacal sectors with the constellations from which they are named, has been caused mainly by the lack of proper allowance for leap days. The old order is nonetheless adhered to.

The traditional 'signs' are:
Aries, the Ram 21 Mar–19 Apr
Taurus, the Bull 20 Apr–20 May
Gemini, the Twins 21 May–21 June
Cancer, the Crab 22 June–22 July
Leo, the Lion 23 July–22 Aug
Virgo, the Virgin 23 Aug–22 Sept
Libra, the Balance 23 Sept–23 Oct
Scorpio, the Scorpion 24 Oct–11 Nov
Sagittarius, the Archer 22 Nov–21 Dec
Capricornus, the Goat 22 Dec–19 Jan
Aquarius, the Water Carrier 20 Jan–18 Feb
Pisces, the Fishes 19 Feb–20 Mar

Standard time

Until the last quarter of last century the time kept was a local affair, or, in the smaller countries, based on the time kept in the capital city. But the spread of railways across the vaster countries caused great time-keeping confusion to the various railway companies and their passengers. In 1880 Greenwich Mean Time (GMT) became the legal time in the British Isles and by 1884 the movement to establish international time zones was successful.

The world, for this purpose, is divided into 24 zones, or segments, each of 15° of longitude, with 12 that, being to the east, are fast on Greenwich time, and 12 that, being to the west, are slow on Greenwich time, due to the West-to-East rotation of the Earth.

Each zone is 7½° on either side of its central meridian. The International Date Line – with some variations due to the convenience of political geography – runs down the 180° meridian. Sunday becomes Saturday when crossing the date line travelling eastward while Sunday becomes Monday when travelling west.

The Chinese zodiac.

A very few countries or divisions of countries do not adhere to the Greenwich system at all and in others no zoning system is used, i.e. the whole nation, despite spanning more than one of the 24 segments, elects to keep the same time. Yet a third group (e.g. India) uses differences of half an hour.

Europe has three zones, part keeping GMT, others mid-European time (i.e. GMT + 1) and the remainder east European time (GMT + 2).

In the United States there are four zones: Eastern, Central, Mountain and Pacific, and these are 5, 6, 7, and 8 hours respectively slow on Greenwich.

The authoritative and complete reference, where the method of time keeping in every place in the world can be found, is *The Nautical Almanac*, published annually by HMSO.

Watches at sea

A watch at sea is four hours except the period between 4 p.m. and 8 p.m., which is, in the Royal Navy, divided into two short watches termed the first dog watch and the last dog watch. The word dog is here a corruption of 'dodge'. The object of

these is to prevent the same men always being on duty during the same hours each day.

Midnight–4 a.m.	Middle Watch
4 a.m.–8 a.m.	Morning Watch
8 a.m.–noon	Forenoon Watch
noon–4 p.m.	Afternoon Watch
4 p.m.–6 p.m.	First Dog Watch
6 p.m.–8 p.m.	*Last Dog Watch
8 p.m.–Midnight	First Watch

* Called Second Dog in Merchant Navy.

Time is marked by bells – one stroke for each half-hour elapsed during a watch which thus ends on eight bells or four bells for a dog watch. The New Year is brought in with 16 bells.

SUNRISE, SUNSET AND TWILIGHT

The Nautical Almanac gives the GMT of sunrise and sunset for each two degrees of latitude for every third day in the year. The sunrise is the instant when the rim of the Sun appears above the horizon, and the sunset when the last segment disappears below the horizon. But because of the Earth's atmosphere, the transition from day to night and vice versa is a gradual process, the length of which varies according to the declination of the Sun and the latitude of the observer. The intermediate stages are called twilight.

There are three sorts of twilight:

Civil twilight. This occurs when the centre of the Sun is 6° below the horizon. Before this moment in the morning and after it in the evening ordinary outdoor activities are impossible without artificial light.

Nautical twilight. This occurs when the Sun is 12° below the horizon. Before this time in the morning and after it in the evening the sea horizon is invisible.

Asronomical twilight. This is the moment when the centre of the Sun is 18° below the horizon. Before this time in the morning or after it in the evening there is a complete absence of sunlight.

Time zones and Relative times

The surface of the Earth is divided into 24 time zones. Each zone represents 15° of longitude or one hour of time. The passage of time follows the path of the Sun moving in a westerly direction so that countries to the east of London and the Greenwich Meridian are ahead of Greenwich Mean Time (GMT) and countries to the west are behind.

All times given are based on noon in London but there may be inconsistencies of one or two hours in some cities caused by the seasonal use of daylight saving.

Wedding anniversaries

The choice of object or material attached to specific anniversaries is in no sense 'official'. The list below is a combination of commercial and traditional usage.

First/Cotton	**Fourteenth**/Ivory
Second/Paper	**Fifteenth**/Crystal
Third/Leather	**Twentieth**/China
Fourth/Fruit, flowers	**Twenty-fifth**/Silver
Fifth/Wooden	**Thirtieth**/Pearl
Sixth/Sugar	**Thirty-fifth**/Coral
Seventh/Wool, copper	**Fortieth**/Ruby
Eighth/Bronze, pottery	**Forty-fifth**/Sapphire
Ninth/Pottery, willow	**Fiftieth**/Golden
Tenth/Tin	**Fifty-Fifth**/Emerald
Eleventh/Steel	**Sixtieth**/Diamond
Twelfth/Silk, linen	**Seventieth**/Platinum
Thirteenth/Lace	

Birthstones

Month	Stone
January	Garnet
February	Amethyst
March	Bloodstone or Aquamarine
April	Diamond
May	Emerald
June	Pearl, Moonstone or Alexandrite
July	Ruby
August	Sardonyx or Peridot
September	Sapphire
October	Opal or Tourmaline
November	Topaz
December	Turquoise or Zircon

When it is 12 noon in London the time in other cities of the world is:

City	Time	City	Time	City	Time
Abu Dhabi	4 p.m.	Darwin	9.30 p.m.	Nicosia	2 p.m.
Accra	Noon	Delhi	5.30 p.m.	Oslo	1 p.m.
Adelaide	9.30 p.m.	Djakarta	8 p.m.	Ottawa	7 a.m.
Algiers	1 p.m.	Dubai	4 p.m.	Panama City	7 a.m.
Amman	2 p.m.	Dublin	Noon	Paris	1 p.m.
Amsterdam	1 p.m.	Frankfurt	1 p.m.	Peking	8 p.m.
Ankara	2 p.m.	Geneva	1 p.m.	Perth	8 p.m.
Athens	2 p.m.	Gibraltar	1 p.m.	Prague	1 p.m.
Auckland	Midnight	Helsinki	2 p.m.	Quebec	7 a.m.
Baghdad	3 p.m.	Hobart	10 p.m.	Rangoon	6.30 p.m.
Bahrain	3 p.m.	Hong Kong	8 p.m.	Rawalpindi	5 p.m.
Bangkok	7 p.m.	Istanbul	2 p.m.	Reykjavik	Noon
Beirut	2 p.m.	Jerusalem	2 p.m.	Rio de Janeiro	9 a.m.
Belgrade	1 p.m.	Johannesburg	2 p.m.	Riyadh	3 p.m.
Berlin	1 p.m.	Karachi	5 p.m.	Rome	1 p.m.
Berne	1 p.m.	Kuala Lumpur	8 p.m.	San Francisco	4 a.m.
Bogota	8 a.m.	Kuwait	3 p.m.	Santiago	8 a.m.
Bombay	5.30 p.m.	Lagos	1 p.m.	Seoul	9 p.m.
Bonn	1 p.m.	Leningrad	3 p.m.	Singapore	7.30 p.m.
Brisbane	10 p.m.	Lima	7 a.m.	Sofia	2 p.m.
Brussels	1 p.m.	Lisbon	1 p.m.	Stockholm	1 p.m.
Bucharest	2 p.m.	Luxembourg	1 p.m.	Sydney	10 p.m.
Budapest	1 p.m.	Madras	5.30 p.m.	Taipei	8 p.m.
Buenos Aires	9 a.m.	Madrid	1 p.m.	Tehran	3.30 p.m.
Cairo	2 p.m.	Manila	8 p.m.	Tokyo	9 p.m.
Calcutta	5.30 p.m.	Melbourne	10 p.m.	Toronto	7 a.m.
Canberra	10 p.m.	Mexico City	6 a.m.	Tunis	1 p.m.
Cape Town	2 p.m.	Monrovia	11 a.m.	Vancouver	4 a.m.
Caracas	8 a.m.	Montevideo	8.30 a.m.	Vienna	1 p.m.
Chicago	6 a.m.	Montreal	7 a.m.	Warsaw	1 p.m.
Colombo	5.30 p.m.	Moscow	3 p.m.	Washington	7 a.m.
Copenhagen	1 p.m.	Nairobi	3 p.m.	Wellington	Midnight
Damascus	2 p.m.	New York	7 a.m.	Winnipeg	6 a.m.

Days of the year: births, deaths and events

January (31 days)

DERIVATION: Latin, *Januarius*, or *Ianuarius*, named after Janus, the two-faced Roman god of doorways (*ianuae*) and archways (*iani*), as presiding over the 'entrance', or beginning, of the year.

1   *Daily Universal Register* became *The Times* 1788; Union of England and Ireland 1801; First full-time fire brigade, the London Fire Engine Establishment, formed in Britain 1833; E. M. Forster b. 1879; Postal Orders introduced 1881; Commonwealth of Australia proclaimed 1901; Old Age Pensions introduced in Britain 1909; Union of Soviet Socialist Republics (USSR) established 1923; Coal industry nationalized 1947; British Railways nationalized 1948; Britain, Ireland, Denmark become members of the EEC 1973
2   Gen. James Wolfe b. 1727
3   Marcus Tullius Cicero b. 106 BC; Clement (later Earl) Attlee b. 1883; J. R. R. Tolkien b. 1892
4   Isaac Pitman b. 1813; Augustus John b. 1878; T. S. Eliot d. 1965; Donald Campbell killed attempting water speed record 1967
5   Edward the Confessor d. 1066; Maiden voyage of the first ocean liner operated on a fixed schedule, *James Monroe*, owned by the US company Black Bull Line 1818; German National Socialist Party founded 1919
6   Richard II b. 1367; Joan of Arc b. *c.* 1412; Jet propulsion invented 1944
7   England lost Calais to France 1558; St Bernadette of Lourdes b. 1844; First crossing of English Channel by balloon, Jean Pierre Blanchard (Fra) and Dr John J. Jeffries (USA) 1785; Emperor Hirohito of Japan d. 1989
8   Marco Polo d. 1324; Galileo Galilei d. 1642; Lord Baden-Powell d. 1941
9   Income Tax in Britain instituted 1799; Richard Nixon b. 1913; Anthony Eden resigned, Harold Macmillan became Prime Minister (10 Jan) 1957
10 Penny Post introduced in Britain by Rowland Hill 1840; First underground railway, the Metropolitan Railway, opened in London 1863; League of Nations founded 1920
11 Thomas Hardy d. 1928
12 Agatha Christie d. 1975
13 James Joyce d. 1941
14 Edmund Halley d. 1742; Albert Schweitzer b. 1875; Charles Lutwidge Dodgson (alias Lewis Carroll) d. 1898
15 Act of Supremacy 1535; First national museum in Britain, the British Museum, opened to the public 1759; Ivor Novello b. 1893; Maternity, sickness and unemployment benefit introduced in Britain 1913; Martin Luther King b. 1929
16 Ivan the Terrible crowned 1547; Federal prohibition of alcohol introduced, USA 1920
17 Benjamin Franklin b. 1706; David Lloyd George b. 1863
18 A. A. Milne b. 1882; Scott reached South Pole 1912; Rudyard Kipling d. 1936; Hugh Gaitskell d. 1963
19 Edgar Allan Poe b. 1809; Paul Cézanne d. 1939
20 John Ruskin d. 1900; King George V d. 1936

21 Louis XVI executed 1793; Vladimir Ulyanov (Lenin) d. 1924; Eric Blair (George Orwell) d. 1950
22 George (later Lord) Byron b. 1788; Queen Victoria d. 1901
23 William Pitt (the younger) d. 1806; Edouard Manet b. 1832; House of Lords televised for first time 1985
24 Gold discovered in California 1848; Sir Winston Churchill d. 1965
25 Robert Burns b. 1759; William Somerset Maugham b. 1874
26 Hong Kong became British colony 1841; Baird's first demonstration of TV, London 1926
27 Wolfgang Amadeus Mozart b. 1756; Charles Lutwidge Dodgson (Lewis Carroll) b. 1832; Guiseppe Verdi d. 1901
28 Charlemagne b. 814; King Henry VIII d. 1547; Sir Francis Drake d. 1596; W. B. Yeats d. 1939; *Challenger* space shuttle exploded on take-off killing all on board 1986
29 George III d. 1820; Victoria Cross instituted 1856; Anton Chekhov b. 1860; W. C. Fields b. 1880
30 King Charles I executed 1649; Franklin Roosevelt b. 1882; John Galsworthy d. 1933; Hitler became German Chancellor 1933; Mohandas Karamchand (Mahatma) Gandhi assassinated 1948; 'Bloody Sunday' in N. Ireland 1972
31 Franz Schubert b. 1797; *Great Eastern* launched 1858; Anna Pavlova b. 1881; US launched *Explorer I* satellite 1958

February (28 or 29 days)

DERIVATION: Latin, *Februarius* (*februare*, to purify), from *februa*, a festival of purification held on 15 Feb.

1   British State Labour Exchanges opened 1910
2   Nell Gwyn b. 1650; James Joyce b. 1882; German capitulation at Stalingrad 1943
3   Felix Mendelssohn-Bartholdy b. 1809; Yalta conference began 1945; Russian *Luna 9* lands on Moon 1966; Bertrand Russell d. 1970
4   Submarine warfare begun by Germany 1915; Mrs Thatcher became leader of Conservative Party 1975; Border between Spain and Gibraltar reopened 1985
5   Sir Robert Peel b. 1788; John Dunlop b. 1840
6   King Charles II d. 1685; Ronald Reagan b. 1911; King George VI d. and Queen Elizabeth II succeeded to throne 1952
7   Sir Thomas More b. 1478; Charles Dickens b. 1812
8   Mary, Queen of Scots, executed 1587; Russo-Japanese War began 1904
9   Fyodor Dostoyevsky d. 1881
10 Académie Française founded 1635; Charles Lamb b. 1775; Harold Macmillan b. 1894; Bertolt Brecht b. 1898
11 Thomas Alva Edison b. 1847; Vatican City established 1929
12 Last invasion of Britain 1797; Abraham Lincoln b. 1809; Charles Darwin b. 1809
13 Massacre of the MacDonald clan at Glencoe 1692; Richard Wagner d. 1883
14 Nicolaus Copernicus b. 1473; Captain James Cook killed 1779; First patient admitted to Great Ormond Street Hospital, London 1852; First regular radio broadcast entertainment in UK 1922

15 Galileo Galilei b. 1564
16 George Macaulay Trevelyan b. 1876
17 Molière d. 1673; International Red Cross founded in Geneva 1863; Geronimo d. 1909
18 Martin Luther d. 1546; Michelangelo d. 1564; John Bunyan's *Pilgrim's Progress* published 1678
19 David Garrick b. 1717
20 King James I of Scotland murdered 1437
21 W. H. Auden b. 1907
22 George Washington b. 1732; Robert (later Lord) Baden-Powell b. 1857
23 Samuel Pepys b. 1633; George Frederick Handel b. 1685; John Keats d. 1821; Benito Mussolini founded Fascist Party 1919; Sir Edward Elgar d. 1934
24 Emperor Charles V b. 1500
25 Sir Christopher Wren d. 1723; Thomas Moore d. 1852; Campaign for Nuclear Disarmament launched in the UK 1958
26 Victor Hugo b. 1802; William F. Cody ('Buffalo Bill') b. 1846; Britain's first atomic bomb announced 1952
27 British Labour Party founded 1900
28 Wesley founds Methodism 1784; Relief of Ladysmith, Boer War, 1900
29 Gioacchino Rossini b. 1792

March (31 days)
DERIVATION: Latin, *Martius*, the month of Mars, the Roman god of war and the protector of vegetation.

1   Frédéric François Chopin b. 1810; Reform Bill introduced 1831; US hydrogen bomb test at Bikini 1954
2   John Wesley d. 1791; D. H. Lawrence d. 1930; First flight of *Concorde* 1969; Rhodesia became a republic 1970
3   Robert Adam d. 1792; Alexander Graham Bell b. 1847; Henry Wood b. 1869
4   US Constitution in force 1789; Comintern formed 1919
5   Churchill's Iron Curtain speech 1946; Marshal Iosif Stalin d. 1953
6   Michelangelo b. 1475; Elizabeth Barrett Browning b. 1806; Ivor Novello d. 1951; Ghana became independent 1957; Social Democratic Party officially launched 1981
7   Maurice Ravel b. 1875; Bell's telephone patented 1876
8   King William III d. 1702; Hector Berlioz d. 1869; Ferdinand von Zeppelin d. 1917; Sir Thomas Beecham d. 1961
9   Yuri Gagarin b. 1934
10 First telephone call 1876
11 Sir Harold Wilson b. 1916; German troops entered Austria 1938; Sir Alexander Fleming d. 1955
12 Russian revolution began 1917; Sun Yat-sen d. 1925; Mahatma Gandhi's civil disturbance campaign in India 1930; 30-mph speed limit introduced in built-up areas in England 1935
13 Uranus discovered by William Herschel 1781; Tsar Alexander II of Russia assassinated 1881; Driving test introduced in Britain 1935
14 Johann Strauss (the elder) b. 1804; Mrs Beeton b. 1836; Maxim Gorki b. 1868; Albert Einstein b. 1879; Karl Marx d. 1883; First trans-Atlantic broadcast 1925
15 Julius Caesar assassinated 44 BC; British clothes rationing ends 1949
16 Tiberius, Emperor of Rome, d. AD 37

17 Marcus Aurelius d. AD 180
18 Ivan the Terrible d. 1584; USSR cosmonaut leaves spacecraft and floats in space 1965
19 David Livingstone b. 1813; Sergey Diaghilev b. 1872
20 Sir Isaac Newton d. 1727; Napoleon's 'Hundred Days' began 1815; Henrik Ibsen b. 1828
21 Johann Sebastian Bach b. 1685
22 Anthony van Dyck b. 1599; Wolfgang von Goethe d. 1832; First public performance of movie show by Auguste and Louis Lumière 1894
23 Stamp Act 1765
24 Queen Elizabeth I d. 1603; Union of English and Scottish Crowns 1603
25 Béla Bartók b. 1881; Claude Debussy d. 1918; Common Market treaty signed by Belgium, France, West Germany, Italy, Luxembourg and Holland to found EEC
26 Ludwig van Beethoven d. 1827; Earl Lloyd-George of Dwyfor d. 1945; Noël Coward d. 1973
27 King James I d. 1625; James Callaghan b. 1912; Yuri Gagarin d. 1968
28 Britain and France entered Crimean War 1854; Spanish Civil War ended 1939; Dwight Eisenhower d. 1969
29 Charles Wesley d. 1788; Canada became a dominion 1867; Last US soldiers left Vietnam 1973
30 Francisco de Goya b. 1746; Ether used as anaesthetic in USA 1842; Vincent van Gogh b. 1853
31 Joseph Haydn b. 1732; John Constable d. 1837; Charlotte Brontë d. 1855

April (30 days)
DERIVATION: Latin, *Aprilis*, from *aperire* (to open), the season when trees and flowers begin to 'open'.

1   First postage stamp introduced in Britain for the London Penny Post 1680; Prince Otto von Bismarck b. 1815; Sergey Rachmaninov b. 1873; Royal Air Force formed 1918; Persecution of Jews began in Germany 1933; School leaving age raised to 15 in 1947; VAT introduced in Britain 1973
2   Charlemagne b. 742; Hans Christian Andersen b. 1805; Emile Zola b. 1840; Argentina invaded Falkland Islands 1982
3   Pony Express established in USA 1860; Johannes Brahms d. 1897
4   First permanent installation of a telephone, by Charles Williams at his home in Massachusetts, USA 1877; North Atlantic Treaty signed 1949; Martin Luther King assassinated 1968
5   Winston Churchill resigns – is succeeded by Eden 1955
6   King Richard I d. 1199; Opening of the first modern Olympic Games held in Athens 1896; Peary reached North Pole 1909; USA entered First World War 1917; PAYE introduced in Britain 1944; Igor Stravinsky d. 1971
7   Dick Turpin hanged 1739; William Wordsworth b. 1770
8   Entente Cordiale signed 1904; Pablo Picasso d. 1973
9   Francis Bacon (Viscount St Albans) d. 1626; Isambard Kingdom Brunel b. 1806; US Civil War ended 1865
10 Evelyn Waugh d. 1966
11 Treaty of Utrecht 1713

12 The Union Jack adopted in Britain 1606; US Civil War began 1861; Franklin Roosevelt d. 1945; Yuri Gagarin (USSR) made first manned Earth orbit 1961; US shuttle *Columbia* launched 1981

13 John Dryden became first Poet Laureate 1668; Thomas Jefferson b. 1743

14 George Frederick Handel d. 1759; First commercial showing of motion pictures, New York 1894; Irish Civil War began 1922

15 Leonardo da Vinci b. 1452; Henry James b. 1843; Abraham Lincoln d. 1865 (wounded by assassin); *Titanic* sank 1912; Jean-Paul Sartre d. 1980

16 Battle of Culloden 1746; Francisco de Goya d. 1828; Charles Chaplin b. 1889

17 Nikita Khrushchev b. 1894; Premium Bonds first issued 1956

18 Judge Jeffreys d. 1689; San Francisco earthquake 1906; League of Nations dissolved 1946; Republic of Ireland established 1949; Albert Einstein d. 1955; Zimbabwe independent 1980

19 War of American Independence started 1775; Lord Byron d. 1824; Benjamin Disraeli (Earl of Beaconsfield) d. 1881; Charles Darwin d. 1882; Pierre Curie d. 1906

20 Napoleon III b. 1808; Adolf Hitler b. 1889

21 Foundation of Rome 753 BC; Charlotte Brontë b. 1816; Mark Twain d. 1910; Queen Elizabeth II b. 1926

22 Vladimir Ulyanov (Lenin) b. 1870; Yehudi Menuhin b. 1916

23 William Shakespeare d. 1616; J. M. W. Turner b. 1775; William Wordsworth d. 1850; Rupert Brooke d. 1915

24 Daniel Defoe d. 1731; Anthony Trollope b. 1815; Stafford Cripps b. 1889; 'Easter Rebellion' in Dublin 1916

25 Oliver Cromwell b. 1599; C. B. Fry b. 1872; Guglielmo Marconi b. 1874

26 Marcus Aurelius b. AD 121

27 Samuel Morse b. 1791; Regent's Park Zoo, London opened 1828

28 Mutiny on the *Bounty* began 1789; Benito Mussolini killed 1945; Japan regained independence 1952; President de Gaulle resigned 1969; Alfred Hitchcock d. 1980

29 Emperor Hirohito of Japan b. 1901

30 George Washington became first US President 1789; Adolf Hitler committed suicide 1945; Potato rationing ended in Britain 1948; End of Vietnamese War 1975

May (31 days)
DERIVATION: Latin, *Maius*, either from Maia, an obscure goddess, or from *maiores* (elders), on the grounds that the month honoured old people, as June honoured the young.

1 Duke of Wellington b. 1769; Great Exhibition opened at Crystal Palace 1851; David Livingstone d. 1873; First May Day (Bank Holiday) in Britain 1978

2 Leonardo da Vinci d. 1519; Catherine the Great of Russia b. 1729

3 Niccolò Machiavelli b. 1469; New Zealand became British colony 1841; Golda Meir b. 1898; General Strike in Britain starts (ends 12th) 1926; King George VI opened Festival of Britain 1951

4 Epsom Derby first run 1780; Work on Panama Canal began 1904; Margaret Thatcher became

first woman Prime Minister of Britain 1979; Marshal Tito d. 1980

5 Karl Marx b. 1818; Napoleon Bonaparte d. 1821; Alan Shepard of USA became second man in space 1961

6 Sigmund Freud b. 1856; First 4-minute mile run by Roger Bannister, Oxford 1954

7 Robert Browning b. 1812; Johannes Brahms b. 1833; Pyotr Tchaikovsky b. 1840; *Lusitania* sunk 1915; Women get right to vote at age 21 1928

8 Paul Gauguin d. 1903; VE-Day in Britain 1945

9 John Brown b. 1800; J. M. (later Sir James) Barrie b. 1860; West Germany admitted to NATO 1955

10 Winston Churchill became Prime Minister 1940; London's heaviest air raid 1941

11 First known printing of a book, *Diamond Sutra*, a Buddhist scripture 868; William Pitt, Earl of Chatham, d. 1778; Trans-Globe expedition reached North Pole, completing first circumnavigation of globe via both Poles 1982

12 Florence Nightingale b. 1820; General Strike ended 1926; Voting age lowered to eighteen 1969

13 Fridtjof Nansen d. 1930

14 Morse transmitted first message on US telegraph 1844; British Legion founded 1921; Home Guard formed in Britain 1940; State of Israel proclaimed 1948; *Skylab* launched 1973

15 Pierre Curie b. 1859; First British hydrogen bomb exploded 1957

16 First film 'Oscars' awarded 1929; Dambusters' raid 1943

17 First colour photograph shown at the Royal Institution, London 1861; Mafeking relieved 1900; Ayatollah Ruhollah Khomeini b. 1900

18 Bertrand (later 3rd Earl) Russell b. 1872; Gustav Mahler d. 1911; Pope John Paul II b. 1920

19 Anne Boleyn executed 1536; W. E. Gladstone d. 1898

20 Christopher Columbus d. 1506; Honoré de Balzac b. 1799

21 Charles Lindbergh completed first solo transAtlantic flight in 37 hours 1927

22 Richard Wagner b. 1813; Sir Arthur Conan Doyle b. 1859; Victor Hugo d. 1885; First public demonstration of motion picture film at Edison Laboratories, USA 1891

23 Henrik Ibsen d. 1906; Italy declared war on Austria-Hungary 1915; Nuclear-generated electric power started from Calder Hall 1956

24 Nicolaus Copernicus d. 1543; Queen Victoria b. 1819

25 Max Aitken (later Lord Beaverbrook) b. 1879; Josip Broz (Tito) b. 1892

26 Samuel Pepys d. 1703; End of American Civil War 1865; Queen Mary b. 1867; Al Jolson b. 1886; Petrol rationing ends in Britain 1950

27 Habeas Corpus Act 1679; Dunkirk evacuation began 1940; Jawaharlal Nehru d. 1964; Guyana became independent 1966

28 King George I b. 1660; William Pitt (the younger) b. 1759; Neville Chamberlain became Prime Minister 1937; Duke of Windsor d. 1972

29 Sir Humphrey Davy d. 1829; John F. Kennedy b. 1917; Hillary and Tenzing first climbed Mount Everest 1953

30 Joan of Arc executed 1431; Peter Paul Rubens d. 1640; Voltaire d. 1778; First hovercraft 'flight'

at Cowes, England 1959
31 Pepys' Diary ended 1669; Joseph Haydn d. 1809; End of Boer War 1902; Battle of Jutland 1916; South Africa leaves the Commonwealth 1961

June (30 days)

DERIVATION: Latin, *Junius*, either from the goddess Juno or from *iuniores* (young people), on the grounds that the month is dedicated to youth.

1 John Masefield b. 1878; First telephone public call-box installed in USA 1880; Clothes rationing introduced in Britain 1941; First TV licences introduced in Britain 1946
2 Thomas Hardy b. 1840; Edward Elgar b. 1857; Apartheid programme began in S. Africa 1949; Coronation of Queen Elizabeth II 1953
3 Johann Strauss (the younger) d. 1899
4 King George III b. 1738; Giacomo Casanova d. 1798; First Trooping of the Colour, Horse Guards, London 1805; Ex-Kaiser Wilhelm II d. 1941; Rome liberated 1944; Profumo resigned from British Parliament after scandal 1963
5 Marshall Plan launched 1947; Six-day War between Israel and Arab nations 1967; Robert Kennedy shot and died 1968
6 Aleksandr Pushkin b. 1799; D-Day invasion in Normandy 1944
7 Robert I ('The Bruce') d. 1329; George ('Beau') Brummell b. 1778
8 Muhammad d. 632; Edward, the Black Prince, d. 1376; Robert Schumann b. 1810
9 Book of Common Prayer adopted throughout England 1549; George Stephenson b. 1781; Charles Dickens d. 1870; Cole Porter b. 1893; First atomic-powered submarine launched in US 1959; First live radio broadcast of House of Commons sitting 1975
10 André Marie Ampère d. 1836; Prince Philip, Duke of Edinburgh b. 1921; Frederick Delius d. 1934; NHS prescription charges introduced 1968
11 Ben Jonson b. 1573; John Constable b. 1776; Richard Strauss b. 1864
12 Charles Kingsley b. 1819; Anthony Eden (later Earl of Avon) b. 1897; First flying bomb (V1) dropped on London 1944; Nelson Mandela sentenced to life imprisonment in S. Africa 1964
13 Alexander the Great d. 323 BC; W. B. Yeats b. 1865; Boxer Rising in China 1900
14 G. K. Chesterton d. 1936; John Logie Baird d. 1946; Cessation of hostilities agreed in Falkland Islands between Britain and Argentina 1982
15 Magna Carta sealed 1215; Edward, the Black Prince, b. 1330; Edward Greig b. 1843; First non-stop air crossing of the Atlantic completed in 16 hr 27 min by Capt. John William Alcock and Lieut. Arthur Whitten Brown 1919
16 Duke of Marlborough d. 1722; Valentina Tereshkova first woman in space (USSR) 1963; 'Watergate' scandal began in USA 1972
17 John Wesley b. 1703; Battle of Bunker Hill 1775; Igor Stravinsky b. 1882; China detonates her first H-bomb 1967
18 USA declared war on Britain 1812; Battle of Waterloo 1815
19 Sir James Barrie d. 1937
20 First municipal fire brigade in Britain, founded at Beverley, Yorkshire 1726; British

captives held in Black Hole of Calcutta 1756; King William IV d. 1837; Bomb plot to assassinate Hitler failed 1944
21 Edward III d. 1377; Niccolò Machiavelli d. 1527; Jean-Paul Sartre b. 1905; Nikolay Rimsky-Korsakov d. 1908
22 Slaves reaching Britain were declared free 1772; Germany invaded the USSR 1941
23 King Edward VIII (later Duke of Windsor) b. 1894
24 Battle of Bannockburn 1314; Lucrezia Borgia d. 1519; St John Ambulance Brigade founded as Ambulance Association by the Red Cross 1877
25 Custer's Last Stand 1876; Louis of Battenburg (later Earl Mountbatten of Burma) b. 1900; Korean War began 1950
26 King George IV d. 1830; Corn Laws repealed 1946; Duke of Windsor marries Wallis Simpson 1937; UN Charter signed 1945
27 Charles Stewart Parnell b. 1846
28 Henry VIII b. 1491; Peter Paul Rubens b. 1577; Archduke Franz Ferdinand assassinated 1914; Germans signed Peace Treaty at Versailles 1919
29 Elizabeth Barrett Browning d. 1861; Thomas Huxley d. 1895
30 Stanley Spencer b. 1891; Bikini atom bomb exploded 1946; Nancy Mitford d. 1973

July (31 days)

DERIVATION: Latin, *Julius*, after Gaius Julius Caesar (b. 12 July, probably in 100 BC, d. 15 March 44 BC), the Roman soldier and statesman. (Formerly known by the Romans as *Quintilis*, the fifth month.)

1 Aurore Dupin (alias George Sand) b. 1804; First registration of births, deaths and marriages in Britain 1837; South Africa became a dominion 1910; Battle of the Somme began 1916; Princess of Wales b. 1961; Algeria became independent 1962
2 Sir Robert Peel d. 1850; Salvation Army founded 1865; Anton Chekhov d. 1904; First flight by German Zeppelin airship 1900; Joseph Chamberlain d. 1914; Ernest Hemingway d. 1961; US Civil Rights Acts ratified 1964
3 Robert Adam b. 1728; First television transmission in colour in London 1928; First transatlantic crossing in hot-air balloon by Richard Branson 1987
4 US Declaration of Independence approved 1776; Thomas Jefferson d. 1826; First regular scheduled bus service in Britain introduced in London with rear entrance buses drawn by three horses 1829
5 Britain's National Health Service inaugurated 1948
6 Henry II d. 1189; Last tram ran in London 1952; Aneurin Bevan d. 1960; Malawi became a republic 1964
7 Edward I d. 1307; Gustav Mahler b. 1860; Sir Arthur Conan Doyle d. 1930
8 Percy Bysshe Shelley d. 1822; Joseph Chamberlain b. 1836
9 Betrothal of Princess Elizabeth to Lieut. Philip Mountbatten announced 1947
10 Rodrigo Díaz de Vivar ('El Cid') d. 1099; Battle of Britain began 1940; *Telstar* satellite launched 1962
11 Robert I ('The Bruce') b. 1274; George Gershwin d. 1937; Aga Khan III d. 1957; *Skylab I* disintegrated 1979

12 Julius Caesar b. 100 BC; Erasmus d. 1536
13 Arnold Schoenberg d. 1951
14 Storming of the Bastille began 1789; The Home Guard in G.B. was established 1940
15 Anton Chekhov d. 1904; National Health Insurance Act passed 1912
16 Joshua Reynolds b. 1723; First atomic bomb exploded 1945
17 Adam Smith d. 1790; *Punch* published 1841
18 William Makepeace Thackeray b. 1811; Jane Austen d. 1817; Spanish Civil War began 1936
19 Lady Jane Grey deposed 1553; Edgar Degas b. 1834; Hitler became Führer 1934
20 Guglielmo Marconi d. 1937; First regular hovercraft passenger service introduced in Britain 1962; First Moon landing by man, Armstrong and Aldrin 1969
21 Robert Burns d. 1796; First Royal Command Film Performance, held in London 1896; Ernest Hemingway b. 1899; Bread rationing in Britain 1946
22 Battle of Salamanca 1812
23 Gen. Ulysses S. Grant d. 1885
24 Simón Bolívar b. 1783; Alexandre Dumas b. 1802; Robert Graves b. 1895
25 Arthur Balfour b. 1848; Louis Blériot (Fra) completed first plane crossing of English Channel in 36½ min 1909; Hovercraft crossed English Channel in 2 hr 1959; World's first 'test-tube' baby born in England 1978
26 George Bernard Shaw b. 1856; Carl Jung b. 1875; Aldous Huxley b. 1894
27 Korean War ended 1953
28 Antonio Vivaldi d. 1741; Johann Sebastian Bach d. 1750; Austria-Hungary declared war on Serbia 1914
29 Spanish Armada defeated 1588; Robert Schumann d. 1856; Benito Mussolini b. 1883; Vincent van Gogh d. 1890; Prince Charles and Lady Diana Spencer married 1981
30 Henry Ford b. 1863; Prince Otto von Bismarck d. 1898; England won World Cup at football 1966
31 First public postal service (inland) established in Britain 1635; St Ignatius of Loyola d. 1556; Franz Liszt d. 1886

August (31 days)

DERIVATION: Latin, *Augustus*, after Augustus Caesar (born Gaius Octavius), the first Roman emperor. (Originally called *Sextilis*, the sixth month.)

1 Queen Anne d. 1714; Battle of the Nile 1798; Abolition of slavery in British Empire 1834; Parcel post introduced in Britain 1883; Germany declared war on Russia 1914
2 King William II d. 1100; Thomas Gainsborough d. 1788; Arthur Bliss b. 1891; USSR explodes hydrogen bomb 1953
3 Rupert Brooke b. 1887; Germany declared war on France 1914; Joseph Conrad d. 1924; Colette d. 1954
4 Percy Bysshe Shelley b. 1792; British Red Cross Society founded 1870; Queen Elizabeth the Queen Mother b. 1900; Britain declared war on Germany 1914; Amin ordered expulsion of British Asians in Uganda 1972
5 First cinema opened in Britain 1901; Neil Armstrong b. 1930; Britain, USSR and USA sign nuclear test-ban treaty 1963
6 End of Holy Roman Empire 1806; Alfred (later Lord) Tennyson b. 1809; Alexander Fleming b.

1881; First atomic bomb dropped on Hiroshima 1945
7 British Summer Time Act 1925
8 Mont Blanc first climbed 1786; Emiliano Zapata b. 1879; Great Train Robbery 1963; US President Nixon resigns 1974; Dmitri Shostakovich d. 1975
9 John Dryden b. 1631; Canada/US border defined 1842; Second atomic bomb, dropped on Nagasaki 1945
10 Royal Observatory founded at Greenwich 1675
11 Cardinal John Henry Newman d. 1890
12 George Stephenson d. 1848; British–Zulu Wars 1879
13 Battle of Blenheim 1704; Florence Nightingale d. 1910; Fidel Castro b. 1927; H. G. Wells d. 1946; E. Germany seals off border and (17–18 Aug) builds 'Berlin Wall' 1961
14 John Galsworthy b. 1867; Bertolt Brecht d. 1956
15 Napoleon Bonaparte b. 1769; Sir Walter Scott b. 1771; T. E. Lawrence (Lawrence of Arabia) b. 1888; Panama Canal opened 1914; Japan surrendered to Allies and ended Second World War (VJ Day) 1945; India and Pakistan independent 1947
16 Peterloo Massacre 1819; Sir Alexander Fleming b. 1881; Menachem Begin b. 1913; Cyprus became independent 1960; Elvis Presley d. 1977
17 Frederick the Great d. 1786; Davy Crocket b. 1786; Registration of Births Act 1836; Honoré de Balzac d. 1850; Mae West b. 1892
18 Berlin Wall completed 1961
19 Blaise Pascal d. 1662; Sir Jacob Epstein d. 1959
20 Groucho Marx d. 1977
21 Princess Margaret b. 1930; Leo Trotsky d. 1940 (wounded by assassin); Invasion of Czechoslovakia 1968
22 English Civil War began 1642; Claude Debussy b. 1862
23 Rudolph Valentino d. 1926; World Council of Churches formed 1948
24 Vesuvius erupted AD 79; North Atlantic Treaty effective 1949
25 Uruguay became independent 1825; Michael Faraday d. 1867; Paris liberated 1944
26 Battle of Crécy 1346; Sir Robert Walpole b. 1676; Prince Albert b. 1819
27 Confucius b. 551 BC; Titian d. 1576; Krakatoa erupted 1883; Earl Mountbatten assassinated 1979
28 St Augustine of Hippo d. 430; Wolfgang von Goethe b. 1749; Leo Tolstoy b. 1828
29 Sergei Diaghilev d. 1929; Eamon de Valera d. 1975
30 Mary Shelley b. 1797
31 John Bunyan d. 1688

September (30 days)

DERIVATION: Latin, from *septem* (seven), as it was originally the seventh month.

1 King Louis XIV of France d. 1715; Earthquake in Japan devastated Tokyo and Yokohama 1923; Germany invaded Poland 1939
2 Great Fire of London began 1666 (ended 6 Sept); J. R. R. Tolkien d. 1973
3 Oliver Cromwell d. 1658; Peace of Versailles recognized independence of USA 1783; France became constitutional monarchy 1791; Britain and France declared war on Germany 1939

4 Edward Grieg d. 1907; First night raid by German planes on London in First World War 1917; Albert Schweitzer d. 1965
5 King Louis XIV of France b. 1638; Jesse James b. 1847
6 *Mayflower* sailed from Plymouth 1620; First free public lending library opened in Britain 1852; Dr Hendrik Verwoerd assassinated 1966
7 Elizabeth I b. 1533; London Blitz began 1940
8 King Richard I b. 1157; Antonín Dvořák b. 1841; First V2 rocket landed in England 1944; Richard Strauss d. 1949
9 William the Conqueror d. 1087; Battle of Flodden Field 1513; Cardinal Richelieu b. 1585; Leo Tolstoy b. 1828; Mao Zedong (Mao Tse-tung) d. 1976
10 Mungo Park b. 1771
11 D. H. Lawrence b. 1885; Jan Smuts d. 1950
12 Jesse Owens b. 1913; Death of Stephen Biko in S. Africa 1977
13 J. B. Priestley b. 1894
14 Gregorian Calendar adopted in Britain 1752; Crimean War began 1854
15 Isambard Kingdom Brunel d. 1859
16 King Henry V b. 1387; Post Office Savings bank instituted in Britain 1861; Two-tier postal charges introduced 1968; Maria Callas d. 1977
17 Circumnavigation of Earth by Juan le Elcano, captain of *Vittoria*, arrived in Spain after three-year voyage 1522; Abraham Lincoln declared that from 1 Jan 1863 all slaves in US to be free 1862; Francis Chichester b. 1901
18 Samuel Johnson b. 1709; Greta Garbo b. 1905
19 Battle of Poitiers 1356; Dr Thomas Barnardo d. 1905; Emil Zátopek b. 1922.
20 Eton College founded 1440; Jean Sibelius d. 1957; *QEII* launched 1967
21 John McAdam b. 1756; Sir Walter Scott d. 1832; H. G. Wells b. 1866; BP struck oil in North Sea 1965
22 Michael Faraday b. 1791; Commercial television (ITV) began in Britain 1955
23 Augustus, Emperor of Rome, b. 63 BC; Sigmund Freud d. 1939
24 Horatio (Horace) Walpole b. 1717
25 Relief of Lucknow 1857; Dmitri Shostakovich b. 1906; Transatlantic telephone service in operation 1956
26 Arrival of Sir Francis Drake in Plymouth after 33-month voyage to circumnavigate the Earth 1580; T. S. Eliot b. 1888; Giovanni Montini (later Pope Paul VI) b. 1897; RMS *Queen Mary* launched 1934
27 St Vincent de Paul d. 1660; Stockton–Darlington Railway opened 1825; RMS *Queen Elizabeth* launched 1938
28 St Wenceslas d. 929; Louis Pasteur d. 1895; W. H. Auden d. 1973
29 Battle of Marathon 490 BC; Horatio Nelson b. 1758; Emile Zola d. 1902; Turkish Republic proclaimed under Kemal 1923; Gamal Abdel Nasser d. 1970
30 St Thérèse d. 1897; First BBC TV broadcast 1929; Nuremburg Trials end 1946

October (31 days)
DERIVATION: Latin, from *octo* (eight), originally the eighth month.

1 First official postcard issued by the Post Office in Britain 1870; Vladimir Horowitz b. 1904; Communist People's Republic of China proclaimed under Mao Tse-tung 1949
2 Mohandas (Mahatma) Gandhi b. 1869; Groucho Marx b. 1890; Graham Greene b. 1904
3 St Francis of Assisi d. 1226; William Morris d. 1896; Boer War started 1899
4 Rembrandt van Rijn d. 1669; Buster Keaton b. 1895; *Sputnik I* launched 1957; *Lunik III* photographed Moon 1959
5 Tea rationing ended in Britain 1952
6 Charles Stewart Parnell d. 1891; Lord Tennyson d. 1892; Arab–Israeli War started 1973; President Anwar Sadat assassinated 1981
7 Edgar Allan Poe d. 1849
8 Henry Fielding d. 1754; Juan Perón b. 1895; Earl Attlee d. 1967; Drink-and-drive laws came into force in UK 1967
9 Battle of Ypres began 1914; Pope Pius XII d. 1958
10 Giuseppe Verdi b. 1813; Fridtjof Nansen b. 1861
11 Vatican Council opened 1962; *Mary Rose*, warship of Henry VIII (sank 1545), raised 1982
12 Ralph Vaughan Williams b. 1872
13 Emilie Le Breton (Lillie Langtry) b. 1853; Sir Henry Irving d. 1905; Margaret Thatcher b. 1925; Bank rate abolished 1972
14 Battle of Hastings 1066; William Penn b. 1644; Dwight Eisenhower b. 1890; Degrees open to women at Oxford for first time 1920
15 Publius Vergilius Maro (Virgil) b. 70 BC; Marie Stopes b. 1880; *Graf Zeppelin* crosses Atlantic 1928
16 Marie Antoinette executed 1793; Oscar Wilde b. 1854; Eugene O'Neill b. 1888; Revolution in China 1911; China exploded atomic bomb 1964; Pope John Paul II elected 1978
17 Frédéric Chopin d. 1849
18 Viscount Palmerston d. 1865; Charles Gounod d. 1893; Pierre Trudeau b. 1919; Thomas Alva Edison d. 1931
19 King John d. 1216; Jonathan Swift d. 1745; Lord Rutherford d. 1937
20 Sir Christopher Wren b. 1632
21 Samuel Taylor Coleridge b. 1772; Battle of Trafalgar, Nelson mortally wounded 1805; Alfred Bernhard Nobel b. 1833; Welsh Aberfan mining disaster 1966
22 Franz Liszt b. 1811; Sarah Bernhardt b. 1844; Pablo Casals d. 1973
23 W. G. Grace d. 1915; Battle of El Alamein began 1942; Al Jolson d. 1950
24 Sybil Thorndike b. 1882; UN Organization established 1945
25 Battle of Agincourt 1415; Charge of the Light Brigade at Balaklava 1854; Pablo Picasso b. 1881
26 King Alfred d. 899; William Hogarth d. 1764; George Stephenson d. 1848; First public demonstration of the telephone in Frankfurt, Germany 1861; Lev Bronstein (Trotsky) b. 1879; Chinese Republic proclaimed 1911
27 Erasmus b. 1466; Capt. James Cook b. 1728; Theodore Roosevelt b. 1858
28 Toulouse-Lautrec b. 1864; Evelyn Waugh b. 1903; Pope John XXIII elected 1958
29 Sir Walter Raleigh executed 1618; New York Wall Street stock market crash 1929
30 King George II b. 1683; First successful television experiment by John Logie Baird 1925
31 John Keats b. 1795; Chiang Kai-shek b. 1887; Augustus John d. 1961

November (30 days)
DERIVATION: Latin, from *novem* (nine), originally the ninth month.

1 Lisbon earthquake killed 30 000 in 1755; Turkish republic proclaimed 1922; First hydrogen bomb exploded 1952
2 Marie Antoinette b. 1755; First television broadcasts by BBC from Alexandra Palace 1936; George Bernard Shaw d. 1950
3 Karl Baedeker b. 1801; Henri Matisse d. 1954; *Sputnik II* containing a dog launched by USSR 1957
4 Felix Mendelssohn-Bartholdy d. 1847; Abraham Lincoln elected US President 1860
5 Gunpowder Plot to blow up Houses of Parliament discovered 1605; Vivien Leigh b. 1913
6 Pyotr Tchaikovsky d. 1893; National Health Act comes into effect 1946; US exploded first hydrogen bomb 1952
7 Marja Sklodowska (later Marie Curie) b. 1867; Bolshevik revolution 1917; Lady Astor became first woman MP to take her seat 1919
8 John Milton d. 1674; F. D. Roosevelt elected US President 1932; Richard Nixon elected President of USA 1968
9 Edward VII b. 1841; Neville Chamberlain d. 1940; John F. Kennedy elected President of USA 1960; General Charles de Gaulle d. 1970
10 Martin Luther b. 1483; H. M. Stanley met David Livingstone at Ujiji 1871; First motor cycle, invented by Gottlieb Daimler, driven in Germany 1885
11 Fyodor Dostoyevsky b. 1821; Armistice Day 1918; Sir Edward German d. 1936; Rhodesia Declaration of Independence 1965
12 King Canute d. 1035; Sir John Hawkins d. 1595; Auguste Rodin b. 1840
13 St Augustine b. 354; Edward III b. 1312; Robert Louis Stevenson b. 1850
14 Nell Gwyn d. 1687; Claude Monet b. 1840; Jawaharlal Nehru b. 1889; Prince of Wales b. 1948; Colour programmes started on television on BBC1 and ITV 1969
15 William Pitt (the elder) b. 1708; Erwin Rommel b. 1891
16 Tiberius b. 42 BC; King Henry III d. 1272; Suez Canal opened 1869
17 Catherine the Great d. 1796; Bernard (later Viscount) Montgomery b. 1887
18 W. S. (later Sir William) Gilbert b. 1836
19 Charles I b. 1600; Franz Schubert d. 1828; Mrs Indira Gandhi b. 1917
20 Count Leo Tolstoy d. 1910; Wedding of Princess (now Queen) Elizabeth to Philip Mountbatten 1947
21 François-Marie Arouet (Voltaire) b. 1694; Henry Purcell d. 1695
22 Charles de Gaulle b. 1890; John F. Kennedy assassinated by Lee H. Oswald in Dallas 1963
23 First pillar box in Britain put into public use in Jersey 1852; Billy the Kid b. 1859; First Royal Command Film Performance before the Sovereign, Queen Victoria, at Windsor Castle 1897
24 Charles Darwin's *Origin of Species* published 1859
25 Angelo Roncalli (later Pope John XXIII) b. 1881; Dame Myra Hess d. 1965
26 John McAdam d. 1836
27 Quintus Horatius Flaccus (Horace) d. 8 BC; Alexander Dubček b. 1921
28 Royal Society founded 1660; William Blake b. 1757
29 Cardinal Thomas Wolsey d. 1530; Louisa May Alcott b. 1832; European Free Trade Association (EFTA) treaty ratified by Britain, Norway, Sweden, Portugal, Switzerland, Austria and Denmark 1959
30 Francis Drake returned from circumnavigating the world in the *Golden Hind* 1580; Jonathan Swift b. 1667; Samuel Clemens (Mark Twain) b. 1835; Winston Churchill b. 1874; Oscar Wilde d. 1900

December (31 days)
DERIVATION: Latin, from *decem* (ten), originally the tenth month.

1 King Henry I d. 1135; Queen Alexandra b. 1844; Beveridge Report 1942; First Christmas stamp introduced in Britain by Post Office 1966
2 Hernán Cortés d. 1547; Sir Christopher Wren's St Paul's Cathedral opened 1697; Battle of Austerlitz 1805; Maria Callas b. 1923; First nuclear chain reaction 1942
3 Joseph Conrad b. 1857; R. L. Stevenson d. 1894; First human heart transplant 1967
4 Thomas Carlyle b. 1795; Samuel Butler b. 1835; Benjamin Britten d. 1976
5 Wolfgang Amadeus Mozart d. 1791; Claude Monet d. 1926; First British motorway opened, Preston bypass section of the M6 1958
6 Anthony Trollope d. 1882; Will Hay b. 1888; Peace treaty sets up Irish Free State 1921
7 Mary, Queen of Scots b. 1542; Japanese attacked Pearl Harbor 1941; John Lennon killed in New York 1980
8 Britain and USA declared war on Japan 1941; Golda Meir d. 1978
9 John Milton b. 1608; Joel Chandler Harris ('Uncle Remus') b. 1848
10 Royal Academy founded 1768; Alfred Nobel d. 1896
11 Hector Berlioz b. 1803; Aleksandr Solzhenitsyn b. 1918; USA declared war on Germany and Italy 1941
12 Robert Browning d. 1889; First transatlantic radio signal 1901
13 Dr Samuel Johnson d. 1784; First permanent electric street lighting introduced in Britain on the Victoria Embankment, London 1878
14 George Washington d. 1799
15 Sitting Bull killed 1890; BBC incorporated 1922; Queen Salote of Tonga d. 1965; Walt Disney d. 1966
16 Boston Tea Party 1773; Jane Austen b. 1775; Noël Coward b. 1899; Roald Amundsen reached South Pole 1911; House of Commons voted for abolition of death penalty 1969
17 Ludwig van Beethoven bapt. 1770; Sir Humphry Davy b. 1778; Vincent van Gogh b. 1853; First petrol-powered aircraft flight 1903
18 Antonio Stradivari d. 1737; Slavery abolished in USA 1865
19 J. M. W. Turner d. 1851; Leonid Brezhnev b. 1906
20 Robert Menzies b. 1894; John Steinbeck d. 1968
21 Pilgrim Fathers landed 1620; Benjamin Disraeli b. 1804; Iosif Stalin b. 1879; Charles de Gaulle elected President of France 1958
22 Jean Racine b. 1639; James Wolfe b. 1726
23 Samuel Smiles b. 1812; Helmut Schmidt b. 1918
24 St Ignatius of Loyola b. 1491; First advertised

radio broadcast from Brant Rock, Massachusetts, USA 1906

25 Isaac Newton b. 1642; Anwar Sadat b. 1918; W. C. Fields d. 1946; Sir Charles Chaplin d. 1977
26 Thomas Gray b. 1716; Mao Zedong (Mao Tsetung) b. 1893; Radium discovered by the Curies 1898; Harry Truman d. 1972
27 Johannes Kepler b. 1571; Louis Pasteur b. 1822; Charles Lamb d. 1834; Soviet forces intervened in Afghanistan 1979
28 Queen Mary II d. 1694; Woodrow Wilson b. 1856; First driving licence issued in Britain 1903
29 St Thomas à Becket killed 1170; Madame de Pompadour b. 1721; William E. Gladstone b. 1809; Pablo Casals b. 1876; Jameson Raid 1895; Irish Free State became Eire 1937; London severely damaged by incendiary bombing 1940
30 Rudyard Kipling b. 1865; Grigori Rasputin assassinated 1916
31 Charles Edward Stuart (the Young Pretender) b. 1720; Henri Matisse b. 1869

Charles Chaplin (1899–1977) – his first appearance in his tramp costume – in *Kid Auto Race at Venice*. (British Film Institute)

THE PLANT WORLD

Glossary

abscission The shedding of a leaf, fruit, flower, etc., by a plant.

absorption Taking up of water, solutes and other substances by both active and passive mechanisms. The taking up of radiant energy (from the sun) by pigments in plants.

achene A simple one-seeded indehiscent dry fruit.

acid rain Rain containing high levels of acidity caused by nitrogen and sulphur oxides – pollution from the burning of coal and oil.

active transport The transport of substances across a membrane, e.g. cell membrane, against a concentration gradient.

ADP Abbreviation for adenine diphosphate. The conversion of ADP to ATP is of central importance in the storage of light energy absorbed during photosynthesis.

adventitious Organs that arise in unexpected sites, e.g. leaves that grow roots.

aerial root A root that appears above soil level, usually hanging down in moist air.

aerobe Organism that can live only in the presence of oxygen.

aerobic respiration Respiration involving the oxidation of oranic substrates and the associated absorption of free oxygen.

alcoholic fermentation Anaerobic respiration in which glucose is broken down to form ethanol and carbon dioxide. Carried out by yeasts.

algae Simple and diverse plant group. They are largely aquatic and many are unicellular.

alpine A regional community of plants found in high mountainous regions and on high plateaus.

alternation of generations The occurrence of an asexual and a sexual reproductive form during the life cycle of a plant.

amino acid These form the basic building blocks of proteins. About 20 commonly occur in proteins.

anaerobe An organism that can live in the absence of free oxygen.

anaerobic respiration This covers a number of chemical pathways by which chemical energy is obtained from various substrates without the use of free oxygen.

androdioecious Male and hermaphrodite flowers borne on separate plants.

androecium Male component of a flower, consisting of several stamens.

andromonoecius Male and hermaphrodite flowers carried on the same plant.

anemophily Wind pollination.

angiosperms The flowering plants.

annual Plant that germinates from seed, grows, flowers, produces seeds and then dies, all within a single year.

annual ring The ring of new wood added to the existing core of wood in a tree in a single year.

anther The tip of the stamen that produces the pollen grains.

antheridium Male sex organ in lower plants.

aphids Insects that feed by sucking plant juices.

apomixis Asexual reproduction.

arboretum An area in which woody plants are grown.

asexual reproduction The formation of new individuals from the parent without the fusion of gametes.

ATP Abbreviation for adenosine triphosphate. It has one more phosphate grouping than ADP and it is the addition of this grouping that acts as an energy store.

auricle A small projection from the base of a leaf or petal.

auxin Plant growth substances that promote the elongation of shoots and roots.

axil The upper angle formed where the leaf or a similar organ joins the stem.

backcross Cross between an individual and one of its parents. Backcrossing is used to introduce desirable genes into a cultivated variety of a plant.

bacteria Microscopic unicellular plants with cell nuclear material not separated from the rest of the cell contents by a nuclear membrane.

bark All the tissues outside the vascular cambium in the stems and roots showing secondary growth.

benthos Plants that live on the seabed or a lake bed.

berry Many-seeded fleshy indehiscent fruit.

biennial A plant that takes two years to complete its life cycle, growing vegetatively in the first year, then flowering, seeding and dying in the second year.

binomial nomenclature System of naming plants using a generic name and a specific epithet. Developed by Linnaeus.

biochemistry Study and use of metabolism and metabolic chemicals.

biological control Control of pests by making use of their natural predators.

blight Plant disease in which leaf damage is sudden and acute.

bloom A noticeable increase in the numbers of a species in the plankton. Usually refers to algae.

bolting Premature production of flowers and seeds.

bract Small leaflike structure that subtends a flower or inflorescence.

bracteole Small bract, typically on a flower stalk.

bud A short axis bearing a densely-packed series of leaf or flower primordia produced by an apical meristem.

budding Asexual reproduction in which a new individual is produced by an outgrowth of the parent.

bud grafting A bud and a small piece of bark is removed and inserted into a slit in the bark of the root-stock.

bulb A fleshy underground modified shoot, made up of swollen scale leaves or leaf bases. It is a perennating organ, allowing the plant to survive for many years.

bulbil Small bulb found on an aerial bud, functioning as a means of vegetative propagation.

callus Parenchymatous cells formed at the site of a wound.

calyx The sepals; the outer whorl of the perianth.

cambium A meristem that occurs parallel with the long axis of an organ. It is responsible for secondary growth.

canker Plant disease in which there is an area of necrosis which becomes surrounded by layers of callus tissue.

capillary action The effect of surface tension on a liquid in a fine tube, causing the liquid to rise up the tube. The supply of water throughout a plant is largely due to capillary action.

carbohydrates Contain carbon, hydrogen and oxygen, often in the formula $(CH_2O)_n$. They are energy storage molecules and form structural components.

carbon dioxide Makes up 0·03% of the air, and is converted to carbohydrates by photosynthesis.

carpel This carries and encloses the ovules in flowering plants. It consists of the ovary, style and stigma.

catkin Hanging unisexual inflorescence, designed for wind pollination.

cellulose A carbohydrate consisting solely of glucose units. It is present in plant cell walls as highly organized microfibrils.

chlorophyll The main class of photosynthetic pigment. They absorb red and blue light and reflect green light; hence the characteristic green colour of photosynthetic plants.

chloroplast Green bodies in plant cells, that contain photosynthetic pigment molecules.

chlorosis Condition in plants in which the chlorophyll levels drop, producing a yellow or pale unhealthy plant.

ciliate Describing a part of the plant fringed with hairs.

circadian rhythm A cycle in which physiological responses occur at 24-hourly intervals, e.g. opening and closing of stomata, change in position of leaves.

cladode A stem structure resembling a leaf, usually produced as an adaptation to dry conditions. The leaves will be reduced when a plant bears cladodes.

cleistogamy When flowers do not open to reveal the reproductive organs, thus preventing cross-pollination.

climacteric Rise in respiration rate in some fruits during ripening.

club root Fungal disease in which roots become swollen and malformed, causing wilting, yellowing and stunting.

coenocarpium Fruit that includes ovaries, floral parts and receptacles of a number of flowers on a fleshy axis.

collenchyma Long cells with thickened but non-lignified primary cell walls. A supporting tissue.

contractile root Specialized thickened root that pulls a rhizome, bulb, corm, etc., down into the soil.

coppicing Cutting trees back to ground level every 10–15 years. New shoots from the base are therefore encouraged and can be harvested when the coppice is next cut back.

cordate Heart-shaped, e.g. leaves.

corm Short swollen underground stem, acting as an organ of perennation and vegetative propagation.

corolla The petals.

corolla tube Fusion of the edges of the petals.

corona Crownlike out-growing of a corolla tube.

corymb Flat-topped cluster of flowers on lateral stalks of different lengths.

cotyledon The first leaf or leaves of the embryo in seed plants. In non-endosperm seeds they are used as food storage organs.

cross-pollination In which pollen from one individual is transferred to the stigma of another individual.

cultivar Variety or strain produced artificially and not found in the natural population.

cuticle Layer of cutin on the surface of aerial parts of a plant, broken only by stomata and lenticels. It acts to conserve water.

cutin Forms the waxy cuticle.

cutting A common form of artificial propagation whereby a portion of a living plant is detached and grown in soil or culture medium.

cymose Inflorescence in which apical tissues of the main and lateral stems differentiate into flowers.

cryptophyte Plant with perennating buds below ground or water.

2,4-D Abbreviation for 2,4-dichlorophenoxyacetic acid, a synthetic auxin widely used in selective weedkillers.

damping off Disease of seedlings in which they rot at soil level and then die. Caused by crowded conditions and cold wet soil.

dark reactions Part of the photosynthetic process that is not light dependent. Stored energy in ATP is used to convert carbon dioxide to carbohydrate.

deciduous Woody perennial trees that shed their leaves before the winter or dry season.

decumbent A stem that lies along the ground.

deficiency disease Disease caused by lack of an essential nutrient, especially minerals.

definite growth A maximum size is reached, beyond which the plant can grow no more.

dehiscence The bursting open of certain plant organs at maturity, especially reproductive structures, to release their contents.

denitrification Loss of nitrate from the soil due to the action of denitrifying bacteria.

dentate A leaf margin that is toothed.

desert Regional community with low rainfall.

dichogamy Anthers and stima maturing at different times on the same plant, thus reducing the chance of self-fertilization.

dicliny Male and female reproductive parts in different flowers.

dicotyledons Those angiosperms with embryos with two cotyledons. The group includes hardwood trees, shrubs and many herbaceous plants.

diffusion The movement of ions or molecules in solution down a concentration gradient. It is involved in, for example, transpiration and the uptake of carbon dioxide.

dioecious Male and female reproductive organs on different individuals, making cross-fertilization necessary and ensuring genetic variation.

DNA Abbreviation for deoxyribonucleic acid. The chemical constituent of genes. It determines the inherited characteristics of a plant.

dormancy An inactive phase of seeds, spores and buds, often in order to survive adverse conditions.

double fertilization In most flowering plants two male gametes participate in fertilization. One fuses with the female gamete to give the zygote which grows into the embryo, while the other fuses with the polar nuclei or definitive nucleus to give the endosperm.

double flower A flower with more than the usual number of petals, either due to the stamens or stamens and carpels forming petals.

drupe Fleshy indehiscent fruit with seed or seeds surrounded by woody tissue.

embryo Young plant after fertilization has taken place.

endocarp Innermost layer of the pericarp of an angiosperm fruit, outside the seeds. It can sometimes be woody.

endosperm Storage tissue in seeds of angiosperms.

entomophily Insect pollination.

enzyme A large protein molecule that can catalyse specific biochemical reactions.

epicalyx Calyx-like extra ring of floral appendages below the calyx, resembling a ring of sepals.

epicotyl Apical end of the axis of an embryo, immediately above the cotyledon or cotyledons. It grows into the stem.

epidermis Outer layer of cells of a plant.

epigeal Germination of the seed in which the cotyledons are raised above the surface of the ground by elongation of the hypocotl, thus forming the first leaves.

epigyny Floral parts found above the ovary.

epiphyte Plant with no roots in the soil. It is usually supported by another plant, and gets its nutrients from the air, rain and organic material on the surface of the other plant.

etiolation When plants are grown in insufficient light they become pale and elongated as they grow towards what light there is.

eukaryotic Organisms with cells that have nuclei.

evergreen Woody perennial plants that keep their leaves throughout the year, shedding and replacing leaves on a continuous basis.

exocarp Outermost layer of an angiosperm fruit, usually forming a skin.

To calculate the age of a tree, one light and one dark ring together equal 1 year's growth. The light wood is spring growth, the dark wood summer growth. (Popperfoto)

F₁ generation First filial generation obtained in breeding experiments.

F₂ generation Second filial generation, obtained by crossing the F₁ generation.

F₁ hybrid First filial generation produced by crossing two selected parental pure lines. They do not breed true.

fen Flat area of land originating from peaty marshes.

fermentation Anaerobic respiration of glucose and other organic substrates to obtain energy.

floral diagram Representation of flower structure. The whorls of floral parts are shown as a series of concentric circles.

floral formula Use of symbols, numbers and letters to record floral structure.

floret A small flower.

flower Sexual reproductive unit of angiosperms, consisting of perianth, androecium and gynoecium, all arising from the receptacle.

forest Community in which the dominant species are trees.

fragmentation Asexual reproduction in which the parent splits into two or more pieces which develop into new individuals.

frond Large leaf or leaflike structure.

fruit The ripened ovary of a flower, plus any accessory parts associated with it.

fungi Saprophytic, parasitic and symbiotic eukaryotic organisms, lacking chlorophyll, whose plant body is typically a mycelium.

gall Abnormal swelling or outgrowth on a plant caused by an attack by a parasite.

gamete A cell or nucleus that can undergo sexual fusion with another gamete to form a zygote, which in turn develops into a new individual.

gametophyte The generation in the life cycle of a plant that produces the gametes.

gamopetalous Petals fused along their margins forming a corolla tube.

gamosepalous Sepals that are fused to form a tubular calyx.

garigue Scrub woodland on limestone areas with low rainfall and thin soils.

gemma Multicellular structure for vegetative reproduction found on some mosses and liverworts.

gene Unit of inheritance.

genotype Genetic make-up of an organism, as opposed to its physical appearance.

genus A group of obviously homologous species.

germination Changes undergone by a reproductive body, e.g. zygote, spore, pollen, grain, seed, before and during the first signs of growth.

glabrous A surface that has no hairs.

glaucous Surfaces with a waxy blue-grey bloom on them.

gley Waterlogged soil lacking in oxygen.

glume Bracts subtending each spikelet in the flowers of grasses.

grafting Artificial means of propagation by which a segment of the plant to be propagated is attached to another plant so that their vascular tissues combine.

grassland Community in which grasses are the dominant group.

green manure Fast-growing crop grown at the end of the season and then ploughed or dug in, thus increasing the amount of organic matter in the soil.

growth ring Secondary xylem produced in a growing period in the stems and roots of many plants. When the stem or root is sliced across this ring is visible.

guard cells Pair of bow-shaped cells surrounding each stomatal pore and forming the stoma. The opening of the stoma is controlled by changes in the turgidity of the guard cells.

guttation Exudation from plants of water in liquid form.

gymnosperms Vascular plant with naked seeds borne on a sporophyll and not in an ovary.

gynandrous Stamens on the gynoecium.

gynodioecious Plants that bear female and hermaphrodite flowers on separate individuals.

gynoecium Female part of the angiosperm flower, consisting of one or more carpels.

gynomonoecious Plants that bear female and hermaphrodite flowers on the same individual.

halophyte Plant that can live in soil with a high salt concentration.

hardening The gradual exposure of plants to lower temperatures in order to increase the resistance to frost, prior to planting out.

hard seed A seed with a hard coat that is impervious to water.

hastate A leaf shaped like a three-lobed spear.

haustorium Organ produced by a parasite to absorb nutrients from the host plant.

heartwood Central part of secondary xylem in some woody plants. It is derived from the sapwood that has deteriorated with age.

heath A region of poor sandy soils exposed to strong winds.

helophyte Marsh plant with perennating buds in the mud at the bottom of the lake.

hemicellulose Carbohydrate found in plant cell walls, often in association with cellulose. Unlike cellulose, it can be broken down by enzymes and thus used as a nutrient reserve.

hemicryptophyte Plants with perennating buds just below the soil surface.

herbaceous perennial Lives for many years, surviving each winter as an underground storage or perennating organ, the leaves and flowers dying back.

herbarium Dried pressed plants kept in a collection.

herbicide Chemical that kills plants.

hermaphrodite Male and female reproductive parts in the same flower.

hesperidium Berry with a leathery epicarp, e.g. citrus fruit.

heteroblastic development Progressive development in the form and size of successive organs such as leaves.

heterophylly Having two or more leaf types differing in morphology and function.

heterostyly Having two or more different arrangements of the reproductive parts in the flowers of a single species.

hilium Scar on the seed coat at the point of abscission.

hip Type of pseudocarp fruit.

homogamy The maturation of anthers and stigmas at the same time.

honey guide Dots or lines on petals that guide pollinating insects to the nectaries.

humus Soft moist organic matter in soil, derived from rotting plant and animal matter.

hybrid Individual produced by genetically distinct parents.

hybrid sterility Inability of some hybrids to produce gametes.

hydrophily Pollination by water transport of pollen grains.

hydrophyte Plant that is adapted to living in water or in waterlogged conditions.

hydroponics Growth of plants, for example in sand, to which nutrients are added in a liquid fertilizer.

hypha Branched filament of fungi. Many hyphae make up the mycelium of fungi.

hypocotl That part of the stem between the cotyledons and the radicle in the embryo.

hypogeal Seed germination in which the cotyledons remain below ground due to lack of growth of the hypocotl.

hypogyny Floral parts inserted below the ovary.

indefinite growth Unlimited growth, i.e. the plant or parts of the plant continue to grow throughout their lives.

indehiscent Fruit or fruiting body that does not open to disperse its seeds.

inflorescence A group of flowers borne on the same stalk.

insectivorous plant A plant that can obtain its nutrients by digesting insects and other tiny animals, in addition to photosynthesizing.

integument Protective envelope around the ovule of seed plants. Most gymnosperms have one integument, while most angiosperms have two.

keel The pair of fused lower petals in pea flowers.

key List of characteristics enabling rapid identification of species.

kingdom All organisms were at one time placed in the plant or animal kingdom. There is now a move to identify other kingdoms, e.g. for the fungi, unicellular organisms.

labellum Distinct lower three petals of an orchid.

lamina Flattened bladelike section of a leaf.

lanceolate Narrow; tapering at both ends.

layering Plant propagation in which runners or stolons are pegged down to the ground encouraging roots to form at that point.

leaching Washing out of minerals and other nutrients from the soil.

leaf Principal photosynthetic organ of green plants. It is formed as a lateral outgrowth from the stem, and consists of the lamina, petiole and leaf base.

leaf base Point of attachment of leaf to stem.

leaf spot Disease involving spots of dead tissue on the leaves.

legume A dry dehiscent fruit containing one or more seeds. It is also a general name for the plants in the family *Leguminosae* (pea family), whose fruit is a legume of one description or another.

lemma Lower of a pair of bracts beneath each flower in a grass.

lenticel Small pore containing loose cells in the periderm of plants. Gaseous exchange takes place through the lenticel.

lichen Plants composed of a fungus and algae in symbiotic relationships. The lichen is distinct from either of its constituents.

life cycle Various stages an organism passes through, from fertilized egg in one generation to fertilized egg in the next generation.

light reactions Those reactions in the photosynthetic chain of reactions that are dependent on light.

lignin Carbohydrate polymer making up about a quarter of the wood of a tree.

liming Addition of lime to the soil to decrease the acidity of the soil and to improve the soil structure.

linear Leaves that are flat and parallel-sided.

lipid Water-insoluble fatty acids, consisting of carbon, hydrogen and oxygen plus some other ele-

A Venus Fly Trap's rose-tinted digestive glands entice the fly into the trap. (Popperfoto)

ments. Their functions vary, but they can be for storage and as structural molecules.

lipoprotein Association of lipid and protein usually found in plant cell membranes.

lithophyte Plant that grows on rocky ground.

littoral The seashore between low and high tide.

loam Soil with even mixture of fine clay and coarser sand particles.

loess Fine yellowish soil, consisting of clay and silt particles.

macronutrient A chemical element required by a plant in relatively large amounts.

maquis Stunted woodland in semi-arid areas that have been deforested.

meadow Moist grassland maintained by mowing.

meristem Region of a plant containing actively- or potentially actively-dividing cells.

mesocarp Middle layer of the pericarp of an angiosperm fruit. It may be absent.

mesophyte Plant with no adaptations to environmental extremes.

microflora Small plants found in a given area.

micronutrient Chemical element required in small quantities, i.e. a trace element.

midrib Vein running down the middle of a leaf.

mildew Fungal disease of plants in which the fungus is seen on the plant surface.

monadelphous Stamen filaments fused to form a tube.

monochasium Cymose inflorescence in which only one axillary bud develops into a lateral branch at each node.

monocotyledons Angiosperms possessing one cotyledon in the embryo. The group includes palms, grasses, orchids, lilies.

monoecious Female and male reproductive parts in separate floral structures on the same plant.

monopodial branching Secondary shoots or branches arise behind the main growing tip and remain subsidiary to the main stem.

moor Wet exposed land where soil water seeps away very slowly.

morphology Branch of biology concerned with the form and structure of organisms.

mould Fungus that produces a velvety growth on the surface of its host.

multiple fruit Fleshy fruit incorporating the ovaries of many flowers and derived from a complete inflorescence.

muskeg Peat bog in coniferous forest of N. America.

mycelium Loose mass of branching and interwoven fungal hyphae.

mycorrhiza Symbiotic relationship between a fungus and the roots of a plant.

nastic movement A plant response caused by an external stimulus. The stimulus acts merely as a trigger, and does not control the plant's response.

necrosis Death of part of a plant while the rest of the plant continues to live.

nectaries Glands at the base of flower that secrete nectar in order to attract insect pollinators.

node Point on the plant stem at which one or more leaves develop.

offset A sort of runner. A short shoot that develops from an axillary bud near the base of the stem and goes on to form a daughter plant.

ontogeny All the changes that occur during the life cycle of an organism.

opposite Pairs of leaves arising at each node.

ornithophily Bird pollination.

osmosis Passage of certain molecules in a solution, down a concentration gradient and across a semipermeable membrane that prevents the passage of other molecules. In plants it is usually water molecules that pass across the membrane, equalizing solute concentrations on either side of the membrane.

ovary Swollen basal part of the carpel in angiosperms containing the ovule or ovules.

ovule Female gamete and its protective and nutritional tissues. It develops into the seed after fertilization.

palea Upper bract of the pair found beneath each floret in a grass inflorescence.

panicle Racemose inflorescence in which the flowers are formed on stalks arising spirally or alternately from the main stem.

pappus Modified calyx consisting of a fine ring of hairs or teeth that persists after fertilization, aiding wind dispersal of the seeds.

parasitism Relationship between two organisms in which one is wholly dependent on the other for food, shelter, etc.

parenchyma Unspecialized tissue in the plant, often forming a ground tissue in which other tissues are located.

parthenocarpy Production of a fruit without the process of fertilization.

pasture Moist grassland maintained by grazing.

peat Partially decomposed plant material, built up in poorly-drained areas.

pedalfer Acid soil from which soluble lime has been leached by rainfall.

pedicel Stalk attaching flowers to the main stem of the inflorescence.

pedocal Alkaline soil in which lime has built up in the surface layers.

pepo Berry with a hard exterior.

perennate To live from one growing season to another, usually with a period of reduced activity between seasons.

perennial A plant that lives for many years.

perianth The protective structure encircling the reproductive parts, consisting of the calyx and corolla or a ring of petals.

pericarp The wall of the fruit, derived from the ovary wall.

periderm Protective secondary tissue replacing the epidermis as the outer cellular layer of stems and roots.

perigyny Floral parts inserted on the receptacle at about the same level as the ovary.

permanent wilting point The point at which the amount of water in the soil is so low that a plant wilts and will not recover unless water is added to the soil.

petal A unit of the corolla, thought to be a modified leaf.

petiole Stalk that attaches the leaf lamina to the stem.

phanerophyte Plant with perennating buds on upright stems well above soil level.

phellem Compact protective tissue replacing the epidermis as the outer layer in plants with secondary growth.

phloem Vascular tissue in plants responsible for translocation of nutrients.

photic zone Surface waters of lakes and seas, in which light penetrates and which is inhabited by plankton.

photoperiodism Alternation of day and night, controlling the physiological mechanisms of many plants.

photorespiration Respiration that occurs in plants in the light.

photosynthesis Series of reactions in green plants in which light energy from the sun is used to drive reactions which convert carbon dioxide and water to carbohydrates and thence to other materials.

phycobiont Algal partner in a lichen.

phyllode Flattened petiole which performs the functions of a leaf.

phyllody Transformation of parts of a flower into leaflike structures.

pileus Cap of a mushroom or toadstool.

piliferous layer The absorbing region of the root

epidermis. It is covered with root hairs.

pinna A first-order leaflet in a compound leaf.

pinnule Second-order leaflet in a compound leaf, i.e. each pinna is divided into a number of pinnules.

pistil A single carpel or group of carpels.

pith Region of parenchyma in the centre of many plant stems.

plankton Microorganisms floating in surface waters of seas and lakes.

plumule Embryonic shoot derived from the epicotyl.

podsol Acid infertile soil found in regions of heavy rainfall and long cold winters.

pollard To prune back a tree to the main trunk.

pollen The microspores, containing the male gamete, released in large numbers as a fine powder by gymnosperms and angiosperms.

pollen sac The chambers on the anther in which pollen is formed.

pollination Transfer of pollen from the male to the female parts in seed plants, i.e. from the anthers to the stigma.

pome A fleshy pseudocarp in which tissues develop from the receptacle and enclose the true fruit.

prickle Short pointed outgrowth from the epidermis.

primary growth Size increase due to cell division at apical meristems.

procumbent Plant that trails loosely along the ground.

prokaryotic Organisms in which the nuclear material is not separated from the rest of the cell contents.

proteins Large molecules consisting of carbon, hydrogen, nitrogen, oxygen and other elements. Plant proteins can largely be grouped as enzymes or structural and contractile proteins.

pruning Cutting back of some or all of the branches of woody plants, usually to promote growth in selected areas of the plant.

pseudocarp Fruit consisting of tissues other than those derived from the gynoecium.

raceme Inflorescence in which flowers are formed on individual pedicels on the main axis.

radicle Embryonic root, normally the first organ to emerge on germination.

receptacle The region at the end of the main axis of the flower, to which the floral parts are attached.

respiration The breakdown of food substances, utilizing molecular oxygen, in order to release energy.

rhizome Underground stem that acts as a means of vegetative propagation.

root Usually underground section of a plant involved with fixing the plant in position and absorbing water and nutrients. It can be used as a food storage organ.

root hair Projections from single cells in the root epidermis. They increase the surface area for absorption.

root nodule Lumpy growth that develops on the roots of leguminous plants as a result of symbiotic infections involved with nitrogen fixation.

rosette plant Plant with its leaves radiation outwards on the surface of the soil.

runner A creeping stem arising from an axillary bud, giving rise to new plants at the nodes.

rusts Fungal infections causing dark rust-coloured spots on the leaves or stem.

samara Achene with pericarp extended into a wing.

sap Liquid containing mineral salts and sugars dissolved in water, found in xylem and phloem vessels.

saprophyte Plant that feeds on dead and decaying organic material.

sapwood Outer functional part of the secondary xylem.

scape Leafless stem of a solitary flower or inflorescence.

schizocarp Dry fruit formed from two or more one-seeded carpels that divide into one-seeded units when mature.

scion Shoot or bud cut from one plant and grafted or budded on to another.

sclerenchyma Strengthening tissue.

seaweed Group of large algae found in the littoral zone and floating freely in the sea.

secondary growth Increase in diameter of a plant organ as a result of cell division in the cambium.

seed The structure that develops from the fertilized ovule in seed plants. It usually contains the embryo and a food store.

seedling A young plant.

self-incompatability Inability of gametes from the same plant to fertilize each other or form a viable embryo.

self-pollination Pollen transferred to the stigma of the same flower or flowers on the same plant.

seminal root Roots growing from the base of the stem and taking over from the radicle during early seedling growth.

sepal Individual unit of the calyx, usually green. They may be coloured and take over the function of petals.

sessile Unstalked.

shade plant Able to flourish in conditions of low light.

silicula Broad dry dehiscent fruit developed from two carpels fused together.

siliqua Longer than a silicula, but otherwise the same.

smut Fungal disease with a black spore mass on the host.

soil The surface layer of the earth's crust, consisting of water, air, living organisms, dead and decaying organisms and mineral particles.

species A single breeding group differentiated from other breeding groups by marked characteristics.

spine Modified leaf or part of a leaf, forming a pointed structure.

spore Simple asexual unicellular reproductive unit.

stamen Male reproductive organ in flowering plants. Together the stamens make up the androecium and produce the pollen on the anthers.

starch Most common and important food reserve carbohydrate in plants.

stele The vascular cylinder responsible for transport of water and solutes in the stems and roots of vascular plants.

stem That part of the plant above ground that carries the leaves, buds and reproductive parts.

stigma The tip of the carpel that receives the pollen at the time of pollination and on which the pollen germinates.

stock Plant on to which shoots or buds are grafted.

stolon Long branch that bends over and touches the ground, at which point a new plant may develop.

stoma Pore in the epidermis of the aerial parts of a

plant, especially the leaves, through which gaseous exchange occurs.

style That portion of the carpel between the ovary and stigma.

substrate Molecules on which enzymes act.

succulent A plant that conserves water by storing it in a swollen stem or leaves.

sucker A shoot that develops from the roots and that develops its own root system.

swamp Vegetation found in stagnant or slow-flowing water.

symbiosis Intimate relationship between two (or more) organisms, in which both benefit.

sympodial branching The apical bud dies at the end of one season and growth continues in the next season from the lateral bud immediately below.

syncarpous Gynoecium with fused carpels.

syngenesious Androecium with fused anthers.

2,4,5-T Selective weedkiller and defoliant.

tap-root A tough primary root, often penetrating deep into the soil. It can sometimes be a specialized food store.

taxis A directional movement of a whole plant in response to external stimuli.

tendril Modified inflorescence, branch or leaf of a climbing plant that can coil around objects to support the plant.

terra rossa Clayey soil, rich in lime, with a bright red colour from iron oxides.

testa Protective outer covering of a seed.

thallus Plant body undifferentiated into leaves, stem and roots.

thorn Modified reduced branch forming a pointed woody structure. It has a vascular structure within it.

tiller Shoot that grows from the base of the stem when the main stem has been cut back, as in coppicing.

toadstool Inedible fruiting body of fungi.

transpiration Loss of water by evaporation from a plant's surfaces, especially through the stoma. This water loss sucks up water through the rest of the plant, from the roots upwards.

trifoliate Compound leaf with three leaflets.

trimerous Arrangement, especially in monocotyledons, in which the floral parts in each whorl are inserted in threes or multiples of three.

tropism Directional growth of a plant in response to an external stimulus. It can be positive or negative.

tuber Swollen underground part of a stem or root, used for food storage and lasting only one year.

turgor Pressure of cell contents on cell walls, swelling them out, due to the cell taking in water by osmosis. Turgidity is the main effect that keeps non-woody plants erect.

umbel Racemose inflorescence in which flowers are borne on undivided stalks that arise from the main stem. The arrangement of these stalks is such that the flowers form a flat-topped plate or umbrella.

variegation Streaks of different colouring in a plant organ, especially leaves and petals.

vascular bundle A strand of primary vascular tissue, consisting largely of xylem and phloem.

vegetative reproduction Asexual reproduction in which specialized multicellular organs are formed and detached from the parent, generating new individuals.

vein Vascular bundle in a leaf.

venation The pattern of veins in a leaf.

vernalization Promotion of flowering by exposing young plants to cold.

vernation Pattern of rolling and folding of leaves in a bud.

vivipary Young plants forming at the axils of flowers, or the germination of seeds on the parent plant before release.

weed Any plant growing where it is not wanted.

wilt Any plant disease causing inadequate water supply and thus wilting.

witches' broom Mass of twigs grown in response to an infection.

xylem Vascular tissue responsible for transporting water and solutes from the roots up to the leaves and other aerial parts. It constitutes the woody tissues.

zygote Product of the fusion of two gametes, before it undergoes subsequent cell division.

The beginnings of life

It is generally assumed by scientists who study the beginnings of life that its creation is a logical event, the result of conditions that existed on this planet more than 3 500 million years ago.

The raw materials and conditions for the creation of life must have been present at the time: temperature, humidity, chemicals, and the catalyst of violent electrical discharges, as in storms. After millions of years of the Earth's formation, the temperature of its atmosphere dropped to below $100°C$, and the vapour or humidity fell as rain, making lakes and seas in which were dissolved the chemicals from the rocks forming a rich solution, or 'primeval soup'. In this 'soup' life was created.

Due to ultra-violet ray bombardment from the Sun, intense volcanic activity and electrical storms, parts of this 'soup' were chemically changed into the components of living things: proteins and nucleic acids. How these two essentials combined is still a matter of conjecture, but they probably existed alongside each other for a long time before combining together.

The first living organisms derived from this combination were probably similar to viruses, but able to reproduce themselves in the environment in which they existed. The development to a cellular existence requires a membrane and this could have been constructed out of the phosphates in the 'soup', forming phospholipids, which are present in modern cell structure.

The first true cells probably resembled bacteria. These would obtain energy by breaking down the chemicals in the 'soup', probably by a kind of fermentation. As they evolved, they would extract energy from the phosphates around them, as do modern cells.

The next prerequisite for the development of living organisms was their ability to photosynthesize, the process by which carbon dioxide and water are chemically changed by the action of sunlight into glucose, releasing oxygen into the surrounding atmosphere. At first the rocks and minerals of the Earth absorbed the oxygen, forming the oxides we find in the Earth today, but gradually the oxygen became part of the atmosphere and with it ozone, the three-atom structure of oxygen. Ozone absorbs ultra-violet light, and protects the Earth's surface from these rays. Although ultra-violet rays were necessary in the first instance, they are lethal to living cells. Thus the screen of ozone in the atmosphere ameliorated conditions on the planet for life to evolve. This allowed increased photosynthesis by the organisms, leading to the evolution of more advanced plants and animals.

The first organisms to employ photosynthesis probably resembled the blue-green algae today found in ponds. The oldest-known fossils, dated as far back as 3 100 million years ago, resemble these algae, which have no separate nucleus. Eukaryotic cells (those possessing a separate nucleus) probably evolved 1 300 million years ago. Between the period of the discovery of the earliest fossils of 3 100 million years ago, and the period when fossils are abundant, the Cambrian period of 570 million years ago, little fossil evidence has been found to show us the development of life, but the Cambrian period has yielded more than 600 different organisms to show that life was, by then, truly established on this planet.

Biological classification

The founder of modern taxonomy (the classification of organisms into groups based on similarities of structure, origin etc.) is usually regarded as Carolus Linnaeus of Sweden. He drew up rules for botanists and zoologists for the assigning of names to both plants and animals. The binomial system was introduced by him in 1758 with the still standard hierarchy of class, order and genus.

International codes were established for nomenclature in botany in 1901; in zoology in 1906 and for bacteria and viruses in 1948. The 5-kingdom Schemes of Classification is as follows: Kingdom Procaryota, Kingdom Protista, Kingdom Fungi, The Plant Kingdom and The Animal Kingdom.

Kingdom Procaryota

The organisms in this kingdom are characterized by an absence of distinct nuclei. Class Microtatobistes comprise viruses and the rickettsias, which are intermediate between the viruses and bacteria in size and biochemistry.

Order Rickettsiales comprises some 60 species, four families, and were named after the virologist Howard T. Ricketts (US) (1871–1910). No general classification of the 1000 plus viruses identified has yet been adopted. Eventual classification is expected to be based on the capsid (coat protein) symmetry in divisions between forms containing DNA (deoxyribonucleic acid) and RNA (ribonucleic acid). These infectious agents measure down to a minute 1.4×10^{-5} mm in diameter.

Bacterial unicellular micro-organisms, often spherical or rod-like, generally range from a micron in diameter to filaments several millimetres in length. They belong to the class Schizomycetes (Greek Schizo=I split; Mykes=a fungus) in some 1500 species in ten orders.

Blue-green algae (Cyano phyta; Greek Kyana= corn-flower hence dark blue; phyton=a plant) have no motile flagellated cells and no sexual reproduction. Some 1500 species have been identified.

Kingdom Protista

This kingdom, first suggested by Ernst Haeckel in 1866, accommodates the mostly microscopic protozoa (Greek protos=first; zoon=an animal) of which some 30000 unicellular species have been described embracing flagellates (Latin Flagellum, diminutive of flagrum=a whip), ciliates (Latin Ciliatus=furnished with hairs), amoeba, ciliates and parasitic forms.

Algae possessing the nuclear mitochondrial and chloroplast membranes are also included among the protophyta in this kingdom.

Kingdom Fungi

The fungus group of some 80000 species because of dissimilarities to both plants and animals are now usually placed in a separate kingdom.

Sac fungi (Order Endomycetales) comprise yeasts (division mycota); moulds, mildews; truffles (class asomycetes) and lichen (Order Lecanorales) which have both an algal and a fungal component.

Club fungi include smuts (Order Ustilaginales) so called because of black and dusty masses of spores; rusts (Order Uredinales) parasitic on vascular plants and hence destructive to agriculture; mushrooms (Order Agaricales); puff-balls (Order Lycoperdales and Order Sclerodermatales) and stinkhorns (Order Phallales).

The Plant Kingdom

Kingdom Plantae (Metaphyta) embraces mosses, liverworts, hornworts, whisk ferns, club mosses, horsetails, ferns, cycads, conifers and flowering plants in 11 divisions. These were listed together with their Greek or Latin derivatives on pp. 33–37 Guinness Book of Answers (2nd Edition). The most advanced clan among the vascular plants is Class Angiospermae.

Class Angiospermae (from Greek, angeion=receptacle; sperma=seed). The true flowering plants, of which there are more than 250000 species. The Angiosperms have ovules enclosed within the ovary of a pistil (gynoecium) and the seeds are enclosed within the ripened ovary, which, when matured, becomes a fruit that may be single-seeded or many-seeded. The angiosperms usually have fibrous roots and soft herbaceous stem tissue. The leaves contain extensive mesophytic tissue (i.e. requiring only an average amount of moisture). The reproductive unit is the flower, which typically consists of a very short central axis bearing one or more apical megasporophylls, commonly called carpels, subtended by microsporophylls (termed stamens) and by two sets of sterile bract-like appendages collective termed the perianth (composed of petals and sepals). In the simplest form of the flower, the ovules are borne along the inner margin of the megasporophyll – like peas in the pod. In all modern angiosperms the megasporophyll is closed and fused marginally, with the ovules in the loculus (cavity) thus formed. In this form, the carpel is termed the pistil and consists of the ovary (the ovule-containing organ) and its apical stigma (the pollen-receiving part). The microsporophylls are closed until maturity, when they open and their pollen is released. The pollen-producing part is the anther and the supporting stalk the filament. The fertilization (which follows pollination) takes place entirely within the carpel of the flower. After the pollen grain (microgametophyte) reaches the receptive stigmatic surface of the pistil, a pollen tube is developed within, and into it moves the generative nucleus, which divides to form two male nuclei, each of which is a male gamete. Stimulated by the environment created in the stigma, the pollen tube grows through the wall of the pollen grain and into the tissue of the stigma and its style (i.e. the usually attenuated part of a pistil between the ovary and the stigma). This growth continues down the style until the tube penetrates the ovary. Growth continues and when the tube reaches the ovule it enters the micropyle (a pore at the tip of the ovule) or elsewhere through the integuments (i.e. the two outer layers of the ovule) and finally the female gametophyte (enclosed within the ovule). As pollen-tube growth progresses from stigma to female gametophyte it carries with it both male nuclei. On approach to the egg nucleus, within the female gametophyte, the two haploid male nuclei are released. One unites with the haploid egg nucleus and forms a diploid sporophyte, called the zygote, and the other unites with the polar nuclei to form a triploid endosperm nucleus. The zygote thus formed is a new generation, and becomes the embryo within the seed. The zygote (enclosed by a membrane) undergoes a series of divisions leading to wall formation (either transverse or longitudinal) separating the terminal cell from the basal cell. The terminal cell continues to divide to produce the axis or hypocotyl of the embryo, from which are later produced the cotyledons (Greek, *kotyledon*=cup-shaped hollow) or seed leaves (either one or two – see below under sub-classes). The basal cell divides to form a chain of cells that functions as a suspensor, and the lowest is attached to the embryo and ultimately gives rise to the root and root cap of the embryo. The endosperm nucleus, together with the embryo sac, multiplies to form the endosperm tissue of the seed. This tissue multiplies as the embryo develops, but the bulk of it is digested by the embryo. The angiosperms may be divided into two groups:

Sub-class Dicotyledonae
(Greek, *di*=two). The dicotyledons – over 200 000 species. This sub-class contains angiosperms in which the embryo has two cotyledons (seed leaves). The stems produce a secondary growth by successive cylinders of xylem tissue (Greek, *xyle*=wood), the wood element which, in angiosperms, contains vessels for water conduction and wood fibres for support. The veins of the leaves are typically arranged in a network, i.e. reticular venation. Leaves may be simple, with entire or toothed margins, or compound with leaflets arranged on either side of, or radiation from a petiole, or footstalk. The petals and sepals of the flowers number mostly four

or five, or multiples of four or five, and the pollen grains are mostly tricolpate (with three furrows). This group may be sub-divided into 40 or more orders of which the following are among the larger and more important. They are listed in the general sequence of primitive to advanced.

Order Ranales (or Magnoliales) – Buttercup, magnolia, tulip tree, marsh marigold, barberry, lotus, custard apple, nutmeg, etc.
Order Rosales – Rose, strawberry, blackberry, apple, cherry, legumes, saxifrages, witch hazel, plane tree, etc.
Order Papaverales (or Rhoeadales) – Poppy, cabbage and relatives, mignonette, bleeding heart, the mustard family (Cruciferae), etc.
Order Geraniales – Geranium, flax, castor bean, the citrus group, rubber, etc.
Order Umbellales – The carrot family, English ivy, the dogwoods, etc.
Order Rubiales – Madder, honeysuckle, coffee, cinchona, teasel, etc.
Order Campanulales – The bellflowers, the aster family (Compositae), etc.
Order Caryophyllales – Tne pinks, pigweed, spinach, buckwheat, sea lavender, thrift, etc.
Order Ericales – Heath, rhododendron, mountain laurel, blueberry, cranberry, etc.
Order Gentianales – Gentian, buddleia, olive, privet, ash, dogbane, milkweed, etc.
Order Polemoniales – Polemonium, morning-glory, phlox, forget-me-not, potato, tobacco, petunia, etc.
Order Lamiales – The mints, salvia, verbena, teak, lantana, etc.
Order Scrophulariales – Snapdragon, mimulus, trumpet vine, gloxinia, bladderwort, acanthus, etc.
There are several families of dicotyledons which appear to have no direct relationship with any other group. These include the Salicaceae (willows and poplars), Casuarinaceae (the Australian pine, not a true pine), Fagaceae (beeches and oaks) and the Proteaceae.

Sub-class Monocotyledonae
(Greek, *monos*=one). The monocotyledons – about 50 000 species. The embryo has one cotyledon. The members of this sub-class have stems without any secondary thickening; the vascular strands are scattered through the stem and no cylinders of secondary xylem tissue are produced. The leaves have entire margins, the blades generally lack a petiole, and the veins are arranged in parallel form. The flower parts are always in multiples of three, and the sepals are often petal-like. The pollen grains are always monocolpate (i.e. with one furrow). This sub-class contains 15 orders, of which the Liliales (Lily order) is considered the most primitive, and the Orchidales (Orchid order) the most advanced. This sub-class also contains palms, grasses, and bamboos.

Fruit

Common name	Scientific name	Geographical origin	Date first described or known
Apple	*Malus pumila*	Southwestern Asia	Early times; Claudius 450 BC
Apricot	*Prunus armeniaca*	Central and western China	BC (Piling and Dioscoridês)
Avocado (Pear)	*Persea americana*	Mexico and Central America	Early Spanish explorers, Clusius 1601
Banana	*Musa sapientum*	Southern Asia	Intro: Africa 1st century AD, Canary Is 15th century

Fruit continued

Common name	Scientific name	Geographical origin	Date first described or known
Blackcurrants	Ribes nigrum	Northern Europe	First recorded in Britain in 17th century herbals
Carambola	Averrhoa carambola	Malaysia and Indonesia	—
Cherry	Prunus avium	Europe (near Dardanelles)	Prehistoric times
Coconut	Cocus nucifera	Pacific	Active planting since 12th century
Cranberry	Oxycccus macrocarpus	America	—
Custard Apple	Annona squamosa	Peru and Ecuador	—
Date	Phoenix dactylifera	unknown	Prehistoric times
Fig	Ficus carica	Syria westward to the Canary Is	c. 4000 BC (Egypt)
Gooseberry	Ribes grossularia	Europe	Fruiterer's bills from France (1276–92) of Edward I
Grape	Vitis vinifera	around Caspian and Black Seas	c. 4000 BC
Grapefruit	Citris grandis	Malay Archipelago and neighbouring islands	12th or 13th century
Kiwifruit	Actinidia chinensis	China	—
Lemon	Citrus limon	Southeastern Asia	11th–13th centuries
Lime	Citrus aurantifolia	Northern Burma	11th–13th centuries
Lychee	Litchi chinensis	Southern China	—
Mandarin (Orange)	Citrus reticulata	China	220 BC in China; Europe 1805
Mango	Mangifera indica	Southeastern Asia	c. 16th century; Cult. India 4th 5th century BC
Olive	Olea europaea	Syria to Greece	Prehistoric times
Orange	Citrus sinensis	China	2200 BC (Europe 15th century)
Papaya	Carica papaya	West Indian Islands or Mexican mainland	14th–15th centuries
Passion Fruit	Passiflora edulis	South America	—
Peach	Prunus persica	China?	300 BC (Greece)
Pear	Pyrus communis	Western Asia	Prehistoric times
Persimmon	Diospyros kaki	China/Japan	Thousands of years
Pineapple	Ananas comosus	Guadeloupe	c. (Columbus)
Plum	Prunus domestica	Western Asia	Possibly AD 100
Pomegranate	Punica granatum	Iran	—
Pomelo	Citrus grandis	Java and Malaysia	17th century
Quince	Cydonia oblonga	Northern Iran	BC
Raspberry	Rubus idaeus	Europe	Turner's Herbal of 1548
Redcurrants	Ribes species	Europe/Northern Asia	First description in German 17th century herbals
Rhubarb	Rheum rhaponticum	Eastern Mediterranean lands and Asia Minor	2700 BC (China)
Strawberry	Fragaria species	Europe	Rome 200 BC
Ugli	Citrus reticulata	Jamaica	—
Water Melon	Citrullus laratus	Central Africa	c. 2000 BC (Egypt)

Vegetables

Common name	Scientific name	Geographical origin	Date first described or known
Asparagus	Asparagus officinalis	Eastern Mediterranean	c. 200 BC
Aubergine	Solanum melongena	Asia	India 4000 years ago
Beetroot	Beta vulgaris	Mediterranean Area	2nd century BC
Broad Bean	Vicia faba	—	Widely cultivated in prehistoric times
Broccoli	Brassica oleracea (Variety Italica)	Eastern Mediterranean	1st century AD
Brussels Sprout	Brassica oleracea (variety gemmifera)	Northern Europe	1587 (Northern Europe)
Cabbage	Brassica oleracea (variety capitata)	Eastern Mediterranean lands and Asia Minor	c. 600 BC
Carrot	Daucus carota	Afghanistan	c. 500 BC
Cauliflower	Brassica oleracea (variety botrytis)	Eastern Mediterranean	6th century BC
Celeriac	Apium graveolens rapaceum	Mediterranean	Wild plant first used by Greeks. By 17th century garden celery distinct from wild plant
Celery	Apium graveolens	Caucasus	c. 850 BC
Chicory	Cichorium intybus	Mediterranean	Ancient Greek or Rome
Chive	Allium schoenoprasum	Eastern Mediterranean	c. 100 BC
Courgette	Cucurbita pepo	Italy	—
Cucumber	Cucumis sativus	Northern India	2nd century BC (Egypt 1300 BC)

Vegetables continued

Common name	Scientific name	Geographical origin	Date first described or known
Dasheen	Colocasia esculenta	Indo-Malaya	Inportant food crop in China about 100 BC
Eddoe	Colocasia antiquorum	Probably Africa	China 2000 years ago
Egg Plant	Solanum melongena	India, Assam, Burma	c. 450 AD (China)
Endive	Cichorium endivia	Eastern Mediterranean lands and Asia Minor	BC
Florence Fennel	Foeniculum vulgare dulce	Italy	Brought to England in Stuart time
Garden Pea	Pisum sativum	Central Asia	3000–2000 BC
Garlic	Allium sativum	Middle Asia	c. 900 BC (Homer)
Gherkin (W. Indian)	Cucumis anguria	Northern India	2nd century BC
Ginger	Zingiber officinale	S.E. Asia	Thousands of years old
Green Beans	Phaseolus vulgaris	South America	Reached England by 1594
Globe Artichoke	Cynara scolymus	Western and Central Mediterranean	c. 500 BC
Jerusalem Artichoke	Helianthus tuberosus	Canada	1616
Kale	Brassica oleracea (variety acephala)	Eastern Mediterranean lands and Asia Minor	c. 500 BC
Kohlrabi	Brassica oleracea caulorapa	Asia	Taken from Italy to Germany mid 16th century
Lamb's Tongue-Lettuce	Valerianella locusta	Europe	—
Leek	Allium porrum	Middle Asia	c. 1000 BC
Lettuce	Lactuca sativa	Asia Minor, Iran and Turkistan	4500 BC (Egyptian tomb)
Mange Tout	Pisum sativum saccharatum	Near East	17th century
Marrow	Cucurbita pepo	America?	16th–17th century (Mexican sites 7000–5500 BC)
Mushrooms	Psalliota compestris	unknown	Mentions in Ancient Rome and Greece
Musk Melon	Cucumis melo	Iran	2900 BC (Egypt)
Okra	Hibiscus esculentus	Tropical Africa	Egypt 13th century
Olives	Olea europaea	Eastern Mediterranean	Found on coast of Syria and dated 4th millenium BC
Onion	Allium cepa	Middle Asia	c. 3000 BC (Egypt)
Parsley	Petroselinum crispum	Southern Europe	Used by Greeks and Romans
Parsnip	Pastinaca sativa	Caucasus	1st century BC
Peas	Psium sativum	The Near East	9570 BC Burma and Thailand
Pepper	Capsicum frutescens	Peru	Early burial sites, Peru; intro. Europe 1493
Potato	Solanum tuberosum	Southern Chile	c. 1530 Intro: Ireland 1565
Pumpkin	Cucurbita maxima	Northern Andean Argentina	1591
Radicchio	Cichorium intybus	Europe	Roman times
Radish	Raphanus sativus	Western Asia, Egypt	c. 3000 BC
Red Cabbage	Brassica oleracea	Mediterranean area and/or Asia Minor	England 14th century
Red Kidney Beans	Phaseolus vulgaris	Probably South American	—
Runner Beans	Phaseolus vulgaris	Central America	c. 1500 (known from Mexican sites 7000–5000 BC)
Soybean	Soja max	China	c. 2850 BC
Spinach	Spinacia oleracea	Iran	AD 647 in Nepal
Spring Onion	Allium cepa	Central Asia	Collected by 19th century botanists (reference to onions can be traced to 1st Egyptian dynasty 3200 BC)
Swede	Brassica napobrassica	Europe	1620
Sweet Corn	Zea mays	Andes	Cult. early times in America; intro. Europe after 1492
Sweet Potato	Ipomoea batatas	Tropical America	Prehistoric Peru
Tomato	Lycopersicon esculentum	Bolivia–Ecuador–Peru area	Italy c. 1550
Turnip	Brassica rapa	Greece	2000 BC
Water Chestnuts	Eleocharis dulcis	S. China	Neolithic times
Watercress	Nasturtium officinale	—	John Gerarde's Herball of 1597
White Cabbage	Brassica oleracea capita	Mediterranean area and/or Asia Minor	Greek kales 600 BC. Germany 1150
Yams	Discorea rotundra	Africa	Arrived in England in 16th century

THE ANIMAL WORLD

Glossary

abdomen The rear section of an arthropod, often divided into segments. Alternatively, in vertebrates, the body cavity in which are found the principal digestive organs.

abomasum The fourth chamber of a ruminant's stomach.

accommodation The adjustments to the eye by which an object is brought into focus.

acetyl choline A neurotransmitter chemical found in the nervous systems of both vertebrates and invertebrates.

acoelomate Animals lacking any form of coelom.

adipose tissue Fatty tissue occurring under the skin in mammals.

adrenaline Hormone secreted in many groups of higher animals. It prepares the body for 'fight and flight'. It is also found in the nervous system acting as a neurotransmitter.

afferent A nerve that passes information back to the central nervous system, i.e. a sensory nerve.

aggression Animal behaviour designed to frighten off another animal, usually of the same species, from a designated territory.

agonistic Behaviour associated with aggression, but actually involving little violence.

air sac Extension of a bird's respiratory system into other parts of the body. Expansion and contraction of these sacs, with movement of the body, speed up the movement of air in and out of the bird's lungs. The air sacs also cut down the bird's weight.

albinism Absence of pigments in the hair, skin and eyes.

alimentary canal The tube down which food passes, and in which it is broken down and digested.

alveolus An air sac at the end of a bronchiole in the lungs of reptiles and mammals. It is in the alveoli that gas exchange occurs between the air and the blood.

amino acid The constituent molecular 'building brick' of proteins.

amnion Membrane containing the embryo and the fluid in which it is bathed.

amphibia Animals that can live both in water and on land. They represent the first group of animals to develop two pairs of pentadactyl limbs.

antenna Jointed appendage found on the heads of many arthropods. It is usually sensory.

anticoagulent A chemical that prevents blood from clotting.

anus The final opening of the alimentary tract.

aorta Large blood vessel that carries blood from the heart to the body. It is found in the higher four-limbed animals.

arteriole Small artery linking an artery to the capillaries.

artery Blood vessel taking blood away from heart.

arthropod An invertebrate having an exoskeleton made of chitin, jointed limbs and a segmented body, e.g. arachnids, insects, crustaceans and centipedes.

articulation Movement of one part of a skeleton over another, often at a joint.

asexual reproduction Occurs only in the lower animals, e.g. the protozoa. It is a form of reproduction by budding.

assimilation Incorporation of the simple molecules resulting from digestion into more complex molecules.

atlas vertebra First vertebra, allowing free movement of the head.

autonomic nervous system Vertebrate nervous system concerned with controlling bodily functions. It consists of the sympathetic and parasympathetic nervous system.

axis vertebra The second vertebra. Its articulation with the atlas vertebra allows rotational movement of the head.

barb A hair-like structure attached to the shaft of a feather.

barbule One of the 'teeth' on the barb of a feather. The barbules interlock, linking the barbs together.

bilateral symmetry Arrangement of the body and organs of an animal in only one plane of symmetry.

bile Secretion of the liver in vertebrates. It is formed from the breakdown of blood cells, and helps in digestion of fats.

bivalves A group of molluscs in which the body is enclosed within a shell consisting of two hinged halves, or valves, e.g. clams, cockles, oysters and mussels.

bladder A fluid- or gas-filled sac, often taken to mean the muscular sac into which urine drains from the kidneys.

blastula Early stage in the development of an animal embryo after fertilizaticn.

blood Fluid that occupies the vascular system. It carries respiratory gases, digestive and excretory products and other biochemicals.

blubber Thick layer of subcutaneous fat found in many marine mammals.

bone A form of tissue, rich in calcium, that forms the endoskeleton of the higher vertebrates.

brain The forward section of the nervous system. In invertebrates it consists of ganglia; in vertebrates it consists of an enlarged part of the neural tube.

bronchiole Tube leading to the alveoli in the lungs.

bronchus One of two tubes, each tube leading to one of the lungs in vertebrates.

buccal cavity The mouth cavity.

caecum An outgrowth of the alimentary canal.

canine tooth Pointed tooth found in mammals. It is used for gripping and tearing, and is prominent in carnivores.

capillary Fine blood vessels forming a network in vertebrate tissues. They carry respiratory gases, nutrients and waste products to and from the tissues.

carapace Shell of some crustaceans, e.g. crabs, and reptiles, e.g. tortoise.

carnassial teeth Modified molar and premolar teeth in many carnivores. They have sharp cutting edges for dealing with meat, bones, ligaments, etc.

carnivore Meat-eating animal.

carpals Bones found in the pentadactyl limb of the higher vertebrates.

cartilage Tough slippery flexible tissue, found in all vertebrates. It has skeletal functions; indeed, some of the lower vertebrates have skeletons consisting entirely of cartilage.

central nervous system That part of the nervous system which coordinates the activities of the other parts of the nervous system. It ranges in complexity from a simple series of paired ganglia to the brain and spinal cord of vertebrates.

cephalopods A marine mollusc with well-developed head and eyes and sucker-bearing tentacles, e.g. octopuses, squids and cuttlefish.

chaeta A stiff bristle found on the body segments of worms.

chela Pincers found in arthropods.

chitin The polymeric chemical that comprises the exoskeleton of arthropods.

chordates Animals which have a notochord, either in the embryo or adult form.

chromatophore Cell containing pigment that is involved in colour changes.

chrysalis Pupal form of butterflies and moths.

cilium (plural cilia) A very fine hair, capable of independent movement. Unlike flagella, cilia are usually found in groups. They can only beat in one direction, and usually move in synchrony.

class In taxonomy a primary grouping or classification into which a phylum or division is divided, e.g. Amphibia, Reptilia and Mammalia are three classes of phylum Chordata.

clitellum The 'saddle' of earthworms, involved in copulation.

cloaca Chamber into which the alimentary canal, the kidneys and the reproductive organs open.

coccyx Fused group of vertebrae at the base of the spine in tailless primates.

cocoon Protective covering around the eggs or larvae of many invertebrates.

coelenteron Body cavity in lower animals that functions as a digestive cavity. There is one opening, and the cavity itself is lined with two layers of cells.

coelom Body cavity in higher animals.

compound eye Simple eye found in crustaceans and insects. It is formed from hundreds of single light receptors, which build up a compound image.

cone Light-sensitive cell in the eyes of vertebrates. It detects colour and detail.

cranium The skull of vertebrates.

crop A section of the alimentary canal capable of being distended in order to store food.

crustacean A (mainly) aquatic arthropod protected by a shell-like cover, e.g. crab, lobster, shrimp, woodlice, barnacles and water flea.

deciduous teeth First set of teeth in mammals. These are shed to make way for the adult teeth.

defaecation The discharge of waste from the body through the anus.

demersal Inhabiting the sea or lake floor.

dental formula Expression of the arrangement of teeth in mammals. It indicates the number of incisors, canines, premolars and molars in one side of the upper and lower jaw.

dentine The main bulk of a tooth. It is served by blood vessels and covered with enamel.

diaphragm Dome of muscle separating the thoracic and abdominal cavities in mammals.

diastole The phase of the heart beat in which the

heart muscle is relaxed.

digestion Breakdown of foodstuffs into simple molecules that can be absorbed and used by the organism.

digit A finger or toe of the vertebrate pentadactyl limb.

dorsal The surface of an animal nearest to the notochord or spinal cord.

ear Vertebrate organ, primarily of balance but subsequently adapted as an organ of hearing.

ecdysis Moulting. The shedding of the exoskeleton in arthropods to allow for growth, or the shedding of the outer layer of skin in reptiles.

efferent Nerve that passes information from the central nervous system out to the tissues and organs of the body.

egg A structure containing the ovum and in which the embryo develops. It contains yolk, which nourishes the embryo during its development, and a number of membranes enclosing the contents, including an outer protective membrane, sometimes calcareous.

embryo Structure that develops from the zygote prior to birth or hatching.

enamel Hard white material that encases the exposed surface of a mammalian tooth.

endocrine gland Type of gland found in vertebrates and some invertebrates, in which the secretion passes into the bloodstream and passes in this way to the organ or organs on which it acts.

endoskeleton A rigid and often articulated structure that lies within the body tissues. It provides support and shape, and often sites of attachment for muscles.

epiglottis Found in mammals, it is a cartilaginous flap that closes off the windpipe during the swallowing reflex.

excretion The elimination of waste chemicals from the body. This is *not* the same as defaecation.

exocrine gland A gland, found in vertebrates, in which the secretion is carried down a duct to the site of activity.

exoskeleton A rigid articulated structure that lies outside the body tissues. It provides protection, support and often sites of attachment for muscles.

faeces Remains of undigested food, bile, dead cells and bacteria, expelled through the anus.

fat body In amphibians the fat body consists solely of fat, and provides them with food reserves during hibernation. In insects it consists of fat, protein and other reserves, and provides nourishment during metamorphosis as well as during hibernation.

feather Birds have three types of feathers. Contour feathers have barbs and barbules that lock together; they are the feathers on the wings and tail associated with flight. Down feathers and filoplumes are fluffy feathers more important for heat retention.

fibrin A protein that forms a fibrous matrix as the basis of a blood clot.

filoplume Hairlike feathers scattered over the surface of a bird. They are important in heat retention.

fin The lateral fins of fishes are based on the pentadactyl limb, the two pectoral fins corresponding to fore limbs, the pelvic fins to the hind limbs. These, and the median and anal fin, are used for steering and balance. The caudal fin on the tail is used for propulsion.

flagellum A hairlike filament found on a cell surface. Its movement causes the cell, or the fluid around it, to move.

follicle A small sac or cavity.

gall bladder Storage organ for bile produced in the liver.

gamete Reproductive cell that can undergo fertilization.

ganglion Mass of nervous tissue, rich in nerve cell bodies. In invertebrates, ganglia form the central nervous system.

gestation Time between conception, i.e. fertilization, and birth.

gill Respiratory organ in marine and freshwater animals. Each gill has a rich blood supply, promoting gas exchange between the blood and the surrounding water.

gizzard Part of the alimentary canal designed to break up hard foods.

gland Organ that secretes a specific chemical or group of chemicals, either into the bloodstream or into a specific site of activity.

glottis Opening of the larynx into the pharynx.

glycogen Storage compound in animals. It is a polymer of glucose.

gonad Organ which produces ova or sperm.

grey matter Region of the vertebrate brain that contains nerve cell bodies and synapses.

gut The alimentary canal.

haem The basis of many respiratory pigments, e.g. haemoglobin, as it can combine reversibly with oxygen.

haemocoel Body cavity containing the blood in arthropods and crustaceans.

hair Cornified threads produced by follicles in the skin of mammals. The colour is due to melanin pigment. The function of hair is largely heat retention.

hallux The often-vestigial digit on the inside of the rear limbs of the higher terrestrial vertebrates.

haltere A modified wing of flies that provides information on stability in flight.

haw The nictitating membrane found in reptiles, birds and some domestic animals, e.g. horse, cat, that can be drawn upwards across the eye.

heart Organ found in all vertebrates and many invertebrates that drives blood around the body unidirectionally.

herbivore Plant-eating animal.

heterocercal Fish in which the vertebral column extends into the tail fin. It is upturned, giving the fin a larger dorsal lobe than ventral lobe.

hibernation Period of time during winter when an animal becomes inactive and the basal metabolic rate drops, thus conserving energy.

hominid A primate in the family *Hominidae*, including early and modern man.

homiothermy Maintenance of the body temperature at a relatively constant temperature. Often referred to as being warm-blooded.

homocercal Fish in which the tail fin does not contain the vertebral column, but is supported merely with fin rays.

hormone Chemical secreted by endocrine glands. It is secreted into the bloodstream, which carries it to the organ it acts on, on which it usually has a specific and often regulatory effect.

ileum Section of the small intestine in mammals, immediately before the colon.

imago Sexually mature adult form of an insect.

implantation Attachment of a vertebrate fertilized ovum to the wall of the uterus.

impulse Passage of an electric current along a nerve fibre.

incisor Front teeth in mammals. They are sharp and are used for biting and gnawing off food.

instar The form adopted by an insect between moults.

insulin Important animal hormone responsible for the control of glucose levels in the blood.

intestine That part of alimentary canal in which food is digested and absorbed.

invertebrate Lacking a backbone or spinal column or notochord, e.g. molluscs, worms, jellyfish, coral.

iris A ring of pigmented tissue which lies over the lens of the eye in invertebrates and cephalopods.

joint Point of contact between two body elements in invertebrates or between two bony or cartilaginous elements in vertebrates.

keel Large blade or projection from the sternum of bats and birds. It provides a large surface area for the attachment of the flight muscles.

keratin The structural protein found in horn, claws, beaks, nails, hair, etc., and in the outer cells of the epidermis of vertebrates.

kidney One of two excretory organs found in vertebrates.

labrum The upper 'lip' in insects that helps in feeding.

lactation Milk production. One of the chief characteristics of mammals.

lacteal Lymph vessels in vertebrates, involved in the absorption of digested fats in the intestine.

larva Form many animals take between hatching from the egg and metamorphosing into the adult, e.g. caterpillars, tadpole.

larynx Area of the throat that controls the swallowing reflex and that contains the vocal chords.

lateral line System of receptors for the detection of vibration (sound) and movement, arranged in a line down each side of fish and some amphibians.

lens Transparent body in the eye designed to focus light on to the retina in vertebrates.

ligament Band of fibre holding two bones together at a vertebrate joint.

liver Largest internal organ found in vertebrates. It is responsible for the major metabolic functions.

lung Respiratory organ found in vertebrates.

lung book Respiratory organ found in some insects.

lymphatic system System of tubes containing lymph, found in vertebrates. It collects tissue fluid and returns it to the blood system, transports digested fats, and is involved in the immune system. Flow in the lymphatic system is effected by lymph hearts in some vertebrates, and by muscular and respiratory movements in mammals.

mammals Group of vertebrates characterized by being homiothermic, having hair on the skin, giving birth to well-developed young which have been nourished within the womb by a placenta and which are subsequently suckled at the mammary glands.

mammary gland Milk-producing gland found in all female mammals.

mandible Lower jaw in invertebrates.

mantle Folds of skin in molluscs which secretes the shell, if present, and protects the gills.

marsupium Pouch found on female marsupials. The mammary glands are found within the pouch, and the young finish their development there after birth.

maxilla Either a feeding appendage found in arthropods, or the upper jawbone of vertebrates.

meatus Passage leading from the outer ear to the eardrum.

median eye A third eye in the top of the head found in many invertebrates. It is formed from an outgrowth of the brain, and is represented vestigially in vertebrates by the pineal body.

medulla Central part of an organ.

medusa Another name for jellyfish. It is a free-swimming form of a group of coelenterates.

melanin Pigment found in skin, hair, etc.

meninges Membranes surrounding the central nervous system of vertebrates and the spaces within it.

metacarpals Bones found in the pentadactyl limb of the higher vertebrates.

metameric segmentation Division of the body into a number of similar segments along its length.

metamorphosis Change from the larval to the adult stage. A process found in insects and amphibians.

metatarsals Bones found in the vertebrate pentadactyl limb. They are greatly elongated in running animals.

migration Movement of whole populations of animal species between two regions, often at roughly the same time each year.

mimicry Ability of one animal to resemble another, usually for the protection of the first animal.

mitral valve Heart valve of the higher vertebrates.

molar A chewing tooth occurring at the rear of the jaw in animals.

mucous membrane Surface membrane that secretes mucus.

mucus Slimy substance that does not dissolve in water.

muscle Contractile tissue that produces movement in invertebrates and vertebrates.

myelin sheath Membranous sheath around nerve fibres.

nasal cavity Cavity in the head of vertebrates containing the organs of smell.

nephridium Excretory organ in invertebrates.

nerve fibre The long thin unbranched section of a nerve cell that transmits the nerve messages over long distances within the body.

nerve net Simple form of nervous system found in the invertebrates.

neurone The chief nerve cell in the nervous system. It consists of a cell body, a number of finger-like dendrites which link up with other nerve cells, and one or more nerve fibres or axons which transport impulses over relatively long distances.

nidiculous Birds that hatch in an undeveloped state and need a lot of care.

nidifugous Birds that hatch in a well-developed state and are soon able to fend for themselves.

notochord A form of primitive cartilaginous spinal column. It is found in adult forms of the lower vertebrates, and in embryonic forms of the higher vertebrates.

nymph Immature form of some insects, in which the wings and reproductive organs are not fully developed.

ocellus A simple form of eye, consisting of a collection of light-sensitive cells, found in some invertebrates, especially insects. It is not capable of forming an image.

oesophagus The gullet. The tube by which food passes from the mouth to the digestive tract.

oestrous cycle The reproductive cycle of female mammals.

oestrus Period of the oestrous cycle when the female mammal is 'on heat', i.e. copulation can occur.

olfactory organs Organs of smell.

omasum Third chamber of a ruminant's stomach.

ommatidium A single unit in the compound eye of arthropods.

omnivore Plant- and animal-eating animal.

operculum Muscular flap covering the gills in bony fish.

optic chiasma Point at which the optic nerves cross over between the vertebrate eyes and brain. It is important in binocular vision.

optic nerve The nerve connecting the vertebrate eye with the brain.

orbit Socket of the vertebrate skull in which the eye lies.

order In taxonomy a group into which a class is divided, e.g. Carnivora, Primates and Rodentia are three orders of the class Mammalia.

ossification Process by which bone is formed from cartilaginous or other tissue.

ovary Reproductive organ of female animals, producing ova and female sex hormones.

oviparous Fertilized ova are laid as eggs and the embryo develops within the egg.

ovoviviparous The fertilized ova develop within the female's body but do not make contact with the body and do not receive nourishment from it (in certain reptiles, fish etc).

ovulation Release of an ovum from the ovary.

ovum (plural ova) Unfertilized non-motile female gamete.

pacemaker Group of cells that provide a rhythmic series of electrical impulses that drives an organ. Most commonly applied to the cells in the vertebrate heart that are responsible for providing the electrical impulses for the heartbeat.

palate The roof of the mouth in vertebrates.

palp A head or mouth appendage found in many vertebrates.

parasympathetic nervous system Part of the autonomic nervous system in vertebrates.

parturition The passage of the foetus out of the female's body at the end of pregnancy in mammals.

pecking order Social hierarchy found in many animals that live in groups.

pectoral fins Forward pair of lateral fins found in fishes.

pectoral girdle Ring of bones in vertebrates to which the fore limbs articulate.

pelagic Inhabiting the open waters of the sea or a lake.

pelvic fins Rear pair of lateral fins in fishes.

pelvic girdle Ring of bones in vertebrates to which the hind limbs articulate.

pentadactyl limb The characteristic limb of the vertebrates, with five digits or 'fingers'.

peripheral nervous system Those parts of the nervous system not included in the central nervous system.

peristalsis Waves of contraction that pass down tubular organs, particularly the digestive tract.

phalange One of the types of bones of the pentadactyl limb.

pheromone Chemical produced by one animal,

designed to elicit a response in another animal of the same species.

phylum Second taxonomic grouping after kingdom and before class.

pineal body Downgrowth of the vertebrate brain with endocrine functions. In some lower vertebrates it functions as the median eye.

pinna Outermost part of the outer ear in some mammals.

pituitary gland The major endocrine gland in vertebrates, occurring as downgrowth of the brain. It produces a wide range of hormones, many of them controlling other endocrine glands.

placenta The series of membranes within the uterus of viviparous animals that nourishes the developing foetus. It allows a close association of the foetal and maternal blood systems.

pleural membranes Membranes enclosing the mammalian lungs.

plexus A network of nerve cells.

poikilothermy Inability to regulate the body temperature, which therefore assumes that of the surroundings.

pollex The inner digit on the forelimbs of the higher vertebrates. It is often vestigial, or may be adapted for a variety of purposes.

polymer Naturally occurring or synthetic compound, e.g. starch.

polyp Non-motile form of those coelenterates that have the medusoid motile form.

premolar Grinding and chewing teeth occurring between the canines and molars in the jaws of mammals.

pupa A non-feeding form in which metamorphosis from a larva to an adult occurs in insects.

pupil Opening in the iris of the eye of vertebrates and some invertebrates, through which light enters the eye.

rachis The shaft of a feather.

radial symmetry Form of symmetry found in sedentary animals, e.g. the coelenterates, in which the body is symmetrical about a number of planes passing through a central axis.

radula A strip on the tongue of molluscs that carries teeth to rasp food off rocks, etc. As the teeth are worn away they are replaced.

reflex Automatic response to a stimulus.

regeneration Regrowth or replacement of tissues and body parts lost due to injury. Extensive regeneration is possible in many invertebrates, but regeneration is much more limited in the vertebrates.

retina Layer of sensory cells in the eyes of vertebrates and some molluscs.

rod Light-sensitive cell in the retina of vertebrate eyes.

rumen The first chamber in the stomach of ruminants.

ruminants Group of higher mammals, including cattle and sheep, in which the digestive system allows food to be swallowed and then digested later.

saliva Secretion of mucus and enzymes which moistens the food and starts off the process of digestion.

scolex The head of a tapeworm, which anchors it to the intestinal wall of the host.

sebum A greasy material produced by the sebaceous glands in the skin of mammals. It greases the hair and protects the skin.

sessile Animals attached to a fixed surface or to another animal.

sibling One of a number of offspring of the same two parents.

sinus A cavity or recess.

smooth muscle Vertebrate muscle tissue, under involuntary control, usually found around hollow organs. It can produce long-term contractions.

sperm Motile male gamete formed in the testes of male animals.

sphincter Ring of muscle around the opening to a hollow organ.

spinal cord That part of the central nervous system in vertebrates enclosed within the spinal column.

spinneret The openings on the abdomen of a spider out of which silk is produced to make webs, tie up prey, spin cocoons, etc.

spiracle Gill slit in fish, or opening of the tracheae in insects.

striated muscle Vertebrate muscle with a striped appearance. It is under voluntary control, important in locomotion. It produces rapid powerful contractions.

stridulation The production of sound by insects, usually by rubbing body parts together.

succus entericus Digestive secretions of the walls of the small intestine in vertebrates.

swim bladder An air bladder found in many fish. It is used in maintaining depth when swimming.

sympathetic nervous system Part of the vertebrate autonomic nervous system.

synapse Point of contact between nerve cells at which the nerve impulse passes from one cell to another.

systole The phase of the heart beat in which the heart muscle is contracted.

tarsals Bones in the rear pentadactyl limbs of vertebrates.

telson The tail appendage found in some arthropods.

tendon Fibrous band connecting a muscle to a bone.

testis Male reproductive organ that produces sperms and male sex hormones.

tetrapod Vertebrate having four limbs.

thorax The middle section of arthropods, particularly of insects. In vertebrates the thorax is the body cavity containing the heart and lungs.

tone State of partial contraction of a muscle which maintains body posture.

trachea In arthropods the tracheae are tubes that take air to the tissues. In vertebrates the trachea is the windpipe, taking air from the larynx to the lungs.

umbilical cord The connection between the embryo and the placenta in pregnant mammals.

ungulate Group of mammals that graze, that have hooves and that walk on the tips of elongated and adapted pentadactyl limbs.

urea Waste product of mammals and many other animals.

uric acid Waste product of birds and some other animals.

urine Liquid produced in the kidney, containing waste products such as urea or uric acid.

uterus The womb in mammals.

vascular system Fluid-filled spaces in the body, e.g. the blood vascular system.

vasoconstriction Constriction of a blood vessel.

vasodilatation Increase in the diameter of a blood vessel.

vein Blood vessel that carries blood from the tissues to the heart.

venation Arrangement of veins in an insect's wing.

ventral Surface of an animal furthest away from the notochord or spinal column.

venule Small blood vessel linking a vein to the capillary network.

vertebra Separate bone of the vertebral column.

vertebral column Bones or cartilage in close apposition, running in a line from the skull to the tail of vertebrates and enclosing the spinal cord.

vertebrate Having a backbone or vertebral column or notochord e.g. fishes, amphibians, reptiles, birds, mammals.

villus A projection from a body surface. It is usually designed to increase the surface area of a tissue.

viviparous Embryos develop within and are nourished by the mother.

vocal cords Elastic fibres in the larynx that produce sounds in vertebrates.

white matter Region of the vertebrate central nervous system consisting of nerve cell fibres.

yolk Nutrient store in eggs.

zoology Study of animals and their behaviour including their classification, structure, physiology and history.

zoonosis Any disease or infection that can be passed on to man from animals.

Animal dimensions by species

Mollusca – 128 000 species: ranging in size between the minute coin shell *Neolepton sykesi* 1·2 mm (*0·047 in*) long, and a giant octopus weighing 6–7 tonnes, which is the heaviest of all invertebrates.

Insecta – 950 000 (1974) described species of a suspected total of perhaps some 3 million: ranging in size between the Battledore wing fairy fly (*Hymenoptera mymaridae*) 0·2 mm (*0·008 in*) long to the bulky 100 g (*3·5 oz*) African goliath beetle (*Goliathus goliathus*).

Crustacea – 25 000 species: ranging in size from the water flea *Alonella* species at 0·25 mm (*0·01 in*) long to the Giant Japanese Spider crab (*Macrocheira kaempferi*) with a spread of 3·66 m (*12 ft*) between claws.

Pisces – 30 000 species: ranging in size between the 12–16 mm (*0·47–0·63 in*) long *Schindleria praematurus* at 2 mg or 17 750 to the oz and the 43 tonne 18·5 m (*60 ft*) long Whale shark (*Rhiniodon typus*).

Amphibia – 3000 species: ranging in size between minute poisonous frogs 12·5 mm (*0·05 in*) long and the 1·5 m (*5 ft*) long giant salamander (*Andrias davidianus*) weighing up to 45 kg (*100 lb*).

Reptilia – 6000 species: ranging in size between 38 mm (*1·5 in*) long geckoes and the South American snake anaconda (*Eunectes murinus*), which has been reported to attain 13·7 m (*45 ft*) in length.

Aves – c. 8950 species: ranging in size from the 1·6 g (*0·06 oz*) Bee humming bird (*Calypte helenae*) up to the 156·5 kg (*345 lb*), 2·7 m (*9 ft*) tall ostrich (*Struthio camelus*).

Mammalia – c. 4500 species: ranging in size, on land, between the 2 g (*0·07 oz*) Kitti's hog-nosed bat (*Craseonycteris thonglongyai*) and the African elephant (*Loxodonta africana africana*) which may very rarely attain 12 tons; and, at sea, between the 35 kg (*77 lb*) Commerson's dolphin (*Cephalorhynchus commersoni*) and the 190 tonne (*187 ton*) Blue Whale (*Balaenoptera musculus*).

Animal longevity

Age determination based on ring-producing structures (e.g. teeth) or length of time animal kept in captivity.

Maximum life span (years)	Species
152+	(a) Marion's Tortoise (*Testudo sumeirii*)
c. 150	Quahog (*Venus mercenaria*)
120+	Man (*Homo sapiens*) – highest proven age
116+	Spur-thighed tortoise (*Testudo graeca*)
c. 100	Deep sea clam (*Tindaria callistiformis*)
>90	Killer whale (*Orcinus orca*)
80–90	Sea anemone (*Cereus pedunculatus*)
88	European eel (*Anguilla anguilla*)
82	(b) Lake sturgeon (*Acipenser fulvescens*)
70–80	Freshwater mussel (*Margaritana margaritifera*)
78	Asiatic elephant (*Elephans maximus*)
77	Tuatara (*Sphenodon punctatus*)
72+	(a) Andean condor (*Vultur gryphus*)
c. 70	African elephant (*Loxodonta africana*)
69¾	Sterlet (*Acipenser ruthenus*)
68+	Great eagle-owl (*Bubo bubo*)
66	American alligator (*Alligator mississipiensis*)
64	Blue macaw (*Ara macao*)
62+	Siberian white crane (*Grus leucogeranus*)
62	Horse (*Equus caballus*)
62	Ostrich (*Struthio camelus*)
60+	European catfish (*Silurus glanis*)
58¾	Alligator snapping turtle (*Macrochelys temminckii*)
58+	(d) Royal albatross (*Diomedea immutabilis*)
57+	Orang-utan (*Pongo pygmaeus*)
56	(c) Sulphur-crested cockatoo (*Cacatua galerita*)
55½+	Chimpanzee (*Pan troglodytes*)
55	Pike (*Esox lucius*)
54⅓	Hippopotamus (*Hippopotamus amphibius*)
54+	Slow-worm (*Anguis fragilis*)
53½+	Gorilla (*Gorilla gorilla*)
53⅓	Stinkpot (*Sternotherus odoratus*)
51+	Japanese giant salamander (*Andrias japonicus*)
51	White pelican (*Pelecanus onocrotalus*)
50+	Green turtle (*Chelonia mydas*)
>50	Koi carp (*Cyprinus carpio*)
c. 50	North American lobster (*Homarus americanus*)
49¾	Domestic goose (*Answer a. domesticus*)
49+	Short-nosed echidna (*Tachyglossus aculeatus*)
49	(e) Grey parrot (*Psittacus erythacus*)
49	Indian rhinoceros (*Rhinoceros unicornis*)

47	European brown bear (*Ursus a. arctos*)
46+	White-throated capuchin (*Cebus capucinus*)
46+	Grey seal (*Halichoerus gypus*)
c. 46	Mandrill (*Mandrillus sphinx*)
c. 45	Blue whale (*Balaenoptera musculus*)
44	Herring gull (*Larus argentatus*)
42+	(d) Emu (*Dromaius novaehollandiae*)
42	Metallic wood borer (*Buprestis aurulenta*)
41	Goldfish (*Carassius auratus*)
40¼	Common boa (*Boa constrictor*)
>40	Common toad (*Bufo bufo*)
36¼	Cape giraffe (*Giraffa camelopardalis*)
35+	Bactrian camel (*Camelus ferus*)
34+	Hoffman's two-toed sloth (*Choloepus hoffmanni*)
34	Domestic cat (*Felis catus*)
34	Canary (*Severius canaria*)
33	American bison (*Bison bison*)
32⅓	Bobcat (*Lynx rufus*)
32+	Australian school shark (*Galeorhinus australis*)
31+	Indian flying fox (*Pteropus giganteus*)
30+	(d) American manatee (*Trichechus manatus*)
c. 30	Red kangaroo (*Macropus rufus*)
29½	African buffalo (*Syncerus caffer*)
29½	Domestic dog (*Canis familiaris*)
29+	Budgerigar (*Melopsittacus undulatus*)
29+	Neptune crab (*Neptunus pelagines*)
c. 29	Lion (*Panthera leo*)
28	African civet (*Viverra civetta*)
c. 28	Theraphosid spider (*Mygalomorphae*)
27¼	Sumatran crested porcupine (*Hystrix brachyura*)
27	Medicinal leech (*Hirudo medicinalis*)
27	Domestic pig (*Sus scrofa*)
26¾	Red deer (*Cervus elephus*)
26¼	Tiger (*Panthera tigris*)
26+	(d) Giant panda (*Ailuropoda melanoleuca*)
26	Common wombat (*Vombatus ursinus*)
24¾	Vicuna (*Vicugna vicugna*)
23½	Grey squirrel (*Sciurus carolinensis*)
21+	Coyote (*Canis latrans*)
21	Canadian otter (*Lutra canadensis*)
20¾	Domestic goat (*Captra hircus domesticus*)
20¼	Blue sheep (*Pseudois nayaur*)
20+	Feather-star (*Promachocrinus kerguelensis*)
18+	Queen ant (*Myrmecina graminicola*)
18+	Common rabbit (*Oryctolagus cuniculus*)
16+	Hedgehog (*Echinops telfairi*)
15	Land snail (*Helix spiriplana*)
c. 15	Brittlestar (*Amphiura chiajei*)
14⅞	Guinea pig (*Cavia porcellus*)
13½	Indian pangolin (*Manis crassicaudata*)
12	Capybara (*Hydrochoerus hydrochoaeris*)
11½	Philippine tree shrew (*Urogale everetti*)
>10	Giant centipede (*Scolopendra gigantea*)
10	Golden hamster (*Mesocricetus auratus*)
9+	Purse-web spider (*Atypus affinis*)
8⅔	Fat dormouse (*Glis glis*)
8+	Greater Egyptian gerbil (*Gerbillus pyramidum*)
7+	Spiny starfish (*Marthasterias glacialis*)
7	Millipede (*Cylindroiulus londinensis*)
6	House mouse (*Mus musculus*)
5+	Segmented worm (*Allolobophora longa*)
4½	Moonrat (*Echinosorex gymnurus*)
3¾	Siberian flying squirrel (*Pteromys volans*)
2	Pygmy white-toothed shrew (*Suncus etruscus*)
1⅛	Monarch butterfly (*Danaus plexippus*)

0·5	Bedbug (*Cimex lectularius*)
0·27	(f) Black widow spider (*Latrodectus mactans*)
0·04	(f) Common housefly (*Musca domestica*)

(a) *Fully mature at time of capture*
(b) *Still actively growing when caught*
(c) *Unconfirmed claims up to 120 years*
(d) *Still alive*
(e) *Another less well substantiated record of 72 years*
(f) *Males*

Velocity of animal movement

The data on this topic are notoriously unreliable because of the many inherent difficulties of timing the movement of most animals – whether running, flying, or swimming – and because of the absence of any standardisation of the method of timing, of the distance over which the performance is measured, or of allowance for wind conditions.

The most that can be said is that a specimen of the species below has been timed to obtain the maximum speed given.

kph	mph	Species
362	225	(a) Peregrine falcon (*Falco peregrinus*)
240+	150+	(b) Golden eagle (*Aquila chrysaetos*)
171	106·25	White-throated spinetail swift (*Hirundapus caudacutus*)
c. 160	c. 100	Alpine swift (*Apus melba*)
154	95·7	Magnificent frigatebird (*Fregata magnificens*)
142	88	Spur-winged goose (*Plectropterus gambensis*)
129	80	Red-breasted merganser (*Mergus serrator*)
124	77	White-rumped swift (*Apus caffer*)
116	72	Canvasback duck (*Aythya valisineria*)
113	70	Common eider (*Somateria mollissima*)
96·5–113	60–70	(c) Racing pigeon (*Columba livia*)
109	68	Sailfish (*Istiophorus platypterus*)
105	65	Mallard (*Anas platyrhynchos*)
96·5+	60+	Cheetah (*Acinonyx jubatus*)
96·5	60	Golden plover {*Pluvialis apricaria*)
92	57	Common quail (*Coturnix coturnix*)
92	57	Common swift (*Apus apus*)
90	56	Red grouse (*Lagopus lagopus*)
88·5+	55+	Pronghorn antelope (*Antilocapra americana*)
88·5	55	Green violetear (*Colibri thalassinus*)

88·5	55	Whooper swan (Cygnus cygnus)	46	28·75	Minke whale (Balaenoptera acutorostrata)
85	53	Grey partridge (Perdix perdix)	45	28	Black rhinoceros (Diceros bicornis)
80+	50+	Blackbuck (Antilope cervicapra)	44·88	27·89	(h) Man (Homo sapiens)
80+	50+	Mongolian gazelle (Procapra gutturosa)	44·4	27·6	Common dolphin (Delphinus delphis)
80	50	House martin (Delichon urbica)	40·7	25·3	Short-finned pilot whale (Globicephala macrorhynchus)
80	50	Marlin (Istophoridae)	40	25	Californian sea-lion (Zalophus californianus)
80	50	Springbok (Antidorcas marsupialis)			
79	49	Royal albatross (Diomedea epomophora)	39	24·5	African elephant (Loxodonta africana)
77·48	48·15	Wahoo (Acanthocybium solandri)	37	23	Salmon (Salmo salar)
			36·5	22·8	Blue whale (Balaenoptera musculus)
75·9	47·2	Long-tailed sylph (Aglaiocercus kingi)	34	21	Mountain goat (Oremnos americanus)
75·5	47	Grant's gazelle (Gazella granti)	32	20	Arabian camel (Camelus dromedarius)
75	46·61	Yellowfin tuna (Thunnus albacares)	c. 29	c. 18	Pacific leatherback turtle (Dermochelys coriacea schlegeli)
72	45	Ostrich (Struthio camelus)			
72	45	Brown hare (Lepus europaeus)	29	18	Six-lined race-runner (Cnemidophorus sexlineatus)
69·8	43·4	(d) Bluefin tuna (Thunnus thynnus)	c. 27	c. 17	Gentoo penguin (Pygosterlis papua)
69·62	43·26	(e) Race horse (Equus caballus) (mounted)	21·5	13·39	Hornet (Vespa crabro)
67·5	42	Red deer (Cervus elephus)	18·9	11·8	Crabeater seal (Lobodon carcinophagus) (land)
67·14	41·72	(f) Greyhound (Canis familiaris)	16–17·5	10–11	Black mamba (Dendroaspis polylepis)
64+	40+	Red fox (Vulpes vulpes)	16	10	N American porcupine (Erithizon dorsatum)
64	40	Bonefish (Albula vulpes)	11·5	7·26	Honey-bee (Apis mellifera)
64	40	(g) Eastern grey kangaroo (Macropus giganteus)	9·5	6	House rat (Rattus rattus)
64	40	Emu (Dromaius novahollandiae)	8·23	5·12	Common house-fly (Musca domestica)
64	40	Mountain zebra (Equus zebra)	7·24	4·5	Common flea (Pulex irritans) (jumping)
c. 64	c. 40	Swordfish (Xiphias gladius)	4·02	2·5	Common shrew (Sorex araneus)
56–64	35–40	American free-tailed bat (Tadarida brasiliensis)	3·6	2·24	Yellow-bellied sea snake (Pelamis platurus) (swimming)
61	38	Barn swallow (Hirundo rustica)	1·88	1·17	House spider (Tegenaria atrica)
59·5	37	Blue wildebeeste (Connochaetes taurinus)	1·80	1·12	Centipede (Scutiger coleoptrata)
58	36	Dragonfly (Austrophlebia costalis)	1·72	1·07	Millipede (Diopsiulus regressus) (jumping)
57	35·5	Whippet (Canis familiaris)	0·37	0·23	Giant tortoise (Geochelone gigantea)
56	35	Coyote (Canis latrans)	0·36	0·224	Rosy boa (Lichanura roseofusca)
48–56	30–35	Deer bot-fly (Cephenemiya pratti)	0·109–0·151	0·068–0·098	(i) Three-toed sloth (Bradypus tridactylus)
55·5	34·5	Killer whale (Orcinus orca)	0·049	0·031	Common garden snail (Helix aspersa)
53·9	33·5	Hawk-moth (Sphingidae)	0·00062	0·00039	(j) Neptune crab (Neptunus pelagines)
51·5	32	Giraffe (Giraffa camelopardalis)			
50·2	31·25	Horse-fly (Tabanus bovinus)			
49·8	31	Mako shark (Isurus oxyrinchus)			
48+	30+	Butterfly (Prepona)			

(a) 45-deg angle of stoop in courtship display. Cannot exceed 100·5 kph (62·5 mph) in level flight.

(b) Vertical dive.

(c) *Wind-assisted speeds up to 177·1 kph* (110·07 mph) *recorded.*
(d) *Credited with burst speeds up to 104 kph* (65 mph).
(e) *Average over 402 m* (440 yd).
(f) *Average over 375 m* (410 yd).
(g) *Young mature females.*
(h) *Over 13·7 m* (15 yd) (*flying start*)
(i) *Can double this speed in an emergency.*
(j) *Travelled 163·3 km* (101·5 miles) *in 29 years.*

The Animal Kingdom

The Animal Kingdom Metazoa (Greek, *meta* =later in time, *zoon* =an animal) is composed of multicellular animals that may lose their boundaries in the adult state, and with at least two layers of cells. The Kingdom contains 21 Phyla, with over a million species identified and described. Animals inhabit most of the planet's seas and land surfaces. As far as its classification is concerned, an animal's full modern hierarchy can extend to 20 strata:

Kingdom	*Order*
Sub-kingdom	Sub-order
Phylum	Super-family
Sub-phylum	*Family*
Super-class	Sub-family
Class	Tribe
Sub-class	Genus
Infra-class	*Species*
Cohort	Sub-species
Super-order	

Animal classification

The Molluscs

PHYLUM Mollusca is a large group of soft-bodied animals with shells, found on land, in freshwater and the sea. A typical mollusc consists of a head, a muscular foot, and a hump containing the viscera. The skin covering the hump is folded and secretes the shell. It has a heart, with an open blood system, and a simple nervous system.

Class Amphineura
A group of sea water molluscs, with elongated bodies and shells consisting of a number of plates. For example, the chitons.

Class Gastropoda
The gastropods are a group of land, sea and freshwater molluscs. There is usually a coiled shell and a distinct head with eyes and tentacles. For example: *Patella*, the limpet; *Buccinium*, the whelk; *Helix*, the land snail; *Planorbis*, the freshwater snail; *Limax*, the slug; *Littorina*, the winkle.

Class Scaphopoda
Long worm-like seawater molluscs, with tubular shells open at both ends. The head is little developed, with a number of tentacles. For example, the elephant's-tusk shells.

Class Lamellibranchia
In the lamellibranchs the body is compressed sideways and completely enclosed in the bivalved shell. They are largely found in seawater, although some inhabit freshwater. For example: *Mytilus*, the mussel; *Ostrea*, the oyster; *Anodonta*, the freshwater mussel; *Pecten*, the scallop; *Teredo*, the shipworm.

Class Cephalopoda
The cephalopods are highly-organized seawater molluscs. They have a well-developed head with complex eyes, tentacles, probably formed from the foot, and often a much reduced shell. For example: *Loligo*, the squid; *Sepia*, the cuttle-fish; *Octopus*; *Nautilus*.

The Arthropods

PHYLUM Arthropoda is a very large and varied group of animals. In general they have hard exoskeletons and a number of body segments. They have a number of segmented limbs, one pair at least serving as jaws. There is a heart and an open blood system, with a more complex nervous system than in the molluscs.

Class Onychophora
A terrestrial group, with a thin soft cuticle (skin). The head is divided into three segments, with one pair of jaws. The remaining body segments are all identical. For example, *Peripatus*.

Class Crustacea
The crustaceans are a mainly aquatic group, breathing via gills. There is often a thickened exoskeleton. Three pairs of appendages are found on the head, with many other diverse appendages on the rest of the body.

Order *Phyllopoda*
A primitive order, with many similar paired appendages. For example, *Chirocephalus*, the fairy shrimp.

Order *Isopoda*
Flattening from top to bottom; many similar paired appendages. For example, the woodlice.

Order *Amphipoda*
The amphipods show side-to-side flattening. For example, *Gammarus*, the freshwater shrimp.

Order *Decapoda*
Five pairs of legs, plus other jointed appendages. For example: *Cancer*, a crab; *Astacus*, a crayfish.

Class Arachnida
The arachnids have bodies divided into two regions. The first region carries, among other jointed appendages, four pairs of legs. The second region consists of 13 segments. For example: *Scorpio*, a scorpion; *Limulus*, a king-crab; *Epeira*, a spider; *Boophilus*, a cow-tick.

Class Myriapoda
A terrestrial group of animals, consisting of many similar limb-bearing segments. There is a clearly-observed head with one pair of jaws.

Order *Chilopoda*
Carnivores with one pair of appendages on each segment. The centipedes.

Order *Diplopoda*
Herbivores with two pairs of appendages on each segment. The millipedes.

Class *Insecta*
The insects are a large, mainly terrestrial group. An insect consists of three regions; a head, thorax and abdomen. The head has a pair of antennae, the body three pairs of legs and two pairs of wings, while the abdominal segments carry no appendages. The two dozen or so orders include the following.

Order *Lepidoptera*
The butterflies and moths.

Order *Coleoptera*
The beetles.

Order *Hymenoptera*
The ants, wasps and bees.

Order *Diptera*
The flies.

Order *Orthoptera*
The cockroaches, grasshoppers, locusts and stick insects.

Order *Anisoptera*
The dragonflies.

The Chordates

PHYLUM Chordata contains the most sophisticated animals. All chordates possess a notochord (a sort of skeletal rod) at some stage in their embryological development. There is a tubular central nervous system, and a closed blood system.

SUB-PHYLUM *PROTOCHORDATA*
A group with no true brain, skull, heart or kidneys. For example: *Balanoglossus*, a burrowing marine worm; *Cionia*, a sea-squirt; *Amphioxus*, a lancelet.

SUB-PHYLUM *VERTEBRATA*
In the vertebrates a vertebral column replaces the notochord of the protochordates, along with a true internal skeleton of bone and/or cartilage. There are usually two pairs of limbs. The kidneys are the organs of excretion. There is a central nervous system, with a brain enclosed in a protective skull.

Class *Pisces*
The fish. A large aquatic class, with gills for breathing, pectoral and pelvic fins as limbs, and scales as a pseudo-exoskeleton.

Sub-class *Chondrichthyes*
A cartilaginous endoskeleton.

Order *Selachii*
There is no operculum covering the gills. There are many teeth, which are constantly being replaced. For example: *Scyliorhinus*, the dogfish; *Selache*, the basking shark; *Raia*, the ray; *Torpedo*, the electric ray.

Sub-class *Teleostomi*
The endoskeleton is entirely of bone, with an exoskeleton of bony scales. An air bladder is usually present.

Order *Dipnoi*
The lung-fishes; there are lungs as well as gills. For example: *Ceratodus*, the Burnett salmon; *Protopterus*, the mud-fish.

Order *Teleostei*
The modern bony fish, in which the endoskeleton is reduced and the exoskeleton consists of bony scales. For example: *Salmo*, the salmon; *Gadus*, the cod; *Exocoetus*, the flying fish; *Hippocampus*, the seahorse.

Class *Amphibia*
Suited for life both in the water and on land. Gills are present in the larvae (tadpoles), lungs in the adult. The legs are modelled on the pentadactyl (five-fingered) limb.

Order *Urodela*
Limbs are short and there is often a tail. The gills often persist into adulthood. For example: *Triton*, the newt; *Salamandra*, the salamander; *Amblystoma*, the axolotl.

Order *Anura*
The frogs and toads. The adults have neither gills nor tails. For example: *Rana*, the frog; *Bufo*, the toad.

Class *Reptilia*
The reptiles have dry skin with scales or bony plates. They breath with lungs. Typically they have two pairs of pentadactyl limbs. They lay yolk-filled eggs with calcareous (calcium-rich) shells.

Order *Chelonia*
The tortoises and turtles.

Order *Lacertilia*
The lizards.

Order *Ophidia*
The snakes.

Order *Crocodilia*
The crocodiles and alligators.

Class *Aves*
The birds are warm-blooded. Of the two pairs of pentadactyl limbs, the front pair is formed into wings. The skin bears feathers, except on the legs, where there are horny scales, linking them with the reptiles. Lungs are the respiratory organs. They lay yolky eggs with calcareous shells, and show parental care of the young.

Order *Ratitae*
Large running birds with rudimentary wings. For example: *Struthio*, the ostrich; *Dromaeus*, the emu; *Casuarius*, the cassowary; *Apteryx*, the kiwi.

Order *Carinatae*
The flying birds, from wrens up to eagles.

Class *Mammalia*
The mammals are warm-blooded, with pentadactyl limbs. The skin has hair. The respiratory organs are lungs, and the thoracic and abdominal cavities are separated by the diaphragm. In most cases they give birth to live young, which they suckle on milk from the mammary glands and to which they show an often well-developed sense of parental care.

Sub-class *Prototheria*
A primitive group of mammals which lay eggs and have no mammary glands. For example: the duck-billed platypus; the spiny anteater.

Sub-class *Metatheria*
The marsupials of Australia and South America. They give birth to only partly-developed young, which are then suckled in the pouch on the body of the mother. For example: the kangaroos; the koala bears; the opossums.

Sub-class *Eutharia*
These are the placental mammals, whose offspring are born at a more developed stage than those of the other two sub-classes.

Order *Insectivora*
The hedgehogs, shrews and moles.

Order *Chiroptera*
The bats.

Order *Rodentia*
The rats, mice, squirrels, lemmings, beavers and porcupines.

Order *Lagomorpha*
The rabbits and hares.

Order *Cetacea*
The whales and dolphins.

Order *Carnivora*
The cats, lions, dogs, weasels, otters, badgers, bears and seals.

Order *Perissodactyla*
The horses, zebras, tapirs and rhinosceroses.

Order *Artiodactyla*
The cows, goats, deer, giraffe and sheep.

Order *Primates*
The lemurs, monkeys, apes and man.

Gestation periods

Please note the figures in brackets are approximate conversions. The months have been calculated on a 30 day month.

Shortest – American Opossum, Water Opossum and Eastern Native Cat, all 12/13 days but may be 8 days.

Longest – Asiatic elephant – 609 days or just over 20 months

aardvark	210 days (7 months)
alpaca	342–345 days (11¼ months)
anteater, giant	190 days (6¼ months)
antelope	280 days (9 months)
armadillo	from 60–120 days (2–4 months)
ass	about 11½ months
baboon	5–6 months
badger	3½–12 months incl. period of delayed implantation*

bear, grizzly	210–255 days (7 months)
bear, polar	about 8 months
bear, American black	210–215 days (7 months)
beaver	about 105 days (3½ months)
bison, American	270–300 days (9 months)
boar, wild	115 days (3¾ months)
bobcat	60–63 days (2 months)
buffalo, wild water	310–330 days (10¼ months)
bushbaby	110–193 days (3½–6¼ months)
capybara	150 days (5 months)
cat	52 day (2 months)
cattle	about 283 days (9¼ months)
cavies	from 50–90 days (3 months)
chamois	160–170 days (5¼ months)
cheetah	91–95 days (3 months)
chimpanzee	230–240 days (7½ months)
civet	70 days (2¼ months)
civet, African	80 days (2½ months)
civet, palm	90 days (3 months)
coati	77 days (2¼ months)
coyote	63 days (2 months)
deer, fallow	229–240 days (7½ months)
deer, musk	150–180 days (5 months)
dhole	60–62 days (2 months)
dingo	63 days (2 months)
dog	53–71 days (2 months)
dog, African wild	70–73 days (2¼ months)
dolphin	10–12 months
dormouse	21–32 days
dromedary	390–410 days (13 months)
elephant, Asiatic	608 days (20 months)
ermine	about 28 days
ferret	40–76 days (1–2½ months)
fox, red	60–63 days (2 months)
gazelle	up to 188 days
gerbil	21–28 days
gibbon	7–8 months
giraffe	453–464 days (15¼ months)
goat	150 days (5 months)
gopher	12–20 days
gorilla	250–270 days (8½ months)
guinea pig	63 days (2 months)
hamster	from 15–37 days
hare	28–35 days
hare, mountain	50 days (1½ months)
hedgehog	30 days
hippo, pygmy	190–210 days (6¼ months)
hippopotamus	about 240 days (8 months)
horse	about 11½ months
hyena	93 days (3 months)
hyena, striped	about 84 days (2¾ months)
jackal	63 days (2 months)
jaguar	93–110 days (3½ months)
kangaroo	6–11 months in pouch
koala	34–36 days (1¼ months)
lemming	20–22 days
lemur	60–160 days where known
leopard	90–105 days (3¼ months)
leopard, snow	98–103 days (3¼ months)
lion	100–119 days (3½ months)
llama	348–368 days (11½–12¼ months)
lynx	60–74 days (2 months)

macaque	5–6 months	panda, red	150 days
marmoset	130–170 days (2¼–5½ months)	peccary, collared	142 days (4¾ months)
meerkat	77 days (2½ months)	pig	101–129 days (3¼ months)
mink	34–70 days (1½ months)	porcupine	205–217 days (6½ months)
mole	28–42 days	porcupine, North American	210 days (7 months)
mongoose	mostly 60 days (2 months)		
moose	264 days (8½ months)	porpoise	183 days (6 months)
mouse	about 20–30 days	puma	90–96 days (3 months)
narwhal	14–15 months	rabbit	30 days
		rabbit, European	28–33 days
ocelot	70 days (2¼ months)	raccoons	63 days (2 months)
opossum, American	12–13 days	rat, black	21 days
orang-utan	210–270 days (8½ months)	reindeer	210–240 days (7–8 months)
otter	49–62 days	rhinoceros, black	15 months
panda, giant	125–150 days (4½ months)	seal, common	245 days (8 months)
panda, Himalayan	90 days (3 months)	seal, eared	12 months incl. period of delayed implantation*

A baby tapir, only a few days old, and his watchful mother at the Hagenback Zoo in Hamburg, West Germany. (Popperfoto)

sea lion	330–365 days (11 months)
serval	75 days (approx.) (2½ months)
sheep	135–160 days (4½–5 months)
shrew	13–24 days
skunks, striped	62–66 days (2 months)
sloth	from 6–11 months
squirrel	about 40 days (1⅓ months)
tapir	335–400 days (11–13 months)
tenrec	50–64 days (2¼ months)
tiger	103 days (3½ months)
vole	90 days
vicuna	330–350 days (11 months)
wallaby	40 days
walrus	15–16 months incl. 4–5 months of delayed implantation*
warthog	170–175 days (5½ months)
weasel	35–45 days (1½ months)
whale	305–365 days (10–12 months)
whale, beluga	14–15 months
whale, sperm	14–15 months
wolf	61–63 days (2 months)
wolf, maned	about 65 days (2 months)
wolverine	about 9 months
yak	258 days (8½ months)
zebra	340 days (about 11½ months)
zorilla	42–44 days

* Delayed implantation = after mating the fertilized egg travels to the uterus developing as it goes into a ball of cells called the blastocyst. In most mammals the blastocyst implants into the uterus wall within a few days and development of the embryo proceeds. But in the 16 or more mustelid species (weasel family) it floats free in the uterus for periods from a few days up to 10 months, and implants only when certain conditions are met.

Collective nouns

Angel Fish	Host
Animals	Menagerie, Tribe
Antelope	Herd, Troop
Ants	Army, Column, State, Swarm
Apes	Shrewdness
Asses	Herd, Pace
Baboons	Troop
Badger	Cete, Colony
Barracuda	Battery
Bass	Fleet
Bears	Sloth
Beavers	Colony
Bees	Cluster, Erst, Hive, Swarm
Birds	Congregation, Dissimulation (young), Flight, Flock, Volery, Volley
Bison	Herd
Bitterns	Sedge, Siege
Bloodhounds	Sute
Boars	Herd, Singular, Sounder
Budgerigars	Chatter
Buffalo	Herd
Bustard	Flock

Camels	Caravan, Flock
Capercaillie	Tok
Caterpillars	Army
Cats	Chowder, Clowder, Cluster
Cats, Wild	Dout
Cattle	Drove, Herd
Chamois	Herd
Chickens	Brood, Clutch, Peep
Choughs	Chattering
Clams	Bed
Cockles	Bed
Colts	Race, Rag, Rake
Coots	Covert, Raft
Cormorants	Flight
Cranes	Herd, Siege
Crows	Clan, Hover, Murder
Curlews	Herd
Deer	Herd, Leash
Dogfish	Brood, Troop
Dogs	Cowardice, Kennel, Pack
Dogs (Hunting)	Cry
Dolphins	Pod, School
Donkeys	Herd, Drove
Dottrel	Trip
Doves	Dole, Flight, Prettying
Ducklings in Nest	Clutch
Ducklings off Nest	Clatch
Ducks (Diving)	Dopping, Dropping
Ducks (Flying)	Flush, Plump, Team
Ducks (on land)	Flight, Flock, Leash, Mob, Sail
Ducks (on water)	Badeling, Paddling, Sail
Eagles	Convocation
Eels	Swarm
Elephants	Herd
Elk (Europe)	Gang
Falcons	Cast
Ferrets	Business, Cast, Fesynes
Finches	Charm, Flight
Fish	Haul, Run, School, Shoal
Flamingoes	Flurry, Regiment, Skein
Flies	Business, Cloud, Scraw, Swarm
Foxes	Earth, Lead, Skulk
Foxhounds	Pack
Frogs	Army, Colony
Geese (Flying)	Flock, Gaggle, Skein
Geese (on land)	Gaggle
Geese (on water)	Gaggle, Plump
Giraffes	Corps, Herd, Troop
Gnats	Cloud, Horde, Swarm
Goats	Flock, Herd, Tribe, Trippe
Goldfinch	Charm, Chattering, Chirp, Drum
Goldfish	Troubling
Goshawks	Flight
Grasshoppers	Cloud
Greyhounds	Brace, Leash, Pack
Grouse	Brood, Covey, Pack
Guillemots	Bazaar
Gulls	Colony
Hares	Down, Drove, Husk, Lie, Trip
Hart	Herd, Stud
Hawks	Cast
Hedgehogs	Array
Hens	Brood, Flock

A parliament of owls impersonating the House of Lords! (Popperfoto)

Heron	Scattering, Sedge, Siege	Monkeys	Troop
Herring	Army, Gleam, Shoal	Moose	Gang, Herd
Hippopotami	Herd, School	Mules	Barren, Cartload, Pack, Span
Hogs	Herd, Drove, Sounder		
Horses	Harass, Herd, Stable, Stud, Troop	Mussels	Bed
Horses (race)	Stable, String	Nightingale	Match, Puddling, Watch
Hounds	Brace, Couple, Cry, Mute, Pack, Stable		
		Ostrich	Flock, Troop
Ibis	Crowd	Otters	Bevy, Family
Insects	Swarm	Owls	Parliament, Stare
		Oxbirds	Fling
Jays	Band, Party	Oxen (domestic)	Drove, Rake, Team, Yoke
Jellyfish	Brood, Smuck	Oxen (wild)	Drove, Herd
		Oyster	Bed
Kangaroos	Herd, Mob, Troop		
Kittens	Brood, Kindle, Litter	Parrots	Flock
		Partridges	Covey
Lapwing	Deceit, Desert	Passenger Pigeons	Roost
Larks	Exultation	Peacocks	Muster
Lemurs	Troop	Peafowl	Muster, Ostentation, Pride
Leopards	Leap	Penguins	Colony, Rookery
Lice	Flock	Perch	Pack, Shoal
Lions	Flock, Pride, Sawt, Souse, Troop	Pheasants	Brook, Ostentation, Pride, Nye
Locusts	Cloud, Horde, Plague, Swarm	Pigeons	Flight, Flock
		Piglets	Farrow
Mackerel	School, Shoal	Pigs	Litter, Herd, Sounder
Magpies	Tiding, Tittering	Pilchards	Shoal
Mallards (on land)	Bord, Flock, Flush, Suite, Sute	Plover	Congregation, Flight, Stand, Wing
Mallards (on water)	Sord	Polecats	Chine
Mares	Flock, Stud	Ponies	Herd
Marten	Raches, Richesse	Porpoises	Gam, Pod, School
Mice	Nest	Poultry	Flock
Minnows	Shoal, Steam, Swarm	Poultry (domestic)	Run
Moles	Company, Labour, Movement, Mumble	Ptarmigan	Covey
		Pups	Litter

Quail	Bevy, Covey	Swans	Bank, Bevy, Game, Herd, Squadron, Teeme, Wedge, Whiteness
Rabbits	Bury, Colony, Nest, Warren		
Racoons	Nursery	Swifts	Flock
Racehorses	Field, String	Swine	Doyet, Dryft
Rats	Colony	Swine (wild)	Sounder
Ravens	Unkindness		
Redwings	Crowd	Teal (on land)	Bunch, Coil, Knab, Raft
Rhinoceros	Crash	Teal (on water, rising from water)	Spring
Roach	Shoal		
Roe Deer	Bevy	Thrush	Mutation
Rooks	Building, Clamour, Parliament	Tigers	Ambush
		Toads	Knab, Knot
Ruffs	Hill	Trout	Hover
		Turkeys	Dule, Raffle, Rafter
Sandpipers	Fling	Turtles	Bale, Dole
Sardines	Family	Turtle Doves	Pitying
Seals, Elephant	Rookery, Team, Troop		
Seals	Harem, Herd, Pod, Rookery	Vipers	Den, Nest
Sheep	Down, Drove, Flock, Hurtle, Trip		
		Walrus	Herd, Pod
Sheldrakes	Dapping, Dropping	Wasps	Herd, Nest, Pladge
Smelt	Quantity	Weasels	Pack, Pop
Snakes	Den, Pit	Whales	Colony, Gam, Herd, Pod, School
Snakes (young)	Bed		
Snipe	Walk, Whisper, Wish, Wisp	Whiting	Pod
Spaniels	Couple	Widgeon	Coil, Company, Flight, Knob
Sparrows	Host, Surration, Quarrel	Wildfowl	Plump, Sord, Sute, Trip
Spiders	Cluster, Clutter	Wolves	Pack, Rout
Squirrels	Drey	Woodcocks	Covey, Fall, Flight, Plump
Starlings	Chattering, Crowd, Murmuration	Woodpeckers	Descent
		Wrens	Herd
Sticklebacks	Shoal		
Stoats	Pack	Young Animals	Kindle, Litter
Storks	Herd, Mustering		
Swallows	Flight	Zebras	Herd

THE HUMAN WORLD

Anthropology

Anthropology, the study of the differences and similarities between the various races of mankind, contains two autonomous sciences: physical anthropology (the study of blood groups and genetic differences) and social anthropology or ethnology (the study of custom).

PHYSICAL ANTHROPOLOGY

The classification of the races or gene pools of man is complex and is vulnerable to political controversy. Many terms which have been used to describe racial groupings are hypothetical, being based either upon cultural and linguistic considerations which are not genetically linked (*e.g.* the term 'the Semitic race'), or upon physical similarities (*e.g.* the term negroid).

Formerly classifications of mankind were attempted based purely upon outward physical characteristics such as skin colour (black, brown, white, yellow); body proportions (anthropometry), the shape of the head (craniometry), hair form, teeth and eyelids. A widely adopted system was that based on hair form which recognized three main types: the straight haired, woolly haired and curly haired groups. Although this remains of value no modern description of race relies solely on hair form. External bodily differences are not ignored in the definition of races but are of less scientific importance than such simply inherited or single gene traits as can be easily and precisely quantified.

One of the major factors in modern anthropological studies is the blood group. Certain blood groups predominate in some races but are almost absent in others; *e.g.* B group is very rare in Amerinds. As well as blood groups various related factors are of racial consequence: abnormal haemoglobins and pigments and deficiencies in some type of cell are all known to be racially linked.

Many metabolic differences are now used in anthropological classification: abnormalities in the sense of taste (some races cannot taste phenylthiocarbamide), the incidence of colour blindness, differences in the secretion of amino acids and other biochemical traits have all been scientifically investigated and shown to be excellent aids in the definition of gene pools. Certain medical disorders of genetic origin are useful to the science; *e.g.* thalassemia is confined to the Mediterranean type of the Caucasoid race. The Japanese have studied earwax types and found them to be genetically significant. Thus blood and other genetic traits have taken first place over body measurements and hair types in the definition of races.

The study of genetically transmitted traits has allowed anthropologists to divide man into about ten major types – the exact number depends upon individual interpretation of the scientific evidence. These major divisions, often referred to as geographical races, account for over 99% of mankind. Each geographical race contains many local groupings which, although forming breeding units separate from others to a greater or lesser degree, are nevertheless genetically related to the whole. The remaining groups are sometimes (inaccurately) termed microraces and consist of either small local genetically distinct populations, (*e.g.* the Ainu of Hokkaido) or peoples whose place in the anthropological jigsaw is still the subject of much controversy (*e.g.* the Bushmen of Southern Africa).

The Geographical Races

(1) The Asiatic or Mongoloid Race

Extent: most of Asia north and east of India.
Classic appearance: 'yellow-brown' skin, straight hair, round head, high cheek bones and flat face.

A northern group includes Lapps, Yakuts and Koreans; a southern group – 'Oceanic Mongoloids' or Indonesians – is very mixed with a tendency to broader heads. The central (Pareoean) type with, in general, less prominent cheek bones and broader noses, includes both Chinese and Japanese.

(2) The Amerindian Race

Extent: the Americas.
Classic appearance: Similar to Asiatics though the Eskimos tend to have longer skulls, broader faces and narrower noses, and the Fuegans have curly hair.

Although there are undoubted links between the Indians of the New World and the Asiatics there is sufficient genetic reason to recognize them as separate races.

(3) The African or Negroid Race

Extent: Africa south of the Sahara.
Classic appearance: tall, woolly hair, black or dark brown skin, broad nose, thickened lips.

Many sub-groups include Nilotics and the much shorter lighter skinned Pygmies (Negrillos). It is debatable whether the Bushmen belong to this geographical race.

(4) The Polynesian Race

Extent: Polynesia including New Zealand.
Classic appearance: similar to 'Oceanic Mongoloids' though with longer heads and some Caucasoid traits.

The ancestral home of the Polynesians was probably South-East Asia.

(5) The Melanesian Race

Extent: Melanesia including New Guinea.
Classic appearance: similar to Africans but some Melanesian islanders tend to be lighter skinned.

This group contains isolated pockets in Asia including Semang tribes in Sumatra and Malaysia, possibly the Andaman Island Negritos, and debatably the short Aeta of the Philippines.

(6) The Micronesian Race

Extent: Micronesia.
Classic appearance: slight of stature, light brown skins, curly hair.

Genetically realted to 'Oceanic Mongoloids'.

Major anthropological discoveries

Year	Scientific Name	Period and Estimated Date BC	Location	Description	Anthropologist or Discoverer
1856[1]	Homo neanderthalensis	Middle Palaeolithic c.70000	Neander Valley, nr Hochdal, Germany	skull cap, 15 bones	von Fuhlrott
1868[2]	Homo sapiens sapiens (Cro-Magnon man)	Upper Palaeolithic 35000	Cro-Magnon, Les Eyzies, France	4 skeletons, 1 foetus	Lartet
1891	Homo erectus (Java man)	Middle Pleistocene c.600000	Kabuh beds, Trinil, Java	calotte, femoral bones	Dubois
1907	Homo heidelbergensis	Lower Palaeolithic c.400000	Mauer, nr Heidelberg, Germany	mandible	Schoetensack
1912[3]	Eoanthropus dawsonii	Holocene (Recent) (fraud)	Piltdown, East Sussex	composite skull	Dawson
1921	Homo rhodesiensis	Late Middle Pleistocene c.125000	Broken Hill, Kabwe, Zambia	skull, humerus, femora	Zwigelaar
1921	Sinanthropus pekinensis	Lower Palaeolithic c.480000	Choukoutien, nr Peking, China	32 skeletons	Andersson
1924	Australopithecus africanus	Early Pleistocene c.1000000	Baxton, Taung, Bophuthatswana	skull and mandible	Dart (de Brayn)
1926[4]	Proconsul nyanzae	Miocene c.25000000	Koru, Kenya	fragments (non-hominoid)	Hopwood
1929–34	Neanderthaloid man	Late Middle Palaeolithic or Mousterian 30000–60000	Tabun and Skhul, Mt Carmel, Israel	part 16 skeletons	Garrod
1932	Ramapithecus	Miocene c.8–13000000	Siwalik Hills, N India	jaws, teeth	G. E. Lewis
1935[5]	Homo sen sapiens	Lower Palaeolithic 225000	Boyn Hill, Swanscombe, Kent	parts skull	Marston
1935[6]	Gigantopithecus blacki	Middle Pleistocene 450000	from Kwangsi, China (Hong Kong druggist)	teeth only	von Koenigswald
1936–39	Pleisianthropus transvaalensis	Early Pleistocene 1000000	Sterkfontein, Transvaal	skull, part femur	Broom (Barlow)
1938	Paranthropus robustus	Early Pleistocene 1200000	Kromdraai, Transvaal	skull part, bones	Broom (Terblanche)
1947	Australopithecus prometheus	Pleistocene 900000	Makapansgat, Transvaal	fragments[7]	Dart
1948	Paranthropus crassidens	Pleistocene c.1250000	Swartkrans, Transvaal	crania and teeth	Broom
1954	Atlanthropus or mauritanicus	Early Middle Pleistocene 1000000	Ternifine, Algeria	parietal, 3 mandibles	Arambourg
1957	Neanderthaloid man	Upper Palaeolithic c.65000 (Layer D)	Shanidar, Iraq	parts of 8 skeletons	Solecki
1959	Zinjanthropus boisei	Pliocene Pleistocene c.1750000	Olduvai, Tanzania	skull	Dr Mary Leakey
1960	Homo habilis	as above c.1800000	Olduvai, Tanzania	fragments	Louis Leakey
1961	Kenyapithecus wickeri	Mid-Miocene c.14000000	Fort Ternan, Kenya	palate, teeth (non-hominoid)	Leakey (Mukiri)
1963	Sinanthropus lantianensis	Middle Pleistocene c.650000	Chenchiawo, Lantien, NW China	mandible	Ju Kang Wu
1969	Pithecanthropus (Homo erectus)	Middle Pleistocene 650000–710000	Sangiran, Java	cranium	Sartono
1972	Homo habilis	Plio-Pleistocene 1900000	East Turkana, Kenya	cranial bones	R. E. F. Leakey (Ngeneo)
1974	Australopithecus afarensis	Pliocene c.3000000	Hadar, Afar region, Ethiopia	skull parts, jaws, teeth, skeleton known as 'Lucy'	Johanson and Gray
1975	Homo erectus	Early Pleistocene 1500000	Turkana, Kenya	skull**	R. E. F. Leakey
1975	Homo	Plio-Pleistocene 3350000–3750000	Laetoli, Tanzania	8 adults, 3 children	Dr Mary Leakey
1977	Ramapithecus	Mid-Miocene c.9–11 million	Potwar Plateau, Pakistan	radius	Pilbeam
1978	Hominid	Plio-Pleistocene 3.6–3.75 million	Laetoli, Tanzania	footprints (24 m, 80 ft)	Dr Mary Leakey (Abell)
1984	Australopithecine	Pliocene 5.4–5.6 million	Lake Baringo, Kenya	mandible with 2 molars	Leakey (Chepoi)
1985	Homo erectus	Plio-Pleistocene 1.6 million	Nariokotome, Kenya	almost complete young male	R. E. F. Leakey (Kimea)

[1] Female skull discovered in Gibraltar in 1848 but unrecognized till 1864.
[2] Earliest specimen found at Engis, near Liège, Belgium, in 1832 by Schmerling.
[3] Exposed by X-ray and radio-activity tests in Nov 1953 as an elaborate fraud.
[4] Non-hominoid. Complete skull discovered 1948 by Mrs Leakey.
[5] Further part discovered 1955.
[6] Since 1957 all the evidence is that these relate to a non-hominoid giant ape.
[7] Complete skull in 1958 (Kitching).
** Of great importance because of its uncanny resemblance to Peking man which Leakey believes is more correctly datable to triple the age advanced by the Chinese.

(7) The Australoid Race
Extent: mainland Australia.
Classic appearance: curly hair, dark brown to black skin, massive skull with protruding jaws and retreating forehead, slender limbs.
The Australian aboriginals are distantly related to the Indic race, in particular to the Veddah of Sri Lanka, but long isolation has resulted in some special features.

(8) The Indic Race
Extent: Indian sub-continent.
Classic appearance: medium height, curly hair, prominent forehead, light brown skin but considerable variation in colour.
Local races include the north Indian Caucasoid type, the south Indian 'Dravidians', Singhalese Veddah and some isolated peoples in Sumatra and Sulawesi.

(9) The Caucasoid Race
Extent: Europe, Asia west of India and north Africa. Also widely diffused to the Americas and Australasia.
Classic appearance: considerable variation in height and build, and hair colour and form although there is a tendency to curly hair; 'white' or light skin, prominent forehead.
Sub-groups include Proto-Nordics (from Turkestan), Somalis, Ethiops and other Caucasoid peoples of the Horn of Africa and the Red Sea, Eurafricans, Arabs (including Bedouins), the Mediterranean or Romance peoples, the Nordic peoples (of Britain, Scandinavia, the Low Countries and Germany), the Pamiri, the Eurasiatics (including the Alpine type) found from central Europe to the Himalayas, and possibly the Ainu of Hokkaido, who are often categorized as a 'microrace'.

Human genetics

Within the nucleus of every cell in the body there are 46 chromosomes. These are microscopic thread-like structures which each have thousands of genes – the chemicals which carry the code for hereditary factors. The 46 chromosomes are made up of 22 pairs of non-sex chromosomes (one chromosome of each pair is derived from the mother and one from the father) and two sex chromosomes. In the female both sex chromosomes are Xs (one from the father and one from the mother); in the male the sex chromosomes are XY (the X from the mother, the Y from the father).
The branch of genetics which fascinates most people is identifying the various dominant and recessive characteristics of their own children, and even predicting how their first or next child will look.

Colour of Eyes
Dark eyes are dominant and pale or light-coloured eyes recessive. Thus, if there are *all* dark eyes on one side of a family (e.g., among the husband's ancestors) then *almost all* the children will be dark-eyed regardless of having a blue-eyed mother. If, however, both parents are light-eyed, *almost all* the children will be light-eyed. Geneticists, however, always caution that occasionally legitimate brown-eyed children have been born to two blue-eyed parents. In genetics there is a saying, *'Pater est semper incertus'* – the true identity of the father is always uncertain.

Hair Form
Curly or wavy hair forms are dominant.

Parentage and Ascendants
1. Two straight-haired parents.
2. All curly-haired on one side.

3. Both parents curly-haired but each with some straight-haired relatives.
4. A curly-haired parent with straight-haired relatives and the other parent straight-haired.

Result in Children
Almost all straight-haired.
Almost all curly-haired regardless of hair form of the other side.
Odds are 3:1 that children will have curly hair.

A 50-50 chance between curly-haired and straight-haired children.

Hair Colour
Dark hair *tends* to be dominant and light hair recessive.

Parentage and Ascendants
1. All dark-haired on one side.
2. Both parents blond.
3. Both parents dark-haired but each with some fair-haired relatives.
4. A dark-haired parent with light-haired relatives and the other parent fair-haired.

Result in Children
Almost all dark-haired.
Almost all children blond.
Odds are 3:1 on dark-haired children.

A 50-50 chance between dark and fair hair.

Note: Red hair genes are often masked by dark hair. Two red-headed parents will almost always produce red-haired children.

The 26 civilizations of man

If the duration of the evolution of Homo, now estimated at 3 750 000 years, is likened to a single year, then the earliest of all history's known civilizations began after 5 p.m. on 30 Dec. Put another way, 289/290ths of man's existence has been uncivilized.
Few historians have attempted to classify the world's civilizations because of the natural tendency to specialize. An early attempt was that of the Frenchman, Count de Gobineau, in his four-volume *L'Inégalité des Races Humaines* (Paris, 1853–5). His total was ten. Since that time western archaeologists have rescued five more ancient civilizations from oblivion – the Babylonic, the Hittite, the Mayan, the Minoan, and the Sumeric. This would have brought his total to 15 compared with a more modern contention of 26.
The most authoritative classification now available is the revised twelve-volume life work of Professor Arnold Joseph Toynbee, *A Study of History*, published between 1921 and 1961. This concludes

The 26 civilizations of man

No.	Name	Dawn	Final Collapse	Duration in Centuries	Cradle	Dominant States	Religion and Philosophy	Derivation
1	Sumeric or Sumerian	ante 3500 BC	c. 1700 BC	c. 18	Euphrates–Tigris Delta	Sumer and Akkad Empire c. 2298–1905 BC	Tammuz-worship	Spontaneous
2	Egyptiac	ante 3400 BC	c. AD 280	c. 43	Lower Nile	Middle Empire c. 2065–1660 BC	Osiris-worship Philosophy of Atonism	Sumerian
3	Indic	ante 3000 BC	c. AD 500	35	Mohenjo-Daro, Harappa, Indus and Ganges valleys	Mauryan Empire 322–185 BC Gupta Empire AD 390–475	Hinduism, Jainism, Hinayána Buddhism	Possibly of Sumeric origin
4	Mayan[1]	c. 2500 BC	AD 1550	c. 45	Guatemalan forests	First Empire AD c. 300–690	Human sacrifice and human penitential self-mortification	Spontaneous
5	Minoan	ante 2000 BC	c. 1400 BC	6	Cnossus, Crete and the Cyclades	Thalassocracy of Minos c. 1750–1400 BC	Goddess worship	w. Anatolia
6	Hittite	2000 BC	c. 1200 BC	8	Boghazköi, Anatolia, Turkey	—	Pantheonism	Related to Minoan
7	Sinic	c. 1600 BC[3]	AD 220	18	Yellow River Basin	Ts'in and Han Empire 221 BC–AD 172	Mahayana Buddhism, Taoism, Confucianism	Believed unrelated
8	Micronesian	c. 1550 BC	c. AD 1775	33	Marianas	—	Ancestor spirits Mana – supernatural power	—
9	Babylonic	c. 1500 BC	538 BC	10	Lower Mesopotamia	Babylonian Empire 610–539 BC	Judaism, Zoroastrianism Astrology	Related to Sumeric
10	Hellenic	c. 1300 BC	AD 558	18½	Greek mainland and Aegean Is	Roman Empire 31 BC–AD 378	Mithraism, Platonism, Stoicism, Epicureanism Pantheonism, Christianity	Related to Minoan
11	Syriac	c. 1200 BC	AD 970	22	Eastern Cilicia	Achaemenian Empire c. 525–332 BC	Islam and Philosophy of Zervanism	Related to Minoan
12	Eskimo	c. 1100 BC	c. AD 1850	c. 30	Umnak, Aleutian Islands	Thule AD c. 1150–1850	Includes Sila, sky god; Sedna, seal goddess	E. Siberia
13	Spartan	c. 900 BC	AD 396	13	Laconia	620–371 BC	—	Hellenic
14	Andean	c. 100 BC	AD 1783	19	Chimu, N Peru and Nazca, S Peru	Inca Empire AD 1430–1533	Philosophy of Viracochaism	Spontaneous
15	Khmer[4]	c. AD 100	AD 1432	13	Cambodian coast	Angkor Kingdom AD 802–1432	Hinduism	Possibly related to Indic and Sinic
16	Far Eastern (main)	AD 589	Scarcely survives	14 to date	Si Ngan (Sian-fu) Wei Valley	Mongol Empire AD 1280–1351 Manchu Empire AD 1644–1912	Muhayaniah Buddhism	Related to Sinic
17	Far Eastern (Japan and Korea)	AD 645	Survives	13 to date	Yamato, Japan via Korea	Tokugawa Shogunate AD 1600–1868	Mikado-worship, Shintoism, Buddhism and Zen Philosophy	Related to Sinic
18	Western	c. AD 675	Flourishes	13 to date	Ireland Iona Lindisfarne	Habsburg Monarchy AD 1493–1918 and French (Napoleonic) Empire AD 1792–1815 The British Empire 1757–1931	Philosophy of Christianity	Related to Hellenic

The 26 civilizations of man continued

No.	Name	Dawn	Final Collapse	Duration in Centuries	Cradle	Dominant States	Religion and Philosophy	Derivation
19	Orthodox Christian (main)	c. AD 680	•Survives	13 to date	Anatolia, Turkey	Byzantine Empire AD 395–1453	Bedreddinism Orthodox Church, Imami	Related to Hellenic and Western
20	Hindu	c. AD 775	Survives	11 to date	Kanauj, Jumna-Ganges Duab	Mughul Raj AD c. 1572–1707 British Raj 1818–1947	Hinduism, Sikhism	Related to Indic
21	Orthodox Christian (Russia)	c. AD 950	Survives	10 to date	Upper Dnieper Basin	Muscovite Empire AD 1478–1917	Orthodox Church Sectarianism	Related to Hellenic
22	Arabic	c. AD 975	AD 1525	5½	Arabia, Iraq, Syria	Abbasid Caliphate of Baghdad	Islam (post AD 1516)	Related to Syriac
23	Mexic	c. AD 1075	AD 1821	7½	Mexican Plateau	Aztec Empire AD 1375–1521	Quetzalcoatl	Related to Mayan
24	Ottoman	c. AD 1310	AD 1919	6	Turkey	Ottoman Empire AD 1372–1919	Islam	—
25	Iranic (now Islamic)	c. AD 1320	Survives	6½ to date	Oxus-Jaxartes Basin	—	Islam (post AD 1516)	Related to Syriac
26	Communist	1848	Declining	1½ to date	Western Europe	USSR and China	Atheism, Marxist-Leninism, Maoism	—

[1] Toynbee regards a Yucatec civilization (c. AD 1075–1680) as a separate entity. Archaeological discoveries in 1960 indicate that Dzibilchaltun, on the Yucatan Peninsula, was in fact the cradle of the whole Mayan civilization.
[2] There is evidence of links with Egyptiac. The early classic period at Tikal dates from c. AD 250–550.
[3] The earliest archaeologically acceptable dynasty was that of Shang, variously dated 1766–1558 BC. The historicity of the First, or Hsia dynasty, allegedly founded by Yu in 2205 BC. is in decided doubt.
[4] Not regarded by Toynbee as a separate civilization but as an offshoot of the Hindu civilization. Modern evidence shows, however, that the Khmer origins antedate those of the Hindu civilization by 7 centuries.

that there have been 21 civilizations of which eight still survive. Those surviving are the Arabic (Islamic), the Far Eastern (began in AD 589 and now split into two), the Orthodox Christian (now also split into two), the Hindu (begun c. AD 775), the Western civilization and the Communist civilization. The term 'civilization' in the context of classifications relates purely to entities with separate imperial designs rather than a differing culture or ethos.

Archaeological discoveries in 1960 showed that the Yucatec and Mayan civilizations had the same cradle. The compilation above gives details. The Eskimo, Spartan, Micronesian, and Ottoman civilizations have been listed though Toynbee excludes these from his total on the grounds that they were 'arrested civilizations'. Spontaneous derivations, once favoured by 'isolationists', are under increasing attack by archaeologists of the 'diffusionist' school, who believe there were trans-oceanic contacts at very early dates.

PREDICTION OF HEIGHT

The table below can be used to estimate the height to which children may be expected to grow if their height and age at present are known:

Age in Years	Boys %	Girls %
Birth	28·6	30·9
¼	33·9	36·0
½	37·7	39·8
¾	40·1	42·2
1	42·2	44·7
1½	45·6	48·8
2	49·5	52·8
2½	51·6	54·8
3	53·8	57·0
4	58·0	61·8
5	61·8	66·2
6	65·2	70·3
7	69·0	74·0
8	72·0	77·5
9	75·0	80·7
10	78·0	84·4
11	81·1	88·4
12	84·7	92·9
13	87·3	96·5
14	91·5	98·3
15	96·1	99·1
16	98·3	99·6
17	99·3	100·0
18	99·8	100·0

Thus a boy measuring 137 cm (54 in) on his ninth birthday could be expected to be

$$137 (54) \times \frac{100}{75 \cdot 0} = 183 \text{ cm} (72 \text{ in}) \text{ as a man.}$$

Human Energy Expenditure

Energy intake as food, and expenditure are measured in 'calories'. The following table gives an indication of how much energy is expended in different activities for an individual of average weight:

	Rate in calories per hour
Rest in bed (basal metabolic rate)	60
Sitting at ease (man)	108
Sitting and writing	114
Standing at ease	118
Driving a car	168
Washing up (woman)	198
Driving a motor cycle	204
Dressing, washing, shaving	212
Bed making (woman)	420
Walking 6·4 kph (4 mph)	492
Climbing 15 cm (6 in) stairs at 2·4 kph (1·5 mph)	620
Tree felling	640
Bicycling at 21 kph (13 mph)	660
Running at 8 kph (5 mph) (slow jogging)	850
Running at 12 kph (7½ mph)	975
Rowing at 33 strokes/min	1140
Swimming breaststroke at 56 strokes/min	1212
Nordic skiing (level snow) at 14·7 kph (9·15 mph)	1572

MEDICINE

Medical and surgical specialities

There are in medicine many specialities. It is possible to have Departments of Neurology, Paediatrics and Paediatric Neurology in the same hospital. This list provides an explanation of medical departments.

Allergy – reaction of a patient to an outside substance, e.g. pollen or penicillin, producing symptoms which may vary between being inconvenient, e.g. hay fever or rashes, to fatal, e.g. asthma.
Anaesthetics – loss of sensation (especially pain) or consciousness caused by drugs.
Anatomy – the study of the structure of the body.
Anthropology – the study of man in his environment. Physical anthropology embraces blood grouping and genetic variations.
Apothecary – a pharmacist or, in its old-fashioned sense, a general practitioner was once described as an apothecary.
Audiology – the assessment of hearing.
Aurology – the study of ear disease.
Bacteriology – the study of bacterial infections. This usually includes viruses.
Biochemistry – the study of the variation of salts and chemicals in the body.
Bio-engineering – the study of the mechanical workings of the body, particularly with reference to artificial limbs and powered appliances which the body can use.
Biophysics – the study of electrical impulses from the body. This can be seen with assessment of muscle disease etc,
Cardiology – the study of heart disease.
Community medicine – the prevention of the spread of disease and the increase of physical and mental well-being within a community.
Cryo-surgery – the use of freezing techniques in surgery.
Cytogenetics – the understanding of the particles within a cell which help to reproduce the same type of being.
Cytology – the microscopic study of body cells.
Dentistry – the treatment and extraction of teeth.
Dermatology – the treatment of skin diseases.
Diabetics – the treatment of diabetes.
Embryology – the study of the growth of the baby from the moment of conception to about the 20th week.
Endocrinology – the study of the diseases of the glands which produce hormones.
E.N.T. *see* Otorhinolaryngology.
Entomology – the study of insects, moths, with particular reference to their transmission of disease.
Epidemiology – the study of epidemics and the way that diseases travel from one person to another.
Forensic medicine – the study of injury and disease caused by criminal activity and the detection of crime by medical knowledge.
Gastro-enterology – the study of stomach and intestinal diseases.

Genetics – the study of inherited characteristics, disease and malformations.
Genito-urinary disease – the study of diseases of the sexual and urine-producing organs.
Geriatrics – the study of diseases and condition of elderly people.
Gerontology – the study of diseases of elderly people and in particular the study of the ageing process.
Gynaecology – the study of diseases of women.
Haematology – the study of blood diseases.
Histochemistry – the study of the chemical environment of the body cells.
Histology – the microscopic study of cells.
Histopathology – the microscopic study of diseased or abnormal cells.
Homoeopathy – a form of treatment by administering minute doses which in larger doses would reproduce the symptoms of the disease that is being treated.
Immunology – the study of the way the body reacts to outside harmful diseases and influences, e.g. the production of body proteins to overcome such diseases as diphtheria or the rejection of foreign substances like transplanted kidneys.
Laryngology – the study of throat diseases.
Metabolic disease – diseases of the interior workings of the body, e.g. disorders of calcium absorption, etc., thyroid disease or adrenal gland disease.
Microbiology – the study of the workings of cells.
Nephrology – the study of kidney disease.
Neurology – the study of a wide range of diseases of the brain or nervous system.
Neurosurgery – operations on the brain or nervous system.
Nuclear medicine – treatment of diseases with radio-active substances.
Obstetrics – the care of the pregnant woman and the delivery of the child.
Oncology – study of cancer.
Ophthalmic Optician (Optometrist) – a practitioner specially trained to assess any visual disorder and examine eyes and provide corrective treatment in the form of visual aids, e.g. spectacles, contact lenses.
Optician, dispensing – a registered dispensing optician is only allowed to dispense spectacles. The prescription is provided either by an Optometrist or an Ophthalmic Medical Practitioner.
Orthodontology – a dental approach to producing teeth that are straight.
Orthopaedics – fractures and bone diseases.
Orthoptics – treatment of squints of the eye (by an orthoptist – medically unqualified but trained practitioner).
Orthotist – an orthopaedic appliance technician.
Otology – the study of diseases of the ear.
Otorhinolaryngology – the study of diseases of the ear, nose and throat, often referred to as E.N.T.
Paediatrics – diseases of children.
Parasitology – the study of infections of the body by worms and insects.
Pathology – the branch of medicine concerned with the cause, origin and nature of disease.
Pharmacology – the study of the use of drugs in relation to medicine.

Physical medicine – the treatment of damaged parts of the body with exercises, electrical treatments, etc., or the preparation of the body for surgery, e.g. breathing exercises and leg exercises.

Physiology – the study and understanding of the normal workings of the body.

Physiotherapist – a trained person who works in the physical medicine department.

Plastic surgery – the reconstruction and alteration of damaged or abnormal parts of the body.

Proctology – the study of diseases of the rectum or back passage.

Prosthetics – the making of artificial limbs and appliances.

Psychiatry – the study and treatment of mental disease.

Psychoanalysis – the investigation of the formation of mental illness by long-term repeated discussion.

Psychology – the study of the mind with particular reference to the measurement of intellectual activity.

Psychotherapy – treatment of mental disorder.

Radiobiology – the treatment or investigation of disease using radioactive substances.

Radiography – the taking of X-rays.

Radiology – the study of X-rays.

Radiotherapy – the treatment of disease with X-rays.

Renal diseases – the diseases of the kidney or urinary tract.

Rheumatology – the study of diseases of muscles and joints.

Rhinology – the study of diseases of the nose.

Therapeutics – curative medicine, the healing of physical and/or mental disorder.

Thoracic surgery – surgery on the chest or heart.

Toxicology – the understanding and analysis of poisons.

Urology – the study of diseases of the kidney or urinary tract.

Vascular disease – diseases of the blood vessels.

Venereology – the study of sexually transmitted disease.

Virology – the study of virus diseases.

Glossary

abdomen The space enclosing the digestive tract and organs, in addition to various other organs. The top of the abdomen is limited by the diaphragm, the lower limit being the pelvis.

abortion Ending of a pregnancy before the foetus can survive outside the uterus.

abscess A local infection causing inflammation and the production of pus.

accommodation The action of focusing the eye, caused by altering the thickness of the lens.

acetylsalicylic acid Aspirin. It relieves pain, lowers a raised temperature and reduces inflammation.

Achilles tendon Tendon in the heel, linking the muscles in the calf to the heel-bone.

achondroplasia A form of dwarfism, caused by defective development of the bones of the skull and limbs.

acne An overproduction of grease by the sebaceous glands. The openings of the glands get blocked and act as foci of infection.

acromegaly An excess of growth hormone, resulting in, among other symptoms, enlargement of the hands and feet.

ACTH Adrenocorticotrophic hormone, produced by the pituitary gland and acting on the adrenals.

acute Describing a disease of rapid onset and short duration.

addiction A craving for a drug, resulting in tolerance of the drug and then physical dependence on it.

adenoid Lymph tissue at the back of the nose.

ADH Antidiuretic hormone, produced by the pituitary and affecting the kidneys.

adrenalin Produced by the adrenal glands. It stimulates the heart, circulatory system and respiratory system and inhibits digestion.

adrenals The adrenal glands are endocrine glands attached to the upper part of each kidney. They produce adrenalin (prepares body for 'fight and flight'), cortisol (affects storage of glucose) and aldosterone (affects kidneys).

afterbirth The placenta.

AIDS Acquired Immune Deficiency Syndrome, disease transmitted sexually or by exchange of blood or other body fluids. As yet (1988) no known cure.

aldosterone A hormone produced by the adrenals, affecting the kidneys. It regulates the excretion of salt.

alimentary canal The mouth, oesophagus, stomach and intestines.

alveolus Air sac in the lungs where oxygen and carbon dioxide are exchanged between the air and the blood.

amenorrhoea Lack of menstrual periods.

amniocentesis Taking a sample of the amniotic fluid from around the foetus in a pregnant woman. Analysis of the sample gives many indications as to the state of the foetus.

amnion Bag of membranes containing the foetus and amniotic fluid during pregnancy.

anaemia Lack of haemoglobin in the blood, due to loss of blood or to defective production of haemoglobin. Haemoglobin carries oxygen in the bloodstream, so anaemia gives rise to symptoms of tiredness and malaise.

anaesthetic A drug that removes sensation in a particular area or throughout the body.

analgesic A drug used to relieve pain.

anastomosis Joining two cut tubes, e.g. two lengths of intestine, from which a diseased section has been removed.

aneurysm A bulge in an artery wall, caused by an area of weakness.

angina Pain in the chest caused by insufficient supply of blood (and therefore oxygen) to the heart muscle. It is due to diseased coronary arteries.

ankylosis Loss of movement in a joint, usually caused by arthritis.

anorexia A neurosis involving loss of appetite and rejection of food.

antibiotic Naturally occurring or synthetic drug that kills bacteria. Antibiotics are thus used to treat bacterial infections.

antibody A chemical produced by the body's immune system in order to neutralise a specific harmful chemical or substance, e.g. microorganism.

anticoagulant Drug that prevents blood from clotting.

antigen A chemical against which an antibody is formed and which the antibody 'attacks'.

antiserum Serum extracted from the blood of an animal that is immune to a specific microorganism, e.g. hepatitis.

antitoxin Antibody that neutralises a specific toxin or antigen.

arrhythmia An alteration in the natural rhythm of the heart.

arteriosclerosis A loss of elasticity in the arteries.

artery Blood vessels carrying oxygenated blood away from the heart.

arthritis Inflammation of a joint, giving pain and restricted movement.

aspirin (see acetylsalicylic acid).

asthma Contraction of the air tubes in the lungs, caused by infection, allergy or stress. The result is very difficult breathing.

athlete's foot Fungal infection of the skin between the toes.

bacteria Microorganisms, capable of being seen with a light microscope, that live off living, dead or inorganic material.

barbiturates Group of drugs used as sedatives, as anaesthetics and to promote sleep. They are potentially addictive drugs.

bed-sore Pressure of skin and tissue against bone caused by prolonged time spent in bed. The blood supply to the area is reduced and eventually a slow-healing ulcer is formed.

benign Mild, usually self-limiting, form of a disease.

bile A secretion of the liver, formed by the breakdown of haemoglobin. It helps in the digestion of fats in the small intestine.

biopsy Removal of a piece of living tissue for examination.

bladder Muscular bag into which urine drains from the kidneys, before being passed out via the urethra.

blood pressure The pressure in the arteries, caused by the pumping action of the heart. It fluctuates with the heartbeat.

breech delivery Delivery of a baby at birth bottom first (instead of head first).

bronchitis Inflammation, often due to infection, of the airways in the lungs, i.e. the bronchi and the bronchioles. Overproduction of mucus is a common symptom.

bruise Bump or knock causing bleeding into the skin and surface tissues. As the blood decomposes, it gives the characteristic colours of a bruise.

calcitonin Hormone produced by the thyroid. It lowers the concentration of calcium in the blood.

callus A hard area of skin, formed as a result of pressure or friction.

calorie The use of the calorie to indicate energy value of foods is common. A calorie indicates the amount of energy required to warm 1 kg of water by 1°C; the calorific value of a food indicates the amount of such energy liberated if the food were completely burnt.

cancer An uncontrolled cell growth, in which the body's usual checks and controls are absent for some reason.

capillary Blood vessel of one cell diameter. Capillaries form a network within the tissues and act as a link between the arteries and veins.

carcinogen A substance or drug with the potential of causing cancer.

cardiac Pertaining to the heart.

cataract An opaque area that develops on the lens of the eye.

cautery A small burn, caused electrically or by use of a laser, used to seal small cut blood vessels.

cerebrospinal fluid Fluid, derived from blood, which surrounds, and is found within cavities of, the brain and spinal cord.

cervical Either pertaining to the cervix of the womb or pertaining to the neck of the womb.

chemotherapy Treating a disease with chemicals.

cholesterol A fatty chemical, found throughout the body. However, it can be deposited in the blood vessels, causing blockages.

chorea Uncontrolled jerky muscular contractions.

chromosome That part of the cell which contains genetic material.

chronic Describing a disease of slow onset and long duration.

cirrhosis Disease of the liver caused by scarring. The scar tissue is hard and fibrous and eventually is liable to affect the whole liver.

clavicle Collar-bone.

cold An infection, initially viral, of the mucous membranes of the nose and throat.

cold sore An infection with the herpes virus around the mouth, causing raised blisters.

colitis Inflammation of the colon or large intestine, either due to infection or, in the case of ulcerative colitis, due to an unknown cause.

colon The large intestine, from the ileum to the rectum.

congenital An abnormality or disease is congenital if the baby is born with it.

conjunctivitis Inflammation of the conjunctiva of the eye, usually caused by viral or bacterial infection.

consumption Traditionally an alternative name for tuberculosis.

corn A form of callus on the foot.

coronary arteries Arteries providing the blood supply to the heart muscle.

costal Pertaining to the ribs.

cramp A spasm of a muscle or group of muscles.

Crohn's disease Inflammation of the final section of the small intestine (the ileum), due to an unknown cause.

cystitis Inflammation of the bladder, usually due to a bacterial infection.

dandruff Condition in which flakes of skin are shed from the scalp.

diabetes In full, diabetes mellitus. A disease due to a deficiency of, or inability to use properly, insulin formed in the pancreas.

diagnosis The identification of a disease from various signs and symptoms.

dialysis Removal of harmful waste products from the blood by an osmotic process in an artificial kidney.

diaphragm A domed sheet of muscle separating the thoracic cavity from the abdominal cavity.

dilatation A process of widening, either as one of the body's reflexes or by mechanical means.

disc A cartilaginous pad between each vertebra, acting as a shock absorber and imparting flexibility to the spinal column as a whole.

diuretic A drug used to increase the flow of urine.

drug A chemical given to help relieve the symptoms of a disease or to modify any of the body's natural processes.

duodenum The first section of the small intestine, between the stomach and the jejunum.

dysmenorrhoea Painful menstrual periods.

dyspnoea Difficulty in breathing.

ECG Electrocardiogram or measurement of the electrical changes in the heart muscle.

ECT Electroconvulsive therapy. Application of an electric shock to the scalp, used to treat certain mental illnesses, especially depression.

ectopic pregnancy A pregnancy in an abnormal position, e.g. in the Fallopian tube.

eczema An inflammatory condition of the skin, often due to an allergy.

EEG Electroencephalogram or measurement of electrical changes in the brain.

embolism Blockage of an artery by an air bubble or, more commonly, a blood clot.

emetic A drug given to induce vomiting.

emphysema Damage to the lungs whereby the tiny air sacs at the ends of the airways break down, leading to breathlessness.

encephalitis A viral infection of the brain.

endemic A disease that is always present in a given area.

endocrine gland A ductless gland that releases secretions (hormones) into the bloodstream, rather than into a duct for local use.

endoscopy Examination of internal organs using a tube lit from the inside; fibre-optics are invariably used now.

enteritis Inflammation of the intestine, usually due to an infection.

epilepsy Convulsive attacks or fits, of an unknown cause.

erythrocyte A red blood cell.

Eustachian tube A passage leading from the back of the nose to the middle ear.

expectorant A drug that loosens mucus in the respiratory tract, particularly the lungs, and aids coughing.

faeces Waste residue of food, dead and live bacteria, and water, expelled from the rectum.

farmer's lung An allergic response to fungi found in hay, straw, etc.

fibrin A protein produced in the blood during the clotting process. It forms the matrix within which the clot forms.

fibroid A lumpy benign tumour of the uterus.

fistula A passage between two parts of the body, either as a result of a wound, e.g. a stab wound, or as a result of a deliberate operation.

foetus Unborn baby, more advanced than an embryo in that it is recognisably human.

forearm The part of the arm between the elbow and the wrist.

fracture A broken bone, either completely or partially broken.

frostbite Damage to the skin and deeper tissues due to ice crystals forming.

fungi Very simple plant forms with parasitic or saprophytic lifestyle. Some forms cause infections, usually of the skin but sometimes internally.

gall bladder Sac under the lower side of the liver that acts as a storage organ for bile.

gall stone Solid crystalline lump precipitated from the bile in the gall bladder.

gamma globulin Blood proteins responsible for immunity to specific diseases. They can be separated and given to non-immune patients, thus conferring short-term immunity.

gangrene Death and bacterial decay of tissue.

gastric Pertaining to the stomach.

gastric ulcer A stomach ulcer.

gastritis Inflammation of the stomach lining.

gastro-enteritis Inflammation of the stomach and intestine.

gingivitis Inflammation of the gums, caused by infection.

glaucoma High pressure within the eyeball resulting in defects in vision.

goitre Swelling of the thyroid gland.

gout Formation of uric acid crystals around joints.

gullet The oesophagus.

haemoglobin The complex protein molecule that gives red blood cells their colour. It transports oxygen in the bloodstream.

haemolysis The breakdown of red blood cells.

haemophilia An inherited disease characterised by an inability of the blood to form clots.

haemorrhage Bleeding.

halothane An anaesthetic gas.

hamstring muscles Muscles at the back of the thigh that flex the knee.

hay fever An allergy to pollen, particularly grass pollens. It causes acute irritation to the mucous membranes of the nose and to the conjunctiva of the eye.

hemiplegia Paralysis of one half of the body caused by damage or disease in the opposite half of the brain.

hepatic Pertaining to the liver.

hepatitis Inflammation of the liver, usually viral.

hernia A rupture, or protrusion of an organ from one body compartment into another compartment.

herpes One group of herpes viruses, *Herpes simplex*, causes cold sores and venereal herpes; the other group, *Herpes zoster*, causes shingles.

hiatus hernia Protrusion of a section of the stomach through the oesophageal opening in the diaphragm.

Hodgkin's disease A form of cancer of the lymph tissues, resulting in lowered resistance to infections.

hormone A chemical, released directly into the bloodstream by one organ (an endocrine gland) in order to regulate other organs or body functions.

hyper- Prefix meaning too much.

hypertension Raised blood pressure.

hyperthermia High body temperature.

hypo- Prefix meaning too little.

hypochondria A preoccupation with or anxiety about one's health.

hypoglycaemia Too low a level of glucose in the blood.

hypothermia Lowered body temperature.

iatrogenic Disease or condition produced as a result of treatment given for another disease or condition.

ileum Latter section of the small intestine, leading into the large intestine.

ilium The haunch-bone; part of the pelvis.

immunity The natural or acquired resistance of a body to invading, i.e. 'foreign', chemicals. The immune system can deal with 'invaders' larger than chemicals, e.g. microorganisms, transplants, but this is because it reacts to chemicals on the surface of the microorganism or transplant.

immunisation The production of immunity to a specific disease.

incontinence Inability to control the emptying of the bladder or bowels.

incubation period The time it takes between infection with a disease-carrying microorganism and the production of disease symptoms.

infarct An area of dead tissue resulting from a

blocked blood vessel.

infection The entry of microorganisms into the body, their subsequent multiplication and the production of disease symptoms.

inflammation Heat, redness, pain and swelling produced as defensive reaction by the body to infection or damage.

inoculation Form of immunisation in which a live harmless variant of the disease-causing microorganism is used to infect the body, producing immunity to both the harmless and harmful microorganisms.

insulin Hormone produced in the pancreas which regulates the metabolism of sugars by controlling the uptake of glucose from the blood by the body's cells.

intercostal muscles Muscles between the ribs.

ischaemia Lack of blood to part of the body.

islets of Langerhans Groups of cells in the pancreas responsible for the production of insulin.

IUD Intrauterine device. A form of contraception; a coil or loop implanted in the uterus prevents a fertilised ovum from embedding in the uterus wall and developing into an embryo.

jaundice Yellowing of skin. It is caused by a build-up of bile pigments in the blood.

jejunum The middle section of the small intestine, between the duodenum and the ileum.

jugular Pertaining to the neck.

lacrimal Pertaining to tears, e.g. lacrimal gland above the eye.

laparotomy Incision in the abdominal wall, usually for purposes of examination.

large intestine The latter part of the intestine, between the small intestine and the rectum.

larynx The voice box, at the front of the throat.

lesion An injury, wound or harmful disturbance to an organ or tissue.

leucocyte White blood cell.

leukaemia A form of cancer in which there is overproduction of underdeveloped, and therefore useless, white blood cells.

lice Insects which infest the hair of the body. Their eggs are called nits.

ligament A fibrous band of tissue holding two bones together at a joint.

linctus A syrupy medicine given to soothe coughing.

lumbar Pertaining to the lower back.

lymph Fluid from the blood which leaks out of the capillaries, bathes the tissues and returns to the blood system via the lymphatic system.

lymphatic system A network of vessels and glands which collect and filter the lymph before returning it to the blood system.

malignant Severe, often fatal, form of a disease.

malnutrition Deficiency in the quality or quantity of food.

meconium Fluid consisting largely of mucus and bile, passed out of an infant's bowels soon after birth.

menarche The appearance of menstruation at puberty.

meninges Membranes enclosing the brain and spinal cord.

meningitis Inflammation of the meninges due to viral or bacterial infection.

menopause The disappearance of menstruation, usually between the ages of about 40 and 50.

menorrhagia Heavy bleeding during menstruation.

metabolism The sum total of the chemical reactions in the body by which nutrients are converted to energy, tissues are renewed, replaced and regenerated and waste products are broken down.

microorganism Any organism too small to be seen with the naked eye. Usually taken to mean viruses, bacteria and some fungi and protozoans.

migraine Acute form of headache, perhaps allergic in origin, sometimes causing nausea and visual disturbances.

miscarriage Accidental abortion.

multiple sclerosis A chronic disease in which areas of the central nervous system degenerate. A variety of symptoms can be involved, depending on the areas of degeneration, and these symptoms can appear and disappear at random, it seems.

myasthenia gravis Progressive form of muscle disease in which voluntary muscles become weaker.

myocardial Pertaining to the heart muscle.

narcolepsy Disease characterised by periods of uncontrollable sleepiness.

narcotic Drug producing dulling or loss of consciousness.

nausea Urge to vomit.

neonatal Pertaining to newborn babies.

nephritis Inflammation of the kidney, due to infection, chemical poisoning or other reasons.

neuralgia Acute pain originating in a nerve.

neuritis Inflammation of a nerve.

nit The egg of a louse, found firmly attached to a hair or to fibres of clothing.

nystagmus Reflex rapid movements of the eyes, designed to keep moving objects in view.

obesity An excess of body fat.

oedema An excess of fluid in the tissues, either generally or locally, causing swelling.

oesophagus That section of the digestive tract between the pharynx and the stomach.

organ A distinct structure in the body designed to perform a particular function.

osteoarthritis Destruction of the cartilaginous surfaces that allow bones to move over each other.

osteoporosis Weakening of the bones in old age due to a reduction in the calcium content of the bones.

oxytocin Hormone produced by the pituitary gland that stimulates contractions of the uterus during labour.

palate The roof of the mouth. The hard palate is at the front, the soft palate at the back.

pancreas A gland at the back of the abdomen. It secretes digestive juices into the small intestine, and also acts as an endocrine gland, producing insulin from the islets of Langerhans.

pandemic A widespread epidemic.

paracetamol An analgesic.

paraplegia Paralysis of the lower half of the body.

parathyroids A group of small endocrine glands associated with the thyroid gland. They produce parathormone which controls the level of calcium in the blood.

Parkinson's disease A form of paralysis in which the muscles become stiff, movement awkward, and a rhythmic twitching affects the muscles locally or generally.

patella The kneecap.

pectoral Pertaining to the chest.

pelvis Ring of bone which forms the base of the

abdominal cavity and which forms the hip joint on each side.

peptic ulcer Ulcer of the stomach or duodenum.

pericarditis Inflammation of the pericardium or fibrous sheath surrounding the heart.

perinatal Pertaining to the period shortly before, during and shortly after birth.

peristalsis Rhythmic contractions producing flow along the digestive tract.

peritoneum The membrane lining the abdominal cavity.

peritonitis Inflammation of the peritoneum.

pharynx That part of the throat, from the back of the nose to the opening of the oesophagus, concerned with both breathing and swallowing.

phlebitis Inflammation of a vein, usually due to blockage of the vein by a clot.

phlegm Mucus.

phrenic Pertaining to the diaphragm.

piles Haemorrhoids; distended varicose veins just inside the anus.

pituitary An endocrine gland on the underside of the brain. It produces a number of hormones: ACTH, which controls the adrenal glands; thyrotrophic hormone which controls the thyroid gland; gonadotrophic hormones, which control the ovaries and testes; growth hormone, controlling growth; prolactin, controlling milk production in the breasts; oxytocin, controlling contraction of the uterus during labour; and ADH, controlling loss of water from the body in the urine.

plasma The fluid component of blood.

platelet Small particle found in blood. Platelets are involved in the clotting mechanism.

pleura A double membrane surrounding the lungs.

pleurisy Inflammation of the pleura, usually due to infection.

pneumonia Inflammation of the lungs, due to infection. It affects the alveoli or air pockets at the ends of the airways.

pneumothorax Air between the lungs and chest wall, impairing breathing.

polycythaemia The opposite of anaemia; an excess of red blood cells.

polyp Tumour, usually benign, growing out of mucous membrane and attached to the membrane by a stalk.

poultice A hot dressing applied to inflamed surfaces.

prickly heat Blockage of sweat glands and production of tiny blisters and an irritating rash.

progesterone Hormone produced in the ovaries; it acts on the uterus in such a way that it prepares itself to receive fertilised ovum.

prognosis Forecast of the course a disease will take.

prolactin Hormone produced by the pituitary that stimulates the breasts to secrete milk.

prolapse Displacement of an organ from its normal position, usually due to gravity.

prophylaxis Prevention of disease.

prostate gland Gland found only in males. It secretes part of the seminal fluid into the urethra.

prosthesis Artificial replacement for part of the body.

psoriasis Scaly red blotches formed on the skin. The complaint tends to come and go, for unknown reasons.

puerperal Pertaining to childbirth.

pulmonary Pertaining to the lungs.

pus Dead cells, dead white blood cells, dead bacteria and tissue fluid.

pyloric stenosis A constriction of the outlet from the stomach to the duodenum.

rabies A disease of a variety of animals. Humans can be infected via an animal bite. Symptoms include fever, delirium, muscle spasms and paralysis. Spasm of the throat muscles causes the inability to drink or hydrophobia.

rectum The last section of the digestive tract, between the large intestine and anus.

referred pain Pain which occurs in a different part of the body from the site of injury or trauma.

reflex An automatic response to a stimulus.

remission Temporary subsidence of the symptoms of a disease.

renal Pertaining to the kidneys.

rheumatic fever Acute disease, generally of children and adolescents, involving raised temperature and inflammation of various parts of the body at different times, including the joints and the valves and lining of the heart.

rheumatism Pain or inflammation of the joints or muscles.

rheumatoid arthritis Formation of inflamed knots of fibrous tissue, usually around joints.

rickets Faulty bone growth due to a lack of vitamin D.

rodent ulcer A type of skin cancer in which a hard lump appears on the face. The centre of the lump subsequently breaks down to form an ulcer.

sciatica Pain in the region of the sciatic nerve at the back of the thigh, calf and foot.

sclerosis Thickening or hardening of a particular tissue.

scoliosis Curvature of the spine sideways.

sebum Greasy material formed by the sebaceous glands of the skin.

sedative A drug that calms or renders someone sleepy.

senility Changes in the brain in old age.

sepsis Infection of tissues, causing damage.

septicaemia Spread of an infection into the blood, which carries the infecting agent throughout the body.

serum Straw-coloured fluid that separates from the blood as it clots.

shingles Another name for *Herpes zoster*; a viral infection of nerves, causing painful blisters on the skin in the area that the infected nerve serves.

shock Sudden drop in blood pressure causing failure of the blood circulation system.

sign Any indication of a disease observed by the doctor, nurse, etc.

sinew A tendon or ligament.

sinus A hollow cavity opening off a passageway, e.g. the nasal sinuses opening off the nose. It can also mean merely a bulge in a tube.

sinusitis Inflammation of the mucous membrane of the nasal sinuses.

spasm Uncontrolled contraction of a muscle or group of muscles.

spastic paralysis Loss or limitation of controlled movement in various muscles, due to disease of the nervous system.

sphincter Ring of muscle around an opening to a hollow or tubular organ.

spina bifida Congenital disease in which the vertebrae do not close over the spinal column, allowing the meninges to protrude.

spleen An organ at the top of the abdominal cavity, responsible for white blood cell production, breakdown of red blood cells and some control of immunity.

spondylitis Inflammation of the vertebrae, often

with loss of mobility.

sputum Mucus.

squint Poor alignment of the eyes; they either turn inwards (convergent squint) or outwards (divergent squint).

stenosis Constriction or narrowing of a tube, e.g. part of the digestive tract.

stroke Interruption of blood supply to part of the brain.

subcutaneous Beneath the skin.

suture The surgical stitching used to close a wound or incision.

symptom Any indication of a disease observed by the patient.

syndrome A group of symptoms that frequently occur together, although they may not always be caused by the same disease.

systemic Pertaining to the body as a whole.

temperature The 'normal' body temperature is between 36°C and 37·5°C (97–9°F) when taken in the mouth. However, it will vary between these limits during the day and, for women, during their menstrual cycle.

tendon Fibre joining muscle to bone.

tetanus Infection of a wound with the bacterium *Clostridium tetani*. The bacteria produces a poison which causes the characteristic muscle spasms.

thorax The space enclosing the heart, lungs and oesophagus. It is bounded by the rib-cage and the diaphragm.

thrombosis Partial or complete blockage of a blood vessel by a blood clot.

thrombus A blood clot formed on the inside surface of a blood vessel.

thrush Infection of a mucous membrane, usually of the mouth, by a fungus.

thyroid Endocrine gland in the neck. It produces thyroxine, which controls energy production in the tissues; and calcitonin, which controls the calcium levels in the blood.

tissue A collection of cells, usually of the same type, specialised to perform a particular function.

tolerance The need to administer larger and larger doses of a drug over time, as the body gets used to it.

tomography n X-ray examination in which a 'slice' of the body is looked at.

tonsil Lymph tissue at the back of the mouth.

topical Pertaining to the surface of the body.

tourniquet A constricting strap or band applied to a limb to stop arterial bleeding.

toxaemia Poisoning of the blood by toxins from infecting bacteria.

toxin Poisonous substance, usually produced by bacteria.

toxoid A toxin that has been chemically modified to render it harmless. It is still able to produce an immune response when used to immunise against the original toxin.

trachea The windpipe. A tube strengthened with cartilage that runs between the larynx and the bronchi that pass into the lungs.

tranquilliser Drug used to calm the mood without inducing sleepiness.

transfusion Transfer of blood from a healthy to an ill person.

transplantation Transfer of a healthy organ to a patient to replace a diseased organ.

trauma Physical damage to tissue, e.g. a wound.

tropical ulcer Ulceration of the skin, usually on the leg, commonly found in the tropics. It is very slow to heal.

tubal pregnancy A form of ectopic pregnancy occurring in the Fallopian tubes.

tumour A group of cells that starts to divide without the usual checks and controls imposed by the body. It may be malignant or benign.

ulcer Breakdown of the skin or mucous membrane that heals very slowly or not at all.

ultrasound Sound waves at a frequency well above the range of human hearing, used to provide an image of internal structures.

ureter Tube leading from the kidney to the bladder.

urethra Tube leading from the bladder to the exterior.

uvula The soft projection hanging down at the back of the mouth.

vaccination Use of dead or a harmless form of microorganism to produce artificial immunity to the harmful form of the microorganism.

vaccine The dead or harmless microorganisms used in a vaccination.

varicose veins Swollen veins, usually in the legs, due to collapse of the valves in the veins allowing backflow of blood.

vascular Pertaining to blood vessels.

vein Blood vessel returning blood from the tissues to the heart. Apart from the vein carrying blood from the lungs to the heart, all veins carry deoxygenated blood.

venereal disease Sexually transmitted disease.

vertigo A form of dizziness in which the subject feels the surroundings are spinning round.

viruses Microorganisms, smaller than bacteria and incapable of being seen with a light microscope. They can only reproduce inside living cells.

vitamins Chemicals found in foodstuffs or synthesised by the body. They are not nutrients, but are essential for the normal functioning of growth, repair and reproduction.

wart A small tumour of the outer layer of the skin caused by a virus.

Drugs in common usage pre-1900

Before this century the number of drugs available was limited. Most were derived from plant sources and only a few of these (or their derivatives) remain in use today:

DIGITALIS

Extract of foxglove leaves used to treat heart failure by herbalists in the 16th century and introduced into scientific medicine by William Withering in Britain in 1785. Its derivative digoxin is still widely used to treat atrial fibrillation (a rapid and irregular heart rhythm) and cardiac failure.

MORPHINE

An addictive narcotic analgesic derived from opium – the dried fluid which is exuded from unripe poppy capsules. First recognised by Friedrich Sertürner in Germany in 1805, but not used in medical practice until 1821. Synthesised in 1952.

ATROPINE
A drug derived from belladonna (deadly nightshade) with a variety of effects on different body tissues, including: speeding up of heart rate; dilating the pupil of the eye; reducing stomach secretions, reducing vomiting, or to treat peptic ulcers, biliary and renal colic, etc. Isolated in 1819 by Rudolph Brondes.

ANAESTHETIC AGENTS:
Ether, Nitrous Oxide and Chloroform
These were all first used in the 1840s. Ether was the first general anaesthetic to be administered (by Dr Crawford W. Long, in Jefferson, Georgia, on 30 Mar 1842).

Nitrous oxide (laughing gas) was discovered in 1776 by Joseph Priestley (GB) but first used as an anaesthetic in 1844 by an American dentist, Horace Wells.

Chloroform was introduced in 1847 by Sir James Simpson (GB), an obstetrician.

PHENOL (carbolic acid)
The discovery by Joseph Lister (GB) in 1865 that phenol had disinfectant properties led to the development of antiseptic surgery with dramatic reduction in mortality.

Post-1900

The 20th century has seen the development of vast numbers of potent drugs. Milestones in therapeutic advances have been:

1917
Oxygen first used therapeutically.

1921
Insulin (used to treat diabetes) isolated by Frederich Banting and C. H. Best in Toronto, Canada.

1929
Progesterone and testosterone isolated.

1935
Tubocurarine isolated by Harold King, a muscle-relaxing drug.

1937
Sulphonamides – the first antibiotics and hence the first effective treatment for infection. The most used early drug was sulphapyridne (May and Baker 693).

1938
Phenytoin introduced – an anticonvulsant used to treat epilepsy.

1939
DDT (dichloro-dephenyl-trichloroethane), a powerful insecticide, developed by Dr Paul Muller which vastly lowered malarial death rate by killing malaria-carrying mosquitoes.

1940
Penicillin first used therapeutically by Sir Howard Florey and E. B. Chain. Developed following the discovery in 1928 by Sir Alexander Fleming that penicillin would inhibit bacterial growth on a Petri dish.

1943
Streptomycin – the first antibiotic effective against tuberculosis.

1948
Imipramine introduced – an anti-depressant.

1949
Cortisone – one of a number of steroid hormones secreted by the adrenal gland. First extracted in 1939, and first used therapeutically in 1949 (to reduce inflammation in rheumatoid arthritis).

1951
Halothane introduced – a safer anaesthetic gas.

1954
Methyldopa and Reserpine – the first effective treatments for high blood pressure.

1955
Oral contraceptives – the first field studies of a pill which could prevent ovulation were in Puerto Rico by Pincus.

Early 1960s
Chlordiazepoxide (Librium) and diazepam (Valium) introduced – tranquillisers for the treatment of tension and anxiety.

Modern usage

There follows a classification of the most commonly prescribed drugs according to their use. The classification follows the order Cardio-vascular system, Respiratory system, Gastro-intestinal system, Musculo-skeletal system, Central nervous system and Hormonal agents. The preparations listed include the vast majority of drugs currently prescribed with the exception of antibiotics and contraceptives. Both of these categories are available in a variety of formulations. Drugs are normally listed here using the so-called 'generic names' rather than the trade names given to the preparations by the various manufacturers.

Cardio-vascular system

BETA-BLOCKERS
Slow heart rate, reduce high blood pressure, reduce anginal pain, particularly if precipitated by exercise. Examples: propranolol, atenolol, metoprolol, pindolol.

CALCIUM ANTAGONISTS
Relax the muscle layer in the walls of blood vessels; used in the treatment of high blood pressure, angina, and in some disorders of heart rhythm. Examples: nifedipine, verapamil, diltiazem, nicardipine.

ACE INHIBITORS
These drugs are used in the treatment of high blood pressure, and recently also for cardiac failure. They act on an enzyme within the kidney and hence modify levels of a chemical which controls blood pressure by constricting blood vessels (the angiotensin-converting enzyme – ACE). Examples are captopril, enalapril and lisinopril.

NITRATES

Derived from the explosive agent nitroglycerine and known to dilate blood vessels and hence ease anginal pain. Glyceryl trinitrate is the simplest form and is absorbed quickly if the tablet is dissolved under the tongue (first used in 1846 by Asconio Sobrero of Italy). Longer-acting preparations can be absorbed through the skin if worn as Elastoplast-like patches.

DIGOXIN (see Pre-1900, Digitalis)

DIURETICS

So-called 'water pills' which stimulate urinary production and are used to treat cardiac failure by removing excess fluid from the lungs, by reducing congestion in the liver, and by reducing fluid retention in the legs. Some can also be used to treat high blood pressure. Examples are frusemide, bumetanide and bendrofluazide (tend to excrete potassium); amiloride, triamterene and spironolactone (tend to retain potassium).

Respiratory system

BETA$_2$ AGONISTS

These drugs act by relaxing the muscle in the walls of the bronchial tubes, and hence relieve the spasm which occurs in these airways in asthma. Formerly given orally, they are now given mainly by inhalation, either from an aerosol, or in devices designed to deliver a small amount of powder by inhalation. Examples are salbutamol, terbutaline and rimiterol, which have replaced the older drugs such as isoprenaline, orciprenaline and ephedrine.

SODIUM CROMOGLYCATE

This drug is used by inhalation to treat asthma caused by allergy (mainly asthma of childhood). It does so by blocking the release of histamine from the cells which produce it (mast cells). This in turn reduces inflammation in the bronchial tubes.

INHALED STEROIDS

When given by inhalation, steroids can be used in very low dosage to treat asthma. The steroid effect reduces the sensitivity of the bronchial tubes but it is not absorbed into the rest of the body. Examples are Beclomethasone and budesonide.

Gastro-intestinal system

ANTACIDS

There are a large number of preparations all of which are basically alkaline and which can neutralise gastric acids and hence reduce indigestion. Some are combined with a seaweed derivate (alginate) which forms a sticky protective layer on the lining of the upper stomach or lower gullet to reduce heartburn.

H$_2$ ANTAGONISTS

These drugs block the nerve endings in the stomach which are responsible for the secretion of gastric acid (these nerves can be stimulated by histamine, hence the term H$_2$ antagonist). They have proved a very effective treatment for duodenal ulcers – a condition which until the mid-1970s frequently required surgery. The original compound cimetidine has been followed by other agents – ranitidine, and more recently nizatidine and famotidine.

ANTI-EMETICS

The principal anti-sickness drugs in current use are prochlorperazine and metoclopramide.

Musco-skeletal system

NON-STEROIDAL ANTI-INFLAMMATORY AGENTS (NSAIs)

Steroid drugs have a very potent effect in reducing joint and muscle pain when this is caused by an inflammation (e.g. rheumatoid arthritis), but have unfortunate side effects (see Hormonal agents, below). Drugs in the NSAI group have a similar but less potent effect, without the same side effects. Most of them act by reducing the production of prostaglandin (a chemical which stimulates inflammation) within the joints. All have the disadvantage that they can cause gastric irritation or even bleeding. Examples include ibuprofen, indomethacin, naproxen, diclofenac, mefenamic acid and ketoprofen, but there are many others.

DRUGS USED IN RHEUMATOID ARTHRITIS

While NSAI-type drugs reduce the symptoms of this condition, there are a number of drugs which, over longer periods of time, can modify the disease process. They do so by altering the body's immune reaction against itself which is occurring in the joints. Examples are sulphasalazine, penicillamine and gold (given by injection).

Central nervous system

SEDATIVES

The benzodiazepine group of drugs are effective for the short-term relief of anxiety which is causing distress. In recent years it has been increasingly recognised that their long-term use produces dependence, and abruptly stopping these drugs can cause withdrawal effects. Examples include diazepam (Valium), lorazepam (Ativan) and chlordiazepoxide (Librium). Excessive anxiety can also be treated with low doses of phenothiazines (see below), or with beta-blockers (see above).

HYPNOTICS

These drugs induce sleep. Older drugs such as barbiturates have now been replaced by the drugs of the benzodiazepine group – these differ from the benzodiazepine sedatives by having a quicker onset and shorter duration of action. Examples are temazepam, nitrazepam and triazolam.

ANTIDEPRESSANTS

The most commonly used drugs are chemically related, and are classified as tricyclic and tetracyclic antidepressants. They act by affecting the levels of chemicals such as noradrenaline and serotonin within the brain. (These chemicals are neurotransmitters, i.e. they pass between nerve cells carrying nerve impulses from one to the next.) Some drugs are more sedative than others. The commonest side effect is dryness of the mouth. Examples are amitriptyline, imipramine, clomipramine, dothiepin and mianserin.

Lithium salts are used to treat patients who have mood swings from depression to manic overactivity.

ANTICONVULSANTS

Used to treat epilepsy, these drugs reduce the excitability of brain tissue. Examples are phenytoin, carbamazepine, sodium valproate and phenobarbitone.

PHENOTHIAZINES

These drugs have sedative properties and can be used to treat anxiety and agitation. The same drugs in larger dosages, or other related drugs can be used in schizophrenia, and in states of mania. Examples are chlorpromazine and thioridazine.

Hormonal agents

STEROIDS

Steroid drugs are drugs chemically related to the hormones produced by the adrenal gland. Those most commonly used in medical treatment are cortico-steroids, i.e. cortisone-like. These vary in potency from hydrocortisone (weak) to prednisolone and dexamethasone (strong). They reduce inflammation but may have long-term side effects (weight gain, thinning of bones and skin tissues, fluid retention, a tendency to cause high blood pressure and diabetes and reduced immune reaction). However, when used in the correct way these drugs can be dramatically beneficial. Creams and ointments containing steroid agents are widely used for treating eczema, dermatitis and other skin conditions. Anabolic steroids are chemically related and have been used by sportsmen and others to build body muscle. Their use is generally outlawed by sporting organisations in part because they may have serious side effects.

HORMONE REPLACEMENT THERAPY

Deficiency of many hormones can now be treated very successfully. Examples are thyroid hormone, hydrocortisone, insulin (by injection), growth hormone, testosterone and oestrogen. The use of combined oestrogen and progesterone therapy to women after the menopause will relieve symptoms such as flushing and sweating and may also prevent bone thinning in later life.

Major communicable diseases

AIDS

Acquired immune deficiency syndrome, first identified in Los Angeles in 1981. The virus responsible for causing AIDS was isolated in 1983 and is now known as HIV (human immunodeficiency virus). It is spreading rapidly throughout the Western world, and has already reached epidemic proportions in Central Africa. The virus attacks one particular type of white cell in the body (the helper/inducer lymphocytes) and this causes immunosuppression (reduced ability to combat infection). It may also attack the nervous system and cause dementia (memory failure: see p. 129).

Acute infection with HIV after exposure leads to the production of antibodies – sero-conversion. These antibodies are detected by blood tests which become positive on average within three months of the virus being acquired, but may take up to 12 months to appear. There may be no symptoms at all during the period of sero-conversion, or there may be a transient flu-like illness with gland swelling and muscle aches.

Not all patients who sero-convert go on to have chronic infection. Of those who do, the infection may be asymptomatic, or may give rise to illness of varying degrees of severity – known as PGL, ARC or AIDS itself. Current knowledge suggests that 10–30 per cent of HIV-antibody positive patients progress to AIDS within five years.

PGL – persistent generalised lymphodenopathy – is the mildest illness caused by HIV infection. There is swelling of lymph glands at various sites of the body but there are no other symptoms. Many patients with PGL remain well for several years.

ARC – AIDS related complex. In this stage of the disease there is some impairment of the immune system as well as lymph gland enlargement. Symptoms may include episodes of fever, weight loss, night sweats, diarrhoea, cough, skin rashes and profound fatigue. Blood tests may show reduced numbers of white blood cells, anaemia, or changes in blood proteins. ARC is usually only diagnosed if such symptoms or blood test abnormalities persist over a three-month period.

AIDS itself is diagnosed once certain specific infections or types of tumour begin to appear. The most common infection is an unusual form of pneumonia (pneumocystis carinii); the most common tumour is Kaposi's sarcoma – a form of skin cancer which may spread to the internal organs. The course of the disease is usually of increasingly serious episodes of infection and it is often fatal within two years. Approximately 30 per cent of subjects suffer dementia by the later stages of their disease. Recent advances in treatment have included better treatments for the episodes of infection, and the development of a drug known as AZT which shows promise in modifying the disease itself. By June 1988, 1598 cases of AIDS had been reported in the UK, 56 per cent of whom had died of the disease; 97 per cent were male. Some estimates put the figure of those who are HIV-antibody positive at 50 000.

The only ways of acquiring HIV infection or AIDS are:

1. by having intimate sexual contact with someone who carries the virus, particularly if this is homosexual contact;
2. by sharing needles or other instruments contaminated with the blood of someone carrying the virus;
3. by receiving blood or blood products from someone with the virus (in the past some haemophiliacs have got the AIDS virus from treatment with blood products, but all blood products and blood transfusions in the UK are now thoroughly tested before use);
4. mothers who have the virus may pass it on to their babies.

In the UK and Europe AIDS is at present more common in homosexual men and intravenous drug users, but the danger of spread to the heterosexual community will increase unless the general population becomes more aware of the problem and how to avoid putting themselves at risk.

ANTHRAX

A (usually) fatal form of blood poisoning in cattle, sheep and horses, this rare condition can be passed to vets or butchers disposing of infected carcases or (more often) to those handling infected animal hides, wool or bone meal. The initial lesion is usually on the hand – a painful swollen boil with a black crust and surrounding redness. If untreated, blood poisoning (septicaemia) may result. Penicillin is curative, and a vaccine exists for those in high-risk occupations.

CHICKENPOX (VARICELLA)
Caused by the same virus as shingles (herpes zoster). This is a mild disease, infectious from 4 days before the rash until 7 days after the rash appears. Incubation period is usually 14 days. Rash may be preceded by mild headache or fever. The rash begins as red spots which over a few hours become raised and topped by a clear blister. Over 2–3 days these small blisters become opalescent and then scab over. Several crops of these appear over 5–7 days. The rash can be all over the body including the mouth and scalp but tends to be most profuse on the trunk. About 80 per cent of adults have had chickenpox. No specific treatment is needed, except to relieve itch and prevent scratching with dirty finger nails. Complications are rare. There is no vaccine.

CHOLERA
Cholera causes profuse watery diarrhoea and dehydration. The last epidemic in Britain was in Cleethorpes in 1879. John Snow first suggested it was transmitted in water contaminated by faeces and in 1854 proved his theory when he stopped an epidemic by removing the pump handle from a well which he suspected was the source of infection. Protection for travellers to areas where the disease still occurs is achieved by two injections at an interval of 2–4 weeks. Booster doses are needed after 6 months.

CORYZA (COMMON COLD)
Many different viruses (at least 40) can cause the same symptoms – sneezing, running eyes and nose, headache, mild fever. Aspirin or antihistamines may help reduce the symptoms.

GASTRO-ENTERITIS
Most short-lasting cases of sickness or diarrhoea are due to viral gastro-enteritis. Children under the age of three are particularly susceptible. In this group the commonest cause is human rotavirus. The treatment is to stop all solid food intake, but to concentrate instead on fluid intake to prevent dehydration. In babies feeds of boiled water are given instead of milk. Breast-fed babies are less likely to get gastro-enteritis.

In salmonella gastro-enteritis the source of infection is food. Raw meat, poultry or eggs can be contaminated by the salmonella organism which can survive deep freezing. If thawing is not complete, or if the cooking time or temperature is inadequate, the cooked food remains infected. Symptoms of diarrhoea, fever and vomiting usually begin 12–48 hours after eating. Complications include septicaemia (blood poisoning) or later an asymptomatic carrier state. Antibiotics are only used if there is septicaemia. Campylobacter gastro-enteritis is similar.

Other forms of food poisoning are due to a toxic chemical being released from the contaminating organism, rather than infection by the organism itself. Symptoms usually begin within 1–6 hours of ingestion. Examples are staphylococcal toxin (often from infected cream, sometimes meat or poultry) and the toxin of *Bacillus cereus* (from fried rice).

GERMAN MEASLES (RUBELLA)
A mild infectious disease causing mild fever, a pink blotchy rash first on the face then on the body, and swelling of the lymph glands at the back of the neck. Cases are mildly infectious for 5 days before, until 5 days after, the rash appears. The incubation period is usually 17–18 days. There may be transient joint soreness particularly in adults, but serious complications almost never occur. However, rubella in a woman in the first three months of pregnancy can cause foetal damage – in the first month the risk of congenital abnormalities of eyes, ears or heart is 50 per cent. This falls to about four per cent by the fourth month (twice the expected risk). Immunisation programmes have previously been mainly aimed at teenage girls but the measles, mumps and rubella vaccine, which has been used for some years in North America, has now been introduced in the UK (October 1988) and is recommended from age 14 months.

DIPHTHERIA
Because of immunisation programmes this disease has now been eradicated in the UK, but as recently as 1941 there were 1622 UK deaths. The initial sore throat is complicated by the formation of a membrane of dead tissue which can totally obstruct the airway and necessitate a tracheotomy – a surgical opening in the neck over the windpipe to allow breathing. Immunisation is with a series of three injections in infancy (combined with tetanus and with or without whooping cough) and booster doses at school age.

DYSENTERY
Two types exist – bacillary dysentery caused by *Shigella* and amoebic dysentery caused by *Entamoeba hystolytica*. Both types cause profuse diarrhoea (often containing blood) and colicky abdominal pain. Amoebic dysentery is a disease of the tropics, only very occasionally seen in returning travellers. Complications include liver problems. Bacillary dysentery occurs in the UK as a result of contamination of food by faeces. The disease can be mild and even after complete recovery the organism can still be excreted for several weeks. Prevention is therefore by good hygiene. No immunisation exists.

GLANDULAR FEVER
(also called Infectious mononucleosis)
Caused by the Epstein-Barr virus. The mode of transmission is now known, but because it mainly affects young adults (age 15–25) one theory has suggested it can be contracted by kissing! Initial feature is a particularly sore throat which often produces a thick white coating over the tonsillar area. There is fever, enlargement of the lymph glands of the neck and sometimes also of the liver and spleen. This enlargement can last 10 or more days and is often followed by a period of severe fatigue and mild depression before complete recovery. No treatment other than rest is available. Diagnosis can be confirmed by blood tests which show a particular pattern of white blood cells and a positive 'Paul Bunnel' test. No immunisation available.

GONORRHOEA

Caused by *Neisseria gonorrhoea*. A venereal disease with an incubation of, on average, 4 days. In men it almost always causes a purulent discharge at the tip of the penis. Complications include infection of the epididymis (structure lying behind the testicle) and prostate gland or later a narrowing of the urethra (urine tube). Some 50 per cent of women may initially have no symptoms. Others may have vaginal discharge, urinary symptoms or abdominal pain due to infection spreading to the pelvic organs including the Fallopian tubes which may become scarred and blocked (can cause infertility). Penicillin is usually curative. No immunisation exists.

HEPATITIS

Hepatitis is inflammation of the liver and has various causes, e.g. alcohol or drug consumption as well as infectious causes. Viral hepatitis is classified as A, B, and Non A, Non B.

Hepatitis A

Also called Infectious Hepatitis. Incubation 2–6 weeks (average 4 weeks). Infection is by close contact or faecal contamination of food or water. Symptoms: fever, nausea, weakness, discomfort and tenderness over the liver area. After some 4 days, jaundice (yellow skin) develops with dark urine and pale faeces. Jaundice lasts 1–2 weeks and then appetite returns. A complete recovery is usual. An injection of human immunoglobulin gives temporary protection to travellers to areas where the disease is endemic.

Hepatitis B

Transmitted by blood-to-blood contact, e.g. sharing contaminated needles, or sexual contact. Incubation period 1–5 months. Symptoms identical to Hepatitis A may develop but a high percentage of cases are 'sub-clinical', i.e. the illness is mild without evidence of jaundice. Some 19 out of 20 cases settle completely and the patient becomes virus-free within 4–6 months. One in 20 goes on to become a chronic carrier, liable to pass on infection by blood or sexual contact, and liable to develop late liver complications such as cirrhosis. Only 1 in 1000 die in the phase of acute hepatitis. Immunisation by a series of three injections is now available for those at high risk, e.g. nurses, doctors and dentists.

HERPES SIMPLEX

Type I – The commonest lesion produced by this virus is the 'cold sore' – a small crop of painful blisters which usually develop around the lips or nose and last for several days before fading. The virus may then be latent and flare up again in response to such events as another infection, trauma, emotional upset or exposure to sunlight. Other infections include blisters of the fingers (whitlow), ulceration of the cornea of the eye, and rarely a serious encephalitis (brain infection) to which infants are vulnerable. Those suffering from 'cold sores' should therefore avoid close contact with infants.

Type II – A variety of the same virus causes genital herpes, a painful recurrent blistering eruption of the genitalia similar in appearance to a 'cold sore' but caused through sexual contact. Treatment with Acyclovir limits attacks but does not prevent recurrence. No immunisation exists.

INFLUENZA

Symptoms are fever, muscle pain, sore throat and cough. Complications include viral pneumonia which can progress to a rapidly progressive pneumonia due to further infection by staphylococci. Pandemics occur such as in April–November 1918 (deaths estimated at 21·6 million). Various types of influenza virus exist and the virus has the capacity to change through time. Immunity from previous exposure or indeed from vaccination is therefore never complete and second or further attacks in the one individual can occur.

LEPROSY

The features are very variable. Mild cases may show only a small area of altered skin pigmentation which may heal spontaneously. Other cases progress to thickening of superficial nerves, areas of skin anaesthesia and muscle paralysis. In extreme forms there is distortion of the skin by nodule formation, thickening, fissuring and ulceration – hence the appearance so feared in Biblical times. The drug dapsone and some drugs used for tuberculosis (e.g. rifampicin), as well as plastic surgery, have improved the treatment dramatically.

MALARIA

Malaria is caused by a protozoa of one of four types – *P. ovale, P. malaria, P. vivax* and *P. falciparum* – and is transmitted to the bloodstream of man by the anopheles mosquito. This mode of transmission was first proved in 1895 by Sir Ronald Ross (GB). The incubation period and the severity of the disease depends on the infecting species. Intermittent fever is the main symptom. *P. falciparum* is the most dangerous infection, and causes malignant tertian malaria in which the brain can be affected, causing fits or coma or even sudden death.

The drugs used to prevent malaria are becoming more complex because in certain areas of the world malaria has become resistant to the drugs which were previously effective. Whatever drug is used must be started one week before travel into the endemic area and should be continued for 4–6 weeks after leaving the area. In North Africa and the Middle East chloroquine taken once per week or proguanil taken daily are the drugs of choice. For the Indian sub-continent, China, Africa and South America both drugs are advised in combination. For some other parts of South-East Asia pyrimethamine and chloroquine are advised.

MEASLES (RUBEOLA)

A viral infection. Incubation period usually 10 days (8–14) before the onset of fever and catarrhal symptoms which exist for 3 days before the rash appears. The rash is red and blotchy, usually starting behind the ears and spreading to the face and trunk. Running eyes and nose are a feature. The inside of the cheeks may be red and little white spots in this area above the lower back teeth (like grains of salt) confirm the diagnosis (Koplik's spots). The rash fades in 3–4 days. Cases are *highly* infectious from the onset of the fever and the catarrhal phase until the rash fades. Bacterial infections of the ears, sinuses and chest are the most immediate complications. A progressive serious brain disease known as subacute sclerosing panencephalitis can occur 4 or more years later.

Immunisation is recommended from the age of 14 months and, since October 1988 in the UK, is combined with a vaccine for mumps and rubella.

The intensive use of this vaccine has made measles an extremely rare condition in Canada in recent years.

MENINGITIS
Bacterial meningitis
This can be caused by a number of organisms: the three commonest are mengingococcal meningitis, pneumococcal meningitis and haemophilus meningitis. E. coli meningitis occurs mainly in newborn infants, and tuberculosis meningitis has a rather more gradual onset.

The symptoms of bacterial meningitis are fever, severe headache, neck stiffness, intolerance of bright lights and vomiting. The speed of onset depends on the infecting organism. Meningococcal meningitis is particularly rapid and can cause sudden collapse and the rapid appearance of a rash looking like small bruises or blood blisters. Antibiotic therapy must be started with the utmost urgency.

Viral meningitis
A great number of viruses can cause meningitis with similar but less severe symptoms to bacterial meningitis (e.g. flu or mumps). Spontaneous recovery can be expected without specific treatment.

MUMPS
Caused by a paramyxovirus. Incubation period usually 21 days. Initial symptoms 3–5 days of mild fever and vague malaise followed by tender swelling of the parotid glands (salivary glands on the side of the face, in front of and below the ears). Usually both sides are affected but one side may become swollen 1–2 days before the other. The swelling lasts several days. Cases are infectious for 1 week before the swelling and until the swelling subsides.

Complications include inflammation of the testicles (orchitis) in adult males, pancreatitis and a mild viral meningitis.

Immunisation: single injection now available combined with measles and rubella.

MYALGIC ENCEPHALOMYELITIS
A condition developing as a sequel probably to various viral infections but more notably to Coxsackie virus infection. The symptoms are diverse but include muscle fatigue and muscle pain provoked by minimal exercise and relieved or prevented by adequate rest. The condition is similar to the fatigue encountered after glandular fever but may last for months – other names are post-viral syndrome and Royal Free disease, so called because of an apparent epidemic in the Royal Free Hospital, London, in the 1950s. No treatment is available.

POLIO
A viral infection no longer seen in the UK but which in 1948 caused 241 deaths in England and Wales. Many cases were no more than a flu-like illness with some gastro-intestinal symptoms lasting only a few days. However, some cases went on to develop meningitis or paralysis of muscles. This could affect the breathing muscles and cause respiratory failure, or the limb muscles resulting in permanent muscle thinning and weakness.

The oral vaccine (Sabin, USA) was first introduced in 1957 and is now given from infancy with later booster doses. An earlier vaccine given by injection was the Salk vaccine which was the first polio vaccine to be used on a large scale.

RABIES
Transmitted in the saliva of warm-blooded animals through broken skin as a result of a bite (e.g. from dogs, foxes, bats). The symptoms include spasm of the throat muscles when swallowing is attempted (hence the term hydrophobia), maniacal behaviour, and finally involvement of other muscles to cause paralysis and death. Vaccine is available for those in high-risk occupations. The last case occurring in the UK was in 1922.

RHEUMATIC FEVER
Like scarlet fever (see below), this can occur as a sequel to tonsillitis caused by streptococcal bacteria. The symptoms are fever and an arthritis which seems to move from one joint to another, causing swelling and pain. Occasionally it can cause chorea (St Vitus's dance) – a type of involuntary movement. The importance of this condition is that it may cause damage to the heart valves which only becomes apparent in later years. The disease can recur, but is today very much less common than 50 years ago. No immunisation exists.

RUBELLA
(see German measles)

SCARLET FEVER (SCARLATINA)
A throat infection caused by a particular bacterium (Streptococcus pyogenus), complicated by the appearance of a uniform pink blush of the skin which on close inspection appears as many fine red points. The face is less affected, but the cheeks are usually flushed and the area round the lips is white (circum-oral pallor). The tongue has a strawberry-like appearance. About a week after the rash there is often peeling of the skin, especially on the hands and feet. Incubation period 2–5 days. Infectious for up to 10 days unless treated with penicillin.

In recent years this disease seems to have become much milder, whether because of antibiotic use or improved social conditions etc. – hence the term scarlatina rather than scarlet fever. Complications are now accordingly rare.

SHINGLES
Caused by the herpes zoster virus (as in chickenpox). The virus is present and dormant in the nerve root for a period of time (perhaps years) before flaring up. This condition is therefore not truly infectious – but it is possible to pass it on as chickenpox by close physical contact. Groups of small blisters on a red base appear in the skin area supplied by a particular nerve root, for example in a narrow band round one side of the chest or abdomen but stopping in the mid line, or in a band on one side of the face, or on one limb. The condition is painful. Pain may precede the rash by 2–3 days and pain and sensitivity at the site take an average of 6 weeks to settle, but may last for months (postherpetic neuralgia).

SMALLPOX
The World Health Organisation has declared the world free of smallpox from 1 January 1980. Vaccination is only needed for research scientists.

SYPHILIS
A venereal disease caused by Treponema pallidum.

The disease has three stages. The primary stage begins after an incubation phase of usually 2–4 weeks and is characterised by a firm ulcer on the site of infection, usually the genitalia, with lymph gland swelling in the nearest lymph glands (e.g. the groin). The secondary stage is 6 weeks later, and can have various effects including skin rashes, mouth ulcers, gland swelling, and fever with muscle aches. The tertiary stage follows after a long period of inactivity (up to 25 years) and can affect any organ of the body but particularly the brain and nerves (can cause insanity and loss of balance). It may also cause localised swellings (gumma) in the skin, bones or heart. Diagnosis is by blood tests and treatment by penicillin.

TETANUS
Tetanus spores can gain access to the body through wounds contaminated particularly with soil. Intense muscle spasm ('lockjaw') results. Prevention is by immunisation with tetanus toxoid – given as three doses in infancy with booster doses at school age and then every 5 years. If immunity has waned the intial three doses are repeated.

TUBERCULOSIS
Tuberculosis is caused by the bacterium *Mycobacterium tuberculosis*, first discovered by Koch (Germany) in 1882. Evidence of this disease has been found in an Egyptian mummy from the 10th century BC. The mortality rate in England and Wales in the 1850s was 60 000 per year, both adults and children dying of what was known as consumption. Two strains of organism exist – human and bovine. The main source of bovine tuberculosis was infected milk and this has now been eliminated in the UK. The source of the human strain is the respiratory tract of an 'open' case of pulmonary tuberculosis – i.e. the organism is coughed up or breathed out by the sufferer. The initial infection is in the lungs and the lymph glands in the middle of the chest cavity. In the majority of cases this is asymptomatic and heals without treatment but may leave a scar on the lung. During this primary infection the body develops an immunity which can be detected by means of the Mantoux test. In this test a tiny amount of killed tubercle is injected just under the skin surface and if immunity is present a raised red lump develops. In a minority of primary infections, insufficient immunity develops and the infection spreads either all through the lungs (consumption or miliary pulmonary tuberculosis) or to other organs, e.g. meningitis, kidney or bone infection. In cases where the primary illness has resolved, the infection can flare up again years later, particularly if there is undernourishment or general debility. This is known as chronic tuberculosis and most commonly affects the lungs, but can affect any organ.

Modern drug treatment is very effective for all forms of the disease but 'open' cases are still kept in isolation until their sputum becomes free of the infecting organism.

B.C.G. (Bacille Calmette-Guérin) is a live attenuated vaccine (i.e. a very mild form of TB) first used in 1906 and still in use. It is given by injection into the skin and results in a small ulcer which heals after several weeks, leaving a scar.

TYPHOID
Caused by *Salmonella typhi* and transmitted by food or water contaminated by an ill patient or healthy carrier of the disease. Symptoms begin with fever and progress to a rash and profuse diarrhoea with blood loss. Untreated, the mortality rate is 10–15 per cent, the remainder recover after about three weeks and some three per cent become chronic carriers without symptoms. The last major epidemic in Britain was in 1964 (Aberdeen – 414 cases). Immunisation is with two injections at an interval of one month and immunity lasts for five years.

WHOOPING COUGH (PERTUSSIS)
Whooping cough is a nasty infection caused by the bacterium *Bordetella pertussis*. In developing countries, where poor nutrition exists, it has a considerable death rate. It can affect any age group and is most severe in young babies. The illness begins with what seems to be an ordinary cold, but instead of improving after a few days, the cough becomes progressively worse and is particularly bad through the night. There are spasms of coughing, with one cough after another, until the child is forced to take a breath in rapidly with a loud whooping sound. In the attack the child becomes red in the face (or even blue) with streaming eyes and the spasm usually ends with a bout of vomiting. These symptoms may persist for several weeks (average 3–4 weeks) before easing, but often a cough at night may persist for several months after the infection. Complications include middle ear infection, pneumonia and encephalitis (brain infection).

The disease is highly infectious. Incubation period is 7–10 days and it is infectious from 7 days after exposure to 3 weeks after the symptoms develop. Before the introduction of vaccine in 1957 there were on average some 100 000 cases per year in the UK. By 1973 when vaccine acceptance was 80 per cent this had fallen to 2400. In the mid-1970s levels of vaccination fell to about 30 per cent and major epidemics followed in 1977, 1979, 1981 and 1983. Mortality from whooping cough in the UK in the 1970s remained about 1 per 1000 notified cases with a higher death rate for infants under 1 year. There are a series of three vaccinations usually given in combination with diphtheria and tetanus vaccine. Complications of vaccination are very rare. The best estimate of risk for a normal infant suffering a reaction is about 1 in 100 000. Almost all of these would be a fever complicated by a single seizure and *without* any permanent ill effects. Permanent neurological (brain) complications are much more common after the infection itself than after the immunisation. Vaccination is contra-indicated in some children who have pre-existing brain damage, who have epilepsy, or who have a close relative with epilepsy. Allergy is not a contra-indication to vaccination.

PHOBIAS

Acerophobia	Sourness
Acarophobia	Itching
Achluophobia	Night, darkness
Acrophobia	Heights
Aerophobia	Flying, air
Agoraphobia	Open spaces
Aichurophobia	Points
Ailurophobia	Cats
Akousticophobia	Sound
Alektorophobia	Chickens
Algophobia	Pain
Altophobia	Heights
Amathophobia	Dust

Term	Meaning
Amaxophobia	Vehicles
Amychophobia	Being scratched
Ancraophobia	Wind
Androphobia	Men
Anemophobia	Draught
Anginaphobia	Narrowness
Anglophobia	England or things English
Anthophobia	Flowers
Anthropophobia	Human beings
Antlophobia	Flood
Apeirophobia	Infinity
Apiphobia	Bees
Arachnophobia	Spiders
Asthenophobia	Weakness
Astraphobia	Lightning
Ataxiophobia	Disorder
Atelophobia	Imperfection
Atephobia	Ruin
Aulophobia	Flute
Auroraphobia	Auroral lights
Automysophobia	Being dirty
Autophobia	Being alone, being egotistical
Bacilliphobia	Microbes
Bacteriophobia	Bacteria
Ballistophobia	Missiles
Barophobia	Gravity
Basiphobia	Walking
Bathophobia	Depth
Batophobia	Passing high objects
Batrachophobia	Reptiles
Belonophobia	Needles
Bibliophobia	Books
Blennophobia	Slime
Brontophobia	Thunder
Cainophobia	Novelty
Cancerophobia	Cancer
Carcinophobia	Cancer
Cardiophobia	Heart condition
Carnophobia	Meat
Chaetophobia	Hair
Cheimatophobia	Cold
Cherophobia	Cheerfulness
Chionophobia	Snow
Cholerophobia	Cholera
Chromatophobia	Colour
Chrometophobia	Money
Chromophobia	Colour
Chronophobia	Duration
Claustrophobia	Enclosed spaces
Clinophobia	Going to bed
Cnidophobia	Stings
Coitophobia	Sexual intercourse
Coprophobia	Faeces
Cremnophobia	Precipices
Cryophobia	Ice, frost
Crystallophobia	Crystals, glass
Cypridophobia	Venereal disease
Cymophobia	Sea swell
Cynophobia	Dogs
Demonophobia	Demons
Demophobia	Crowds
Dendrophobia	Trees
Dermatophobia	Skin
Dermatosiophobia	Skin diseases
Dikephobia	Justice
Dipsophobia	Drinking
Domatophobia	Home
Doraphobia	Fur
Dromophobia	Crossing streets
Dysmorphophobia	Deformity
Ecclesiaphobia	Churches
Ecophobia	Home surroundings
Eisoptrophobia	Mirrors
Electrophobia	Electricity
Eleutherophobia	Freedom
Emetophobia	Vomiting
Enetephobia	Pins
Entomophobia	Insects
Eosophobia	Dawn
Eremitophobia	Solitude
Eremophobia	Solitude, stillness
Ereuthophobia	Blushing
Ergasiophobia	Surgical operations, work
Ergophobia	Work
Erotophobia	Physical love
Eyrythrophobia	Blushing
Frigophobia	Cold
Gallophobia	France or things French
Gamophobia	Marriage
Gatophobia	Cats
Genophobia	Sex
Genuphobia	Knees
Gephyrophobia	Crossing a bridge
Germanophobia	Germany or things German
Geumatophobia	Taste
Graphophobia	Writing
Gymnophobia	Nudity
Gynophobia	Women
Hadephobia	Hell
Haematophobia	Blood
Halophobia	Speaking
Haphephobia	Touching or being touched
Haptophobia	Touch
Harpaxophobia	Robbers
Hedonophobia	Pleasure
Heliophobia	Sun
Helminthophobia	Worms
Hierophobia	Sacred things
Hippophobia	Horses
Hodophobia	Travel
Homichlophobia	Fog
Hormephobia	Shock
Hyalinopygophobia	Glass bottoms
Hydrophobia	Water
Hygrophobia	Dampness, moisture
Hypegiaphobia	Responsibility
Hypnophobia	Sleep
Hypsophobia	High places
Ichthyophobia	Fish
Ideophobia	Ideas
Iophobia	Rust
Kakorraphiaphobia	Failure
Katagelophobia	Ridicule
Kenophobia	Void
Keraunophobia	Thunder
Keraunothnetophobia	Fall of man-made satellites
Kinesophobia	Motion
Kinetophobia	Motion
Kleptophobia	Stealing
Koniphobia	Dust
Kopophobia	Fatigue
Kyphophobia	Stooping
Lalophobia	Speech
Leprophobia	Leprosy
Limnophobia	Lakes
Linonophobia	String
Logophobia	Words
Lyssophobia	Insanity
Maieusiophobia	Pregnancy
Maniaphobia	Insanity
Mastigophobia	Flogging
Mechanophobia	Machinery
Melissophobia	Bees
Merinthophobia	Being bound

Metallophobia	Metals	Sciophobia	Shadows
Meteorophobia	Meteors	Scopophobia	Being looked at
Microphobia	Bacteria	Selaphobia	Flashes
Monophobia	One thing, being alone	Siderodromophobia	Travelling by train
Musicophobia	Music	Siderophobia	Stars
Musophobia	Mice	Sinophobia	China or things Chinese
Mysophobia	Dirt, infection	Sitophobia	Food
Mythophobia	Making false statements	Spermatophobia	Semen
Myxophobia	Slime	Spermophobia	Germs
Necrophobia	Death, corpse	Spheksophobia	Wasps
Negrophobia	Negroes	Stasiphobia	Standing upright
Nelophobia	Glass	Stasophobia	Standing
Neophobia	New	Stygiophobia	Hell
Nephophobia	Clouds	Syphilophobia	Syphilis
Nomatophobia	Names	Tachophobia	Speed
Nosemaphobia	Illness	Taphophobia	Buried alive, grave
Nosophobia	Disease	Teratophobia	Monsters, monstrosities
Nyctophobia	Darkness/night	Terdekaphobia	Number 13
Ochlophobia	Crowds	Thaasophobia	Sitting idle
Ochophobia	Vehicles	Thalassophobia	Sea
Odontophobia	Teeth	Thanatophobia	Death
Odynophobia	Pain	Theophobia	God
Oikophobia	Home	Thermophobia	Heat
Olfactophobia	Smell	Thixophobia	Touching
Ombrophobia	Rain	Tocophobia	Childbirth
Ommatophobia	Eyes	Topophobia	Places
Oneirophobia	Dreams	Toxiphobia	Poison
Onomatophobia	Certain name	Traumatophobia	Wounds, injury
Ophidiophobia	Snakes	Tremophobia	Trembling
Ophiophobia	Snakes	Triskaidekaphobia	Number 13
Ornithophobia	Birds	Trypanophobia	Inoculations, injections
Osmophobia	Odours	Xenophobia	Foreigners
Osphresiophobia	Odours (body)	Zelophobia	Jealousy
Ouranophobia	Heaven	Zenophobia	Foreigners
Paediphobia	Children	Zoophobia	Animals
Pantophobia	Everything		
Paralipophobia	Neglect of duty		
Parasitophobia	Parasites		
Parthenophobia	Young girls		
Pathophobia	Disease		
Patroiophobia	Heredity		
Peccatophobia	Sinning		
Pediculophobia	Lice		
Pediophobia	Dolls		
Peniaphobia	Poverty		
Phagophobia	Eating		
Phasmophobia	Ghosts		
Pharmacophobia	Drugs		
Phengophobia	Daylight		
Phobophobia	Fears		
Phonophobia	Speaking aloud/noise		
Photophobia	Strong light		
Phronemophobia	Thinking		
Phthisiophobia	Tuberculosis		
Phyllophobia	Leaves		
Pnigerophobia	Smothering, choking		
Pogonophobia	Beards		
Poinephobia	Punishment		
Polyphobia	Many things		
Ponophobia	Fatigue		
Potamophobia	Rivers		
Potophobia	Drink, alcohol		
Psychophobia	Mind		
Psychrophobia	Cold		
Pteronophobia	Feathers		
Pyrophobia	Fire		
Rhabdophobia	Being beaten		
Russophobia	Russia or things Russian		
Rypophobia	Soiling		
Satanophobia	Satan		
Scabiophobia	Itching		
Scholionophobia	School		

Psychiatric conditions

actual neurosis Term coined by Freud to describe the physiological results of current disturbances.

affective disorder Psychosis in which disturbances of mood occur.

agitated An adjective used to describe depressions when they make the patient anxious, tense and restless.

alienation Being set apart from or removed from either oneself or others.

amnesia Inability to remember.

anhedonia An inability to experience pleasure.

anorexia An absence of appetite.

anxiety An irrational fear, often in response to an unrecognised stimulus.

apathy An absence of emotion.

aphanisis The fear of losing the ability to experience pleasure.

autism A childhood disorder, often persisting into adulthood, in which the patient appears to be cut off from his environment; the senses function normally, but there appears to be little perception.

behaviour disorder A group of conditions in which the behaviour of the patient is frowned on by society.

boredom A condition, distinct from apathy in that the patient is irritable and restless in his search for an activity or interest with which to occupy himself.

catatonia Schizophrenic condition in which the patient suffers periods of excitement and/or stupor, during which he seems out of touch with his environment.

conversion hysteria One of the psychoneuroses in which the patient's symptoms are physical complaints, i.e. the symptoms are physical in their expression but psychoneurotic in their origin.

delusion A fixed idea, held by a patient, that is at variance with beliefs and ideas held by normal people.

dementia A physical deterioration in the brain, resulting in mental deterioration and disorder.

depersonalisation A feeling of unreality.

depression A disorder of mood in which the patient suffers from low spirits (the traditional 'melancholy'), an impairment of some mental processes and often a lack of sleep, appetite, etc.

disassociation Existence of two or more mental processes which lack any connection.

elation A feeling of high spirits accompanying mania.

engulfment An extreme form of anxiety in which all relationships with others are seen as threatening.

exhibitionism Usually taken to mean the sexual perversion, invariably on the part of the male, in which the sex organs are exposed to a female. It can also be taken more widely to mean showing off.

extraversion Outgoing behaviour. This is a component, to a greater or lesser extent, of most people's behaviour; it only becomes a problem when taken to extremes.

fixation Attachment to a concept, object or person, usually appropriate to an earlier stage of development.

frigidity An inability for a woman to be sexually aroused. It may involve an aversion to sexual arousal.

fugue Seemingly automatic behaviour which the subject subsequently cannot remember.

guilt Guilt is attached to an action that has already occurred. It becomes neurotic when the action has not transgressed any value systems of the patient.

hallucination A sensation with no physical origin. Hallucinations can occur as a result of physical illness, or they can be psychotic, usually associated with schizophrenia.

hebephrenia A form of schizophrenia in which the sufferer neglects his person and appears withdrawn, often with unusual mannerisms.

hypochondriasis An imagined belief on the patient's part that he is ill, often with an incurable complaint.

hypomania A mild form of mania.

hysteria A form of neurosis, involving anxiety, physical symptoms, usually attaching to a part of the body about which the patient is concerned, and an absence of any physical foundation for these symptoms.

illusion A misinterpretation of something that has actually occurred.

implosion Fear of being destroyed by reality.

impotence Inability of a man to perform sexual intercourse, either for physical or psychological reasons.

inferiority complex A feeling of inadequacy.

inhibition The suppression of a function by the operation of another function.

introversion Introspective behaviour. This is a component, to a greater or lesser extent, of most people's behaviour; it only becomes a problem when taken to extremes.

involutional melancholia Severe depression occurring at the time of the menopause.

mania A psychosis in which elation, excitement, insomnia and perhaps exhaustion eventually lead to rapid and aimless thought.

manic depressive psychosis A psychosis in which a cycle of depression and elation repeats itself, the patient seemingly unable to control the cycle.

melancholia Another term for depression.

neuralgia Pain originating in a nerve.

neurasthenia An ill-defined form of tiredness that can almost be seen as a neurosis.

neuritis Inflammation of a nerve or nerves.

neurosis Mental disorder of the personality in which there is no organic damage to the nervous system. Someone suffering from a neurosis is aware that something is wrong.

obsessional neurosis Neurosis characterised by obsessions, i.e. ideas that constantly impose themselves on the patient's thinking. The resulting behaviour is repetitive, even ritualistic.

organic mental illness Mental illness resulting from damage to or a disorder of the brain.

paranoia A psychosis in which the patient suffers from delusions of persecution, often organised into a complex and coherent system which controls the patient's life.

phobia An unrealistic and excessive fear of an object or situation. A form of anxiety.

psychomotor acceleration The speeding up of thoughts and actions that occurs in mania.

psychomotor retardation The slowing down of thoughts and actions that occurs in depression.

psychopathy Antisocial irresponsible aggressive behaviour that is often impulsive.

psychosis Mental disorder which leaves the patient out of touch with reality; he is unaware of his disorder. Psychoses can either be organic, in which case disease of the brain can be shown, or functional, in which no damage to the brain can be observed.

psychosomatic illness Physiological symptoms and disturbances of function caused by the patient's personality and psychological disturbances.

regression Behaviour more appropriate to an earlier stage of life, often sparked off by stress.

schizophrenia Functional psychosis characterised by disturbances of thinking, motivation and mood, coupled with hallucinations and delusions.

stupor Complete lack of movement and responsiveness, either due to organic or psychiatric causes.

traumatic neurosis Neurosis which develops shortly after an unexpected and traumatic experience. The neurosis involves the periodic reliving of the traumatic experience.

Schools of psychology

Adler, Alfred Psychoanalyst who developed individual psychology.

analytical psychology That branch of psychology developed by Jung.

behavioural psychology This school of psychology is largely based on the work of B. S. Skinner. Its central tenet is that human behaviour can be modified by reinforcement, i.e. the provision of a 'reward', either physical or social, or the avoidance of punishment. It assumes that the symptom is the illness and that the patient can be 'cured' by deconditioning and reconditioning.

body-centred psychology This is not so much a school of psychology as a loose grouping of therapies and ideas in which work on the physical body results in an alteration in the personality or the image of self. It includes such diverse philosophies and therapies as yoga, the Alexander technique, Rolfing, bioenergetics, T'ai Chi and Feldenkrais.

clinical psychology An essentially practically-based area of psychology in which research findings and methods are applied to human behaviour, both normal and abnormal. It is now a very broadly-based discipline, encompassing experimental psychology, social psychology, environmental psychology and ethology.

developmental psychobiology The study of biological processes and systems that affect the development of behaviour. In particular, interest focuses on the behavioural characteristics which enable species to cope with environmental challenges, and the behaviour and development of the young as they relate to their environment.

ego psychology This is a branch of psychoanalytical theory that has developed from Freud's book *The Ego and the Id*. It is now associated with Freud's daughter, Anna Freud, who developed the thinking in her *The Ego and the Mechanisms of Defence*. It concentrates on the manner in which the individual develops and acquires functions which enable him to control his impulses and his environment and to act independently.

existential analysis This area of psychology is heavily influenced by the existential philosophers such as Sartre and Heidegger. Essentially it lays emphasis on the here and now, expecting the patient to take responsibility for his actions, through which his life will take on meaning. There is little emphasis on the unconscious mental processes dwelt on by other schools of psychology.

Freudian psychoanalysis Psychoanalysis was developed in the first place by Sigmund Freud. It has subsequently been adapted by various psychoanalysts so that there are now many branches of psychoanalysis. However, classical psychoanalysis can be traced back directly to Freud's teachings and writings, particularly to his *An Outline of Psychoanalysis*.

Fromm, Erich One of the neo-Freudians, he at first subscribed to Freud's ideas but subsequently broke away to develop his own thinking. He was much affected by existential philosophy and came to emphasise the part that society as a whole – its structures, expectations, etc. – has to play in determining the way in which an individual copes with basic human needs.

Horney, Karen Another of the neo-Freudians who at first subscribed to Freud's thinking, then later broke away to develop their own ideas. Horney concentrated on the experience of childhood as the basis for neurosis, postulating that such neuroses can be avoided by good child care.

individual psychology This was the name Alfred Adler gave to his branch of psychoanalysis, formed when he departed from Freud's thinking. Adler saw the individual as responsible for his own actions and able to work towards his own goals.

Jungian theory Carl Jung was at first associated with Sigmund Freud in the development of psycholanalysis, but subsequently developed his own ideas. These cover a very wide spectrum of psychology, but one of his most important contributions was to develop a 16-category typology of character, e.g. introversion, extraversion, thinking, feeling, etc.

Kleinian theory Melanie Klein's theories lie within the mainstream of Freudian psychoanalysis, but there are important departures. Primarily she lays emphasis on the first year of a child's life as being a time rich in fantasy and a time during which the origins of neurosis occur.

Lacan, Jacques A French psychoanalyst who introduced elements of structuralism and linguistics into psychoanalysis and psychology.

Laing, R. D. Scottish psychiatrist responsible for much pioneering work in the area of radical therapy and for bringing a more humanistic approach to psychology.

learning theory Psychological theories which aim to explain individual behaviour and personality arising as a result of learned reactions and responses to the environment. This is in contrast to psychoanalysis, which sees behaviour and personality arising as a result of developmental processes.

neo-Freudian theory This encompasses a wide variety of psychological thought. The common thread running through the ideas is that those who have formulated the ideas have at first espoused Freud's ideas on psychoanalysis. They have subsequently broken away from or modified or added to Freud's thinking. In general they have put forward ideas that emphasise the social needs of individuals more than Freud did.

neurolinguistics A combination of psychology, linguistics and neurology that looks at the acquisition of language, its production and processing, and its disruption or disturbances, especially those disturbances related to organic brain disease.

neuropsychiatry The study of organic brain disorders and the effects they have on behaviour and personality.

phenomenology Literally, the study of phenomena, i.e. of the experiences that we have and the effect they have on personality and behaviour.

psychiatry The treatment and study of mental, emotional, personality and behavioural disorders.

psychoanalysis A method of treating mental illness,

originated by Sigmund Freud. Psychoanalysis aims to bring to the surface those fears and conflicts between instinct and conscience that have been pushed into the unconscious.

psychology The study of the mind, of behaviour and of thinking.

psychopathology The study of the abnormal workings of the mind and of abnormal behaviour.

psychosynthesis Psychological thinking developed by the Italian Roberto Assagioli, who trained under Freud. His ideas diverged widely from Freud's, in that he recognised that mental disturbance can arise when the elements of personality are at odds with each other, and that a release occurs when these elements can be merged. Psychosynthesis aims to bring these elements together in a greater whole.

psychotherapy Treatment of mental disturbance, personality problems, behavioural difficulties, etc., by psychological means. Invariably a strong link is forged between the therapist and the patient, who often meet on a one-to-one basis.

radical therapy A relatively recent move in psychology has been to call into question society's definitions of such words as 'sane' and 'insane', undermining the medical model of psychology. This move was catalysed by R. D. Laing, and owes a lot to the existentialists and humanists; insanity, if there is such a thing, is seen as a social problem needing social solutions.

Rogers, Carl Ransom Rogers developed what is known as humanistic psychology, in which the self-image the patient (client) has of himself is paramount. The therapist should therefore be open and honest with the patient, and not seek to change the patient by any approval or disapproval.

social psychiatry The examination of mental disorder as a part of society. Both the social causes of such disorders and the social methods of prevention are looked at.

Sullivan, Harry Stack One of the neo-Freudians who at first subscribed to Freud's thinking, Sullivan subsequently broke away to develop his own ideas of personality. These ideas are based on his observations of the patterns existing in social and interpersonal relations, and development of personality with these patterns.

Nobel prizewinners in physiology and medicine since 1950

1950 Philip S. Hench, Edward C. Kendall, both US; Tadeus Reischstein, Swiss.
1951 Max Theiler, US.
1952 Selman A. Waksman, US.
1953 Hans A. Krebs, British; Fritz A. Lipmann, US.
1954 John F. Enders, Frederick C. Robbins, Thomas H. Weller, all US.
1955 Alex H. J. Theorell, Swedish.
1956 André F. Cournand, US; Werner Forssmann, German; Dickinson W. Richards, Jr, US.
1957 Daniel Bovet, Italian.
1958 George W. Beadle, US; Edward L. Tatum, US; Joshua Lederberg, US.
1959 Arthur Kornberg, US; Severo Ochoa, US.

1960 Sir F. MacFarlane Burnet, Australian; Peter B. Medawar, British.
1961 Georg von Bekesy, US.
1962 Francis H. C. Crick, British; James D. Watson, US; Maurice H. F. Wilkins, British.
1963 Sir John C. Eccles, Australian; Alan L. Hodgkin, British; Andrew F. Huxley, British.
1964 Konrad E. Bloch, US; Feodor Lynen, German.
1965 François Jacob, André Lwoff, Jacques Monod, all French.
1966 Charles B. Huggins, Francis Peyton Rous, both US.
1967 Ragnar Granit, Swedish; Haldan Keffer Hartline, US; George Wald, US.
1968 Robert W. Holley, H. Gobind Khorana, Marshall W. Nirenberg, all US.
1969 Max Delbruck, Alfred D. Hershey, Salvador Luria, all US.
1970 Julius Axelrod, US; Sir Bernard Katz, British; Ulf von Euler, Swedish.
1971 Earl W. Sutherland, Jr, US.
1972 Gerald M. Edelman, US; Rodney R. Porter, British.
1973 Karl von Frisch, German; Konrad Lorenz, German-Austrian; Nikolaas Tinbergen, British.
1974 Albert Claude, Luxembourg-US; George Emil Palade, Romanian-US; Christian René de Duve, Belgian.
1975 David Baltimore, Howard Temin, both US; Renato Dulbecco, Italian-US.
1976 Baruch S. Blumberg, US; Daniel Carleton Gajdusek, US.
1977 Rosalyn S. Yalow, Roger C. L. Guillemin, Andrew V. Schally, all US.
1978 Daniel Nathans, Hamilton O. Smith, both US; Werner Arber, Swiss.
1979 Allan M. Cormack, US; Geoffrey N. Hounsfield, British.
1980 Baruj Benacerraf, George Snell, both US; Jean Dausset, French.
1981 Roger W. Sperry, David H. Hubel, Tosten N. Wiesel, all US.
1982 Sune Bergstrom, Bengt Samuelsson, both Swedish; John R. Vane, British.
1983 Barbara McClintock, US.
1984 Cesar Milstein, British/Argentine; George J. F. Kohler, W. German; Neils K. Jerne, British/Danish.
1985 Michael Brown, Joseph Goldstein, both US.
1986 Rita Levi-Montalcini, Italian.
1987 Susumu Tonegawa, Japanese.
1988 Sir James Black, British; Dr Gertrude Elion, US; Dr George Hitchings, US.

The human body

Bones in the human body

Skull	Number
Occipital	1
Parietal – 1 pair	2
Sphenoid	1
Ethmoid	1
Inferior Nasal Conchae – 1 pair	2
Frontal – 1 pair, fused	1
Nasal – 1 pair	2
Lacrimal – 1 pair	2
Temporal – 1 pair	2
Macilla – 1 pair	2
Zygomatic – 1 pair	2
Vomer	1
Palatine – 1 pair	2
Mandible – 1 pair, fused	1
	22

The Ears	
Malleus	2
Incus	2
Stapes	2
	6

Vertebrae	
Cervical	7
Thoracic	12
Lumbar	5
Sacral – 5, fused to form the Sacrum	1
Coccyx – between 3 and 5, fused	1
	26

Vertebral Ribs	
Ribs, 'true' – 7 pairs	14
Ribs, 'false' – 5 pairs of which 2 pairs are floating	10
	24

Sternum	
Manubrium	1
'The Body' (sternebrae)	1
Xiphisternum	1
	3

Hyoid (in the throat)	1

Pectoral Girdle	
Clavicle – 1 pair	2
Scapula (including Coracoid) – 1 pair	2
	4

Upper Extremity (each arm)	
Humerus	1
Radius	1
Ulna	1
Carpus:	
Scaphoid	1
Lunate	1
Triquetral	1
Pisiform	1
Trapezium	1
Trapezoid	1
Capitate	1
Hamate	1
Metacarpals	5
Phalanges:	
First Digit	2
Second Digit	3
Third Digit	3
Fourth Digit	3
Fifth Digit	3
	30

Pelvic Girdle	
Ilium, Ischium and Pubis (combined) – 1 pair of hip bones (innominate)	2

Lower Extremity (each leg)	
Femur	1
Tibia	1
Fibula	1
Tarsus:	
Talus	1
Calcaneus	1
Navicular	1
Cuneiform, medial	1
Cuneiform, intermediate	1
Cuneiform, lateral	1
Cuboid	1
Metatarsals	5
Phalanges:	
First Digit	2
Second Digit	3
Third Digit	3
Fourth Digit	3
Fifth Digit	3
	29

Total	
Skull	**22**
The Ears	**6**
Vertebrae	**26**
Vertebral Ribs	**24**
Sternum	**3**
Throat	**1**
Pectoral Girdle	**4**
Upper Extremity (arms) – 2 × 30	**60**
Hip Bones	**2**
Lower Extremity (legs) – 2 × 29	**58**
	206

Organs of the human body

ALIMENTARY (DIGESTIVE) SYSTEM

Food passes from the mouth and oesaphagus to the stomach which acts as a collecting bag and begins the process of digestion by its churning action, and by secreting hydrochloric acid and other juices (pepsin). Food then passes to the small intestine (small bowel) comprising the duodenum, jejunum and ileum (lengths: duodenum 25 cm (10 in); jejunum 2·5 m (8 ft); ileum 4 m (13 ft)). The liver (via the gall bladder) and the pancreas gland also secrete digestive juices into the duodenum. Both digestion and absorption of nutrients take place in the small intestine before the large intestine (colon) is reached (length 1·5 m, 5 ft), where reabsorption of body fluids is the main function before excretion via the rectum.

THE LIVER

This vital organ weighs about 2 kg (4 lb). Its functions are:

1. Produces bile which emulsifies fat in the bowel and hence allows its absorption.
2. Receives all the products of food absorption and controls the storage and release of these as energy sources. Carbohydrates are stored as glycogen and the liver, in conjunction with insulin from the pancreas gland, controls the body's glucose (sugar) level.

THE SKELETON

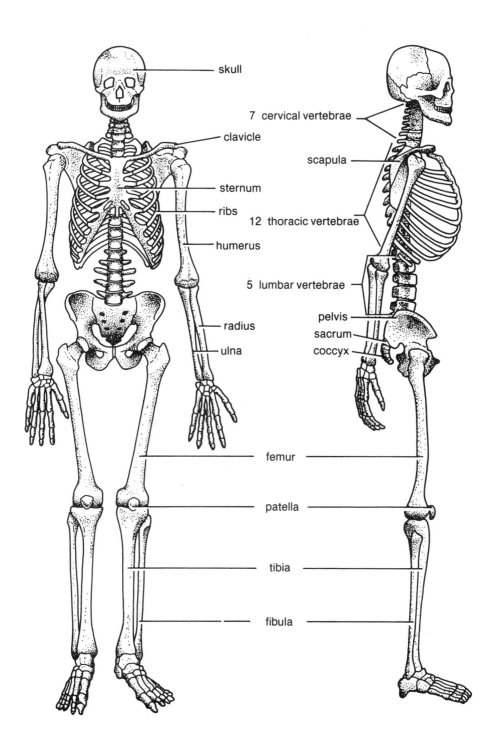

skull

7 cervical vertebrae

clavicle

scapula

sternum

ribs

12 thoracic vertebrae

humerus

5 lumbar vertebrae

radius

pelvis

ulna

sacrum

coccyx

femur

patella

tibia

fibula

THE HUMAN BODY

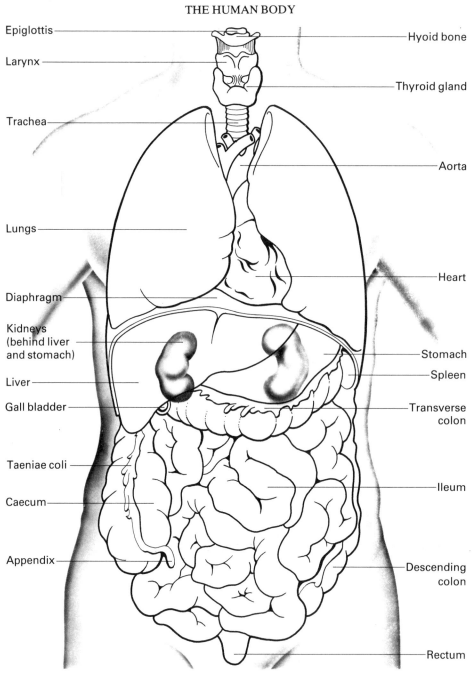

Epiglottis

Larynx

Trachea

Lungs

Diaphragm

Kidneys
(behind liver
and stomach)

Liver

Gall bladder

Taeniae coli

Caecum

Appendix

Hyoid bone

Thyroid gland

Aorta

Heart

Stomach

Spleen

Transverse
colon

Ileum

Descending
colon

Rectum

3. Purifies blood by removing toxins and worn-out red cells.
4. Produces proteins needed for blood clotting.

CIRCULATION AND RESPIRATORY SYSTEM

The ribs enclose the thoracic cavity within which lie the heart and the two lungs. The heart weighs 250–300 g (*9–11 oz*) and is approximately the size of a clenched fist. It is a muscular pump which squeezes blood out through the arteries with each beat. The arteries carry blood away from the heart through a series of branching and progressively smaller blood vessels (capillaries) which then join together again to form the veins which return blood to the heart. The heart is divided into four compartments or chambers (atria and ventricles). The right atrium collects blood from the veins and passes it to the right ventricle which then pumps the blood to the lungs. In the capillaries of the lungs the process of breathing (respiration) replaces the blood's oxygen content, before the blood returns to the left side of the heart. It collects in the left atrium, then passes through the mitral valve to the left ventricle (largest heart chamber) which pumps it out to the rest of the body via the aortic valve and aorta (largest blood vessel of the body, 2·5 cm or *1 in* in diameter).

The heart beats 2500 million times in an average lifetime. At a heart rate of 70 per minute it pumps approximately 5 l (*9 pt*) of blood per minute, but it can pump 20 l (*35 pt*) per minute during vigorous exercise when the heart rate increases to about 150 per minute. The average total lung volume is about 5 l but normal breathing only draws about ½ l (*⅘ pt*) of air in and out with each breath. The oxygen in the air is passed into the bloodstream in exchange for carbon dioxide which is exhaled.

URINARY SYSTEM
The two kidneys lie behind the abdominal organs, below the ribs on either side of the spine. They measure about 15 cm (*6 in*) in length, and each weighs 150 g (*5 oz*). They purify the blood in a complex system of microscopic syphons (glomeruli and nephrons) before passing the urine so produced through drainage tubes (ureters) to the bladder. There urine is stored before excretion through the urethra.

BLOOD AND LYMPHATIC SYSTEM
The average blood volume is 5·5 l (*10 pt*); 55 per cent of the blood is plasma, and 45 per cent consists of blood cells of three types. Red blood cells (erythrocytes) are biconcave discs which contain the chemical haemoglobin and carry oxygen. There are approximately 5 million red cells per mm³ of blood, each with a lifespan of about 120 days. The white cells (leucocytes) are fewer in number (8000 per mm³) and act to combat infection. The platelets help in the normal process of blood clotting.

ENDOCRINE ORGANS
The chemicals which these glands secrete directly into the bloodstream are hormones – they regulate many aspects of the body's performance.

Pituitary: situated at the base of the brain, produces hormones which control the other endocrine glands; a hormone which regulates growth; a hormone which causes the uterus to contract during childbirth; a hormone which causes the mammary glands (breasts) to produce milk; and a hormone which regulates the concentration of the urine.

Thyroid: situated in the neck in front of the windpipe. Thyroid hormone controls the rate of chemical reactions in body cells (the metabolic rate).

Parathyroid Glands: there are four in number (embedded within the thyroid). They control calcium levels in the body.

Pancreas: the hormone insulin regulates glucose levels in the body. Deficiency causes diabetes mellitus (sugar diabetes).

Adrenal Glands: they produce adrenalin which prepares the body for stress by increasing heart rate and blood pressure. They also produce cortisone which has a variety of metabolic effects.

Ovaries: they produce the female sexual hormones oestrogen and progesterone and in addition release one egg (ovum) per month from the menarche to menopause (the woman's reproductive life).

Testes: the testes produce sperms and the male hormone testosterone.

SKIN
The skin can also be classed as an organ and accounts for 16 per cent of the body's weight (surface area 18 000 cm², *2800 in²*). Among its functions is the control of heat loss.

BRAIN AND NERVOUS SYSTEM
The human brain weighs about 1·4 kg (*3 lb*) and contains 10 000 million nerve cells each of which has a potential 25 000 inter-connections with other cells. The brain relays and receives electrical impulses through the special senses and the nerves and spinal cord. There are 12 pairs of cranial nerves supplying the face and head. Nerves in other areas of the body can be classified as motor (supply movement), sensory (recognise touch, pain, temperature and sense body position) and autonomic (regulate the internal body activities of which we are not normally aware, e.g. bowel activity, breathing, heart rate etc.).

HUMAN DENTITION
Man has two sets of teeth during his lifetime. The primary set (milk or deciduous teeth) number 20, and are usually acquired between the ages of 6 months and 2 years. The primary set are lost from about age 6 onwards when the permanent teeth begin to appear. There are 32 in all:

Eight incisors – the central (front) teeth, four upper and four lower, which have a cutting function.

Four canine teeth – the pointed fang-like teeth on either side of the incisors.

Eight pre-molars – two in each quadrant of the mouth; each has two cusps.

12 molars – three in each quadrant of the mouth; the upper molars have four cusps, and the lower molars five cusps, to allow efficient grinding of food. The furthest back molar in each gum is the wisdom tooth, which usually only appears at age 18–20.

Alternative medicine

Introduction
The term used to cover any therapy outside orthodox Western medicine. Currently cooperation between the two schools of thought is increasing rapidly and where they are combined, the term 'complementary' medicine is preferred. Most therapies have their roots in very ancient civilisations and many involve as much art and intuition as science, sometimes with super-sensory powers on the part of the practitioner. Alternative therapies tend to have greater success for patients with stress-related psychosomatic illnesses,

psychogenic pain, chronic disease caused by emotional or spiritual suffering or imbalances, where the line between the physical and metaphysical is often blurred.

Characteristics common to virtually every discipline are: a holistic approach (i.e. considering the state of the individual's 'body, mind and spirit' and his environmental factors); identifying the root causes of the diseases and enabling the patient's own natural healing processes to restore and maintain internal balances over time, rather than suppressing the symptoms more immediately; encouraging the patient to participate in his healing; concern with diet, breathing and exercise, lifestyle and stress levels, and the ecology; and taking preventive measures, to avoid the need for drugs and surgery.

ACUPUNCTURE

The traditional Chinese system of medicine, more than 2000 years old, based on the belief that health depends on the individual's ability to maintain a balanced and harmonious internal environment. It is expressed through the principles of *Yin* and *Yang*, with the flow of vitality or 'life force' (*Chi*), where spiritual, mental, emotional or physical blockages may cause pain or disease. Our organs are associated with specific 'acupuncture' points, which lie along 12 pairs of channels or 'meridians' plus two single ones where *Chi* is concentrated. By stimulating these points with massage or fine needles (sometimes also by warming a dried herb called 'moxa' to generate heat on the skin), the flow of *Chi* is restored, and the imbalances that caused the illness corrected. The stimulation of acupuncture points induces the release of morphine-like substances by the brain, known as endorphins, which are pain-relieving. This technique is therefore also frequently used for anaesthesia in the East – usually following through psychological preparation of the patient.

ALEXANDER TECHNIQUE

A process of re-education by highly trained teachers (usually one to one pupil), in posture, breathing, balance, while performing habitual movements. This leads to physical lengthening, inner harmony and freedom of movement, as well as a sense of well-being and confidence, from which good health flows. Developed by F. Matthias Alexander, b. Tasmania 1869, who moved to London in 1904 and died in 1955. He wrote *The Use of Self* 1932.

ANTHROPOSOPHICAL MEDICINE

An extension of the medicine and practice of the Austrian Rudolph Steiner, Ph.D., 1861–1925. Called a mystic, he regarded himself as a 'spiritual scientist'. He worked and lectured in Berlin and Basle and believed the modern 'reductionist' approach to Western medicine limited the spirit. Steiner described the four 'bodies' of man as the basic 'plumbing', the etheric, the astral and the 'I'. He believed it was essential for the doctor to attain the highest levels of understanding and perception, both of the spiritual nature of his patients and the plants he administered. The system also uses homoeopathic medicine, prescribes mainly vegetarian diet, eurhythmy (the art of movement) and painting therapy and movement.

AROMATHERAPY

A combination of body and facial massage, using essential oils extracted from various parts of plants, each with specific restorative effects. These can also be taken internally or inhaled. Originally developed by the ancient Egyptians, and since by English botanist William Turner (15th century) and four Frenchmen: Gattefosse, who coined the term aromatherapy in his first publication, 1928; Goddissart in Los Angeles, 1938, and Dr Valnet during the Second World War, who all achieved great results in skin cancer and wound healing. Lately this has been extended to cosmetology and rejuvenation by biochemist Mme Maury.

Aromatherapy is often used with radiesthesia, when specific diagnosis is not always necessary.

AYURVEDA

Very metaphysical system of sacred medicine of ancient India, developed between 3000 and 1000 BC, from which most modern Western, Chinese and Japanese medicine is derived. Ayurvedics view the Universe and the human body and mind as an intricately balanced and interacting system of energies, processes and activities, each with their particular qualities. As long as the seven tissues, *Dhatus*, in the human body are in balance and in context, the patient will be healthy. The patient is approached as a unique individual, great emphasis is put on good diet and cleansing, the use of mantras, ceremonies and yogic breathing. Ayurveda also includes branches of surgery, gynaecology and psychology, especially with sexual disorders. Astrology is used for diagnosis, and an enormous pharmacopoeia of drugs is called upon.

BACH FLOWER REMEDIES

A system of 38 herbal remedies developed by Dr Edward Bach, 1880–1936, a successful Harley Street pathologist and bacteriologist. He published *Heal Thyself*, 1931. The remedies have been widely used in the UK only very recently. Spring water or dew is impregnated with the properties of the different plants whilst left in sunshine. Each corrects a specific disharmony of personality or emotions. Particularly effective for depression, anxiety and schizophrenia – having no side effects. 'Rescue Remedy' is a combination of five remedies to be used in emergencies.

BIOCHEMICS or Tissue Salts

A branch of homoeopathy, developed by the German chemist Dr W. H. Schuessler in the 19th century who maintained that signs and symptoms are associated with specific imbalances in the body's 12 inorganic salts and oxides. Dr Eric Powell has since discovered 30 more essential trace elements. Combinations of these are widely available in Europe, USA and Asia, given in homoeopathic doses, often used for self-treatment.

BIOFEEDBACK TRAINING

The use of electrical equipment such as EEGs (electroencephalograms) and ECGs (electrocardiograms) to train patients to positively modify and control specific bodily responses such as blood flow and respiration by instantaneously feeding back their progress. Particularly good for relaxation and stress-management. Man's ability to control his brain alpha rhythms at will was first discovered by Joe Kamiya in USA, 1958. There is evidence from the USA that it can cure and prevent disease, even cancers.

CHIROPRACTIC

A manipulative therapy which, by correcting the alignment of the bones of the spine and joints of the whole body, aims to restore nerve function, alleviate pain and promote natural health and well-being. As well as back, neck and other musculo-skeletal pains, chiropractic can help migraine, allergies, indigestion, arthritis and emotional imbalances, especially those that are stress-related. Spinal manipulation was widely used by ancient Egyptians, Hindus, Chinese etc., but this lapsed until 1895 when the Canadian D. D. Palmer redeveloped it. Today it is the most widely recognised alternative medical profession in the world. The two schools in the UK are McTimoney and Anglo-European schools.

COLOUR THERAPY

A very ancient therapy using different colours (usually in the form of light, including sunlight) to restore body, mind and spirit. It is believed that the colours' specific energies act on the cells and energy fields of the patient. Whilst some practitioners can see auras psychically, others use indigo Kilner screens to observe more acutely the patient's aura to determine which colours are needed to rebalance his energies. (Auras can be photographed by the Kirlian method.) Associated with gem and rainbow therapy in the USA. Particularly good for arrested personality development in children and adults, anxiety states and rheumatoid arthritis.

HERBALISM

The use of plants to prevent and cure disease, probably as old as man himself. These are prescribed according to the individual rather than the disease, aiming to restore the body's natural balance and to stimulate its own healing mechanisms. Only small doses are needed, but the whole plant must be used as this seems to contain side-effect-eliminating substances, which are absent in isolated manufactured form. The new pharmacopoeia is now officially recognised by the Department of Health in the UK.

HOMOEOPATHY

A system based on the following principles: 'Like cures like' – agents which produce the signs and symptoms of a disease in a healthy person will cure that disease; 'minimum dose' – the more diluted a drug, the more powerful or 'potentised' it becomes; 'the Law of Cure' – symptoms may get worse before they get better, they move from the vital organs peripherally, and disappear in the reverse order of appearance; the whole patient is looked at very specifically rather than his disease. Developed by Dr Samuel Hahnemann, 1755-1843, from Leipzig. Today more than 2000 active substances are known. Homoeopathy is today fully recognised under law and available on the National Health Service. The method is combined with both modern and ancient treatment. Also used for animals. The remedy is ground up (*trituration*), serially diluted (*potentisation*) and shaken vigorously (*succussion*).

HYDROTHERAPY

The use of water to heal – especially by stimulating the circulation and by elimination, through sweating, excretion and relaxation. First made into a science by the Romans, still popular in Germany today. Techniques include pressure hosing, salt rubs, sitz-baths, bathing in muds, colonic irrigation and the drinking of mineral water as part of an elimination diet.

HYPNOTHERAPY

Hypnosis is the art of inducing an altered state of consciousness and heightened suggestibility, during which the subject is neither awake nor asleep. It was first popularised in the 1760s by Franz Anton Mesmer in the fairgrounds and theatres of Europe and even today it is tarnished with associations of quackery due to his approach. However, it is one of the most acceptable of the fringes of medicine, used since the times of the ancient Greeks and Druids to cure anxiety and hysterical states. Today, it is also successfully used for asthma, insomnia, many phobias and to stop habits such as smoking. Its anaesthetic powers, first developed by James Braid in the 1890s, are frequently used in dentistry and sometimes for major surgery and control of pain in childbirth. Hypnosis is often practised by trained doctors in conjunction with other treatments; patients themselves can be trained in self-hypnosis. Under hypnosis, the subject can be made to regress through life, even to infancy, with almost perfect memory recall. This is widely used for psychotherapy as well as for police work in the USA.

IRIDOLOGY

A diagnostic technique whereby potential weaknesses on all levels of the patient can be pinpointed early, by examining the irises of the eyes, different areas of which relate to specific areas and systems of the body. Carved stone representations of irises testify to this science being used in 1000 BC by the Chaldeans of Babylonia and also by Hippocrates. Iridology was rediscovered by neurosurgeon Dr Ignatz von Pecezeli (1822-1911) (Hungary), who confirmed the science by examining bodies post mortem.

MACROBIOTICS

A wide (macro) view or philosophy of life (biotics) based on keeping the contrasting yet complementary principles of *yin* (feminine, passive) and *yang* (masculine, active) in balance, intuitively and through wholesome diet and behaviour, so as to remain happy and healthy. More than half the diet comprises grains. Foods should be grown locally, used as fresh as possible and carefully prepared.

MEGAVITAMIN THERAPY
or 'orthomolecular' medicine

Developed in the 1960s and 1970s out of Dr Linus Pauling's (double Nobel Prize winner) work, using megadoses of Vitamin C. In the USA other vitamins are now given, some up to 'body tolerance', to patients whose poor digestive absorption has caused deficiencies. For example, Vitamin A for osteoarthritis and neuropsychiatric disorders; D for bone thinning; E for sterility and heart disease. But the danger of overdoses and lack of clinical trials make this therapy still very controversial. Cures for alcoholism, hyperactivity in children, schizophrenia and depression are claimed.

NATUROPATHY

Healing by encouraging the healing forces naturally present in everybody – a fact already appreciated by Hippocrates in 400 BC. (See introduction for general principles.) A naturopath is more of a teacher than a doctor, encouraging patients to correct their diet, lifestyle and posture. Naturopathy is often combined in the UK with osteopathy or Alexander Technique. A greater understanding of healing forces, vital energies and auras has been gained through Kirlian photography in the USSR since the 1950s. Diseases in the pre-clinical phase can also be detected.

NEGATIVE ION THERAPY
The replacement of negatively charged air particles which are naturally present in pure country air, but absent in air-conditioned or polluted environments. Much work done by NASA has shown that negative ions beneficially affect heart rate and blood pressure, brain rhythms and endocrine system, and good results have been achieved, healing burns and skin diseases, migraine, respiratory allergies and catarrh.

OSTEOPATHY
A system of manipulation of the spine, joints and connective tissues (see also Chiropractic) developed in the USA from 1874 by Dr Andrew Still. He was also an engineer and believed the body cannot function properly if the fabric is in bad condition, or has 'lesions' (structural deviations). Although Dr Still was a devout Christian, osteopathy also had a mystical and spiritual dimension for him. He stressed the 'Total Lesion' – a state where the patient is disturbed biochemically, psychologically as well as structurally. This state is remedied by the 'Total Adjustment'. Osteopathy also focuses on correcting diet, posture etc.

Cranial osteopathy
Developed in the 1930s by Still's disciple William Garnet Sutherland. The bones of the skull are gently adjusted, correcting the flow of cerebrospinal fluid and improving the endocrine system. Successful with migraine, some eye conditions and general debilitation.

RADIESTHESIA, RADIONICS AND PSIONIC MEDICINE
Radiesthesia – the use of dowsing or divining to diagnose diseases and choose the appropriate remedies. Radionics involves the ability to heal spiritually, but at a distance, with the healer having only a spot of the patient's blood, hair or nail. Psionics, developed by Dr George Laurence in England between 1904 and 1964, combines orthodox medicine and radiesthesia to discover the fundamental causes of diseases. All acknowledge a higher level of intuition or 'etheric force' and psionics, the theory of 'miasms' hypothesised by Hahnemann. It is thought to work through energy fields and magnetic patterns beyond explanation in terms of conventional physics. Particularly good for chronic diseases and detecting disease at a very early stage.

REFLEXOLOGY or 'zone therapy'
An ancient Chinese and Egyptian system, dating back about 5000 years, of deeply massaging specific reflex points of the feet (or hands) to diagnose early, prevent and cure disease in the rest of the body. These reflexes relate to each organ and every part of the body. Troubled areas feel tender. Most successful with functional disorders. Developed in the West by Dr William H. Fitzgerald and Eunice D. Ingham in the USA earlier this century.

ROLFING
A kind of deep body massage which breaks down connective tissues that have become thickened and coarsened by bad posture and the stresses of the modern environment. Once freed, the patient becomes more supple, posture improves permanently, height may increase and a sense of wellbeing will follow. Developed by Ida Rolf in 1920s to 1940s in New York.

SHIATSU
Literally meaning 'finger pressure', it is an ancient Japanese form of deep massage, which works on all levels of body, mind and spirit by stimulating acupuncture points and meridians (see Acupuncture). Commonly practised among members of Japanese families. Self-treatment is called *Do-in*. Shiatsu is used as a preventive, as well as curative treatment.

TOUCH FOR HEALTH or Applied Kinesiology
A diagnostic and curative technique from the USA using 'muscle testing' to identify and balance weak muscles or organs. Frequently used with chiropractic.

YOGA
A Hindu system of philosophy and health care meaning 'union' or 'oneness', dating beyond 3000 BC. Breathing, posture, suppleness and meditation

A photographic reproduction of an Electro-Image picture of the human physical aura of a healthy male hand. This demonstrates the effects as reported by Kilner and other researchers from their observation, using complementary colour method (Kilner screen; see glossary).
(The Society of Metaphysicians)

are essential. *Hatha* yoga is the branch concerned with optimum health through mastery of the body and 'controlling the waves of the mind' as described by the yogi Patanjali. Very beneficial for hypertension.

Glossary

alpha rhythms Electrical energy produced by the brain whilst very relaxed. The rhythms of this energy can be measured by an electroencephalograph (EEG) and vary from *c.* 7–14 cycles per second (CPS). Slower brain frequencies, called Theta (4–7 CPS), are produced during light sleep and Delta during deep sleep. When wide awake, the brain vibrates at *c.* 14–20 CPS (Beta).

Chi The Chinese concept of life, that we are all at one with the world, working within the rhythm of the natural order. This is represented by two forces, the *Yin* and the *Yang*. For good health it is essential that the Chi circulates in a balanced and unbroken manner.
connective tissue One of the main tissue types in the body, including bone, cartilage and fat. It acts to bind and support other tissues. It plays important roles in the body, especially structural and protective.

endorphins Morphine-like substances – a group of peptides (sequences of amino-acids), which are produced naturally in the brain and suppress pain.

hyperactivity A pattern of restless, inattentive and impulsive behaviour.

Kilner screens (aura goggles) A complementary colour method of seeing the aura, developed in 1908–11 by Dr Walter Kilner of St Thomas's Hospital, London. The physical aura is seen with physical vision and appears as a grey smoke or 'bundles of sticks', as described by Kilner. (This is not the same aura as that which many clairvoyants claim to be able to see by 'psychic vision': that aura seems to appear in many different colours and patterns.)
Kirlian photography Developed in 1939 by Semyon Kirlian, a Soviet electronics engineer, and his wife. The level of corona discharge is measured with a high-frequency spark-generator. The photography is used medically to identify illnesses such as cancer and tumours at a very early stage, before X-rays.

metaphysical medicine That which is concerned with the nature and origin of matter and the interaction between the mind, body, spirit and the Universe.
miasm The theory expounded by Christian Hahnemann (1755–1843), founder of homoeopathy, that chronic illness is caused by an underlying weakness, or 'miasm', which can be handed down through generations, eventually causing serious illness. It is necessary to find and treat this miasm in order to prevent further recurrences of the disease.
morphine The main substance, found in the juice of the unripe poppy plant, upon which the action of opium depends. Its primary effect when taken is on the central nervous system and it is used primarily in the medical profession as a narcotic to alleviate severe pain and relieve depression.

neuropsychiatric disorders Disorders relating to neuropsychiatry, the branch of medical science which deals with the treatment of nervous and mental conditions.

pathology The science which deals with the causes of and changes produced in the body by disease.
pharmacopoeia A official publication giving recognised drugs and their uses, preparation, sources and tests.
potentisation In homoeopathy, the production of potency in a drug by dilution.

reductionist The view that a complex system can be adequately understood by the analysis of its separate parts in isolation of the whole.

schizophrenia A mental disorder characterised by the apparent 'splitting' of the mind into fragments. Ideas are disconnected and thought processes are disrupted. The illness can take various forms, and delusions, hallucinations, odd speech and behaviour are all symptoms.
succussion In homoeopathy, a method of mixing by shaking vigorously.

trace elements Chemical elements, such as iodine and iron, which are distributed throughout the body in very small amounts. They are essential for the chemistry and nutrition of the body.
trituration In homoeopathy, the mixing by grinding of a medicinal substance with a suitable inert material to produce an evenly distributed, finely divided product.

Yang One of the two forces contained within *Chi*, the Chinese concept of life, the other being *Yin*. It is the positive force in man and nature – powerful elements such as heat, energy, virility, the fertile period of summer.
Yin One of the two forces contained within *Chi*, the Chinese concept of life, the other being *Yang*. It is the passive, almost negative force, for example winter when plant growth is negligible and certain animals hibernate.

See also Medical glossary.

LANGUAGE

World's principal languages

The world's total of languages is estimated to be about 5000. The most widely spoken, together with the countries in which they are used, are as follows.

1. Guoyu (standardized Northern Chinese or Beifanghua)
Alphabetized into *Zhùyīn fúhào* (37 letters) in 1918 and converted to the *Pinyin* system of phonetic pronunciation in 1958. Spoken in China (Mainland). Language family: Sino-Tibetan. 900 000 000.

2. English
Evolved from an Anglo-Saxon, Norman-French and Latin amalgam *c.* 1350. Spoken in Australia, Bahamas, Canada, Sri Lanka (3rd), Cyprus (3rd), The Gambia, Ghana, Guyana, India (non-constitutional), Ireland, Jamaica, Kenya (official with Swahili), Malaysia, Malta (official with Maltese), New Zealand, Nigeria (official), Pakistan (now only 1 per cent), Sierra Leone (official), Singapore (2nd at 24 per cent), South Africa (38 per cent of white population), Tanzania (official with Swahili), Trinidad and Tobago, Uganda (official), UK, USA, Zimbabwe and also widely as the second language of educated Europeans and of citizens of the USSR. Language family: Indo-European. 426 000 000.

3. Hindustani (a combination of Hindi and Urdu)
Foremost of the 845 languages of India of which 15 are 'constitutional'. Hindi (official) is spoken by more than 25 per cent, Urdu by nearly 4 per cent and Hindustani, as such, by 10 per cent. In Pakistan, Hindustani is the third most prevalent language (7½ per cent). Language family: Indo-European. 313 000 000.

4. Spanish
Dates from the 10th century AD; spoken in Argentina, Bolivia, Canary Islands, Chile, Colombia, Costa Rica, Cuba, Dominican Republic, Ecuador, El Salvador, Guatemala, Honduras, Mexico, Nicaragua, Panama, Paraguay, Peru, The Philippines, Puerto Rico, Spain, Uruguay, Venezuela. Language family: Indo-European. 308 000 000.

5. Great Russian
The foremost of the official languages used in the USSR and spoken as the first language by 60 per cent of the population. Language family: Indo-European. 287 000 000.

6. Arabic
Dates from the early sixth century. Spoken in Algeria, Bahrain, Egypt, Iraq (81 per cent), Israel (16 per cent), Jordan, Kuwait, Lebanon, Libya, Maldives, Morocco (65 per cent), Oman, Qatar, Saudi Arabia, Somalia, Sudan (52 per cent), Syria, Tunisia, United Arab Emirates and both Yemens. Language family: Hamito-Semitic. 182 000 000.

7. Bengali
Widely spoken in the Ganges delta area of India and Bangladesh. Language family: Indo-European. 175 000 000.

8. Portuguese
Distinct from Spanish by 14th century and, unlike it, was more influenced by French than by Arabic. Spoken in Angola, Brazil, Goa, Guinea-Bissau, Macao, Mozambique, Portugal, East Timor (Indonesia). Language family: Indo-European. 166 000 000.

9. Malay-Indonesian
Originated in Northern Sumatra, spoken in Indonesia (form called Bahasa is official), Malaysia, Sabah, Sarawak, Thailand (southernmost parts). Language family: Malayo-Polynesian. 132 000 000.

10. Japanese
Earliest inscription (in Chinese characters) dates from the 5th century. Spoken in Japan, Formosa (Taiwan), Hawaii and some formerly colonized Pacific islands. Unrelated to any other language. 123 000 000.

11. German
Known in written form since the 8th century AD. Spoken in the Federal Republic of Germany (West) and the German Democratic Republic (East), Austria, Liechtenstein, Luxembourg and Switzerland plus minorities in the USA, USSR, Hungary, Poland, Romania and in formerly colonized German territories in eastern and southern Africa and the Pacific. Language family: Indo-European. 118 000 000.

12. French
Developed in 9th century as a result of Frankish influence on Gaulish substratum. Fixed by Académie Française from 17th century. Spoken in France, French Pacific Is., Belgium, Guadeloupe, Haiti, Luxembourg, Martinique, Monaco, Switzerland, the Italian region of Aosta, Canada, USA (Louisiana) and widely in former French colonies in Africa. Language family: Indo-European. 115 000 000.

13. Urdu
One of the 15 official languages of India. Also spoken in parts of Pakistan and Bangladesh. 85 000 000.

14. Punjabi
One of the 15 constitutional languages of India spoken by the region of that name. Also spoken in parts of Pakistan. 74 000 000.

15. Korean
Not known to be related to any other tongue. 67 000 000.

16. Telugu
Used in south India. Known in a written,

grammatic form from the 11th century. Language family: Dravidian. 64 000 000.

17. Italian
Became very distinct from Latin by 10th century. Spoken in Eritrea, Italy, Libya, Switzerland and widely retained in USA among Italian population. Language family: Indo-European. 63 000 000.

18. Tamil
The second oldest written Indian language. Cave graffiti date from the 3rd century BC. Spoken in Sri Lanka, southern India, and among Tamils in Malaysia. Language family: Dravidian. 62 000 000.

19. Marathi
A language spoken in west and central India, including Goa and part of Hyderabad and Poona with written origins dating from about AD 500. Language family: Indo-European. 61 000 000.

20. Cantonese
A distinctive dialect of Chinese spoken in the Kwang-tung area. Language family: Sino-Tibetan. 60 000 000.

21. Wu
A dialect in China spoken, but not officially encouraged, in the Yang-tse delta area. Language family: Sino-Tibetan. 59 000 000.

=22. Javanese
Closely related to Malay. Serves as the language of 50 per cent of Indonesian population. Language family: Malayo-Polynesian. 53 000 000.

=22. Vietnamese
Used in the whole of eastern Indo-China. Classified as a Mon-Khmer by some and as a Thai language by other philologists. 53 000 000.

24. Turkish
Spoken in European and Asian Turkey – a member of the Oghuz division of the Turkic group of languages. 52 000 000.

25. Min (Fukien)
A dialect in China which includes the now discouraged Amoy and Fuchow dialects and Hainanese. Language family: Sino-Tibetan. 45 000 000.

26. Ukrainian (Little Russian)
Distinction from Great Russian discernible by 11th century, literary zenith late 18th and early 19th century. Banned as written language in Russia 1876–1905. Discouraged since 1931 in USSR. Spoken in Ukrainian SSR, parts of Russian SFSR and Romania. Language family: Indo-European. 44 000 000.

27. Polish
A western Slavonic language with written records back to the 13th century, 300 years before its emergence as a modern literary language. Spoken in Poland, and western USSR and among émigré populations notably in the USA. Language family: Indo-European. 41 000 000.

Origins of the English language

The three Germanic dialects on which English is based are descended from the Indo-Germanic or Aryan family of languages, spoken since c. 3000 BC by the nomads of the Great Lowland Plain of Europe, which stretches from the Aral Sea in the Soviet Union to the Rhine in West Germany. Now only fragments of Old Lithuanian contain what is left of this ancestral tongue.

Of the three inherited Germanic dialects, the first was Jutish, brought into England in AD 449 from Jutland. This was followed 40 years later by Saxon, brought from Holstein, and Anglian, which came from the still later incursions from the area of Schleswig-Holstein.

These three dialects were superimposed on the 1000-year-old indigenous Celtic tongue, along with what Latin had survived in the towns from nearly 15 generations of Roman occupation (AD 43–410)., The next major event in the history of the English language was the first of many Viking invasions, beginning in 793, from Denmark and Norway. Norse and Danish left permanent influences on the Anglo-Frisian Old English, though Norse never survived as a separate tongue in England beyond 1035, the year of the death of King Canute (Cnut), who had then reigned for 19 years over England, 16 years over Denmark and seven years over Norway.

The Scandinavian influence now receded before Norman French, though Norse still struggled on in remote parts of Scotland until about 1630 and in the Shetland Islands until c. 1750. The Normans were, however, themselves really Vikings, who in five generations had become converts to the Latin culture and language of northern France.

For three centuries after the Norman conquest of 1066 by William I, descendant of Rollo the Viking, England lived under a trilingual system. The mother tongue of all the first 13 kings and queens, from William I (1066–87) until as late as Richard II (1377–99), was Norman. English became the language of court proceedings only during the reign of Edward III, in October 1362, and the language for teaching in the universities of Oxford and Cambridge in c. 1380.

English did not really crystallize as an amalgam of Anglo-Saxon and Latin root forms until the 14th century, when William Langland (c. 1330–c. 1400) and Geoffrey Chaucer (c. 1340–1400) were the pioneers of a literary tradition, which culminated in William Shakespeare, who died in 1616, just four years before the sailing of the *Mayflower*.

Artificial languages

Of the several hundred artificial, or auxiliary, languages Esperanto is regarded to be the most successful, spoken by 2–10 million people.

MILESTONES
1887 Esperanto constructed by Ludwik Lejzer Zamenhof, a Polish oculist. *Lingvo Internacia* by Doktoro Esperanto – pseudonym of Dr L. L. Zamenhof – was published in Warsaw for Russian speakers.
1889 First Esperanto journal *La Esperantisto*.

1905 First international Congress of Esperanto at Boulogne sur Mer, France (*c.* 700 delegates from 20 countries).
Publication of the magazine *Esperanto* (rules of the structure and vocabulary).

1908 Universala Esperanto-Asocio (membership 83 countries).

1923 Radio stations began broadcasting in Esperanto.

1925 Postage stamps with Esperanto text first appeared.

1938 The worldwide Esperanto Youth Organization was founded.

1954 UNESCO passed a resolution in favour of Esperanto.

1970s Esperanto was taught in over 600 schools and 31 universities. President Franz Jonas of Austria, himself speaking Esperanto, opened the 55th World Esperanto Congress in Vienna in 1970.

1972 National association in 60 states and over 1250 local societies.

1979 World Esperanto Association had *c.* 31 000 members, mainly in Eastern Europe.

1987 The centenary World Esperanto Congress in Warsaw attracted over 6000 delegates from 70 countries.

1988 To date, over 100 periodicals and more than 30 000 books have been published in Esperanto. There are fifty national Esperanto associations and twenty-two international professional associations using Esperanto. The World Esperanto Congress is held annually.

The Tower of Babel which, according to the Bible, is the origin of the world's many different languages. (After Pieter Brueghel the Elder after the original painting in the Kunsthistorisches Museum, Vienna. Photo: Images)

LITERATURE

Glossary

abridged edition Condensed or shortened version of a work.

acrostic Poem in which the initial letters of the word of each line makes a word or words when read downwards.

act Major division in a dramatic work.

adage Maxim or proverb.

addendum Addition or appendix to a book.

allegory Story or tale with double meaning.

alliteration Figure of speech where consonants at the beginning of words, or stressed syllables, are repeated.

almanac Book or table comprising a calendar of days, weeks and months indicating special occasions or events.

anagram Letters or word or phrase which, when re-arranged, form a new word.

anecdote Brief account or story about an individual.

annotation Textual comment on a book.

anthology Collection of poetry or prose from diverse sources.

aphorism Short statement of a truth or dogma couched in memorable terms.

argot Slang or coarse vernacular language.

assonance Repetition of similar vowel sounds in speech in writing to achieve a particular effect.

autobiography An account of a person's life by himself or herself.

avant-garde Advanced (in style or thought); ahead of its time.

ballad Story that tells a narrative.

belles lettres Essays on literary studies and the aesthetics of literature.

bibliography List of works on a particular subject or author.

biography An account of a person's life by someone else.

blank verse Poetry with unrhymed line endings.

blurb Brief description of a book printed on the dust cover or jacket.

bowdlerize To 'cleanse' a work by omitting or cutting out indecent passages, phrases or words.

canon Collection of works established as genuine.

canto Division of an epic or narrative poem.

caption Short description accompanying an illustration.

catalogue List of books or works.

chronicle A compilation of events in sequence, either actual or fictional.

cipher Writing that employs substitution or transposition of letters.

cliché Over-used expression that has become trite.

colloquialism Word, phrase or expression in everyday use.

concordance Alphabetical index of words in a work, or works by a single author.

copyright Protective law to prevent pirating or plagiarism of an author's work.

couplet Two successive rhyming lines in poetry.

cycle Group of works united by an overall theme.

dialect Manner of speaking pertaining to a particular class or geographical region.

dialogue The speech of characters in a story or play; part of a work in which characters speak.

diary Sequential private record of personal and other events kept by an individual.

dictionary Book containing the words of a language, and their definitions, alphabetically; two-language dictionaries contain the corresponding words of both languages and their meanings, also alphabetically; any book that gives words and phrases about a particular subject, arranged alphabetically.

digest Publication where works are abridged.

documentary Form of fiction or drama based on documentary evidence provided by newspapers, recent historical reports or other contemporary or recent factual evidence.

doggerel Rough, ill-constructed verse.

double entendre Ambiguity in a word or expression, one of which meanings is usually bawdy or frivolous.

drama Work to be performed on a stage by actors.

dramatis personae Characters in a play.

duologue Conversation between two characters in a play, story or poem.

edition Total number of copies of a book printed from unchanged set of type.

elegy Serious meditative poem; lament.

encyclopedia Comprehensive work encompassing and describing many aspects of knowledge; specialist work covering comprehensively a subject or discipline.

epic Long narrative poem incorporating myth, legend, folklore and history, about the deeds of heroes, warriors, important people; a grandiose treatment of an individual's or nation's story.

epigram Short witty statement in verse or prose.

epistle Direct address to another person; a 'letter' in the form of verse.

epitaph Valediction to dead person or persons; inscription on a tomb or grave.

eponymous Person whose name becomes the title of the work.

essay Composition, usually in prose, discussing a topic or variety of topics.

euphemism Substitution of a bland expression for a harsh or blunt one.

exposition Summary of plot and events given at the beginning of a play.

expurgate To remove obscene or offensive sections from book or text.

fable A short narrative in prose or verse that points a moral.

fiction General term for an imaginative work, usually in prose.

foreword Short introduction to a work.

gazetteer Geographical dictionary or index.

ghost writer Person who undertakes literary work for another who takes the credit.

glossary Alphabetical list of unfamiliar or uncommon words, usually appended to work in which they appear.

hyperbole Figure of speech that contains exaggeration for emphasis.

idiom Form of expression of phrase peculiar to its language and possessing a meaning other than its literal one.

introduction Essay stating author's intention to reader.

jingle Verse or verses with strong rhyme and rhythm.

journal Paper, periodical or magazine.

legend Story about a particular person containing myth and historical fact; explanation of symbols on a map or chart.

lexicon Dictionary, especially for Classical and Middle Eastern languages.

libretto Text of an opera or operetta.

limerick Type of light or amusing verse, of five lines.

linguistics The scientific study of language.

lyric Words to a song.

manuscript Book or work written by hand.

maxim Short statement or even sentence containing a general truth about human conduct and human nature.

melodrama Exaggeratedly and emotionally written story, usually tragic.

metaphor Figure of speech in which one thing is described in terms of another, by implication.

meter Patterns of stressed and unstressed syllables in verse.

monologue Single person addressing an audience alone, in drama, verse or prose. *Interior* monologue; unspoken but thought speech in verse or prose.

myth Non-factual story that embodies explanation of how something comes to exist, usually involving supernatural or superhuman creatures.

narrative Story or tale in prose or verse.

neologism Newly-coined word.

nom de plume Term used to indicate a fictitious name used by a writer to represent his work.

novel Extended piece of prose fiction.

novella Prose fiction, longer than a short story, shorter than a novel, concentrating upon a single event.

ode Lyric poem describing an event or feelings about a person, object or event.

onomatopoeia Word whose sound is imitative of the meaning e.g. hiss.

paradox Apparently self-contradicting statement that, on closer examination, is found to contain a truth reconciling the two opposites.

parody Imitation of words, style, sense, subject of a writer to make them appear ridiculous.

patois Local dialect.

periodical Magazine or journal published regularly.

philology Study of literature, language and linguistics.

plagiarism Wrongful appropriation and publica-

tion of another's work as one's own.

plot Plan or organization of events and characters in a play, work of fiction or poem as to induce curiosity and suspense in the audience or reader.

poem Literary work which may be in rhyme, blank verse or a combination of the two.

poetry Any kind of metrical composition in a literary work.

pornography Work in which there is a deliberate emphasis on the sexual behaviour of characters, in order to arouse sexual excitement.

potboiler Work written essentially to gain the author a livelihood.

précis Concise statement; short summary of a work.

preface Introduction to a work.

prologue Opening section of the work itself.

propaganda Work devoted to the dissemination of an idea or belief, usually biased.

pseudonym Name other than the true one used by an author to represent his work.

pun Figure of speech that involves a play upon the words used.

refrain Phrase, line or lines repeated at intervals or at the end of a stanza in poetry.

review Notice or critical article on musical, artistic or literary work.

revue Theatrical entertainment made up of sketches, dances, songs, recitals and improvised pieces, usually humorous, satirical or topical.

rhetoric Art of using language, in speaking or writing, to persuade. The persuasive style (rather than the content) of a work.

rhyme Echoing sound or audible similarity in two or more words, especially at endings. Device used to construct much poetry.

riddle Puzzle, question or enigma; conundrum.

saga Lengthy prose work, sometimes in several parts, describing the history and events surrounding medieval kings, warriors and, recently, fictitious families.

satire Any work in which wickedness, folly, vice and corruption in individuals and society is exposed by ridicule and scorn.

semantics Branch of linguistics dealing with meaning, and the change of meaning, in words.

semiology General study or science of signs with which humans communicate with each other (including words and their use in every context).

sic Included in brackets after a printed word or quoted passage to indicate that it is quoted accurately, however actually incorrect.

simile Figure of speech where one thing is likened to another explicitly.

slang Colourful and vernacular language of the street, marketplace, barrackroom, workplace, sportsplace and playground.

soliloquy Kind of monologue in which a stage character expresses his thoughts and feelings.

song Poem or verse set to music.

sonnet Formal poem of 14 lines.

style Characteristic manner of expression in prose or verse; the way in which a thing is written by an author.

synonym A word similar in meaning to another.

synopsis Outline of the main points of a work; summary.

tale Spoken or written narrative.

tautology Overuse of synonyms or repetition of ideas in sentence.
theme Central idea of a work, rather than its subject.
thesis Long essay or treatise on a subject, usually expository; work presented to examiners for academic qualification.
tract Short printed treatise on religious or political subject.
tragedy Serious dramatic composition in prose or verse in which the principal character or characters are victims, often fatally so, of circumstance, or of a fatal flaw of character, of a crime of violence, especially one involving the death of an innocent person.
translation Rendering of a work into another language.
treatise Formal work examining a subject and the principles underlying it.

vade-mecum Manual or handbook carried for frequent reference.
vernacular Domestic or native language.

yarn Story or tale, sometimes improbable and far-fetched.

English literature

Nothing definite has survived of the stories or songs possessed by the ancient Britons who were invaded by Julius Caesar on 26 Aug 55 BC. Barely anything has survived from the 376-year Roman occupation until AD 410. English literature thus begins at least by being English.

The earliest known British born author was Pelagius (fl. 400-18) from whom survive some remains of theological disputations written in Rome.

The earliest English poem known to us is Widseth, about a wandering minstrel of the 6th century. In the Exeter Book 150 lines of this poem survive.

The oldest surviving record of a named English poet who composed on British soil is from the paraphrase by Bede (673-735) of a hymn attributed to Caedmon of Streaneshalch (Whitby, North Yorkshire), who was living in 670. This survives in the Cambridge mansucript of Bede (or Baeda) in a hand possibly of the 8th century.

The first great book in English prose is the Anglo-Saxon Chronicle supervised by King Alfred until 892. Alfred himself translated some of the writings of Bede and of Gregory the Great's *Pastoral Care* into West Saxon.

The Lindisfarne Gospels, a beautiful vellum quarto Latin manuscript now in the British Library, London, was written *c.* 696-8. In *c.* 950 Alred, Bishop of Durham, added an interlinear gloss in Northumbrian dialect.

The leading authors of the Old English Period are:

Alfric	*c.* 955–*c.* 1020
King Alfred	849–99
Venerable Bede	*c.* 673–735
Caedmon	fl. 670
Cynewulf	? 9th century
Wulfstan	d. 1023

Bibliography

Below are brief notes and a list of the major works of the 10 British writers who have the longest entries in the *Oxford Dictionary of Quotations.* They are listed in order of length of their entry.

SHAKESPEARE, WILLIAM (1564-1616)
The greatest contribution to the world's store of poetry and drama has been made by William Shakespeare (1564-1616). Born at Stratford-upon-Avon, this eldest surviving child of an alderman and trader produced in the space of the seventeen years between 1594 (*Titus Andronicus*) and 1611 (*The Tempest*) thirty-seven plays which total 814 780 words.

Shakespeare's outpourings of sheer genius has excited and amazed critics of every age since. His contemporary Ben Jonson called him 'The applause! delight! the wonder of our stage!' Milton refers to him as 'Sweetest Shakespeare, Fancy's child'. To Thomas Carlyle, looking at his massive brow, he was 'The greatest of intellects'. Matthew Arnold refers to him as 'out-topping knowledge'. (See **Theatre** for list of plays.)

TENNYSON, ALFRED, FIRST BARON (1809-92)

Poems [including *The Lotos Eaters* and *The Lady of Shalott* (dated 1833)]	1832
Poems (two volumes) (including *Ulysses, Sir Galahad, Morte d'Arthur, Locksley Hall*)	1842
In Memoriam A.H.H. (Arthur Henry Hallam)	1830
Ode on the Death of the Duke of Wellington	1852
Charge of the Light Brigade	1854
Maud and Other Poems	1859
Idylls of the King	1857–85
(completed edition 1889)	
Enoch Arden (including *Old Style*)	1864
Holy Grail	1869
The Revenge: A Ballad of the Fleet	1878
Becket	1884
Locksley Hall 60 Years After	1886
Demeter and Other Poems (including *Crossing the Bar*)	1889

MILTON, JOHN (1608-74)

On the Death of Fair Infant Dying of a Cough	1625
L'Allegro and Il Penseroso	1632
Arcades	1633
Comus (2 Masques)	1634
Lycidas	1638
A Tractate of Education	1644
Doctrine and Discipline of Divorce	1644
Areopagitica (a Tract)	1644
Tenure of Kings and Magistrates (a Pamphlet)	1649
Paradise Lost (written *c.* 1640-57)	1657
Paradise Regained (written 1665-66)	1671
Samson Agonistes	1671

KIPLING, JOSEPH RUDYARD (1865-1936)

Departmental Ditties	1886
Plain Tales from The Hills	1888
Soldiers Three	1888
Wee Willie Winkie	1888
The Light That Failed	1891
Barrack Room Ballads	1892

Many Inventions	1893
Jungle Books (two volumes)	1894–95
The Seven Seas (including *Mandalay*)	1896
Captains Courageous	1897
Recessional	1897
Stalky & Co.	1899
Kim	1901
Just So Stories for Children	1902
Puck of Pook's Hill	1906
Rewards and Fairies	1910
A School History of England	1911

WORDSWORTH, WILLIAM (1770–1850)

The Evening Walk (written 1787–92)	1793
Descriptive Sketches (written 1787–92)	1793
Guilt and Sorrow	1794
Lyrical Ballads (with Coleridge)	1798 & 1800
Prelude	1805
Poems in Two Volumes (including *Ode to Duty* and *Ode on Intimations of Immortality*)	1807
Excursion: a portion of the *Recluse*	1814
Poems, including the Borderers	1842

SHELLEY, PERCY BYSSHE (1792–1822)

Alastor	1816
Ode to The West Wind	1819
The Cenci	1819
Prometheus Unbound	1820
The Witch of Atlas	1820
To a Skylark	1820
The Cloud	1820
Epipsychidion	1821
Adonais	1821
Queen Mab	1821
Hellas	1822
Defence of Poetry (uncompleted)	

JOHNSON, DR SAMUEL (1709–84)

A Voyage to Abyssinia by Father Jerome Lobo (Translation)	1735
London: a Poem, in Imitation of the Third Satire of Juvenal (anon.)	1738
Parliamentary Reports disguised as Debates in the Senate of Magna Lilliputia (Senate of Lilliput) July 1741–Mar 1744	
Life of Savage	1744
Plan of a Dictionary of the English Language	1747
Irene (Theatrical tragedy produced by Garrick at Drury Lane)	1748
The Vanity of Human Wishes	1749
The Rambler (essays in 208 bi-weekly issues) Mar 1750–Mar 1752	
A Dictionary of the English Language (8 years' work, 1747–55)	1755
The Prince of Abyssinia, A Tale	1759
The Idler (essays in the *Universal Chronicle* or the *Weekly Gazette*) Apr 1758–Apr 1760	
Rasselas	1759
Shakespeare, a new Edition	1765
A Journey to the Western Highlands	1775
The Lives of the Poets vols. i–iv 1779, vols. v–x	1781
Dr Johnson's Diary, posthumously published	1816

BROWNING, ROBERT (1812–89)

Paracelsus	1835
Sordello	1840
Christmas-Eve and Easter-Day	1850
Men and Women (including *One Word More* and *Bishop Blougram's Apology*)	1855

Dramatis Personae (including *Rabi ben Ezera* and *Caliban upon Setebos*)	1864
The Ring and The Book	1868–69
A Grammarian's Funeral	
Soliloquy of the Spanish Cloister	
The Pied Piper of Hamelin	
Asolando	posthumously 1890
New Poems (with Elizabeth Barrett Browning)	posthumously 1914

BYRON, GEORGE GORDON, SIXTH BARON (1788–1824)

Fugitive Pieces (privately printed) originally called *Juvenilia*	1806
Hours of Idleness (reprint of the above with amendments)	1807
English Bards and Scotch Reviewers	1809
Childe Harold (began at Janina, 1809), Cantos i and ii	1812
The Giaour	1813
The Corsair	1814
Lora	1814
The Siege of Corinth	1816
The Prisoner of Chillon	1816
Childe Harold (written in Switzerland), Canto iii	1816
Childe Harold (written in Venice), Canto iv	1817
Manfred	1817
Don Juan (first five cantos)	1818–20
Autobiography	(burnt 1824)
Cain	1821
Don Juan (later cantos)	1821–22
Contribution to *The Liberal* newspaper 'Vision of Judgement'	1822
The Island	1823
Heaven and Earth	1824

DICKENS, CHARLES JOHN HUFFAM (1812–70)

Sketches of Young Gentlemen, Sketches of Young Couples, The Mudfog Papers	unpublished
A Dinner at Poplar Walk (re-entitled *Mr Minns and his Cousin*)	Dec 1833
Sketches by Boz. Illustrative of Every-Day Life and Every-Day People published in *Monthly Magazine* (1833–35) and *Evening Chronicle*	1835
The Posthumous Papers of the Pickwick Club	from Apr 1836
Oliver Twist (in Bentley's *Miscellany*)	1837–39
Nicholas Nickleby (in monthly numbers)	1838–39
Master Humphrey's Clock (Barnaby Rudge and *The Old Curiosity Shop)*	1840–41
The Old Curiosity Shop (as a book)	1841
Barnaby Rudge (as a book)	1841
American Notes	1842
Martin Chuzzlewit (parts)	1843–44
A Christmas Carol	1843
The Chimes (written in Italy)	1844
The Cricket on the Hearth	1845
Pictures from Italy	1846
Daily News (later the *News Chronicle*) Editor	Jan–Feb 1846
The Battle of Life	1846
The Haunted Man	1847
Dombey and Son (parts) (written in Switzerland	1847–48
Household Words (weekly periodical) Editor (included *Holly-Tree*)	1848–59

David Copperfield	1849–50
Bleak House (in parts)	1852–53
A Child's History of England	1852–3–4
(in three volumes)	
Hard Times. For These Times	
(book form)	1854
Little Dorrit	1857–58
All the Year Round (Periodical) Editor	1859–70
Great Expectations	1860–61
The Uncommercial Traveller (collected	1861
parts of *A Tale of Two Cities*)	
Our Mutual Friend	1864–65
The Mystery of Edwin Drood	1870
(unfinished)	

Other British writers (14th to 20th centuries)

The writers below are listed in chronological order of year of birth, together with their best known work or works.

14th CENTURY
Langland, William (*c.* 1330–*c.* 1400). *Vision of Piers Plowman.*
Chaucer, Geoffrey (*c.* 1340–1400). *Canterbury Tales.*

15th CENTURY
Malory, Sir Thomas (*c.* 1400–1470). *Morte d'Arthur.*
More, Sir Thomas (1478–1535). *Utopia.*

16th CENTURY
Leland or Leyland (*c.* 1506–1552) *Itinerary.*
Spenser, Edmund (1552–99). *The Faerie Queene.*
Lyly, John (*c.* 1554–1606). *Euphues.*
Sidney, Sir Philip (1554–86). *The Countesse of Pembrokes Arcadia; Astrophel and Stella; The Defence of Poesie.*
Bacon, Francis (Baron Verulam, Viscount St Albans) (1561–1626). *The Advancement of Learning.*
Marlowe, Christopher (1564–1593). *Tamburlaine The Great; Dr Faustus.*
Donne, John (1572–1631). *Poems; Songs and Sonnets; Satyres; Elegies.*
Jonson, Benjamin (1572–1637). *Every Man in His Humour* (produced 1598, published 1601); *Every Man out of his Humour* (1600); *Volpone: or The Foxe* (1607); *The Alchemist* (1610, published 1612); *Bartholomew Fayre* (1614, published 1631).
Burton, Robert (1577–1640). *Anatomy of Melancholy.*
Beaumont, Francis (1584–1616) and Fletcher, John (1579–1625). *The Scornful Lady; Philaster; The Maid's Tragedy; A King and No King.*
Hobbes, Thomas (1588–1679). *Leviathan; Behemoth.*
Herrick, Robert (1591–1674). *Hesperides.*
Walton, Izaak (1593–1683). *The Compleat Angler.*

17th CENTURY
Clarendon, Edward Hyde, Earl of (1608–74). *History of the Rebellion and Civil Wars in England.*
Butler, Samuel (1612–80). *Hudibras.*
Evelyn, John (1620–1706). *Diary.*
Bunyan, John (1628–88). *The Pilgrim's Progress.*
Dryden, John (1631–1700). *All For Love.*
Locke, John (1632–1704). *Essay Concerning Human Understanding.*
Pepys, Samuel (1633–1703). *Diary.*
Newton, Sir Isaac (1643–1727). *Philosophiae Naturalis Principia Mathematica; Opticks.*

Ottway, Thomas (1652–85). *Venice Preserved.*
Defoe, Daniel (1660–1731). *The Life and Adventures of Robinson Crusoe.*
Swift, Jonathan (1667–1745). *Gulliver's Travels.*
Congreve, William (1670–1729). *The Way of the World.*
Addison, Joseph (1672–1719). *The Spectator.*
Pope, Alexander (1688–1744). *An Essay on Criticism; The Rape of the Lock; The Dunciad; An Essay on Man.*
Richardson, Samuel (1689–1761). *Pamela; Clarissa.*

18th CENTURY
Fielding, Henry (1707–54). *Tom Thumb; The History of Tom Jones.*
Sterne, Laurence (1713–68). *Tristram Shandy.*
Gray, Thomas (1716–71). *An Elegy Written in a Country Churchyard.*
Walpole, Horace, 4th Earl of Orford (1717–97). *Letters.*
Smollett, Tobias George (1721–71). *Roderick Random; Peregrine Pickle; Humphrey Clinker.*
Smith, Adam (1723–1790). *Wealth of Nations.*
Goldsmith, Oliver (1728–74). *The Vicar of Wakefield; She Stoops to Conquer; The Deserted Village.*
Burke, Edmund (1729–97). *Reflections on the Revolution in France.*
Cowper, William (1731–1800). *Poems.*
Gibbon, Edward (1737–94). *A History of the Decline and Fall of the Roman Empire.*
Paine, Thomas (1737–1809). *Rights of Man.*
Boswell, James (1740–95). *Life of Johnson.*
Sheridan, Richard Brinsley (1751–1816). *The Rivals; The School For Scandal.*
Burney, Frances 'Fanny' (Madame D'Arblay), (1752–1840). *Evelina.*
Blake, William (1757–1827). *Songs of Innocence; Songs of Experience.*
Burns, Robert (1759–96). *Poems chiefly in the Scottish dialect; Tam O'Shanter; The Cotters Saturday Night; The Jolly Beggars.*
Cobbett, William (1762–1835). *Rural Rides.*
Smith, Rev Sydney (1771–1845). *The Letters of Peter Plymley; Edinburgh Review.*
Scott, Sir Walter (1771–1832). *Waverley; Rob Roy; Ivanhoe; Kenilworth; Quentin Durward; Redgauntlet; Lady of the Lake.*
Coleridge, Samuel Taylor (1772–1834). *Lyrical Ballads (Ancient Mariner); The Kubla Khan.*
Southey, Robert (1774–1843). *Quarterly Review* (contributions); *Life of Nelson.*
Austen, Jane (1775–1817). *Sense and Sensibility; Pride and Prejudice; Mansfield Park; Emma; Northanger Abbey; Persuasion.*
Lamb, Charles (1775–1834). *Tales from Shakespeare* [largely by his sister, Mary Lamb (1764–1947)]; *Essays of Elia.*
Hazlitt, William (1778–1830). *My First Acquaintance with Poets; Table Talk; The Plain Speaker.*
Hunt, James Henry Leigh (1784–1859). *The Story of Rimini; Autobiography.*
De Quincey, Thomas (1785–1859). *Confessions of an English Opium Eater.*
Peacock, Thomas Love (1785–1866). *Headlong Hall; Nightmare Abbey.*
Marryat, Frederick (1792–1848). *Mr Midshipman Easy.*
Clare, John (1793–1864). *Poems Descriptive of Rural Life.*
Keats, John (17905–1821). *Endymion; Ode to a Nightingale; Ode on a Grecian Urn; Ode to Psyche; Ode to*

Autumn; Ode on Melancholy; La Belle Dame sans Merci; Isabella.
Carlyle, Thomas (1795–1881). *The French Revolution; Oliver Cromwell's Letters and Speeches.*
Shelley, Mary Wollstonecraft (Godwin) (1797–1851). *Frankenstein.*
Hood, Thomas (1799–1845). *The Song of the Shirt; The Bridge of Sighs; To The Great Unknown.*
Macaulay, Thomas Babington (Lord) (1800–59). *Lays of Ancient Rome; History of England.*

19th CENTURY
Newman, John Henry, Cardinal (1801–90). *The Dream of Gerontius.*
Surtees, Robert Smith (1803–64). *Handley Cross.*
Borrow, George (1803–1881). *Lavengro.*
Disraeli, Benjamin (Earl of Beaconsfield) (1804–81). *Coningsby; Sybil; Tancred.*
Browning, Elizabeth Barrett (1806–61). *Poems; Aurora Leigh.*
Mill, John Stuart (1806–1873). *Liberty.*
Darwin, Charles Robert (1809–82). *On the Origin of Species; The Descent of Man.*
Fitzgerald, Edward (1809–83). *Rubáiyát of Omar Khayyám.*
Gaskell, Mrs (Elizabeth Cleghorn Stevenson) (1810–65). *Mary Barton; Cranford; North and South.*
Thackeray, William Makepeace (1811–63). *Vanity Fair; The History of Henry Esmond Esq.*
Smiles, Samuel (1812–1904). *Self-Help.*
Lear, Edward (1812–88). *A Book of Nonsense; Nonsense Songs.*
Read, Charles (1814–84). *The Cloister and the Hearth.*
Trollope, Anthony (1815–82). *The six Barsetshire novels (The Warden; Barchester Towers; Doctor Thorne; Framley Parsonage; The Small House at Allington; The Last Chronicle of Barset).*
Brontë, (later Nicholls), Charlotte (1816–55). *Jane Eyre; Shirley; Vilette.*
Brontë, Emily Jane (1818–48). *Wuthering Heights.*
Ruskin, John (1819–1900). *Modern Painters.*
'Eliot, George' (Mary Ann [or Marian] Evans, later Mrs J. W. Cross) (1819–80). *Adam Bede; The Mill on the Floss; Silas Marner; Middlemarch.*
Kingsley, Charles (1819–75). *Westward Ho!; The Water Babies.*
Brontë, Anne (1820–49). *Tenant of Wildfell Hall.*
Arnold, Matthew (1822–88). *The Strayed Reveler; Poems.*
Collins, William Wilkie (1824–89). *The Woman in White; The Moonstone.*
Bagehot, Walter (1826–77). *The English Constitution.*
Meredith, George (1828–1909). *Modern Love; Diana of the Crossways.*
Rossetti, Dante Gabriel (1828–82). *Poems; Ballads and Sonnets.*
'Carroll, Lewis' (Rev. Charles Lutwidge Dodgson) (1832–98). *Alice's Adventures in Wonderland; Through The Looking Glass.*
Morris, William (1834–96). *News from Nowhere.*
Gilbert, Sir William Schwenck (1836–1911). *The Mikado; The Gondoliers, HMS Pinafore; The Pirates of Penzance; The Yeomen of the Guard; Patience.*
Swinburne, Algernon Charles (1837–1909). *Poems and Ballads; Rosamund.*
Hardy, Thomas (1840–1928). *Under The Greenwood Tree; Tess of the D'Urbervilles; Far From the Madding Crowd; The Return of the Native; The Mayor of Casterbridge; Jude the Obscure.*
Hudson, W(illiam) H(enry) (1841–1922). *Green Mansions.*

Bridges, Robert Seymour (1844–1930). *The Testament of Beauty.*
Hopkins, Gerard Manley (1844–89). *The Notebooks and Papers of Gerard Manley Hopkins.*
Stoker, Bram (Abraham) (1847–1912). *Dracula.*
Jefferies, Richard (1848–1887). *The Amateur Poacher.*
Stevenson, Robert Louis (1850–94). *Travels with a Donkey in the Cévennes; New Arabian Nights; Treasure Island; Strange Case of Dr Jekyll and Mr Hyde; Kidnapped; Catriona; The Black Arrow; The Master of Ballantrae; Weir of Hermiston (unfinished).*
Moore, George (1852–1933). *Esther Waters.*
Wilde, Oscar Fingal O'Flahertie Wills (1854–1900). *The Picture of Dorian Gray; Lady Windermere's Fan; The Importance of Being Ernest.*
Haggard, Sir Henry Rider (1856–1925). *King Solomon's Mines; She; Alain Quartermain.*
Shaw, George Bernard (1856–1950). *Plays Pleasant and Unpleasant (including Mrs Warren's Profession, Arms and the Man, Candida); Three Plays for Puritans (The Devil's Disciple, Caesar and Cleopatra and Captain Brassbound's Conversion); Man and Superman; John Bull's Other Island; Major Barbara; Androcles and the Lion; Pygmalion; Saint Joan; Essays in Fabian Socialism.*
Gissing, George (Robert) (1857–1903). *The Private Papers of Henry Ryecroft.*
Conrad, Joseph (né Teodor Józef Konrad Nalecz Korzeniowski) (1857–1924). *Almayer's Folly; An Outcast of the Islands; The Nigger of the 'Narcissus'; Lord Jim; Youth; Typhoon; Nostromo; The Secret Agent; Under Western Eyes.*
Doyle, Sir Arthur Conan (1859–1930). *The White Company; The Adventures of Sherlock Holmes; The Hound of the Baskervilles; The Exploits of Brigadier Gerard; The Lost World.*
Thompson, Francis (1859–1907). *The Hound of Heaven; The Kingdom of God.*
Housman, Alfred Edward (1859–1936). *A Shropshire Lad.*
Grahame, Kenneth (1859–1932). *The Wind in the Willows.*
Barrie, Sir James Matthew (1860–1937). *Quality Street; The Admirable Crichton; Peter Pan.*
Quiller-Couch, Sir Arthur Thomas ('Q') (1863–1944). *On the Art of Writing; Studies in Literature.*
Yeats, William Butler (1865–1939). *Collected Poems; The Tower; Last Poems; The Hour Glass.*
Wells, Herbert George (1866–1946). *The Invisible Man; The History of Mr Polly; Kipps; The Shape of Things to Come; The War of the Worlds.*
Murray, George Gilbert Aimé (1866–1957). *History of Ancient Greek Literature.*
Bennett, Enoch Arnold (1867–1931). *Anna of the Five Towns; The Old Wives' Tale; Clayhanger; Card; Riceyman Steps.*
Galsworthy, John (1867–1933). *The Forsyte Saga; Modern Comedy; The White Monkey.*
Douglas, Norman (1868–1952). *Old Calabria; South Wind.*
Belloc, Joseph Hilaire Pierre (1870–1953). *The Path to Rome; The Bad Child's Book of Beasts; Cautionary Tales.*
Synge, John Millington (1871–1909). *The Playboy of the Western World.*
Beerbohm, Sir Max (1872–1956). *Zuleika Dobson.*
Powys, John Cowper (1872–1963). *Weymouth Sands.*
Ford, Ford Madox (1873–1939). *The Good Soldier.*
De La Mare, Walter (1873–1956). *Poems; Come Hither; O Lovely England.*
Chesterton, Gilbert Keith (1874–1936). *The Inno-*

cence of Father Brown; The Ballad of The White Horse.

Churchill, Sir Winston Spencer (1874-1965). Life of Marlborough; The Second World War; A History of The English-Speaking Peoples; The World Crisis.

Maugham, William Somerset (1874-1965). Of Human Bondage; The Moon and Sixpence; The Razor's Edge.

Buchan, John (1st Baron Tweedsmuir) (1875-1940). Montrose; The Thirty-Nine Steps; Greenmantle; Prester John; Huntingtower.

Powys, Theodore Francis (1875-1953). Mr Weston's Good Wine.

Trevelyan, George Macaulay (1876-1962). History of England; English Social History.

Masefield, John (1878-1967). Salt-Water Ballads; The Everlasting Mercy; So Long to Learn; Jim Davis; Collected Poems.

Thomas, Edward (1878-1917). Poems.

Forster, Edward Morgan (1879-1970). Where Angels Fear to Tread; A Room with a View; Howard's End; A Passage to India.

O'Casey, Sean (1880-1964). Juno and the Paycock; The Plough and the Stars.

Wodehouse, Sir Pelham Grenville (1881-1975). Summer Lightning; Much Obliged Jeeves.

Joyce, James (1882-1941). Ulysses; Finnegans Wake; Portrait of the Artist as a Young Man.

Woolf (née Stephen), Virginia (1882-1941). The Voyage Out; Night and Day; Jacob's Room; The Years.

Milne, Alan Alexander (1882-1956). Winnie the Pooh; The House at Pooh Corner.

Keynes, John Maynard (Baron) (1883-1946). The Economic Consequences of the Peace; The General Theory of Employment.

Mackenzie, Sir Compton (1883-1972). Whisky Galore; Sinister Street.

Lewis, (Percy) Wyndham (1884-1957). The Apes of God.

Ransome, Arthur Michell (1884-1967). Swallows and Amazons.

Walpole, Sir Hugh Seymour (1884-1941). Herries Chronicle.

Flecker, James Elroy (1884-1915). The Golden Journey to Samarkand.

Lawrence, David Herbert (1885-1930). Sons and Lovers; Love Poems and Others.

Sassoon, Siegfried (1886-1967). Memoirs of a Fox-Hunting Man; Memoirs of an Infantry Officer.

Sitwell, Dame Edith (1887-1964). Collected Poems; Aspects of Modern Poetry.

Brooke, Rupert Chawner (1887-1915). 1914 and Other Poems; Letters from America.

Muir, Edwin (1887-1959). First Poems.

Cary, (Arthur) Joyce (Lunel) (1888-1957). The Horse's Mouth.

Eliot, Thomas Stearns (1888-1965). Murder in the Cathedral; The Waste Land.

Lawrence, Thomas Edward (later Shaw) (1888-1935). Seven Pillars of Wisdom.

Mansfield, Katherine (Beauchamp) (1888-1923). In a German Pension: The Dove's Nest and Other Stories.

Toynbee, Arnold Joseph (1889-1975). A Study of History.

Herbert, Sir Alan Patrick (1890-1971). Misleading Cases.

Rosenberg, Isaac (1890-1918). Poems.

Christie, Agatha Mary Clarissa (1891-1976). The Murder of Roger Ackroyd.

Tolkien, J(ohn) R(onald) R(euel) (1892-1973). The Hobbit; The Lord of the Rings.

Owen, Wilfred (1893-1918). Poems.

Sayers, Dorothy Leigh (1893-1957). The Nine Tailors.

Priestley, John Boynton (1894-1985). The Good Companions; The Linden Tree; An Inspector Calls.

Huxley, Aldous Leonard (1894-1963). Brave New World; Point Counter Point.

Hartley, Leslie Poles (1895-1972). The Go-Between.

Graves, Robert Ranke (b. 1895). I Claudius; Goodbye to All That.

Blunden, Edmund (1896-1974). Poems 1914-1930.

Sheriff, Robert Cedric (1896-1975). Journey's End.

Williamson, Henry (1897-1977). Tarka the Otter.

Coward, Sir Noel (1899-1973). Hay Fever; Private Lives; Blithe Spirit.

Hughes, Richard (1900-1976). A High Wind in Jamaica.

20th CENTURY

Orwell, George (Eric Arthur Blair) (1903-50). Animal Farm; 1984.

Waugh, Evelyn (1903-66). Scoop; Men at Arms; Officers and Gentlemen; Unconditional Surrender; Brideshead Revisited.

Day-Lewis, Cecil (1904-72). Collected Poems.

Isherwood, Christopher (b. 1904). Goodbye to Berlin.

Greene, Graham (b. 1904). Brighton Rock; Our Man in Havana; The Power and the Glory.

Green, Henry (pseud. of Henry Vincent Yorke) (1905-73). Living; Loving; Concluding.

Snow, Sir Charles Percy (1905-80). Strangers and Brothers.

Bates, Herbert Ernest (1905-74). 'Flying-Officer X' Stories.

Powell, Anthony (b. 1905). The Music of Time novel sequence.

Beckett, Samuel (b. 1906). Waiting for Godot.

Betjeman, John (1906-84). Mount Zion; Collected Poems.

Fry, Christopher (b. 1907). The Lady's Not for Burning; Venus Observed.

MacNeice, Louis (1907-63). Autumn Journal; Collected Poems.

Auden, Wystan Hugh (1907-73). Poems; Look Stranger; The Dance of Death.

Fleming, Ian (Lancaster) (1908-65). Dr No; Goldfinger.

Lowry, (Clarence) Malcolm (1909-57). Under the Volcano.

Golding, William (b. 1911). Lord of the Flies.

Rattigan, Terence (1911-77). French Without Tears; The Winslow Boy.

Durrell, Lawrence (b. 1912). Selected Poems; The Alexandria Quartet.

Thomas, Dylan (1914-53). Portrait of the Artist as a Young Dog; Under Milk Wood.

Burgess, Anthony (b. 1917). A Clockwork Orange; Napoleon Symphony.

Wilson, Angus (b. 1913). Hemlock and After; The Old Men at the Zoo.

Lessing, Doris (May) (b. 1919). Children of Violence; The Golden Notebooks.

Murdoch, Iris (b. 1919). An Unofficial Rose; The Italian Girl; An Accidental Man.

Amis, Kingsley (b. 1922). Lucky Jim.

Larkin, Phillip (b. 1922). High Windows.

Osborne, John (b. 1929). Look Back in Anger.

Arden, John (b. 1930). Serjeant Musgrave's Dance.

Hughes, Ted (b. 1930). The Hawk in the Rain; Lupercal.

Pinter, Harold (b. 1930). The Caretaker; The Birthday Party.

Wesker, Arnold (b. 1932). *Roots; Chips with Everything.*
Stoppard, Tom (b. 1937). *Rosencrantz and Guildenstern are Dead; Dirty Linen.*
Ayckbourn, Alan (b. 1939). *How the Other Half Loves; The Norman Conquests.*
Rushdie, Salman (b. 1947). *Midnight's Children; The Satanic Verses.*

Poets Laureate

The office of poet laureate is one of great honour, conferred on a poet of distinction. In 1616, James I granted a pension to the poet Ben Jonson, but it was not until 1668 that the laureateship was created as a royal office. When the position of poet laureate falls vacant, the prime minister is responsible for putting forth names for a new laureate, to be chosen by the sovereign. The sovereign then commands the Lord Chamberlain to appoint the poet laureate, and he does so by issung a warrant to the laureate-elect. The Chamberlain also arranges for the appointment – for life – to be announced in the *London Gazette.*

John Dryden (1631–1700; laureate 1668–88)
Thomas Shadwell (1642?–92; laureate 1688–92)
Nahum Tate (1652–1715; laureate 1692–1715)
Nicholas Rowe (1674–1718; laureate 1715–18)
Laurence Eusden (1688–1730; laureate 1718–30)
Colley Cibber (1671–1757; laureate 1730–57)
William Whitehead (1715–85; laureate 1757–85)
  (Appointed after Thomas Gray declined the offer)
Thomas Warton (1728–90; laureate 1785–90)
Henry James Pye (1745–1813; laureate 1790–1813)
Robert Southey (1774–1843; laureate 1813–43)
William Wordsworth (1770–1850; laureate 1843–50)
Alfred, Lord Tennyson (1809–92; laureate 1850–92)
  (Appointed after Samuel Rogers declined the offer)
Alfred Austin (1835–1913; laureate 1896–1913)
Robert Bridges (1844–1930; laureate 1913–30)
John Masefield (1878–1967; laureate 1930–67)
Cecil Day-Lewis (1904–72; laureate 1968–72)
Sir John Betjeman (1906–84; laureate 1972–84)
Ted Hughes (b. 1930 laureate 1984–)

Some well-known writers

Listed by country.

ARGENTINA
Borges, Jorge Luis (b. 1899). *The Labyrinth; Ficciones.*

AUSTRIA
Kafka, Franz (1883–1924). *The Trial; The Castle.*

BELGIUM
Maeterlinck, Maurice (1862–1949). *The Blue Bird.*

CANADA
Atwood, Margaret (b. 1939). *Surfacing; The Handmaid's Tale.*

CHILE
Neruda, Pablo (pseudo. of Neftali Ricardo Reyes) (b. 1904). *Poems.*

COLOMBIA
Marques, Gabriel Garcia (b. 1920). *One Hundred Years of Solitude.*

DENMARK
Anderson, Hans Christian (1807–75). *The Emperor's New Clothes.*

FRANCE
Rabelais, François (1494?–1553?). *Gargantua; Pantagruel.*
Corneille, Pierre (1606–84). *Le Cid.*
Molière, *nom de théâtre* of Jean-Baptiste Poquelin (1622–73). *Tartuffe; La Malade Imaginaire.*
Racine, Jean (1639–99). *Phèdre.*
Voltaire, pseud. of François-Marie Arouet (1694–1778). *Candide.*
Stendhal, pseud. of Henri Beyle (1783–1842). *The Red and the Black.*
Balzac, Honoré de (1799–1850). *La Comedie Humaine.*
Dumas, Alexandre (père) (1802–70). *The Three Musketeers.*
Hugo, Victor Marie (1802–85). *Les Misérables.*
Baudelaire, Charles-Pierre (1821–67). *Les Fleurs du Mal.*
Flaubert, Gustave (1821–1880). *Madame Bovary.*
Zola, Emile (1840–1902). *Nana; Germinal.*
Maupassant, Guy de (1850–93). *Stories.*
Rimbaud, Arthur (1854–91). *Illuminations.*
Gide, André (1869–1951). *Strait is the Gate.*
Proust, Marcel (1871–1922). *Remembrance of Things Past.*
Colette, Sidonie Gabrielle (1873–1954). *Cheri.*
Sartre, Jean-Paul (1905–80). *The Age of Reason.*
Genet, Jean (b. 1910). *The Thief's Journal; The Maids.*

GERMANY
Goethe, Johann Wolfgang von (1749–1832). *Faust.*
Schiller, Friedrich (1759–1805). *Poems; Wallenstein.*
Heine, Heinrich (1797–1856). *Poems.*
Mann, Thomas (1875–1955). *Death in Venice; The Magic Mountain.*
Rilke, Rainer Maria (1875–1926). *Poems.*
Hesse, Hermann (1877–1962). *Steppenwolf.*
Brecht, Bertolt (1898–1956). *Mother Courage.*
Grass, Günter (b. 1927). *The Tin Drum.*

INDIA
Tagore, Radindranath (1861–1941). *Poems.*

ITALY
Dante Alighieri (1265–1321). *Divine Comedy.*
Petrarch (Petrarca), Francesco (1304–74). *Sonnets.*
Machiavelli, Niccolo (1469–1527). *The Prince.*
D'Annunzio, Gabriele (1863–1938). *Francesca da Rimini.*
Pirandello, Luigi (1867–1936). *Six Characters in Search of an Author; The Rules of the Game.*
Lampedusa, Giuseppe Tomasi de (1896–1957). *The Leopard.*
Silone, Ignazio, pseud. of Secondo Tranquilli (1900–78). *Bread and Wine.*
Moravia, Alberto, pseud. of Alberto Pincherle (b. 1907). *The Woman of Rome.*
Calvino, Italo (b. 1923). *Adam One Afternoon and Other Stories.*

An accolade to Friedrich von Schiller in Rome in 1859 to celebrate his 100th birthday. (Popperfoto)

JAPAN

Murasaki Shikibu (c. 980–c. 1030). *Tale of Genji.*
Sei Shonagon (fl. 1000). *The Pillow-Book of Sei Shonagon.*

NORWAY

Ibsen, Henrik (1828–1906). *Ghosts; A Doll's House; Hedda Gabler.*
Hamsun, Knut (1859–1952). *The Growth of the Soil.*

RUSSIA

Pushkin, Aleksandr Sergeyevich (1799–1837). *Eugene Onegin; Stories.*
Turgenev, Ivan (1818–83). *A Month in the Country.*
Dostoyevsky, Fyodor Mikhailovich (1821–1881). *The Idiot; The Brothers Karamazov; Crime and Punishment.*
Tolstoy, Count Leo Nikolayevich (1828–1910). *War and Peace; Anna Karenina.*
Chekhov, Anton Pavlovich (1860–1904). *The Seagull; The Cherry Orchard.*
Pasternak, Boris Leonidovich (1890–1960). *Dr Zhivago.*
Solzhenitsyn, Aleksandr Isayevich (b. 1918). *One Day in the Life of Ivan Denisovich.*

SPAIN

Cervantes, Saavedra, Miguel de (1547–1616). *Don Quixote.*
Lorca, Federico Garcia (1898–1936). *Poems; Blood Wedding.*

SWEDEN

Strindberg, August (1849–1912). *Miss Julie.*

UNITED STATES

Hawthorne, Nathaniel (1804–64). *The Scarlet Letter.*
Longfellow, Henry Wadsworth (1807–82). *The Wreck of the Hesperus; The Song of Hiawatha.*
Poe, Edgar Allan (1809–49). *The Murders in the Rue Morgue; The Raven.*
Thoreau, Henry David (1817–62). *Walden.*
Melville, Herman (1819–91). *Moby Dick; Billy Budd.*
Whitman, Walt (1819–92). *Leaves of Grass.*
Twain, Mark (Samuel Langhorne Clemens) (1835–1910). *Adventures of Tom Sawyer; Adventures of Huckleberry Finn.*
James, Henry (1843–1916). *The Turn of the Screw; The Golden Bowl; Portrait of a Lady.*
Frost, Robert (1874–1963). *Poems.*
London, Jack (John Griffith London) (1876–1916). *The Call of the Wild; White Fang.*
O'Neill, Eugene (1888–1953). *The Iceman Cometh; Long Day's Journey into Night.*
Fitzgerald, F. Scott (1896–1940). *The Great Gatsby; Tender is the Night; The Last Tycoon.*
Faulkner, William (1897–1962). *The Sound and the Fury.*
Hemingway, Ernest (1898–1961). *A Farewell to Arms; For Whom the Bell Tolls; The Old Man and the Sea.*
Nabokov, Vladimir (b. 1899). *Pale Fire; Lolita.*
Pound, Ezra (b. 1900). *Pisan Cantos; Hugh Selwyn Mauberley.*
Steinbeck, John (1902–68). *The Grapes of Wrath; Of Mice and Men.*
O'Hara, John (1905–70). *Appointment in Samarra; Pal Joey.*
Williams, Tennessee (1911–83). *A Streetcar Named Desire; The Glass Menagerie.*
Bellow, Saul (b. 1915). *Herzog; The Dean's December.*

Miller, Arthur (b. 1915). *Death of a Salesman; The Crucible.*
Lowell, Robert (1917–80). *Poems.*
Mailer, Norman (b. 1923). *The Naked and the Dead.*
Roth, Philip (b. 1933). *Portnoy's Complaint; Letting Go.*

Nobel prizewinners in literature since 1950

1950 Bertrand Russell, British
1951 Pär F. Lagerkvist, Swedish
1952 François Mauriac, French
1953 Sir Winston Churchill, British
1954 Ernest Hemingway, US
1955 Halldor K. Laxness, Icelandic
1956 Juan Ramon Jimenez, Puerto Rican-Span.
1957 Albert Camus, French
1958 Boris L. Pasternak, Russian (Prize declined)
1959 Salvatore Quasimodo, Italian
1960 Saint-Jean Perse, French
1961 Ivo Andric, Yugoslavian
1962 John Steinbeck, US
1963 Giorgos Seferis, Greek
1964 Jean-Paul Sartre, French (Prize declined)
1965 Mikhail Sholokhov, Russian
1966 Samuel Joseph Agnon, Israeli
     Nelly Sachs, Swedish
1967 Miguel Angel Asturias, Guate.
1968 Yasunari Kawabata, Japanese
1969 Samuel Beckett, Irish
1970 Aleksandr I. Solzhenitsyn, Russian
1971 Pablo Naruda, Chilean
1972 Heinrich Boll, W. German
1973 Patrick White, Australian
1974 Eyvind Johnson, Harry Edmund Martinson, both Swedish
1975 Eugenio Montale, Italian
1976 Saul Bellow, US
1977 Vincente Aleixandre, Spanish
1978 Isaac Bashevis Singer, US (Yiddish)
1979 Odysseus Elytis, Greek
1980 Czeslaw Milosz, Polish-US
1981 Elias Canetti, Bulgarian-British
1982 Gabriel Garcia Marquez, Colombian-Mex.
1983 William Golding, British
1984 Jaroslav Seifert, Czechoslovakian
1985 Claude Simon, France
1986 Wole Soyinka, Nigeria
1987 Joseph Brodsky, US
1988 Naguib Mahfouz, Egypt

Booker prizewinners

1969 P. H. Newby, *Something to Answer For*
1970 Bernice Rubens, *The Elected Member*
1971 V. S. Naipaul, *In a Free State*
1972 John Berger, *G*
1973 J. G. Farrell, *The Siege of Krishnapur*
1974 (joint prizewinners)
     Nadine Gordimer, *The Conservationist*
     Stanley Middleton, *Holiday*
1975 Ruth Prawer Jhabvala, *Heat and Dust*
1976 David Storey, *Saville*
1977 Paul Scott, *Staying On*
1978 Iris Murdoch, *The Sea, The Sea*
1979 Penelope Fitzgerald, *Offshore*

Wole Sayinka, the first African to win the Nobel Prize for Literature, arriving at Lagos Airport. (Popperfoto)

1980 William Golding, *Rites of Passage*
1981 Salman Rushdie, *Midnight's Children*
1982 Thomas Keneally, *Schindler's Ark*
1983 J. M. Coetzee, *Life and Times of Michael K.*
1984 Anita Brookner, *Hotel du Lac*
1985 Keri Hulme, *The Bone People*
1986 Kingsley Amis, *The Old Devils*
1987 Penelope Lively, *Moon Tiger*
1988 Peter Carey, *Oscar and Lucinda*

Whitbread Literary Award-winners

1971 **Novel:** Gerda Charles, *The Destiny Waltz*
   Biography: Michael Meyer, *Henrik Ibsen*
   Poetry: Geoffrey Hill, *Mercian Hymns*
1972 **Novel:** Susan Hill, *The Bird of Night*
   Biography: James Pope-Hennessey, *Trollope*
   Children's Book: Rumer Godden, *The Diddakoi*
1973 **Novel:** Shiva Naipaul, *The Chip Chip Gatherers*
   Biography: John Wilson, *CB: A Life of Sir Henry Campbell-Bannerman*
   Children's Book: Alan Aldridge and William Plomer, *The Butterfly Ball and the Grasshopper's Feast*
1974 **Novel:** Iris Murdoch, *The Sacred and Profane Love Machine*
   Biography: Andrew Boyle, *Poor Dear Brendan*
   Joint Children's Books: Russell Hoban and Quentin Blake, *How Tom Beat Captain*

Najork and His Hired Sportsmen
Jill Paton Walsh, *The Emperor's Winding Sheet*
First Book: Clare Tomalin, *The Life and Death of Mary Wollstonecraft*
1975 **Novel:** William McIlvanney, *Docherty*
   Autobiography: Helen Corke, *In Our Infancy*
   First Book: Ruth Spalding, *The Improbable Puritan: A Life of Bulstrode Whitelock*
1976 **Novel:** William Trevor, *The Children of Dynmouth*
   Biography: Winifred Gerin, *Elizabeth Gaskell*
   Children's Book: Penelope Lively, *A Stitch in Time*
1977 **Novel:** Beryl Bainbridge, *Injury Time*
   Biography: Nigel Nicolson, *Mary Curzon*
   Children's Book: Shelagh Macdonald, *No End to Yesterday*
1978 **Novel:** Paul Theroux, *Picture Palace*
   Biography: John Grigg, *Lloyd George: The People's Champion*
   Children's Book: Philippa Pearce, *The Battle of Bubble and Squeak*
1979 **Novel:** Jennifer Johnston, *The Old Jest*
   Autobiography: Penelope Mortimer, *About Time*
   Children's Novel: Peter Dickinson, *Tulku*
1980 **Novel:** David Lodge, *How Far Can You Go?*
   Biography: David Newsome, *On the Edge of Paradise: A. C. Benson the Diarist*
   Children's Novel: Leon Garfield, *John Diamond*
   Book of the Year: David Lodge, *How Far Can You Go?*

1981 **Novel:** Maurice Leitch, *Silver's City*
Biography: Nigel Hamilton, *Monty: The Making of a General*
Children's Novel: Jane Gardam, *The Hollow Land*
First Novel: William Boyd, *A Good Man in Africa*
1982 **Novel:** John Wain, *Young Shoulders*
Biography: Edward Crankshaw, *Bismarck*
Children's Novel: W. J. Corbett, *The Song of Pentecost*
First Novel: Bruce Chatwin, *On the Black Hill*
1983 **Novel:** William Trevor, *Fools of Fortune*
Joint Biography: Victoria Glendinning, *Vita*
Kenneth Rose, *King George V*
Children's Novel: Roald Dahl, *The Witches*
First Novel: John Fuller, *Flying to Nowhere*
1984 **Novel:** Christopher Hope, *Kruger's Alp*
First Novel: James Buchan, *A Parish of Rich Women*
Biography: Peter Ackroyd, *T. S. Eliot*
Children's Novel: Barbara Willard, *Queen of the Pharisees Children*
Short Story: Diana Rowe, *Tomorrow is Our Permanent Address*
1985 **Novel:** Peter Ackroyd, *Hawksmoor*
First Novel: Jeanette Winterson, *Oranges Are Not the Only Fruit*
Children's Novel: Janni Howker, *The Nature of the Beast*
Biography: Ben Pimlott, *Hugh Dalton*
Poetry: Douglas Dunn, *Elegies*
Book of the Year: Douglas Dunn, *Elegies*
1986 **Novel:** Kazuo Ishiguro, *An Artist of the Floating World*
First Novel: Jim Crace, *Continent*
Children's Novel: Andrew Taylor, *The Coal House*
Poetry: Peter Reading, *Stet*
Biography: Richard Mabey, *Gilbert White*
Book of the Year: Kazuo Ishiguro, *An Artist of the Floating World*
1987 **Novel:** Ian McEwan, *The Child in Time*
First Novel: Francis Wyndham, *The Other Garden*
Children's Novel: Geraldine McCaughrean, *A Little Later than the Angels*
Poetry: Seamus Heaney, *The Haw Lantern*
Biography: Christopher Nolan, *Under the Eye of the Clock*
Book of the Year: Christopher Nolan, *Under the Eye of the Clock*
1988 **Novel:** Salman Rushdie, *The Satanic Verses*
First Novel: Paul Sayer, *The Comforts of Madness*
Children's Novel: Judy Allen, *Awaiting Developments*
Poetry: Peter Porter, *The Automatic Oracle*
Biography: A. N. Wilson, *Tolstoy*
Book of the Year: Paul Sayer, *The Comforts of Madness*

Pulitzer Fiction Award-winners

1917 No award
1918 Ernest Poole, *His Family*
1919 Booth Tarkington, *The Magnificent Ambersons*
1920 No award

1921 Edith Wharton, *The Age of Innocence*
1922 Booth Tarkington, *Alice Adams*
1923 Willa Cather, *One of Ours*
1924 Margaret Wilson, *The Able McLaughlins*
1925 Edna Ferber, *So Big*
1926 Sinclair Lewis, *Arrowsmith*
1927 Louis Bromfield, *Early Autumn*
1928 Thornton Wilder, *The Bridge at San Luis Rey*
1929 Julia Peterkin, *Scarlet Sister Mary*
1930 Oliver La Farge, *Laughing Boy*
1931 Margaret Ayer Barnes, *Years of Grace*
1932 Pearl S. Buck, *The Good Earth*
1933 T. S. Stribling, *The Store*
1934 Caroline Miller, *Lamb in His Bosom*
1935 Josephine Winslow Johnson, *Now in November*
1936 Harold L. Davis, *Honey in the Horn*
1937 Margaret Mitchell, *Gone With the Wind*
1938 John Phillips Marquand, *The Late George Apley*
1939 Marjorie Kinnan Rawlings, *The Yearling*
1940 John Steinbeck, *The Grapes of Wrath*
1941 No award
1942 Ellen Glasgow, *In This Our Life*
1943 Upton Sinclair, *Dragon's Teeth*
1944 Martin Flavin, *Journey in the Dark*
1945 John Hersey, *A Bell For Adano*
1946 No award
1947 Robert Penn Warren, *All the King's Men*
1948 James A. Michener, *Tales of the South Pacific*
1949 James Gould Cozzens, *Guard of Honor*
1950 A. B. Guthrie, Jr, *The Way West*
1951 Conrad Richter, *The Town*
1952 Herman Wouk, *The Caine Mutiny*
1953 Ernest Hemingway, *The Old Man and the Sea*
1954 No award
1955 William Faulkner, *A Fable*
1956 Mackinley Kantor, *Andersonville*
1957 No award
1958 James Agee, *A Death in the Family*
1959 Robert Lewis Taylor, *The Travels of Jamie McPheeters*
1960 Allen Drury, *Advise and Consent*
1961 Harper Lee, *To Kill a Mockingbird*
1962 Edwin O'Connor, *The Edge of Sadness*
1963 William Faulkner, *The Reivers*
1964 No award
1965 Shirley Ann Grau, *The Keepers of the House*
1966 Katherine Anne Porter, *The Collected Stories of Katherine Anne Porter*
1967 Bernard Malamud, *The Fixer*
1968 William Styron, *The Confession of Nat Turner*
1969 N. Scott Momaday, *House Made of Dawn*
1970 Jean Stafford, *Collected Stories*
1971 No award
1972 Wallace Stegner, *Angle of Repose*
1973 Eudora Welty, *The Optimist's Daughter*
1974 No award
1975 Michael Shaara, *The Killer Angels*
1976 Saul Bellow, *Humboldt's Gift*
1977 No award
1978 James Alan McPherson, *Elbow Room*
1979 John Cheever, *The Stories of John Cheever*
1980 Norman Mailer, *Executioner's Song*
1981 John Kennedy Toole, *Confederacy of Dunces*
1982 John Updike, *Rabbit is Rich*
1983 Alice Walker, *The Color Purple*
1984 William Kennedy, *Ironweed*
1985 Alison Lurie, *Foreign Affairs*
1986 Larry McMurtry, *Lonesome Dove*
1987 Peter Taylor, *A Summons to Memphis*
1988 Toni Morrison, *Beloved*

PHILOSOPHY

'Philosophy' is a word derived from the Greek words meaning 'love of wisdom', and philosophy in the Western world began with the ancient Greeks. It is used to cover a wide area: the scientific arrangement of those principles which underlie all knowledge and existence.

The sphere of philosophy can be roughly delineated by stating how it is distinct from other areas of thought. It differs from religion since its quest for the underlying causes and principles of being and thinking does not depend on dogma and faith; and from science, since it does not depend solely on fact, but leans heavily on speculation. Its interrelation with both science and religion can be seen in the large number of philosophers who were also either theologians or scientists, and the few such as Blaise Pascal and Roger Bacon, who were all three. Philosophy developed from religion, becoming distinct when thinkers sought truth independent of theological considerations. Science in turn developed from philosophy and eventually all the branches of science from physics to psychology broke away – psychology being the last to do so in the 20th century.

Philosophy can be split into three particularly important categories: ethics, metaphysics and epistemology. Such a division leaves out some important areas of philosophical speculation, including logic, which is the increasingly formalized technique of exact analysis of reasoning, but it serves to introduce a few of the most important writings.

Ethics is the study of human conduct and morality. Philosophers have held many points of view about ideal human conduct but their opinions tend to resolve into an opposition between two main schools. One school, the 'Idealist', considers that the goodness or badness of a course of action must be judged by standards dictated from the other world – from God or from some force for good – external to man. The second school, who might be grouped under the term 'Utilitarians', feels that the effect which a course of action produces in this world makes it good or bad.

The Idealist school was represented quite early in the history of Western philosophy by the Greek philosopher Plato, who wrote in the 4th century BC. Plato, in a series of dialogues, has his ex-teacher Socrates discuss the problems of philosophy with friends and opponents.

Socrates' procedure is to draw out the wisdom from the gentleman with whom he is discussing the question. Socrates, in fact, rarely makes a statement, rather he asks questions which compel the others either to make the statement he wants them to make or to appear foolish.

In three of these dialogues, especially – *The Protagoras, The Phaedo*, and *The Gorgias* – Plato develops a system of ethics which is essentially idealistic. Socrates propounds that the good comes from the realm of 'ideas' or 'forms'. This is a sort of perfect other world which projects distorted copies of everything good down to the world we have to contend with. For Plato, individual conduct is good in so far as it is governed by the emanated spirit from above. Plato does not, of course, use the word 'heaven' for the world of ideas, but he was adapted – after being modified by Aristotle, Plotinus, and others – for Christian purposes. One of the ways in which the knowledge from the realm of the 'ideas' was communicated to mortals was by a voice or 'demon'. In the *Apology*, Socrates describes how this individual conscience has prevented him from wrongdoing.

Another important work which has to be classed with the Idealists is Aristotle's *Nicomachean Ethics*. Aristotle was a pupil of Plato and, like Plato, he thinks of the good as a divine emanation, or overflow, but his ethics have a more 'practical' bent. He equates happiness with the good and is responsible for the doctrine of the 'golden mean'. This states that every virtue is a mean, or middle-point, between two vices. Generosity, for instance, is the mean between prodigality and stinginess.

The same tendency to give idealism a practical bent is found in a more modern philosopher, Immanuel Kant. His idealistic aspect may be compared with Socrates' 'demon'. Kant maintains that there is in each man a voice which guides him as to right or wrong.

But the part of Kant's ethics which is most famous is that connected with the phrase 'categorical imperative'. In Kant's own words: 'Act only according to a maxim by which you can at the same time will that it shall become a general law'. In other words, before acting in a certain way, the individual must ask himself: 'If everybody did the same thing what would be the moral condition of the universe?'

Immanuel Kant, 18th century philosopher of the Idealist school. (Popperfoto)

This is a practical consideration in the sense that it concerns the *result* of an action, but Kant's concern is for the morality of the universe and not its happiness or earthly welfare. Kant's principal ethical works are *The Critique of Pure Reason, The Critique of Practical Reason, The Metaphysics of Morality,* and *The Metaphysics of Ethics.*

The opposing group of 'utilitarian' ethics is concerned with the matter of earthly welfare. The earliest Western philosopher to represent this tradition is Epicurus, a Greek philosopher of the 4th century BC.

Instead of deriving ideas of right and wrong from above, as did the Socratics for example, Epicurus maintained that 'we call pleasure the beginning and end of the blessed life'. The term 'Epicurean' was used – and often still is used – to describe one who indulges in excessive pleasure, but this usage is neither accurate nor just. Epicurus did not condone excesses. On the contrary, he said that pleasure was only good when moderate or 'passive'. 'Dynamic' pleasure, which caused painful after-effects, was not good.

The utilitarian tradition has on the whole had more adherents than the idealistic tradition in modern philosophy. Jeremy Bentham, for example, writing in the 18th century, acknowledged his debt to Epicurus in his *Principles of Morals and Legislation.* Bentham agreed that pain and pleasure were the 'sovereign masters' governing man's conduct. He added to this a doctrine of *utility* which argued that 'the greatest happiness of the greatest number is the measure of right and wrong'.

John Stuart Mill is perhaps the most famous of the Utilitarians. He extended Bentham's doctrines pointing out that there were different *qualities* of pleasure and pain; and that 'some *kinds* of pleasure are more valuable than others'. These articles were later put out in a book called *Utilitarianism.*

In the USA the Utilitarians made an impact on the Pragmatists, who held that 'the *right* is only the expedient in our way of thinking' – to quote William James, whose *Pragmatism* is the best-known book produced by this school.

Metaphysics. The term 'metaphysics' originated as the title of one of Aristotle's treatises. It probably meant only that he wrote it after his *Physics,* but it was once thought to signify study beyond the realm of physics. Today it is usually employed to describe the speculation as to the ultimate nature of reality and the structure of the universe.

The sort of questions asked by metaphysicians concern the origin and condition of the universe in which man lives, and, as we might expect, they came up early in the history of philosophy. Before Aristotle had invented the term 'metaphysics' – as early as the 6th century BC – pre-Socratic Greek philosophers were offering their solutions of the mysteries of the universe.

Much of the speculation of these pre-Socratic philosophers was centred on speculation about the four *elements* which they thought made up the universe. Empedocles, who, according to legend, threw himself into the volcano at Mt Etna to prove his immortality – and failed – first defined earth, air, fire and water as the four basic elements. Others attempted to make one of these the most important, or *primary,* element from which the others were derived. Thales – one of the seven wise men of Greece – thought water was the primary element. Heraclitus' primary element was fire. Anaximander

reasoned that none of the four was primary. They must, he said, exist in perpetual balance.

Epistemology is the study of the nature, grounds and validity of man's knowing – how we come to know and how far we can rely on what we think we have discovered.

Some epistemologists assert that knowledge is born in the individual and has only to be drawn forth. The other point of view is that at birth the mind is a *tabula rasa* – blank sheet – on which knowledge is imprinted.

The first school is represented classically by Plato. In the *Theaetetus* especially, he discusses various theories of knowledge and discards those built on the shifting sands of sense perception. The senses are, he feels, too fallible. True knowledge comes from those general notions which are derived from the realm of the *ideas* – which the soul possesses prior to birth.

The classic representative of the second school is John Locke – a 17th-century English philosopher. In his *Essay Concerning Human Understanding,* Locke defines what is really the opposite point of view to Plato's. He is the pioneer proponent of the *tabula rasa.* Locke regards the mind at birth as comparable to an empty cabinet with two compartments. As we live, one compartment is filled with our *perceptions* and the other with our *sensations.* From these two combined we get our *ideas.*

This theory tends to make knowledge a matter of experience and mental processing rather than one of religious insight. As one might expect, Locke's theories are important influences in those fields which investigate the processes of mental activity – such as psychology and education.

Philosophical Terms

a posteriori Used to describe knowledge that comes from experience.

a priori Used to describe knowledge that can be acquired independently of experience through pure reason.

aesthetics The science of feelings and sensations; a branch of philosophy concerned with value – judgements about beauty and taste, especially in art.

analytic A system of logical analysis; that which discovers the function of pure reason; describes a judgement whose truth is found by analysing the concepts involved.

axiom A necessary and self-evident proposition, requiring no proof.

causality The relationship between a cause and its effect.

deduction The act of reaching a conclusion by arguing from the general to the particular.

dialectic Means of discovering the truth by proceeding from a thesis to a denial of it or antithesis and finally reconciling the two through a synthesis.

empirical Knowledge derived from experience rather than by logic.

epistemology Branch of philosophy that attempts to answer questions about the nature of knowledge and the means by which it is acquired. Study of the origins of human knowledge.

ethics Branch of inquiry that attempts to answer questions about right and wrong, good and evil; pertaining to how human life should be lived.

induction The logic of drawing general conclusions from particular instances.

logic Branch of philosophy (and especially mathematics) that, by abstracting the subject matter of statements and deductive arguments, seeks to investigate their structure and form.

metaphysics Branch of philosophy concerned with systems of ideas that attempt to explain a general theory of the universe and man's place in it, relying on *a priori* arguments rather than empirical proofs.

paradox, logical Any conclusion that at first sounds ridiculous but has an argument to sustain it; e.g. the Cretan philosopher Epimenides said 'All Cretans are liars.' As he was Cretan himself, is his statement true or false?

predestination Postulation that all the events of a human's life are determined beforehand.

sense datum (data) What one actually sees, hears, touches, smells, tastes of an object, from which the receiver of such data projects his understanding of and identification of the whole object.

sophistry Containing a fallacious argument.

synthesis The outcome of the confrontation of two arguments, by which a truth is discovered.

teleology Argument or theory that postulates that things can be explained better in terms of what they will become rather than what they are now or have been.

thesis A proposition or argument.

value-judgement Assessment of a thing's worth in aesthetic terms.

Schools and Theories

Since the days of the early Greeks, philosophers have been divided into different schools and have advanced opposing theories. Among the many basic outlooks and theories not already discussed but which have developed since Thales of Miletus (624–550 BC) first questioned the nature of ultimate reality, the following may be listed:

Absolutism: the theory that there is an ultimate reality in which all differences are reconciled.

Agnosticism: the position that the ultimate answer to all fundamental enquiries is that we do not know.

Altruism: the principle of living and acting in the interest of others rather than oneself.

Antinomianism: the view that ordinary moral laws are not applicable to Christians, whose lives are governed, it is said, solely by divine grace.

Asceticism: the belief that withdrawal from the physical world into the inner world of the spirit is the highest good attainable.

Atheism: rejection of the concept of God as a workable hypothesis.

Atomism: the belief that the entire universe is composed of distinct and indivisible units.

Conceptualism: the doctrine that universal ideas are neither created by finite (human) minds, nor

entirely apart from an absolute mind (God).

Critical idealism: the concept that man cannot determine whether there is anything beyond his own experience.

Critical realism: the theory that reality is tripartite, that in addition to the mental and physical aspects of reality, there is a third aspect called essences.

Criticism: the theory that the path to knowledge lies midway between dogmatism and scepticism.

Determinism: the belief that the universe follows a fixed or pre-determined pattern.

Dialectical materialism: the theory that reality is strictly material and is based on a struggle between opposing forces, with occasional interludes of harmony.

Dogmatism: assertion of a belief without authoritative support.

Dualism: the belief that the world consists of two radically independent and absolute elements, e.g. good and evil, spirit and matter.

Egoism: in ethics the belief that the serving of one's own interests is the highest end.

Empiricism: rejection of all *a priori* knowledge in favour of experience and induction.

Evolutionism: the concept of the universe as a progression of interrelated phenomena.

Existentialism: denial of objective universal values – man must create values for himself through action; the self is the ultimate reality.

Fatalism: the doctrine that what will happen will happen and nothing we do or do not do will make any difference.

Hedonism: the doctrine that pleasure is the highest good.

Humanism: any system that regards human interest and the human mind as paramount in the universe.

Hylozoism: the view that all objects in the universe are invested with life and are responsive to each other.

Idealism: any system that regards thought or the idea as the basis either of knowledge or existence; in ethics, the search for the best of the highest.

Instrumentalism: the concept of ideas as instruments, rather than as goals of living.

Interactionism: a theory of the relationship between mind and body – physical events can cause mental events, and vice versa.

Intuitionism: the doctrine that the perception of truth is by intuition, not analysis.

Materialism: the doctrine that denies the independent existence of spirit, and asserts the existence of only one substance – matter; belief that physical well-being is paramount.

Meliorism: the belief that the world is capable of improvement, and that man has the power of helping in its betterment, a position between optimism and pessimism.

Monism: belief in only one ultimate reality, whatever its nature.

Mysticism: belief that the ultimate reality lies in direct contact with the divine.

Naturalism: a position that seeks to explain all phenomena by means of strictly natural (as opposed to supernatural) categories.

Neutral monism: theory that reality is neither physical nor spiritual, but capable of expressing itself as either.

Nominalism: the doctrine that general terms have no corresponding reality either in or out of the mind, and are, in effect, nothing more than words (cf. Realism).

Optimism: any system that holds that the universe is

the best of all possible ones, and that all will work out for the best.

Panpsychism: the theory that the world is rendered more comprehensible on the assumption that every object has a soul or mind.

Pantheism: the belief that God is identical with the universe.

Personalism: the theory that ultimate reality consists of a plurality of spiritual beings or independent persons.

Pessimism: belief that the universe is the worst possible and that all is doomed to evil.

Phenomenalism: theory that reality is only appearance.

Pluralism: belief that there are more than two irreducible components of reality.

Positivism: the doctrine that man can have no knowledge except of phenomena, and that the knowledge of phenomena is relative, not absolute.

Pragmatism: a method that makes practical consequences the test of truth.

Rationalism: the theory that reason alone, without the aid of experience, can arrive at the basic reality of the universe.

Realism: the doctrine that general terms have a real existence (cf. Nominalism).

Relativism: rejection of the concept of the absolute.

Scepticism: the doctrine that no facts can be certainly known.

Sensationalism: the theory that sensations are the ultimate and real components of the world.

Structuralism: a method of approach. In linguistics, the theory that language is best described in terms of its structural units; in the social sciences, the view that the key to the understanding of observed phenomena lies in the underlying structures and systems of social organization.

Theism: acceptance of the concept of God as a workable hypothesis.

Transcendentalism: belief in an ultimate reality that transcends human experience.

Voluntarism: the theory that will is the determining factor in the universe.

Chronology of philosophers and their theories

PRE-SOCRATIC GREEKS

Thales of Miletus (624–550 BC). Regarded as the starting point of Western philosophy; the first exponent of monism.

Anaximander of Miletus (611–547 BC). Continued Thales' quest for univesal substance, but reasoned that substance need not resemble known substances.

Anaximenes of Miletus (588–524 BC). Regarded air as the ultimate reality.

Pythagoras of Samos (527–497 BC). Taught a dualism of body and soul.

Heraclitus of Ephesus (533–475 BC). Opposed concept of a single ultimate reality; held that one permanent thing is change.

Anaxagorus of Clazomenae (500–428 BC). Believed in an indefinite number of basic substances.

Empedocles of Acragas (c. 495–435 BC). Held that there were four irreducible substances (water, fire, earth and air) and two forces (love and hate).

Parmenides of Elea (c. 495 BC). Formulated the basic doctrine of idealism; member of Eleatic school, so called because based as Elea in southern Italy.

Zeno of Elea (c. 495–430 BC). Argued that plurality and change are appearances, not realities.

Protagoras of Abdera (481–411 BC). An early relativist and humanist; doubted human ability to attain absolute truth.

CLASSIC GREEK PHILOSOPHERS

Socrates (c. 470–399 BC). Developed Socratic method of enquiry; teacher of Plato, through whose writings his idealistic philosophy was disseminated.

Democritus of Abdera (460–370 BC). Began tradition in Western thought of explaining universe in mechanistic terms.

Antisthenes (c. 450–c. 360 BC). Chief of group known as the Cynics; stressed discipline and work as the essential good.

Plato (c. 428–347 BC). Founded the Academy at Athens; developed the idealism of his teacher Socrates; teacher of Aristotle.

Diogenes of Sinope (c. 412–c. 325 BC). Famous Cynic.

Aristotle (384–322 BC). Taught that there are four factors in causation: the interrelated factors of form and matter; motive cause, which produces change; and the end, for which a process of change occurs. Perhaps the greatest influence on Western civilization.

HELLENISTIC PERIOD

Pyrrho of Elis (c. 365–275 BC). Initiated the Sceptic school of philosophy; believed that man could not know anything for certain.

Epicurus (341–270 BC). Taught that the test of truth is in sensation; proponent of atomism and hedonism.

Zeno of Citium [Cyprus] (c. 335–263 BC). Chief of the Stoics, so called because they met in the Stoa Poikile or Painted Porch at Athens; proponent of pantheism, evolutionism; taught that man's role is to accept nature and all it offers, good or bad.

Plotinus (AD 205–270). Chief expounder of Neo-Platonism, a combining of the teachings of Plato with Oriental concepts.

Augustine of Hippo (AD 354–430). Known to history as St Augustine; expounder of optimism and absolutism; believed that God transcends human comprehension; one of greatest influences on medieval Christian thought.

Boethius (c. AD 480–524). Late Roman statesman and philosopher. A Neo-Platonist, his great work, *The Consolations of Philosophy*, served to transmit Greek philosophy to medieval Europe.

MEDIEVAL PERIOD

Avicenna (980–1037). Arabic follower of Aristotle and Neo-Platonism; his works led to a revival of interest in Aristotle in 13th-century Europe.

Anselm (1033–1109). Italian Augustinian; known to history as St Anselm; a realist, he is famous for his examination of the proof of God's existence.

Peter Abelard (1079–1142). Leading theologian and philosopher of medieval France; his nominalism caused him to be declared a heretic by the Church.

Averroes (1126–98). Great philosopher of Muhammadan Spain, and leading commentator on Aristotle; regarded religion as allegory for the common man, philosophy as the path to truth.

Maimonides (1135–1204). Leading Jewish student of Aristotle in medieval Muhammadan world; sought to combine Aristotelian teaching with that of the Bible.

Roger Bacon (*c.* 1214–92). English student of Aristotle, advocated return to Hebrew and Greek versions of Scripture; an empiricist.

St Bonaventure (1221–74). Born John of Fidanza in Italy; friend of Thomas Aquinas; student of Plato and Aristotle; a mystic and ascetic.

St Thomas Aquinas (1225–74). Italian; leading philosopher of the Scholastics or Christian philosophers of the Middle Ages; evolved a compromise between Aristotle and Scripture, based on the belief that faith and reason are in agreement; his philosophical system is known as Thomism.

THE RENAISSANCE
Desiderius Erasmus (1466–1536). Greatest of the humanists, he helped spread the ideas of the Renaissance in his native Holland and throughout Northern Europe.

Niccolò Machiavelli (1469–1527). Italian politician and political thinker; a realist, he placed the state as the paramount power in human affairs. His famous book *The Prince*, brought him a reputation of amoral cynicism.

Thomas More (1478–1535). Statesmen and later saint; early influence in the English Renaissance. Stressed a return to Greek sources and political and social reform. All these traits appeared in his famous *Utopia* (1516).

TRANSITION TO MODERN THOUGHT
Francis Bacon (1561–1626). English statesman and philosopher of science; in his major work, *Novum Organum*, he sought to replace the deductive logic of Aristotle with an inductive system in interpreting nature.

Thomas Hobbes (1588–1679). English materialist who believed the natural state of man is war; outlined a theory of human government in his book *Leviathan*, whereby the state and man's subordination to it form the sole solution to human selfishness and aggressiveness.

René Descartes (1596–1650). French; dualist, rationalist, theist. Descartes and his system, Cartesianism, are at the base of all modern knowledge. What he furnished is a theory of knowledge that underlies modern science and philosophy. 'All the sciences are conjoined with one another and interdependent' he wrote.

Blaise Pascal (1623–62). French theist who held that sense and reason are mutually deceptive; truth lies between dogmatism and scepticism.

Benedict de Spinoza (1632–77). Dutch rationalist metaphysician, he developed ideas of Descartes while rejecting his dualism.

John Locke (1632–1704). English dualist, empiricist; in his great *Essay Concerning Human Understanding* he sought to refute the rationalist view that all knowledge derives from first principles. His influence in political, religious, educational and philosophical thought was wide and deep.

18TH CENTURY
Gottfried Wilhelm von Leibniz (1646–1716). German idealist, absolutist, optimist (his view that this is the best of all possible worlds was ridiculed by Voltaire in *Candide*), held that reality consisted of units of force called monads.

George Berkeley (1685–1753). Irish idealist and theist of English ancestry who taught that material things exist only in being perceived; his system of subjective idealism is called Berkeleianism.

Emmanuel Swedenborg (1688–1772). Swedish mystic, scientist, theologian; author of *Principia Rerum Naturalium*, 1734.

David Hume (1711–76). Scottish philosopher and historian. An empiricist who carried on ideas of Locke, but developed a system of scepticism (Humanism) according to which human knowledge is limited to experience of ideas and sensations, whose truth cannot be verified.

Jean-Jacques Rousseau (1712–78). French political philosopher whose concepts have had a profound influence on modern thought; advocated a 'return to nature' to counteract the inequality among men brought about by civilized society.

Adam Smith (1723–90). Founder of modern political economy and a leader of the 'Scottish Renaissance'. His *Wealth of Nations* (1776), with its emphasis on economic liberalism and natural liberty, has had a more profound influence than almost any other philosophical work.

Immanuel Kant (1724–1804). German founder of critical philosophy. At first influenced by Leibniz, then by Hume, he sought to find an alternative approach to the rationalism of the former and the scepticism of the latter; in ethics, formulated the Categorical Imperative – which states that what applies to oneself must apply to everyone else unconditionally – a restatement of the Christian precept 'Do unto others as you would have them do unto you'.

Jeremy Bentham (1748–1832). English Utilitarian. Believed, like Kant, that the interests of the individual are at one with those of society, but regarded fear of consequences rather than basic principle as the motivation for right action.

Johann Gottlieb Fichte (1762–1814). German; formulated a philosophy of absolute idealism based on Kant's ethical concepts.

19TH CENTURY
Georg Wilhelm Friedrich Hegel (1770–1831). German; his metaphysical system, known as Hegelianism, was rationalist and absolutist, based on the belief that thought and being are one, and nature is the manifestation of an Absolute Idea.

Arthur Schopenhauer (1788–1860). German who gave the will a leading place in his metaphysics. The foremost exponder of pessimism, expressed in *The World as Will and Idea*. Rejected absolute idealism as wishful thinking, and taught that the only tenable attitude lay in utter indifference to an irrational world; an idealist who held that the highest ideal was nothingness.

Auguste Comte (1798–1857). French founder of positivism, a system which denied transcendant metaphysics and stated that the Divinity and man were one, that altruism is man's highest duty, and that scientific principles explain all phenomena.

John Stuart Mill (1806–73). English; major exponent of Utilitarianism, who differed from Bentham by recognizing differences in quality as well as quantity in pleasure. Most famous work *On Liberty* (1859).

Søren Kierkegaard (1813–55). Danish religious existentialist, whose thought is the basis of modern (atheistic) existentialism; taught that 'existence precedes essence' that only existence has reality, and the individual has a unique value.

Karl Marx (1818–83). German revolutionist, from whom the movement known as Marxism derives its name and many of its ideas; his works became, in the late 19th century, the basis of European socialism; published *The Communist Manifesto* with Friedrich Engels in 1848.

Herbert Spencer (1820–1903). English evolutionist whose 'synthetic philosophy' interpreted all phenomena according to the principle of evolutionary progress.

Charles S. Peirce (1839–1914). American physicist and mathematician who founded the philosophical school called pragmatism; regarded logic as the basis of philosophy and taught that the test of an idea is whether it works.

William James (1842–1910). American psychologist and pragmatist who held that reality is always in the making and that each man should choose the philosophy best suited to him.

Friedrich Wilhelm Nietzsche (1844–1900). German philosopher and poet. An evolutionist who held that the 'will to power' is basic in life, that the spontaneous is to be preferred to the orderly; attacked Christianity as a system that fostered the weak, whereas the function of evolution is to evolve 'supermen'.

20TH CENTURY

Samuel Alexander (1859–1938). Australian-born philosopher. One of the most influential figures in the realist reaction against idealism. He held that knowledge, generally, consists in the 'compresence' of a mental act and an object, that is, it is essentially of a mind-independent world.

Henri Bergson (1859–1941). French evolutionist who asserted the existence of a 'vital impulse' that carries the universe forward, with no fixed beginning and no fixed end – the future is determined by the choice of alternatives made in the present.

John Dewey (1859–1952). American; basically a pragmatist, he developed a system known as instrumentalism. Saw man as continuous with, but distinct from, nature.

Edmund Husserl (1859–1938). German who developed a system called 'phenomenology', which asserts that realities other than mere appearance exist – called essences.

Alfred North Whitehead (1861–1947). British evolutionist and mathematician who held that reality must not be interpreted in atomistic terms, but in terms of events; that God is intimately present in the universe, yet distinct from it, a view called panentheism, as opposed to pantheism, which simply equates God and Nature.

George Santayana (1863–1952). American born in Spain; a foremost critical realist who held that the ultimate substance of the world is matter in motion – and the mind itself is a product of matter in motion.

Benedetto Croce (1866–1952). The best-known Italian philosopher of the 20th century. Noted for his role in revival of historical realism in Italy 1900–1920.

Bertrand Russell (1872–1970). British agnostic who adhered to many systems of philosophy before becoming chief expounder of scientism, the view that all knowledge is solely attainable by the scientific method.

George Edward Moore (1873–1958). Rigorous British moral scientist. Developed doctrine of Ideal Utilitarianism in *Principia Ethica*, 1903.

Karl Jaspers (1883–1969). German existentialist who approached the subject from man's practical concern with his own existence.

Martin Heidegger (1889–1976). German student of Husserl, he furthered development of phenomenology and greatly influenced atheistic existentialists.

Gabriel Marcel (1889–1973). French philosopher, initially a student of the English-speaking Idealists, he had a preoccupation with the Cartesian problem of the relation of mind and matter. Latterly, he considered the implications of parapsychological phenomena.

Ludwig Wittgenstein (1889–1951). Austrian; developed the philosophy of language.

Friedrich von Hayek (b. 1899). Austrian economist and philosopher. Argues that social science must not try to ape the method of physics. What can be predicted and used for analysis is an abstract pattern which leaves the details unspecified.

Gilbert Ryle (1900–76). British philosopher. Studied the nature of philosophy and the concept of mind and the nature of meaning and the philosophy of logic.

Karl Popper (b. 1902). British of Austrian extraction. Exponent of critical rationalism arguing that scientific laws can never be proved to be true; the most that can be claimed is that they have survived attempts to disprove them. Writer from liberal and individualistic standpoint.

Jean-Paul Sartre (1905–1980). French; developed existentialist thought of Heidegger; atheistic supporter of a subjective, irrational human existence, as opposed to an orderly overall reality.

Claude Lévi-Strauss (b. 1908). French anthropologist and proponent of structuralism. His writings investigate the relationship between culture (exclusively an attribute of humanity) and nature, based on the distinguishing characteristics of man – the ability to communicate in a language.

Sir Isaiah Berlin (b. 1909). British moral and political philosopher and historian. Has argued against determinist philosophies of history and emphasises the importance of moral values, and the necessity of rejecting determinism if the ideas of human responsibility and freedom are to be retained.

Alfred J. Ayer (b. 1910). British, principal advocate of logical positivism, a modern extension of the thinking of Hume and Comte.

RELIGION

Religions of The World

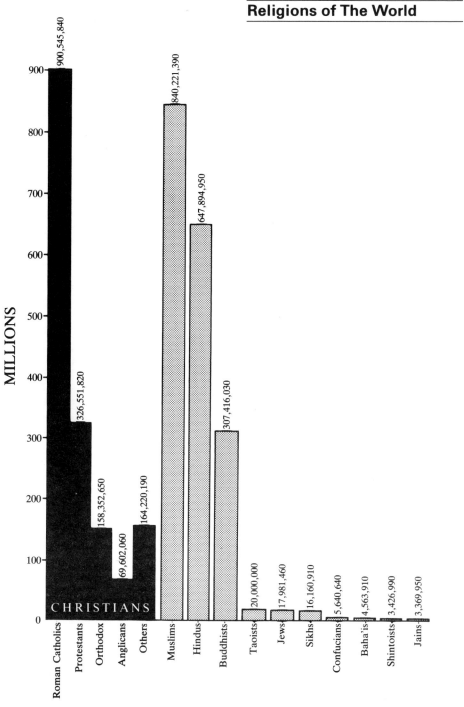

MILLIONS

900,545,840 — Roman Catholics
326,551,820 — Protestants
158,352,650 — Orthodox
69,602,060 — Anglicans
164,220,190 — Others
CHRISTIANS

840,221,390 — Muslims
647,894,950 — Hindus
307,416,030 — Buddhists
20,000,000 — Taoists
17,981,460 — Jews
16,160,910 — Sikhs
5,640,640 — Confucians
4,563,910 — Baha'is
3,426,990 — Shintoists
3,369,950 — Jains

Christianity

The religion Christianity takes its name from Jesus Christ*, son of the Virgin Mary, whose subsequent husband, Joseph of Nazareth, was 27 generations descended from David. His birth is now regarded as occurring at Bethlehem in the summer of 4 BC or earlier. The discrepancy is due to an error in the 6th century by Dionysius Exiguus in establishing the dating of the Christian era.

The principles of Christianity are proclaimed in the New Testament which was written in Greek and of which the earliest complete surviving manuscript dates from AD c. 350.

Christ was crucified in the reign of the Roman emperor Tiberius during the procuratorship in Judaea of Pontius Pilate in AD 29 or according to the Roman Catholic chronology, 7 April, AD 30.

The primary commandment of Jesus was to love God. His second commandment (Mark xii, 31) was to 'love thy neighbour' in a way that outward performance alone did not suffice.

Hate was prohibited and not only adultery but evil lust (Matt. v, 21).

Unselfishness and compassion are central themes in Christianity.

Jesus appointed 12 disciples; the following are common to the lists in the books of Matthew, Mark, Luke and the Acts.

1. Peter, Saint Peter (brother of Andrew)
2. Andrew, Saint Andrew (brother of Peter)
3. James, son of Zebedee (brother of John)
4. John, Saint John (the Apostle) (brother of James)
5. Philip
6. Bartholomew
7. Thomas
8. Matthew, Saint Matthew
9. James, of Alphaeus
10. Simon the Canaanean (in Matthew and Mark) or Simon Zelotes (in Luke and the Acts)
11. Judas Iscariot (not an apostle)

Thaddaeus in the book of Matthew and Mark is the twelfth disciple, while in Luke and the Acts the twelfth is Judas of James. The former may have been a nickname or place name to distinguish Judas of James from the Iscariot. Matthias succeeded to the place of the betrayer Judas Iscariot.

Christianity is a world-wide religion.

ROMAN CATHOLICISM

Roman Catholic Christianity is that practised by those who acknowledge the supreme jurisdiction of the bishop of Rome (the Pope) and recognize him as the lawful successor of St Peter who was appointed by Christ Himself to be head of the church. Peter visited Rome c. AD 42 and was mar-

* Jesus (the Saviour, from Hebrew root yasha', to save) Christ (the anointed one, from Greek, Χριω, chrio, to anoint).

tyred there c. AD 67. Pope John Paul II is his 263rd successor.

The Roman Catholic Church claims catholicity inasmuch as she was charged (de jure) by Christ to 'teach all nations' and de facto since her adherents are by far the most numerous among Christians. The Roman Catholic Church is regarded as the infallible interpreter both of the written and the unwritten word of God. The organization of the Church is the Curia, the work of which is done by 11 permanent departments or congregations.

The great majority of Catholics are of the Roman rite and use the Roman liturgy. While acknowledging the hierarchical supremacy of jurisdiction of the Holy See some Eastern Churches or Uniate Rites continue to use the Byzantine or Greek rite, the Armenian rite, and the Coptic rite.

The doctrine of the Immaculate Conception was proclaimed on 8 Dec 1854, and that of Papal Infallibility was adopted by the Ecumenical Council by 547 votes to 2 on 18 July 1870. The 21st Council was convened by Pope John XXIII. The election of Popes is by the College of Cardinals.

The Pope

Otherwise known as the Bishop of Rome, the Pope is the chief bishop of the Roman Catholic Church, considered by Catholics to be the Vicar of Christ on earth and the successor of St Peter, the first Bishop of Rome. He is thus looked upon as the supreme head of the Church on earth and the chief pastor of the whole Church.

The Pope is elected by the College of Cardinals in the Vatican City, meeting in secret conclave. The election is by scrutiny and requires a two-thirds majority.

The Popes over the last 300 years have been as follows.

Benedict XIV	(Lambertini)	elected 1740
Clement XIII	(Rezzonico)	elected 1758
Clement XIV	(Ganganelli)	elected 1769
Pius VI	(Braschi)	elected 1775
Pius VII	(Chiaramonti)	elected 1800
Leo XII	(della Genga)	elected 1823
Pius VIII	(Castiglioni)	elected 1829
Gregory XIV	(Cappellari)	elected 1831
Pius IX	(Mastai-Ferretti)	elected 1846
Leo XIII	(Pecci)	elected 1878
Pius X	(Sarto)	elected 1903
Benedict XV	(della Chiesa)	elected 1914
Pius XI	(Ratti)	elected 1922
Pius XII	(Pacelli)	elected 1939
John XXIII	(Roncalli)	elected 1958
Paul VI	(Montini)	elected 1963
John Paul I	(Luciani)	elected 1978
John Paul II	(Wojtyla)	elected 1978

EASTERN ORTHODOX

The church officially described as 'The Holy Orthodox Catholic Apostolic Eastern Church' consists of those churches which accepted all the decrees of the first seven General Councils and such churches as have since sprung up in that tradition and are in communion with the Patriarchate of Constantinople. The Orthodox Church maintains that it is the 'one true Church of Christ which is not and has not been divided'. It views the Roman Catholic Church as in schism.

Coptic manuscript on goat skin, Church of Ganeta Mariam, Ethiopia. (Popperfoto)

Some features of this branch of Christianity are that bishops must be unmarried; the dogma of the immaculate conception is not admitted; icons are venerated in the churches and fasts are frequent and rigorous.

PROTESTANTISM

*This is the system of Christian faith and practice based on acceptance of the principles of the Reformation. The term is derived from the 'Protestatio' of the reforming members of the Diet of Speyer (1529) against the decisions of the Catholic majority. The word has retained a strongly anti-Roman flavour and is commonly repudiated by those who minimize their difference from Rome.

The chief branches of original Protestantism were Lutheranism, Calvinism and Zwinglianism. The position of the Church of England is disputed. Here strong Calvinist influences have intermingled with older traditions, but it is often contended that these have not effected any intrinsic modification of the pre-Reformation faith. The term is not used in any edition of the Book of Common Prayer, but from the beginning of the 17th century it was adopted as opposed to both Roman Catholicism and Puritanism, e.g. by Charles I when he affirmed his allegiance to the Protestant religion. After the Restoration, however, it was generally extended to include also the Nonconformists. In this enlarged sense it is now widely used in popular parlance, though a large body of Anglicans deny the Protestant character of the Church of England.

The chief characteristics of original Protestantism, common to all its denominations, are the acceptance of the Bible as the only source of revealed truth, the doctrine of justification by faith only, and the universal priesthood of all believers. Protestantism has tended to stress the transcendence of God, laying corresponding emphasis on the effects of the Fall and Original Sin, and the impotence of the unaided human intellect to obtain any knowledge of God, to minimize the liturgical aspects of Christianity, to put preaching and hearing of the Word before Sacramental faith and practice, and, while rejecting asceticism, to uphold for the individual a high, if at times austere, standard of personal morality. The principle of 'private judgement' in the interpretation of Scripture accounts for the great variety of sects and Churches typical of Protestantism, in which many shades of doctrine and practice are found.

THE CHURCH OF ENGLAND

The church in England renounced the supremacy of the Pope in favour of royal supremacy in 1534, but the episcopal form of church government was retained.

The Church of England is the established church with the Sovereign consecrated as its Head by his or her coronation oath. The authority of Parliament is acknowledged where secular authority is competent to exercise control.

The Church is organized into two provinces, each under an Archbishop. Canterbury has 29 dioceses listed in order of antiquity of consecration.

* This article is reprinted from *The Oxford Dictionary of the Christian Church* (2nd ed 1974) by permission of Oxford University Press.

Canterbury	597	Rochester	604
London	501	Winchester	662

Lichfield	664	Peterborough	1541
Hereford	669	Bristol	1542
Leicester	679–	Oxford	1542
	c. 888, 1926	Truro	1877
Worcester	680	St Albans	1877
Bath and Wells	909	Birmingham	1905
(Wells)		Southwark	1905
Exeter	1046	Chelmsford	1914
Lincoln	1067	St Edmundsbury	
Chichester	1070	and Ipswich	1914
(Selsey)		Coventry	1918
Salisbury	1078	Guildford	1927
Norwich	1090	Portsmouth	1927
Ely	1109	Derby	1927
Gloucester	1541		

York has 14 dioceses listed in order of antiquity of consecration.

York	625	Liverpool	1880
Durham	635	Newcastle	1882
(Lindisfarne)		Southwell	1884
Carlisle	1133	Wakefield	1888
Sodor and Man	1387	Sheffield	1914
Chester	1541	Bradford	1920
Ripon	1836 (678)	Blackburn	1926
Manchester	1847		

The governing body of the Church is the General Synod of the Church of England. This has three houses: the House of Bishops, consisting of 43 diocesan bishops and 9 suffragan bishops; the House of Clergy, comprising the Lower House of the Convocations of the Provinces of Canterbury and York (251 members); and the House of Laity, consisting of 248 elected diocesan representatives.

THE CHURCH IN WALES
The Province of Wales consists of six dioceses under the Archbishop of Wales, who is also the Bishop of St David's. The other dioceses are St Asaph, Bangor, Llandaff, Monmouth, and Swansea & Brecon.

THE ROMAN CATHOLIC CHURCH IN GREAT BRITAIN
There are six Archbishops: those of Westminster, Birmingham, Liverpool, Cardiff, St Andrew's and Edinburgh, and Glasgow. There are Episcopal Conferences of England and Wales, and of Scotland.

THE CHURCH OF SCOTLAND
The Church of Scotland is an established church, Presbyterian in constitution, presided over by a Moderator, who is chosen annually by the General Assembly, at which the Sovereign is represented by a Lord High Commissioner. The Church is divided into 16 synods and 46 presbyteries.

Versions of the Bible in English

The Bible was first brought in Latin form to England by Aidan in the north and St Augustine in the south. After that various parts were translated or summarized: the poem of *Caedmon* (8th century?); the works of *Bede* and *Alfred* are considered to have advanced the cause, but little, if anything remains of their efforts.

The *Lindisfarne Gospels* of the 10th century represent the first extant translation of the gospels into English. From then on, various parts of the Bible as we know it were translated notably by Aelfric and Richard Rolle (d. 1349).

The first complete version of the bible in English was translated by William Wycliffe, whose translations were completed in 1384. A list of versions to the present day is given below.

Tyndale's version (New Testament only) c. 1526.
Coverdale's Bible (Old and New Testaments) 1535.
Matthew's Bible 1537.
Taverner's Bible 1539.
The Great Bible 1539.
The Geneva Bible 1557.
The Bishop's Bible 1568.
The Rheims and Douai Bible 1582.
The Authorized Version (King James' Version) 1611.

Since the Authorized Version, there have been many versions in English translation. A list of some of the more well-known is given below.

The Revised Version 1885.
The American Standard Version 1901.
The revised Standard Version 1946.
The Jerusalem Bible 1966.
The New English Bible 1976.
The Jerusalem Bible 1976.
The Good News Bible (Today's English Version) 1976.

Religions in Britain

The *UK Christian Handbook** (1989/90 Edition) gives two sets of statistics for Christian churches and other faiths (1987). The first consists of *church members* (not counting children under 14 or people on the fringe) as follows:

Roman Catholics	2 059 240
Anglicans	1 927 506
Presbyterians	1 346 366
Methodists	516 739
Baptists	241 451
Orthodox	231 070
Others (including Afro-West Indians: 65 211)	604 458
Total	6 926 830

which is 15% of the total adult (15 & over) UK population of 45 966 000.

On the same basis it gives the following figures for other faiths:

Muslims	900 000
Jews	108 800
Hindus	150 000
Sikhs	200 000
Buddhists	25 000

The second set of statistics consists of the following '*Community figures*' in millions:

Anglicans	26·9
Roman Catholics	5·2
Presbyterians	1·7
Methodists	1·3
Baptists	0·6
Orthodox	0·5
Others	1·3
Total	37·5

which is 66% of the total United Kingdom population of 56 764 000.

On the same basis it gives the following figures for other faiths:	
Muslims	1·5
Jews	0·3
Hindus	0·3
Sikhs	0·5

Islam

Islam is the world's second largest religion with its emphasis on an uncompromising monotheism and a strict adherence to certain religious practices. The Arabic term *islam* means 'the act of resignation' to God. The root word is *slm* pronounced salm, which means 'peace' from which comes the word *aslama* which means he submitted or resigned. Islam (or Al-Islam) is the religion which brings peace to mankind when man commits himself to God and submits himself to His will. Muslims believe that God's will was made known through the Qur'an (Koran), the book revealed to his messenger, Muhammad (572–632).

Muhammad was a member of the Quraysh tribe which guarded the sacred shrine known as the Ka'ba in the Arab trading city of Makka (Mecca). In 616, Muhammad received his first revelations, which commissioned him to preach against the idolatry and polytheism of the Arab tribes. In 622, he led his followers to Madina (Medina) where political power was added to his spiritual authority. Before Muhammad died in 632, the whole of Arabia had embraced Islam or entered into a peace-treaty with the Prophet.

The revelations which Muhammad received over a period of 20 years, from God (Allah) via, Muslims believe, the Archangel Gabriel, form the Qur'an (lit. 'The Recitation'), Islam's scripture. Muhammad also accepted the inspiration of the Hebrew scriptures. Next in importance are the Hadith, the collections of Muhammad's sayings and doings, for the prophet is the best model for mankind of obedience to God's will. Muslims teach that Islam was the religion of Adam and of all the prophets God sent man to call him back to his path. Muslims revere Abraham, Moses and Jesus amongst other prophets but Muhammad is the final prophet, because the Qur'an completed and superseded earlier revelations.

The basic belief of Islam is expressed in the Shahada, the Muslim confession of faith: 'There is no God but Allah and Muhammad is his Prophet!' From this fundamental belief are derived beliefs in (1) angels (particularly Gabriel), (2) the revealed Books (of the Jewish and Christian faiths in addition to the Qur'an), (3) a series of prophets and (4) the Last Day, the Day of Judgement. Acceptance of

this essential creed involves further duties that are to be strictly observed: five daily prayer sessions, a welfare tax called the zakat, fasting during the month of Ramadan and a pilgrimage (*hajj*) at Mecca, all of which – including the profession of faith – are called the Five Pillars. Ramadan is the ninth month of the Muslim lunar calendar.

Shi'ism and Sunnism are the two main forms of Islam. Although the majority of Muslims are Sunnis, the Shi'ah (who number only about 40 000 000) are dominant in Iran, which is about 93 per cent Shi'ah. The main difference between Sunni and Shi'ah Islam lies in the latter's belief that the charisma of the prophet was inherited by his descendants, in whom they invest supreme spiritual and political authority. The Sunni believe that orthodoxy is determined by the Ijma' (consensus) of the community. Their caliphs exercised political but not spiritual authority. The historic caliphate ceased to exist in 1924. Shi'ism has produced a variety of sects, including the Ismailis, the Bohras and the Khojas though the majority are known as 'Twelvers' (Ithna 'Ashariyah). They believe that the 12th Imam or successor to Muhammad in linear descent disappeared as the Mahdi, who is now the hidden Imam. The doctors of the law, especially the Mujtahid, interpret the Hidden Imam and share his infallibility. The Ayatollah (lit. sign of God) Khomeini was regarded, in Iran, as such a Mujtahid. Others revere living Imams, such as the Aga Khan Khojas whose leader claims to be a descendant of Muhammad through Ismail, the 7th Imam.

Islam's mystical or Sufi tradition has both Sunni and Shi'ah adherents. Many of its orders or circles have appointed or hereditary *pirs* (spiritual guides) and venerate their predecessors as saints. Sufi missionaries played an important role in Islam's expansion into Africa and Asia.

Though the sheer variety of races and cultures embraced by Islam has produced wide differences, all segments of Muslim society are bound by a common faith and a sense of belonging to a single community. With the loss of political power during the period of Western colonialism in the 19th and early 20th centuries, the concept of the Islamic community, instead of weakening, became stronger. This, in harness with the discovery of immense oil reserves, helped various Muslim peoples in their struggle to gain political freedom and sovereignty in the mid-20th century.

Islam as a total way of life is a missionary religion committed to bringing all men into the Household of Faith (Dar-al-Islam). However, it affords special status to followers of its sister faiths, Jews and Christians, who have existed as protected minority communities in many Muslim lands and who are not regarded as part of Dar-al-Harb (lit. House of War – territory not yet surrendered to God).

Hinduism

* This information from the *UK Christian Handbook* is by permission of MARC Europe (1987 statistics).

The word Hindu was first used by Arab invaders in the 8th century AD to describe those who lived beyond the Sind or Indus Valley. Hinduism is now used to describe the religion and social institutions of the great majority of the people of India, though strictly speaking it is an English word. The origins of Hinduism (or Sanatam-Dharma: ancient way of life) lie in the Arya-Dharma (Aryan way of life) of the light skinned Nordic people who invaded the Indus from Asia Minor and Iran c. 1500 BC. They wrote the Vedas (Rig-Veda, Yajur-Veda, Sama-Veda, Atharva-Veda) which are collections of prayers, hymns and formulas for worship. The Aryans worshipped nature-deities, including Agni (fire) and Surya (sun). Their traditions intermingled with those of the Dravidians, who had settled in India c. 3000 BC. This process of assimilation resulted in the great epic poems which were composed between 200 BC and AD 200, the *Ramayana* and the *Mahabharata*, which includes the famous *Bhagavad-Gita*.

Three forms of the deity dominate these epics:

Goddess Shiva, 'the destroyer', one of three main divinities of the Hindu religion (the other two being Brahma and Vishnu). (Photograph by William MacQuitty)

Brahma, Vishnu and Shiva, representing creation, preservation and destruction. There are other gods and demi-gods and also important avatars (incarnations), such as Krishna (a form of Vishnu). Shiva, a male principle (represented by the lingam or phallus) is also consorted by Shakti, the female principle, represented by the yoni or circle. Within philosophical Hinduism, which developed originally in the 5th century BC with its 13 Upanishads (philosophical scriptures), the dominant concept is Brahman, an impersonal, all embracing spirit. The law of Manu (written during the first two centuries AD) contains the concept that God created distinct orders of men, priests (Brahmans), soldiers and rulers (Kshatriyas), farmers (Vaisyas) and artisans and labourers (Sudras). The so-called caste system thus developed. Hinduism tolerates a great variety of beliefs and practices and there is absolute freedom with regard to the choice and mode of one's philosophy. The Brahmans recognize six schools as orthodox of which the best known are yoga, sankhya and vedanta of which the great philosopher, Shankara (Sankara) (AD 788–820) was an exponent. The Brahmans regard Buddhism and Jainism as heterodox.

The aim of most Hindus is to be reunited with the absolute (Atman or Brahman) and thereby to escape the wheel of existence (Samsara) which is determined by Karma (lit. deeds or actions). Moksa (release) may be gained through yoga, through Gyan (knowledge) or through Bhakti (devotion to ones God).

Hinduism traditionally divides life into four ideal periods

(1) Brahmacharya (celibate period)
(2) Grahastha (householder)
(3) Vanprasthu (retired stage)
(4) Sanyas (renunciation)

Hinduism embraces many local as well as national traditions and has numerous pilgrim centres, temples, ashrams and orders of monks. The concept of the Holy Man, or guru, is important and many contemporary gurus attract European as well as Indian devotees. In the 19th century several reform movements began, such as the Rama Krishna Mission, founded by Swami Vivekananda (1862–1902), the Arya Samaj of Dayananda Saraswati (1824–83) and the Brahma Samaj of Ram Mohan Roy (1772–1833). Ghandhian 'Ahimsa' (non-violence) was inspired by Hindu philosophy. The International Society of Krishna Consciousness founded by Swami Prabhupada (1896–1977) in 1966 has attracted Western devotees. Nepal is the world's only officially Hindu nation.

Buddhism

Buddhism is based on the teaching of the Indian prince Siddhartha (later called Gautama) (c. 563–

483 BC) of the Gautama clan of the Sakyas, later named Gautama Buddha (*buddha* meaning 'the enlightened one').

After seeing in c. 534 BC for the first time a sick man, an old man, a holy man and a dead man, he wandered fruitlessly for six years, after which he meditated for 49 days under a Bodhi tree at Gaya in Magadha. He achieved enlightenment or *nirvana* and taught salvation in Bihar, west of Bengal, until he died, aged 80. Gautama's teaching was essentially a protesting offshoot of early Hinduism. It contains four Noble Truths:

(1) Dukkha: Man suffers from one life to the next;
(2) Samudaya: the origin of suffering is craving; craving for pleasure, possessions and the cessation of pain;
(3) Nirodha: the cure for craving is non-attachment to all things including self;
(4) Magga: the way to non-attachment is the Eight-fold path of right conduct, right effort, right intentions, right livelihood, right meditations, right mindfulness, right speech and right views. This is represented in the Wheel of Law (Dharma Chakra) which has eight spokes for the eight steps towards Nirvana.

Buddhism makes no provisions for God and hence has no element of divine judgement or messianic expectation. It provides an inexorable law or *dharma* of cause and effect which determines the individual's fate.

The vast body or *sangha* of monks and nuns practise celibacy, non-violence, poverty and vegetarianism.

Therevada Buddhism (the school of the elders) is practised in Sri Lanka, Burma and Thailand. It was the original Buddhism of India where by AD 1200 Buddhism had vanished, except for remote parts of East Bengal (now Bangladesh) and Assam. It remains non-theistic and emphasizes the importance of the celibate life to gain nirvana. In 1956, Dr Bhimrao Ramji Ambedkar (1891–1956), the leader of India's untouchables, converted to Buddhism and approximately four million of his disciples followed his example.

Mahayana (self-styled, the 'Greater Vehicle') which, pejoratively, calls the Therevada 'Hinayana' or the 'Lesser Vehicle', is practised in Indo-China, China and Japan. It has several sub-divisions, including Zen in which enlightenment or Satori is achieved only by prolonged meditation and mental and physical shock.

In Mahayana, the concept of the Bodhisattva (lit. one bound for enlightenment, but who delays entering nirvana to help others) developed to include many such heavenly beings alongside, but subordinate to, the Buddha, who is regarded as quasi-divine at least. Mahayana is sometimes described as pantheistic.

Vajrayana (the 'Diamond Vehicle') or Tantric Buddhism developed in Tibet. This makes much use of mantras (sacred chants) and also of images, which depict the Bodhisattvas as very active in the world, opposing evil. The male quality of compassion is often united with the female quality of wisdom. In the West, Buddhism in all forms has attracted a significant following. The Friends of the Western Buddhist Order was formed in 1968 and seeks to find forms of expression amenable to the West, which some call 'Navayana' (a 'New Vehicle').

Taoism

Lao-tzu (Lao-tze or Lao-tse), the Chinese philosopher and founder of Taoism, was, according to tradition, born in the sixth century BC. Lao-tzu taught that Taoism (Tao = the Ultimate and Unconditioned Being) could be attained by virtue if thrift, humility and compassion were practised.

Taoism has the following features – numerous gods (though Lao-tzu did not himself permit this); a still persisting, though now decreasing, body of superstition; and two now declining schools – the 13th-century Northern School with its emphasis on man's life, and the Southern School, probably of 10th century origin, stressing the nature of man. Various Taoist societies have been formed more recently by laymen, who, though worshipping deities of many religions, promote charity and a more moral culture. The moral principles of Taoism consist of simplicity, patience, contentment and harmony. Since the decline of its espousal by the T'ang dynasty (AD 618–906), it has proved to be chiefly the religion of the semi-literate.

Philosophical Taoism or Tao-chia advocates naturalism and is thus opposed to regulations and organizations of any kind. After the 4th century BC when Buddhism and Taoism began to influence each other there was a weakening of this anti-collectivist strain but the philosophy still has a strong hold over the way of life and culture in parts of China.

The religion imitates Buddhism in the matter of clergy and temple, the chief of which is the White Cloud temple in Peking, China.

Judaism

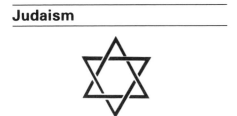

Judaism is the oldest monotheistic religion. The word Jew is derived from the Latin *Judaeus*, from the Hebrew *Yehudhi*, signifying a descendant of Jacob, Abraham's grandson. The Exodus of the Jews from Egypt is believed to have occurred c. 1290 BC and was the decisive event or watershed in Israel's history. Even today, Jews understand themselves in the light of the Exodus. This resulted in their emerging as a distinct nation (Israel). The observance of the Passover (*Pesach*) makes every believing Jew a participant in the event which delivered their ancestors from bondage and established a special relationship between themselves and the One True God (The God of Abraham, Isaac and Jacob).

The Torah is the Hebrew name for the Law of Moses (the Pentateuch) which was divinely revealed to Moses on Mount Sinai, soon after the Exodus. The Talmud contains civic and religious laws and is a collection of originally oral traditions. The two main versions were completed in Jerusalem in the 5th century BC and in Babylon at the end of the 6th century. The *Mishnah* is the oral law dating from between the 1st century BC to the 3rd century AD. The Hebrew scriptures (Old Testament) also contain the books of the prophets, the wisdom literature (e.g. Solomon) and the historical writings (e.g. Kings).

At the beginning of the Christian era, Judaism was divided into several sects, including the Pharisees, the Sadducees and the Essenes. The fall of Jerusalem (AD 70) resulted in the diaspora (though there were dispersed Jewish communities before AD 70) and until 1790 Jews lived throughout Europe, Africa and Asia Minor under severe discrimination and disabilities. During this period, the Yiddish language evolved in Central Europe from German and Hebrew elements and Jewish philosophy developed, as did Cabala (mysticism) especially in Spain, where, under the tolerant Muslim Moors, there was much interaction between Jewish, Muslim and Christian scholars.

Jewish emancipation began with the enfranchisement of Jews in France in September 1791. The new climate stimulated the growth of the Reform movement, founded by David Friedlander (1756–1834) which accepted for Judaism the status of a religious sect within the European nations, loyal to their countries of adoption. Another movement, called Conservatism, stands midway between Orthodoxy and Reformed Judaism. Associated with the name of Solomon Schechter (1830–1915) it also teaches that the faith must find its place in the contemporary world. There are also Liberal and Progressive Jews. During the Second World War, Nazi anti-semitism resulted in the holocaust, the murder of six million Jews. Thousands, escaping Nazi tyranny, fled to Palestine to fulfil their dream of Israel's restoration to the Jewish people, which the Balfour declaration of 2 November 1917 had favoured. The British had captured Palestine from the Turks in 1917. The first Zionist Congress, calling for a return to Israel, had been held at Basle, Switzerland, in 1897. The modern state of Israel was created on 14 May 1948 as a Jewish homeland, which resulted in the dispossession of the Arab Palestinians and in recurring wars with Israel's neighbouring Arab states. The majority of Jews still live in the diaspora but the state of Israel (although officially secular) is important to most Jews as a symbol of the hope and pride which sustained their faith during centuries of persecution. Israeli Judaism is very cosmopolitan. Different groups from the diaspora preserve their distinctive traditions – including the Sephardim (Portugal, Spain and North African communities), the Ashkenazi (Central Europe) and most recently, the Falasha from Ethiopia.

Judaism as a total way of life revolves around the family as its main institution. Jews cannot surrender their religion. A boy becomes a man for religious purposes at his bar mitzvah at the age of 13 but is circumcised eight days after birth. Festivals include the Passover, Shavuot (Pentecost), Rosh Hashanah (New Year) and Yom Kippur (Day of Atonement).

Sikhism

Sikhism is a reformed Hindu sect founded by Guru Nanak (1479-1539) at the end of the 15th century. It originated in Pakistan and north-west India – an area called the Punjab (meaning 'land of the five rivers').

Sikhs believe in the idea of the guru: that God is the true Guru; the Sikh community is called the guru; and the scriptures, the *Granth*, are said to be a guru. Sikhs believe in the existence of only one true God and that through worship and meditation the most devoted Sikhs can experience and know him. They believe that each person is trapped in his own failings and weaknesses and the only hope is that the true Guru is merciful.

The religion was developed under Nanak who came to be called a guru, having provided such a vital strength for early followers, and his nine successive Sikh orthodox gurus. Each guru was chosen by his predecessor on the basis of his spiritual enlightenment. The succession of gurus is as follows:

Nanak	1469-1539
Angad	1504-1552
Amar Das	1479-1574
Ram Das	1534-1581
Arjan	1563-1606
Har Govind	1595-1644
Har Rai	1630-1661
Har Krishan	1656-1664
Tegh Bahadur	1621-1675
Gobind Singh	1666-1708

The first five gurus developed the majority of the Sikh doctrines. After the ten gurus the religion centred on a community (the *Guru Panth*) rather than individual men, and the scriptures (the *Guru Granth*). This community was to defend the faith and establish a strict moral society.

The holy scriptures, the *Granth*, is the central document to all Sikh rituals and ceremonies. It is mostly Guru Arjan's work although Guru Gobind Singh produced the final edition, the *Adi Granth*. The Sikhs worship in their own temples, known as a *gurdwara* (the guru's door). There are no priests to conduct the services – anyone can lead the worship, although some are specially trained to read the *Granth*.

Sikhism has spread outside the Punjab during the 20th century to Britain, the USA, Canada and parts of South and East Africa.

The Sikh religion is an ethnic religion in that it attempts to keep the community intact and does not aim to convert members from outside. It does not deny the existence of other faiths but strives for its members to be devoted to God.

Confucianism

Confucius (551-479 BC) was not the sole founder of Confucianism but was rather a member of the founding group of *Ju* or meek ones. Confucius is the Latinized version of K'ung Fu-tzo or Master K'ung who was a keeper of accounts from the province of Lu. He became the first teacher in Chinese history to instruct the people of all ranks in the six arts:

(1) ceremonies
(2) music
(3) archery
(4) charioteering
(5) history
(6) numbers.

Confucius taught that the main ethic is *jen* (benevolence), and that truth involves the knowledge of one's own faults. He believed in altruism and insisted on filial piety. He decided that people could be led by example and aimed at the rulers of his own time imitating those in a former period of history, where he attributed the prosperity of the people to the leadership of the Emperors. Confucianism included the worship of Heaven and revered ancestors and great men, though Confucius himself did not advocate prayer, believing that man should direct his own destiny.

Confucius' Ideal Man (Chun-tzu) was a pattern of good faith, sincerity and rightmindedness. Confucius hoped for the appearance of a true King (Wang) who would rule with moral example, not constraint. He stressed the idea of the 'Golden mean' and was not impressed by heroic deeds or by unusual people. He equated novelty with impiety. His aim was to bring back the golden age of the past. Confucius' great successor, Meng-tzu (377-289 BC), known as the second inspired one, accepted the prevailing worship of spirits and ancestors and imbued Confucianism with a more speculative interest.

Confucianism can be better described as a religious philosophy or code of social behaviour, rather than a religion in the accepted sense, since it has no church or clergy and is in no way an institution. For many years it had a great hold over education, its object being to emphasize the development of human nature and the person. During the early 19th century, attempts were made by followers to promote Confucianism to being a state religion, and though this failed, a good deal of the Confucian teachings still remain despite the onslaught of Communist ideology in the traditional area of its influence.

Chinese communists regard Confucius as 'Forefather of all reactionaries'.

Baha'ism

Baha'ism was founded in 1863 and evolved from the teachings of two visionaries in Persia in the 19th century. The first was Mirza Ali Muhammed (1820–50) who called himself Bab ('gateway') and the second was Mirza Husain Ali (1817–92) who called himself Baha'u'llah ('Glory of God'). Baha'u'llah was a follower of Bab, and in 1863 he announced that he was the manifestation of God sent to redeem the world, as earlier prophesied by Bab. He proclaimed this message and was imprisoned and exiled many times. He developed his teachings into a religion based on a new scripture, the *Kitab Akdas*.

After his death the followers of this faith grew in number until, today, it is present in over 70 000 centres in various parts of the world, predominantly in south-west Asia. About two-thirds of its followers are converts from Islam or the descendants of such, and the remainder are mostly west Europeans and Americans.

Baha'u'llah followers see him as a divine healer, relieving human suffering and uniting mankind. The Baha'i faith does not predict an end to this world or any intervention by God but declares that there will be a change within man and society, by which the world will return to peace and recover from the deterioration of moral values.

Baha'ism is not a minor sect but a universal religion, emphasizing the value of all religion and the spiritual unity of all mankind.

Shinto

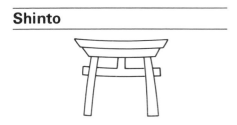

Shinto ('the teaching' or 'the way of the gods') came into practice during the 6th century AD to distinguish the Japanese religion from Buddhism which was reaching the islands by way of the mainland. The early forms of Shinto were a simple nature worship, and a religion for those who were not impelled by any complicated religious lore. The help of the deities was sought for the physical and spiritual needs of the people and there was great stress laid upon purification and truthfulness.

The more important national shrines were dedicated to well-known national figures, but there were also those set up for the worship of deities of mountain and forest.

During the 19th century, 13 Sect Shinto denominations were formed and these were dependent on private support for their teaching and organization. They had very little in common and varied widely in beliefs and practices. Some adhered to the traditional Shinto deites while others did not. Of the 13 denominations *Tenrikyo* is the one with the greatest following outside Japan.

Theories of Shinto have been greatly influenced by Confucianism, Taoism and Buddhism. In 1868, however, the Department of Shinto was established and attempts were made to do away with the Shinto and Buddhist coexistence, and in 1871 Shinto was proclaimed the Japanese national religion. Following the Second World War the status was discontinued.

Jainism

Jainism (from Hindi jaina 'saint') is an ancient Hindu sect which probably evolved sometime during the 7th to 5th centuries BC – it dates well back into Indian pre-history. It spread from east to west across India, but with the rise of Hinduism in the Middle Ages declined and became concentrated in two different regions, where it still exists today – Gujarat and Rajasthan and the Deccan. There are approximately two million Jains in India today.

Jainism has its own scriptures, passed down orally from Mahavira (b. c. 540 BC), one of the great teachers of Jainism. Its belief is that the material world is eternal, moving on in a never-ending series of vast cycles. Like all Indian religion it upholds the universal law of *karma*, which states that all actions, thoughts, words and deeds produce an effect which initiates another action, forming a chain of cause and effect.

A Jain is atheistic, believing in no one but himself to help man in his efforts – in practice the faith of Jainism is very pessimistic, the world is full of misery. The dismissal of God does not mean dismissal of prayer and worship; these are practices but are known as contemplation. To attain freedom and salvation (*moksha*) man must free his soul from matter and thus acquire god-like omniscience.

Greek Gods and Goddesses

Adonis God of vegetation and re-birth.
Aeolus God of the winds.
Alphito Barley goddess of Argos.
Aphrodite Goddess of love and beauty.
Apollo God of prophecy, music and medicine.
Ares God of war.
Arethusa Goddess of springs and fountains.
Artemis Goddess of fertility.
Asclepius God of healing.

Athene Goddess of prudence and wise council; and protectress of Athens.
Atlas A Titan who bears up the earth.
Attis God of vegetation.
Boreas God of the Northern wind.
Cronus Father of the God *Zeus*.
Cybele Goddess of the earth.
Demeter Goddess of the harvest.
Dionysus God of wine and the 'good life'.
Eos Goddess of the dawn.
Eros God of love.
Gaia Goddess of the earth.
Ganymede God of rain.
Hebe Goddess of youth.
Hecate Goddess of the moon.
Helios God of the sun.
Hera Goddess of the sky.
Hermes God of trade and travellers.
Hestia Goddess of fire.
Hypnos God of sleep.
Iris Goddess of the rainbow.
Morpheus God of dreams.
Nemesis God of destiny.
Nereus God of the sea.
Nike Goddess of victory.
Oceanus Ruler of the sea.
Pan God of male sexuality and of herds.
Persephone Goddess of the underworld and of corn.
Pluto God of the underworld.
Poseidon God of the sea.
Prometheus God of creation.
Rhea The original Mother Goddess; wife of Cronus.
Selene Goddess of the moon.
Thanatos God of death.
Zeus The overlord of the Olympian gods and goddesses; God of the sky and all its properties.

Roman Gods and Goddesses

Bacchus God of wine and ecstasy.
Bellona Goddess of war.
Ceres Goddess of corn.
Consus God of seed sowing.
Cupid God of love.
Diana Goddess of fertility and hunting.
Dis Pater God of the underworld.
Egreria Goddess of fountains and childbirth.
Epona Goddess of horses.
Fauna Goddess of fertility and herds.
Faunus God of crops and herds.
Feronia Goddess of spring flowers.
Fides God of honesty.
Flora Goddess of fruitfulness and flowers.
Fortuna Goddess of chance and fate.
Genius Protective god of individuals, groups and the state.
Janus God of entrances, travel, the dawn.
Juno Goddess of marriage, childbirth, light.
Jupiter God of the sky and its attributes (sun, moon, thunder, rain, etc.).
Lar God of the house.
Liber Pater God of agricultural and human fertility.
Libitina Goddess of funeral rites.
Maia Goddess of fertility.
Mars God of war and agriculture.
Mercury The messenger god; also god of merchants.
Minerva Goddess of war, craftsmen, education.

Mithras The sun god; god of regeneration.
Neptune God of the sea.
Ops Goddess of the harvest.
Orcus God of death.
Pales Goddess of flocks.
Penates Gods of food and drink.
Picus God of agriculture.
Pomono Goddess of fruit trees.
Portunus God of husbands.
Rumina Goddess of nursing mothers.
Saturn God of the vine, and of working men.
Silvanus God of trees and forests.
Venus Goddess of spring, gardens (later, goddess of love).
Vertumnus God of fruit trees.
Vesta Goddess of fire.
Victoria Goddess of victory.
Vulcan God of fire and thunderbolts.

Norse Gods and Goddesses

Aegir God of the sea.
Alcis Twin gods of the sky.
Baldur Son of Odin.
Bor Father of Odin.
Bragi God of poetry.
Donar God of thunder.
Fafnir A dragon god.
Fjorgynn Mother of Thor.
Freyja Goddess of libido.
Freyr God of fertility.
Frigg Goddess of fertility; wife of Odin.
Gefion Goddess who received virgins after death.
Heimdall Guardian of the bridge Bifrost.
Hel Goddess of death; Queen of Niflheim, the land of mists.
Hermod Son of Odin.
Hoder Blind god who killed Baldur.
Idunn Guardian goddess of the golden apples of youth; wife of Bragi.
Ing Founder God of the Anglo-Saxons and of the dynasty of Berenicia.
Kvasir God of wise utterances.
Logi The fire-god.
Loki God of mischief.
Mimir God of wisdom.
Nanna Goddess wife of Baldur.
Nehallenia Goddess of plenty.
Nerthus Goddess of earth.
Njord God of ships and the sea.
Odin (Woden, Wotan) Chief of the Aesir family of gods, the 'father' god, the god of battle, death, inspiration.
Otr The otter-god.
Ran Goddess of the sea.
Sif Goddess wife of Thor.
Sigyn Goddess wife of Loki.
Thor God of thunder and the sky; god of crops.
Tiwaz God of battle.
Valkyries Female helpers of the gods of war.
Weland (Volundr, Weiland, Wayland) The craftsman god.

Religious and other Festivals

MUSLIM FESTIVALS
Weekly (Friday) Day of Assembly
1 Muharram New Year's Day

1–10 Muharram New Year Festival (*Muharram*)
12 Rabi' ul-Awwal Festival of the Prophet's Birthday
26 Rajab Festival of the Prophet's Night Journey and Ascension
15 Sha'ban Night of Forgiveness
1–29/30 Ramadan Annual Fast (*Ramadan*)
1 Shawal Festival of Breaking the Fast (*Eid-ul-Fitr*)
9 Dhul-Hijjah Day of Arafat
10 Dhul-Hijjah Festival of Sacrifice (*Eid-ul-Adha*)
NB The dates vary against the Gregorian calendar, from year to year (see Islamic Calendar).

BUDDHIST FESTIVALS
Weekly Uposatha Days
Different festivals and, in some cases, different dates for similar festivals, are observed in the different countries where Buddhism is practised.

BURMA
16/17 April New Year
May/June The Buddha's Birth, Enlightenment and Death
July The Buddha's First Sermon/Beginning of the Rains Retreat
October End of the Rains Retreat
November Kathina Ceremony

CHINA
June/August Summer Retreat
August Festival of Hungry Ghosts
Gautama Buddha's Birth
Kuan-Yin

SRI LANKA
13 April New Year
May/June The Buddha's Birth, Enlightenment and Death
June/July Establishment of Buddhism in Sri Lanka
July The Buddha's First Sermon
July/August Procession of the Month of Asala
September The Buddha's First Visit to Sri Lanka
December/January Arrival of Sanghamitta

THAILAND
13–16 April New Year
May The Buddha's Enlightenment
May/June The Buddha's Cremation
July–October Rains Retreat
October End of the Rains Retreat
November Kathina Ceremony
November Festival of Lights
February All Saints' Day

TIBET
February New Year
May The Buddha's Birth, Enlightenment and Death
June Dzamling Chisang
June/July The Buddha's First Sermon
October The Buddha's Descent from Tushita
November Death of Tsongkhapa
January The Conjunction of Nine Evils and the Conjunction of Ten Virtues

CHRISTIAN FESTIVALS
1 January The Solemnity of Mary Mother of God
6 January Epiphany
25 January Conversion of St Paul
February Shrove Tuesday; Ash Wednesday

2 February Hypapante
The Presentation of Christ in the Temple
February–March/April Lent (The Great Fast)
19 March St Joseph
25 March The Annunciation of the Lord
March/April Holy Week; Palm Sunday; Maundy Thursday; Good Friday; Holy Saturday; Easter
25 April St Mark
May Ascension
1 May St Philip and St James
14 May St Matthias
31 May The Visitation of the Blessed Virgin Mary
May/June The Fathers of the First Ecumenical Council Pentecost; Trinity Sunday; All Saints; Corpus Christi
11 June St Barnabas
29 June St Peter and St Paul
July The Sacred Heart of Jesus
3 July St Thomas
25 July St James
6 August The Transfiguration
24 August St Bartholomew
1 September New Year (Eastern Orthodox Church)
8 September The Nativity of the Blessed Virgin Mary
14 September The Exaltation of the Holy Cross
21 September St Matthew
29 September St Michael and All Angels (Michaelmas)
18 October St Luke
28 October St Simon and St Jude
1 November All Saints
21 November Presentation of the Blessed Virgin Mary in the Temple
30 November St Andrew
November–December Advent
7 December St John
8 December The Immaculate Conception of the blessed Virgin Mary
25 December Christmas
26 December St Stephen
27 December St John
28 December Holy Innocents

JEWISH FESTIVALS
Weekly Sabbath (*Shabat*)
Monthly New Moon (*Rosh Hodesh*)
January/February (15 Shevat) Festival of 15 Shevat/New Year for Trees (*Tu B'shevat*)
February/March (13 Adar) Fast of Esther (*Taanit Ester*), (14 Adar) Festival of Lots (*Purim*)
March/April (14 Nisan) Fast of the First-born (*Taanit Behorim*), (15/16–21/22 Nisan) Passover (*Pesah*), (27 Nisan) Holocaust Day (*Yom Ha-Shoah*)
April/May (4 Iyyar) Remembrance Day (*Yom Ha'Zikharon*), (5 Iyyar) Independence Day (*Yom Ha'Atzmaut*), (18 Iyyar) 33rd Day of Counting the Omer, (28 Iyyar) Jerusalem Day (*Yom Yerushalayim*)
May/June (6/7 Sivan) Festival of Weeks (*Shavuot*), (20 Sivan) Fast of 20 Sivan
June/July (17 Tammuz) Fast of 17 Tammuz
July/August (9 Av) Fast of 9 Av (*Tisha B'Av*), (15 Av) Festival of 15 Av (*Tu B'Av*)
August/September (1 Ellul) Festival of 1 Ellul/New Year for Cattle
September/October (1/2 Tishri) New Year (*Rosh Hashanah*), (3 Tishri) Fast of Gedaliah (*Tsom Gedaliah*), (10 Tishri) Day of Atonement (*Yom Kippur*), (15/16–22/23 Tishri) Festival of Tabernacles (*Sukkot*), (22/23 Tishri) Eighth Day of Conclu-

sion (*Shemini Atzeret*), (23 Tishri) Rejoicing in the Torah (*Simhat Torah*)
November/December (25 Kislev–2 Tevet) Festival of the Dedication of the Temple/Festival of Lights (*Hanukah*)
December/January (10 Tevet) Feast of 10 Tevet

HINDU FESTIVALS

January Makar Sankranti/Til Sankranti/Lohri, Pongal, Kumbha Mela at Prayag (every twelve years)
January/February Vasanta Panchami/Shri Panchami/Saraswati Puja, Bhogali Bihu, Mahashivratri
20 February Ramakrishna Utsav
February/March Holi
March/April Ugadi, Basora, Rama Navami, Hanuman Jayanti
April Vaisakhi
April/May Akshaya Tritiya, Chittrai
May/June Ganga Dasa-hara, Nirjala Ekadashi, Snan-yatra
June/July Ratha-yatra/Jagannatha, Ashadhi Ekadashi/Toli Ekadashi
July/August Teej, Naga Panchami, Raksha Band-han/Shravana Purnima/Salono/Rakhi Purnima
August/September Onam, Ganesha Chaturthi, Janamashtami/Krishna Jayanti
September/October Mahalaya/Shraddha/Pitri Paksha/Kanagat, Navaratri/Durga Puja/Dassehra, Lakshmi Puja (West Bengal and Himachal Pradesh)
2 October Gandhi Jayanti
October/November Divali/Deepavali, Chhath, Karttika Ekadashi/Devuthna Ekadashi/Tulsi Ekadashi Karttika Purnima/Tripuri Purnima, Hoi, Skanda Shasti
November/December Vaikuntha Ekadashi, Lakshmi Puja (Orissa)

CHINESE FESTIVALS

January/February Chinese New Year
February/March Lantern Festival
March/April Festival of Pure Brightness
May/June Dragon Boat Festival
July/August Herd Boy and Weaving Maid
August All Souls' Festival
September Mid-Autumn Festival
September/October Double Ninth Festival
November/December Winter Solstice

Yemenite Jewish family celebrating a traditional Passover (*c.* 1950) and contemporary style seder plate used during the Passover meal. (Popperfoto)

PAINTING AND SCULPTURE

DRAWING is the process of artistic depiction on a two-dimensional surface by linear (and sometimes tonal) means, of objects or abstractions.

PAINTING is the visual and aesthetic expression of ideas and emotions primarily in two dimensions, using colour, line, shapes, texture and tones.

SCULPTURE describes the processes of carving, or engraving, modelling and casting so as to produce representations or abstraction of an artistic nature in relief, in intaglio, or in the round.

Styles and movements

PALAEOLITHIC ART from 24 000 BC
Cave painting of the Perigordian (Aurignacian period) and the later Solutrean and Magdalenian periods (18 000–11 000 BC) first discovered at Chaffaud, Vienne, France in 1834. Lascaux examples discovered 1940. Cave paintings also discovered in Czechoslovakia, the Urals, USSR, India, Australia (Mootwingie dates from c. 1500 BC) and North Africa (earliest is from the Bubulus period in the Sahara *post* 5400 BC).

MESOPOTAMIAN ART 3600–6000 BC
Covering the Sumerian, Assyrian and Babylonian epochs, it is epitomised by many styles which incorporate figures, animals, plants and mythical animals. Is seen now mainly in the sculptural works on palaces (Nineveh) and on tiles.

EGYPTIAN ART (3100–341 BC)
It is essentially a decorative tomb art, based on the notion of immortality, and provided that a deceased was recorded and equipped for the afterlife in writing (heiroglyph), pictures and material wealth and goods.

ANCIENT GREEK 2000–27 BC
Minoan and Mycenaean art (2800–1100 BC) consists mainly of sculptured engravings, decorated pottery and some frescoes. The Archaic period (800–500 BC) saw the development of sculpture, especially human figures. This tendency was developed in the Classical period (500–323 BC) where the body was glorified and drapery carved to imitate movement. The Hellenistic period (323–27 BC) expressed the emotions and was noticeable for its portraits. Throughout the entire period pottery was decorated with figures and scenes from story and legend.

ROMAN ART (100 BC–AD 400)
Based on Greek art, it excelled in copying Greek sculpture and relief carving of a very high quality. Portraiture also was popular. Roman painting was mainly executed in fresco in a naturalistic style (Pompeii). Mosaic floors were also highly decorative.

EARLY CHRISTIAN AD 200
Funerary fresco painting in the Roman catacombs ended with Constantine.

MIGRATION PERIOD 150–1000
A general term covering the art of the Huns with strong Asian influence and the Revised post-Roman Celtic art in Ireland and Britain, the pre-Carolingian Frankish art and the art of the Vikings.

A remarkable prehistoric cave drawing of reindeer from Font de Gaume, France. (Popperfoto)

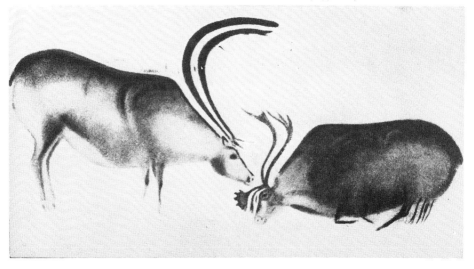

BYZANTINE ART c. 330–c. 1450

At first an admixture of Hellenic, Roman, Middle Eastern and Oriental styles, it dates from and has its first centre in the establishment of Constantinople as capital of the Roman Empire in the East. The First Golden Age was reached in the 6th century, when Hagia Sophia (St Sophia) was built in the city. The Second Golden Age occurred between 1051 and 1185 when Western Europe was influenced by its severe, spiritually uplifted style. These two Ages are chiefly artistically dominated by the use of mosaic work, but by the Third Golden Age (1261–1450) this expensive medium was being replaced by fresco painting.

ISLAMIC ART 7th century–17th century

Originally based on superb Koranic calligraphy, it is a highly decorative art form which reaches its apotheosis in the miniature painting, the ceramic tile, and carpetmaking in which floral and geometric motives reach a high peak of formal perfection.

ROMANESQUE ART 1050–1200

A widespread European style, mainly architectural, distinguished by the use of rounded arches. The sculpture is mainly church work intended to inspire awe of the divine power by depicting scenes of heaven and hell, demons and angels and the omnipotent deity. Illuminated manuscripts of high quality include the Winchester Bible.

GOTHIC ART (1125–1450)

The style of architecture, painting and sculpture which succeeded Romanesque art in Europe. The first Gothic building was St Denis, outside Paris, which differed from the previous style mainly by having ribbed vaulting to its roofs which were held up by pointed arches. The sculpture is narrative and realistic, in painting the style evolved more slowly and is seen in manuscripts, which developed into the most decorative style seen in International Gothic.

INTERNATIONAL GOTHIC c. 1380–c. 1470

A mixture of styles of painting and sculpture in Europe due to the movements of notable peripatetic artists and the increase in trade, travel and court rivalry. The main influences were Northern France, The Netherlands and Italy, and its main features are rich and decorative colouring and detail, and flowing line.

THE RENAISSANCE c. 1300–1545

Meaning 'rebirth', the term describes the revival of classical learning and art. At first centred in Florence, it marked the end of the Middle Ages and was probably the outstanding creative period in the history of the arts. Architecture, painting, sculpture, deriving from Greek and Roman models, moved into an unparalleled vigour and prominence, and the artist gained a role in society hitherto unknown, mainly due to the rival city states that employed them. Artistic invention included perspective and painting with oil. Latterly, the Renaissance style moved towards Mannerism.

MANNERISM c. 1520–1700

A style emerging from the Renaissance, it exaggerated the styles of Michelangelo and Raphael into contorted and extravagantly gestured figures, to achieve a more intense emotional effect. This style influenced the later Baroque movement.

THE BAROQUE c. 1600–1720

Centred on the new stability of the Roman Catholic faith, its main artistic aim was to unite the main parts of building, sculpture and painting into an overall dramatic effect. It is mainly 'frontal', that is it is best seen from one, rather than many, viewpoints. Its exuberance and monumentality make it one of the most robust movements in art history.

ROCOCO c. 1735–65

A mainly French style, it is characterized by a wealth of elaborate and superficial decoration. Elegance was the keynote and Rococo reflected the extravagance and brilliance of Court Life.

NEO-CLASSICISM (c. 1750–1850)

More of a discipline than a movement, it expresses the qualities of harmony, clarity and order associated with Greek and Roman Art. The antithesis of Romanticism, it espouses accepted notions of beauty and rejects individual inspiration.

ROMANTICISM c. 1780–1850

A mainly literary movement, it was a reaction to Classicism and the growing Industrial Revolution. deriving its inspiration from untamed nature, the Romantic belief centred on the importance of spontaneity of individual feeling towards the natural world.

THE PRE-RAPHAELITE BROTHERHOOD 1848–1856

A brotherhood of seven London artists formed to make a return to the pre-Raphael (hence the name) Italian forms as a protest against the frivolity of the prevailing English School of the day. The founders and most important demonstrators of the style were William Holman Hunt, John Everett Millais and Dante Gabriel Rossetti.

ARTS AND CRAFTS MOVEMENT c. 1870–1900

Based on the revival of interest in the mediaeval craft system led by William Morris, its aims were to fuse the functional and the decorative, and to restore the worth of handmade crafts in the face of the growing mass-produced wares of the late 19th century.

SYMBOLISM c. 1880–1905

Influenced by the Pre-Raphaelites and the Romantics, it was a movement that provided an intellectual alternative to the straight visual work of the Impressionists. Its twin sources were either literary or pictorially formal and the results were intended to engage the emotions. Symbolism influenced the Surrealists and was the forerunner of Expressionist and abstract art.

IMPRESSIONISM 1875–1886

The term was inadvertently introduced by the journalist Leroy in *Charivari* to describe the work of Monet, Sisley, Pissarro and others, taking the name from Monet's *Impression: Soleil levant.* The painters in this manner were concerned with light and its effects, and the use of 'broken' colour.

POINTILLISM c. 1880–1915

Based on the colour theories of Chevreul, its aim was to achieve greater pictorial luminosity by placing small marks of pure primary colour on the surface, allowing them to merge at a viewing distance to create an optical mixture. Sometimes called Divisionism.

POST-IMPRESSIONISM c. 1880-1910
Term used to describe any breakaway tendencies from pure impressionism that took place during the period, and embraces Pointillism and the beginnings of Expressionism, especially the works of Gauguin, Van Gogh and Cézanne.

ART NOUVEAU c. 1890-1915
A decorative style deriving from the Arts and Crafts movement of the UK, it is represented by two streams, one of fluid asymmetry and flowing linear rhythms inspired by nature, the other of a geometrical austerity. Called Jugendstil (Germany) and Sezessionstil (Austria).

20th century forms

FAUVISM c. 1905-7
A short-lived but highly influential French movement of artists surrounding Matisse, it is summarized by the daring and spontaneous handling of paint in bold, brilliant, sometimes non-representational colour, in a subjective, joyous response to the visual world. 'Fauve' means 'wild beast', a critic's response to seeing paintings by Matisse and others at the 1905 Salon d'Automne.

DIE BRUCKE (The Bridge) c. 1905-13
A group of German Expressionist artists, including Kirchner, whose manifesto was to overthrow the concept of art as an end in itself and to integrate art and life by using art as a means of communication. Influenced by tribal art and Van Gogh, the founders lived and worked communally, forcing the intensity of their work by using clashing colours and aggressive distortions.

EXPRESSIONISM c. 1905-25
Used loosely, a term that denotes an emphasis on pictorial distortion or chromatic exaggeration within a work of art of any given period. More specifically it is used to define certain 20th century North European art where the emphasis is on stress or heightened emotion, as portrayed through the artists' subjective vision. Influenced by Gauguin, Van Gogh, Munch and Fauvism, the movement includes the most specific groups of Die Brucke and Der Blaue Reiter.

CUBISM c. 1907-23
The style formulated from investigations by Picasso and Braque into Cézanne's late works and African tribal sculpture. The first painting to combine these influences was Picasso's 'Les Demoiselles d'Avignon'. The term 'Cubist' was coined by a French critic on seeing Braque's work in that style of 1908. 'Analytic' (early) Cubism presents the subject from a variety of viewpoints; 'Synthetic' (late) Cubism introduced decorative elements such as lettering and applied materials such as newspaper (collage) to achieve a balance between the depiction of reality and the picture as an object in its own right. The movement had many followers, but in a few years Picasso and Braque moved away from it to independent paths.

FUTURISM c. 1909-19
Initially a literary movement, its manifesto con-

cerned itself with incorporating the thrust of modern technology with art. Anti art-establishment, it approached abstract art, especially cubism, to express its dynamism. Its founder-member Marinetti described speed as 'a new form of beauty'.

SCHOOL OF PARIS c. 1910-50
Term used to distinguish the large international group of Paris-based artists which made the city the centre of the Art World until the emergence of the New York School.

DER BLAUE REITER (the Blue Rider) c. 1911-14
A loosely-knit group of Expressionist painters including Kandisky, Klee and Marc, united by a dictum of Kandinsky that stated 'the creative spirit is concealed within matter'.

DADA c. 1915-23
A total rejection of established values; anti-aesthetic and anti-rational, by European and American artists, sculptors and photographers.

BAUHAUS c. 1919-33
A post-First World War resolution to re-integrate the disparate visual arts and crafts within the discipline of architecture, function dictating the form. It exerted, and still exerts a profound influence on 20th century architecture and crafts.

SURREALISM c. 1924-
A French avant-garde movement of literary origin inspired by Dada, and greatly influenced by Freud's theories of psychoanalysis. Irrational association, spontaneous techniques and an elimination of premeditation to free the workings of the unconscious mind, as well as an interest in dreams, were the main motivations of its practitioners.

KINETIC ART c. 1930-
A term which broadly covers art which incorporates movement, in the work in space, generated by air currents, motors, artificial lights, etc.

ABSTRACT IMPRESSIONISM c. 1940-
Placing emphasis on spontaneous personal expression, it rejects contemporary, social and aesthetic values. Recognized as the first movement in the USA to develop independently of and actually influence Europe. Notable practitioners include Jackson Pollock and De Kooning. Includes Action Painting (USA), and Tachisme (Europe).

NEW YORK SCHOOL c. 1945-60
A group of avant-garde artists whose aim was to find a uniquely American mode of expression. The group included such artists as Pollock, De Kooning and Rothko.

OP ART c. 1950-
An abstract art that bases itself on creating optical effects which appear to move on a flat surface.

POP ART c. 1955-
A reaction against Abstract Expressionism, the movement started almost simultaneously in UK and USA and uses the images of mass media, advertising and pop culture, presenting the common, everyday object as art.

MINIMAL ART c. 1960-

A rejection of the aesthetic qualities of art in favour of the physical reality of the art object. The material used is important, as are their strictly geometrical formats and placings within settings. A famous (some might say, notorious) example was Andre's *Equivalent VIII*, 120 firebricks arranged in a solid rectangle on the Tate Gallery floor in 1966.

Media

AIRBRUSH TECHNIQUE

A system of spraying varnish, fixative or colour with an airbrush, an implement which resembles a fountain pen and which has a small container near the nozzle. Air pressure is applied via a mechanical compressor and can be minutely controlled to create fine, delicate lines or a wide sweep.

ACRYLIC RESIN

A quick-drying waterproof emulsion that can be mixed with dry pigments to give paints that can be applied with heavy knife-laid impasto or diluted with water to wash-like consistency.

ETCHING

The process of biting out a design on a metal plate with acid, so that the resultant indentations hold ink, which will subsequently print the image on to paper.

FRESCO

(Ital.: *fresco*, fresh.) Developed by Minoan and other ancient civilizations. *Buon fresco* is executed with pigments ground in water or lime-water on to a freshly prepared lime-plaster wall while the plaster is still damp.

GOUACHE

A water-colour painting carried out with opaque colours as opposed to pure water colour which employs transparent colours.

INKS

Liquids for drawing or painting; generally the colours are a suspension or present as a dye. Sometimes, as with Indian ink or white ink, there may be opaque pigments in suspension. Inks may be applied with different types of pen or soft hair brushes.

INTAGLIO

Any method where a metal plate is bitten into, etched or cut to hold ink for a design to be printed from it. Engraving, Drypoint, Etching, Aquatint and Mezzotint fall into this category.

LITHOGRAPHY

Planar printing method where design is drawn on limestone or metal plate with greasy ink or crayon. The surface is then wetted; the ink applied to it

Highest price paintings – Progessive records

Price	Painter, title, sold by and sold to	Date
£6 500	Antonio Correggio's *The Magdalen Reading* (in fact spurious) to Elector Friedrich Augustus II of Saxony	1746
£8 500	Raphael's *The Sistine Madonna* (1513–14) from Placenza to Elector Friedrich Augustus II of Saxony	1759
£16 000	Van Eyck's *Adoration of the Lamb*, 6 outer panels of Ghent altarpiece by Edward Solby to the Government of Prussia	1821
£24 600*	Murillo's *The Immaculate Conception* by estate of Marshal Soult to the Louvre (against Czar Nicholas I) in Paris	1852
£70 000	Raphael's *Ansidei Madonna* (1506) from Perugia by the 8th Duke of Marlborough to the National Gallery	1885
£100 000	Raphael's *The Colonna Altarpiece* (1503–05) from Perugia by Seldemeyer to J. Pierpont Morgan	1901
£102 880	Van Dyck's *Elena Grimaldo-Cattaneo* (portrait) by Knoedler to Peter Widener (1834–1915)	1906
£102 880	Rembrandt's *The Mill* by 6th Marquess of Lansdowne to Peter Widener	1911
£116 500	Raphael's smaller *Panshanger Madonna* by Joseph (later Baron) Duveen (1869–1939) to Peter Widener	1913
£310 400	Leonardo da Vinci's *Benois Madonna* (c. 1477) to Czar Nicholas II in Paris	1914
£821 429*	Rembrandt's *Aristotle Contemplating the Bust of Homer* by estate of Mr and Mrs Alfred W. Erickson to New York Metropolitan Museum of Art	1961
£1 785 714	Leonardo da Vinci's *Ginerva de' Benci* (c. 1475) by Prince Franz Josef II of Liechtenstein to National Gallery of Art, Washington DC, USA	1967
£2 310 000*	Velázquez's *Portrait of Juan de Pareja* by the Earl of Radnor to the Wildenstein Gallery, New York	1970
£2 729 000*	Turner's *Juliet and Her Nurse* by Whitney Museum, New York to undisclosed bidder at Sotheby Parke Bernet, New York	1980
£7 470 500*	Turner's *Seascape: Folkestone* from estate of Lord Clark (1903–83) to Leggatt's of London for an unknown buyer	1984
£8 100 000*	Mantegna's *The Adoration of the Magi* by the Marquess of Northampton to the J. Paul Getty Museum, Malibu, California	1985
£22 500 000	Van Gogh's *Sunflowers* at Sotheby's, London, from Lady Beatty to Yasuda Fire and Marine Insurance Co., Tokyo	1987
£30 187 623*	Van Gogh's *Irises* from John Whitney Payson to an undisclosed bidder at Sotheby's, New York	1987

* *Indicates price at auction, otherwise prices were by private treaty.*

adheres only to the greasy part, the wetted part repelling it. A print is then taken from the surface.

MONOTYPE
Single print taken from a design painted on a flat surface while the paint is still wet.

OIL
Dry pigments ground in an oil; this is generally linseed, but may be poppy, walnut or other similar oils. It is a technique that gradually evolved during the latter part of the Middle Ages. The Van Eyck brothers did much to perfect the medium.

PASTEL
A stick of colour made from powdered pigment bound with gum. Applied dry to paper the colours can be blended and mixed but the result can be fragile and impermanent unless fixed with spray varnish (fixative).

TEMPERA
A loose term in painting in which the dry pigments are mixed with such substances as egg white, egg yolk, glue, gelatine or casein. True tempera is when the colours are ground with egg yolk only.

WATER COLOUR
Pigments are ground with gum arabic and thinned in use with water. The technique as used today started with Albrecht Dürer but did not achieve widespread use until the emergence of the English School of water-colourists in the first half of the 19th century. Applied with squirrel or sable brushes on white or tinted paper.

WOODCUT
Design incised on wood, the grain of which runs lengthwise. The negative areas are cut away, leaving the raised design to take ink, from which is taken the paper print. The Japanese perfected this medium.

WOOD ENGRAVING
As in woodcut, except that the printing surface is on the end grain of the wood block, allowing fine detail to be cut with a graver or burin. Extensively used in book illustration until the invention of photomechanical engraving.

Renowned painters by country

Some of the world's most renowned painters with well-known examples of their work:

AUSTRALIA
Nolan, Sidney (b. 1917) *Themes from the Career of Ned Kelly.*

AUSTRIA
Klimt, Gustav (1862-1918) *Mosaic mural for the Palais Stoclet in Brussels.*
Kokoschka, Oskar (b. 1886) *View of the Thames.*
Schiele, Egon (1890-1918) *The Artist's Mother Sleeping.*

BELGIUM
Brueghel, Pieter (The Elder) (c. 1525-69) *The Adoration of the Kings, The Peasant Dance.*

Ensor, James (1860-1949) *Entry of Christ into Brussels.*
Gossaert, Jan (c. 1478-1533) *Adoration.*
Jordaens, Jacob (1593-1678) *The Bean King.*
Magritte, René (1898-1967) *The Key of Dreams.*
Memlinc, Hans (c. 1430-94) *Mystic Marriage of St. Catherine.*
Rubens, Peter Paul (1577-1640) *Adoration of the Magi, Battle of the Amazons*
Teniers, David (The Younger) (1610-90) *Peasants Playing Bowls.*
Van der Weyden, Rogier (c. 1400-64) *Deposition, The Magdalen Reading.*
Van Eyck, Anthony (1599-1641) *Charles I of England, Elena Grimaldi-Cattaneo.*
Van Eyck, Hubert (c. 1370-c. 1426) Jan (c. 1390-1441) *Ghent Altarpiece, The Three Mary's at the Open Sepulchre.* Jan alone *The Arnolfini Marriage, Adoration of the Lamb.*

CZECHOSLOVAKIA
Kupka, Frank (Frantisek) (1871-1957) *Amorpha, fugue in two colours.*

FRANCE
Arp, Hans (Jean) (1887-1966) *Berger et Nuage.*
Bonnard, Pierre (1867-1947) *The Window.*
Boucher, François (1703-70) *Diana Bathing.*
Braque, Georges (1882-1963) *Vase of Anemones.*
Cézanne, Paul (1839-1906) *Mont Sainte-Victoire, Bathers.*
Chagall, Marc (1887-1985) *I and the Village, Calvary.*
Chardin, Jean-Baptiste Siméon (1600-1779) *The Skate, The Lesson.*
Corot, Jean-Baptiste Camille (1796-1875) *Ponte de Mantes, Sens Cathedral.*
Courbet, Gustave (1819-77) *A Burial at Ornans.*
Daumier, Honoré (1808-79) *The Third-Class Carriage.*
David, Jacques Louis (1748-1825) *The Rape of the Sabines.*
Degas, Hilaire-Germain-Edgar (1834-1917) *La Danseuse au Bouquet.*
Delacroix, Eugène (1798-1863) *The Massacre of Chios.*
Derain, André (1880-1945) *Mountains at Collioure.*
Fouquet, Jean (c. 1420-c. 1480) *Etienne Chevalier with St Stephen.*
Fragonard, Jean-Honoré (1732-1806) *The Love Letter, Baigneuses.*
Gauguin, Paul (1848-1903) *Ta Matete.*
Gellée, Claude (called Claude Lorraine) (1600-82) *Ascanius and the Stag.*
Gericault, Theodore (1791-1824) *The Raft of the Medusa.*
Ingres, Jean-Auguste Dominique (1780-1867) *Odalisque.*
La Tour, George de (1593-1652) *St Sebastian tended by the Holy Women.*
Leger, Fernand (1881-1955) *Three Women.*
Lorraine, Claude (1600-82) *Embarkation of St Ursula.*
Manet, Edouard (1823-83) *Déjeuner sur l'Herbe.*
Matisse, Henri (1869-1954) *Odalisque.*
Millet, Jean-François (1814-75) *Man with the Hoe, Angelus.*
Monet, Claude (1840-1926) *Rouen Cathedral, Water-lilies.*
Pissarro, Camille (1830-1903) *The Harvest, Montfoucault.*
Poussin, Nicolas (1593/4-1665) *Worship of the Golden Calf.* (Damaged Mar. 1978)

The Skaters by Pieter Brueghel, one of Belgium's best-known artists. (Popperfoto)

Renoir, Pierre August (1841–1919) *Luncheon of the Boating Party.*
Rouault, Georges (1871–1958) *Christ Mocked.*
Rousseau, Henri Julien ('Le Douanier') (1844–1910) *The Dream.*
Seurat, Georges (1859–91) *Sunday Afternoon on the Grande Jatte.*
Stael, Nicholas de (1914–55) *The Roofs.*
Toulouse-Lautrec, Henri de (1864–1901) *At the Moulin Rouge.*
Utrillo, Maurice (1883–1955) *Port of St Martin.*
Vlaminck, Maurice de (1876–1958) *The Bridge at Chatou.*
Watteau, Antoine (1684–1721) *The Embarkation for Cythera.*

GERMANY
Altdorfer, Albrecht (c. 1480–1538) *Battle of Arbela.*
Beckmann, Max (1884–1950) *The Night.*
Beuys, Joseph (b. 1921) *Fond IV/4.*
Cranach, Lucas (The Elder) (1472–1553) *Venus, Rest on Flight into Egypt.*
Dix, Otto (1891–1969) *The War.*
Ernst, Max (1891–1976) *The Elephant Celebes.*
Dürer, Albrecht (1471–1528) *The Four Apostles, Apocalypse.*
Friedrich, Caspar David (1774–1840) *The Cross in the Mountains.*
Grosz, George (1893–1959) *Suicide.*
Grunewald, Mathias (c. 1460–1528) *Isenheim Altarpiece.*
Holbein, Hans (The Younger) (c. 1497–1543) *Henry VIII, The Ambassadors.*
Kirchner, Ernst Ludwig (1880–1938) *Self-portrait with Model.*
Marc, Franz (1880–1916) *The Blue Horse.*

Nolde, Emil (Emil Hansen) (1867–1956) *Masks and Dahlias.*

GREAT BRITAIN
Auerbach, Frank (b. 1931) *E.O.W. Nude.*
Bacon, Francis (b. 1909) *Three Studies at the Base of a Crucifixion.*
Blake, William (1757–1827) *The Book of Job: Divine Comedy.*
Bonington, Richard Parkes (1801–28) *A Sea Piece.*
Constable, John (1776–1837) *The Hay Wain.*
Crome, John (1768–1821) *The Slate Quarries.*
Dobson, William (1610–46) *Endymion Porter.*
Freud, Lucian (b. 1922) *Francis Bacon.*
Fuseli, Henry (Johann Heinrich Fussli) (1741–1825) *Nightmare.*
Gainsborough, Thomas (1727–88) *Blue Boy.*
Girtin, Thomas (1775–1802) *Kirkstall Abbey: Evening.*
Hamilton, Richard (b. 1922) *Portrait of Hugh Gaitskell as a Famous Monster of Filmland.*
Hilliard, Nicholas (c. 1537–1619) *Elizabeth I, Sir Walter Raleigh.*
Hockney, David (b. 1937) *Mr & Mrs Clark and Percy.*
Hogarth, William (1697–1764) *Rake's Progress, Marriage à la Mode.*
Hunt, William Holman (1827–1910) *The Scapegoat, Light of the World.*
John, Augustus Edwin (1878–1961) *The Smiling Woman.*
John, Gwen (1876–1939) *Self Portrait.*
Landseer, Sir Edwin (1802–73) *The Old Shepherd's Chief Mourner, Shoeing.*
Millais, Sir John Everett (1829–96) *Order of Release.*
Nash, Paul (1889–1946) *British. Dead Sea.*
Nicholson, Ben (b. 1894) *White Relief.*

Raeburn, Sir Henry (1756-1823) *Sir John Sinclair.*
Ramsay, Allan (1713-84) *The Artist's Wife.*
Reynolds, Sir Joshua (1723-92) *Mrs Siddons as the Tragic Muse, The Three Graces.*
Rossetti, Dante Gabriel (1828-82) *Beata Beatrix.*
Sickert, Walter Richard (1860-1942) *Ennui.*
Sisley, Alfred (1839-99) *Flood at Port Marly.*
Smith, Sir Matthew (1879-1959) *Fitzroy Street Nudes.*
Spencer, Sir Stanley (1891-1959) *The Resurrection, Cookham.*
Stubbs, George (1724-1806) *Horse Frightened by a Lion.*
Sutherland, Graham (1903-80) *Christ in Glory, Coventry Cathedral.*
Turner, Joseph Mallord William (1775-1851) *The Grand Canal, Venice, Shipwreck, Juliet and Her Nurse.*
Wilson, Richard (1713-82) *Okehampton Castle.*

HUNGARY
Moholy-Nagy, Laszlo (1895-1946) *Light prop.*
Vasarely, Victor (b. 1908) *Timbres II.*

ITALY
Balla, Giacomo (1871-1958) *Dynamism of a Dog on a Leash.*
Bellini, Giovanni (c. 1429-1561) *Pieta, Coronation of the Virgin, Agony in the Garden.*
Botticelli, Sandro (Alessandro di Mariano Filipepi) (1445-1510) *Birth of Venus, Mystic Nativity.*
Canaletto, Giovanni Antonio Canal (1697-1768) *Venice: A Regatta on the Grand Canal.*
Caravaggio, Michelangelo Merisi (1573-1610) *St Matthew, Deposition.*
Carra, Carlo (1881-1966) *Metaphysical Muse.*
Del Castagno, Andrea (Andrea di Bartolo di Bargilla) (1421-57) *The Vision of St Jerome.*
Chirico, Giorgio de (1888-1978) *Mystery and Melancholy of a Street: Nostalgia of the Infinite.*
Corregio, Antonio Allegri (c. 1489-1534) *Jupiter and Io, Assumption of the Virgin, The Magdalen reading* (attributed but spurious).
Duccio (Di Buoninsegna) (active 1278-1318) *The Rucellai Madonna.*
Da Fabriano Gentile (1370-1427) *The Adoration of the Magi.*
Francesca, Piero della (c. 1415-92) *Nativity.*
Fra Angelico, Giovanni da Fiesole (1387-1455) *Annunciation.*
Fra Filippo Lippi (c. 1406-69) *Tarquinia Madonna.*
Giorgione, Giorgio da Castelfranco (1475-1510) *Sleeping Venus.*
Giotto di Bondone (c. 1267-1337) *Life of St Francis.*
Leonardo da Vinci (1452-1519) *Mona Lisa (La Gioconda), Last Supper, Cinerva de' Benci, Benois Madonna.*
Lorenzetti, Ambrogio (active c. 1319-48?) *Good and Bad Government, Palazzo Pubblico, Siena.*
Mantegna, Andrea (c. 1430-1506) *The Triumph of Caesar.*
Martini, Simone (c. 1285-1344) *Annunciation.*
Masaccio (1401-28?) *Scenes from the Life of St Peter, Brancacci Chapel.*
Da Messina, Antonello (1430-79) *Salvador Mundi.*
Michelangelo, Buonarroti (1475-1564) *Creation of Adam.*
Modigliani, Amedeo (1884-1920) *Portrait of Madame Zborowski.*
Morandi, Giorgio (1890-1964) *Still Life.*
Orcagna (Andrea di Cione) (active 1343-68) *The Redeemer with the Madonna and Saints.*

Parmigianino (Girolamo Francesco Maria Mazzola) (1503-40) *The Vision of St Jerome.*
Raphael (1483-1520) *Sistine Madonna, Panshanger Madonna, The Colonna Altarpiece, Ansidei Madonna.*
Romano, Giulio (1499?-1546) *The Hall of the Giants.*
Del Sarto, Andrea (Andrea d'Agnolo) (1486-1530) *The Madonna of the Harpies, A Young Man.*
Signorelli, Luca (active 1470-1523) *The Last Judgment, Orvieto.*
Tiepolo, Giovanni Battista (1696-1770) *The Finding of Moses.*
Tintoretto, Jacopo Robusti (1518-94) *Last Supper, Il Paradiso.*
Titian (c. 1487-1576) *The Tribute Money, Bacchus and Ariadne.*
Uccello, Paolo (1396/7-1475) *The Battle of San Romano, The Night Hunt.*
Veronese, Paolo Caliari (1528-88) *Marriage at Cana.*

JAPAN
Hiroshige, Ando (1797-1858) *A Hundred Famous Views of Edo.*
Hokusai, Katsushika (1760-1849) *Thirty-six Views of Mount Fuji.*
Motonobu, Kano (1476-1559) *Eight Views of Hsiao-hsiang.*
Utamaro, Kitagawa (1753-1806) *Mushierabi (Book of Insects).*

MEXICO
Orozco, José Clemente (1883-1949) *Hidalgo and Castillo.*
Rivera, Diego (1886-1957) *Creation.*
Siqueiros, David Alfaro (1896-1974) *The March of Humanity on Earth, Towards the Cosmos.*

NETHERLANDS
Appel, Karel (b. 1921) *Cry of Liberty.*
Bosch, Hieronymus (c. 1450-1516) *Christ Crowned with Thorns, The Garden of Earthly Delights.*
Hals, Frans (c. 1580-1666) *Laughing Cavalier.*
Hooch, Pieter de (1629-83) *An Interior.*
Leyden, Lucas van (1494-1533) *Last Judgment.*
Mondrian, Piet (1872-1944) *Composition.*
Rembrandt, Harmensz van Rijn (1606-69) *The Night Watch, The Anatomy Lesson, Aristotle Contemplating the Bust of Homer, The Mill.*
Ruisdael, Jacob van (c. 1628-82) *View of Haarlem.*
Van Gogh, Vincent (1853-90) *Road with Cypresses, Old Peasant, L'Eglise d'Auvers.*
Vermeer, Jan (1632-75) *Woman with a Water Jug.*

NORWAY
Munch, Edvard (1863-1944) *Dance of Death, Shriek.*

SPAIN
Dali, Salvador (1904-89) *Crucifixion, The Persistence of Memory.*
El Greco (1541-1614) *The Burial of Count Orgaz, View of Toledo.*
Goya, Francisco de (1746-1828) *The Naked Maja, The Shootings of May 3rd.*
Gris, Juan (José Gonsalez) (1887-1927) *Violin and Fruit Dish.*
Murillo, Bartolomé Esteban (1617-82) *Virgin and Child, Immaculate Conception.*
Picasso, Pablo (1881-1973) *Guernica, Les Demoiselles d'Avignon.*
Ribera, José (1591-1652) *The Martyrdom of St Bartholomew.*

Tapies, Antonio (b. 1923) *Large Painting.*
Velázquez, Diego (1599–1660) *Rokeby Venus, The Water-Carrier, Juan de Pareja.*

SWITZERLAND
Klee, Paul (1879–1940) *Twittering Machine.*

USSR
Kandinsky, Wassily (1866–1944) *Compositions, Improvisations and Impressions.*
Larionov, Mikhail Fedorovich (1881–1964) *Glass.*
Malevich, Kasimir Severinovich (1878–1935) *Black Square.*
Soutine, Chaim (1893–1943) *The Madwoman.*
Tatlin, Vladimir (1885–1953) *Constructivist Sculptures.*

UNITED STATES OF AMERICA
Audubon, John James (1785–1851) *Birds of America.*
Cassatt, Mary (1845–1926) *The Bath.*
Eakins, Thomas (1844–1916) *The Gross Clinic.*
Homer, Winslow (1836–1910) *Northeaster.*
O'Keeffe, Georgia (b. 1887) *Cityscapes of New York.*
De Kooning, Willem (b. 1904) *Woman Series.*
Lichtenstein, Roy (b. 1923) *Wham!*
Moses, Grandma (Anna Mary Robertson) (1860–1961) *The Thanksgiving Turkey.*
Pollock, Jackson (1912–56) *Autumn Rhythm.*
Rauschenberg, Robert (b. 1925) *Monogram.*
Rothko, Mark (1903–70) *Green on Blue.*
Ray, Man (1890–1978) *The Rope Dancer Accompanies Herself With Her Shadows.*
Sargent, John Singer (1856–1925) *Carnation, Lily, Lily, Rose.*
Warhol, Andy (1930–87) *Campbell's Soupcans.*
Whistler, James Abbott McNeill (1834–1903) *Arrangement in Grey and Black – The Artist's Mother.*
Wyeth, Andrew (b. 1917) *Christina's World.*

Renowned sculptors by country

FRANCE
Brancusi, Constantin (1876–1957) Romanian French.
Gaudier-Brzeska, Henri (1891–1915).
Pevsner, Antoine (1886–1962).
Pigalle, Jean-Baptiste (1714–85).
Rodin, Louis-François (c. 1705–62).

GREAT BRITAIN
Caro, Anthony (b. 1924).
Epstein, Sir Jacob (1880–1959).
Flaxman, John (1755–1826).
Hepworth, Barbara (1903–75).
Moore, Henry (1898–1986).
Paolozzi, Eduardo (b. 1924).

GREECE
Phidias (died c. 432 BC).
Praxiteles (active mid-4th century BC).

ITALY
Bernini, Gianlorenzo (1598–1680).
Cellini, Benvenuto (1500–71).
Donatello (Donato di Niccolo) (1386–1466).
Ghiberti, Lorenzo (1378–1455).

Michelangelo, Buonarroti (1475–1564).
Pisano, Giovanni (active c. 1265–1314).
Pisano, Nicola (active c. 1258–84).
Robbia, Luca della (1400–82).

SPAIN
Gonzalez, Julio (1876–1942).

SWITZERLAND
Giacometti, Alberto (1901–66).

USSR
Archipenko, Alexander (1887–1964).
Gabo, Naum (Naum Neemia Pevsner) (1890–1977).
Zadkine, Ossip (1890–1967).

UNITED STATES OF AMERICA
Calder, Alexander (1898–1976).
Nevelson, Louise (b. 1900).
Smith, David (1906–65).

Photography

The camera obscura (Latin, 'darkened room') and its principles were familiar as far back in times as the 4th century BC, when Aristotle observed that if a very small aperture was made in one wall of an otherwise light-free room, the scene outside the wall was cast, but inverted, on the opposite inside wall of the room. Perfected with lenses in the aperture during the 19th century, this device was used as an aid to artists.

In 1725 the German, Johann Heinrich Schultze, discovered that silver salts darken in ratio to the strength of light exposed to them. The first actual use of this phenomenon was made in England by Thomas Wedgwood and Sir Humphrey Davy, who coated silver salts onto paper and produced silhouette images on it from leaves and other natural sources. They published a joint paper on their findings in 1802.

In 1826, a Frenchman, Joseph Nicéphore Niepce, made and fixed permanently the first photographic image, a view from his workroom. His camera obscura lens resolved the image onto a bituminous, light-sensitive coating supported by a plate of pewter. Development of the image was obtained by acid etching the unexposed bitumen, the relief image left on the pewter giving a printing surface to obtain copies. Niepce then went into partnership with Louis Jacques Mandé Daguerre. Adapting Schultze's discovery, they used copper plates covered with silver iodide. In 1835 Daguerre succeeded in developing his images with mercury vapour; two years later he was able to permanently fix the images by immersing the plates in a solution of common salt (sodium chloride). Announcing his discovery in 1839, he patented it, using the name Daguerrotype, for which the French government awarded him an annual pension on condition that his process be made public.

Numerous experiments using silver salts then took place, the most important being those of William Henry Fox Talbot in England who, by using impregnated paper with silver salts, obtained negative images from which multiple positives could be made. The process was called Calotype, but was not as sharp and brilliant as Daguerrotype, which remained the more popular.

In 1850 an English sculptor, Frederick Scott Archer, invented the wet-plate process. The image was formed on a glass plate coated with light-sensitive collodion, a jelly-like substance that remained wet for some time. While still wet, the plate was exposed in the camera and immediately developed. Such methods were cumbersome and technical and it was not until the introduction of the dry-plate process, invented in 1871 by Englishman, Richard L. Maddox, that amateur photography caught on.

By 1884 George Eastman in the United States was manufacturing silver bromide printing papers; in 1891 the Belgian, Leo Backland, marketed the first commercially successful contact papers, calling them Velox papers.

Dry-plate photography, though a great improvement on previous processes, was still awkward and cumbersome. John Carbutt, an American, coated sheets of celluloid with emulsion. Eastman was quick to realize its commercial aspects and in 1888 introduced the first Kodak, a simple hand camera already loaded at the factory with celluloid film for 100 shots. After the film was exposed the whole equipment was returned to the factory; the film developed and printed, and the camera reloaded. Eastman introduced paper-backed roll film for daylight loading in 1891, and, together with camera improvements, photography became a hobby for the masses.

Colour in photography is based on the principle that an admixture in varying ratios of the three primary colours, red, blue and green, will give any colour in the spectrum. In 1810 a German physicist found that wet silver chloride exposed to a spectrum would reproduce faintly the spectrum colours but would disappear when the image was dried. In 1860 James Clark Maxwell, a British physicist, made three wet-collodion photographs of a tartan ribbon, each one through a red, blue and green filter. He then projected them through similar filters, superimposing the images on a screen. A crude colour reproduction resulted, but lacking in sensitivity to red and green.

After various experiments the three-layer emulsion method, each layer being sensitive to a different primary colour, was perfected in the Kodachrome film, marketed in 1935. The film was developed layer by layer, each being dyed in the appropriate complementary colours yellow, magenta and cyan blue, thus giving a transparency of the true image colours. About the same time

Agfacolour was introduced, the difference between it and Kodachrome being that the three layers contained not only the sensitive emulsions but also colour formers, all of which reacted with a special developer to produce an accurate colour image in one step, instead of the separate three-step development of Kodachrome. From these two methods, most modern colour film has been developed.

CAMERAS

From the camera obscura to a light-free box with a lens was an obvious step. Camera development followed that of the development of the image plate, and it was not until dryplate and celluloid roll film was introduced that the camera became truly portable. However, the first single-lens reflex camera had been patented in 1861 by Thomas Sutton, and in 1880 the British firm of R. & J. Beck produced a twin-lens reflex camera. A factory-loaded roll-film camera, the Kodak, was brought out in 1888 by George Eastman, followed in 1891 by the first daylight-loading camera. In 1900 the first of a long line of 'Brownie' cameras was introduced.

In 1914 Oscar Bernak of Germany invented the Leica principle, a small precision instrument of considerable sophistication using 35 mm roll film. This was marketed successfully in 1925 and is still the most widely used format, there being a host of refinements from Germany and later Japan up to the present day. Beck's twin-lens reflex camera was marketed in 1928 under the name Rolleiflex.

In 1963 Edwin Land introduced the revolutionary Polaroid camera, which was able to produce black-and-white and colour pictures in less than a minute after exposure. After the picture is taken, the negative forms a sandwich with the positive, which is passed through rollers that break open plastic pods containing developer and fixer. After an appropriate time lapse, the camera back is opened and the print is peeled away from the negative, giving a positive image of the picture.

1963 was also the year that Kodak launched its line of Instamatic Cameras which was to become the most popular range in the history of photography.

In 1982 Kodak launched the innovative Disc Camera which relied on a revolutionary disc of film that rotated in the camera, unlike other cameras where spools of film had to be wound through the camera from one chamber to another.

ARCHITECTURE

Glossary of terms

abacus Flat top of the capital of a column.
apse Semicircular termination or recess at the end of a church chancel.
architrave The beam which extends across the top of the columns in classical architecture.
baptistry Building used for baptisms. Sometimes merely a bay or chapel reserved for baptisms.
barrel vault A continuous vault, either semicircular or pointed in section. Used from Roman times to the present. (Also called tunnel vault.)
bay Compartment or unit of division of an interior or of a façade – usually between one window or pillar and the next.
belvedere Open-sided structure designed to offer extensive views, usually in a formal garden.
boss Projection, usually carved, at the intersection of stone ribs of Gothic vaults and ceilings.
buttress Vertical mass of masonry built against a wall to strengthen it and to resist the outward pressure of a vault.
campanile Bell-tower.
capital Top of a column, usually carved.
caryatid Sculptured female figure serving as a supporting column.
cornice Projecting upper part of the entablature in classical architecture.
cross vault Vault with arched diagonal groins, formed by the intersection of two barrel vaults. (Also called groin vault.)
dado Lower part of an interior wall when panelled or painted separately from the main part.
drum Cylindrical lower part of a dome or cupola.
entablature In classical architecture, the beam-like division above the columns, comprising architrave, frieze and cornice.
flying buttress Arch conveying the thrust of a vault towards an isolated buttress.
frieze Decorated central division of an entablature, between the architrave and the cornice.
groin vault See cross vault.
keystone Central, wedge-shaped stone of an arch, so called because the arch cannot stand up until it is in position.
lancet window Window with a single, sharply pointed arch. The style is associated with the Early English period of Gothic architecture, around the 13th century.
mezzanine Low storey introduced between two loftier ones, usually the ground and first floors.
order Basic elements of classical and Renaissance architecture, comprising the base, column, capital and entablature.
oriel Bay window on an upper floor, supported by projecting stonework.
pediment In classical architecture, the low-pitched gable above the entablature, usually filled with sculpture.
pendentive Curved triangular surface to support a circular dome over a square or polygonal base.
pier Vertical masonry support for a wall arch.
rustication Heavy stonework with the surface left rough, or with deeply channelled joints, used principally on Renaissance buildings.
spandrel Triangular space between the curves of two adjacent arches and the horizontal moulding above them.
tracery Ornamental stonework in the upper part of a Gothic window.
tunnel vault See barrel vault.
tympanum Triangular space bounded by the mouldings of a pediment; also, the space, often carved, between the lintel and arch of a Gothic doorway.
vault A roof or ceiling built in stone, brick or concrete, as opposed to wood.

SOME NOTABLE ARCHITECTS
Aalto, Alvar (1898–1976) Finnish.
Adam, Robert (1728–72) Scottish.
Alberti, Leone Battista (1404–72) Italian.
Barry, Sir Charles (1795–1860) English.
Bernini, Gianlorenzo (1598–1680) Italian.
Borromini, Francesco (1599–1667) Italian.
Brunelleschi, Filippo (1377–1446) Italian.
Burlington, Richard Boyle (Earl of) (1694–1753) English.
Campbell, Colen (1660?–1729) Scottish.
Gibbs, James (1682–1754) Scottish.
Hawksmoor, Nicholas (1661–1736) English.
Jones, Inigo (1573–1652) English.
Kent, William (1685–1748) English.
Le Corbusier (Charles Edouard Jeanmerat) (1887–1965) French.
Le Vau, Louis (1612–70) French.
Maderna, Carlo (1556–1629) Italian.
Mansart, François (1598–1666) French.
Mansart, Jules (1646–1708) French.
Michelangelo, Buonarroti (1475–1564) Italian.
Mies van der Rohe, Ludwig (1886–1969) German.
Nash, John (1752–1835) English.
Niemeyer, Oscar (b. 1907) Brazilian.
Palladio, Andrea (1508–80) Italian.
Paxton, Sir Joseph (1801–65) English.
Pugin, Augustus (1812–52) English.
Saarinen, Eero (1910–61) Finnish.
Soane, Sir John (1753–1837) English.
Vanbrugh, Sir John (1664–1726) English.
Wren, Sir Christopher (1632–1723) English.
Wright, Frank Lloyd (1869–1959) American.
Wyatt, James (1746–1813) English.

Egyptian (c. 2700–c. 1200 BC)

All of the important buildings were built for the Pharaohs. Historians have divided the Pharaohs into 30 dynasties and three historic periods, the Ancient Kingdom, the Middle Kingdom and the New Empire. During the Ancient Kingdom at the time of the Third Dynasty (2778–2723 BC) 'mastabas' or tomb houses were built – small, flat-topped buildings with sloping sides. From the mastabas developed the pyramids. The first known pyramid, the oldest still in existence and the world's first large-scale monument in stone, was the Djozer step pyramid at Sakkâra, built c. 2778 BC by

Queen Hatshepsut's Terraced Temple at Deir-el-Bahri in Thebes, Egypt. (Popperfoto)

Imhotep, who is considered to be the first architect in history. During the Fourth Dynasty (2723–2563 BC) many pyramids were constructed. The three famous pyramids of Cheops, Chephren and Mykerinos around Gizeh demonstrate the fascination the Egyptians had for such an elementary architectural form.

It was during the Middle Kingdom that the monolithic formations were replaced by a trabeated system of construction as represented by the mortuary temples of Mentuhetep at Deir el-Bahari (11th Dynasty, 2133–1992 BC) and the great temple of Amun at Karnak (12th Dynasty, 1991–1928 BC).

The new capital of Thebes was founded in the period of the New Empire. At the beginning of the 18th Dynasty, Thothmes I (1530 BC) commenced additions to the temple at Karnak which was continued by successive Pharaohs, making Thebes the most imposing city in Egypt. Other notable buildings from this period are the great Hypostyle Hall at Karnak by Rameses I (1350 BC), the mortuary temple of Rameses III (1198–1166 BC) at Medinet Habu in Thebes, and the funerary temple at Deir el-Bahari for Queen Hatshepsut (1511–1480 BC).

West Asiatic
(c. 4000–300 BC)

West Asiatic architecture can be divided into three periods: the Babylonian (c. 4000–c. 1275 BC), the Assyrian (c. 1275–538 BC) and the Persian (538–333

BC). In the Babylonian period, temples formed the centre of religious as well as commercial and social life. Remarkable stepped pyramids, known as ziggurats, were built, an example of which is the largest surviving Ziggurat of Ur (now Muquyyar, Iraq) built c. 2113–2096 BC, with a base of 61 × 45·7 m (200 × 150 ft) built to three storeys surmounted by a summit temple. The first and part of the second storeys now survive to a height of 18 m (60 ft).

The city of Babylon which was situated on the banks of the river Euphrates became the capital of the Empire around 2000 BC. It was planned with a gridiron pattern of roads. Towers and giant walls surrounded the city and protected its inhabitants. Temples were of vast dimensions; the greatest of these was the temple of Marduk. The palace of Nebuchadnezzar was the site of the famous 'Hanging Gardens of Babylon'. The whole city was made of mud bricks, giving little resistance to the ravages of time; now only mounds show where the city stood.

In the Assyrian period the palaces of warrior kings were the major buildings in Assyria. Examples are those built by Sennacherib (705–681 BC), Esarhaddon (681–668 BC) and Ashur-Bani-Pal (668–626 BC) in the capital Ninevah. The palaces were enormous and were planned around internal courtyards with numerous rooms connected by corridors. They stood high above the ground on platforms of sun-dried bricks faced with stone and were reached by broad stairs and ramps. The buildings were decorated with bas-reliefs of sculptured monsters and coloured glazed bricks.

Three types of masonry walls, used in the Early Greek period. From left to right: cyclopean, rectangular and polygonal.

The palace of Xerxes (485 BC), built during the Persian period in the capital Susa, displayed features from the preceding Assyrian period such as the raised platforms, bas-relief sculptures and coloured glazed bricks.

Greek (*c.* 3000–*c.* 146 BC)

Greek architecture has two discernible periods: the Early and the Hellenic. Buildings of the Early period (*c.* 3000–*c.* 700 BC) are characterized by the distinct appearance of the masonry wall used in their construction. There are three types, firstly cyclopean which is built with large stone piles with gaps filled with smaller stones held together with clay; secondly walls built of hewn blocks of stone in a regular course with joints which are not always vertical; and thirdly polygonal, where many-sided blocks are worked together to form a strong structure. An example of the architecture of the Early period is King Minos's palace at Knossos on the island of Crete (*c.* 2000 BC). Here cyclopean masonry was used and simple downward-tapering wooden columns in the form of colonnades. Rooms were decorated with frescoes and the columns brightly painted.

The architecture of the Hellenic period (*c.* 700–146 BC) is distinguished by the use of the column. The columnar type of building gave Greek architecture an uncomplicated appearance. Temples were the most important buildings. The masterpieces of Greek temple architecture were built during this period. They were located on the most important sites in a city. The prime example of this is the Parthenon (447 BC) on the Acropolis in Athens. The typical temple was rectangular with a low-pitched roof supported by a colonnade of columns. The three orders were Doric (*c.* 640–*c.* 300 BC), Ionic (*c.* 560–*c.* 200 BC) and Corinthian (*c.* 420–*c.* 100 BC) (an order is the design of an entire column consisting of base, shaft and capital with an entablature over the top as the horizontal element). The Doric order is the oldest and the simplest of the three orders and the Parthenon in Athens is a fine example of this. The most distinguishing feature of the Ionic order is the capital which is ornamented with four spiral motifs called volutes. The Ionic order is more slender and more ornamental than the Doric order. The temple of Artemis in Ephesus (*c.* 356 BC) and the Erechtheion in Athens (*c.* 420–393 BC) are fine examples of Ionic architecture. The Corinthian order is the lightest and most ornamental of the three Greek orders and the least used. The two main motifs used in the capital are the leaf generally based on the acanthus and the scroll open volutes. There was a reasonable amount of variation in the design of the Corinthian capital but one of the most representative examples is that of the Olympeion in Athens (174 BC–AD 131).

Doric   Ionic   Corinthian

Roman (*c.* 753 BC–AD 475)

The Romans adopted the central concept of Greek architecture, that of the three orders, adding two of their own, the Tuscan and the Composite, but they changed the manner in which they were expressed. They had to find a way in which to use this architectural idea which had been developed for temples, on arched, domed and vaulted buildings, sometimes of enormous size and built for a new range of building types. A basic architectural form which is also a structural form was the semicircular arch. By placing a number of arches side by side a tunnel vault is produced, and if semicircular arches are built in a circle a dome is generated. However, huge thick walls and buttresses are also needed to support the outward thrust created by the weight on the arches. By intersecting two tunnel vaules it is possible to gorm a groin vault; this structural form helped to reduce the amount of wall surface which was necessary, and thus allowing more light into the building.

The great baths of Rome, such as the Thermae of Caracalla (AD 211–17), were a fifth of a mile across and incorporated in one section of their design a

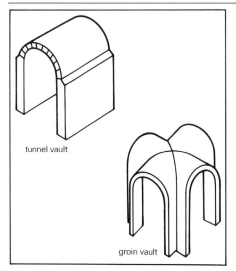

tunnel vault

groin vault

The tunnel vault (also called barrel vault) has been used since Roman times. The groin vault is also known as the cross vault.

vast rectangular space which in effect was built of several colossal groin vaults. The baths needed a large supply of water and again the arch was used as the main structural form for the aqueduct. The finest of these is still to be seen in southern France, the Pont du Gard (AD 14) – it is 270 m (*900 ft*) long and 54 m (*180 ft*) above the river.

One of the most impressive Roman buildings still intact is the Pantheon (AD 120–4) in Rome. It is a great circular structure with a height and diameter of 43·2 m (*142 ft*) with a magnificent colonnaded portico. The structure is capped with a hemispherical dome, with a small opening at the top to provide natural light.

The famous Colosseum (AD 70–82) in Rome is a multi-storey building, 47·8 m (*157 ft*) in height. It is a fine example of the use of orders on a large building several storeys high. Each storey is given an appropriate order – the strong, plain Doric at ground level, the slender Ionic at the first floor, the grace of the Corinthian at the second floor and the luxurious Composite at the top.

Byzantine (324–1453)

With the approach of the fall of the Roman Empire the Emperor Constantine fled Rome to the old Hellenic town of Byzantium, where the city remained Christian until it was overthrown by the Turks in 1453. The city was renamed Constantinople (now called Istanbul) but its culture is referred to as Byzantine. Byzantium inherited the artistry of the Greeks and combined it with the engineering skills of the Romans. The Byzantines' main architectural problem was to build a dome on a square base. This problem was solved by the use of pendentives, small spherical segments inserted between the dome and the square base, usually supported on arches. The advantage of a square base over a circular or polygonal base was that vaulted aisles, semi-

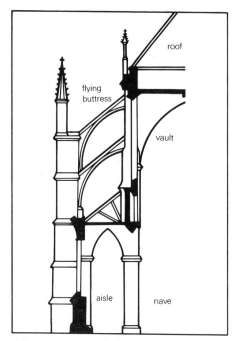

roof

flying buttress

vault

aisle

nave

Half cross section through a Gothic cathedral.

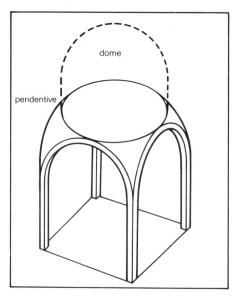

dome

pendentive

Circular dome on a square base using pendentives.

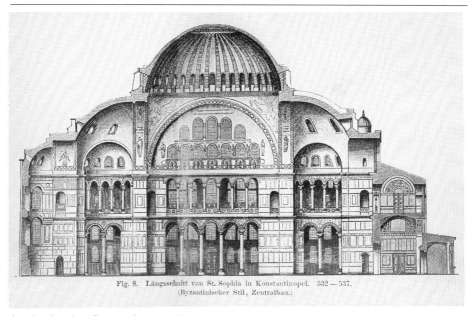

Fig. 8.   Längsschnitt von St. Sophia in Konstantinopel.   532 — 537.
(Byzantinischer Stil, Zentralbau.)

A section through the Byzantine Cathedral of St. Sophia in Constantinople. (Popperfoto)

domed apses and other domes could be easily erected adjacent to a central dome. The best example of this type of structure is Hagia Sophia (AD 537) in Constantinople. The building is a vast rectangle 76 m (*250 ft*) by 67 m (*220 ft*), with a large central dome 33 m (*107 ft*) in diameter. To the east and west, abutting the central dome, are two large semi-domes, and to the north and south, vaulted aisles with galleries above.

The Byzantines decorated their buildings with mosaics made from marble, which was in abundant supply. The dome of the Hagia Sophia was covered in blue and gold mosaic which was lit up by sunlight penetrating through the windows at the base of the dome.

Byzantine architecture spread throughout Asia Minor and as far north as Kiev in Russia, Armenia and the Balkans. To the west, Venetians were the only people in direct contact with the Byzantine Empire. St Mark's in Venice was begun in 1063 and is essentially a Byzantine church with a plan form based on a Greek cross surmounted by five domes, and low in proportion.

Romanesque
(*c.* 1000–*c.* 1200)

With the spread of Christianity in western Europe came the urgent need for the construction of places of worship. Romanesque architecture was formed by the preceding architecture of the Roman and early Christian period in western Europe. The churches were based on the form of the Roman basilicas which were simple places of assembly.

The typical Romanesque church consisted of a high central nave with windows at a high level and a row of columns or piers forming an arcade at ground level which divided it from two narrow side-aisles. In its earliest form the nave terminated at the

eastern end in an apse but this basic plan was changing – transepts and the chancel (the space between the crossing formed by the transepts and the original apse) were added. The Romanesque church was generally tall with a tower, or towers, making it clearly visible on the skyline.

The two main characteristics of Romanesque architecture are the awareness of the built enclosure being of massive dimensions, and the manifest verticality expressed in the design. Although the walls and piers were large their surfaces began to be animated with shafts and mouldings, and because of the desire for height, extra elements began to appear, such as the gallery storey, between the arcade and the high-level windows, or clerestory. An endless number of variations were evolved but they were all based on these basic themes.

The most celebrated Christian shrine in Europe, besides Jerusalem and Rome, was Santiago de Compostela, that of St James. Pilgrimages were a fundamental part of Christian life during this period. Because Santiago de Compostela was so venerated, a whole series of beautiful Romanesque churches arose along the several principal pilgrimage routes to the shrine. They can be found at such places as Tours, Orléans, Poitiers, Saintes, Vézelay, Le Puy, Conques, Arles and Toulouse.

Gothic (*c.* 1150–*c.* 1500)

In 1140 Abbot Suger rebuilt the choir at St Denis in Paris and it is generally accepted that it was there that the Gothic style was invented. Following St Denis, new cathedrals were built in the Île de France region between 1140 and 1220 at Sens, Noyan, Senlis and Paris. These were followed by others at Laon, Chartres, Reims, Amiens and Beauvais. There were many others but these are the

Florence Cathedral, seen from the Palazzo Vecchio, is one of the most beautiful of Italian cathedrals and second in size only to St Peter's in Rome. Dedicated to Santa Maria del Fiore, it was begun in 1296 and finished by the 15th century. The dome by Brunelleschi was built in 1420-36. (Popperfoto)

chief examples, which comprise what is termed the Île de France Gothic.

The main theme expressed in Gothic architecture is the resolution of the horizontal and vertical movement, whereby a totally unified structure is achieved. Gothic architects interpret the wall, the pier and the vault in a new way. The structural components which form the wall, pier and vault are reduced in size to such an extent that they become a system of structural stress lines combining together into a skeleton of stone, infilled with a thin shell of stone in the roof area, stained glass in the wall area and the pier standing clear defying deflection. Cathedral exteriors lose any traces of positive enclosure and the feeling of mass disappears.

It is generally accepted that England's first truly Gothic building was the rebuilt choir and retrochoir of Canterbury cathedral after it was destroyed by fire in 1174. The architects involved were the Frenchman William of Sens and his successor William the Englishman. The Gothic style in England is usually divided into three main periods: Early English, Decorated and Perpendicular. The style-names are based on somewhat arbitrary characteristics but for all this they have now become acceptable architectural descriptions. The distinguishing features of English cathedrals are the very long and low naves, the extended eastern ends and the pronounced transepts, sometimes two in number. The idea of structural clarity was not pursued by the English; their interests lay in the possibilities of decoration. The primary examples

of English Gothic can be seen at Wells, Lincoln, York, Ely, Canterbury and Winchester.

Italian Renaissance (c. 1420–c. 1530)

The Renaissance style began in Florence at the beginning of the 15th century. This was a period when the architect gained high status in society and approached his work more academically. One of the main figures of the early Renaissance period was Filippo Brunelleschi (1377–1446). He was one of the first to comprehend classical architecture, study, at first hand, surviving classical buildings, and to understand the constructional ideas behind their designs. His greatest achievement was the dome of Florence cathedral (1420-36), which consists of a double shell dome of brickwork supported on ribs.

Leone Battista Alberti (1404–72), also a Florentine architect, was the theorist of the style in its early years and he wrote the 'Ten Books of Architecture', the first part of which dealt with geometry and perspective. One of his most famous buildings was St Andrea in Mantua (1470–2).

As a consequence of the growing wealth and power of merchants and bankers such as the Medici, the city of Florence saw the growth of magnificent palace buildings. They were very large and built right up to the edge of the street with regular windows and bold rusticated wall surfaces. All the important rooms opened into cool internal courtyards. An example is the Palazzo Strozzi begun in 1489.

Italian High Renaissance evolved in Rome at the end of the 15th century and the beginning of the 16th century. Donato Bramante (1444-1514) was the leading architect of this period and his famous building in Rome, although very small, is the Tempietto at St Pietro in Montorio (1502). However, his greatest achievement was the original design for St Peter's in Rome.

Mannerism (c. 1520–c. 1630)

As Michelangelo (1475-1564) developed as an architect, his style changed into what is now known as Mannerism, which expresses the wish to move from the sober High Renaissance style to something more dynamic and complex. A young contemporary of Michelangelo was Giulio Romano (1492-1546), who designed one of the best examples of Mannerist architecture, the Palazzo del Te (1526-34) in Mantua for the Gonzaga family. It maintains the formal plan of the High Renaissance but handles the details in a new, rather perverse, manner.

One of the most influential Mannerist buildings was the Gesù in Rome designed by Giacomo Vignola (1507-73). It was the main church of the Jesuits in Rome, who were the most powerful religious force of the 16th century. The interior is dominated by the nave because the aisles are reduced to side chapels and the lofty domed crossing which was to be repeated by many Baroque architects.

The most original of the Mannerist architects was Andrea Palladio (1508-80) of Vicenza, who built many villas and palazzos in and around Vicenza, the most famous being the Villa Rotunda (1550-1). However, his churches in Venice, especially St Giorgio Maggiore (begun 1566), show Palladio at the height of his career.

Italian Baroque (c. 1600–c. 1760)

At the end of the 16th century and the beginning of the 17th century a new architectural style evolved in Rome known as Baroque. The leading figure of the style in Italy was Gianlorenzo Bernini (1598-1680). Typical of his work was the baldacchino over the high altar in St Peter's, an extravagant piece of work expressing the essence of the Baroque style. He also designed the dignified oval-shaped double colonnade around the piazza in front of St Peter's which contrasts so well with the complexities of the church.

The Baroque style can best be described as work that utilized movement, whether actual (such as curving walls) or implied (such as figures portrayed in vigorous action). It was a style that produced striking visual effects in buildings and decorations. Although perhaps at times over-ornate and theatrical, it still possessed the seriousness of other styles.

As the movement progressed, the buildings became even more extravagant and complex. Examples are the churches of St Ivo della Sapienza

(1642-60) and the delightful St Carlo alle Quattro Fontane (1633-67), both in Rome and designed by Francesco Borromini (1599-1667).

English Renaissance (c. 1530–c. 1750)

For a long time England was oblivious to the developments of the Italian Renaissance. Renaissance details first appeared in the mid-Tudor period when John Thynne (d. 1580) designed the Old Somerset House in London – it was a symmetrical building with pedimented windows and a crowning balustrade. Thynne's other work of note was the mansion at Longleat (begun 1553), a wonderful essay in the art of fenestration.

Between 1575 and 1620 great stylish country houses were built, the so-called 'prodigy houses' – Hardwick Hall (Derbyshire), Wollaton Hall (Nottingham) and Burghley House (Northamptonshire) – represent some of the very best examples of this style. All possessed the very English feature of the 'long gallery' with its pictures and furniture on one side and a wall of almost all windows on the other.

The man who changed the course of English architecture by introducing the Renaissance style into England was Inigo Jones (1573-1652). His designs had restraint and fine proportion heavily influenced by Palladio. His finest work is the Banqueting House in Whitehall which was completed in 1622.

After the Great Fire of London 1666, Old St Paul's cathedral needed to be replaced. This work was undertaken by Christopher Wren (1632-1723). The plan was based on a Baroque idea with a giant dome over the crossing inspired by the work of Bramante. Wren designed a great number of parish churches in and around the City of London most of which were based in some way on the Baroque style.

Around this time Sir John Vanbrugh (1664-1726) together with Nicholas Hawksmoor were designing great country houses. They incorporated the whole of the Baroque vocabulary in their designs, combined with a natural sense of the monumental. Blenheim Palace (1705-24) in Oxfordshire and Castle Howard (1699) in Yorkshire are the most notable products of this partnership. Hawksmoor alone was the designer of some remarkable Baroque churches in London – St Anne at Limehouse (1715-24), Christ Church at Spitalfields (1717-29) and St Mary at Woolnoth (1716-27). James Gibbs (1682-1754) was another prominent architect of the time who would have gained more notoriety if he had not been accused of Catholicism and Jacobitism; however, he did design St Martin-in-the-Fields in London (1722-6) and the magnificent rotundity of Radcliffe Camera at Oxford (1739-49).

The Palladian Movement (1710-50)

Soon after the first decade of the 18th century, English architecture became subject to what was known as the 'Rule of Taste'. It was a set of widely held standards which basically said what a building should look like. The leading figures in the movement were Lord Burlington (1694-1753), Colen Campbell (1660-1729) and William Kent (1685-1748). The means by which the movement was established was through the publication of two books in 1715, namely the first volume of *Vitruvius Britannicus*, a folio of 100 engravings of classical buildings in Britain, and an English version of Palladio's *I Quattro Libri dell Architettura* (originally published in 1570). Three typical buildings of the Palladian period are Houghton Hall (1722-35) by Colen Campbell, Chiswick House (1725) by Lord Burlington, and Holkham Hall (1734) by William Kent.

19th Century

The architecture of the 19th century in Britain was dominated by two architectural styles: Neo-Classicism and Gothic Revival. There was also a third very important area of building activity which was solely controlled by Engineers. Robert Smirke's (1780-1867) British Museum (1823-47) in London represents a good example of the Neo-Classical style and the Houses of Parliament (1840-65) by Charles Barry (1795-1860) and Augustus Pugin (1812-52) demonstrates the British affection for Gothic architecture. Undoubtedly the most famous example of Engineering architecture is the Crystal Palace designed by Joseph Paxton (1803-65), which was originally erected in Hyde Park, London, for the Great Exhibition of 1851 but came to an unhappy end in south London.

The Modern Movement (c. 1890)

Towards the end of the 19th century, the United States became the forerunner of the utilization of new inventions and developments. In Chicago the first 'skyscraper' was constructed using a steel frame and hung masonry. This method meant that a large amount of floor space could be built on a relatively small ground area; however, this also limited the aesthetics of a building. Louis Sullivan (1856-1924) overcame this problem, as demonstrated by his design of the Guaranty Building in Buffalo (1894-5).

Meanwhile, in Europe, the use of ductile metal was being exploited in a style known as Art Nouveau. In Paris the most obvious example of this was the Eiffel Tower, created in 1887 by Gustave Eiffel (1832-1923). The three greatest Art Nouveau architects were Antoni Gaudí (1852-1926) from Barcelona, best remembered for his unfinished transept of the Sagrada Familia begun in 1883; Victor Horta (1861-1947) from Belgium, whose aesthetic use of iron and glass can be seen in the department store 'A l'Innovation' in Brussels; and Charles Rennie Mackintosh (1868-1928), whose greatest work stands in his home town of Glasgow, the School of Arts built in two stages between 1897 and 1909.

The first replacement of the wall with a matrix of steel and glass was seen at the Fagus factory at Alfeld in Germany, designed by Walter Gropius and Adolf Meyer in 1911. This could be achieved by having floors cantilevered, supported by columns set back within the building. In 1919 Gropius (1883-1969) established the Bauhaus in Weimar, later to move to Dessau, in Germany. It became the most influential school of design in the 20th century and taught architects and designers that they should work to understand man's psychological and physical needs. However, due to continual pressure by the Nazis in 1933, the school was closed and in 1937 Gropius moved to America to take the Chair of Architecture at Harvard and began to influence American architectural education.

The Mila y Camps, a famous example of the Catalan architect Anthonio Gaudi. (Popperfoto)

MUSIC AND DANCE

Orchestral instruments

Woodwind

Piccolo or Octave Flute
Earliest concerto: Vivaldi, *c.* 1735. *Earliest orchestral use:* 1717 Handel's Water Music. *History:* Name 'piccolo' dates from 1856, but the origin goes back to prehistory via flute and sopranino recorder.

Flute – transverse or cross-blown
Earliest concerto: Vivaldi, *c.* 1729. *Earliest orchestral use:* 1672 Lully. *History:* Prehistoric (*c.* 18 000 BC); the modern Boehm flute dates from 1832.

Oboe
Earliest concerto: Marcheselli, 1708. *Earliest orchestral use:* 1657 Lully's *L'amour malade*. *History:* Originated Middle Ages in the schalmey family. The name comes from Fr. *hautbois* (1511) = high wood.

Cor anglais
Earliest concerto: J. M. Haydn, *c.* 1755? *Earliest orchestral use:* 1760 in Vienna. *History:* Purcell wrote for 'tenor oboe' *c.* 1690; this *may* have originated the name English Horn. Alternatively, it may be from 'angled horn', referring to its crooked shape.

Clarinet
Earliest concerto: Vivaldi, *c.* 1740?: two clarinets; Molter, *c.* 1747: one clarinet. *Earliest orchestral use:* 1726 Faber: Mass. *History:* Developed by J. C. Denner (1655–1707) from the recorder and schalmey families.

Bass Clarinet
Earliest orchestral use: 1838 Meyerbeer's *Les Huguenots*. *History:* Prototype made in 1772 by Gilles Lot of Paris. Modern Boehm form from 1838.

Bassoon
Earliest concerto: Vivaldi, *c.* 1730? *Earliest orchestral use:* *c.* 1619. *History:* Introduced in Italy *c.* 1540 as the lowest of the double-reed group.

Double Bassoon
Earliest orchestral use: *c.* 1730 Handel. *History:* 'Borrowed' from military bands for elemental effects in opera.

Saxophone
Earliest concerto: Debussy's *Rhapsody*, 1903. *Earliest orchestral use:* 1844 Kastner's *Last King of Judah*. *History:* Invented by Adolphe Sax, *c.* 1840.

Brass

Trumpet
Earliest concerto: Torelli, before 1700, Haydn, 1796: keyed trumpet. *Earliest orchestral use:* *c.* 1800, keyed, 1835 valved, in Halévy's *La Juive*. *History:* The natural trumpet is of prehistoric origin; it formed the basis of the earliest orchestras.

Horn
Earliest concerto: Bach, 1717–21, or Vivaldi, Bach . . . Vivaldi: two horns; Telemann, before 1721: one horn. *Earliest orchestral use:* 1639, Cavalli. *History:* Prehistoric. The earliest music horns were the German helical horns of the mid-16th century. Rotary valve horn patented in 1832.

Trombone
Earliest concerto: Wagenseil, *c.* 1760. *Earliest orchestral use:* *c.* 1600, as part of bass-line. *History:* From Roman *buccina* or slide-trumpet, via the mediaeval sackbut to its modern form, *c.* 1500.

Tuba
Earliest concerto: Vaughan Williams, 1954. *Earliest orchestral use:* 1830, Berlioz's *Symphonie Fantastique*. *History:* Patented by W. Wieprecht and Moritz, Berlin, 1835.

Percussion

Anvil
History: Used for musical effect since 1528.

Bass Drum
Earliest orchestral use: 1748, Rameau's *Zais*. *History:* Originated in the ancient Orient.

Bells
History: Date back to Ancient Egypt *c.* 3500 BC. Bells first used in 'art' music in a funeral cantata by G. M. Hoffman *c.* 1730.

Castanets
History: Known to the Egyptians by 730 BC. Made of chestnut (castaña = chestnut in Spanish).

Celesta
Earliest orchestral use: 1880, Widor's *Der Korrigane*. *History:* Invented by Mustel in 1880.

Cymbals
Earliest orchestral use: 1680, Strungk's *Esther*. *History:* From Turkish military bands of antiquity.

Glockenspiel
Earliest orchestral use: 1739, Handel's *Saul*. *History:* Today strictly a keyboard instrument, in the 19th century the metal plates were struck by hand-held hammers. The original instrument dates from fourth-century Rome.

Gong or Tam Tam
Earliest orchestral use: 1791, Gossec's *Funeral March*. *History:* Originating in the ancient Far East.

Side or Snare Drum
Earliest orchestral use: 1749, Handel's *Fireworks Music*. *History:* Derived from the small drums of prehistory, via the mediaeval tabor. Achieved its modern form in the 18th century.

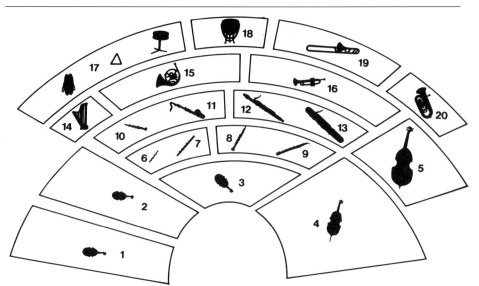

The standard arrangement of a modern symphony orchestra: 1) 1st violins; 2) 2 violins; 3) violas; 4) cellos; 5) double basses; 6) piccolos; 7) flutes; 8) oboes; 9) cor anglais; 10) clarinets; 11) bass clarinets; 12) bassoons; 13) double bassoons; 14) harps; 15) horns; 16) trumpets; 17/18) percussion; 19) trombones; 20) tubas.

Tambourine
Earliest orchestral use: 1820. *History:* Dates back to the mediaeval Arabs; prototype used by Assyrians and Egyptians. Earliest use of the word 1579.

Tenor Drum
Earliest orchestral use: 1842.

Timpani/Kettle Drum
Earliest concerto: Masek, *c.* 1790: one set, Tausch, *c.* 1870: six timpani. *Earliest orchestral use:* 1607, Monteverdi's *Orfeo. History:* Originated in the ancient Orient.

Triangle
Earliest orchestral use: 1774, Glantz: Turkish Symphony. *History:* From Turkish military bands of antiquity.

Vibraphone
Earliest orchestral use: 1934. *History:* First used in dance bands in the 1920s.

Xylophone
Earliest orchestral use: 1873, Lumbye's *Traumbilder. History:* Primitive; earliest 'art' mention 1511.

Strings

Violin
Earliest concerto: Torelli, 1709. *Earliest orchestral use: c.* 1600. *History:* Descended from the lyre via the sixth-century crwth, rebec and fiddle. Modern instruments of Lombardic origin *c.* 1545. The words violin and fiddle derive ultimately from Roman *vitulari* ('to skip like a calf').

Violoncello/Cello
Earliest concerto: Jacchini, 1701. *Earliest orchestral use: c.* 1600. *History:* As violin.

Viola
Earliest concerto: Telemann *ante* 1722. *Earliest orchestral use: c.* 1600. *History:* As violin.

Double Bass
Earliest concerto: Vanhal, *c.* 1770. *Earliest orchestral use: c.* 1600. *History:* Developed alongside the violin family, but is a closer relative to the bass viol or violone.

Harp
Earliest concerto: Handel, 1738. *Earliest orchestral use: c.* 1600. *History:* Possibly prehistoric: attained its modern form by 1792.

Popular and folk instruments

Accordion/Concertina
Accordion invented as Handäoline in Germany, 1822. Concertina invented in England, 1829. When operated by hand the accordion produces two notes, one drawn, the other pressed, to a key, the concertina only one; further, the accordion sometimes has a keyboard, the concertina never has.

Bagpipes
A prehistoric Middle Eastern or Chinese instrument made by shepherds of a lamb or goat skin with pipes attached. The bag acts as a bellows to actuate chanter and drone pipes. First concerto, 1755. Much used today as a military instrument in Scotland and elsewhere. Irish form of bagpipes, uillean pipes, prevalent in Celtic folk music; unlike Scots pipes, these are not played with the mouth but purely through external pressure.

Balalaika
East European (predominantly Russsian) triangular development of the long-necked lute, reaching its present form about a century ago. Currently made in six sizes, each with three strings.

Guitar
A fretted six-stringed development of the antique lute (q.v.), possibly introduced into Europe by the Moors (eighth century) and settling as Spain's national instrument, attaining its present basic form *c.* 1750. Earliest printed music, 1546. Earliest concerto, 1808.

Harmonium
Keyboard instrument invented (as orgue expressif) in France, 1830s. A bellows reed organ, perfected during the 1840s as a modest-sized keyboard instrument for church, cinema and home use (known in England sometimes as 'cottage organ').

Harpsichord
Evolved from the psaltery during the 14th century; earliest surviving example dated 1521. Mainly a domestic instrument, it also supported the bass line in early orchestras. First solo concerto, *c.* 1720. Eclipsed *c.* 1800 by pianoforte (q.v.), but reintroduced progressively since 1903.

Keyboards
Generic term for keyboard instrument(s) often connected to electronic device which produces extensive variations in tone-colour and note duration.

Kora
Twenty-one-string instrument fashioned from hollow gourd covered with cured cowhide and played via a rosewood fingerboard. Developed in 17th-century West Africa, popularized in 19th-century Kaabu (now Guinea).

Lute
Extremely ancient (*c.* 3000 BC or before) source of all subsequent bowed and plucked stringed instruments, including violin, guitar, sitar, mandolin, etc. Earliest published music, 1507. Popularity subsided during 18th century, but currently revived for performance of early music.

Mouth Organ/Harmonica
Invented in Germany by Buschmann, 1821, as 'Mund Aeoline'. First concerto 1951. Diatonic harmonica's metal reeds give an octave range of different tones by alternately sucking or blowing, while chromatic gives up to four octaves by means of extra reeds and a finger-operated slide.

Organ
Ultimate origin lies in the antique panpipes (q.v.), but subsequent developments make it the biggest and most powerful of all instruments. First concerto by Handel, *c.* 1730. Saint-Saëns first used it in a symphony, 1886.

Panpipes
Named after the god Pan, this – the simplest and most primitive organ – is held in the hand and operated by mouth. Each pipe is of graduated length. Important in Balkan folk music, it has recently achieved more widespread recognition.

Pianoforte
Descended from the dulcimer. Invented by

Ravi Shankar with his sitar which he helped to popularise in the West in the mid-60s. (Popperfoto)

Cristofori, *c.* 1709. Earliest printed music, 1732; first concert use in London, 1767; first concerto by J. C. Bach, 1776. Attained its modern basic form *c.* 1850.

Recorder
End-blown flute, developed from prehistoric pipes. First mentioned 1388. Popular during 17th and 18th centuries until being succeeded by the transverse flute.

Sitar
High-pitched stringed instrument from the Indian sub-continent popularized in West by Beatle George Harrison in 1965 and subsequently Ravi Shankar. In Indian music, plays *ragas*, modal melodies over a continuous drone.

Synthesizer
Electronic device, invented *c.* 1950 to create pitch, tone-colour and duration of any note or notes or sounds. Used especially in popular and jazz music, where it is often attached to a keyboard.

Tabla
Pair of small drums, *dahina* (the higher, on the right-hand side) and *bahina* (a mini kettle drum, on the left). Tuned to the tonic (ground note) of the *raga*, the pitch may be varied by the heel of the hand.

Ukulele
'Jumping flea' in Hawaiian, it was introduced to Hawaii in the 1870s by the Portuguese. Has been played in Europe and the US as a jazz and solo instrument in the 20th century.

Famous conductors

Spontini, Gasparo (1774–1851)
Spohr, Louis (1784–1859)
Berlioz, Hector (1803–69)
Mendelssohn-Bartholdy, Felix (1809–47)
Wagner, Richard (1813–83)
von Bulow, Hans (1830–94)
Nikisch, Arthur (1855–1922)
Mahler, Gustav (1860–1911)
Weingartner, Felix (1863–1942)
Strauss, Richard (1864–1949)
Toscanini, Arturo (1867–1967)
Monteux, Pierre (1875–1964)
Walter, Bruno (1876–1962)
Beecham, Sir Thomas (1879–1961)
Klemperer, Otto (1885–1973)
Furtwängler, Wilhelm (1886–1954)
Stokowski, Leopold (1887–1977)
Boult, Sir Adrian (1889–1983)
Barbirolli, Sir John (1890–1970)
Sargent, Sir Malcolm (1895–1967)
Mitropoulos, Dimitri (1896–1960)
Schmidt-Isserstedt, Hans (1900–1973)
von Karajan, Herbert (b. 1908)
Solti, Sir Georg (b. 1912)
Bernstein, Leonard (b. 1918)
Pritchard, Sir John (b. 1921)
Marriner, Sir Neville (b. 1924)
Rozhdestvensky, Gennadi (b. 1926)
Davis, Sir Colin (b. 1927)
Previn, André (b. 1929)
Abbado, Claudio (b. 1933)
Ozawa, Seiji (b. 1935)
Rattle, Simon (b. 1955)

History and development of music

PREHISTORIC
Improvisatory music-making. Music and magic virtually synonymous.

PRIMITIVE (Ancient Greece and Rome; Byzantium) 8th century BC to AD 4th century
Improvisatory music-making in domestic surroundings. Competitive music-making in the arena.

AMBROSIAN (AD 4th to 6th century)
The beginnings of plainsong and the establishment of order in liturgical music.

Principal composer
Bishop Ambrose of Milan (c. 333–97) established four scales.

GREGORIAN (6th to 10th century)
Church music subjected to strict rules, e.g. melodies sung only in unison.

Principal composer
Pope Gregory I, 'The Great' (540–604), extended the number of established scales to eight.

MEDIAEVAL (1100–1300)
Guido d'Arezzo (c. 980–1050) was called 'the inventor of music': his teaching methods and invention of a method of writing music transformed the art.

Beginning of organized instrumental music; start of polyphony in church music.

Principal composers
Minstrels (10th–13th centuries). Goliards (travelling singers of Latin songs: 11th–12th centuries). Troubadours (c. 1100–1210). Trouvères (from 1100). Bernart de Ventadorn (c. 1150–95) encouraged singing in the vernacular.

RENAISSANCE (1300–1600)
The great age of polyphonic church music. Gradual emergence of instrumental music. Appearance of madrigals, chansons, etc. The beginnings of true organization in music and instruments.

Principal composers
Guillaume de Machut (c. 1300–77)
John Dunstable (c. 1380–1453)
Guillaume Dufay (c. 1400–74)
Johannes Ockeghem (1430–95)
Josquin des Prés (c. 1450–1521)
John Taverner (c. 1495–1545)
Giovanni da Palestrina (c. 1525–94)
Orlando di Lasso (c. 1530–94)
Thomas Morley (1557–1603)
John Dowland (1563–1626)
Michael Praetorius (1571–1621)

BAROQUE (1600–1750)
Beginnings of opera and oratorio. Rise of instrumental music; the first orchestras, used at first in the opera house but gradually attaining separate existence. Beginnings of sonata, concerto, suite and symphony. The peak of polyphonic writing.

Principal composers
Giovanni Gabrieli (1557–1612)
Claudio Monteverdi (1567–1643)
Orlando Gibbons (1583–1625)
Pietro Cavalli (1602–76)
Jean-Baptiste Lully (1632–87)
Arcangelo Corelli (1653–1713)
Henry Purcell (c. 1659–95)
Alessandro Scarlatti (1660–1725)
François Couperin (1668–1733)
Reinhard Keiser (1674–1739)
Antonio Lucio Vivaldi (1678–1741)
Georg Philipp Telemann (1681–1767)
Jean-Philippe Rameau (1683–1764)
Domenico Scarlatti (1685–1757)
Johann Sebastian Bach (1685–1750)
George Frideric Handel (1685–1759)

CLASSICAL (1750–1800+)
The age of the concert symphony and concerto. Beginning of the string quartet and sinfonia concertante. Decline of church music. Important developments in opera.

Principal composers
Giovanni Battista Sammartini (c. 1700–75)
Christoph Willibald von Gluck (1714–87)
Carl Philipp Emanuel Bach (1714–88)
Franz Joseph Haydn (1732–1809)
Wolfgang Amadeus Mozart (1756–91)
Luigi Cherubini (1760–1842)

EARLY ROMANTIC (1800–50)
High maturity of the symphony and concerto etc. in classical style. Romantic opera. The age of the piano virtuosi. Invention of the nocturne. Beginnings of the symphonic poem (lieder). Beginnings of nationalism.

Principal composers
Ludwig van Beethoven (1770–1827)
Nicolo Paganini (1782–1840)
Carl Maria von Weber (1786–1826)
Gioacchino Rossini (1792–1868)
Franz Schubert (1797–1828)
Hector Berlioz (1803–69)
Mikhail Glinka (1804–57)
Jakob Ludwig Felix Mendelssohn-Bartholdy (1809–47)
Frédéric François Chopin (1810–49)
Robert Schumann (1810–56)

HIGH ROMANTICISM (1850–1900)
The development of nationalism. Maturity of the symphonic and tone poems. Emergence of music drama.

Principal composers
Franz Liszt (1811–86)
Richard Wagner (1813–83)
Giuseppe Verdi (1813–1901)
César Franck (1822–90)
Bedřich Smetana (1824–84)
Anton Bruckner (1824–96)
Johannes Brahms (1833–97)
Peter Ilyitch Tchaikovsky (1840–93)
Antonin Dvořák (1841–1904)
Edvard Hagerup Grieg (1843–1907)
Gustav Mahler (1860–1911)

MODERN (1900–)
Impressionism and post-romanticism. Gigantism. Neo-classicism and other reactionary movements. Atonalism.

Principal composers
Giacomo Puccini (1858–1924)
Claude Debussy (1862–1918)
Richard Strauss (1864–1949)
Carl Nielsen (1865–1931)
Jean Sibelius (1865–1957)
Alexander Scriabin (1872–1915)
Ralph Vaughan Williams (1872–1958)
Sergei Rachmaninov (1873–1943)
Arnold Schoenberg (1874–1951)
Charles Ives (1874–1954)
Maurice Ravel (1875–1937)
Béla Bartók (1881–1945)
Igor Stravinsky (1882–1971)
Anton Webern (1883–1945)
Alban Berg (1885–1935)
Sergei Prokofiev (1891–1953)
Aaron Copland (b. 1900)
Sir William Walton (1902–82)
Sir Michael Tippett (b. 1905)
Dmitri Shostakovich (1906–75)
Samuel Barber (b. 1910)
Benjamin Britten (1913–77)

AVANT-GARDE (Today)
Avant-garde is history in the making and any list of composers would be arbitrary since one cannot tell which of the many directions taken by modern music will prove most influential. There have always been avant-garde composers, without which the art of music would never have developed: we would take many of the above names as good examples. Here are some names of avant-gardistes of prominence.

Principal composers
Luigi Dallapiccola (1904–75)

Oliver Messiaen (b. 1908)
John Cage (b. 1912)
Witold Lutoslawski (b. 1913)
Iannis Xenakis (b. 1922)
Luigi Nono (b. 1924)
Pierre Boulez (b. 1925)
Hans Werner Henze (b. 1926)
Karlheinz Stockhausen (b. 1928)
Steve Reich (b. 1936)

A chart of the main works of 72 of history's major composers from the 13th to the 20th century was published in the *Guinness Book of Answers* (2nd Edition), pages 94–97.

Composers of musicals

Kern, Jerome (1885–1945) *Show Boat; Swing Time*
Berlin, Irving (b. 1888) *Annie Get Your Gun; Call Me Madam*
Porter, Cole (1891–1964) *Kiss Me Kate; Can Can*
Novello, Ivor (1893–1969) *The Dancing Years; King's Rhapsody*
Warren, Harry (1893–1981) *42nd Street*
Gershwin, George (1898–1937) *Lady Be Good; Porgy and Bess*
Gay, Noel (Reginald Armitage, 1898–1954) *Me and My Girl*
Coward, Noël (1899–1973) *Bitter Sweet; Sail Away; Cowardy Custard*
Weill, Kurt (1900–50) *Threepenny Opera; One Touch of Venus*
Rodgers, Richard (b. 1902) *The King and I; Oklahoma; South Pacific*
Loesser, Frank (1910–69) *Guys and Dolls*
Bernstein, Leonard (b. 1918) *On the Town; West Side Story; Candide*

Ivor Novello, Welsh composer of such classics as *King's Rhapsody*. (Moniter)

Wilson, Sandy (b. 1924) *The Boy Friend*
Sondheim, Stephen (b. 1930) *Company*; *A Little Night Music*; *Follies*
Bart, Lionel (b. 1930) *Oliver!*
Schönberg, Claude-Michel (b. 1944) *Les Misérables*
Ulvaeus, Björn (b. 1945)/Andersson, Benny (b. 1946) *Chess*
Lloyd Webber, Andrew (b. 1948) *Jesus Christ Superstar*; *Evita*; *Cats*; *Phantom of the Opera*

Jazz musicians and composers

Handy, William Christopher (1873–1958) Composer
Bolden, Buddy (1878–1931) Cornet
Morton, (Ferdinand la Menthe) 'Jellyroll' (1885–1941) Piano
Oliver, Joe 'King' (1885–1938) Cornet
Ory, Edward 'Kid' (1886–1973) Trombone
Bechet, Sidney (1891–1959) Soprano saxophone
Smith, Bessie (1895–1937) Singer
Ellington, Edward Kennedy (Duke) (1899–1974) Pianist, bandleader
Armstrong, Louis 'Satchmo' (1900–71) Trumpet, singer
Beiderbecke, Leon 'Bix' (1903–31) Cornet
Miller, Glenn (1904–44) Trombone, composer
Basie, William 'Count' (1904–84) Pianist, bandleader
Dorsey, Thomas (Tommy) (1905–56) Trombone, bandleader
Goodman, Benjamin David, 'Benny' (b. 1909) Clarinet, bandleader
Tatum, Arthur 'Art' (1910–56) Piano
Evans, Gil (1912–88) Pianist, composer
Herman, Woodrow Charles, 'Woody' (b. 1913) Clarinet, bandleader
Holiday, Billie (1915–59) Singer
Cole, Nat 'King' (Nathaniel Coles) (1919–65) Pianist, singer
Monk, Theolonius Sphere (1917–82) Piano
Gillespie, John Birks, 'Dizzy' (b. 1917) Trumpet
Fitzgerald, Ella (b. 1918) Singer
Parker, Charles Christopher 'Bird' (1920–55) Saxophone
Peterson, Oscar Emmanuel (b. 1925) Piano
Roach, Maxwell, 'Max' (b. 1925) Drums
Coltrane, John (1926–67) Saxophone
Davis, Miles (b. 1926) Trumpet
Coleman, Ornette (b. 1930) Alto saxophone
Zawinul, Josef (b. 1932) Keyboards
Shorter, Wayne (b. 1933) Tenor saxophone
Hancock, Herbie (b. 1940) Keyboards

Musical terms

a cappella Without instrumental accompaniment.
adagio Slow and leisurely.
aleatory music Allowing performers freedom of interpretation or which introduces other random elements.
allegro Quick, lively.
andante Gently moving, flowing.
anthem Church choral work.
aria Solo sung in opera or oratorio.

arpeggio Notes of a chord played upward or downward in quick succession.
atonal music Use of all 12 semitones; having no key.
cadence Musical punctuation used to end phrases, sections or complete works.
cadenza Solo virtuoso piece before the final cadence in an aria, or at any stated place in a concerto.
canon Repetition of tune or tunes that overlap each other.
chord Notes played together simultaneously.
chromatic Relating to notes and chords comprising the 12-note scale.
coda Theme introduced at the end of a movement to emphasize its finality.
concrete music (Musique concrète). Music constructed from previously recorded natural sounds.
continuo Keyboard augmentation of a 17th- or 18th-century orchestral work.
counterpoint Two or more independent tunes sung or played at the same time.
diatonic Relating to notes of the major and minor scales.
dominant key Key whose keynote is the fifth note of the tonic solfa.
electronic music Consisting of electronically produced sounds.
forte (f) Loudly.
fortissimo (ff) Very loudly.
fugue A polyphonic composition. The first tune is in the tonic; the second, introduced later, in the dominant key, and so on.
interval Difference in pitch between two notes.
largo Slow, stately.
libretto Text of oratorio or opera.
lieder German romantic songs of the 19th century.
madrigal Secular composition for voices.
Mass Roman Catholic sung service of Communion.
motet Unaccompanied part song of a religious nature.
movement A division of a long musical work.
obbligato Accompaniment by solo instrument.
opera Drama set to music.
operetta Light opera, often with dialogue.
oratorio Religious equivalent of opera without costume or scenery.
overture Instrumental introduction to opera or oratorio.
pentatonic scale A primitive five-note scale.
pianissimo (pp) Very soft.
piano (p) Soft.
pitch The height or depth of a note, measured according to its vibrations (e.g. A above middle C equals 440 vibrations a second).
pizzicato Notes played by plucking strings of normally bowed instruments.
polyphonic 'Many voiced', combining independent melodic lines. As in motets and fugues.
recitative Solo vocal music that follows speech patterns.
Requiem Mass for the dead.
rondo Music composition where the first and main sections return alternately after different contrasting sections.
scherzo Lively movement.
serial music Compositions of the 12-tone scale using all notes with equal importance, and each once only before all have been used.
sonata form A form of musical composition devel-

oped during the 18th century. The first part sets out two main themes, each in a different key. The second part develops these two themes. The third is a recapitulation in which both themes are presented in the key of the first theme.

suite A work made up of several movements.

symphony Major orchestral work, usually made up of four movements.

syncopation Accentuation of a beat in each bar that is normally not accentuated.

tempo Pace at which a work is performed.

tertiary form A simple three-part musical structure in which the central part contrasts with the first and third, which are similar (ABA form).

theme A basic tune.

tutti Passage for whole orchestra.

vibrato Wavering of a note's pitch in singing, string playing and wind playing, to give vibrancy.

vivace Lively.

History and development of dance

Main Trends	Types of Dance Popular at the Time
Prehistory Unorganized or loosely organized dances for warlike and communal purposes. Courtship, harvest, rain or religion. Egypt and Peru just two places where surviving art suggests processions and religious ceremonies incorporated elements of dance.	
500 BC Greek theatre provides origins of theatrical dance.	
12th Century Court dancing in Provence: the processional *estampies* give way to *danses à deux*, the first recorded instances of couples dancing together.	
14th Century Danse basse: low, slow, gliding steps. Hault danse: with high, fast steps.	Pavane; derived from instrumental music from Padua; possibly the first stylized dance. Galliard, also from Italy, where the name implies gaiety.
15th Century First true ballet, with settings by Leonardo da Vinci, danced at Tortona, 1489. Introduced at the court of Henry VIII of England as masque. 1416, Domenico de Piacenza publishes first European dance manual, *De Arte Saltandi et Choreas Ducendi* (on the art of dancing and directing choruses).	Court ballet: Branle, English clog dance with circular figures. Allemande, i.e. 'from Germany'. Courante, i.e. 'running', from It. *corrente* (current). Volta, very lively (It. *volta*: vault).
16th Century Ballet comique. First complete printed account (15 Oct 1581) of a ballet to celebrate the marriage of duc de Joyeuse and Marguerite of Lorraine. It was based on the story of Circe and choreographed by Baltazarini di Belgioioso.	Morisca, moresque: dances from Moorish Spain first recorded 1446 by Bohemian traveller who visited Burgos. No relation to Morris dance, which developed from religious cult.
17th Century Ballet masquerade, often with hideous and elaborate masks.	Mazurka, Polish round dance for eight couples, with second beat accentuated. Gigue, originally from English jig, the word from German *Geige*: 'fiddle'. Sarabande, slow and graceful, introduced to Spain *c.* 1588 from Morocco or West Indies. Bouree, lively dance, starting on the upbeat.
Playford's *English Dancing Master* published 1651, a collection of tunes and steps.	Chaconne, graceful dance introduced from Peru (*guacones, c.* 1580) via Spain. Gavotte, medium pace, from Provence; *gavoto*: a native of the Alps. Minuet, named after French *pas menu* or 'small steps'; first recorded by Lully in 1663. Passacaglia, as chaconne above, but in minor key. Rigaudon: rigadoon, lively French dance.

History and development of dance *continued*

Main Trends	Types of Dance Popular at the Time
First waltz, developed from minuet and Ländler in 1660; word 'waltz' first used in 1754 in Austria. Ballet systematique: Louis XIV established the Académie Royale de Danse 1661. Five classic positions codified by Pierre Beauchamp. Paris Opéra succeeds Académie in 1671. First history of dancing published in 1682.	Ländler, rustic dance, from *Ländl*: 'small country'. Matelot, Dutch sailors' clog dance. Contredanse, from English 'country dance', but mistranslated as 'counterdance', i.e. for opposing groups, and reintroduced into England in this form. Cotillion, from French word for 'petticoat', for two groups of four pairs each; developed into quadrille at the end of the 19th century.

18th Century
Jean-Georges Noverre's *Lettres sur la danse et sur les ballets* (1760) starts movement towards dance as expression.
Gaetano Vestris perfects *grand jeté* at the Paris Opera as pirouettes and leaps push forward the physical frontiers of ballet. Employment of Italian acrobats and comic dancers assists process.
Vestris's abandonment of customary leather masks in *Medée et Jason* (1770) opens ballet to possibility of showing emotion through movement, validating Noverre's *lettres*.

19th Century
Court dances superseded by professional dancers. Audience for dance now mixes commoners and nobility in public theatres.
Square dance (*c.* 1815).
La Sylphide (1832, chor. Filippo Tuglione) ushers in era of true European ballet, abandoning Greek myths and featuring female dancers *sur les pointes* symbolizing sylphs, nymphs, etc.
Can-can (*c.* 1835), high-kicking exhibitionist female dance popular on Parisian stages.

Quadrille, a French derivation of 17th-century contredanse. A series of five 'figure' dances for four couples.

Age of the great waltz composers: Josef Lanner; Johann Strauss; Emil Waldteufel, etc.

Polka, introduced to Paris in 1843 from Bohemian courtship dance.
Cakewalk, graceful walking dance of competitive type with cakes as prizes, popular in Black America in 1872; introduced into ballrooms *c.* 1900.

20th Century
Ballets Russes established in Paris by Diaghilev, 1909; took Russian ballet to the West and offshoots establish ballet companies in UK, US, Australia, etc.

New free dance forms emerging. Isadora Duncan, Ruth St Denis and others incorporate elements of other cultures – Greece, Far Eastern – into abstract dance. Rudolf Laban and disciples extend range of dance movement. Emile Jaques-Dalcroze develops eurythmics, a system of musical rhythm in movement.

Samba emerged from Brazil, 1885; known *c.* 1920 as Maxixe; resumed name 'samba' *c.* 1940. Quickstep invented in America 1900; reached peak of popularity in 1920s. Tango, syncopated dance popular in 1920s, emerged from Buenos Aires and developed from Cuban *habañera*. Barn dance, associated in America with festivities surrounding the completion of a new barn. Two-step.
Boston, predecessor of the foxtrot.
Turkey trot.
Foxtrot, slow and quick varieties, introduced in 1912 in America, allegedly named after Harry Fox. The slow foxtrot evolved *c.* 1927 into 'blues' dance.

Ballroom dance craze, mostly couples dancing to small instrumental groups (*c.* 1920).

Younger choreographers like Alvin Ailey, Twyla Tharp incorporate rock, African, West Indian, jazz music into their work.

Doing the Charleston, energetic and highly popular dance of the 20s. (Rex Features)

Growth of very energetic dancing, often to jazz or pseudo-jazz groups (from 1939). Modern discotheque style, i.e. recorded music for dancing; originated in Parisian clubs (c. 1951).

Charleston, side kick from the knee. Named after a Mack and Johnson song (1923) about the town that saw the first ballet in America in 1735.
Pasodoble, Spanish-style two-step.
Rumba, authentic Cuban dance popularized in 1923.
Black Bottom, first mentioned in *New York Times* (19 Dec 1926), a type of athletic and jerky foxtrot.
Conga, single-file dance developed in 1935 from rumba and from aboriginal African dances.
Jive, developed from jitterbug.
Mambo, an off-beat rumba (1948) of Cuban origin.

Popularity of dances closely linked to the record charts and the consequent invention of many new dance styles.

Rock 'n' roll, introduced in 1953 by Bill Haley and his Comets in America; heavy beat and simple melody for energetic and free dancing.
Cha cha cha (1954), a variation of the mambo, couples dancing with lightly linked hands.
Twist (1961), body-torsion and knee-flexing lively dance, with partners rarely in contact.
Bossa nova, lively Latin American dance.
Go-go (1965), repetitious dance of verve, often exhibitionist.
Reggae (1969), introduced from Jamaica, strong accentuations off-beat.
Pogo (1976), introduced by 'punk rockers'; dancers rise vertically from the floor in imitation of a pogo stick.
Disco dancing, flamboyant freestyle, often with exaggerated hand movement, popularized by film *Saturday Night Fever* (1977).
Break dancing (1980); dancers perform acrobatic feats while dancing.
Robotics-dancers imitate clockwork dolls with rigid limb movements.

Rock and pop

The combination of elements of black music with country and western, as exemplified by Elvis Presley in his earliest recordings in 1954, became known as rock 'n' roll: less 'pure' forms were later known as rock.

The establishment of best-selling charts, initially of sheet music but then of 45 rpm records (replacing 78 rpm discs at the beginning of the sixties) and the growing influence of television led to popular (pop) music and its performers becoming a youth cult and displacing the old guard such as Frank Sinatra and Dean Martin. Country, soul/blues and, later, reggae remained minority interests by comparison, though each wielded occasional influence on pop music fashions. The emergence of the Beatles in the sixties turned the spotlight from individual performers to self-contained groups.

The advent of punk rock in the late seventies gave a new energy to the music with its up-tempo drive.

Live Aid (1985) presented rock as a force for humanitarian causes.

Major artists

Guthrie, Woody (1912–67)
Williams, Hank (1923–53)
Haley, Bill (1925–1981)
Domino, Antoine 'Fats' (b. 1928)
Cooke, Sam (1931–64)
Berry, Chuck (b. 1931)
Cash, Johnny (b. 1932)
Charles, Ray (b. 1932)
Brown, James (b. 1933)
Presley, Elvis (1935–77)
Lewis, Jerry Lee (b. 1935)
Holly, Buddy (1936–59)
Everly Brothers (Don b. 1937; Phil b. 1939)
Turner, Tina (b. 1938)
Richard, Cliff (b. 1940)
Baez, Joan (b. 1941)
Dylan, Bob (b. 1941)
Franklin, Aretha (b. 1942)
Ross, Diana (b. 1944)
Marley, Bob (1945–81)
Van Morrison (b. 1954)
Parton, Dolly (p. 1946)
Bowie, David (b. 1947)
John, Elton (b. 1947)
Springsteen, Bruce (b. 1949)
Wonder, Stevie (b. 1950)
Jackson, Michael (b. 1958)
Beatles (formed 1959; split 1970)
Beach Boys (formed 1961)
Simon & Garfunkel (formed 1962; split 1970)
The Rolling Stones (formed 1962)
The Who (formed 1964)
The Byrds (formed 1964)
Pink Floyd (formed 1965)
The Jimi Hendrix Experience (formed 1966; Hendrix d. 1970)
Genesis (formed 1966)
Fleetwood Mac (formed 1967)
Crosby, Stills, Nash & Young (formed 1968)
Little Feat (formed 1969)
Steely Dan (formed 1972; split 1981)
Abba (formed 1973; split 1982)
The Sex Pistols (formed 1975; split 1978)
The Police (formed 1977; split 1986)

Ballet terms

à terre Steps which do not entail high jumps. They include the *glissade, pas balloné* and *pas brisé*.
battement Ballet exercises.
batterie, battu Jump during which a dancer beats the calves sharply together.
corps de ballet Group of dancers who support the principal dancers.
divertissement Self-contained dance within a ballet, designed purely as entertainment or to show off a dancer's technique.
elevation Any high jump in ballet. Elevations include the *entrechat, rivoltade, pas de chat* and *cabriole*.
enchaînement Sequence of steps linked to make a harmonious whole.
entrechat Vertical jump during which the dancer changes the position of the legs after beating the calves together.
fouetté Spectacular pirouette in which the dancer throws his raised leg to the front and side in order to achieve momentum for another turn.
jeté Jump from one leg to the other, basic to many ballet steps. These include the *grand jeté en avant*, in which the dancer leaps forward as if clearing an obstacle, and the *jeté fouetté* where the dancer performs a complete turn in mid-air.
pas Basic ballet step in which the weight is transferred from one leg to another. The term is also used in combination to indicate the number of performers in a dance; a *pas seul* is a solo and a *pas de deux* a dance for a pair of dancers.
pirouette Complete turn on one leg, performed either on the ball of the foot or on the toes.
plié Bending the legs from a standing position; *demi-plié* involves bending the knees as far as possible while keeping the heels on the floor.
relevé Bending the body from the waist to one side or the other during a turn or a pirouette.
rivoltade, revoltade Step in which a dancer raises one leg in front, jumps from the other and turns in the air, landing in the original position but facing the other way.
saut A plain jump in the air without embellishment.
soutenu Movement executed at a slower tempo than usual.
sur les pointes On the toes.
variation Solo by a male dancer in a *pas de deux*.

Some well-known ballet companies

Royal Danish Ballet
Founded 1748.
Royal Swedish Ballet
Founded 1773 by Louis Gallodier.
Bolshoi Ballet
Founded in Moscow in 1776.
Kirov Ballet Formerly the Imperial Russian Ballet of St Petersburg (Leningrad)
Founded 1860.
Ballets Russes
Founded by Diaghilev in Paris 1909.
Martha Graham Dance Company
Founded by Graham in 1930.

Ballet Rambert
Founded by Marie Rambert in 1930.
Vic-Wells Ballet (afterwards Sadlers Wells Ballet)
Founded in 1931 by Dame Ninette de Valois.
Ballets Jooss
Founded by Kurt Jooss in 1932.
Ballet Russe de Monte Carlo
Founded 1932 by W. de Basil. Dissolved 1947 and reconstituted 1965 as Ballet de Monte Carlo.
New York City Ballet
Founded in 1934 as School of American Ballet.
American Ballet Theatre
Founded in 1940 by Lucia Chase as the Ballet Theatre; American added in 1957.
National Ballet of Canada
Founded in 1951.
Merce Cunningham Dance Company
Founded by Cunningham in 1952.
Royal Ballet Successor to Sadlers Wells Ballet
Founded 1956.
The Joffrey Ballet
Founded 1956 as the Robert Joffrey Ballet.
Alvin Ailey Dance Theatre
Founded in 1957.
Stuttgart Ballet
Founded in 1961 by John Cranko.
Dance Theatre of Harlem
Founded in 1968 by Arthur Mitchell.

Notable choreographers

Pierre Beauchamp (d. 1695)
Weaver, John (1673-1760)
Noverre, Jean-Georges (1727-1810)
Tuglione, Filippo (1777-1871)
Delsarte, François (1811-71)
Petipa, Marius (1819-1910)
Jaques-Dalcroze, Emile (1865-1950)
Duncan, Isadora (1877-1927)
St Denis, Ruth (1877-1968)
Laban, Rudolf (1879-1958)
Folkine, Michel (1880-1942)
Diaghilev, Sergei (1872-1929)
Lopukhov, Fyodor (1886-1973)
Wigman, Mary (1886-1973)
Nijinska, Brorislava (1891-1972)
Graham, Martha (b. 1893)
Humphrey, Doris (1895-1958)
Massine, Léonide (1895-1979)
De Valois, Dame Ninette (b. 1898)
Jooss, Kurt (1901-79)
Balanchine, George (1904-83)
Ashton, Sir Frederick (b. 1906)
Tudor, Antony (b. 1909)
Sokolow, Anna (b. 1912)
Cunningham, Merce (b. 1919)
Béjart, Maurice (b. 1927)
Cranko, John (1927-73)
Grigorovich, Yuri (b. 1927)
MacMillan, Kenneth (b. 1929)
Ailey, Alvin (b. 1931)
Tharp, Twyla (b. 1942)

Notable ballet dancers

Dupré, Louis (1697-1744)
Salle, Marie (1707-56)

Camargo, Marie (1710-70)
Campanini, Barberina (1721-99)
Vestris, Gaetano (1729-1808)
Pavlova, Anna (1881-1931)
Nijinsky, Vaslav (1890-1950)
Markova, Alicia (b. 1910)
Fonteyn, Dame Margot (b. 1919)
Shearer, Moira (b. 1926)
Nerina, Nadia (b. 1927)
Nureyev, Rudolf (b. 1938)
Seymour, Lynn (b. 1939)
Baryshnikov, Mikhail (b. 1948)

Notable opera singers

Basile, Adriana (*c.* 1580–*c.* 1640)
Lablache, Luigi (1794-1858)
Sontag, Henriette (1806-54)
Petrov, Ossip (1806-78)
Malibran, Maria (1808-36)
Lind, Jenny (1820-87)
Viardot Garcia, Pauline (1821-1910)
Stolz, Teresa (1836-1902)
Nilsson, Christine (1843-1921)
Maurel, Victor (1848-1923)
Melba, Dame Nellie (1861-1931)
Caruso, Enrico (1873-1921)
Pears, Sir Peter (b. 1910)
Callas, Maria (1923-77)
Sutherland, Dame Joan (b. 1926)
Caballé, Montserrat (b. 1933)
Pavarotti, Luciano (b. 1935)
Domingo, Placido (b. 1941)
te Kanawa, Kiri (b. 1944)

Notable opera composers and their works

Monteverdi, Claudio (1567-1643) *La Favola d'Orfeo, Arianna*
Mozart, Wolfgang Amadeus (1756-91) *Le Nozze Di Figaro, Don Giovanni, Cosí Fan Tutti, The Magic Flute*
Beethoven, Ludwig van (1770-1827) *Fidelio*
Rossini, Gioacchino (1792-1868) *La Gazza Ladra, The Barber of Seville, William Tell*
Wagner, Richard (1813-83) *Lohengrin, Tristan und Isolde, Die Meistersinger, The Ring Cycle, Parsifal*
Verdi, Giuseppe (1813-1901) *Otello, Rigoletto, Falstaff, La Traviata*
Strauss, Johann (1825-99) *Die Fledermaus, Wiener Blut*
Bizet, Georges (1838-75) *Carmen*
Mussorgsky, Modest (1839-81) *Boris Godunov*
Sullivan, Sir Arthur (1842-1900) *HMS Pinafore, The Pirates of Penzance, The Mikado, Iolanthe*
Puccini, Giacomo (1858-1924) *Tosca, Madame Butterfly, La Bohème, Turandot*
Strauss, Richard (1864-1949) *Der Rosenkavalier, Salomé*
Gershwin, George (1898-1937) *Porgy and Bess*
Britten, Benjamin (1913-76) *Peter Grimes, Billy Budd*

THE CINEMA

Origins of the cinema

The creation of the cinema as we know it today was preceded by various developments in photography and the study of movement that go back to the early 19th century. The illusion of movement was first obtained by projecting images mechanically in rapid succession and was used in toys made in the 1830s.

The first motion picture films were taken on a camera patented in Britain by French-born Louis Le Prince, who used sensitized paper roll film, developed in 1885, to obtain images. In 1889 Eastman celluloid film was available in Britain and Le Prince used this to develop the commercial aspects of his patent.

The kinetoscope, invented in 1891 at the laboratories of Edison in the USA, was the first apparatus for viewing cine film: the intermittent 'gate', which holds each frame of film stationary while it is being exposed was invented in Britain by William Friese-Greene in 1888. Rapidly, all these experiments and inventions were integrated into one apparatus, a combined movie camera and projector, by the French brothers, Auguste and Louis Lumière. They started the first movie shows, the first public performance before a paying audience taking place in Paris on 28 Dec 1895. The cinema, as we know it, was born.

The public's interest in the new medium became unassuageable, and showmen were quick to exploit its commercial potential. Programmes were shown in fairgrounds and hired halls; soon permanent cinemas were being established and by 1912 there were over 4000 in Britain alone.

At first, cinema presentations were confined to the showing of a number of short films, but in 1906 the first feature film was made in Australia. Lasting 60–70 minutes, it was made by Charles Tait and was called *The Story of the Kelly Gang*. Europe and the United States did not follow Australia's lead until *c.* 1912, but by the outbreak of World War I in 1914, 24 countries were producing feature films.

Colour movies

Colour photography experiments were being carried out throughout the latter half of the 19th century, and in July 1906 the first commercially successful colour film was made. Developed by G. A. Smith in Britain, he called his process Kinemacolor, and the first public presentation of a film in this new process was shown in a programme of 21 films on 26 Feb 1909. Britain led the United States in the production of Kinemacolor films, producing the first full-length feature in colour in 1914. The first (non-subtractive) Technicolor film was made in the United States in 1917, using (like Kinemacolor) colour filters on both camera and projector. Two-colour subtractive Technicolor film was made and used in 1922.

By 1932, three-colour subtractive Technicolor film was available and was first used for a Walt Disney cartoon shown on 17 July 1932. Meanwhile, two-colour processes continued to be developed, the most notable being Cinecolor. Eastman Color was introduced in 1952 and steadily displaced its rivals. It is now almost universally used in Western countries.

The introduction of sound

Although *The Jazz Singer*, starring Al Jolson, made in Hollywood in 1927, is credited with being the first 'talkie', there is a long list of precedents stretching back to 1896. Short sound films were shown in Berlin in September of that year, using synchronized discs for the sound. Sound-on-disc continued to be used in various forms until 1929, and as far back as 1906 the first sound-on-film process was patented by French-born Eugene Lauste of London, but it was not until 1910 that he succeeded in recording and reproducing speech on film. By 1913 he had perfected the apparatus to record and reproduce sound on films, but World War I put an end to his hopes of commercially exploiting his invention. Sound track was added to Technicolor film in 1924. The first presentation of a sound-on-film production before a paying audience was shown in New York on 15 Apr 1923. *The Jazz Singer* takes its place in the record books as being the first talking feature film, and used the sound-on-disc system. The first sound-on-film feature, *The Air Circus*, was shown on 1 Sept 1928, in New York.

Stereophonic sound was patented in France in 1932 and its first use was three years later.

Dolby sound, a high fidelity noise reduction sys-

Kinemacolour produced this first ever full length feature film in colour as early as 1914. (Science Museum)

tem described by inventor Ray Dolby as a means of 'reproducing the silence as accurately as the sound', came to fruition with the release of Ken Russell's 1975 *Lisztomania*, the first film with a Dolby encoded stereo optical soundtrack. By 1986 a thousand feature films had been produced in Dolby stereo.

Even more advanced is digital sound, first applied to motion picture presentation when a specially recorded version of Disney's 1941 *Fantasia* was shown before paying audiences at Century City, California, in 1985. The process enables the exact reproduction of sound.

Other technical developments

The first wide screen showings date back to the 1890s, when film stock of exceptional width was used. It was first used in a feature film in Italy in 1923. Anamorphic lenses – used to contract a wide image onto standard film (as in Cinemascope) – were first used in France in 1927. 70 mm film for use with a wide screen was used in the United States in 1929. The first system to combine wide-gauge film and anamorphic lenses was called Ultra-Panavision and was first used in 1957. Cinemascope was developed by the Frenchman, Henri Chrétien, from an anamorphic system he invented in 1927. The patent rights were acquired by 20th Century Fox and used in the first Cinemascope feature in 1953, *The Robe*.

Cinerama was shown at the New York World Fair in 1939, but was not launched commercially until 1952.

Three-dimensional films date from 1915, using red and green spectacles worn by the viewers.

As early as 1936 the Italians produced a full-length talkie in 3-D titled *Nozze Vagabonde*, but it was not until 1952 that Hollywood took up the idea in an attempt to win back audiences staying at home to watch TV. During the next three years there were 45 American features produced in 3-D as well as a number from other countries, but the fad was shortlived. Sporadic production resumed in 1960 and there have been about 60 3-D films made since then.

A recent innovation expected to become significant in the 1990s is HDVS, a system developed jointly by the Italians and the Japanese which enables feature films to be shot on high definition video and transferred to film without loss of picture quality. It is claimed to cut below-the-line production costs by up to 30 per cent.

Cinemas worldwide

USA	22719	(1987)
India	8409	(1988)
USSR	5257	(1987)
France	5063	(1988)
China	3100	(1988)
Italy	3000	(1988)
Mexico	2995	(1988)
Spain	2234	(1988)
Indonesia	2215	(1987)
Japan	2109	(1986)
Canada	2004	(1984)
UK	1250	(1987)

Film production (1987)

(Feature films of 1 hour or more)	
India	806
USA	331
Japan	286
Philippines	167
USSR	151
Turkey	c. 150
China	140
France	133
Thailand	130
Italy	115
Hong Kong	113
Mexico	82
South Africa	78
Spain	77
Pakistan	76
Germany, West	74
Egypt	70
Bangladesh	65
Canada	61
Brazil	60
Indonesia	52
UK	30

Motion Picture Academy Awards (Oscars)

The year given is the year the award was made.

1929
Actor: Emil Jannings, *The Way of All Flesh*.
Actress: Janet Gaynor, *Seventh Heaven*.
Director: Frank Borzage, *Seventh Heaven*; Lewis Milestone, *Two Arabian Knights*.
Picture: *Wings*, Paramount.

1930
Actor: Warner Baxter, *In Old Arizona*.
Actress: Mary Pickford, *Coquette*.
Director: Frank Lloyd, *The Divine Lady*.
Picture: *Broadway Melody*, MGM.

1931
Actor: George Arliss, *Disraeli*.
Actress: Norma Shearer, *The Divorcee*.
Director: Lewis Milestone, *All Quiet on the Western Front*.
Picture: *All Quiet on the Western Front*, Univ.

1932
Actor: Lionel Barrymore, *Free Soul*.
Actress: Marie Dressler, *Min and Bill*.
Director: Norman Taurog, *Skippy*.
Picture: *Cimarron*, RKO.

1933
Actor: Fredric March, *Dr Jekyll and Mr Hyde*; Wallace Beery, *The Champ* (tie).
Actress: Helen Hayes, *Sin of Madelon Claudet*.
Director: Frank Borzage, *Bad Girl*.
Picture: *Grand Hotel*, MGM.
Special: Walt Disney, *Mickey Mouse*.

1934
Actor: Charles Laughton, *Private Life of Henry VIII.*
Actress: Katharine Hepburn, *Morning Glory.*
Director: Frank Lloyd, *Cavalcade.*
Picture: *Cavalcade*, Fox.

1935
Actor: Clark Gable, *It Happened One Night.*
Actress: Claudette Colbert, *It Happened One Night.*
Director: Frank Capra, *It Happened One Night.*
Picture: *It Happened One Night*, Columbia.

1936
Actor: Victor McLaglen, *The Informer.*
Actress: Bette Davis, *Dangerous.*
Director: John Ford, *The Informer.*
Picture: *Mutiny on the Bounty*, MGM.

1937
Actor: Paul Muni, *Story of Louis Pasteur.*
Actress: Luise Rainer, *The Great Ziegfeld.*
Sup. Actor: Walter Brennan, *Come and Get It.*
Sup. Actress: Gale Sondergaard, *Anthony Adverse.*
Director: Frank Capra, *Mr Deeds Goes to Town.*
Picture: *The Great Ziegfeld*, MGM.

1938
Actor: Spencer Tracy, *Captains Courageous.*
Actress: Luise Rainer, *The Good Earth.*
Sup. Actor: Joseph Schildkraut, *Life of Emile Zola.*
Sup. Actress: Alice Brady, *In Old Chicago.*
Director: Leo McCarey, *The Awful Truth.*
Picture: *Life of Emile Zola*, Warner.

1939
Actor: Spencer Tracy, *Boys Town.*
Actress: Bette Davis, *Jezebel.*
Sup. Actor: Walter Brennan, *Kentucky.*
Sup. Actress: Fay Bainter, *Jezebel.*
Director: Frank Capra, *You Can't Take It With You.*
Picture: *You Can't Take It With You*, Columbia.

1940
Actor: Robert Donat, *Goodbye, Mr Chips.*
Actress: Vivien Leigh, *Gone With the Wind.*
Sup. Actor: Thomas Mitchell, *Stage Coach.*
Sup. Actress: Hattie McDaniel, *Gone With the Wind.*
Director: Victor Fleming, *Gone With the Wind.*
Picture: *Gone With the Wind*, Selznick International.

1941
Actor: James Stewart, *The Philadelphia Story.*
Actress: Ginger Rogers, *Kitty Foyle.*
Sup. Actor: Walter Brennan, *The Westerner.*
Sup. Actress: Jane Darwell, *The Grapes of Wrath.*
Director: John Ford, *The Grapes of Wrath.*
Picture: *Rebecca*, Selznick International.

1942
Actor: Gary Cooper, *Sergeant York.*
Actress: Joan Fontaine, *Suspicion.*
Sup. Actor: Donald Crisp, *How Green Was My Valley.*
Sup. Actress: Mary Astor, *The Great Lie.*
Director: John Ford, *How Green Was My Valley.*
Picture: *How Green Was My Valley*, 20th Century-Fox.

1943
Actor: James Cagney, *Yankee Doodle Dandy.*
Actress: Greer Garson, *Mrs Miniver.*
Sup. Actor: Van Heflin, *Johnny Eager.*
Sup. Actress: Teresa Wright, *Mrs Miniver.*
Director: William Wyler, *Mrs Miniver.*
Picture: *Mrs Miniver*, MGM.

1944
Actor: Paul Lukas, *Watch on the Rhine.*
Actress: Jennifer Jones, *The Song of Bernadette.*
Sup. Actor: Charles Coburn, *The More the Merrier.*
Sup. Actress: Katina Paxinou, *For Whom the Bell Tolls.*
Director: Michael Curtiz, *Casablanca.*
Picture: *Casablanca*, Warner.

1945
Actor: Bing Crosby, *Going My Way.*
Actress: Ingrid Bergman, *Gaslight.*
Sup. Actor: Barry Fitzgerald, *Going My Way.*
Sup. Actress: Ethel Barrymore, *None But the Lonely Heart.*
Director: Leo McCarey, *Going My Way.*
Picture: *Going My Way*, Paramount.

1946
Actor: Ray Milland, *The Lost Weekend.*
Actress: Joan Crawford, *Mildred Pierce.*
Sup. Actor: James Dunn, *A Tree Grows in Brooklyn.*
Sup. Actress: Anne Revere, *National Velvet.*
Director: Billy Wilder, *The Lost Weekend.*
Picture: *The Lost Weekend*, Paramount.

1947
Actor: Fredric March, *The Best Years of Our Lives.*
Actress: Olivia de Havilland, *To Each His Own.*
Sup. Actor: Harold Russell, *The Best Years of Our Lives.*
Sup. Actress: Anne Baxter, *The Razor's Edge.*
Director: William Wyler, *The Best Years of Our Lives.*
Picture: *The Best Years of Our Lives*, Goldwyn, RKO.

1948
Actor: Ronald Colman, *A Double Life.*
Actress: Loretta Young, *The Farmer's Daughter.*
Sup. Actor: Edmund Gwenn, *Miracle on 34th Street.*
Sup. Actress: Celeste Holm, *Gentleman's Agreement.*
Director: Elia Kazan, *Gentleman's Agreement.*
Picture: *Gentleman's Agreement*, 20th Century-Fox.

1949
Actor: Laurence Olivier, *Hamlet.*
Actress: Jane Wyman, *Johnny Belinda.*
Sup. Actor: Walter Huston, *Treasure of Sierra Madre.*
Sup. Actress: Claire Trevor, *Key Largo.*
Director: John Huston, *Treasure of Sierra Madre.*
Picture: *Hamlet*, Two Cities Film, Universal International.

1950
Actor: Broderick Crawford, *All the King's Men.*
Actress: Olivia de Havilland, *The Heiress.*
Sup. Actor: Dean Jagger, *Twelve O'Clock High.*
Sup. Actress: Mercedes McCambridge, *All the King's Men.*

Director: Joseph L. Mankiewicz, *Letter to Three Wives.*
Picture: *All the King's Men,* Columbia.

1951
Actor: Jose Ferrer, *Cyrano de Bergerac.*
Actress: Judy Holliday, *Born Yesterday.*
Sup. Actor: George Sanders, *All About Eve.*
Sup. Actress: Jopsephine Hull, *Harvey.*
Director: Joseph L. Mankiewicz, *All About Eve.*
Picture: *All About Eve,* 20th Century-Fox.

1952
Actor: Humphrey Bogart, *The African Queen.*
Actress: Vivien Leigh, *A Streetcar Named Desire.*
Sup. Actor: Karl Malden, *A Streetcar Named Desire.*
Sup. Actress: Kim Hunter, *A Streetcar Named Desire.*
Director: George Stevens, *A Place in the Sun.*
Picture: *An American in Paris,* MGM.

1953
Actor: Gary Cooper, *High Noon.*
Actress: Shirley Booth, *Come Back, Little Sheba.*
Sup. Actor: Anthony Quinn, *Viva Zapata!*
Sup. Actress: Gloria Grahame, *The Bad and the Beautiful.*
Director: John Ford, *The Quiet Man.*
Picture: *Greatest Show on Earth,* C. B. DeMille, Paramount.

1954
Actor: William Holden, *Stalag 17.*
Actress: Audrey Hepburn, *Roman Holiday.*
Sup. Actor: Frank Sinatra, *From Here to Eternity.*
Sup. Actress: Donna Reed, *From Here to Eternity.*
Director: Fred Zinnemann, *From Here to Eternity.*
Picture: *From Here to Eternity,* Columbia.

1955
Actor: Marlon Brando, *On the Waterfront.*
Actress: Grace Kelly, *The Country Girl.*
Sup. Actor: Edmond O'Brien, *The Barefoot Contessa.*
Sup. Actress: Eva Marie Saint, *On the Waterfront.*
Director: Elia Kazan, *On the Waterfront.*
Picture: *On the Waterfront,* Horizon-American, Columbia.

1956
Actor: Ernest Borgnine, *Marty.*
Actress: Anna Magnani, *The Rose Tattoo.*
Sup. Actor: Jack Lemmon, *Mister Roberts.*
Sup. Actress: Jo Van Fleet, *East of Eden.*
Director: Delbert Mann, *Marty.*
Picture: *Marty,* Hecht and Lancaster's Steven Prods., U.A.

1957
Actor: Yul Brynner, *The King and I.*
Actress: Ingrid Bergman, *Anastasia.*
Sup. Actor: Anthony Quinn, *Lust for Life.*
Sup. Actress: Dorothy Malone, *Written on the Wind.*
Director: George Stevens, *Giant.*
Picture: *Around the World in 80 Days,* Michael Todd, U.A.

1958
Actor: Alec Guinness, *The Bridge on the River Kwai.*

Actress: Joanne Woodward, *The Three Faces of Eve.*
Sup. Actor: Red Buttons, *Sayonara.*
Sup. Actress: Miyoshi Umeki, *Sayonara.*
Director: David Lean, *The Bridge on the River Kwai.*
Picture: *The Bridge on the River Kwai,* Columbia.

1959
Actor: David Niven, *Separate Tables.*
Actress: Susan Hayward, *I Want to Live.*
Sup. Actor: Burl Ives, *The Big Country.*
Sup. Actress: Wendy Hiller, *Separate Tables.*
Director: Vincente Minnelli, *Gigi.*
Picture: *Gigi,* Arthur Freed Production, MGM.

1960
Actor: Charlton Heston, *Ben-Hur.*
Actress: Simone Signoret, *Room at the Top.*
Sup. Actor: Hugh Griffith, *Ben-Hur.*
Sup. Actress: Shelley Winters, *Diary of Anne Frank.*
Director: William Wyler, *Ben-Hur.*
Picture: *Ben-Hur,* MGM.

1961
Actor: Burt Lancaster, *Elmer Gantry.*
Actress: Elizabeth Taylor, *Butterfield 8.*
Sup. Actor: Peter Ustinov, *Spartacus.*
Sup. Actress: Shirley Jones, *Elmer Gantry.*
Director: Billy Wilder, *The Apartment.*
Picture: *The Apartment,* Mirisch Co., U.A.

1962
Actor: Maximilian Schell, *Judgment at Nuremberg.*
Actress: Sophia Loren, *Two Women.*
Sup. Actor: George Chakiris, *West Side Story.*
Sup. Actress: Rita Moreno, *West Side Story.*
Director: Jerome Robbins, Robert Wise, *West Side Story.*
Picture: *West Side Story,* United Artists.

1963
Actor: Gregory Peck, *To Kill a Mockingbird.*
Actress: Anne Bancroft, *The Miracle Worker.*
Sup. Actor: Ed Begley, *Sweet Bird of Youth.*
Sup. Actress: Patty Duke, *The Miracle Worker.*
Director: David Lean, *Lawrence of Arabia.*
Picture: *Lawrence of Arabia,* Columbia.

1964
Actor: Sidney Poitier, *Lilies of the Field.*
Actress: Patricia Neal, *Hud.*
Sup. Actor: Melvyn Douglas, *Hud.*
Sup. Actress: Margaret Rutherford, *The VIPs.*
Director: Tony Richardson, *Tom Jones.*
Picture: *Tom Jones,* Woodfall Prod., UA-Lopert Pictures.

1965
Actor: Rex Harrison, *My Fair Lady.*
Actress: Julie Andrews, *Mary Poppins.*
Sup. Actor: Peter Ustinov, *Topkapi.*
Sup. Actress: Lila Kedrova, *Zorba the Greek.*
Director: George Cukor, *My Fair Lady.*
Picture: *My Fair Lady,* Warner Bros.

1966
Actor: Lee Marvin, *Cat Ballou.*
Actress: Julie Christie, *Darling.*
Sup. Actor: Martin Balsam, *A Thousand Clowns.*
Sup. Actress: Shelley Winters, *A Patch of Blue.*

Director: Robert Wise, *The Sound of Music.*
Picture: *The Sound of Music*, 20th Century-Fox.

1967
Actor: Paul Scofield, *A Man for All Seasons.*
Actress: Elizabeth Taylor, *Who's Afraid of Virginia Woolf?*
Sup. Actor: Walter Matthau, *The Fortune Cookie.*
Sup. Actress: Sandy Dennis, *Who's Afraid of Virginia Woolf?*
Director: Fred Zinnemann, *A Man for All Seasons.*
Picture: *A Man for All Seasons*, Columbia.

1968
Actor: Rod Steiger, *In the Heat of the Night.*
Actress: Katharine Hepburn, *Guess Who's Coming to Dinner.*
Sup. Actor: George Kennedy, *Cool Hand Luke.*
Sup. Actress: Estelle Parsons, *Bonnie and Clyde.*
Director: Mike Nichols, *The Graduate.*
Picture: *In the Heat of the Night.*

1969
Actor: Cliff Robertson, *Charly.*
Actress: Katharine Hepburn, *The Lion in Winter*; Barbra Streisand, *Funny Girl* (tie).
Sup. Actor: Jack Albertson, *The Subject Was Roses.*
Sup. Actress: Ruth Gordon, *Rosemary's Baby.*
Director: Sir Carol Reed, *Oliver!*
Picture: *Oliver!*

1970
Actor: John Wayne, *True Grit.*
Actress: Maggie Smith, *The Prime of Miss Jean Brodie.*
Sup. Actor: Gig Young, *They Shoot Horses, Don't They?*
Sup. Actress: Goldie Hawn, *Cactus Flower.*
Director: John Schlesinger, *Midnight Cowboy.*
Picture: *Midnight Cowboy.*

1971
Actor: George C. Scott, *Patton* (refused).
Actress: Glenda Jackson, *Women in Love.*
Sup. Actor: John Mills, *Ryan's Daughter.*
Sup. Actress: Helen Hayes, *Airport.*
Director: Franklin Schaffner, *Patton.*
Picture: *Patton.*

1972
Actor: Gene Hackman, *The French Connection.*
Actress: Jane Fonda, *Klute.*
Sup. Actor: Ben Johnson, *The Last Picture Show.*
Sup. Actress: Cloris Leachman, *The Last Picture Show.*
Director: William Friedkin, *The French Connection.*
Picture: *The French Connection.*

1973
Actor: Marlon Brando, *The Godfather* (refused).
Actress: Liza Minnelli, *Cabaret.*
Sup. Actor: Joel Grey, *Cabaret.*
Sup. Actress: Eileen Heckart, *Butterflies are Free.*
Director: Bob Fosse, *Cabaret.*
Picture: *The Godfather.*

1974
Actor: Jack Lemmon, *Save the Tiger.*
Actress: Glenda Jackson, *A Touch of Class.*
Sup. Actor: John Houseman, *The Paper Chase.*
Sup. Actress: Tatum O'Neal, *Paper Moon.*

Director: George Roy Hill, *The Sting.*
Picture: *The Sting.*

1975
Actor: Art Carney, *Harry and Tonto.*
Actress: Ellen Burstyn, *Alice Doesn't Live Here Anymore.*
Sup. Actor: Robert DeNiro, *The Godfather, Part II.*
Sup. Actress: Ingrid Bergman, *Murder on the Orient Express.*
Director: Francis Ford Coppola, *The Godfather, Part II.*
Picture: *The Godfather, Part II.*

1976
Actor: Jack Nicholson, *One Flew Over the Cuckoo's Nest.*
Actress: Louise Fletcher, *One Flew Over the Cuckoo's Nest.*
Sup. Actor: George Burns, *The Sunshine Boys.*
Sup. Actress: Lee Grant, *Shampoo.*
Director: Milos Forman, *One Flew Over the Cuckoo's Nest.*
Picture: *One Flew Over the Cuckoo's Nest.*

1977
Actor: Peter Finch, *Network.*
Actress: Faye Dunaway, *Network.*
Sup. Actor: Jason Robards, *All the President's Men.*
Sup. Actress: Beatrice Straight, *Network.*
Director: John G. Avildsen, *Rocky.*
Picture: *Rocky.*

1978
Actor: Richard Dreyfuss, *The Goodbye Girl.*
Actress: Diane Keaton, *Annie Hall.*
Sup. Actor: Jason Robards, *Julia.*
Sup. Actress: Vanessa Redgrave, *Julia.*
Director: Woody Allen, *Annie Hall.*
Picture: *Annie Hall.*

1979
Actor: Jon Voight, *Coming Home.*
Actress: Jane Fonda, *Coming Home.*
Sup. Actor: Christopher Walken, *The Deer Hunter.*
Sup. Actress: Maggie Smith, *California Suite.*
Director: Michael Cimino, *The Deer Hunter.*
Picture: *The Deer Hunter.*

1980
Actor: Dustin Hoffman, *Kramer vs Kramer.*
Actress: Sally Field, *Norma Rae.*
Sup. Actor: Melvyn Douglas, *Being There.*
Sup. Actress: Meryl Streep, *Kramer vs Kramer.*
Director: Robert Benton, *Kramer vs Kramer.*
Picture: *Kramer vs Kramer.*

1981
Actor: Robert DeNiro, *Raging Bull.*
Actress: Sissy Spacek, *Coal Miner's Daughter.*
Sup. Actor: Timothy Hutton, *Ordinary People.*
Sup. Actress: Mary Steenburgen, *Melvin & Howard.*
Director: Robert Redford, *Ordinary People.*
Picture: *Ordinary People.*

1982
Actor: Henry Fonda, *On Golden Pond.*
Actress: Katharine Hepburn, *On Golden Pond.*
Sup. Actor: John Gielgud, *Arthur.*
Sup. Actress: Maureen Stapleton, *Reds.*
Director: Warren Beatty, *Reds.*
Picture: *Chariots of Fire.*

1983
Actor: Ben Kingsley, *Gandhi.*
Actress: Meryl Streep, *Sophie's Choice.*
Sup. Actor: Louis Gossett, Jr, *An Officer and a Gentleman.*
Sup. Actress: Jessica Lange, *Tootsie.*
Director: Richard Attenborough, *Gandhi.*
Picture: *Gandhi.*

1984
Actor: Robert Duvall, *Tender Mercies.*
Actress: Shirley MacLaine, *Terms of Endearment.*
Sup. Actor: Jack Nicholson, *Terms of Endearment.*
Sup. Actress: Linda Hunt, *The Year of Living Dangerously.*
Director: James L. Brooks, *Terms of Endearment.*
Picture: *Terms of Endearment.*

1985
Actor: F. Murray Abraham, *Amadeus.*
Actress: Sally Field, *Places in the Heart.*
Sup. Actor: Haing S. Ngor, *The Killing Fields.*
Sup. Actress: Peggy Ashcroft, *A Passage to India.*
Director: Milos Forman, *Amadeus.*
Picture: *Amadeus.*

1986
Actor: William Hurt, *Kiss of the Spider Woman.*
Actress: Geraldine Page, *The Trip to Bountiful.*
Sup. Actor: Don Ameche, *Cocoon.*

Sup. Actress: Anjelica Huston, *Prizzi's Honor.*
Director: Sydney Pollack, *Out of Africa.*
Picture: *Out of Africa.*

1987
Actor: Paul Newman, *The Color of Money.*
Actress: Marlee Matlin, *Children of a Lesser God.*
Sup. Actor: Michael Caine, *Hannah and Her Sisters.*
Sup. Actress: Dianne West, *Hannah and Her Sisters.*
Director: Oliver Stone, *Platoon.*
Picture: *Platoon.*

1988
Actor: Michael Douglas, *Wall Street.*
Actress: Cher, *Moonstruck.*
Sup. Actor: Sean Connery, *The Untouchables.*
Sup. Actress: Olympia Dukakais, *Moonstruck.*
Director: Bertolucci, *The Last Emperor.*
Picture: *The Last Emperor.*

1989
Actor: Dustin Hoffman, *Rain Man.*
Actress: Jodie Foster, *The Accused.*
Sup. Actor: Kevin Kline, *A Fish Called Wanda.*
Sup. Actress: Geena Davis, *The Accidental Tourist.*
Director: Barry Levinson, *Rain Man.*
Picture: *Rain Man.*

The 1989 Oscar winners – (left) Dustin Hoffman for *Rain Man* with co-star Tom Cruise; (right) Jodie Foster for *The Accused.*

THE THEATRE

Glossary

Abbey Theatre Founded in Dublin in 1904 by Lady Gregory and W. B. Yeats and financed by Annie Horniman, a centre for Irish writing in the early 20th century and the first British 'repertory' theatre.

Absurd, Theatre of the Description applied to the work of Ionesco, Adamov, Becket and some other writers of the 1950s because it *presented* the absurdity of the human condition.

anti-pros US equivalent of FOH lights.

apron Extension of the stage in front of a proscenium.

arena theatre Theatre-in-the-round, also originally used to describe open-stage.

ASM See stage manager.

auditorium The audience area.

bar Pipe from which lamps are hung behind borders, numbered from front of stage.

barn doors Hinged flaps at sides of lamps to restrict beam.

batten Horizontal wooden bar or metal pipe from which scenery or lights are suspended; or row of lamps in joined compartments to give diffused light over a long area (usually hung, called ground-rows when on stage floor).

Berliner Ensemble Company formed in East Berlin by Bertolt Brecht and where he produced definitive versions of some of his plays. Long rehearsals helped to develop the accomplished ensemble playing of its actors.

boat truck Wheeled platform on which scenery and furniture can be preset and pushed on-stage.

blocking Fixing actors' movements in rehearsal and entering in prompt copy.

boom Vertical pipe for lighting.

border Horizontal masking to hide lights and anything above stage.

box Separate compartment in auditorium for seating several people, often either side of proscenium but in some old theatres whole tiers are divided into boxes.

box office Place to purchase tickets (originally only boxes reserved).

brace Angled support which hooks through a screw eye on a flat and secured by a weight on its projecting foot.

Bread and Puppet Theater American company formed by Peter Schumann in 1961, often performing processional pieces in the open air using large puppets. Bread was given away to the spectators.

bring in Fade in lights quickly.

bring up Increase intensity of lights.

Broadway Fashionable theatre area of New York, not just a section of the street of that name but defined by American Equity as extending between 5th and 9th Avenues from 34th Street to 56th Street and from 5th to the Hudson River bounded by 56th and 72nd Streets.

bump in/out Australian term for get in/out.

call Message to actors or stage crew that they are needed; also notice of rehearsals, costume fittings etc.; **curtain call** – line-up of actors before audience at end of show.

circle Tier of seating in auditorium.

cleat line Rope for lashing flats together. Nailed to upper part of one flat it is flicked around a projection on another, then wrapped round projections lower down and tied-off with a slip knot making a rapid way of erecting and dismantling scenery.

cloth Hanging canvas scenery. A backcloth is at the rear of the stage; a cut cloth is one with areas cut out so that the audience can see through them.

Comédie Française French national theatre, founded 1680.

comedy A light and amusing play.

corpse To come out of character and laugh at something not part of the play.

crease Like corpse but more successfully suppressed.

cue Words or actions to which an actor answers or which indicate the moment for an effect or scenic or lighting change. Also used to mean the sound or lighting change itself.

cut cloth See cloth.

cyclorama Curved cloth or other backing at rear of stage lit to give impression of sky or continuing space.

dress rehearsal Rehearsal with full scenery, costumes and effects.

director Person who rehearses actors and decides and co-ordinates artistic aspects of a production.

dimmer Rheostat, a device to reduce intensity of lamps.

dip Light plug in stage floor, covered by a small trap.

dress circle First balcony or tier of auditorium seating.

dry To forget one's lines.

effects Any sounds, special lighting devices, etc., required by the play.

el Teatro Campesino (Farmworkers' Theatre) founded by Luis Valdez in 1965 to serve Californian Chicanos.

fade in/out Bring in/take out lights or sounds slowly.

false pros(cenium) Inner frame to narrow proscenium arch.

farce Funny play in which characters usually represent basic types, whose structure relies on mishaps, coincidence, embarrassing disclosures and on visual jokes, including chases.

flat Scenic unit of canvas stretched on a wooden frame. May have opening to take door, window or fireplace.

flies Space above stage where lights and scenery can be hung out of audience view.

float See boat truck.

floats Footlights, because they were originally wicks floating in bowls of oil.

flood Lamp with reflector giving wide beam, not focusable.

FOH Front-of-house: the audience part of the

theatre. Can include foyers, etc. (as in front-of-house staff: box office and ushers), but usually the auditorium, especially of lights placed there.

follow spot Bright spotlight the beam of which an operator moves to keep an actor lit irrespective of general stage lighting.

footlights Lighting batten at front of stage shining upwards. Originally needed to counteract strong shadows from lamps overhead, now infrequently used.

forestage Area in front of house curtain in proscenium theatres.

gallery Highest tier or balcony of seats, traditionally known as 'the gods'.

gauze A cloth of fine weave, transparent when lit from behind, so that any front-lit scene painted on it seems to disappear.

get-in/out Moving scenery and all equipment in/out of theatre.

Glasgow Citizens' Theatre Founded in 1943 and now famous for its adventurous international repertoire and imaginatively designed productions.

go Instruction to operate cues.

gods Gallery or gallery spectators.

grand guignol French genre which piles horror on horror.

grid Framework or scaffold above stage or acting area from which scenery and lights are suspended.

ground row Cut-out scenery on stage floor representing wall, skyline, etc. Usually masking lighting. Also a lighting batten used to light a cyclorama or backcloth.

house The auditorium, or the audience (e.g. 'The house is in': the audience is in the theatre).

in-the-round See theatre-in-the-round.

Kabuki Traditional Japanese form of theatre.
Kathakali Indian form of drama performed by men and boys.
kill Switch off sound or lights or remove something from the set.
koken Unhooded Kabuki stage assistant.
kurogo Hooded Kabuki stage assistant.
kyogen Comic plays which originally developed as interludes in Japanese Noh theatre.

La MaMa American coffee-house theatre club and company founded by Ellen Stewart in 1962 and inspired by ideas of Artaud.
legs Hanging cloth wings.
lime(light) Bright spots, used for follow spots, originally used a piece of lime to create bright incandescence.
lines The words of an actor's part. Also the ropes used for raising and lowering scenery from the flies.
Living Theater American experimental theatre group founded by Julian Beck and Judith Molina in 1947.
lose Remove.

mask To hide equipment or space behind scenes from the audience. For one actor to block the audience view of another. Also covering worn to hide the face or to represent a different face.
melodrama A sensational romantic drama with extremes of character.
Method, The Acting technique developed by Lee Strasberg at the New York Actors' Studio from the teachings of Stanislavsky.

mie Stylized pose with crossed eyes used for emphasis in Kabuki.
mime Acting through gesture and without words.
miracle play Medieval religious drama based on miraculous incidents from the lives and works of the saints and performed on the days dedicated to them.
morality play Medieval allegorical drama showing ordinary humans exposed to temptation.
Moscow Art Theatre Founded by Constantin Stanislavsky and Vladimir Nemirovich-Danchenko in 1897 and closely linked with the plays of Chekhov.
mystery play Medieval religious drama originally presented by members of craft guilds.

National Theatre, British First proposed by David Garrick as an equivalent to the Comédie Française and more definitively planned in 1903. Foundation stones were laid by royalty at several sites before the company eventually came into being at the Old Vic in 1963 under Laurence Olivier, the present building being erected in 1976.
Noh Theatre Classic Japanese theatre. Probably the oldest form of theatre which has been continuously performed in the same traditional manner.

Off-Broadway Those small theatres, usually converted from other spaces, created to provide an opportunity for productions which could not find a home in Broadway commercial theatre. Its use dates from *c.* 1952 in relation to the Circle in the Square theatre. As these theatres came to be used commercially avant garde and experimental work was driven to 'Off-off' Broadway.
Old Vic London theatre, opened as the Coburg in 1818 on the south bank of the river Thames. A popular melodrama house, it changed its name to the Royal Victoria in 1833. Taken over as an entertainment hall for the temperance movement by Emma Cons and then run by her niece Lillian Baylis (1874–1937), it became internationally famous, especially for its Shakespeare and other classical productions and a National Theatre in all but name and financial resources. From it also developed the British national ballet and opera companies.
onnagato Kabuki actor (all male) specializing in female roles. Also known as *oyama*.
OP Opposite-prompt. The right-hand side of the stage facing the audience (left in US).
open stage Stage surrounded by an arc of audience, like the Greek theatre's orchestra.
orchestra Circular dancing floor in ancient Greek theatre where most of play took place.

pantomime Originally all mime performance but generally the popular Christmas entertainments based on fairy stories which originally incorporated the Harlequinade from the Commedia dell'Arte. They traditionally feature transvestite performers in the male romantic roles and the leading comic female part.
pipe Hollow metal bar from which scenery and lighting are suspended.
Piccolo Teatro Opened in Milan in 1947, the first in Italy to be supported by public funds, and acclaimed for the productions of its director Giorgio Strehler (b. 1921).
pit Lower floor of the auditorium, especially when this used to be open benches. Now usually called stalls.

playbill Poster or leaflet advertising a play, also sometimes used for the programme.

plot Story-line of a play.

—— **plot** List of requirements and cues for each technical department, as lighting plot, etc.

'Poor' Theatre Term coined by Jerzy Grotowski (b. 1933) for a theatre which rejects superfluous technical means (lighting, sound, make-up, props) and works directly with the actor's body and the audience relationship, as in the work in his Laboratory Theatre in Poland.

practical Prop or piece of set that can be used, e.g. food that has to be eaten, a door that has to open.

producer Person or company who presents the show, raises the money, and employs the cast and the production team. Until 1960s used for what is now called the director when the producer would have been known as the manager.

promenade Performance in which actors and audience share a space and the action (and audience) move within it, or in which the action moves through several spaces.

prop(erty) Anything used on the stage which does not form part of the scenery, costumes or technical equipment. **Hand props** are those which are carried or handled by the actors.

prompt Rapid delivery of lines which an actor has forgotten.

prompt copy (or prompt book) Copy of script in which positions and moves of scenery, furniture and actors and all cues for changes and effects are recorded.

prompt corner Control centre from which stage management give all cues and prompts.

prompt side Stage left facing the audience (right in US). Usually, but not always, the side on which the prompt corner is placed.

proscenium Originally the shallow platform in front of the skene, or rear building, of the Greek theatre. Now the wall dividing auditorium from stage where the proscenium arch is located.

PS Prompt side.

Public Theater New York theatre and production company founded by Joe Papp presenting classics and modern work of the kind seen in subsidized theatres in Europe.

read through First reading of the whole play by the cast. Often the first rehearsal.

rehearsal Plotting, practising and developing of performance by actors.

repertory theatre Originally a theatre having a repertoire of plays which can be presented but more generally a theatre which presents a succession of plays, usually with the same company, rather than running one single play as long as it attracts an audience.

return A flat joined at right angles to another; also a ticket brought back for resale.

reveal Small return by arch, window or doorway to show thickness of wall.

rostrum Platform, usually collapsible, formed from a top set into a hinged frame.

Royal Court Theatre London theatre famous for seasons under J. V. Vendrenne and Granville Barker which established Shaw as a dramatist, and since 1956 the home of the English Stage Company, led by George Devine (1910–66) (with Bill Gaskill among his successors) with a policy of encouraging new writing.

Royal Shakespeare Company In 1879 Frank Benson (1858–1961) led the company which opened the Shakespeare Memorial Theatre at Stratford-upon-Avon. In 1960, under Peter Hall, this became the Royal Shakespeare Company and it now also has a London theatre at the Barbican as well as studio theatre and a space inspired by the Elizabethan playhouses. It continues to produce outstanding Shakespeare but also produces new writing and revivals of work from all periods.

Schaubüne Theatre Berlin company, originally run as a co-operative, acclaimed for its imaginative productions, especially those of Peter Stein.

shite Principal actor in Noh theatre.

SM Stage manager.

soliloquy A speech, supposedly unheard by others on the stage, in which a character speaks his or her thoughts.

spot(light) Focusable lamp of which both angle and size of beam can be controlled. **Fresnel** spots throw a soft-edged beam, **profile** or mirror spots produce a hard-edged beam of more intense light.

stage manager Person responsible for the organizing and conduct of rehearsals, co-ordination of all technical departments, making and updating of the prompt copy and running performances. There may be more than one stage manager and assistant stage managers. In a large theatre running plays in repertoire a production manager may head the team. Sometimes the term stage director is used.

stock company US term for repertory company.

strobe Lamp which produces short flashes of light, giving impression of freezing movement. If used audiences should be warned since it can be dangerous to epileptics and certain other conditions.

stalls Separate seats, usually with arm rests, originally front of lowest level (pit stalls), now usually the whole of that level.

tabs Curtains. Originally tableau curtains because they would be opened and close on tableaux, moments when the actors froze; **house tabs** are those between stage and audience.

Théâtre du Soleil French co-operative company formed by Ariana Mnouchkine (b. 1938) in 1964, based in a disused munitions factory at Vincennes where its productions use promenade techniques.

theatre-in-the-round Theatre with audience on all sides of the acting area. Used even when shape is rectangular or polygonal.

Théâtre National Populaire (T.N.P.) French company founded as a touring company in 1920 by Firmin Gèmiere and based in the Palais de Chaillot, Paris, since 1937. Directed from 1951 by Jean Vilar (1912–71) and from 1972 by Roger Planchon (b. 1931).

Theatre Workshop British company formed by Joan Littlewood (b. 1914) which eventually became based in Stratford, East London. It gained international acclaim for innovative productions created from minimal resources.

thrust stage Stage projecting into the audience.

tormentor Narrow curtain or flat used to mask wings behind proscenium.

tragedy Serious drama in which protagonist is overcome because of a personal failing or social and psychological circumstances.

trap An opening in the stage floor, covered either by hinged or sliding panels, including **grave-trap** of a size to form a grave and **star trap** with triangular hinged panels forming a circular hole just big enough for an actor to push through – used for sudden appearances, especially of Demon King in pantomime.

trough Lighting ground row, usually with circular filters to give wide beam spread, used to light cyclorama.
traverse Tabs which are drawn across the stage.
traverse staging Rectangular acting area with audience on both its long sides.

wings Areas backstage at the side of the acting area. Also flats or curtains hung facing audience at sides of stage which together mask these areas.
wardrobe Costumes and the staff and premises handling them.
warn To give instructions to actors or technicians to stand by for a cue.

Origins of theatre

The origins of drama can be seen in ancient games and rituals when hunters acted out the hunt to ensure success or to placate the spirit of their prey. Similarly, early farmers sought to ensure the renewal of the seasons or the coming of the annual Nile flood with rituals like that in which the Egyptian Pharaohs re-enacted the murder and resurrection of their god Osiris. Drama was both a kind of magic and a form of worship.

Greek drama

Western drama had its first flowering in ancient Greece, in the festival which honoured Dionysus, god of fertility and wine. From the orgiastic celebrations of his cult developed a form of choral performance, the **dithyramb**, in which a tale of gods and heroes was recounted in song and dance. To this, in the sixth century BC, a priest called Thespis is credited with adding a solo performer who engaged in dialogue with the leader of the chorus, thus inventing the first Greek play. These plays were known as tragedies, a word originally meaning goat-song, perhaps because the song was offered at the same time as a goat was sacrificed to the god. Thespis is said to have taken a troupe of actors around the countryside performing plays, and today actors are sometimes called **thespians** after him.

Within a century, the poets Aeschylus, Sophocles and Euripides had created plays that rank with the greatest and are still performed. To tragedy, with its serious plots of fate and the gods, had been added bawdy 'satyr' plays (satyrs were horse-tailed goat-eared men who were supposed to be Dionysus's followers), which often made fun of the scandalous love-life of the gods, and comedies which were humorous and topical. The actors – all male – had increased in number from a single protagonist (= first actor) to three men. In one play they might each play several roles, each character clearly identified by its costume and a face mask, but no more than three characters could appear in any one scene.

Greek theatres

Touring troupes may have performed in market places but most cities had a hillside theatre where people could stand or later sit on a semicircle of wooden or stone benches to watch the performers on a flattened circle called the **orchestra**, perhaps originally a threshing floor. Later a row of buildings across the back of the orchestra provided a narrow raised platform which the actors could sometimes use.

Large theatres, like that at Epidavros, could hold 14 000 spectators and performances could last all day.

Roman theatre

Roman theatre followed the style of the Greek but with more elaborate buildings and a preference for scabrous plots which drew the disapproval of the growing Christian Church with the result that in the sixth century AD the Emperor Justinian ordered all theatres to be closed.

The Middle Ages

Travelling entertainers probably preserved the elements of theatre but it was in the Church itself that formal drama reappeared as parts of Christian teaching and liturgy began to be given dramatic form. From this developed the performance of plays retelling bible stories – **miracle plays** or **mystery plays** – and then secular moral tales. These were staged in a variety of ways; sometimes with the settings, or 'mansions', for different scenes arranged side by side on a wide outdoor stage, sometimes on and within a ring of platforms or, in Britain and Spain, with each scene on a separate cart or **pageant**, all of which were pulled through the streets for the play to be performed at a number of locations. The **mysteries** were not those of religion but refer to the professional secrets of particular trades, as individual craft guilds became responsible for an appropriate play.

Renaissance theatre

With the renewed interest in classical ideas that came with the Renaissance, schools and universities began to perform some of the plays surviving in Latin texts. Attempts were even made to build theatres like those of ancient Rome, such as the *Teatro Olimpico* (1585) at Vicenza, Italy, though unlike ancient Roman theatres this was roofed over.

Elizabethan theatre

London's first public playhouse opened in 1576. It was built in the fields to the north of the city because the city fathers had forbidden plays within the city boundaries. The playhouse was galleried and circular, with a stage jutting out into the centre of the circle, and open to the sky. Performances were by daylight, starting at two in the afternoon. Although some scenic elements were used and there were colourful costumes and effects, most of the scene-setting was built into the text. This was the kind of theatre for which William Shakespeare wrote his plays. It allowed for rapidly moving drama in which one scene followed straight on from another. The actors were in close contact with the audience, some standing on the ground around the stage, some sitting up in the galleries. Even in the largest London theatre, which could accommodate up to 3000 spectators, no one was more than about 30 feet from the stage.

Performances by boys from London choir schools became fashionable for a time at an indoor theatre which evaded the city's laws by calling itself 'private'; later Shakespeare's company took it over. Lit by candles and lanterns, it probably allowed for more spectacle, though it would hardly have been as lavish as the entertainments, known as **masques**, which the nobility performed at court. Masques, with an emphasis on music, dance and elaborate effects, originated in the courts of Italy and France and from them developed both opera and ballet. Originally scenic elements were arranged around the performance space but later they retreated behind a masking frame, the **proscenium**.

The proscenium stage

In 1642 the English Parliament banned stage plays altogether and theatres were forced to close. When they were allowed again two decades later they were indoors and designed for perspective scenery, following the continental pattern. At first the forestage in front of the proscenium was fairly deep with doors opening on to it for entrances and exits, and some of the audience sitting in 'boxes' on either side.

Many theatres retained this proximity between actors and audience well into the 19th century but as stronger lighting was developed, eventually using gas and electricity, it became possible to light up both actors and scenery more brilliantly even well up-stage. The proscenium advanced further and further forward until it became literally a picture frame for the whole action. The lighting in the auditorium was now turned down during the performance and the audience watched from the darkness.

New theatre forms

In the latter part of the 19th century the picture-frame stage was the kind of theatre most people expected. New lighting methods allowed the side walls of a room to be constructed and even a ceiling to be lowered above it so that the audience appeared to be looking into a room with one wall removed – the 'fourth wall', as the division between actors and audience came to be known.

Today you will still find many theatres with picture-frame prosceniums and tiered horseshoes of seating but all kinds of other arrangements are now used and many performance spaces are designed so that the seating arrangements can be altered to suit a particular production. You may even find that there are no seats and no stage as such but the action moves from place to place among the audience.

Oriental theatre

Western-style theatre now exists in most countries but in the east the traditional forms developed quite separately though, as in Greece, they had their roots in religious ceremony. In India, where the same word was used for dance and drama, a variety of dance styles developed, the main ones being Bharatanatym, Manipuri, Kathak and Kathakali. All incorporate a strong mimetic element and gestures codified to form an elaborate language, but only Kathakali, with its mask-like face make-up and exaggerated costumes, recounts a connected narrative. However, verse plays in Sanskrit survive from a poetic drama which appears to have flourished from before the birth of Christ to the 10th century AD consisting of *nataka*, historical or mythological plays, and *prakarana*, invented stories usually about human love and heroism.

In China theatrical entertainments are recorded as far back as 700 BC but serious theatre dates from the establishment of a drama school in the Pear Garden of the Imperial Park by the Tang Emperor Ming Huang, and up to the present century Chinese actors were still known as 'young persons of the pear garden'. They seemed to have performed simple comedies for only two actors.

Peking Opera, *P'i Huang* or *Ching Psi*, as it is known in China, the form of traditional theatre best known today, became established as a popular and spectacular entertainment in the 19th century. It uses considerable symbolism, though this draws on realistic images (unlike the abstractions of other eastern forms) with costumes and make-up providing immediate information about each character.

The Noh Theatre is the oldest dramatic form in Japan, developing, as in China, from temple festivities and dances until in the 14th century the Kanami family of actors created the form still known today. It uses a simple wooden stage with a fir tree painted on the back wall and other symbolic elements and is still performed in the speech and verse forms of the 14th century. It is very formal with the audience on three sides of the stage and musicians sitting on the stage. The all-male actors wear wooden masks, especially if playing women or elderly characters.

Noh eventually became an art for the nobility and a much freer form, **Kabuki**, became the popular entertainment. Still formal by western standards, and originally performed on a Noh-like stage, it developed spectacular scenery with revolving stages (already used in 1760). A reciter and musicians sit in full view at the side of the stage narrating and commenting on the story and black-robed assistants, who by convention the audience considers invisible, help elaborate costume transformations and move furniture and handle properties.

Entrances and exits are frequently made through the auditorium on the *hana-michi* or flower-way, a walkway at the level of the audience's heads from the back of the auditorium to the left side of the stage. Men again play female roles, but stylized make-up and gesture, not masks, are used. At particular dramatic moments actors freeze and adopt a special cross-eyed look, the *mie*, to draw the attention of the audience.

Plays and playwrights

Classical Theatre

Early Greek tragedies were about gods and heroes of great courage and inner strength. **Euripides** developed individual character more than previous writers and reduced the role of the chorus which commented on the action in song. According to **Aristotle**, watching a tragedy should awaken both fear and pity in spectators so that they go through a purging of such emotions. **Aristophanes**, whose comedies are the earliest surviving, usually makes ordinary people his main characters and later comedy dealt with everyday middle-class life. Only one complete satyr play survives and this form had little direct influence on later theatre.

Classical scholars who revived the drama in the Renaissance mistakenly thought that Greek plays had observed strict rules – what they called the Three Unities: the action should take place in the same day, in a single location and deal with a single story. This had a considerable influence on writers in the 17th and 18th centuries, especially in France, where the plays of Racine are extremes in this form.

Kabuki – the spectacular theatre of Japan.

Shakespeare

In contrast to the classical 'unities', the plays of Shakespeare range widely in location, telescope time, sometimes of many years, have subsidiary plots and may develop several themes. Their vitality is prefigured in some of the mystery plays which intersperse the scriptural stories with humour, such as a hen-pecked Noah in a Flood play from Chester or the sheep-stealing Mak in a Wakefield Nativity play.

Commedia dell'Arte

The popular Italian tradition developed the *Commedia dell'Arte*, an improvised drama performed by travelling players, without a written script and using stock characters such as young lovers, a braggart soldier, an old merchant (Pantelone) and comic, trick-playing servants (Harlequin and Pulchinello). Its influence can be seen in the early work of Molière and both modern pantomime and Punch and Judy shows have links with it, but by the mid-18th century its form had become debased and **Carlo Goldoni** led a change to a more sophisticated Italian drama with witty scripted plays rooted in observation of contemporary society and individual behaviour.

Romanticism and naturalism

European drama of the 18th and 19th centuries broadly reflects literary trends, from classicism to romanticism, and historical dramas. In France, **Marivaux** and **Beaumarchais**, in Britain dramatists such as **Congreve** and **Sheridan** reflected the foibles of contemporary society. **Goethe, Schiller, Hugo, Pushkin** and **Dumas** fils contributed romantic tragedies while a clichéd form of *melodrama* with stock villains and pure heroines satisfied a popular demand for thrills and scenic transformation.

A new kind of realism was introduced, not only in scenery and acting but also in the treatment of characters and ordinary life, in the work of **Tom Robertson** and **Emile Zola** but it was **Henrik Ibsen** who had the most influence in creating a true reflection of life rather than of sentimental emotions. A champion and follower was **Bernard Shaw** but this kind of writing has its culmination in the plays of **Anton Chekhov**.

Modern drama

Most 20th-century writing for the theatre reflects the characteristics of the 'well-made play' (credited originally to the prolific playwright **Eugene Scribe**, 1791–1861): clear exposition of character and situation, careful preparation for future events, continuous and mounting suspense, unexpected but logical reversals and logical and believable resolution. The usual division has been into three acts with strong 'curtains' (dramatic closings to each act).

Modern plays and theatre production now increasingly reject the naturalistic styles of the 'well-made play' for ritualistic, expressionist and deliberately theatrical styles which exploit nature of the theatrical experience or, as in the work of Bertolt Brecht, may seek to distance the audience from sentimental involvement so that they can dispassionately consider the arguments a play presents.

Dramatists

Aeschylus (c. 525–456 BC) *The Persians, The Oresteia, Prometheus Bound.*
Sophocles (496–406 BC) *Ajax, Antigone, Oedipus the King, Philoctetes, Oedipus at Colonus.*
Aristophanes (c. 450–385 BC) *The Clouds, The Wasps, The Birds, Lysistrata, The Frogs.*
Euripides (484–406/7 BC) *Medea, Hippolytus, The Trojan Women, Electra, The Bacchae.*
Titus Maccius Plautus (c. 254–c.184 BC) *Menaechmi, Amphitryon.*
Terence (c. 190–159 BC) *The Brothers, The Eunuch.*
Lucius Annaeus Seneca (c. 4 BC–AD 65) *Medea, Phaedra, Oedipus.*
Niccolo Machiavelli (1469–1527) *Mandragola.*
Nicholas Udall (1505–56) *Ralph Roister Doister.*
Torquato Tasso (1544–95) *Aminta.*
Thomas Kyd (1558–94) *The Spanish Tragedy.*
Lope (Felix) de Vega (Carpio) (1562–1635) *Fuente Ovejuna, The King the Greatest, Alcade* (he wrote 1800 plays; most survive!).
Christopher Marlowe (1564–93) *Dr Faustus, Edward II, Tamburlaine, The Jew of Malta.*
William Shakespeare (1564–1616) (see page 216 for a complete list of plays).
Tirso de Molina (?1571–1648) *The Deceiver of Seville.*
Ben Jonson (1572–1637) *Every Man in his Humour, Volpone, The Alchemist, Bartholomew Fair.*
John Fletcher (1579–1625) *The Wild Goose Chase, The Maid's Tragedy* (with Beaumont).
Francis Beaumont (1584–1616) *The Knight of the Burning Pestle.*
John Webster (?–1634) *The White Devil, The Duchess of Malfi.*
John Ford (c. 1625–33) *'Tis Pity She's a Whore.*
Pedro Calderon de Barca (1600–81) *The Mayor of Zalamea, Life is a Dream, The Constant Prince.*
Pierre Corneille (1606–84) *Le Cid.*
Jean Racine (1639–99) *Britannicus, Phaedre, Andromaque.*
Molière (Jean-Baptiste Poquelin, 1622–73) *L'École des Femmes, L'Avare, Le Misanthrope, La Malade Imaginaire, Le Bourgeois Gentilhomme.*
John Dryden (1631–1700) *All for Love.*
George Etherege (1634–91) *The Man of the Mode.*
Ahra Behn (1640–89) *The Rover, The Lucky Chance, Emperor of the Moon.*
William Wycherley (1640–1716) *The Country Wife, The Plain Dealer.*
Thomas Otway (1652–85) *Venice Preserved, The Orphan.*
John Vanbrugh (1664–1726) *The Relapse, The Provoked Wife.*

William Congreve (1670–1729) *Love for Love, The Way of the World.*
George Farquhar (1678–1707) *The Constant Couple, The Recruiting Officer, The Beaux' Stratagem.*
Voltaire (François-Marie Arouet, 1694–1778) *Zaïre, Alzire.*
Pierre Carlet Chamblain de Marivaux (1688–1763) *La Double Inconstance, Le Jeu de l'Amour et du Hasard, La Dispute.*
Carlo Goldoni (1707–93) *The Servant of Two Masters, Mine Hostess, The Mania for the Country, The Adventure in the Country, The Return from the Country, The Fan.*
Carlo Gozzi (1720–1806) *The King Stag.*
Gotthold Ephraim Lessing (1729–81) *Emilia Galotti, Nathan the Wise.*
Pierre Augustin Caron de Beaumarchais (1732–99) *The Barber of Seville, The Marriage of Figaro.*
Oliver Goldsmith (1739–74) *She Stoops to Conquer.*
Johann Wolfgang von Goethe (1749–1805) *Egmont, Faust.*
Richard Brinsley Sheridan (1751–1816) *The Rivals, The School for Scandal, The Critic, Pizarro.*
Friedrich von Schiller (1749–1832) *The Robbers, Don Carlos, Mary Stuart, William Tell.*
August Friedrich Ferdinand von Kotzebue (1761–1819) *Repentance (The Stranger), The Spaniards in Peru.*
Heinrich von Kleist (1777–1811) *The Broken Jug, Penthesilia, The Prince of Homburg.*
Victor Hugo (1802–85) *Hernani.*
Nikolai Gogol (1809–52) *The Inspector General.*
Georg Büchner (1813–37) *Danton's Death, Woyzeck.*
Alfred de Musset (1810–57) *No Trifling with Love, Lorenzaccio.*
Eugéne Labiche (1815–88) *An Italian Straw Hat.*
Tom Taylor (1817–80) *The Ticket-of-Leave Man.*
Ivan Turgenev (1818–83) *A Month in the Country.*
Alexander Ostrovsky (1832–86) *Diary of a Scoundrel, The Storm, The Forest.*
Dionysus Larner Boucicault (1820–96) *London Assurance, The Vampire, The Corsican Brothers, The Octoroon, The Poor of New York, The Coleen Bawn, The Shaughraun.*
Alexandre Dumas fils (1824–95) *La Dame aux Camellias.*
Henrik Ibsen (1828–1906) *Peer Gynt, Ghosts, A Doll's House, Hedda Gabler, Pillars of Society, The Wild Duck, An Enemy of the People, The Master Builder, When We Dead Awaken.*
Tom W. Robertson (1829–71) *Caste, School.*
Emile Zola (1840–1902) *Thérèse Raquin.*
August Strindberg (1849–1912) *The Father, Miss Julie, The Dream Play, The Ghost Sonata.*
Oscar Wilde (1854–1900) *Lady Windermere's Fan, An Ideal Husband, The Importance of Being Earnest, Salomé.*
Arthur Wing Pinero (1855–1934) *The Magistrate, Dandy Dick, The Second Mrs Tanqueray, Trelawney of the 'Wells'.*
George Bernard Shaw (1856–1950) *Widower's Houses, Arms and the Man, You Never Can Tell, Mrs Warren's Profession, The Philanderer, Caesar and Cleopatra, Man and Superman, Major Barbara, Androcles and the Lion, Heartbreak House, Back to Methuselah, St Joan.*
Anton Chekhov (1860–1904) *The Seagull, Uncle Vanya, The Three Sisters, The Cherry Orchard.*
James Matthew Barrie (1860–1937) *The Admirable Crichton, Peter Pan, Mary Rose.*
Maurice Maeterlinck (1862–1949) *Pelléas and Mélisande, The Bluebird.*

Georges Feydeau (1862-1921) *Hotel Paradiso, Le Dindon, A Flea in Her Ear, The Lady from Maxim's.*

Arthur Schnitzler (1862-1931) *Reigen (La Ronde), Anatol.*

Frank Wedekind (1864-1918) *Spring Awakening, Pandora's Box.*

Luigi Pirandello (1867-1936) *Six Characters in Search of an Author, Henry IV, Tonight We Improvise.*

John Galsworthy (1867-1933) *The Silver Box, Strife, The Skin Game, Loyalties.*

Maxim Gorki (1868-1936) *The Lower Depths, Summer Folk.*

Paul Claudel (1868-1955) *Partage de Midi, Le Soulier de Satin, The Book of Christopher Columbus.*

John Millington Synge (1871-1909) *Riders to the Sea, The Playboy of the Western World, The Tinker's Wedding.*

Alfred Jarry (1873-1907) *Ubu Roi, Ubu Enchaîné, Ubu Cocu.*

William Somerset Maugham (1874-1907) *Penelope, Home and Beauty, The Circle, The Letter, For Services Rendered, Sheppey.*

Harley Granville Barker (1877-1946) *The Voysey Inheritance, Waste, The Madras House.*

Georg Kaiser (1878-1945) *Gas.*

Eugene O'Neill (1888-1953) *Mourning Becomes Electra, Anna Christie, Long Day's Journey into Night, The Iceman Cometh, The Hairy Ape.*

Ernst Toller (1878-1945) *Man and the Masses, The Machine Wreckers.*

Sean O'Casey (1880-1964) *The Shadow of a Gunman, Juno and the Paycock, The Plough and the Stars, The Silver Tassie, The Star Turns Red, Purple Dust, Red Roses for Me.*

Ben Travers (1886-1980) *Rookery Nook, Thark, Plunder, The Bed Before Yesterday.*

Thomas Stearns Eliot (1888-1965) *Murder in the Cathedral, The Family Reunion, The Confidential Clerk.*

Maxwell Anderson (1888-1959) *Key Largo, Winterset.*

Jean Cocteau (1889-1963) *Orphée, The Infernal Machine, The Eagle Has Two Heads.*

Karel Capek (1890-1938) *R.U.R.,* (and with his brother Josef) *The Insect Play, The Makropoulos Secret.*

Elmer Rice (1892-1967) *The Adding Machine.*

Vladimir Vladimirovich Mayakovsky (1893-1930) *The Bedbug, The Bathhouse.*

John Boynton Priestley (1894-1985) *When We Are Married, Dangerous Corner, Johnson Over Jordan, An Inspector Calls.*

Robert Emmet Sherwood (1896-1955) *The Threepenny Opera, Mother Courage, Caucasian Chalk Circle, The Good Woman of Setzuan, Galileo.*

Federico Garcia Lorca (1898-1936) *The Public, Blood Wedding, Yerma, The House of Bernada Alba.*

Noël Coward (1899-1973) *The Vortex, Hay Fever, Private Lives, Present Laughter.*

Marguerite Duras (b. 1904) *The Square, La Musica, L'Amante Anglaise, Havannah Bay.*

Jean-Paul Sartre (1905-80) *The Flies, Huis Clos, The Devil and the Good Lord, Les Mains Sales, Altona, Kean.*

Samuel Beckett (b. 1905) *Waiting for Godot, Endgame, Happy Days.*

Lillian Hellman (1905-84) *The Children's Hour, The Little Foxes, Watch on the Rhine, Toys in the Attic.*

Clifford Odets (1906-63) *Waiting for Lefty, Golden Boy, The Big Knife, The Country Girl.*

Christopher Fry (b. 1907) *The Lady's Not for Burning,* *Venus Observed, The Dark is Light Enough.*

William Saroyan (1908-81) *My Heart's in the Highlands, The Time of Your Life, Hello, Out There.*

Jean Genet (1910-86) *The Maids, The Balcony, Deathwatch, The Blacks, The Screens.*

Jean Anouilh (1910-87) *Thieves' Carnival, Eurydice, Antigone, Ardele, Ring Round the Moon, Waltz of the Toreadors, The Lark, Becket.*

Terence Rattigan (1911-77) *French Without Tears, The Deep Blue Sea, Separate Tables.*

Eugene Ionesco (b. 1912) *The Chairs, The Lesson, The Bald Primadonna, Rhinoceros.*

Albert Camus (1913-60) *Caligula, The Just Assassins.*

William Inge (1913-73) *Come Back Little Sheba, Picnic, Bus Stop.*

Tennessee Williams (b. 1914) *The Glass Menagerie, A Streetcar Named Desire, Summer and Smoke, The Rose Tattoo, Orpheus Descending, Camino Real.*

Arthur Miller (b.1915) *All My Sons, View from the Bridge, Death of a Salesman, The Crucible.*

Peter Ulrich Weiss (1916-82) *The Persecution and Assassination of Jean-Paul Marat as Performed by the Inmates of the Asylum of Charenton under the Direction of the Marquis de Sade, The Investigation, Lusitanian Bogey.*

John Whiting (1917-63) *A Penny for a Song, The Devils, Marching Song.*

Friedrich Dürrenmatt (b. 1921) *Romulus the Great, The Visit, The Physicists.*

Brendan Behan (1923-64) *The Quare Fellow, The Hostage.*

Dario Fo (b. 1926) *Accidental Death of an Anarchist, Can't Pay? Won't Pay!*

Peter Shaffer (b. 1926) *Five-Finger Exercise, The Royal Hunt of the Sun, Black Comedy, Equus, Amadeus, Lettice and Lovage.*

Peter Nichols (b. 1927) *A Day in the Death of Joe Egg, The National Health, Privates on Parade, Passion Play, Poppy.*

Neil Simon (b. 1927) *Barefoot in the Park, Plaza Suite, The Sunshine Boys, Biloxi Blues, Brighton Beach Memoirs, The Odd Couple.*

Edward Albee (b. 1928) *The Zoo Story, Who's Afraid of Virginia Woolf?, Tiny Alice, A Delicate Balance.*

John Osborne (b. 1929) *Look Back in Anger, The Entertainer, Luther, A Patriot for Me, The Hotel in Amsterdam.*

John Arden (b. 1930) *Sergeant Musgrave's Dance, Armstrong's Last Goodnight.*

Lorraine Hansberry (1930-65) *A Raisin in the Sun.*

Harold Pinter (b. 1930) *The Birthday Party, The Caretaker, Homecoming, No Man's Land.*

Peter Barnes (b. 1931) *The Ruling Class, The Bewitched, Red Noses.*

Rolf Hochhüth (b. 1931) *The Representative, Soldiers.*

Arnold Wesker (b. 1932) *Chicken Soup with Barley, Roots, Chips with Everything.*

Athol Fugard (b. 1932) *Blood Knot, Boesman and Lena, Sizwe Banzi is Dead, A Lesson from Aloes, Master Harold . . . and the Boys.*

Joe Orton (1933-67) *Entertaining Mr Sloane, Loot, The Good and Faithful Servant, What the Butler Saw.*

Alan Bennett (b. 1934) *Forty Years On, Habeas Corpus, The Old Country, Enjoy, Kafka's Dick.*

Edward Bond (b. 1934) *Saved, Narrow Road to the Deep North, Early Morning, Lear, Bingo, Restoration.*

Amiri Baraka (b. 1934) *Dutchman* (as Leroi Jones), *A Black Mass.*

Trevor Griffiths (b. 1935) *The Party, Comedians, Real Dreams.*

David Rudkin (b. 1936) *Afore Night Come, Ashes, The Sons of Light*).
Tom Stoppard (b. 1937) *Rosencrantz and Guildenstern are Dead, Jumpers, Travesties, The Real Thing, Hapgood.*
Arthur Kopit (b. 1937) *Oh Dad Poor Dad Mama's Hung You in the Closet and I'm Feelin' So Sad.*
Caryl Churchill (b. 1938) *Light Shining in Buckinghamshire, Vinegar Tom, Cloud Nine, Top Girls, Serious Money.*
Alan Ayckbourn (b. 1939) *Bedroom Farce, The Norman Conquests, Woman in Mind.*
Howard Brenton (b. 1942) *Hitler Dances, Weapons of Happiness, Epsom Downs, The Romans in Britain, Pravda* (with David Hare), *Greenland.*
Sam Shepard (b. 1943) *The Tooth of Crime, Fool for Love, A Lie of the Mind, True West.*
Howard Barker (b. 1946) *Victory, The Castle, The Possibilities, The Last Supper.*
Christopher Hampton (b. 1946) *Total Eclipse, The Philanthropist, Tales from Hollywood.*
David Hare (b. 1947) *Teeth 'n' Smiles, Fanshen, Plenty, Map of the World, Pravda* (with Howard Brenton).
David Mamet (b. 1947) *American Buffalo, Sexual Perversity in Chicago, Glengarry Glen Ross.*
Willy Russell (b. 1947) *Stags and Hens, Educating Rita, Blood Brothers, Shirley Valentine.*
David Edgar (b. 1948) *Destiny, Maydays, Entertaining Strangers.*
Ntozake Shange (b. 1948) *for coloured girls who have considered suicide when the rainbow is enuf, Spel No 7, Three Views of Mt Fuji.*

Hubert Carter plays Othello to Tita Brand's Desdemona in a 1905 production. (Moniter)

SHAKESPEARE'S PLAYS	Publication date
Titus Andronicus	1594
*Henry VI Part 2**	1594
The Taming of the Shrew (see also 1623, First Folio)	1594
*Henry VI Part 3**	1595
Romeo and Juliet	1597
Richard II	1597
Richard III	1597
Henry IV Part 1	1598
Love's Labour's Lost (Revised version, original (?1596) probably lost)	1598
Henry IV Part 2	1600
A Midsummer Night's Dream	1600
The Merchant of Venice	1600
Much Ado About Nothing	1600
Henry V (First 'true' text published 1623 in First Folio)	1600
*Sir John Falstaff and the Merry Wives of Windsor** (First 'true' text published in 1623 in First Folio)	1602
*Hamlet**	1603
Hamlet ('according to the true and perfect copy')	1604
King Lear	1608
Pericles, Prince of Tyre	1609
Troilus and Cressida	1609
Sonnets (1640 in 'Poems')	1609
Posthumously Published	
Othello	1622
First Folio – 36 plays in all including the first publication of *The Taming of the Shrew* (Shakespeare's revised version of the 1594 version)	1623
Henry IV Part 1	

* Bad quartos or unauthorized editions.

The Two Gentlemen of Verona
The Comedy of Errors
King John
As You Like It
Julius Caesar
Twelfth Night
Measure for Measure
All's Well That Ends Well
Macbeth
Timon of Athens
Antony and Cleopatra
Coriolanus
Cymbeline
A Winter's Tale
The Tempest
Henry VIII

Famous actors and directors

Richard Tarlton (d. 1588) English actor.
Will Kempe (c. 1550–c. 1607) English actor.
Richard Burbage (1567–1619) English actor.
Jean-Baptiste Poquelin (Molière) (1622–73) French actor and dramatist.
Thomas Betterton (c. 1635–1710) English actor.
Nell Gwyn (1650–87) English actress.
Michael Baron (1653–1729) French actor.
Andrienne Lecouvreur (1692–1730) French actress.
James Quin (1692–1766) English actor.

Charles Macklin (1699-1797) English actor.
Colley Cibber (1671-1757) English actor.
David Garrick (1717-79) English actor.
Konrad Ekhof (1720-78) German actor.
Sarah Siddons (1755-1831) English actress.
John Phillip Kemble (1757-1823) English actor.
François Joseph Talma (1763-1826) French actor.
Frederich Ludwig Schroeder (1774-1816) German actor.
Edmund Kean (1787-1833) English actor.
Mikhail Shchepkin (1788-1863) Russian actor.
William Macready (1793-1873) English actor.
Joseph Grimaldi (1778-1837) English actor-clown.
Junius Brutus Booth (1796-1852) US actor.
Samuel Phelps (1804-78) English actor.
Ira Aldridge (c. 1805-67) US actor.
Edwin Forrest (1806-72) US actor.
Charles Kean (1811-68) English actor.
Constant-Benoît Coquelin (1841-1909) French actor.
Tommaso Salvini (1829-1915) Italian actor.
Adelaide Ristori (1822-1906) Italian actress.
Charlotte Cushmann (1816-76) US actress.
Helena Modjeska (1840-1909) US actress.
Rachel (1824-48) French actress.
Joseph Jefferson (1829-1905) US actor.
Edwin Booth (1833-93) US actor.
Henry Irving (1838-1905) English actor.
Sarah Bernhardt (1844-1923) French actress.
James O'Neill (1846-1920) US actor.
Ellen Terry (1847-1928) English actress.
Herbert Beerbohm Tree (1853-1917) English actor.
Eleanora Duse)1858-1924) Italian actress.
André Antoine (1858-1943) French director.
Vladimir Nemirovich Danchenko (1859-1943) Russian director.
Constantin Stanislavsky (1863-1938) Russian actor/director.
Mrs Patrick Campbell (1865-1940) English actress.
Olga Knipper (1868-1959) Russian actress.
Max Reinhardt (1873-1943) German director.
Lilian Baylis (1874-1937) English theatre manager.
Vsevolod Emilievich Meyerhold (1874-1940) Russian director.
Harley Granville Barker (1877-1946) English director.
Lionel Barrymore (1878-1954) US actor.
Jacques Copeau (1878-1949) French actor/director.
Ethel Barrymore (1878-1959) US actress.
Alexander Moissi (1880-1935) German actor.
John Barrymore (1882-1942) US actor.
Sybil Thorndike (1882-1976) English actress.
Laurette Taylor (1884-1946) US actress.
Charles Dullin (1885-1949) French actor/director.
Lynne Fontaine (1887-1983) US actor.
Luois Jouvet (1887-1951) French actor.
Edith Evans (1888-1976) English actress.
Alfred Lunt (1892-1977) US actor.
Irwin Piscator (1893-1966) German director.
Katharine Cornell (1893-1974) US actress.
Mei Lanfang (1894-1961) Chinese actor.
Ruth Gordon (1896-1985) US actress.
Maurice Karnovsky (b. 1897) US actor.

Michel St Denis (1897-1971) French director and teacher.
Paul Robeson (1898-1976) US actor.
Bertolt Brecht (1898-1956) German director/dramatist.
Judith Anderson (b. 1898) US actress.
Micheál mac Liammóir (b. 1899-1978) Irish actor.
Madeleine Renaud (b. 1900) French actress.
Katina Paxinon (1900-73) Greek actress.
Helen Hayes (b. 1900) US actress.
Helene Weigel (1900-72) German actress.
Eduardo de Filippo (b. 1900) Italian actor/director.
Maurice Evans (b. 1901) US actor.
Lee Strasberg (1901-82) US director/teacher.
Florentine Eldridge (b. 1901) US actress.
Harold Clurman (1901-80) US director.
Donald Wolfit (1902-68) English actor.
Ralph Richardson (1902-83) English actor.
John Gielgud (b. 1904) English actor/director.
Roger Blin (1907-84) French actor.
Edwige Feuillière (b. 1907) French actress.
Laurence Olivier (b. 1907) English actor/director.
Peggy Ashcroft (b. 1907) English actress.
Anna Magnani (1908-73) Italian actress.
Michael Redgrave (1908-85) English actor.
Jean Louis Barrault (b. 1910) French actor/director.
Hume Cronyn (b. 1911) US actor.
Lee J. Cobb (1911-76) US actor.
Alec Guinness (b. 1914) English actor.
Tadeus Kantor (b. 1915) Polish director.
Orson Welles (1915-85) US actor/director.
Irene Worth (b. 1916) US actress.
Uta Hagen (b. 1919) US actress.
Giorgio Strehler (b. 1921) Italian director.
Joseph Papp (b. 1921) US director/producer.
Paul Scofield (b. 1922) English actor.
Geraldine Page (1924-88) US actress.
Marlon Brando (b. 1924) US actor.
John Dexter (b. 1925) English director.
Peter Brook (b. 1925) English director.
Julian Beck (b. 1925) US actor/director.
Richard Burton (1925-84) Welsh actor.
Judith Malina (b. 1926) US director.
Eric Porter (b. 1928) English actor.
Ekkerhard Schall (b. 1930) German actor.
William Gaskill (b. 1930) English director.
Peter Hall (b. 1930) English director.
Ian Holm (b. 1931) English actor.
Roger Planchon (b. 1931) French director.
Jerzy Grotowski (b. 1933) Polish director.
Alan Bates (b. 1934) English actor.
Jonathan Miller (b. 1934) British director.
Joseph Chaikin (b. 1935) US director.
Judi Dench (b. 1935) English actress.
Glenda Jackson (b. 1936) English actress.
Albert Finney (b. 1936) English actor.
Anthony Hopkins (b. 1937) Welsh actor.
Vanessa Redgrave (b. 1937) English actress.
Dustin Hoffman (b. 1937) US actor.
Peter Stein (b. 1937) German director.
Derek Jacobi (b. 1938) English actor.
Ian McKellan (b. 1939) English actor.
Trevor (Robert) Nunn (b. 1940) British actor/director.
Michael Gambon (b. 1940) English actor.
Robert Wilson (b. 1941) US director.
Anthony Sher (b. 1949) English actor.

SPORT

A-Z of history and development

AMERICAN FOOTBALL
Evolved at American universities in the second half of the 19th century as a descendant from soccer and rugby in Britain. The first professional game was played in 1895 at Latrobe, Pennsylvania. The American Professional Football Association was formed in 1920 and twelve teams contested the first league season. The association became the National Football League (NFL) in 1922. The American Football League (AFL) was formed in 1960. The two leagues merged in 1970, and under the NFL were reorganized into the National Football Conference (NFC) and the American Football Conference (AFC).

The major trophy is the Super Bowl, held annually since 1967 as a competition between firstly champions of the NFL and AFL, and since 1970 between the champions of the NFC and AFC.

The game is 11-a-side (12-a-side in Canada) with substitutes freely used. Pitch dimensions (NFL): $109 \cdot 7 \times 47 \cdot 8$ m ($360 \times 160\,ft$). Ball length 280–286 mm (11–$11\frac{1}{4}$ in), weighing 397–425 g (14–15 oz).

Superbowl winners
1967 Green Bay Packers
1968 Green Bay Packers
1969 New York Jets
1970 Kansas City Chiefs
1971 Baltimore Colts
1972 Dallas Cowboys
1973 Miami Dolphins
1974 Miami Dolphins
1975 Pittsburgh Steelers
1976 Pittsburgh Steelers
1977 Oakland Raiders
1978 Dallas Cowboys
1979 Pittsburgh Steelers
1980 Pittsburgh Steelers
1981 Oakland Raiders
1982 San Francisco 49ers
1983 Washington Redskins
1984 Los Angeles Raiders
1985 San Francisco 49ers
1986 Chicago Bears
1987 New York Giants
1988 Washington Redskins
1989 San Francisco 49ers

ARCHERY
Although developed as an organized sport from the 3rd century AD, archery is portrayed much earlier as a skill in Mesolithic cave paintings. Internationalized as a sport in 1931 with the founding of the governing body, *Fédération Internationale de Tir à l'Arc* (FITA); the most popular form of archery is termed Target Archery. Other forms are Field Archery, shooting at animal figures, and Flight Shooting, which has the sole object of achieving distance.

World Target Championships were first held in Poland in 1931, and biennially since 1957. Competitors shoot Double FITA rounds, 144 arrows from

Gary Clark, Wide Receiver, Washington Redskins. (All-Sport)

four different distances. An Olympic event in 1900, it disappeared between 1920 and 1972. The 1988 champions were: (men) *team* South Korea, *individual* Jay Barrs (USA); (women) *team* South Korea, *individual* Kim Soo-nyung (S. Korea).

ATHLETICS (TRACK AND FIELD)
There is evidence that running was involved in early Egyptian rituals at Memphis *c.* 3800 BC, but organized athletics is usually dated to the ancient Olympic Games *c.* 1370 BC. The earliest accurately known Olympiad was in July 776 BC, where Coroibos of Elis is recorded as winning the foot race, about 180–185 m (*164–169 yd*).

The modern Olympics were revived in 1896 (see Olympic section). The inaugural World Championships were held at Helsinki, Finland in August 1983 and attracted entries from 157 countries, making it the greatest number of nations represented at any sports meeting in history. The Championships were next held in Rome in 1987, when again 157 countries were represented.

Marathon events, held since 1896, commemorate the legendary run of an unknown Greek courier, possibly Pheidippides, who in 490 BC ran some 38·6 km (*24 miles*) from the Plain of Marathon to Athens with news of a Greek victory over the numerically superior Persian army. Delivering his message – 'Rejoice! We have won' – he collapsed and died. Since 1908 the distance has been standardized as 42 195 m (*26 miles 385 yd*).

Dimensions in field events: Shot (men) – weight 7·26 kg (*16 lb*), diameter 110–130 mm (*4·33–5·12 in*); Shot (women) – weight 4 kg (*8 lb 13 oz*), diameter 95–110 mm (*3·74–4·33 in*); Discus (men) – weight 2 kg (*4·409 lb*), diameter 219–221 mm (*8·622–8·701 in*); Discus (women) – weight 1 kg (*2·204 lb*), diameter 180–182 mm (*7·086–7·165 in*). Hammer – weight 7·26 kg (*16 lb*), length 117·5–121·5 cm (*46·259–47·835 in*), diameter of head 110–130 mm (*4·33–5·12 in*); Javelin (men) – weight 800 g (*28·219 oz*), length 260–270 cm (*102·362–106·299 in*); Javelin (women) – weight 600 g (*21·164 oz*), length 220–230 cm (*86·61–90·55 in*).

Track & field athletics world records

Men

	min:sec	
100 m	9·83	Ben Johnson (Can) 1987
200 m	19·72	Pietro Mennea (Ita) 1979
400 m	43·29	Butch Reynolds (USA) 1988
800 m	1:41·73	Sebastian Coe (UK) 1981
1000 m	2:12·18	Sebastian Coe (UK) 1981
1500 m	3:29·46	Saïd Aouita (Mor) 1985
1 mile	3:46·32	Steve Cram (UK) 1985
2000 m	4:50·81	Saïd Aouita (Mor) 1987
3000 m	7:32·1	Henry Rono (Ken) 1978
5000 m	12:58·39	Saïd Aouita (Mor) 1987
10 000 m	27:13·81	Fernando Mamede (Por) 1984
20 km	57:24·19	Jos Hermens (Hol) 1976
1 hour	20 944 m	Jos Hermens (Hol) 1976
25 000 m	1 hr 13:55·8	Toshihiko Seko (Jap) 1981
30 000 m	1 hr 29:18·8	Toshihiko Seko (Jap) 1981
Marathon	2 hr 06:50	Belayneh Dinsamo (Eth) 1988
3 km steeple	8:05·4	Henry Rono (Ken) 1978
110 m hurdles	12·93	Renaldo Nehemiah (USA) 1981
400 m hurdles	47·02	Edwin Moses (USA) 1983
4×100 m relay	37·83	United States 1984
4×400 m relay	2:56·16	United States 1968 & 1988
	metres	
High jump	2·43	Javier Sotomayor (Cub) 1988
Pole vault	6·06	Sergey Bubka (USSR) 1988
Long jump	8·90	Bob Beamon (USA) 1968
Triple jump	17·97	Willie Banks (USA) 1985
Shot	23·06	Ulf Timmermann (GDR) 1988
Discus	74·08	Jürgen Schult (GDR) 1986
Hammer	86·74	Yuriy Sedykh (USSR) 1986
Javelin	87·66	Jan Zelezný (Cs) 1987
Decathlon	8847 pts	Daley Thompson (UK) 1984
Track walking		
	min:sec	
20 km	1 hr 18:40·0	Ernesto Canto (Mex) 1984
50 km	3 hr 41:38·4	Raúl González (Mex) 1979
Road walking – fastest recorded times		
20 km	1 hr 18:54	Yevgeniy Misyulya (USSR) 1989
50 km	3 hr 38:17	Ronald Weigel (GDR) 1986

Women

	min:sec	
100 m	10·49	Florence Griffith-Joyner (USA) 1988
200 m	21·34	Florence Griffith-Joyner (USA) 1988
400 m	47·60	Marita Koch (GDR) 1985
800 m	1:53·28	Jarmila Kratochvilová (Cs) 1983
1000 m	2:30·6	Tatyana Providokhina (USSR) 1978
1500 m	3:52·47	Tatyana Kazankina (USSR) 1980
1 mile	4:16·71	Mary Slaney (USA) 1985
2000 m	5:28·69	Maricica Puica (Rom) 1986
3000 m	8:22·62	Tatyana Kazankina (USSR) 1984
5000 m	14:37·33	Ingrid Kristiansen (Nor) 1986
10 000 m	30:13·74	Ingrid Kristiansen (Nor) 1986
Marathon	2 hr 21:06	Ingrid Kristiansen (Nor) 1985
100 m hurdles	12·21	Yordanka Donkova (Bul) 1988
400 m hurdles	52·94	Marina Stepanova (USSR) 1986
4×100 m relay	41·37	GDR 1985
4×400 m relay	3:15·18	USSR 1988
	metres	
High jump	2·09	Stefka Kostadinova (Bul) 1986
Long jump	7·52	Galina Chistyakova (USSR) 1988
Shot	22·63	Natalya Lisovskaya (USSR) 1987
Discus	76·80	Gabrielle Reinsch (GDR) 1988
Javelin	80·00	Petra Felke (GDR) 1988
Heptathlon	7291 pts	Jackie Joyner-Kersee (USA) 1988
Track walking		
	min:sec	
5000 m	20:32·75	Kerry Saxby (Aus) 1989
10 km	42:14·2	Kerry Saxby (Aus) 1988
Road walking – fastest recorded time		
10 km	41:30	Kerry Saxby (Aus) 1988

OLYMPIC GAMES RECORDS up to 1988

Men

	min:sec	
100 m	9·92	Carl Lewis (USA) 1988
200 m	19·75	Joe DeLoach (USA) 1988
400 m	(A) 43·86	Lee Evans (USA) 1968
800 m	1:43·00	Joaquim Cruz (Bra) 1984
1500 m	3:32·53	Sebastian Coe (UK) 1984
5000 m	13:05·59	Saïd Aouita (Mor) 1984
10 000 m	27:21·46	Brahim Boutayeb (Mor) 1988
Marathon	2 hr 09:21	Carlos Lopes (Por) 1984
3000 m steeple	8:05·51	Julius Kariuki (Ken) 1988
110 m hurdles	12·98	Roger Kingdom (USA) 1988
400 m hurdles	47·19	Andre Phillips (USA) 1988
4×100 m relay	37·83	USA 1984
4×400 m relay	2:56·16	USA 1968(A) & 1988
20 km walk	1 hr 19:57	Jozef Pribilinec (Cs) 1988
50 km walk	3 hr 38:29	Vyacheslav Ivenenko (USSR) 1988
	metres	
High jump	2·38	Gennadiy Avdeyenko (USSR) 1988
Pole vault	5·90	Sergey Bubka (USSR) 1988

10 000 m	31:05·21	Olga Bondarenko (USSR) 1988
Marathon	2hr 24:52	Joan Benoit (USA) 1984
100 m hurdles	12·38	Yordanka Donkova (Bul) 1988
400 m hurdles	53·17	Debbie Flintoff-King (Aus) 1988
4×100 m relay	41·60	GDR 1980
4×400 m relay	3:15·18	USSR 1988
	metres	
High jump	2·03	Louise Ritter (USA) 1988
Long jump	7·40	Jackie Joyner-Kersee (USA) 1988
Shot	22·41	Ilona Slupianek (GDR) 1980
Discus	72·30	Martina Hellmann (GDR) 1988
Javelin	74·68	Petra Felke (GDR) 1988
Heptathlon	7291 pts	Jackie Joyner-Kersee (USA) 1988

AUSTRALIAN RULES FOOTBALL

Originally a hybrid of soccer, Gaelic football and rugby, laws were codified in 1866 in Melbourne, with the oval (rather than round) ball in use by 1867. The first football body in Australia, the Victoria Football Association, was formed in 1877 and the Australian Football Council (AFC) in 1906.

Teams are 18-a-side. Pitch dimensions are: width 110–155 m (*120–170 yd*), length 135–185 m (*150–200 yd*), encompassing an oval boundary line. The oval ball measures 736 mm (*29½ in*) in length, 572 mm (*22¾ in*) in diameter and weighs 452–482 g (*16–17 oz*).

BADMINTON

The modern game is believed to have evolved from Badminton Hall, Avon, England, c. 1870, or from a game played in India at about the same time. Modern rules were first codified in Poona, India in 1876. A similar game was played in China 2000 years earlier.

The International Badminton Federation was founded in 1934, with affiliations in over 70 countries. Main countries today: Canada, China, Denmark, India, Indonesia, Japan, Malaysia, New Zealand, S. Africa, USA, and the UK.

World Championships were instituted in 1977 and are held triennially. Previously, the All England Championships (instituted 1899) was considered premier. International men's teams compete for the Thomas Cup (first held 1949); and women's for the Uber Cup (first held 1957). Both are held triennially and China won both competitions in 1988. Court dimensions: 13·41 × 6·1 m (*44 × 20 ft*) (singles game 3 ft narrower). The net is 1·5 m (*5 ft*) high at the centre; two or four players.

BASEBALL

The modern, or Cartwright, rules were introduced in New Jersey on 19 June 1846, although a game of the same name had been played in England prior to 1700. Baseball is mainly played in America, where there are two leagues, the National (NL) and the American (AL), founded in 1876 and 1901 respectively. It is also very popular in Japan. The winners of each US league meet annually in a best of seven series of games, the World Series, established permanently in 1905.

Recent winner of the World Series:

1980 Philadelphia Phillies (NL)
1981 Los Angeles Dodgers (NL)

Florence Griffith-Joyner (USA), first in the 100-metre final at the 1988 Olympic Games. (All-Sport)

Long jump	(A) 8·90	Bob Beamon (USA) 1968
Triple jump	17·61	Khristo Markov (Bul) 1988
Shot	22·47	Ulf Timmermann (GDR) 1988
Discus	68·82	Jürgen Schult (GDR) 1988
Hammer	84·80	Sergey Litvinov (USSR) 1988
Javelin	*85·90	Jan Zelezný (Cs) 1988
Old javelin	94·58	Miklos Nemeth (Hun) 1976
Decathlon	8847 pts	Daley Thompson (UK) 1984

Women

	min:sec	
100 m	10·54	Florence Griffith-Joyner (USA) 1988
200 m	21·34	Florence Griffith-Joyner (USA) 1988
400 m	48·65	Olga Bryzgina (USSR) 1988
800 m	1:53·43	Nadezhda Olizarenko (USSR) 1980
1500 m	3:53·96	Paula Ivan (Rom) 1988
3000 m	8:26·53	Tatyana Samolenko (USSR) 1988

* performance made in qualifying round.
(A) at high altitude, Mexico City 2240 m.

1982 St Louis Cardinals (NL)
1983 Baltimore Orioles (AL)
1984 Detroit Tigers (AL)
1985 Kansas City Royals (AL)
1986 New York Mets (NL)
1987 Minnesota Twins (AL)
1988 Los Angeles Dodgers (NL)

The game is 9-a-side. A standard ball weighs 148 g (*5-5¼ oz*) and is 23 cm (*9-9½ ins*) in circumference. Bats are up to 7 cm (*2¾ in*) in diameter and up to 1·07 m (*42 in*) in length.

BASKETBALL

A game not dissimilar to Basketball was played by the Olmecs in Mexico in the 10th century BC, but the modern game was devised by (Canadian born) Dr James Naismith in Massachusetts, December 1891.

The governing body is the Fédération Internationale de Basketball Amateur (FIBA), formed in 1932, and the game is played worldwide. By 1989, 178 national federations were members of FIBA. An Olympic sport since 1936 for men, for women since 1976. The 1988 titles were won by the USSR (men) and USA (women). World championships, first held for men in 1950 and for women in 1953, are staged every four years. The USA won both titles in 1986.

Teams are 5-a-side, with seven substitutes allowed. The rectangular court is 26·0 m (*85 ft*) in length, and 14·0 m (*46 ft*) wide, and the ball is 75–78 cm (*30 in*) in circumference and weighs 600–650 g (*21–23 oz*).

BILLIARDS

Probably deriving from the old French word *billiard* (a stick with a curved end), an early reference exists, dated 1429, to the game played on grass. Louis XVI of France (1461-83) is believed to be the first to have played on a table. Rubber cushions were introduced in 1835, and slate beds in 1836.

World Professional and Amateur Championships have been held since 1870 and 1926 respectively.

Dimensions of table: 3·66 × 1·87 m (*12 × 6 ft*).

BOARDSAILING (WINDSURFING)

Following a High Court decision, Peter Chilvers has been credited with devising the prototype boardsail in 1958. As a sport, it was pioneered by Henry Hoyle Schweitzer and Jim Drake in California in 1968. World Championships were first held in 1973 and boardsailing was added to the Olympic Games in 1984.

BOBSLEIGH AND TOBOGGANING

Although the first known sledge dates back to c. 6500 BC in Heinola, Finland, organized bobsleighing began in Davos, Switzerland in 1889.

The International Federation of Bobsleigh & Tobogganing was formed in 1923, followed by the International Bobsleigh Federation in 1957.

World and Olympic Championships began in 1924, and competition is for crews of two or four. The driver steers while the rear man operates brakes and corrects skidding. With the four-man, the middle two riders alter weight transference for cornering.

The oldest tobogganing club is the St Moritz in Switzerland, founded in 1887, and home of the Cresta Run which dates to 1884. The course is 1212·25 m (*3977 ft*) long with a drop of 157 m (*514 ft*). Solo speeds reach 145 km/h (*90 mph*). In Lugeing, the rider sits or lies back, as opposed to lying face down in tobogganing.

BOWLING (TEN-PIN)

Evolved from the ancient German game of nine-pins, which having been exported to America was banned in Connecticut in 1847 and then in other States. Ten pins were introduced to beat the ban. Rules were first standardized by the American Bowling Congress (ABC), formed in September 1895.

Concentrated in the USA, the game is also very popular in Japan and Europe. World Championships were introduced for men in 1954 and women in 1963, under the Fédération Internationale des Quilleurs (FIQ), which governs a number of bowling games.

The ten pins are placed in a triangle at the end of a lane of total length 19·16 m (*62 ft 10¾ in*) and width 1·06 m (*42 in*).

BOWLS

Outdoor bowls goes back as far as 13th century England, but was forbidden by Edward III since its popularity threatened the practice of archery. The modern rules were not framed until 1848-9, in Scotland by William Mitchell. There are two types of greens, the crown and the level, the former being played almost exclusively in Northern England and the Midland counties.

Lawn bowls is played mostly in the UK and Commonwealth countries. The International Bowling Board was formed in July 1905. Men's and Women's World Championships are held every four years, with singles, pairs, triples and fours events. World Championships for Indoor Bowls were introduced in 1979.

BOXING

Competitively, boxing began in Ancient Greece as one of the first Olympic sports. Boxing with gloves was first depicted on a fresco from the Isle of Thera, c. 1520 BC. Prize-fighting rules were formed in England in 1743 by Jack Broughton, but modern day fights evolved from 1867 when the 8th Marquess of Queensberry gave his name to rules. Boxing only became a legal sport in 1901.

Professional boxing has several world governing bodies, the two oldest being the World Boxing Council (WBC) and the World Boxing Association (WBA), based in Mexico City and Manila respectively. Recognized weight categories are: Strawweight (limit 104 lb); Light-flyweight (limit 108 lb); Flyweight (limit 112 lb); Super-flyweight (limit 115 lb); Bantamweight (118 lb); Light-featherweight (122 lb); Featherweight (126 lb); Junior Lightweight (130 lb); Lightweight (135 lb); Light Welterweight (140 lb); Welterweight (147 lb); Light Middleweight (153½ lb); Middleweight (160 lb); Super Middleweight (168 lb); Light Heavyweight (175 lb); Cruiserweight (190 lb) and Heavyweight.

CANOEING

Modern canoes and kayaks originated among the Indians and Eskimos of North America, but canoeing as a sport is attributed to an English barrister, James MacGregor, who founded the Royal Canoe Club in 1866.

With a kayak, the paddler sits in a forward-facing

position and uses a double-bladed paddle, whereas in a canoe the paddler kneels in a forward-facing position and propels with a single-bladed paddle. An Olympic sport since 1936, Olympic titles are now held in nine events for men at 500 m and 1000 m, and three for women each at 500 m.

CHESS

Derived from the Persian word *Shah*, meaning a king or ruler, the game itself originated in India under the name Caturanga, a military game (literally 'four corps'). The first chessmen, of ivory, found in Russia, are dated *c.* AD 200. By the 10th century, chess was played in most European countries. There are today some 40 million enthusiasts in the USSR alone. The governing body, founded in 1922, is the *Fédération Internationale des Echecs* (FIDE), which has been responsible for the World Chess Championship competitions since 1946, although official champions date from 1886 and unofficial before then.

Players are graded according to competitive results on the official ELO scoring system. Bobby Fischer (USA), world champion 1972–5, achieved the highest-ever rating of 2785. The current world champions are men: Gary Kasparov (USSR) and women: Maya Chiburdanidze (USSR), rated at 2775 and 2520 respectively. The highest rated woman player is Judit Polgar (Hungary) at 2555 prior to her 13th birthday (25 July 1976).

CRICKET

A drawing dated *c.* 1250 shows a bat and ball game resembling cricket, although the formal origins are early 18th century. The formation of the MCC (Marylebone Cricket Club) in 1878 resulted in codified laws by 1835.

The International Cricket Conference (ICC), so called since 1965, having allowed membership from non-Commonwealth countries. There are seven full members, 18 associate members and five affiliated members. The seven Test-playing full members are: England, Australia, West Indies, India, Pakistan, New Zealand and Sri Lanka.

There are four domestic competitions. The UK County Championship, a league of the 17 first class counties with matches over three or four days; the one-day knockouts of the Nat. West (previously Gillette) Trophy of 60-over matches and the Benson & Hedges of 55, and the one-day Refuge Assurance League (formerly John Player League) of 40-over matches. The first-class domestic competitions of Australia, New Zealand, India and the West Indies are the Sheffield Shield, the Shell Trophy, the Ranji Trophy and the Red Stripe Cup (formerly Shell Shield) respectively.

The World Cup, the international one day tournament, is held every four years, with the seven Test-playing countries plus the winner of the ICC Trophy which is competed for by non-Test playing countries. Australia won the 1987 tournament, India in 1983, the West Indies the first two in 1975 and 1979.

The first Women's World Cup was held in 1988, with Australia the winners.

Dimensions: Ball circumference 20·79–22·8 cm (8³⁄₁₆–9 in), weight 155–163 g (5½–5¾ oz); pitch 20·11 m (22 yd) from stump to stump.

CURLING

Similar to bowls on ice, curling dates from the 15th century although organized administration only began in 1838 with the Grand (later Royal) Caledonian Curling Club in Edinburgh. The sport is traditionally popular in Scotland and Canada. The International Curling Federation was formed in 1966, and curling was added to the 1988 Olympic Games as a demonstration sport.

CYCLING

The first known race was held over 2 km (*1·2 m*) in Paris on 31 May 1868. The Road Record Association in Britain was formed in 1888, while F. T. Bidlake devised the time trial (by 1890) as a means of avoiding traffic congestion caused by ordinary mass road racing.

Competitive racing, popular worldwide, is now conducted both on road and track. The Tour de France (founded in 1903) is the longest lasting non-motorized sporting event in the world, taking 21 days to stage annually. The yellow jersey, to distinguish the leading rider, was introduced in 1919.

Included since the first of the modern Olympic Games in 1896, there are currently seven men's and two women's events on the Olympic programme.

1988 Olympic champions:

Men

Sprint: Lutz Hesslich (GDR)
1000 m time trial: Aleksandr Kirichenko (USSR) 1:04·499
4000 m individual pursuit: Gintautas Umaras (USSR)
Points: Dan Frost (Denmark)
Road race: Olaf Ludwig (GDR)
100 km road team time trial: GDR
Team pursuit: USSR

Women

Sprint: Erika Salumyae (USSR)
Road race: Monique Knol (Hol)

DARTS

Brian Gamlin of Bury, Lancashire, is credited with devising the present numbering system on the board, although in non-sporting form darts began with the heavily weighted throwing arrows used in Roman and Greek warfare.

Immensely popular in the UK – there are today some 6 000 000 players – the sport is rapidly spreading in America and parts of Europe.

World championships were first held in 1978. Champions have been:

1978 Leighton Rees (Wal)
1979 John Lowe (Eng)
1980 Eric Bristow (Eng)
1981 Eric Bristow (Eng)
1982 Jocky Wilson (Sco)
1983 Keith Deller (Eng)
1984 Eric Bristow (Eng)
1985 Eric Bristow (Eng)
1986 Eric Bristow (Eng)
1987 John Lowe (Eng)
1988 Bob Anderson (Eng)
1989 Jocky Wilson (Sco)

EQUESTRIANISM

Horse riding is some 5000 years old, but schools of horsemanship, or equitation, were not established until the 16th century, primarily in Italy and then in France. The earliest jumping competiton was in Islington, London in 1869.

An Olympic event since 1912, events are held in dressage, show jumping and Three Day Event, with team and individual titles for each. Dressage (the French term for the training of horses) is a test of riders' ability to control horses through various manoeuvres within an area of 60×20 m (66×22 yd). In show jumping riders jump a set course of fences, incurring four faults for knocking a fence down or landing (one or more feet) in the water, three faults for a first refusal, six faults then elimination for 2nd and 3rd, and eight for a fall. The Three Day event encompasses dressage, cross country and jumping.

The governing body is the Fédération Equestre Internationale, founded in May 1921.

FENCING
Fencing (fighting with single sticks) was practised as a sport, or as part of a religious ceremony, in Egypt as early as 1360 BC. The modern sport developed directly from the duelling of the Middle Ages.

There are three types of sword used today. With the foil (introduced 17th century), only the trunk of the body is acceptable as a target. The épée (mid-19th century) is marginally heavier and more rigid and the whole body is a valid target. The sabre (late 19th century) has cutting edges on both sides of the blade and scores on the whole body from the waist upwards. Only with the sabre can points be scored with the edge of the blade rather than the tip.

For men, there are individual and team events for each type of sword in the Olympics. Women compete in foil only. The world governing body is the Fédération Internationale d'Escrime, founded in 1913. Olympic champions in 1988 were:

Men *Individual*   *Team*
Foil   Stefano Cerioni (Ita)   USSR
Épée   Arndt Schmidt (W. Ger)   France
Sabre Jean-François Lamour (Fra)   Hungary

Women
Foil   Anja Fichtel (W. Ger)   West Germany

FIVES
Eton Fives originates from a handball game first recorded as being played against the buttress of Eton College Chapel in 1825. Rules were codified in 1877, and last amended in 1981.

Rugby Fives, a variation, dates from c. 1850. Both are more or less confined to the UK.

FOOTBALL (Association)
Tsu-Chu – Tsu, meaning 'to kick the ball with feet' (*chu* means 'leather'), was played in China around 400 BC. Calcio, closer to the modern game, existed in Italy in 1410. Official references date to Edward II's reign in Britain – he banned the game in London in 1314. Later monarchs issued similar edicts. The first soccer rules were formulated at Cambridge University in 1846; previously football was brutal and lawless. The Football Association (FA) was founded in England on 26 October 1863. Eleven per side became standard in 1870.

The governing body, the Fédération Internationale de Football Association (FIFA) was founded in Paris on 21 May 1904; football is played throughout the world.

Professionally, domestic competitions in England are the League Championship (the Football League was formed in 1888 with 12 teams), now with 4 divisions totalling 92 teams; the FA Challenge Cup, inst. 1871; and the Littlewoods (previously League and Milk) Cup, inst. 1960. 'Non-League' or semi-professional football is also widespread. Internationally, the World Cup has been held every four years since 1930 (not 1942 or 1946); the European Championship, instituted in 1958 as the Nations Cup, held every four years; the European Champions Club Cup, instituted in 1955 as the European Cup, contested annually by the League Champions of the member countries of the Union of European Football Associations (UEFA); the European Cup Winners Cup, instituted in 1960 for National Cup winners (or runners-up if the winners are in the European Cup); the UEFA Cup instituted in 1955 as the Inter-City Fairs Cup, held annually since 1960; the European Super Cup (inst. 1972) played between the winners of the European Champions Club Cup and the Cup Winners Cup; and the World Club Championship (inst. 1960) a contest between the winners of the European Cup and the Copa Libertadores (the S. American championship).

Football is an 11-a-side game; the ball's circumference is 68–71 cm (*27–28 in*) and weight 396–453 g (*14–16 oz*). Pitch length 91–120 m (*100–130 yd*), width 45–91 m (*50–100 yd*).

The World Cup

Year	Winner	Venue
1930	Uruguay	Uruguay
1934	Italy	Italy
1938	Italy	France
1950	Uruguay	Brazil
1954	W. Germany	Switzerland
1958	Brazil	Sweden
1962	Brazil	Chile
1966	England	England
1970	Brazil	Mexico
1974	W. Germany	W. Germany
1978	Argentina	Argentina
1982	Italy	Spain
1986	Argentina	Mexico

The FA Cup (UK)
The FA Cup, or Football Association Challenge Cup, was instituted in 1871, 17 years before the birth of the Football League. The first final was played at Kennington Oval, London in 1872, when the Wanderers defeated Royal Engineers 1–0. Southern amateur clubs dominated the early years and the Cup did not 'go north' until Blackburn Olympic won in 1883. The final has been played at Wembley Stadium since 1923, when Bolton Wanderers defeated West Ham.

1872 Wanderers
1873 Wanderers
1874 Oxford University
1875 Royal Engineers
1876 Wanderers
1877 Wanderers
1878 Wanderers
1879 Old Etonians
1880 Clapham Rovers
1881 Old Carthusians
1882 Old Etonians
1883 Blackburn Olympic
1884 Blackburn Rovers
1885 Blackburn Rovers
1886 Blackburn Rovers

FA Cup Wembley, 1988 final with Wimbledon players (from left to right) Eric Young, Laurie Sanchez, Dave Beasant holding the FA Cup, and Tery Phelan. (All-Sport)

1887	Aston Villa	1929	Bolton Wanderers
1888	West Bromwich Albion	1930	Arsenal
1889	Preston North End	1931	West Bromwich Albion
1890	Blackburn Rovers	1932	Newcastle United
1891	Blackburn Rovers	1933	Everton
1892	West Bromwich Albion	1934	Manchester City
1893	Wolverhampton Wanderers	1935	Sheffield Wednesday
1894	Notts County	1936	Arsenal
1895	Aston Villa	1937	Sunderland
1896	Sheffield Wednesday	1938	Preston North End
1897	Aston Villa	1939	Portsmouth
1898	Nottingham Forest	1946	Derby County
1899	Sheffield United	1947	Charlton Athletic
1900	Bury	1948	Manchester United
1901	Tottenham Hotspur	1949	Wolverhampton Wanderers
1902	Sheffield United	1950	Arsenal
1903	Bury	1951	Newcastle United
1904	Manchester City	1952	Newcastle United
1905	Aston Villa	1953	Blackpool
1906	Everton	1954	West Bromwich Albion
1907	Sheffield Wednesday	1955	Newcastle United
1908	Wolverhampton Wanderers	1956	Manchester City
1909	Manchester United	1957	Aston Villa
1910	Newcastle United	1958	Bolton Wanderers
1911	Bradford City	1959	Nottingham Forest
1912	Barnsley	1960	Wolverhampton Wanderers
1913	Aston Villa	1961	Tottenham Hotspur
1914	Burnley	1962	Tottenham Hotspur
1915	Sheffield United	1963	Manchester United
1920	Aston Villa	1964	West Ham United
1921	Tottenham Hotspur	1965	Liverpool
1922	Huddersfield Town	1966	Everton
1923	Bolton Wanderers	1967	Tottenham Hotspur
1924	Newcastle United	1968	West Bromwich Albion
1925	Sheffield United	1969	Manchester City
1926	Bolton Wanderers	1970	Chelsea
1927	Cardiff City	1971	Arsenal
1928	Blackburn Rovers	1972	Leeds United

1973	Sunderland	
1974	Liverpool	
1975	West Ham United	
1976	Southampton	
1977	Manchester United	
1978	Ipswich Town	
1979	Arsenal	
1980	West Ham United	
1981	Tottenham Hotspur	
1982	Tottenham Hotspur	
1983	Manchester United	
1984	Everton	
1985	Manchester United	
1986	Liverpool	
1987	Coventry City	
1988	Wimbledon	
1989	Liverpool	

GAELIC FOOTBALL

The game developed from inter-parish 'free for all' with no time limit, no defined playing area nor specific rules. The Gaelic Athletic Association established the game in its present form in 1884. Teams are 15-a-side. Played throughout Ireland.

GOLF

A prohibiting law passed by the Scottish Parliament in 1457, which declared 'goff be utterly cryit doune and not usit', is the earliest mention of golf, although games of similar principle date as far back as AD 400. Golf is today played worldwide.

Competition is either 'match play', contested by individuals or pairs, and decided by the number of holes won, or 'stroke play' decided by the total number of strokes for a round. The modern golf course measures total distance 5500–6400 metres, divided into 18 holes of varying lengths. Clubs are currently limited to a maximum of 14, comprising 'irons' Nos. 1–10 (with the face of the club at increasingly acute angles), and 'woods' for driving. Golf balls in the UK have minimum diameter 41·55 mm (*1·62 oz*). In America, the minimum diameter is 42·62 mm (*1·68 in*).

Professionally, the four major tournaments are the British Open, the US Open, the US Masters and the US Professional Golfers' Association (USPGA).

The British Open Golf Championship

The oldest open championship in the world, 'The Open', was first held on 17 October 1860 at the Prestwick Club, Ayrshire. It was then over 36 holes; since 1892 it has been over 72 holes of stroke play. Since 1920, the Royal and Ancient Golf Club have managed the event.

Winners, UK unless specified:	*Score*
1860 Willie Park, Sr	174
1861 Tom Morris, Sr	163
1862 Tom Morris, Sr	163
1863 Willie Park, Sr	168
1864 Tom Morris, Sr	167
1865 Andrew Strath	162
1866 Willie Park, Sr	169
1867 Tom Morris, Sr	170
1868 Tom Morris, Jr	170
1869 Tom Morris, Jr	154
1870 Tom Morris, Jr	149
1871 Not held	
1872 Tom Morris, Jr	166
1873 Tom Kidd	179

1874 Mungo Park	159
1875 Willie Park, Sr	166
1876 Robert Martin	176
1877 Jamie Anderson	160
1878 Jamie Anderson	170
1879 Jamie Anderson	170
1880 Robert Ferguson	162
1881 Robert Ferguson	170
1882 Robert Ferguson	171
1883 Willie Fernie	159
1884 Jack Simpson	160
1885 Bob Martin	171
1886 David Brown	157
1887 Willie Park, Jr	161
1888 Jack Burns	171
1889 Willie Park, Jr	155
1890 John Ball	164
1891 Hugh Kirkcaldy	169
1892 Harold Hilton	305
1893 William Auchterlonie	322
1894 John Taylor	326
1895 John Taylor	322
1896 Harry Vardon	316
1897 Harry Hilton	314
1898 Harry Vardon	307
1899 Harry Vardon	310
1900 John Taylor	309
1901 James Braid	309
1902 Alexander Herd	307
1903 Harry Vardon	300
1904 Jack White	296
1905 James Braid	318
1906 James Braid	300
1907 Arnaud Massy (Fra)	312
1908 James Braid	291
1909 John Taylor	295
1910 James Braid	299
1911 Harry Vardon	303
1912 Edward (Ted) Ray	295
1913 John Taylor	304
1914 Harry Vardon	306
1920 George Duncan	303
1921 Jock Hutchinson (USA)	296
1922 Walter Hagen (USA)	300
1923 Arthur Havers	295
1924 Walter Hagen (USA)	301
1925 James Barnes (USA)	300
1926 Robert T. Jones, Jr (USA)	291
1927 Robert T. Jones, Jr (USA)	285
1928 Walter Hagen (USA)	292
1929 Walter Hagen (USA)	292
1930 Robert T. Jones, Jr (USA)	291
1931 Tommy Armour (USA)	296
1932 Gene Sarazen (USA)	283
1933 Denny Shute (USA)	292
1934 Henry Cotton	283
1935 Alfred Perry	283
1936 Alfred Padgham	287
1937 Henry Cotton	283
1938 Reg Whitcombe	295
1939 Richard Burton	290
1946 Sam Snead (USA)	290
1947 Fred Daly	293
1948 Henry Cotton	284
1949 Bobby Locke (Saf)	283
1950 Bobby Locke (Saf)	279
1951 Max Faulkner	285
1952 Bobby Locke (Saf)	287
1953 Ben Hogan (USA)	282
1954 Peter Thomson (Aus)	283
1955 Peter Thomson (Aus)	281
1956 Peter Thomson (Aus)	286

1957	Bobby Locke (Saf)	279
1958	Peter Thomson (Aus)	278
1959	Gary Player (Saf)	284
1960	Kel Nagle (Aus)	278
1961	Arnold Palmer (USA)	284
1962	Arnold Palmer (USA)	276
1963	Bob Charles (NZ)	277
1964	Tony Lema (USA)	279
1965	Peter Thomson (Aus)	285
1966	Jack Nicklaus (USA)	282
1967	Robert de Vicenzo (Arg)	278
1968	Gary Player (Saf)	299
1969	Tony Jacklin	280
1970	Jack Nicklaus (USA)	283
1971	Lee Trevino (USA)	278
1972	Lee Trevino (USA)	278
1973	Tom Weiskopf (USA)	276
1974	Gary Player (Saf)	282
1975	Tom Watson (USA)	279
1976	Johnny Miller (USA)	279
1977	Tom Watson (USA)	268
1978	Jack Nicklaus (USA)	281
1979	Severiano Ballesteros (Spa)	283
1980	Tom Watson (USA)	271
1981	Bill Rogers (USA)	276
1982	Tom Watson (USA)	284
1983	Tom Watson (USA)	275
1984	Severiano Ballesteros (Spa)	276
1985	Sandy Lyle	282
1986	Greg Norman (Aus)	280
1987	Nick Faldo	279
1988	Severiano Ballesteros (Spa)	273

GLIDING

Leonardo da Vinci around AD 1500 defined the difference between gliding and powered flight in some drawings. However, the first authenticated man-carrying glider was designed by Sir George Cayley in 1853.

In competitive terms, gliders contest various events – pure distance, distance to a declared goal, to a declared goal and back, height gain and absolute altitude. World Championships were first held in 1937 and biennially from 1948.

Hang gliding has flourished in recent years, boosted by the invention of the flexible 'wing' by Professor Francis Rogallo in the early 1960s. The first official World Championships were held in 1976.

GREYHOUND RACING

Greyhounds were first used in sport at coursing – chasing of hares by pairs of dogs – brought to England by the Normans in 1067. Use of mechanical devices was first practised in England, but the sport was popularized in the USA. The first regular track was opened at Emeryville, California in 1919.

Races are usually conducted over distances of between 210 m (*230 yd*) for the sprint and 1096 m (*1200 yd*) for the marathon. The Derby, the major race in Britain, was instituted in 1927.

GYMNASTICS

Tumbling and similar exercises were performed *c.* 2600 BC as religious rituals in China, but it was the ancient Greeks who coined the word gymnastics, which encompassed various athletic contests including boxing, weightlifting and wrestling. A primitive form was practised in the ancient Olympic Games, but the foundations of the modern sport were laid by the German Johann Friedrich Simon

in 1776, and the first national federation was formed in Germany in 1860.

The International Gymnastics Federation was founded in Belgium in 1881, and gymnastics was included in the first modern Olympic Games in 1896. Current events for men are: floor exercises, horse vault, rings, pommel horse, parallel bars and horizontal bar, while those for women are: floor exercises, horse vault, asymmetrical bars and balance beam. Rhythmic Gymnastics for women was introduced for the first time at the 1984 Los Angeles games. The USSR, USA, Romania, China and Japan are now the strongest nations.

At the 1988 Olympics the USSR won both men's and women's team events. The combined exercises individual champions were men: Vladimir Artemov (USSR) and women: Yelena Shushunova (USSR).

HANDBALL

Handball, similar to soccer only using hands not feet, was first played at the end of the 19th century. A growing sport, by 1982 there were 80 countries affiliated to the International Handball Federation (founded 1946) and an estimated 10 million participants.

Handball was introduced into the Olympic Games at Berlin in 1936 as an 11-a-side outdoor game but on its reintroduction in 1972, it became indoor 7-a-side, the standard size of team since 1952. (In Britain it is often 5-a-side.) At the 1988 Olympics the winners were the USSR (men) and South Korea (women).

HARNESS RACING

Trotting races were held in Valkenburg, Netherlands in 1554 but harness racing developed and is most popular in North America. The sulky, the lightweight vehicle, first appeared in 1829. Horses may trot, moving their legs in diagonal pairs, or pace, moving fore and hind legs on one side simultaneously.

HOCKEY

Early Greek wall carvings *c.* 500 BC show hockey-like games, while curved-stick games appear on Egyptian tomb paintings *c.* 2050 BC. Hockey in its modern form, however, developed in England in the second half of the 19th century, with Teddington HC (formed 1871) standardizing the rules. The English Hockey Association was founded in 1886. Hockey was included in the 1908 and 1920 Olympic Games, with England the winners on each occasion. It has been held at every Games from 1928 and the tournaments were dominated for many years by India, winners at all six Games 1928–1956, and also in 1964 and 1980, and by Pakistan, winners in 1960, 1968 and 1984. However their supremacy has been successfully challenged by nations from Europe and Australasia in recent years. Women's hockey was introduced to the Olympics in 1980. The 1988 Olympic champions were Great Britain (men) and Australia (women).

Dimensions: ball circumference 223–224 cm (*8³⁄₁₆–9½ in*) and weight 155–163 g (*5½–5¾ oz*); pitch length 91·44 m (*100 yd*); width 50–55 m (*55–60 yd*).

HORSE RACING

Early organized racing appears to have been confined to chariots – Roman riders had a foot on each of two horses. The first horse-back racing was by the Greeks in the 33rd Ancient Olympiad in 648 BC. The first recognizable race meeting was held at Smithfield, London in 1174, whilst the first known prize money was a purse of gold presented by Richard I in 1195.

The Jockey Club is now the governing body of flat racing, steeplechasing and hurdle racing, having merged with the National Hunt Committee in 1968. The flat racing season in England takes place between late March and early November. Thoroughbreds may not run until they are two years old. The five classic races are the Two Thousand Guineas and the One Thousand Guineas (Newmarket, 1600 m (one mile)), the Derby and the Oaks (Epsom, 2400 m (1½ miles)) and the St Leger (Doncaster, 2800 m (1¾ miles)).

Steeplechase and hurdle races are run over distances of 2 or more miles, with at least one ditch and six birch fences for every mile. The National Hunt season can last from early August to 1st June, and the two most important steeplechases are the Grand National, first run in 1839, at Aintree over a course of 7220 m (4 miles 856 yd) with 30 jumps, and the Gold Cup run over 5·2 km (3¼ miles) at Cheltenham.

The premier hurdle race is the Champion Hurdle, held annually over 3·2 km (2 miles) at Cheltenham.

Recent winners of major races, with jockey in brackets

The Derby
1980 Henbit (W. Carson)
1981 Shergar (W. Swinburn)
1982 Golden Fleece (Pat Eddery)
1983 Teenoso (L. Piggott)
1984 Secreto (C. Roche)
1985 Slip Anchor (S. Cauthen)
1986 Shahrastani (W. Swinburn)
1987 Reference Point (S. Cauthen)
1988 Kahyasi (R. Cochrane)

Grand National
1980 Ben Nevis (C. Fenwick)
1981 Aldaniti (R. Champion)
1982 Grittar (R. Saunders)
1983 Corbiere (B. De Haan)
1984 Hallo Dandy (N. Doughty)
1985 Last Suspect (H. Davies)
1986 West Tip (R. Dunwoody)
1987 Maori Venture (S. Knight)
1988 Rhyme N'Reason (B. Powell)
1989 Little Polveir (J. Frost)

HURLING
An ancient game that has been played in Ireland since pre-Christian times, but standardized only since the founding of the Gaelic Athletic Association in 1884. The hurl, or stick, is similar to a hockey stick only flat on both sides. All-Ireland Championships have been held since 1887.

ICE HOCKEY
A game similar to hockey on ice was played in Holland in the early 16th century, but the birth of modern ice hockey took place in Canada, probably at Kingston, Ontario in 1885. Rules were first formulated by students of McGill University in Montreal who first formed a club, in 1880.

The International Ice Hockey Federation was formed in 1908, and World and Olympic Championships inaugurated in 1920. The USSR have won seven of the last eight Olympic titles. The major professional competition is the National Hockey League (NHL) in North America, founded in 1917, whose teams contest the Stanley Cup.

Teams are 6-a-side; the ideal rink size is 61 m (200 ft) long and 26 m (85 ft) wide.

ICE AND SAND YACHTING
Ice, sand and land yachting require, in basic form, a wheeled chassis beneath a sailing dinghy. Dutch ice yachts date to 1768, but ice yachting today is mainly in North America. Land and sand yachts of Dutch construction go back even further to 1595. The sports are governed by the International Federation of Sand and Land Yacht Clubs who recognize speed records. International championships were first staged in 1914.

ICE SKATING
Second century Scandinavian literature refers to ice skating, although archaeological evidence points to origins ten centuries earlier. The first English account is dated 1180, while the first club, the Edinburgh Skating Club, was formed around 1742. Steel blades, allowing precision skating, were invented in America in 1850. The International Skating Union was founded in the Netherlands in 1892.

Competitively, ice skating is divided into figure skating, speed skating and ice dancing. Figure skating has been an Olympic event since the Winter Games were first organized in 1924, but there were also events at the 1908 and 1920 Games. Ice dancing was not included until 1976.

The first international speed skating competition was in Hamburg, Germany, in 1885, with World Championships officially dated from 1893. Included for men in the 1924 Olympics, women's events were included in 1960.

JUDO
Developed from a mixture of pre-Christian Japanese fighting arts, the most popular of which was ju-jitsu which is thought to be of ancient Chinese origin. 'Ju' means 'soft', i.e. the reliance on speed and skill as opposed to 'hard' brute force. Judo is a modern combat sport first devised in 1882 by Dr Jigoro Kano. Today, students are graded by belt colours from white to black, the 'master' belts. Grades of black belts are 'Dans', the highest attainable being Tenth Dan.

The International Judo Federation was founded in 1951; World Championships were first held in Tokyo in 1956, with women competing from 1980. Included in the Olympics since 1964 (except 1968), there are currently eight weight divisions. Points are scored by throws, locks on joints, certain pressures on the neck, and immobilizations. Women's judo was held as a demonstration sport at the 1988 Olympic Games.

KARATE
Literally meaning 'empty hand' fighting, karate is based on techniques devised from the 6th century Chinese art of Shaolin boxing (Kempo), and was developed by an unarmed populace in Okinawa as a weapon against Japanese oppressors c. 1500. Transmitted to Japan in the 1920s by Funakoshi Gichin, the sport was refined and organized with competitive rules.

There are five major styles in Japan: Shotokan, Wado-ryu, Goju-ryu, Shito-ryu and Kyokushinkai, each placing different emphases on speed and power. The military form of Tae Kwon-do is the Korean martial art. Wu shu is a comprehensive term embracing all Chinese martial arts. Kung fu is one aspect of these arts popularized by the cinema. Many forms of the martial arts have gained devotees in Europe and the Americas.

LACROSSE

North American Indians played *baggataway*, and a French clergyman, likening the curved stick to a bishop's crozier, called it *la crosse*. The French may also have named it after their game *Chouler à la crosse*, known in 1381. Certainly in its recognizable form the game had reached Europe by the 1830s, and was introduced into Britain in 1867.

The International Federation of Amateur Lacrosse (AFAL) was founded in 1928, but the game was not standardized sufficiently to hold World Championships until 1967 for men and 1969 for women. Championships are now held every four years. 1986 champions were USA (men) and Australia (women). It was played in the Olympic Games of 1904 and 1908, and was a demonstration sport in 1928, 1932 and 1948.

The game is 10-a-side (12-a-side for women at international level); pitch dimensions 100 × 64 m (*100 × 70 yd*). Ball weight in England 142 g (*5 oz*), circumference (184–203·2 mm (*7¼–8 in*), colour yellow; in USA weight 142–149 g (*5–5¼ oz*), circumference 196·9–203·2 mm (*7¾–8 in*), colour orange or white.

LAWN TENNIS

Lawn tennis evolved from the indoor game of real tennis; 'field tennis' is mentioned in a 1793 magazine; Major Harry Gem founded the first club in Leamington Spa in 1872. The All England Croquet Club added Lawn Tennis to their title in 1877 when they held their first Championships. The United States Lawn Tennis Association (now USLTA) was founded in 1881, the English in 1888. The International (Lawn) Tennis Federation was formed in Paris in March 1913.

The Wimbledon or All England, Championships have since 1877 been regarded as the most important in the world, alongside the US Open, French and Australian Opens. Together these four make up the 'Grand Slam', the elusive distinction of holding all four titles at once. The US Open (instituted 1881) is now held at Flushing Meadows, New York, and the French at Roland Garros, Paris. The Australian Championships, now held at Flinders Park, Melbourne, were first held in 1905.

Men and women today compete in various 'circuits' in the second richest sport in the world to golf. 'Grand Prix' tournaments are scaled according to a standard, with points accumulated to decide world rankings. The international team competition for men is the Davis Cup, won a record 28 times by the USA. Recent winners have been Sweden, 1984, 1985 and 1987, Australia, 1983 and 1986, and West Germany 1988. The Federation Cup, first held in 1963, is the women's equivalent. The USA has a record 12 wins and Australia 7. West Germany won in 1987 and Czechoslovakia in 1988. The Wightman Cup is an annual USA–GB women's contest. Begun in 1923, in 1988 the USA achieved its 50th win in 60 contests.

Tennis was reintroduced to the Olympic Games in 1988, when the winners were men's singles: Miloslav Mecir (CZ), men's doubles: Ken Flach & Robert Seguso (USA), women's singles: Steffi Graf (W. Germany), women's doubles: Pam Shriver & Zina Garrison (USA). Tennis had last been held as an official sport in 1924, although it had been a demonstration sport in 1968 and 1984.

The Wimbledon Championships

Wimbledon, 'The All England Championships', dates back to 1877 when it comprised just one event, the men's singles. Women's singles and men's doubles were introduced in 1884, with women's doubles and mixed doubles becoming full Championship events in 1913.

Championships since 1947

Men's Singles

1947	Jack Kramer (USA)
1948	Bob Falkenburg (USA)
1949	Ted Schroeder (USA)
1950	Budge Patty (USA)
1951	Dick Savitt (USA)
1952	Frank Sedgman (Aus)
1953	Vic Seixas (USA)
1954	Jaroslav Drobny (Cz)
1955	Tony Trabert (USA)
1956	Lew Hoad (Aus)
1957	Lew Hoad (Aus)
1958	Ashley Cooper (Aus)
1959	Alex Olmedo (USA)
1960	Neale Fraser Aus)
1961	Rod Laver (Aus)
1962	Rod Laver (Aus)
1963	Chuck McKinley (USA)
1964	Roy Emerson (Aus)
1965	Roy Emerson (Aus)
1966	Manuel Santana (Spa)
1967	John Newcombe (Aus)
1968	Rod Laver (Aus)
1969	Rod Laver (Aus)
1970	John Newcombe (Aus)
1971	John Newcombe (Aus)
1972	Stan Smith (USA)
1973	Jan Kodes (Cz)
1974	Jimmy Connors (USA)
1975	Arthur Ashe (USA)
1976	Bjorn Borg (Swe)
1977	Bjorn Borg (Swe)
1978	Bjorn Borg (Swe)
1979	Bjorn Borg (Swe)
1980	Bjorn Borg (Swe)
1981	John McEnroe (USA)
1982	Jimmy Connors (USA)
1983	John McEnroe (USA)
1984	John McEnroe (USA)
1985	Boris Becker (W. Germany)
1986	Boris Becker (W. Germany)
1987	Pat Cash (Aus)
1988	Stefan Edberg (Swe)

Women's Singles

1947	Margaret Osborne (USA)
1948	Louise Brough (USA)
1949	Louise Brough (USA)
1950	Louise Brough (USA)
1951	Doris Hart (USA)
1952	Maureen Connolly (USA)
1953	Maureen Connolly (USA)

1954 Maureen Connolly (USA)
1955 Louise Brough (USA)
1956 Shirley Fry (USA)
1957 Althea Gibson (USA)
1958 Althea Gibson (USA)
1959 Maria Bueno (Bra)
1960 Maria Bueno (Bra)
1961 Angela Mortimer (GB)
1962 Karen Susman (USA)
1963 Margaret Smith (Aus)
1964 Maria Bueno (Bra)
1965 Margaret Smith (Aus)
1966 Billie Jean King née Moffitt (USA)
1967 Billie Jean King (USA)
1968 Billie Jean King (USA)
1969 Ann Jones (GB)
1970 Margaret Smith-Court (Aus)
1971 Evonne Goolagong (Aus)
1972 Billie Jean King (USA)
1973 Billie Jean King (USA)
1974 Chris Evert (USA)
1975 Billie Jean King (USA)
1976 Christ Evert (USA)
1977 Virginia Wade (GB)
1978 Martina Navratilova (Cz)
1979 Martina Navratilova (Cz)
1980 Evonne Goolagong-Cawley (Aus)
1981 Chris Evert-Lloyd (USA)
1982 Martina Navratilova (USA)
1983 Martina Navratilova (USA)
1984 Martina Navratilova (USA)
1985 Martina Navratilova (USA)
1986 Martina Navratilova (USA)
1987 Martina Navratilova (USA)
1988 Steffi Graf (W. Germany)

Women's Doubles
1947 Pat Todd & Doris Hart (USA)
1948 Louise Brough & Margaret Osborne-du Pont (USA)
1949 Louise Brough & Margaret Osborne-du Pont (USA)
1950 Louise Brough & Margaret Osborne-du Pont (USA)
1951 Doris Hart & Shirley Fry (USA)
1952 Doris Hart & Shirley Fry (USA)
1953 Doris Hart & Shirley Fry (USA)
1954 Louise Brough & Margaret Osborne-du Pont (USA)
1955 Angela Mortimer & Anne Shilcock (GB)
1956 Angela Buxton (GB) & Althea Gibson (USA)
1957 Althea Gibson & Darlene Hard (USA)
1958 Maria Bueno (Bra) & Althea Gibson (USA)
1959 Jean Arth & Darlene Hard (USA)
1960 Maria Bueno (Bra) & Darlene Hard (USA)
1961 Karen Hantze & Billie Jean Moffitt (USA)
1962 Karen Hantze-Susman & Billie Jean Moffitt (USA)
1963 Maria Bueno (Bra) & Darlene Hard (USA)
1964 Margaret Smith & Lesley Turner (Aus)
1965 Maria Bueno (Bra) & Billie Jean Moffitt (USA)
1966 Maria Bueno (Bra) & Nancy Richey (USA)
1967 Rosemary Casals & Billie Jean King née Moffitt (USA)
1968 Billie Jean King & Rosemary Casals (USA)
1969 Margaret Smith-Court & Judy Tegart (Aus)
1970 Billie Jean King & Rosemary Casals (USA)
1972 Billie Jean King & Rosemary Casals (USA)
1972 Billie Jean King (USA) & Betty Stove (Hol)
1973 Billie Jean King & Rosemary Casals (USA)
1974 Evonne Goolagong (Aus) & Peggy Michel (USA)

1975 Ann Kiyomura (USA) & Kazuko Sawamatsu (Jap)
1976 Chris Evert (USA) & Martina Navratilova (Cz)
1977 Helen Cawley (Aus) & Joanne Russell (USA)
1978 Kerry Reid & Wendy Turnbull (Aus)
1979 Billie Jean King (USA) & Martina Navratilova (Cz)
1980 Kathy Jordan & Anne Smith (USA)
1981 Martina Navratilova (Cz) & Pam Shriver (USA)
1982 Martina Navratilova & Pam Shriver (USA)
1983 Martina Navratilova & Pam Shriver (USA)
1984 Martina Navratilova & Pam Shriver (USA)
1985 Kathy Jordan (USA) & Liz Smylie (Aus)
1986 Martina Navratilova & Pam Shriver (USA)
1987 Claudia Kohde-Kilsch (W. Ger) & Helena Sukova (Cz)
1988 Steffi Graf (W. Ger) & Gabriella Sabatini (Arg)

Men's Doubles
1947 Bob Falkenburg & Jack Kramer (USA)
1948 John Bromwich & Frank Sedgman (Aus)
1949 Ricardo Gonzales & Frank Parker (USA)
1950 John Bromwich & Adrian Quist (Aus)
1951 Ken McGregor & Frank Sedgman (Aus)
1952 Ken McGregor & Frank Sedgman (Aus)
1953 Lew Hoad & Ken Rosewall (Aus)
1954 Rex Hartwig & Mervyn Rose (Aus)
1955 Rex Hartwig & Lew Hoad (Aus)
1956 Lew Hoad & Ken Rosewall (Aus)
1957 Budge Patty & Gardnar Mulloy (USA)
1958 Sven Davidson & Ulf Schmidt (Swe)
1959 Roy Emerson & Neale Fraser (Aus)
1960 Rafael Osuna (Mex) & Dennis Ralston (USA)
1961 Roy Emerson & Neale Fraser (Aus)
1962 Bob Hewitt & Fred Stolle (Aus)
1963 Rafael Osuna & Antonio Palafox (Mex)
1964 Bob Hewitt & Fred Stolle (Aus)
1965 John Newcombe & Tony Roche (Aus)
1966 Ken Fletcher & John Newcombe (Aus)
1967 Bob Hewitt & Frew McMillan (Saf)
1968 John Newcombe & Tony Roche (Aus)
1969 John Newcombe & Tony Roche (Aus)
1970 John Newcombe & Tony Roche (Aus)
1971 Roy Emerson & Rod Laver (Aus)
1972 Bob Hewitt & Frew McMillan (Saf)
1973 Jimmy Connors (USA) & Ilie Nastase (Rom)
1974 John Newcombe & Tony Roche (Aus)
1975 Vitas Gerulaitis & Sandy Mayer (USA)
1976 Brian Gottfried & Raul Ramirez (Mex)
1977 Ross Case & Geoff Masters (Aus)
1978 Bob Hewitt & Frew McMillan (Saf)
1979 John McEnroe & Peter Fleming (USA)
1980 Peter McNamara & Paul McNamee (Aus)
1981 John McEnroe & Peter Fleming (USA)
1982 Peter McNamara & Paul McNamee (Aus)
1983 John McEnroe & Peter Fleming (USA)
1984 John McEnroe & Peter Fleming (USA)
1985 Balazs Taroczy (Hun) & Heinz Gunthardt (Switz)
1986 Joachim Nystrom & Mats Wilander (Sweden)
1987 Ken Flach & Robert Seguso (USA)
1988 Ken Flach & Robert Seguso (USA)

Mixed Doubles
1947 Louise Brough (USA) & John Bromwich (Aus)
1948 Louise Brough (USA) & John Bromwich (Aus)
1949 Sheila Summers & Eric Sturgess (Saf)
1950 Louise Brough (USA) & Eric Sturgess (Saf)
1951 Doris Hart (USA) & Frank Sedgman (Aus)
1952 Doris Hart (USA) & Frank Sedgman (Aus)

1953 Doris Hart & Vic Seixas (USA)
1954 Doris Hart & Vic Seixas (USA)
1955 Doris Hart & Vic Seixas (USA)
1956 Shirley Fry & Vic Seixas (USA)
1957 Darlene Hard (USA) & Mervyn Rose (Aus)
1958 Lorraine Coghlan & Bob Howe (Aus)
1959 Darlene Hard (USA) & Rod Laver (Aus)
1960 Darlene Hard (USA) & Rod Laver (Aus)
1961 Lesley Turner & Fred Stolle (Aus)
1962 Margaret Osborne-du Pont (USA) & Neale Fraser (Aus)
1963 Margaret Smith & Ken Fletcher (Aus)
1964 Lesley Turner & Fred Stolle (Aus)
1965 Margaret Smith & Ken Fletcher (Aus)
1966 Margaret Smith & Ken Fletcher (Aus)
1967 Billie Jean Moffitt-King (USA) & Owen Davidson (Aus)
1968 Margaret Smith-Court & Ken Fletcher (Aus)
1969 Ann Jones (GB) & Fred Stolle (Aus)
1970 Rosemary Casals (USA) & Ilie Nastase (Rom)
1971 Billie Jean King (USA) & Owen Davidson (Aus)
1972 Rosemary Casals (USA) & Ilie Nastase (Rom)
1973 Billie Jean King (USA) & Owen Davidson (Aus)
1974 Billie Jean King (USA) & Owen Davidson (Aus)
1975 Margaret Smith-Court (Aus) & Marty Riessen (USA)
1976 Françoise Durr (Fra) & Tony Roche (Aus)
1977 Greer Stevens & Bob Hewitt (Saf)
1978 Betty Stove (Hol) & Frew McMillan (Saf)
1979 Greer Stevens & Bob Hewitt (Saf)
1980 Tracey Austin & John Austin (USA)
1981 Betty Stove (Hol) & Frew McMillan (Saf)
1982 Anne Smith (USA) & Kevin Curren (Saf)
1983 Wendy Turnbull (Aus) & John Lloyd (GB)
1984 Wendy Turnbull (Aus) & John Lloyd (GB)
1985 Martina Navratilova (USA) & Paul McNamee (Aus)
1986 Kathy Jordan & Ken Flach (USA)
1987 Jo Durie & Jeremy Bates (GB)
1988 Zina Garrison & Sherwood Stewart (USA)

MODERN PENTATHLON AND BIATHLON

In the ancient Olympic Games, the Pentathlon was the most prestigious event. It then consisted of discus, javelin, running, jumping and wrestling. The modern pentathlon, introduced into the Olympics in 1912, consists of riding (an 800 m course with 15 fences, riders do not choose their mounts); fencing (épée), shooting, swimming (300 m freestyle) and finally a cross-country run of 4000 m. Each event is held on a different day, with scaled points awarded for each activity.

L'Union Internationale de Pentathlon Moderne et Biathlon (UIPMB) was founded in 1948. Originally the UIPM, the administration of Biathlon (cross-country skiing and shooting) was added in 1957. Biathlon has been an Olympic event since 1960.

MOTORCYCLE RACING

The earliest motorcycle race was held at Sheen House, Richmond, Surrey in 1897 over a 1·6 km (*1 mile*) oval course. The first international motorcycle-only race (early races had included motorcars) was held in 1905, the International Cup Race, after the same race had been declared void in 1904 following bad organization and underhand intrigues. The new Fédération Internationale des Club Motocyclistes (FCIM) had organized the 1905 event, but has since been succeeded by the Fédération Internationale Motocycliste (FIM).

World Championships were started in 1949 by the FIM, in which competitors gain points from a series of Grand Prix races. Races are currently held for the following classes of bike: 50 cc, 125 cc, 250 cc, 500 cc and sidecars.

In road racing the Isle of Man TT races (Auto-Cycle Union Tourist Trophy), first held in 1907, are the most important series. The 60·72 km (*37·73 miles*) 'Mountain' course, with 264 corners and curves, has been in use since 1911.

In Moto-Cross, or Scrambling, competitors race over rough country including steep climbs and drops, sharp turns, sand, mud and water.

MOTOR RACING

The first known race between automobiles was over 323 km (*201 miles*) in Wisconsin in 1878, but it is generally accepted that the first 'real' race was the Paris–Bordeaux–Paris run of 1178 km (*732 miles*) in 1895. Emile Levassor (Fra), the winner, averaged 24·15 kph (*15·01 mph*). The first closed circuit race was at Rhode Island, 1896; the oldest Grand Prix is the French, inaugurated in 1906.

Competition in the highest bracket, the Formula One, is over the series of Grand Prix races (each usually about 656 km (*200 miles*) in length) held worldwide, scoring points according to placing. The first World Championships were held in 1950, with the Manufacturers' Championships starting in 1958. Formula Two and Three Championships are held for cars with lesser cubic capacities.

Other forms of competition include the Le Mans circuit, a 24-hour race for touring cars; 'rallying' over public roads through several thousands miles, and drag racing, a test of sheer acceleration, most firmly established in USA.

World drivers champions

1950 Giuseppe Farina (Ita)
1951 Juan Manuel Fangio (Arg)
1952 Alberto Ascari (Ita)
1953 Alberto Ascari (Ita)
1954 Juan Manuel Fangio (Arg)
1955 Juan Manuel Fangio (Arg)
1956 Juan Manuel Fangio (Arg)
1957 Juan Manuel Fangio (Arg)
1958 Mike Hawthorn (UK)
1959 Jack Brabham (Aus)
1960 Jack Brabham (Aus)
1961 Phil Hill (USA)
1962 Graham Hill (UK)
1963 Jim Clark (UK)
1964 John Surtees (UK)
1965 Jim Clark (UK)
1966 Jack Brabham (Aus)
1967 Denny Hulme (NZ)
1968 Graham Hill (UK)
1969 Jackie Stewart (UK)
1970 Jochen Rindt (Aut)
1971 Jackie Stewart (UK)
1972 Emerson Fittipaldi (Bra)
1973 Jackie Stewart (UK)
1974 Emerson Fittipaldi (Bra)
1975 Niki Lauda (Aut)
1976 James Hunt (UK)
1977 Niki Lauda (Aut)
1978 Mario Andretti (USA)
1979 Jody Scheckter (Saf)

Ayrton Senna (Brazilian) in the very successful McLaren Honda in 1988. (All-Sport)

1980 Alan Jones (Aus)
1981 Nelson Piquet (Bra)
1982 Keke Rosberg (Fin)
1983 Nelson Piquet (Bra)
1984 Niki Lauda (Aut)
1985 Alain Prost (Fra)
1986 Alain Prost (Fra)
1987 Nelson Piquet (Bra)
1988 Ayrton Senna (Bra)

NETBALL
Modern netball grew out of basketball, and reached England in 1895, having been invented in America in 1891. Rings instead of baskets date to 1897, and the term netball was coined in 1901 in England. National Associations date to 1924 and 1926 in New Zealand and England; the International Federation was formed in 1960. World Championships are held every four years, since 1963, with the most recent winners being Australia in 1983 and New Zealand in 1987.

Netball is no-contact, 7-a-side and played almost exclusively by females. The court measures 30·48 × 15·24 m (*100 × 50 ft*); ball circumference 68–71 cm (*27–28 in*), weight 397–454 g (*14–16 oz*).

ORIENTEERING
'Orienteering' was first used to describe an event held in Oslo in 1900, based on military exercises, but the founding of the modern sport is credited to Major Ernst Killander (Swe) in 1918.

Basically a combination of cross-country running and map-reading, the sport is very popular in Scandinavia and has a keen band of followers in Britain. The International Orienteering Federation was founded in 1961, with World Championships from 1966, largely dominated by Sweden and Norway.

PELOTA VASCA (Jaï Alaï)
The sport, which originated in Italy as *longue paume* and was introduced into France in the 13th century, is said to be the fastest of all ball games. Various forms of pelota are played according to national character or local custom throughout the world. 'Gloves' and 'chisteras' (curved frames attached to a glove) are of varying sizes, and courts can be open or enclosed with wide differences in dimensions and detail. The Federacion Internacional de Pelota Vasca has staged World Championships every four years since 1952.

PÉTANQUE
Pétanque, or *boules*, originated in France from its parent game Jeu Provençal, where it is still immensely popular. Origins go back over 2000 years, but it was not until 1945 that the Fédération Français de Pétanque et Jeu Provençal was formed, and subsequently the Fédération Internationale (FIPJP).

POLO
Thought to be of Persian origin, having been played as *Pulu c.* 525. Brought to England from India in 1869. Teams are 4-a-side, mounted on horses of any type.

POWERBOAT RACING
Steamboat races date from 1827, petrol engines from 1865, but actual powerboat racing started in about 1900. International racing was largely established by the presentation of a Challenge Trophy by Sir Alfred Harmsworth in 1903, heralding thereafter 'circuit' or shorter course competition (America has been the most prominent winner of the trophy). Offshore events for (planing) cruises began in 1958, and speed records are recognized in various categories by the various governing bodies.

REAL TENNIS

Evolved from the game *jau de paume* ('game of the palm') played in French monasteries in the 11th century, using the hands. The long-handled racket was not invented until about 1500. The world championship at real tennis is the oldest world championship of any sport, dating to approximately 1740. Today, real tennis is only played in five countries – England, Scotland, USA, France and Australia and the total number of courts in use throughout the world has dwindled to approximately 30.

ROLLER SKATING

The first roller skate was devised by Jean-Joseph Merlin of Belgium in 1760, but proved disastrous in demonstration. The present four-wheeled type was patented by New Yorker James L. Plimpton in 1863. Competition is along similar lines to ice skating – speed, figure and dance.

ROWING

A literary reference to rowing is made by the Roman poet Virgil in the *Aeneid*, published after his death in 19 BC; regattas were held in Venice *c.* AD 300. The earliest established sculling race is the Doggett's Coat and Badge, first rowed in August 1716 from London Bridge to Chelsea, and still contested annually.

The governing body, the Fédération Internationale de Sociétés d'Aviron was founded in 1892, with the first major international meeting, the European Championships, held a year later.

Olympic Championships were first held in 1900 for men and 1976 for women. Current events are held for: (men) single, double and coxless quadruple sculls, coxless and coxed pairs, coxless and coxed fours and eights; (women) single and double sculls, coxless pairs, coxless quadruple sculls, coxed fours and eights. With sculling, the sculler has a smaller oar in each hand rather than pulling one oar with both hands.

The Oxford-Cambridge Boat Race was first held in 1829, from Hambledon Lock to Henley Bridge, and won by Oxford. The current course, used continuously since 1864, is from Putney to Mortlake and measures 6·779 km (*4 miles 374 yd*). To 1989, there has been only one dead heat, in 1877.

RUGBY LEAGUE

The game originated as a breakaway from Rugby Union on 29 August 1895, on account of the governing body forbidding northern clubs paying players, who thus lost Saturday wages. Three years later full professionalism came into being. In 1906 the major change from 15-a-side to 13 was made, and the title 'Rugby League' was created in 1922.

Rugby League is played principally in Great Britain, Australia, New Zealand and France. Major trophies in England are the Challenge Cup (inst. 1897), the League Championship (inst. 1907), the Premiership Trophy (inst. 1975) and the John Player Trophy (inst. 1972). Australia won the World Cup in 1988.

Dimensions: Pitch length maximum 100·58 m (*110 yd*), width maximum 68·58 m (*75 yd*). Ball length 27·3–29·2 cm (*10¾–11½ in*), circumference at widest point 584–610 mm (*23–24 in*).

RUGBY UNION

Developed at Rugby School, England. A traditional yarn tells of William Webb Ellis illegally picking up the ball and running with it during a football game, although this may be apocryphal. Certainly the game was known to have been played at Cambridge University by 1839. The Rugby Football Union was formed on 27 January 1871.

The International Rugby Football Board was formed in 1890. Teams representing the British Isles have toured Australia, New Zealand and South Africa since 1888, although they were not composed of players from all the Home Countries until 1924, when the term 'British Lions' was first coined.

The International Championship – between England, Ireland, Scotland, and Wales – was first held in 1884, with France included from 1910. Now also known as the Five Nations tournament, the 'Grand Slam' is prized for winning all four matches. The 'Triple Crown' is achieved for a Home Countries side defeating the other three.

The first World Cup was contested by 16 national teams in Australia and New Zealand in 1987. In the final New Zealand beat France 29–9.

The game is 15-a-side. Dimensions: pitch of maximum 68·58 m (*75 yd*) width, and 91·44 m (*100 yd*) between goal lines. Ball length 27·9–28·5 cm (*10¾–11½ in*) and weight 382–439 g (*13½–15½ oz*).

SHINTY

Shinty (from the Gaelic *sinteag*, a bound) goes back some 2000 years to Celtic history and legend, to the ancient game of *camanachd*, the sport of the curved stick. Having been introduced by the invading Irish Gaels it kept close associations with hurling but is essentially native to Scotland. The governing body, the Camanachd Association, was set up in 1893.

SHOOTING

The first recorded club for gun enthusiasts was the Lucerne Shooting Guild in Switzerland, dating from *c.* 1466, and the first known shooting match took place in Zürich in 1472. The National Rifle Association in Britain was founded in 1860; the Clay Pigeon Shooting Association developed from trap shooting in the USA and descended from the Inanimate Bird S.A. Skeet shooting is a form of clay pigeon designed to simulate a range of bird game and was invented in the USA in 1915. Pistol events, like air rifle, are judged by accuracy in scoring on a fixed target, from various distances and positions.

Shooting events for men were held in the first modern Olympic Games in 1896, but the 1984 Games included two mixed events (men and women) for the first time. Only two other Olympic sports have mixed competition, equestrianism and yachting.

At the 1988 Olympics there were seven men's, four women's and two mixed events.

SKIING

A well preserved ski found in Sweden is thought to be 4500 years old, and various other evidence from Russia and Scandinavia chronicles primitive skiing, but the modern sport did not develop until 1843 with a competition in Tromsø, Norway. The first modern slalom was held at Murren, Switzerland in 1922. The International Ski Federation (FIS) was founded in 1924.

Alpine skiing is racing on prepared slopes, against the clock, whereas Nordic skiing is either cross-country or ski jumping. Alpine world championships date to 1931, and have been included in the Olympics since 1936, as a combination event, but events are now split into Slalom, Giant Slalom and Downhill. Nordic events date to the 1924 Olympics, and include a combination event of cross-country and jump.

The world's best skiers contest a series of events each winter for the World Cups in Alpine skiing and the Nordic events of cross-country and ski jumping.

SNOOKER
Colonel Sir Neville Chamberlain concocted the game of snooker as a cross between 'Black Pool', 'Pyramids' and billiards, in 1875 at Madras, India. The term 'Snooker' came from the nickname given to first-year cadets at the Royal Military Academy, Woolwich. The game reached England in 1885 via world billiards champion, John Roberts who had been introduced to snooker in India.

Rules were codified in 1919, and the World Professional Championship instituted in 1927. Since 1970 the professional game has been controlled by the World Professional Billiards and Snooker Association.

A full size table measures 3·66 × 1·87 m (*12 × 6 ft*); ball values are: red (1), yellow (2), green (3), brown (4), blue (5), pink (6) and black (7).

Recent world champions:
1980 Cliff Thorburn (Can)
1981 Steve Davis (Eng)
1982 Alex Higgins (NI)
1983 Steve Davis (Eng)
1984 Steve Davis (Eng)
1985 Dennis Taylor (NI)
1986 Joe Johnson (Eng)
1987 Steve Davis (Eng)
1988 Steve Davis (Eng)
1989 Steve Davis (Eng)

SOFTBALL
Softball, the indoor derivative of baseball, was invented by George Hancock in Chicago, USA in 1887, and rules were first codified in Minnesota in 1895. The name softball was not adopted until 1930. A 9-a-side game (except in the USA) softball is played in Canada, Japan, the Philippines, most of Latin America, New Zealand and Australia. The ball is as hard as a baseball, but as distinct from baseball must be pitched underarm and released below hip level. The pitching distance is 14 m (*45 ft 11 in*) for men, 11·11 m (*36 ft 5½ in*) for women and 18·3 m (*60 ft ½ in*) between bases for both. 'Slow pitch' softball is a modern variation.

SPEEDWAY
Motorcycle racing on dust track surfaces has been traced back to 1902 in the USA, but the first 'short track' races were in Australia in 1923. Evolving in Britain in the 1920s, the National League was instituted in 1932. The first World Championships were held in September 1936 at Wembley under the auspices of the Fédération Internationale Motocycliste (FIM). A team competition was inaugurated only as late as 1960. Each race is contested by four riders (six in Australia) over four laps; the bikes have no brakes, one gear and are limited to 500 cc.

SQUASH
Squash developed at Harrow School, England in 1817 from a game used for practising rackets but

substituted a softer, 'squashy' ball. There was no recognized champion of any country however until 1907 in the USA. A rapidly growing game in modern times, World Open Championships have been held since 1976, and since 1979 the ISRF (International Squash Rackets Federation), previously for amateurs only, has been open to all players and includes a team event won always by either Australia, Great Britain or Pakistan. The British Open has been held since 1922 for women and 1930 for men.

Court dimensions: 9·75 m (*31 ft 11¾ in*) long and 6·40 m (*21 ft*) wide, with front wall height 4·75 m (*15 ft 7 in*) up to the boundary line. The 'tin' runs along the bottom of the front wall, above which the ball must be hit.

SURFING
Originating in Polynesia, the first reference to surfing on a board dates to 1779 by a Naval Officer in Hawaii. Revived in the early 20th century in Australia, hollow boards were introduced in 1929. World Amateur Championships began in 1964.

SWIMMING
Competitive swimming dates to 36 BC in Japan, the first country to seriously adopt the sport, Emperor G-Yozei decreeing its introduction in schools. In Britain, organized competitive swimming was only introduced in 1837 when the National Swimming Society was formed. Australia led modern developments with an unofficial world 100 yd championship in 1858 at Melbourne.

The first widely-used technique (possibly excepting the 'doggy paddle') was the breaststroke. From this developed the side-stroke, a similar action performed sideways, last used by an Olympic Champion, Emil Rausch (Ger) to win the 1904 one mile event. A style resembling the front crawl had been seen in various parts of the world by travellers in the mid-19th century. Backstroke developed as inverted breaststroke, which modified towards inverted crawl. Butterfly began as an exploitation of a loophole in the rules for breaststroke allowing the recovery of arms from the water, and was recognized as a separate stroke in 1952. The medley event, using all four strokes in turn, came from America in the 1930s.

The world governing body for swimming, diving, water polo and synchronized swimming is the Fédération Internationale de Natation Amateur (FINA), founded in 1908. World Championships in swimming were first held in 1973, and are now held quadrennially.

Swimming has been an integral part of the Olympics since 1896, the first modern Olympic Games, with 100 m, 400 m, 1500 m and 100 m (sailors) freestyle events for men. Women first competed in 1912. Diving was introduced in 1904 (1912 for women), and water polo in 1900.

Synchronized swimming, a form of water ballet, was first recognized internationally in 1952 and was included in the first World Championships in 1973. It appeared in the Olympics for the first time in 1984.

Swimming world records
Men
50 m freestyle: 22·14 Matt Biondi (USA) 1988
100 m freestyle: 48·42 Matt Biondi (USA) 1988
200 m freestyle: 1:47·25 Duncan Armstrong (Aus) 1988

400 m freestyle: 3:46·95 Uwe Dassler (GDR) 1988
800 m freestyle: 7:50·64 Vladimir Salnikov (USSR) 1986
1500 m freestyle: 14:54·76 Vladimir Salnikov (USSR) 1983
4 × 100 m freestyle: 3:16·53 USA 1988
(Chris Jacobs, Troy Dalbey, Tom Jager, Matt Biondi)
4 × 200 m freestyle: 7:12·51 USA 1988
(Troy Dalbey, Matt Cetlinski, Doug Gjertsen, Matt Biondi)
100 m backstroke: 54·51 David Berkoff (USA) 1988
200 m backstroke: 1:58·14 Igor Polyanskiy (USSR) 1985
100 m breaststroke: 1:01·65 Steven Lundquist (USA) 1984
200 m breaststroke: 2:13·34 Victor Davis (Can) 1984
100 m butterfly: 52·84 Pablo Morales (USA) 1986
200 m butterfly: 1:56·24 Michael Gross (FRG) 1986
200 m individual medley: 2:00·17 Tamas Darnyi (Hun) 1988
400 m individual medley: 4:14·75 Tamas Darnyi (Hun) 1988
4 × 100 m medley: 3:36·93 USA 1988
(David Berkoff, Richard Schroeder, Matt Biondi, Chris Jacobs)

Women
50 m freestyle: 24·98 Yang Wenyi (Chn) 1988
100 m freestyle: 54·73 Kristin Otto (GDR) 1986
200 m freestyle: 1:57·55 Heike Friedrich (GDR) 1986
400 m freestyle: 4:03·85 Janet Evans (USA) 1988
800 m freestyle: 8:17·12 Janet Evans (USA) 1988
1500 m freestyle: 15:52·10 Janet Evans (USA) 1988
4 × 100 m freestyle: 3:40·57 GDR 1986
(Kristin Otto, Manuela Stellmach, Sabina Schulz, Heike Friedrich)
4 × 200 m freestyle: 7:55·47 GDR 1987
(Manuela Stellmach, Astrid Strauss, Anke Möhring, Heike Friedrich)
100 m backstroke: 1:00·59 Ines Kleber (GDR) 1984
200 m backstroke: 2:08·60 Betsy Mitchell (USA) 1986
100 m breaststroke: 1:07·91 Silke Hörner (GDR) 1987
200 m breaststroke: 2:26·71 Silke Hörner (GDR) 1988
100 m butterfly: 57·93 Mary T. Meagher (USA) 1981
200 m butterfly: 2:05·96 Mary T. Meagher (USA) 1981
200 m individual medley: 2:11·73 Ute Geweniger (GDR) 1981
400 m individual medley: 4:36·10 Petra Schneider (GDR) 1982
4 × 100 m medley: 4:03·69 GDR 1984
(Ina Kleber, Sylvia Gerasch, Ines Geissler, Birgit Meineke)

Swimming Olympic records
Men
50 m freestyle: 22·14 Matt Biondi (USA) 1988
100 m freestyle: 48·63 Matt Biondi (USA) 1988
200 m freestyle: 1:47·25 Duncan Armstrong (Aus) 1988
400 m freestyle: 3:46·95 Uwe Dassler (GDR) 1988
1500 m freestyle: 14:58·27 Vladimir Salnikov (USSR) 1980
4 × 100 m freestyle: 3:16·53 USA 1988
4 × 200 m freestyle: 7:12·51 USA 1988
100 m backstroke: 54·51 David Berkoff (USA) 1988*
200 m backstroke: 1:58·99 Rick Carey (USA) 1984
100 m breaststroke: 1:01·65 Steven Lundquist (USA) 1984
200 m breaststroke: 2:13·34 Victor Davis (Can) 1984
100 m butterfly: 53·00 Anthony Nesty (Surinam) 1988
200 m butterfly: 1:56·94 Michael Gross (FRG) 1988
* in heat

200 m individual medley: 2:00·17 Tamas Darnyi (Hun) 1988
400 m individual medley: 4:14·75 Tamas Darnyi (Hun) 1988
4 × 100 m medley: 3:36·93 USA 1988

Women
50 m freestyle: 25·49 Kristin Otto (GDR) 1988
100 m freestyle: 54·79 Barbara Krause (GDR) 1980
200 m freestyle: 1:57·65 Heike Friedrich (GDR) 1988
400 m freestyle: 4:03·85 Janet Evans (USA) 1988
800 m freestyle: 8:20·20 Janet Evans (USA) 1988
4 × 100 m freestyle: 3:40·63 GDR 1988
100 m backstroke: 1:00·89 Kristin Otto (GDR) 1988
200 m backstroke: 2:09·29 Krisztina Egerszegi (Hun) 1988
100 m breaststroke: 1:07·95 Tania Dangalakova (Bul) 1988
200 m breaststroke: 2:26·71 Silke Hörner (GDR) 1988
100 m butterfly: 59·00 Kristin Otto (GDR) 1988
200 m butterfly: 2:06·90 Mary T. Meagher (USA) 1984
200 m individual medley: 2:12·64 Tracy Caulkins (USA) 1984
400 m individual medley: 4:36·29 Petra Schneider (GDR) 1980
4 × 100 m medley: 4:03·74 GDR 1988

TABLE TENNIS

Earliest evidence of a game resembling table tennis goes back to London sports goods manufacturers in the 1880s. Known as *gossima*, it was the introduction of the celluloid ball and the noise it made when hit that brought the name 'ping pong' and the Ping Pong Association in 1902. Interest declined until the use of attached rubber mats to the wooden bats (allowing spin) in the early 1920s. The International Table Tennis Association was founded in 1926, with World Championships held since 1927. The Swaythling and Corbillon Cups are held as world team championships, instituted in 1927 and 1934 for men and women respectively. China has been particularly dominant in recent years. Dimensions: ball diameter 37·2–38·2 mm (*1·46–1·5 in*), weight 2·4–2·53 g (*0·08 oz*), table length 2·74 m (*9 ft*), 1·525 m (*5 ft*) wide.

TRAMPOLINING

Equipment similar to today's trampoline was used by a show business group, 'The Walloons', just prior to World War I. The word originates from the Spanish *trampolin*, a springboard, and indeed springboards date to circus acrobats of the Middle Ages. The birth of the sport follows the invention of the prototype 'T' type by the American, George Nissen in 1936. World Championships, administered by the International Trampolining Association, were instituted in 1964 and held biennially since 1968.

VOLLEYBALL

Although an Italian game *pallone* was played in the 16th century, the modern game was invented as *Minnonette* in 1895 by William Morgan at Massachusetts, USA, as a game for those who found basketball too strenuous. The name volleyball came a year later. The game spread rapidly worldwide and reached Britain in 1914. The first international tournament was the inaugural European

Championship in 1948, the year after the founding of the International Volleyball Federation, whose membership reached 175 nations in 1989. USA, volleyball was not included in the Olympics until 1964. The USA won the 1984 and 1988 men's titles as well as the 1986 world title, and the USSR won the 1988 Olympic title for women, after China had won the 1984 Olympic and 1986 world titles.

Court dimensions are 18 × 9 m (89 ft 0¾ × 29 ft 6⅜ in); ball circumference 65–67 cm (25¹⁹⁄₃₂–26⅜ in), 250–260 g (8·85–9·9 oz) in weight. Net height is 2·43 m (7 ft 11¾ in) for men and 2·24 m (7 ft 4¼ in) for women.

WALKING
Walking races have been included in the Olympic events since 1906 but walking matches have been known since 1859. Walking as a sport is defined as 'progression by steps so that unbroken contact with the ground is maintained'. Road walking has become more prevalent than track walking, and the men's Olympic distances are currently 20 km and 50 km.

WATER SKIING
Water skiing as we now know it was pioneered by Ralph Samuelson (USA) on Lake Pepin, Minnesota in 1922. Having tried and failed with snow skis, he gave exhibitions with pine board skis culminating in the first jump, off a greased ramp, in 1925. The Union Internationale de Ski Nautique was set up in July 1946 and the British Water Ski Federation was formed in 1954.

Competitively, the sport is divided into trick skiing, slalom and ski jumping. (Trick skiing, performed at lower speeds, involves gymnastic feats rewarded according to difficulty.) The World Championships, begun in 1947 and held biennially, include an overall title, in which the USA have figured prominently in recent years, both for men and women.

Skiing barefoot brought a new element to the sport and competitions are held for straight speed records.

WEIGHTLIFTING
In China during the Chou Dynasty, which ended in 249 BC, weightlifting became a necessary military test, and as an exercise could date as far back as 3500 BC. Competitions for lifting weights of stone were held in the ancient Olympic Games. The amateur sport, however, is of modern vintage with competitions dating to c. 1850 and the first championship termed 'world' to 1891. The International Weightlifting Federation was established in 1920, and its first official championships held in 1922 in Estonia.

Weightlifting was included in the first modern Olympics in 1896, and then from 1920. In 1988 there were ten weight divisions, from up to 52 kg to over 110. Competition is decided by aggregate of two forms of lifting, the snatch and the clean and jerk. A third form, the press, was dropped in 1976 because of the difficulty in judging it. The Eastern bloc, especially the USSR and Bulgaria, has dominated the sport in which world records have, in recent years, been broken more frequently than in any other.

Women's weightlifting world championships were held in 1987.

Powerlifting involves different techniques which perhaps have greater emphasis on sheer strength rather than technique. The three basic lifts are the squat (or deep knee bend), bench press and dead lift. The International Powerlifting Federation was founded in 1972, with the USA recently dominant as world record holders in 9 of the 11 weight divisions for men stretching to 125+ kg and 7 of the 10 women's weight divisions to 90+ kg.

WRESTLING
One of the oldest sports in the world, organized wrestling may date to c. 2750–2600 BC; certainly it was the most popular sport in the ancient Olympic Games, and victors were recorded from 708 BC. Wrestling developed in varying forms in different countries, with the classical Greco-Roman style popular in Europe, and free style more to the liking of countries in the East and the Americas. The main distinction is that in Greco-Roman style the wrestler cannot seize his opponent below the hips nor grip with the legs. The International Amateur Wrestling Federation (FILA) also recognizes Sambo wrestling, akin to judo and popular in the USSR. FILA was founded in 1912, although the sport was in the first modern Olympics in 1896. There are currently ten weight divisions in both free-style and Greco-Roman events at the Games.

Sumo wrestling is a traditional form in Japan dating to 23 BC. Conducted with ceremony and mysticism, weight and bulk are vital since the object is to force the opponent out of the circular ring, using any hold.

YACHTING
Yachting dates to the race for a £100 wager between Charles II and his brother James, Duke of York, on the Thames in 1661 from Greenwich to Gravesend and back. The first recorded regatta was held in 1720 by the Cork Harbour Water Club (later Royal Cork Yacht Club), the oldest club, but did not prosper until the seas became safe after the Napoleonic Wars in 1815. That year the Yacht Club (later the Royal Yacht Squadron) was formed and organized races at Cowes, Isle of Wight, the beginning of modern yacht racing. The International Yacht Racing Union (IYRU) was established in 1907.

There were seven classes of boat at the 1988 Olympic Games, one of which, the 470, had separate competitions for men and women. Other major competitions include the Admiral's Cup, a biennial inter-nation, 200 mile Channel and inshore race from Cowes to Fastnet Rock, Ireland and back to Plymouth, and the Whitbread Round the World Race, instituted in 1973 and quadrennial. The America's Cup was originally won as an outright prize by the schooner *America* on 22 August 1851 at Cowes and later offered by the New York Yacht Club as a challenge trophy. Since 1870 the Cup has been challenged by Great Britain in 16 contests, by Canada in two, Australia eight and New Zealand one, but the USA were undefeated until 1983 when *Australia II* defeated the American boat *Liberty*. However Denis Conner in *Stars & Stripes* regained the Cup over *Kookaburra III* (Australia) in 1987 and defended it against New Zealand in 1988. The latter victory was, however, annulled by a decision of the US Supreme Court Justice, Carmen Ciparick in 1989.

Speed in sport

kph	mph	Record	Name	Place	Date
1190·377	739·666	Highest land speed – unofficial	Stan Barrett (USA) in *Budweiser Rocket*	Edwards Air Force Base, California, USA	17 Dec 1979
1019·467	633·468	Highest land speed (official one mile record, jet powered)	Richard Noble (UK) in *Thrust II*	Black Rock Desert, Nevada, USA	4 Oct 1983
1006	625·2	Parachuting freefall in mesosphere (military research)	Capt. J. W. Kittinger (USA)	Tularosa, New Mexico, USA	16 Aug 1960
690·909	429·311	Highest land speed (wheel driven)	Donald Campbell (UK) in *Bluebird*	Lake Eyre, South Australia	17 July 1964
673·516	418·504	Highest land speed (4-wheel direct drive)	Robert Summers (USA) in *Golden-rod*	Bonneville Salt Flats, Utah, USA	12 Nov 1965
556	345	Highest water borne speed – estimated	Ken Warby (Aus) in *The Spirit of Australia*	Blowering Dam, NSW, Australia	20 Nov 1977
514·39	319·627	Official water speed record	Ken Warby (Aus) in *The Spirit of Australia*	Blowering Dam, NSW, Australia	8 Oct 1978
513·165	318·866	Highest speed motor cycle	Don Vesco (USA)	Bonneville Salt Flats, Utah	28 Aug 1978
403·878	250·958	Motor Racing – closed circuit	Dr Hans Liebold (FRG)	Nardo, Italy	5 May 1979
368·52	229	Hydroplane record (propeller driven)	Eddie Hill (USA)	Lake Irvine, California	5 June 1983
363·911	262·138	Motor Racing – race lap record	Rick Mears (USA)	Indianapolis (USA)	14 May 1989
302·5	188	Pelota (Fastest ball game)	Jose Areitio	Newport, Rhode Island	3 Aug 1979
273	170	Golf ball	(Electrically timed)	USA	1960
263	163·6	Lawn tennis – serve	Bill Tilden	USA	1931
245·077	152·284	Cycling, motor paced	John Howard (USA)	Bonneville Salt Flats, Utah	20 July 1985
230·26	143·08	Water skiing	Christopher Massey (Aus)	Hawkesbury River, NSW, Australia	6 Mar 1983
230	143	Ice yacht	John D. Buckstaff (USA)	Lake Winnebago, Wisconsin, USA	1938
223·741	139·030	Alpine skiing – Downhill	Michael Prufer (Monaco)	Les Arcs, France	16 Apr 1988
222	138	Lawn tennis – serve (modern equipment)	Steve Denton (USA)	Colorado, USA	29 July 1984
195	121	Gliding (100 km triangular course)	Ingo Renner (Aus) in a Nimbus 3	Tocumwal, NSW, Australia	14 Dec 1982
192·08	119·36	Water skiing, Barefoot	Scott Pelaton (USA)	Chowchilla, California, USA	4 Sep 1983
190·3	118·3	Ice Hockey – puck slap shot	Bobby Hull (Canada)	Chicago, Illinois, USA	1965
162·3	100·9	Baseball (pitch)	Lynn Nolan Ryan (USA)	Anaheim, California, USA	20 Aug 1974
142·26	88·4	Sand Yacht	Nord Embroden (USA) in *Midnight at the Oasis*	Superior Dry Lake, California, USA	14 Apr 1976
107	66·48	Sand Yacht – official record	Christian-Yves Nau (Fra) in *Mobil*	Le Touquet, France	22 Mar 1981
104·53	64·95	Alpine Skiing – Olympic Downhill course (average)	William Johnson (USA)	Sarajevo, Yugoslavia	16 Feb 1984
85·72	53·27	Tobogganing – Cresta Run (1212·25 m *3977 ft* course in 51·75 sec)	Franco Gansser (Sui)	St Moritz, Switzerland	22 Feb 1987
84·60	52·57	Speedway (4 laps of 393 m *430 yd*)	Scott Autrey	Exeter, England	19 June 1978
74·77	46·46	Boardsailing (in 50 knot wind)	Eric Beale (UK)	Saintes Maries de-la-mer, France	17 Nov 1988
71·849	44·645	Track Cycling (200 m unpaced in 10·021 sec)	Lutz Hesslich (GDR)	Moscow, USSR	22 Aug 1984
69·62	43·26	Horse racing (402 m *440 yd* in 20·8 sec)	Big Racket	Mexico City, Mexico	5 Feb 1945
67·14	41·72	Greyhound racing (374 m *410 yd* straight in 26·13 sec)	The Shoe (Aus)	Richmond, NSW, Australia	25 Apr 1968

kph	mph	Record	Name	Place	Date
66·78	*41·50*	Sailing (36·04 knots) *Crossbow II*	Tim Coleman (UK) in	Portland, Dorset, England	17 Nov 1980
56·42	*35·06*	Horse Racing – The Derby (2·41 km *1 mile 885 yd*)	Mahmoud	Epsom, Surrey, England	27 May 1936
56	*35*	Boxing – speed of punch	Sugar Ray Robinson (USA)	USA	Jan 1957
51·151	*31·784*	Cycling – 1 hour, unpaced	Francesco Moser (Italy)	Mexico City, Mexico	23 Jan 1984
49·68	*30·87*	Speed skating on ice (500 m *564 yd* in 36·23 sec on 400 m *437 yd* rink)	Nick Thometz (USA)	Medeo, USSR	26 Mar 1987
47·96	*29·80*	Steeplechasing – The Grand National (7·280 km *4 miles 856 yd* in 9 min 1·9 sec)	Red Rum ridden by Brian Fletcher	Aintree, Liverpool, England	31 Mar 1973
43·37	*26·95*	Sprinting (during 100 m race)	Carl Lewis (USA) and Ben Johnson (Canada)	Seoul, S. Korea	24 Sep 1988
41·48	*25·78*	Roller skating (402 m *440 yd* in 34·9 sec)	Giuseppe Cantarella (Italy)	Catania, Sicily	28 Sep 1963
22·01	*13·68*	Rowing (2000 m)	USA Eight	Lucerne, Switzerland	17 June 1984
19·98	*12·41*	Canoeing (1000 m in 3 min 00·20 sec)	Hungarian Olympic K4	Seoul, S. Korea	1 Oct 1988
19·96	*12·40*	Marathon run (average over 42·195 km *26 miles 385 yd*)	Belayneh Dinsamo (Ethiopia)	Rotterdam, Holland	17 Apr 1988
15·55	*9·66*	Walking, 1 hour	Josef Pribilinec (Cz)	Hildesheim, W. Germany	6 Sep 1986
8·85	*5·50*	Swimming (25 m) – short course in 10·17 sec	Dano Halsall (Swi)	Hendon, England	24 Feb 1989
8·13	*5·05*	Swimming (50 m) – long course in 22·14 sec	Matthew Biondi (USA)	Seoul, S. Korea	24 Sep 1988
0·00135	*0·00084*	Tug of War (2 hr 41 min pull – 3·6 m *12 ft*)	2nd Derbyshire Regt (UK)	Jubbulpore, India	12 Aug 1889

Human limitations in sport

The basic physiological limitations to human performance in physical achievement embrace the following:

1) No human can survive more than 18 days without food and water.
2) Speed limit for transmission of messages through the nervous system is 228 kph (*180 mph*).
3) No human can survive prolonged blood temperatures above 41°C (*105·8°F*) or below 16°C (*60·8°F*) unharmed.
4) No human (except perhaps some asthmatic children) can detect sounds of a frequency above 20 000 Hz.
5) No human can detect sounds below 2×10 pascal and the most sensitive a frequency below 2750 Hz.
6) The human eye cannot resolve an object smaller than 100 microns at 25·4 cm (*10 in*).
7) Visual stimuli rapidly repeated appear fused or continuous at frequencies between 4 and 60 per second according to the level of luminance.
8) No human can detect a vibration with an amplitude of less than 0·02 micron.
9) The human lung volume or vital capacity at maturity tends to a limit of 5·5 litres with up to 300 million alveoli.
10) The heart, as a pump, has a limited capacity above the normal circulatory volume of 5 to 6 litres per minute of which 60 per cent is liquid plasma.

The Olympic Games

The ancient Olympic Games were staged every four years at Olympia, 120 miles west of Athens. The earliest celebration of which there is a certain record is that of July 776 BC, from which all subsequent Games are dated. However, earlier Games were certainly held, perhaps dating back to 1370 BC. These early Games had considerable religious significance.

The Games grew in size and importance to the height of their fame in the 5th and 4th centuries BC. Events included running, jumping, wrestling, throwing the discus, boxing and chariot racing. They were much more than sporting contests, great artistic festivals upholding the Greek ideal of perfection of mind and body. Winners were awarded a branch of wild olive, the Greeks' sacred tree.

The final Olympic Games of the ancient era were held in AD 393 before the Emperor of Rome, Theodosius I, decreed the prohibition of the Games, which were not favoured by the early Christians and which were then long past their great days.

The first modern Games, in Athens in 1896, were at the instigation of Pierre de Fredi, Baron de Coubertin (1863-1937). A far cry from today's huge organization, just 311 competitors (from 13 countries) took part, of whom 230 were from Greece and others were foreign tourists. By contrast, 160 countries were represented by a total of 9581 athletes at the 1988 Games in Seoul, Korea.

Celebration of the Modern Olympic Games

	Year	Venue	Date	Countries	Competitors Male	Female
I	1896	Athens, Greece	6-15 Apr	13	311	—
II	1900	Paris, France	20 May-28 Oct	22	1319	11
III	1904	St Louis, USA	1 July-23 Nov	13[1]	617	8
*	1906	Athens, Greece	22 Apr-2 May	20	877	7
IV	1908	London, England	27 Apr-31 Oct	22	2013	43
V	1912	Stockholm, Sweden	5 May-22 July	28	2491	55
VI	1916	Berlin, Germany	Not held due to war	—	—	—
VII	1920	Antwerp, Belgium	20 Apr-12 Sept	29	2618	74
VIII	1924	Paris, France	4 May-27 July	44	2956	136
IX	1928	Amsterdam, Netherlands	17 May-12 Aug	46	2724	290
X	1932	Los Angeles, USA	30 July-14 Aug	37	1281	127
XI	1936	Berlin, Germany	1-16 Aug	49	3738	328
XII	1940	Tokyo, then Helsinki	Not held due to war	—	—	—
XIII	1944	London, England	Not held due to war	—	—	—
XIV	1948	London, England	29 July-14 Aug	59	3714	385
XV	1952	Helsinki, Finland	19 July-3 Aug	69	4407	518
XVI	1956[2]	Melbourne, Australia	22 Nov-8 Dec	67	2958	384
XVII	1960	Rome, Italy	25 Aug-11 Sept	83	4738	610
XVIII	1964	Tokyo, Japan	10-24 Oct	93	4457	683
XIX	1968	Mexico City, Mexico	12-27 Oct	112	4749	781
XX	1972	Munich, FRG	26 Aug-10 Sept	122	6086	1070
XXI	1976	Montreal, Canada	17 July-1 Aug	92	4834	1251
XXII	1980	Moscow, USSR	19 July-3 Aug	81	4238	1088
XXIII	1984	Los Angeles, USA	28 July-12 Aug	140	5458	1620
XXIV	1988	Seoul, South Korea	20 Sept-5 Oct	160	6892	2410
XXV	1992	Barcelona, Spain				

* This celebration to mark the tenth anniversary of the Modern Games was officially intercalated but is not numbered.
[1] Including newly discovered French national.
[2] The equestrian events were held in Stockholm, Sweden, 10-17 June with 158 competitors from 29 countries.

Table of Olympic medal winners – Summer Games, 1896-1988

		Gold	Silver	Bronze	Total			Gold	Silver	Bronze	Total
1.	USA	746	560	475	1781	26.	South Korea	19	22	29	70
2.	USSR	395	323	299	1017	27.	China	20	19	21	60
3.	Great Britain	174	223	207	604	28.	Cuba	23	21	15	59
4.	Germany[1]	157	207	207	571	29.	New Zealand	26	6	23	55
5.	France	153	167	177	497	30.	South Africa[3]	16	15	21	52
6.	Sweden	131	139	169	439	31.	Turkey	24	13	10	47
7.	GDR[2]	153	129	127	409	32.	Argentina	13	18	13	44
8.	Italy	147	121	124	392	33.	Mexico	9	12	18	39
9.	Hungary	124	112	136	372	34.	Brazil	7	9	20	36
10.	Finland	97	75	110	282	35.	Kenya	11	9	11	31
11.	Japan	87	75	82	244	36.	Iran	4	11	15	30
12.	Australia	71	67	87	225	37.	Spain	4	12	8	24
13.	Romania	55	64	82	201	38.	Jamaica	4	10	8	22
14.	Poland	40	56	95	191	39.	Estonia[4]	6	6	9	21
15.	Canada	39	62	73	174	40.	Egypt	6	6	6	18
16.	Switzerland	40	66	57	163	41.	India	8	3	3	14
17.	Netherlands	43	47	63	153	42.	Ireland	4	4	5	13
18.	Bulgaria	37	62	52	151	43.	Portugal	2	4	7	13
19.	Denmark	33	58	53	144	44.	North Korea[5]	2	5	5	12
20.	Czechoslovakia	45	48	49	142	45.	Mongolia	0	5	6	11
21.	Belgium	35	48	42	125	46.	Ethiopia	5	1	4	10
22.	Norway	42	33	33	108	47.	Pakistan	3	3	3	9
23.	Greece	22	39	39	100	48.	Uruguay	2	1	6	9
24.	Yugoslavia	26	29	28	83	49.	Venezuela	1	2	5	8
25.	Austria	19	26	34	79	50.	Chile	0	6	2	8

		Gold	Silver	Bronze	Total
51.	Trinidad	1	2	4	7
52.	Philippines	0	1	6	7
53.	Morocco	3	1	2	6
54.	Uganda	1	3	1	5
55.	Tunisia	1	2	2	5
56.	Colombia	0	2	3	5
57.	Lebanon	0	2	2	4
=58.	Puerto Rico	0	1	3	4
=58.	Nigeria	0	1	3	4
60.	Peru	1	2	0	3
61.	Latvia[4]	0	2	1	3
=62.	Taipei	0	1	2	3
=62.	Ghana	0	1	2	3
=62.	Thailand	0	1	2	3
65.	Luxembourg	1	1	0	2
66.	Bahamas	1	0	1	2
67.	Tanzania	0	2	0	2
=68.	Cameroun	0	1	1	2
=68.	Haiti	0	1	1	2
=68.	Iceland	0	1	1	2
=71.	Algeria	0	0	2	2
=71.	Panama	0	0	2	2
=73.	Zimbabwe	1	0	0	1

		Gold	Silver	Bronze	Total
=73.	Surinam	1	0	0	1
=75.	Ivory Coast	0	1	0	1
=75.	Singapore	0	1	0	1
=75.	Sri Lanka	0	1	0	1
=75.	Syria	0	1	0	1
=75.	Costa Rica	0	1	0	1
=75.	Indonesia	0	1	0	1
=75.	Netherlands Antilles	0	1	0	1
=75.	Senegal	0	1	0	1
=75.	Virgin Islands	0	1	0	1
=84.	Bermuda	0	0	1	1
=84.	Dominican Repub.	0	0	1	1
=84.	Guyana	0	0	1	1
=84.	Iraq	0	0	1	1
=84.	Niger	0	0	1	1
=84.	Zambia	0	0	1	1
=84.	Djibouti	0	0	1	1

[1] Germany 1896–1964, West Germany from 1968.
[2] GDR, East Germany, from 1968.
[3] South Africa, up to 1960.
[4] Estonia and Latvia, up to 1936.
[5] North Korea, from 1964.

Celebrations of the Winter Games

	Year	Venue	Date	Countries	Competitors Male	Competitors Female
I*	1924	Chamonix, France	25 Jan–4 Feb	16	281	13
II	1928	St Moritz, Switzerland	11–19 Feb	25	468	27
III	1932	Lake Placid, USA	4–15 Feb	17	274	32
IV	1936	Garmisch-Partenkirchen, Germany	6–16 Feb	28	675	80
V	1948	St Moritz, Switzerland	30 Jan–8 Feb	28	636	77
VI	1952	Oslo, Norway	14–25 Feb	22	623	109
VII	1956	Cortina d'Ampezzo, Italy	26 Jan–5 Feb	32	687	132
VIII	1960	Squaw Valley, USA	18–28 Feb	30	521	144
IX	1964	Innsbruck, Austria	29 Jan–9 Feb	36	893	200
X	1968	Grenoble, France	6–18 Feb	37	1065	228
XI	1972	Sapporo, Japan	3–13 Feb	35	1015	217
XII	1976	Innsbruck, Austria	4–15 Feb	37	900	228
XIII	1980	Lake Placid, USA	13–24 Feb	37	833	234
XIV	1984	Sarajevo, Yugoslavia	7–19 Feb	49	1287	223
XV	1988	Calgary, Canada	23 Feb–6 Mar	57	1226	336

* There were Winter Games events included in the Summer Games of 1908 (London) and 1920 (Antwerp) which attracted six countries, 14 males and seven females for the first, and 10 countries, 73 males and 12 females for the latter.

Table of Olympic medal winners – Winter Games, 1924–88

		Gold	Silver	Bronze	Total
1.	USSR	79	57	59	195
2.	Norway	54	60	54	168
3.	USA	42	47	34	123
4.	GDR[1]	39	36	35	110
5.	Finland	33	43	34	110
6.	Austria	28	38	32	98
7.	Sweden	36	25	31	92
8.	Germany[2]	26	26	23	75
9.	Switzerland	23	25	25	73
10.	Canada	14	13	17	44
11.	Netherlands	13	17	12	42
12.	France	13	10	16	39
13.	Italy	14	10	9	33
14.	Czechoslovakia	2	8	13	23
15.	Great Britain	7	4	10	21

		Gold	Silver	Bronze	Total
16.	Liechtenstein	2	2	5	9
17.	Japan	1	4	2	7
18.	Hungary	0	2	4	6
=19.	Belgium	1	1	2	4
=19.	Poland	1	1	2	4
21.	Yugoslavia	0	3	1	4
22.	Spain	1	0	0	1
23.	North Korea[3]	0	1	0	1
=24.	Bulgaria	0	0	1	1
=24.	Romania	0	0	1	1

Total include all first, second and third places, including those events not on the current schedule.
[1] GDR, East Germany, from 1968.
[2] Germany, 1924–64, West Germany, from 1968.
[3] From 1964.

METROLOGY

In essence, measurement involves *comparison:* the measurement of a physical quantity entails comparing it with an agreed and clearly defined *standard.* The result is expressed in terms of a *unit,* which is the name for a standard, preceded by a number which is the *ratio* of the measured quantity of the appropriate fixed unit.

A *system of units* is centred on a small number of *base units.* These relate to the fundamental standards of length, mass and time, together with a few others to extend the system to a wider range of physical measurements, e.g. to electrical and optical quantities. There are also two geometrical units which belong to a class known as *supplementary units.*

These few base units can be combined to form a large number of *derived units.* For example, units of area, velocity and acceleration are formed from units of length and time. Thus very many different kinds of measurement can be made and recorded employing very few base units.

For convenience, *multiples* and *submultiples* of both base and derived units are frequently used, e.g. kilometres and millimetres.

Historically, several systems of units have evolved: in Britain, the imperial system; in the

United States, the US customary units; and forms of the metric system (CGS for centimetre-gram-second and MKS for metre-kilogram-second), employed universally in science and generally in very many countries of the world.

The International System of Units (Système International d'Unités or SI) is a modern form of the metric system. It was finally agreed at the Eleventh General Conference of Weights and Measures in October 1960 and is now being widely adopted throughout the scientific world.

The imperial system

UNIT DEFINITION

The yard (yd). This is equal to 0·914 4 metre exactly (Weights and Measures Act, 1963).

The pound (lb). This is equal to 0·453 592 37 kilogram exactly (Weights and Measures Act, 1963).

The gallon (gal). The space occupied by 10 pounds weight of distilled water of density 0·998 859 gram per millilitre weighed in air of density 0·001 217 gram per millilitre against weights of density 8·136 gram per millilitre (Weights and Measures Act,

The SI units

BASE UNITS

Quantity	Unit	Symbol	Definition
length	metre	m	the length of the path travelled by light in vacuum during a time interval of 1/299 792 458 of a second.
mass	kilogram	kg	the mass of the international prototype of the kilogram, which is in the custody of the Bureau International des Poids et Mésures (BIPM) at Sèvres near Paris, France.
time	second	s	the duration of 9 192 631 770 periods of the radiation corresponding to the transition between the two hyperfine levels of the ground state of the caesium-133 atom.
electric current	ampere	A	that constant current which, if maintained in two straight parallel conductors of infinite length of negligible circular cross-section, and placed 1 metre apart in vacuum, would produce between these conductors a force equal to 2×10^{-7} newton per metre of length.
thermodynamic temperature	kelvin	K	the fraction 1/273·15 of the thermodynamic temperature of the triple point of water. The triple point of water is the point where water, ice and water vapour are in equilibrium.
luminous intensity	candela	cd	the luminous intensity, in a given direction, of a source that emits monochromatic radiation of frequency 540×10^{12} Hz and has a radiant intensity in that direction of (1/683) watts per steradian.
amount of substance	mole	mol	the amount of substance of a system which contains as many elementary entities as there are atoms in 0·012 kilogram of carbon-12.

SUPPLEMENTARY UNITS

plane angle	radian	rad	the plane angle between two radii of a circle which cut off on the circumference an arc equal in length to the radius.
solid angle	steradian	sr	the solid angle which having its vertex in the centre of a sphere, cuts off an area of the surface of the sphere equal to that of a square having sides of length equal to the radius of the sphere.

1963). The definition of the gallon in the meaning of the 1963 Weights and Measures Act uses the 1901 definition of the litre [1 litre (1901) = 1·000 028 dm³].

OTHER UNITS OF LENGTH EMPLOYED

animal stature	the hand = 4 in. *NB* – a horse of 14 hands 3 in. to the withers is often written 14·3 hands.
surveying	the link = 7·92 in or a hundredth part of a chain.
approximate	the span = 9 in (from the span of the hand).
biblical	the cubit = 18 in.
approximate	the pace = 30 in. (from the stride).
nautical	the cable = 120 fathoms or 240 yd.
navigation	the UK nautical mile = 6080 ft at the Equator.
navigation	the International nautical mile

(adopted also by the USA on 1 July 1954) = 6076·1 ft (0·999 36 of a UK nautical mile).

THE CHANGE TO METRIC

The use of the metric system was legalized in the United Kingdom in 1897. The Halsbury Committee recommended the introduction of decimal currency in September 1963. The intention to switch to the metric system was declared on 24 May 1965 by the President of the Board of Trade 'within ten years'. The date for the official adoption of the metric system was announced on 1 Mar 1966 to be 'February 1971'. On Tuesday 23 Mar 1976, the Government decided not to proceed with the second reading of the Weights and Measures (Metrication) Act.

DERIVED UNITS

Quantity	Unit	Symbol	Expression in terms of other SU units
area	square metre	m^2	—
volume	cubic metre	m^3	—
velocity	metre per second	$m \cdot s^{-1}$	—
angular velocity	radian per second	$rad\,s^{-1}$	—
acceleration	metre per second squared	$m \cdot s^{-2}$	—
angular acceleration	radian per second squared	$rad\,s^{-2}$	—
frequency	hertz	Hz	s^{-1}
density	kilogram per cubic metre	$kg \cdot m^{-3}$	—
momentum	kilogram metre per second	$kg \cdot m \cdot s^{-1}$	—
angular momentum	kilogram metre squared per second	$kg \cdot m^2 \cdot s^{-1}$	—
moment of inertia	kilogram metre squared	$kg \cdot m^2$	—
force	newton	N	$kg \cdot m \cdot s^{-2}$
pressure, stress	pascal	Pa	$N \cdot m^{-2} = kg \cdot m^{-1} \cdot s^{-2}$
work, energy, quantity of heat	joule	J	$N \cdot m = kg \cdot m^2 \cdot s^{-2}$
power	watt	W	$J \cdot s^{-1} = kg \cdot m^2 \cdot s^{-3}$
surface tension	newton per metre	$N \cdot m^{-1}$	$kg \cdot s^{-2}$
dynamic viscosity	newton second per metre squared	$N \cdot s \cdot m^{-2}$	$kg \cdot m^{-1} \cdot s^{-1}$
kinematic viscosity	metre squared per second	$m^2 \cdot s^{-1}$	—
temperature	degree Celsius	°C	—
thermal coefficient of linear expansion	per degree Celsius, or per kelvin	$°C^{-1}, K^{-1}$	—
thermal conductivity	watt per metre degree C	$W \cdot m^{-1} \cdot °C^{-1}$	$kg \cdot m \cdot s^{-3} \cdot °C^{-1}$
heat capacity	joule per kelvin	$J \cdot K^{-1}$	$kg \cdot m^2 \cdot s^{-2} \cdot K^{-1}$
specific heat capacity	joule per kilogram kelvin	$J \cdot kg^{-1} \cdot K^{-1}$	$m^2 \cdot s^{-2} \cdot K^{-1}$
specific latent heat	joule per kilogram	$J\,kg^{-1}$	$m^2 \cdot s^{-2}$
electric charge	coulomb	C	$A \cdot s$
electromotive force, potential difference	volt	V	$W \cdot A^{-1} = kg \cdot m^2 \cdot s^{-3} \cdot A^{-1}$
electric resistance	ohm	Ω	$V \cdot A^{-1} = kg \cdot m^2 \cdot s^{-3} \cdot A^{-2}$
electric conductance	siemens	S	$A \cdot V^{-1} = kg^{-1} \cdot m^{-2} \cdot s^3 \cdot A^2$
electric capacitance	farad	F	$A \cdot s \cdot V^{-1} = kg^{-1} \cdot m^{-2} \cdot s^4 \cdot A^2$
inductance	henry	H	$V \cdot s \cdot A^{-1} = kg \cdot m^2 \cdot s^{-2} \cdot A^{-2}$
magnetic flux	weber	Wb	$V \cdot s = kg \cdot m^2 \cdot s^{-2} \cdot A^{-1}$
magnetic flux density	tesla	T	$Wb \cdot m^{-2} = kg \cdot s^{-2} \cdot A^{-1}$
magnetomotive force	ampere	A	—
luminous flux	lumen	lm	$cd \cdot sr$
illumination	lux	lx	$lm \cdot m^{-2} = cd \cdot sr \cdot m^{-2}$
radiation activity	becquerel	Bq	s^{-1}
radiation absorbed dose	gray	Gy	$J \cdot kg^{-1} = m^2 \cdot s^{-2}$

Metric and Imperial Units and Conversions (= exact)*

Column One	Equivalent	Column Two	To convert Col. 2 to Col. 1 Multiply by	To convert Col. 1 to Col. 2 Multiply by
Length				
inch (in)	—	centimetre (cm)	0·393 700 78	2·54*
foot (ft)	12 in	metre	3·280 840	0·3048*
yard (yd)	3 ft	metre	1·093 61	0·9144*
mile	1760 yd	kilometre (km)	0·621 371 1	1·609 344*

Column One	Equivalent	Column Two	To convert Col. 2 to Col. 1 Multiply by	To convert Col. 1 to Col. 2 Multiply by
fathom	6 ft	metre	0·546 80	1·8288*
chain	22 yd	metre	0·049 70	20·1168*
UK nautical mile	6080 ft	kilometre	0·539 611 8	1·853 184*
International nautical mile	6076·1 ft	kilometre	0·539 956 8	1·852*
angstrom unit (Å)	10^{-10} m	nanometre	10	10^{-1}
Area				
square inch	—	square centimetre	0·155 00	6·4516*
square foot	144 sq in	square metre	10·763 9	0·092 903*
square yard	9 sq ft	square metre	1·195 09	0·836 127*
acre	4840 sq yd	hectare (ha) (10^4 m²)	2·471 05	0·404 686*
square mile	640 acres	square kilometre	0·386 10	2·589 988*
Volume				
cubic inch	—	cubic centimetre	0·061 024	16·387 1*
cubic foot	1728 cu in	cubic metre	35·314 67	0·028 317*
cubic yard	27 cu ft	cubic metre	1·307 95	0·764 555*
Capacity				
litre	100 centilitres	cubic centimetre or millilitre	0·001*	1000*
pint	4 gills	litre	1·759 753	0·568 261
UK gallon	8 pints or 277·4 in³	litre	0·219 969	4·546 092
barrel (for beer)	36 gallons	hectolitre	0·611 026	1·636 59
US gallon	0·832675 UK gallons	litre or dm³	0·264 172	3·785 412
US barrel (for petroleum)	42 US gallons	hectolitre	0·628 998	1·589 83
fluid ounce	0·05 pint	millilitre	0·035 195	28·413 074
Velocity				
feet per second (ft/s)	—	metres per second	3·280 840	0·3048
miles per hour (mph)	—	kilometres per hour	0·621 371	1·609 344
UK knot (1·00064 Int knots)	nautical mile/hour	kilometres per hour	0·539 611 8	1·853 184
Acceleration				
foot per second per second (ft/s²)	—	metres per second per second (m/s²)	3·280 840	0·3048*
Mass				
grain (gr)	a 1/480th of an oz troy	milligram (mg)	0·015 432 4	64·798 91
dram (dr)	27·3438 gr	gram	0·564 383	1·771 85
ounce (avoirdupois)	16 drams	gram	0·035 274 0	28·349 523 125
pound (avoirdupois)	16 ounces	kilogram	2·204 62*	0·453 592 37*
stone	14 pounds	kilogram	0·157 473 04	6·350 293 18*
quarter	28 pounds	kilogram	0·078 737 5	12·700 586 36*
hundredweight (cwt)	112 pounds	kilogram	0·019 684 1	50·802 345 44*
ton (long)	2240 pounds	tonne (= 1000 kg)	0·984 206 5	1·016 046 908 8

Note: A pound troy consists of 12 ounces troy each of 480 grains

Column One	Equivalent	Column Two	To convert Col. 2 to Col. 1 Multiply by	To convert Col. 1 to Col. 2 Multiply by
Density				
pounds per cubic inch	—	grams per cubic centimetre	0·036 127 2	27·6799
pounds per cubic foot	—	kilograms per cubic metre	0·062 428 0	16·0185
Force				
dyne (dyn)	10^{-5} newton	newton	10^5	10^{-5}
poundal (pdl)	—	newton	7·233 01	0·138 255
pound-force (lbf)	—	newton	0·224 809	4·448 22
tons-force	—	kilonewton (kN)	0·100 361	9·964 02
kilogram-force (kgf) (or kilopond)	—	newton	0·101 972	9·806 65
Energy (Work, Heat)				
erg	10^{-7} joule	joule	10^7	10^{-7}
horse-power (hp) (550 ft/lbf/s)	—	kilowatt (kW)	1·341 02	0·745 700
therm	—	mega joule (MJ)	0·009 478 17	105·506
kilowatt hour (kWh)	—	mega Joule (MJ)	0·277 778	3·6
calorie (international)	—	joule	0·238 846*	4·1868*
British thermal unit (Btu)	—	kilo-joule (kJ)	0·947 817	1·055 06
Pressure, Stress				
millibar (mbar or mb)	1000 dynes/cm²	Pa	0·01*	100*
standard atmosphere (atm)	760 torrs	kPa	0·009 869 2	101·325
pounds per square inch (psi)	—	Pa	0·000 145 038	6894·76
pounds per square inch (psi)	—	kilogram-force per cm²	14·223 3	0·070 307 0
Temperature				

Degrees Celcius (Centigrade) converted to Degrees Fahrenheit
Multiply °C by 9/5 and add 32

Degrees C		Degrees F
37	=	98·6
50	=	122
100	=	212

Degrees Fahrenheit converted to Degrees Celcius (Centigrade)
Multiply °F by 5/9 after subtracting 32

Degrees F		Degrees C
−40	=	−40
32	=	0
59	=	15

Multiples and Sub-Multiples

In the metric system the following decimal multiples and sub-multiples are used:

Prefix	Symbol	British Equivalent	Factor
atto- (Danish *atten* = eighteen)	a	trillionth part (US quintillionth)	$\times 10^{-18}$
femto- (Danish *femtem* = fifteen)	f	thousand billionth part (US quadrillionth)	$\times 10^{-15}$
pico- (L. *pico* = minuscule)	p	billionth part (US trillionth)	$\times 10^{-12}$
nano- (L. *nanus* = dwarf)	n	thousand millionth part (US billionth)	$\times 10^{-9}$
micro- (Gk. *mikros* = small)	μ	millionth part	$\times 10^{-6}$
milli- (L. *mille* = thousand)	m	thousandth part	$\times 10^{-3}$
centi- (L. *centum* = hundred)	c	hundredth part	$\times 10^{-2}$
deci- (L. *decimus* = tenth)	d	tenth part	$\times 10^{-1}$
deca- (Gk. *deka* = ten)	da	tenfold	$\times 10$
hecto- (Gk. *hekaton* = hundred)	h	hundredfold	$\times 10^{2}$
kilo- (Gk. *chilioi* = thousand)	k	thousandfold	$\times 10^{3}$
mega- (Gk. *megas* = large)	M	millionfold	$\times 10^{6}$
giga- (Gk. *gigas* = mighty)	G	thousand millionfold (US billion)	$\times 10^{9}$
tera- (Gk. *teras* = monster)	T	billionfold (US trillion)	$\times 10^{12}$
peta- (Gk. *penta* = five)	P	thousand billionfold (US quadrillion)	$\times 10^{15}$
exa- (Gk. *hexa* = six)	E	trillionfold (US quintillion)	$\times 10^{18}$

Weights and measures – miscellaneous information

Metric units

Length

10 ångström	=	1 nanometre
1000 nanometres	=	1 micrometre
1000 micrometres	=	1 millimetre
10 millimetres	=	1 centimetre
10 centimetres	=	1 decimetre
1000 millimetres	=	1 metre
100 centimetres	=	1 metre
10 decimetres	=	1 metre
10 metres	=	1 dekametre
10 dekametres	=	1 hectometre
10 hectometres	=	1 kilometre
1000 kilometres	=	1 megametre

Nautical

1852 metres	=	1 int. nautical mile

Area

100 sq millimetres	=	1 sq centimetre
100 sq centimetres	=	1 sq decimetre
100 sq decimetres	=	1 sq metre
100 sq metres	=	1 are
100 ares	=	1 hectare
100 hectares	=	1 sq kilometre

Weight (mass)

1000 milligrams	=	1 gram
10 grams	=	1 dekagram
10 dekagrams	=	1 hectogram
10 hectograms	=	1 kilogram
100 kilograms	=	1 quintal
1000 kilograms	=	1 tonne

Volume

1000 cu millimetres	=	1 cu centimetre
1000 cu centimetres	=	1 cu decimetre
1000 cu decimetres	=	1 cu metre
1000 cu metres	=	1 cu dekametre

Capacity

10 millilitres	=	1 centilitre
10 centilitres	=	1 decilitre
10 decilitres	=	1 litre
1 litre	=	1 cu decimetre

10 litres	=	1 dekalitre
10 dekalitres	=	1 hectolitre
10 hectolitres	=	1 kilolitre
1 kilolitre	=	1 cu metre

Imperial units

Length

12 inches	=	1 foot
3 feet	=	1 yard
5½ yards	=	1 rod, pole or perch
4 rods	=	1 chain
10 chains	=	1 furlong
5280 feet	=	1 mile
1760 yards	=	1 mile
8 furlongs	=	1 mile

Nautical

6 feet	=	1 fathom
100 fathoms	=	1 cable length
6080 feet	=	1 nautical mile

Area

144 sq inches	=	1 sq foot
9 sq feet	=	1 sq yard
304¼ sq yards	=	1 sq rod, pole or perch
40 sq rods	=	1 rood
4 roods	=	1 acre
4840 sq yards	=	1 acre
640 acres	=	1 sq mile

Weight (*avoirdupois*)

437½ grains	=	1 ounce
16 drams	=	1 ounce
16 ounces	=	1 pound
14 pounds	=	1 stone
28 pounds	=	1 quarter
4 quarters	=	1 hundredweight
20 hundredweights	=	1 ton

Volume

1728 cu inches	=	1 cu foot
27 cu feet	=	1 cu yard

5·8 cu feet	=	1 bulk barrel

Shipping

1 register ton	=	100 cubic feet

Capacity

8 fluid drachms	=	1 fluid ounce
5 fluid ounces	=	1 gill
4 gills	=	1 pint
2 pints	=	1 quart
4 quarts	=	1 gallon
2 gallons	=	1 peck
4 pecks	=	1 bushel
8 bushels	=	1 quarter
36 gallons	=	1 bulk barrel

Miscellaneous

Water

1 litre	weighs 1 kilogram
1 cubic metre	weighs 1 tonne
1 UK gallon	weighs 10·022 lb
1 UK gallon salt water	weighs 10·3 lb

Speed

15 mph =	22 feet per second	
1 knot	=	1 nautical mph

Beer, wines and spirits

Proof spirit contains 57·03% pure alcohol by volume (at 50° F).

Proof strength in degrees = % of alcohol by volume (at 50° F) multiplied by 1·7535.

Beer

nip	=	¼ pint
small	=	½ pint
large	=	1 pint
flagon	=	1 quart
anker	=	10 gallons
tun	=	216 gallons

Wines and spirits

tot (whisky)	=	⅙, ⅕, ¼ or ⅓ gill
noggin	=	1 gill
bottle	=	1⅓ pints

Champagne

2 bottles	=	1 magnum
4 bottles	=	1 jeroboam
20 bottles	=	1 nebuchadnezzar

Type sizes

Depth

72¼ (approx)	=	1 inch
1 didot point	=	0·376 mm

Width

The normal unit is a pica em

1 pica em	=	12 points

Book sizes

Crown Quarto	=	246 × 189 mm
Crown Octavo	=	186 × 123 mm
Demy Quarto	=	276 × 219 mm
Demy Octavo	=	216 × 138 mm
Royal Quarto	=	312 × 237 mm
Royal Octavo	=	234 × 156 mm
A4	=	297 × 210 mm
A5	=	210 × 148 mm

Crops

UK (imperial) bushel of

wheat	=	60 lb
barley	=	50 lb
oats	=	39 lb
rye	=	56 lb
rice	=	45 lb
maize	=	56 lb
linseed	=	52 lb
potatoes	=	60 lb

US bushel:

as above except

barley	=	48 lb
linseed	=	56 lb
oats	=	32 lb

Bale (cotton):

US (net)	=	480 lb
Indian	=	392 lb

Energy

1000 British thermal units (Btu)	=	0·293 kW h
100 000 Btu	=	1 therm
1 UK horsepower	=	0·7457 kilowatt

Paper sizes

Large post	=	16½ × 21 in
		419·1 × 533·4 mm
Demy	=	17½ × 22½ in
		444·5 × 571·5 mm
Medium	=	18 × 23 in
		457·2 × 584·2 mm
Royal	=	20 × 25 in
		508 × 635 mm
Double crown	=	20 × 30 in
		508 × 762 mm

'A' Series (metric sizes)

A0	=	841 × 1189 mm
		33⅛ × 46¾ in
A1	=	594 × 841 mm
		23⅜ × 33⅛ in
A2	=	420 × 594 mm
		16½ × 23⅜ in
A3	=	297 × 420 mm
		11¾ × 16½ in
A4	=	210 × 297 mm
		8¼ × 11¾ in
A5	=	148 × 210 mm
		5⅞ × 8¼ in

Petroleum

1 barrel	=	42 US gallons
	=	34·97 UK gallons
	=	0·159 cubic metre

Precious metals

24 carat implies pure metal.

1 metric carat	=	200 milligrams
1 troy (fine) ounce	=	480 grains

Millions and Billions

Some confusion has existed on the nomenclature of high numbers because of differing usage in various countries.

The position is that in the United Kingdom and in Germany it has been customary to advance by increments of a million thus:

million	1 000 000(10⁶)
billion	1 000 000 000 000(10¹²)
trillion	1 000 000 000 000 000 000(10¹⁸)

In France and the United States it is the practice to advance in increments of a thousand thus:

million	1 000 000(10⁶)
billion	1 000 000 000(10⁹)
trillion	1 000 000 000 000(10¹²)

Thus a US trillion is equal to a classic British billion.

Billion began to be used in Britain, in the US sense, as early as 1951 but the latest supplement to the *Oxford English Dictionary*, published in 1972, states that the older sense 'prevails'. In France one thousand million is described as a milliard which term is also permissibly used in Britain, as is the even more rare milliardth.

On 20 Dec 1974 the then Prime Minister (J. H. Wilson) announced that HM Treasury would adhere to their practice of using the billion (made more prevalent by inflationary trends) in financial statistics in the sense of £1000 million. The word million has been in use since 1370 and a trillion was first mentioned *c.* 1484.

The higher degrees of numbers in use together with the date of their earliest usage and number of zeros are:

	First use	US	UK
quadrillion	(1674)	1×10^{15}	1×10^{24}
quintillion	(1674)	1×10^{18}	1×10^{30}
sextillion	(1690)	1×10^{21}	1×10^{36}
septillion	(1690)	1×10^{24}	1×10^{42}
octillion	(1690)	1×10^{27}	1×10^{48}
nonillion	(1828)	1×10^{30}	1×10^{54}
decillion	(1845)	1×10^{33}	1×10^{60}
vigintillion		1×10^{63}	1×10^{120}
centillion		1×10^{303}	1×10^{600}

International Clothing Sizes

The tables below should be used as approximate guides as actual sizes may vary according to manufacturers. **It is wise to check all measurements in centimetres.**

Ladies' coats and jackets

Belgium	38/34N	40/36N	42/38N	44/40N	46/42N	48/44N
France	38/34N	40/36N	42/38N	44/40N	46/42N	48/44N
Germany	34	36	38	40	42	44
Holland	34	36	38	40	42	44
Italy	36	38	40	42	44	46
Japan	7	9	11	13	15	17
Norway/Sweden/Denmark	36	38	40	42	44	46
Spain	40	42	44	46	48	50
UK	8/30	10/32	12/34	14/36	16/38	18/40
USA	6	8	10	12	14	16

Men's Suits and Overcoats

Belgium	46	48	50	52	54	56
France	46	48	50	52	54	56
Germany	46	48	50	52	54	56
Italy	46	48	50	52	54	56
Norway/Sweden/Denmark	46	48	50	52	54	56
Spain	46	48	50	52	54	56
UK	46	48	50	52	54	56
USA	46	48	50	52	54	56

Men's Shirts

Belgium	36	37	38	39	40	41
France	36	37	38	39	40	41
Germany	36	37	38	39	40	41
Holland	36	37	38	39	40	41
Italy	36	37	38	39	40	41
Norway/Sweden/Denmark	36	37	38	39	40	41
Spain	36	37	38	39	40	41
UK	14	14½	15	15½	16	16½
USA	14	14½	15	15½	16	16½

Ladies' shoes

Belgium	36	37	38	39	40
France	36	37	38	39	40
Japan	22	23	24	25	25½
Norway/Sweden/Denmark	36	37	38	39	40
UK	3	4	5	6	7
USA	4½	5½	6½	7½	8½

Men's Shoes

Belgium	39	40	41	42	43
France	39	40	41	42	44½
Norway/Sweden/Denmark	40	41	42	43	44
UK	6	7	8	9	10
USA	6½	7½	8½	9½	10½

MATHEMATICS

Shapes and solids

Rectangle

All the angles of a rectangle are right angles, so the opposite sides are parallel in pairs.
A rectangle which is not a square has two lines of symmetry.

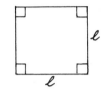

Area $= \ell^2$
Perimeter $= 4\ell$

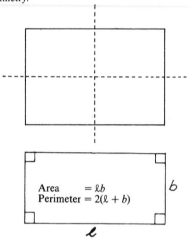

Area $= \ell b$
Perimeter $= 2(\ell + b)$

Copies of a rectangle can be used to tile a plane in many different ways. This is a common pattern.

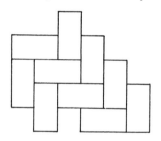

Square

A square is a rectangle whose sides are all equal. It has 4 lines of symmetry, both diagonals and the two lines joining the middle points of pairs of opposite sides.

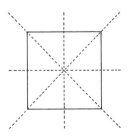

Parallelogram

The opposite sides of a parallelogram are parallel. It has no lines of symmetry, unless it is also a rectangle, but it does have rotational symmetry about its centre, the point where the diagonals meet.
If one angle of a parallelogram is a right angle, then all the angles are right angles, and it is a rectangle.
Any parallelogram can be dissected into a rectangle by cutting a right angled triangle off one end, and sliding it to the opposite end.

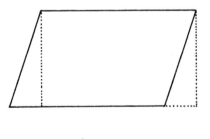

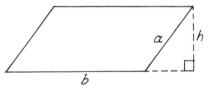

This dissection does not change the area of the parallelogram, or the length of the sides, so the area of any parallelogram is equal to the area of a rectangle with same base and the same height.

Area $= bh$
Perimeter $= 2(a + b)$

Triangle

Triangles have many curious properties. For example, the three lines which join the vertices of a triangle to the middle points of the opposite sides, meet in a point, they are *concurrent*.

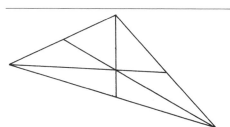

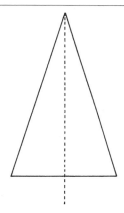

So are the three lines which bisect the sides at right angles. They meet in the point which is the centre of the circle through the vertices of the triangle.

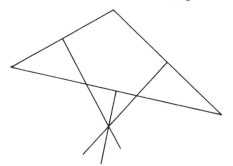

Any triangle can be thought of as one half of a parallelogram, which has been divided in two by one of its diagonals. Here is an example.

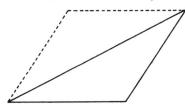

Therefore the area of a triangle is one half of the area of a parallelogram with the same base and the same height.

An *equilateral* triangle has all its sides equal, and all its angles are equal to 60°.

Trapezium

A trapezium has one pair of opposite sides parallel. If the height is measured between the pair of parallel sides, then its area is equal to the height multiplied by the *average* length of the parallel sides.

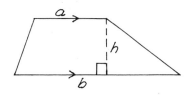

Area $= \frac{1}{2}(a + b)h$

i.e. $= \frac{1}{2}$ (sum of the parallel sides)

$\times$ perp. distance between them

Rhombus

A rhombus is a parallelogram whose sides are all equal in length. Its diagonals are both lines of symmetry, and therefore bisect each other at right angles.

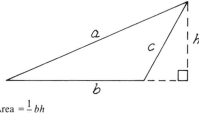

Area $= \frac{1}{2}bh$

The area of a triangle can also be calculated from the lengths of the sides, by a formula discovered by the Greek mathematician Archimedes:

If half the sum of the sides is s, then,

Area $= \sqrt{\{s(s - a)(s - b)(s - c)\}}$

A scalene triangle has sides of three different lengths, and has no axes of symmetry. If two sides of a triangle are equal in length, the triangle is *isosceles*, and has one axis of symmetry, and a pair of equal angles.

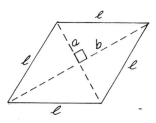

Area $\quad = \frac{1}{2}(2a)(2b)$

i.e. $\quad = \frac{1}{2}$ (product of the diagonals)

Perimeter $= 4\ell$

Circle

A circle is a path of a point which moves at a constant distance (called the radius) from a fixed point (called the centre of the circle).

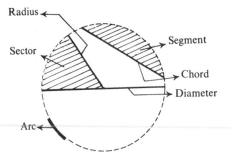

$$\text{Circumference} = 2\pi r \text{ or } \pi d$$
$$\text{Area} \qquad\quad = \pi r^2$$

Ring

$$\text{Area} = \pi(R^2 - r^2)$$
$$\quad\ = \pi(R - r)(R + r)$$

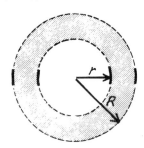

Rectangular block

All the faces are rectangles.

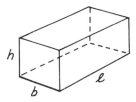

$$\text{Surface Area} = 2(\ell b + bh + h\ell)$$
$$\text{Volume} \qquad\ = \ell bh$$
$$\text{i.e.} \qquad\qquad\ = \text{Area of the base} \times \text{height}$$

The volume of any solid whose sides are perpendicular to its base (or cross-section) and whose ends are parallel is always equal to the
Area of the base × perpendicular height

Prism

A prism has two parallel faces, which are identical polygons, and which are called its ends. These are joined by parallelograms, which could be rectangles.

The volume of a prism equals the area of either of the ends, multiplied by the perpendicular distance between the ends.

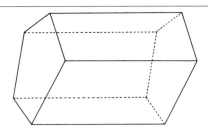

Pyramid

A pyramid has a base which is a polygon, and a special vertex called the apex which is joined to each vertex of the base. Therefore all its faces, apart from the base, are triangles.

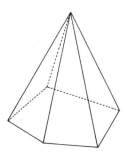

It is possible for the base of a pyramid to be a triangle also. In this case, any of the faces can be thought of as a base, and the solid is called a tetrahedron. Any pyramid can be fitted inside a prism so that the base of the pyramid is one end of the prism, and the apex of the pyramid is on the other end of the prism.

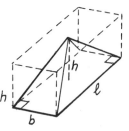

Thus, the volume of a pyramid on a rectangular base $= \dfrac{1}{3}(\ell bh)$

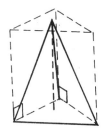

The volume of a pyramid within a triangular prism $= \dfrac{1}{3}$ (Area of the triangular base × height)

The volume of a pyramid is one third of the volume of the prism that it fits into in this way. Therefore,

$$\text{Volume of pyramid} = \frac{1}{3} \times \text{area of base} \times \text{height}$$

Cylinder
The area of the curved surface = $2\pi rh$
If the circles at both ends are included, then the total surface area = $2\pi rh + 2\pi r^2$.
The volume of a cylinder can be found by thinking of it as a special case of a prism. The volume equals the area of the base, multiplied by the height.
Volume of cylinder = $\pi r^2 h$

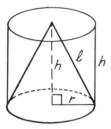

Cone
If the slant height of the cone is 1, the area of the curved surface is πrl.
The volume can be calculated as if the cone were a special case of a pyramid. The volume is one third the volume of the cylinder with the same base and height.

$$\text{Volume of cone} = \frac{1}{3}\pi r^2 h$$

Sphere
Surface Area = $4\pi r^2$

$$\text{Volume} = \frac{4}{3}\pi r^3$$

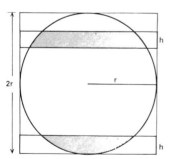

A little-known and interesting fact about the sphere is that the area of any zone of its curved surface lying between two parallel planes is exactly equal to the curved surface of the surrounding cylinder between the same to planes. This fact was discovered by Archimedes, who requested that a sphere inscribed in a cylinder be engraved on his tomb. This applies to any belt of the sphere, or to a cap or to the whole sphere. It thus makes the calculation of what might appear to be a difficult area quite simple.

Thus, either shaded area of the sphere is equal to the curved surface area of a cylinder of radius a and height h, the height of the zone, i.e.
$A = 2\pi rh$ and for the whole sphere
$A = 2\pi 2r$
  $= 4\pi r^2$
which we already know to be the surface area of a sphere.

Conic sections

Ellipse
The path of each of the planets round the Sun is approximately an ellipse. There are many ways to draw an ellipse. One of the simplest is to stretch a loop of thread round two pins, and hold it taut with a pencil. The path of the pencil will be an ellipse. An ellipse can also be thought of as a circle that has been stretched in one direction.

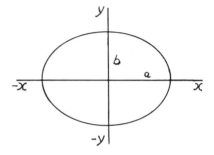

Area = πab

Basic equation (centre at the origin)
$$\frac{x^2}{a^2} + \frac{y^2}{b^2} = 1$$

Parabola
If you throw a ball in the air, then the path of the ball will be approximately a parabola.

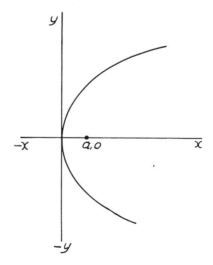

Basic equation (symmetrical about the x-axis, focus at $(a, 0)$)
$y^2 = 4ax$

Hyperbola

Basic equation (centre at the origin)

$$\frac{x^2}{a^2} - \frac{y^2}{b^2} = 1$$

These are called the conic sections because they can all be obtained by the intersection of a plane with a complete, or 'double' cone.

Circle

The circle is a special case of an ellipse.
General equation (centre at $-g, -f$)

$$x^2 + y^2 + 2gx + 2fy + c = 0$$

Basic equation (centre at the origin)

$$x^2 + y^2 = r^2$$

Rectangular Hyperbola

Rectangular hyperbola (referred to the axes of co-ordinates as asymptotes) $xy = k^2$

Basic algebra

$$x^a \times x^b = x^{a+b}$$

$$\frac{x^a}{x^b} = x^{a-b}$$

$(x^a)^b$ or $(x^b)^a = x^{ab}$

$$x^{-a} = \frac{1}{x^a}$$

$$x^{1/n} = \sqrt[n]{x}$$

Important identities
$(x \pm y)^2 \equiv x^2 \pm 2xy + y^2$

$A^2 - B^2 = (A - B)(A + B)$
A difference of two squares

$(x \pm y)^3 \equiv x^3 \pm 3x^2y + 3xy^2 \pm y^3$

$A^3 \pm B^3 \equiv (A \pm B)(A^2 \mp AB + B^2)$
The sum or difference of two cubes

The solutions of the standard quadratic equation

$ax^2 + bx + c = 0$
are given by

$$x = \frac{-b \pm \sqrt{b^2 - 4ac}}{2a}$$

If b^2 is $> 4ac$ the roots are real and different
b^2 is $= 4ac$ the roots are real and equal
b^2 is $< 4ac$ the roots are imaginary (complex)
b is $= 0$ and c is $-ve$, the roots are real, equal and opposite
b is $= 0$ and c is $+ve$, the roots are imaginary (no real part)

If the roots are α and β,

then $\alpha + \beta = -\dfrac{b}{a}$ and $\alpha\beta = \dfrac{c}{a}$

Logarithms

If $N = a^x$
then $\text{Log}_a N = x$ (i.e. Log N to the base 'a' $= x$)
Log NM = Log N + Log M

and Log $\dfrac{N}{M}$ = Log N - Log M

To change the base of a logarithm:

$$\text{Log}_b N = \frac{\text{Log}_a N}{\text{Log}_a b} \text{or} \quad \text{Log}_a N \times \text{Log}_b a$$

$\text{Log} N^p = p \text{ Log} N \qquad \text{Log}_a b = \dfrac{1}{\text{Log}_b a}$

$\text{Log} \sqrt[n]{N} = \dfrac{1}{n} \text{ Log } N$

Basic trigonometry

$$\text{Sin } C = \frac{AB}{AC}$$

$$\text{Cos } C = \frac{BC}{AC}$$

$$\text{Tan } C = \frac{AB}{BC}$$

$$\text{Cosec } \theta = \frac{1}{\text{Sin } \theta}$$

$$\text{Sec } \theta = \frac{1}{\text{Cos} \theta}$$

$$\text{Cot } \theta = \frac{1}{\text{Tan } \theta}$$

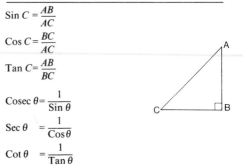

Trigonometrical equivalents of Pythagoras' Theorem (q.v.)

$\text{Sin}^2 \theta + \text{Cos}^2 \theta = 1 \quad \text{Sec}^2 \theta = 1 + \text{Tan}^2 \theta$

$\text{Cosec}^2 \theta = 1 + \text{Cot}^2 \theta$

Formulae for the solution of non-right-angled triangles:

Sine Rule
Given at least one side and the opposite angle:

$$\frac{a}{\text{Sin} A} = \frac{b}{\text{Sin} B} = \frac{c}{\text{Sin} C} (=2R)$$

where R = radius of the circumcircle

Area of a triangle $= \dfrac{1}{2} ab \text{ Sin } C$

Cosine Rules
(1) Given two sides and the included angle (b, c and the angle A)

$$a^2 = b^2 + c^2 - 2bc \text{ Cos } A$$

(2) Given three sides

$$\text{Cos} A = \frac{b^2 + c^2 - a^2}{2bc}$$

Sines, cosines and tangents of angles greater than 90°

2nd quadrant
90° $< \theta <$ 180°
Sin θ = Sin $(180° - \theta)$
Cos θ = $-$ Cos $(180° - \theta)$
Tan θ = $-$ Tan $(180° - \theta)$

3rd quadrant
180° $< \theta <$ 270°
Sin θ = $-$ Sin $(\theta - 180°)$
Cos θ = $-$ Cos $(\theta - 180°)$
Tan θ = Tan $(\theta - 180°)$

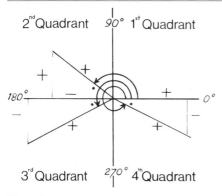

2ndQuadrant   90°   1stQuadrant

180°————————————————— 0°

3rdQuadrant   270°   4thQuadrant

4th quadrant
$270° < \theta < 360°$
$\text{Sin } \theta = -\text{Sin } (360° - \theta)$
$\text{Cos } \theta = \text{Cos } (360° - \theta)$
$\text{Tan } \theta = -\text{Tan } (360° - \theta)$

Radian measure

A radian is the angle subtended at the centre of a circle by a length of arc equal to the radius. Thus
$$1 \text{ radian} = \frac{180}{\pi} \text{ degrees}$$
or approx. $57 \cdot 3°$
$\pi \text{ radians} = 180°$

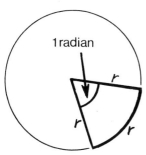

1 radian

Length of an arc of a circle is given by:

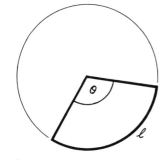

$$\frac{\ell}{2\pi r} = \frac{\theta}{360°}$$

i.e. $\ell = \dfrac{\pi r \theta}{180}$ where θ is in degrees

or $\ell = r\theta$ where θ is in radians

Area of the sector of a circle is given by:

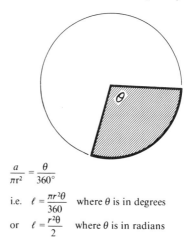

$$\frac{a}{\pi r^2} = \frac{\theta}{360°}$$

i.e. $\ell = \dfrac{\pi r^2 \theta}{360}$ where θ is in degrees

or $\ell = \dfrac{r^2 \theta}{2}$ where θ is in radians

Pythagoras' Theorem
In the triangle ABC right-angled at B
$$AC^2 = AB^2 + BC^2$$

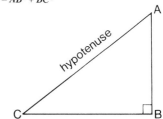

There are an infinite number of right-angled triangles whose sides are integers. Four of the smallest have the sides:

3, 4, 5   5, 12, 13
8, 15, 17   and 7, 24, 25

Such whole-number sets are sometimes called 'Pythagorean Triples'.

In words the theorem states that the area of the square drawn on the hypotenuse of a right-angled triangle is equal to the sum of the areas of the squares drawn on the other two sides.

However, it is also true that the area of any shape drawn on the hypotenuse is equal to the sum of the areas of similar shapes drawn on the other two sides.

Percentages
(1) $x\%$ of a number $(N) = \dfrac{x}{100} \times N$

(2) To find what percentage a quantity A is of a quantity B

$$\% = \frac{A}{B} \times 100$$

(3) To find the percentage increase or decrease of a quantity

$$\% \begin{cases} \text{Increase} \\ \text{Decrease} \end{cases} = \frac{\text{Actual increase}}{\text{Original amount}} \times 100$$

(4) To find the percentage profit or loss

$$\% \begin{Bmatrix} \text{Profit} \\ \text{Loss} \end{Bmatrix} = \frac{\text{Actual profit or loss}}{\text{Cost price}} \times 100$$

(5) To find 100% given that $x\% = N$

$$100\% = \frac{N}{x} \times 100$$

Note that percentages may not be added or subtracted unless they are percentages of the same quantity. Thus successive depreciations of 10% and 15% are not equivalent to a single depreciation of 25%.

Interest

Simple Interest (principal remains constant) $= \dfrac{PRT}{100}$

where P = principal (sum invested)
R = rate % per annum
T = time in years

Compound Interest (interest added to the principal each year)

$$A = PR^n$$

where A = Amount (i.e. Principal + Interest)

$$R = 1 + \frac{r}{100} \quad \text{where } r = \text{rate \%p.a.}$$

n = number of years

Polyhedra

A polyhedron is a solid shape with all plane faces.
The faces of a regular polyhedron, or regular solid, are all identical regular polygons.
There are just five regular polyhedra.

The cube and the octahedron are dual polyhedra. You will notice that the cube has 6 faces and 8 vertices, while the octahedron has 6 vertices but 8 faces.
The regular dodecahedron and regular icosahedron are also duals.

	Faces	Type of face	Vertices	Edges
Regular Tetrahedron	4	equilateral triangles	4	6
Cube	6	squares	8	12
Regular Octahedron	8	equilateral triangles	6	12
Regular Dodecahedron	12	regular pentagons	20	30
Regular Icosahedron	20	equilateral triangles	12	30

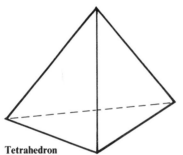

Tetrahedron

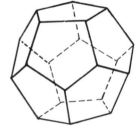

Dodecahedron

Cube

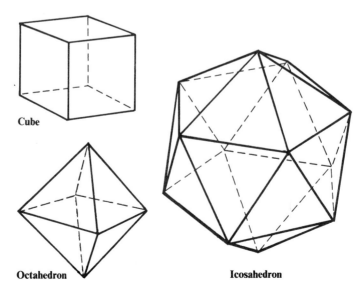

Octahedron

Icosahedron

There are many more less regular polyhedra. The simplest to visualize have faces which are mixtures of two kinds of regular polygons. For example, the faces of this cuboctahedron are equilateral triangles and squares.

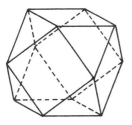

The mathematician Euler made an interesting discovery about the relationship between the number of faces (F), vertices (V) and edges (E) of polyhedra.

The equation $F + V - E = 2$ is true for all 'simple' polyhedra, such as the regular polyhedra, as you can check from the above table.

It is not true for polyhedra with holes in, such as this example, or for many other 'weird' polyhedra.

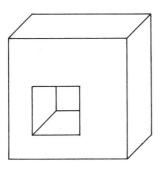

Furthermore, the same relationship is true for an area divided into any number of regions (R) by boundaries or arcs (A) which join at nodes (N).

Then $R + N - A = 2$

For the area shown,
$R = 8$ (the surrounding space counts as a region)
$N = 12$ $A = 18$
Thus $R + N - A$
$= 8 + 12 - 18$
$= 2$

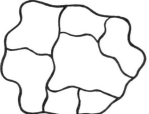

Incidentally, for such a region, or indeed any map, no more than 4 colours are necessary so that no two adjoining regions have the same colour.

Polygons (many-sided figures)

Sum of the interior angles $= (2n - 4) \times 90°$
where n = number of sides.

Each interior angle of a regular polygon $= \dfrac{(2n - 4) \times 90°}{n}$

$$\text{or} = 180° - \frac{360°}{n}$$

Sum of the exterior angles of any polygon $= 360°$, regardless of the number of sides.

Some important polygons
Triangle	3 sides
Quadrilateral	4 sides
Pentagon	5 sides
Hexagon	6 sides
Heptagon	7 sides
Octagon	8 sides
Nonagon	9 sides
Decagon	10 sides
Dodecagon	12 sides

The area of any regular polygon of side 'a' $= \dfrac{1}{4} na^2 \operatorname{Cot} \dfrac{180°}{n}$

Where n = the number of sides

Networks

A series of nodes joined by arcs is called a network. A node is odd or even according to the number of arcs which are drawn from it. The network may represent a road or railway system, an electricity grid and so on. Such a system will be traversable (i.e. can be drawn without covering any arc twice or taking the pencil off the paper) if there are not more than 2 odd nodes. In which case the route must begin and end at an odd node. Here are two simplified networks, one of which is traversable and one is not. The latter was used by Euler to solve the famous Konigsberg Bridge problem.

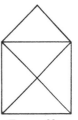

Traversable

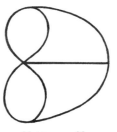

Not traversable

Matrices

A matrix is an array of numbers, of rectangular shape, which presents information in a concise form. Matrices serve many purposes, and according to the circumstances they may be multiplied or added or subtracted.

Two matrices may be multiplied if there are the same number of ROWS in the second matrix as there are COLUMNS in the first, but they may only be added or subtracted if they have the same number of rows and columns. A 2×3 matrix is one with 2 rows and 3 columns. Thus a 2×3 matrix may be multiplied by a 3×4 or a 3×2 or a $3 \times n$ matrix where n is any number.

If $A = \begin{pmatrix} a & b \\ c & d \end{pmatrix}$ and $B = \begin{pmatrix} p & q \\ r & s \end{pmatrix}$

Then, $AB = \begin{pmatrix} a & b \\ c & d \end{pmatrix}\begin{pmatrix} p & q \\ r & s \end{pmatrix}$

$= \begin{pmatrix} ap + br & aq + bs \\ cp + dr & cq + ds \end{pmatrix}$

$A + B = \begin{pmatrix} a & b \\ c & d \end{pmatrix} + \begin{pmatrix} p & q \\ r & s \end{pmatrix}$

$= \begin{pmatrix} a + p & b + q \\ c + r & d + s \end{pmatrix}$

The Transformation Matrices change the position or shape of a geometrical figure, and sometimes both.
The following are the principal transformation matrices:

(1) Reflection in the x-axis $\begin{pmatrix} 1 & 0 \\ 0 & -1 \end{pmatrix}$

(2) Reflection in the y-axis $\begin{pmatrix} -1 & 0 \\ 0 & 1 \end{pmatrix}$

(3) Reflection in the line $y = x$ $\begin{pmatrix} 0 & 1 \\ 1 & 0 \end{pmatrix}$

(4) Reflection in the line $y = -x$ $\begin{pmatrix} 0 & -1 \\ -1 & 0 \end{pmatrix}$

(5) Rotation through $90°$ about the origin in a $+ve$ (anticlockwise) direction $\begin{pmatrix} 0 & -1 \\ 1 & 0 \end{pmatrix}$

(6) Rotation through $180°$ ($+ve$ or $-ve$) $\begin{pmatrix} -1 & 0 \\ 0 & -1 \end{pmatrix}$

(7) $+ve$ rotation of $270°$ ($-ve$ rotation of $90°$) $\begin{pmatrix} 0 & 1 \\ -1 & 0 \end{pmatrix}$

(8) $+ve$ rotation about the origin through an angle θ $\begin{pmatrix} \text{Cos} & -\text{Sin } \theta \\ \text{Sin } \theta & \text{Cos } \theta \end{pmatrix}$

(9) The *identity matrix* $\begin{pmatrix} 1 & 0 \\ 0 & 1 \end{pmatrix}$ leaves the elements of the multiplied matrix unchanged.
The following matrices change the shape of the figure.

(10) An enlargement, factor E $\begin{pmatrix} E & 0 \\ 0 & E \end{pmatrix}$

(e.g. if $E = 3$ the figure will have its linear dimensions trebled)

(11) A stretch, parallel to the x-axis, factor S $\begin{pmatrix} S & 0 \\ 0 & 1 \end{pmatrix}$

(12) A stretch, parallel to the y-axis, factor S $\begin{pmatrix} 1 & 0 \\ 0 & S \end{pmatrix}$

(13) A two-way stretch, parallel to the axes, factors S_1 and S_2 $\begin{pmatrix} S_1 & 0 \\ 0 & S_2 \end{pmatrix}$

(14) A shear, parallel to the x-axis $\begin{pmatrix} 1 & S \\ 0 & 1 \end{pmatrix}$

(15) A shear, parallel to the y-axis $\begin{pmatrix} 1 & 0 \\ S & 1 \end{pmatrix}$

The inverse of matrix A above (denoted by A^{-1}) is

$$\frac{1}{(ad - bc)} \begin{pmatrix} d & -b \\ -c & a \end{pmatrix}$$

The expression $(ad - bc)$ is called the determinant of the matrix.
The value of the determinant of a matrix represents the ratio by which the area of the original figure has been changed. If the determinant is zero, all the points will be moved to lie on a line, and the matrix is said to be 'singular'.
If a matrix is multiplied by its inverse the result is the identity matrix.
A transformation which does not change either the shape or the size of a figure is called an isometric transformation.

Number bases

Our familiar denary system of calculating undoubtedly arose because we have 5 'digits' on each hand. Had we been created with 4 instead, we should have been just as happily working in the Octal scale. A denary number may be easily converted to any other base simply by repeated division by the new base, the remainders being recorded at each step, thus:
8)543_{10}
 8)67 r 7
  8)8 r 3
   1 r 0
Reading from the bottom up, 543_{10} is equivalent to 1037_8 (read 'one nought three seven base eight').

To convert a number in any other base into base 10, however, each digit must be given its appropriate place-value in the given base.

Thus, 1037_8
$= 1 \times 8^3 + 0 \times 8^2 + 3 \times 8^1 + 7$
$= 512 + 0 + 24 + 7$
$= 543_{10}$

Base 2 or the binary scale is the most important non-denary base since it uses only the digits 0 and 1, and these can easily be related to the 'off' and 'on' of an electrical impulse and form the basis for the operation of electronic calculators and computers.

As before, a number may be converted to base 2 by repeated division. Thus, to convert 217_{10}

```
2)217
2)108  r 1
2)54   r 0
2)27   r 0      i.e.    217₁₀ = 11011001₂
2)13   r 1
2) 6   r 1
2) 3   r 0
   1   r 1
```

i.e. $217_{10} = 11011001_2$

The reverse process will be:
11011001_2
$= 1 \times 2^7 + 1 \times 2^6 + 0 \times 2^5 + 1 \times 2^4 + 1 \times 2^3$
$\quad + 0 \times 2^2 + 0 \times 2^1 + 1$
$= 128 + 64 + 0 + 16 + 8 + 0 + 0 + 1$
$= 217_{10}$

A denary-binary conversion table reveals some interesting points about binary numbers. Note the repetitive patterns in the columns of the successive numbers. Since odd numbers always end in 1 while even numbers end in 0, a number is doubled simply by adding a 0 (in the same way that a denary number is multiplied by 10 by adding a nought), and divided by 2, where possible, by removing a terminal 0. Denary numbers which are powers of 2 have a binary equivalent consisting of a 1 followed by the same number of zeros as the appropriate power of 2.

Denary	Binary
1	1
2 (2^1)	10
3	11
4 (2^2)	100
5	101
6	110
7	111
8 (2^3)	1000
9	1001
10	1010
11	1011
12	1100
13	1101
14	1110
15	1111
16 (2^3)	10000

Denary fractions are rendered as negative powers of 2.

Denary		Binary
0·5	(2^{-1})	0·1
0·25	(2^{-2})	0·01
0·125	(2^{-3})	0·001
0·0625	(2^{-4})	0·0001
0·03125	(2^{-5})	0·00001
0·015625	(2^{-6})	0·000001

Thus, to convert a 'bicimal' to a decimal,

$0·1101_2 = 0·5 + 0·25 + 0 + 0·0625$
$\qquad\quad = 0·8125$

Converting from a decimal to a bicimal requires repeated *multiplication* of the *decimal part only* at each stage, the result being given by the whole-number parts read from the top. Thus, to convert 0·3 to a bicimal we proceed as follows:

```
0·3 × 2
0·6 × 2
1·2 × 2
0·4 × 4
0·8 × 2
1·6 × 2
1·2 and so on.
```

Reading the whole-numbers from the top we have: 0·010011. Clearly this could go on until we have the required number of bicimal places or the process comes to a stop.

The check shows that we have only an approximate equivalence.
$0·010011_2$
$= 0 + 0·25 + 0 + 0 + 0·03125 + 0·015625$
$= 0·296875_{10}$

Some important series

Arithmetic progression (AP)
$a, \ a+d, \ a+2d, \ a+3d \ldots [a+(n-1)d]$

Sum to n terms $= \dfrac{n}{2}[2a + (n-1)d]$

or $\qquad\qquad = \dfrac{n}{2}(a+l)$ where l = last term

Geometric series (GP)
$a, \ ar, \ ar^2, \ ar^3 \ldots ar^{n-1}$

Sum to n terms $= a\dfrac{(1-r^n)}{1-r}$ if $r < 1$, or $\dfrac{a(r^n - 1)}{r-1}$ if $r > 1$

When $r < 1$, the sum to infinity $S_\infty = \dfrac{a}{1-r}$

The sum of the first n natural (counting) numbers
$1 + 2 + 3 + 4 + \ldots n$ (i.e. an AP in which $a = 1$ and
$d = 1) = \dfrac{n}{2}(n+1)$

The sum of the squares of the first n natural numbers
$1^2 + 2^2 + 3^2 + 4^2 \ldots n^2 = \dfrac{n}{6}(n+1)(2n+1)$

The sum of the cubes of the first n natural numbers
$1^3 + 2^3 + 3^3 + 4^3 \ldots n^3 = \left[\dfrac{n}{2}(n+1)\right]^2$

i.e. the square of the sum of the first n natural numbers.

The sum of the first n odd numbers.
$1 + 3 + 5 + 7 \ldots$ to n terms $= n^2$
i.e. the square of the numbers of numbers.

The sum of the first n even numbers
$2 + 4 + 6 + 8 \ldots$ to n terms $= n(n+1)$
i.e. twice the sum of an equal number of natural numbers.

Factorial n If a number is multiplied by all the successive numbers between it and 1, this is called Factorial n, and is denoted by $\underline{n}|$ or $n!$ Thus:
$6! = 6.5.4.3.2.1$
$\quad = 720$

Exponential series
$e^x = 1 + x + \dfrac{x^2}{2!} + \dfrac{x^3}{3!} + \dfrac{x4}{4!} + \cdots \dfrac{x^n}{n!} + \cdots$ for all values of x

Hence, when $x = 1$
$e = 1 + 1 + \dfrac{1}{2!} + \dfrac{1}{3!} + \dfrac{1}{4!} + \cdots = 2·71828$

More generally,

$$e^{mx} = 1 + mx + \frac{(mx)^2}{2!} + \frac{(mx)^3}{3!} + \cdots$$

If $m = \log_e a$

$$a^x = 1 + x \log_e a + \frac{(x \log_e a)^2}{2!} + \frac{(x \log_e a)^3}{3!} + \cdots$$

Logarithmic series

$$\log_e(1 + x) = x - \frac{x^2}{2} + \frac{x^3}{3} - \frac{x^4}{4} \cdots (-1)^{n+1} \frac{x^n}{n}$$

when $-1 < x \leqslant 1$

$$\log_e(1 - x) = -\left[x + \frac{x^2}{2} + \frac{x^3}{3} + \frac{x^4}{4} + \cdots\right]$$

when $-1 \leqslant x < 1$

Trigonometrical series

$$\sin \theta = \theta - \frac{\theta^3}{3!} + \frac{\theta^5}{5!} - \frac{\theta^7}{7!} + \cdots$$

where θ is in radians

$$\cos \theta = 1 - \frac{\theta^2}{2!} + \frac{\theta^4}{4!} - \frac{\theta^6}{6!} + \cdots$$

Binomial theorem

$$(1 + x)^n = 1 + nx + \frac{n(n-1)}{1.2} x^2 + \frac{n(n-1)(n-2)}{1.2.3} x^3 + \cdots$$

If n is not a positive integer (whole number) the series is infinite and is only true if x is numerically < 1.
More generally,

$$(a + x)^n = a^n + {}_nC_1 a^{-1} x + {}_nC_2 a^{n-2} x^2 + \cdots {}_nC_r a^{n-r} x^r + \cdots x^n.$$

where $\displaystyle {}_nC_r = \frac{n(n-1)(n-2) \cdots (n-r+1)}{1.2.3 \ldots r}$

or $\displaystyle = \frac{n!}{r! \, (n-r)!}$

Fibonacci Numbers
Fibonacci Numbers were named in the 19th century after Leonardo Fibonacci of Pisa (b. c. 1170 d. ante 1240), who introduced Arabic figures 1 to 9 plus 0 in his *Liber abaci* in 1202. He earned the title of *Stupor mundi* (wonder of the world) from the Holy Roman Emperor. In 1225 he published a recursive sequence of his Arabic numbers 1, 1, 2, 3, 5, 8, 13, 21, 34, 55 etc. in which each number is the sum of the two preceding numbers. In the 19th century this sequence was found to occur in nature – the arrangement of leaf buds on a stem, animal horns, the genealogy of the male bee and spirals in sunflower heads and pine cones.

Number patterns

Rectangular numbers
Another name for composite numbers, that is, numbers which are not prime. Any composite number can be represented in the form of a rectangle of dots.

Thus $6 =$

Square numbers
Numbers with a pair of equal factors, and may therefore be represented as a square.

Thus $4 =$ $\quad$ $9 =$

1 4 9 16 25 36 49 64 81 100 121 144 169 are the squares of the first 13 numbers.
Note that all square numbers are positive.

Triangular numbers
Numbers which can be formed into a series of equilateral triangles. Triangular numbers can be represented by a triangular pattern of dots.

Thus
1 $\quad$ 3 $\quad$ 6 $\quad$ 10 $\quad$ 15

The differences between successive triangular numbers are the natural numbers:

(1)	1	3	6	10	15	21	28
	2	3	4	5	6	7	8

Pascal's Triangle
This is one of the most famous and important of all number patterns.

Although it was known long before Pascal (who died in 1662) he was the first to make ingenious and wide use of its properties.

The numbers in Pascal's Triangle appear in the binomial theorem, in problems about the selection of combinations of objects, and therefore in the theory of probability and in statistics.

The numbers in each row are formed by adding the numbers above and to each side of it.

The numbers in the rows so formed are then the coefficients of the terms in the Binomial Theorem referred to above.

Thus the numbers in the 4th row (1 3 3 1) are the coefficients in the expansion of $(a + x)^3$, while those in the 6th would be those in the expansion of $(a + x)^5$, i.e. 1 5 10 10 5 1.

	Totals
1	$1 = 2^0$
1 1	$2 = 2^1$
1 2 1	$4 = 2^2$
1 3 3 1	$8 = 2^3$
1 4 6 4 1	$16 = 2^4$
1 5 10 10 5 1	$32 = 2^5$

Permutations and Combinations
The number of permutations of a set of items, i.e. the number of different *arrangements* of those items is denoted by ${}_nP_r$. The number of combinations of a set of items is the number of *groups* of those items (i.e. different arrangements do not count) and is denoted by ${}_nC_r$

${}_nP_r$ means the number of permutations of n things taken r at a time.

Thus $\displaystyle {}_nP_r = \frac{n!}{(n-r)!}$

$= n(n-1)(n-2) \ldots (n-r+1)$

and ${}_nP_n = n!$, since $0! = 1$

Note that $_nC_r = \dfrac{_nP_r}{r!}$

$= \dfrac{n!}{r!\,(n-r)!}$

i.e. the number of permutations of n things taken r at a time, divided by the number of permutations of all r things among themselves.

The Real Number System

The set of real numbers includes all the following:
(1) The natural or counting numbers.
(2) The integers (whole numbers) both positive and negative.
(3) The fractions.
All the above are called rational numbers since they can all be expressed as a ratio.
(4) The irrational numbers, i.e. those which cannot be expressed as a ratio.
   For example $\sqrt{10}$, $\sqrt[3]{7}$ and so on.
All the real numbers can be located on a number-line, and will in fact together form the solid line of geometry.

The square of any real number is positive. Therefore a negative number does not have a square root which can be marked on the number line. However, by giving a name to the square root of -1, mathematicians use the letter i, it is possible for every negative real number, like every positive real number, to have two square roots.
   For example: $i^2 = (-i)^2 = -1$
   $(3i)^2 = (-3i)^2 = -9$
   $(i\sqrt{5})^2 = (-i\sqrt{5})^2 = -5$

If x and y are real, and i is the square root of -1, then $x + iy$ is a complex number. Complex numbers can be added, subtracted, multiplied and divided, like real numbers, but they cannot be represented on the number line. Instead, they can be represented on an Argand diagram.

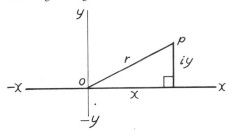

The point P (or the vector OP) represents the complex number $x + iy$. r is called the modulus and θ the amplitude (or 'argument') of the complex number, where:

$r = \sqrt{(x^2 + y^2)}$ and $\tan\theta = \dfrac{y}{x}$

Since $x = r\cos\theta$ and $y = r\sin\theta$ the complex number may also be rendered in the form $r(\cos\theta + i\sin\theta)$

Set symbols

{ }	the set of
$n\{A\}$	the number of elements in the set A
$\{x:\ \}$	the set of elements x such that
$\in$	is an element of
$\mathscr{U}$	is not an element of
(or)	the universal set

Ø	the empty (null set)
∪	union
∩	intersection
⊂	is a subset of
A'	the complement of the set A
$f:x \to y$	the function mapping the set X (the domain) into the set Y
f^{-1}	the inverse of the function f
R	the set of all real numbers
Z	the set of all integers
$\mathbf{Z}_+$	the set of all positive integers
Q	the set of all rationals, e.g. ¾

The relationship between sets may be conveniently represented on a Venn diagram. If the various sets to be represented are shaded differently and the general principle is that *union* is represented by *everything* shaded and *intersection* is represented by cross-hatched shading, quite complicated relationships may be easily clarified.

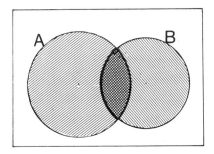

Thus $A \cup B$ = everything shaded and $A \cap B$ = cross-hatched shading and these two areas would contain the appropriate elements.

This illustrates that:
$A \subset B$ and $A \cap B = A$
and $A \cup B = B$

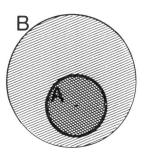

The shaded area represents A'

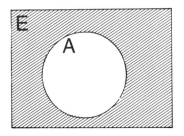

This shows that the elements in $A \cap B'$ will be found in the cross-hatched area. In this case the areas A and B' have been shaded.

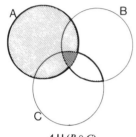

More complicated relationships between several sets may also be conveniently represented in this way, and the equivalence between apparently different relationships clearly illustrated.

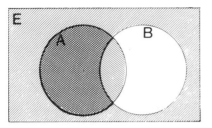

$A \cup (B \cap C)$
Everything shaded

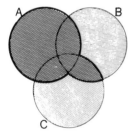

$(A \cup B) \cap (A \cup C)$
Cross-hatched shading

Clearly these (bottom left) two are equivalent, but neither is equivalent to $(A \cup B) \cap C$ illustrated in the third diagram (below).

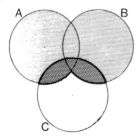

$(A \cup B) \cup C$

The reader should illustrate $A \cap (B \cup C)$, $(A \cap B) \cup (A \cap C)$ and $(A \cap B) \cup C$ in the same way.

Area under any curve

(1) Trapezoidal Rule

$$\text{Area} = \left[\frac{y_1 + y_7}{2} + y_2 + y_3 + y_4 + y_5 + y_6\right] w$$

i.e. = [half the sum of the first and last ordinates + all the others] × the width of the strip

The area may be divided into any number of equal strips.

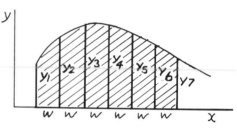

(2) Simpson's Rule

$$\text{Area} = \frac{w}{3}\left[y_1 + y_7 + 4(y_2 + y_4 + y_6) + 2(y_3 + y_5)\right]$$

i.e. = one-third of the width of a strip, multiplied by the sum of the first and last ordinates, + 4 times the even ordinates, + twice the remaining odd ordinates.

For this rule the area must be divided into an *even* number of strips of equal width.

(3) Both the above rules give very good approximations, but the exact area is found by calculus provided the equation of the curve is known. Then:

$$\text{Area} = \int_{x_1}^{x_2} y\,dx$$

Basic calculus

If y is any function of x, and Δy, Δx are corresponding increments of y and x, then the differential coefficient of y with respect to x

$$\left(\text{written } \frac{dy}{dx}\right) \text{is defined as } \underset{\Delta x \to 0}{\text{Lt}} \frac{[f(x + \Delta x) - f(x)]}{\Delta x}$$

$\frac{dy}{dx}$ gives the gradient of a curve, i.e. it measures the rate of change of one variable with respect to another.

Thus, since velocity is the rate of change of distance with respect to time, it may be expressed in calculus terms as $\frac{ds}{dt}$ where s is the distance of a body from a fixed point and the equation of motion of the body is of the form $s = f(t)$.

Similarly, since acceleration is the rate of change of *velocity* with time, it may be expressed as $\frac{dv}{dt}$ or as $\frac{d^2s}{dt^2}$, i.e. as the second differential of s with respect to t. Acceleration may also be expressed as $v\frac{dv}{ds}$, i.e. as the velocity multiplied by the rate of change of velocity with distance. In general, if: $y = ax^n$

then $\frac{dy}{dx} = nax^{n-1}$

Since $\dfrac{dy}{dx}$ gives the gradient of a curve it may be used to find the maximum and minimum values of a function. Thus if $y = f(x)$, then when $\dfrac{dy}{dx} = 0$, the tangents to the curve will be parallel to the x axis, and will indicate the positions of the critical values (the maximum or minimum) but without distinguishing them. However,

if $\dfrac{d^2y}{dx^2}$ is +ve the critical value of x gives a *minimum* value of the function, while

if $\dfrac{d^2y}{dx^2}$ is −ve the critical value gives a *maximum* value of the function, and

if $\dfrac{d^2y}{dx^2} = 0$, and changes sign as x increases through the point, the curve is passing through a point of inflection

| Minimum | Maximum | Point of inflection |

Differential coefficient of a product
If $y = uv$ where u and v are functions of x, then
$$\frac{dy}{dx} = u\frac{dv}{dx} + v\frac{du}{dx}$$

Differential coefficient of a quotient

If $y = \dfrac{u}{v}$ where u and v are functions of x, then
$$\frac{dy}{dx} = \frac{v\dfrac{du}{dx} - u\dfrac{dv}{dx}}{v^2}$$

Integration
Integration is the reverse of differentiation. In general, $\int ax^n dx$ where a is a constant,
$$= \frac{ax^{n+1}}{n+1} + c \text{ where } c \text{ is constant.}$$

However, whereas in general differentiation is a straightforward process, integration may be difficult and require the knowledge of a number of standard results.

Integration may be used, among other things, for finding the area under a curve, the volume of revolution of a curve about an axis, and the length of the arc of a curve.

Thus, if the curve is represented by $y = f(x)$, then the area between it and the x-axis between the limits x_1 and x_2 is given by
$$A = \int_{x_1}^{x_2} y\,dx.$$

The volume of revolution about the x-axis between the same limits is given by
$$V = \pi \int_{x_1}^{x_2} y^2 dx$$

and the length of arc between the same limits is given by
$$L = \int_{x_1}^{x_2}\sqrt{1 + \left(\frac{dy}{dx}\right)^2}\,dx$$

Among the various processes used in integration an important one is *integration by parts*. If u and $\dfrac{dv}{dx}$ are functions of x, then
$$\int\left(u\frac{dv}{dx}\right)dx = uv - \int\left(v\frac{du}{dx}\right)dx$$

Basic applied mathematics

Newton's Laws of Motion were first published in his *Principia* in 1687.
(1) Every body continues in its state of rest, or of uniform motion in a straight line, unless it be compelled by external impressed forces to change that state.
(2) The rate of change of momentum is proportional to the impressed force, and takes place in the direction of the straight line which the force acts.
(3) To every action there is an equal and opposite reaction.
Newton's famous Law of Gravitation states that Every particle of matter attracts every other particle of matter with a force which varies directly as the product of the masses of the particles, and inversely as the square of the distance between them. This may be expressed as
$$F \propto \frac{m_1 m_2}{d^2}$$

Law 2 leads to the definition of a unit of force as that which, acting on a unit of mass, generates in it unit acceleration.
This leads to the fundamental equation
$F = ma$.

Basic equation of motion with constant acceleration

$s = \dfrac{1}{2}t(u + v)$ | $v^2 = u^2 + 2as$

$v = u + at$ | $s = ut + \dfrac{1}{2}at^2$

where

u = initial velocity $\qquad v$ = final velocity
s = distance (space) $\qquad a$ = acceleration
$\qquad\qquad\qquad\qquad\quad t$ = time

For constant velocity,
Distance = velocity × time.

Relative velocity
To find the velocity (and direction) of a body A relative to a body B, combine with the velocity of A a velocity equal and opposite to that of B. The sides of the triangle represent the velocities in magnitude and direction.
Thus to a person on a ship B, the ship A would *appear* to be moving in the direction (and at the speed) represented by the double-arrowed line.

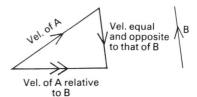

Triangle of velocities
The triangle ABC shows how the track (i.e. the actual direction) and velocity relative to the ground (the ground speed) of an aircraft or boat may be found from the course set and the wind or current.

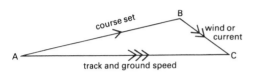

In vector terms, $\overrightarrow{AB} + \overrightarrow{BC} = \overrightarrow{AC}$

Projectiles
For simple cases, in which air resistance is neglected and the vertical velocity is subject only to the force of gravity, the following results may be derived from the fundamental equations of motion:

(1) The time of flight
$$T = \frac{2u \sin \theta}{g}$$
(2) The time to the greatest height
$$= \frac{T}{2}$$
$$= \frac{u \sin \theta}{g}$$

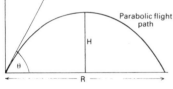

Parabolic flight path

(3) The greatest height attained
$$H = \frac{u^2 \sin^2 \theta}{2g}$$
(4) The range on a horizontal plane
$$R = \frac{u^2 \sin 2\theta}{g}$$
For a given velocity of projection u there are, in general, two possible angles of projection to obtain a given horizontal range. These directions will make equal angles with the vertical and horizontal respectively. For maximum range the angle makes 45° with the horizontal.
Note that
(1) the time taken for a body moving freely under gravity is the same to rise as it is to descend.
(2) the velocity at any point on its upward path is equal to that at the same point on its downward path, and that consequently . . .
(3) its velocity (and direction) on striking the ground at the same horizontal level are equal to that with which it was projected.

Impact of elastic bodies
If the bodies are smooth (e.g. two billiard balls) and only the forces between the bodies are considered, then the following equations will determine the velocities and directions of the bodies after the impact.
(1) Momentum (i.e. product of the individual masses and velocities) along the line of centres after impact = momentum *in the same direction* before impact.
(2) The velocity of separation = the velocity of approach (also measured along the line of centres) multiplied by the coefficient of elasticity between the two bodies.
If the impact is oblique (and the bodies are smooth) the velocities at right-angles to the line of centres are unchanged.
If u_1 and u_2, m_1 and m_2 are the initial velocities and masses of the two spheres, and α, β the angles these velocities make with the line of centres, and v_1 and v_2 the components of velocities *along the line of centres* after impact, then the above statements are represented by the following equations:
(1) $m_1 v_1 + m_2 v_2 = m_1 u_1 \cos \alpha + m_2 u_2 \cos \beta$
(2) $v_2 \pm v_1 = e (u_1 \cos \alpha - u_2 \cos \beta)$

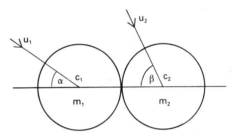

where e is the coefficient of elasticity between the two bodies. Note that in equation 2, v_1 and v_2 will be added or subtracted to get the 'velocity of separation' according to whether the bodies are considered to be going in the opposite or same direction respectively. The conditions of the problem will determine this for the 'velocity of approach'. In the example m_1 is 'catching up' on m_2 and therefore we take the difference in their velocities to obtain velocity of approach.

Motion in a circle
If a body is moving in a circle with uniform speed, then its linear velocity v is given by the equation $v = r\omega$ where r is the radius of the circle, and ω is the angular velocity. The body will nevertheless have an acceleration (since a force is acting on it to make it move in a circle) but this will be directed *towards* the centre.
The acceleration will be $\frac{v^2}{r}$ or $r\omega^2$ and the force producing it will be $\frac{mv^2}{r}$ or $mr\omega^2$ where m is the mass of the body.

Note that if a body is whirled round on the end of a string there is no tendency for it to move outwards along the *radius* of the circle. If the string breaks it will instead move straight on along the *tangent* to the circle.

In the case of a train going round a curve the necessary force is provided by the flanges on the wheels, while in the case of a car going round a track it is provided by the friction between the wheels and the ground. By banking the rails or road the weight of the train or car may be made to provide the necessary force.

The required angle to prevent any tendency to skid is given by the equation

$$\tan \theta = \frac{v^2}{gr}$$

where θ is the angle made with the horizontal by the banking. It is the same angle by which a cyclist would have to lean over from the *vertical* when going round a corner.

Simple harmonic motion

If a particle moves so that its acceleration is directed towards a fixed point in its path, and is proportional to its distance from that point, it is said to move with simple harmonic motion.

The fundamental equation is $\dfrac{d^2x}{dt^2} = -\omega^2 x$, and by integrating the corresponding equation $v\dfrac{dv}{dx} = -\omega^2 x$ the velocity at any displacement x is given by

$v = \omega\sqrt{a^2 - x^2}$ where a is the maximum value of x.

By solving the first equation we find that
$x = a \cos \omega t$ (if $t = 0$ when $x = a$) or
$x = a \sin \omega t$ (if $t = 0$ when $x = 0$)

The period of the motion is given by $T = \dfrac{2\pi}{\omega}$

Statics

Some fundamental principles of **statics** (the study of the forces acting on bodies at rest, as opposed to

dynamics, the study of bodies in motion) are:
(1) The *moment of a force* about a point is the product of the force and the perpendicular distance of the line of action of the force from the point.
(2) For a body to be at rest under a system of forces in one plane,
   (a) the algebraic sum of the resolved parts of the forces in any two directions which are not parallel must be zero, and
   (b) the algebraic sum of the moments of the forces about any point must be zero (i.e. clockwise moments = anticlockwise moments).
(3) For a system of particles of weights w_1, w_2, w_3 etc. whose distances from a fixed axis are x_1, x_2, x_3, etc., the position of the centre of gravity from

that axis is given by $x = \dfrac{\sum wx}{\sum w}$ where $\sum wx$ is the

sum of all the weights of the particles.

From this, the centres of gravity of irregular shapes, or shapes with portions missing, can be found by the principles that
the Moment of the whole = the sum of the moments of the parts
and the Moment of the remainder = the moment of the whole − the sum of the moments of the parts removed

The positions of the centres of gravity of some important shapes are as follows:
(a) A triangle   at the intersection of the medians (i.e. the lines joining the vertices to the mid-points of the opposite sides) or at one-third of the length of the median from the base.

(b) Square, rectangle, parallelogram, rhombus   at the intersection of the diagonals.

(c) Sector of a circle of angle 2θ radians   at a distance $\dfrac{2}{3}\dfrac{r\sin\theta}{\theta}$ from the centre along the line bisecting the sector, where r = the radius.

For a semi-circle $\theta = \dfrac{\pi}{2}$ and the distance of the centre of gravity from the centre of the circle will $= \dfrac{4r}{3\pi}$

(d) A solid pyramid on any base   at a point one-quarter of the height of the pyramid above the base.

(e) A hollow cone   at a point one-third of the height from the base.

(f) A solid hemisphere   at a point along the axis distant $\dfrac{3r}{8}$ from the centre where r is the radius.

(g) A hollow hemisphere   at a point distant $\dfrac{r}{2}$ along the axis from the centre.
[Note that this is the same as for the centre of gravity of the cylinder which would surround, or contain, the hemisphere.]

(h) A solid, or hollow closed cylinder   Half-way along the axis.

(4) If a rigid body is in equilibrium under the action of three forces in a plane, the lines of action of these forces must either all be parallel, or must meet at a common point. The sum of the three forces must be zero, and therefore it must thus always be possible to draw a triangle to represent the forces.
(5) The Laws of Friction.
   (a) The direction of the frictional force is opposite to that in which the body tends to move.
   (b) The magnitude of the friction is, up to a certain point, exactly equal to the force tending to produce motion.
   (c) Only a certain amount of friction can be called into play. This is called 'limiting friction'.
   (d) The magnitude of the limiting friction for a given pair of surfaces bears a constant ratio to the normal (i.e. perpendicular) pressure between the surfaces. This ratio is denoted by μ and is called the Coefficient of Friction.
   (e) The amount of friction is independent of the areas and shape of the surfaces in contact provided the normal pressure remains unaltered.
   (f) When motion takes place, the friction still opposes the motion. It is independent of the velocity, and is proportional to the normal pressure, but is less than the limiting friction.
If F is the limiting friction (i.e. the force of friction when motion is about to occur), and R is the normal (perpendicular) force, then

$F = \mu R$ where μ is the coefficient of friction

The resultant of the forces F and R makes an angle (usually denoted by λ) with R, and thus

$$\tan \lambda = \frac{F}{R}$$

$$= \mu$$

λ is called the Angle of Friction.
These relationships are illustrated in the following diagrams:

λ = Angle of Friction

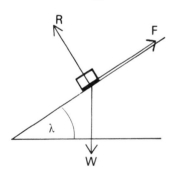

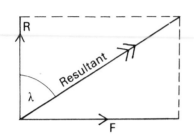

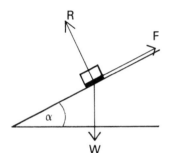

Mathematical symbols

=	equal to
≠	not equal to
≡	identically equal to; congruent
>	greater than
<	less than
≯	not greater than
≮	not less than
⩾	equal to or greater than
⩽	equal to or less than
≏	approximately equal to
+	plus
−	minus
±	plus or minus
×	multiplication (times)
÷	divided by
( ) [ ] { }	brackets, square brackets, enveloping brackets
‖	parallel
∦	not parallel
#	numbers to follow (USA)
%	per cent(um) (hundred)
‰	per mille (thousand)
∝	varies with
∞	infinity
$r!$ or $\angle r$	factorial r
$\sqrt{}$	square root
$\sqrt[n]{}$	nth root
r^n	r to the power n
Δ	triangle, finite difference or increment
~	difference
Σ	summation
∫	integration sign
° ′ ″	degree, minute, second ($1° = 60'$, $1' = 60''$)
→	appropriate limit of; tends to
∴	therefore
∵	because
⇒	implies that
⇐	is implied by
⇔	is equivalent to

If a body is placed on an inclined plane, then if the angle of the plane (α) is less than the angle of friction, it will not slide down.
If the angle of the plane is equal to λ, the angle of friction, the body will be just on the point of sliding. If the angle of the plane is greater than the angle of friction the body will slide.

COMPUTERS

History

The story of computers is the story of human efforts to solve problems. It required discoveries in several directions to lay the groundwork for computing as we know it; in speeding up calculations, in automating repetitive processes, and in learning to code and store information in ways that speeded up its handling.

In the history of computing the first invention was probably the abacus. From around 3000 BC traders living around the Mediterranean worked out their prices and profits using this simple device of rods and beads – the beads in different sections representing different units of value.

In 17th-century Europe the ferment of interest in the new sciences, such as astronomy and navigation, spurred creative minds to simplify computations. It could take years for early scientists to calculate the vast quantities of numerical data whose patterns they were trying to unravel. In 1614 the Scotsman John Napier reported his discovery of logarithms, enabling the products of complex multiplications to be reduced to a process of simple addition. Very soon after, in the 1620s, the slide rule was invented, based upon the mathematical principles Napier had discovered.

In the later 1600s the Frenchman Blaise Pascal and the German Gottfried Wilhelm von Leibniz devised simple calculators – they were not easy to use reliably but the logical problems underlying the devices continued to challenge advanced thinkers over the next centuries. It was not until the 19th century that inventors were moving towards the design of a prototype computer.

The desire of a French cloth manufacturer to automate the weaving of complex patterns advanced the technology needed for computing. Joseph Jacquard, in 1804, began using a loom which used punched cards to control the creation of complex fabric designs. (The same technique came to be used in pianolas or 'player pianos', which utilized punched cards to play back piano music, both popular and classical, and which were able to reproduce the performances recorded by famous artists.)

Here a most surprising name appears in the cast of computer enthusiasts – the Lady Augusta Byron, daughter of the poet, Lord Byron. Her active interest in and promotion of a machine devised by the 19th-century inventor, Charles Babbage, have led some to describe her as 'the first computer programmer'. She saw Babbage's machine as a sort of mathematical loom, that could carry out any pattern of calculations which had been punched onto cards. Babbage never succeeded in manufacturing his 'Analytical Engine' which conventional wisdom declared to be 'too advanced for the technology of his time'. However, the Swedish inventor, Scheutz, demonstrated a simpler version (based on Babbage's earlier 'Difference Engine') at the Paris Exposition of 1855.

Building on similar ideas in the USA, for the 1890 census Herman Hollerith devised a punched card machine to record census information on every citizen. To public amazement, the census results were ready in only six weeks' time. Hollerith's success in selling his machine – he even sold one to Czarist Russia – led him to found the company which eventually became known as IBM.

From Leibniz's time, advanced thinkers had seen the merits of a simple logic system such as 'EITHER–OR' or 'TRUE–FALSE', to test a series of logical propositions. In calculating devices, such dualities could be converted into 'SWITCH ON or SWITCH OFF' choices to record data.

After Jacquard, punched cards could be used to indicate the presence or absence of information on any point – a perforation showing the presence of data and non-perforation showing its absence. The cards were manipulated by cogs and wheels or, on Hollerith's census machine, by pins, which recorded the answers given by every citizen on every question included in the census.

In 1930, Vannevar Bush (USA) at MIT designed the 'differential analyser', marking the start of our computer age; the 'analyser' was an electromechanical machine which measured degrees of change in a model. The machine took up most of a large room. In order to analyse a new problem, engineers had to change the gear ratios, and they would emerge two or three days later, hands coated in oil. Nevertheless, the machine's ability to handle complex calculations far surpassed any previous invention. In 1936 the maverick scientist, Alan Turing of Britain, captured scientific attention with his influential paper 'On Computable Numbers with an Application to the Entscheidungsproblem' suggesting that if his vision of a universal computer were implemented, solutions might now be found to previously unsolvable problems.

The Second World War saw Germany and the Western countries in competition to develop the capacity for faster calculation, along with better capabilities for creating codes and for decoding the enemies' messages. In response to this pressure, the US developed the enormous Mark I computer at Harvard, which stood 2·5 m (8 ft) high and which held 15·5 m (51 ft) of relays, wires and switches. Its designer, Howard Aiken, had used Babbage's ideas as a guide, and Mark I became dedicated to solving the Navy's ballistics problems. In Germany, Konrad Zuse was testing the projected aerodynamics of rockets in the computer he had first set up in his parents' living room. In England, the 'Colossus' decoder (based on Alan Turing's ideas) succeeded in cracking the German Enigma codes in 1943, scanning code messages at a rate of 5000 characters per second.

Also from 1943 the ENIAC computer was being developed in the States to help gunners improve their targeting under varying weather and ground conditions. Only completed after the war's end, this giant – 5·5 m (18 ft) high, 24 m (80 ft) long and weighing 30 tons – worked a thousand times faster than the Mark I.

In early computers (including the one used by

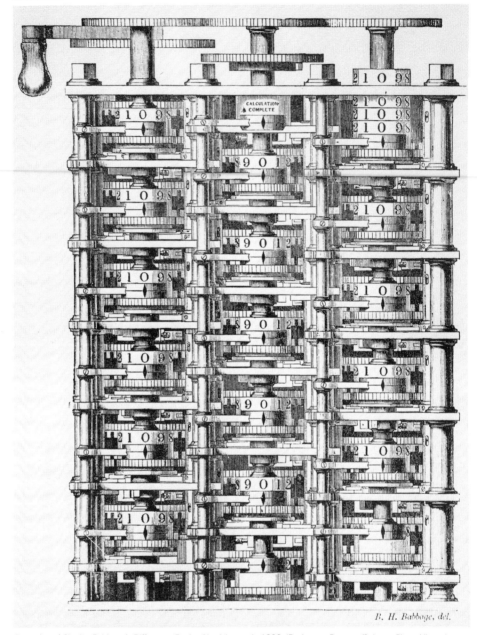

B. H. Babbage, del.

Engraving of Charles Babbage's Difference Engine No. 1 begun in 1823. (Dr Jeremy Burgess/Science Photo Library)

Zuse to test feasibility of rockets) information had been passed by mechanical relay switches. These were coil-wrapped iron bars which, when magnetized by a flow of electricity, attracted a pivot – thereby completing a circuit that allowed the electrical pulse to proceed through the system. The switches were noisy and subject to constant mechanical failure.

In Britain's 'Colossus' decoder, the mechanical relay devices had been replaced by vacuum tubes, enabling far speedier passage of information within the computer. This was said to be the first 'electronic' computer. But vacuum tubes had their own weaknesses – they required huge sources of electrical power and burned out constantly. Engineers working with the giant ENIAC computer found the vacuum tubes could cause overheating to a temperature of 49°C (120°F).

As a 1949 newspaper article reported: 'Edsac (Electronic Delay Storage Automatic Calculator) – a gigantic high speed ready reckoner – works some 15 000 times faster than the human brain. The photo shows the mechanical 'brain' with its racks of valves (3500) and cathode tubes (left). In front of the machine are the designers, M. V. Wilkes (left) and W. Renwick.' (Popperfoto)

And even on the ENIAC, wires had to be hand-set to solve each new problem. The process might take two days, during which the technicians disconnected and reconnected hundreds of wires.

For the industry to advance, computers had to be able to transfer and amplify electrical current more efficiently, using better conductors and resistors. In 1948 development in the US of the transistor – in one early form a sort of 'electronic sandwich' only about 13 mm (½ in) long – was the breakthrough to the increasing miniaturization of computers.

Three Bell Laboratories' scientists, William Shockley, John Bardeen and Walter Brattain, shared credit for the transistor's invention, jointly receiving a Nobel Prize in physics in 1956. Shockley is credited with the transistor's entry into the marketplace, a workable transistor appearing in 1951.

The 'fifties saw a ferment in innovation, much of which occurred in Palo Alto, California, where the brightest minds had set up their own companies.

The next development was the integrated circuit or 'IC', soon to be nicknamed the 'chip'. Robert Noyce of Fairchild is credited with its invention. Manufacture of the microchip, 6·45 mm² (a tenth of an inch square), was soon followed by the capacity to crowd as many as 10 miniaturized transistors – and eventually a thousand varied parts – into the same space.

By 1971, the microprocessor had been developed by Noyce's new company, Intel. This innovation put onto a single microchip the circuitry for all of a computer's usual functions. Circuits which had formerly been 'hard-wired' to perform a single function could now be engraved on the chips in a series of wafer-thin layers. These made computing faster and more flexible, the improved circuitry allowed the computer to perform several tasks at once and to allocate memory more efficiently.

The contribution of these inventions has been immeasurable in providing personal computers that are easy to use. Users take for granted fast and reliable responses to commands and a vast store of memory both in terms of current working memory – RAM – and hard disk space to store completed work. 'Old hands' tell how, using mainframes in the early 1960s, they were limited to 4K of working memory – about 1½ typed pages. Writing programs, they had to keep command lines short; their commands were sent through 'memory devices' which could retain only a limited amount before the surplus was lost. Program writers would have to 'catch' electronically some of the commands before they vanished to avoid having to rewrite that line of program.

In the 1960s a programmer, walking into the heart of a mainframe computer, like the Ferranti 'Deuce', could watch the commands – represented by 'blips' of light – pass through a glowing tube; and the last 'blip' needed to be 'caught' before it vanished. If one blinked, the 'blip' would be lost and

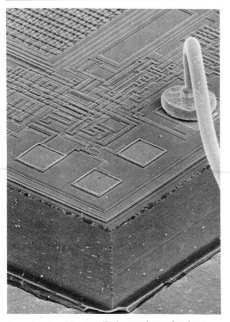

An early microchip, magnified many times, showing a connecting pin. The chip (or integrated circuit) reproduced in miniature form a circuitry that had occupied roomfuls of circuits in previous models. Its development enabled long sets of coded instructions to be stored in memory rather than having to be created anew each time a problem was to be solved. (Dr Jeremy Burgess, Science Photo Library)

one would have to rewrite the line of instructions.

Two types of computer, the analogue and the digital, have developed to serve quite different needs. The analogue computer responds instantly to events in 'real-time' using a model of the test product, and has been used to test factors such as voltage, angle and speed in order to improve the design of existing products. Its memory storage, however, was limited, and it was not capable of being programmed. The prototype built in 1930 at MIT by Vannevar Bush was of this type.

The digital computer is the one normally associated with the word 'computer', having a large memory store to hold data that has been fed in by operators and translated into a code for speed of data manipulation. The computer responds to the sequence of commands previously stored which are termed 'programs'. Recently, hybrid computers have come into use, taking the best features of the two systems. They can simulate flight of guided missile systems and spacecraft.

Leibniz originated, and in the 19th century George Boole developed, the logic of the universal language used by computers known as binary code. This language has enabled data – whether alphabets, number systems, logical statements or, most recently, visual and sound units – to be represented in unique patterns of On–Off pulses. The 'On' pulse is written as 1 and the 'Off' as 0.

A total os 128 permutations of these patterns are available. In one coding system the letter 'A' carries 1 'On' pulse and 6 'Off' pulses; the letter 'Z' codes as 4 pulses 'On' and 3 'Off'. (An 8th pulse is kept in reserve to check the accuracy of transmission.) These pulses are termed 'bits' (shorthand for 'binary digits') and the 8 'bits' make 1 'byte'. The byte is the basic unit of measurement for memory storage capacity in computers.

Much of the world's store of knowledge has now been committed to computers, and mankind looks to computers to help in the conquest of disease, of global environmental problems – and to further exploration of everything from chromosomes to outer space. Organizations now require more and more information to be held on computer; in business, people often complain that documents and contracts have become longer and often more complex. It has come as something of a surprise that many people working with computers find themselves doing repetitive work that they thought computers were designed to replace. Increased use of scanners and voice recognition systems may enable more data to be fed to computers without operators having to type it in, but the need for manual 'keying in' of information will continue until the cost of such alternative systems falls.

While the early milestones in computing resulted in a device to ease work, recent milestones have come from people's attempts to protect themselves against the dangers, the intrusions and authority of computers over their working and personal lives. Man's creativity has been vastly spurred by such a powerful servant; it would appear that his well-being depends upon his keeping control over the uses to which computers are put.

Milestones

3000 BC. The abacus, widely used in the Mediterranean area; possibly of Babylonian origin.

1614 Napier's logarithms, forerunner to slide rule.

1642 Blaise Pascal's adding machine consisting of wheels and cogs, each wheel representing a decimal column.

1666 Leibniz proposed a 'universal language' which would enable all rational thought to be treated mathematically. He went on to refine the binary system.

1673 Leibniz's calculator, adding a movable element to Pascal's device to speed repetitive calculations. It could divide and multiply sums.

1804 Jacquard loom – first punched cards in machine processes.

1822 Babbage's design of the 'Difference Engine' which he hoped would be used to eradicate mathematical errors, e.g. in navigational calculations.

1847 George Boole's paper on a universal language, 'The Mathematical Analysis of Logic'.

1890 Hollerith tabulator – used for US census.

1930 Forerunner to analogue computer built by Vannevar Bush at Massachusetts Institute of Technology (USA).

1936 Alan Turing published his influential paper proposing a universal machine: 'On Computable Numbers with an Application to the Entscheidungsproblem'.

1941 The German Konrad Zuse developed his home-made model Z3, an operational binary system computer, to test German rockets.

1943 Mark I computer, Harvard University (USA). The 'Colossus' code-breaking machine at Bletchley Park (UK) decoded German

Enigma codes as part of a highly secret project with which Alan Turing was connected. First device to use valves rather than relay switches.

1946 Unveiling of ENIAC computer (USA), the first large digital computer. Its first use was assessing feasibility of hydrogen bomb.

1948 First computer with a memory – the Manchester University Mark 1 (USA).

1949 Invention of the transistor (USA).

Konrad Zuse marketed successors to his Z4 computer in Germany.

The Edsac (electronic delay storage automatic calculator), Cambridge University, England, was designed by M. V. Wilkes and W. Renwick. It was said to work some 15 000 times faster than the human brain.

In England, Lyon's Corner Houses installed the world's first Electronic Office under the name of LEO for accounting and stock control.

1951 EDVAC computer, first US computer to use binary code and to write part of program for its own development.

1952 First national election in which a computer analysed voting patterns to predict election results (USA).

1954 IBM began mass-production of computers.

1956 The term 'artificial intelligence' was first used in the USA.

1958 First computer-matched couple married in Hollywood.

1959 Invention of the microchip.

1965 Digital Equipment produced the first widely marketed minicomputer.

Computerized typesetting first used in Germany.

PROLOG programming language devised to advance development of computers with Artificial Intelligence.

1971 A coin-operated computer (Hewlett-Packard) gave 2½ minutes of computer time for 25 cents in a California public library.

Invention of the microprocessor, enabling many of a computer's parts to be held on a single chip. The 4004 microprocessor was designed by Ted Hoff of Intel.

1975 The American company MITS marketed Altair, the first personal computer, also available in kit form.

1977 Steven Jobs marketed the Apple II microcomputer, developed in partnership with Stephen Wozniak. From a start-up capital of $1300, in three years Apple became a company selling $117 million of computers.

The Swedish National Bureau of Statistics reported health problems among VDU operators: 75 per cent suffered eyestrain; 55 per cent back and shoulder problems; 35 per cent head and neck problems; 25 per cent arm and wrist problems; 15 per cent leg problems. In Canada and Italy similar problems of vision impairments, postural problems, stress and also birth defects were reported.

1978 A 'hacker' was charged with defrauding a Los Angeles bank of $10·2 million.

1979 The University of Loughborough's Human Sciences and Advanced Technology research group (HUSAT) published the VDU Manual, widely regarded as the ' "ergonomic bible" for VDU work'.

1980 Norway's Labour Inspectorate instituted draft standards for VDU workplaces, which were generally felt to have set the standard for Europe. Draft regulations included eye tests and provision of lenses if required, limits of four hours per day during intensive keying in, and maintenance to ensure good image quality of screens.

British Telecom began marketing Prestel, the world's first videotex information service, offering 'electronic mail' and bulletin boards to subscribers.

1981 IBM introduced IBM-PC to personal computer market, which led to acceptance of desktop (micro)computers in the business world and to the development of easy-to-use programs designed for non-technicians. An example is the Lotus 1-2-3 spreadsheet program.

West Germany passed national regulations regarding VDU workstations. Regulations required VDU designs to conform to national standards, and adjustability of displays, document holders, tables and chairs. Regular eye tests for operators were also required.

1984 The Apple Macintosh appeared with mouse (movable desktop pointing device) and user-friendly screen that enabled users to carry out standard procedures by pointing at pictures (ikons) rather than having to type commands.

A New York Workers' Compensation Board Panel found a connection between a youthful employee's development of cataracts in both eyes and her use of VDUs.

Apricot (UK) released a portable microcomputer, capable of limited voice recognition.

A British Industrial Tribunal decided that a woman library assistant's fears of using a video screen during pregnancy were 'not ill-founded' and required that she be given alternative work.

1985 Japan's General Council of Trade Unions reported that, on average, one-third of women users of VDUs experienced problems during pregnancy or delivery. Among the 250 women surveyed, two-thirds of those using the screen for six hours a day or more reported problems during pregnancy.

The transputer, devised by Ian Barron of Inmos (UK), enabled a single computer to handle parallel processing of information. (This is distinct from multi-tasking: division of the task into such minute fractions of time that the computer appears to handle them simultaneously.)

1986 Data Protection Act passed in Britain, requiring disclosure of computer-held information to anyone requesting it.

1987 In Britain, draft standards were set by the British Standards Institute (BSI) requiring conformity to minimal standards of video screen clarity and keyboards.

1988 First USA bill passed to regulate use in the workplace of visual display units, requiring regular rest breaks from screen use.

British and American Press reported alleged computer-held blacklists, being maintained to block employment of political activists and to prevent tenancies being given to tenant rights activists.

EEC proposed a directive to set guidelines on trianing, eye examinations, employers' provision of spectacles where recommended, and design elements of computer and work-station, along with noise limitation. In December 1988 the House of Lords Select Committee vetoed the directive, placing British workers outside its protection. ICL and Tender Electronic Systems jointly designed an improved laser disk for general-purpose computing.

Most innovative new product: Wang's Free-style computer, recording both handwritten data – written with an electronic pen – and spoken messages.

Japanese devise programming language to facilitate use of PROLOG in Artificial Intelligence research.

1989 Britain's Museum of Science began fund-raising campaign to construct Babbage's 'Difference Engine': the target sum £250 000, for completion in 1991. (This compares with £17 000 funding – in today's terms £435 000 – given to Babbage by the British government in the early 1800s before they lost patience with his inability to produce a working model.)

Breakthrough by British Telecom in develop-ment of computers to run on light instead of electricity. Their new switch will manipulate pulses of light, enabling faster transmission over great distances.

Performing at ten times the speed of previous chips, the RISC (Reduced Instruction Set Computer) chip (RISCi 860) was developed by INTEL (USA). This breakthrough brings 'Artificial Intelligence' to business computers at a fraction of the price of the former multi-million dollar super-computers.

Human Computer – Mrs Shakuntala Devi of India multiplied two 13-digit numbers in 28 seconds. The numbers were picked at random by the Computer Department of Imperial College, London. They were 7 686 369 774 870 × 2 465 099 745 779 and her answer was 18 947 668 177 995 426 462 773 730.

Glossary

Analogue (analog) computer Deals with data having physical quantity and which is constantly changing. The output may be graphed instantly by a plotting pen, and this output may in turn drive another device. Analogue computers operate in 'real time', as events occur, rather than handling previously stored and coded data.

Archive Stored data, usually held separately from that held on-line.

Artificial Intelligence Refers to computer programs intended to simulate human learning and decision-taking abilities.

Binary code Representation of symbols or characters by patterns of 0s and 1s.

Bit From BInary digiT. The smallest unit of information that can be recognized by a computer.

Bulletin board A computer-linked database for holding messages and information.

Byte A byte usually contains eight bits. Each byte corresponds to one character of data; a single letter, number or symbol. A unit of measurement for computer memory capacity.

Character Any symbol capable of being stored and processed by a computer.

Chip Small piece of crystal (usually silicon) etched in a pattern to form a logical circuit or circuits.

Circuit Complete path of an electrical current.

Conductor Substance that enables passage of electricity.

Data Factors such as characters or symbols stored by a computer from which 'information' is derived after processing.

Database Structured collection of data which can be analysed and interrogated on computer to retrieve items (or combinations of items) that match selected criteria.

Digital computer One that processes previously stored and coded data.

Electronic Referring to the flow of electrons; in computing, typically in devices employing vacuum tubes, transistors or chips.

Electronic mail Information directed to specific users' screens or held in 'computer mailboxes' for access by users typing in codes. Information held on a 'bulletin board' can be accessed by any user.

Hacker One that explores a computer system, possibly with criminal intent.

Hard disk A magnetic storage disk typically installed permanently in the computer and holding many times the data which can be held on removable disks.

Hard-wired Restricted functioning of a computer limited by soldered connections, and not responsive to varying software commands.

Ikon Screen picture that represents a standard computer function; a typical ikon is an onscreen 'wastebasket' that a user can point to when he wants to delete a file.

K Usually translated as thousands of bytes; actually 1K = 1024 bytes.

Keying in Typing at a computer keyboard.

Laser disk Disk capable of storing vast quantities of archive files in a minute area, prepared by focusing a narrow beam of light on to it. Its main use is archive storage of data, though it can be used interactively.

Mainframe A large computer whose stored data may be accessed by 100 or more terminals.

Memory Usually refers to currently accessible store (RAM), but sometimes can refer to disk storage capabilities.

Microchip Circuit formed on a small semiconductor, usually by etching and chemical treatment.

Microprocessor Device capable of holding memory and instructions, comprising a basic unit of a microcomputer.

Microcomputer Low-cost, independent computer unit based on the microprocessor, requiring low power and, unless linked into a network, having limited memory.

Minicomputer Small computer standing between capabilities of the microcomputer and the mainframe in speed, power and data handling. Developed during the US space research programme to meet the need for a small computer which could be moved on site.

Mouse Hand-held device that rolls across a tabletop, used as an alternative to the computer keyboard to access a screen.

Network A system of computers connected to each other through cable, telephone, data communication technology, or even radio.

Program A set of instructions that a system follows to carry out tasks.

Prestel The British Telecom videotex information service, designed to be received on home televisions and computers, the communications carried on public telephone lines.

RAM Random Access Memory. Memory available for current work, which is lost when computer is switched off, unless work is transferred out of RAM on to permanent store such as disk.

Relay switches Switches controlled electromagnetically, typically used in analogue computers.

Resistor Substance impeding the flow of a current.

Scanner Device that transforms an image into coded signals that can be stored on computer and redisplayed. Using scanners, printed text can be stored directly on to disk without having to be keyed in.

Screen The display device on a computer, also called a monitor, VDU or VDT.

Semiconductor A material like silicon whose qualities as a conductor of electricity lie between metals and insulators. High temperatures increase its conductivity and low temperatures impede its conductivity.

Software The programs that give instructions to, or run on, a computer.

Spreadsheet Popular type of program enabling speedy analysis of financial data.

Terminal Device linked to a computer, comprising a keyboard, a VDU, or both.

Transistor Device that transfers current across a resistor.

Transputer Large, fast and powerful chip which, when paired with another, enables a computer to carry out two tasks simultaneously.

User-friendly Describes simple and easy-to-use computer products.

Vacuum tube An airless tube facilitating electronic passage of a current.

Videotex Information service designed for access by television screen or transmitted down telephone lines.

VDT – VDU Visual Display Terminal or Visual Display Unit.

Voice recognition A computer's ability to respond to spoken words.

Workstation The equipment used by a computer operator, and, increasingly, the associated furniture, lighting and working environment.

The latest development in micro-miniaturization, a wafer containing many chips densely packed. Their circuits are almost too small to be seen except under a microscope. (Science Photo Library)

INVENTIONS

The invention and discovery of drugs, and musical instruments are treated separately (see Index)

Object	Year	Inventor	Notes
Adding Machine	1623	Wilhelm Schickard (Ger)	Earliest commercial machine devised by William Burroughs (US) in St Louis, Missouri, in 1885
Aeroplane	1903	Orville (1871–1948) and Wilbur Wright (1867–1912) (US)	Kitty Hawk, North Carolina (17 Dec). First sustained controlled flight
Airship (non-rigid)	1852	Henri Giffard (Fr) (1825–82)	Steam-powered propeller, near Paris (24 Sept)
(rigid)	1900	Graf Ferdinand von Zeppelin (Ger) (1838–1917)	Bodensee (2 July)
Bakelite	1907	Leo H. Baekeland (Belg/US) (1863–1944)	First use, electrical insulation by Loando & Co, Boonton, New Jersey
Balloon	1783	Jacques (1745–99) and Joseph Montgolfier (1740–1810) (Fr)	Tethered flight, Paris (15 Oct) manned free flight, Paris (21 Nov) by François Pilâtre de Rozier and Marquis d'Arlandes. Father Bartolomeu de Gusmaõ (né Lourenço) (b. Brazil, 1685) demonstrated toy hot air balloon in Portugal on 8 Aug 1709
Ball-Point Markers	1888	John J. Loud (US)	First practical and low cost writing pens by Lazlo and Georg Biro (Hungary) in 1938
Barbed Wire	1867	Lucien B. Smith (patentee) (25 June)	Introduced to Britain in 1880 by 5th Earl Spencer in Leicestershire
Barometer	1644	Evangelista Torricelli (It) (1608–47)	Referred to in a letter of 11 June
Battery (Electric)	1800	Alessandro Volta (1745–1827)	Demonstrated to Napoleon in 1801
Bicycle	1839–40	Kirkpatrick Macmillan (Scot) (1810–78)	Pedal-driven cranks. First direct drive in March 1861 by Ernest Michaux (Fr)
Bicycle Tyres (pneumatic)	1888	John Boyd Dunlop (GB) (1840–1921)	Principle patented but undeveloped by Robert William Thomson (GB), 10 June 1845
			First motor car pneumatic tyres adapted by André and Edouard Michelin (Fr) 1895 (see Rubber tyres)
Bifocal Lens	1780	Benjamin Franklin (1706–90) (US)	His earliest experiments began c. 1760
Bronze (copper with tin) Working	c. 3700 BC	Pre-dynastic, Maidum, Egypt	Copper smelting with arsenical ores was practised earlier
Bunsen Burner	1855	Robert Wilhelm von Bunsen (1811–99) (Ger) at Heidelberg	Michael Faraday (1791–1867) (UK) had previously designed an adjustable burner
Burglar Alarm	1858	Edwin T. Holmes (US)	Electric, installed, Boston, Mass (21 Feb)
Car (steam gun tug)	1769	Nicolas Cugnot (Fr) (1725–1804)	Three-wheeled military tractor. Earliest for passengers was Richard Trevithick's eight-seater in Camborne, Cornwall, in 1801 (22 Dec).
(internal combustion)	1826	Samuel Brown (GB)	First powered with internal combustion engine was gas-powered carriage on Shooter's Hill, Blackheath, S.E. London.
(petrol)	1885	Karl Benz (Ger) (1844–1929)	First successful run Mannheim Nov or Dec. Patented 29 Jan 1886.
Carburettor	1876	Gottlieb Daimler (Ger) (1834–1900)	Carburettor spray: Charles E. Duryea (US) (1892)
Carpet Sweeper	1876	Melville R. Bissell (US)	Grand Rapids, Mich (Patent, 19 Sept)
Cash Register	1879	James Ritty (US) (Patent 4 Nov)	Built in Dayton, Ohio. Taken over by National Cash Register Co 1884
Cellophane	1908	Dr Jacques Brandenberger (Switz), Zurich	Machine production not before 1911
Celluloid	1861	Alexander Parkes (GB) (1813–90)	Invented in Birmingham, England; developed and trade marked by J. W. Hyatt (US) in 1870

Object	Year	Inventor	Notes
Cement (Portland)	1824	Joseph Aspdin (GB) (1779–1885)	Wakefield, Yorkshire (21 Oct)
Chronometer	1735	John Harrison (GB) (1693–1776)	Received in 1772 Government's £20 000 prize on offer since 1714
Cinema (see also Film)	1895	Auguste Marie Louis Nicolas Lumière (1862–1954) and Louis Lumière (1864–1948) (Fr)	Development pioneers were Etienne Jules Marey (Fr) (1830–1903) and Thomas A. Edison (US) (1847–1931). First public showing, Blvd des Capucines, Paris (28 Dec)
Clock (mechanical)	725	I-Hsing and Liang-Tsan (China)	Earliest escapement. Clockwork known in Greece by 80 BC
(pendulum)	1656	Christiaan Huygens (Neth) (1629–95)	
Compact Disc	1978	Philips (Netherlands) and Sony (Japan)	Needleless laser beam-read discs. First marketed in October 1982
Copper working	c. 7100 BC	A hammered reamer, Çayönü Tepesi, Turkey	Earliest smelting sites, Rudna Glava, Yugoslavia (Vinça culture) (c. 4500 BC)
Dental Plate	1817	Anthony A. Plantson (US) (1774–1837)	
Dental Plate (rubber)	1855	Charles Goodyear (US) (1800–60)	
Diesel Engine	1895	Rudolf Diesel (Ger) (1858–1913)	Diesel's first commercial success, Augsburg, 1897
Disc Brake	1902	Dr F. Lanchester (GB) (1868–1946)	First used on aircraft 1953 (Dunlop Rubber Co)
Dynamo	1832	Hypolite Pixii (Fr), demonstrated, Paris 3 Sept	Rotative dynamo, demonstrated by Joseph Saxton, Cambridge, England, June 1833
Electric Blanket	1883	Exhibited Vienna, Austria Exhibition	
Electric Flat Iron	1882	H. W. Seeley (US)	New York City, USA (Patent 6 June)
Electric Lamp	1879	Thomas Alva Edison (US) (1847–1931)	First practical demonstration at Menlo Park, New Jersey, USA, 20 Dec. Pioneer work on carbon filaments, Sir Joseph Swan (1828–1914), 1860
Electric Motor (DC)	1873	Zénobe Gramme (Belg) (1826–1901)	Exhibited in Vienna. Patent by Thomas Davenport (US) of Vermont, 25 Feb 1837
Electric Motor (AC)	1888	Nikola Tesla (b. Yugoslavia) (US) (1856–1943)	
Electromagnet	1824	William Sturgeon (GB) (1783–1850)	Improved by Joseph Henry (US) (1797–1878)
Electronic Computer (see Integrated Circuit)	1938	John Vincent Atanasoff (USA) (b. 1903) and Clifford E. Berry	Built the 300-valve ABC machine at Ames, Iowa: Alterable stored program Manchester University Mark I by Sir Frederick Williams and Prof T. Kilburn 1948: Point-contact transistor invented by John Bardeen (b. 1908) and Walter Brattain (1902–87) 16 Dec 1958
Film (moving outlines)	1885	Louis le Prince	Institute for the Deaf, Washington Hts, New York City, USA
(talking)	1922	Josef Engl, Josef Mussolle and Hans Vogt (Germany)	Der Brandstifter, Alhambra, Berlin (17 Sept)
(musical sound)	1923	Dr Lee de Forest (US) (1873–1961)	New York demonstration (13 Mar)
Fountain Pen	1884	Lewis E. Waterman (US) (1837–1901)	Patented by D. Hyde (US), 1830, undeveloped
Galvanometer	1834	André-Marie Ampère (1755–1836)	First measurement of flow of electricity with a free-moving needle
Gas Lighting	1792	William Murdoch (GB) (1754–1839)	Private house in Cornwall, 1792; Factory Birmingham, 1798; London streets, 1807
Glass (stained)	ante 850	St Paul's, Jarrow, Durham	Earliest complete window Augsburg, Germany, c. 1080
Glassware	c. 2600 BC	Eshanna, Mesopotamia	Glass blowing, Sidon, Syria, c. 50 BC
Glider	1853	Sir George Cayley (GB) (1773–1857)	Near Brompton Hall, Yorkshire. Passenger possibly John Appleby. Emmanuel Swedenborg (1688–1772) sketches dated 1716.
Gramophone	1878	Thomas Alva Edison (US) (1847–1931)	Hand-cranked cylinder at Menlo Park, NJ. Patent, 19 Feb. First described on 30 Apr 1877 by Charles Cros (1842–88) (Fr)

Object	Year	Inventor	Notes
Gyro-compass	1911	Elmer A. Sperry (US) (1860–1930)	Tested on USS *Delaware*, (28 Aug). Gyroscope devised 1852 by Jean Foucault (Fr) (1819–68)
Helicopter	1924	Etienne Oehmichen (Fr)	First FAI world record set on 14 Apr 1924. Earliest drawing of principle Le Mans Museum, France *c*. 1460. First serviceable machine by Igor Sikorsky (US), 1939
Hovercraft	1955	Sir Christopher Cockerell (GB) (b. 1910)	Patented 12 Dec. Earliest air-cushion vehicle patent was in 1877 by J. I. Thornycroft (1843–1928) (GB). First 'flight' Saunders Roe SRN-1 at Cowes, England, 30 May 1959
Integrated Circuit	1952	Concept by Geoffrey Dummer (GB) (b. 1909)	First reduced to practice Harwick Johnson (US), Princeton, NY, May 1953
Iron Working (Carburised iron)	*c*. 1323 BC	Unknown foreign ironsmith	Regular working initiated by the Hittites, in Anatolia, Turkey, *c*. 1250 BC. Tutankhamun's ceremonial dagger. He reigned from 1361 to 1352 BC
Jet Engine	1937	Sir Frank Whittle (GB) (b. 1907)	First test bed run, Rugby (12 Apr). Principles announced by Merconnet (Fr) 1909 and Maxime Guillaume (Fr) 1921. First flight 27 Aug 1939 by Heinkel He-178
Laser	1960	Dr Charles H. Townes (US) (b. 1915). First demonstration by Theodore Maiman (US) (b. 1927)	Demonstrated at Hughes Research, Malibu, California, in July. Abbreviation for Light amplification by stimulated emission of radiation
Launderette	1934	J. F. Cantrell (US)	Fort Worth, Texas (18 Apr)
Lift (Mechanical)	1852	Elisha G. Otis (US) (1811–61)	Earliest elevator at Yonkers, NY
Lightning Conductor	1752	Benjamin Franklin (US) (1706–90)	Philadelphia, Pennsylvania, USA, in Sept.
Linoleum	1860	Frederick Walton (GB)	
Locomotive (railed)	1804	Richard Trevithick (GB) (1771–1833)	Penydarren, Wales, 14·4 km (*9 miles*) (21 Feb)
Loom, power	1785	Edmund Cartwright (GB) (1743–1823)	
Loudspeaker	1900	Horace Short (GB) patentee	A compressed air Auxetophone. First used atop the Eiffel Tower, summer 1900. Earliest open-air electric public address system used by Bell Telephone on Staten Island, NY, USA, on 30 June 1916
Machine Gun	1718	James Puckle (GB) patentee, 15 May 1718. White Cron Alley factory in use 1721	Richard Gatling (US) (1818–1903) model dates from 1861
Maps	*c*. 2250 BC	Sumerian (clay tablets of river Euphrates)	Earliest measurement by Eratosthenes *c*. 220 BC. Earliest printed map printed in Bologna, Italy, 1477
Margarine	1869	Hippolyte Mège-Mouries (Fr)	Patented 15 July
Match, safety	1826	John Walker (GB), Stockton, Teesside	
Microphone	1876	Alexander Graham Bell (1847–1922) (US)	Name coined 1878 by Prof David Hughes, who gave demonstration in London in January 1878
Micro-processor	1971	Marcian E. Hoff (US) (b. 1937) June	Launched by US company Intel (Robert Noyce) Dec
Microscope	1590	Zacharias Janssen (Neth)	Compound convex-concave lens
Motor Cycle	1885	Gottlieb Daimler (1834–1900) of Cannstatt, Germany, patent 29 Aug	First rider Paul Daimler (10 Nov 1885); first woman rider Mrs Edward Butler near Erith, Kent, 1888
Neon Lamp	1910	Georges Claude (Fr) (1871–1960)	First installation at Paris Motor Show (3 Dec)
Night Club	1843	Paris, France	First was Le Bal des Anglais, Paris 5me. (Closed *c*. 1960)
Nylon	1937	Dr Wallace H. Carothers (US) (1896–1937) at Du Pont Labs, Seaford, Delaware, USA (Patent, 16 Feb)	First stockings made about 1937. Bristle production 24 Feb 1938. Yarn production Dec 1939
Paper	AD 105	Mulberry-based fibre, China	Introduced to West *via* Samarkand, 14th century
Parachute	1785	Jean-Pierre F. Blanchard (Fr) (1753–1809)	Dropped small mammal over London. Earliest jump from aircraft 1 Mar 1912 by Albert Berry (US) over St Louis, Missouri, USA

Object	Year	Inventor	Notes
Parchment	c. 1300 BC	Egypt	Modern name from Pergamum (now Bergama), Asia Minor, c. 250 BC
Parking Meter	1935	Carlton C. Magee (US)	Oklahoma City (16 July)
Pasteurisation	1867	Louis Pasteur (1822–1895)	Destruction of pathogenic micro-organisms by heat. Effective against tuberculous milk
Photography			
(on metal)	1826	J. Nicéphore Niépce (Fr) (1765–1833)	Sensitised pewter plate, 8-hr exposure at Chalon-sur-Saône, France
(on paper)	1835	W. H. Fox Talbot (GB) (1807–77)	Lacock Abbey, Wiltshire (Aug)
(on film)	1888	John Carbutt (US)	Kodak by George Eastman (US) (1854–1932), Aug 1888
Plastics	c. 1852	Alexander Parkes (1813–90)	Discovered pyroxylin, the first plastic
Pocket Calculator	1971	Jack St Clair Kilby (b. 1924); James van Tassell and Jerry D. Merryman (b. 1932) (US)	Texas Instrument Inc., Dallas 'Pocketronic' (14 Apr)
Porcelain	851	Earliest report from China	Reached Baghdad in ninth century
Potter's Wheel	c. 6500 BC	Asia Minor	Used in Eridu, Mesopotamia
Printing Press	c. 1455	Johann Gutenberg (Ger) (c. 1400–68)	Wooden block printing in Korea (Dharani sutra, AD 704)
Printing (rotary)	1846	Richard Hoe (US) (1812–86)	Philadelphia Public Ledger rotary printed, 1847
Propeller (ship)	1837	Francis Smith (GB) (1808–74)	Hand propeller screw used in 1776 submarine (q.v.)
Pyramid	2850 BC	Imhotep (Egypt)	Earliest was Djoser step pyramid, Sakkara, Egypt
Radar	1922	Dr Albert H. Taylor and Leo C. Young	Radio reflection effect first noted. First harnessed by Dr Rudolph Kühnold, Kiel, Germany, 20 Mar 1934. Word coined in 1940 by Cdr S. M. Tucker USN
Radio Telegraphy	1879	David Edward Hughes (1830–1900) 500 yds, Great Portland St, London	First advertised radio broadcast by Prof R. A. Fessenden (b. Canada, 1868–1832) at Brant Rock, Massachusetts on 24 Dec 1906
Radio Telegraphy (Transatlantic)	1901	Guglielmo Marconi (It) (1874–1937)	Morse signals from Poldhu, Cornwall, to St John's, Newfoundland (12 Dec)
Rayon	1883	Sir Joseph Swan (1828–1914) (GB)	Production at Courtauld's Ltd, Coventry, England, November 1905. Name 'Rayon' adopted in 1924
Razor			
(electric)	1931	Col Jacob Schick (US)	First manufactured Stamford, Conn (18 Mar)
(safety)	1895	King C. Gillette (US) Patented 2 Dec 1901	First throw-away blades. Earliest fixed safety razor by Kampfe
Record (long-playing)	1948	Dr Peter Goldmark (US)	Micro-groove developed in the CBS Research Labs and launched 21 June by Columbia, so ending 78 rpm market supremacy
Refrigerator	1850	James Harrison (GB) and Alexander Catlin Twining (US)	Simultaneous development at Rodey Point, Victoria, Australia and in Cleveland, Ohio. Earliest domestic refrigerator 1913 in Chicago, Illinois
Rubber			
(latex foam)	1928	Dunlop Rubber Co (GB)	Team led by E. A. Murphy at Fort Dunlop, Birmingham
(tyres)	1846	Thomas Hancock (GB) (1786–1865)	Introduced solid rubber tyres for vehicles (1847) (see also Bicycle)
(vulcanised)	1841	Charles Goodyear (US) (1800–60)	
(waterproof)	1823	Charles Macintosh (GB) (1766–1843)	First experiments in Glasgow with James Syme. G. Fox in 1821 had marketed a Gambroon cloth, but no detail has survived
Rubik Cube	1975	Prof Ernö Rubik (Hungary)	Patented device with $4 \cdot 3 \times 10^{22}$ combinations
Safety Pin	1849	Walter Hunt (US)	First manufactured New York City, NY (10 Apr)
Scotch Tape	1930	Richard Drew (US) (1899–1980)	Developed from opaque masking tape
Self-Starter	1911	Charles F. Kettering (US) (1876–1958)	Developed at Dayton, Ohio, sold to Cadillac

Object	Year	Inventor	Notes
Sewing Machine	1829	Barthélemy Thimmonnier (Fr) (1793–1854)	A patent by Thomas Saint (GB) dated 17 July 1790 for an apparently undeveloped machine was found in 1874. Earliest practical domestic machine by Isaac M. Singer (1811–75) of Pittstown, NY, USA, in 1851. A. B. Wilson machine of 1850, Farrington Museum, Conn., USA, Sept 1938
Ship (sea-going)	c. 50 000 BC	Possibly double dug-out canoes	Traversed Indonesia to northern Australia
(steam)	1775	J. C. Périer (Fr) (1742–1818)	On the Seine, near Paris. Propulsion achieved on river Saône, France, by Marquis d'Abbans, 1783. First successful steam-powered vessel was the *Charlotte Dundas* by William Symington in 1801–2
(turbine)	1894	Hon Sir Charles Parsons (GB) (1854–1931)	*SS Turbinia* attained 34·5 knots on first trial. Built at Heaton, Tyne and Wear
Silk Manufacture	c. 50 BC	Reeling machines devised, China	Silk mills in Italy c. 1250, world's earliest factories
Skyscraper	1882	William Le Baron Jenny (US)	Home Insurance Co. Building, Chicago, Ill, 10 storey (top four with steel beams)
Slide Rule	1621	William Oughtred (1575–1660) (GB)	Earliest slide between fixed stock by Robert Bissaker, 1654
Spectacles	c. 1286	Pisa, Italy (convex)	Concave lens for myopia Nicholas of Cusa (1401–64) c. 1450
Spinning Frame	1769	Sir Richard Arkwright (GB) (1732–92)	
Spinning Jenny	1764	James Hargreaves (GB) (1745–78)	
Spinning Mule	1779	Samuel Crompton (GB) (1753–1827)	
Steam Engine	1698	Thomas Savery (GB) (c. 1650–1715)	Recorded on 25 July. Denis Papin (Fr) (1647–1712) had invented the pressure cooker 1679
Steam Engine (condenser)	1769	James Watt (Scot) (1736–1819)	Ford patent (5 Jan)
Steam Engine (piston)	1712	Thomas Newcomen (GB) (1663–1729)	Hero of Alexandria (*fl.* AD 62) devised his toy-like aeropile.
Steel Production	1855	Henry Bessemer (GB) (1813–1898)	At St Pancras, London. Cementation of wrought iron bars by charcoal contact known by Chalybes people of Asia Minor c. 1400 BC
Steel (stainless)	1913	Harry Brearley (GB)	First cast at Sheffield (20 Aug). Krupp patent, Oct 1912 for chromium carbon steel; failed to recognise corrosion resistance
Submarine	1776	David Bushnell (US), Saybrook, Conn	Hand-propelled screw, one man crew, used off New York. A 12- man wooden and leather submersible devised by Cornelius Drebbel (Neth) demonstrated in Thames in 1624
Superconductivity	1911	Heike Kamerling Onnes (Neth) (1853–1926), Leiden at 4K	Karl Müller and Georg Bednorz in Zürich in Dec 1985 found a barium, copper, lanthanum compound was superconductive at 35K. In Feb 1987 Paul Chu (US) in Houston with yttrium added found 98K was attainable.
Tank	1914	Sir Ernest Swinton (GB) (1868–1951)	Built at Lincoln, designed by William Tritton. Tested 8 Sept 1915
Telegraph (mechanical)	1787	M Lammond (Fr) demonstrated a working model, Paris	
Telegraph Code	1837	Samuel F. B. Morse (US) (1791–1872)	The real credit belonged largely to his assistant Alfred Vail (US) who first transmitted at Morristown, NJ on 8 Jan 1838
Telephone	1849	Antonio Meucci (It) in Havana, Cuba	Caveat not filed until 1871. Instrument worked imperfectly by electrical impulses
	1876	Alexander Graham Bell (US) (1847–1922). Patented 7 Mar 1876	First exchange at Boston, Mass, 1878
Telescope (refractor)	1608	Hans Lippershey (Neth)	Miuldleburg (2 Oct)

Object	Year	Inventor	Notes
Television (mechanical)	1926	John Logie Baird (GB) (1888-1946)	First successful experiment 2 Oct 1925 First public demonstration 27 Jan 1926, London, of moving image with gradations of light and shade both at 22 Frith Street, London. First tranmission in colour on 3 July 1928 at 133 Long Acre, London
Television (electronic)	1927	Philo Taylor Farrnsworth (US) (1906-71)	First images (Nov) 202 Green St, San Francisco. Patent granted 26 Aug 1930
Terylene	1941	J. R. Whinfield (1901-66), J. T. Dickson (GB) at Accrington, Lancashire	First available 150, marketed in USA as 'Dacron'
Thermometer	1593	Galiléo Galilei (It) (1564-1642)	
Transformer	1831	Michael Faraday (GB) (1791-1867)	Gas thermoscope built at Royal Institution, London (29 Aug)
Transistor	1948	John Bardeen, William Shockley and Walter Brattain (US)	Researched at Bell Telephone Laboratories. First application for a patent was by Dr Julius E. Lilienfeld in Canada on October 1925 (see Electronic Computer)
Typewriter	1808	Pellegrine Tarri (It)	First practical 27 character keyed machine with carbon paper built in Reggio Emilia, Italy
Washing Machine (electric)	1907	Hurley Machine Co (US)	Marketed under the name of 'Thor' in Chicago, Illinois, USA
Watch	1462	Bartholomew Manfredi (It)	Earliest mention of a named watchmaker (November) but in reference to an earlier unnamed watchmaker
Water Closet	1589	Designed by Sir John Harington (GB)	Installed at Kelston, near Bath. Built by 'T C' (full name unknown)
Welder (electric)	1877	Elisha Thomson (US) (1853-1937)	
Wheel	c.3580 BC	Sumerian civilization, Uruk, Iraq	Pottery cup with 3 four-wheeled waggons; Brónócice, Poland c. 3500 BC
Windmill	c. 600	Persian corn grinding	Oldest known English post mill, 1191,
Writing	c.3600 BC	Sumerian civilization, Pictographs	Earliest evidence found in SE Iran, 1970
X-Ray	1895	Wilhelm Konrad Röntgen (Ger)	University of Würzburg (8 Nov)
Zip Fastener	1891	Whitcomb L. Judson (US) Exhibition 1893 at Chicago Exposition	First practical fastener invented in USA by Gideon Sundback (Sweden) in 1913

John Logie Baird (1888-1946) and one of the commercial forms of the Baird television, for home use.
Behind the grill on the left is a loud speaker, with the screen on the right.

CHEMISTRY

Glossary

ablation Degradation due to heat.

absolute temperature Temperature on the absolute scale is measured in kelvins (K), 1 K being equal to 1°C. Zero on the absolute scale is −273·16°C.

absorptiometer A device used to measure the absorption of light.

acetal A compound derived from an alcohol and an aldehyde or a ketone, with the general formula:

acetin An acetate derived from glycerol.

acetylation The introduction of one or more acetyl groups, $CH_3 \cdot CO—$, into organic compounds.

acid A substance able to form hydrogen ions when in solution, whether in water or in a non-aqueous solvent.

acid-base indicator An indicator that has a markedly different colour in acid and base solutions. The difference in colour is between the ionized and non-ionized form of the indicator.

actinides A group of radioactive elements, many of them artificially produced by irradiation: actinium, thorium, protactinium, uranium, neptunium, plutonium, americium, curium, berkelium, californium, einsteinium, fermium, mendelevium nobelium, lawrencium.

acyl Group left after the —OH group has been removed from carboxylic acid.

addition reaction Reaction by which unsaturated carbon bonds, e.g. $C≡C$; $C=C$ are saturated to give single bonds.

adhesive A substance which wets surfaces that are to be stuck together and then solidifies to form the actual joint.

adiabatic Process by which heat is neither added to nor allowed to leave a system.

adsorbate Substance which is adsorbed on to an adsorbent.

adsorbent The substance that provides an absorption surface.

adsorption Process by which free atoms or molecules become attached to surface.

aerosol Fine particles of a solid suspended in air.

alcohol Organic compound in which hydroxyl —OH, group or groups are attached to carbon atoms.

aldehyde Organic compound in which a —CHO group is attached to a carbon atom.

aliphatic Organic compounds with carbon atoms arranged in chains rather than rings.

alkali Strictly speaking, a hydroxide of one of the alkali metals, although generally taken to mean a substance which gives a pH of greater than 7 in water.

alkanes Otherwise known as paraffins, these organic compounds have the general formula

$C_nH_{2n} + _2$ and form the principal constituents of petroleum.

alkenes Aliphatic hydrocarbons containing one double $C=C$ bond. They have the general formula C_nH_{2n}.

alkyd resins Compounds used extensively in paints and other coatings. They are formed by condensation reactions between polybasic acids and polyhydric alcohols.

alkyls An aliphatic hydrocarbon with the final hydrogen atom removed.

allotropy An element existing in more than one physical form, e.g. carbon as diamond and graphite.

alloy A combination of two or more metals, or of metallic and non-metallic elements. The physical characteristics of this combination are metallic.

alum Potassium alum, $KAl(SO_4)_2 \cdot 12H_2O$, used in a variety of industrial processes including dyeing, paper manufacture, and waterproofing.

alumina Aluminium oxide, Al_2O_3.

aluminates Compounds containing an Al^{3+} ion in anions that are hydroxide or oxide based.

amalgam Compounds of a metal and mercury. They can be both liquid and solid.

amides Organic compounds based on ammonia. One or more of the hydrogen atoms in the ammonia molecule is substituted by organic acid groups:

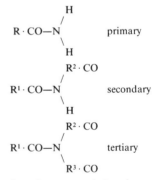

amines Organic compounds based on ammonia. One or more of the hydrogen atoms in the ammonia molecule is substituted by hydrocarbon groups. As with amides, primary, secondary and tertiary amines can be formed.

amino acids Organic compounds containing the amino group, $—NH_2$, and the carboxyl group, $—COOH$. Proteins are built up from amino acids.

ammonium A cation, $(NH_4)^+$, which behaves similarly to the alkali metal cations.

amphoteric Having both acid and basic properties.

aniline An important organic chemical used in the dye industry. Based on the benzene ring, its formula is $C_6H_5 \cdot NH_2$.

anisotropic Having different properties in different directions, e.g. an anisotropic crystal has different physical properties along different crystal axes.

annealing Reduction of the stresses within a metal by heating then cooling it in controlled fashion.

aromatic Organic compounds based on the benzene ring, C_6H_6. The benzene ring is stable, even though the carbon atoms within it are unsaturated. It therefore undergoes substitution reactions rather than addition reactions.

aryls An aromatic hydrocarbon with a hydrogen atom removed.

asbestos A group of silicate minerals. The SiO_4 groups are linked together into chains, giving the characteristic fibrous texture.

atomic mass unit One-twelfth of the mass of carbon-12 atom. Approximately the mass of a proton or neutron.

atomic number The number of protons in the nucleus of an atom of the element.

atomic weight The average mass of atoms in an element, in atomic mass units.

Avogardro's number The number of particles in one mole of any pure substance is $L = 6.023 \times 10^{23}$.

azo dyes A group of dyes containing the group $-N=N-$ linking two aromatic groups.

base An aqueous solution of a compound which, with an acid, gives a salt and water only.

benzene C_6H_6. The six carbon atoms are arranged in a ring. The bonds between the carbon atoms have characteristics between single and double bonds; they are said to resonate between the two, and as such are stable.

benzyl The C_6H_5. CH_2- group.

Bessemer converter Large vessel in which pig iron is refined to steel. Air is blown through the molten mixture and impurities are oxidized and removed as slag.

Bimolecular reaction A reaction in which only two molecular types react together, e.g.:
$2Cu + O_2 = 2CuO$.

biuret reaction A test for peptides and proteins, whereby the peptide linkage gives a pinkish colour with sodium hydroxide, NaOH, and copper sulphate, $CuSO_4$.

body-centred lattice A crystal structure in which atoms or molecules occur at the corners of each crystal cell and at the centre of the body of the crystal cell.

bond The link that holds atoms together in molecules and that is also the basis of crystal structure.

bond energy Energy involved in holding a bond together. When the bond is broken, this energy is released in a variety of forms.

borates Boric acid (H_3BO_3) salts.

borax A naturally-occurring source of boron, $Na_2(B_4O_5(OH)_4 \cdot 8H_2O)$.

Bordeaux mixture Copper sulphate, $CuSO_4$, and calcium hydroxide, $Ca(OH)_2$, mixed in water. It is used as a fungicide.

brass An alloy of copper and zinc. Two principal forms of brass are made, one containing less than 30% zinc, the other between 30% and 40% zinc.

brine A solution of sodium chloride, NaCl.

bromates Salts with bromium oxy-anions. Commonly this is taken to mean the BrO_3^- oxy-anion, but BrO^- and BrO_4^- oxy-anions are also found.

bromides Salts of HBr, hydrogen bromide, based on the bromide ion, Br^-.

bronze A group of alloys of copper and, originally, tin, often with smaller amounts of other elements. The term can now mean copper alloys with no tin, e.g. aluminium bronze.

buffer A mixture of acid, or alkali, and an associated salt, whose pH alters only gradually with addition of more acid or alkali. The salt acts as a supply of anions or cations, which combine with hydrogen or base ions.

butane The lowest member of the paraffin series, C_4H_{10}. It is widely used in cylinders and canisters as camping gas.

carboxylic acid Organic acid containing a carboxyl group, $-COOH$.

calcite A form of naturally-occurring calcium carbonate, $CaCO_3$, found as chalk, limestone and marble.

calcium carbonate The most commonly occurring salt of calcium, $CaCO_3$.

camphor $C_{10}H_{16}O$. Camphor occurs naturally, being extracted from the wood of the camphor tree. It is also manufactured.

carbohydrates General formula $C_xH_{2y}O_y$. Naturally-occurring compounds used as energy compounds, energy stores and for structural uses.

carbonates Salts of carbonic acid, H_2CO_3. The carbonate ion is CO_3^{2-} and forms a number of commercially-important salts, including calcium carbonate.

carbon dioxide CO_2. A product of respiration and a constituent of air. It represents the complete combustion of carbon.

carbon monoxide CO. Formed by the incomplete combustion of carbon. It is a toxic gas.

carotene $C_{40}H_{55}$. It occurs naturally in plants as one of the chief colouring pigments, and is also found in many animal tissues. It is a precursor of vitamin A.

cast iron A partly-refined form of iron containing 2–4% carbon. It is a brittle alloy.

catalyst A substance that speeds up the rate of a chemical reaction without being permanently chemically altered by the reaction.

cathode In electrolysis, this is the negative electrode.

cation A positively-charged ion, occurring in crystals, solutions and melts.

cellulose $(C_6H_{10}O_5)_n$. It is the principal structural component of cell walls, formed by the polymerization of glucose.

cement Common builders' cement, or Portland cement, consists of a mixture of calcium silicates, calcium aluminates and calcium sulphate. It is made by heating limestone and clay and grinding the product with gypsum. When mixed with water it hardens to a solid mass.

ceramic Hard high-melting point non-metallic inorganic materials, e.g. enamels, pottery, porcelain, abrasives.

chain reaction A process by which the product of one reaction takes part in a further reaction, the products of which take part in yet more reactions, etc.

chalk Naturally-occurring form of calcium carbonate, $CaCO_3$.

charcoal A form of carbon produced by the slow burning of wood in a shortage of air.

chlorates Chlorine oxy-acid salts, formed from the ClO^-, ClO_2^-, ClO_3^- and ClO_4^- ions.

chlorides Compounds containing the Cl^- ion.

chlorophyll A complex organic chemical colouring matter found in green plants. It is an essential constituent of the photosynthetic process, by which carbohydrates are produced in plants from carbon dioxide and water.

cholesterol $C_{27}H_{46}O$. A complex organic chemical

based on the sterol ring structure. It is found in animals, particularly in membranes.

chromates Salts based on chromic acid, i.e. containing the CrO_4^{2-} and $Cr_2O_7^{2-}$ ions.

clay Naturally-occurring aluminosilicates consisting of $AlSiO_4$, together with $Mg(OH)_2$ and $Al(OH)_3$.

coenzymes Compounds necessary for the action of enzymes. They may be altered during the course of the reaction, but will be reformed during later reactions.

colloid Small particles, larger than atoms or molecules but too small to be seen by a light microscope, usually found in suspension or solution.

concrete The hardened material formed from mixing cement, sand or gravel, and water.

condensation reaction Reaction in which two molecules react together to give one product molecule plus water, H_2O.

conformation The shape a molecule has due to the positioning a group may have in relation to a bond. In complex organic molecules the conformation may affect physical properties.

copolymer A polymer resulting from the combination of two or more monomers.

covalent bond Two atoms linked by sharing two electrons, one electron originating from each atom.

crude oil A naturally-occurring mixture of hydrocarbons, often mixed with water, sulphur and other inorganic impurities.

crystal A solid particle with a regular geometric shape caused by the regular arrangement of atoms or ions or molecules.

crystallization Process by which crystals of a substance are removed from a solution by increasing the concentration above the saturation point.

cyanates Salts formed from the cyanate ion, NCO^-.

cyanides Salts formed from the cyanide ion, CN^-.

deliquescence Absorption of water by a solid to give a solution.

detergent A water-soluble surface-active agent which can wet surfaces and help to loosen oil and grease. Detergents invariably consist of a hydrophobic group that allows them to dissolve the oils and grease, and a hydrophilic group that promotes water-solubility.

dialysis Separation of mixtures by selective diffusion through a semipermeable membrane.

diamond Naturally-occurring crystalline form of carbon.

dicarboxylic acids Organic acids containing two carboxyl groups $—COOH$.

dienes Organic chemicals with two carbon–carbon double bonds.

diffusion Movement of a gas or liquid caused by the random movement of its atoms or molecules.

diketones Organic compounds with two keto groups $—CO—$.

dimer A polymer consisting of two molecules of a monomer.

distillation The separation of two liquids or a liquid from a solid by evaporation and recondensation.

doping The introduction of impurities into a crystal lattice, giving different electrical or other properties to the crystal.

double bond Two atoms sharing two pairs of electrons, i.e. two covalent bonds.

dry ice Solid CO_2.

EDTA Ethylenediaminetetra-acetic acid, it forms complexes with most elements.

efflorescence Formation of a powdery solid from crystals, by the loss of water of crystallization, or from liquids, by evaporation.

elastomer A material with elastic properties, e.g. rubber.

electrochemical series A series in which the elements are placed in decreasing order of oxidation potential. Among other things, an element higher up the series will displace from solution an element lower down the series.

electrolysis Decomposition of substance in solution by the passage of an electric current.

electrolyte A substance which, when in solution, dissociates into ions. It can thus act as an electric conductor.

electronegativity The degree to which an atom in a molecule attracts electrons to itself. In general, values of electronegativity decrease from right to left and from top to bottom of the periodic table of elements.

element A substance formed of atoms, all with the same atomic number.

emulsion A dispersed colloid of one liquid in another.

enantiomers Isomers that are mirror images of each other in the spatial arrangement of their constituent atoms.

endothermic reaction A reaction in which heat is absorbed.

enthalpy Symbol H. Thermodynamic function of a system equal to the sum of its internal energy and the product of its pressure and volume.

entropy Symbol S. The disorder of a system. The greater the disorder of a system, the greater the entropy.

enzyme A protein which catalyses one specific chemical reaction.

epimer A type of isomer which differs in the configuration around only one of a number of atoms.

epoxy Indicating a $C—O—C$ ring in the form:

equilibrium Any state in which the properties do not change with time, e.g. in a reversible reaction it is the stage at which the rate of the forward reaction equals the rate of the reverse reaction.

equivalent The weight of a substance that will combine with or displace eight parts by weight of oxygen.

ester Product of a condensation reaction between an organic acid and an alcohol.

ethane CH_3. CH_3, a naturally-occurring constituent of natural gas, as well as being extensively synthesized.

ethanoic acid CH_3. COOH, otherwise known as acetic acid.

ethanol CH_3CH_2OH, ethyl alcohol or merely alcohol. Although originally produced as result of fermentation, most ethanol is now synthesized.

ethene $CH_2 = CH_2$, otherwise known as ethylene.

ether $(CH_3CH_2)_2O$, otherwise known as diethyl ether and diethyl oxide.

ethers Compounds with the general formula $R^1—O—R^2$, where R^1 and R^2 are alkyl or aryl groups.

ethyne $C_2H_2 \cdot HC{\equiv}CH$, otherwise known as acetylene.

eutectic A mixture of two substances which shows a clearly-defined melting point.

evaporation Conversion of a liquid to a vapour at a temperature below its boiling point.

fats Esters of fatty acids and glycerol with the general formula:

$$CH_2 \cdot OOC \cdot R^1$$
$$CH \cdot OOC \cdot R^2$$
$$CH_2 \cdot OOC \cdot R^3$$

R^1, R^2 and R^3 being the fatty acid residues.

fatty acids Organic acids consisting of an alkyl group attached to a carboxyl group, with the general formula $C_nH_{2n}O_2$.

Fehling's solution A solution of copper sulphate, sodium potassium tartrate and sodium hydroxide, used for testing for reducing sugars.

fermentation Use of micro-organisms to break down substances and release, generally, useful products, e.g. fermentation of sugar by yeasts, yielding alcohol and carbon dioxide.

ferrates Oxy-anions of iron, incorporating the FeO_4^{2-} ion.

ferric compounds Compounds incorporating Fe(III) iron.

ferrous compounds Compounds incorporating Fe(II) iron.

flash point Temperature to which a substance must be heated before it can be ignited.

flavones Yellow pigments found in plants.

flocculation Coagulation of a colloid into larger particles.

flourescein $C_{20}H_{12}O_5$. A red crystalline substance that flouresces bright green.

flourides The salts of hydrogen flouride, HF.

flourocarbons A group of hydrocarbons in which hydrogen atoms are replaced by flourine atoms. They are widely used as refrigerants and as aerosols.

foams A dispersion of bubbles of gas in a liquid or solid.

fractional crystallization Separation of two or more substances by using changes in solubility with temperature. As the temperature is lowered, first one substance will crystallize out, then another, and so on.

fractional distillation Separation of two or more substances by evaporating the mixture, allowing the vapours to pass up a fractionating column and collecting the various fractions as they condense at different points up the column, depending on their volatility.

free radical An atom or group of atoms with unpaired electrons. It is therefore very reactive.

galvanizing The protection of steel by covering it with a thin layer of zinc.

gas Gases will expand spontaneously to fill a container. The intermolecular attractions are very weak and the constituent atoms or molecules show random movement.

gasification Conversion of a solid or liquid to a lower molecular weight gas. Usually applied to the conversion of hydrocarbon solids and liquids to fuel gases.

gasoline A mixture of various hydrocarbons used as motor fuel or aviation fuel.

gel A colloid suspension in which the particles are linked by a form of partial coagulation to form a jelly.

gelatin A protein made by boiling collegen in dilute acid.

glucose $C_6H_{12}O_6$, otherwise known as dextrose. It is the most common hexose sugar, found in plants and animals. It is the constituent monomer of cellulose, starch, glycogen, etc.

glue Proteins in a colloid mixture. It is prepared from animal waste containing collagen.

gluten Proteins from wheat dough.

glycerides The esters produced from glycerol. Depending on how many of the hydroxyl groups in the glycerol molecule combine with acid radicals, the glycerides are called mono-, di- or tri-glycerides.

glycerol Otherwise known as glycerin or 1,2,3-trihydroxypropane, with the structure:

$$CH_2 \cdot OH$$
$$CH \cdot OH$$
$$CH_2 \cdot OH$$

gram molecular volume Volume occupied by 1 mole of a substance in the gaseous state. At STP this equals 22·414 litres.

gram molecule A mole.

graphite A crystalline form of carbon, occurring naturally. It consists of flat sheets of hexagonal cells, which slip easily over each other, giving graphite its characteristic properties.

group In the periodic table of elements, a group is a vertical column of elements. A group will have distinct properties and characteristics in common.

haem A complex three-dimensional molecule with the formula $C_{34}H_{32}FeN_4O_4$. Haem is an important constituent of a number of active biochemicals, including haemoglobin. It has an iron atom at its centre which can act as an electron carrier, changing from the ferrous to the ferric state and back again.

haematite One of the iron ores, Fe_2O_3.

halogenation The addition or substitution of halogen atoms to a molecule.

halogens Group VII in the periodic table, consisting of flourine, chlorine, bromine, iodine and astatine.

hexanes A group of chemicals with the formula C_6H_{14}.

hexose A carbohydrate with a ring of six carbon atoms. Glucose is the most important of the hexoses.

hydration The addition of water to a substance, particularly to ions, e.g.:
$$H^+ + H_2O = H_3O^+$$

hydrocarbons Compounds of hydrogen and carbon.

hydrochloric acid An aqueous solution of hydrogen chloride, HCl.

hydrogenation A form of reduction in which hydrogen gas is used to add hydrogen to a compound.

hydrogen bond A weak bond between an electronegative atom, e.g. oxygen, and a hydrogen atom covalently bonded to another electronegative atom.

hydrolysis Reaction in which water combines with a compound.

hydroxylation Introduction of a hydroxyl group, OH^-, into a molecule.

imides Organic compounds containing the —CO—NH—CO— group.

imines Organic compounds containing the —NH— group. The nitrogen atom is not linked to a carbonyl group or hydrogen atom.

indicator Generally, an indicator shows the presence of a particular compound or group of compounds by a characteristic colour. More specifically, indicators are used to show precisely when the end-point in a titration has occurred.

indole An organic double-ring structure based on the formula C_8H_7N.

inorganic chemistry The chemistry of all elements other than carbon.

ion An atom or molecule that has lost or gained one or more electrons, thereby carrying a positive or negative charge.

isocyanates Organic compounds containing the group $-N=C=O$.

isomers Compounds with the same chemical formula, but existing in different three-dimensional structures due to differing orientation about certain atoms.

isomorphism Compounds having the same crystal structure.

isonitriles Organic compounds having the group $-N-C$. Otherwise known as isocyanides or carbylamines.

isotonic Solutions with the same osmotic pressure.

isotopes Atoms having the same number of protons but differing numbers of neutrons.

ketones Organic compounds with the general formula R^1-CO-R^2, where R^1 and R^2 are generally hydrocarbons.

lactose A disaccharide sugar with the formula $C_{12}H_{22}O_{11}$. It occurs in varying amounts in the milk of all animals.

lanthanides A series of metallic elements: lanthanum, cerium, praseodymium, neodymium, promethium, samarium, europium, gadolinium, terbium, dysprosium, holmium, erbium, thulium, ytterbium, lutetium.

lattice The regular three-dimensional arrangement of atoms in a crystal.

lime water Calcium hydroxide, $Ca(OH)_2$.

liquefied petroleum gas Hydrocarbon gases produced as a result of the refining of petroleum. Butane and propane are the two alternatives available, although neither are pure forms of the gas.

litmus Colouring obtained from lichens. It is used as an indicator to detect pH changes.

macromolecules Large molecules with molecular weight in excess of 10 000.

magnesium alloys A very light group of alloys.

manganates Salts containing the ion MnO_4^{2-}.

marble A form of calcium carbonate, $CaCO_3$.

mercaptans Otherwise known as thiols. A group of organic compounds containing the $-SH$ group linked to a carbon atom.

meta A prefix denoting the position of groups attached to the benzene ring. It means that the substituents are separated by one carbon atom, i.e. they occur at the 1,3 positions.

metal Elements that are malleable, lustrous, and conduct heat and electricity. They tend to form cations.

methane CH_4, otherwise known as marsh gas. It occurs naturally as a result of the decay of vegetable matter.

methanol CH_3OH, otherwise known as methyl alcohol.

methanol HCHO, otherwise known as formaldehyde.

methylation The addition of a methyl group, $-CH_3$, to an organic compound.

micelle A colloidal particle.

miscibility The ability of one substance to mix with another.

molarity The number of moles of a substance dissolved in 1 litre of solution.

mole Otherwise known as a gram molecule, it is the amount of substance that contains the same number of elementary entities (molecules, ions, atoms, etc.) as there are in 0·012 kg of carbon-12.

molecular weight Ratio of the mass per molecule of a substance to 1/12 of the mass of a carbon-12 atom.

molecule The smallest independent particle of a substance.

monotropy A substance that exists in only one stable crystalline form.

naphthalene $C_{10}H_8$. A double benzene ring structure.

natural gas A mixture of over 90% methane with other hydrocarbon gases, as well as nitrogen and carbon dioxide.

ninhydrin $C_9H_4O_3.H_2O$. It gives a blue colour on heating with amino acids and proteins and is therefore widely used as an indicator.

nitrates Salts of nitric acid, containing the ion NO_3^-.

nitric acid HNO_3. It has many important industrial uses, including the manufacture of fertilizers.

nitrides Compounds of nitrogen and other elements.

nitrites Salts of nitrous acid, containing the ion NO_2^-.

nitro compounds Group of aromatic compounds with the basic formula $R-NO_2$.

noble gases Inert group of gases: helium, neon, argon, krypton, xenon, radon. Traces of all these gases are found in the atmosphere.

nylon A group of synthetic plastics and fibres, largely formed by condensation polymerization.

octanes Group of hydrocarbons with eight carbon atoms and the basic formula C_8H_{18}. The group falls in the alkane series, and the constituents are all found in crude oil.

optical activity The ability of certain substances to rotate the polarization plane of polarized light, due to the assymetry of the molecules.

organic Related to the compounds of carbon.

ortho A prefix denoting the position of groups attached to the benzene ring. It means that the substituents occur in the 1,2 positions.

oxidation Process by which the proportion of an electronegative constituent of a compound is increased. This invariably means the addition of oxygen to a compound.

oxide A compound containing oxygen and other elements.

oximes Group of organic compounds containing $=N.OH$ linked to a carbon atom.

oxonium A positive ion with the basic formula R_3O^+, where R is hydrogen or an organic group, e.g. the hydroxonium ion H_3O^+.

ozone O_3. An allotrope of oxygen.

para A prefix denoting the position of groups attached to the benzene ring. It means that the substituents occur in 1,4 positions.

patina An oxide layer formed on metals and alloys.

pentanes Group of hydrocarbons with five carbon atoms and the basic formula C_5H_{12}. The constituents are all found in crude oil.

pentose A carbohydrate with a ring of five carbon atoms.

peptides Chains of two or more amino acids linked by a peptide linkage, $-CO-NH-$. Peptide chains are arranged in three-dimensional structures to form proteins.

period A period in the periodic table of elements is a horizontal series of elements, from an alkali metal to a noble gas.

periodic table Arrangement of elements in a table so that similarities between elements are emphasized.

permanganates A group of salts containing the MnO_4^- ion.

peroxides Derivatives of hydrogen peroxide, H_2O_2, containing linked pairs of oxygen atoms.

pewter An alloy of tin and lead.

pH The logarithm (base 10) of the reciprocal of the concentration of hydrogen ions in a solution, giving a measure of the acidity or alkalinity of a solution.

phenol $C_6H_5 \cdot OH$, an aromatic hydroxy compound.

phenolphthalein $C_{20}H_{14}O_4$. An aromatic compound used as an indicator.

phenyl The atomatic group C_6H_5-.

phosphates Salts based on the PO_4^{3-} and PO_7^{4-} ions.

phosphoric acid There are a number of oxy-acids of phosphorus, the best known being H_3PO_4. They are based on phosphorus (V).

phosphors Substances that phosphoresce.

phosphorus acid Oxy-acids of phosphorus (III), the best known being H_3PO_3.

pig iron Iron produced by a blast furnace, before it is cast to shape.

plastics Artificial organic polymers that can be moulded to shape.

polycarbonates A group of hard thermoplastics based on carbonic acid.

polyesters Polymers formed by condensation reactions between polybasic acids and polyhydric alcohols.

polymers A compound consisting of long-chain molecules made up of repeating molecular units.

polymorphism A substance existing in more than one crystalline form.

polysaccharides Carbohydrates formed by condensation reactions between monosaccharides.

precipitation Production of an insoluble compound in a solution by a chemical reaction.

propane $CH_3.CH_2.CH_3$. A constituent of natural gas.

proteins A large group of naturally-occurring organic compounds consisting of chains of amino acids folded into complex three-dimensional molecules.

radical Atom or molecule which has one or more free valencies.

rare earths Otherwise known as the lanthanide series of elements.

rectification Fractional distillation used to separate an organic liquid into its constituent parts.

redox Simultaneous oxidation and reduction occurring in one chemical reaction.

reduction Process by which the proportion of an electronegative constituent of a compound is decreased. This invariably means a reduction in the amount of oxygen in a compound or an addition of hydrogen.

resins A solid natural or synthetic polymer.

reversible reaction A reaction that can proceed in either direction. Such a reaction usually attains an equilibrium, depending on the concentrations of the reactants and the physical conditions.

ribose A pentose sugar, $C_5H_{10}O_5$, found in nucleic acids.

rust The coating of $Fe_2O_3.H_2O$ found on iron.

salt Salt commonly refers to sodium chloride, $NaCl$. However, in chemistry it refers to the product of the reaction between a base and an acid.

sand A mixture of SiO_2 and other minerals, formed by the degradation of rocks.

saponification Hydrolysis of an ester using an alkali.

saturated compound A compound in which there are no double or triple bonds, only single bonds.

silica Silicon dioxide, SiO_2, one of the most common constituents of the earth's crust.

silicates At their simplest, silicates are compounds containing the SiO_4^{4-} ion. However, the term extends to cover a wide range of minerals based on the SiO_4 tetrahedral crystal structure.

silicones Organic polymers containing $-SiO-Si-$ linkages.

two electrons in a single bonding orbital.

sintering Fusion of two or more substances by heating powders together under pressure at a temperature below their melting point.

soap The salt of a fatty acid.

solders Alloys used to join metals together. The solder melts at a temperature below that of the metals.

solution A single-phase homogeneous mixture of two or more compounds, one of them invariably being liquid (the solvent) in which the solute is dissolved.

standard temperature and pressure Abbreviated to STP, it indicates a temperature of $273 \cdot 15$ K and a pressure of $101 \cdot 325$ kPa.

starch A naturally-occurring polymer of glucose.

steel A group of alloys of iron and carbon, often with other elements.

strength The strength of an acid or alkali indicates its ability to give hydroxonium ions, H_3O^+.

sublimation The change from solid to gaseous state without passing through a liquid state.

substitution A displacement reaction in which one atom or group in a molecule is replaced by another atom or group.

substrate The substance on which an enzyme acts.

sucrose A disaccharide carbohydrate with the formula $C_{12}H_{22}O_{11}$.

sugars Carbohydrates invariably based on six- or twelve-carbon atoms. They are crystalline, soluble in water and sweet to taste.

sulphates Salts based on the SO_4^{2-} ion.

sulphides Compounds of elements and sulphur, usually based on the S^{2-} ion.

sulphites Salts based on the SO_3^{2-} ion.

sulphuric acid A colourless liquid, H_2SO_4.

superphosphates A mixture of calcium hydrogen phosphate, $Ca(H_2PO_4)_2$, and calcium sulphate, $CaSO_4$. It is used as a fertilizer.

surface active agents Otherwise known as surfactants. Mainly organic substances which, when dissolved in water, reduce the surface tension.

2,4,5-T Otherwise known as 2,4,5-trichlorophenoxyacetic acid, $C_8H_5Cl_3O_3$. Widely used as a selective weedkiller.

tellurates Salts containing oxyanions of tellurium, i.e. TeO_6^{6-} and TeO_3^{2-} ions.

terpenes Volatile aromatic hydrocarbons with the formula $(C_5H_8)_n$. They are naturally occurring in the essential oils of many plants.

thermoplastics Plastics which can be softened by heating and then hardened by cooling many times.

thio- Containing sulphur.

tinning Coating the surface of iron with tin in order to prevent corrosion.

titration The determination of the amount of one substance needed to react with a fixed amount of another substance. The endpoint is determined by a change in property, e.g. change in colour.

toluene An aromatic compound, $C_6H_5 \cdot CH_3$.

transition elements A series of elements with an incomplete inner shell of electrons: scandium to zinc, yttrium to cadmium, and lanthanum to mercury.

triple bond A bond formed by three pairs of electrons shared between two atoms.

valency Another name for the oxidation state. It is the difference between the number of electrons attached to an atom of the free element and the number of electrons associated with an atom of the element in a compound.

van der Waals' bonds Weak forces between molecules due to electronic coupling, acting over short distances.

vapour pressure The pressure of a vapour produced by a solid or liquid. In a closed system a saturated vapour pressure will eventually be established, at which the vapour will be in equilibrium with the solid or liquid.

verdigris Copper carbonate, $CuCO_3$, coating on surface of copper or bronze, due to exposure to the atmosphere.

vinegar A dilute solution of ethanoic acid.

vinyl The $CH_2=CH-$ group, otherwise known as ethenyl.

washing soda Sodium carbonate, $Na_2CO_3 \cdot 10H_2O$.

water Oxygen hydride, H_2O.

Carbohydrates

These are an important source of energy for living organisms as well as a means by which chemical energy can be stored. The name originally indicated the belief that compounds of this group could be represented as hydrates of carbon of general formula $C_x(H_2O)_y$, but it is now realized that many important carbohydrates do not have the required 2 to 1 hydrogen to oxygen ratio while other compounds which conform to this structure, such as methanal (formaldehyde) (HCHO) and ethanoic acid (acetic acid) (CH_3COOH) are obviously not of this group. Further, other carbohydrates contain sulphur and nitrogen as important constituents. Carbohydrates can be defined as polyhydroxy aldehydes or ketones or as a substance which yields these compounds on hydrolysis. Glucose and fructose (both of general formula $C_6H_{12}O_6$) are typical examples, respectively, of an 'aldose' and a 'ketose', e.g.

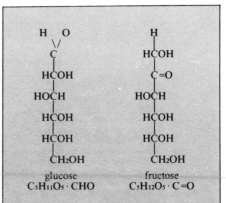

glucose $C_5H_{11}O_5 \cdot CHO$

fructose $C_5H_{12}O_5 \cdot C=O$

Carbohydrates are defined by the number of carbon atoms in the molecule using the usual multiplying affixes, i.e. tetrose for 4 carbon atoms, pentose for 5, hexose for 6, etc. They are divided into two main groups known as sugars and polysaccharides, where the former is subdivided into monosaccharides of general formula $C_nH_{2n}O_n$ (where n = 2 to 10) which cannot be hydrolysed into smaller molecules, and oligosaccharides such as disaccharides ($C_{12}H_{22}O_{11}$), trisaccharides ($C_{18}H_{32}O_{16}$), and tetrasaccharides ($C_{24}H_{42}O_{21}$) which yield two, three, and four monosaccharide molecules respectively on hydrolysis.

The polysaccharides yield a large number of monosaccharides on hydrolysis and have molecular weights ranging from thousands to several million. The most widely spread polysaccharides are of the general formula $(C_6H_{10}O_5)_n$ and include *starch*, which occurs in all green plants and is obtained from maize, wheat, barley, rice and potatoes, and from which dextrins are produced by boiling with water under pressure; *glycogen*, which is the reserve carbohydrate of animals and is often known as 'animal starch'; and *cellulose*, the main constituent of the cell walls of plants.

Of the naturally-occurring sugars (which are all optically active), the most familiar monosaccharides are the dextrorotary (D+) aldohexose *glucose* (dextrose or grape sugar) and the laevorotary (D−) ketohexose *fructose* (laevulose or fruit sugar), both of formula $C_6H_{12}O_6$.

The most important disaccharides are those of the formula $C_{12}H_{22}O_{11}$ and include *sucrose* (cane sugar or beet sugar) obtained from sugar cane or sugar beet after chemical treatment; *maltose* (malt sugar) produced by the action of malt on starch; and *lactose* (milk sugar) which occurs naturally in the milk of all mammals.

Nobel prizewinners in chemistry since 1950

1950 Kurt Alder, German; Otto P. H. Diels, German

1951 Edwin M. McMillan, US; Glen T. Seaborg, US

1952 Archer J. P. Martin, British; Richard L. M. Synge, British
1953 Hermann Staudinger, German
1954 Linus C. Pauling, US
1955 Vincent du Vigneaud, US
1956 Sir Cyril N. Hinshelwood, British; Nikolai N. Semenov, USSR
1957 Sir Alexander R. Todd, British
1958 Frederick Sanger, British
1959 Jaroslav Heyrovsky, Czech
1960 Willard F. Libby, US
1961 Melvin Calvin, US
1962 John C. Kendrew, British; Max F. Perutz, British
1963 Giulio Natta, Italian; Karl Ziegler, German
1964 Dorothy C. Hodgkin, British
1965 Robert B. Woodward, US
1966 Robert S. Mulliken, US
1967 Manfred Eigen, German; Ronald G. W. Norrish, British; George Porter, British
1968 Lars Onsager, US
1969 Derek H. R. Barton, British; Odd Hassel, Norwegian
1970 Luis F. Leloir, Argentinian
1971 Gerhard Herzberg, Canadian

1972 Christian B. Anfinsen, US; Stanford Moore, US; William H. Stein, US
1973 Ernst Otto Fischer, German; Geoffrey Wilkinson, British
1974 Paul J. Flory, US
1975 John Cornforth, Austral.-Brit.; Vladimir Prelog, Yugo.-Swiss
1976 William N. Lipscomb, US
1977 Ilya Prigogine, Belgian
1978 Peter Mitchell, British
1979 Herbert C. Brown, US; George Wittig, German
1980 Paul Berg, US; Walter Gilbert, US; Frederick Sanger, British
1981 Kenichi Fukui, Japanese; Roald Hoffmann, US
1982 Aaron Klug, S. African
1983 Henry Taube, US
1984 R. Bruce Merrifield, US
1986 Herbert A. Hauptman, US; Jerome Karle, US
1987 Donald J. Cram, US; Jean-Marie Lehn, French; Charles J. Pedersen, US
1988 Johann Diesenhofer, German; Robert Huber, German; Hartmut Michel, German

M. and Mme Curie in their laboratory. Marie Curie was an early Nobel Prizewinner for Chemistry in 1911. (The Mansell Collection)

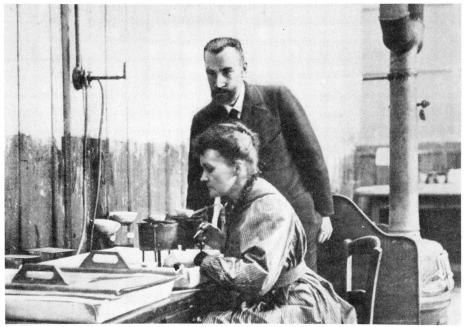

NOTES (for the following table)

1. The former spelling 'sulphur' is not recommended under International Union of Pure and Applied Chemistry (I.U.P.A.C.) rules on chemical nomenclature.
2. Provisional I.U.P.A.C. names for elements 104 to 109. The names rutherfordium (Rf) and kurchatovium (Ku) have been proposed for element 104 and hahnium (Ha) and nielsbohrium (Ns) for element 105. Competing, but less substantiated, USSR claims have been made for elements 104 (G. N. Flerov et al 1964), 105 (G. N. Flerov et al 1970) and 106 (Yu. Ts. Oganessian et al 1974).
3. A value in brackets is the atomic mass of the isotope with the longest known half-life.
4. For the highly radioactive elements the density value has been calculated for the isotope with the longest known half-life.
5. This value is the minimum pressure under which liquified helium can be solidified.
6. The melting and boiling points of carbon are based on the assumption that 'carbynes' form the stable structures above 2300°C. This is disputed and an alternative suggestion is that graphite remains stable at high temperatures, subliming directly to vapour at 3720°C and can only be melted at a pressure of 100 atm at 4730°C.

Atomic Number	Symbol	Element Name	Derived From	Discoverers	Year	Atomic Weight (Note 3)	Density At 20°C (Unless Otherwise Stated) (g/cm³) (Note 4)	Melting Point (°C)	Boiling Point (°C)	Number Of Nuclides
1	H	Hydrogen	Greek 'hydro genes' = water producer	H. Cavendish (UK)	1766	1·007 94	0·0871 (solid at mp) 0·000 089 89 (gas at 0°C)	−259·192	−252·753	3
2	He	Helium	Greek 'helios' = sun	J. N. Lockyer (UK) and P. J. C. Jannsen (France)	1868	4·002 602	0·190 8 (solid at mp) 0·000 178 5 (gas at 0°C)	−272·375 at 24·985 atm (Note 5)	−268·928	8
3	Li	Lithium	Greek 'lithos' = stone	J. A. Arfwedson (Sweden)	1817	6·941	0·5334	180·57	1339	8
4	Be	Beryllium	Greek 'beryllion' = beryl	N. L. Vauquelin (France)	1798	9·012 182	1·846	1287	2471	9
5	B	Boron	Persian 'burah' = borax	L. J. Gay Lussac and L.J. Thenard (France) and H. Davy (UK)	1808	10·811	2·333 (β Rhombahedral)	2130	3910	13
6	C	Carbon	Latin 'carbo' = charcoal	Prehistoric	—	12·011	2·266 (Graphite) 3·515 (Diamond)	3530 (Note 6)	3870 (Note 6)	15
7	N	Nitrogen	Greek 'nitron genes' = saltpetre producer	D. Rutherford (UK)	1772	14·006 74	0·9426 (solid at mp) 0·001 250 (gas at 0°C)	−210·004	−195·806	12
8	O	Oxygen	Greek 'oxys genes' = acid producer	C. W. Scheele (Sweden) and J. Priestley (UK)	1772–1774	15·9994	1·359 (solid at mp) 0·001 429 (gas at 0°C)	−218·789	−182·962	14
9	F	Fluorine	Latin 'fluo' = flow	H. Moissan (France)	1886	18·998 403	1·780 (solid at mp) 0·001 696 (gas at 0°C)	−219·669	−188·200	14
10	Ne	Neon	Greek 'neos' = new	W. Ramsay and M. W. Travers (UK)	1898	20·1797	1·434 (solid at mp) 0·000 899 9 (gas at 0°C)	−248·588	−246·048	15
11	Na	Sodium	English 'soda'	H. Davy (UK)	1807	22·989 768	0·9688	97·819	882	17
12	Mg	Magnesium	Magnesia, a district of Thessaly	H. Davy (UK)	1808	24·3050	1·737	650	1095	17
13	Al	Aluminium	Latin 'alumen' = alum	H. C. Oerstedt (Denmark) and F. Wöhler (Germany)	1825–1827	26·981 539	2·699	660·457	2516	18
14	Si	Silicon	Latin 'silex' = flint	J.J. Berzelius (Sweden)	1824	28·0855	2·329	1414	3190	20
15	P	Phosphorus	Greek 'phosphorus' = light bringing	H. Brand (Germany)	1669	30·973 762	1·825 (White) 2·361 (Violet) 2·708 (Black)	44·14 597 at 45 atm 606 at 48 atm	277 431 sublimes 453 sublimes	19
16	S	Sulfur (Note 1)	Sanskrit 'solvere': Latin 'sulfurum'	Prehistoric	—	32·066	2·070 (Rhombic)	115·21	444·674	20
17	Cl	Chlorine	Greek 'chloros' = green	C. W. Scheele (Sweden)	1774	35·4527	2·038 (solid at mp) 0·003 214 (gas at 0°C)	−100·98	−33·99	19
18	Ar	Argon	Greek 'argos' = inactive	W. Ramsay and Lord Rayleigh (UK)	1894	39·948	1·622 (solid at mp) 0·001 784 (gas at 0°C)	−189·352	−185·855	20
19	K	Potassium (Kalium)	English 'potash'	H. Davy (UK)	1807	39·0983	0·8591	63·60	758	20
20	Ca	Calcium	Latin 'calx' = lime	H. Davy (UK)	1808	40·078	1·526	842	1495	19
21	Sc	Scandium	Scandinavia	L. F. Nilson (Sweden)	1879	44·955 910	2·989	1541	2831	14
22	Ti	Titanium	Latin 'Titanes' = sons of the earth	M. H. Klaproth (Germany)	1795	47·88	4·504	1672	3360	17
23	V	Vanadium	Vanadis, a name given to Freyja, the Norse goddess of beauty and youth	N. G. Sefström (Sweden)	1830	50·9415	6·119	1929	3410	18

Atomic Number	Symbol	Element Name	Derived From	Discoverers	Year	Atomic Weight (Note 3)	Density At 20°C (Unless Otherwise Stated) (g/cm³)(Note 4)	Melting Point (°C)	Boiling Point (°C)	Number Of Nuclides
24	Cr	Chromium	Greek 'chromos' = colour	N.L. Vauquelin (France)	1798	51·9961	7·193	1860	2680	21
25	Mn	Manganese	Latin 'magnes' = magnet	J.G. Gahn (Sweden)	1774	54·93805	7·472	1246	2051	20
26	Fe	Iron(Ferrum)	Anglo-Saxon 'iren'	Earliest smelting	c. 4000 BC	55·847	7·874	1538	2837	21
27	Co	Cobalt	German 'kobold' = goblin	G. Brandt (Sweden)	1737	58·93320	8·834	1495	2944	21
28	Ni	Nickel	German abbreviation of 'Kupfernickel' (devil's 'copper') or niccolite	A. F. Cronstedt (Sweden)	1751	58·69	8·905	1455	2887	24
29	Cu	Copper(Cuprum)	Cyprus	Prehistoric (earliest known use)	c. 8000 BC	63·546	8·934	1084·88	2573	23
30	Zn	Zinc	German 'zink'	A.S. Marggraf (Germany)	1746	65·39	7·140	419·58	908	25
31	Ga	Gallium	Latin 'Gallia' = France	L. de Boisbaudran (France)	1875	69·723	5·912	29·772	2203	22
32	Ge	Germanium	Latin 'Germania' = Germany	C. A. Winkler (Germany)	1886	72·61	5·327	938·3	2772	22
33	As	Arsenic	Latin 'arsenicum'	Albertus Magnus (Germany)	c. 1220	74·92159	5·781	817 at 38 atm	603 sublimes	22
34	Se	Selenium	Greek 'selene' = moon	J.J. Berzelius (Sweden)	1818	78·96	4·810 (Trigonal) 3·937 (solid at mp)	221·18	685	23
35	Br	Bromine	Greek 'bromos' = stench	A.J. Balard (France)	1826	79·904	3·119 (liquid at 20°C)	-7·25	59·76	23
36	Kr	Krypton	Greek 'kryptos' = hidden	W. Ramsay and M. W. Travers (UK)	1898	83·80	2·801 (solid at mp) 0·003749 (gas at 0°C)	-157·386	-153·353	25
37	Rb	Rubidium	Latin 'rubidus' = red	R. W. Bunsen and G. R. Kirchhoff (Germany)	1861	85·4678	1·534	39·29	687	27
38	Sr	Strontium	Strontian, a village in Highland region, Scotland	W. Cruikshank (UK)	1787	87·62	2·582	768	1388	25
39	Y	Yttrium	Ytterby, in Sweden	J. Gadolin (Finland)	1794	88·90585	4·468	1522	3300	23
40	Zr	Zirconium	Persian 'zargun' = gold coloured	M. H. Klaproth (Germany)	1789	91·224	6·506	1855	4360	22
41	Nb	Niobium	Latin 'Niobe' daughter of Tantalus	C. Hatchett (UK)	1801	92·90638	8·595	2473	4860	23
42	Mo	Molybdenum	Greek 'molybdos' = lead	P. J. Hjelm (Sweden)	1781	95·94	10·22	2624	4710	22
43	Tc	Technetium	Greek 'technetos' = artificial	C. Perrier (France) and E. Segrè (Italy/USA)	1937	(97·9072)	11·40	2157	4270	22
44	Ru	Ruthenium	Ruthenia (the Ukraine, in USSR)	K. K. Klaus (Estonia/USSR)	1844	101·07	12·37	2334	4310	23
45	Rh	Rhodium	Greek 'rhodon' = rose	W. H. Wollaston (UK)	1804	102·90550	12·42	1963	3700	23
46	Pd	Palladium	The asteroid Pallas (discovered 1802)	W. H. Wollaston (UK)	1803	106·42	12·01	1555·3	2975	24
47	Ag	Silver(Argentum)	Anglo-Saxon 'seolfor'	Prehistoric (earliest silversmithery)	c. 4000 BC	107·8682	10·50	961·93	2167	29
48	Cd	Cadmium	Greek 'kadmeia' = calamine	F. Stromeyer (Germany)	1817	112·411	8·648	321·108	768	33
49	In	Indium	indigo spectrum	F. Reich and H. T. Richter (Germany)	1863	114·82	7·289	156·635	2019	31

Atomic Number	Symbol	Element Name	Derived From	Discoverers	Year	Atomic Weight (Note 3)	Density At 20°C (Unless Otherwise Stated) (g/cm³) (Note 4)	Melting Point (°C)	Boiling Point (°C)	Number Of Nuclides
50	Sn	Tin (Stannum)	Anglo-Saxon 'tin'	Prehistoric (intentionally alloyed with copper to make bronze)	c. 3500 BC	118·710	7·288	231·968	2595	33
51	Sb	Antimony (Stibium)	Lower latin 'antimonium'	Near historic	c. 1000 BC	121·75	6·693	630·755	1635	29
52	Te	Tellurium	Latin 'tellus' = earth	F. J. Muller (Baron von Reichenstein) (Austria)	1783	127·60	6·237	449·87	989	33
53	I	Iodine	Greek 'iodes' = violet	B. Courtois (France)	1811	126·90447	4·947	113·6	185·1	33
54	Xe	Xenon	Greek 'xenos' = stranger	W. Ramsay and M. W. Travers (UK)	1898	131·29	3·410 (solid at mp) 0·005897 (gas at 0°C)	-111·760	-108·096	36
55	Cs	Caesium	Latin 'caesius' = bluish-grey	R. W. von Bunsen and G. R. Kirchoff (Germany)	1860	132·90543	1·896	28·47	668	36
56	Ba	Barium	Greek 'barys' = heavy	H. Davy (UK)	1808	137·327	3·595	729	1740	31
57	La	Lanthanum	Greek 'lanthano' = conceal	C. G. Mosander (Sweden)	1839	138·9055	6·145	921	3410	30
58	Ce	Cerium	The asteroid Ceres (discovered 1801)	J. J Berzelius and W. Hisinger (Sweden) and M. H. Klaproth (Germany)	1803	140·115	6·688 (beta) 6·770 (gamma)	799	3470	30
59	Pr	Praseodymium	Greek 'prasios didymos' = green twin	C. Auer von Welsbach (Austria)	1885	140·90765	6·772	934	3480	29
60	Nd	Neodymium	Greek 'neos didymos' = new twin	C. Auer von Welsbach (Austria)	1885	144·24	7·006	1021	3020	30
61	Pm	Promethium	Greek demi-god 'Prometheus' - the fire stealer	J. Marinsky, L. E. Glendenin, and C. D. Coryell (USA)	1945	(144·9127)	7·141	1042	3000	28
62	Sm	Samarium	The mineral Samarskite (named after Col. M. Samarski, a Russian engineer)	L. de Boisbaudran (France)	1879	150·36	7·517	1077	1794	29
63	Eu	Europium	Europe	E. A. Demarçay (France)	1901	151·965	5·243	822	1556	26
64	Gd	Gadolinium	Johan Gadolin (1760–1852)	J. C. G. de Marignac (Switzerland)	1880	157·25	7·899	1313	3270	27
65	Tb	Terbium	Ytterby, in Sweden	C. G. Mosander (Sweden)	1843	158·92534	8·228	1356	3230	25
66	Dy	Dysprosium	Greek 'dysprositos' = hard to get at	L. de Boisbaudran (France)	1886	162·50	8·549	1412	2573	28
67	Ho	Holmium	Holmia, a Latinized form of Stockholm	J. L. Soret (France) and P. T. Cleve (Sweden)	1878–1879	164·93032	8·794	1474	2700	27
68	Er	Erbium	Ytterby, in Sweden	C. G. Mosander (Sweden)	1843	167·26	9·064	1529	2815	28
69	Tm	Thulium	Latin and Greek 'Thule' = Northland	P. T. Cleve (Sweden)	1879	168·93421	9·319	1545	1950	30
70	Yb	Ytterbium	Ytterby, in Sweden	J. C. G. de Marignac (France)	1878	173·04	6·967	817	1227	30
71	Lu	Lutetium	Lutetia, Roman name for the city of Paris	G. Urbain (France)	1907	174·967	9·839	1665	3400	34

Atomic Number	Symbol	Element Name	Derived From	Discoverers	Year	Atomic Weight (Note 3)	Density At 20°C (Unless Otherwise Stated) (g/cm³)(Note 4)	Melting Point (°C)	Boiling Point (°C)	Number Of Nuclides
72	Hf	Hafnium	Hafnia = Copenhagen	D. Coster (Netherlands) and G. C. de Hevesy (Hungary/Sweden)	1923	178·49	13·28	2230	4700	31
73	Ta	Tantalum	'Tantalus' - a mythical Greek king	A. G. Ekeberg (Sweden)	1802	180·9479	16·67	3020	5490	30
74	W	Tungsten (Wolfram)	Swedish 'tung sten' = heavy stone	J. J. de Elhuyar and F. de Elhuyar (Spain)	1783	183·85	19·26	3420	5860	33
75	Re	Rhenium	Latin 'Rhenus' = the river Rhine	W. Noddack, Fr. I. Tacke and O. Berg (Germany)	1925	186·207	21·01	3185	5610	32
76	Os	Osmium	Greek 'osme' = odour	S. Tennant (UK)	1804	190·2	22·59	3137	5020	34
77	Ir	Iridium	Latin 'iris' = a rainbow	S. Tennant (UK)	1804	192·22	22·56	2447	4730	33
78	Pt	Platinum	Spanish 'platina' = small silver	A. de Ulloa (Spain)	1748	195·08	21·45	1768·7	3870	34
79	Au	Gold (Aurum)	Anglo-Saxon 'gold'	Prehistoric	—	196·96654	19·29	1064·43	2875	32
80	Hg	Mercury (Hydrargyrum)	'Hermes' (Latin 'Mercurius'), the divine patron of the occult sciences	Near historic	c. 1600 BC	200·59	14·17 (solid at mp) 13·55 (liquid at 20°C)	−38·836	356·661	33
81	Tl	Thallium	Greek 'thallos' = a budding twig	W. Crookes (UK)	1861	204·3833	11·87	303	1468	29
82	Pb	Lead (Plumbum)	Anglo-Saxon 'lead'	Prehistoric	—	207·2	11·35	327·502	1748	33
83	Bi	Bismuth	German 'weissmuth' = white matter	C. F. Geoffroy (France)	1753	208·98037	9·807	271·442	1566	28
84	Po	Polonium	Poland	Mme. M. S. Curie (Poland/France)	1898	(208·9824)	9·155	254	948	27
85	At	Astatine	Greek 'astatos' = unstable	D. R. Corson and K. R. Mackenzie (USA) and E. Segré (Italy/USA)	1940	(209·9871)	7·0	302	377	24
86	Rn	Radon	Latin 'radius' = ray	F. E. Dorn (Germany)	1900	(222·0176)	4·7 (solid at mp) 0·01004 (gas at 0°C)	−64·9	−61·2	30
87	Fr	Francium	France	Mlle. M. Perey (France)	1939	(223·0197)	2·8	24	650	31
88	Ra	Radium	Latin 'radius' = ray	P. Curie (France), Mme. M. S. Curie (Poland/France), and M. G. Bemont (France)	1898	(226·0254)	5·50	707	1530	28
89	Ac	Actinium	Greek 'aktinos', genetive of 'aktis' = a ray	A. Debierne (France)	1899	(227·0278)	10·04	1230	3600	26
90	Th	Thorium	'Thor', the Norse god of thunder	J. J. Berzelius (Sweden)	1829	232·0381	11·72	1760	4660	25
91	Pa	Protactinium	Greek 'protos' = first, plus actinium	O. Hahn (Germany) and Fr. L. Meitner (Austria); F. Soddy and J. A. Cranston (UK)	1917	(231·0359)	15·41	1570	4490	24
92	U	Uranium	The planet Uranus (discovered 1781)	M. H. Klaproth (Germany)	1789	238·0289	19·05	1134	4160	17

Atomic Number	Symbol	Element Name	Derived From	Year	Discoverers	Atomic Weight (Note 3)	Density At 20°C (Unless Otherwise Stated) (g/cm³) (Note 4)	Melting Point (°C)	Boiling Point (°C)	Number Of Nuclides
93	Np	Neptunium	The planet Neptune	1940	E. M. McMillan and P. H. Abelson (USA)	(237·0482)	20·47	637	4090	16
94	Pu	Plutonium	The planet Pluto	1940–1941	G. T. Seaborg, E. M. McMillan, J. W. Kennedy and A. C. Wahl (USA)	(244·0642)	20·26	640	3270	15
95	Am	Americium	America	1944–1945	G. T. Seaborg, R. A. James, L. O. Morgan and A. Ghiorso (USA)	(243·0614)	13·76	1176	2023	13
96	Cm	Curium	Pierre Curie (1859–1906) (France) and Marie Curie (1867–1934) (Poland/France)	1944	G. T. Seaborg, R. A. James and A. Ghiorso (USA)	(247·0703)	13·67	1340	3180	14
97	Bk	Berkelium	Berkeley, a town in California. USA	1949	S. G. Thompson, A. Ghiorso and G. T. Seaborg (USA)	(247·0703)	14·61	1050	2710	11
98	Cf	Californium	California	1950	S. G. Thompson, K. Street Jr., A. Ghiorso and G. T. Seaborg (USA)	(251·0796)	15·16	900	1612	18
99	Es	Einsteinium	Dr Albert Einstein (1879–1955) (USA. b. Germany)	1952	A. Ghiorso et al (USA)	(252·0829)	9·05	860	996	14
100	Fm	Fermium	Dr Enrico Fermi (1901–1954) (Italy)	1953	A. Ghiorso et al (USA)	(257·0951)	—	—	—	18
101	Md	Mendelevium	Dmitriy I. Mendeleyev (1834–1907) (Russia)	1955	A. Ghiorso, B. G. Harvey, G. R. Choppin, S. G. Thompson and G. T. Seaborg (USA)	(258·0986)	—	—	—	13
102	No	Nobelium	Alfred B. Nobel (1833–1896) (Sweden)	1958	A. Ghiorso, T. Sikkeland, J. R. Walton and G. T. Seaborg (USA)	(259·1009)	—	—	—	10
103	Lr	Lawrencium	Dr Ernest O. Lawrence (1901–1958) (USA)	1961	A. Ghiorso, T. Sikkeland, A. E. Larsh and R. M. Latimer (USA)	(262·11)	—	—	—	9
104	Unq	Unnilquadium (Note 2)	Un-nil-quad (1-0-4)	1969	A. Ghiorso, M. Nurmia, J. Harris, K. Eskola and P. Eskola (USA/Finland)	(261·1087)	—	—	—	10
105	Unp	Unnilpentium (Note 2)	Un-nil-pent (1-0-5)	1970	A. Ghiorso, M. Nurmia, K. Eskola, J. Harris and P. Eskola (USA/Finland)	(262·1138)	—	—	—	7
106	Unh	Unnilhexium (Note 2)	Un-nil-hex (1-0-6)	1974	A. Ghiorso et al (USA)	(263·1182)	—	—	—	4
107	Uns	Unnilseptium (Note 2)	Un-nil-sept (1-0-7)	1981	G. Münzenberg et al (Federal Republic of Germany)	(262·1229)	—	—	—	2
108	Uno	Unniloctium (Note 2)	Un-nil-oct (1-0-8)	1984	G. Münzenberg et al (Federal Republic of Germany/Finland)	(265·1302)	—	—	—	2
109	Une	Unnilennium (Note 2)	Un-nil-enn (1-0-9)	1982	G. Münzenberg et al (Federal Republic of Germany)	(266·1376)	—	—	—	1

PHYSICS

Glossary

Å Ångstrom, 0·1 nm.

absolute zero Lowest temperature theoretically possible, at which the random motion of the particles in a system is zero. It is equal to $-273.15\,^{\circ}\mathrm{C} = 0\ \mathrm{K} = -459.67\,^{\circ}\mathrm{F}$.

absorption spectrum If light of a continuous frequency is passed through a medium into a spectroscope, dark regions appear in the spectrum, due to the absorption of light by the medium. The medium will absorb the wavelengths which it would normally emit if it were raised to a high enough temperature, i.e. the absorbed radiation excites atoms from the ground state to an excited state.

acceleration Rate of increase of velocity with time.

accelerator A large machine in which an electric field is used to increase the kinetic energy of charged particles such as electrons and protons by accelerating them. The stream of accelerated particles is guided into the desired path by a magnetic field.

acoustics The study and use of sound waves.

allotropy The existence of a substance in more than one form (allotropes), differing in physical rather than chemical properties.

alpha (α) particle A helium nucleus, consisting of two protons and two neutrons and carrying a positive charge.

alpha rays A stream of alpha particles, emitted by many radioactive substances. The alpha particles can be stopped by a piece of paper, i.e. they have a very low penetrating power.

alternating current An electric current that regularly reverses its direction in a circuit.

ammeter An instrument for measuring electric current.

ampere Symbol A. Unit of electric current.

anion A negatively charged ion.

anode Positive electrode.

antimatter Matter consisting of anti-particles. Anti-matter has never actually been detected.

Archimedes' principle A body floating in a fluid displaces a weight of fluid equal to its own weight.

atom Smallest particle of a pure element that can take part in a chemical reaction.

atomic mass unit Symbol u. One-twelfth of the mass of carbon-12 atom. Approximately the mass of a proton or neutron.

atomic number Symbol Z. Number of protons in the nucleus.

atomic weight Symbol A_r. The average mass of atoms in an element, in atomic mass units.

Avogadro's hypothesis Equal volumes of all gases measured at the same temperature and pressure contain the same number of molecules.

background radiation Low-intensity radiation resulting from bombardment of the earth by cosmic rays and from naturally occurring isotopes in soil, air, buildings, etc.

bar A unit of pressure equal to 10^5 pascals. The millibar is used by meteorologists.

barometer A device for measuring atmospheric pressure.

Becquerel rays Alpha, beta and gamma rays emitted by uranium compounds.

beta (β) particle An electron emitted by a radioisotope during beta decay.

beta rays A stream of beta particles, emitted by nuclei of certain radioisotopes. They can penetrate thin metal foil.

betatron An accelerator producing high-energy electrons. They are accelerated by means of magnetic induction.

black body A body that absorbs all radiation falling on it.

boiling point The temperature at which the saturated vapour pressure of a liquid equals the external pressure.

breeder reactor A nuclear reactor in which more fissile material is produced than is used.

Brownian movement Irregular movement of smoke particles, or of very small particles, e.g. pollen, in a liquid. It is due to molecular bombardment by moving molecules.

c The velocity of light; 2.99792458×10^8 m/s.

calorimeter A device in which thermal measurements can be made.

candela Symbol cd. Unit of luminous intensity.

capacitance Symbol C. The ability of an isolated electrical conductor to store electrical charge.

capacitor A device containing one or more pairs of electrical conductors separated by insulators (the dielectric). It is used to store electrical charge.

capillarity The effect of surface tension on a liquid in a fine tube, causing the liquid to rise or fall in the tube.

cathode Negative electrode.

cathode ray tube Electrons from a heated cathode are projected on to a phosphor screen. The intensity and movement of the beam can be controlled, and the phosphor screen converts the kinetic energy of the electrons into a bright spot of light. This is the basis of a TV.

Celsius scale The official name of the centigrade temperature scale. The ice point is $0\,^{\circ}\mathrm{C}$ and the boiling point $100\,^{\circ}\mathrm{C}$.

centrifugal force The inertial force directed radially outwards, in equilibrium with the applied centripetal force.

centripetal force A lateral force that makes a body move in a circular path. It is directed towards the centre of the circle.

CGS System of units based on the centimetre, gram and second. It has now been superseded by the more coherent SI system.

charge Symbol Q. The ability of some elementary particles, such as electrons and protons, to exert forces on one another. Like forces repel, unlike forces attract.

concave Curving inwards. Concave mirrors converge rays of light, concave lenses diverge them.

conductor A substance that offers a relatively low resistance to an electric current.

conservation of mass and energy In any system the

sum of the mass and energy is always constant.

conservation of momentum In any system, the linear or angular momentum remains the same unless there is an external force acting on the system.

convection Transfer of heat in a fluid by movement of the fluid.

convex Curving outwards. A convex mirror diverges rays of light, a convex lens converges them.

cosmic rays Particle radiation reaching the earth from space.

cryogenics The study and production of very low temperatures.

curie Symbol Ci. The unit of activity of a radioactive substance. It corresponds to 3.7×10^{10} disintegrations per second, and is about equal to the activity of 1 g of radium.

current Symbol I. The rate of flow of electricity. The unit is the ampere.

cyclotron An accelerator in which the beam of charged particles follows a spiral path.

decay The breakdown of a radioactive nuclide into a daughter product by disintegration.

decibel A bel is a logarithmic unit for comparing two amounts of power. A decibel is one-tenth of a bel. One decibel represents an increase in intensity of about 26 per cent – about the smallest increase that the ear can detect. (The decibel is *not* a measure of loudness, as the sensitivity of the ear varies with frequency.)

densitometer Instrument for measuring the density of a substance.

density Symbol ρ. Mass per unit volume of a substance.

dielectric An insulator.

diffraction The phenomenon of waves appearing to travel round corners. It occurs when a wavefront meets a narrow slit or obstacle.

diffractometer An instrument used to measure the intensities of diffracted X-rays or neutron beams at different angles to each other.

diffusion Process by which substances mix due to the kinetic motions of the particles, be they atoms, molecules or groups of molecules.

diode An electronic device with only two electrodes.

direct current An electric current that flows in one direction only and is reasonably constant in magnitude.

discharge Passage of electric current through a gas-discharge tube, usually with luminous effects.

disintegration In which a nucleus emits particles, either after a collision or spontaneously.

dispersion The process by which a beam of white light is spread out to produce spectra.

Döppler effect Apparent change in frequency (of light or sound) when there is relative motion along a line between the source and the observer.

e The charge on an electron.

earth The electric potential of the earth is taken as being zero.

efficiency Symbol η. The ratio of the useful energy output of a machine to the energy input. A perfect machine would have an efficiency of 1.

Einstein's law $E = mc^2$, the law of equivalence of mass and energy, whereby a mass m has energy E, and vice versa.

elasticity The ability of a substance to return to its original size and shape after being deformed.

electric field strength Symbol E. The strength of an electric field at a given point, measured in volts per metre.

electric flux Symbol ψ. The quantity of electricity displaced across a given area in a dielectric, measured in coulombs.

electric potential Symbol V. The work done in bringing a unit positive charge from infinity to a point.

electrolyte A substance that conducts electricity in solution because of the presence of ions.

electron An elementary particle, found spinning around the nuclei of atoms. As free electrons they are responsible for electrical conduction.

electronics Nowadays, the study and use of electricity in semiconductors.

electronvolt Symbol eV. The energy acquired by an electron in falling freely through a potential difference of 1 volt.

elementary particle Any particle of matter that cannot be subdivided into smaller particles.

energy Symbol E. A measure of a systems capacity to do work.

enthalpy Symbol H. Thermodynamic function of a system equal to the sum of its internal energy and the product of its pressure and volume.

entropy Symbol S. The disorder of a system; the greater the disorder of a system, the greater the entropy.

evaporation Conversion of a liquid to a vapour at a temperature below the boiling point.

Fahrenheit scale Temperature scale on which the ice point is 32°F and the steam point is 212°F.

fallout Radioactive material that falls to earth after a nuclear explosion.

farad Symbol F. Unit of capacitance, in which a charge of 1 coulomb is acquired when 1 volt is applied.

ferromagnetism Solids that can be magnetized by weak magnetic fields, e.g. iron, cobalt, nickel.

fibre optics The study and use of the transmission of light by very fine flexible glass rods.

fission Splitting of a heavy nucleus into two or more fragments, normally accompanied by the emission of neutrons or gamma rays.

fluid A liquid or gas.

fluidics Study and use of jets of fluid in circuits to perform tasks usually carried out by electronic circuits.

fluorescence When electromagnetic radiation, e.g. X-rays, UV light, etc., strikes a fluorescent substance, radiation of a longer wavelength, e.g. light, is emitted.

flux The strength of a field of force through a specified area.

force Symbol F. Any action that tends to alter a body's state of rest or uniform motion.

free fall Downward motion in a gravitational field, unimpeded by any bouyancy effects.

freezing point The same as the melting point. The temperature at which both the solid and liquid phases of a substance can exist in equilibrium.

frequency Symbol v or f. The number of complete cycles or oscillations that occur in a unit of time.

fusion Change of state from liquid to solid at the melting point.

g Symbol for the acceleration due to free fall. On the earth it is 9.81 m s^{-2}.

gain The efficiency of an electronic system.

galvanometer An instrument for measuring or detecting electrical currents.

gamma (γ) rays Electromagnetic radiation emitted by certain radioactive substances. They can penetrate much greater distances than alpha and beta rays, and form the extreme short-wave end of the electromagnetic spectrum.
Geiger counter Device for detecting ionizing radiation, especially alpha particles. Because it can count the particles it can therefore measure the strength of radioactivity.
gravitation The attraction which all bodies have for one another.

h Symbol for Planck's constant.
half-life The time in which a radioactive substance decays to half its original quantity or half its original activity.
harmonic A simple multiple of a fundamental frequency.
heat That form of energy transferred between bodies as a result of differences in their temperature.
heat pump A device for extracting heat from large quantities of a substance, e.g. water, air, at a low temperature and supplying it at a higher temperature, e.g. to a building. Mechanical work must be performed for the pump to work.
hertz Symbol Hz. The unit of frequency; 1 cycle or oscillation per second.
holography A laser technique for producing stereoscopic images without cameras or lenses.
hydrodynamics The study and use of the motion of fluids.
hysteresis Lagging of effect behind cause when cause varies in amount, e.g. magnetic induction lagging behind an applied cycle of magnetic changes.

ice point The temperature at which ice and water are in equilibrium at standard pressure.
induction When an electrical conductor is moved so that it cuts the flux of a magnetic field, a potential difference is induced between the ends of the conductor.
inertia The tendency for a body to remain at rest or in a state of uniform motion in a straight line.
infrared rays Electromagnetic radiation (heat) emitted by hot bodies. It consists of radiation of longer wavelengths than the red end of the visible spectrum.
integrated circuit A complete circuit in a single package, usually in or on a single chip of silicon.
interference If light or sound waves of the same wavelength but from different sources cross over, areas of minimum and maximum intensity occur where the waves superimpose on each other.
ion Electrically charged atom, group of atoms, molecular or group of molecules.
isobar Line joining places with the same atmospheric pressure.
isotopes Atoms having the same number of protons but different numbers of neutrons.

joule Symbol J. Unit of energy; 1 newton moved through 1 metre in the direction of the applied force.

kelvin Symbol K. Unit of thermodynamic temperature; the temperature difference on the Kelvin and Celsius scale, where $1 K = 1°C$.
kinetic energy Symbol T. Energy possessed by virtue of a body's motion.

laminar flow Steady flow in which a fluid moves in parallel layers (laminae), although the velocities of the fluid particles in each lamina are not necessarily equal.
laser Abbreviation for Light Amplification by Stimulated Emission of Radiation. A source of intense coherent radiation of a single wavelength in the infrared, visible and ultraviolet regions of the spectrum.
latent heat The quantity of heat released or absorbed when a substance changes phase at a fixed temperature.
lattice A regularly-repeated three-dimensional array of points that determines the positions of atoms or molecules in a crystalline structure.
lens A piece of transparent material, bounded by two regularly curved surfaces and designed to focus light to a fixed point.
light A narrow section of the electromagnetic spectrum.
longitudinal waves Waves in which displacement of the transmitting medium is in the same plane as the direction of travel, e.g. sound waves.
lumen Symbol lm. Unit of luminous flux, i.e. the rate of flow of radiant energy.
lux Symbol lx. Unit of illumination.

machine A device for doing work, in which a small effort is used to overcome a larger force or load.
Mach number Symbol M. Ratio of the relative velocity of a body in a fluid to the velocity of sound in the fluid. Mach 1 thus indicates the speed of sound.
magnetic bottle An arrangement of magnetic fields designed to contain a plasma.
magnetic field A field of force containing magnetic flux.
magnetism Attractive and repulsive forces due to the motion of electrons around the atoms in a substance.
magnifying power Ratio of the size of the image produced by an instrument to the size of the image as seen by the naked eye.
maser Abbreviation for Microwave Amplification by Stimulated Emission of Radiation. The microwave equivalent of a laser.
mass The quantity of matter in a body; the reluctance of a body to accelerate when acted on by a force. It is measured in grams.
mass number Symbol A. The number of nucleons in a nucleus.
mass spectrometer An instrument for measuring atomic masses of elements which can be formed into a beam of ions.
mechanics The study of motion and the equilibrium of bodies.
metrology The study of the accurate measurement of mass, length and time.
microscope An instrument, containing converging lenses, that produces an enlarged image of small objects.
microwave An electromagnetic wave with a wavelength between infrared radiation and radio waves.
mil One-thousandth of an inch.
mm HG Abbreviation for millimetres of mercury. A unit of pressure measured by the height in mm of a column of mercury supported by the pressure.
mole Symbol mol. The amount of substance that contains the same number of elementary entities (molecules, ions, atoms, etc.) as there are in 0·012 kg of carbon-12.

moment A turning effect, equal to the magnitude of the force and the perpendicular distance from the line of action of the force to the axis.

momentum Symbol p. The product of the mass and the velocity of a body.

monochromatic radiation Radiation of one wavelength or, at worst, of a very narrow band of wavelengths.

motor A machine that converts electrical energy into mechanical energy.

neutron A constituent of the nucleus, with zero charge and about the same mass as the proton.

neutron number Symbol N. The number of neutrons present in the nucleus of an atom.

neutron star A massive star consisting largely of neutrons.

newton Symbol N. Unit of force that gives 1 kilogram an acceleration of 1 metre per second per second.

Newton's rings Circular interference fringes formed between a lens and a glass plate with which the lens is in contact.

NTP Abbreviation for normal temperature and pressure.

nuclear fusion A nuclear reaction in which light atomic nuclei combine to form a heavier atomic nucleus with the release of energy.

nuclear isomer Nuclei with the same mass number and atomic number but different radioactive properties.

nuclear magnetic resonance An effect observed when radio-frequency radiation is absorbed by matter. It is due to the spin of atomic nuclei developing characteristic magnetic moments.

nucleon Collective name for the constituents of the atomic nucleus, i.e. proton and neutron.

nucleus The most massive part of an atom, consisting of neutrons and protons held together by binding forces.

ohm Symbol Ω. Unit of resistance. The resistance between two points if an applied potential difference of 1 volt produces a current of 1 amp.

optics The study and use of light.

orbit A curved path described, for example, by a planet or comet around the sun or a particle such as an electron in a field of force such as that encountered around an atomic nucleus.

oscillation A vibration with a regular frequency; a movement backwards and forwards between two points with a regular frequency.

osmosis The use of a semipermeable membrane that allows certain kinds of molecule in a liquid to pass down a hydrostatic pressure gradient but that prevents the passage of other molecules.

parallax Apparent displacement of an object caused by an actual change of point of observation.

parity Symbol P. Parity invariance states that no distinction can be made between laws of physics for a right-handed system of coordinates and for a left-handed system of coordinates.

pascal Symbol Pa. Unit of pressure resulting from 1 newton acting uniformly over 1 m².

Pascal's principle Pressure applied at any point to a fluid at rest is transmitted without loss to all other parts of the fluid.

Pauli exclusion principle No two fermions can exist in identical quantum states, e.g. no two electrons in an atom can have the same quantum number.

pendulum A mass suspended from a fixed point that oscillates with a known and fixed period.

period Symbol T. Time occupied by one complete vibration or oscillation.

permeability Symbol μ. Ratio of magnetic flux density in a body to the external magnetic field strength inducing it.

phase The proportion of a period that has elapsed, taken from a fixed point in the cycle.

photoemission Release or emission of electrons due to bombardment of the substance by electromagnetic radiation, e.g. light.

piezoelectric effect Production of an electrical potential difference across a piece of crystal, e.g. quartz, when subjected to pressure.

pitch The frequency of a sound.

Planck's constant A universal constant, $h = 6.626 \times 10^{-34}$ J s.

Planck's law Electromagnetic radiation consists of small indivisible packets called photons or quanta whose energy $= hf$, where h is Planck's constant and f is the frequency of the radiation.

plasma Gas of positive ions and free electrons with roughly equal positive and negative charges.

pneumatics Study and use of dynamic properties of gases.

polarization The restriction of particle displacement to a single plane. It can only occur in transverse waves, e.g. electromagnetic radiation.

pole Point towards which lines of magnetic flux converge.

positron Positive electron, the antiparticle of the electron.

potential difference The potential difference between two points is the work done per coulomb of positive electrical charge taken from one point to the other, measured in volts.

power Symbol P. Work done per second, measured in watts.

pressure Symbol p. Force per unit area, measured in pascals.

prism A refracting substance, such as glass, with two plane intersecting surfaces. It deviates a beam of light and disperses it into its constituent colours.

proton A positively-charged elementary particle about 1836 times as heavy as an electron. All atomic nuclei contain protons, and the hydrogen nucleus consists solely of one proton.

quantum mechanics A mathematical physical theory based on Planck's quantum theory and the probability of finding an elementary particle at any particular point.

quantum theory Theory based on Planck's idea of discrete quanta of electromagnetic radiation.

rad Unit of absorbed radiation equal to 0.01 joule per kilogram of absorbing material.

radiation Any energy propagated as rays, streams of particles or waves.

radioactivity Spontaneous disintegration of the nuclei of some isotopes of certain elements, with the emission of alpha or beta particles, sometimes together with gamma rays.

radiopaque Opaque to radiation, especially gamma rays and X-rays, e.g. bones are radiopaque to X-rays but other body tissues are not.

radio waves Electromagnetic radiation of radio frequency.

rectifier Electrical device that allows current to flow in only one direction and thus converts alternating to direct current.

Hasylab, a German particle physics laboratory in Hamburg, which uses radiation to provide a useful source of ultraviolet and X-rays which are used for a variety of experiments. (Science Photo Library)

reflection When light or sound strikes a surface between two different media, some is thrown back into the original medium.

refraction The change of direction a ray of light or sound wave undergoes when it passes from one medium to another.

relativity A theory developed by Einstein, confirming the unification of mass and energy, the former being a 'congealed' form of the latter.

resistance Symbol R. The ratio between the potential difference across a conductor and the current passing through it, measured in ohms.

resistivity Symbol ρ. Resistance per unit length of unit cross-sectional area of a conductor, measured in ohm-metres.

resonance Maximum response which occurs when a driving frequency applied to a system is equal to the natural frequency of the system.

rheology Study and use of the deformation and flow of matter.

saturated vapour A vapour in dynamic equilibrium with its liquid at a given temperature – it can hold no more substance in the gaseous phase at that temperature.

scattering Deflection of radiation by interaction with nuclei or electrons. Deflection of sound waves

by a reflecting surface. Deflection of light waves by fine particles.

Schrödinger wave equation The basic equation of wave mechanics. It shows the behaviour of a particle moving in force field.

scintillation The emission of small flashes of light when radiation strikes certain substances.

second Symbol s. The basic unit of time in the SI units.

semiconductor A substance with a resistivity between that of conductors and insulators. Junctions between semiconductors form the basis of modern electronics industry.

semipermeable membrane A membrane that allows the passage of certain molecules in a fluid while preventing the passage of other molecules.

shells Electrons moving round the atomic nucleus exist in different energy states. The sets of states corresponding to the same energy are called shells.

simple harmonic motion The periodic motion of a body subjected to a restoring force proportional to the displacement from the centre. The period of oscillation is independent of amplitude and the displacement varies sinusoidally with time.

sinusoidal Having a waveform the same as that of a sine function.

SI units Abbreviation for *Système International*

d'Unités. An internationally-agreed coherent system of units based on the metre, kilogram and second.

solenoid A coil of wire with a greater length than diameter. When an electric current is passed through the wire it forms an electromagnet.

specific When applied to an extensive physical property, specific restricts the meaning to 'per unit mass' of the substance.

spectrometer An instrument for producing, recording or examining a spectrum of radiation.

spectrum A distribution of electromagnetic radiation. It is usually applied to the visible display of colours, but can be applied to any part of the range of electromagnetic radiation.

speed Rate of increase of distance travelled with time.

spin An electron travels round the atomic nucleus and as it does it spins on its own axis.

standard atmosphere Symbol atm. Unit of pressure equal to 101 325 pascals.

standard temperature and pressure A standard condition for the reduction of gas pressures and temperatures. It is equal to $0°C$ and 101 325 pascals.

steam point Temperature at which the liquid and vapour phases of water are in equilibrium at standard pressure, i.e. $100°C$.

strain Change of shape and/or volume of a body due to applied forces.

stress Forces in equilibrium acting on a body and tending to produce strain.

superconductivity When many metals and alloys are cooled to near absolute zero $(0 K, -273°C)$, their electrical resistance almost vanishes.

supercooling Slow and continuous cooling of liquids, taking them down below their normal freezing point.

superfluid A fluid, at a very low temperature, that has very high thermal conductivity and can flow through very fine channels without friction.

telescope An instrument for producing a magnified or intensified image of a distant object. Optical telescopes use lenses or lenses and mirrors; radio telescopes use electronic circuitry to amplify radio signals from distant sources.

temperature Symbol T. The hotness of a body that determines which direction heat flows when the body is in contact with other bodies.

thermodynamics The study and use of the interrelationships between heat and other forms of energy.

tone The quality of a musical sound, caused by the presence of harmonics.

transducer A device for converting a non-electrical variable into a proportionately variable electrical signal.

transformer A device, consisting of two electrical circuits magnetically coupled together such that an alternating voltage in one circuit is transformed into an alternating voltage (usually different) in the other.

transistor A semiconductor device in which a small base current or voltage can control or modulate a larger collector current or voltage.

transverse waves Waves in which displacement of the transmitting medium is perpendicular to the direction of travel, e.g. electromagnetic waves.

tribology The study of friction, lubrication and wear of surfaces.

triple point The temperature at which, for any substance, the three physical states of the substances can exist at equilibrium. For water this occurs at $0°C$.

ultrasonics The study and use of frequencies beyond the limits of human hearing, i.e. above about 20 khz.

ultraviolet radiation Electromagnetic radiation lying beyond the violet end of the visible spectrum and before the X-ray region.

unified field theory Theory, yet to be developed, that seeks to link together the properties of gravitational, nuclear and electromagnetic fields.

vacuum Space or vessel devoid of matter or from which all air has been removed.

valence electrons Those electrons in the outermost shell of an atom that are involved in chemical changes.

vapour Substance in gaseous form but below its critical temperature. It can thus be liquefied merely by pressure, without the need for cooling.

vector A quantity that has direction as well as magnitude.

velocity Symbol v. Rate of increase of distance travelled by a body in a particular direction.

viscosity The ability of fluids to offer resistance to flow.

visible spectrum Visible electromagnetic radiation between 380 and 780 nm.

volt Symbol V. The potential difference between two points such that 1 joule of work is done by every coulomb of positive charge moved from one point to the other.

watt Symbol W. The unit of power resulting from the dissipation of 1 joule in 1 second.

wave A curve of an alternating quantity plotted against time, giving rise to a disturbance travelling through a medium.

wavelength Symbol λ. The distance between one vibrating particle in a wave train and the next particle that is vibrating in the same phase.

wave mechanics A form of quantum mechanics.

weight The pull of gravity on a body, measured in newtons.

work Symbol w or W. Work is carried out when a force moves its point of application. It is measured in joules, i.e. 1 newton moved through 1 metre.

X-rays Electromagnetic radiation lying between ultraviolet radiation and gamma rays.

Milestones in physics

Physics is very much concerned with fundamental particles – the building blocks out of which the Universe is constructed – and the forces which bind and regulate them. Many theories have been proposed from time to time to provide a better understanding of the vast number of facts and observations which have accumulated. The main development of physics is essentially a series of unifications of these theories.

1687 Sir Isaac Newton (1642–1727) produced the great unifying theory of **gravitation** which linked the falling apple with the force which keeps the stars and planets in their courses. This made available for further scientific investigation one of the basic universal forces of nature, the force of gravity. The gravitational force, F, between two bodies of masses, m_1, m_2, distance, r, apart is given by

$$F = G \frac{m_1 m_2}{r^2}$$

where G is a Universal constant. Though he first derived his inverse square law of gravity in the summer of 1666, at Woolsthorpe, Lincolnshire, Newton did not publish it until 1687 in his *Principia*.

By Newton's time there existed two rival theories to explain the passage of light from source to observer. One was the **particle theory** which maintained that light consists of vast numbers of minute particles ejected by the luminous body in all directions. Newton, who made so many brilliant advances in optics, favoured this theory. It accounted in a particularly simple way for the transmission of light through the vacuum of space, for its rectilinear propagation, and for the laws of reflection. The alternative was the **wave theory**, which assumed that light was transmitted by means of a wave motion. This would imply that light would bend round corners, but when it was discovered that the wavelength of the light was very small (about 1/2000th of a millimetre), it was realized that the effect would be small as is in fact observed. Light does not cast a perfectly sharp shadow. Further phenomena were discovered which demonstrated the wave nature of light and added support to that theory, e.g. interference and diffraction.

1820   Hans Christian Oersted (1777–1851) of Denmark discovered that the flow of electric current in a conductor would cause a nearby compass needle to be deflected.

1831   Michael Faraday (1791–1867) the English physicist, uncovered the principle of magnetic induction which led to the invention of the dynamo. He showed that a change in the magnetic field surrounding a conductor could cause a flow of electrical current.

1865   The unification between magnetism and electricity was brought to full flower by the Scottish physicist, James Clerk Maxwell (1831–79), in his great **electromagnetic theory**, which described every known field of magnetic and electric behaviour. The set of equations named after him showed that electromagnetic waves travel at the velocity of light and confirmed that light is, in fact, an electromagnetic radiation. This provided further support for the wave theory of light.

1887   Heinrich Rudolph Hertz (1857–94), the German physicist, performed a classic experiment in which electromagnetic waves were produced and transmitted across the laboratory. This laid the foundation for radio transmission and provided ample vindication for Maxwell's theory.

As the 19th century drew to a close many of the problems of physics appeared to have been solved and there was a belief that, in principle, if all the observations and calculations could be made, the destiny of the Universe could be revealed in full detail. However, following on Hertz's experiment, a quick succession of phenomena presented themselves which threatened to destroy the orderly structure which had been so painstakingly built up over the preceding centuries.

1895   **X-rays** were discovered by Wilhelm Konrad von Röntgen (1845–1923) the German physicist.

When experimenting with the passage of electrical discharges through gases, he noticed that fluorescent material near his apparatus glowed. He won the first Nobel prize for physics in 1901 for this work.

1896   Antoine Henri Becquerel (1852–1908), the French physicist, discovered that uranium salts, even in the dark, emit a radiation similar to Röntgen's X-rays and would fog a photographic plate. This was **radioactivity**.

1898   Marie Curie (1867–1934), of Poland, working with her French husband, Pierre, (1859–1906) announced the existence of two new chemical elements which powerfully emit radiation. She named the elements radium and polonium. The active phenomenon she gave the name radioactivity. She won the Nobel prize for physics in 1903 with Becquerel and her husband, and in 1911, for chemistry on her own.

Ernest Rutherford (1871–1937), New Zealand born British physicist and Frederick Soddy (1877–1956), British chemist, formulated a theory of radioactivity which forms the basis of our present understanding of the phenomenon. Three types of radioactivity were identified, α-rays, β-rays, and γ-rays. The γ-rays turned out to be like X-rays, more powerful than those of Röntgen. The β-rays were streams of fast moving electrons. The α-rays were found to consist of electrically charged particles being the nuclei of the element helium. The particles emitted from radioactive materials at such speed provided a means of investigating the structure of the atom itself, and enabled Rutherford to propose in 1911 a model of the atom which is the basis of our modern ideas of atomic structure.

A further important discovery which contributed to a revision of the ideas of classical physics was the **photoelectric effect**. It was observed that a polished zinc plate, when illuminated with ultra-violet light acquired a positive electric charge. In **1897** Joseph John Thomson (1856–1940), the British physicist, discovered the first of the fundamental particles, the **electron**, which is the basic unit of negative electricity. It became clear that the photoelectric effect was the result of electrons being knocked out of the metal surface by the incident light. It was further discovered that, firstly, the number of electrons emitted was greater for a greater intensity of light and, secondly, that their energy was related only to the wavelength of the light, being greater for shorter wavelengths. The first result was as expected but the second was a mystery.

Modern physics

Modern physics could be said to have been born at the beginning of the 20th century, during the course of which a number of radical ideas have been formulated and developed into theories which have completely revolutionized the thinking in physics.

1900   The quantum theory was the first of these, put forward by the German physicist Max Karl Ernst Ludwig Planck (1858–1947). This arose out of yet another problem which had been insoluble up to that time. Calculations showed that the energy emitted from a hot body should be, at very short wavelengths, practically infinite: this was clearly not so. The calculations were satisfactory for radiation of longer wavelengths in that they agreed with

Einstein, author of the *Special Theory of Relativity*, at home in his study. (Popperfoto)

experiment. To resolve this difficulty, Planck made the very novel suggestion that energy was radiated from the body, not in a continuous flow of waves as had been supposed up to then, but rather in distinct individual bundles. He called a bundle of energy a **quantum**. The energy of the quantum, E, is given by

$$E = \frac{hc}{\lambda}$$

where λ is the wavelength of the radiation, c is the velocity of light *in vacuo* and h is a fixed, universal constant called Planck's constant. On this theory, energy at the shorter wavelengths would require to

be emitted in bigger bundles and thus there would be less of them available for emission in accordance with experimental results. Planck's constant is small and so quantum effects are also small, occurring only in the domain of atomic phenomena.

1905 Albert Einstein (1879–1955), a Swabian Jew, published his theory of the photoelectric effect and for which he was to win the Nobel prize in 1921. Einstein followed Planck's ideas and could see that the incident light must consist of a stream of quanta, that is, bundles of light, which came to be known as **photons**. A photon striking a metal surface is absorbed by an electron in it, the electron having more energy as a result. This causes it to jump from the surface, and since photons have greater energy at shorter wavelengths, so shorter wavelength light causes the emission of higher energy electrons. And, of course, the greater the intensity of the light the more quanta will be striking the surface and so more electrons will be emitted. Thus, the idea of the quantum enabled Einstein to account for the phenomena of the photoelectric effect and this was an early triumph for the new quantum theory which was to become a ground force in the subsequent developments in physics.

1905   This year also saw the publication of Einstein's **Special (or Restricted) Theory of Relativity**. It has been said that as a child he had wondered what would happen if it were possible to travel fast enough to catch a ray of light and that this led him some years later to formulate his celebrated theory. This theory arises from an apparent contradiction between two basic postulates:

1. The velocity of light *in vacuo* is a constant for all observers regardless of their state of motion relative to the light source.
2. The special principle of relativity which states that the laws of physics are the same for all observers in uniform motion relative to each other.

Imagine for a moment a train travelling with a uniform velocity *v* relative to the railway embankment, and a ray of light transmitted with velocity *c* along the embankment parallel, and in the direction of the train. For an observer in the train the velocity of the light should appear to be *c-v*: obviously less than *c*. But this violates the special principle of relativity above: the velocity of light must be the same for an observer on the embankment and an observer on the train. The reconciliation of these two apparently contradictory conclusions is the basis for the special theory and is achieved by surrendering the concepts of absolute time, absolute distance and of the absolute significance of simultaneity. From these ideas, fairly straightforward algebraic manipulation leads to equations which show that when a body is in uniform motion relative to an observer, the length of the body is diminished in the direction of travel and its mass is increased. The equations are:

$$l = l_0 \sqrt{(1 - v^2/c^2)} \quad \text{and} \quad m = \sqrt{\frac{m_0}{(1 - v^2/c^2)}}$$

where *l* and *m* are the length and mass respectively of a body as seen by an observer, and moving at volocity *v* in the direction of its length relative to him. l_0 is the velocity of the body at rest and m_0 is its mass at rest.

Thus, if a 20 m rocket came past you in space at 149 896 km per sec (i.e. 0·5c) it would (if you could measure it) be only about 17 m long.

If two observers are moving at a constant velocity relative to each other, it appears to each that the other's clocks are slowed down and this is expressed in the equation:

$$t = t_0 / \sqrt{(1 - v^2/c^2)}$$

where *t* is one observer's time as read by the other, and t_0 is his own time as read by himself, *v* being the constant relative velocity of the two observers.

From the theory it can be shown that, at rest, a body possesses energy, *E*, given by

$$E = m c^2$$

Relativity theory thus confirms an important unification in physics between two of its very basic concepts: mass and energy with the former being a congealed form of the latter with a transmission constant being the speed of light (*c*) squared. This most famous of formulae was first published in Leipzig on 14 May 1907.

1911   Ernest Rutherford proposed a model of the atom which is the basis of our ideas of atomic structure to this day. He had from the first recognized the value of the fast moving α-particles emitted naturally from radioactive materials as probes for discovering the nature of the atom. He arranged for α-particles to bombard a thin gold foil and found that while many passed straight through a few were deflected at comparatively large angles, some even 'bouncing' back towards the source. He concluded from this that the mass of the atom was concentrated at its centre in a minute nucleus consisting of positively charged particles called **protons**. Around the nucleus and at a relatively large distance from it revolved the negatively charged electrons rather like a miniature solar system. The combined negative charges of the electrons exactly balanced the total positive charge of the nucleus. This important model of the atom suffered from a number of defects. One of these was that from Maxwell's electromagnetic theory the atom should produce light of all wavelengths whereas, in fact, atoms of each element emit light consisting of a number of definite wavelengths – a spectrum – which can be measured with great accuracy. The spectrum for each element is unique.

A further major difficulty was that the electrons, moving round the nucleus, should yield up their energy in the form of radiation and so would spiral into the nucleus bringing about the collapse of the atom. In fact, nothing of the sort occurs: under normal conditions at atom is a stable structure which does not emit radiation.

1913   The difficulties of the Rutherford atom were overcome by the Danish physicist, Niels Hendrik David Bohr (1885-1962) who proposed that electrons were permitted only in certain orbits but could jump from one permitted orbit to another. In so jumping the electron would gain or lose energy in the form of photons, whose wavelength followed from Planck's rule:

$$\lambda = \frac{hc}{E}$$

In this way the spectrum of light emitted, or absorbed, by an atom would relate to its individual structure. The theoretical basis to Bohr's work was confirmed by Einstein in 1917 and the Bohr theory went on successfully to explain other atomic phenomena. However, after many outstanding successes over a number of years, an increasing number of small but important discrepancies appeared with which the Bohr theory could not cope.

1919   Rutherford performed the first artificial nuclear disintegration when he bombarded nitrogen atoms with α-particles from radon-C. He demonstrated that protons were emitted as a result of the disintegration and this confirmed that the proton was, indeed, a nuclear particle.

1924 Louis-Victor de Broglie (1892–1976), French physicist, postulated that the dual wave-particle nature of light might be shown by other particles and particularly by electrons. The wavelength, λ, would be given by

$$\lambda = \frac{h}{mv}$$

where m is the mass of the particle, and v is its velocity. Electron waves were demonstrated experimentally in 1927 by C. J. Davisson (1881–1958) and L. H. Germer (b. 1896) of the USA. Subsequently, de Broglie's idea of matter waves was extended to other particles, protons, neutrons, etc. All matter has an associated wave character, but for the larger bodies of classical mechanics, the wavelengths are too small for their effects to be detectable.

1926 Erwin Schrödinger (1887–1961), a physicist from Vienna, took up the idea of de Broglie waves and applied them to the Bohr atom. The solutions to the resulting wave equation gave the allowed orbits or energy levels more accurately than the quantized orbits in the Bohr atom. Max Born (1882–1970), the German physicist, interpreted these solutions in terms of probability, i.e. they gave the probability of finding an electron in a given volume of space within the atom.

1927 The German physicist, Werner Karl Heisenberg (1901–76) formulated his celebrated and profound Uncertainty Principle: this states that there is a definite limit to the accuracy with which certain pairs of measurements can be made. The more accurate one quantity is known, the less accurate is our knowledge of the other. Position and momentum is an example of such a pair of measurements. The more exactly we know the position of, say, an electron, the less will we know about its momentum. This can be expressed:

$$\Delta x \,.\, \Delta p \sim h$$

where Δx represents the uncertainty in position, Δp the uncertainty in momentum and h is Planck's constant. A further important example relates to time and energy: it is not possible to know how much energy E is possessed by a particle without allowing sufficient time t for the energy to be determined.

$$\Delta E \,.\, \Delta t \sim h$$

The uncertainty principle provides the main reason why the classical mechanics of Newton do not apply to atomic and subatomic phenomena.

1928 Paul Adrien Maurice Dirac (b. 1902), the Cambridge mathematician, introduced a theory of the electron which successfully brought together the ideas of quantum mechanics thus far developed with those of relativity. As a result of this, the important concept of electron spin previously advanced by Bohr became theoretically justified.

Dirac's equations revealed a negative quantity which led to the prediction of the existence of the antielectron, a particle identical to the electron, of the same mass but of opposite electric charge. This major idea, that there could exist **antimatter** in the universe composed of antiparticles arises from Dirac's bold prediction.

Heisenberg's uncertainty principle led to the idea of the instantaneous creation and annihilation of short-lived 'virtual' particles in the vicinity of stable particles. The basic uncertainty in the energy of a particle enables it to acquire a loan, as it were, of energy for a short time: the length of time, in fact, being inversely related to the amount of energy lent. Provided the loan is repaid in the time available, there is no violation of the law of conservation of energy. The action of forces could now be seen in terms of these 'virtual' particles, which behave as force-carriers travelling rapidly from one particle to the other. So, it comes about that particles, not in direct contact, respond each to the presence of the other.

1932 Ernest Orlando Lawrence (1901–58), an American physicist, developed the **cyclotron**. This was one of the first machines constructed for accelerating charged particles artificially to high velocities for research. The particles, which in the first instance were protons, were caused to move with ever increasing velocity in a spiral path by the suitable application of magnetic and electric fields. Lawrence was awarded the Nobel prize in 1939 for this work.

1932 Carl David Anderson (b. 1905), an American physicist of California, announced the discovery of the antielectron predicted a few years previously by Dirac. This was the first particle of antimatter to be discovered and he named it the **positron**.

1932 James Chadwick (1891–1974), the English physicist, discovered the **neutron**, a constituent of the atomic nucleus of zero charge and only slightly heavier than the proton.

1933 Wolfgang Pauli (1900–58) of Austria postulated the existence of the **neutrino**, a neutral particle of negligible mass in order to explain the fact that in β-emission in radioactivity, there was a rather greater loss of energy than could be otherwise explained.

In 1956 Fred Reines and Clyde Cowan in Los Alamos succeeded in detecting neutrinos (electron neutrinos). In 1962 Lederman and Melvin Schwarz of Columbia University demonstrated the existence of the other neutrino, the muon neutrino.

1934 Hideki Yukawa, the Japanese physicist, sought to explain the forces which held the particles in the nucleus together – the **strong force** – and called the force-carrying particles in this case **mesons**. The meson predicted by Yukawa, the **pion**, was discovered by Cecil F. Powell of Bristol University in 1947.

1938 **Nuclear fission** was discovered by Otto Hahn (1879–1968) and Fritz Strassman by bombarding uranium with neutrons, when trying to produce transuranic elements. They succeeded in producing elements lighter than uranium from the mineral of the periodic table. The incident neutron causes the target nucleus to split into two pieces of almost equal mass. Each of the fragments consists of protons and neutrons and an enormous amount of energy is released in the process. Enrico Fermi (1901–54) suggested that the neutrons released in fission could themselves induce further fission and that it should be possible to sustain a chain reaction.

1942 The first nuclear reactor, set up by Fermi in the University of Chicago, became critical.

1945 The first atomic explosion which was experimental took place in July followed by bombs dropped on Hiroshima and Nagasaki in August.

1952 The first hydrogen bomb was exploded in November. This derived its energy from the process of nuclear fusion in which two or more relatively light nuclei combined to form a heavier atomic nucleus releasing thereby a very considerable amount of energy. Considerable effort is being made to develop a fusion reactor and the main difficulty is the problem of containing the enormously high temperatures involved within the reactor for long enough to allow the reaction to proceed. In June 1954 the world's first nuclear powered generator produced electricity at Obnisk near Moscow, and in August 1956 the first large scale nuclear power generating station, Calder Hall, Cumberland (Cumbria), started up. It was officially opened by Her Majesty Queen Elizabeth II in October when power first flowed into the national grid.

1953 Murray Gell-Mann (b. 1929) of the USA, introduced a concept he called **strangeness**, a quality akin in some ways to electric charge, which helped to account for the increased lifetimes of the strange particles. Aided by this idea, it was found that particles could be fitted into patterns according to the amount of strangeness they possessed. This led to the prediction of the existence of a rather unusual particle and it was a great triumph for these theories when in 1964 the omega-minus particle was discovered.

1963 From considerations of these patterns Gell-Mann was led to the idea that hadrons were composed of more basic particles called 'quarks' (a name he borrowed from the writings of the Irish author, James Joyce). There were three kinds of quarks, 'up', 'down' and 'strange' and, for each, a corresponding anti-quark. Quarks could only be combined in two ways – either as a quark-antiquark pair known as a 'meson' or a three quark combination known as a 'baryon'. Thus the proton consists of two up quarks and a down quark and the neutron consists of one up quark and two down quarks, whilst a meson such as the charged pion consists of an up quark and an anti-down quark.

1965 It was realized that quarks with exactly the same quantum numbers cannot exist together and therefore must possess an extra degree of freedom known as 'colour', a concept introduced by M. Y. Han and Y. Nambu. Each quark can exist in three colours, but in such a way as to give zero net colour in hadrons (i.e. they are 'colourless'). This concept was developed in to the theory known as 'quantum chromodynamics' and in 1973 H. Fritzsch suggested that quarks were held together by exchanging massless particles known as 'gluons' which carry the enormously strong force known as the 'colour force'.

1974 It was suggested in 1964 that a further quark in addition to the three already known was required to preserve quark-lepton symmetry, i.e. the muon and electron neutrino corresponded to the up and down quarks but the muon and muon neutrino corresponded only to the strange quark. The name 'charm' was suggested for the new quark in 1970 by S. L. Glashow and others who presented firmer evidence for this quark on theoretical grounds. However this suggestion would have remained academic but in November 1974 a heavy meson was discovered which had a lifetime which was much longer than would be expected at this mass level and such a phenomena is usually explained in terms of the existence of a unique quantum number. The particle was named 'psi' or 'J' and only a fortnight later a similar but much heavier meson was discovered, while a number of other similar particles were discovered within the next twelve months.

1977 The unexpected discovery in 1975 of a heavy lepton (the 'tau') led immediately to the suggestion of the existence of a tau neutrino and of two very heavy quarks in order to preserve quark-lepton symmetry. The new quarks were given the names 'bottom' and 'top' (the alternative names 'beauty' and 'truth' now appeared to have been dropped). The discovery in November 1977 of two very heavy mesons with masses close to 10 000 MeV but with very long lifetimes similar to those of the psi mesons was considered as confirmation of the existence of the bottom quark, although the mesons consisted of bottom quarks and their anti-quarks and therefore showed zero net bottom. Mesons exhibiting net bottom flavour (the neutral B consisting of a down quark and an anti-bottom quark and the charged B consisting of an up quark and an anti-bottom quark) were discovered at Cornell University New York in January 1983.

1983 Following original concepts developed by C. N. Yang and R. Mills in 1954 and J. Schwinger in 1957, the standard model to describe electroweak interactions was introduced by S. Weinberg and A. Salam in 1967–68 and generalized by S. L. Glashow in 1970. In this model both weak and electromagnetic interactions are described in a unified theory which requires the existence not only of the massless photon but also of very massive intermediate particles which are both charged (the $W^{\pm}$) and neutral (the Z^0). The existence of both the $W^{\pm}$ (in January 1983) and the Z^0 (in August 1983) were established at the European Laboratory of Particle Physics (CERN), Geneva, Switzerland. Current experimental values of the masses at 81·0 GeV and 92·4 GeV respectively are in excellent agreement with theoretical values calculated from the electroweak theory.

1986 Experiments in January led to a revolution in the development of superconductive materials. Superconductivity is defined as 'a complete lack of electrical resistance' and was discovered by H. Kamerlingh Onnes in 1911. Over the next 75 years it was considered to be a very low temperature effect with the maximum superconducting temperature attained being 23 K ($-250°$C) so the technique was extremely limited in use. However, in the January experiments by K. A. Muller and J. G. Bednorz of IBM, Zurich, superconductivity was observed at 35 K ($-238°$C) in a mixed oxide of barium, lanthanum, and copper. The results were not published until September but these immediately led to a frenzy of activity and in February 1987 two groups in the USA and China independently reported attaining superconductive temperatures of about 90 K ($-183°$C) in a mixed oxide of yttrium, barium, and copper. Research continues and the current record holder is 125 K ($-148°$C) for a mixed oxide of thallium, barium, calcium, and copper. Such temperatures are within the range of liquid nitrogen and will dramatically reduce the cost of using **superconductivity in engineering applications.**

to explain the manifest different behaviour of the electromagnetic and weak interaction mechanisms).

Newton's laws of motion

These three self-evident principles were discovered experimentally before Newton's time but were first formulated by him.

Law 1. The law of inertia
A particle will either remain at rest or continue to move with uniform velocity unless acted upon by a force.
Law 2
The acceleration of a particle is directly proportional to the force producing it and inversely proportional to the mass of the particle.
Law 3. The law of action and reaction
Forces, the results of interactions of two bodies, always appear in pairs. In each pair the forces are equal in magnitude and opposite in direction.

Equations of motion

Where
u is the initial velocity of a body;
v is its final velocity after time t;
s is the distance it travels in this time;
a is the uniform acceleration it undergoes, then

$$v = u + at$$
$$s = ut + \tfrac{1}{2}at^2$$
$$v^2 = u^2 + 2as$$

Laws of Thermodynamics

Thermodynamics (Greek, *thermos*, hot; *dynamis*, power) is the quantitative treatment of the relation of heat to natural and mechanical forms of energy.
There are three Laws of Thermodynamics.
The **First Law**, derived from the principle of Conservation of Energy, may be stated 'Energy can neither be created nor destroyed, so that a given system can gain or lose energy only to the extent that it takes it from or passes it to its environment'. This is expressed as

$$E_f - E_i = \Delta$$

where E_i is the initial energy, E_f the final content of energy and Δ the change of energy. The impossibility of useful mechanical perpetual motion follows directly from this. The law applies only to systems of constant mass.
The **Second Law** concerns the concept of entropy (Gk. *en*, into; *tropos*, a changing) which is the relation between the temperature of and the heat content within any system. A large amount of lukewarm water may contain the same amount of heat as a little boiling water. The levelling out (equalizing) of heat within a system (i.e. the pouring of a kettle of boiling water into a lukewarm bath) is said to increase the entropy of that system of two vessels. Any system, including the Universe, naturally tends to increase its entropy, i.e. to distribute its heat. If the Universe can be regarded as a closed system, it follows from the Law that it will have a finite end, i.e. when it has finally dissipated or unwound itself

to the point that its entropy attains a maximal level – this is referred to as the 'Heat Death' of the Universe. From this it would also follow that the Universe must then have had a finite beginning for if it had had a creation an infinite time ago heat death would by now inevitably have set in. The second Law, published in Berlin in 1850 by Rudolf Clausius (1822–88) states 'Heat cannot of itself pass from a colder to warmer body'. This is mathematically expressed by the inequality.

$$\Delta > 0$$

i.e. the change of entropy in any heat exchanging system and its surroundings taken together is always greater than zero.
The **Third Law** is not a general law but applies only to pure crystalline solids and states that at absolute zero the entropies of such substances are zero.

Celsius and Fahrenheit compared

The two principal temperature scales are Celsius and Fahrenheit. The former was devised in 1743 by J. P. Christen (1683–1755) but is referred to by its present name because of the erroneous belief that it was invented by Anders Celsius (1701–44). The latter is named after Gabriel Daniel Fahrenheit (1686–1736), a German physicist.
To convert C to F, multiply the C reading by 9/5 and add 32.
To convert F to C, subtract 32 from the F reading and multiply by 5/9.
Useful comparisons are:

(1) Absolute Zero	=	−273·15°C	=	−459·67°F
(2) Point of Equality	=	−40·0°C	=	−40·0°F
(3) Zero Fahrenheit	=	−17·8°C	=	−0·0°F
(4) Freezing Point of water	=	0·0°C	=	32·0°F
(5) Normal Human Blood Temperature	=	36·9°C	=	98·4°F
(6) 100 Degrees F	=	37·8°C	=	100·0°F
(7) Boiling Point of Water (at standard pressure)	=	100·0°C	=	212·0°F

Scientists in a non-meteorological context most frequently employ the Kelvin Scale in which kelvin (K) = fraction 1/273·16 of the triple point of water (where ice, water and water vapour are in equilibrium). Thus absolute zero is zero K, the ice-point of water (0°C or 32°F) is 273·15 K and boiling point (100°C or 212°F) is 373·15 K.

The fundamental physical constants

The constants are called 'fundamental' since they are used universally throughout all branches of science. Increasing experimental accuracy as well as advances in theory require a complete revision of the constants during each decade, the last revision being carried out in 1986. Values are reported so that the figures in brackets following the last digits are the estimated uncertainties of those digits. Note that the speed of light is now *exactly* defined.

	Quantity	Symbol	Value	Units
General	speed of light in vacuo	c	$2 \cdot 99792458 \times 10^8$	$m \cdot s^{-1}$
Constants	elementary charge	e	$1 \cdot 60217733(49) \times 10^{-19}$	C
	Planck constant	h	$6 \cdot 6260755(40) \times 10^{-34}$	$J \cdot s$
	gravitational constant	G	$6 \cdot 67259(85) \times 10^{-11}$	$m^3 \cdot s^{-2} \cdot kg^{-1}$
Matter In	Avogadro constant	N_A	$6 \cdot 0221367(36) \times 10^{23}$	mol^{-1}
Bulk	atomic mass constant	m_u	$1 \cdot 6605402(10) \times 10^{-27}$	kg
			$9 \cdot 3149432(28) \times 10^2$	MeV
	Faraday constant	$F = N_A e$	$9 \cdot 6485309(29) \times 10^4$	$C \cdot mol^{-1}$
	molar gas constant	R	$8 \cdot 314510(70)$	$J \cdot mol^{-1} \cdot K^{-1}$
			$8 \cdot 205783(70) \times 10^{-5}$	$m^3 \cdot atm \cdot mol^{-1} \cdot K^{-1}$
	molar volume of ideal gas	V_m	$2 \cdot 241410(19) \times 10^{-2}$	$m^3 \cdot mol^{-1}$
	Boltzmann constant	$k = R/N_A$	$1 \cdot 380658(12) \times 10^{-23}$	$J \cdot K^{-1}$
Electron	electron rest mass	m_e	$9 \cdot 1093897(54) \times 10^{-31}$	kg
			$0 \cdot 51099906(15)$	MeV
	electron specific charge	e/m_e	$1 \cdot 75881962(53) \times 10^{11}$	$C \cdot kg^{-1}$
Proton	proton rest mass	m_p	$1 \cdot 6726231(10) \times 10^{-27}$	kg
			$9 \cdot 3827231(28) \times 10^2$	MeV
Neutron	neutron rest mass	m_n	$1 \cdot 6749286(10) \times 10^{-27}$	kg
			$9 \cdot 3956563(28) \times 10^2$	MeV
Energy	million electron volt unit	MeV	$1 \cdot 78266270(54) \times 10^{-30}$	kg
Conversion			$1 \cdot 60217733(49) \times 10^{-13}$	J

The forces of nature

Four basic forces that exist in Nature are firmly established and are listed below in ascending order of strength. They all involve the exchange of force carrying particles or 'quanta' which are known as 'bosons' since they have integral spin, i.e. 0, 1, or 2. The strong force is explained by the theory known as 'quantum chromodynamics' which requires the existence of eight gluons, six carrying the 'colour' charge and two which are colour neutral. The weak and electromagnetic forces have been successfully described in terms of a single 'electroweak' theory while efforts continue to produce a unified theory for all four forces.

The particles of physics

In addition to the quanta which carry the various forces of Nature, matter is made up of leptons and quarks which can be associated into generations or families as shown in the table below. The existence of a fourth family is predicted from the observed amount of deuterium and helium in the Universe while a fifth family may also exist.

Leptons have zero baryon number (B) while quarks have $B = \frac{1}{3}$ and both types of entity have half-integral spin ($J = \frac{1}{2}$). Leptons and quarks are believed to differ in the property known as 'colour' - leptons being 'colourless' while quarks exist in three 'colours'. However both types of particles are

Force	Range	Quanta	Mass (MeV)	Spin	Notes
gravity	very long	graviton	0?	2	acts on all matter, weak within the atom
weak	less than 10^{-16} cm	charged $W^\pm$	81 000	1	acts on all the basic particles,
		neutral Z^0	92 400	1	leptons and quarks, involved in radioactive processes
electromagnetic	very long	photon (γ)	0	1	acts on all charged particles; provides the basis to the reactions of chemistry and hence biology
strong	less than 10^{-13} cm	gluon (g)	0?	1	acts on the quarks allowing them free movement within the hadrons, i.e. the mesons and baryons, but confines them within these particles

Generation		Leptons			Quarks					
	Name	Electric Charge	Mass (MeV)	Quark Flavour	Electric Charge	Mass (MeV)*	Strangeness	Charm	Bottomness	Topness
First Family	e (electron)	−1	0·511	d (down)	−⅓	350	0	0	0	0
	v_e (electron neutrino)	0	0?	u (up)	+⅔	350	0	0	0	0
Second Family	μ (muon)	−1	105·658	s (strange)	−⅓	500	−1	0	0	0
	v_μ (muon neutrino)	0	0?	c (charm)	+⅔	1 500	0	+1	0	0
Third Family	τ (tau)	−1	1784·1	b (bottom)	−⅓	5 000	0	0	−1	0
	v_τ (tau neutrino)	0	0?	t (top)	+⅔	50 000	0	0	0	+1

*Because of the strong colour force the masses of quarks depend on the distance over which they are measured. The approximate values given in the table are those which appear to sum to the masses of the hadrons (the 'long distance' masses) while the 'short distance' or Lagrangian masses are those that are required by the theory of quantum chromodynamics, i.e. for the u, d, s, and c quarks are approximately 6, 10, 200, and 1300 MeV respectively, whilst the masses of the bottom and top quarks are too approximately known to distinguish between the long and short distance masses.

believed to be composed of more simpler entities known as 'preons'.

For each lepton and quark there is an equivalent anti-particle with opposite charge. Composites of quarks are known as 'hadrons', mesons being composed of quark and anti-quark pairs (but not necessarily of the same flavour) while baryons consist of three quarks. Hadrons may be associated into groups known as 'multiplets' which is governed by the property known as 'isospin' (I) such that there are (2I + 1) states in a multiplet. Thus the proton and neutron with I = ½ form a two particle multiplet while the delta baryon resonances with I = ³⁄₂ form four particle multiplets. While it is possible to form thousands of particles from a combination of six quarks, at the end of 1987 the existence was accepted of 71 meson multiplets and 59 baryon multiplets representing the discovery of 238 particles and an equal number of anti-particles.

Nobel prizewinners in physics since 1950

1950 Cecil F. Powell, British.
1951 Sir John D. Cockroft, British; Ernest T. S. Walton, Irish.
1952 Felix Bloch, US; Edward M. Purcell, US.
1953 Frits Zernike, Dutch.
1954 Max Born, British; Walter Bothe, German.
1955 Polykarp Kusch, US; Willis E. Lamb, US.
1956 John Bardeen, US; Walter H. Brattain, US; William Shockley, US.
1957 Tsung-dao Lee, US; Chen Ning Yang, US.
1958 Pavel Cherenkov, USSR; Ilya Frank, USSR; Igor Y. Tamm, USSR.
1959 Owen Chamberlain, US; Emilio G. Segre, US.
1960 Donald A. Glaser, US.
1961 Robert Hofstadter, US; Rudolf L. Mossbauer, German.

1962 Lev. D. Landau, USSR.
1963 Maria Goeppert-Mayer, US; J. Hans D. Jensen, German; Eugene P. Wigner, US.
1964 Nikolai G. Basov, USSR; Aleksander M. Prochorov, USSR; Charles H. Townes, US.
1965 Richard P. Feynman, US; Julian S. Schwinger, US; Shinichiro Tomonaga, Japanese.
1966 Alfred Kastler, French.
1967 Hans A. Bethe, US.
1968 Luis W. Alvarez, US.
1969 Murray Gell-Mann, US.
1970 Louis Neel, French; Hannes Alfven, Swedish.
1971 Dennis Gabor, British.
1972 John Bardeen, US; Leon N. Cooper, US; John R. Schrieffer, US.
1973 Ivar Giaever, US; Leo Esaki, Japanese; Brian D. Josephson, British.
1974 Martin Ryle, British; Antony Hewish, British.
1975 James Rainwater, US; Ben Mottelson, US-Danish; Aage Bohr, Danish.
1976 Burton Richter, US; Samuel C. C. Ting, US.
1977 John H. Van Vleck, US; Philip W. Anderson, US; Nevill F. Mott, British.
1978 Pyotr Kapitsa, USSR; Arno Penzias, US; Robert Wilson, US.
1979 Steven Weinberg, US; Sheldon L. Glashow, US; Abdus Salam, Pakistani.
1980 James W. Cronin, US; Val L. Fitch, US.
1981 Nicolass Boembergen, US; Arthur Schlawlow, US; Kai M. Siegbahn, Swedish.
1982 Kenneth G. Wilson, US.
1983 Subrahmanyam Chandrasekhar, US; William A. Fowler, US.
1984 Carlo Rubbia, Italian; Simon van der Meer, Dutch.
1985 Klaus von Klitzing, W. German.
1986 Ernest Ruska, W. German; Heinrich Rohrer, Swiss; Gerhard Binnig, W. German.
1987 Georg Bednorz, W. German; K. Alex Muller, Swiss.
1988 Leon Lederman, US; Melvin Schwartz, US; Joel Steinberger, US.

TRANSPORT

Shipping

World's largest ships

The largest passenger vessel of all-time was the liner *Queen Elizabeth* (UK) of 82 998 gross tons and 314 m (*1031 ft*) completed in 1940 and destroyed by fire in Hong Kong as *Seawise University* on 9 Jan 1972. The largest active liner is the *Norway* of 70 202·19 grt and 315·66 m (*1035 ft 7½ in*) in length. She was built as the *France* in 1961 and put out of service in 1975. In June 1979 she was bought by the Norwegian Knut Kloster, renamed *Norway*, and recommissioned as a cruise ship in August 1979.

Shipping tonnages

There are four tonnage systems in use, namely gross tonnage (GRT), net tonnage (NRT), deadweight tonnage (DWT) and displacement tonnage.

(1) *Gross Registered Tonnage*, used for merchantmen, is the sum in cubic ft of all the enclosed spaces divided by 100, such that 1 grt=100 ft³ of enclosed space.

(2) *Net Registered Tonnage*, also used for merchantmen, is the gross tonnage (above) less deductions for crew spaces, engine rooms and ballast which cannot be utilized for paying passengers or cargo.

(3) *Deadweight Tonnage*, mainly used for tramp ships and oil tankers, is the number of UK long tons (of 2240 lb) of cargo, stores, bunkers and, where necessary, passengers which is required to bring down a ship from her height line to her load-water line, i.e. the carrying capacity of a ship.

(4) *Displacement Tonnage*, used for warships and US merchantmen, is the number of tons (each 35 ft³) of sea water displaced by a vessel charged to its load-water line, i.e. the weight of the vessel and its contents in tons.

OIL TANKERS (OVER 450 000 TONS DWT)

Name	Flag	High DWT	GRT	Length m	ft	Breadth m	ft
Seawise Giant	Liberia	564 763	238 558	458	*1504*	63	*209*
Pierre Guillaumat	France	555 051	274 838	414	*1359*	62	*206*
Prairial	France	554 974	274 838	414	*1359*	62	*206*
Bellamya	France	553 662	275 276	414	*1359*	62	*206*
Batillus	France	553 662	273 550	413	*1358*	62	*206*
Esso Atlantic	Liberia	516 893	234 638	406	*1333*	71	*233*
Esso Pacific	Liberia	516 423	234 626	406	*1333*	71	*233*
King Alexander	Sweden	491 120	245 140	363	*1194*	78	*259*
Nissei Maru	Japan	484 337	238 517	379	*1243*	62	*203*
Globtik London	Liberia	483 933	213 894	379	*1243*	62	*203*
Globtik Tokyo	Liberia	483 662	213 886	379	*1243*	62	*203*
Burmah Enterprise	UK	457 927	231 629	378	*1241*	68	*224*
Burmah Endeavour	UK	457 841	231 629	378	*1241*	67	*223*

BULK ORE, BULK OIL AND OIL CARRIERS (OVER 250 000 TONS DWT)

Name	Flag	High DWT*	GRT*	Length m	ft	Breadth m	ft
World Gala	Liberia	282 462	133 748	338	*1109*	55	*179*
Dode Canyon	Liberia	275 588	131 473	340	*1114*	54	*180*
Mary R. Koch	Liberia	270 656	136 991	335	*1099*	51	*171*
Weser Ore	Liberia	270 000	139 401	335	*1099*	51	*171*
Rhine Ore	Panama	270 000	139 406	335	*1099*	51	*171*
Jose Bonifacio	Brazil	266 088	126 760	337	*1106*	55	*179*
Castor	Liberia	264 484	132 305	335	*1101*	53	*176*
Licorne Atlantique	France	260 429	131 619	335	*1101*	53	*176*
Alkisima Alarabia	Saudi Arabia	260 412	143 959	335	*1101*	53	*176*

*NB Seagoing carriers are subject to modification and change, which is why high DWT and GRT's differ from previous information.

Main commercial aircraft in airline service*

Name of Aircraft**	Nationality	No. in service	Wingspan	Length	Max. cruising speed	Range with max. payload	Max. takeoff weight	Max. seating capacity
Yakolev YAK-40	USSR	2641	25·00 m (82 ft 0 in)	20·36 m (66 ft 9½ in)	550 kph (297 knots)	1450 km (782 naut miles)	16 000 kg (35 275 lb)	32
Boeing 727 (−200)	USA	1769	32·92 m (108 ft 0 in)	46·69 m (153 ft 2 in)	964 kph (520 knots)	3966 km (2140 naut miles)	95 025 kg (209 500 lb)	189
McDonnell Douglas DC9 (Super 81)	USA	1091	32·87 m (107 ft 10 in)	45·06 m (147 ft 10 in)	902 kph (487 knots)	4925 km[1] (2657 naut miles)	63 500 kg (140 000 lb)	172
Boeing 737 (−200)	USA	1011	28·35 m (93 ft 0 in)	30·53 m (100 ft 2 in)	927 kph (500 knots)	4262 km (2300 naut miles)	56 472 kg (124 500 lb)	130
Boeing 747 (−200)	USA	597	59·46 m (195 ft 8 in)	70·66 m (231 ft 10 in)	964 kph (520 knots)	10 562 km[2] (5700 naut miles)	377 840 kg (833 000 lb)	516
Fokker F27 (Mk 500)	Netherlands	495	29·00 m (95 ft 2 in)	25·06 m (82 ft 2½ in)	480 kph (259 knots)	1741 km (935 naut miles)	20 410 kg (45 000 lb)	60
McDonnell Douglas DC8 (Srs 63)	USA	402	45·23 m (148 ft 5 in)	57·12 m (187 ft 5 in)	965 kph (521 knots)	7240 km (3907 naut miles)	158 000 kg (350 000 lb)	259
McDonnell Douglas DC10 (Srs 40)	USA	357	50·41 m (165 ft 5 in)	55·50 m (182 ft 1 in)	992 kph (498 knots)	7505 km (4050 naut miles)	259 450 kg (572 000 lb)	380
Boeing 707/720 (707-320)	USA	310	44·42 m (145 ft 9 in)	46·61 m (152 ft 11 in)	973 kph (525 knots)	9265 km[3] (5000 naut miles)	151 315 kg (333 600 lb)	219
Lockheed L-1011 Tristar (−500)	USA	242	47·34 m (155 ft 4 in)	50·05 m (164 ft 2½ in)	973 kph (525 knots)	9653 km (5209 naut miles)	224 980 kg (496 000 lb)	400
Airbus A300B (A300B4-200)	International	238	44·84 m (147 ft 1 in)	53·62 m (175 ft 11 in)	911 kph (492 knots)	5095 km[4] (2750 naut miles)	165 000 kg (363 760 lb)	336
BAC One-eleven (Srs 500)	UK	210	28·50 m (93 ft 6 in)	32·61 m (107 ft 0 in)	871 kph (470 knots)	2744 km (1480 naut miles)	47 400 kg (104 500 lb)	119
Antonov AN 24/-26 (An 26)	USSR	107	29·20 m (95 ft 10 in)	23·80 m (78 ft 1 in)	440 kph (237 knots)	1100 km (594 naut miles)	24 000 kg (52 911 lb)	40
Tupolev Tu-154 (−154B)	USSR	49	37·55 m (123 ft 3 in)	47·90 m (157 ft 1¾)	950 kph (513 knots)	2750 km (1485 naut miles)	96 000 kg (211 650 lb)	169
Ilyushin IL-18 (11-18D)	USSR	47	37·40 m (122 ft 9 in)	35·90 m (117 ft 9½ in)	675 kph (364 knots)	3700 km (1997 naut miles)	64 000 kg (141 095 lb)	110[5]
BAC/Aérospatiale Concorde	International	14	25·56 m (83 ft 10 in)	62·10 m (203 ft 9 in)	2179 kph (1176 knots)	6230 km (3360 naut miles)	185 065 kg (408 000 lb)	128

* No details available for Fokker F28.
** Scheduled and non-circulated services including all-freight. Specifications apply to version in brackets.
1 Range quoted with max. fuel.
2 With 442 passengers.
3 With 147 passengers.
4 With 269 passengers.
5 122 seats in summer with wardrobes deleted.

Major world airlines 1986

Airline	Passenger km (000)	Aircraft km (000)	Passengers carried (000)	Aircraft departures
Aeroflot, USSR	194 349 000	113 000 (est.)	115 761 000	47 000 (est.)
United Airlines, USA	95 349 000	815 000	50 698 000	627 000
American Airlines, USA	78 510 739	679 009	46 139 172	520 933
Eastern Airlines, USA	56 141 110	556 409	43 011 502	558 373
Delta Airlines, USA	50 467 322	507 840	41 114 644	533 010
Transworld Airlines (TWA), USA	43 986 676	343 421	20 064 231	244 522
North-west Orient Airlines, USA	43 537 898	354 034	20 526 794	277 959
British Airways, UK	40 315 862	252 141	16 949 985	198 148
Japan Airlines (JAL), Japan	34 510 684	198 223	15 147 659	80 246
Pan American World Airways, USA	35 531 751	224 928	12 570 600	128 932
Continental Airlines, USA	33 655 627	338 555	20 498 636	253 820
Air France, France	27 570 377	197 461	12 025 229	143 293
Lufthansa, Germany	26 640 283	253 475	15 173 954	234 080
Singapore Airlines, Singapore	22 875 778	86 789	4 990 315	31 643
Air Canada, Canada	21 764 113	211 350	10 895 822	167 026
All Nippon Airways (ANA), Japan	20 116 045	122 977	24 637 700	166 813
Qantas, Australia	20 103 271	87 001	2 901 495	21 208
KLM Royal Dutch Airlines, Netherlands	19 099 570	115 625	5 070 239	63 602
Iberia, Spain	18 332 658	142 765	13 592 921	152 543
US Airlines, USA	17 947 823	244 174	22 097 306	373 957
Western Airlines, USA	17 665 919	194 246	12 369 380	174 929
Republic Airlines, USA	17 235 017	275 690	17 520 047	365 993
People Express Airlines, USA	16 856 798	141 812	13 081 391	139 852
Saudia Airlines, Saudi Arabia	15 018 102	105 331	9 929 409	95 532
Alitalia, Italy	13 993 799	103 998	8 383 375	99 757
Cathay Pacific Airways, Hong Kong	13 928 323	58 185	4 161 503	23 627
Korean Airlines, Korea	13 405 595	85 152	7 211 367	53 071
Swiss Air, Switzerland	12 874 128	105 701	6 316 993	90 517
SAS, Scandinavia	12 538 821	136 365	11 868 961	198 208
Varig International, Brazil	12 039 522	100 565	5 834 963	81 172
CP Air, Canada	11 158 182	88 452	3 735 202	49 276
Thai International, Thailand	10 573 608	57 998	3 049 748	22 775
Méxicana, Mexico	9 118 920	92 410	7 783 847	94 946
Philippine Airlines, Philippines	8 920 371	53 563	4 879 595	62 902
Garuda Indonesian Airlines, Indonesia	8 747 584	86 714	5 412 602	92 898
Air New Zealand, New Zealand	8 731 876	54 785	4 281 497	80 520
South African Airways, South Africa	8 682 464	66 712	4 207 326	55 093
Indian Airlines, India	7 817 061	67 312	9 695 349	111 831
Aeromexico, Mexico	7 766 230	83 372	6 040 674	98 115
Air India, India	7 608 528	42 077	1 789 870	16 872
British Caledonian, UK	7 207 260	56 883	2 353 850	33 830
Frontier Airlines, USA	7 146 129	101 686	6 978 146	128 207
Pakistan International, Pakistan	7 126 269	51 095	4 127 236	52 008
PSA-Pacific Southwest, USA	6 896 330	99 271	10 688 033	170 381
Aerolineas, Argentina	6 653 996	56 900	3 412 440	60 251
Olympic Airways, Greece	6 385 446	48 579	6 479 519	75 849
Malaysian Airline System, Malaysia	6 252 345	47 305	6 310 531	94 073

World's major airports 1987

Airport name and location	Terminal passengers (000)	International passengers (000)	Air transport movements (000)	Cargo (000 tonnes)
O'Hare International, Chicago, USA	56 281	1 211	753·4	678·9
Hartsfield International, Atlanta, USA	47 649	n.a.	766·2	363·9
Los Angeles International, USA	44 783	7 517	599·3	909·9
Dallas/Fort Worth Regional, Texas, USA	41 875	n.a.	600·7	360·0
Heathrow Airport, London, UK	34 743	28 615	308·0	574·1
Stapleton International, Denver, USA	32 355	n.a.	478·7	n.a.
John F. Kennedy International, New York, USA	30 192	17 405	259·5	1072·6
Tokyo International (Haneda), Japan	29 927	n.a.	n.a.	396·7
San Francisco International, California, USA	29 812	n.a.	419·4	442·2
La Guardia Airport, NY, USA	24 226	195	321·6	45·8

Airport name and location	Terminal passengers (000)	International passengers (000)	Air transport movements (000)	Cargo (000 tonnes)
Miami International, Florida, USA	24 025	7 668	302·1	565·3
Newark, NY, USA	23 475	1 307	332·9	295·2
Logan International, Boston, Mass., USA	23 283	2 085	373·1	264·9
Frankfurt International, Germany	22 521	16 771	234·8	784·3
Orly, Paris, France	20 427	7 929	169·5	202·2
Honolulu International, Oahu, USA	20 380	2 775	368·0	218·3
Lambert International, St Louis, Missouri, USA	20 363	n.a.	360·7	n.a.
Metropolitan, Detroit, USA	19 747	801	398·8	85·7
Gatwick, London, UK	19 380	18 248	173·3	163·8
Osaka International, Japan	19 291	3 523	126·7	349·3
Toronto International (Pearson), Canada	18 602	8 903	301·2	216·7
Minneapolis-St Paul International, USA	17 859	n.a.	288·3	n.a.
Pittsburg International, USA	17 458	n.a.	339·7	n.a.
Charles de Gaulle, Paris, France	16 044	14 450	157·6	546·3
Washington National, USA	15 440	n.a.	n.a.	n.a.

Milestones in aviation

1717 Earliest 'rational' design published by Emmanuel Swedenborg (1688–1772) in Sweden.

1785 7 Jan. First crossing of English Channel by balloon Jean-Pierre Blanchard (FRA) and Dr John J. Jeffries (USA).

1852 24 Sept. First flight by navigable airship, in France.

1900 2 July. First flight by German Zeppelin airship.

1903 17 Dec. First sustained flight in an aeroplane, by Wright Brothers, near Kitty Hawk, N. Carolina, United States.

1906 12 Nov. First public aeroplane flight in Europe. Alberto Santos-Dumont covers a distance of 220 m (722 ft) near Paris, France.

1909 25 July. Louis Blériot (FRA) completes first aeroplane crossing of the English Channel in 36½ min.

1910 27-8 Aug. Louis Paulhan completes first flight from London to Manchester, in 4 hr 12 min with an overnight stop.

1919 14–15 June. Capt. John William Alcock and Lieut. Arthur Whitten Brown complete first non-stop crossing of the Atlantic in 16 hr 27 min.

1919 12 Nov.–10 Dec. Capt. Ross Smith and Lieut. Keith Smith complete first flight from Britain (Hounslow) to Australia (Darwin).

1924 1 Apr. Imperial Airways formed in Great Britain.

1927 20–21 May. First solo non-stop transatlantic flight (eastbound) by Capt. Charles A. Lindbergh (US) in Ryan monoplane in 33 hr 39 min.

1928 15 May. Inauguration of Australia's Flying Doctor Service.

1928 31 May–9 June. First trans-Pacific flight from San Francisco to Brisbane, by Capt. Charles Kingsford Smith and C. T. P. Ulm.

Blériot's aeroplane lands safely on Dover's cliffs after the first Channel flying. (Popperfoto)

International information: distance in kilometres between airports

	Athens	Bahrain	Bangkok	Bombay	Buenos Aires	Cairo	Chicago	Copenhagen	Frankfurt	Hong Kong	Johannesburg	Karachi	Lagos	Lima	London	Madrid	Manila	Mexico City	Montreal	Moscow	Nairobi	New York	Paris	Peking (Beijing)	Rio de Janeiro	Rome	San Francisco	Singapore	Sydney	Tehran	Tokyo	Vancouver
Athens		2829	7916	5164	11699	1117	8758	2136	1807	8541	7131	4320	4043	11762	2414	2359	9637	11274	7616	2251	4564	7914	2093	7617	9704	1047	10918	9053	15315	2458	9543	9792
Bahrain	2829		5358	3008	13293	1929	16877	4461	4437	6389	6297	1661	5457	14333	5090	5185	7364	13963	7069	3399	10614	4822	6182	11460	3862	12730	6326	12504	1048	8314	11782
Bangkok	7916	5358		3008	16877	7249	13912	8601	8963	1719	8989	3701	10604	19676	9540	10157	2199	15717	13378	7069	7207	13912	9433	3296	16073	8814	12730	1443	7538	5457	4642	11782
Bombay	5164	3008	3008		14935	4339	11844	6564	6564	4298	6974	876	9165	18344	7207	7512	5132	14122	12069	5047	4529	12523	6999	4763	14019	6160	12523	3917	10152	2803	6782	11170
Buenos Aires	11699	13293	16877	14935		11844	9043	12086	11494	18443	8109	14716	7934	3151	11129	10079	14218	7391	9051	13488	10411	8528	11062	19277	1996	11170	10395	15867	11760	13781	18285	11297
Cairo	1117	1929	7249	4339	11844		9866	3197	2922	8123	6258	3556	3927	12435	3540	3349	9162	12363	8722	2913	3540	9009	3204	7530	9893	2125	11994	8255	14395	1955	9588	10835
Chicago	8758	16877	13912	11844	9043	9866		6849	6966	12425	14009	12363	14009	6847	6349	7512	13062	2718	1198	7968	13486	1187	6665	10554	7734	7734	2962	15039	14857	10067	10554	2828
Copenhagen	2136	4461	8601	6564	12086	3197	6849		678	8662	9204	5537	5511	11086	982	2058	9780	9507	5799	1539	6699	6184	1035	7191	10178	1535	8801	9959	16031	3657	8706	7657
Frankfurt	1807	4437	8963	6564	11494	2922	6966	678		9165	8684	5690	4853	10717	654	1420	10290	9545	5851	2021	6312	6185	471	7783	9560	966	9142	10270	16484	3765	9360	8057
Hong Kong	8541	6389	1719	4298	18443	8123	12425	8662	9165		10694	4775	11835	18344	9640	10519	1125	14122	12956	7149	8750	12822	9627	1985	17687	9271	11097	2576	7374	6186	2936	10245
Johannesburg	7131	6297	8989	6974	8109	6258	14009	9204	8684	10694		7041	4522	10901	9068	8097	10975	14588	12962	9164	2910	14588	8707	11699	7146	7718	16966	8649	11019	7283	13506	11706
Karachi	4320	1661	3701	876	14716	3556	12363	5537	5690	4775	7041		7041	11835	6334	6658	5716	14588	11241	4202	4367	11675	6128	2910	13004	5303	12983	4736	11160	1930	6969	11706
Lagos	4043	5457	10604	9165	7934	3927	14009	5511	4853	11835	4522	7041		10901	5000	3827	10759	5716	8498	6251	3828	8440	6334	4367	11675	5303	4149	11373	2373	5850	13506	11938
Lima	11762	14333	19676	18344	3151	12435	6847	11086	10717	18344	10901	11835	10901		10143	9520	11644	4241	6419	12620	10143	5861	5000	14588	2506	5303	6022	18812	11003	5850	15413	8154
London	2414	5090	9540	7207	11129	3540	6349	982	654	9640	9068	6334	5000	10143		1244	10759	8901	5213	2506	6830	5536	365	8148	9245	1460	8610	10873	17008	4411	9585	7574
Madrid	2359	5185	10157	7512	10079	3349	7512	2058	1420	10290	8097	6658	3827	9520	1244		11644	9063	5550	3418	6189	5758	1031	9199	8140	1360	9142	11373	17661	4753	10764	8422
Manila	9637	7364	2199	5132	14218	9162	13062	9780	10290	1125	10975	5716	10759	11644	10759	11644		14218	13686	8273	9401	13686	10752	2873	18107	11097	11221	2373	6258	7247	2993	3940
Mexico City	11274	13963	15717	14122	7391	12363	2718	9507	9545	14122	14588	14588	5716	4241	8901	9063	14218		3712	10683	14218	3366	9195	12427	7661	10052	3027	16587	16002	11829	11247	3926
Montreal	7616	7069	13378	12069	9051	8722	1198	5799	5851	12956	12962	11241	8498	6419	5213	5550	13686	3712		7036	11701	536	5523	10440	8189	6605	4072	14794	16011	10384	11247	3679
Moscow	2251	3399	7069	5047	13488	2913	7968	1539	2021	7149	9164	4202	6251	12620	2506	3418	8273	10683	7036		6366	7477	2479	5802	11526	2397	9219	8443	6313	2486	7502	8180
Nairobi	4564	4822	7207	4529	10411	3540	13486	6699	6312	8750	2910	4367	3828	10143	6830	6189	9401	14218	11701	6366		11828	6475	9219	8937	5380	9219	7456	12128	4374	11296	11206
New York	7914	10614	13912	12523	8528	9009	1187	6184	6185	12822	14588	11675	8440	5861	5536	5758	13686	3366	536	7477	11828		5829	10971	7723	6886	4149	15329	16002	10824	10824	3926
Paris	2093	4822	9433	6999	11062	3204	6665	1035	471	9627	8707	6128	6334	5000	365	1031	10752	9195	5523	2479	6475	5829		8214	9144	1100	8971	10728	16954	4198	9736	8971
Peking (Beijing)	7617	6182	3296	4763	19277	7530	10554	7191	7783	1985	11699	2910	4862	14588	8148	9199	2873	12427	10440	5802	9219	10971	8214		17302	8120	9186	4486	15738	4486	2132	11206
Rio de Janeiro	9704	11460	16073	14019	1996	9893	7734	10178	9560	17687	7146	13004	11526	2506	9245	8140	18107	7661	8189	11526	8937	7723	9144	17302		9186	10633	15738	13516	10633	18519	11206
Rome	1047	3862	8814	6160	11170	2125	7734	1535	966	9271	7718	5303	5303	5303	1460	1360	11097	10052	6605	2397	5380	6886	1100	8120	9186		10052	10010	16302	3396	9880	9007
San Francisco	10918	12730	12730	12523	10395	11994	2962	8801	9142	11097	16966	12983	4149	6022	8610	9142	11221	3027	4072	9219	9219	4149	8971	9186	10633	10052		13579	11941	11829	8222	1286
Singapore	9053	6326	1443	3917	15867	8255	15039	9959	10270	2576	8649	4736	11373	18812	10873	11373	2373	16587	14794	8443	7456	15329	10728	4486	15738	10010	13579		6296	6615	5361	11206
Sydney	15315	12504	7538	10152	14857	14395	14857	16031	16484	7374	11019	11160	2373	11003	17008	17661	6258	16002	16011	6313	12128	16002	16954	15738	13516	16302	11941	6296		12909	7826	12492
Tehran	2458	1048	5457	2803	13781	1955	10067	3657	3765	6186	7283	1930	5850	5413	4411	4753	7247	11829	10384	2486	4374	10824	4198	4486	10633	3396	11829	6615	12909		7713	10556
Tokyo	9543	8314	4642	6782	18285	9588	10067	8706	9360	2936	13513	6969	13506	15413	9585	10764	2993	11247	11247	7502	11296	10824	9736	2132	18519	9880	8222	5361	7826	7713		7500
Vancouver	9792	11782	11782	11170	11297	10835	2828	7657	8057	10245	11938	11706	11938	8154	7574	8422	3940	3926	3679	8180	11206	3926	8971	11206	11206	9007	1286	11206	12492	10556	7500	

To convert kilometres to miles multiply by 0.62137

1929 30 Mar. First commercial air route between London and Karachi inaugurated by Imperial Airways.

1929 8-29 Aug. The first airship flight around the world was made by the German *Graf Zeppelin*, captained by Dr Hugo Eckener.

1934 8 Dec. The first weekly air mail service between England and Australia was started.

1935 13 Apr. The first through passenger air service by Imperial Airways and Qantas Empire Airways from England to Australia was initiated.

1935 22 Nov. The first scheduled air mail flight across the Pacific was flown, from San Francisco to Manila, Philippines.

1937 12 Apr. First test-bed run of a jet engine by Fl. Off. Frank Whittle (GB).

1939 28 June. Inauguration of Pan American's transatlantic New York–Southampton flying-boat service.

1939 27 Aug. First turbo-jet test flight by Fl. Kapt. Erich Warsitz in He 178 at Marienche, Germany.

1947 14 Oct. First supersonic flight by Capt. Charles E. Yeager USAF in Bell XS-1 over Maroc, California, USA.

1949 27 July. First flight of a turbojet-powered airliner, the de Havilland Comet 1. (Entered service 2 May 1952.)

1950 29 July. A Vickers V630 Viscount made the world's first scheduled passenger service by a gas-turbine powered airliner.

1957 19 Dec. The first transatlantic passenger service to be flown by turbine-powered airliners was inaugurated by BOAC with Bristol Britannia 312 aircraft.

1958 4 Oct. The first transatlantic passenger service to be flown by a turbojet-powered airliner was inaugurated by a de Havilland Comet 4 of BOAC.

1968 31 Dec. First flight of the Soviet supersonic airliner, the Tupolev Tu-144.

1969 9 Feb. First flight of the Boeing 747 'Jumbojet'. (Entered service 22 Jan. 1970.)

1969 2 Mar. First flight of BAC/Aérospatiale Concorde. (Entered scheduled service with Air France and British Airways 21 Jan 1976.)

1974 1 Sept. Lockheed SR-71A flew the North Atlantic in 1 hr 54 min 56·4 sec.

1977 26 Sept. Laker Airways inaugurated transatlantic cheap fare Skytrain.

1978 12–17 Aug. First crossing of the North Atlantic by a balloon, the American Yost HB-72 *Double Eagle II*, crewed by Ben L. Abruzzo, Maxie L. Anderson and Larry M. Newman, in 137 hr 5 min.

1979 12 June. First crossing of the English Channel by a man-powered aircraft, Dr Paul MacCready's *Gossamer Albatross*, powered/piloted by Bryan Allen. The flight took 2 hr 49 min.

1980 5 Dec. Dr Paul MacCready's solar-powered aircraft, *Solar Challenger*, recorded a first significant solar-powered flight of 1 hr 32 min.

1981 12 Apr. The NASA space shuttle *Columbia* made an unpowered, but otherwise conventional landing by a heavier-than-air craft, on the dry bed of Rogers Lake at Edwards Air Force Base, California, after a space mission involving 54 hr 21 min in Earth orbit.

1981 7 July. Piloted by Steve Ptacek, Dr Paul MacCready's *Solar Challenger* became the first solar-powered aircraft to make a crossing of the English Channel, flying from Cormeilles-en-Vexin, France, to Manston aerodrome, Kent.

1986 14 Dec. The strange-looking 900 kg (*2000 lb*) *Voyager*, piloted by Dick Rutan and Jeana Yeager, became the first plane to fly around the World without stopping and without refuelling. It took off from the Mojave Desert and landed back there 9 days 3 min and 44 sec later, on the day before Christmas Eve.

1987 2 July. First transatlantic crossing by hot-air balloon, the *Virgin Atlantic Flyer*, crewed by Richard Branson and Per Lindstrand. It left from Sugar Loaf, Maine, USA and first touched land on 3 July near Limavady, Northern Ireland, finally landing in the sea, just off the coast.

Rail

A railway may be defined as a track which guides vehicles travelling along it. Such tracks, formed of parallel lines of stone blocks with grooves in the centre, date back to Babylonian times, about 2245 BC, and can still be found in south-eastern Europe. The word 'railway' was first recorded in 1681 at Pensnett near Stourbridge, West Midlands. 'Railroad' was first used at Rowton near Coalport, Shropshire, in 1702. Both words were used in Britain until about 1850 after which 'railway' was adopted. In the USA 'railroad' became widely, though not universally, used. The first positive record of the use of steam power on a railway was in 1804 when a locomotive built by Richard Trevithick hauled a train at Penydarren Ironworks in South Wales. The first railway to be operated entirely by steam engines from its opening was the Liverpool & Manchester, on 15 Sept 1830.

The 'standard gauge' of 1435 mm (*4 ft 8½ in*) was first established at the Willington Colliery wagonway near Newcastle-upon-Tyne in 1764–5. Today this gauge is standard in Great Britain, Canada, the USA, Mexico, Europe (except Ireland, Spain, Portugal, Finland and the USSR), North Africa, the Near Eastern countries, Australian National Railways and New South Wales, China and South Korea, also some lines in Japan, Western Australia and Victoria. In South America it is found in Paraguay, Uruguay, the Argentine Urquiza system, Central and Southern Railways of Peru, Venezuela and short lines in Brazil.

The modern standard system of railway electrification at 25 kV 50 Hz was first used in France in 1950 and in England, on the Colchester–Clacton-Walton lines, on 16 Mar 1959.

The world's first railway tunnel was an underground line at Newcastle-upon-Tyne, England, which was built in 1770. The first underwater public railway tunnel was the Thames Tunnel on the East London Railway, opened in 1843. The Channel Tunnel's twin-bore railway will be 7·6 m (*25 ft*) diameter and 49·4 km (*30·7 miles*) long of which 38 km (*23·6 miles*) will be under the sea.

Principal railway systems of the world

Railway system	Year of first railway	Gauge mm	ft	in	Route km	length miles
Argentina	1857	1676	5	6	22 101	13 733
		1435	4	8½	3 088	1 919
		1000	3	3⅜	11 844	7 359
		750	2	5½	285	177
					37 318	23 188
Australia	1854	1600	5	3	8 396	5 217
		1435	4	8½	14 243	8 850
		1067	3	6	16 749	10 407
					39 388	24 474
Brazil	1854	1600	5	3	1 736	1 079
		1000	3	3⅜	21 711	12 286
		762	2	6	202	125
					23 649	13 490
Canada	1836	1435	4	8½	68 023	42 267
		1067	3	6	1 146	712
		915	3	0	178	111
					69 347	43 090
Chile	1851	1676	5	6	4 282	2 661
		1435	4	8½	370	230
		1000	3	3⅜	3 300	2 050
					7 952	4 941
China	1880	1435	4	8½	c.50 000	c.31 000
Czecho- slovakia	1839	1520	4	11⅞	101	63
		1435	4	8½	13 039	8 102
		1000	3	3⅜ ⎱	177	110
		600	1	11½ ⎰		
					13 317	8 275
France	1832	1435	4	8½	34 362	21 351
Germany	1835					
Federal (West)		1435	4	8½	28 450	17 678
State (East)		1435	4	8½	14 215	8 833
					42 665	26 511
Great Britain	1830	1435	4	8½	17 248	10 718
		600	1	11½	19	12
					17 267	10 730
India	1853	1676	5	6	31 789	19 753
		1000	3	3⅜	25 209	15 664
		762	2	6	3 521	2 188
		610	2	0	390	242
					60 909	37 847
Italy	1839	1435	4	8½	16 133	10 024
Japan	1872	1435	4	8½	1 177	731
		1067	3	6	20 145	12 517
					21 322	13 248
Mexico	1850	1435	4	8½	14 151	8 793
		914	3	0	457	280
		mixed			72	45
					14 680	9 118
Pakistan	1861	1676	5	6	7 754	4 818
		1000	3	3⅜	444	276
		762	2	6	610	379
					8 808	5 473

Railway system	Year of first railway	Gauge mm	ft	in	Route km	length miles
Poland	1842	1435	4	8½	23 855	14 822
Romania	1869	1435	4	8½	10 515	6 534
		762	2	6 ⎱	568	353
		610	2	0 ⎰		
					11 083	6 887
South Africa	1860	1065	3	6	22 891	14 223
		610	2	0	706	439
					23 597	14 662
Spain	1848	1676	5	6	13 531	8 407
Sweden	1856	1435	4	8½	11 158	6 933
		891	2	11	182	113
					11 340	7 046
Turkey	1896	1435	4	8½	8 140	5 847
USA	1830	1435	4	8½	294 625	183 077
		1520	4	11⅞	c.141 800	c.88 110
		1435	4	8½	73	45
		1067	3	6	761	473
		up to 1 metre			2 571	1 598
					c.439 830	c.273 303

Road transport

AVERAGE MILEAGE
The average estimated mileage for a car in the UK rose from 13 000 km (*8100 miles*) per year in 1977 to 14 000 km (*8700 miles*) per year in 1987.

CAR OWNERSHIP
Car ownership per 1000 inhabitants in the UK at the end of 1987 was 324, or a total of 17 856 000 cars.

PETROL PRICES
Petrol prices for four-star petrol rose from 32½p in 1970 to 76½p per gallon in 1978. The price reached its peak in the 1985 Budget when it reached £2 a gallon, then dropped sharply in 1986 as crude oil prices plummetted as a result of a world recession and overproduction. Since then the price has fluctuated according to market trends, in December 1988 standing at 171p per gallon (*37.6p per litre*).

ACCIDENTS
The cumulative total of fatalities since the first in the UK on 17 Aug 1896 surpassed 250 000 in 1959 and by the end of 1987 it had reached about 414 500. (There are only estimated figures for Northern Ireland during the period 1923–30.)

The peak year for fatalities was 1941 when there were wartime restrictions on the use of headlamps; in that year 9444 people were killed, an average of 26 per day, in Great Britain alone. L plates were introduced in May 1935.

Motor vehicles and roads – Great Britain

Year	No. of vehicles (all types)	Roads kilometres	miles	Motorways kilometres	miles	Road per vehicle metres	yards	Fatalities
1904	c. 18 000	c. 283 200	c. 176 000	–	–	–	–	–
1914	388 860	c. 283 200	c. 176 000	–	–	727·8	796	–
1920	c. 652 000	c. 283 200	c. 176 000	–	–	434·3	475	–
1925	1 538 235	c. 286 400	c. 178 000	–	–	185·6	203	–
1930	2 309 515	288 532	179 286	–	–	124·9	136·7	c. 7400
1939	3 208 410	290 530	180 527	–	–	90·5	99·0	8419
1945	1 654 364	c. 294 500	c. 183 000	–	–	178	194·7	5380
1950	4 511 626	317 163	197 076	–	–	70·5	77.1	5156
1960	9 610 432	334 645	207 939	152·8	95	34·8	38·1	7142
1980	19 210 000	339 633	211 038	2556	1588	17·7	19·3	5953
1981	19 347 000	342 320	212 707	2646	1644	17·7	19·3	5844
1982	19 762 000	343 942	213 715	2692	1673	17·4	19·0	5934
1983	20 209 000	345 776	214 855	2741	1703	17·1	18·7	5445
1984	20 765 000	347 482	215 915	2823	1754	16·7	18·3	5599
1985	21 157 000	348 837	216 757	2853	1773	16·5	18·0	5165
1986	21 699 000	350 798	217 975	2925	1818	16·2	17·7	5382
1987	22 152 000	352 292	218 904	2980	1852	15·9	17·4	5125

Notes: Vehicles surpassed 1 million early in 1923. Cars surpassed 1 million early in 1930, 5 million early in 1949. Motor cycles (including mopeds, scooters and three-wheelers) surpassed 1 million in 1953. Trams reached their peak in 1927 with 14 413 and sank by 1965 to 110. Diesel vehicles surpassed 25% of all goods vehicles in 1961 (2·1% in 1935) and 35% in 1965. The road mileage includes Trunk roads, Class I, Class II and Unclassified. The earliest dual carriageway was the Southend arterial in 1937 though parts of both the Great West Road and the Kingston bypass were converted to separate carriageways in 1936.

TRAFFIC SIGNALS
1868 Parliament Square, Westminster, London; semaphore-arms with red and green gas lamps for night use.
1914 First electric system erected by the American Traffic Signal Co. in Cleveland, Ohio, USA. Standing 4·5 m (*15 ft*) high, red and green lights were used with a warning buzzer.
1918 First system with red, green and amber lights, New York, USA.
1925 Piccadilly Circus, London, police-operated.
1926 Wolverhampton, Staffordshire, modern-type electric.
1932 First vehicle actuation sets introduced.

RIGHT AND LEFT HAND DRIVING
Of the 221 separately administered countries and territories in the world 58 drive on the left and 163 on the right. In Britain it is believed that left hand driving is a legacy from the preference of passing an approaching horseman or carriage right side to right side to facilitate right armed defence against sudden attack. On the Continent the postillions were mounted on the rearmost left horse in a team and thus preferred to pass left side to left side. While some countries have transferred from left to right the only case recorded of a transfer from right to left is in Okinawa, Japan, on 30 July 1978.

INTERNATIONAL VEHICLE REGISTRATION LETTERS
A Austria
ADN Yemen, People's Democratic Republic
AFG Afghanistan
AL Albania
AND Andorra
AUS Australia

B Belgium
BD Bangladesh
BDS Barbados
BG Bulgaria

BH Belize
BR Brazil
BRN Bahrain
BRU Brunei
BS Bahamas
BUR Burma

C Cuba
CDN Canada
CH Switzerland
CI Ivory Coast
CL Sri Lanka
CO Colombia
CR Costa Rica
CS Czechoslovakia
CY Cyprus

D Germany, Federal Republic
DDR German Democratic Republic
DK Denmark
DOM Dominican Republic
DY Benin
DZ Algeria

E Spain, Balearic Islands, Canary Islands, Spanish Guinea, Spanish Sahara
EAK Kenya
EAT Tanzania
EAU Uganda
EAZ Zanzibar (Tanzania)
EC Ecuador
ES El Salvador
ET Egypt
ETH Ethiopia

F France and territories
FJI Fiji
FL Liechtenstein
FR Faeroe Islands

GB United Kingdom
GBA Alderney
GBG Guernsey

GBJ	Jersey	RC	Taiwan
GBM	Isle of Man	RCA	Central African Republic
GBZ	Gibraltar	RCB	Congo
GCA	Guatemala	RCH	Chile
GH	Ghana	RH	Haiti
GR	Greece	RI	Indonesia
GUY	Guyana	RIM	Mauritania
		RL	Lebanon
H	Hungary	RM	Madagascar
HK	Hong Kong	RMM	Mali
HKJ	Jordan	RN	Niger
		RO	Romania
I	Italy	ROK	Korea
IL	Israel	ROU	Uruguay
IND	India	RP	Philippines
IR	Iran	RSM	San Marino
IRL	Republic of Ireland	RU	Burundi
IRQ	Iraq	RWA	Rwanda
IS	Iceland		
		S	Sweden
J	Japan	SD	Swaziland
JA	Jamaica	SF	Finland
		SGP	Singapore
K	Kampuchea	SME	Suriname
KWT	Kuwait	SN	Senegal
		SU	Union of Soviet Socialist Republics
L	Luxembourg	SWA	Namibia
LAO	Laos	SY	Seychelles
LAR	Libya	SYR	Syria
LB	Liberia		
LS	Lesotho	T	Thailand
		TG	Togo
M	Malta	TN	Tunisia
MA	Morocco	TR	Turkey
MAL	Malaysia	TT	Trinidad and Tobago
MC	Monaco		
MEX	Mexico	USA	United States of America
MS	Mauritius		
MW	Malawi	V	Vatican City
		VN	Vietnam
N	Norway		
NA	Netherlands Antilles	WAG	Gambia
NIC	Nicaragua	WAL	Sierra Leone
NL	Netherlands	WAN	Nigeria
NZ	New Zealand	WD	Dominica
		WG	Grenada
P	Portugal, Cape Verde Islands,	WL	St Lucia
	Mozambique, Portuguese Guinea,	WS	Western Samoa
	Portuguese Timor, Angola, São Tome and	WV	St Vincent and the Grenadines
	Principe Islands		
PA	Panama	YU	Yugoslavia
PAK	Pakistan	YV	Venezuela
PE	Peru		
PL	Poland	Z	Zambia
PNG	Papua New Guinea	ZA	South Africa
PY	Paraguay	ZRE	Zaire
		ZW	Zimbabwe
RA	Argentina		
RB	Botswana		

SPACEFLIGHT

Manned spaceflights (to 31 March 1989)

1 USSR 1
12 April 1961
Vostok 1
Yuri Gagarin
1 hr 48 min
Landed separately
from craft.

2 USA 1
5 May 1961
Freedom 7
Alan Shepard
15 min 28 sec
Suborbital;
splashdown.

3 USA 2
21 July 1961
Liberty Bell 7
Gus Grissom
15 min 37 sec
Spacecraft sank.

4 USSR 2
6 August 1961
Vostok 2
Gherman Titov
1 day 1 hr 18 min
At 25, youngest person
in space.

5 USA 3
20 February 1962
Friendship 7
John Glenn
4 hr 55 min 23 sec
First American to
orbit.

6 USA 4
24 May 1962
Aurora 7
Scott Carpenter
4 hr 56 min 5 sec
Landing overshoot of
250 miles.

7 USSR 3
11 August 1962
Vostok 3
Andrian Nikolyev
3 day 22 hr 22 min
First bachelor in
space.

8 USSR 4
12 August 1962
Vostok 4
Pavel Popovich
2 day 22 hr 57 sec
Came to within 6·4 km
(*4 miles*) of Vostok 3.

9 USA 5
3 October 1962
Sigma 7
Wally Schirra
9 hr 13 min 11 sec
Pacific splashdown.

10 USA 6
15 May 1963
Faith 7
Gordon Cooper
1 day 10 hr 19 min
49 sec
Final US one-man
flight.

11 USSR 5
14 June 1963
Vostok 5
Valeri Bykovsky
4 day 23 hr 6 min
Solo flight record-
holder.

12 USSR 6
16 June 1963
Vostok 6
Valentina Tereshkova
2 day 22 hr 50 min
First woman in space.

13 USSR 7
12 October 1964
Voskhod 1
Vladimir Komarov,
Konstantin Feoktistov,
Boris Yegerov
1 day 0 hr 17 min 3 sec
Riskiest flight, no
spacesuits, no ejection
seats, inside a 'Vostok'.

14 USSR 8
18 March 1965
Voskhod 2
Pavel Belyayev, Alexei
Leonov
1 day 2 hr 2 min 17 sec
Leonov makes first
walk in space.

15 USA 7
25 March 1965
Gemini 3
Gus Grissom, John
Young
4 hr 52 min 51 sec
Grissom first man in
space twice.

Valentina Tereschkova, the first woman in space in 1963.

16 USA 8
3 June 1965
Gemini 4
James McDivitt,
Edward White
4 day 1 hr 56 min
12 sec
White walks in space.

17 USA 9
21 August 1965
Gemini 5
Gordon Cooper,
Charles Conrad
7 day 22 hr 55 min
14 sec
Breaks endurance
record.

18 USA 10
4 December 1965
Gemini 7
Frank Borman, James
Lovell
13 day 18 hr 35 min
1 sec
Acted as rendezvous
target; breaks
endurance record.

19 USA 11
15 December 1965
Gemini 6
Wally Schirra, Tom
Stafford
1 day 1 hr 51 min
54 sec
First rendezvous in
space.

20 USA 12
16 March 1966
Gemini 8
Neil Armstrong, David
Scott
10 hr 41 min 26 sec
Emergency landing
after first space
docking.

21 USA 13
3 June 1966
Gemini 9
Tom Stafford, Eugene
Cernan
3 day 0 hr 20 min
50 sec
Rendezvous;
spacewalk; bullseye
splashdown.

Eugene Cernan – spacewalker in 1966.

26 USA 17
11 October 1968
Apollo 7
Wally Schirra, Donn
Eisele, Walt
Cunningham
10 day 20 hr 9 min
3 sec
Earth orbit shakedown
of Command and
Service Module.

27 USSR 10
26 October 1968
Soyuz 3
Georgi Beregovoi
3 day 22 hr 50 min 45
sec
Failed to dock with
unmanned Soyuz 2.

USSR
December 1968
Zond Pavel Belyayev
Circumlunar flight
cancelled.

28 USA 18
21 December 1968
Apollo 8
Frank Borman, James
Lovell, William
Anders
6 day 3hr 0 min 42 sec
Ten lunar orbits over
Christmas.

29 USSR 11
14 January 1969
Soyuz 4
Vladimir Shatalov
2 day 23 hr 20 min
47 sec
Launched with one
man, returned with
three.

30 USSR 12
15 January 1969
Soyuz 5
Boris Volynov, Alexei
Yeleseyev, Yevgeny
Khrunov
3 day 0 hr 54 min
15 sec
Yeliseyev and
Khrunov spacewalk to
Soyuz 4 after docking.

31 USA 19
3 March 1969
Apollo 9
James McDivitt, David
Scott, Russell
Schweickart
10 day 1 hr 0 min
54 sec
Test of Lunar Module
in Earth orbit;
spacewalk.

32 USA 20
18 May 1969
Apollo 10
Tom Stafford, John
Young, Eugene
Cernan
8 day 0 hr 3 min 23 sec
Lunar Module tested
in lunar orbit; came to
14·5 km (9 miles) of
surface of Moon.

33 USA 21
17 July 1969
Apollo 11
Neil Armstrong,
Michael Collins,
Edwin Aldrin
8 day 3 hr 18 min
35 sec
Armstrong and Aldrin
walk on Moon for over
2 hours.

34 USSR 13
11 October 1969
Soyuz 6
Georgi Shonin, Valeri
Kubasov
4 day 22 hr 42 min
47 sec
Welding tests.

35 USSR 14
12 October 1969
Soyuz 7
Anatoli Filipchenko,
Vladislav Volkov,
Viktor Gorbatko
4 day 22 hr 40 min
23 sec
Rendezvous to within
488 m (1600 ft) of
Soyuz 8.

36 USSR 15
13 October 1969
Soyuz 8
Vladimir Shatalov,
Alexei Yeliseyev
4 day 22 hr 50 min
49 sec
Third flight in strange
troika mission by
Soviets.

37 USA 22
14 November 1969
Apollo 12
Charles Conrad,
Richard Gordon, Alan
Bean
10 day 4 hr 36 min
25 sec
Pinpoint landing near
Surveyor.

22 USA 14
18 July 1966
Gemini 10
John Young, Michael
Collins
2 day 22 hr 46 min
39 sec
Docking; spacewalk;
record altitude of 763
km (474 miles).

23 USA 15
12 September 1966
Gemini 11
Charles Conrad,
Richard Gordon
2 day 23 hr 17 min
8 sec
Docking; spacewalk;
altitude of 1368 km
(850 miles); automatic
landing.

24 USA 16
11 November 1966
Gemini 12
James Lovell, Edwin
Aldrin
3 day 22 hr 34 min
31 sec
Docking; record
spacewalk of over 2 hr.

USA
27 January 1967
Apollo 1
Gus Grissom, Edward
White, Roger Chaffee
Killed in spacecraft
fire.

25 USSR 9
23 April 1967
Soyuz 1
Vladimir Komarov
1 day 2 hr 47 min
52 sec
Komarov killed when
parachute fails;
intended to dock with
Soyuz 2.

USSR
24 April 1967
Soyuz 2
Valeri Bykovsky,
Alexei Yeliseyev and
Yevgeny Khrunov
Flight cancelled; was
to have docked with
Soyuz 1 but this craft
had problems.

38 USA 23
11 April 1970
Apollo 13
James Lovell, Jack
Swigert, Fred Haise
5 day 22 hr 54 min
41 sec
Service module
exploded 55 hours into
mission; crew limped
home using Lunar
Module as lifeboat.

39 USSR 16
1 June 1970
Soyuz 9
Andiran Nikolyev,
Vitali Sevastyanov
17 day 16 hr 58 min
50 sec
Crew carried from
craft on stretchers
suffering acute stress
of readapting to
gravity after longest
flight.

40 USA 24
31 January 1971
Apollo 14
Alan Shepard, Stuart
Roosa, Edgar Mitchell
9 day 0 hr 1 min 57 sec
Shepard only Mercury
astronaut to walk on
Moon.

41 USSR 17
23 April 1971
Soyuz 10
Vladimir Shatalov,
Alexei Yeliseyev,
Nikolai
Ruckavishnikov
1 day 23 hr 45 min
54 sec
Failed to enter Salyut 1
space station after soft
docking.

42 USSR 18
6 June 1971
Soyuz 11
Georgi Dobrovolsky,
Vladislav Volkov,
Viktor Patsayev
23 day 18 hr 21 min
43 sec
Crew died as craft
depressurized before
re-entry; not wearing
spacesuits.

43 USA 25
26 July 1971
Apollo 15
David Scott, Alfred
Worden, James Irwin
12 day 7 hr 11 min
53 sec
First lunar rover.

44 USA 26
16 April 1972
Apollo 16
John Young, Ken
Mattingly, Charles
Duke
11 day 1 hr 51 min
5 sec
Space Shuttle
approved during
mission; Mattingly in
lunar orbit makes
longest solo US flight.

45 USA 27
7 December 1972
Apollo 17
Eugene Cernan, Ron
Evans, Jack Schmitt
12 day 13 hr 51 min
59 sec
Last manned
expedition to Moon
this century?

46 USA 28
25 May 1973
Skylab 2
Charles Conrad, Joe
Kerwin, Paul Weitz
28 day 0 hr 49 min
49 sec
Spacewalk to repair
severely disabled
Skylab 1 space station.

47 USA 29
28 July 1973
Skylab 3
Alan Bean, Owen
Garriott, Jack Lousma
59 day 11 hr 9 min
4 sec
Stranded in space
temporarily as
Command Module
malfunctions.

48 USSR 19
27 September 1973
Soyuz 12
Vasili Lazarev, Oleg
Makarov
1 day 23 hr 15 min 32
sec
Test of space-station
ferry.

49 USA 30
16 November 1973
Skylab 4
Gerry Carr, Edward
Gibson, Bill Pogue
84 day 1 hr 15 min
31 sec
Longest US manned
spaceflight.

50 USSR 20
18 December 1973
Soyuz 13
Pyotr Klimuk, Valetin
Lebedev
7 day 20 hr 55 min
35 sec
Russians and
Americans in space
together for first time,
although they don't
meet.

51 USSR 21
3 July 1974
Soyuz 14
Pavel Popvich, Yuri
Artyukhin
15 day 17 hr 30 min
28 sec
First space spies, on
Salyut 3.

52 USSR 22
26 August 1974
Soyuz 15
Gennadi Serafanov,
Lev Demin
2 day 0 hr 12 min
11 sec
Failed to dock with
Salyut 3.

53 USSR 23
2 December 1974
Soyuz 16
Anatoli Filipchenko,
Nikolai
Ruckavishnikov
5 day 22 hr 23 min
35 sec
Rehearsal for US–
USSR joint flight,
ASTP.

54 USSR 24
11 January 1975
Soyuz 17
Alexei Gubarev,
Georgi Grechko
29 day 13 hr 19 min
45 sec
Aboard Salyut 4.

55 USSR 25
5 April 1975
Soyuz 18-1
Vasili Lazarev, Oleg
Makarov
21 min 27 sec
Second stage failed;
flight aborted.

56 USSR 26
24 May 1975
Soyuz 18
Pyotr Klimuk, Vitali
Sevastyanov
62 day 23 hr 20 min 8
sec
Aboard Salyut 4.

57 USSR 27
15 July 1975
Soyuz 19
Alexei Leonov, Valeri
Kubasov
5 day 22 hr 30 min
51 sec
Docked with Apollo 18
in joint ASTP mission.

58 USA 31
15 July 1975
Apollo 18
Tom Stafford, Vance
Brand, Deke Slayton
9 day 1 hr 28 min
24 sec
Docked with Soyuz 19;
flight for Mercury
astronaut Slayton at
51; crew gassed during
landing, recovered.

59 USSR 28
6 July 1976
Soyuz 21
Boris Volynov, Vitali
Zholobov
49 day 6 hr 23 min
32 sec
Evacuated Salyut 5.
(Soyuz 20 was Progress
tanker test,
unmanned.)

60 USSR 29
22 September 1976
Soyuz 22
Valeri Bykovsky,
Vladimir Aksyonov
7 day 21 hr 52 min
17 sec
Independent Earth
survey flight.

61 USSR 30
14 October 1976
Soyuz 23
Vyacheslav Zudov,
Valeri Rozhdestvensky
2 day 0 hr 6 min 35 sec
Failed to dock with
Salyut 5; splashed
down in lake.

62 USSR 31
7 February 1977
Soyuz 24
Viktor Gorbatko, Yuri
Glazkov
17 day 17 hr 25 min
50 sec
Aboard Salyut 5.

63 USSR 32
9 October 1977
Soyuz 25
Vladimir Kovalyonok,
Valeri Ryumin
2 day 0 hr 44 min
45 sec
Failed to dock with
Salyut 6.

64 USSR 33
10 December 1977
Soyuz 26
Yuri Romanenko,
Georgi Grechko
96 day 10 hr 0 min
7 sec
Aboard Salyut 6; broke
endurance record.

65 USSR 34
10 January 1978
Soyuz 27
Vladimir
Dzhanibekov, Oleg
Makarov
5 day 22 hr 58 min
58 sec
Visitors to Salyut 6.

66 USSR 35
2 March 1978
Soyuz 28
Alexei Gubarev,
Vladimir Remek
7 day 22 hr 16 min
Remek was from
Czechoslovakia, first
non-American, non-
Russian in space; visit
to Salyut 6.

67 USSR 36
15 June 1978
Soyuz 29
Vladimir Kovalyonok,
Alexander
Ivanchenkov
139 day 14 hr 47 min
32 sec
Aboard Salyut 6;
landed in Soyuz 31.

68 USSR 37
27 June 1978
Soyuz 30
Pyotr Klimuk,
Miroslaw
Hermaszewski
7 day 22 hr 2 min
59 sec
Visit to Salyut 6;
Hermaszewski from
Poland.

69 USSR 38
26 August 1978
Soyuz 31
Valeri Bykovsky,
Sigmund Jahn
7 day 29 hr 49 min 4
sec
Visit to Salyut 6; Jahn
from East Germany;
landed in Soyuz 29.

70 USSR 39
25 February 1979
Soyuz 32
Vladimir Lyakhov,
Valeri Ryumin
175 day 0 hr 35 min
37 sec
Visit to Salyut 6;
landed in Soyuz 34
which was launched
unmanned.

71 USSR 40
10 April 1979
Soyuz 33
Nikolai
Ruckavishnikov,
Georgi Ivanov
1 day 23 hr 1 min 6 sec
Failed to dock with
Salyut 6; Bulgarian
Ivanov only
Intercosmos visitor not
to reach space station.

72 USSR 41
9 April 1980
Soyuz 35
Leonid Popov, Valeri
Ryumin
184 day 20 hr 11 min
35 sec
Salyut 6 mission takes
Ryumin to 361 days
space experience.

73 USSR 42
26 May 1980
Soyuz 36
Valeri Kubasov,
Bertalan Farkas
7 day 20 hr 45 min
44 sec
Visit to Salyut 6;
Farkas from Hungary;
landed in Soyuz 35.

74 USSR 43
5 June 1980
Soyuz T2
Yuri Malyshev,
Vladimir Aksyonov
3 day 22 hr 19 min
30 sec
Test of new Soyuz
model to Salyut 6.
(Soyuz T1 was
unmanned.)

75 USSR 44
23 July 1980
Soyuz 37
Viktor Gorbatko,
Pham Tuan
7 day 20 hr 42 min
Visit to Salyut 6; Tuan
from Vietnam; landed
in Soyuz 36.

76 USSR 45
18 September 1980
Soyuz 38
Yuri Romanenko,
Arnaldo Mendez
7 day 20 hr 43 min
24 sec
Visit to Salyut 6;
Mendez from Cuba.

77 USSR 46
27 November 1980
Soyuz T3
Leonid Kizim, Oleg
Makarov, Gennadi
Strekalov
12 day 19 hr 7 min
42 sec
Maintenance crew to
Salyut 5; first three-
man Soyuz since
Soyuz 11 accident.

78 USSR 47
12 March 1981
Soyuz T4
Vladimir Kovalyonok,
Viktor Savinykh
74 day 17 hr 37 min
23 sec
Final Salyut 6 long-
stay crew; Savinykh
100th person in space.

79 USSR 48
22 March 1981
Soyuz 39
Vladimir
Dzhanibvekov,
Jugderdemidyin
Gurragcha
7 day 20 hr 42 min
3 sec
Salyut 6 visit;
Gurragcha from
Mongolia.

80 USA 32
12 April 1981
Columbia STS 1
John Young, Bob
Crippen
2 day 6 hr 20 min 52
sec
Maiden flight of Space
Shuttle.

81 USSR 49
15 May 1981
Soyuz 40
Leonid Popov,
Dumitru Prunariu
7 day 20 hr 41 min 52
sec
Final visiting crew to
Salyut 6; Prunariu
from Romania.

82 USA 33
12 November 1981
Columbia STS 2
Joe Engle, Dick Truly
2 day 6 hr 13 min
11 sec
First manned flight of
used vehicle.

83 USA 34
22 March 1982
Columbia STS 3
Jack Lousma, Gordon
Fullerton
8 day 0 hr 4 min 46 sec
Third test flight.

84 USSR 50
13 May 1982
Soyuz T5
Anatoli Berezevoi,
Valentin Lebedev
211 day 9 hr 4 min 32
sec
First, record-breaking,
visit to Salyut 7.

85 USSR 51
24 June 1982
Soyuz T6
Vladimir
Dzhanibekov,
Alexander
Ivanchenkov, Jean-
Loup Chretien
7 day 21 hr 50 min
52 sec
Visit to Salyut 7;
Chrétien from France,
first Western European
in space.

86 USA 35
27 June 1982
Columbia STS 4
Ken Mattingly, Hank
Hartsfield
7 day 1 hr 9 min 31 sec
Military flight; final
test flight.

87 USSR 52
19 August 1982
Soyuz T7
Leonid Popov,
Alexander Serebrov,
Svetlana Savitskaya
7 day 21 hr 52 min
24 sec
Savitskaya second
woman in space after
20 years.

88 USA 36
11 November 1982
Columbia STS 5
Vance Brand, Robert
Overmyer, Joe Allen,
William Lenoir
5 day 2 hr 14 min 26
sec
First commercial
mission of Shuttle;
deployed two
communications
satellites; first four-
person flight.

89 USA 37
4 April 1983
Challenger STS 6
Paul Weitz, Karol
Bobko, Don Peterson,
Story Musgrave
5 day 0 hr 23 min
42 sec
Deployed TDRS 1;
limped into orbit after
upper stage failure;
performed spacewalk.

90 USSR 53
20 April 1983
Soyuz T8
Vladimir Titov,
Gennadi Strekalov,
Alexander Serebrov
2 day 0 hr 17 min
48 sec
Failed to dock with
Salyut 7; Titov first
spaceman with same
name as previous one;
Serebrov first person
to fly consecutive
missions.

91 USA 38
18 June 1983
Challenger STS 7
Bob Crippen, Rick
Hauck, John Fabian,
Sally Ride, Norman
Thagard
6 day 2 hr 24 min
10 sec
Satellite deployment
mission is first by five
people; includes first
US woman in space.

92 USSR 54
27 June 1983
Soyuz T9
Vladimir Lyakhov,
Alexander Alexandrov
149 day 10 hr 46 min
Trouble with space
station, Salyut 7, halts
flight.

93 USA 39
30 August 1983
Challenger STS 8
Richard Truly, Dan
Brandenstein, Guoin
Bluford, Dale
Gardner, William
Thornton
6 day 1 hr 8 min 40 sec
Night launch and
landing.

USSR
27 September 1983
Soyuz T10-1
Vladimir Titov,
Gennadi Strekalov
Launcher explodes on
pad; crew saved by
launch escape system.

94 USA 40
28 November 1983
Columbia STS 9
John Young, Brewster
Shaw, Owen Garriott,
Robert Parker, Byron
Lichtenberg, Ulf
Merbold
10 day 7 hr 47 min
23 sec
Flight of European
Spacelab 1; Merbold
from West Germany;
first six-up flight.

95 USA 41
3 February 1984
Challenger STS 41B
Vance Brand, Robert
Gibson, Bruce
McCandless, Robert
Stewart, Ronald
McNair
7 day 23 hr 15 min
54 sec
First independent
spacewalk using MMU
by McCandless; first
space mission to end
at launch site
(Kennedy/Canaveral).

96 USSR 55
8 February 1984
Soyuz T10
Leonid Kizim,
Vladimir Solovyov,
Oleg Atkov
236 day 22 hr 49 min
Longest manned space
mission to date; Kizim
and Solovyov made
record six spacewalks.

97 USSR 56
3 April 1984
Soyuz T11
Yuri Malyshev,
Gennadi Strekalov,
Rakesh Sharma
7 day 21 hr 40 min
Visit to Salyut 7;
Sharma from India

98 USA 42
6 April 1984
Challenger STS 41C
Bob Crippen, Dick
Scobee, George
Nelson, Terry Hart,
James van Hoften
6 day 23 hr 40 min
5 sec
Repaired Solar Max;
with Soyuz T10 and
T11 crews in space, 11
people are up at once.

99 USSR 57
17 July 1984
Soyuz T12
Vladimir
Dhzanibekov,
Svetlana Savitskaya,
Oleg Volk
11 day 19 hr 14 min
36 sec
Savitskaya becomes
first woman
spacewalker, outside
Salyut 7.

100 USA 43
30 August 1984
Discovery STS 41D
Hank Hartsfield,
Michael Coats, Judy
Resnik, Steven
Hawley, Michael
Mullane, Charlie
Walker
6 day 0 hr 56 min 4 sec
Launch pad abort in
June; three satellites
deployed; Walker first
industry-engineer
astronaut.

101 USA 44
5 October 1984
Challenger STS 41G
Bob Crippen, Jon
McBride, Sally Ride,
Kathy Sullivan, David
Leestma, Marc
Garneau, Paul Scully
Power.
8 day 5 hr 23 min
33 sec
First seven-up flight;
first carrying two
women; first US woman
in space twice; Sullivan
first US woman to
spacewalk; Garneau
from Canada.

102 USA 45
8 November 1984
Discovery STS 51A
Rick Hauck, Dave
Walker, Joe Allen,
Dale Gardner, Anna
Fisher
7 day 23 hr 45 min
54 sec
Two spacewalks to
retrieve lost
communications
satellites and return
them to Earth.

103 USA 46
24 January 1985
Discovery STS 51C
Ken Mattingly, Loren
Shriver, Ellison
Onizuka, James
Buchli, Gary Payton
3 day 1 hr 33 min
13 sec
Military mission;
Payton first USAF
Manned Space Flight
Engineer.

104 USA 47
12 April 1985
Discovery STS 51D
Karol Bobko, Don
Williams, Rhea
Seddon, Jeff Hoffman,
David Griggs, Charlie
Walker, Jake Garn
6 day 23 hr 55 min
23 sec
Deployed three
communications
satellites; unscheduled
EVA to attempt repair
of one; Senator Jake
Garn first passenger
observer in space.

105 USA 48
29 April 1985
Challenger STS 51B .
Bob Overmyer, Fred
Gregory, Don Lind,
William Thornton,
Norman Thagard,
Lodewijk van den
Berg, Taylor Wang
7 day 0 hr 8 min 50 sec
Spacelab 3 research
mission; Lind in space
after 19-year wait.

106 USSR 58
6 June 1985
Soyuz T13
Vladimir
Dzhanibekov, Viktor
Savinykh
112 day 3 hr 12 min
Complete overhaul of
Salyut 7 after systems
failures; Savinykh
came home in Soyuz

T14 and Georgi Grechko in Soyuz T13.

107 USA 49
17 June 1985
Discovery STS 51G
Dan Brandenstein,
John Creighton,
Shannon Lucid, Steve
Nagel, John Fabian,
Patrick Baudry, Abdul
Aziz Al-Saud
7 day 1 hr 38 min 58
sec
Satellite deployment
and research mission;
first with three nations
represented, Baudry
from France (first non-
US, non-USSR nation
to make two flights), Al
Saud a Sultan Prince
from Saudi Arabia.

108 USA 50
20 July 1985
Challenger STS 51F
Gordon Fullerton, Roy
Bridges, Karl Henize,
Anthony England,
Story Musgrave, John-
David Bartoe, Loren
Acton
7 day 22 hr 45 min
27 sec
Launch pad abort on
July 12; one engine
shutdown during
launch, causing abort-
to-orbit; Henize oldest
man in space at 58;
Spacelab 2 research
mission.

109 USA 51
27 August 1985
Discovery STS 51I
Joe Engle, Dick Covey,
William Fisher, James
van Hoften, Mike
Lounge
7 day 2 hr 14 min
42 sec
Three satellites
deployed; Leasat 3
captured, repaired and
redeployed.

110 USSR 59
17 September 1985
Soyuz T14
Vladimir Vasyutin,
Georgi Grechko,
Alexander Volkov
64 day 21 hr 52 min

Mission cut short after
Vasyutin becomes
mentally disturbed;
Grechko returned in
Soyuz T13; Savinykh
stayed with Soyuz T14
and clocked up
mission time of 168
days.

111 USA 52
3 October 1985
Atlantis STS 51J
Karol Bobko, Ron
Grabe, Dale Hilmers,
Bob Stewart, William
Pailes
4 day 1 hr 45 min
30 sec
Military mission.

112 USA 53
30 October 1985
Challenger STS 61A
Hank Hartsfield, Steve
Nagel, Bonnie
Dunbar, Guion
Gluford, James Buchli,
Ernst Messerschmitt,
Reinhard Furrer,
Wubbo Ockels
7 day 0 hr 44 min
51 sec
West German-funded
Spacelab D1 mission;
Messerschmitt and
Furrer from West
Germany; Ockels from
Holland; first eight-up
mission.

113 USA 54
27 November 1985
Atlantis STS 61B
Brewster Shaw, Bryan
O'Connor, Mary
Cleave, Jerry Ross,
Sherwood Spring,
Rudolpho Neri Vela,
Charlie Walker
6 day 21 hr 4 min
50 sec
Neri Vela from
Mexico; Walker's third
flight as Shuttle
payload specialist;
Ross and Spring
assemble structures
during EVAs.

114 USA 55
12 January 1986
Columbia STS 61C
Robert Gibson,
Charles Bolden,

Franklin Chang-Diaz,
George Nelson, Steve
Hawley, Robert
Cenker, Bill Nelson
6 day 2 hr 4 min 9 sec
Much-delayed flight;
first with crew
members of same
name; Bill Nelson, a
Congressman, second
political passenger.

USA
28 January 1986
Challenger STS 51L
Dick Scobee, Mike
Smith, Judith Resnik,
Ronald McNair,
Ellison Onizuka,
Christa McAuliffe,
Gregory Jarvis
73 sec
Exploded at 14330 m
(*47000 ft*); crew killed;
first flight to take off
but not to reach space;
first American in-flight
fatalities.

115 USSR 60
13 March 1986
Soyuz T15
Leonid Kizim,
Vladimir Solovyov
125 day 0 hr 1 min
First mission to new
space station Mir 1;
also docked with
Salyut 7; Kizim clocks
up over a year in space
experience.

116 USSR 61
5 February 1987
Soyuz TM2
Yuro Romanenko,
Alexander Laveikin
326 day 11 hr 37 min
59 sec
Record duration
mission by
Romanenko aboard
Mir 1. Landed in
Soyuz TM3 (Soyuz
TM1 was unmanned).
Laveikin, 200th person
in space, returned after
174 days.

117 USSR 62
22 July 1987
Soyuz TM3
Alexander Viktorenko,
Alexander Alexandrov,

Muhammed Faris
7 day 23 hr 4 min 5 sec
Faris from Syria.
Alexandrov remains
on Mir for 160 days.
Viktorenko and Faris
land in Soyuz TM2
with Laveikin.

118 USSR 63
21 December 1987
Soyuz TM4
Vladimir Titov, Musa
Manarov, Anatoli
Levchenko
365 day 22 hr 39 min
Levchenko returns in
Soyuz TM3 with
Romanenko and
Alexandrov after flight
of 7 days. Titov and
Manarov return in
Soyuz TM6.

119 USSR 64
7 June 1988
Soyuz TM5
Anatoli Solovyov,
Viktor Savinykh,
Alexander Alexandrov
9 day 20 hr 10 min
Alexandrov second
Bulgarian in space.
Crew returns in Soyuz
TM4.

120 USSR 65
31 August 1988
Soyuz TM6
Vladimir Lyakhov,
Valeri Polyakov,
Abdol Mohmand
8 day 20 hr 27 min
Mohmand from
Afghanistan. Polyakov
remains on Mir.
Lyakhov and
Mohmand land in
Soyuz TM5 after
'stranded in space'
scare.

121 USA 56
29 September 1988
Discovery STS 26
Rick Hauck, Dick
Covey, Mike Lounge,
David Hilmers,
George Nelson
4 day 1 hr 0 min
America's return to
space 32 months after
Challenger disaster.
Nelson first American
to make successive
national spaceflights.

122 USSR 66
26 November 1988
Soyuz TM7
Alexander Volkov,
Sergei Krikalev, Jean-
Loup Chretien.
Visit to Mir. First non-
US, non-USSR to
make two spaceflights,
Chretien is also the
first to make a
spacewalk. Volkov,
Krikalev and Polyakov
returned on 27 April
1989. Krikalev
returned in TM6.

123 USA 57
2 December 1988
Atlantis STS 27
Robert Gibson, Guy
Gardner, Jerry Ross,
Mike Mullane,
William Shepherd
4 day 9 hr 6 min
DoD mission to
deploy Lacrosse spy
satellite. With six
cosmonauts on Mir, 11
people are in space at
once, for the third
time.

124 USA 58
13 March 1989

Discovery STS 29
Michael Coats, John
Blaha, James Buchli,
James Bagian, Robert
Springer
4 day 23 hr 39 min
Deployed TDRS
satellite. STS 28
delayed.

Planned flights for 1989

19 April (mission
delayed)
Soyuz TM8
Alexander Viktorenko
and Alexander
Balandin
Six month mission to
Mir

4 May
Atlantis STS 30
Five man crew
deployed Magellan
Venus radar mapping
satellite

Aug STS 28 Columbia
Oct STS 34 Atlantis
Nov STS 33 Discovery
Dec STS 32 Columbia

SPACEWOMEN

Savitskaya	19 day 17 hr 06 min	USSR	2
Ride	14 day 07 hr 46 min	USA	2

National manned spaceflight totals*

Country	Days	No. of Flights
USSR	2683*	66*
USA	492	58
West Germany	17	2 (USA)
France	40	3 (2 USSR, 1 USA)
Bulgaria	12	2 (USSR)
Afghanistan	10	1 (USSR)
Canada	8	1 (USA)
Syria	8	1 (USSR)
Czechoslovakia	8	1 (USSR)
Poland	8	1 (USSR)
India	8	1 (USSR)
East Germany	8	1 (USSR)
Hungary	8	1 (USSR)
Romania	8	1 (USSR)
Cuba	8	1 (USSR)
Mongolia	8	1 (USSR)
Vietnam	8	1 (USSR)
Saudi Arabia	7	1 (USA)
Holland	7	1 (USA)
Mexico	7	1 (USA)

TOTALS: 20 countries, 3362 days

* To nearest day. Does not include uncompleted flight by Polyakov,
Volkov and Krikalev.

Most experienced spacemen

Name	Experience	Country	No. of Flights
Romanenko	430 day 18 hr 20 min	USSR	3
Kizim	374 day 17 hr 57 min	USSR	3
V. Titov	367 day 22 hr 56 min	USSR	2
Manarov	365 day 22 hr 39 min	USSR	1
V. Solovyov	361 day 22 hr 50 min	USSR	2
Ryumin	361 day 21 hr 31 min	USSR	3
Lyakhov	333 day 05 hr 48 min	USSR	3
Alexandrov	309 day 18 hr 02 min	USSR	2
Savinykh	252 day 17 hr 38 min	USSR	3
Polyakov	240 day 22 hr 36 min	USSR	1
Atkov	236 day 22 hr 49 min	USSR	1
Lebedev	219 day 05 hr 59 min	USSR	2
Kovalyonok	216 day 09 hr 09 min	USSR	3
A. Volkov	216 day 09 hr 02 min	USSR	2
Berezovoi	211 day 09 hr 04 min	USSR	1
Popov	200 day 14 hr 44 min	USSR	3
Laveikin	174 day 03 hr 25 min	USSR	1
Krikalev	151 day 11 hr 10 min	USSR	1
Ivanchenkov	147 day 03 hr 37 min	USSR	2
Dzhanibekov	145 day 15 hr 56 min	USSR	5
Grechko	134 day 20 hr 32 min	USSR	3
Carr	84 day 01 hr 15 min	USA	1
Gibson	84 day 01 hr 15 min	USA	1
Pogue	84 day 01 hr 15 min	USA	1

NATIONAL MAN-DAYS IN SPACE

Country	Days
USSR	5676*
USA	1832
France	40
West Germany	24

Rest: see National Manned Spaceflight Totals

* Does not include uncompleted mission by Polyakov, Volkov and
Krikalev.

PEOPLE WHO HAVE FLOWN INTO SPACE
214 in total
125 USA (8 women)
67 USSR (2 women)
3 West Germany
2 France
2 Bulgaria
1 each from: Canada, Poland, India, East Germany, Hungary, Cuba, Mongolia, Vietnam,
Romania, Czechoslovakia, Saudi Arabia, Mexico,
Holland, Afghanistan and Syria.

People who have flown two missions:
93 (54 USA, 38 USSR, 1 France). Includes two
women, Sally Ride (USA) and Svetlana Savitskaya
(USSR)

People who have flown three missions:
35 (17 USA, 18 USSR)

People who have flown four missions:
7 (5 USA, 2 USSR)

In-flight fatalities

Vladimir Komarov	USSR	Soyuz 1	24 April 1967
Georgi Dobrovolsky	USSR	Soyuz 11	6 June 1971
Vladislav Volkov	USSR	Soyuz 11	
Viktor Patsayev	USSR	Soyuz 11	
Dick Scobee	USA	Space Shuttle* Challenger STS 51L	28 January 1986
Mike Smith	USA	Space Shuttle* Challenger STS 51L	
Judith Resnik	USA	Space Shuttle* Challenger STS 51L	
Ellison Onizuka	USA	Space Shuttle* Challenger STS 51L	
Ronald McNair	USA	Space Shuttle* Challenger STS 51L	
Gregory Jarvis	USA	Space Shuttle* Challenger STS 51L	
Christa McAulliffe	USA	Space Shuttle* Challenger STS 51L	

* Did not reach space

Deceased spacepersons

Gus Grissom	USA	27 January 1967	Spacecraft fire on launch pad
Edward White	USA	27 January 1967	Spacecraft fire on launch pad
Vladimir Komarov	USSR	24 April 1967	Soyuz 1
Yuri Gagarin	USSR	27 March 1968	Air crash
Pavel Belyayev	USSR	20 January 1970	Peritonitis
Georgi Dobrovolsky	USSR	26 June 1971	Soyuz 11
Vladislav Volkov	USSR	26 June 1971	Soyuz 11
Viktor Patsayev	USSR	26 June 1971	Soyuz 11
Jack Swigert	USA	27 December 1982	Cancer
Dick Scobee	USA	28 January 1986	Challenger
Judith Resnik	USA	28 January 1986	Challenger
Ellison Onizuka	USA	28 January 1986	Challenger
Ronald McNair	USA	28 January 1986	Challenger
Donn Eisele	USA	1 December 1987	Heart attack
Anatoli Levchenko	USSR	6 August 1988	Brain tumour
David Griggs	USA	16 June 1989	Air crash

Note: This listing includes only those astronauts and cosmonauts who made spaceflights.

People who have flown five missions:
2 John Young, USA and Vladimir Dzhanibekov, USSR

People who have flown six missions:
1 John Young, USA

Youngest and oldest in space

Oldest: Karl Henize, 58, USA.
Oldest Russian: Georgi Grechko, 53.
Oldest other country: Jean-Loup Chrétien, 51, France*
Oldest woman: Shannon Lucid, 42, USA.
Oldest Russian woman: Svetlana Savitskaya, 35.
Youngest: Gherman Titov, 25, USSR.
Youngest American: Sally Ride, 32.
Youngest American male: Eugene Cernan, 32.
Youngest Russian woman: Valentina Tereshkova, 26.
Youngest other country: Dumitru Prunariu, 28, Romania.

* on second space flight: oldest on first flight, Reinhard Forrer, 44, West Germany

Spacewalking records

38 flights have involved EVAs: 14 USSR, 23 USA
64 people have walked in space once: 41 USA, 22 USSR, 1 France
34 people have walked in space twice: 25 USA, 9 USSR
16 people have walked in space three times: 11 USA, 5 USSR
5 people have walked in space four times: 3 USA, 2 USSR

2 people have walked in space five, six, seven and eight times: 2 USSR (Kizim and Solovyov)
Longest spacewalk: Cernan and Schmitt on Moon, Apollo 17, 7 hr 37 min.
Longest spacewalk in Earth orbit: Nelson and van Hoften,* STS 41C, 7 hr 18 min.
Most experienced spacewalkers: Kizim and Solovyov, eight **EVAs, 31 hr 40 min.
Untethered spacewalker (with manned manoeuvring units): McCandless, Stewart, Nelson, van Hoften, Allen and Gardner (all USA).

* Space Transportation System
** Extra Vehicular Activity

Moon travellers

24 Americans have travelled to the Moon.
22 Americans have orbited the Moon.
12 Americans have walked on the Moon: Armstrong, Aldrin, Conrad, Bean, Shepard, Mitchell, Scott, Irwin, Young, Duke, Cernan, Schmitt.
3 Americans have travelled to the Moon twice: Lovell, Young, Cernan.
2 Americans have orbited to the Moon twice: Young, Cernan.
Moonwalk totals: 3 days 8 hrs 22 min.
Lunar stay time total: 12 days 11 hrs 40 min.
Weight of Moon returned to Earth: 386·0 kg (*850·2 lb*).

Space Shuttle logs

Flight hours: 165 day 0 hr 51 min 4 sec on 27 missions (does not include Challenger's final ill-fated 73 sec ascent).

Note: based on launch to main gear touchdown times, not nose wheel or stop times.

Orbiter flight experience

Challenger 62 day 07 hr 55 min 2 sec (not including 51L)
Discovery 47 day 06 hr 45 min 16 sec
Columbia 42 day 01 hr 54 min 26 sec
Atlantis 15 day 7 hr 56 min 20 sec

105 individuals have flown on a Space Shuttle space mission (does not include Challenger which did not reach space), 35 have flown twice, 8 have flown three times, 3 have flown four times, 1 (Bob Crippen) has flown four missions.

SPACE SHUTTLE ASTRONAUT EXPERIENCE TABLE (OVER 14 DAYS)

Crippen	23 day 13 hr 49 min 19 sec
Hartsfield	23 day 02 hr 50 min 24 sec
C. Walker	19 day 21 hr 56 min 17 sec*
Gibson	18 day 10 hr 25 min 04 sec
Hauck	18 day 03 hr 08 min 55 sec
G. Nelson	17 day 02 hr 45 min 04 sec
Shaw	17 day 01 hr 52 min 13 sec
Bobko	16 day 02 hr 04 min 35 sec
Fullerton	15 day 22 hr 50 min 13 sec
Buchli	15 day 01 hr 57 min 04 sec
Ride	14 day 07 hr 27 min 32 sec
Nagel	14 day 02 hr 23 min 49 sec
van Hoften	14 day 01 hr 57 min 47 sec
D. Gardner	14 day 01 hr 53 min 36 sec

* Charlie Walker is a non-NASA astronaut payload specialist

Famous firsts in manned spaceflight

		Date of Launch
First in space:	Yuri Gagarin USSR	12 Apr 1961
First to make two flights:	Gus Grissom USA	25 Mar 1965
First non-US, non-Soviet to make two flights:	Jean-Loup Chrétien France	26 Nov 1988
First to make three flights:	Wally Schirra USA	11 Oct 1968
First to make four flights:	James Lovell USA	11 Apr 1970
First to make five flights:	John Young USA	12 Apr 1981
First to make six flights:	John Young USA	28 Nov 1983
First to walk in space:	Alexei Leonov USSR	18 Mar 1965
First to walk in space twice:	Buzz Aldrin USA	16 July 1969
First to walk in space three times:	David Scott USA	26 July 1971
First to walk in space four times:	Gene Cernan USA	7 Dec 1972
First to walk in space five times:	Vladimir Solvyov USSR	
	Leonid Kizim USSR	13 Mar 1986
	(Also the first to walk in space six, seven and eight times)	
First to walk in space independently:	Bruce McCandless USA	3 Feb 1984
First male–female spacewalk:	Vladimir Dzhanibekov and Svetlana Savitskaya USSR	17 July 1984
First spacewalk between Moon and Earth:	Alfred Worden USA	26 July 1971
First spacewalk by non-US, nonSoviet:	Jean-Loup Chretien France	26 Nov 1988
First aborted ascent:	Soyuz 18-1 USSR	5 Apr 1975
First aborted launch:	Gemini 6 USA	12 Dec 1965
First spacecraft manoeuvres:	Gemini 3 USA	25 Mar 1965
First over 50 years of age in space:	Deke Slayton USA	15 July 1975
First to touch another spacecraft:	Mike Collins USA	18 July 1966
First to fly on on birthday:	Richard Truly USA	12 Nov 1981
First bachelor:	Andrian Nikolyev USSR	11 Aug 1961
First to fly consective missions:	Alexander Serebrov USSR	20 Apr 1983
First crew transfer:	Alexei Yeleseyev USSR Yevgeni Khrunov USSR	15 Jan 1969
First curtailed flight:	Gemini 5 USA	21 Aug 1965
First satellite deployment:	Faith 7 USA	15 May 1963
First docking:	Gemini 8 USA	16 Mar 1966
First dual flight:	Vostok 3 and 4 USSR	12 Aug 1961
First launch explosion: (crew saved by escape system)	Soyuz T10-1 USSR Vladimir Titov USSR Gennadi Strekalov USSR	27 Sept 1983
First extended mission:	Voskhod 2 USSR	18 Mar 1965
First spaceman to become father while in space:	Leonid Kizim USSR	8 Feb 1984
First two crew flight:	Voskhod 2 USSR	18 Mar 1965
First three crew flight:	Voskhod 1 USSR	12 Oct 1964
First four crew flight:	STS 5 USA	11 Nov 1982
First five crew flight:	STS 7 USA	18 Jun 1983
First six crew flight:	STS 9 USA	28 Nov 1983
First seven crew flight:	STS 41G USA	5 Oct 1984
First eight crew flight:	STS 61A USA	30 Oct 1985
First grandfather in space:	Lev Demin USSR	24 Aug 1974

First landing at launch base:	STS 41B USA	3 Feb 1984
First military mission:	Soyuz 14 USSR	3 July 1974
First flight to the Moon:	Apollo 8 USA	21 Dec 1968
First flight to land on the Moon:	Apollo 11 USA	16 July 1969
First men on Moon:	Neil Armstrong USA	16 July 1969
	Buzz Aldrin USA	
First mother in space:	Anna Fisher USA	8 Nov 1984
First black man in space:	Guion Bluford USA	30 Aug 1983
First non-US, non-Soviet spaceman:	Vladimir Remek Czechoslovakia	2 Mar 1978
First night launch:	Soyuz 1 USSR	23 Apr 1967
First night landing:	Soyuz 10 USSR	23 Apr 1971
First rendezvous in space:	Gemini 6 and 7 USA	16 Dec 1965
First satellite repair:	Solar Max, STS 41C USA	6 Apr 1984
First to sleep in space:	Gherman Titov USSR	6 Aug 1961
First to fly solo in lunar orbit:	John Young USA	18 May 1969
First telecast from space:	Vostok 3 USSR	11 Aug 1962

First person to fly to Moon twice:	James Lovell USA	11 Apr 1970
First woman in space:	Valentina Tereshkova USSR	16 Jun 1963
First woman spacewalker:	Svetlana Savitskaya USSR	17 Jul 1984
First passenger-observer:	Jake Garn USA	12 Apr 1985
First reactivation of dead space station:	Soyuz T13 USSR Vladimir Dzhanibekov Viktor Savinykh	6 Jun 1985
First mission with three nationalities:	STS 51G USA	17 Jun 1965
First return due to illness:	Vladimir Vasyutin USSR	17 Sep 1985
First flight with crew with same name:	STS 61C USA George Nelson Bill Nelson	12 Jan 1986
First flight to take off but not reach space:	Challenger 51L USA	28 Jan 1986
First landing with each crewmember having been launched in separate spacecraft:	Yuri Romanenko USSR Alexander Alexandrov USSR Anatoli Levchenko USSR	29 Dec 1987*

* Date of landing

Left to right: Neil Armstrong, Michael Collins and Edwin Aldrin, crew of the history-making Apollo II. (NASA)

DEFENCE

Nuclear weapons and warfare

For nearly four decades, direct conflict between the major powers has been avoided largely through deterrence – the prevention of aggression by means of threats of such overwhelming destruction that potential aggressors can see no worthwhile gains to be had from their actions. Deterrence is based upon the existence of nuclear weapons of proven capability, backed by a belief that, in certain mutually understood circumstances, such weapons would be used. Since the atom-bomb attacks on Japan by the USA in August 1945, a further four countries have openly joined the 'nuclear club' – the USSR (1949), Britain (1952), France (1960) and China (1964). They deploy weapons that may be used either on the battlefield (tactical), in a theatre of war (inter-mediate/medium range) or between continents (strategic). The latter apply principally to the Superpowers (the USA and USSR), who operate a system of deterrence known as Mutual Assured Destruction (MAD): if one side should attack the other using nuclear weapons, the victim has the ability to absorb such a 'first strike' and to hit back using 'second-strike' retaliatory weapons invulnerable to surprise attack – chiefly in submarines, hiding in deep-ocean areas of the world.

Eight major systems of nuclear delivery exist:

Intercontinental ballistic missiles (ICBMs) with ranges up to 14 800 km (*9200 miles*) – strategic.
Submarine-launched ballistic missiles (SLBMs) on board sub-surface ballistic nuclear (SSBN) sub-marines, with ranges up to 9100 km (*5650 miles*) – strategic.
Long-range bombers with ranges up to 12 800 km (*7450 miles*) – strategic/theatre.
Intermediate/medium-range ballistic missiles (I/MRBMs) with ranges up to 5000 km (*3100 miles*) – theatre.
Medium-range bombers with ranges up to 11 000 km (*6800 miles*) – theatre.
Short-range ballistic missiles (SRBMs) with ranges up to 900 km (*570 miles*) – tactical/theatre.
Short-range aircraft with ranges up to 3800 km (*2360 miles*) – tactical/theatre.
Artillery with ranges up to 21·6 km (*13·2 miles*) – tactical.

Warheads fitted to such weapons may produce explosions ranging between 1 Megaton (MT) in the Soviet SS-11 Sego ICBM, with its range of 13 000 km (*8000 miles*), to 0·5 Kiloton (KT) in the American M-110 203 mm self-propelled howitzer artillery, with its range of 18 km (*11 miles*). One KT is equivalent to 1000 tons of TNT and one MT to one million

Force comparison of major nuclear systems

INTERCONTINENTAL BALLISTIC MISSILES (ICBMs)

	Total Number of Launchers	Number and Yield of Warheads	Range (km)
USA			
Minuteman II	450	1 × 1–2 MT	11 300
Minuteman III	527	1 × 170 KT/3 × 335 KT	14 800
MX Peacekeeper	23	10 × 300 KT	11 000
TOTAL:	1000		
USSR			
SS-11 Sego	420	1 × 1 MT/3 × 300 KT	13 000
SS-13 Savage	60	1 × 600 KT	9 400
SS-17 Spanker	138	4 × 500 KT	10 000
SS-18 Satan	308	10 × 500 KT	11 000
SS-19 Stiletto	350	6 × 550 KT	10 000
SS-24 Scalpel	10	10 × 100 KT	10 000
SS-25 Sickle	100	1 × 550 KT	10 500
TOTAL:	1386		
China			
DF-4	4	1 × 3 MT	7 000
DF-5	2	1 × 5 MT	15 000
TOTAL:	6		

tons of TNT. ICBMs and SLBMs are fitted with multiple warheads known as MIRVs (multiple independently targetable re-entry vehicles): the Soviet SS-18 Satan has 10 MIRV'd warheads on each missile.

The deterrent balance may be upset by a variety of factors, not least the ability by one side to defend itself against attack while retaining the capability to inflict damage on the enemy. In March 1983 President Ronald Reagan of the USA announced an intention to deploy a space-based defensive system – the Strategic Defense Initiative (SDI, or 'Star Wars') – using laser and charged particle beam weapons designed to destroy incoming Soviet warheads as they followed an orbital trajectory towards the United States. Dependent on enormous research and funds, SDI is unlikely to be deployed until the 21st century. Meanwhile, the Soviets are conducting their own research.

Fears of imbalance leading to the possibility of one side 'winning' a nuclear exchange have produced arms control negotiations and agreements. Between 1969 and 1972, the Superpowers conducted Strategic Arms Limitation Talks (SALT), producing a package known as SALT I (1972) which placed a common 'ceiling' on the number of weapons deployed by both sides. SALT II (1979) attempted to reduce that ceiling, but was not accepted by the USA once the Soviets had invaded Afghanistan (December 1979). Further negotiations, known as the Strategic Arms Reduction Talks (START) failed to reach agreement, although in December 1987 the Superpowers signed the Intermediate Nuclear Forces (INF) agreement, cutting the number of theatre weapons in Europe.

SUBMARINE-LAUNCHED BALLISTIC MISSILES (SLBMs)

	Total missiles	Total warheads
USA	900	10 632
UK	64	192
France	96	176
TOTAL:	1060	11 000
USSR TOTAL:	967	2–3000
China TOTAL:	24	2200–3000

LONG-RANGE AIRCRAFT
(nuclear-armed)

	Numbers deployed	Range (km)
USA		
B-52G	98	12 000
B-52H	96	12 000
B-1B	54	12 000
TOTAL:	248	
USSR		
Tu-95 Bear	150	12 800
Mya-4 Bison	15	11 200
TOTAL:	165	

INTERMEDIATE/MEDIUM-RANGE BALLISTIC MISSILES (I/MRBMs)
(NB US/NATO and Soviet systems being withdrawn from Europe under terms of the INF Agreement, December 1987)

	Numbers deployed	Range (km)
US/NATO		
GLCM	256	2500
Pershing II	150	1800
TOTAL:	406	
USSR		
SS-4 Sandal	112	2000
SS-20 Saber	441	5000
TOTAL:	553	
China		
DF-2	50	1200
DF-3	60	2700
TOTAL:	110	

MEDIUM-RANGE AIRCRAFT
(nuclear-armed)

	Numbers deployed	Range (km)
USA		
FB-111A	56	4 700
USSR		
Tu-16 Badger	502	4 800
Tu-22 Blinder	165	6 200
Tu-26M Backfire	290	11 000
TOTAL:	957	
China		
H-6	120	5000

SHORT-RANGE BALLISTIC MISSILES
(SRBMs)

	Numbers deployed	Range (km)
USA/NATO		
Lance	107	110
Pershing 1A	72	160–720
TOTAL:	179	
France		
Pluton	32	120
USSR/Warsaw Pact		
FROG-7	760	70
SS-21 Scarab	138	120
SS-1c Scud B	735	300
SS-23 Spider	20	500
SS-12	130	900
TOTAL:	1783	

SHORT-RANGE AIRCRAFT (including carrier-based; nuclear capable)

USA/NATO	France	USSR/Warsaw Pact
TOTALS: 2954	150	2863

ARTILLERY (nuclear capable)

USA/NATO	USSR/Warsaw Pact
TOTALS: 6560	9910

Conventional war

Military conflict conducted without access or recourse to nuclear weapons is known as conventional war, if fought between the armed forces of recognized states. Conventional war in the 20th century has taken a number of forms.

Total War: Wars fought for the complete destruction of the enemy, using all available weapons against both military and civilian targets, wherever they may be found. World War I (1914–18) had elements of totality, but World War II (1939–45) was the closest to total war yet fought. With the advent of nuclear weapons, total war has become equated with complete nuclear devastation, although it is still possible for non-nuclear powers to fight such conflicts.

Limited War: Wars fought under conscious restraint, usually by nuclear-capable countries choosing not to use their nuclear arsenals. Other limitations may include geography, force levels and targetting. Examples are the Korean War (1950–53), the American War in Vietnam (1965–73) and the Falklands/Malvinas War (1982).

Local War: Wars fought between non-nuclear countries. Examples are the various Arab–Israeli Wars (1948, 1956, 1967, 1973 and 1982) and the Iran–Iraq War (1980–88). Despite a lack of nuclear weapons, such wars can be devastating for the countries involved, which may be fighting to the full capability of their forces.

There is always a danger of conventional wars escalating into nuclear confrontations, either because nuclear-capable countries are directly involved or because they are dragged in by non-nuclear allies. The greatest danger seems to lie in Europe, where forces of the North Atlantic Treaty Organization (NATO) and the Warsaw Pact face each other, each centred upon a rival Superpower.

NATO North Atlantic Treaty Organization

NATO, an idea first broached by the Secretary of State for External Affairs for Canada on 28 Apr 1948, came into existence on 4 Apr 1949 and into force on 24 Aug 1949, with Belgium, Canada, Denmark, France, Iceland, Italy, Luxembourg, the Netherlands, Norway, Portugal, the United Kingdom and the USA as founder-members. Greece and Turkey were admitted on 18 Feb 1952, the Federal Republic of Ger-

many on 5 May 1955, and Spain on 30 May 1982, bringing the total of countries involved to 16. France withdrew from NATO's military affairs on 1 July 1966 and NATO HQ was moved from Paris to Brussels. Greece left the military command structure on 14 Aug 1974 but its reintegration was approved by NATO's Defence Planning Committee on 20 Oct 1980.

WARSAW PACT The Warsaw Pact Treaty Organization

The Warsaw Pact refers to a treaty of friendship and non-aggression signed between the USSR and its eastern European satellite countries on 14 May 1955. The aim was to set up a joint military command structure and to ensure that all members of the Pact would come to the defence of any one member who suffered aggression. The original members were Albania, Bulgaria, Czechoslovakia, Hungary, Poland, Romania and the USSR. The Democratic Republic of Germany, initially only an observer, achieved full membership in late 1955. From 1962 Albania began to distance itself from the Pact, withdrawing completely in 1968.

CONVENTIONAL ARMED FORCE COMPARISON (global figures)

	NATO	Warsaw Pact
Total ground forces	2 992 000	2 829 000
Total ground-force reserves	5 502 000	5 348 000
Main battle tanks	30 500	68 300
Artillery pieces	21 500	50 400
Armed helicopters	2 020	2 130
Land combat aircraft	7 438	9 506
Submarines	238	301
Surface ships	1 207	1 280
Naval aircraft	2 102	1 191
(NB NATO figures include French and Spanish forces)		

Insurgency and terrorism

Many countries face the threat of insurgency and terrorism, being forced to react to levels of violence which do not constitute full-scale war. Insurgency involves politico-military actions (including guerrilla warfare) within a country by groups intent on the overthrow of the established government; terrorism involves the use of indiscriminate force to instil fear into both government and people, usually coupled to political demands. International terrorism arises when groups from different countries co-operate to increase the level and nature of the threat, using techniques such as bomb attacks, kidnaps and hijacks.

A meeting of the Chiefs of Staff at NATO HQ in Brussels. (Popperfoto)

Major terrorist groups currently active

Abu Nidal Faction – Palestinian group, led by Abu Nidal (Sabri al-Banna) and based in Libya.

Action Directe – European anti-NATO group, based in France and led by Jean-Marc Rouillan; linked to CCC and RAF (qv).

CCC – Communist Fighting Cells; European anti-NATO group based in Belgium, led by Pierre Carette.

DFLP – Democratic Front for the Liberation of Palestine, led by Naif Hawatmeh.

ETA/Basques – Basque separatist group, founded in 1959 in Spain, led by Domingo Iturbo.

Hezbollah – The Party of God, founded in Lebanon in 1982 and dedicated to the Islamic Revolution.

INLA – Irish National Liberation Army; left-wing breakaway group from the IRA (qv) in Ireland.

IRA – Irish Republican Army; nationalist group dedicated to the unification of an independent Ireland; split in 1970 into Official and Provisional wings.

PFLP – Popular Front for the Liberation of Palestine, founded by George Habash and Wadi Haddad to further the Palestinian cause through international terrorism. Has splintered into the PFLP-General Command under Ahmed Jibril, and the PFLP-Special Command under Abu Mohammed (Salim Salem).

PLO – Palestine Liberation Organisation, founded in 1964 but dominated since 1969 by *Fatah* under Yassir Arafat. Defeated in southern Lebanon in 1982 by Israeli forces but still active as the 'government-in-exile' of the Palestinian people.

RAF – Red Army Faction, West German group which emerged from the Baader-Meinhof Group of the early 1970s; contacts with the CCC and Action Directe (qv).

Red Brigades – left-wing Italian group, recently weakened by effective police action.

Sendero Luminoso – 'Shining Path'; Peruvian Marxist group formed by Abimael Guzman.

UDA – Ulster Defence Association, 'Loyalist' group in Northern Ireland dedicated to attacks on the Provisional IRA (qv) and Roman Catholic population.

Principal conflicts since 1945

It is estimated that more than 130 conflicts have taken place worldwide since 1945, ranging in intensity from low-scale insurgency (I) to full-scale conventional war (C). The following are the most important.

1945–48 Palestine (I): Jewish groups versus Britain; British withdrawal and creation of the State of Israel.

1945–49 Chinese Civil War (I/C): Nationalist Chinese (with US assistance) versus Communist Chinese. Fighting lapsed October 1949 with establishment of Communist state and withdrawal of Nationalists to Taiwan.

1945–49 Greek Civil War (I/C): Nationalists versus Communists; Nationalist victory.

1946–54 Philippines (I): Government versus Communists; Government victory.

1946–54 First Indochina War (I/C): French versus Communist Viet Minh, culminating in the battle of Dien Bien Phu and French defeat.

1948–49 Israeli War of Independence (C): Israel versus Egypt, Transjordan, Syria, Iraq and Lebanon; Israeli victory.

1948–60 Malaya (I): Britain versus Malayan Communists; Government victory and independence.

1950-53 Korean War (C): North Korea and China versus United Nations forces; 25 June 1950 North Korean invasion of South Korea; November 1950 Chinese intervention; armistice 27 July 1953.

1952-60 Kenya (I): Britain versus Mau Mau insurgents; Government victory and independence.

1954-62 Algeria (I): Nationalists versus the French; Algerian independence 1962; French withdrawal.

1955-59 Cyprus (I): Britain versus Greek Cypriot EOKA insurgents; Cypriot independence after British withdrawal to Sovereign Base Areas.

1956 Suez (C): Britain, France and Israel versus Egypt; ceasefire agreed under international (mainly US) pressure.

1956-59 Cuba (I): Government versus insurgents under Fidel Castro; insurgent victory.

1957-80 Rhodesia/Zimbabwe (I): Nationalists versus British/Rhodesian governments; Nationalist victory.

1959-75 Second Indochina War (I/C): North Vietnamese and Viet Cong versus South Vietnamese and Americans; American intervention 1965-73; North Vietnamese victory 1975.

1960-67 Congo/Zaire (C): Nationalist factions; UN intervention.

1961-75 Angola (I): Nationalists versus the Portuguese; Nationalist victory followed by a civil war.

1962 Sino-Indian War (C): Communist China versus India; various border incidents; ceasefire.

1962-66 Brunei/Borneo (I/C): Malaysia (with British assistance) versus Indonesia; ceasefire 1966.

1964-67 Aden (I): Nationalists versus Britain; British withdrawal and independence followed by civil war.

1964-75 Mozambique (I): Nationalists versus the Portuguese; Nationalist victory followed by civil war.

1965 Indo-Pakistan War (C): India versus Pakistan; UN-policed ceasefire.

1965-75 Oman/Dhofar (I): Government (with British assistance from 1970) versus Marxist insurgents; Government victory.

1967 Six-Day War (C): Israel versus Egypt, Jordan and Syria; Israeli occupation of Sinai, the West Bank and Golan Heights; UN ceasefire.

1967-70 Nigerian Civil War (C): Nigeria versus secessionist Biafra; Nigerian victory.

1969- Northern Ireland (I): Britain versus Republican insurgents.

1971 Indo-Pakistan War (C): India versus Pakistan; Indian victory and creation of Bangladesh (from East Pakistan).

1973 Yom Kippur War (C): Israel versus Egypt and Syria; Israeli victory.

1975- Lebanese Civil War (I/C): Christian versus Moslem factions; Syrian intervention 1976; Israeli invasion of southern Lebanon 1982.

1976- Cambodian (Kampuchean) Civil War (I/C): Communist factions; genocide under Pol Pot 1976-79; Vietnamese invasion 1978.

1979- Afghanistan (I/C): Communists (with Soviet assistance) versus Mujahaddin Nationalists; Soviet invasion 1979, withdrawal 1989.

1979- Nicaragua (I): Sandinista government versus US-aided 'Contras'.

1980-88 Iran–Iraq (Gulf) War (C): Iran versus Iraq; Iraqi invasion of Iran September 1980; ceasefire 1988.

1980-to date El Salvador (I): Government (with US assistance) versus Communist insurgents.

1982 Falklands/Malvinas War (C): Britain versus Argentina; British victory.

The British ship HMS Antelope was one of the casualties of the Falklands/Malvinas War in 1982. (UPI)

The United Nations

'A general international organization . . . for the maintenance of international peace and security' was recognized as desirable in Clause 4 of the proposals of the Four-Nation Conference of Foreign Ministers signed in Moscow on 30 Oct 1943 by Anthony Eden, later the Earl of Avon (UK), Cordell Hull (USA), Vyacheslav M. Skryabin, alias Molotov (USSR) and Ambassador Foo Ping-sheung (China).

Ways and means were resolved at the mansion of Dumbarton Oaks, Washington DC, USA, between 21 Aug and 7 Oct 1944. A final step was taken at San Francisco, California, USA, between 25 Apr and 26 June 1945 when delegates of 50 participating states signed the Charter (Poland signed on 15 Oct 1945). This came into force on 24 Oct 1945, when the four above-mentioned states, plus France and a majority of the other 46 states, had ratified the Charter. The first regular session was held in London on 10 Jan–14 Feb 1946. Thereafter, the organization moved to New York, USA.

Of the 170 de facto sovereign states of the world, 157 are now in membership, plus the two USSR republics of Byelorussia and the Ukraine which have separate membership. The non-members are:

Andorra	Monaco
China (Taiwan)	Nauru
Kiribati	San Marino
Korea, Democratic People's Republic of	Switzerland
	Tonga
Korea, Republic of	Tuvalu
Liechtenstein	Vatican City (Holy See)

UN member states, with year of joining

Afghanistan	1946
Albania	1955
Algeria	1962
Angola	1976
Antigua and Barbuda	1981
Argentina*	1945
Australia*	1945
Austria	1955
Bahamas	1973
Bahrain	1971
Bangladesh	1974
Barbados	1966
Belgium*	1945
Belize	1981
Benin	1960
Bhutan	1971
Bolivia*	1945
Botswana	1966
Brazil*	1945
Brunei	1984
Bulgaria	1955
Burkina Faso (Upper Volta)	1960
Burma	1948
Burundi	1962
Byelorussia*	1945
Cambodia (Kampuchea)	1955
Cameroon	1960
Canada*	1945
Cape Verde	1975
Central African Republic	1960
Chad	1960
Chile*	1945
China*	1945
Colombia*	1945
Comoros	1975
Congo	1960
Costa Rica*	1945
Cuba*	1945
Cyprus	1960
Czechoslovakia*	1945
Denmark*	1945
Djibouti	1977
Dominica	1978
Dominican Republic*	1945
Ecuador*	1945
Egypt*	1945
El Salvador*	1945
Equatorial Guinea	1968
Ethiopia*	1945
Fiji	1970
Finland	1955
France*	1945
Gabon	1960
Gambia	1965
German Democratic Republic	1973
German Federal Republic	1973
Ghana	1957
Greece*	1945
Grenada	1974
Guatemala*	1945
Guinea	1958
Guinea-Bissau	1974
Guyana	1966
Haiti*	1945
Honduras*	1945
Hungary	1955
Iceland	1946
India*	1945
Indonesia	1950
Iran*	1945
Iraq*	1945
Ireland	1955
Israel	1949
Italy	1955
Ivory Coast	1960
Jamaica	1962
Japan	1956
Jordan	1955
Kenya	1963
Kuwait	1963
Laos	1955
Lebanon*	1945
Lesotho	1966
Liberia*	1945
Libya	1955
Luxembourg*	1945
Madagascar	1960
Malawi	1964
Malaysia	1957
Maldives	1965
Mali	1960
Malta	1964
Mauritania	1961
Mauritius	1968
Mexico*	1945
Mongolia	1961
Morocco	1956
Mozambique	1975
Nepal	1955
Netherlands*	1945
New Zealand*	1945
Nicaragua*	1945
Niger	1960

Nigeria	1960
Norway*	1945
Oman	1971
Pakistan	1947
Panama*	1945
Papua New Guinea	1975
Paraguay*	1945
Peru*	1945
Philippines*	1945
Poland*	1945
Portugal	1955
Qatar	1971
Romania	1955
Rwanda	1962
St Christopher and Nevis	1983
St Lucia	1979
St Vincent and the Grenadines	1980
Samoa, Western	1976
São Tome and Principe	1975
Saudi Arabia*	1945
Senegal	1960
Seychelles	1976
Sierra Leone	1961
Singapore	1965
Solomon Islands	1978
Somalia	1960
South Africa*	1945
Spain	1955
Sri Lanka	1955
Sudan	1956
Suriname	1975
Swaziland	1968
Sweden	1946
Syria*	1945
Tanzania	1961
Thailand	1946
Togo	1960
Trinidad and Tobago	1962
Tunisia	1956
Turkey*	1945
Uganda	1962
Ukraine*	1945
USSR*	1945
United Arab Emirates	1971
UK*	1945
USA*	1945
Uruguay*	1945
Vanuatu	1981
Venezuela*	1945
Vietnam	1977
Yemen Arab Republic	1947
Yemen, People's Democratic Republic	1967
Yugoslavia*	1945
Zaire	1960
Zambia	1964
Zimbabwe	1980

*Original Member

The United Nations' principal organs are:

The General Assembly consisting of all member nations, each with up to five delegates but one vote, and meeting annually in regular sessions with provision for special sessions. The Assembly has seven main committees, on which there is the right of representation by all member nations. These are (1) Political and Security, (2) Economic and Financial, (3) Social, Humanitarian and Cultural, (4) Decolonization, (5) Administration and Budgetary, (6) Legal, and (7) Special Political.

The Security Council, consisting of 15 members, each with one representative, of whom there are five permanent members (China, France, the USSR, the UK and the USA) and 10 elected members serving a two-year term. Apart from procedural questions, an affirmative majority vote of at least nine must include that of all five permanent members. It is from this stipulation that the so-called veto arises.

The Economic and Social Council, consisting of 54 members elected for three-year terms, is responsible for carrying out the functions of the General Assembly's second and third Committees, viz. economic, social, educational, health and cultural matters. It has the following Functional Commissions: (1) Statistical, (2) Population, (3) Social Development, (4) Narcotic Drugs, (5) Human Rights, (6) Status of Women. The Council has also established Economic Commissions, as follows: (1) for Europe (ECE), (2) for Asia and the Pacific (ESCAP), (3) for Latin America (ECLA), (4) for Africa (ECA) and (5) for Western Asia (ECWA).

The International Court of Justice or World Court, comprising 15 judges (quorum of nine) of different nations, each serving a nine-year term and meeting at 's-Gravenhage (The Hague), Netherlands. All members of the UN plus Liechtenstein, San Marino and Switzerland are parties to the Statute of the Court. Only states may be parties in contentious cases. In the event of a party's failing to adhere to a judgement, the other party may have recourse to the Security Council. Judgements are final and without appeal but can be reopened on grounds of a new decisive factor within ten years.

The Secretariat. The principal administrative officer is the Secretary General who is appointed by the General Assembly for a five-year term. This office has been held by:

Trygve Halvdan Lie (1896–1968) (Norway) 1 Feb 1946–10 Nov 1952.

Dag Hjalmar Agne Carl Hammarskjold (1905–61) (Sweden) 10 Apr 1953–18 Sept 1961.

U Maung Thant (1909–74) (Burma) (acting) 3 Nov 1961–30 Nov 1962, (permanent) 30 Nov 1962–31 Dec 1971.

Kurt Waldheim (b. 21 Dec 1918) (Austria) 1 Jan 1972–31 Dec 1981.

Javier Perez de Cuellar (b. 19 Jan 1920) (Peru) 1 Jan 1982 (in office).

UN Peacekeeping

In the event of a dispute between member states, the Security Council or, in special circumstances, the General Assembly, may offer to mediate or negotiate a ceasefire. If requested, armed forces may be provided, under the control of the Secretary General, to supervise the ceasefire or monitor the disengagement, but these peacekeeping units, drawn from member states who volunteer their services and are acceptable to the states in conflict, have only limited powers. Only once, during the Korean War (1950–53) did the UN provide forces to fight, although during the Congo troubles (1960–64) they were used to intervene to put down an illegal revolt. In all other cases, if the host state requests it, the forces must be withdrawn and, if fighting breaks out anew, they cannot do more than defend themselves. The major UN Peacekeeping operations have been:

UNEF I	UN Emergency Force on the Egypt–Israel border 1956–67
UNOGIL	UN Observer Group in Lebanon 1958
ONUC	UN Congo Operation 1960–64
UNSF	UN Security Force, West Irian 1962–63
UNYOM	UN Yemen Observation Group 1963–64
UNFICYP	UN Force in Cyprus 1964-to date
UNIPOM	UN India and Pakistan Observer Mission 1965–66
UNEF II	UN Emergency Force on the Syrian–Israeli border, 1973-to date
UNIFIL	UN Interim Force in Lebanon 1978-to date

Specialized Agencies of the UN

There are 15 specialized agencies, which in order of absorption or creation, are:

ILO	International Labour Organization, concerned with social justice.
FAO	Food and Agriculture Organization, to improve the production and distribution of agricultural products worldwide.
UNESCO	UN Educational, Scientific and Cultural Organization, to stimulate popular education and the spread of culture.
ICAO	International Civil Aviation Organization, to encourage safety measures and co-ordinate facilities for international flight.
IBRD	International Bank for Reconstruction and Development (The World Bank), to aid development through capital investment.
IMF	International Monetary Fund, to promote international monetary co-operation.
UPU	Universal Postal Union, to unite members in a single postal territory.
WHO	World Health Organization, to promote the attainment by all peoples of the highest possible standards of health.
ITU	International Telecommunication Union, to allocate frequencies and standardize procedures.
WMO	World Meteorological Organization, to standardize meteorological observations and apply the information to the greatest international benefit, for shipping, agriculture, etc.
IFC	International Finance Corporation, to promote the flow of private capital internationally and to stimulate the capital markets.
IMCO	Inter-Governmental Maritime Consultative Organization, to co-ordinate safety at sea.
IDA	International Development Association, to assist less developed countries by providing credits on special terms.

WIPO	World Intellectual Property Organization, to promote the protection of intellectual property (inventions, designs, copyright, etc).
IFAD	International Fund for Agricultural Development, to generate grants or loans to increase food production in developing countries.

Defence abbreviations

AAM	air-to-air missile
ABM	anti-ballistic missile
ACDA	Arms Control and Disarmament Agency
ACM	Advanced Cruise Missile
ADCOM	Air Defense Command (US)
ADP	Automatic Data Processing
AEA	Atomic Energy Authority
AEC	Atomic Energy Commission
AERE	Atomic Energy Research Establishment
AEW	airborne early warning
AFCENT	Allied Forces Central Europe (NATO)
AFNORTH	Allied Forces Northern Europe (NATO)
AFSOUTH	Allied Forces Southern Europe (NATO)
AFV	armoured fighting vehicle
AGM	air-to-ground missile
ALB (2000)	AirLand Battle (2000)
ALBM	air-launched ballistic missile
ALCM	air-launched cruise missile
APC	armoured personnel carrier
APFSDS	armour-piercing fin-stabilized discarding sabot (tank round)
ASALM	advanced strategic air-launched missile
ASAT	anti-satellite
ASBM	air-to-surface ballistic missile
ASM	air-to-surface missile
ASROC	anti-submarine rocket
ASW	anti-submarine warfare
ATB	advanced technology bomber (Stealth)
ATGW	anti-tank guided weapon
AWACS	airborne warning and control system
AWDREY	atomic weapons detection, recognition and estimation of yield
AWRE	Atomic Weapons Research Establishment
BMD	ballistic missile defence
BMEWS	ballistic missile early warning system
C³I	command, control, communication and information
CBM	confidence-building measures
CBW	chemical and biological warfare
CCD	Conference of the Committee on Disarmament
CD	Committee on Disarmament
CENTO	Central Treaty Organization
CEP	circular error probable
CINCUSEUR	Commander-in-Chief US Forces Europe
CINCPAC	Commander-in-Chief Pacific (US)
CLGP	cannon-launched guided projectile
CND	Campaign for Nuclear Disarmament

CSCE	Conference on Security and Co-operation in Europe	NADGE	NATO Air Defence Ground Environment
CTB	comprehensive test ban	NATO	North Atlantic Treaty Organization
DIVADS	divisional air defence system	NBC	nuclear, biological, chemical
ECM	electronic counter-measures	NFZ	nuclear free zone
ELINT	electronic intelligence	NND	non-nuclear defence
EMP	electro-magnetic pulse	NOP	nuclear operations plans
END	European Nuclear Disarmament	NORAD	North American Aerospace Defense Command
ENDC	Eighteen Nation Disarmament Committee	NPG	Nuclear Planning Group (NATO)
ER-RB	enhanced radiation – reduced blast	NPT	non-proliferation treaty
ERW	enhanced radiation weapon	OAS	Organization of American States
EW	electronic warfare	OAU	Organization of African Unity
FBS	forward based systems	PGW	precision guided weapon
FOBS	fractional orbital bombardment system	PLSS	Precision Location Strike System
		PTBT	partial test-ban treaty
FOFA	Follow-On Forces Attack	RDJTF	Rapid Deployment Joint Task Force (US)
FROG	free rocket over ground		
GCC	Gulf Co-operation Council	RPV	remotely piloted vehicle
GLCM	ground-launched cruise missile	RV	re-entry vehicle
GSFG	Group of Soviet Forces Germany	SAC	Strategic Air Command (US)
GZ	ground zero	SACEUR	Supreme Allied Commander Europe (NATO)
HEAT	high explosive anti-tank (tank round)		
HESH	high explosive squash head (tank round)	SALT	Strategic Arms Limitation Talks/Treaty
HLG	High Level Group (NATO)	SAM	surface-to-air missile
IAEA	International Atomic Energy Agency	SCG	Special Consultative Group (NATO)
ICBM	intercontinental ballistic missile	SDI	Strategic Defense Initiative ('Star Wars')
IFV	infantry fighting vehicle		
IISS	International Institute for Strategic Studies	SEATO	South East Asia Treaty Organization
		SHAPE	Supreme Headquarters Allied Powers Europe (NATO)
INF	intermediate-range nuclear forces		
IRBM	intermediate-range ballistic missile	SIGINT	signals intelligence
JOINT-STARS	Joint surveillance and target attack radar system	SIOP	single integrated operational plan
		SIPRI	Stockholm International Peace Research Institute
KT	kiloton		
LNO	limited nuclear options	SLBM	submarine-launched ballistic missile
LNW	limited nuclear war	SLCM	submarine-launched cruise missile
LORAN	long-range navigation	SOSUS	sound surveillance system
LOW	launch on warning	SRAM	short-range attack missile
LRTNF	long-range theatre nuclear force	SRBM	short-range ballistic missile
LRTNW	long-range theatre nuclear weapons	SSBN	sub-surface ballistic nuclear (submarine)
MAD	mutual assured destruction		
MARV	manoeuvrable re-entry vehicle	SSM	surface-to-surface missile
MBFR	mutual and balanced force reductions	SSN	sub-surface nuclear (submarine)
MBT	main battle tank	START	Strategic Arms Reduction Talks
MICV	mechanized infantry combat vehicle	SUBROC	submarine rocket
MIRV	multiple independently targetable re-entry vehicle	TAC	Tactical Air Command
		TEL	transporter-erector-launcher
MLF	multi-lateral force	TERCOM	terrain contour-matching guidance system
MLRS	multi-launch rocket system		
MNF	multi-national force	TNF	theatre nuclear forces
MRASM	medium-range air-to-surface missile	TNW	theatre nuclear weapons
MRBM	medium-range ballistic missile	TTBT	Threshold Test Ban Treaty
MRL	multiple rocket launcher	UNSSD	United Nations Special Session on Disarmament
MRTNF	medium-range theatre nuclear force		
MRV	multiple re-entry vehicle	UNO	United Nations Organization
MT	megaton	USAF (E)	United States Air Force (Europe)
M-X	missile experimental	WTO	Warsaw Treaty Organization

ECONOMICS

Economics is a relatively recent development when considered amongst the history of sciences. The word *economics* was earlier (since 1393) used for the art of housekeeping. Its modern sense of the practical and theoretical science of the production and distribution of wealth was first used in the context of rural economics in 1792. The earliest attempt at a rigorous treatment, however, dates from Galiani's *Della Moneta* published in 1751.

The first major landmark in the history of economic thought was in 1776 with the publication of the handbook of the Industrial Revolution, *An Enquiry into the Nature and Causes of the Wealth of Nations* by Adam Smith (1723–90), the Scottish professor of logic and moral philosophy. He propounded the theory that a whole community achieves the benefit of the largest possible total wealth through the delicate market balance of free competition and man's conflicting self-interests. Further major stages in the development of economic theory are:

1798 Thomas Malthus (1766–1834) *An Essay on the Principle of Population.* Over-population was the death knell of economic growth and prosperity.
1848 John Stuart Mill (1806–73) *Principles of Political Economy.* Value of any commodity depended upon the amount of all factors going into its production.
1848 Karl Marx (1818–83) *The Communist Manifesto.* Written with Friedrich Engels.
1867 Karl Marx *Das Kapital* Vol 1 (Vol 2, 1885, Vol 3, 1894). Theory of 'surplus value' accruing to the insatiable capitalist. Free enterprise system is self-destructive and a 'dictatorship of the proletariat' would follow.
1890 Alfred Marshall (1842–1924) *Principles of Economics.* Utility and costs are the joint determinants of value.
1936 John Maynard Keynes (1883–1946) *The General Theory of Employment, Interest and Money.* Duty of state to dispel depressions by higher public expenditure, even at the price of persistent inflation.
1962 Milton Friedman (b. 1912) *Capitalism and Freedom.* Duty of states with large inflationary public sector economies to restore prosperity by cutting public spending and borrowing.

Glossary

annuity An asset for which the owner receives a regular annual income of a specified figure.
arbitrage Process of making a buying or selling margin out of differences in commodity prices or currency values in different markets.
assets Resources employed within an enterprise to conduct its business.
asset stripping Purchasing a business with the motive of selling off its assets at a profit above the purchase price instead of perpetuating it.
Austrian School A group of University of Vienna

deductive economists led by Carl Menger (1840–1921), von Wieser (1851–1926) and von Böhm-Bawerk (1851–1914). Followed in the 20th century by Ludwig von Mises (1881–1973) and Friedrich Hayek (b. 1899) who oppose the Keynesian ascendancy of macro-economics.
authorized capital The share capital registered when a company is set up under the Companies Acts.
averaging If the price of shares falls below the price brought at, more can be bought at this price and so reduce the average cost per share.

backwardation A percentatge charge paid by the seller of stock for the right to delay delivery.
balance of payments Balance of international transactions and transfers for goods (imports and exports) and services (invisibles).
balance of trade The solely *current* account sector of the balance of payments. This latter also embraces the capital account.
bank rate The rate at which a central bank will lend to its national banking system. In Britain this rate was pivotal to interest levels until replaced by Minimum Lending Rate or MLR (now discontinued).
banks, joint stock Banks whose principal function is to receive deposits and make short-term loans, mainly for working capital. Also described as commercial banks.
base rate Banks lend money to borrowers where there are no risks attached at base rate. For borrowers who are less creditworthy a higher rate of interest above the base rate is charged.
bear Speculators who sell on a falling market in the hope that they may buy back at a lower level.
'big bang' The name given to 27 Oct 1986 when the London Stock Exchange's new regulations took effect. Fixed commissions charged by stockbrokers for share transactions were abolished. The term has also been extended to refer to the merger between different types of financial institutions following the liberalization of City demarcation lines by the British authorities.
bill of exchange A transferable and unconditional order drawn by a creditor on a debtor for discharge on an agreed fixed date – hence a 90 day bill.
blue chip Originally an American expression originating from gambling where the highest value chips were coloured blue. Now the expression is widely used to describe an equity share of a company with a good financial reputation.
bridging loan Often applied to bank or other loans where the borrower is prepared to bear interest for a fixed period, to avoid losing an intended new investment, while anticipating the sale of another.
bull Speculators who buy stock in the belief that they will be able to sell it at a profit (see bear).

capitalism A social system in which work is undertaken for individual reward, under a system of free contract, and capital is ownable by private persons.
cartels Associations which limit competition by price-fixing and/or market-sharing.

The statue of Karl Marx and Friedrich Engels, authors of *The Communist Manifesto*, in Karl Marx Stadt, a county capital in the south of the German Democratic Republic. (Popperfoto)

CIF Cost, insurance, freight. The inclusion of these on-costs in the quoted price.

communism The official doctrine, originating from Lenin's interpretation of the writings of Marx, which controls the USSR, China, Eastern European and other countries. A system of society with vesting of property in the community, each member working for the common benefit according to his capacity and receiving according to his needs.

debenture A fixed-interest security which is issued by a company in return for a loan. It can be traded on the Stock Exchange.

deferred shares A share issued by a company which has a fixed or very stable dividend pay-out to its equity shareholders. After the dividend payments have been made, any profits outstanding accrue to the holders of the deferred shares. Because of the risk attached they are now seldom seen.

deflation When prices are forced up because demand exceeds supply of goods (inflation), the country's economy is sometimes deflated. The normal way of achieving this is to reduce demand by, for example, raising interest rates, increasing taxation and reducing public spending.

demurrage Payment by a shipper to a shipowner for discharging or loading delays beyond the stipulated time contracted.

depreciation The decrease in the value of an asset due to wear and tear, age, obsolescence or fall in market price.

devaluation Reducing the value of the nation's currencies thereby cheapening exports and raising the price of imports.

discounted cash flow The discounting of cash flows to present value to determine or compare the viability of a project.

disinflation Measures to relieve inflationary stress such as running a budget surplus, credit squeezes or hire purchase controls.

dividend Money yield per share from the profits or reserves of a company.

dumping The often criticized practice of exporting goods at prices below the cost of production, thereby selling at prices lower than that offered by the country's home market.

elasticity of demand Responsiveness or sensitivity of demand to a change in price. Inelastic demand is insensitive.

entrepreneur One who risks his own capital in an enterprise.

equity Ordinary (as opposed to preference) shares holding in a limited company.

Euro-currency A currency which is deposited in banks in a foreign country on a large scale. The main Euro-currency is the Euro-dollar. Euro-dollars are dollar deposits held outside the US banks.

exchange rate The price at which one particular currency can be exchanged for another.

exports Sales overseas or abroad of a country's goods (visible exports) or services (invisible exports).

factoring A means of raising money on debts. If supplier A owes money to supplier B and is unlikely to pay in the immediate future, then supplier B can sell the debt to a further supplier for less than face value.

fiduciary issues Issue of notes 'in faith' unbacked by gold or tangible assets.

floating exchange rate Exchange rates which are not fixed and which fluctuate according to foreign exchange market supply or demand.

foreign exchange market Financial centres in which foreign currency is bought and sold by dealers. In Britain these include banks, finance houses and exchange brokers.

forward market A market where contracts for dealings in commodities, currencies or securities for future delivery can be fixed at the time the deal is made.

free trade Trade which flows freely and without tariffs or other distortions so that the benefit of international specialisation is globally maximized.

funded debt Perpetual loans or debts with no fixed repayment date.

galloping inflation A condition of rapidly rising prices.

general agreement on tariffs and trade (GATT) Established in Geneva in 1947 it aims to eliminate all barriers to trade through non-discrimination and a negotiated reduction in tariffs.

gilt-edged securities Those considered absolutely safe for purposes of interest and redemption at par when they mature.

gold standard A monetary system in which the gold value of the currency is fixed by law.

Gresham's Law Tendency for money of lower intrinsic value to circulate more freely than money of higher intrinsic and equal nominal value.

hard currency Currency is 'hard' if it has an underlying strength based on internal stability and external surplus on balance of trade.

hedge The way in which investors reduce the risk in a contract by making purchases in forward markets.

hyper-inflation Inflation so rapid that contracts can be shortened no further and flight from the currency is total, thus leading to a total economic breakdown, e.g. Germany (1922–23), Hungary (1946), China (1948–49).

indexed pension Pension rates annually or periodically adjusted to preserve value by allowing for rises (and falls) in the Retail Price Index.

indirect taxes Taxes on goods and services collected indirectly through traders or manufacturers (as opposed to direct collection as in case of income tax).

inflation A fall in the value of money caused by expansion of money supply, high public spending, credit creation, high wage settlements etc.

interest The price payable for the use of loanable funds or credit.

invisibles The international trade in services as opposed to visible goods. It includes banking, insurance and shipping as well as, for example, air transport, tourism, royalties from goods sold abroad, etc.

issued capital When a company is legally set up it is entitled to borrow a certain amount of money by issuing shares. This entitlement cannot be taken out in full. The part which is issued is known as its issued capital.

Keynesianism The doctrine of the macro-economist Lord Keynes (1883–1946), adopted by the British Government in 1944, that generation of demand

Gas oil dealers in US style trading 'pits' at Commodity Quay, new home of the International Exchange or London Commodity Exchange. (Popperfoto)

by public spending (or budget deficit) will promote faster expansion, more private investment and higher employment levels.

liquidity The ease and speed with which an asset can be exchanged. Cash has 'perfect' liquidity whereas a deposit account requiring notice of withdrawal has not.

M1 Total money supply in its most liquid form (coin, banknotes, and immediately encashable assets).

M2 (Not used since 1972) M1 plus clearing bank and discount house deposits.

M3 M1 plus assets liquefiable in the short term, *viz* Building Society deposits and shares enchashable within the account period.

market economy Conditions of competitive, noncentralized supply and demand that operates like a continuous referendum, between consumers and manufacturers, buyers and sellers, and lenders and borrowers.

Marxism The doctrine of the co-author of *The Communist Manifesto* (1848), Karl Marx (1818–1883). He advocated the abolition of private property, and State provision of work and subsistence for all.

minimum lending rate (MLR) The rate of interest charged by the central bank in any country.

monetarism The doctrine that the avoidance of inflation and deflation is better achieved by monetary rather than fiscal methods, i.e. by control over money supply (*via* interest rates, hire purchase and other credit creations, and levels of public spending and borrowing).

monopoly A company which is the only supplier of a certain good. In order to achieve maximum profits the company will keep prices above the cost of production and restrict output. Most governments try to control this practice.

national income The total of incomes of all residents, companies and government bodies derived from goods and services produced through economic activity.

negative income tax A device for alleviating poverty by 'topping up' the lowest band of incomes by fiscal rebate rather than by conventional social benefits.

nominal value The face value of an asset – usually a share or a bond. This is usually the value of the asset when it first appeared.

oligopoly A market where there is a small number of firms competing for a share in one particular product.

option In the context of stock markets, the purchase of a choice whether to buy or sell a share. In order to take advantage of a predicted change in the price of a share, an option can be bought, normally at a fraction of the cost of the share price. This option enables the shares to be bought or sold in the future at a price agreed now. An option to buy is known as a call option; to sell a put option; to buy or sell a double option.

ordinary shares An owner of this type of share is entitled to income from them, known as dividends. This is not guaranteed since if the company makes no profits there will be no pay out.

overmanning The employment of more labour than required to achieve efficient production due to

unfulfilled expectations of rising demand, anxiety to deny skilled workers to a competitor, or trade union pressure to prevent job losses.

par value The nominal or face value of a particular share. In the case of a government security with no risk of default the issue price is normally 100. If the price falls below 100 it is known to be below par and, conversely, above 100, above par.

PAYE Pay As You Earn system of collection of income tax from current earnings. developed from a German model by Sir Paul Chambers. Introduced into Britain in 1944.

preference shares These are fixed-interest shares and rank immediately after debentures (if issued) for dividends, and thus come before holders of ordinary shares. If a company does not pay dividends, holders of preference shares are entitled to receive extra dividends in future years when the company's position improves.

public sector borrowing requirement (PSBR) The amount by which the revenue of public sector organizations falls short of expenditure. This deficit, by central and local authorities and nationalized industries, is financed by sales of securities, increases in currency, borrowing from overseas and bank lending to the public sector.

reflation The initial and temporary phase in the upturn from a slump in which extra spending is matched by increased supply. Reflation ends and inflation starts if demand continues or grows to the point of raising prices.

retail price index (RPI) Commonly known as the cost of living index, it is a measure of the increase in prices in the shops. The UK's index is compiled by the Department of Employment each month.

reverse income tax *See* Negative Income Tax.

rights issue If a public company wants to raise more finance it can offer a new issue of its shares to existing shareholders. If, however, the shareholders do not wish to invest any more money with the company, they may sell the rights to the new issue to someone else. This type of issue is therefore known as a rights issue.

spot rate The rate of exchange of a currency or price of a commodity for immediate settlement and delivery.

stagflation A simultaneous presence of rises in prices and rises in unemployment levels once thought by economists to be mutually exclusive.

syndicalism A doctrine whereunder industry is controlled by workers.

treasury bills Bills issued by the Treasury (originating in 1873) in multiples of £5000 for short term (3 months) funding of Government debt.

value added tax A tax levied on the basis of the cost of 'inputs' of materials and labour as opposed to a turnover or sales tax.

zero price Economists jargon for a state service supplied at no cost to the eligible recipient at the time. The tax-price, paid by most people, is paid only later and indirectly.

Gross national product

The best means of measuring the economic power of a country is in its gross national product (GNP) and its national income.

GNP is derived from the gross domestic product plus income received from abroad, less payments made abroad.

Gross domestic product (GDP) is the sum of all output produced domestically. It is equal to domestic expenditure plus exports less imports. Estimates of GDP can be made in three ways: on an expenditure basis (how much money has been spent); on an output basis (how many goods have been sold); and on an income basis (how much income has been earned).

National income is the sum of all income received in an economy during a particular period of time. It is equal to the GNP product less depreciation.

World statistics

Country	Mid-1985 population ('000)	1985 Gross national product ($ million)	1985 GNP per head ($)
Afghanistan	18 136	2 290	160
Albania	2 962	1 930	740
Algeria	20 841	55 230	2 530
American Samoa	36	190	5 410
Andorra	47	n.a.	n.a.
Angola	8 754	3 320	470
Antigua and Barbuda	80	160	2 030
Argentina	30 564	65 080	2 130
Aruba	67	n.a.	n.a.
Australia	15 758	171 170	10 840
Austria	7 555	69 060	9 150
Bahamas	234	1 670	7 150
Bahrain	412	4 040	9 560
Bangladesh	98 657	14 770	150
Barbados	253	1 180	4 680
Belgium	9 859	83 230	8 450
Belize	166	180	1 130
Benin	3 932	1 080	270
Bermuda	68	1 030	13 070
Bhutan	1 165	190	160
Bolivia	6 429	3 010	470
Botswana	1 088	900	840
Brazil	135 564	222 010	1 640
Brunei	224	3 940	17 580
Bulgaria	8 959	37 390	4 150
Burkina Faso	7 747	1 080	140
Burma	39 411	7 080	190
Burundi	4 718	1 110	240
Cameroon	10 186	8 300	810
Canada	25 379	347 360	13 670
Cape Verde	334	140	430
Central African Republic	2 608	700	270
Chad	5 018	360	80
Channel Islands	136	1 350	10 390
Chile	12 122	17 230	1 440
China, People's Republic	1 045 320	318 920	310
China (Taiwan)	19 136	59 135	3 090

Country	Mid-1985 population ('000)	1985 Gross national product ($ million)	1985 GNP per head ($)
Colombia	27 867	37 610	1 320
Comoros	476	110	280
Congo	1 854	1 910	1 020
Costa Rica	2 489	3 340	1 290
Cuba	10 098	12 330	1 270
Cyprus	665	2 650	3 790
Czechoslovakia	15 500	89 260	5 820
Denmark	5 114	57 330	11 240
Djibouti	430	180	480
Dominica	83	90	1 160
Dominican Republic	6 243	5 050	810
East Timor	631	100	150
Ecuador	9 378	10 880	1 160
Egypt	48 503	32 220	680
El Salvador	4 819	3 940	710
Equatorial Guinea	300	62	180
Ethiopia	43 350	4 630	110
Faeroe Islands	46	500	10 930
Fiji	715	1 190	1 700
Finland	4 902	53 450	10 870
France	55 172	526 630	9 550
French Guiana	83	210	3 230
French Polynesia	170	1 370	7 840
Gabon	1 206	3 330	3 340
Gambia	688	170	230
German Democratic Republic	16 644	120 940	7 180
Germany, Federal Republic	61 020	667,970	10 940
Ghana	12 206	4 960	390
Gibraltar	29	130	4 370
Greece	9 934	35 250	3 550
Greenland	53	390	7 270
Grenada	89	90	970
Guadeloupe	331	1 370	4 330
Guam	120	670	5 470
Guatemala	7 963	9 890	1 240
Guinea	5 781	1 950	320
Guinea-Bissau	810	150	170
Guyana	790	460	570
Haiti	5 273	1 900	350
Honduras	4 372	3 190	730
Hong Kong	5 456	33 770	6 220
Hungary	10 649	20 720	1 940
Iceland	241	2 580	10 720
India	750 900	194 820	250
Indonesia	163 416	86 590	530
Iran	47 820	69 170	2 060
Iraq	14 110	39 500	3 020
Ireland	3 541	17 250	4 840
Isle of Man	64	380	5 910
Israel	4 233	21 140	4 920
Italy	57 128	371 050	6 520
Ivory Coast	9 300	6 250	620
Jamaica	2 190	2 090	940
Japan	120 754	1 366 040	11 330
Jordan	3 515	4 010	1 560
Kampuchea	7 284	570	70
Kenya	20 333	5 960	290
Kiribati	64	30	450
Korea, Democratic People's Republic	20 385	17 040	1 000
Korea, Republic	41 056	88 440	2 180
Kuwait	1 712	24 760	14 270
Laos	3 585	290	80
Lebanon	2 668	3 290	1 070

Country	Mid-1985 population ('000)	1985 Gross national product ($ million)	1985 GNP per head ($)
Lesotho	1 528	730	480
Liberia	2 189	1 040	470
Libya	3 637	27 000	7 500
Liechtenstein	27	n.a.	n.a.
Luxembourg	367	4 900	13 380
Macau	392	810	2 710
Madagascar	9 985	2 510	250
Malawi	7 058	1 160	170
Malaysia	15 681	31 930	2 050
Maldives	189	50	290
Mali	8 206	1 070	140
Malta	360	1 190	3 300
Martinique	328	1 320	4 260
Mauritania	1 339	700	410
Mauritius	1 020	1 110	1 070
Mexico	79 938	163 790	2 080
Monaco	27	n.a.	n.a.
Mongolia	1 891	1 100	700
Morocco	21 941	13 390	610
Mozambique	14 174	2 810	270
Namibia	1 550	1 660	1 520
Nauru	7	n.a.	n.a.
Nepal	16 625	2 610	160
Netherlands	14 484	132 920	9 180
Netherlands Antilles	172	1 610	6 110
New Caledonia	145	860	5 760
New Zealand	3 307	23 720	7 310
Nicaragua	3 058	2 760	850
Niger	5 686	1 250	200
Nigeria	95 198	75 940	760
Norway	4 153	57 580	13 890
Oman	1 242	8 360	7 080
Pacific Islands (Trust Territory)	142	160	1 100
Pakistan	96 180	36 230	380
Panama	2 180	4 400	2 020
Papua New Guinea	3 329	2 470	710
Paraguay	3 681	3 180	940
Peru	19 698	17 830	960
Philippines	54 668	32 630	600
Poland	37 203	78 960	2 120
Portugal	10 157	20 140	1 970
Puerto Rico	3 282	15 940	4 850
Qatar	257	5 110	15 980
Réunion	537	1 890	3 580
Romania	22 725	57 030	2 540
Rwanda	6 274	1 730	290
St Christopher and Nevis	46	70	1 520
St Lucia	134	160	1 210
St Vincent and the Grenadines	108	100	840
San Marino	22	n.a.	n.a.
São Tomé and Príncipe	108	30	310
Saudi Arabia	11 542	102 120	8 860
Senegal	6 397	2 400	370
Seychelles	65	160	2 430
Sierra Leone	3 700	1 380	370
Singapore	2 558	18 970	7 420
Solomon Islands	221	140	510
Somalia	4 653	1 450	270
South Africa	32 392	65 320	2 010
Spain	38 505	168 820	4 360
Sri Lanka	15 837	5 980	370
Sudan	20 564	7 350	330

Country	Mid-1985 population ('000)	1985 Gross national product ($ million)	1985 GNP per head ($)
Suriname	389	1 010	2 570
Swaziland	647	490	650
Sweden	8 350	99 050	11 890
Switzerland	6 472	105 180	16 380
Syria	10 268	17 060	1 630
Tanzania	21 733	5 840	270
Thailand	51 683	42 100	830
Togo	2 747	750	250
Tonga	97	70	730
Trinidad and Tobago	1 181	7 140	6 010
Tunisia	7 261	8 730	1 220
Turkey	50 664	56 060	1 130
Tuvalu	7	5	680
Uganda	13 225	3 290	230
USSR	277 540	1 212 030	4 550
United Arab Emirates	1 206	26 400	19 120
United Kingdom	56 618	474 190	8 390
USA	239 283	3 915 350	16 400
US Virgin Islands	108	1 030	9 280
Uruguay	2 983	4 980	1 660
Vanuatu	140	40	350
Venezuela	17 317	53 800	3 110
Vietnam	59 713	7 750	160
Western Samoa	159	110	660
Yemem Arab Republic	9 274	4 140	520
Yemen, People's Democratic Republic	2 294	1 130	540
Yugoslavia	23 123	47 900	2 070
Zaire	30 363	5 220	170
Zambia	6 242	2 620	400
Zimbabwe	8 175	5 450	650

Car ownership (1987)

	Persons per car	Total no. of cars
EUROPE		
Germany, Federal Republic	2·2	28 304 184
Iceland	2·3	105 000
Luxembourg	2·3	162 481
Switzerland	2·3	2 732 720
France	2·5	21 970 000
Italy	2·5	22 500 000
Sweden	2·5	3 366 570
Norway	2·6	1 623 137
United Kingdom	2·7	20 605 514
Austria	2·8	2 684 780
Belgium	2·8	3 497 818
Netherlands	2·8	5 117 748
Finland	2·9	1 698 671
Denmark	3·2	1 587 641
Gibraltar	3·3	9 500
Spain	4·0	9 750 000
German Democratic Republic	4·8	3 462 184
Ireland	4·8	736 595
Malta	4·8	80 000
Cyprus	5·1	130 000
Czechoslovakia	5·7	2 700 000
Greece	7·2	1 378 493

	Persons per car	Total no. of cars		Persons per car	Total no. of cars
Yugoslavia	7·8	2 972 807	Oman	11·0	112 500
Portugal	7·9	1 290 000	Malaysia	14·0	1 125 000
Hungary	8·4	1 660 300	Taiwan	20·2	945 000
Poland	10·2	3 650 000	Jordan	25·0	140 000
Bulgaria	12·0	775 000	Iran	28·0	1 575 000
USSR	24·0	11 750 000	Hong Kong	33·2	166 977
Romania	27·0	850 000	Iraq	45·0	350 000
Turkey	45·3	1 087 815	Korea, Republic of	48·8	844 360
Total*	5·2	158 238 958	Yemen Arab Republic	70·0	100 000
			Thailand	98·0	525 000
			Syria	102·0	100 000
			Sri Lanka	107·1	147 837
AMERICA			Philippines	155·0	350 000
USA	1·7	139 041 000	Indonesia	169·3	965 245
Canada	2·2	11 477 314	Yemen, People's Democratic		
Cayman Islands	2·4	8 500	Republic	190·0	12 000
Bermuda	2·7	21 000	Pakistan	240·0	400 000
Falkland Islands	2·7	750	Kampuchea	485·0	15 000
Puerto Rico	3·1	1 125 000	India	500·0	1 506 000
Bahamas	3·5	66 000	Laos	515·0	8 000
French Guiana	3·7	22 000	Afghanistan	605·0	30 000
French West Indies	3·8	175 000	Burma	1250·0	30 000
Netherlands (Antilles)	3·9	67 500	Bangladesh	3100·0	31 948
Barbados	7·6	33 500	China	3850·0	275 000
Argentina	7·9	3 928 000	Total*	62·1	42 992 418
Antigua	8·8	11 790			
Venezuela	11·0	1 800 000			
Suriname	12·0	32 500	**AFRICA**		
Brazil	13·5	10 025 000	Réunion	4·2	127 500
Panama	14·8	147 562	Libya	8·7	415 000
Mexico	15·0	5 200 000	South Africa	10·5	3 078 635
Uruguay	17·0	180 000	Seychelles	18·0	3 600
St Kitts	18·0	2 500	Swaziland	20·0	35 000
St Lucia	20·0	6 500	Algeria	30·0	725 000
Chile	24·0	500 000	Mauritius	33·0	31 000
Jamaica	24·0	100 000	Tunisia	40·0	175 000
St Vincent	24·0	4 316	Djibouti	45·0	10 000
Dominica	30·0	2 500	Zimbabwe	45·0	180 000
Costa Rica	32·5	80 000	Morocco	49·0	450 000
Guyana	39·0	20 250	Ivory Coast	60·0	165 000
Belize	48·0	3 500	Gabon	65·0	17 500
Colombia	48·0	600 000	Congo	70·0	25 000
Peru	50·4	390 520	Zambia	70·0	95 000
Dominican Republic	57·0	110 000	Senegal	75·0	87 500
Guatemala	64·0	125 000	Botswana	77·0	14 000
Paraguay	80·0	82 000	Egypt	115·0	425 000
Bolivia	85·8	74 848	Cameroon	120·0	85 000
El Salvador	88·0	55 000	Gambia	120·0	5 500
Nicaragua	105·0	31 500	Nigeria	125·0	750 000
Honduras	145·0	30 000	Equatorial Guinea	130·0	3 000
Ecuador	149·6	62 702	Togo	130·0	23 000
Haiti	220·0	30 000	Sierra Leone	150·0	24 000
Cuba	520·0	19 406	Kenya	155·0	130 000
Total*	3·8	175 713 058	Angola	175·0	50 000
			Mozambique	185·0	75 000
			Benin	200·0	20 000
			Madagascar	200·0	50 000
ASIA			Ghana	225·0	60 000
Kuwait	3·0	575 000	Mauritania	236·0	8 000
Brunei	3·2	70 000	Sudan	270·0	80 000
Qatar	3·7	85 392	Liberia	275·0	8 000
Japan	4·1	29 478 342	Guinea-Bissau	300·0	3 000
Arab Emirates	5.5	240 000	Central African Republic	325·0	8 000
Lebanon	6·0	450 000	Niger	340·0	18 000
Israel	6·5	655 827	Zaire	340·0	90 000
Saudi Arabia	8·7	1 325 000	Burkina Faso	430·0	11 000
Bahrain	8·9	108 000	Somalia	465·0	10 000
Singapore	10·2	250 000	Malawi	475·0	14 911

	Persons per car	Total no. of cars
Tanzania	485·0	45 000
Uganda	485·0	32 000
Rwanda	505·0	12 000
Guinea	510·0	12 000
Mali	550·0	15 000
Chad	630·0	8 000
Burundi	675·0	7 000
Ethiopia	985·0	44 000
Total*	70·8	7 761 146

OCEANIA

	Persons per car	Total no. of cars
Guam	1·0	110 000
New Zealand	2·1	1 550 000
Australia	2·2	7 072 800
New Caledonia	3·8	43 000
French Polynesia	4·8	34 000
Fiji	21·0	33 000
Vanuatu	40·0	3 500
Papua New Guinea	111·0˙	30 000
Total*	2·7	8 876 300
Grand Total*	12·0	393 581 880

* Total of countries listed only

Home ownership

Country/Area	Householders owning their dwellings (%)
Mongolia	100·0
Burundi	98·7
Tokelau	97·7
Pacific Islands	94·3
Samoa	93·4
Bangladesh	92·4
Thailand	88·6
Philippines	87·7
Indonesia	87·0
Cyprus	86·3
Tonga	85·1
India	84·6
Faeroe Islands	84·5
Cameroon	83·4
Iraq	83·0
Haiti	82·9
Paraguay	81·8
Syria	81·6
St Pierre and Miquelon	81·4
Turkey	80·7
Pakistan	78·4
Yemen	78·4
Bulgaria	77·3
Niue Island	76·0
Nepal	75·8
Cuba	74·7
St Vincent and the Grenadines	74·7
Tunisia	73·9
Barbados	73·5
Puerto Rico	73·4
San Marino	72·8
Dominican Republic	72·0
Honduras	71·8
New Zealand	70·9
Venezuela	70·9
American Samoa	70·7

Country	Householders owning their dwellings (%)
Yugoslavia	70·7
Greece	70·6
Israel	70·6
Iceland	70·3
Turks and Caicos	70·3
Iran	70·2
Bolivia	69·6
Peru	69·5
Sri Lanka	69·4
Montserrat	69·2
Argentina	69·1
Ireland	68·8
Hungary	68·5
Vietnam	68·4
Australia	68·1
Cayman Islands	67·8
Israel	67·2
Mexico	66·8
Norway	66·6
Nicaragua	66·1
Norfolk Island	66·0
Guadeloupe	64·6
USA	64·4
St Lucia	63·8
Canada	63·7
Channel Islands: Guernsey	63·5
Finland	62·9
Panama	62·9
Libya	62·5
Ecuador	60·8
Bahrain	60·6
Brazil	60·4
Japan	59·8
Martinique	59·6
Trinidad and Tobago	59·3
Sudan	59·2
Korea, Republic	58·6
Belize	57·9
St Helena	57·7
St Christopher and Nevis	57·2
Spain	57·2
El Salvador	56·9
Guyana	56·8
Guatemala	56·7
Costa Rica	56·3
Congo, People's Republic	56·2
Antigua	55·9
Luxembourg	55·9
Bahamas	55·1
Singapore	55·0
Denmark	54·9
Sweden	54·9
British Virgin Islands	54·5
Réunion	54·5
Belgium	53·6
Colombia	53·5
Austria	52·9
Chile	52·3
Jamaica	52·1
Italy	50·9
Brunei	50·3
Turkey	49·3
Channel Islands: Jersey	48·8
New Caledonia	48·8
Jordan	48·5
Mauritius	48·5
Zimbabwe	48·0
Zaire	47·4
France	46·7

Home ownership *continued*

Country/Area	Householders owning their dwellings (%)
Guam	46·0
UK: Northern Ireland	45·6
Czechoslovakia	44·7
Portugal	44·5
Suriname	44·0
Egypt	43·0
UK: England and Wales	43·0
Netherlands Antilles	40·5
Bermuda	39·6
Malawi	39·6
Uruguay	39·4
French Guiana	37·9
Seychelles	37·2
Morocco	37·0
Poland	36·3
Greenland	36·1
Germany, Federal Republic	36·0
Sweden	35·2
UK: Scotland	34·7
Malta	32·4
US Virgin Islands	30·5
Kuwait	29·9
Ethiopia	28·1
Switzerland	28·1
Hong Kong	27·9
Monaco	26·3
Netherlands	25·7
Tanzania	25·7
Germany, Democratic Republic	23·0
Papua New Guinea	16·3
Nigeria	8.0
Gibraltar	4·4
Cocos (Keeling) Islands	0·7
Christmas Island	0·6
USSR	n.a.

Life expectancy, years at birth, 1985

Males

Country	Life expectancy
Japan	74·84
Iceland	73·96
Hong Kong	73·80
Sweden	73·79
Switzerland	73·50
Faeroe Islands	73·30
Israel	73·10
Netherlands	72·94
Norway	72·80
Cuba	72·66
Spain	72·55
Australia	72·32
Cyprus	72·26
Greece	72·15
Canada	71·88
United Kingdom	71·80
Denmark	71·60
USA	71·20
Germany, Federal Republic	71·18
Italy	71·05
France	71·04
New Zealand	70·97
Malta	70·76

Country	Life expectancy
Puerto Rico	70·53
Costa Rica	70·50
Austria	70·40
Jamaica	70·30
Ireland	70·14
Brunei	70·13
Finland	70·07
UK: Scotland	70·05
Belgium	70·04
Luxembourg	70·00
Kuwait	69·60
German Democratic Republic	69·52
UK: Northern Ireland	69·25
Panama	69·20
Bermuda	68·81
Singapore	68·70
Albania	68·51
Bulgaria	68·35
Portugal	68·35
Sri Lanka	67·78
Yugoslavia	67·69
Malaysia	67·64
Romania	67·42
St Lucia	67·20
Barbados	67·15
Czechoslovakia	67·11
Martinique	67·00
Trinidad and Tobago	66·88
China	66·70
Venezuela	66·68
Poland	66·50
Guadeloupe	66·40
Seychelles	66·16
Bahrain	65·90
Guyana	65·80
Uruguay	65·66
Hungary	65·60
Suriname	65·60
Réunion	65·50
Argentina	65·43
Qatar	65·40
United Arab Emirates	65·40
Chile	65·03
Korea, Democratic People's Republic	64·60
Mauritius	64·38
Syrian Arab Republic	63·77
Cook Islands	63·17
Lebanon	63·10
USSR	62·87
Paraguay	62·80
Korea, Republic	62·70
El Salvador	62·60
Mexico	62·10
Jordan	61·90
Algeria	61·57
Iraq	61·50
Colombia	61·40
Samoa	61·00
Brazil	60·90
Fiji	60·72
Dominican Republic	60·70
Greenland	60·40
Philippines	60·20
Tunisia	60·10
Mongolia	60·00
Turkey	60·00
Ecuador	59·51
Saudi Arabia	59·20
Pakistan	59·04

Country	Life expectancy
Cape Verde	58·95
Burma	58·93
Nicaragua	58·70
Thailand	57·63
Peru	56·80
Vietnam	56·70
Libya	56·60
Morocco	56·60
Iran	55·75
Guatemala	55·11
Bangladesh	54·90
Zimbabwe	54·00
Maldives	53·44
Honduras	53·38
India	52·50
Botswana	52·32
Indonesia	52·20
South Africa	51·80
Haiti	51·20
Kenya	51·20
Papua New Guinea	51·20
Oman	51·00
Nepal	50·88
Ghana	50·30
Zambia	49·60
Tanzania	49·30
Cameroon	49·20
Madagascar	48·90
Ivory Coast	48·80
Togo	48·80
Bolivia	48·60
Comoros	48·30
Laos	48·30
Zaire	48·30
Gabon	47·40
Uganda	47·40
Liberia	47·36
Mali	46·90
Nigeria	46·90
Yemen Arab Republic	46·90
Yemen, People's Democratic Republic	46·90
Bhutan	46·60
Namibia	46·60
Sudan	46·60
Lesotho	46·30
Rwanda	45·10
Burundi	44·90
Congo	44·90
Mozambique	44·40
Burkina Faso	43·70
Swaziland	42·90
Benin	42·40
Equatorial Guinea	42·40
Mauritania	42·40
Kampuchea	42·00
Senegal	41·70
Central African Republic	41·40
Chad	41·40
Guinea-Bissau	41·40
Niger	40·90
Angola	40·40
Ethiopia	39·30
Somalia	39·30
East Timor	39·20
Guinea	38·70
Malawi	38·12
Afghanistan	36·60
Gambia	33·50
Sierra Leone	32·50

Life expectancy, years at birth, 1985

Females

Country	Life expectancy
Japan	80·46
Iceland	80·20
Switzerland	80·00
Sweden	79·68
Netherlands	79·67
Faeroe Islands	79·60
Norway	79·51
France	79·19
Hong Kong	79·19
Canada	78·98
Australia	78·76
Spain	78·59
Finland	78·49
USA	78·20
Germany, Federal Republic	77·79
Italy	77·78
United Kingdom	77·74
Denmark	77·50
Puerto Rico	77·39
Austria	77·36
Belgium	76·79
Luxembourg	76·70
Israel	76·60
Greece	76·35
Bermuda	76·28
Cuba	76·10
Malta	76·01
Cyprus	75·99
UK: Scotland	75·83
Costa Rica	75·70
Jamaica	75·70
UK: Northern Ireland	75·65
Ireland	75·62
German Democratic Republic	75·42
St Lucia	75·30
Portugal	75·20
Poland	74·81
Czechoslovakia	74·31
Réunion	74·00
Singapore	74·00
Albania	73·78
Kuwait	73·70
Hungary	73·57
Bulgaria	73·55
Martinique	73·50
Seychelles	73·46
Yugoslavia	73·23
Panama	72·85
Venezuela	72·80
USSR	72·73
Malaysia	72·70
Brunei	72·69
Barbados	72·46
Uruguay	72·41
Guadeloupe	72·40
Romania	72·18
Argentina	72·12
Chile	71·69
Sri Lanka	71·66
Trinidad and Tobago	71·62
Mauritius	71·23
Korea, Democratic People's Republic	71·00
Guyana	70·80
Suriname	70·60
Qatar	69·80

Life expectancy, years at birth, 1985 continued

Country	Life expectancy
United Arab Emirates	69·80
Korea, Republic	69·07
Bahrain	68·90
China	68·90
Paraguay	67·50
El Salvador	67·10
Cook Islands	67·09
Lebanon	67·00
Greenland	66·30
Brazil	66·00
Colombia	66·00
Mexico	66·00
Jordan	65·50
Syrian Arab Republic	64·70
Dominican Republic	64·40
Samoa	64·30
Mongolia	64·10
Fiji	63·87
Philippines	63·70
Burma	63·66
Thailand	63·56
Algeria	63·32
Iraq	63·30
Turkey	63·30
Saudi Arabia	62·70
Ecuador	61·83
Tunisia	61·10
Vietnam	61·10
Cape Verde	61·04
Nicaragua	61·00
Peru	60·50
Libya	60·00
Morocco	60·00
Botswana	59·70
Egypt	59·50
Guatemala	59·43
Pakistan	59·20
Zimbabwe	57·60
Honduras	56·93
South Africa	55·20
Iran	55·04
Indonesia	54·90
Bangladesh	54·70
Kenya	54·70
Haiti	54·40
Ghana	53·80
Oman	53·70
Zambia	53·10
Bolivia	53·00
Papua New Guinea	52·70
Tanzania	52·70
Cameroon	52·60
Lesotho	52·30
Ivory Coast	52·20
Togo	52·20
India	52·10
Comoros	51·70
Zaire	51·70
Laos	51·20
Gabon	50·70
Uganda	50·70
Liberia	50·69
Madagascar	50·40
Nigeria	50·20
Namibia	49·90
Yemen Arab Republic	49·90

Country	Life expectancy
Yemen, People's Democratic Republic	49·90
Mali	49·66
Maldives	49·51
Swaziland	49·50
Sudan	49·00
Burundi	48·10
Congo	48·10
Nepal	48·10
Rwanda	47·70
Burkina Faso	46·80
Mozambique	46·20
Benin	45·60
Equatorial Guinea	45·60
Mauritania	45·60
Bhutan	45·10
Kampuchea	44·90
Senegal	44·90
Central African Republic	44·60
Chad	44·60
Guinea-Bissau	44·60
Niger	44·10
Angola	43·60
Ethiopia	42·50
Somalia	42·50
Guinea	41·80
Malawi	41·16
East Timor	40·70
Afghanistan	37·30
Gambia	36·50
Sierra Leone	35·50

Alcoholic liquor consumption (Average per annum)

Country	Wine (litres per head)	Beer (litres per head)	Spirits (litres per head of 100% alcohol)
Argentina	73.2	7.9	1.3
Australia	18·2	134·1	1·1
Austria	35·1	104·8	1·5
Belgium	21·0	124·0	2·1
Brazil	2·6	19·0	n.a.
Bulgaria	25·2	60·9	3·2
Canada	8·9	86·4	3·4
Chile	43·7	17·0	n.a.
Czechoslovakia	16·0	140·1	3·6
Denmark	16·1	131·0	1·6
Finland	8·8	57·1	2·8
France	89·0	44·0	2·5
German Democratic Republic	10·3	141·4	4·8
Germany, Federal Republic	24·7	147·0	2·8
Greece	44·9	34·6	n.a.
Hungary	29·7	88·0	5·0
Ireland	3·6	116·4	1·9
Italy	92·9	17·9	1·9
Japan	0·6	39·4	1·8
Mexico	0·3	40·0	0·9
Netherlands	13·0	89·6	2·5
New Zealand	14·5	117·7	2·0
Norway	4·2	44·8	1·6
Peru	1·1	28·7	1·4
Poland	7·5	28·6	4·3

Country	Wine (litres per head)	Beer (litres per head)	Spirits (litres per head of 100% alcohol)	Country	Wine (litres per head)	Beer (litres per head)	Spirits (litres per head of 100% alcohol)
Portugal	71·7	36·6	0·8	Switzerland	48·2	71·0	2·1
Romania	28·9	45·0	2·0	United Kingdom	8·6	111·5	1·7
South Africa	9·4	34·6	1·4	USA	8·2	93·3	3·0
Spain	59·0	55·2	3·0	USSR	12·8	23·4	3·3
Sweden	9·7	45·2	2·5	Yugoslavia	26·9	44·2	2·0

United Kingdom Expectation of Remaining Length of Life (1982–84)

Age	England and Wales Males	Females	Scotland Males	Females	Northern Ireland Males	Females
0	71·6	77·4	69·6	75·6	70·2	76·2
5	67·5	73·2	65·6	71·4	66·3	72·2
10	62·6	68·3	60·7	66·5	61·4	67·3
15	57·7	63·4	55·8	61·6	56·4	62·3
20	52·9	58·5	51·0	56·7	51·7	57·4
25	48·1	53·6	46·2	51·7	47·0	52·5
30	43·3	48·7	41·5	46·9	42·2	47·7
35	38·5	43·8	36·7	42·0	37·5	42·8
40	33·7	39·0	32·0	37·2	32·8	38·0
45	29·1	34·2	27·4	32·6	28·2	33·3
50	24·6	29·7	23·1	28·1	23·8	28·7
55	20·4	25·3	19·1	23·8	19·8	24·3
60	16·6	21·1	15·6	19·9	16·0	20·2
65	13·2	17·2	12·4	16·2	12·8	16·4
70	10·3	13·6	9·7	12·8	9·9	12·8
75	7·9	10·4	7·4	9·8	7·4	9·7
80	5·9	7·7	5·6	7·2	5·5	7·1
85	4·4	5·5	4·3	5·2	4·2	5·1

Changes in OECD Consumer Prices (%)
(Organisation for Economic Cooperation and Development)

	1982	1983	1984	1985	1986	1987
Australia	11·1	10·1	3·9	6·8	9·1	8·5
Austria	5·4	3·3	5·6	3·2	1·7	1·4
Belgium	8·7	7·7	6·3	4·9	1·3	1·6
Canada	10·8	5·9	4·3	4·0	4·2	4·4
Denmark	10·1	6·9	6·3	4·7	3·6	4·0
Finland	9·6	8·3	7·1	5·9	3·6	3·7
France	11·8	9·6	7·4	5·8	2·7	3·1
Germany, Federal Republic	5·3	3·3	2·4	2·2	−0·2	0·2
Greece	21·0	20·2	18·5	19·3	23·0	16·4
Iceland	49·1	86·5	30·9	31·9	22·2	n.a.
Ireland	17·1	10·5	8·6	5·4	3·8	3·2
Italy	16·6	14·6	10·8	8·6	6·1	4·6
Japan	2·7	1·9	2·2	2·1	0·4	−0·2
Luxembourg	9·4	8·7	5·6	4·1	0·3	−0·1
Netherlands	6·0	2·8	3·3	2·3	0·2	−0·5
New Zealand	7·8	7·4	6·2	15·4	13·2	15·7
Norway	11·3	8·4	6·2	5·7	7·2	8·7
Portugal	22·4	25·5	29·3	19·3	11·7	n.a.
Spain	14·4	12·2	11·3	8·8	8·8	5·3
Sweden	8·6	8·9	8·0	7·4	4·3	4·2
Switzerland	5·6	3·0	3·0	3·4	0·7	1·5
Turkey	32·7	28·8	45·6	45·0	34·6	38·9
UK	8·6	4·6	5·0	6·1	3·4	4·2
USA	6·1	3·2	4·3	3·6	1·9	3·7

COUNTRIES OF THE WORLD

Afghanistan

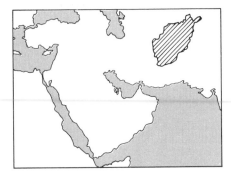

Official name: Jamhuria Afghanistan (Pushtu): The Republic of Afghanistan.
Population: 18 614 000 (official estimate of 1986) – this includes estimates for nomadic population (2 734 000) but takes no account of refugees living in Pakistan (estimated in 1988 at 2 800 000) and other countries (a further 2 200 000).
Area: 652 225 km² (*251 773 miles²*).
Languages: Dari (a Persian dialect), Pushtu (Pushtu or Pakhto).
Religion: Islam (mostly Sunni).
Capital city: Kabul, population 1 036 407 (including suburbs) at 1982 estimate.
Other principal towns (1982): Qandahar (Kandahar) 191 345; Herat 150 497; Mazar-i-Sharif 110 367; Jalalabad 57 824; Kunduz 57 824.
Highest point: Noshaq, 7492 m (*24 581 ft*) (first climbed 17 Aug 1960).
Principal mountain ranges: Hindu Kush, Koh-i-Baba, Band-i-Baian, Band-i-Baba, Paropamisus, Paghman.
Principal rivers: Helmand, Bandihala-Khoulm, Kabul, Murghab, Kunduz, Hari Rud, Farah Rud, Ab-i-Panja.
Head of State: Dr Sayid Mohammed Najibullah, President of the Revolutionary Council and General Secretary of the Central Committee of the People's Democratic Party.
Prime Minister: Dr Mohammed Hasan Sharq.
Climate: Wide variations between highlands and lowlands. Average annual rainfall 300 mm (*12 in*). In Kabul, July (16°C *61°F* to 33°C *92°F*) and August (15°C *59°F* to 33°C *91°F*) hottest; January (−8°C (*18°F*) to 2°C (*36°F*)) coldest; March rainiest (7 days). Maximum temperature up to 49°C (*120°F*); minimum below −23°C (−*10°F*).
Labour force: 3 868 081 (settled population only) aged 8 and over (1979 census): Agriculture, forestry and fishing 61·3%; Industry (mining, manufacturing, utilities) 12·8% (manufacturing 10·9%); Services 24·6%. Figures exclude persons seeking work for the first time.
Net material product: 100 400 million afghanis (1985/6): Agriculture, forestry, fishing 64·8%; mining, quarrying, manufacturing 16·2%.
Exports: US$ 846 million in 1983/4: Natural gas 41·96%; dried fruit 26·3%; fresh fruit 9·1%.
Monetary unit: Afghani. 1 afghani = 100 puls (puli).
Denominations:
Coins 25, 50 puls; 1, 2, 5 afghanis.
Notes 10, 20, 50, 100, 500, 1000 afghanis.
Political history and government: Formerly an hereditary kingdom, under British influence until 1919. Afghanistan became a limited constitutional monarchy, without political parties, on 1 Oct 1964. A bicameral parliament was inaugurated on 16 Oct 1965. The last king, Zahir Shah, was deposed by a military *coup* on 17 July 1973, when the Republic of Afghanistan was proclaimed, the constitution abrogated and parliament dissolved. The king abdicated on 24 Aug 1973. Government was

AFGHANISTAN
assumed by a 13-man Central council of the Republic, led by Lt-Gen. Muhammad Da'ud, a former Prime Minister, who became President. Da'ud was deposed and killed in another *coup* (known, from the month, as the 'Saur Revolution') on 27 Apr 1978, when power was assumed by an Armed Forces Revolutionary Council (AFRC). On 30 Apr 1978 the Democratic Republic of Afghanistan (DRA) was proclaimed and the AFRC incorporated into a new Revolutionary Council. Nur Muhammad Taraki, imprisoned leader of the formerly banned People's Democratic Party of Afghanistan (PDPA), was released and installed as President of the Revolutionary Council. The 1977 republican constitution was abolished. On 16 Sept 1979 Taraki was overthrown and succeeded as President by the Prime Minister, Hafizullah Amin. On 27 Dec 1979 Amin was deposed and killed in a Soviet-backed *coup*, supported by the entry into Afghanistan of thousands of USSR troops, which brought Babrak Karmal into office as Head of State. Since then opponents of the government have waged a guerrilla war.

A provisional constitution, 'Basic Principles of the DRA', was ratified by the PDPA on 13 Apr 1980 and by the Revolutionary Council on the following day. This provided for the establishment of a *Loya Jirgah* (National Assembly), to be directly elected by adult suffrage. Pending elections to the Assembly, supreme power was vested in the 57-member Revolutionary Council. This body rules by decree and appoints the Council of Ministers. Political power is held by the Central Committee of the pro-Communist PDPA. In February 1989 Soviet forces were withdrawn. A civil war between the central Government and nationalist forces continues.

Afghanistan has 29 provinces, each administered by an appointed governor.
Length of roadways: 18 752 km (*11 652 miles*) (31 Dec 1978).

Universities: 2 – and 1 polytechnic.
Adult illiteracy: 76·3% (1985).
Defence: Military service three years; total armed forces 45 000 (1987 estimate); defence expenditure: 37·5% of total government expenditure in 1980–81.
Foreign tourists: 9200 in 1982.

Albania

Official name: Republika Popullore Socialiste e Shqipërisë (Socialist People's Republic of Albania).
Population: 3 022 000 (official estimate 1986).
Area: 28 748 km² (*11 100 miles²*).
Language: Albanian.
Religions: Albania is officially an atheist state. All mosques and churches were closed in 1967. Before that date 70% of the population adhered to Islam (Sunni) with Greek Orthodox and Roman Catholic minorities.
Capital city: Tiranë (Tirana), population 206 100 (estimate for 1983).
Other principal towns (1983): Shkodër (Scutari) 71 200; Durrës (Durazzo) 72 400; Vlorë (Valona) 61 100; Elbasan 69 900; Korçë (Koritsa) 57 100; Berat 36 600; Fier 37 000.
Highest point: Mount Korabi, 2751 m (*9028 ft*).
Principal mountain ranges: Albanian Alps, section of the Dinaric Alps.
Principal rivers: Semani 253 km (*157 miles*), Drini 280 km (*174 miles*), Vjosa 236 km (*147 miles*), Mati 105 km (*65 miles*), Shkumbini 146 km (*91 miles*).
Head of State: Ramiz Alia, President of the Presidium of the People's Assembly.
Head of Government: Adil Çarçani, Chairman of the Council of Ministers.
Climate: Mild, wet winters and dry, hot summers along coast; rainier and colder inland. Maximum temperature 45·3°C (*113·5°F*), Lezhe, 23 Aug 1939; minimum −25·0°C (*−13·0°F*), Voskopje, 29 Jan 1942.
Labour force: 1 398 000 (1985 estimate): Agriculture, forestry and fishing 50·6%.
Gross national product: No figures given.
Exports: No figures have been published for the value of trade since 1964.
Monetary unit: New Lek. 1 new lek = 100 qindarka (qintars).
Denominations:
Coins 5, 10, 20, 50 qintars; 1 lek.
Notes 1, 3, 5, 10, 25, 50 and 100 leks.
Political history and government: Formerly part of Turkey's Ottoman Empire. On 28 Nov 1912 a group of Albanians established a provisional government and declared the country's independence. Albania was occupied by Italy in 1914 but its independence

ALBANIA

was re-established in 1920. A republic was proclaimed on 22 Jan 1925 and Ahmet Beg Zogu was elected President. He was proclaimed King Zog on 1 Sept 1928 and reigned until invading Italian forces occupied Albania on 7 Apr 1939. Italian rule ended in 1943 but German forces then occupied Albania. After they withdrew a provisional government was established in October 1944. The Communist-led National Liberation Front, a wartime resistance group, took power on 29 Nov 1944. A Communist-dominated assembly was elected on 2 Dec 1945. This body proclaimed the People's Republic of Albania on 12 Jan 1946. The new régime's first constitution was adopted in March 1946. The Communist Party was renamed the Albanian Party of Labour (APL) in 1948. A new constitution, introducing the country's present name, was adopted by the People's Assembly on 27 Dec 1976. In April 1985 Enver Hoxha, who had led Albania since the Second World War, died. At the time of his death he was the world's longest serving head of state.

The supreme organ of state power is the unicameral People's Assembly, with 250 members elected for four years by universal adult suffrage. The assembly elects a Presidium (13 members) to be its permanent organ. Executive and administrative authority is held by the Council of Ministers, elected by the Assembly.

Political power is held by the APL (or Worker's Party), the only permitted political party, which dominates the Democratic Front. The Front presents a single list of approved candidates for elections to all representative bodies. The APL's highest authority is the Party Congress, convened every five years. The Congress elects a Central Committee (88 full members and 40 candidate members were elected on 7 Nov 1981) to supervize Party work. To direct its policy the Committee elects a Political Bureau (Politburo), with 14 full and five candidate members.

For local governments Albania is divided into 26 districts, each with a People's Council elected for three years.
Length of roadways: 21 000 km (*13 040 miles*).
Length of railways: 408 km (*253·6 miles*).
Universities: 1.
Adult illiteracy: No recent figures.
Defence: Military service: Army two years, Air Force, Navy and special units three years; total armed forces 42 000 (20 000 conscripts) in 1987; defence expenditure: 10·6% of total government expenditure in 1986.
Foreign tourists: about 10 000 each year.

Algeria

Official name: El Djemhouria El Djazaïria Demokratia Echaabia, or la République algérienne démocratique et populaire (the Democratic and Popular Republic of Algeria).
Population: 22 972 000 (1987 census).
Area: 2 381 741 km² (*919 595 miles²*).
Languages: Arabic; Berber; French.
Religion: Islam (Sunni).
Capital city: El Djazaïr or Alger (Algiers), population 1 721 607 (1983 estimate).
Other principal towns (1983): Ouahran (Oran) 663 504; Qacentina (Constantine) 448 578; Annaba (Bône) 348 322; El Boulaïda (Blida) 191 314; Sétif 186 978; Sidi-Bel-Abbès 146 653.

Highest point: Mt Atakor, 2918 m (*9573 ft*).
Principal mountain ranges: Atlas Saharien, Ahaggar (Hoggar), Hamada de Tinrhert.
Principal river: Chéliff 692 km (*430 miles*).
Head of State: Col Bendjedid Chadli (b. 14 Apr 1929), President.
Prime Minister: Abdelhamid Brahimi (b. 2 Apr 1936).
Climate: Temperate (hot summers, fairly mild winters, adequate rainfall) along the coast, more extreme inland, hot and arid in the Sahara. In Algiers, August hottest (22°C to 29°C 71°F to 85°F), January coldest (9°C to 15°C 49°F to 59°F), December rainiest (12 days). Maximum temperature 53·0°C (*127·4°F*), Ouargla, 27 Aug 1884.
Labour force: 3 567 000 in 1983; Agriculture, Forestry and Fishing 26·9%; Mining and Manufacturing 13·3%; Construction 17·1%; Trade and transport 4·4%; services 38·3%.
Gross domestic product: 231 900 million dinars in 1983.
Exports: 59 106 million dinars in 1984; Energy and lubricants 97·5%; Primary products and raw materials 1·65%; Food and tobacco 0·4%.
Monetary unit: Algerian dinar. 1 dinar = 100 centimes.
Denominations:
Coins 1, 2, 5, 10, 20, 50 centimes; 1, 5 dinars.
Notes 5, 10, 100 dinars.
Political history and government: A former French possession, 'attached' to metropolitan France. A nationalist revolt, led by the *Front de libération nationale* (FLN) or National Liberation Front, broke out on 1 Nov 1954. This ended with a cease-fire and independence agreement on 18 Mar 1962. A provisional government was formed on 28 Mar 1962. Following a referendum on 1 July 1962, Algeria became independent on 3 July 1962. The provisional government transferred its functions to the Political Bureau of the FLN on 7 Aug 1962. A National Constituent Assembly was elected, from a single list of candidates adopted by the Bureau, on 20 Sept 1962. The Republic was proclaimed on 25 Sept 1962 and a new government was formed with Ahmed Ben Bella as Prime Minister. The government's draft constitution, providing for a presiden-

tial régime with the FLN as sole party, was adopted by the Assembly on 28 Aug 1963 and approved by popular referendum on 8 Sept 1963. Ben Bella was elected President on 15 Sept 1963 and a new National Assembly elected on 20 Sept 1964. The President was deposed by a military *coup* on 19 June 1965, when the Assembly was dissolved and power was assumed by a Revolutionary Council, led by Col. Houari Boumédienne, Minister of Defence.

The régime's National Charter, proclaiming Algeria's adherence to socialism, was approved by referendum on 27 June 1976. A new constitution, embodying the principles of the Charter, was similarly approved on 19 Nov 1976 and promulgated on 22 Nov 1976. It continued the one-party system, with the FLN as sole party. Executive power is vested in the President, who is Head of State and Head of Government. He was nominated by the FLN and elected by universal adult suffrage. The President appoints the Council of Ministers. Legislative power is held by the National People's Assembly, with 261 members elected by popular vote for five years (subject to dissolution by the Head of State). Boumédienne was elected President (unopposed) on 10 Dec 1976 and members of the Assembly elected (from 783 candidates – three per constituency – nominated by the FLN) on 25 Feb 1977. President Boumédienne died on 27 Dec 1978. His successor was elected on 7 Feb 1979, and sworn in two days later. A Prime Minister was appointed on 8 Mar 1979. Legislation approved on 30 June 1979 shortened the President's term of office from 6 to 5 years. A referendum in 1989 was held to approve constitutional changes including multiparty elections.

Algeria comprises 48 *wilayaat* (regions), each *wilaya* having an appointed governor (*wali*).
Length of roadways: 82 000 km (*50 922 miles*).
Length of railways: 3761 km (*2335 miles*).
Universities: 16.
Adult illiteracy: 50·4% in 1985.
Defence: Military service six months; total armed forces 169 000 (1987); defence expenditure: 9·2% of total government expenditure in 1987.
Foreign tourists: 450 000 (1986).

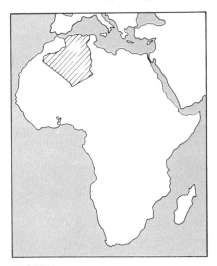

ALGERIA

Andorra

Official name: Les Valls d'Andorrà (Catalan); also Los Valles de Andorra (Spanish), or Les Vallées d'Andorre (French).
Population: 46 976 (1986 census).
Area: 467 km² (*180 miles²*).
Languages: Catalan (official), French, Spanish.
Religion: Roman Catholic.
Capital city: Andorra la Vella, population 18 463 in 1986.
Other principal towns: Les Escaldes; Sant Julià de Lòria.
Highest point: Pla del'Estany, 3011 m (*9678 ft*).
Principal mountain range: Pyrenees.
Principal river: Valira.
Head of State: Co-Princes (the Bishop of Urgel Dr Joan Martí Alanis and the President of France), each represented by a Permanent Delegate and, in Andorra, by the Viguier Episcopal and the Viguier Français.
First Syndic: Francesc Cerqueda-Pascuet.
Head of Government: Josef Pintat Solans.

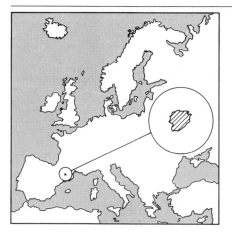

ANDORRA

Climate: Mild (cool summers, cold winters) and dry. May–October are rainiest months.
Monetary unit: French and Spanish currencies (*q.v.*).
Political history and government: In 1278 Andorra was placed under the joint suzerainty of the Bishop of Urgel, in Spain, and the Comte de Foix, in France. The rights of the Comte passed to France in 1589. Andorra is an autonomous principality (*seigneurie*) in which legislative power is held by the unicameral General Council of the Valleys, with 28 members (four from each of the seven parishes) elected by adult Andorran citizens for four years, half the seats being renewable every two years. Female suffrage was introduced by decree on 23 Apr 1970. The Council elects the First Syndic to act as chief executive for a three-year term. Political parties are technically illegal but one sought recognition in 1979.
In January 1982 an Executive Council was appointed, following elections held in 1981. Legislative and executive powers were thus separated.
Foreign tourists: 6 000 000 in 1982.

Angola

Official name: A República Popular de Angola (the People's Republic of Angola).
Population: 8 981 000 (1986 estimate).
Area: 1 246 700 km² (*481 354 miles²*).
Languages: Portuguese (official), Ovimbundu, Kimbundu, Bakongo, Chokwe.
Religions: Catholic 55%; Protestant 9%; animist 34%.
Capital city: São Paulo de Luanda, population 1 200 00 (1982 estimate).
Other principal towns (1970): Huambo (Nova Lisboa) 61 885; Lobito 59 258; Benguela 40 996; Lubango (Sá de Bandeira) 31 674; Malanje 31 559.
Highest point: Serra Môco, 2610 m (*8563 ft*).
Principal mountain ranges: Rand Plateau, Benguela Plateau, Bié Plateau, Humpata Highlands, Chela mountains.
Principal rivers: Cunene (Kunene), Cuanza (Kwanza), Congo (Zaire), Cuando (Kwando), Cubango (Okavango), Zambezi, Casssai (Kasai).
Head of State: José Eduardo dos Santos (b. 28 Aug 1942), President.

Climate: Tropical, tempered locally by altitude. Two distinct seasons (wet and dry) but with little variation in temperature. Very hot and rainy in lowlands, with lower temperatures inland. Rainy season October to May; average annual rainfall 1780 mm (*70 in*) Cabina, 280 mm (*11 in*) in Lobito. Average annual temperature 26°C (*79°F*) at Santo António do Zaire, 19°C (*67°F*) at Huambo.
Labour force: 3 719 000 (1985 estimate): Agriculture 71·6%.
Gross domestic product: 201 970 million kwanza (1982).
Exports: 39 531 million kwanza in 1979: Crude petroleum 74%; Petroleum products 10%; Coffee 5%; Diamonds 10%.
Monetary unit: Kwanza. 1 kwanza = 100 lwei.
Denominations:
Coins 50 lwei; 1, 2, 5, 10, 20 kwanza.
Notes 20, 50, 100, 500, 1000 kwanza.
Political history and government: A former Portuguese territory, independent since 11 Nov 1975. Before and after independence, rival nationalist groups fought for control of the country. By February 1976 the dominant group was the *Movimento Popular de Libertação de Angola* (MPLA), the Popular Movement for the Liberation of Angola, supported by troops from Cuba. the MPLA's first Congress, on 4–11 Dec 1977, restructured the Movement into a Marxist-Leninist political party called MPLA-*Partido de Trabalho* (MPLA-PT) or MPLA-Party of Labour. No other parties are permitted. The supreme organ of state is the National People's Assembly, with 206 members serving a three-year term. Members are chosen by electoral colleges composed of representatives elected by 'loyal citizens'. The first Assembly was installed on 11 Nov 1980. Executive power is vested in the President, who is also Chairman of the Council of Ministers and Chairman of the MPLA-PT. Angola has 18 provinces, each with a legislature elected by 'loyal citizens'.
An agreement was reached in 1988 for the gradual withdrawal of the Cuban forces in Angola which are aiding Government troops in the civil

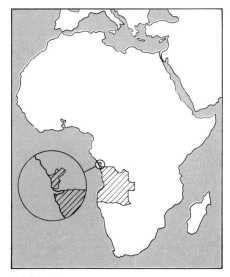

ANGOLA

war against the *Unita* forces which control much of the south of the country. This withdrawal agreement includes provision for the independence of neighbouring Namibia and the removal of South African forces from that territory.
Length of roadways: 72 323 km (*44 939 miles*) (31 Dec 1974).
Length of railways: 2952 km (*1833 miles*).
Universities: 1.
Adult illiteracy: 59% in 1985.
Defence: Military service two years; total armed forces 53 000 (1985); also about 28 000 Cuban troops who are to be withdrawn according to a timetable yet to be finalized; defence expenditure: 35·8% of total government expenditure in 1984.

Antigua and Barbuda

Population: 76 295 (1986 estimate).
Area: 442 km² (*170·5 miles²*).
Language: English.
Religion: Christian (mainly Anglican).
Capital city: St John's (St John City), population 36 000.
Highest point: Boggy Peak, 402 m (*1319 ft*).
Head of State: HM Queen Elizabeth II, represented by Sir Wilfred Ebenezer Jacobs, KCVO, OBE (b. 19 Oct 1919), Governor-General.
Prime Minister: Vere Cornwall Bird (b. 7 Dec 1910).
Climate: Generally warm and pleasant. Temperatures range from 15°C (*60°F*) to 34°C (*93°F*), with an average of 27°C (*81·5°F*). Average annual rainfall 1090 to 1140 mm (*43 to 45 in*).
Labour force: 32 254 (1985).
Gross domestic product: EC$509·9 million in 1985.
Exports: EC$47·5 million in 1984.
Monetary unit: East Caribbean dollar (EC$). 1 dollar = 100 cents.
Denominations:
Coins 1, 2, 5, 10, 25, 50 cents; 1 dollar.
Notes 1, 5, 20, 100 dollars.
Political history and government: A former British dependency, comprising Antigua, Barbuda (formerly Dulcina) and Redonda. The islands (collectively known as Antigua) were administered as part of the Leeward Islands, under a federal arrangement. Antigua became a separate Crown Colony on

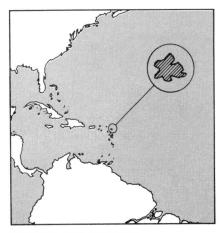

ANTIGUA AND BARBUDA

30 June 1956, although under the Governor of the Leeward Islands until 31 Dec 1959. From 1 Jan 1960 the colony had a new constitution, with its own Administrator. On 27 Feb 1967 Antigua became one of the West Indies Associated States, with full internal self-government. The Administrator was replaced by a Governor and the Chief Minister was restyled Premier.

Following a constitutional conference on 4–16 Dec 1980, the islands became fully independent, within the Commonwealth, on 1 Nov 1981, when the Governor became Governor-General and the Premier took office as Prime Minister. Executive power is vested in the British monarch and is exercisable by the Governor-General, who is appointed on the advice of the Prime Minister and acts in almost all matters on the advice of the Cabinet. Legislative power is vested in the bicameral Parliament, comprising a Senate (17 members appointed by the Governor-General) and a House of Representatives (17 members elected by universal adult suffrage for 5 years, subject to dissolution). The Governor-General appoints the Prime Minister and, on the latter's recommendation, other Ministers. The Cabinet is responsible to the House.
Length of roadways: 960 km (*600 miles*).
Adult illiteracy: No recent figures.
Defence: Total armed forces: about 700; there are also two US bases on Antigua.
Foreign tourists: 149 300 in 1986.

Argentina

Official name: República Argentina (the Argentine Republic).
Population: 31 029 694 (1986 estimate).
Area: 2 766 889 km² (*1 068 302 miles²*) (this figure excludes the Falkland Islands – Malvinas – its dependencies and the Antarctic territory claimed by Argentina).
Language: Spanish.
Religions: Roman Catholic; Protestant minority of 0·5 million; Jewish 0·3 million.
Capital city: Buenos Aires, population (including suburbs) 9 967 826 (1980 census).
Other principal towns (1980): Córdoba 983 900; Rosario 957 300; Mendoza 605 600; La Plata 564 700; San Miguel de Tucumán 498 500; Mar del Plata 414 600.
Highest point: Cerro Aconcagua, 6960 m (*22 834 ft*) (first climbed 14 Jan 1897).
Principal mountain range: Cordillera de los Andes.
Principal rivers: Paraná (4000 km *2485 miles*), Negro, Salado.
Head of State: Dr Raul Alfonsin, President. (President elect: Carlos Menem).
Climate: Sub-tropical in Chaco region (north), sunny and mild in pampas, cold and windy in southern Patagonia. In Buenos Aires, January hottest (17°C to 29°C *63°F to 85°F*), June coldest (5°C to 14°C *41°F to 57°F*), August, October and November rainiest (each 9 days). Absolute maximum temperature 48·8°C (*119·8°F*), Rivadavia, 27 Nov 1916; minimum −33·0°C (−27·4°F), Sarmiento.
Labour force: 11 467 983 (1985); in 1983 28% were involved in community, social and personal services (including business), 19·9% in manufacturing, 17% in trade, restaurants and hotels, 12% in agriculture, forestry and fishing.

ARGENTINA

Gross domestic product: 92360 million pesos in 1984: Agriculture, forestry and fishing 15%; Manufacturing 25%; Trade, restaurants and hotels 13%; Transport and communications 12%; Community, social and personal services 24%.

Exports: $8107 million in 1984: Vegetable products 42·8%; Prepared foodstuffs 13·7%.

Monetary unit: Austral (=1000 pesos): 1 austral = 100 centavos.

Denominations:
Coins 1, 5, 10, 50 centavos.
Notes 1, 5, 10, 100, 1000 australes.

Political history and government: A federal republic of 22 states, a federal district and two centrally administered territories. Lt-Gen. Juan Perón was elected President on 23 Sept 1973 and took office on 12 Oct 1973. Gen. Perón died on 1 July 1974 and was succeeded by his wife, the former Vice-President. She was deposed by an armed forces *coup* on 24 Mar 1976, when a three-man military junta took power. The bicameral Congress (a Senate and a Chamber of Deputies) and provincial legislatures were dissolved and political activities suspended. In 1982 Argentina invaded the British-ruled Falkland Islands (Islas Malvinas). After early success they were defeated and the Argentine troops forced to surrender. This brought about the collapse of the military junta, and elections in 1983 ushered in a civilian government. Each province is administered by an elected Governor.

Length of roadways: 211 369 km (*131 260 miles*) (31 Dec 1978).

Length of railways: 34 544 km (*21 145 miles*).

Universities: 52.

Adult illiteracy: 5·5% in 1980.

Defence: Military service: Army 6–12 months; Air Force one year, Navy 14 months; total armed forces 78000 in 1987; defence expenditure: 7·3% of total government expenditure in 1987.

Foreign tourists: 1 608 000 (1984).

Australia

Official name: The Commonwealth of Australia.
Population: 15 973 900 (census June 1986).
Area: 7 682 300 km² (*2 966 150 miles²*).
Language: English.
Religions: Church of England; Roman Catholic; Methodist; Presbyterian.
Capital city: Canberra, population 273 600 (1985 estimate) (includes suburbs in New South Wales).
Other principal towns (1985): Sydney 3 391 600; Melbourne 2 916 600; Brisbane 1 157 200; Perth 1 001 000; Adelaide 987 100; Newcastle 423 300; Wollongong 236 800; Gold Coast 208 100; Hobart 178 100; Geelong 147 100; Townsville 103 700.
Highest point: Mt Kosciusko, 2230 m (*7316 ft*).
Principal mountain ranges: Great Dividing Range, Macdonnell Ranges, Flinders Ranges, Australian Alps.
Principal rivers: Murray (with Darling), Flinders, Ashburton, Fitzroy.
Head of State: HM Queen Elizabeth II, represented by Bill Hayden, Governor-General.
Prime Minister: The Rt. Hon. Robert Hawke.
Climate: Hot and dry, with average temperatures of about 27°C (*80°F*). Very low rainfall in interior. In Sydney, January and February warmest (each average 18°C to 25°C *65°F to 78°F*), July coldest (8°C to 15°C *46°F to 60°F*), each month has an average of between 11 and 14 rainy days. In Perth, average daily maximum of 17°C (*63°F*) (July) to 29°C (*85°F*) (January, February), minimum 9°C (*48°F*) (July, August) to 17°C (*63°F*) (January, February), July and August rainiest (each 19 days), January and February driest (each 3 days). In Darwin, average maximum 30°C (*87°F*) (July) to 34°C (*94°F*) (November), minimum 19°C (*67°F*) (July) to 25°C (*78°F*) (November, December), January rainiest (20 days), no rainy days in July or August. Absolute maximum temperature 53·1°C (*127·5°F*), Cloncurry, 13 Jan 1889; absolute minimum −22·2°C (*−8·0°F*), Charlotte Pass, 14 July 1945 and 22 Aug 1947.
Labour force: 6 885 700 in 1986: Agriculture, forestry and fishing 5·7%; Mining 1·4%; Manufacturing 16·4%; Construction 6·1%; Trade 18%; Services 34·7%.
Gross domestic product: A$202 397 million in 1985–6.
Exports: A$32 795·3 million in 1986: Food and live animals 24·6%; Wool 8·6%; Metal ores and scrap 14·8%; Mineral fuels etc 24·4%; Basic manufactures 10%.
Monetary unit: Australian dollar (A$). 1 dollar = 100 cents.
Denominations:
Coins 1, 2, 5, 10, 20, 50 cents; 1 dollar.
Notes 1, 2, 5, 10, 20, 50, 100 dollars.
Political history and government: Britain's six Australian colonies merged to form a federation of states as the Commonwealth of Australia, a dominion under the British Crown, on 1 Jan 1901. The Northern Territory was separated from South Australia, and the Australian Capital Territory was acquired from New South Wales, on 1 Jan 1911. The capital was transferred from Melbourne to Canberra in May 1927. Australia became fully independent, within the Commonwealth, under the Statute of Westminster, a law promulgated in Britain on 11 Dec 1931 and adopted by Australia on 9 Oct 1942 (with effect from 3 Sept 1939).

Executive power is vested in the Queen and exercised by her representative, the Governor-General, advised by the Federal Executive Council (the Cabinet), led by the Prime Minster. The Governor-General appoints the Prime Minister and, on the latter's recommendation, other Ministers. Legislative power is vested in the Federal Parliament. This consists of the Queen, represented by the Governor-General, and two chambers elected by universal adult suffrage (voting is compulsory). The Senate has 64 members (10 from each state and two from each of the federal territories) elected by proportional representation for six years (half the seats renewable every three years). The House of Representatives has 125 members elected for three years (subject to dissolution) from single-member constituencies. The Cabinet is responsible to Parliament. Australia comprises six states (each with its own Government and judicial system) and two federally-administered territories.
Length of roadways: 852 986 km (*529 704 miles*) (1982).
Length of railways: 40 807 km (*25 362 miles*) (1982).
Universities: 19.
Defence: Military service voluntary; total armed forces 70 500 (1985); defence expenditure, 1986–7; A$7420 million.
Foreign tourists: 1 430 000 in 1985.

New South Wales

Population: 5 543 500 (1986 census).
Area: 801 600 km² (*309 500 miles²*).
Capital city: Sydney, population 3 391 600 (1986 census).
Other principal towns (1984): Newcastle 423 300; Wollongong 423 800; (1985 estimates) Lake Macquarie* 165 300; Shoalhaven* 61 700; Wagga Wagga 50 900; Shellharbour* 47 400; Albury 40 400. *These country municipalities include a number of settlements and the figures given do not represent the population of a single town.
Highest point: Mt Kosciusko, 2230 m (*7316 ft*).
Principal mountain ranges: Great Dividing Range, Australian Alps, New England Range, Snowy Mountains, Blue Mountains, Liverpool Range.
Principal rivers: Darling, Murray.
Governor: Air Marshal Sir James Anthony Rowland, KBE, DFC, AFC (b. 1 Nov 1922).
Premier: B. J. Unsworth.
Climate: Most of the state has hot summers and mild winters, with rainfall well distributed, but in the east drought and storms sometimes occur.
Length of roadways: 195 548 km (*121 534 miles*).
Length of railways: 10 030 km (*6228 miles*) (1986).
Universities: 6.

Queensland

Population: 2 592 600 (1986 census).
Area: 1 727 200 km² (*666 875 miles²*).
Capital city: Brisbane, population 1 157 200 (1986 census).
Other principal towns (1986): Gold Coast 208 100; Townsville 103 700; Sunshine Coast 90 300; Cairns 69 500; Rockhampton 57 000.
Highest point: Mr Bartle Frere, 1611 m (*5287 ft*).
Principal mountain ranges: Great Dividing Range, Selwyn, Kirby.
Principal rivers: Brisbane, Mitchell, Fitzroy, Barcoo, Flinders.

Governor: Sir Walter Benjamin Campbell, QC.
Premier: Michael John Ahern.
Length of roadways: 167 681 km (*104 130 miles*) (1986).
Length of railways: 10 225 km (*6349 miles*) (1983).
Universities: 3.

South Australia

Population: 1 373 100 (1986 census).
Area: 984 000 km² (*379 925 miles²*).
Capital city: Adelaide, population 987 100 (1986 census).
Other principal towns (1986): Whyalla 27 100; Mount Gambier 18 730; Port Augusta 15 620; Port Pirie 14 600.
Principal mountain ranges: Middleback, Mt Lofty Range, Flinders Range, Musgrave Range.
Principal river: Murray.
Governor: Lt-Gen. Sir Donald Dustan, KBE, CB.
Premier: John Charles Bannon.
Climate: Mediterranean type.
Length of roadways: 102 866 km (*63 931 miles*) (1986).
Length of railways: 5591 km (*3472 miles*).
Universities: 2.

Tasmania

Population: 446 900 (1986 census).
Area: 67 800 km² (*26 175 miles²*).
Capital city: Hobart, population 178 100 (1986 census).
Other principal towns (1986): Launceston 88 500; Devonport* 21 424; Burnie-Somerset* 20 368. (*1981 estimate).
Highest point: Cradle Mountain, 1545 m (*5069 ft*).
Principal mountain range: Highlands.
Principal rivers: Derwent, Gordon, Tamar.
Governor: Sir Philip Bennett, AO, KBE, DSO.
Premier: R. T. Gray.
Length of roadways: 22 210 km (*13 804 miles*) (1983).
Length of railways: 985 km (*612 miles*) (1983).
Universities: 1.

Victoria

Population: 4 164 700 (1986 census).
Area: 227 600 km² (*87 875 miles²*).
Capital city: Melbourne, population 2 916 600 (1986 census).
Other principal towns (1986): Geelong 147 100; Ballarat 75 200; Bendigo 62 400; Shepparton 37 100.
Principal mountain ranges: Australian Alps, Great Dividing Range.
Principal rivers: Murray, Yarra-Yarra.
Governor: Rev. Dr Davis McCaughey.
Premier: John Cain.
Length of roadways: 157 311 km (*97 690 miles*) (1984).
Length of railways: 5780 km (*3592 miles*) (1985).
Universities: 4.

Western Australia

Population: 1 440 600 (1986 census).
Area: 2 525 500 km² (*975 100 miles²*).
Capital city: Perth, population 1 001 000 (1986 census).
Other principal towns (1986): Bunbury 25 000; Geraldton 20 400. (The city of Fremantle had 24 000 and is included in the suburbs of Perth).
Highest point: Mt Meharry, 1244 m (*4082 ft*).
Principal mountain ranges: Darling, Hamersley.

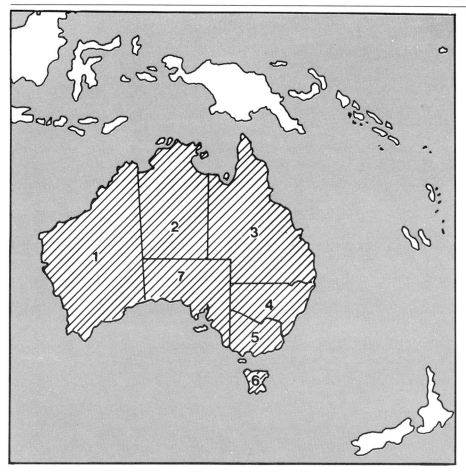

AUSTRALIA—1. Western Australia   2. Northern Territory   3. Queensland
4. New South Wales   5. Victoria   6. Tasmania   7. South Australia.

Principal rivers: Fitzroy, Ashburton, Fortescue, Swan, Murchison.
Governor: Prof. Gordon Stanley Reid (b. 26 Sept 1923).
Premier: Hon. Brian Thomas Burke.
Length of roadways: 119 941 km (*74 483 miles*) (1986).
Length of railways: 7518 km (4672 miles) (1986).
Universities: 2.

The Northern Territory of Australia

Population: 148 100 (1986 census).
Area: 1 346 200 km² (*519 750 miles²*).
Capital: Darwin, population 68 500 (1986 census).
Other principal town: Alice Springs, population 22 800 (1986).
Highest point: Mount Ziel, 1510 m (*4955 ft*).
Principal mountain range: MacDonnell Ranges.
Principal rivers: Victoria, Roper.
Climate: Tropical, but with considerable variations. Dry in the south, with very hot summers. On the coast, the rainy season is from November to April and the dry season from May to October.
Length of roadways: 20 080 km (*12 479 miles*).

Length of railways: 2266 km (*1407 miles*) (1987).
University college: 1.

The Australian Capital Territory

Population: 264 400 (1986 census).
Area: 2400 km² (*925 miles²*).
Principal town: Canberra, (as above).
Principal river: Murrumbidgee.
Climate: (see New South Wales).
Length of roadways: 2182 km (*1356 miles*).
Length of railways: 8 km (*5 miles*).
Universities: 1.

Australian Territories

Ashmore and Cartier Islands

Location: In the Timor Sea, respectively 850 km (*527 miles*) and 790 km (*490 miles*) west of Darwin.
Area: 5 km² (*2 miles²*).
Population: uninhabited.

Christmas Island

Location: In the Indian Ocean, 360 km (*223 miles*) south of Java Head.
Area: Approximately 135 km² (*52 miles²*).
Population: 3214 (1983 estimate) (1967 Chinese, 800 Malays, 341 Europeans, 106 others).
Principal settlement: Flying Fish Cove.

Territory of Cocos (Keeling) Islands

Location: In the Indian Ocean, about 2768 km (*1720 miles*) north-west of Perth. The territory contains 27 islands. North Keeling Island lies about 24 km (*15 miles*) north of the main group.
Area: Apprximately 14 km² (*5·5 miles²*).
Population: 584 (1984).
Principal settlement: Bantam Village (on Home Island).

Coral Sea Islands Territory

Location: East of Queensland, between the Great Barrier Reef and 157° 10′ E longitude.
Area: 8 km² (*5 miles²*) plus 780 000 km² (*300 000 miles²*) of sea.
Population: 3 meteorologists on an island in the Willis Group.

Territory of Heard and MacDonald Islands

Location: In the southern Indian Ocean, south-east of the Kerguelen Islands, and about 4023 km (*2500 miles*) south-west of Fremantle.
Area: 292 km² (*113 miles²*).
Population: No permanent inhabitants.

Norfolk Island

Location: In south-west Pacific Ocean 1676 km (*1042 miles*) from Sydney and about 643 km (*400 miles*) from New Zealand. Philip Island is about 6 km (*4 miles*) south of Norfolk Island.
Area: 34·55 km² (*13·34 miles²*).
Population: 2367 (1986). Figures include visitors. Philip Island and Nepean Island are uninhabited.
Seat of Government: Kingston.

Austria

Official name: Republik Österreich (Republic of Austria).
Population: 7 565 000 (1986 estimate).
Area: 83 855 km² (*32 367 miles²*).
Language: German.
Religions: Roman Catholic (84%), Protestant minority.
Capital city: Wien (Vienna), population 1 489 153 (1985).
Other principal towns (1981): Graz 243 166; Linz 199 910; Salzburg 139 426; Innsbruck 117 287.
Highest point: Grossglockner, 3798 m (*12 462 ft*) (first climbed in 1800).
Principal mountain range: Alps.
Principal rivers: Donau (Danube) (2850 km *1770 miles*), Inn, Mur.
Head of State: Dr Kurt Waldheim (b. 21 Dec 1918), Federal President.
Head of Government: Dr Franz Vranitzky (b. 4 Oct 1937), Acting Federal Chancellor.

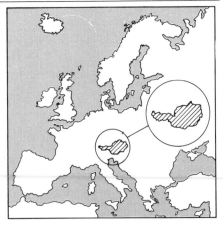

AUSTRIA

Climate: Generally cold, dry winters and warm summers, with considerable variations due to altitude. Average annual temperature 7°C (*45°F*) to 9°C (*48°F*). Most of rain in summer. In Vienna, July hottest (15°C to 24°C *59°F to 75°F*), January coldest (−3°C to 1°C *26°F to 34°F*), August rainiest (10 days). Absolute maximum temperature 39·4°C (*102·9°F*), Horn, 5 July 1957; absolute minimum −36·6°C (*−33·9°F*), Zwettl, 11 Feb 1929.
Labour force: 3 388 000 in 1986: Agriculture and forestry 8·4%; Industry and manufacturing 28·2%; Commerce 13·9%; Services 32·4%.
Gross domestic product: 1·432 billion Schilling in 1986: Agriculture and forestry 3·2%; Mining and material goods production 27·5%; Construction 6·9%; Commerce, hotels and restaurants 15·9%; Transport and communications 5·7%.
Exports: 407 954 million Schilling in 1986: Machinery and transport equipment 33·8%; Basic manufactures 19·2%; Chemicals and related products 10·2%.
Monetary unit: Schilling. 1 Schilling = 100 Groschen.
Denominations:
 Coins 1, 2, 5, 10, 50 Groschen; 1, 5, 10, 20, 25, 50, 100, 500, 1000 Schilling.
 Notes 20, 50, 100, 500, 1000 Schilling.
Political history and government: Formerly the centre of the Austro-Hungarian Empire. In 1918 the Empire was dissolved and Austria proper became a republic. Troops from Nazi Germany entered Austria on 11 Mar 1938. It was annexed on 12 Mar 1938 and incorporated in the German Reich. After liberation by Allied forces, a provisional government was established on 27 Apr 1945. Austria was divided into four occupation zones, controlled by France, the USSR, the United Kingdom and the USA. It regained independence by the Austrian State Treaty, signed on 15 May 1955 and effective from 27 July 1955. Occupation forces were withdrawn on 25 Oct 1955.

Austria is a federal state, divided into nine provinces. Legislative power is vested in the bicameral Federal Assembly, comprising the *Nationalrat* (National Council) of 183 members, directly elected by universal adult suffrage for four years (subject to dissolution), and the *Bundesrat* (Federal Council) of 63 members elected for varying terms by the provincial assemblies. The Federal President is a constitutional Head of State, elected by direct popular vote for six years. He normally acts on the advice of the Council of Ministers, led by the Federal Chancellor, which is responsible to the National Council. The President appoints the Chancellor and, on the latter's advice, other Ministers.

Length of roadways: 146 250 km (*90 821 miles*) (1986).
Length of railways: 5766 km (*3584 miles*) (1986).
Universities: 18.
Defence: Military service six months, followed by 60 days' reservist training; total armed forces 54 700 (27 000 conscripts) in 1987; defence expenditure, 1987: $18 290 million Schilling.
Foreign tourists: More than 15·5 million in 1986.

The Bahamas

Official name: The Commonwealth of the Bahamas.
Population: 235 000 (1986 estimate).
Area: 13 939 km² (*5382 miles²*).
Language: English.
Religions: Anglican, Baptist, Roman Catholic, Methodist, Saints of God and Church of God.
Capital city: Nassau (on New Providence Island), population 110 000 (1980).
Highest point: Mount Alvernia, Cat Island.
Head of State: HM Queen Elizabeth II, represented by Sir Christopher Cash, KCVO, OBE (b. 28 May 1917), Governor-General.
Prime Minister: The Rt Hon. Lynden Oscar Pindling (b. 22 Mar 1930).
Climate: Equable. Winter averages of 21°C to 24°C (*70°F to 75°F*). Summer averages of 26°C to 32°C (*80°F to 90°F*). Highest recorded temperature is 34°C (*94°F*) and the lowest 10°C (*51°F*). Rainfall mainly between May and September.
Labour force: 87 052 (1980): Construction 7·6%; Trade, restaurants and hotels 28·1%; Community, social and personal services 27·6%.
Gross domestic product: B$1448·8 million in 1982.
Exports: B$2252·3 million in 1985.
Monetary unit: Bahamian dollar (B$). 1 dollar = 100 cents.
Denominations:
Coins 1, 5, 10, 15, 25, 50 cents; B$ 1, 2, 5.
Notes 50 cents; B$ 1, 3, 5, 10, 20, 50, 100.
Political history and government: A former British

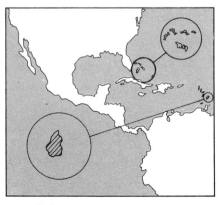

centre: **THE BAHAMAS**
right **BARBADOS**

colony, with internal self-government from 7 Jan 1964. Following a constitutional conference on 12–20 Dec 1972, the Bahamas became independent, within the Commonwealth, on 10 July 1973. Executive power is vested in the Queen and exercisable by her appointed representative, the Governor-General, advised by the Cabinet. The Governor-General appoints the Prime Minister and, on the latter's advice, other members of the Cabinet. Legislative power is vested in the bicameral Parliament, comprising the Senate (16 appointed members) and the House of Assembly, with 49 members elected for five years by universal adult suffrage. The Cabinet is responsible to Parliament.
Length of roadways: 2334 km (*1450 miles*).
Defence: The security forces consist of a paramilitary Coastguard numbering nearly 500 (1987). Defence budget (1987): US$ 60 million.
Foreign tourists: 2 500 000 in 1986.

Bahrain

Official name: Daulat al-Bahrain (State of Bahrain).
Population: 411 700 (1986 estimate).
Area: 691 km² (*267 miles²*).
Language: Arabic.
Religions: Islam (Sunni and Shia), Christian minority.
Capital city: Manama, population 121 986 (1981 census).
Other principal towns (1981): Muharraq 61 853; Rifa'a 28 150; Isa Town 21 275; Hidd 7111.
Highest point: Jabal ad-Dukhan, 134 m (*440 ft*).
Head of State: HH Shaikh Isa bin Sulman al-Khalifa, Hon GCMG (b. 3 July 1933), Amir of Bahrain (succeeded to the Throne on 2 Nov 1961). The Crown Prince is HH Shaikh Hamad bin Isa al-Khalifa, (son of the Amir).
Prime Minister: Shaikh Khalifa bin Sulman al-Khalifa (b. 1935).
Climate: Very hot and humid. Average maximum 20°C (*68°F*) (January) to 38°C (*100°F*) (August), minimum 14°C (*57°F*) (January) to 29°C (*85°F*) (July, August); December and February rainiest (each two days).
Labour force: 81 503 (1984): Agriculture 1·8%; Manufacturing 12·5%; Construction 33·8%; Trade 13·8%.
Gross domestic product: 1877·5 million Bahrain dinars in 1984.
Exports: 2781·1 million Bahrain dinars in 1985: Refined petroleum 26·6%.
Monetary unit: Bahrain dinar. 1 dinar = 1000 fils.
Denominations:
Coins 1, 5, 10, 25, 50, 100 fils.
Notes 500 fils; 1, 5, 10, 20 dinars.
Political history and government: A shaikhdom under British protection from 1882 until full independence on 15 Aug 1971. Now an amirate, with a Cabinet appointed by the Ruler. A new constitution came into force on 6 Dec 1973. This provided for a National Assembly, containing Cabinet ministers and 30 elected members serving a four-year term. Elections were held on 7 Dec 1973 but the Assembly was dissolved by Amiri decree on 26 Aug 1975.
Adult illiteracy: 27·3% (1985).
Defence: Military service voluntary; total armed forces 2800 (1985).
Foreign tourists: 154 000 (largely from other Gulf states) in 1984.

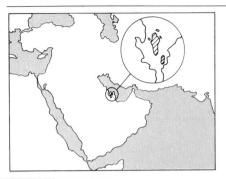

BAHRAIN

Bangladesh

Official name: Gana Praja Tantri Bangla Desh (People's Republic of Bangladesh).
Population: 100 616 000 (1986 estimate).
Area: 143 998 km² (55 598 miles²).
Language: Bengali.
Religions: Islam (Sunni), with Hindu, Christian and Buddhist minorities.
Capital city: Dhaka (Dacca), population 3 430 312 (1981 census) – includes Narayanganj 298 400.
Other principal towns (1981): Chittagong 1 391 877; Khulna 646 359; Rajshahi 253 740; Comilla 184 132.
Principal rivers: Ganga (Ganges), Jumna, Meghna.
Head of State: Lt-Gen. Hossain Mohammad Ershad, President.
Prime Minister: Moudud Ahmed.
Climate: Tropical and monsoon. Summer temperature about 30°C (86°F); winter 20°C (68°F). Rainfall is heavy, varying from 1270 to 3430 mm (50 to 135 in) per year in different areas, and most falling from June to September (the monsoon season).
Labour force: 27 972 000 employed in 1983–4: Agriculture, forestry and fishing 58·6%; Trade, hotels and restaurants 11·7%; Manufacturing 7·5%.
Gross domestic product: 481 622 million taka in 1985–6: Agriculture, forestry and fishing 46·7% (agriculture 41%); Manufacturing 8%.
Exports: 20 441·3 million taka in 1983: Jute and jute products 44%.
Monetary unit: Taka. 1 taka = 100 poisha.
Denominations:
Coins 1, 2, 5, 10, 25, 50 poisha.
Notes 1, 5, 10, 50, 100 taka.
Political history and government: Formerly the eastern wing of Pakistan, formed by the partition of British India on 15 Aug 1947. In elections for a Pakistan National Assembly on 7 Dec 1970 the Awami League, led by Sheikh Mujibur Rahman, won all but two seats in East Pakistan and an overall majority in the Assembly. The League advocated autonomy for East Pakistan within a loose federation but this was unacceptable to the main party in West Pakistan. When constitutional talks failed, the League declared East Pakistan's independence as Bangladesh on 26 Mar 1971. Civil war broke out and the League was outlawed. Mujib was arrested but the League announced on 11 Apr 1971 that he was President of Bangladesh. After Indian intervention, Pakistani forces surrendered and Bangladesh's secession became effective on 16 Dec

1971. Mujib was released and became Prime Minister on 12 Jan 1972. Bangladesh joined the Commonwealth on 18 Apr 1972. Mujib was deposed by a *coup* and killed on 15 Aug 1975, when martial law was imposed. Political parties were banned on 30 Aug 1975. After an army mutiny on 3 Nov 1975, the new President resigned on 6 Nov 1975, when the Chief Justice of the Supreme Court became President and Chief Martial Law Administrator. He immediately dissolved Parliament and on the next day the mutiny was crushed. Political parties were again legalized by a regulation of 28 July 1976. The President's deputy, Maj-Gen. Ziaur Rahman, took over martial law powers on 29 Nov 1976 and became President on 21 Apr 1977. A Presidential proclamation of 22 Apr 1977 amended the constitution to change Bangladesh from a secular to an Islamic state. Zia was elected President by a large majority of the popular vote on 3 June 1978 and sworn in for a 5-year term on 12 June. On 29 June 1978 he formed a cabinet in place of his Council of Advisers. Elections were held on 18 Feb 1979 for 300 members to serve a 5-year term in a new *Jatiya Sangsad* (Parliament). In a further 30 seats, reserved for women, candidates were unopposed. The state of emergency was revoked on 27 Nov 1979. President Zia was killed on 30 May 1981, during an attempted insurrection, and the Vice-President became acting Head of State. He was elected President on 15 Nov 1981. The elected President was deposed and the Jatiya Sangsad (Parliament) dissolved following promulgation of martial law and the take-over of power by Lt-Gen. H. M. Ershad on 24 Mar 1982. Gen. Ershad appointed a retired judge to be President on 27 March 1982, but assumed the Presidency himself on 11 Dec 1983. Parliamentary elections were held in 1986 and 1988 and a presidential election held on 15 Oct 1986, in which Ershad was voted to the presidency.
Length of roadways: 6240 km (3875 miles).
Length of railways: 4551 km (2828 miles) (1984).
Universities: 6.
Adult illiteracy: 74% in 1986.
Defence: Military service voluntary; total armed forces 101 500 (1987); paramilitary forces 55 000; estimated defence expenditure, 6640 million taka (1986–7).
Foreign tourists: 129 000 in 1986.

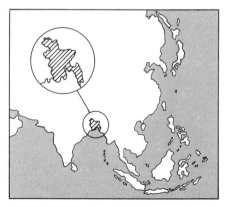

BANGLADESH

Barbados

Population: 253 055 (estimate 1985).
Area: 430 km² (*166 miles²*).
Language: English.
Religions: Anglican, with Methodist, Roman Catholic and Moravian minorities.
Capital city: Bridgetown, population 7517 (parish of Bridgetown and St Michael 97 872) at 1980 census.
Other principal town: Speightstown.
Highest point: Mount Hillaby, 340 m (*1115 ft*).
Head of State: HM Queen Elizabeth II, represented by Sir Hugh Springer, GCMG, KA, CBE (b. 22 June 1913), Governor-General.
Prime Minister: Erskine Sandiford.
Climate: Pleasant, with temperatures rarely rising above 30°C (*86°F*) or falling below 18°C (*67°F*). Average annual rainfall, which varies from district to district, 1270 to 1778 mm (*50 to 75 in*). Subject to hurricanes.
Labour force: 116 900 (1986): Agriculture, forestry and fishing 6·8%; Manufacturing and mining 9·9%; Trade 17·7%; Community, social and personal services 38·1%.
Gross domestic product: B$2676·9 million in 1986.
Exports: B$796·5 million in 1985: Sugar 6·5%; Basic manufactures 9·8%; Machinery and transport equipment 33·4%.
Monetary unit: Barbados dollar (B$). 1 dollar = 100 cents.
Denominations:
  Coins 1, 5, 10, 25 cents; B$1.
  Notes B$ 1, 2, 5, 10, 20, 100.
Political history and government: A former British colony, with internal self-government from 16 Oct 1961. A member of the West Indies Federation from 3 Jan 1958 to 31 May 1962. Following a constitutional conference on 20 June–4 July 1966, Barbados became independent, within the Commonwealth, on 30 Nov 1966. Executive power is vested in the Queen and exercisable by her appointed representative, the Governor-General, advised by the Cabinet. The Governor-General appoints the Prime Minister and, on the latter's advice, other members of the Cabinet. Legislative power is vested in the bicameral Parliament, comprising the Senate (21 appointed members) and the House of Assembly, with 27 members elected by universal adult suffrage for five years (subject to dissolution) from 27 constituencies. The Cabinet is responsible to Parliament.
Length of roadways: 1642 km (*1020 miles*).
Universities: 1.
Defence: The Barbados Defence Force was established in April 1978 with 154 regular personnel; defence expenditure: 3·4% of total government expenditure in 1986.
Foreign tourists: 370 000 in 1986.

Belgium

Official name: Royaume de Belgique (in French), Koninkrijk België (in Dutch) or Königreich Belgien (in German): Kingdom of Belgium.
Population: 9 867 751 (1986 estimate).
Area: 30 519 km² (*11 783 miles²*).
Languages: Dutch (Flemish), French, German.
Religion: Roman Catholic.

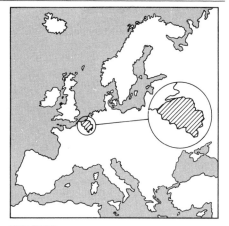

BELGIUM

Capital city: Bruxelles (Brussel, Brussels), population 973 499 (1986 estimate): includes suburbs.
Other principal towns (1985): Antwerpen (Anvers, Antwerp) 479 748; Gent (Gand, Ghent) 233 856; Charleroi 209 395; Liège (Luik) 200 891; Brugge (Bruges) 117 755; Namur (Namen) 102 670; Mons (Bergen) 89 693.
Highest point: Botrange, 694 m (*2277 ft*).
Principal mountain range: Ardennes.
Principal rivers: Schelde, Meuse (925 km *575 miles*).
Head of State: HM Baudoin Ier (Albert Charles Léopold Axel Marie Gustave), KG (b. 7 Sept 1930), King of the Belgians. The King's name is also written Boudewijn (in Dutch) or Balduin (in German). King Baudoin Ier succeeded 17 July 1951. The Crown Prince is HRH Albert, Prince of Liège (b. 6 June 1934), brother of the king.
Prime Minister: Wilfried Martens.
Climate: Mild and humid on coast. Hotter summers, colder winters inland. In Brussels, January coldest (−0·5°C to 5°C *31°F to 42°F*), July hottest (12°C to 23°C *54°F to 73°F*), December rainiest (13 days). Absolute maximum temperature 40·0°C (*104°F*) on the coast, 27 June 1947; absolute minimum −29·8°C (−*21·6°F*), Vieselm, 10 Dec 1879.
Labour force: 4 211 600 in 1986. Manufacturing 19%; Trade 17%; Services 29·9%.
Gross domestic product: 4812·1 billion Belgian francs in 1984: Agriculture 2·4%; Manufacturing 22·9%; Trade 5·4%; Services 32%.
Exports: 3 066 578 billion Belgian francs in 1986 (includes figures for the Grand Duchy of Luxembourg): Food and live animals 8·9%; Chemicals and related products 12·5%; Basic manufactures 29·8%; Machinery and transport equipment 25·8%.
Monetary unit: Belgian franc (frank). 1 franc = 100 centimes (centiemen).
Denominations:
  Coins 50 centimes; 1, 5, 20, 250 francs.
  Notes 50, 100, 500, 1000, 5000 francs.
Political history and government: A constitutional and hereditary monarchy, comprising nine provinces. Legislative power is vested in the King and the bicameral Parliament, comprising the Senate (181 members, including 106 directly elected by universal adult suffrage, 50 elected by provincial councils and 25 co-opted by the elected members) and the Chamber of Representatives (212 members directly elected. using proportional representation).

Members of both Houses serve for up to four years. Executive power, nominally vested in the King, is exercised by the Cabinet. The King appoints the Prime Minister and, on the latter's advice, other Ministers. The Cabinet is responsible to Parliament.
Length of roadways: 130 311 km (*80 989 miles*) (1984).
Length of railways: 3618 km (*2246 miles*) (1986).
Universities: 19 including university centres.
Defence: Military service 10 months (in Germany) or 12 months (in Belgium); total armed forces 90 800 in 1987; defence expenditure, 1987: 124·340 million Belgian francs.
Foreign tourists: 6 630 000 (1983).

Belize

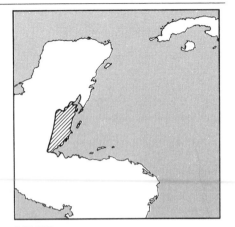

BELIZE

Population: 166 000 (1986 estimate).
Area: 22 965 km² (*8867 miles²*).
Languages: English (official), Spanish.
Religion: Christian (Roman Catholic 55%, Protestant 43%).
Capital city: Belmopan, population 4500 (1985 estimate).
Other principal towns (1985): Belize City 47 000; Orange Walk 9600; Dangriga (Stann Creek) 7700.
Highest point: Victoria Peak, 1122 m (*3681 ft*).
Principal mountain range: Maya Mountains.
Principal rivers: Hondo (on Mexican border), Belize, New River.
Head of State: HM Queen Elizabeth II, represented by Dame Elmira Minita Gordon, GCMG, Governor-General.
Prime Minister: Manuel Amades Esquivel.
Climate: Sub-tropical. At Belize City, on the coast, temperatures range from 10°C to 36°C (*50°F to 96°F*), with an annual average of 31°C (*78·5°F*). There are greater variations inland. Rainfall increases from north (annual average 1295 mm (*51 in*) at Corozal) to south (4445 mm (*175 in*) at Toledo).
Labour force: 33 121 (census of 7 Apr 1970).
Gross domestic product: BZ$385 million in 1984.
Exports: BZ$128·8 million in 1985: Sugar 35·6%; Bananas 5·1%; Citrus products 18·8%; Fish products 11·6%; Garments 24·1%.
Monetary unit: Belizean dollar (BZ$). 1 dollar = 100 cents.
Denominations:
Coins 1, 5, 10, 25, 50 cents.
Notes 1, 2, 5, 10, 20, 100 dollars.
Political history and government: Formerly British Honduras, a dependency of the United Kingdom. The colony was granted internal self-government on 1 Jan 1964, when the First Minister became Premier, and was renamed Belize on 1 June 1973. There has been a continuing territorial dispute with Guatemala.

Following a constitutional conference on 6–14 Apr 1981, Belize became independent within the Commonwealth, on 21 Sept 1981, when the Premier was restyled Prime Minister. Executive power is vested in the British monarch and is exercisable by the Governor-General, who is appointed on the advice of the Prime Minister and acts in almost all matters on the advice of the Cabinet. Legislative power is vested in the bicameral National Assembly, comprising a Senate (8 members appointed by the Governor-General) and a House of Representatives (28 members elected by universal adult

suffrage for 5 years, subject to dissolution). The Governor-General appoints the Prime Minister and, on the latter's recommendation, other Ministers. The Cabinet is responsible to the House.
Length of roadways: 4180 km (*2600 miles*).
Adult illiteracy: 7% (estimate).
Defence: The Belize Defence Force was formed on 1 Jan 1978. In 1987 the armed forces numbered 600; there are currently about 1400 British forces in Belize. Defence expenditure: about 2% of total government expenditure in 1987.
Foreign tourists: 93 440 in 1985.

Benin

Official name: La République populaire du Bénin (the People's Republic of Benin).
Population: 4 042 000 (1986 estimate).
Area: 112 622 km² (*43 484 miles²*).
Languages: French (official), Fon, Adja, Bariba, Yoruba.
Religions: Animist, with Christian and Muslim minorities.
Capital city: Porto-Novo, population 208 258 (1982 estimate).
Other principal towns (1982): Cotonou 487 020; Natitingou 50 800; Abomey 41 000; Kandi 31 000; Ouidah 30 000.
Highest point: 635 m (*2083 ft*).
Principal mountain range: Châine de l'Atakora.
Principal rivers: Ouémé, Niger (4184 km *2600 miles*) on frontier.
Head of State: Brig.-Gen. Mathieu Kerekou (b. 2 Sept 1933), President and Head of the Government.
Climate: Tropical (hot and humid). Average temperatures 20°C to 34°C (*68°F to 93°F*). Heavy rainfall near the coast, hotter and drier inland. In Cotonou the warmest month is April (daily average high 28°C *83°F*), coldest is August (23°C *73°F*).
Labour force: 1 775 000 (1980).
Gross domestic product: 385 300 million CFA francs in 1983: Agriculture, forestry and fishing 48%; Manufacturing 6%; Trade 19·3%; Transport and communications 7·6%; Public administration and defence 8·7%.
Exports: 62 000 million CFA francs in 1980.

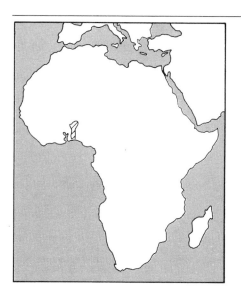

BENIN

Monetary unit: Franc de la Communauté financière africaine.
Denominations:
Coins 1, 2, 5, 10, 25, 50, 100 CFA francs.
Notes 50, 100, 500, 1000, 5000 CFA francs.
Political history and government: Formerly part of French West Africa, became independent as the Republic of Dahomey on 1 Aug 1960. The latest in a series of *coups* took place on 26 Oct 1972, when power was assumed by army officers, led by Maj. Mathieu Kerekou. On 1 Sept 1973 President Kerekou announced the creation of a National Council of the Revolution (CNR), with 69 members (including 30 civilians), under his leadership, to develop state policy. The military régime proclaimed its adherence to Marxist-Leninist principles and on 1 Dec 1975 it introduced the country's present name, with a single ruling political party. In August 1977 the CNR adopted a *Loi fondamentale* (Fundamental Law) providing for the establishment of a National Revolutionary Assembly comprising 196 People's Commissioners representing socio-professional classes. The first Assembly was elected by universal adult suffrage on 20 Nov 1979, from a single list of candidates, and the CNR was disbanded. The Assembly elects the President, who appoints the National Executive Council (Cabinet).
Length of roadways: 8645 km (*5369 miles*).
Length of railways: 1230 km (*764 miles*) (1988).
Universities: 1.
Adult illiteracy: 74·1% in 1985.
Defence: Total armed forces 4350; defence expenditure: 9367 million CFA francs.
Foreign tourists: 48 000 in 1983.

Bhutan

Official name: Druk-yul or, in Tibetan, Druk Gyalkhap (Realm of the Dragon). The name Bhutan is Tibetan for 'the End of the Land'.
Population: 1 286 275 (1985 estimate).
Area: 46 500 km² (*17 954 miles²*).

Languages: Dzongkha, Bumthangka, Sarchapkkha.
Religions: Buddhist, with Hindu minority.
Capital city: Thimphu, population 15 000 (1985 estimate).
Other principal towns: Paro Dzong; Punakha; Tongsa Dzong.
Highest point: Khula Kangri 1, 7554 m (*24 784 ft*).
Principal mountain range: Himalaya.
Principal rivers: Amo-Chu, Wang-chu, Machu, Manas.
Head of State: HM Jigme Singye Wangchuk (b. 11 Nov 1955), King of Bhutan. (In Dzongkha, 'Druk Gyalpo' meaning 'Dragon King'). The King succeeded on 21 July 1972. The Crown Prince is HRH Prince Gesar Wangchuk (b. 1979), son of the King.
Climate: Steamy hot in lowland foothills. Cold most of the year in higher areas.
Labour force: 650 000 in 1981–2: Agriculture, forestry and fishing 94·3%; Public services 3·4%.
Gross domestic product: 2012·8 million ngultrum (1984).
Monetary unit: Ngultrum. 1 ngultrum = 100 chetrums (Indian currency is also legal tender).
Denominations:
Coins 5, 10, 25, 60 chetrums; 1 ngultrum.
Notes 1, 2, 5, 10, 20, 50, 100 ngultrums.
Political history and government: A hereditary monarchy, under the Wangchuk dynasty since 1907. The Treaty of Punakha in 1910 provided that Bhutan's external relations were to be guided by British India. After the independence of India in 1947, an Indo-Bhutan Treaty of 8 Aug 1949 transferred this protection to India.
The King is Head of State and Head of Government but a Royal Advisory Council (nine members), established in 1965, is the principal policy-making body. Bhutan's first Cabinet was formed in May 1968. The government is assisted by the unicameral National Assembly (*Tsogdu*), established in 1953. The Assembly has 151 members, of whom 110 are indirectly elected by village headmen, 10 represent ecclesiastical bodies and 30 are appointed officials. Members of the Assembly serve a three-year term. The Royal Advisory Council and the Council of Ministers are responsible to the Assembly.
Length of roadways: 2050 km (*1271 miles*) (1986).
Adult illiteracy: 80% (1987 estimate).
Defence: Army: 4000 men, Indian trained.
Foreign tourists: 2500 in 1986.

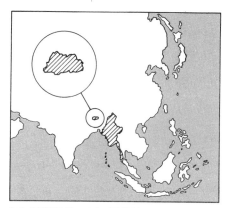

left: **BHUTAN**   *right:* **BURMA**

Bolivia

Official name: República de Bolivia.
Population: 6 611 351 (1986 estimate).
Area: 1 098 581 km² (*424 164 miles²*).
Languages: Spanish, Amyará, Quéchua.
Religion: Roman Catholic.
Capital city: La Paz (de Ayacucho), population 1 033 288 (1986 estimate). La Paz is the administrative capital of Bolivia. Sucre is the legal capital and is the seat of the judiciary.
Other principal towns (1986): Santa Cruz de la Sierra 457 619; Cochabamba 329 941; Oruro 184 101; Potosi 117 010; Sucre (legal capital) 88 774.
Highest point: Nevado Sajama, 6520 m (*21 391 ft*) (first climbed in 1937).
Principal mountain ranges: Cordillera de los Andes, Cordillera Real, Cordillera Oriental, Cordillera Central.
Principal rivers: Beni, Mamoré, Pilcomayo, Paraguai (Paraguay) (2410 km *1500 miles*) on frontier.
Head of State: Dr Victor Paz Estenssoro, President.
Climate: Dry, with cold winds on Altiplano, hot and humid in eastern lowlands. In La Paz, average maximum 17°C (*62°F*) (June, July) to 19°C (*67°F*) (November), minimum 0·5°C (*33°F*) (July) to 6°C (*43°F*) (January, February), January rainiest (21 days).
Labour force: 1 661 426 (1986).
Gross domestic product: 105 977 million pesos (1986): Agriculture 19·8%; Mining (inc. petroleum) 10·5%; Industry 10%; Commerce and finance 28·7%.
Exports: US$637·5 million in 1983: Minerals 30·9%; Natural gas 51·5%; Wood 3·7%.
Monetary unit: In January 1987 the peso was replaced by the boliviano whose value is equivalent to 1 000 000 former pesos. (The figures below are given in the former currency).
100 centavos = 1 boliviano.
Denominations:
 Coins 2, 5, 10, 20, 50 centavos; 1 boliviano.
 Notes 2, 5, 10, 20, 50, 100, 200 bolivianos.
Political history and government: A republic, divided into nine departments. A series of military régimes held power from 1969 to 1979. Elections were held on 1 July 1979 for a President and for a bicameral Congress. No candidate gained a majority in the presidential election. Congress was convened on 1 Aug 1979 but it also failed to give a majority to any presidential candidate. On 8 Aug 1979 the President of the Senate was sworn in to serve as interim President. He was deposed by a military *coup* on 1 Nov 1979. The *coup* leader resigned on 16 Nov. Congress elected the President of the Chamber of Deputies to be interim Head of State until fresh elections for a President and Congress, to hold office for four years. These were held on 29 June 1980 but the presidential election again proved inconclusive. Congress, comprising a Senate (27 members) and a Chamber of Deputies (117 members), was due to meet on 4 Aug 1980 to elect a President but an armed forces junta again seized power on 17 July 1980. The *coup* leader, Gen. Luis García Meza, was sworn in as President on the next day and Congress was suspended. On 4 Aug 1981 President García resigned and ceded power to the junta. In 1982 the junta handed back power to the Congress elected in 1980, and Dr Siles Suazo was elected President for a four-year term. Elections were eventually held in 1985 after labour unrest.
Length of roadways: 40 987 km (*25 473 miles*).
Length of railways: 3838 km (*2383 miles*).
Universities: 10.
Adult illiteracy: 25·8% (1985).
Defence: Military service 12 months, selective; total armed forces 27 600 in 1985; defence expenditure: (1986) equivalent of 180·5 million bolivianos.
Foreign tourists: 163 000 in 1984.

Botswana

Official name: The Republic of Botswana.
Population: 1 131 000 (1986 estimate).
Area: 582 000 km² (*224 711 miles²*).
Languages: Setswana, English.
Religions: Christian, ancestral beliefs.
Capital city: Gaborone, population 59 657 (1981 census).
Other principal towns (1981): Francistown 31 065; Selebi-Pikwe 29 469; Kanye 20 215; Lobatse 19 034; Mochudi 18 386; Molepole 20 565; Mahalapye 20 712; Maun 14 925.
Principal rivers: Chobe, Shashi.
Head of State: Dr Quett Ketumile Joni Masire (b. 23 July 1925), President.
Climate: Sub-tropical but variable. Hot summers. In winter, warm days and cold nights in higher parts. Average annual rainfall 457 mm (*18 in*), varying from 635 mm (*25 in*) in north to 228 mm (*9 in*) or less in western Kalahari. Sand and dust blown by westerly wind in August.
Labour force: 367 949 in 1985: Agriculture 48·5%; Mining 3·5%; Trade 3·8%.
Gross domestic product: 1523·6 million pula in 1985: Agriculture 3·9%; Mining and quarrying 46·9%;

left: **BOLIVIA** *right:* **BRAZIL**

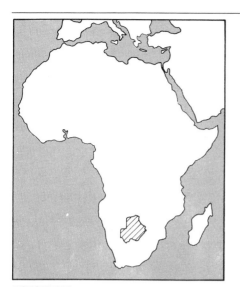

BOTSWANA

Trade, restaurants and hotels 17·6%; Finance etc 5·1%.

Exports: 1963 million pula (1986): Meat and meat products 7·5%; Diamonds 74·1%; Copper-nickel matte 15·3%.

Monetary unit: Pula. 1 pula = 100 thebe.

Denominations:
Coins 1, 5, 10, 25, 50 thebe; 1 pula.
Notes 1, 2, 5, 10, 20 pula.

Political history and government: Formerly the Bechuanaland Protectorate, under British rule. In February 1965 the seat of government was moved from Mafeking (now Mafikeng), in South Africa, to Gaberones (now Gaborone). The first elections were held on 1 Mar 1965, when internal self-government was achieved, and the first Prime Minister was appointed two days later. Bechuanaland became the independent Republic of Botswana, within the Commonwealth, on 30 Sept 1966, when the Prime Minister became President.

Legislative power is vested in the unicameral National Assembly, with 38 members, including 32 directly elected by universal adult suffrage from single-member constituencies. Members of the Assembly serve for up to five years. Executive power is vested in the President, who is the leader of the majority party in the Assembly. He governs with the assistance of an appointed Cabinet, responsible to the Assembly. The government is also advised by the House of Chiefs, with 15 members, including the chiefs of the eight principal tribes, four sub-chiefs and three others.

Length of roadways: 15 000 km (*9300 miles*) (1986).

Length of railways: 710 km (*441 miles*).

Universities: 1.

Adult illiteracy: 29·2% in 1985.

Defence: Total armed forces 3250 (1987); defence expenditure (1987) 45·3 million pula.

Foreign tourists: 60 000 in 1986.

Brazil

Official name: A República Federativa do Brasil (the Federative Republic of Brazil).

Population: 138 493 000 (1986 estimate).

Area: 8 511 965 km² (*3 286 488 miles²*).

Language: Portuguese.

Religion: Roman Catholic.

Capital city: Brasília, population 1 576 657 (1985 estimate).

Other principal towns (1985): São Paulo 10 099 086; Rio de Janeiro 5 615 149; Belo Horizonte 2 122 073; Salvador 1 811 367; Fortaleza 1 588 709; Nova Iguaçu 1 324 639; Recife 1 289 627; Curitiba 1 285 027; Port Alegre 1 275 483; Belém 1 120 777; Goiânia 928 046.

Highest point: Pico da Bandira, 2890 m (*9482 ft*).

Principal mountain ranges: Serra do Mar, Serra Geral, Serra de Mantiqueira.

Principal rivers: Amazonas (Amazon) (6448 km *4007 miles*) and tributaries, Paraná, São Francisco.

Head of State: José Sarney, President.

Climate: Hot and wet in tropical Amazon basin; sub-tropical in highlands; temperate (warm summers and mild winters) in southern uplands. In Rio de Janeiro, average maximum 24°C (*75°F*) (July, September) to 29°C (*85°F*) (February), minimum 17°C (*63°F*) (July) to 23°C (*73°F*) (January, February), December rainiest (14 days). In São Paulo, maximum 22°C (*71°F*) (June, July) to 28°C (*82°F*) (February), minimum 9°C (*49°F*) (July) to 18°C (*64°F*) (February), January rainiest (19 days). Absolute maximum temperature 43·9°C (*111·0°F*), Ibipetuba, 16 Sept 1927; absolute minimum −11°C (*12·2°F*), Xanxerê, 14 July 1933.

Labour force: 50 940 700 in 1985: Agriculture, forestry and fishing 25·7%; Manufacturing 13·3%; Construction 9·1%; Trade 10%; Services (inc. hotels and restaurants) 15·5%.

Gross domestic product: 1 406 077 million cruzeiros in 1985.

Exports: US$29 309 million in 1984: Coffee 10·5%; Food, beverages, vinegar and tobacco 19·4%; Mineral products 11·3%; Machinery and transport equipment 10%.

Monetary unit: 1 cruzado = 1 centavos. (The cruzado was introduced in 1986. 1 cruzado is equivalent to 1000 cruzeiros. Some figures given in this section are in the former currency).

Denominations:
Coins 1, 5, 10 and 50 centavos; 1 cruzado.
Notes 100, 200, 500, 1000, 5000, 10 000, 50 000 and 100 000 cruzeiros stamped with their equivalent value in cruzados.

Political history and government: Under a military-backed government since the army revolution of 31 Mar–1 Apr 1964. Existing political parties were banned on 27 Oct 1965. Two new parties (one pro-government, one against) were formed in December 1965. New constitutions were introduced on 15 Mar 1967 and 20 Oct 1969. Brazil is a federal republic comprising 23 States, four Territories and a Federal District (Brasília). Legislative power is exercised by the National Congress, comprising the Chamber of Deputies (487 members, elected for four years) and the Federal Senate (69 members, elected in rotation for eight years). One-third of the Senate is elected indirectly. All literate adults may vote. Executive power is exercised by the President, elected for six years by an electoral college composed of members of Congress and representatives

of State legislatures. He is assisted by a Vice-President and an appointed Cabinet. The President has far-reaching powers. On 22 Nov 1979 Congress approved legislation to end the two-party system. Several opposition parties were later formed and have been represented in Congress since elections in November 1986. In February 1987 the Congress became a Constituent Assembly to draft a new Constitution. A referendum in 1993 will decide, among other issues, whether Brazil will retain its republican form of government or restore the monarchy (overthrown in 1889).
Length of roadways: 1 593 653 km (*989 659 miles*) (1986).
Length of railways: 29 901 km (*18 584 miles*).
Universities: 68.
Adult illiteracy: 21·8% in 1984.
Defence: Military service one year; total armed forces 295 700 in 1987; defence expenditure: 44 030 million cruzados in 1987.
Foreign tourists: 1 900 000 in 1986.

Brunei

Population: 221 900 (1985 estimate).
Area: 5765 km² (*2226 miles²*).
Languages: Malay, English.
Religion: Islam (Sunni).
Capital city: Bandar Seri Begawan, population 55 000 (1985 estimate).
Principal river: Brunei River.
Head of State: HM Sir Muda Hassanal Bolkiah Mu'izzadin Waddaulah, Sultan of Brunei (b. 15 July 1946). Succeeded 5 Oct 1967 (crowned 1 Aug 1968).
Head of Government: HM The Sultan.
Climate: Hot and wet, tropical marine, rainfall ranging from 2500 mm (*100 in*) on the coast to 5000 mm (*200 in*) inland. Bandar Seri Begawan, January 27°C (*80°F*), July 28°C (*82°F*).
Labour force: 81 535 (1985). In 1981: Construction 17·9%; Trade 10·4%; Transport, storage and communications 6·4%; Community, social and personal services 41·4%; Unemployed 3·6%.
Gross domestic product: BS\$6977 million in 1986.
Exports: B\$ 6532·9 million in 1985: Crude petroleum 54·4%; Natural gas 42·6%.
Currency: Brunei dollar = 100 cents.
Coins 1, 5, 10, 50 cents.
Notes 1, 5, 10, 50, 100, 500, 1000 dollars.
Political history and government: The Sultanate of Brunei once controlled all of the island of Borneo, as well as parts of the Sulu Islands and the Philippines. After the 16th century its power declined until, by the middle of the 19th century, it had been reduced to its present boundaries, under the protection of Great Britain.
 The present Sultan formed a constitution in 1959, whereby there would be a Privy Council, an Executive and a Legislative Council. On 6 Jan 1965 amendments were made to the constitution so that elections could be made to the Legislative Council. The Executive Council was renamed the Council of Ministers. The Council of Ministers is presided over by the Sultan and consists of six ex-officio members and four other members, all of whom, except one, are members of the Legislative Council. The Mentri Besar, or Acting Chief Minister (one of the ex-officio members of the Legislative Council

and the Council of Ministers) is responsible to the Sultan for the exercise of executive authority in the State.
 On 7 Jan 1979 the Sultan and the British government signed a treaty by which Brunei became an independent state on 31 Dec 1983.
Length of roadways: 1511 km (*938 miles*).
Universities: 1.
Adult illiteracy: 29% (1981).
Defence: Total armed forces, 4050 (1985); defence expenditure: B\$505 million in 1986. A Gurkha battalion of the British Army is stationed in Brunei.
Foreign tourists: 6400 in 1985.

Bulgaria

Official name: Narodna Republika Bulgariya (People's Republic of Bulgaria).
Population: 8 942 976 (1985 census).
Area: 110 912 km² (*42 823 miles²*).
Languages: Bulgarian 88%; Turkish and Macedonian minorities.
Religions: Eastern Orthodox, with Muslim, Roman Catholic and Protestant minorities.
Capital city: Sofiya (Sofia), population 1 093 752 (1983 estimate).
Other principal towns (1983): Plovdiv 373 235; Varna 295 218; Ruse 181 185; Burgas 183 477; Stara Zagora 144 904; Pleven 140 440; Shumen 104 089.
Highest point: Musala, 2925 m (*9596 ft*).
Principal mountain range: Stara Planina (Balkan Mountains).
Principal rivers: Dunav (Danube) (2850 km *1770 miles*), Iskûr (Iskar) (368 km *229 miles*), Maritsa (524 km *326 miles*), Tundzha.
Head of State: Todor Zhivkov (b. 7 Sept 1911), Chairman of the State Council and General Secretary of the Central Committee of the Bulgarian Communist Party.
Head of Government: Georgi Atanasov, Chairman of the Council of Ministers.
Climate: Mild in the south, more extreme in the north. In Sofia, July (14°C to 28°C *57°F to 82°F*), August (13°C to 28°C *56°F to 82°F*) hottest, January (−5°C to 1°C *22°F to 34°F*) coldest, May rainiest (11 days).
Labour force: 4 802 005 in 1985: Agriculture 22·4%; Industry 34·3%; Construction 8·6%; Commerce 8·7%; Education and culture 7·4%; Public health, welfare and sports 4·8% (1983 figures).
Net material product: 25 450·5 million leva in 1985: Agriculture and livestock 13·8%; Industry 59·6%; Construction 9·8%; Transport, storage, communications 7·1%.
Exports: 12 987·3 million leva in 1984: Machinery and equipment 47·7%; Fuels, mineral raw materials and metals 10·8%; Foodstuffs, beverages and tobacco products 17·5%.
Monetary unit: Lev. 1 lev = 100 stotinki (singular: stotinka).
Denominations:
Coins 1, 2, 5, 10, 20, 50 stotinki; 1, 2, 5 leva.
Notes 1, 2, 5, 10, 20 leva.
Political history and government: Formerly part of Turkey's Ottoman Empire, becoming an autonomous principality in 1878. Bulgaria became a fully independent kingdom on 22 Sept 1908. The government allied with Nazi Germany in the Second World War. On 9 Sept 1944 the Fatherland Front, a

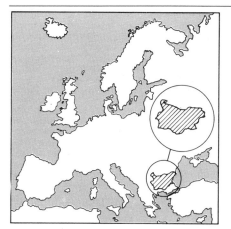

BULGARIA

Communist-dominated coalition, seized power in a *coup*. The monarchy was abolished by a popular referendum on 8 Sept 1946 and a republic proclaimed on 15 Sept 1946. A constitution for a People's Republic was adopted on 4 Dec 1947. A new constitution was promulgated, after approval by referendum, on 18 May 1971.

The supreme organ of state power is the unicameral National Assembly, with 400 members elected for five years (unopposed) by universal adult suffrage in single-member constituencies. The Assembly elects the State Council (28 members were elected on 17 June 1981) to be its permanent organ. The Council of Ministers, the highest organ of state administration, is elected by (and responsible to) the Assembly.

Political power is held by the Bulgarian Communist Party (BCP), which dominates the Fatherland Front. The Front presents an approved list of candidates for elections to all representative bodies. The BCP's highest authority is the Party Congress, convened every five years. The Congress elects a Central Committee (197 members were elected in April 1981) to supervise Party work. To direct its policy, the Committee elects a Political Bureau (Politburo), with 11 full members and six candidate members in 1988.

Bulgaria comprises nine regions, 29 urban areas and 299 other districts each with a council elected for 30 months. Since 1984–5 there have been attempts to forcibly 'Bulgarianize' ethnic minorities, particularly the Turks.

Length of roadways: 37 397 km (*23 223 miles*) (1987).
Length of railways: 6430 km (*3996 miles*) (1986).
Universities: 3.
Defence: Military service: Army and Air Force two years, Navy three years; total armed forces 152 800 (94 000 conscripts in 1987; defence expenditure: 5·5% of total government expenditure in 1985.
Foreign tourists: 7 567 000 in 1986.

Burkina Faso

Official name: Burkina Faso (previously Upper Volta).
Population: 7 976 019 (1985 census).

Area: 274 200 km² (*105 869 miles²*).
Languages: French (official), Mossi, other African languages.
Religions: Animist; Islam (Sunni) and Christian minorities.
Capital city: Ouagadougou, population 442 223 (1985 census).
Other principal towns (1985): Bobo-Dioulasso 231 162; Koudougou 51 670; Ouahigouya 38 604.
Highest point: Mt Tema, 749 m (*2457 ft*).
Principal rivers: Volta Noire (Black Volta), Volta Rouge (Red Volta), Volta Blanche (White Volta).
Head of State: Capt. Blaise Compaoré, President.
Climate: Hot (average temperature 28°C (*83°F*). Dry from November to March. Very dry in north and north-east. Rainy season June to October in south. In Ouagadougou, average maximum temperature 30°C (*87°F*) (August) to 40°C (*104°F*) (March), minimum 15°C (*60°F*) to 26°C (*79°F*).
Labour force: 3 537 000 in 1984: Agriculture, forestry and fishing 79%.
Gross domestic product: 346 451 million CFA francs in 1983. Agriculture, forestry and fishing 38·7%; Manufacturing 14·2%; Trade 12·9%.
Exports: 34 872 million francs CFA: Cotton 55%.
Monetary unit: Franc de la Communauté financière africaine.
Denominations:
Coins 1, 2, 5, 10, 25, 50, 100 CFA francs.
Notes 50, 100, 500, 1000, 5000 and 10 000 CFA francs.
Political history and government: Formerly a part of French West Africa, independent since 5 Aug 1960. The civilian President was deposed on 3 Jan 1966 in a military *coup* led by Lt.-Col. (later Maj.-Gen.) Sangoulé Lamizana, the army Chief of Staff. He took office as President and Prime Minister, constitution was suspended, the National Assembly dissolved and a Supreme Council of the Armed Forces established. Political activities were suspended on 21 Sept 1966 but the restriction was lifted in November 1969. A new constitution was approved by popular referendum on 14 June 1970 and introduced on 21 June. This provided for a four-year transitional régime, under joint military and civilian control, leading to the return of civilian rule. Elections for a unicameral National Assembly of 57 members were held on 20 Dec 1970. The leader of the majority party was appointed Prime Minister by the President, took office on 13 Feb 1971 and formed a mixed civilian and military Council of Ministers. On 8 Feb 1974, after a dispute between the Premier and the Assembly, the President dismissed the former and dissolved the latter. The army again assumed power, with the constitution and political activity suspended. The Head of State also became President of the Council of Ministers on 11 Feb 1974. Political parties were banned on 30 May. The Assembly was replaced by a National Consultative Council for Renewal, formed on 2 July 1974, with 65 members nominated by the President.

Political parties were allowed to resume activities from 1 Oct 1977. A referendum on 27 Nov 1977 approved a draft constitution providing for a return to civilian democratic rule, with legislative elections on a multi-party basis, a President directly elected for a 5-year term and a separate Prime Minister nominated by the President. Elections held on 30 Apr 1978 for a new National Assembly (57 members serving a 5-year term). Under the constitution, only the three parties which obtained most votes were allowed to continue their activities (other parties being obliged to merge with them). A presidential election was held on 14 May 1978 but no candidate gained an overall majority. A 'run-off' election between the two leading candidates on 28 May was won by Lamizana. On 7 July 1978 the Assembly elected the President's nominee for Prime Minister. The President appointed other Ministers on the Prime Minister's recommendation. On 29 May 1979 the Assembly passed a law limiting the number of authorized political parties to the three strongest in the 1978 elections.

On 25 Nov 1980 the government was overthrown in a military *coup*, led by Col Saye Zerbo, military commander of the capital region. He was overthrown in November 1982, Maj. Jean-Baptiste Oedraogo assuming power, who was himself overthrown by Capt. Thomas Sankara in August 1983. Sankara subsequently survived a number of attempts to overthrow him but was killed in a *coup* on 15 Oct 1987. A new Military council was formed on 31 Oct 1987.

The country is divided into 30 provinces.
Length of roadways: 16 574 km (*10 299 miles*).
Length of railways: 550 km (*342 miles*).
Universities: 1.
Adult illiteracy: 86·8% in 1985.
Defence: Total armed forces 8700 (1987); defence expenditure (1987) 14 280 million francs CFA. There is voluntary military service (two years).
Foreign tourists: 60 000 in 1986.

Burma

Official name: Pyidaungsu Thammada Myanma Nainggnan (The Republic of the Union of Burma). (Since 30 May 1989 the official name of the country has been the Union of Myanma.)
Population: 36 392 000 (1984 estimate).
Area: 676 552 km² (*261 218 miles²*).
Languages: Burmese, English.
Religions: Buddhist, with Muslim, Hindu and Animist minorities.
Capital city: Yangon (Rangoon), population 2 458 712 (1983 census).
Other principal towns (1983): Mandalay 532 895; Moulmein 219 991; Bassein 335 000; Akyab 143 000.
Highest point: Hkakado Razi, 5881 m (*19 296 ft*).
Principal mountain ranges: Arakan Yoma, Pegu Yoma.
Principal rivers: Irrawaddy (including Chindwin), Salween, Sittang, Mekong (4180 km *2600 miles*) on frontier.
Head of State: Maung Maung, President.
Prime Minister: Saw Maung.
Climate: Hot March–April, monsoon May–October, cool November–February. In Rangoon, average maximum 29°C (*89°F*) (July, August) to 36°C (*97°F*) (April), minimum 18°C (*65°F*) (January) to 25°C (*77°F*) (May), July (26 days) and August (25 days) rainiest. Absolute maximum temperature 45·56°C (*114°F*), Mandalay, 29 Apr 1906, Monywa, 15 May 1934; absolute minimum −0·56°C (*31°F*), Maymyo, 29 Dec 1913.
Labour force: 14 792 000 in 1985: Agriculture, forestry and fishing 66·1%; Manufacturing 8·3%; Trade 9·8%; Administration 3·9%.
Gross domestic product: 57 148 million kyats in 1985–6: Agriculture, forestry and fishing 48%; Manufacturing 9·4%; Transport 3·4%; Financial institu-

tions 2·3%; Social and administrative services 4·7%.
Exports: 3419·5 million kyats in 1983–4: Rice and rice products 40·8%; Teak 24·6%; Base metals and ores 8·8%.
Monetary unit: Kyat. 1 kyat = 100 pyas.
Denominations:
Coins 1, 5, 10, 25, 50 pyas; 1 kyat.
Notes 1, 5, 10, 15, 45, 90 kyats.
Political history and government: Formerly part of British India. Burma became a separate British dependency, with limited self-government, in 1937. It was invaded and occupied by Japanese forces in February 1942 but re-occupied by British forces in May 1945. Burma became independent, outside the Commonwealth, on 4 Jan 1948. The government was deposed by a military *coup* on 2 Mar 1962 and Parliament was dissolved the next day. Power was assumed by a Revolutionary Council, led by Gen. Ne Win. The military régime established the Burmese Socialist Programme Party (BSPP), the only permitted party from March 1964 until 1988.

A new one-party constitution, approved by popular referendum on 15–31 Dec 1973, was introduced on 4 Jan 1974, when the country's present name was adopted. Legislative power is vested in the People's Assembly, with 475 members elected for four years by universal adult suffrage. The first Assembly was elected on 27 Jan–10 Feb 1974 and inaugurated on 2 Mar 1974, when the Revolutionary Council was dissolved. The Assembly elects a Council of State (29 members) to be the country's main policy-making body. The Chairman of the Council of State is President of the Republic. The Council of Ministers, elected by the Assembly, has executive responsibility. Following widespread public disorder, Ne Win resigned in 1988 as party chairman during a congress called to discuss Burma's political and economic crisis. The President and Prime Minister were also replaced. The government does not have control over large areas of the country. Over ten minority and other movements control large areas of the country particularly along the Thai border. The main revolts against the central authorities are those of the Karen, Mon, Kachin, Shan and Chin.

The country is divided into seven states and seven administrative divisions.
Length of roadways: 23 067 km (*14 333 miles*) (1985).
Length of railways: 3156 km (*1961 miles*) (1985).
Universities: 3.
Adult illiteracy: 34% in 1980.
Defence: Military service voluntary; total armed forces 186 000 (1985); defence expenditure: 1900 million kyats (1987).
Foreign tourists: 32 900 in 1985.

Burundi

Official name: La République du Burundi or Republika y'Uburundi (the Republic of Burundi).
Population: 4 852 000 (1986 estimate).
Area: 27 834 km² (*10 747 miles²*).
Languages: French, Kirundi, Kiswahili.
Religions: Roman Catholic, with Animist and Protestant minorities.
Capital city: Bujumbura (formerly Usumbura), population 272 600.
Other principal town: Gitega (Kitega), population 95 300 (1986).
Highest point: 2685 m (*8809 ft*).
Principal rivers: Kagera, Ruzizi.

Head of State: Major Pierre Buyoya. President.
Prime Minister: Adrien Sibomana.
Climate: Hot and humid in lowlands, cool in highlands.
Labour force: 2 480 841 in 1983: Agriculture and fishing 93·7%; Traditional trades 0·9%; Private sector 1·5%; Public sector 3·8%.
Gross domestic product: 142 606 Burundi francs in 1986: Agriculture, forestry and fishing 56·8%; Trade 8%; Government services 12·5%.
Exports: 19 306·2 million Burundi francs in 1986: Coffee 93·7%; Tea 2·8%.
Monetary unit: Burundi franc. 1 franc = 100 centimes.
Denominations:
Coins 1, 5, 10 francs.
Notes 10, 20, 50, 100, 500, 1000, 5000 francs.
Political history and government: Formerly a monarchy, ruled by a *Mwami* (King). Part of German East Africa from 1899. Occupied in 1916 by Belgian forces from the Congo (now Zaire). From 1920 Burundi was part of Ruanda-Urundi, administered by Belgium under a League of Nations mandate and later as a UN Trust Territory. Became independent on 1 July 1962. A one-party state since 24 Nov 1966. The monarchy was overthrown, and a republic established, by a military *coup* on 28 Nov 1966, when the Prime Minister, Col. (later Lt.-Gen.) Michel Micombero, took power and became President. Another military *coup* deposed Micombero on 1 Nov 1976. A Supreme Revolutionary council (SRC) with 30 members, all military officers, was established on 2 Nov 1976 and its leader became President of the Second Republic. The office of Prime Minister was abolished on 13 Oct 1978. The ruling party's National Congress, opening on 26 Dec 1979, elected a Central Committee to take over the SRC's functions. President Bagaza was deposed in September 1987.
Length of roadways: 5144 km (*3196 miles*).
Universities: 1.
Adult illiteracy: 66·2% in 1982.
Defence: Total armed forces 7200 (1987); defence expenditure: 4780 million Burundi francs in 1986.
Foreign tourists: 38 000 in 1982.

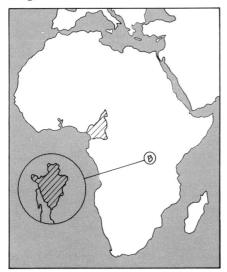

above: **CAMEROON** *encircled:* **BURUNDI**

Cameroon

Official name: La République unie du Cameroun (the United Republic of Cameroon).
Population: 10 446 000 (1986 estimate).
Area: 475 442 km² (*183 569 miles²*).
Languages: French, English (both official).
Religions: Animist, with Christian and Islamic minorities.
Capital city: Yaoundé, population 583 470 (1985 estimate).
Other principal towns (1985): Douala 852 705; Nkongsamba (1981) 86 870; Garoua (1981) 77 856; Bafoussam (1981) 75 832.
Highest point: Cameroon Mt, 4069 m (*13 350 ft*).
Principal mountain ranges: Massif de Ladamaoua.
Principal rivers: Sanaga, Nyong.
Head of State: Paul Biya (b. 13 Feb 1933), President.
Climate: Hot and rainy on the coast; cooler and drier inland. Average temperature 27°C (*80°F*). In Yaoundé average maximum 27°C to 29°C (*80°F to 85°F*), minimum around 19°C (*66°F*).
Labour force: 3 876 588 (1984–5).
Gross domestic product: 3195 billion CFA francs in 1983–4: Agriculture, forestry and fishing 22%; Mining 16·3%; Manufacturing 11·2%; Construction 6%; Trade 13%; Financial services 12·4%.
Exports: 440 470 million CFA francs in 1984: Cocoa 22·8%; Coffee 21·3%; Cotton fibre 2·3%; Cotton fabric 2·1%; Timber 4·2%; Aluminium 6·8%; Petroleum 21·6%.
Monetary unit: Franc de la Communauté financière africaine (CFA).
Denominations:
Coins 1, 2, 5, 10, 25, 50, 100, 500 CFA francs.
Notes 10, 500, 1000, 5000, 10 000 CFA francs.
Political history and government: The former German colony of Cameroon was divided into British and French zones, both parts becoming UN trust Territories. The French zone became independent as the Republic of Cameroon on 1 Jan 1960. The northern part of the British zone joined Nigeria on 1 June 1961 and the southern part became West Cameroon when it joined the former French zone (renamed East Cameroon) to form a federal republic on 1 Oct 1961. A one-party state since 8 Sept 1966. After approval by a referendum on 21 May 1972, the federal arrangement ended and Cameroon became a unitary state on 2 June 1972. The legislature is a unicameral National Assembly of 120 members elected for five years by universal suffrage. The President, elected by the people every five years, appoints the Prime Minister, other Ministers and a governor for each of the ten provinces.
Length of roadways: 64 065 km (*39 784 miles*) (1985).
Length of railways: 1173 km (*729 miles*).
Universities: 1.
Adult illiteracy: 43·8% in 1985.
Defence: Total armed forces 6600 (1987); defence expenditure: 45 000 million francs CFA (1987).
Foreign tourists: 124 000 in 1985.

Canada

Official name: Canada.
Population: 25 354 054 (1986 census).
Area: 9 976 139 km² (*3 851 809 miles²*).
Languages: English, French (28·9%).

Religions: Roman Catholic, United Church of Canada, Anglican.
Capital city: Ottawa, population 819 263 (1986 census) includes Hull and suburbs.
Other principal towns (1986 census): Toronto 3 427 168; Montreal 2 921 357; Vancouver 1 380 729; Edmonton 785 465; Calgary 671 326; Winnipeg 623 304; Quebec 603 267; Hamilton 557 029.
Highest point: Mt Logan, 6050 m (*19 850 ft*) (first climbed 23 June 1925).
Principal mountain ranges: Rocky Mts, Coast Mts, Mackenzie Mts.
Principal rivers: Mackenzie (4240 km *2635 miles*, including Peace 1923 km *1195 miles*), Yukon (3185 km *1979 miles*), St Lawrence (3130 km *1945 miles*), Nelson (2575 km *1600 miles*, including Saskatchewan 1940 km *1205 miles*), Columbia (1850 km *1150 miles*), Churchill (1609 km *1000 miles*).
Head of State: HM Queen Elizabeth II, represented by Mme Jeanne Sauvé (b. 1922), Governor-General.
Prime Minister: The Rt Hon Martin Brian Mulroney (b. 1939).
Climate: Great extremes, especially inland. Average summer temperature 18°C (*65°F*), very cold winters. Light to moderate rainfall, heavy snowfalls. Below are listed a selection of towns showing the extreme monthly variations in average maximum and minimum daily temperatures and the month with the maximum number of rainy days.

Calgary: Average maximum −4°C (*24°F*) (January) to 24°C (*76°F*) (July). Average minimum −17°C (*2°F*) (January) to 8°C (*47°F*) (July).
Halifax: Average maximum −0·5°C (*31°F*) (February) to 23°C (*74°F*) (July, August). Average minimum −9°C (*15°F*) (January, February) to 13°C (*56°F*) (August). Rainiest month (rainy days) January (17).
Ottawa: Average maximum −6°C (*21°F*) (January) to 27°C (*81°F*) (July). Average minimum −16°C (*3°F*) (January, February) to 14°C (*58°F*) (July). Rainiest month (rainy days) December (14).
St John's: Average maximum −2°C (*28°F*) (February) to 20°C (*69°F*) (August). Average minimum −9°C (*16°F*) (February) to 12°C (*53°F*) (August). Rainiest months (rainy days) November, December (17).
Vancouver: Average maximum 5°C (*41°F*) (January) to 23°C (*74°F*) (July). Average minimum 0°C (*32°F*) (January) to 12°C (*54°F*) (July, August). Rainiest month (rainy days) December (22).
Winnipeg: Average maximum −14°C (*7°F*) (January) to 26°C (*79°F*) (July). Average minimum −25°C (*−13°F*) (January) to 13°C (*55°F*) (July). Rainiest months (rainy days) January, June (12).
Yellowknife: Average maximum −23°C (*−10°F*) (January) to 20°C (*69°F*) (July). Average minimum −33°C (*−26°F*) (January) to 11°C (*52°F*) (July). Rainiest month (rainy days) December (13).

Absolute maximum temperature 46·1°C (*115°F*), Gleichen, Alberta, 28 July 1903; absolute minimum −62·8°C (*−81°F*), Snag, Yukon, 3 Feb 1947.
Labour force: 12 870 000 in 1986: Agriculture 3·7%; Manufacturing 15·9%; Trade 15·6%; Services 40·6%.
Gross domestic product: C$509 898 million (1986).
Exports: C$116 561·7 million in 1986: Raw materials 13·2%; Fabricated goods 45·1%.
Monetary unit: Canadian dollar (C$). 1 dollar = 100 cents.

Denominations:
Coins 1, 5, 10, 25, 50 cents; $1.
Notes $1, 2, 5, 10, 50, 100, 1000.
Political history and government: The Dominion of Canada, under the British Crown, was established on 1 July 1867 by the British North America Act. It was originally a federation of four provinces (Quebec, Ontario, Nova Scotia and New Brunswick). These were later joined by Manitoba (15 July 1870), British Columbia (20 July 1871), Prince Edward Island (1 July 1873), Albert and Saskatchewan (1 Sept 1905). Canada acquired its Arctic islands from the United Kingdom on 1 Sept 1880. The country acheived full independence, within the Commonwealth, by the Statute of Westminster on 11 Dec 1931. Newfoundland, previously a separate British dependency, became the tenth province on 1 Apr 1949.

In November 1981 the Canadian government agreed on the provisions of an amended constitution, to the end that it should replace the British North America Act and that its future amendment should be the prerogative of Canada. These proposals were adopted by the Parliament of Canada and were enacted by the UK Parliament as the Canada Act of 1982.

The Act gave to Canada the power to amend the Constitution according to procedures determined by the Constitutional Act 1982, which was proclaimed in force by the Queen on 17 Apr 1982. The Constitution Act 1982 added to the Canadian Constitution a charter of Rights and Freedoms, and provisions which recognize the nation's multicultural heritage, affirm the existing rights of native peoples, confirm the principle of equalization of benefits among the provinces, and strengthen provincial ownership of natural resources.

Canada is a federal parliamentary state. Executive power is vested in the Queen and exercisable by her representative, the Governor-General, whom she appoints on the advice of the Canadian Prime Minister. The Federal Parliament comprises the Queen, a nominated Senate (104 members, appointed on a regional basis) and a House of Commons (282 members elected by universal adult suffrage). A Parliament may last no longer than 5 years. The Governor-General appoints the Prime Minister and, on the latter's recommendation, other Ministers to form the Cabinet. The Prime Minister must have majority support in Parliament, to which the Cabinet is responsible. Canada contains 10 provinces (each with a Lieutenant-Governor and a legislature from which a Premier is chosen) and two (soon to be three) centrally-administered territories – the Northwest Territories are to be divided into two separate territories.
Length of roadways: 928 258 km (*575 520 miles*) (1982).
Length of railways: 66 370 km (*41 150 miles*).
Universities: 66.
Defence: Military service voluntary; total armed forces 84 600 (1987); defence expenditure for 1987–8 estimated at C$ 10 200 million.
Foreign tourists: 38 200 000 in 1986.

Alberta

Population: 2 365 825 (1986 census).
Area: 661 199 km² (*255 285 miles²*).
Languages: English, German, Ukrainian, French.
Religions: United Church of Canada, Roman Catholic, Anglican, Lutheran.

**CANADA—1. Yukon Territory   2. Northwest Territories   3. British Columbia
4. Alberta   5. Saskatchewan   6. Manitoba   7. Ontario   8. Quebec   9. Newfoundland
10. New Brunswick   11. Nova Scotia   12. Prince Edward Island**

Capital city: Edmonton, population 785 465 (1986) includes suburbs).
Other principal towns (1986): Calgary 671 326; Lethbridge 60 610; Red Deer 54 309; Medicine Hat 41 804.
Principal mountain range: Rocky Mountains.
Principal rivers: Peace, Athabasca.
Lieutenant-Governor: Helen Hunley.
Premier: Hon. Donald Getty.
Length of roadways: 151 785 km (*94 335 miles*).
Length of railways: 9031 km (*5613 miles*).

Other principal towns (1984): Vancouver 1 380 729; Prince George 67 621; Kamloops 61 773; Kelowna 61 213; Nanaimo 49 029.
Principal mountain range: Rocky Mountains.
Principal rivers: Fraser, Thompson, Kootennay, Columbia.
Lieutenant-Governor: Robert Gordon Rogers.
Premier: William Vander Zalm.
Length of roadways: 43 939 km (*27 308 miles*).
Length of railways: 7766 km (*4826 miles*).

British Columbia

Population: 2 889 207 (1986 census).
Area: 948 596 km² (*366 255 miles²*).
Languages: English, German.
Religions: United Church of Canada, Anglican, Roman Catholic, Lutheran.
Capital city: Victoria, population 255 547 (1986 census).

Manitoba

Population: 1 063 016 (1986 census).
Area: 650 087 km² (*251 000 miles²*).
Languages: English, Ukrainian, German, French.
Religions: United Church of Canada, Roman Catholic, Anglican, Lutheran.
Capital city: Winnipeg, population 623 304 (1986 census).

Other principal towns (1986): Brandon 38 708; Thompson 14 701; Portage la Prairie 13 198.
Highest point: Duck Mountain, 831 m (2727 ft).
Lieutenant-Governor: Dr George Johnson.
Premier: Howard Pawley.
Length of roadways: 19 007 km (11 813 miles).
Length of railways: 7886 km (4900 miles).

New Brunswick

Population: 709 442 (1986 census).
Area: 73 437 km² (28 354 miles²).
Languages: English, French.
Religions: Roman Catholic, Baptist, United Church of Canada, Anglican.
Capital city: Fredericton, population 44 352 (1986 census).
Other principal towns (1986): Saint John 76 381; Moncton 55 468; Bathurst 14 683; Edmundston 11 497.
Highest point: Mt Carleton, 820 m (2690 ft).
Principal river: St John.
Lieutenant-Governor: Gilbert Finn.
Premier: Francis J. McKenna.
Length of roadways: 20 686 km (12 854 miles).

Newfoundland (Terre-Neuve) and Labrador

Population: 568 349 (1986 census).
Area: 404 517 km² (156 185 miles²).
Language: English.
Religions: Roman Catholic, Anglican, United Church of Canada, Salvation Army.
Capital city: St John's, population 161 901 (1986 census).
Other principal towns (1986): Corner Brook 22 719; Gander 10 207; Grand Falls 9121; Labrador City 8664.
Highest point: Mt Gras Morne, 812 m (2666 ft).
Principal mountain range: Long Range Mountain.
Principal rivers: Humber, Exploits, Gander.
Lieutenant-Governor: James McGrath.
Premier: (Alfred) Brian Peckford (b. 27 Aug 1942).
Length of roadways: 8713 km (5415 miles) (1984).
Length of railways: 1458 km (906 miles) (1984).

Nova Scotia

Population: 873 176 (1986 census).
Area: 55 490 km² (21 425 miles²).
Language: English.
Religions: Roman Catholic, United Church of Canada, Anglican, Baptist.
Capital city: Halifax, population 295 990 (1986 census).
Other principal towns (1986): Dartmouth 65 243; Sydney 27 754; Glace Bay 20 467; Truro 12 124.
Lieutenant-Governor: Alan R. Abraham.
Premier: John MacLennan Buchanan (b. 22 Apr 1931).
Length of roadways: 25 582 km (15 899 miles) (1984).
Length of railways: 1432 km (890 miles) (1984).

Ontario

Population: 9 101 694 (1986 census).
Area: 1 068 582 km² (412 582 miles²).
Languages: English, French, Italian, German.
Religions: Roman Catholic, United Church of Canada, Anglican, Presbyterian.
Capital city: Toronto, population 3 427·168 (1986 census).

Other principal towns (1986): Ottawa 819 263 (includes suburbs across the river in Quebec province); Hamilton 557 029; St Catharine's-Niagara 343 258; London 342 302; Kitchener 311 195; Windsor 253 988.
Principal rivers: St Lawrence, Ottawa.
Lieutenant-Governor: Rt. Hon. Lincoln M. Alexander.
Premier: David Peterson.
Length of roadways: 153 613 km (95 471 miles) (1984).
Length of railways: 16 693 km (10 375 miles) (1984).

Prince Edward Island

Population: 126 646 (1986 census).
Area: 5657 km² (2184 miles²).
Languages: English, French.
Religions: Roman Catholic, United Church of Canada, Presbyterian.
Capital city: Charlottetown, population 15 776 (1986).
Other principal town: Summerside 8020 (1986).
Lieutenant-Governor: Lloyd G. MacPhail.
Premier: Joseph A. Ghiz, QC.
Length of roadways: 5278 km (3280 miles) (1984).
Length of railways: 441 km (274 miles) (1984).

Quebec

Population: 6 532 461 (1986 census).
Area: 1 540 680 km² (594 860 miles²).
Languages: French, English.
Religion: Roman Catholic.
Capital city: Quebec, population 603 267 (1986 census).
Other principal towns (1986): Montréal 2 921 357; (Laval – part of Montréal – 284 164); Sherbrooke 74 438; (Verdun – part of Montréal – 60 246); (Hull – included in figure for Ottawa – 58 722); Trois-Rivières 50 122.
Highest point: Mt Jacques Cartier, 1268 m (4160 ft).
Principal mountain ranges: Notre Dame, Appalachian.
Principal river: St Lawrence.
Lieutenant-Governor: Hon. Gilles Lamontagne.
Premier: Robert Bourassa.
Length of roadways: 57 602 km (35 800 miles) (1984).
Length of railways: 4507 km (2801 miles) (1984).

Saskatchewan

Population: 1 009 613 (1986 census).
Area: 651 900 km² (251 700 miles²).
Languages: English, German, Ukrainian.
Religions: United Church of Canada, Roman Catholic, Lutheran, Anglican.
Capital city: Regina, population 175 064 (1986 census).
Other principal towns (1986): Saskatoon 200 665; Moose Jaw 35 073; Prince Albert 33 686; Swift Current 15 666.
Highest point: 1385 m (4546 ft).
Principal rivers: N. Saskatchewan, Cree, Geokie.
Lieutenant-Governor: Frederick W. Johnson.
Premier: Grant Devine.
Length of roadways: 207 500 km (128 962 miles) (1985).
Length of railways: 11 800 km (7330 miles) (1984).

Northwest Territories

Population: 52 238 (1986 census).
Area: 3 379 683 km² (1 304 903 miles²).

Languages: Eskimo and Indian languages, English, French.
Religions: Roman Catholic, Anglican, United Church of Canada.
Capital city: Yellowknife, population 11077 (1986 census).
Other principal towns: Inuvik 3166; Hay River 3142; Frobisher Bay 2954.
Principal mountain range: Mackenzie.
Principal river: Mackenzie.
Commissioner: John Havelock Parker (b. 2 Feb 1929).
NB The Northwest Territories are to be divided into two – east and west. Two bodies have been created, one for each area to develop constitutions for each area, choose their names and negotiate a dividing boundary.

Yukon Territory

Population: 23504 (1986 census).
Area: 482515 km² (*186299 miles²*).
Languages: English, Indian languages.
Religions: Anglican, Roman Catholic, United Church of Canada.
Capital city: Whitehorse, population 18385 (1986 census).
Other principal towns (1986): Watson Lake 1595; Dawson City 1553.
Highest point: Mt Logan, 6050 m (*19850 ft*).
Principal mountain range: St Elias.
Principal river: Yukon.
Commissioner: Ken McKinnon.
Length of roadways: 4695 km (*2918 miles*) (1984).

Cape Verde

Official name: A República de Cabo Verde (the Republic of Cape Verde).
Population: 334000 (1985 estimate).
Area: 4033 km² (*1557 miles²*).
Languages: Portuguese, Crioulo (a patois).
Religions: Roman Catholic 98·7% (1965).
Capital city: Praia, population 57748 (1980 census).
Other principal town: Mindelo 36746 (1980).
Highest point: 2829 m (*9285 ft*).
Head of State: Aristides Maria Pereira (b. 17 Nov 1924) President.
Prime Minister: Maj. Pedro Verona Rodrigues Pires (b. 29 Apr 1934).
Climate: Hot and semi-arid, tempered by oceanic situation. Average temperature in Praia varies from 22°C to 27°C (*72°F to 80°F*). Prevailing north-easterly wind. Rainfall is scarce (falling almost entirely between August and October) and drought sometimes chronic.
Labour force: 102000 (1980 estimate): Agriculture 51·9%.
Gross domestic product: 3350 million escudos Caboverdianos in 1980: Agriculture and forestry 17%; Fishing 5·5%; Construction 17·6%; Trade and transport 40·5%.
Exports: 147 million escudos Caboverdianos in 1981: Vegetables and vegetable products 58·9%; Animals and animal products 11·4%; Foodstuffs and beverages 9·5%.
Monetary unit: Escudo Capoverdianos. 1 escudo = 100 centavos.
Denominations:
Coins 20, 50 centavos; 1, 2½, 10, 20, 50 escudos.
Notes 100, 500, 1000 escudos.

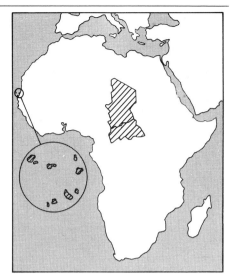

encircled: **CAPE VERDE** *top:* **CHAD**
immediately below: **THE CENTRAL AFRICAN REPUBLIC**

Political history and government: A former Portuguese territory, the Cape Verde Islands were part of Portuguese Guinea (now Guinea-Bissau) until 1879 and formed a separate territory from then until independence on 5 July 1975. The independence movement was dominated by the *Partido Africano da Independência da Guiné e Cabo Verde* (PAIGC), the African Party for the Independence of Guinea and Cape Verde. At independence Portugal transferred power to a PAIGC régime. The country's first constitution was approved on 7 Sept 1980. Legislative power is vested in the National People's Assembly, with 56 members elected by universal adult suffrage for five years. Executive power is held by the President, elected for five years by the Assembly. He appoints and leads a Council of Ministers. Following the *coup* in Guinea-Bissau on 14 Nov 1980, the Cape Verde branch of the PAIGC was renamed the African Party for the Independence of Cape Verde on 20 Jan 1981. Constitutional articles relating to the proposed union with Guinea-Bissau were revoked on 12 Feb 1981.
Length of roadways: 2250 km (*1398 miles*) (1981).
Adult illiteracy: 52·6% (1987).
Defence: Total armed forces 1185 in 1987.

The Central African Republic

Official name: La République centrafricaine.
Population: 2740000 (1986 estimate).
Area: 622984 km² (*240535 miles²*).
Languages: Sangho, French (official).
Religions: Protestant, Roman Catholic, Animist.
Capital city: Bangui, population 473800 (1984).
Other principal towns (1982): Berberati 100000; Bouar 55000.
Highest point: Mt Gaou, 1420 m (*4659 ft*).
Principal mountain range: Chaîne des Mongos.
Principal river: Oubangui.
Head of State: Gen. André Kolingba, Chairman of

the Military Committee for National Recovery.
Prime Minister: Gen. André Kolingba.
Climate: Tropical (hot and humid). Heavy rains
June to October, especially in south-western forest
areas. Average temperature 26°C (79°F). Daily
average high temperature 29°C to 34°C (85°F to
93°F), low 19°C to 22°C (66°F to 71°F).
Labour force: 1 200 000 (1980): Agriculture 72·3%.
Gross domestic product: 318 677 million CFA francs
in 1985: Agriculture, forestry and fishing 41·1%;
Manufacturing 7·3%; Wholesale and retail 21·3%;
Other services 20·5%.
Exports: 35 454 million CFA francs in 1982: Dia-
monds 24·4%; Cotton 6·4%; Coffee 33·2%; Wood
20·1%.
Monetary unit: Franc de la Communauté
financière africaine.
Denominations:
Coins 1, 2, 5, 10, 25, 50, 100 FCA francs.
Notes 100, 500, 1000, 5000, 10 000 CFA francs.
Political history and government: Formerly Ubangi-
Shari (Obangui-Chari), part of French Equatorial
Africa. Became the Central African Republic
(CAR) on achieving self-government, 1 Dec 1958.
Independent since 13 Aug 1960. The first President,
David Dacko, was deposed on 31 Dec 1965 by a mil-
itary *coup*, led by his uncle, Col. (later Marshal)
Jean-Bédel Bokassa. The National Assembly was
dissolved on 1 Jan 1966 and the constitution
revoked on 4 Jan. Bokassa assumed full powers and
became 'President for life' in February 1972. On 4
Dec 1976 he proclaimed the Central African
Empire with himself as Emperor. He crowned himself on 4 Dec 1977. Bokassa was deposed on 20–21
Sept 1979, when ex-President Dacko and the CAR
were restored. The imperial constitution was abrogated. A new constitution, providing for a multi-
party system, was approved by referendum on 1 Feb
1981 and promulgated on 6 Feb. Dacko was elected
President on 15 Mar and sworn in for a six year
term on 3 Apr. On 21 July he declared a 'state of
siege', to be administered by Gen. André Kolingba,
the Army Chief of Staff. On 1 Sept 1981 President
Dacko was deposed in a military *coup* by Gen.
Kolingba as leader of a 23-man *Comité militaire
pour le redressement national* (CMRN). The constitution and political parties were suspended, and all
legislative and executive powers assumed by the
CMRN. An all-military Council of Ministers was
formed.
Length of roadways: 20 278 km (*12 593 miles*) (1986).
Universities: 1.
Adult illiteracy: 59·5% (1985).
Defence: Total armed forces 4300 (1987); defence
expenditure: 6500 million francs CFA.
Foreign tourists: 7000 in 1983.

Chad

Official name: La République du Tchad (the
Republic of Chad).
Population: 5 061 000 (1985 estimate).
Area: 1 284 000 km² (*495 750 miles²*).
Languages: French (official), Arabic, African lan-
guages.
Religions: Muslim, Animist, Christian.
Capital city: N'Djaména (formerly Fort-Lamy),
population 511 700 (1985 estimate).
Other principal towns (1985): Sarh (formerly Fort-

Archambault) 124 000; Moundou 87 000; Abéché
71 000; Bongor 69 000.
Highest point: Emi Koussi, 3415 m (*11 204 ft*).
Principal mountain ranges: Tibesti, Ennedi.
Principal rivers: Chari, Bahr Kéita.
Head of State: Hissène Habré, President.
Climate: Hot and dry in the Sahara desert (in the
north) but milder and very wet (annual rainfall
4980 mm *196 in*) in the south. In N'Djaména, average maximum 30°C (*87°F*) (August) to 42°C
(*107°F*) (April), minimum 14°C (*57°F*) (December,
January) to 25°C (*77°F*) (May), August rainiest (22
days).
Labour force: 1 738 000 in 1981: Agriculture, forestry
and fishing 83%.
Gross domestic product: 226 200 million CFA francs
in 1982: Agriculture, hunting, forestry, fishing
48·9%; Manufacturing 7·3%; Trade, restaurants,
hotels 22·9%; Public administration and defence
12·2%.
Exports: 4120 million CFA francs in 1983: Raw cotton 91·1%; Live cattle 1·2%.
Monetary unit: Franc de la Communauté
financière africaine.
Denominations:
Coins 1, 2, 5, 10, 25, 50, 100, 500 CFA francs.
Notes 500, 1000, 5000, 10 000 CFA francs.
Political history and government: Former province
of French Equatorial Africa, independent since 11
Aug 1960. From the time of independence the central government was opposed by Muslim rebels,
who formed the *Front de libération nationale du
Tchad* (FROLINAT), or Chad National Liberation
Front, in 1966. The Front later split into several factions but most insurgent groups remained linked to
it. On 13 Apr 1975 the central government was
overthrown by a military *coup*. The new régime
formed a Supreme Military Council (SMC), led by
Gen. Félix Malloum. On 25 Aug 1978 the SMC
signed a 'fundamental charter' with a section of one
of Chad's rebel groups, the Northern Armed Forces
Command Council (CCFAN). The charter was to
serve as the country's interim constitution. On 29
Aug 1978 the SMC was dissolved. Gen. Malloum
was confirmed as President and a CCFAN leader
became Prime Minister. Following a peace conference between the various factions, the President
and Prime Minister resigned on 23 Mar 1979 and a
Provisional State Council was formed. Fighting
continued, however, and this body was replaced by
a transitional Council of Ministers on 29 Apr 1979.
After a further reconciliation conference, this Government resigned on 29 Aug 1979 to make way for a
new régime dominated by FROLINAT, whose
Chairman Goukouni Oueddei, became Head of
State. A Provisional Administrative Committee
(including only northern guerrilla representatives)
was set up on 3 Sept 1979 but this was replaced on 10
Nov by a Transitional Government of National
Unity, including most faction leaders.
In 1980 a treaty of friendship was signed with
Libya, who supported the northern rebels, and in
1981 there was even talk of a merger between the
two countries. The country was effectively divided
between government forces in the south and rebel
forces in the north for a time but by Spring 1987
most of the rebel-held areas had been regained by
the government and the Libyans were forced back
into the extreme northern Aozou Strip (over 110 000
km² *42 480 miles²*) which they had occupied since
1973.

Length of roadways: 30 725 km (*19 092 miles*) (1976).
Universities: 1.
Adult illiteracy: 74·7% (1985).
Defence: Total armed forces 17 200 (1987); defence expenditure: 16 850 million CFA francs (1986). France has an estimated 2500 troops in Chad.

Chile

Official name: República de Chile.
Population: 12 536 383 (1987 estimate).
Area: 756 945 km² (*292 258 miles²*).
Language: Spanish.
Religions: Roman Catholic, Protestant minority.
Capital city: Santiago, population 4 630 000 (1986 estimate).
Other principal towns (1986 estimates): Viña del Mar 286 000; Valparaíso 280 000; Concepción 240 000; Talcahuano 210 000; Antofagasta 170 000; Temuco 180 000.
Highest point: Ojos del Salado, 6885 m (*22 588 ft*) (first climbed 1937).
Principal mountain range: Cordillera de los Andes.
Principal rivers: Loa (439 km (*273 miles*)), Maule, Bio-Bio, Valdiva.
Head of State: Gen. Augusto Pinochet Ugarte (b. 25 Nov 1915), President.
Climate: Considerable variation north (annual rainfall 1mm *0·04 in*) to south (2665 mm *105 in*). Average temperatures 12°C (*53°F*) winter, 17°C (*63°F*) summer. In Santiago, December (10°C to 28°C *51°F to 83°F*). January (12°C to 29°C *53°F to 85°F*), and February (11°C to 29°C *52°F to 84°F*) hottest, June (3°C to 14°C *37°F to 58°F*) and July (3°C to 15°C *37°F to 59°F*) coldest and rainiest (6 days each). Absolute maximum temperature 41·6°C (*106·9°F*), Los Angeles, February 1944; absolute minimum −21·2°C (*−6·16°F*), Longuimay, July 1933.
Labour force: 3 895 700 in 1986: Agriculture, forestry and fishing 20·6%; Manufacturing 13·6%; Commerce 16·7%; Services 31·6%.
Gross domestic product: 1557·7 billion pesos in 1983: Mining and quarrying 10·1%; Manufacturing 20·6%; Trade 15·0%; Services 36·0%.
Exports: US$3823 million in 1985: Copper 46·1%; Meat and fish meal 7·2%; Chemical wood pulp 3·4%.
Monetary unit: Chilean peso. 1 peso = 100 centavos.
Denominations:
Coins 1, 5, 10, 50 pesos.
Notes 100, 500, 1000, 5000 pesos.
Political history and government: A republic, divided into 12 regions and one metropolitan region (Santiago). The last civilian President was deposed by a military *coup* on 11 Sept 1973. A 'state of siege' was proclaimed; the bicameral National Congress (a Senate and a Chamber of Deputies) was dissolved on 13 Sept 1973, and the activities of political parties were suspended on 27 Sept 1973. Power is held by the *Junta Militar de Gobierno*, whose leader was proclaimed President of the Republic on 17 Dec 1974. All political parties were banned on 12 Mar 1977. The state of siege was lifted on 11 Mar 1978 but a state of emergency remained in force. A new constitution was approved in a plebiscite on 11 Sept 1980, signed by the President on 21 Oct 1980 and entered into force on 11 Mar 1981. It provided for the separation of the junta and presidency, with

CHILE

the military régime retaining power for a 'transitional' period of eight years. Legislative elections are scheduled for 1990, when the junta is to submit a single presidential candidate to referendum. Gen. Pinochet stood as the nomination for single presidential candidate in a plebiscite in October 1988 – his nomination was rejected by the voters. During 1987–8 a number of political parties sought legal registration (under a law of March 1987 restoring the right to form political parties).
Length of roadways: 79 000 km (*49 059 miles*) (1986).
Length of railways: 8570 km (*5322 miles*) (1986).
Universities: 8.
Defence: Military service two years; total armed forces 97 500 in 1987; defence expenditure: 101 090 million pesos in 1987.
Foreign tourists: 459 000 in 1985.

China

Official name: Zhonghua Renmin Gongheguo (People's Republic of China).
Population: 1 060 080 000 (1986 estimate).
Area: 9 561 000 km² (*3 691 500 miles²*).
Languages: Chinese (predominantly Mandarin dialect).
Religions: Confucianism, Buddhism, Daoism (Taoism); Roman Catholic and Muslim minorities.
Capital city: Beijing (Peking), population 5 860 000 (1985).
Other principal towns (1986): Shanghai 6 980 000; Tianjin 5 380 000; Shenyang 4 200 000; Wuhan 3 400 000; Guangzhou (Canton) 3 290 000; Chongquin 2 780 000; Harbin 2 630 000; Chengdu 2 580 000; Xian 2 330 000; Zibo 2 300 000; Nanjing (Nanking) 2 250 000; Taiyuan 1 880 000; Changchun 1 860 000; Dalian (Dairen) 1 630 000;

Zhengzhou 1 590 000; Kunming 1 490 000; Jinan 1 430 000; Tangshan 1 390 000: Guiyang 1 380 000; Lanzhou 1 350 000; Anshan 1 280 000; Qidihar 1 260 000; Hangzhou 1 250 000; Qingdao 1 250 000; Fushun 1 240 000; Fuszhou 1 190 000; Changsha 1 160 000; Shijazhuang 1 160 000; Jilin 1 140 000; Nanchang 1 120 000; Baotau 1 100 000; Huainan 1 070 000; Luoyang 1 050 000; Ningbo 1 020 000; Datong 1 000 000; Urumqi 1 000 000.

(*NB* Some of these municipalities include considerable rural areas as well as the urban area – thus a number of these figures are artificially high).

Highest point: Mt Everest (on Tibet-Nepal border), 8848 m *(29 028 ft)* (first climbed 29 May 1953).

Principal mountain ranges: Himalaya, Kunlun Shan, Tien Shan, Nan Shan, Astin Tagh.

Principal rivers: Changjiang (Yangtze Kiang) (5530 km *3436 miles*), Huanghe (Yellow), Mekong.

Head of State: Yang Shangkun, State President.

Political Leader: Zhao Ziyang (b. 1919), General Secretary of the CPC.

Head of Government: Li Peng, Premier of the State Council.

Climate: Extreme variations. Warm, humid summers and long cold winters in north (annual average below 10°C *50°F*); sub-tropical in extreme south; monsoons in the east; arid in the north-west. In Beijing, July hottest (22°C to 32°C *72°F to 89°F*) and rainiest (13 days), January coldest (−9°C to 2°C *15°F to 35°F*).

Labour force: 498 727 000 in 1985: Industry 16·7%; Construction 4·4%; Agriculture, forestry etc 62·5%; Commerce, trade, etc 4·7%.

Net material product: 68 2 200 million yuan in 1985: Agriculture 41·5%; Industry 41·5%; Construction 5·5%; Transport 3·5%; Commerce 8%.

Exports: 58 056 million yuan in 1985: Food and live animals 12·4%; Crude materials 9·2%; Mineral fuels 23%; Basic manufactures 19·3%; Machinery 5·8%; Miscellaneous manufactured articles 18%.

Monetary unit: Yuan. 1 yuan (or renminbiao) = 10 jiao (chiao) = 100 fen.

Denominations:
Coins 1, 2, 5 fen.
Notes 1, 2, 5 jiao; 1, 2, 5, 10 yuan.

Political history and government: Under Communist rule since September 1949. The People's Republic was inaugurated on 1 Oct 1949. The present constitution was adopted on 5 Mar 1978. China is a unitary state comprising 21 provinces, 5 'autonomous' regions (including Tibet) and 3 municipalities. The Communist Party is the 'core of leadership' and the Chairman of the Party's Central Committee commands the People's Liberation Army (PLA), which includes naval and air forces. The highest organ of state power is the National People's Congress, (in 1980) 3478 deputies indirectly elected for 5 years by provinces, regions, municipalities and the PLA. The Congress, under the leadership of the Party, elects a Standing Committee (196 members in March 1978) to be its permanent organ. The executive and administrative arm of government is the State Council (a Premier, Vice-Premiers and other Ministers), appointed by and accountable to Congress.

Political power is held by the Communist Party of China (CPC). The CPC's highest authority is the Party Congress, convened normally every five years. The 11th Congress, meeting on 12–18 Aug 1977, elected a Central Committee (201 full and 132 alternate members) to supervise Party work. To direct its policy, the Committee elects a Political

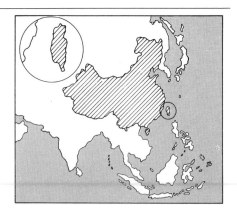

CHINA (MAINLAND)

encircled: **CHINA (TAIWAN)**

bureau (Politburo), with 24 full and two alternate members in 1980. The Politburo has a five-member Standing Committee (the Chairman and four Vice-Chairmen).

A new constitution was introduced in 1982 which, among other things, restored the post of State President.

Length of roadways: 940 000 km *(583 740 miles)* (1985).

Length of railways: 52 000 km *(32 300 miles)* (1984).

Universities: 37.

Adult illiteracy: 23% in 1983.

Defence: Military service selective (Army three years, Air and Army technicians four years, Navy five years); total regular forces 3 200 000 (1987); defence expenditure: 20 376 million yuan.

Foreign tourists: 22 800 000 in 1986.

China (Taiwan)

Official name: Chung-hua Min Kuo (Republic of China).

Population: 19 454 610 (1986 estimate).

Area: 35 981·4 km² *(13 892·5 miles²)*.

Language: Northern Chinese (Amoy dialect).

Religions: Buddhist, with Muslim and Christian minorities.

Capital city: Taipei, population 2 575 180 (1986 estimate).

Other principal towns (1986): Kaohsiung 1 320 552; Taichung 695 562; Tainan 646 298; Panchiao 491 721.

Highest point: Yü Shan (Mt Morrison), 3997 m *(13 113 ft)*.

Principal mountain ranges: Chunyang Shanmo.

Principal rivers: Hsia-tan-shui Chi (159 km *99 miles*), Choshui Chi (170 km *106 miles*), Tanshui Ho (144 km *89 miles*), Wu Chi (113 km *70 miles*).

Head of State: Lee Teng-hui, President.

Prime Minister: Yu Kuo-hwa.

Climate: Rainy summers and mild winters, average temperature 23°C *(73°F)*, average annual rainfall 2565 mm *(101 in)*. In Taipei, July (24°C to 34°C *74°F to 93°F*) and August (24°C to 33°C *75°F to 91°F*) warmest, January (12°C to 19°C *54°F to 66°F*) and February (12°C to 18°C *53°F to 65°F*) coolest, April rainiest (14 days).

Labour force: 7 945 000 in 1986: Agriculture, forestry and fishing 16·6%; Manufacturing 32·9%; Commerce 17·4%; Construction 6·6%; Transport, storage and communications 5·1%; Other services 15·2%.
Gross domestic product: NT$2 701 773 million in 1986: Agriculture 4·1%; Manufacturing 42·9%; Government services 9·3%; Trade etc. 14·1%.
Exports: NT$1 504 348·8 million in 1986: Plastic articles 8·9%; TV receivers 1·5%; Calculating machines 5·9%; Clothing 6%; Synthetic fabrics 2%.
Monetary unit: New Taiwan dollar (NT$). 1 dollar = 100 cents.
Denominations:
Coins 50 cents; 1, 5, 10 dollars.
Notes 10, 50, 100, 500, 1000 dollars.
Political history and government: After the Republic of China was overthrown by Communist forces on the mainland, the government withdrew to Taiwan on 8 Dec 1949. As it claims to be the legitimate administration for all China, the régime continues to be dominated by mainlanders who came to the island in 1947–49. The first elections since the Communist victory were held in Taiwan on 23 Dec 1972. There are five governing bodies (*yuans*). The highest legislative organ is the Legislative Yuan, comprising (in 1989) 329 members. This body submits proposals to the National Assembly (964 life members and 62 elected for 6 years), which elects the President and Vice-President for 6 years. The Executive Yuan (Council of Ministers) is the highest administrative organ and is responsible to the Legislative Yuan.
Length of roadways: 19 885 km (*12 348 miles*).
Length of railways: 3036 km (*1887 miles*).
Universities: 16.
Defence: Military service two years; total armed forces 424 000 (1987); defence expenditure: NT$175 900 million in 1987–8.
Foreign tourists: 1 610 385 in 1986.

Colombia

Official name: La República de Colombia.
Population: 27 867 326 (1985 census).
Area: 1 138 914 km² (*439 737 miles²*).
Language: Spanish.
Religion: Roman Catholic.
Capital city: Bogotá, population 4 185 174 (1985 census).
Other principal towns (1985): Medellín 1 468 089; Cali 1 350 565; Barranquilla 899 781; Cartagena 531 426; Cúcuta 379 478.
Highest point: Pico Cristóbal Colón, 5775 m (*18 947 ft*) (first climbed 1939).
Principal mountain range: Cordillera de los Andes.
Principal rivers: Magdalena, Cauca, Amazonas (Amazon, 6448 km *4007 miles*) on frontier.
Head of State: Dr Virgilio Barco, President.
Climate: Hot and humid on the coasts and in the jungle lowlands, temperate in the Andean highlands, with rainy seasons March–May and September–November. In Bogotá, daily average low temperature 9°C to 10°C (*48°F to 51°F*), high 18°C to 20°C (*64°F to 68°F*), April and October rainiest (20 days).
Labour force: 8 467 000 in 1980: Agriculture, forestry and fishing 28·5%; Manufacturing 13·4%; Trade 14·9%; Community, social and personal services 23·6%.

COLOMBIA

Gross domestic product: 4 728 439 million pesos in 1985: Agriculture 17·2%; Industry 22·9%; Wholesale and retail trade 13·8%; Services 24·6%.
Exports: US$4·79 billion in 1986: Coffee 62·3%; Fuel oil 4·3%; Bananas 4·1%; Cotton 1·9%.
Monetary unit: Colombian peso. 1 peso = 100 centavos.
Denominations:
Coins 1, 2, 5, 10, 20, 50 pesos.
Notes 20, 50, 100, 200, 500, 1000, 2000, 5000 pesos.
Political history and government: A republic. Legislative power is vested in Congress, which is composed of the Senate (112 members) and the House of Representatives (199 members). Members of both Houses are elected for 4 years. Executive power is exercised by the President (elected for 4 years by universal adult suffrage), assisted by a Cabinet. The country is divided into 23 departments, 4 intendancies and 5 commissaries.
Length of roadways: 106 218 km (*65 961 miles*) (1986).
Length of railways: 3403 km (*2115 miles*).
Universities: 98.
Adult illiteracy: 11·9% in 1985.
Defence: Military service two years; total armed forces 70 200 in 1987; defence expenditure: 66 230 million pesos in 1987.
Foreign tourists: 732 200 in 1986.

The Comoros

Official name: La République fédérale islamique des Comores (the Federal Islamic Republic of the Comoros).
Population: 422 500 (1987 estimate).
Area: 2171 km² (*838 miles²*) (including Mayotte, 373 km² (*144 miles²*).

Languages: French (official), Comoran (a blend of Swahili and Arabic).
Religions: Islam, with a Christian minority.
Capital city: Moroni, population 17 267 (1980 census).
Other principal town: Mutsamudu 13 000 (1980 census).
Highest point: Mt Kartala, 2361 m (*7746 ft*).
Head of State: Ahmed Abdallah Abderemane (b. 1918), President.
Climate: Tropical climate with two distinct seasons. Dry between May and October, hot and humid from November to April. Most rain in January (up to 380 mm *15 in*). Cyclones, water-spouts and tidal waves occur in the summer. The November monsoon brings the maximum temperature of 28°C (*82°F*), while the minimum temperature (July) falls to 20°C (*68°F*).
Labour force: 181 000 (1980): Agriculture, forestry and fishing 82·8%; Industry 5·5%.
Gross domestic product: 32 580 million Comoros francs in 1982: Agriculture, fishing etc. 39·8%; Construction 10·2%; Trade 13·2%.
Exports: 7048 million Comoros francs in 1985: Vanilla 66·5%; Cloves 19·5%; Ylang-ylang 9·3%.
Monetary unit: Comoros franc. 1 Comoros franc = 100 centimes.
Denominations:
Coins 1, 2, 5, 10, 20 francs.
Notes 50, 100, 500, 1000, 5000 francs.
Political history and government: A former French dependency. Attached to Madagascar in 1912, the Comoro Islands became a separate French Overseas Territory in 1947. The Territory acheived internal self-government by a law of 29 Dec 1961, with a Chamber of Deputies (in place of the Territorial Assembly) and a Government Council to control local administration. Ahmed Abdallah, President of the Council from 26 Dec 1972, was restyled President of the Government on 15 June 1973. In a referendum on 22 Dec 1974 the Comorans voted 95·6% in favour of independence, though on the island of Mayotte the vote was 65% against. The French Government wanted each island to ratify its new constitution separately by referendum. To avoid the expected separation of Mayotte, the Chamber of Deputies voted for immediate independence on 6 July 1975. A unilateral declaration of independence, as the *Etat Comorien* (Comoran State), was made on the same day. On 7 July the Chamber elected Abdallah as President of the Comoros and constituted itself as the National Assembly. France kept its hold on Mayotte but the three other main islands achieved *de facto* independence. On 3 Aug 1975 Abdallah was deposed in a *coup*. France recognized the independence of the three islands on 31 Dec 1975. The new régime was overthrown by a *coup* on 12–13 May 1978. A Political-Military Directory was formed and on 23 May ex-President Abdallah and his former deputy were appointed its co-presidents. On 24 May 1978 the country's present name was announced. A new constitution was approved by referendum on 1 Oct 1978 and Abdallah was elected President (unopposed) for a 6-year term on 22 Oct 1978. A 39-member Federal Assembly was elected for a 5-year term on 8 and 15 Dec 1978, and in 1979 the assembly approved the formation of a one-party state.
A referendum on Mayotte on 8 Feb 1976 resulted in a 99·4% vote for retaining links with France. In a second referendum, on 11 Apr 1976, Mayotte voted against remaining a French Overseas Territory. In

December 1976 France enacted legislation to give the island a special status as a *collectivité particulière*. It is thus an integral part of the French Republic and administered by a Government Commissioner.
Length of roadways: 750 km (*466 miles*) (1986).
Defence: About 800 personnel; defence expenditure: 768 million Comoros francs in 1984.
Foreign tourists: About 2000 per year.

The Congo

Official name: La République populaire du Congo (the People's Republic of the Congo).
Population: 1 912 429 (1985 census).
Area: 342 000 km² (*132 047 miles²*).
Languages: French (official), Bantu languages.
Religions: Animist, Christian minority.
Capital city: Brazzaville, opopulation 595 102 (1985 census).
Other principal towns (1985 census): Pointe-Noire 297 392; N'kayi (formerly Jacob) 49 458; Loubomo (formerly Dolisie) 35 628.
Highest point: 1040 m (*3412 ft*).
Principal mountain range: Serro do Crystal.
Principal rivers: Zaïre (Congo) (4700 km *2920 miles*), Oubangui.
Head of State: Col. Denis Sassou-Nguesso (b. 1943), President.
Prime Minister: Ange-Edouard Poungi.
Climate: Tropical (hot and humid). Equatorial rains for seven to eight months per year. In Brazzaville, daily average low temperature 17°C to 21°C (*63°F to 70°F*), high 28°C to 33°C (*82°F to 91°F*).
Labour force: 649 000 (1980): Agriculture 62·4%; Industry 11·9%; Services 25·6%.
Gross domestic product: 958 509 million CFA francs in 1984: Agriculture, forestry and fishing 7·4%; Mining 43·2%; Manufacturing 4·3%; Trade 10·9%; Transport, storage and communications 7·1%; Government services 9·3%.
Exports: 488 365·7 million CFA francs in 1985:

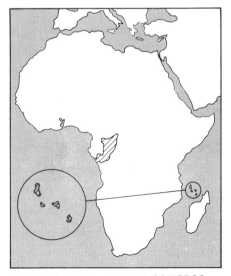

left: **THE CONGO** *right:* **THE COMOROS**

Petroleum and petroleum products 93·3%; Wood 2·5%.

Monetary unit: Franc de la Communauté financière africaine.

Denominations:

Coins 1, 2, 5, 10, 25, 50, 100 CFA francs.

Notes 100, 500, 1000, 5000, 10 000 CFA francs.

Political history and government: Formerly, as Middle Congo, a part of French Equatorial Africa. Became independent as the Republic of the Congo on 15 Aug 1960. A one-party state since 2 July 1964. Present name adopted on 3 Jan 1970. On 18 Mar 1977 the President was assassinated and the Central Committee of the ruling party transferred its powers to an 11-member Military Committee. The new régime suspended the 1973 constitution on 5 Apr 1977 and dissolved the National Assembly the next day. On 5 Feb 1979 the Military Committee resigned and handed over powers to the party's Central Committee. On 8 July 1979 a new constitution was approved by referendum and a National People's Assembly of 89 members elected (unopposed). The Congress of the ruling party elects a Central Committee (60 members) whose Chairman is also the country's President (serving a five-year term). The President leads the Council of Ministers, including a Prime Minister who is responsible to the party. The Assembly is responsible to the Prime Minister.

Length of roadways: 8246 km (*5124 miles*) (1980).

Length of railways: 795 km (*494 miles*).

Universities: 1.

Adult illiteracy: 37·1% in 1985.

Defence: Military service voluntary; total armed forces 8750 (1985), plus 500 Cuban troops; defence expenditure: 25 000 million CFA francs in 1985.

Foreign tourists: 62 000 in 1981.

Costa Rica

Official name: República de Costa Rica (the 'rich coast').

Population: 2 489 000 (1985 estimate).

Area: 51 100 km² (*19 730 miles²*).

Language: Spanish.

Religion: Roman Catholic.

Capital city: San José, population 245 370 (1984 census).

Other principal towns (1984): Limón (43 158; Puntarenas 47 851; Alajuela 33 929; Heredia 20 867; Cartago 23 884.

Highest point: Chirripó, 3820 m (*12 533 ft*).

Principal mountain ranges: Cordillera del Guanacaste, Cordillera de Talamanca.

Principal river: Río Grande.

Head of State: Dr Oscar Arias Sánchez, President.

Climate: Hot and wet on Caribbean coast, hot but drier on Pacific coast, cooler on central plateau. In San José, May hottest (17°C to 27°C *62°F to 80°F*), December and January coolest (14°C to 24°C *58°F to 75°F*), rainy season May–November, October rainiest (25 days). Absolute maximum temperature 42°C (*107·6°F*), Las Cañas de Guanacaste, 26 Apr 1952; absolute minimum −1·1°C (*30°F*), Cerro Buena Vista, 11 Jan 1949.

Labour force: 887 456 in 1985: Agriculture 26·8%; Mining and manufacturing 16%; Commerce 18·6%; Services 25·1%.

Gross domestic product: 238 468 million colones in 1986.

Exports: US$1074 million in 1986: Coffee 34·4%; Bananas 29·6%; Cattle and meat 6·2%.

Monetary unit: Costa Rican colón. 1 colón = 100 céntimos.

Denominations:

Coins 5, 10, 25, 50 céntimos; 1, 2, 5, 10, 20 colónes.

Notes 5, 10, 20, 50, 100, 500, 1000 colónes.

Political history and government: A republic. Legislative power is vested in the unicameral Legislative Assembly (57 deputies elected for four years by compulsory adult suffrage). Executive power is vested in the President, similarly elected for four years. He is assisted by two Vice-Presidents and a Cabinet. There are 7 provinces, each administered by an appointed governor.

Length of roadways: 29 093 km (*18 081 miles*) (1984).

Length of railways: 883 km (549 miles) (1984).

Universities: 3.

Adult illiteracy: 6%. Highest rate of literacy in Central America.

Defence: There have been no armed forces since 1948. Paramilitary forces number about 9500.

Foreign tourists: 273 901 in 1984.

Cuba

Official name: Le República de Cuba.

Population: 10 245 913 (1986 estimate).

Area: 110 860 km² (*42 803 miles²*).

Languages: Spanish, English.

Religions: Roman Catholic, Protestant minority.

Capital city: Ciudad de la Habana (Havana), population 2 036 799 (1986 estimate).

Other principal towns (1986): Santiago de Cuba 364 554; Camagüey 265 588; Holguín 199 861; Santa Clara 182 349; Guantánamo 179 091; Cienfuegos 112 225; Bayamo 108 716; Pinar del Rio 108 109; Matanzas 106 954.

Highest point: Pico Turquino, 1971 m (*6467 ft*).

Principal mountain range: Sierra Maestra.

Principal river: Cauto (249 km *155 miles*).

Head of State: Dr Fidel Castro Ruz (b. 13 Aug 1927), President of the State Council and Chairman of the Council of Ministers; also First Secretary of the Communist Party of Cuba.

Climate: Semi-tropical. Rainy season May–October. High winds, hurricanes frequent. In Havana, July and August warmest (24°C to 32°C *75°F to 89°F*), January and February coolest (18°C to 26°C *65°F to 79°F*), September and October rainiest (11 days each).

Labour force: 3 262 700 in 1986: Industry 22·3%; Agriculture 17·5%; Trade 11·4%; Services 23·2%.

Net material product: 12 853·9 million pesos in 1986: Agriculture, forestry and fishing 11%; Industry 37·5%; Construction 9·2%; Trade 33·7%.

Exports: 5 325 million pesos in 1986: Sugar 77% approx.

Monetary unit: Cuban peso. 1 peso = 100 centavos.

Denominations:

Coins 1, 5, 20, 40, centavos; 1 peso.

Notes 1, 3, 5, 10, 20, 50 pesos.

Political history and government: On 1 Jan 1959 the dictatorship of Gen. Fulgencio Batista was overthrown by revolutionary forces, led by Dr Fidel Castro. The constitution was suspended and a Fundamental Law of the Republic was instituted from 7 Feb 1959. Executive and legislative authority was vested in the Council of Ministers, led by a Prime Minister, which appointed the Head of State. A

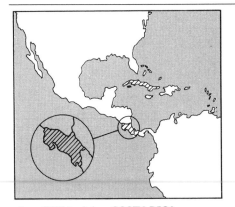

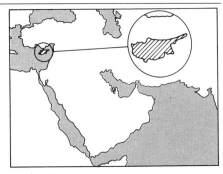

CYPRUS

above: **CUBA** *below:* **COSTA RICA**

'Marxist-Leninist programme' was proclaimed on 2 Dec 1961 and revolutionary groups merged into a single political movement, called the Communist Party of Cuba (CPC) since 2 Oct 1965. On 24 Nov 1972 the government established an Executive Committee (including the President and Prime Minister) to supervise State administration. The first elections since the revolution were held for municipal offices in one province on 30 June 1974.

A new constitution, approved by referendum on 15 Feb 1976 and in force from 24 Feb 1976, provides for assemblies at municipal, provincial and national levels. On 10 Oct 1976 elections were held for 169 municipal assemblies, with 'run-off' elections a week later. Members are elected by universal adult suffrage for 2½ years. On 31 Oct 1976 the municipal assemblies elected delegates to 14 provincial assemblies. The municipal assemblies elect 499 deputies to the National Assembly of People's Power, inaugurated on 2 Dec 1976. The National Assembly, whose members hold office for five years, is the supreme organ of state. The Assembly elects 31 of its members to form a Council of State, its permanent organ. The Council's President is Head of State and Head of Government. Executive power is vested in the Council of Ministers, appointed by the National Assembly on the proposal of the Head of State, who presides over it. The CPC, the only permitted political party, is 'the leading force of society and the state'. To direct its policy, the Central Committee of the CPC appoints a Political Bureau (Politburo).

Length of roadways: 34 000 km (*21 114 miles*) (1984).
Length of railways: 12 654 km (*7858 miles*) (1986).
Universities: 4.
Adult illiteracy: estimated 4%.
Defence: Military service three years; total armed forces 175 500 (1987); defence expenditure, 1987: 1300 million pesos.
Foreign tourists: 201 000 in 1984.

Cyprus

Official name: Kypriaki Dimokratia (in Greek), or Kibris Cumhuriyeti (in Turkish), meaning Republic of Cyprus.
Population: 673 100 (1986 estimate) including 157 894 in Turkish Republic of Northern Cyprus (1984 estimate).

Area: 9251 km² (*3572 miles²*), including Turkish area of 3355 km² (*1295 miles²*).
Languages: Greek 77%; Turkish 18%; English 3% (1960).
Religions: Greek Orthodox 77·0%; Islam 18·3%.
Capital city: Nicosia, population: Government-controlled, 164 400 (1985 estimate); Turkish 68 286 (1978).
Other principal towns (1982): Limassol 107 200; Famagusta 39 500; Larnaca 48 400.
Principal mountain ranges: Troödos, Kyrenian Mts.
Principal rivers: Seranhis, Pedieas.
Head of State: Georgios Vassiliou, President; Head of State of Turkish Republic of Northern Cyprus: Rauf Denktash, President.
Climate: Generally equable. Average rainfall is about 380 mm (*15 in*) but the summers are often rainless. The average daily high temperature in Nicosia reaches 36°C (*97°F*) (July) and the average daily low 5°C (*42°F*) (January).
Labour force: 220 089 (in 1983, for whole island): Agriculture, forestry, fishing 19·7%; Manufacturing 18·9%; Trade, restaurants and hotels 17·4%; Transport, storage and communication 4·8%; Services 18·1%.
Gross domestic product: C£1525·6 million in 1986, for Government-controlled area.
Exports: C£260·16 million in 1986, for Government-controlled area: Potatoes 11·4%; Citrus fruit 8%; Beverages 2·8%; Basic manufactures 6%; Clothing 23·2%; Footwear 8·1%.
Monetary unit: Cyprus pound. C£1 = 100 cents; Turkish lira (q.v.) in Turkish area.
Denominations:
Coins ½, 1, 2, 5, 10, 20, 50 cents; £1
Notes 50 cents, £1, £5, £10.
Political history and government: A former British dependency, independent since 16 Aug 1960 and a member of the Commonwealth since 13 Mar 1961. Under the 1960 constitution, Cyprus is a unitary republic with executive authority vested in one President (who must be a Greek Cypriot) and the Vice-President (who must be a Turkish Cypriot). They are elected for 5 years by universal suffrage (among the Greek and Turkish communities respectively) and jointly appoint a Council of Ministers (seven Greeks, three Turks). The national legislature is the unicameral House of Representatives, comprising 50 members (35 Greek and 15 Turkish, separately elected for 5 years). Each community was also to have a communal chamber.

The first President of Cyprus was Archbishop Makarios III, who proposed amendments to the constitution on 30 Nov 1963. These were unacceptable to the Turks, who have ceased to participate in the central government since December 1963. After the Turkish withdrawal, the all-Greek House of Representatives abolished the Greek Communal Chamber and the separate electoral rolls. The Turkish community continued to elect a Vice-President for Cyprus (not recognized by the Greeks) and established separate administrative, legal and judicial organs.

After the temporary overthrow of President Makarios in a *coup* in July 1974, the armed forces of Turkey intervened and occupied northern Cyprus. On 17 Feb 1975 the Turkish Cypriots unilaterally proclaimed this area the Turkish Federated State of Cyprus, for which a constitution was approved by referendum on 8 June 1975. Makarios died on 3 Aug 1977, when Spyros Kyprianou, President of the House of Representatives, became acting Head of State. On 31 Aug 1977 he was elected unopposed to complete Makarios's term of office. He was returned unopposed as President on 26 Jan 1978 and inaugurated on 1 Mar. He was again re-elected for a further five year term on 13 Feb 1983 but defeated by Georgios Vassiliou in an election on 21 Feb 1988.

In November 1983 the Turkish Cypriot leadership declared the Turkish-held area of Cyprus to be the Turkish Republic of Northern Cyprus. To date this action remains unrecognized by the world community. UN sponsored talks between the Greek and the Turkish Cypriot sides have made no progress in resolving the Cyprus problem.

Length of roadways: 11 227 km (*6978 miles*) (1983).
Defence: *Greek Cypriots:* military service 26 months; total armed forces 13 000 (1987); *Turkish Cypriots:* 36 500 (1985). Cyprus also has a UN peace-keeping force of 2300 (1987) and two Sovereign British military bases (Akrotiri and Episkopi).
Foreign tourists: 900 727 to Government-controlled area in 1986; 131 492 to Turkish-controlled area in 1986.

Czechoslovakia

Official name: Československá Socialistická Republika (Czechoslovak Socialist Republic).
Population: 15 500 088 (1985 estimate).
Area: 127 881 km² (*49 375 miles²*).
Languages: Czech 64%; Slovak 30%; Hungarian 4%.
Religions: Roman Catholic 70%; Protestant 15%.
Capital city: Praha (Prague), population 1 193 513 (1986 estimate).
Other principal towns (1986): Bratislava 417 103; Brno 385 684; Ostrava 327 791; Košice 222 175; Plzeň 175 244; Olomouc 106 086; Liberec 100 917; Hradec Králové 99 571.
Principal mountain ranges: Bohemian–Moravian Highlands, Krkonoše (Giant Mountains), High Tatras, Low Tatras.
Principal rivers: Labe (Elbe, 845 km *525 miles*), Vltava (Moldau), Dunaj (Danube, 2850 km *1770 miles*), Morava, Váh, Nitra, Hron.
Head of State: Dr Gustáv Husák (b. 10 Jan 1913), President.
Prime Minister: Ladislav Adamec.
General Secretary of the Communist Party of Czechoslovakia: Mitos Jakes.

Climate: Cold winters and warm, rainy summers. Average temperature 9°C (*49°F*). In Prague, July warmest (14°C to 23°C *58°F to 74°F*), January coldest (−4°C to 1°C *25°F to 34°F*). June and July rainiest (14 days each). Absolute maximum temperature 39·0°C (*102·2°F*), Hurbanovo, 5 Aug 1905; absolute minimum −41·0°C (−*41·8°F*), Vigláš-Pstruša, 11 Feb 1929.
Labour force: 7 950 000 in 1985: Agriculture and forestry 11·9%; Construction 9·1%; Trade 8·6%; Education and culture 7%.
Net material product: 560 billion Kčs in 1985: Agriculture, forestry and fishing 6·6%; Industry 59·6%; Construction 11·2%; Trade 16·1; Transport and storage 4·2%.
Exports: 119 818 million Kčs in 1985: Mineral fuels and lubricants 4·3%; Chemicals 6·0%; Basic manufactures 16·8%; Machinery and transport equipment 53·6%; Miscellaneous manufactures 11·2%.
Monetary unit: Koruna (Kčs) or Czechoslovak crown. 1 koruna = 100 haléřu (singular: halér).
Denominations:
Coins 5, 10, 20, 50 haléřu; 1, 2, 5 korunas.
Notes 10, 20, 50, 100, 500, 1000 korunas.
Political history and government: Formerly part of Austria-Hungary, independent since 28 Oct 1918. Under the Munich agreement, made on 29 Sept 1938 by France, Germany, Italy and the United Kingdom, Czechoslovakia ceded the Sudetenland to Germany and other areas to Hungary and Poland. German forces entered Czechoslovakia on 1 Oct 1938. On 16 Mar 1939 Germany invaded and occupied the rest of the country. At the end of the Second World War in May 1945 the pre-1938 frontiers were restored but Czechoslovakia ceded Ruthenia to the USSR in June 1945. The Communist Party won 38% of the vote at the 1946 election and dominated the government. After Ministers of other parties resigned, Communist control became complete on 25 Feb 1948. A People's Republic was established on 9 June 1948. A new constitution, introducing the country's present name, was proclaimed on 11 July 1960. Czechoslovakia has been a federal republic since 1 Jan 1969.

The country comprises two nations, the Czechs and the Slovaks, each forming a republic with its own elected National Council and government. Czechoslovakia comprises 10 administrative regions and two cities.

The supreme organ of state power is the bicameral Federal Assembly, elected for 5 years by universal adult suffrage. Its permanent organ is the elected Presidium. The Assembly comprises the Chamber of the People, with 200 members (136 Czechs and 64 Slovaks), and the Chamber of Nations, with 150 members (75 from each republic). The Assembly elects the President of the Republic for a 5-year term and he appoints the Federal Government, led by the Chairman of the Government (Prime Minister), to hold executive authority. Ministers are responsible to the Assembly.

Political power is held by the Communist Party of Czechoslovakia, which dominates the National Front (including four other minor parties). All candidates for representative bodies are sponsored by the Front. The Communist Party's highest authority is the Party Congress, which elects the Central Committee to supervise Party work. The Committee elects a Presidium (11 full members and 6 alternate members were elected in 1988) to direct policy.

Length of roadways: 74 064 km (*46 031 miles*) (excluding local roads).
Length of railways: 13 141 km (*8167 miles*) (1983).
Universities: 5 (plus 12 technical universities).
Defence: Military service: Army 2 years, Air Force 3 years; total regular forces 212 000 in 1987; defence expenditure: 29 260 million Korunas in 1987. Soviet forces are present on Czech territory.
Foreign tourists: 19 000 000 in 1986.

Denmark

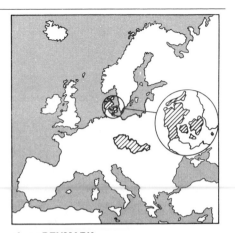

above: **DENMARK**
below: **CZECHOSLOVAKIA**

Official name: Kongeriget Danmark (Kingdom of Denmark).
Population: 5 124 794 – metropolitan Denmark (1987 estimate); plus 46 000 – Faroes (1986 estimate) and 53 733 – Greenland (1987 estimate).
Area: Denmark and the Faroes 44 500 km² (*17 180 miles²*) of which Faroes 1400 km² (*540 miles²*); Greenland 341 700 km² (*131 930 miles²*).
Language: Danish.
Religions: Evangelical Lutheran 94%, other Christian minorities.
Capital city: København (Copenhagen), population 1 358 540 (including suburbs) (1986).
Other principal towns (1 Jan 1986): Aarhus 253 650; Odense 172 751; Aalborg 154 905; Esbjerg 80 639.
Capital of Faroes: Tórshavn 13 408 (1984 estimate).
Capital of Greenland: Nuuk (formerly Godthåb 11 209 (1987).
Highest point: Yding Skovhøj, 173 m (*568 ft*).
Principal river: Gudenå.
Head of State: HM Queen Margrethe II (b. 16 Apr 1940). Queen Margrethe succeeded on the death of her father King Frederik IX on 14 Jan 1972. Crown Prince: HRH Prince Frederik b. 26 May 1968, eldest son of Queen Margrethe.
Prime Minister: Poul Schlüter (b. 3 Apr 1929).
Climate: Temperate: Mild summers (seldom above 21°C *70°F*) and cold winters (although seldom below freezing). The days are often foggy and damp. In Copenhagen, July warmest (13°C to 22°C (*55°F to 72°F*), February coldest (−2°C to 2°C (*28°F to 36°F*), August rainiest (12 days). Absolute maximum temperature 35·8°C (*96·4°F*), Antvorskov, 13 Aug 1911; absolute minimum −31·0°C (*−23·8°F*), Løndal, 26 Jan 1942.
NB: The figures which follow are for metropolitan Denmark only, that is excluding the Faroes and Greenland.
Labour force: 2 585 100 in 1986: Agriculture, fishery etc 6·6%; Manufacturing 20·5%; Construction 6·7%; Trade 13·3%; Transport 7%; Finance 9·3%; Community services 35·9%.
Gross domestic product: 667 186 million kroner in 1986: Agriculture, forestry and fishing 4·8%; Manufacturing 20·4%; Construction 6·4%; Trade 13·3%; Transport, storage and communications 8·1%; Government services 21·3%.
Exports: 171 613 900 000 kroner in 1986: Agriculture/fisheries 27·6%; Crude materials 6·3%; Chemicals 9·1%; Machinery 24%; Basic manufactures 11·4%.
Monetary unit: Danish krone. 1 krone = 100 øre.
Denominations:
Coins 5, 10, 25 øre; 1, 5, 10 kroner.
Notes 20, 50, 100, 500, 1000 kroner.
Political history and government: A constitutional monarchy since 1849. Under the constitutional charter (*Grundlov*) of 5 June 1953, legislative power is held jointly by the hereditary monarch (who has

no personal political power) and the unicameral Parliament (*Folketing*), with 179 members (175 from metropolitan Denmark and two each from the Faroe Islands and Greenland). Members are elected by universal adult suffrage for 4 years (subject to dissolution), using proportional representation. Executive power is exercised by the monarch through a Cabinet, led by the Prime Minister, which is responsible to Parliament. Denmark comprises 14 counties, one city and one borough plus the external territories of the Faroes and Greenland. The Faroese have control over their internal affairs (under the Home Rule Act of 1948) – they have a local Parliament (løgting) but also send two members to the Danish Parliament which is responsible for defence, foreign policy, the constitution, judiciary and monetary matters. The Faroes are not part of the EEC. Greenland, like the Faroes, is part of the Kingdom of Denmark – it has its own Parliament (Landsting) although responsibility for foreign policy and defence remain with Denmark. Greenland is represented in the Danish Parliament by two members, and like the Faroes, is not part of the EEC (having withdrawn with effect from 1 Feb 1985).
Length of roadways: 70 190 km (*43 588 miles*) (1987).
Length of railways: 2552 km (*1586 miles*).
Universities: 5 (plus 3 technical universities).
Defence: Military service nine months; total armed forces 29 300 in 1987; defence expenditure: 12 671 million kroner in 1987.
Foreign tourists: 2 042 908 in 1986.

Djibouti

Official name: Jumhuriya Jibuti (Arabic) or République de Djibouti (French): Republic of Djibouti.
Population: 456 000 (1986 estimate).
Area: 23 000 km² (*8880 miles²*).
Languages: Somali, Afar, Arabic, French (official).
Religions: Islam; Christian minority.
Capital city: Djibouti (Jibuti), population 200 000 (1985 estimate).
Other principal towns: Tadjoura, Obock, Dikhil, Ali-Sabieh.

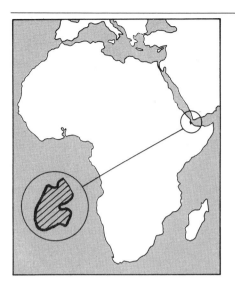

DJIBOUTI

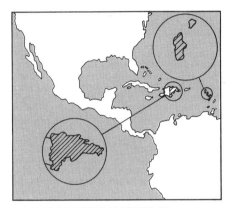

left: **THE DOMINICAN REPUBLIC**
right: **DOMINICA**

Head of State: Gouled Aptidon Hassan (b. 1916), President.
Prime Minister: Gourad Hamadou Barkat.
Climate: Very hot and dry.
Gross domestic product: 60 234 million Djibouti francs in 1984.
Exports: 20 830 million Djibouti francs in 1982.
Monetary unit: Djibouti franc. 1 franc = 100 centimes.
Denominations:
    Coins 1, 2, 5, 10, 20, 50, 100 francs.
    Notes 500, 1000, 5000, 10 000 francs.
Political history and government: Formerly a dependency of France. Known as French Somaliland until 5 July 1967 and from then until independence as the French Territory of the Afars and the Issas. Also in 1967 the Territorial Assembly became the Chamber of Deputies. A provisional independence agreement was signed on 8 June 1976. A popular referendum approved independence on 8 May 1977, when an enlarged Chamber of Deputies (65 members) was also elected. The Chamber elected a Prime Minister on 16 May 1977. The Territory

became independent on 27 June 1977, when the Prime Minister became President and the Chamber became a Constituent Assembly. Executive power is held by the President, directly elected for a six-year term as Head of State and Head of Government. The President appoints the Prime Minister and, on the latter's recommendation, other members of the Council of Ministers. The Assembly is to draw up a new constitution.
Length of roadways: 2906 km (*1806 miles*).
Length of railways: 100 km (*62 miles*).
Adult illiteracy: over 50% (estimate).
Defence: Total armed forces 2870 (1987); Defence expenditure: US$32·2 million (1985).
Foreign tourists: 17 037 in 1985.

Dominica

Official name: The Commonwealth of Dominica.
Population: 83 266 (1984 estimate).
Area: 751 km² (*289·8 miles²*).
Language: English.
Religion: Roman Catholic 80%.
Capital city: Roseau, population 28 346 (1981).
Other principal towns: Portsmouth, Marigot.
Highest point: Imray's View, 1447 m (*4747 ft*).
Principal river: Layou.
Head of State: Sir Clarence A. Seignoret, President.
Prime Minister: Mary Eugenia Charles (b. 1919).
Climate: Warm and pleasant. Cool from December to May. Rainy season generally June to October, dry February to May. Sometimes in the path of severe hurricanes.
Labour force: 25 333 in 1981: Agriculture 31%; Manufacturing 5·6%; Construction 9·1%; Trade 6·4%; Services 19·7%.
Gross domestic product: EC$ 230·7 million in 1984.
Exports: EC$50·3 million in 1986: major categories in 1982 were Bananas 43·7%; Soap 38·1%; Copra 4·9%.
Monetary unit: East Caribbean dollar (EC$). 1 dollar = 100 cents.
Denominations:
    Coins 1, 2, 5, 10, 25, 50 cents.
    Notes 1, 5, 20, 100 dollars.
Political history and government: A former British dependency, Dominica was part of the Leeward Islands until 31 Dec 1939, when it was transferred to the Windward Islands. The federal arrangement in the British-ruled Windward Islands ended on 31 Dec 1959. Under a new constitution, effective from 1 Jan 1960, Dominica achieved a separate status, with its own Administrator. On 1 Mar 1967 Dominica became one of the West Indies Associated States, gaining full autonomy in internal affairs. The Administrator became Governor and the Chief Minister was restyled Premier.
  Dominica became an independent republic on 3 Nov 1978, with the Premier as Prime Minister. Legislative power is vested in the unicameral House of Assembly, with 31 members (21 elected by universal adult suffrage, 9 appointed by the President and 1 *ex officio*) serving a term of five years (subject to dissolution). Executive authority is vested in the President, elected by the House, but he generally acts on the advice of the Cabinet. The President appoints the Prime Minister, who must be supported by a majority in the House, and (on the Prime Minister's recommendation) other Ministers. The Cabinet effectively controls government and is responsible to the House.

Length of roadways: 752 km (*467 miles*) (31 Dec 1976).
Universities: 1 (a branch of the University of the West Indies).
Defence: The Dominican Defence Force was disbanded in 1981. There is a police force (including a coastguard service with one patrol boat) of 300.
Foreign tourists: 36 310 (1986).

The Dominican Republic

Official name: La República Dominicana.
Population: 6 416 000 (1986 estimate).
Area: 48 442 km² (*18 703 miles²*).
Language: Spanish.
Religion: Roman Catholic.
Capital city: Santo Domingo de Guzmán, population 1 313 172 (1981 census).
Other principal towns (1981): Santiago de los Caballeros 278 638; La Romana 91 571; San Pedro de Macoris 78 562; San Francisco de Macoris 64 906; La Vega 52 432.
Highest point: Pico Duarte (formerly Pico Trujillo), 3175 m (*10 417 ft*).
Principal mountain range: Cordillera Central.
Principal river: Yaque del Norte.
Head of State: Dr Joaquín Balaguer, President.
Climate: Sub-tropical. Average temperature 27°C (*80°F*). The west and south-west are arid. In the path of tropical cyclones. In Santo Domingo, August is hottest (23°C to 31°C (*73°F to 88°F*)), January coolest (19°C to 29°C (*66°F to 84°F*), June rainiest (12 days). Absolute maximum temperature 43°C (*109· 4°F*), Valverde, 31 Aug 1954; absolute minimum −3·5°C (*25·7°F*), Valle Nuevo, 2 Mar 1959.
Labour force: 1 784 157 in 1981: Agriculture, forestry, fishing 23·6%; Manufacturing 12·6%; Trade 10·8%; Services 20·4%.
Gross domestic product: RD$9497·8 million in 1984: Agriculture, forestry and fishing 11·9%; Manufacturing 16·5%; Trade 17·3%, Government services 7·9%.
Exports: US$722 144 000 in 1986: Raw sugar 18·5%; Cocoa beans 8·2%; Coffee 15·6%; Ferro-nickel 10·8%; Gold and silver (alloy) 15·5%.
Monetary unit: Dominican Republic peso. 1 peso = 100 centavos.
Denominations:
  Coins 1, 5, 10, 25, 50 centavos; 1 peso.
  Notes 1, 5, 10, 20, 50, 100, 500, 1000 pesos.
Political history and government: A republic comprising 27 provinces (each administered by an appointed governor) and a *Distrito Nacional* (DN) containing the capital. Legislative power is exercised by the bicameral National Congress, with a Senate of 28 seats (one for each province and one for the DN) and a Chamber of Deputies (120 members). Members of both houses are elected for four years by universal adult suffrage. Executive power lies with the President, elected by direct popular vote for four years. He is assisted by a Vice-President and an appointed Cabinet containing Secretaries of State.
Length of roadways: 17 120 km (*10 632 miles*).
Length of railways: 588 km (*365 miles*).
Universities: 6.
Adult illiteracy: 22·7% in 1985.
Defence: Military service is voluntary; 4 years; total armed forces 21 400; defence expenditure: 255·3

million RD$.
Foreign tourists: 800 000 in 1986.

Ecuador

Official name: La República del Ecuador ('the equator').
Population: 9 922 514 (1987 estimate).
Area: 283 561 km² (*109 484 miles²*).
Language: Spanish.
Religion: Roman Catholic.
Capital city: Quito, population 1 509 108 (1986 estimate).
Other principal towns (1986): Guayaquil 1 093 278; Cuenca 193 012; Machala 137 321; Portoviejo 134 393; Manta 129 578; Ambato 122 139; Esmeraldas 115 138.
Highest point: Chimborazo, 6267 m (*20 561 ft*) (first climbed 1879).
Principal mountain range: Cordillera de los Andes.
Principal rivers: Napo, Pastaza, Curaray, Daule.
Head of State: Dr Rodrigo Borja Cevallos (b. 1936), President.
Climate: Tropical (hot and humid) in coastal lowlands. Temperate (mild days, cool nights) in highlands, average temperatures 13°C (*55°F*), rainy season November–May. In Quito, average maximum 21°C (*70°F*) (April, May) to 23°C (*73°F*) (August, September), minimum 7°C (*44°F*) (July) to 8°C (*47°F*) (February–May), April rainiest (22 days). Absolute maximum temperature 38°C (*100·4°F*), Babahoyo, 4 Jan 1954; absolute minimum −3·6°C (*25·5°F*), Cotopaxi, 9 Sept 1962.
Labour force: 3 017 650 in 1984: Agriculture, forestry and fishing 46·4%; Manufacturing 10·9%; Trade

ECUADOR

11·7%; Community, social and personal services 16·2%.

Gross domestic product: 1 366 304 million sucres in 1986: Agriculture, hunting and fishing 15·3%; Mining and quarrying 15·1%; Manufacturing 16·9%; Trade 14·7%.

Exports: US$2185·9 million in 1986: Petroleum 41·8%; Bananas 12·5%; Coffee 13·7%; Fish and fish products 3·3%.

Monetary unit: Sucre. 1 sucre = 100 centavos.

Denominations:
Coins 10, 20, 50 centavos; 1 sucre.
Notes 5, 10, 20, 50, 100, 500, 1000 sucres.

Political history and government: A republic comprising 19 provinces (each administered by an appointed governor) and a National Territory, the Archipiélago de Colón (the Galapagos Islands). On 22 June 1970 the President dismissed the National Congress (a Senate of 54 members and a 72-member Chamber of Deputies) and assumed dictatorial powers. He was deposed by the armed forces on 15 Feb 1972 and a National Military Government was formed. All political activity was suspended on 11 July 1974. A three-man military junta took power on 11 Jan 1976 as the Supreme Council of Government. On 2 June 1976 the régime announced plans for a return to civilian rule. A referendum on 15 Jan 1978 approved a new constitution providing for an executive president and a unicameral Congress with legislative power, both to be directly elected by universal adult suffrage. A presidential election was held on 16 July 1978 but no candidate obtained a majority of the votes. A 'run-off' election between the two leading candidates was held on 29 Apr 1979, when the new Congress (69 members) was also elected. Jaime Roldós Aguilera was elected President and took office for a 4-year term on 10 Aug 1979, when the Congress was inaugurated and the new constitution came into force. President Roldós was killed in an air crash on 24 May 1981 and his Vice-President succeeded him for the remainder of his term. Elections in 1984 were won by León Cordero and in 1988 by Dr Rodrigo Borga Cevallos. The President appoints and leads the Council of Ministers.

Length of roadways: 36 187 km (*22 472 miles*) (1986).
Length of railways: 971 km (*606 miles*) (1984).
Universities: 8 (plus 8 technical universities).
Defence: Military service: two years, selective; total armed forces 37 000 (1987); defence expenditure: 20 400 million sucres in 1986.
Foreign tourists: 250 000 (1985).

Egypt

Official name: Jumhuriyat Misr al-'Arabiya (Arab Republic of Egypt).
Population: 51 000 000 (1987 estimate).
Area: 1 101 449 km² (*386 662 miles²*).
Language: Arabic.
Religions: Islam (mainly Sunni) 92·6%; Christian 7·3% (1960).
Capital city: El Qahira (Cairo), population 13 300 000 (1987 estimate).
Other principal towns (1985): El-Iskandariyah (Alexandria) 2 821 000; (El-Giza 1 230 446 included in Greater Cairo); Shubrâ al-Khayma 515 500; Bur

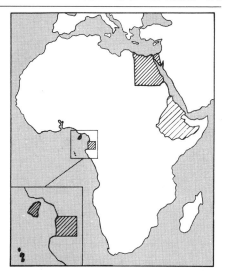

left: **EQUATORIAL GUINEA**
top right: **EGYPT** *lower right:* **ETHIOPIA**

Sa'id (Port Said) 374 000; Tantâ 364 700; El Mahalla al-Kubrâ 362 700; Hulwan 345 600; El Mansura 328 700.

Highest point: Jebel Katherina, 2609 m (*8651 ft*).
Principal mountain ranges: Sinai, Eastern Coastal Range.
Principal river: Nile (6670 km *4145 miles*).
Head of State: Lt-Gen. (Muhammad) Husni Mubarak (b. 1928), President.
Prime Minister: Dr Atef Sedki.
Climate: Hot and dry. Over 90% is arid desert. Annual rainfall generally less than 50 mm (*2 in*), except on Mediterranean coast (maximum of 200 mm (*8 in*) around Alexandria). Mild winters. In Cairo, average maximum 18°C (*65°F*) (January) to 35°C (*96°F*) (July), minimum 8°C (*47°F*) (January) to 22°C (*71°F*) (August). In Luxor, average maximum 23°C (*74°F*) (January) to 42°C (*107°F*) (July), minimum 5°C (*42°F*) (January) to 23°C (*73°F*) (July, August), rain negligible.
Labour force: 12 890 600 in 1985: Agriculture, fishing etc 34·6%; Manufacturing and mining 13·4%; Construction 7·6%; Trade 9·4%; Services 7·4%; Government services 19·9%.
Gross domestic product: No figures are published by the Government.
Exports: US$6396 million in 1986: (in 1983) – Raw cotton and cotton products 22·7%; Edible fruits 2·7%; Crude petroleum 47·6%; Fuel oils 9·2%.
Monetary unit: Egyptian pound (£E). £E1 = 100 piastres = 1000 millièmes.
Denominations:
Coins 1, 2, 5, 10, 20 piastres.
Notes 5, 10, 25, 50 piastres; 1, 5, 10, 20, 100 pounds.
Political history and government: A former British protectorate, Egypt became independent, with the Sultan as King, on 28 Feb 1922. Army officers staged a *coup* on 23 July 1952 and the King abdicated, in favour of his son, on 26 July 1952. Political parties were dissolved on 16 Jan 1953. The young King was deposed, and a republic proclaimed, on 18 June 1953. Egypt merged with Syria to form the United Arab Republic on 1 Feb 1958. Syria broke

away and resumed independence on 29 Sept 1961 but Egypt retained the union's title until the present name was adopted on 2 Sept 1971. A new constitution, proclaiming socialist principles, was approved by referendum on 11 Sept 1971. Legislative authority rests with the unicameral People's Assembly of 458 members (10 appointed and 400 elected according to the list system and 48 individual system for 5 years). Half the elected members must be workers or peasants. The Assembly nominates the President, who is elected by popular referendum for six years. He has executive authority and appoints one or more Vice-Presidents, a Prime Minister and a Council of Ministers to perform administrative functions. The Arab Socialist Union (ASU), created on 7 Dec 1962, was the only recognized political organization of the state until the formation of political parties was again legalized on 29 June 1977. The three parties initially permitted were based on the three 'platforms' of the ASU which presented separate candidates at the Assembly elections of 28 Oct and 4 Nov 1976. Elections were again held in 1984 to the People's Assembly, but the electoral requirements for the opposition parties were very tightly drawn. The country is composed of 26 governorates (5 cities, 16 provinces, 5 frontier districts).

Length of roadways: 90 083 km (*55 890 miles*) (1984).
Length of railways: 5983 km (*3715 miles*) (1986).
Universities: 12.
Adult illiteracy: 55·5% in 1985.
Defence: Military service; 3 years (selective); total armed forces 445 000 (1985); defence expenditure: £E3650 million in 1986–7.
Foreign tourists: 1 518 000 in 1985.

El Salvador

Official name: La República de El Salvador ('The Saviour').
Population: 4 913 000 (1986 estimate).
Area: 21 041 km² (*8124 miles²*).
Language: Spanish.
Religion: Roman Catholic.
Capital city: San Salvador, population 462 652 (1985 estimate).
Other principal towns (1981): Santa Ana 208 322; San Miguel 161 156; Zacatecoluca 78 751; Ahuachapán 69 852; Usulutain 65 462.
Highest point: 2804 m (*9200 ft*).
Principal river: Lempa (402 km *250 miles*), San Miguel.
Head of State: Alfredo Cristiani, President.
Climate: Tropical (hot and humid) in coastal lowlands, temperate in uplands. In San Salvador, maximum temperature is 32°C (*90°F*) (April and May), minimum around 15°C (*60°F*) (December, January, February).
Labour force: 2 490 000 in 1984: Agriculture 50%; Industry 22%; Services 27%.
Gross domestic product: 14 330·8 million colónes in 1985: Agriculture, forestry and fishing 18·1%; Manufacturing 16·4%; Commerce 27·2%; Public administration 11·1%; Personal services 8·9%.
Exports: 1 697 400 million colones in 1985: Coffee 66·9%.
Monetary unit: Salvadorian colón. 1 colón = 100 centavos.

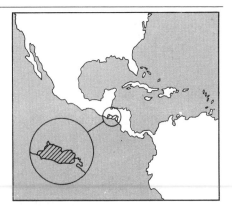

EL SALVADOR

Denominations:
Coins 1, 2, 3, 5, 10, 25, 50 centavos; 1 colón.
Notes 1, 2, 5, 10, 50, 100 colónes.
Political history and government: A republic composed of 14 departments. From 1932 a series of military officers held power, either as elected Presidents (often after disputed polls) or by means of a *coup*. On 20 Feb 1977 Gen. Carlos Humberto Romero Mena was elected President (despite allegations of fraud) and on 1 July 1977 he was sworn in. On 15 Oct 1979 President Romero was deposed in a military *coup*. The unicameral Legislative Assembly was dissolved. The new régime formed a 5-member junta (including 3 civilians). On 15 Oct 1980 the junta announced that elections to a constituent assembly would be held in 1982 and general elections in 1983. On 22 Dec 1980 two members of the junta were sworn in as President and Vice-President. Presidential elections were held in 1984. The country remains in a state of considerable unrest with large areas being under the control of insurgents. Guerrilla activity occurs in both town and country led by the FDR-FMLN opposition front.
Length of roadways: 12 164 km (*7553 miles*) (1986).
Length of railways: 600 km (*372 miles*) (1985).
Universities: 34.
Adult illiteracy: 27·9% (1985).
Defence: Total armed forces 59 000 (1987); military service compulsory – two years; defence expenditure, US$125·4 million US military aid (1987) plus expenditure of 885 million colónes (1987).
Foreign tourists: 133 000 (1985).

Equatorial Guinea

Official name: La República de Guinea Ecuatorial.
Population: 384 000 (1987 estimate).
Area: 28 051 km² (*10 831 miles²*).
Languages: Spanish (official), Fang, Bubi.
Religions: Roman Catholic, Protestant minority.
Capital city: Malabo (formerly Santa Isabel), population 15 253 (1983 census).
Other principal town: Bata, population 24 100 (1983).
Highest point: Pico de Moca (Moka), 2850 km (*9350 ft*).
Principal rivers: Campo, Benito, Muni.
Head of State: Lt-Col. Teodoro Obiang Nguema Mbasogo (b. 1946), President.

Prime Minister: Cristino Seriche Bioke Malabo.
Climate: Tropical (hot and humid), with average temperatures of over 26°C (*80°F*) and heavy rainfall (about 2000 mm (*80 in*) per year).
Labour force: 169 000 in 1985: Agriculture 60·9%.
Gross domestic product: 5450 million bipkwele in 1982: Agriculture 38·8%; Trade 8·8%; Public administration 28·6%.
Exports: 3837 million bipkwele in 1982: Cocoa 47%; Coffee 1·8%; Timber 16·1%.
Monetary unit: Franc de la Commonauté financière africaine. (Until 1985 it was the epkwele, plural bipkwele, linked to the Spanish peseta at 1 peseta = 2 epkwele since 1980.)
Denominations:
  Coins 1, 2, 5, 10, 25, 50, 100, 500 CFA francs.
  Notes 100, 500, 1000, 5000, 10 000 CFA francs.
Political history and government: Formed on 20 Dec 1963 by a merger of two Spanish territories, Río Muni on the African mainland and the adjacent islands of Fernando Póo (later renamed Macías Nguema Biyogo, then Bioko) and Annobón (now Pagalu). Became an independent republic, as a federation of two provinces, on 12 Oct 1968. All political parties were merged into one on 2 Feb 1970. The first President, Francisco Macías Nguema, was proclaimed 'President for Life' on 14 July 1972. A revised constitution, approved by referendum on 29 July 1973 and effective from 4 Aug 1973, gave absolute power to the President and established a unitary state, abolishing the provincial autonomy of the islands. President Macías was deposed by a *coup* on 3 Aug 1979, when a Supreme Military Council assumed power.
Length of roadways: 1175 km (*730 miles*).
Adult illiteracy: 63% (1985).
Defence: Total armed forces: 2200 (1985); defence expenditure US$6 million in 1982.

Ethiopia

Official name: Hebretesebawit Ityopia (People's Democratic Republic of Ethiopia).
Population: 44 927 000 (1986 estimate).
Area: 1 221 900 km² (*471 800 miles²*).
Languages: Amharic, Galla, Somali.
Religions: Islam (mainly Sunni) 50%, Christian (mainly Coptic).
Capital city: Addis Ababa, population 1 412 577 (1984 census).
Other principal towns (1984): Asmara 275 385; Dire Dawa 98 104; Gondar/Azesso 80 886; Nazret 76 284; Dessie 68 848; Harar 62 160; Mekele 61 583.
Highest point: Ras Dashen, 4620 m (*15 158 ft*).
Principal mountain ranges: Eritrean highlands, Tigre Plateau, Eastern Highlands, Semien mountains.
Principal rivers: Abbay, Tekeze, Awash, Omo, Sagan, Webi, Shebele.
Head of State: Lt-Col. Mengistu Haile Mariam (b. 1937), President of the Derg (Provisional Military Administrative Council).
Climate: Mainly temperate and cool on the high plateau, with average annual temperature of 13°C (*55°F*), abundant rainfall (June to August) and low humidity. Very hot and dry in desert lowlands and valley gorges. In Addis Ababa, average maximum 21°C (*69°F*) (July, August) to 25°C (*77°F*) (March–May), minimum 5°C (*41°F*) (December) to 10°C (*50°F*) (April–August). Absolute maximum 47·5°C

(*117·5°F*), Kelaffo, May 1959; absolute minimum −5·6°C (*−22·0°F*), Maichew, November 1956.
Labour force: 18 492 300 in 1984: Agriculture, forestry and fishing 76·8%.
Gross domestic product: 9881·3 million birr in 1984–5: Agriculture, forestry and fishing 39·7%; Manufacturing 6·9%; Trade 9·8%; Transport and communications 4·8%; Public administration 7·8%.
Exports: 861 759 000 birr in 1984: Coffee 63·3%; Sheepskins 6·9%.
Monetary unit: Birr (formerly Ethiopian dollar). 1 birr = 100 cents.
Denominations:
  Coins 1, 5, 10, 25, 50 cents.
  Notes 1, 2, 10, 50, 100 birr.
Political history and government: Formerly a monarchy, ruled by an Emperor with near-autocratic powers. Political parties were not permitted. The former Italian colony of Eritrea was merged with Ethiopia, under a federal arrangement, on 15 Sept 1952. Its federal status was ended on 14 Nov 1962.
  The last Emperor was deposed by the armed forces on 12 Sept 1974. The constitution and the bicameral Parliament (a Senate and a Chamber of Deputies) were suspended. The *coup* was engineered by the Armed Forces Coordinating Committee (the Derg). The Committee established a Provisional Military Government and on 28 Nov 1974 created the Provisional Military Administrative Council (PMAC) as its executive arm. Ethiopia was declared a socialist state on 20 Dec 1974 and the monarchy was abolished on 21 Mar 1975. Under a government re-organization, announced on 29 Dec 1976 and modified by proclamation on 11 Feb 1977, the PMAC was renamed the Derg and was reconstituted. In 1979 all political groupings were replaced by a Commission for Organizing the Party of the Working People in Ethiopia. In 1984 this was in turn replaced by the Workers' Party of Ethiopia, modelled on the Communist Party in the USSR. Ethiopia has 14 provinces. Nationalist guerrillas control large areas of Eritrea and of Tigre, the former seeking independence from Ethiopia, the latter autonomy within Ethiopia.
Length of roadways: 37 871 km (*23 517 miles*) (1985).
Length of railways: 988 km (*614 miles*).
Universities: 2.
Adult illiteracy: 45% (1983).
Defence: Military service: conscription; total armed forces 320 000, plus an estimated 4000 Cubans; defence expenditure: 925 million birr in 1984–5.
Foreign tourists: 69 000 in 1983–4.

Fiji

Population: 715 375 (1985 census).
Area: 18 274 km² (*7056 miles²*).
Languages: English, Fijian, Hindi.
Religions: Christian 50·8% (mainly Methodist), Hindu 40·3%, Muslim 7·8%.
Capital city: Suva, population 69 481 (1986 census).
Other principal towns (1982): Lautoka 26 000; Vatukoula 7000; Ba 7000; Nausori 6000; Labasa 5000.
Highest point: Mt Victoria (Tomaniivi) on Viti Levu, 1323 m (*4341 ft*).
Principal rivers: Rewa, Sigatoka, Navua, Nadi, Ba.
Head of State: Ratu Sir Penaia Ganilau, GCMG, KCVO, KBE, DSO.

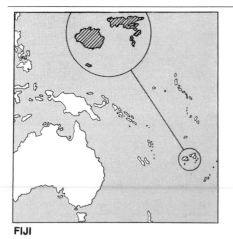

FIJI

Prime Minister: Ratu the Rt Hon Sir Kamisese Kapaiwai Tuimacilai Mara, GCMG, KBE (b. 13 May 1920).
Climate: Temperate, with temperatures rarely falling below 15·5°C (60°F) or rising above 32·2°C (90°F). Copious rainfall on windward side; dry on leeward side. Rainy season November–March, driest month July.
Labour force: 241 160 in 1986: Agriculture 44·2%; Manufacturing 7·5; Trade 10·8%.
Gross domestic product: $F1160 million in 1986: Agriculture, forestry and fishing 24·3%; Manufacturing 12·2%; Distribution (inc. tourism) 16·8%; Government services 17·8%.
Exports: $F280 141 000 in 1986: Sugar 47·7%; Gold 13·8%; Prepared fish 6·9%.
Monetary unit: Fiji dollar (F$). 1 dollar = 100 cents.
Denominations:
Coins 1, 2, 5, 10, 20, 50 cents.
Notes 1, 2, 5, 10, 20 dollars.
Political history and government: A former British colony, an independent member of the Commonwealth since 10 Oct 1970. On independence executive power was vested in the Queen and exercisable by her personal representative, the Governor-General, appointed on the recommendation of the Cabinet. A bicameral legislature comprised a Senate (22 members nominated for staggered six-year terms) and a House of Representatives (52 members elected for five years, subject to dissolution). Elections to the House were on three rolls: Fijian (22), Indian (22) and general (8). A military *coup* took place in May 1987 when the Government was removed from office by the Governor-General who took charge of the administration. A second *coup*, led by Col. Rabuka, took place in September 1987 – following this the country was declared a Republic and membership of the Commonwealth lapsed. Civilian rule was restored (when a 21-man Cabinet was appointed) in December 1987. A new Constitution will guarantee permanent Melanesian majority in the legislature. There are 14 provinces, each headed by a chairman.
Length of roadways: 595 km (*369 miles*).
Length of railways: 725 km (*450 miles*).
Universities: 1.
Defence: Military service voluntary; total armed forces 2600 (1987); defence expenditure, 1987: $F16·9 million.
Foreign tourists: 200 000 in 1987.

Finland

Official name: Suomen Tasavalta (Republic of Finland).
Population: 4 925 644 (1986 estimate).
Area: 338 145 km² (*130 557 miles²*).
Languages: Finnish 93·6%; Swedish 6·2%.
Religions: Lutheran 90·1%; Orthodox 1·1%.
Capital city: Helsinki (Helsingfors), population 965 233 (including suburbs) (1986).
Other principal towns (1986): Tampere (Tammerfors) 256 080 (including suburbs); Turku (Åbo) 260 532 (including suburbs); (Espoo/Esbo 160 406 included in Helsinki metropolitan area); (Vantaa/Vanda 146 425 included in Helsinki metropolitan area); Oulu (Uleåborg) 97 869; Lahti 94 205; Kuopio 78 529; Pori (Björneborg) 77 805.
Highest point: Haltiatunturi, 1324 m (*4344 ft*).
Principal mountain ranges: Suomenselkä, Maanselkä.
Principal rivers: Paatsjoki, Torniojoki, Kemijoki, Kokemäenjoki.
Head of State: Dr Mauno Henrik Koivisto (b. 25 Nov 1923), President.
Prime Minister: Harri Holkeri (b. 1937).
Climate: Warm summers, very cold winters. Average annual temperature 17°C (*62°F*). Winters are long and extreme in the north. In Helsinki, July warmest (14°C to 22°C *57°F to 71°F*), February coldest (−9°C to −3°C (*15°F to 26°F*), August and October rainiest (12 days each). Absolute maximum temperature 35·9°C (*96·6°F*), Turku, 9 July 1914; absolute minimum −48·4°C (*−55·8°F*), Sodankylä, January 1868.
Labour force: 2 569 000 in 1986: Agriculture, forestry and fishing 10·4%; Manufacturing 21·4%; Trade 16·4%; Community, personal and social services 31·8%.
Gross domestic product: 357 236 million markkaa in 1986: Agriculture, forestry, fishing etc 6·7%; Manufacturing 21%; Trade 10·3%; Financial services 9·9%; Other services 16%.
Exports: 82 579·3 million markka in 1986: Paper and paperboard 25·1%; Machinery and transport equipment 27·6%; Wood and wood pulp 11·7%.
Monetary unit: Markka (Finnmark). 1 markka = 100 penniä (singular: penni).
Denominations:
Coins 5, 10, 20, 50 penniä; 1, 5, 10 markkaa.
Notes 5, 10, 50, 100, 500, 1000 markkaa.
Political history and government: Formerly a Grand Duchy within the Russian Empire. After the Bolshevik revolution in Russia, Finland's independence was declared on 6 Dec 1917. A republic was established by the constitution of 17 July 1919. This combines a parliamentary system with a strong presidency. The unicameral Parliament (*Eduskunta*) has 200 members elected by universal adult suffrage for 4 years (subject to dissolution by the President), using proportional representation. The President, entrusted with supreme executive power, is elected for 6 years by a college of 301 electors, chosen by popular vote in the same manner as members of Parliament. Legislative power is exercised by Parliament in conjunction with the President. For a general administration the President appoints a Council of State (Cabinet), headed by a Prime Minister, which is responsible to Parliament. Finland has 12 provinces, each administered by an appointed Governor.
Length of roadways: 76 223 km (*47 334 miles*) (1986).

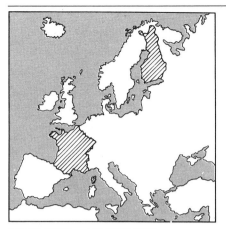

left: FRANCE *right:* FINLAND

Length of railways: 5883 km (*3653 miles*) (1987).
Universities: 17 universities, 3 technical univesities and 5 institutions of university equivalent status.
Defence: Military service: 8 to 11 months; total armed forces 34 400 (1987); defence expenditure: 1987 was 5528 million markkaa.
Foreign tourists: 451 000 (1983).

France

Official name: La République française (the French Republic).
Population: 55 392 000 (1986 estimate), the population figure for metropolitan (European) France. The following overseas departments and *collectivités territoriales* are integral parts of the French Republic: Guyane, population 84 177 (1986 estimate); Guadeloupe 333 378 (1985 estimate); Martinique 328 281 (1985 estimate); Réunion 560 000 (1987 estimate); Mayotte 67 167 (1985 census); St Pierre and Miquelon 6041 (1982 census). This gives a total population of the French Republic of 56 771 000.
Area: 547 026 km² (*211 208 miles²*) for metropolitan France. The following overseas departments and *collectivités territoriales* are integral parts of the French Republic: Guyane (French Guiana) 90 000 km² (*34 750 miles²*); Guadeloupe 1780 km² (*687·3 miles²*); Martinique 1100 km² (*424·7 miles²*); Réunion 2512 km² (*970 miles²*); Mayotte 376 km² (*145 miles²*); St Pierre and Miquelon 242 km² (*93·4 miles²*). This gives a total area of the French Republic of 643 041 km² (*248 278 miles²*).
Language: French; Breton and Basque minorities.
Religions: Roman Catholic, Protestant, Jewish, Islam.
Capital city: Paris, population 8 706 973 including suburbs (1982 census).
Capital of Guyane Cayenne, population 38 091 (1985).
Capital of Guadeloupe Basse-Terre, population 13 656 (1981).
Capital of Martinique Fort-de-France, population 97 814 (1982).
Capital of Réunion Saint-Denis, population 109 068 (1982).
Capital of Mayotte Dzaoudzi, population 5865 (1982).

Capital of St Pierre and Miquelon Saint-Pierre 5415 (1982).
Other principal towns (1982): Lyon 1 220 844; Marseille 1 110 511; Lille 936 295; Bordeaux 640 012; Toulouse 541 271; Nantes 464 857; Nice 449 496; Grenoble 392 021; Rouen 379 879; Toulon 410 393; Strasbourg 373 470; Valenciennes 349 505; St-Étienne 317 228; Lens 327 383; Nancy 306 982; Cannes 295 525; Tours 262 786; Béthune 258 383; Clermont-Ferrand 256 189; Le Havre 254 595; Rennes 234 418; Montpellier 221 307; Mulhouse 220 613; Orléans 220 478; Dijon 215 865; Douai 202 366; Brest 201 145.
Highest point: Mont Blanc, 4807 m (*15 771 ft*) (first climbed on 8 Aug 1786).
Principal mountain ranges: Alps, Massif Central, Pyrenees, Jura Mts, Vosges, Cévennes.
Principal rivers: Rhône, Seine, Loire (1006 km *625 miles*), Garonne, Rhin (Rhine).
Head of State: François Mitterand (b. 26 Oct 1916), President.
Prime Minister: Michel Rocard (b. 1931).
Climate: Generally temperate, with cool summers in the west and warm summers elsewhere. Mediterranean climate (warm summers, mild winters) in the south. In Paris, average maximum 5°C (*42°F*) (January) to 24°C (*76°F*) (July), minimum 0°C (*32°F*) (January) to 13°C (*55°F*) (July, August), December rainiest (17 days). Absolute maximum temperature 44·0°C (*111·2°F*), Toulouse, 8 Aug 1923; absolute minimum −33°C (*−27·4°F*), Langres, 9 Dec 1879.
NB: The following details apply only to metropliltan France.
Labour force: 23 573 300 in 1984: Agriculture, forestry and fishing 7%; Manufacturing 21·2%; Construction 6·7%; Trade, restaurants and hotels 14·7%; Finance and business services 7·0%; Community, social and personal services 26·3%.
Gross domestic product: 5014·9 million francs in 1986: Agriculture 3·7%; Manufacturing 26·7%; Construction 5·9%; Trade 10%; Finance 18·9%; Government services 13·5%; Community and personal services 8·8%.
Exports: 813 537 million francs in 1984: Agriculture 12·6%; Chemicals 13·5%; Basic manufactures 19·5%; Machinery and transport equipment 33·5%.
Monetary unit: French franc. 1 franc = 100 centimes.
Denominations:
Coins 5, 10, 20, 50 centimes; 1, 2, 5, 10 100 francs.
Notes 10, 50, 100, 200, 500 francs.
Political history and government: A republic whose present constitution (establishing the Fifth Republic and the French Community) was approved by referendum on 28 Sept 1958 and promulgated on 6 Oct 1958. Legislative power is held by a bicameral Parliament. The Senate has 319 members (296 for metropolitan France, 13 for the overseas departments and territories and 10 for French nationals abroad) indirectly elected for 9 years (one third renewable every three years). The National Assembly has 577 members directly elected by unviersal adult suffrage (using two ballots if necessary) for 5 years, subject to dissolution. In 1986 the elections were held under the departmental list system of proportional representation according to the principle of the highest average. The system has now been changed back to direct election by universal adult suffrage, using two ballots if necessary. Executive power is held by the President. Since 1962 the President has been directly elected by universal

adult suffrage (using two ballots if necessary) for 7 years. The President appoints a Council of Ministers, headed by the Prime Minister, which governs the country and is responsible to Parliament. Metropolitan France comprises 22 adminstrative regions containing 96 departments. There are also four overseas departments (French Guiana, Guadeloupe, Martinique, La Réunion) and two *collectivités territoriales* (Mayotte and St Pierre and Miquelon), which are integral parts of the French Republic. Each department is administered by an elected President of the Regional Council.
Length of roadways: 1 508 015 km *(936 477 miles)* (1987).
Length of railways: 34 640 km *(21 362 miles)* (1986).
Universities: 69 plus 3 National Polytechnics with university status.
Defence: Military service; 12 months (18 months for overseas); total armed forces 546 900 (1987); defence expenditure: 177 860 million francs in 1987.
Foreign tourists: 36 080 000 (1986).

French External Territories

Details for Guyane, Guadeloupe, Martinique, Réunion, Mayotte and St Pierre and Miquelon are listed in the main entry for France.

Polynesia

Official name: Polynesie française.
Population: 176 543 (1985 estimate).
Area: 4200 km² *(1622 miles²)*.
Capital city: Papeete, population 23 496 (1983).

French Southern and Antarctic Territories

Official name: Terres Australes et Antarctiques françaises.
Population: fluctuating population of scientific missions, of which 140 were in the Southern Territories in 1985.
Area: Kerguelen Archipelago 18 130 km² *(7000 miles²)*; Croqet Archipelago 1295 km² *(500 miles²)*; Amsterdam Island 155 km² *(60 miles²)*; St Paul Island 18 km² *(7 miles²)*.
Principal settlement: Port-aux-Français, population 100 (1985).
NB: For details of French Antarctic Territories see Antarctica in the 'Other Territories' listing following the directory of Sovereign Countries.

New Caledonia

Official name: Nouvelle-Calédonie.
Population: 145 368 (1983 census).
Area: 19 103 km² *(7376 miles²)*.
Capital city: Nouméa, population 60 112 (1983).

Wallis and Futuna Islands

Official name: Îles de Wallis et Futuna.
Population: 12 391 (1983).
Area: 710 km² *(274 miles²)*.
Capital city: Mata-Utu, population 815 (1983).

Gabon

Official name: La République gabonaise (the Gabonese Republic).
Population: 1 224 000 (1987 estimate).
Area: 267 667 km² *(103 347 miles²)*.
Languages: French (official), Fang, Eshira, Mbété.
Religions: Christian 60%, Animist minority.
Capital city: Libreville, population 350 000 (1983).
Other principal towns (1978): Port-Gentil 123 300; Lambaréné 26 257.
Highest point: Mon Iboundji, 1580 m *(5185 ft)*.
Principal river: Ogooué (Ogowe).
Head of State: *El Hadj* Omar Bongo (b. Albert-Bernard Bongo, 30 Dec 1935), President and Head of Goverment.
Prime Minister: Léon Mébiame (b. 1 Sept 1934).
Climate: Tropical (hot and humid). Average temperature 26°C *(79°F)*. Heavy rainfall (annual average 2490 mm *98 in)*. In Libreville, average maximum 30°C to 34°C *(86°F to 94°F)*, minimum 18°C to 22°C *(65°F to 71°F)*.
Labour force: 502 000 in 1980: Agriculture 75·5%; Industry 10·7%; Services 13·8%.
Gross domestic product: 1 148 000 million CFA francs in 1986: Mining and quarrying, crude petroleum and natural gas 24%; Construction 8·9%; Trade 11·3%; Public administration 13·7%.
Exports: 887 000 million CFA francs in 1985: Crude petroleum 82·8%; Timber 6·2%; Manganese ores and concentrates 6·2%.
Monetary unit: Franc de la Communauté financière africaine.
Denominations:
Coins 1, 2, 5, 10, 25, 50, 100 CFA francs.
Notes 100, 500, 1000, 5000, 10 000 CFA francs.
Political history and government: Formerly part of French Equatorial Africa, independent since 17 Aug 1960. A one-party state since March 1968. The legislature is a unicameral National Assembly of 111 members, of whom nine are nominated by the President and the rest directly elected by universal adult suffrage for five years. Executive power is held by the President, directly elected for seven years. He

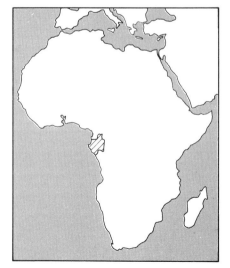

GABON

appoints, and presides over, a Council of Ministers, including a Prime Minister. Gabon comprises nine regions, each administered by an appointed Prefect.
Length of roadways: 7535 km (*4679 miles*) (1986).
Length of railways: 1042 km (*647 miles*).
Universities: 1.
Adult illiteracy: 38·4% (1985).
Defence: Military service voluntary; total armed forces 2850 (1987); defence expenditure: 22% of total government expenditure in 1988. France maintains some 600 troops in Gabon.
Foreign tourists: 16000 in 1983.

The Gambia

Official name: The Republic of the Gambia.
Population: 698 817 (1986 estimate).
Area: 11 295 km² (*4361 miles²*).
Languages: English (official), Mandinka, Fula, Wollof.
Religions: Islam (Sunni), Christian minority.
Capital city: Banjul (formerly Bathurst), population 145 692 (1983 census) – comprising Banjul city 44 188; Kombo St Mary urban area 101 504.
Other principal towns (1983): Serekunda 64 494; Birkama 19 584; Bakau 19 309.
Principal river: Gambia.
Head of State: *Alhaji* Sir Dawda Kairaba Jawara (b. 11 May 1924), President.
Climate: Long dry season, normally November to May, with pleasant weather on coast (best in West Africa) due to effect of the *harmattan*, a northerly wind. Hotter up-river, especially February to May. Average annual rainfall 1000 mm (*40 in*) on coast, less inland. Rainy season June to October. Average annual temperature in Banjul 27°C (*80°F*).
Labour force: 300 000 in 1984: Agriculture, forestry and fishing 76·3%.
Gross domestic product: 414·1 million dalasi in 1986: Agriculture, forestry and fishing 26·1%; Trade 22·6%; Services 34·2%.
Exports: US$87·3 million in 1986.
Monetary unit: Dalasi. 1 dalasi = 100 butut.
Denominations:
Coins 1, 5, 10, 25, 50 butut; 1 dalasi.
Notes 1, 5, 10, 25 dalasi.
Political history and government: A former British dependency, an independent member of the Commonwealth since 18 Feb 1965. A republic since 24 April 1970. Legislative power is held by a unicameral House of Representatives containing 43 members (35 directly elected for 5 years by universal adult suffrage, 4 Chiefs' Representative Members elected by the Chiefs in Assembly, 3 non-voting nominated members and the Attorney-General). Executive power is held by the President, the leader of the majority party in the House. He appoints a Vice-President (who is leader of government business in the House) and a Cabinet from elected members of the House. The country has four political parties. On 1 Feb 1982 The Gambia and Senegal formed a confederation named Senegambia.
Length of roadways: 3083 km (*1916 miles*) (1983).
Adult illiteracy: 74·9% (1985).
Defence: Military service voluntary; total armed forces 600 in 1987.
Foreign tourists: 77 039 (1985–6).

encircled left: **THE GAMBIA**
GHANA

Germany (East)

Official name: Deutsche Demokratische Republik (German Democratic Republic).
Population: 16 624 000 (1986 estimate).
Area: 108 333 km² (*41 828 miles²*).
Language: German.
Religions: Protestant 50%, Roman Catholic 8%.
Capital city: (East) Berlin, population 1 215 600 (1985 estimate).
Other principal towns (1985): Leipzig 553 700; Dresden 519 800; Karl-Marx-Stadt (Chemnitz) 315 500; Magdeburg 285 000; Rostock 244 400; Halle an der Saale 235 200; Erfurt 216 000.
Highest point: Fichtelberg, 1214 m (*3983 ft*).
Principal mountain ranges: Thüringer Wald, Erz Gebirge.
Principal rivers: Elbe (845 km *525 miles*) (with Havel and Saale), Oder (with Neisse).
Head of State: Erich Honecker (b. 25 Aug 1912), Chairman of the Council of State; also General Secretary of the Central Committee of the Socialist Unity Party.
Head of Government: Willi Stoph (b. 9 July 1914), Chairman of the Council of Ministers.
Climate: Temperate (warm summers, cool winters), greater range inland. In Berlin, July warmest (13°C to 23°C *55°F to 74°F*), January coldest (−3°C to 2°C *26°F to 35°F*), December rainiest (11 days). Absolute maximum temperature 38·3°C (*102·7°F*), Blankenberg, 7 July 1957; absolute minimum −33·8°C (*−28·8°F*), Zittau-Hirschfelde, 11 Feb 1939.
Labour force: 8 540 000: Industry 41%; Agriculture 10·8%; Construction 6·8%; Commerce 10·2%; Transport 7·5%.
Net material product: 233 620 million DDR-marks (1985): Agriculture and forestry 8·5%; Industry and productive crafts 74·7%; Trade 9·3%.
Exports: 93 490 million DDR Valuta-marks in 1985: Machinery 48·5%; Fuels, raw materials, metals 18·5%; Durable consumer goods 14·2%; Chemical products, building materials etc 11·9%.

Monetary unit: Mark der Deutschen Demo-kratischen Republik (DDR-Mark). 1 Mark = 100 Pfennige.
Denominations:
Coins 1, 5, 10, 20, 50 Pfennige; 1, 2, 5, 10, 20 DDR-Marks.
Notes 5, 10, 20, 50, 100 DDR-Marks.
Political history and government: The territory was the USSR's Zone of Occupation in Germany from May 1945. The Republic, a 'people's democracy' on the Soviet pattern, was proclaimed on 7 Oct 1949. The USSR granted full sovereignty on 25 Mar 1954. The present constitution was promulgated on 9 Apr 1968. The supreme organ of state power is the *Volkskammer* (People's Chamber), with 500 members elected for 5 years by universal adult suffrage (from a single list of candidates). The Chamber elects a 25-member *Staatsrat* (Council of State) to be its permanent organ. The executive branch of government is the *Ministerrat* (Council of Ministers), under a Chairman (Minister-President) appointed by the Chamber, which also approves his appointed Ministers. The Council's work is directed by a Presidium of 16 members. Political power is held by the (Communist) Socialist Unity Party of Germany (SED), formed in 1946 by a merger of the Communist Party and the Social Democratic Party in the Soviet Zone. The SED dominates the National Front of Democratic Germany, which also includes four minor parties and four mass organizations. The SED's highest authority is the Party Congress. The Congress elects the Central Committee to supervise Party work; the Central Committee elects a Political Committee (Politburo), with 22 full members and 5 candidate members in 1987, to direct its policy. The country is divided into 14 districts (*Bezirke*) and the city of East Berlin.
Length of roadways (classified): 124 610 km (*77 382 miles*) (1986).
Length of railways: 14 005 km (*8697 miles*) (1986).
Universities: 7 plus 47 institutions of university status.
Defence: Military service 18–24 months; total regular forces 176 000 in 1987; defence expenditure: 20 897 million DDR marks; some 380 000 Soviet troops are stationed in the GDR.
Foreign tourists: 933 889 in 1983.

Germany (West)

Official name: Bundesrepublik Deutschland (Federal Republic of Germany).
Population: 61 047 700 (1986 estimate).
Area: 248 706 km² (*96 025 miles²*).
Language: German.
Religions: Protestant 49%, Roman Catholic 44·6%.
Capital city: Bonn, population 290 800 (estimate 1986).
Other principal towns (1986): Berlin (West) 1 868 700; Hamburg 1 575 700; München (Munich) 1 269 400; Köln (Cologne) 914 000; Essen 617 700; Frankfurt 593 400; Dortmund 569 800; Stuttgart 564 500; Düsseldorf 561 200; Bremen 524 700; Duisberg 516 600; Hannover 506 400; Nürnberg 466 500; Bochum 381 000; Wuppertal 375 300; Bielefeld 299 200; Mannheim 295 500; Gelsenkirchen 284 400; Münster 268 900; Karlsruhe 267 600; Wiesbaden 266 700; Mönchengladbach 254 700; Braunschweig (Brunswick) 247 300;

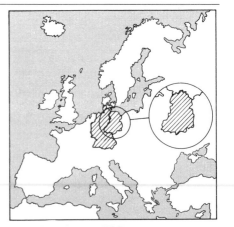

left: **GERMANY (WEST)**
encircled right: **GERMANY (EAST)**

Augsburg 245 600; Kiel 244 700; Aachen (Aix-la-Chapelle) 238 600; Oberhausen 222 100; Krefeld 216 700; Lübeck 209 800; Hagen 206 100.
Highest point: Zugspitze, 2963 m (*9721 ft*) (first climbed 1820).
Principal mountain ranges: Alps, Schwarzwald (Black Forest).
Principal rivers: Rhein (Rhine) (1320 km *820 miles*), Ems, Weser, Elbe, Donau (Danube) (2850 km *1770 miles*).
Head of State: Dr Richard von Weizsäcker (b. 15 Mar 1920), Federal President.
Head of Government: Dr Helmut Kohl (b. 3 Apr 1930), Federal Chancellor.
Climate: Generally temperate (average annual temperature 9°C (*48°F*)) with considerable variations from northern coastal plain (mild) to Bavarian Alps (cool summers, cold winters). In Hamburg, July warmest (13°C to 20°C *56°F to 69°F*), January coolest (−2°C to 2°C *28°F to 35°F*), January, July and December rainiest (each 12 days). Absolute maximum temperature 39·8°C (*103·6°F*), Amerg, 18 Aug 1892; absolute minimum −35·4°C (*−31·7°F*), 12 Feb 1929.
Labour force: 27 835 000 in 1985: Agriculture, forestry and fishing 5·4%; Production 41%; Trade, transport and communications 18·3%; Others 35·3%; Unemployed 8·3%.
Gross domestic product: 1944 billion DM in 1986: Agriculture and forestry 1·7%; Producing industries 41·5%; Trade, transport and communications 14·4%; Services 25·8%.
Exports: 537 164 million DM in 1985: Road vehicles 17·1%; Products of mechanical engineering 14·7%; Chemical products 13·9%.
Monetary unit: Deutsche Mark (DM). 1 Deutsche Mark = 100 Pfennige.
Denominations:
Coins 1, 2, 5, 10, 50 Pfennige; 1, 2, 5, 10 DM.
Notes 5, 10, 20, 50, 100, 500, 1000 DM.
Political history and government: The territory was the British, French and US Zones of Occupation in Germany from May 1945. A provisional constitution, the *Grundgesetz* (Basic Law), came into force in the three Zones (excluding Saarland) on 23 May 1949 and the Federal Republic of Germany (FRG)

was established on 21 Sept 1949. Sovereignty was limited by the continuing military occupation, and subsequent defence agreements, until 5 May 1955, when the FRG became fully independent. Saarland (under French occupation) was rejoined with the FRG administratively on 1 Jan 1957 and economically incorporated on 6 July 1959. The FRG is composed of 10 states (*Länder*) – each *Land* having its own constitution, parliament and government – plus the city of West Berlin which retains a separate status. The country has a parliamentary régime, with a bicameral legislature. The Upper House is the *Bundesrat* (Federal Council) with 45 seats, including 41 members of *Land* governments (which appoint and recall them) and 4 non-voting representatives appointed by the West Berlin Senate. The term of office varies with *Land* election dates. The Lower House, and the FRG's main legislative organ, is the *Bundestag* (Federal Assembly), with 520 deputies, elected for four years by universal adult suffrage (using a mixed system of proportional representation and direct voting) – the total includes 22 members (with limited voting rights) elected by the West Berlin House of Representatives. Executive authority rests with the *Bundesregierung* (Federal Government), led by the *Bundeskanzler* (Federal Chancellor) who is elected by an absolute majority of the *Bundestag* and appoints the other Ministers. The Head of State, who normally acts as the Chancellor's advice, is elected for a five-year term by a Federal Convention, consisting of the *Bundestag* and an equal number of members elected by the *Land* parliaments.

Length of roadways: 491 240 km (*305 060 miles*) (1984).

Length of railways: 27 484 km (*17 068 miles*). (1985).

Universities: 48 (and 17 institutions of university status, including 9 technical universities).

Defence: Military service 18 months; total armed forces 488 400 (including 223 450 conscripts) in 1987; defence expenditure: DM50 850 million in 1987.

Foreign tourists: 12 600 000 in 1985.

GERMAN STATES

Baden-Württemberg Population (1986): 9 295 100; Area: 35 751 km² (*13 803 miles²*); Capital: Stuttgart.

Bayern (Bavaria) Population (1986): 10 993 400; Area: 70 553 km² (*27 241 miles²*); Capital: München (Munich).

Bremen Population (1986): 657 500; Area: 404 km² (*156 miles²*); Capital: Bremen.

Hamburg Population (1986): 1 575 700; Area: 755 km² (*292 miles²*); Capital: Hamburg.

Hessen (Hesse) Population (1986): 5 531 300; Area: 21 114 km² (*8152 miles²*); Capital: Wiesbaden.

Niedersachsen (Lower Saxony) Population (1986): 7 194 300; Area: 47 438 km² (*18 316 miles²*); Capital: Hannover.

Nordrhein-Westfalen (North Rhine-Westphalia) Population (1986): 16 665 300; Area: 34 068 km² (*13 154 miles²*); Capital: Düsseldorf.

Rheinland-Pfalz (Rhineland-Palatinate) Population (1986): 3 610 400; Area: 19 848 km² (*7663 miles²*); Capital: Mainz.

Saarland Population (1986): 1 043 400; Area 2569 km² (*992 miles²*); Capital: Saarbrücken.

Schleswig-Holstein Population (1986): 2 612 700; Area: 15 727 km² (*6072 miles²*); Capital: Kiel.

West-Berlin Population (1986): 1 868 700; Area: 480 km² (*185 miles²*); Capital: West Berlin.

Ghana

Official name: The Republic of Ghana ('land of gold').

Population: 14 045 000 (1986 estimate).

Area: 238 537 km² (*92 100 miles²*).

Languages: English (official), Asante, Ewe, Fante, Ga, and Dagbani.

Religions: Christian, Islam (Sunni), Animist.

Capital city: Accra, population 964 879 (1984 census).

Other principal towns (1984): Kumasi 399 300; Tamale 136 800; Tema 99 600; Takoradi 61 500; Cape Coast 57 700; Sekondi 32 400.

Highest point: Afadjato 872 m (*2860 ft*).

Principal rivers: Volta (formed by the confluence of the Black Volta and the White Volta) and its tributaries (principally the Oti, Tano, Ofin).

Head of State: Flight-Lieutenant Jerry John Rawlings (b. 1947), Chairman Provisional National Defence Council.

Climate: Tropical. In north hot and dry. Forest areas hot and humid. Eastern coastal belt warm and fairly dry. In Accra average maximum 27°C (*80°F*) (August) to 31°C (*88°F*) (February to April and December), average minimum 22°C (*71°F*) (August) to 24°C (*76°F*) (March, April), June rainiest (10 days).

Labour force: 4 353 000 in 1980: Agriculture 55·8%; Industry 17·8%; Services 26·4%.

Gross domestic product: 344 182 million new cedis in 1985.

Exports: 55 814 million new cedis in 1984: Cocoa 75·1%; Gold 21·4%; Manganese ore 1·6%.

Monetary unit: New cedi. 1 cedi = 100 pesewas.

Denominations:

Coins ½, 1, 2½, 5, 10, 20 pesewas; 1, 5 cedis.

Notes 1, 2, 5, 10, 50, 100, 200, 500 cedis.

Political history and government: On 6 Mar 1957 the British dependency of the Gold Coast merged with British Togoland to become independent, and a member of the Commonwealth, as Ghana. Became a republic on 1 July 1960. The President, Dr Kwame Nkrumah, was deposed by a military *coup* on 24 Feb 1966. Civilian rule was restored on 30 Sept 1969 but again overthrown by the armed forces on 13 Jan 1972. The 1969 constitution was abolished, the National Assembly dissolved and political parties banned. Power was assumed by the National Redemption Council (NRC), comprising military commanders and Commissioners of State with ministerial responsibilities. The first Chairman of the NRC was Lt.-Col. (later Gen.) Ignatius Acheampong. On 14 Oct 1975 a 7-man Supreme Military Council (led by Acheampong) was established, with full legislative and administrative authority, to direct the NRC. Acheampong was removed from office by the SMC on 5 July 1978. A constitutional drafting commission, appointed by the military government, reported on 17 Nov 1978. Its recommendations were debated by a Constituent Assembly of 120 members (64 elected by local councils, the remainder nominated by the SMC and other national bodies), which was inaugurated on 21 Dec 1978 and presented its final report on 15 May 1979. The ban on political parties had been lifted on 1 Jan 1979 and the return to civilian rule planned for 1 July. The régime was overthrown by another military *coup* on 4 June 1979, when an Armed Forces Revolutionary coun-

cil (AFRC) took power. The AFRC postponed the return to civilian rule but on 14 June it promulgated the new constitution, providing for an executive President (serving a four-year term) and a unicameral parliament (with a five-year term) both to be elected by universal adult suffrage. Elections were held on 18 June 1979 for a President and the 140 members of Parliament. No presidential candidate received a majority of votes and a 'run-off' election between the two leading candidates was held on 9 July. Civilian rule was restored, and the President took office, on 24 Sept 1979, but was subsequently overthrown in a bloodless coup by Flt.-Lt. Rawlings on 31 Dec 1981. Ghana comprises ten regions, each the responsibility of a Minister.
Length of roadways: 53 100 km (*33 000 miles*) (1985).
Length of railways: 947 km (*588 miles*) (1986).
Universities: 3.
Adult illiteracy: 46·8% (1985).
Defence: Military service voluntary; total armed forces 10 600 (1987); defence expenditure: 343 million cedis in 1985.
Foreign tourists: 92 500 in 1986.

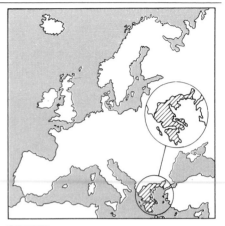

GREECE

Greece

Official name: Elleniki Dimokratia (Hellenic Republic).
Population: 9 965 830 (1986 estimate).
Area: 131 944 km² (*50 944 miles²*).
Language: Greek.
Religions: Eastern Orthodox Church 97%; Roman Catholic and other minorities.
Capital city: Athínai (Athens), population 3 027 331 (1981).
Other principal towns (1981): Thessaloniki (Salonika) 406 413; (Piraeus 196 389 – included in Athens metropolitan area); Patras 142 163; Heraklion 102 398; Larisa 102 426; Volos 71 378; Kavála 56 705; Canea 47 451.
Highest point: Óros Ólimbos (Olympus), 2911 m (*9550 ft*).
Principal mountain range: Pindus Mountains.
Principal rivers: Aliákmon (314 km *195 miles*), Piniós, Akhelóös.
Head of State: Christos Sartzetakis (b. 1929), President.
Prime Minister: Tzannis Tzannetakis.
Climate: Mediterranean (hot, dry summers and mild, wet winters). Colder in the north and on higher ground. In Athens, July and August hottest (22°C to 32°C *72°F to 90°F*), January coolest (5°C to 12°C *42°F to 54°F*), December and January rainiest (seven days each). Absolute maximum temperature 45·7°C (*114·3°F*), Heraklion, Crete, 16 June 1914; absolute minimum −25°C (−13°F), Kavála, 27 Jan 1954.
Labour force: 3 761 300 in 1986: Agriculture, fishing 27·4%; Manufacturing 19·9%; Construction 6·7%; Trade, restaurants, hotels 15·4%; Transport 6·8%; Services 16·9%.
Gross domestic product: 5 495 747 million drachmae in 1986: Agriculture, forestry and fishing 17·1%; Manufacturing 18·7%; Trade 16·1%.
Exports: 789 994 million drachmae in 1986: Fruit and vegetables 14·3%; Beverages and tobacco 5·1%; Crude materials 5·9%; Mineral fuels, lubricants, etc. 6·6%; Basic manufactures 27·4%; Clothing 19·2%.

Monetary unit: Drachma. 1 drachma = 100 leptae (singular: lepta).
Denominations:
Coins 10, 20, 50 leptae; 1, 2, 5, 10, 20 drachmae.
Notes 50, 100, 500, 1000 drachmae.
Political history and government: While Greece was a monarchy a *coup* by army officers, led by Col. Georgios Papadopoulos, deposed the constitutional government on 21 Apr 1967. Parliament was suspended and political parties banned. Papadopoulos became Prime Minister on 13 Dec 1967, a Regent was appointed and the King left the country the next day. A Republic was proclaimed on 1 June 1973 and Papadopoulos became President. He was deposed by another military *coup* on 25 Nov 1973. Civilian rule was re-established on 24 July 1974, when a Government of National Salvation took office. The ban on political parties was lifted and free elections for a Parliament were held on 17 Nov 1974. A referendum on 8 Dec 1974 rejected the return of the monarchy. A new republican constitution, providing for a parliamentary democracy, came into force on 11 June 1975. Greece became a full member of the EEC in 1981. Executive power rests with the President, elected for 5 years by the legislature, a unicameral parliament (*Vouli*) of 301 members directly elected by universal adult suffrage for 4 years. The President appoints a Prime Minister and, on his recommendation, the other Ministers to form a Cabinet to govern the country. The Cabinet is accountable to Parliament. The country is divided into 51 prefectures (*Nomoi*). The district of Mount Athos, with its autonomous monastic community, has a privileged status as a self-governing part of the Greek state – (Mount Athos – an autonomous monks' republic – had a population of 1472 in 1981, an area of 336 km² (*130 miles²*) and the settlement of Karyai as its capital).
Length of roadways: 34 492 km (*21 419 miles*) (1985).
Length of railways: 2577 km (*1602 miles*).
Universities: 14.
Adult illiteracy: 7·7% (1986).
Defence: Military service 21–25 months; total armed forces 209 000 (1987); defence expenditure: 289 000 million drachmae in 1987.
Foreign tourists: 7 400 000 in 1986.

Grenada

Official name: State of Grenada.
Population: 92 000 (1987 estimate).
Area: 344 km² (*133 miles²*).
Language: English.
Religion: Christian.
Capital city: St George's, population 29 369 (1981 census).
Other principal towns: Grenville, Victoria, Sauteurs, Gouyave (Charlotte Town), Hillsborough.
Highest point: Mount St Catherine's, 840 m (*2756 ft*).
Head of State: HM Queen Elizabeth II, represented by Sir Paul Scoon, GCMG, GCVO, OBE (b. 4 July 1935), Governor-General.
Prime Minister: Rt Hon. H. A. Blaize.
Climate: Tropical maritime, with equable temperature averaging 28°C (*82°F*) in the lowlands. Annual rainfall averages 1524 mm (*60 in*) in coastal area and 3810–5080 mm (*150–200 in*) in mountain areas. Rainy season June to December (November wettest), dry season January to May.
Labour force: 45 000 (1986).
Gross domestic product: EC$260·4 million in 1985.
Exports: EC$50·7 in 1983: Cocoa 31·7%; Bananas 16·2%; Nutmeg 15·2%; Fruit 25·2%.
Monetary unit: East Caribbean dollar (EC$). 1 dollar = 100 cents.
Denominations:
  Coins 1, 2, 5, 10, 25, 50 cents.
  Notes 1, 5, 20, 100 dollars.
Political history and government: A former British dependency. An Associated State, with internal self-government, from 3 Mar 1967 until becoming fully independent, within the Commonwealth, on 7 Feb 1974. Executive power is vested in the Queen and exercised by the Governor-General, who acts on the advice of the Cabinet, led by the Prime Minister. At independence the Grenada United Labour Party (GULP) was in power. The GULP government was overthrown on 13 Mar 1979 in a *coup* by supporters of the main opposition party, the New Jewel Movement. A 'People's Revolutionary Government' took power, dissolved Parliament, suspended the constitution and announced plans to create a people's Consultative Assembly to draft a new one. Maurice Bishop, the Prime Minister was subsequently killed in a power struggle, whereupon the army took control (19 Oct 1983). At the request of other Caribbean countries, the US then led an invasion of the island, and a state of emergency was declared. An interim government took over, to be succeeded by an elected government in December 1984.
Length of roadways: 980 km (*610 miles*) (1983).
Defence: A Special Security Unit.
Foreign tourists: 171 159 in 1986.

Guatemala

Official name: República de Guatemala.
Population: 8 990 000 (1987 estimate).
Area: 108 889 km² (*42 042 miles²*).
Languages: Spanish, with some twenty Indian dialects (most important is Quiché).
Religion: Roman Catholic 90%.
Capital city: Ciudad de Guatemala (Guatemala City), population 1 300 000 (1983 estimate).
Other principal towns (1983): Quezaltanango 65 733; Puerto Barrios 38 956; Mazatenango 38 319; Antigua 26 631; Zacapa 35 769; Coban 53 538.
Highest point: Volcán Tajumulco, 4220 m (*13 881 ft*).
Principal mountain ranges: Sierra Madre, Sierra de las Minas, Sierra de los Cuchumatanes, Sierra de Chuacús.
Principal rivers: Motagua (400 km (*249 miles*)), Usumacinta (1107 km (*688 miles*)).
Head of State: Vinicio Cerezo Arevalo, President.
Climate: Tropical (hot and humid) on coastal lowlands, with average temperature of 28°C (*83°F*). More temperate in central highlands, with average of 21°C (*68°F*). Mountains cool. In Guatemala City, average maximum 22°C (*72°F*) (December) to 29°C (*84°F*) (May), minimum 12°C (*53°F*) (January) to 16°C (*61°F*) (June), June rainiest (23 days). Absolute maximum temperature 45°C (*113°F*), Guatemala City, 17 Dec 1957; absolute minimum −7·1°C (*19·2°F*), Quezaltenango, 15 Jan 1956.
Labour force: 2 448 502 in 1985: Agriculture, forestry and fishing 58·1%; Manufacturing 13·6%; Trade 7·3%; Services 12%.
Gross domestic product: 2926·3 million quetzales in 1986: Agriculture, forestry and fishing 25·6%; Manufacturing 16·2%; Trade 24·9%; Community, social and personal services 6·4%.
Exports: 1119·1 million quetzales in 1986: Coffee 44·1%; Cotton 3·1%; Bananas 6·8%; Sugar 5%; Cardamom 5·4%.
Monetary unit: Quetzal. 1 quetzal = 100 centavos.
Denominations:
  Coins 1, 5, 10, 25 centavos.
  Notes 50 centavos; 1, 5, 10, 20, 50, 100 quetzales.
Political history and government: A republic comprising 22 departments. Under the constitution, promulgated on 15 Sept 1965 and effective from 1 July 1966, legislative power is vested in the unicameral National Congress, with 61 members elected for 4 years by universal adult suffrage. Executive power is held by the President, also directly elected for 4 years. If no candidate obtains an absolute majority of votes, the President is chosen by Congress. He is assisted by a Vice-President and an appointed Cabinet. There is guerrilla activity in parts of the country.
Length of roadways: 18 000 km (*11 200 miles*) (1985).
Length of railways: 820 km (*510 miles*) (1985).
Universities: 5.
Adult illiteracy: 45% in 1985.

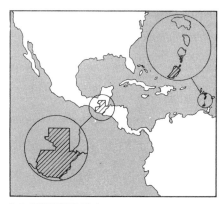

left: **GUATEMALA**
right: **GRENADA**

Defence: Military service: 2 years; total armed forces 40 200 (1987); defence expenditure 265·8 million quetzales in 1987.
Foreign tourists: 287 460 in 1986.

Guinea

Official name: La République populaire et révolutionnaire de Guinée (the People's Revolutionary Republic of Guinea).
Population: 6 225 000 (1986 estimate).
Area: 245 857 km² (94 926 miles²).
Languages: French (official), Fulani (Poular), Susu, Malinké.
Religions: Islam (Sunni), Animist minority.
Capital city: Conakry, population 705 280 (1983 census).
Other principal towns (1983): Kankan 88 760; Labé 65 439; Kindia 55 904.
Highest point: Mt Nimba, 1752 m (5748 ft).
Principal mountain ranges: Fouta Djalon.
Principal rivers: Niger (4184 km 2600 miles), Bafing, Konkouré, Kogon.
Head of State: Brig.-Gen. Lansana Conté.
Climate: Hot and moist, with heavy rainfall in coastal areas. Cooler in higher interior. In Conakry, average maximum 28°C to 32°C (82°F to 90°F), minimum around 23°C (74°F), annual rainfall 4300 mm (169 in).
Labour force: 2 846 000: Agriculture, forestry and fishing 78·1%.
Gross domestic product: 45 660 million sylis in 1982: Agriculture 39%; Mining and quarrying 12·2%; Trade 11·9%; Public administration and defence 11·6%.
Exports: 8852 million sylis in 1980: Bauxite and alumina 96·8%; Pulses and oilseeds 2·9%.
Monetary unit: In 1986 the syli was replaced by the Guinea Franc and the currency devalued by about 90%. 1 franc guineén = 100 centimes.
Denominations:
Notes 25, 50, 100, 500, 1000, 5000 francs.
Political history and government: Formerly French guinea, part of French West Africa. Became independent as the Republic of Guinea, outside the French Community, on 2 Oct 1958. A provisional constitution was adopted on 12 Nov 1958. Legislative power is vested in the unicameral National Assembly, with 210 members elected by univesal adult suffrage for 7 years. The Assembly elects a Commission to be its permanent organ. Full executive authority is vested in the President, also directly elected for 7 years. He appoints and leads a Cabinet, including a Prime Minister. Guinea has a single political party, the Parti démocratique de Guinée (PDG), which exercises 'sovereign and exclusive control of all sections of national life'. The party's directing organ is the Central Committee, 25 members elected for 5 years at Congress. The PDG Congress of 17–22 Nov 1978 decided to alter the country's name from 1 Jan 1979. It was also decided to increase the PDG Central Committee to 75.
Elections were held in 1980, and in 1984 the government was overthrown by the military on the death of President Sekou Touré. The military have held on to power since then.
Length of roadways: 28 400 km (17 650 miles).
Length of railways: 1038 km (645 miles).

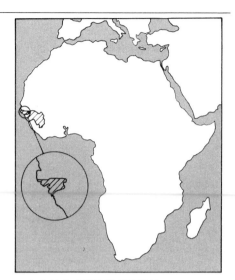

encircled left: **GUINEA-BISSAU**
right: **GUINEA**

Universities: 1.
Adult illiteracy: 71·7% in 1985.
Defence: Military service compulsory – two years; total armed forces 9900 (1987).

Guinea-Bissau

Official name: República da Guiné-Bissau (the Republic of Guinea-Bissau).
Population: 935 000 (1987 estimate).
Area: 36 125 km² (13 948 miles²).
Languages: Portuguese (official), Creole, Balante, Fulani, Malinké.
Religions: Animist; Islamic (Sunni) minority.
Capital city: Bissau, population 109 486 (1979 census).
Other principal towns (1979): Oio 135 114; Cacheu 130 227; Bafatá 116 032; Gabú 104 227.
Principal rivers: Cacheu, Mansôa, Géba, Corubel.
Head of State: Maj. João Bernardo Vieira (b. 1939), President of the Council of the Revolution.
Climate: Tropical, with an average annual temperature of 25°C (77°F). Rainy season June to November. In dry season (December to May) the northerly harmattan, a dust-laden wind, blows from the Sahara.
Labour force: 403 000 in 1980: Agriculture 82·4%; Industry 3·5%; Services 14·1%.
Gross domestic product: 6490 million Guinea pesos in 1982.
Exports: US$9·6 million in 1986: Palm kernels 10·4%; Cashew nuts 53·1%; Fish 11·5%; Timber 10·4%.
Monetary unit: Guinea peso. 1 peso = 100 centavos.
Denominations:
Coins 5, 10, 20, 50 centavos; 1, 2½, 5, 10, 20 pesos.
Notes 50, 100, 500 pesos.
Political history and government: Formerly Portuguese Guinea. Independence declared on 24 Sept 1973, recognized by Portugal on 10 Sept 1974. The

independence movement was dominated by the *Partido Africano da Independência da Guiné e Cabo Verde* (Paigc), the African Party for the Independence of Guinea and Cape Verde. In 1973 the PAIGC established a National People's Assembly as the supreme organ of the state and formulated the independence constitution, which provided for the eventual union of Guinea-Bissau with Cape Verde (*q.v.*). In elections held between 19 Dec 1976 and January 1977 voters chose regional councils from which a new National Assembly of 150 members was subsequently selected. The Assembly, to hold office for up to four years, was convened on 13 Mar 1977. The Head of State was elected for a four-year term by the Assembly. The constitution proclaimed the PAIGC, the only permitted party, to be 'the supreme expression of the sovereign will of the people'. Executive power was vested in the State Council, with 15 members elected for three years from deputies to the Assembly. Administrative authority lay with the Council of State Commissioners, appointed by the Head of State. On 10 Nov 1980 the Assembly approved a new constitution, increasing the powers of the Head of State, but on 14 Nov he was overthrown in a *coup*. A nine-member Revolutionary council, led by the former Chief State Commissioner, took power. The Assembly and State Council were dissolved on 19 Nov 1980 and a Provisional Government announced on the next day. A New People's Assembly (of 150 members) was elected in 1984.

Length of roadways: 5058 km (*3144 miles*) (1982).
Adult illiteracy: 68·6% (1985).
Defence: Total armed forces 9150 (1987); estimated defence expenditure for 1982, 375 million pesos.

Guyana

Official name: The Co-operative Republic of Guyana.
Population: 812000 (1987 estimate).
Area: 214969 km² (*83000 miles²*).
Languages: English (official), Hindu, Urdu.
Religions: Christian 56·7%; Hindu 33·4%; Islam 8·8% (1960).
Capital city: Georgetown, population 188000 (1983 estimate).
Other principal towns (1970): Linden 29000; New Amsterdam 23000; Mackenzie 20000; Corriverton 17000.
Highest point: Mt Roraima 2772 m (*9094 ft*), on the Brazil-Venezuela border.
Principal mountain ranges: Pakaraima, Serra Acarai, Kanuku, Kamoa.
Principal rivers: Essequibo, Courantyne (on the frontier with Suriname), Mazaruni, Berbice, Demarara.
Head of State: Hugh Desmond Hoyte, President.
Prime Minister: Hamilton Green.
Climate: Generally warm and pleasant. Average temperature 27°C (*80°F*), with daily range of about 10°C (*18°F*) on coast, increasing inland. Average annual rainfall 2360 mm (*93 in*), 2030–2540 mm (*80 to 100 in*) on coast (mainly April to August and November to January), 1520 mm (*60 in*) inland (May to August).
Labour force: 239331 in 1980: Agriculture, forestry and fishing 20·3%; Mining 3·9%; Manufacturing 11·7%; Trade 6·1%; Transport, storage and commu-

GUYANA

nications 3·8%; Community, social and personal services 24%; Unemployed 18·7%.
Gross domestic product: $G2219 million in 1986.
Exports: $G548·7 million in 1983: Bauxite 39·9%; Sugar 39·2%; Rice 11·8%.
Monetary unit: Guyana dollar ($G). 1 dollar = 100 cents.
Denominations:
Coins 1, 5, 10, 25, 50 cents.
Notes 1, 5, 10, 20 dollars.
Political history and government: Formerly the colony of British Guiana. Became independent, within the Commonwealth, on 26 May 1966, taking the Guyana. A republic since 23 Feb 1970. Legislative power is held by the unicameral National Assembly. Following a referendum on 10 July 1978, which gave the Assembly power to amend the constitution, elections to the Assembly were postponed for 15 months. It assumed the role of a Constituent Assembly, established on 6 Nov 1978, to draft a new constitution. A new constitution was promulgated on 6 Oct 1980. Elections took place in 1980 and 1985, in which the ruling Peoples' National Congress party were accused of malpractice on both occasions.

The National Assembly has 65 members, including 12 regional representatives and 53 members elected for five years by universal adult suffrage, using proportional representation. Executive power is vested in the President, who is leader of the majority party in the Assembly and holds office for its duration. The President appoints and leads a Cabinet, responsible to the Assembly.
Length of roadways: 4830 km (*3000 miles*).
Length of railways: 187 km (*116 miles*).
Universities: 1.
Adult illiteracy: 4·1% in 1985.
Defence: Total armed forces 5425 (1987); defence

expenditure US$65 million (1986); military service was introduced in 1974.

Haiti

Official name: République d'Haïti.
Population: 5 358 000 (1986 estimate).
Area: 27 750 km² (*10 714 miles²*).
Languages: French (official), Créole 90%.
Religions: Roman Catholic, Vodum (Voodoo).
Capital city: Port-au-Prince, population 738 342 (including suburbs) (1984 estimate).
Other principal towns (1982): Cap Haïtien 64 406; Gonaïves 34 209; Les Cayes 34 090; Port de Paix 21 733 (1975).
Highest point: Pic La Selle, 2680 m (*8793 ft*).
Principal mountain range: Massif de la Hotte.
Principal river: Artibonite (237 km *147 miles*).
Head of State: Prosper Avril, President.
Climate: Tropical but cooled by sea winds. Rainy season May to September. North warmer than south. In Port-au-Prince, average maximum 31°C (*87°F*) (December, January) to 34°C (*94°F*) (July), minimum 20°C (*68°F*) (January, February) to 23°C (*74°F*) (July), May rainiest (13 days).
Labour force: 2 016 200 in 1982–3: Agriculture, forestry and fishing 65·9%; Manufacturing 6·8%; Trade 17·9%; Community, social and personal services 7·1%.
Gross domestic product: 6867 million gourdes in 1986.
Exports: 969·3 million gourdes in 1985–6; Coffee 31·5%; Cocoa 2·9%; Light industrial products 6·6%; Manufactured articles 47·7%.
Monetary unit: Gourde. 1 gourde = 100 centimes.
Denominations:
Coins 5, 10, 20, 50 centimes.
Notes 1, 2, 5, 10, 50, 100, 250, 500 gourdes.
US currency is also used.
Political history and government: A republic comprising 9 departments. Dr François Duvalier was elected President on 22 Sept 1957 and took office on 22 Oct 1957. Under the constitution of June 1964, the unicameral Legislative Chamber has 58 members elected for 6 years by universal adult suffrage. The constitution granted absolute power to the President, who took office for life on 22 June 1964. On 14 Jan 1971 the constitution was amended to allow the President to nominate his own successor. The President named his son, Jean-Claude, to succeed him as President for life. Dr Duvalier died on 21 Apr 1971 and his son was sworn in on the following day.

However, popular feeling against Jean-Claude Duvalier increased and in February 1986 he was forced to flee the country. Government was subsequently assumed by a ruling council in which the military figured strongly. Following a general strike in November 1986 and the approval of a new Constitution in a referendum in March 1987, elections were scheduled, but widespread disorder including a massacre of peasants in Jean Rabel and the murder of presidential candidates led to the cancellation of elections and the dissolution of the Provisional Electoral Council in November 1987. Fresh elections were held in January 1988 and were won by Prof. Leslie Manigat.
Length of roadways: 4000 km (*2500 miles*).
Universities: 1.

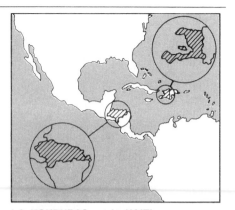

left: **HONDURAS**   *right:* **HAITI**

Adult illiteracy: 62·5% in 1985 – the highest in the Western Hemisphere.
Defence: Total armed forces 7600 (1987); defence expenditure: US$30·5 million in 1985.
Foreign tourists: 208 092 in 1985–6.

Honduras

Official name: Republica de Honduras.
Population: 3 826 200 (1985 estimate).
Area: 112 088 km (*43 277 miles*).
Language: Spanish, some Indian dialects.
Religion: Roman Catholic.
Capital city: Tegucigalpa, population 604 600 (1986 estimate).
Other principal towns (1986): San Pedro sula 399 700; La Ceiba 63 800; Choluteca 60 700; El Progreso 58 300.
Highest point: Cerro las Minas 2865 m (*9400 ft*).
Principal rivers: Patuca, Ulúa.
Head of State: José Azcona Hoyo, President.
Climate: Tropical (hot and humid) and wet on coastal plains. Rainy season May to November. More moderate in central highlands. In Tegucigalpa, average maximum 25°C (*77°F*) (December, January) to 30°C (*86°F*) (June), September and October rainiest (each 14 days). Absolute maximum temperature 43·3°C (*110°F*), Nueva Octepeque, 13 Mar 1958; absolute minimum −0·6°C (*31°F*), La Esperanza, 17 Feb 1956.
Labour force: 1 140 600 in 1986: Agriculture, forestry and fishing 53·6%; Manufacturing 13·2%; Trade 9·6%; Services 13·8%.
Gross domestic product: 7565 million lempiras in 1986: Agriculture, forestry and fishing 19·8%; Manufacturing 12·7%; Trade 12%; Services 10·7%.
Exports: 1708·5 million lempiras in 1986: Bananas 30·1%; Coffee 37·7%; Shellfish 5·3%.
Monetary unit: Lempira. 1 lempira = 100 centavos.
Denominations:
Coins 1, 2, 5, 10, 20, 50 centavos.
Notes 1, 2, 5, 10, 20, 50, 100 lempiras.
Political history and government: A republic comprising 18 departments and a federal district. The last elected President was deposed on 4 Dec 1972 by a military *coup*, led by a former President, Brig.-Gen. Oswaldo López Arellano. The military régime suspended the legislature, a unicameral Congress

of Deputies, and introduced government by decree. On 22 Apr 1975 Gen. López was overthrown by army officers and replaced by Col. (later Gen.) Juan Melgar Castro. On 7 Aug 1978 Gen. Melgar was deposed by another *coup* and a 3-man military junta took power. Its leader became President and rules with the assistance of an appointed Cabinet. On 20 Apr 1980 a 71-member Constituent Assembly was elected by universal adult suffrage. On 20 July 1980 the junta transferred power to the Assembly and on 25 July the Assembly elected the President to continue in office as interim Head of State. A presidential election on 29 Nov 1981 was won by Dr Roberto Suazo Córdova, who took office on 27 Jan 1982. His government was still dominated by the military however, a situation that continued to a varying degree until the next elections in 1985.
Length of roadways: 14 167 km (*8798 miles*) (1986).
Length of railways: 1780 km (*1106 miles*).
Universities: 1.
Adult illiteracy: 40·5% in 1985.
Defence: Military service: 8 months; total armed forces 16 950; defence expenditure: 143·2 million lempiras in 1986/7.
Foreign tourists: 170 599 in 1986.

Hungary

Official name: Magyar Népköztársaság (Hungarian People's Republic).
Population: 10 621 000 (1987 estimate).
Area: 93 036 km² (*35 921 miles²*).
Language: Magyar.
Religions: Roman Catholic; Protestant, Orthodox and Jewish minorities.
Capital city: Budapest, population 2 093 487 (1987).
Other principal towns (1987): Debrecen 214 836; Miskolc 211 156; Szeged 185 559; Pécs 179 051; Győr 130 194; Nyíregyháza 118 179; Székesfehérvár 112 703; Kecskemét 103 944; Szombathely 86 682.
Highest point: Kékes, 1015 m (*3330 ft*).
Principal mountain ranges: Cserhát, Mátra, Bükk, Bakony.
Principal rivers: Duna (Danube) (2850 km *1770 miles*, 439 km *273 miles* in Hungary), with its tributaries (Drava, Tisza, Rba).
Head of State: Bruno Ferenc Straub, President of the Presidential Council.
Political Leader: Károly Grósz, General Secretary of the Hungarian Socialist Workers' Party.
Head of Government: Miklos Nemeth, Chairman of the Council of Ministers.
Climate: Continental (long, dry, hot summers, cold winters). In Budapest, July warmest (16°C to 28°C *61°F to 82°F*), January coldest (−3°C to 2°C *26°F to 35°F*), May and December rainiest (each nine days). Absolute maximum temperature 41·3°C (*106·3°F*), Pécs, 5 July 1950; absolute minimum −34·9°C (*−30·8°F*), Asófügöd, 16 Feb 1940.
Labour force: 4 885 200 in 1987: Industry 32·9%; Agriculture and forestry 19·3%; Trade 10·5%; Services 22·1%.
Net material product: 881 300 million forint in 1986: Industry 38·1%; Agriculture and forestry 12·6%; Trade 13%.
Exports: 420 303·1 million forint in 1986: Agriculture 16·6%; Chemical and related products 10·9%; Basic manufacturers 13%; Machinery and transport equipment 35·1%.

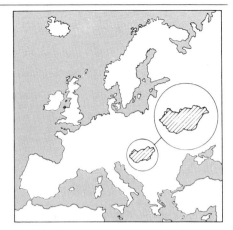

HUNGARY

Monetary unit: Forint. 1 forint = 100 fillér.
Denominations:
Coins 10, 20, 50 fillér; 1, 2, 5, 10, 20 forints.
Notes 20, 50, 100, 500, 1000 forints.
Political history and government: After occupation by Nazi Germany, a Hungarian provisional government signed an armistice on 20 Jan 1945. Following elections in October 1945, a republic was proclaimed on 1 Feb 1946. The Communist Party took power in May–June 1947. A new constitution was introduced on 18 Aug 1949 and a People's Republic established two days later.
The highest organ of state is the unicameral National Assembly which currently has 387 members elected for 5 years by universal adult suffrage; 352 of these members represent territorial constituencies, all of which must be contested in a general election under the amended electoral law of 1983. In addition there are 35 members who are presented on a national list. The Assembly elects from its members a Presidential Council (21 members) to be its permanent organ and the state's executive authority, responsible to the Assembly. The Council of Ministers, the highest organ of state administration, is elected by the Assembly on the recommendation of the Presidential Council.
Political power is held by the (Communist) Hungarian Socialist Workers' Party (HSWP). The Front presents a list of candidates for elections for representative bodies, nominations being made in public nomination meetings in the various constituencies and local council wards. The HSWP's highest authority is the Party Congress, which elects a Central Committee to supervise Party work. The Central Committee elects a Political Committee (Politburo) of 13 members to direct policy. In March 1989 the formation of other political parties was allowed and these will be permitted to contest elections in future. A new Constitution, which is expected to provide for an executive Presidency is to be drafted.
Hungary comprises 19 counties and the capital city.
Length of roadways: 95 004 km (*58 997 miles*) (1986).
Length of railways: 7881 km (*4894 miles*) (1986).
Universities: 10 (plus 9 technical universities plus an open university).

Defence: Military service: 18 months; total regular forces 106 000 (58 000 conscripts) in 1987; defence expenditure: 56 400 million forint in 1988.
Foreign tourists: 19 000 000 in 1987.

Iceland

Official name: Lýdveldid Island (Republic of Iceland).
Population: 244 009 (1986).
Area: 103 000 km² (39 784 miles²).
Language: Icelandic.
Religion: Lutheran.
Capital city: Reykyavik, population 106 003 (1986) – includes Kópavogur 14 609.
Other principal towns (1986): Akureyri 13 750; Hafnarfjordur 13 431; Keflavik 6993; Akranes 5373; Gardbaer 6231; Vestmannaeyjar 4785.
Highest point: Hvannadalshnúkur, 2119 m (6952 ft).
Principal rivers: Thrórsá (193 km 120 miles), Skjálfandafljót, Jökulsa á Fjöllum.
Head of State: Mme Vigdís Finnbogadóttir (b. 15 Apr 1930), President.
Prime Minister: Steingrimur Hermannsson.
Climate: Cold. Long winters with average temperature of 1°C (34°F). Short, cool summers with average of 10°C (50°F). Storms are frequent. In Reykjavik, average maximum 2°C (36°F) (January) to 14°C (58°F) (July), minimum −2°C (28°F) (January, February) to 9°C (48°F), (July), December rainiest (21 days). Absolute maximum temperature 32·8°C (91·0°F) May 1901; absolute minimum −44·6°C (−48·2°F), Grímsstaoir, 22 Mar 1918.
Labour force: 116 559 in 1984: Agriculture and fishing 20·4%; Manufacturing 23·9%; Trade, finance and services 14·5%; Other services 23·8%.
Gross domestic product: 159 375 million krónur in 1986.
Exports: 813·8 million US$ in 1985: Fish products 65·5%; Manufacturing products 15·7%.
Monetary unit: New Icelandic króna. 1 króna = 100 aurar (singular: eyrir).
Denominations:
Coins 5, 10, 50 aurar; 1, 5 krónur.
Notes 10, 50, 100, 500 krónur.
Political history and government: Formerly ruled by Denmark. Iceland became a sovereign state, under the Danish Crown, on 1 Dec 1918. An independent republic was declared on 17 June 1944. Legislative power is held jointly by the President (elected for 4 years by universal adult suffrage) and the Althing

(Parliament), with 63 members elected by universal suffrage for 4 years (subject to dissolution by the President), using a mixed system of proportional representation. The Althing chooses 21 of its members to form the Upper House, the other 42 forming the Lower House. For some purposes, the two Houses sit jointly as the United Althing. Executive power is held jointly by the President and the Cabinet, although the President's functions are mainly titular. The President appoints the Prime Minister and, on the latter's recommendation, other Ministers. The Cabinet is responsible to the Althing. Iceland has 23 counties.
Length of roadways: 11 649 km (7238 miles) (1986).
Universities: 1.
Defence: Iceland has no forces but is a member of NATO.
Foreign tourists: 113 500 in 1986.

India

Official name: Bharatiya Ganrajya or Bharat ka Ganatantra (the Republic of India). India is called Bharat in the Hindi language.
Population: 766 135 000 (1986 estimate).
Area: 3 287 263 km² (1 269 213 miles²) (provisional, 31 March 1982) includes Indian-held part of Jammu and Kashmir, plus Sikkim.
Languages: Assamese; Bengali 7%; Gujarati; Hindi (official) 24%; Kannada; Kashmiri; Malayalam; Marathi 6%; Oriya; Punjabi; Sanskrit; Sindhi; Tamil; Telugu 7%; Urdu.
Religions: Hinduism 82·7%; Ismal 11·2%; Christianity 2·6%; Sikhism 1·9%; Buddhism 0·7%; Jainism 0·5%; plus others (1971).
Capital city: New Delhi, population 5 729 283 (1981 census).
Other principal towns (1981): Calcutta 9 194 018; Bombay 8 243 405; Madras 4 289 347; Bangalore 2 921 751; Ahmedabad 2 548 057; Hyderabad 2 545 836; Pune (Poona) 1 686 109; Kanpur 1 639 064; Nagpur 1 302 066; Jaipur 1 015 160; Lucknow 1 007 604; Coimbatore 920 355; Patna 918 903; Surat 913 806; Madurai 907 732; Indore 829 327; Varanasi (Banaras) 797 162; Jabalpur 757 303; Agra 747 318.
NB: These are figures for the cities plus their suburbs.
Highest point: Nanda Devi, 7816 m (25 645 ft) (first climbed 29 Aug 1936), excluding Kashmir.
Principal mountain ranges: Himalaya, Gravalti, Sappura, Vindhya, Western Ghats, Chota Nagpur.
Principal rivers: Ganga (Ganges) (2510 km 1560 miles) and tributaries, Brahmaputra (2900 km 1800 miles), Sutlej, Narmeda, Tapti, Godavari, Krishna, Cauvery.
Head of State: R. Venkataraman, President.
Prime Minister: Rajiv Gandhi (b. 20 Aug 1944).
Climate: Ranges from temperate in the north (very cold in the Himalayas) to tropical in the south. The average summer temperature in the plains is about 29°C (85°F). The full weight of the monsoon season is felt in June and July but the rainfall figures vary widely according to locality. Average daily high temperature in Bombay 28°C (83°F) (January, February) to 33°C (91°F) (May); average daily low temperature 19°C (67°F) (January, February) to 27°C (80°F) (May); rainiest month July (21 days). Aver-

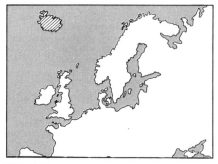

ICELAND

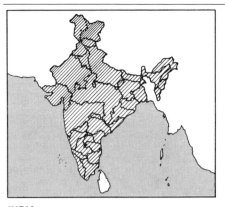

INDIA

which is responsible to Parliament. The President appoints the Prime Minister and, on the latter's recommendation, other Ministers.

India comprises 25 self-governing States (including the disputed territory of Jammu-Kashmir) and 7 Union Territories. Each State has a Governor (appointed by the President for 5 years), a legislature elected for 6 years (to be reduced to 5 years under legislation of 30 Apr 1979) and a Council of Ministers. The Union Territories are administered by officials appointed by the President.

Length of roadways: 1 675 000 km (*1 041 000 miles*) (1983).
Length of railways: 61 836 km (*38 400 miles*) (1986).
Universities: 132.
Adult illiteracy: 63·8% in 1981.
Defence: Military service voluntary; total armed forces: 1 262 000 in 1987; defence expenditure: 125 120 million rupees in 1987–8.
Foreign tourists: 1 080 500 in 1986.

age daily high temperature in Calcutta 26°C (*79°F*) (December) to 36°C (*97°F*) (April); average daily low 13°C (*55°F*) (December, January) to 26°C (*79°F*) (June, July); rainiest months July, August (each 18 days).
Labour force: 220 100 000 (excluding unemployed) at 1981 census: Agriculture 66%; Manufacturing 3%.
Gross domestic product: 2762·6 billion rupees in 1986–7: Agriculture, forestry and fishing 30·6%; Manufacturing 16·7%; Trade 14·8%.
Exports: 110 119·6 million rupees in 1985–6: Fish 3·5%; Tea 5·6%; Cotton fabrics 3·4%; Ready-made garments 9·2%; Leather, leather goods 4·4%; Pearls, precious stones 13%; Iron ore 5%; Machinery and transport equipment 5·5%; Mineral fuels 4·7%.
Monetary unit: Indian rupee. 1 rupee = 100 paisa (singular: paise).
Denominations:
Coins 5, 10, 20, 25, 50 paisa; 1, 2 rupees
Notes 1, 2, 5, 10, 20, 50, 100 rupees.
Political history and government: On 15 Aug 1947 former British India was divided on broadly religious lines into two independent countries, India and Pakistan, within the Commonwealth.

India was formed as a Union of States, with a federal structure. A republican constitution was passed by the Constituent Assembly on 26 Nov 1949 and India became a republic, under its present name, on 26 Jan 1950. France transferred sovereignty of its five Indian settlements on 2 May 1950 (Chandernagore) and 1 Nov 1954 (Pondicherry, Karikal, Yanam and Mahé). The Portuguese territories of Goa, Daman and Diu were invaded by Indian forces on 19 Dec 1961 and incorporated in India. Sikkim, formerly an Associated State, became a State of India on 26 Apr 1975.

Legislative power is vested in a Parliament, consisting of the President and two Houses. The Council of States (*Rajya Sabha*) has 244 members, including 232 indirectly elected by the State Assemblies for 6 years (one third retiring every two years) and 12 nominated by the President. The House of the People (*Lok Sabha*) has 546 members, including 532 elected by universal adult suffrage for 5 years (subject to dissolution) and 13 nominated. The President is a constitutional Head of State elected for 5 years by an electoral college comprising elected members of both Houses of Parliament and the State legislatures. He exercises executive power on the advice of the Council of Ministers,

Indonesia

Official name: Republik Indonesia.
Population: 164 046 988 (1985) including East Timor (630 676).
Area: 2 034 255 km² (*785 766 miles²*) includes East Timor 14 874 km² (*5743 miles²*).
Languages: Bahasa Indonesia (official), Javanese, Madurese, Sundanese, Bugis, Makassar, Batak.
Religions: Islam (Sunni) 85%; Christian, Buddhist and Hindu minorities.
Capital city: Jakarta, population 7 347 800 (1983).
Other principal towns (1983): Surabaya 2 223 600; Medan 1 805 500; Bandung 1 566 700; Semarang 1 205 800; Palembang 873 900; Ujung Pandang (Makassar) 840 500; Padang 656 800; Malang 547 100; Surakarta 490 900; Banjarmasin 423 600; Yogyakarta 420 700.
Highest point: Puncak Jaya (formerly Ngga Pulu and Mt Sukarno), 4883 m (*16 020 ft*) (first climbed on 13 Feb 1962).
Principal mountain ranges: Bukit, Barisan, Pegunungan Jayawijaya.
Principal rivers: Kapuas (1150 km *715 miles*), Digul (896 km *557 miles*), Barito (900 km *560 miles*), Mahakam, Kajan, Hari.
Head of State: Gen. Suharto (b. 8 June 1921), President and Prime Minister.
Climate: Tropical (hot and rainy). Average temperature 27°C (*80°F*). Mountain areas cooler. In Jakarta, average maximum 29°C (84°F) (January, February) to 31°C (*88°F*) (September), minimum 23°C (*73°F*) (July, August) to 24°C (*75°F*) (April, May) January rainiest (18 days).
Labour force: 62 457 138 in 1985: Agriculture, forestry and fishing 54·7%; Manufacturing 9·3%; Trade 15%; Community, social and personal services 13·3%.
Gross domestic product: 96 066·4 million rupiahs in 1985: Agriculture, forestry and fishing 23·6%; Mining and quarrying 16·2%; Manufacturing 13·5%; Trade 15·4%.
Exports: US$14 805 million in 1986: Oil and gas 56·1%; Coffee 8·1%; Rubber 4·8%.
Monetary unit: Rupiah. 1 rupiah = 100 sen.
Denominations:
Coins 5, 10, 25, 50, 100 rupiah.
Notes 100, 500, 1000, 5000, 10 000 rupiahs.

INDONESIA

Political history and government: Excluding East Timor (see below), Indonesia was formerly the Netherlands East Indies. The islands were occupied by Japanese forces in March 1942. On 17 Aug 1945, three days after the Japanese surrender, a group of nationalists proclaimed the independence of the Republic of Indonesia. The Netherlands transferred sovereignty (except for West New Guinea) on 27 Dec 1949. West New Guinea remained under Dutch control until 1 Oct 1962, when a UN Temporary Executive Authority took over administration of the territory until it was transferred to Indonesia on 1 May 1963.

Military commanders, led by Gen. Suharto, assumed emergency executive powers on 11–12 Mar 1966. The President handed all power to Suharto on 22 Feb 1967. On 12 Mar 1967 the People's Consultative Assembly removed the President from office and named Gen. Suharto as acting President. He became Prime Minister on 11 Oct 1967 and, after being elected by the Assembly, was inaugurated as President on 27 Mar 1968.

The highest authority of the state is the People's Consultative Assembly, with 1000 members who serve for 5 years. The Assembly, which elects the President and Vice-President for 5 years, includes 500 members of the House of Representatives, which is the legislative organ. The House has 400 members and 100 nominated by the President. The President is assisted by an appointed Cabinet.

Indonesia comprises 27 provinces, including East (formerly Portuguese) Timor, unilaterally annexed on 17 July 1976.

Length of roadways: 219 009 km (*136 005 miles*) (1986).

Length of railways: 6877 km (*4273 miles*).

Universities: 71 (46 state – including institutions of university equivalent – and 25 private).

Adult illiteracy: 25·9% in 1985.

Defence: Military service selective; total armed forces 284 000 (1986); defence expenditure: 2 188 000 million rupiahs in 1987/8.

Foreign tourists: 700 000 in 1985.

Iran

Official name: Jomhori-e-Islami-e-Irân (Islamic Republic of Iran).
Population: 49 857 384 (1986 census).
Area: 1 648 000 km² (*636 296 miles²*).
Languages: Farsi (Persian), Azerbaizhani, Kurdish, Arabic.
Religions: Islam (Shia) 98%; Christian, Jewish, Zoroastrian minorities.
Capital city: Tehrān (Teheran), population 6 022 029 (1886).
Other principal towns (1986): Mashad 1 500 000 (1986); Isfahan 1 000 000 (1986); Tabriz 852 296 (1982); Shiraz 800 416 (1982); Bakhtaran (formerly Kermanshah) 531 350 (1982); Karaj 526 272 (1982); Ahwaz 470 927 (1982); Qom 424 048 (1982).
Highest point: Qolleh-ye Damâvand (Mt Demavend), 5604 m (*18 386 ft*).
Principal mountain ranges: Reshteh-ye Alborz (Elburz Mts), Kūhhā-ye-Zagros (Zagros Mts).
Principal rivers: Kārūn, Safid (Sefid Rud), Atrak, Karkheh, Zāyandeh.
National Leader and President: Hojatoleslam Ali Khamenei (b. 1939).
Prime Minister: Hossein Mousavi Khameini (b. 1941).
Climate: Extremely hot on Persian Gulf, cooler and dry on central plateau, subtropical on shore of Caspian Sea. In Teheran, July hottest (25 °C to 37 °C 77 °F to 99 °F), January coldest (−3 °C to 7 °C 27 °F to 45 °F), March rainiest (5 days). Absolute maximum temperature 52 °C (*126 °F*), Abādān, 6 July 1951.
Labour force: 33 183 174 in 1986: Agriculture 29·1%; Industry 25·5%; Services 42%.
Gross domestic product: No figures produced by the Government.
Exports: 1218·6 million rials in 1985.
Monetary unit: Iranian rial. 1 rial = 100 dinars.
Denominations:
Coins 50 dinars; 1, 2, 5, 10, 20, 50 rials.
Notes 100, 200, 500, 1000, 5000, 10 000 rials.
Political history and government: Formerly the Empire of Persia, renamed Iran on 21 Mar 1935. The country was an absolute monarchy until the adoption of the first constitution, approved by the Shah (Emperor) on 30 Dec 1906. On 31 Oct 1925 the National Assembly deposed the Shah and handed power to the Prime Minister, Reza Khan. He was elected Shah on 13 Dec 1925 and took the title Reza Shah Pahlavi. During the Second World War Reza Shah favoured Nazi Germany. British and Soviet forces entered Iran on 25 Aug 1941, forcing the Shah to abdicate in favour of his son, Mohammad Reza Pahlavi, on 16 Sept 1941.

Under the Pahlavi dynasty, Iran was a limited constitutional monarchy and executive power remained with the Shah. On 2 Mar 1975 Shah Mohammad dissolved existing political parties and announced the formation of a single party. Opposition to the Shah's rule later grew and, in response to increasing political violence and demonstrations, other parties were granted the freedom to resume their activities on 29 Aug 1978. Protests against the Shah intensified and a mainly military government was appointed on 6 Nov 1978. After further unrest, another civilian Prime Minister was appointed on 4 Jan 1979. The new Cabinet was approved by the legislature on 16 Jan, when the Shah left the country.

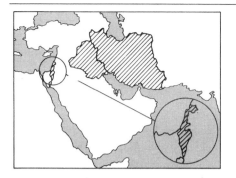

encircled: **ISRAEL** *centre:* **IRAQ** *right:* **IRAN**

new Prime Minister was approved by the *Majlis* on 29 Oct 1981. Ali Khameini was re-elected as president in 1985.

Iran and Iraq have been at war since 1980, originally over a border dispute but a ceasefire arranged by the United Nations was declared in 1988.
Length of roadways: 136372 km *(84 687 miles)* (1985).
Length of railways: 4567 km *(2838 miles)*.
Universities: 22.
Adult illiteracy: 38% in 1986.
Defence: Military service 24 months; total regular armed forces 654 500 (1987); defence expenditure: 465 000 million rials (1986–7).
Foreign tourists: 171 837 in 1986–7.

Iraq

Popular opposition to the Shah grouped behind the Islamic traditionalist movement, dominated by the Ayatollah Ruhollah Khomenei, a spiritual leader of the Shi'a Muslims, who had been exiled by the Shah since 1963. Khomeini established a Revolutionary Islamic Council on 13 Jan 1979, returned to Iran on 1 Feb and appointed a provisional government on 5 Feb. After heavy fighting, the Shah's government fell, and power was surrendered to Khomeini's movement, on 11 Feb 1979. Both houses of Parliament requested their own dissolution.

Following a referendum on 30–31 Mar, a republic was proclaimed on 1 Apr 1979. A draft constitution officially published on 18 June, was submitted to a Constituent Council of Experts, with 73 members elected by popular vote on 3 Aug 1979. The council, inaugurated on 19 Aug, completed its work on 14 Nov 1979. The constitution, including the Council's far-reaching amendments, was approved by a referendum on 2–3 Dec 1979. In accordance with Ayatollah Khomeini's principle of *Wilayat e Faqih* ('Rule of the Theologian'), supreme authority is vested in the *Wali Faqih*, a religious leader (initially Khomeini) agreed by the Muslim clergy, with no fixed term of office. The President is chief executive, elected by universal adult suffrage for a four-year term. Legislative power is vested in the unicameral Islamic Consultative Assembly (*Majlis*), with 270 members, also directly elected for four years. A 12-member Council of Guardians ensures that legislation conforms with Islamic precepts. Abolhasan Bani-Sadr was elected first President on 25 Jan 1980 and assumed office on 4 Feb. The *Majlis* was elected on 14 Mar and 9 May 1980.

The Prime Minister appointed by Khomeini had resigned on 5 Nov 1979. On the next day power was assumed by the 14-man Revolutionary Council. After the transfer of legislative power from this Council to the *Majlis*, the President was formally sworn in on 22 July 1980. The *Majlis* approved a new Prime Minsiter, Muhammad Ali Rajai, on 11 Aug 1980 and he was appointed on 20 Aug. A list of Ministers was approved on 10 Sept 1980 and the Revolutionary Council dissolved itself. After a dispute between the *Majlis* and President Bani-Sadr, the *Wali Faqih* dismissed the President on 22 June 1981. Rajai was elected President on 24 July and sworn in by the *Majlis* on 3 Aug. President Rajai and his Prime Minister were assassinated on 30 Aug. Another presidential election was held on 2 Oct and the winning candidate sworn in on 13 Oct. A

Official name: Al-Jumhuriya al-'Iraqiya (the Republic of Iraq).
Population: 17 093 000 (1987 estimate).
Area: 434 924 km² *(167 925 miles²)*.
Languages (1965): Arabic 81·1%; Kurdish 15·5%; Turkoman 1·7%.
Religions: Islam (both Shia and Sunni), Christian minority.
Capital city: Baghdad, population 3 844 608 (1987 census).
Other principal towns (1977): Al-Basrah 1 540 000; Mosul 1 220 000; Kirkuk 535 000.
Highest point: 3658 km *(12 000 ft)*.
Principal mountain range: Kurdistan Mts.
Principal rivers: Tigris, Euphrates (2740 km *1700 miles*).
Head of State: Saddam Husain (b. 1937), President and Prime Minister.
Climate: Extremely hot, dry summers, humid near coast. Cold, damp winters with severe frosts in highlands. In Baghdad, average maximum 15°C *(60°F)* (January) to 43°C *(110°F)* (July, August), minimum −1°C *(39°F)* (January) to 24°C *(76°F)* (July, August), December rainiest (5 days). Absolute maximum temperature 52°C *(125°F)*, Shaiba, 8 Aug 1937; minimum −14°C *(6°F)*, Ar Rutbah, 6 Jan 1942.
Labour force: 3 059 214 (excluding 74 725 unemployed) at 1977 census: Agriculture, forestry and fishing 31·5%; Construction 10·7%; Community, social and personal services 31·9%.
Gross domestic product: No figures are published by the Government.
Exports: 3041·8 million Iraqi dinars in 1983: Crude petroleum 98·6%.
Monetary unit: Iraqi dinar. 1 dinar = 5 riyals = 20 dirhams = 1000 fils.
Denominations:
Coins 1, 5, 10, 25, 50, 100 fils; 1 dinar.
Notes 250, 500 fils; 1, 5, 10 dinars.
Political history and government: Formerly part of Turkey's Ottoman Empire, captured by British forces during the 1914–18 war. After the war Iraq became a Kingdom under a League of Nations mandate, administered by Britain. The mandate was ended on 3 Oct 1932, when Iraq became independent. In an army-led revolution on 14 July 1958 the King was murdered, the bicameral parliament dissolved and a republic established. A succession of military régimes then held power. The latest of these was established on 17 July 1968. A provisional constitution, proclaiming socialist principles, was

introduced on 16 July 1970. A National Charter, to be the basis of a permanent constitution, was issued on 15 Nov 1971.

An elected National Assembly was envisaged but, before it was formed, the highest authority in the state was the Revolutionary Command Council (RCC). Legislation published on 5 Dec 1979, and ratified by the RCC on 16 Mar 1980, provided for a National Assembly, with a four-year term, to perform legislative duties alongside the RCC. The 250 members of the Assembly were elected on 20 June 1980. Executive power remains with the RCC, whose President is Head of State and Supreme Commander of the Armed Forces. The RCC, whose membership in 1988 was 9, elects the President and the Vice-President. The President appoints and leads a Council of Ministers to control administration. The dominant political organization is the Arab Socialist Renaissance (Ba'ath) Party.

Iraq comprises 18 governorates, each administered by an appointed governor. Three of the governorates form the (Kurdish) Autonomous Region, which has an elected Legislative Council.

Iraq and Iran have been at war since 1980, originally over a border dispute but a ceasefire arranged by the United Nations was declared in 1988.

Length of roadways: 33 238 km (*20 640 miles*) (1986).
Length of railways: 2029 km (*1260 miles*) (1986).
Universities: 6.
Defence: Military service 21–24 months; total armed forces 1 000 000 in 1987; defence expenditure: US$11 580 million in 1986.
Foreign tourists: 2 020 000 in 1982.

Ireland

Official name: Poblacht na h'Éireann (Republic of Ireland), abbreviated to Éire (Ireland).
Population: 3 540 643 (1986 census).
Area: 70 282·6 km² (*27 136·3 miles²*).
Languages: English, Irish Gaelic.
Religions: Roman Catholic 94·9% (1961); Church of Ireland, Presbyterian, Methodist, Jewish minorities.
Capital city: Dublin (Baile Átha Cliath), population 920 956 (1986 census) includes Dún Laoghaire and suburbs.
Other principal towns (1986): Cork (Corcaigh) 173 694 including suburbs; Limerick (Luimneach) 76 557 including suburbs; Galway (Gaillimh) 47 104 including suburbs; Waterford (Port Lairge) 41 054 including suburbs.
Highest point: Carrantuohill, 1041 m (*3414 ft*), in Co. Kerry.
Principal mountain ranges: Macgillycuddy's Reeks, Wicklow Mts.
Principal rivers: Shannon (360 km *224 miles*), Suir (136 km *85 miles*), Boyne (112 km *70 miles*), Barrow (191 km *119 miles*), Erne (115 km *72 miles*).
Head of State: Dr Patrick John Hillery (Pádraig Ó hIrighile) (b. 2 May 1923). *An Uachtaran* (President).
Head of Government: Charles Haughey, *Taoiseach* (Prime Minister).
Climate: Mild (generally between 0°C and 21°C (*32°F and 70°F*). In Dublin, average maximum 8°C (*47°F*) (December, January, February) to 19°C (*67°F*) (July, August), minimum 2°C (*35°F*) (January, February) to 10°C (*51°F*) (July, August); December rainiest (14 days). Absolute maximum

temperature 33°C (*92°F*), Dublin (Phoenix Park), 16 July 1876; absolute minimum −19°C (*−2°F*), Markee Castle, Co. Sligo, 16 Jan 1881.
Labour force: 1 075 000 in 1986: Agriculture, forestry and fishing 15·6%; Manufacturing 19·2%; Construction 6·7%; Commerce, insurance and finance 19·7%; Transport and communications 6·0%; Public administration and defence 6·6%.
Gross domestic product: I£16 280 million in 1986: Agriculture, forestry and fishing 9·9%; Mining, manufacturing and construction 37·5%; Public administration and defence 6·8%; Transport, communication and trade 18·2%; Other services 32·6%.
Exports: I£9388·2 million in 1986: Food and live animals 23·2%; Chemicals 13·3%; Machinery and transport equipment 30·5%; Miscellaneous manufactures 11·8%.
Monetary unit: Irish pound (punt or IR£). 1 pound = 100 pence.
Denominations:
Coins 1, 2, 5, 10, 50 pence.
Notes 1, 5, 10, 20, 50, 100 pounds.
Political history and government: The whole of Ireland was formerly part of the United Kingdom. During an insurrection against British rule in April 1916 a republic was proclaimed but the movement was suppressed. After an armed struggle, beginning in 1919, a peace agreement was signed on 6 Dec 1921 and became operative on 15 Jan 1922. It provided that the six Ulster counties of Northern Ireland should remain part of the UK while the remaining 26 counties should become a dominion under the British Crown. Southern Ireland duly achieved this status as the Irish Free State on 6 Dec 1922. A new constitution, giving full sovereignty within the Commonwealth, became effective on 29 Dec 1937. Formal ties with the Commonwealth were ended on 18 Apr 1949, when the 26 counties became a republic.

Legislative power is vested in the bicameral National Parliament (*Oireachtas*): a Senate (*Seanad Éireann*) of 60 members (11 nominated by the Prime Minister, 49 indirectly elected for 5 years) with restricted powers; and a House of Representatives (*Dáil Éireann*) with 166 members elected by universal adult suffrage for 5 years (subject to dissolution), using proportional representation. The President is a constitutional Head of State elected

IRELAND

by universal adult suffrage for 7 years. Executive power is held by the Cabinet, led by a Prime Minister, appointed by the President on the nomination of the *Dáil*. The President appoints other Ministers on the nomination of the Prime Minister with the previous approval of the *Dáil*. The Cabinet is responsible to the *Dáil*.

In 1985 the Anglo-Irish Agreement was signed, providing for participation of Eire in political, legal, security and cross-border matters in N. Ireland, via an Intergovernmental Conference.
Length of roadways: 92 303 km (*57 320 miles*) (1986).
Length of railways: 1876 km (*1165 miles*).
Universities: 4.
Defence: Military service voluntary; total armed forces 13 600 (1987); defence expenditure: I£311 million in 1987.
Foreign tourists: 2 464 000 in 1986.

Israel

Official name: Medinat Israel (State of Israel).
Population: 4 331 000 (1986 estimate) (includes East Jerusalem and Israeli residents in other occupied territories).
Area: 21 942 km² (*8572 miles²*) (includes Golan Heights but not the other occupied territories).
Languages (1983): Hebrew (official) 68·8%; Arabic 18·3%; Yiddish 2·6%.
Religions (1984): Jewish 82·7%; Islam (Sunni) 13·3%.
Capital city: Yerushalayim (Jerusalem), population 468 900 (1986 estimate), including East Jerusalem (Jordanian territory under Israeli occupation since 1967).
Other principal towns (1985): Tel Aviv/Jaffa 322 800; Haifa 224 600; Ramat Gan 116 000; Bat-Yam 131 200; Holon 138 800; Petah Tikva 129 300; Beersheba 115 000.
Highest point: Mt Atzmon (Har Meron), 1208 m (*3963 ft*).
Lowest point: The Dead Sea, 395 m (*1296 ft*) below sea level.
Principal mountain range: Mts of Judea.
Principal rivers: Jordan (321 km *200 miles*), Qishon.
Head of State: Chaim Herzog, President.
Prime Minister: Yitzhak Shamir.
Climate: Mediterranean (hot, dry summers and mild, rainy winters). More extreme in the south. Sub-tropical on coast. In Jerusalem, average maximum 12°C (*55°F*) (January) to 30°C (*87°F*) (July, August), minimum 5°C (*41°F*) (January) to 17°C (*64°F*) (August), February rainiest (11 days). Absolute maximum temperature 54°C (*129°F*), Tirat Zevi, 22 June 1942; absolute minimum −16°C (*2°F*), Tel ha Tanim, 8 Nov 1950.
Labour force: 1 471 900 in 1986: Agriculture, forestry and fishing 4·8%; Manufacturing 21·5%; Trade 12·1%; Financial services 9%; Public and community services 27·6%.
Gross domestic product: 25 966 million new Shekels in 1985: Mining and manufacturing 23·4%; Trade 14·5%; Financial services 16·1%; Community services 21·8%.
Exports: US$7135·6 million in 1986: Diamonds 26·3%; Chemicals 13·1%; Machinery 10·7%; metals and metal products 12·3%.
Monetary unit: New Israel shekel (=1000 old shekels). 1 shekel = 100 agorot (singular: agora).

Denominations:
Notes 5, 10, 50, 100 shekels.
Political history and government: Palestine (of which Israel forms part) was formerly part of Turkey's Ottoman Empire. During the First World War (1914–18) Palestine was occupied by British forces. After the war it was administered by Britain as part of a League of Nations mandate, established in 1922. The British Government terminated its Palestine mandate on 14 May 1948, when Jewish leaders proclaimed the State of Israel. After armed conflict with neighbouring Arab states, Israel's borders were fixed by armistice agreements in 1949. During the war of 5–10 June 1967 Israeli forces occupied parts of Egypt, Syria and Jordan, including East Jerusalem (which Israel unilaterally incorporated into its territory by legislation on 27 June 1967).

Israel is a republic. Supreme authority rests with the unicameral *Knesset* (Assembly), with 120 members elected by universal suffrage for 4 years, using proportional representation. The *Knesset* elects the President, a constitutional Head of State, for 5 years. Executive power rests with the Cabinet, led by the Prime Minister. The Cabinet takes office after receiving a vote of confidence in the *Knesset*, to which it is responsible. Israel comprises 6 administrative districts.
Length of roadways: 13 280 km (*8247 miles*) (1985).
Length of railways: 573 km (*358 miles*).
Universities: 6 (plus 2 specialized).
Defence: Military service: men 36 months, women 24 months (Jews and Druses only), Christians and Arabs may volunteer; annual training for reservists thereafter up to age 54 for men, 38 (or marriage) for women; total armed forces 141 000 (including 110 000 conscripts) in 1987, defence expenditure: US$5110 million in 1987–8.
Foreign tourists: 1 101 481 in 1986.

Italy

Official name: Repubblica Italiana (Italian Republic), abbreviated to Italia.
Population: 57 290 519 (1986 estimate).
Area: 301 263 km² (*116 318 miles²*).
Languages: Italian; small German and other minorities.
Religions: Roman Cathoic; Protestant and Jewish minorities.
Capital city: Roma (Rome), population 2 815 457 (1986 estimate).
Other principal towns (1986): Milano (Milan) 1 495 260; Napoli (Naples) 1 204 211; Torino (Turin) 1 035 565; Genova (Genoa) 727 427; Palermo 723 732; Bologna 432 406; Firenze (Florence) 425 835; Catania 372 486; Bari 362 524; Venezia (Venice) 331 454; Messina 268 896; Verona 259 151; Taranto 244 997; Trieste 239 031; Padova (Padua) 225 769; Cagliari 222 574.
Highest point: On Monte Bianco (Mont Blanc), 4760 m (*15 616 ft*).
Principal mountain ranges: Appennini (Appenines), Alps.
Principal rivers: Po (672 km *418 miles*), Tevere (Tiber), Arno, Volturno, Garigliano.
Head of State: Francesco Cossiga, President.
Head of Government: Ciriaco de Mita, President of the Council of Ministers (Prime Minister) (resigned May 1989 – no successor appointed at time of going to press).

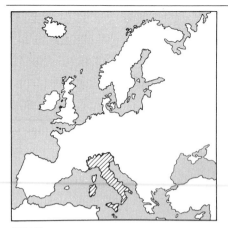

ITALY

Climate: Generally Mediterranean, with warm, dry summers (average maximum 26°C *80°F*) and mild winters. Cooler and rainier in the Po Valley and the Alps. In Rome, average maximum 12°C *(54°F)* (January) to 31°C *(88°F)* (July, August), minimum 4°C *(39°F)* (January, February) to 17°C *(64°F)* (July, August), February rainiest (11 days). Absolute maximum temperature 46°C *(114°F)*, Foggia, 6 Sept 1946; absolute minimum −34°C *(−29°F)*, Pian Rosa, 14 Feb 1956.
Labour force: 23 467 000 in 1986: Agriculture, forestry and fishing 9·5%; Manufacturing 20·1%; Construction 8·0%; Commerce 18·8%; Other services 23·5%.
Gross domestic product: 889 360 billion lire in 1986: Agriculture 5%; Industry 34·4%; Public administration 12·6%.
Exports: 145 323 billion lire in 1986: Food and live animals 5·2%; Chemicals 7·2%; Basic manufactures 22·6%; Machinery and transport equipment 33·9%; Miscellaneous manufactures 24·5%.
Monetary unit: Italian lira. 1 lira = 100 centesimi.
Denominations:
Coins 5, 10, 20, 50, 100, 500 lire.
Notes 1000, 2000, 5000, 10 000, 20 000, 50 000, 100 000 lire.
Political history and government: Formerly several independent states. The Kingdom of Italy, under the House of Savoy, was proclaimed in 1861 and the country unified in 1870. Italy was under Fascist rule from 28 Oct 1922 to 25 July 1943. A referendum on 2 June 1946 voted to abolish the monarchy and Italy became a republic on 10 June 1946. A new constitution took effect on 1 Jan 1948.
Legislative power is held by the bicameral Parliament (*Parlamento*), elected by universal suffrage for 5 years (subject to dissolution), using proportional representation. The Senate has 315 elected members (seats allocated on a regional basis) and 7 life Senators. The Chamber of Deputies has 630 members. The minimum voting age is 25 years for the Senate and 18 for the Chamber. The two houses have equal power. The President of the Republic is a constitutional Head of State elected for 7 years by an electoral college comprising both Houses of Parliament and 58 regional representatives. Executive power is exercised by the Council of Ministers. The Head of State appoints the President of the Council (Prime Minister) and, on the latter's recommenda-

tion, other Ministers. The Council is responsible to Parliament.
Italy has 20 administrative regions, each with an elected legislature and a regional executive.
Length of roadways: 301 307 km (*187 112 miles*).
Length of railways: 16 105 km (*10 001 miles*) (1984).
Universities: 59.
Defence: Military service: Army and Air Force 12 months, Navy 18 months; total armed forces 388 300 (including 266 200 conscripts) (1987); defence expenditure: 15 815 000 million lire in 1987.
Foreign tourists: 53 300 000 in 1986.

The Ivory Coast

Official name: La République de la Côte d'Ivoire (the Republic of the Ivory Coast).
Population: 10 595 000 (1986 estimate).
Area: 322 463 km² (*124 504 miles²*).
Languages: French (official), many African languages.
Religions: Animist, Islam (Sunni), Christian.
Capital city: Yamoussoukro, population 70 000 in 1983.
Other principal towns (1983): Abidjan 1 850 000; Bouaké 200 000, Daloa 70 000; Man 50 000; Gagnoa 45 000.
Highest point: Mont Toukui, *c.* 2100 m (*6900 ft*).
Principal mountain ranges: Man Mountains, Guinea Highlands.
Principal rivers: Bandama, Sassandra, Komoé.
Head of State: Félix Houphouët-Boigny (b. 18 Oct 1905), President.
Climate: Generally hot, wet and humid. Temperatures from 14°C to 39°C (*57°F to 103°F*). Rainy seasons May to July, October to November. In Abidjan, average maximum 28°C to 32°C (*82°F to 90°F*), minimum around 23°C (*74°F*).
Labour force: 4 053 000 in 1985: Agriculture 58·8%.
Gross domestic product: 2855·8 billion CFA francs in 1984: Agriculture 26·2%; Manufacturing 12·1%; Trade 18·4%.
Exports: 1 318 060 000 million CFA francs: Coffee 21·1%; Cocoa 30·2%; Fuels 9%; Wood 6·9%.
Monetary unit: Franc de la Communauté financière africaine. 1 franc = 100 centimes.
Denominations:
Coins 1, 5, 10, 25, 50, 100 CFA francs.
Notes 500, 1000, 5000, 10 000 CFA francs.
Political history and government: Formerly part of French West Africa, independent since 7 Aug 1960. The ruling *Parti démocratique de la Côte d'Ivoire* has been the only organized political party since its establishment in 1946.
Under the constitution, promulgated on 31 Oct 1960, legislative power is vested in the unicameral National Assembly, elected for five years by universal adult suffrage. The first multi-candidate elections were held in two rounds on 9 and 23 Nov 1980, the Assembly being increased from 120 to 147 members and since to 175 members. Executive power is held by the President, also directly elected for five years. On 25 Nov 1980 the Assembly adopted a constitutional amendment creating the post of Vice-President. The President rules with the assistance of an appointed council of Ministers, responsible to him. The country comprises 34 departments. The Government wishes the country to be known as Côte d'Ivoire. Since January 1986 Côte d'Ivoire has

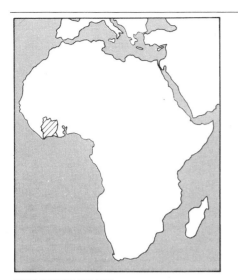

THE IVORY COAST

been the only correct title for the republic but in the English-speaking world the state is almost universally still known as Ivory Coast.
Length of roadways: 53 736 km (*33 370 miles*) (1984).
Length of railways: 1156 km (*718 miles*).
Universities: 1.
Adult illiteracy: 57·3% in 1985.
Defence: Military service voluntary; total armed forces 7120 (1987); defence expenditure: 5·9% of budget.
Foreign tourists: 194 869 in 1984.

Jamaica

Population: 2 346 700 (1986 estimate).
Area: 10 991 km² (*4244 miles²*).
Language: English.
Religion: Christian (Anglican and Baptist in majority).
Capital city: Kingston, population 524 638 (1982 census).
Other principal towns (1982): Spanish Town 89 097; Montego bay 70 265.
Highest point: Blue Mountain Peak (2256 m *7402 ft*).
Principal mountain range: Blue Mountains.
Principal river: Black River.
Head of State: HM Queen Elizabeth II, represented by Sir Florizel Augustus Glasspole, GCMG (b. 25 Sept 1909), Governor-General.
Prime Minister: Michael Manley.
Climate: The average rainfall is 1956 mm (*77 in*), and the rainfall is far greater in the mountains than on the coast. In Kingston, average maximum 30°C (*86°F*) (January to March) to 32°C (*90°F*) (July, August), minimum 19°C (*67°F*) (January, February) to 23°C (*74°F*) (June), wettest month is October (nine days). In the uplands the climate is pleasantly equable.
Labour force: 1 055 500 in 1986: Agriculture, forestry and fishing 25·3%; Manufacturing 10·9%; Transport, communications and public utilities 3·6%;

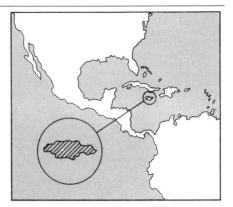

JAMAICA

Commerce 11·9%; Public administration 7·6%; Other services 14·2%.
Gross domestic product: J$13 328 million in 1986.
Exports: J$3 089 238 000 in 1986: Food and live animals (including sugar) 22·6%; Crude materials (including bauxite) 53·2%.
Monetary unit: Jamaican dollar (J$). 1 dollar = 100 cents.
Denominations:
Coins 1, 5, 10, 20, 25, 50 cents.
Notes 50 cents; 1, 2, 5, 10, 20, 100 dollars.
Political history and government: A former British colony. Became independent, within the Commonwealth, on 6 Aug 1962. Executive power is vested in the British monarch and exercised by the Governor-General, who is appointed on the recommendation of the Prime Minister and acts in almost all matters on the advice of the Cabinet. Legislative power is held by the bicameral Parliament: the Senate has 21 members, appointed by the Governor-General (13 on the advice of the Prime Minister and 8 on that of the Leader of the Opposition), and the House of Representatives has 60 members elected by universal adult suffrage for 5 years (subject to dissolution) in single-member constituencies. The Governor-General appoints the Prime Minister and, on the latter's recommendation, other Ministers. The Cabinet is responsible to the House.
Length of roadways: 16 638 km (*10 332 miles*) (1984).
Length of railways: 294 km (*183 miles*).
Universities: 1.
Defence: Total armed forces 3265 (1987); defence expenditure: US$5 million (1985/6).
Foreign tourists: 954 621 in 1986.

Japan

Official name: Nippon or Nihon (land of the Rising Sun).
Population: 121 672 326 (1986 estimate).
Area: 377 765 km² (*145 817 miles²*).
Language: Japanese.
Religions: Shinto, Buddhist.
Capital city: Tōkyō, population 11 829 363 (1987).
Other principal towns (1986): Yokohama 2 992 926; Osaka 2 636 249; Nagoya 2 116 381; Sapporo 1 542 979; Kyoto 1 479 218; Kobe 1 410 834; Fukuoka 1 160 440; Kawasaki 1 088 624; Kitakyushu

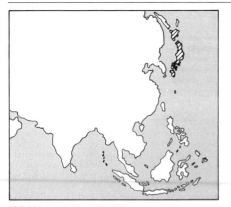

JAPAN

1 056 402; Hiroshima 1 044 118; Sakai 818 271.
Highest point: Fuji, 3776 m (*12 388 ft*) (first climbed before AD 806).
Principal mountain range: Hida.
Principal rivers: Tone (321 km *200 miles*), Ishikarai (365 km *227 miles*), Shinano (368 km *229 miles*), Kitakami (251 km *156 miles*).
Head of State: HIM Akihito (b. 23 Dec 1933), Emperor of Japan *Nihon-koku Tennō*, succeeded upon the death of his father Emperor Hirohito (Showa) 7 Jan 1989. The Emperor's era name is *Heisei*. Crown Prince: HIH Prince Naruhito (b. 23 Feb 1960), elder son of the Emperor.
Prime Minister: Sosuke Uno (b. 1923).
Climate: Great variation, from north (warm summers with long, cold winters) to south (hot, rainy summers with mild winters). In Tōkyō, August warmest (22°C to 30°C *72°F to 86°F*), January coldest (−6°C to 8°C *20°F to 47°F*), June and September rainiest (each 12 days). Absolute maximum temperature 41°C (*105°F*), Yamagata, 25 July 1933; absolute minimum −41°C (−*42°F*), Asahikawa, 25 Jan 1902.
Labour force: 60 200 000 in 1986: Agriculture and forestry 7·5%; Construction 8·9%; Manufacturing 24%; Commerce and finance 29·1%; Services 20·1%.
Gross domestic product: 317 305 billion yen in 1985: Manufacturing 33·3%; Trade 14·3%; Construction 7·5%; Transport and communications 6·3%; Agriculture 3·2%; Others, including services 35·3%.
Exports: US$209 151·2 million in 1986: Chemicals 4·5%; Basic manufactures 14·2%; Machinery and transport equipment 63·8%.
Monetary unit: Yen. 1 yen = 100 sen.
Denominations:
Coins 1, 5, 10, 50, 100 yen.
Notes 500, 1000, 5000, 10 000 yen.
Political history and government: An hereditary monarchy, with an Emperor as Head of State. After being defeated in the Second World War, Japanese forces surrendered on 14 Aug 1945. Japan signed an armistice on 2 Sept 1945, agreeing to give up many outer islands, and the country was placed under US military occupation. A new constitution was promulgated on 3 Nov 1946 and took effect from 3 May 1947. Following the peace treaty of 8 Sept 1951, Japan regained its sovereignty on 28 Apr 1952. The Tokara Archipelago and the Amami Islands (parts of the Ryukyu group) were restored on 5 Dec 1951 and 25 Dec 1953 respectively. The Bonin Islands were restored on 26 June 1968 and the rest of the

Ryukyu Islands (including Okinawa) on 15 May 1972.
Japan is a constitutional monarchy, with the Emperor as a symbol of the state. He has formal prerogatives but no power relating to government. Legislative power is vested in the bicameral Diet (*Kokkai*), elected by universal adult suffrage. The House of Councillors (*Sangiin*), with limited delaying powers, has 252 members elected for 6 years (half retiring every three years) and the House of Representatives (*Shugiin*) has 512 members elected for 4 years (subject to dissolution). Executive power is vested in the Cabinet. The Prime Minister is appointed by the Emperor (on designation by the Diet) and himself appoints the other Ministers. The Cabinet is responsible to the Diet.
Japan has 47 prefectures, each administered by an elected Governor.
Length of roadways: 1 168 000 km (*725 916 miles*) (1986).
Length of railways: 26 899 (*16 704 miles*) (1986).
Universities: 400 (public and private).
Defence: Military service voluntary; total armed forces 246 000 (1987); defence expenditure: 3 670 600 million yen in 1987.
Foreign tourists: 2 061 526 in 1986.

Jordan

Official name: Al-Mamlaka al-Urduniya al-Hashimiyah (the Hashemite Kingdom of Jordan).
Population: 2 796 100 (1986 estimate) – figure for East Bank only. [For West Bank see other territories section at the end of the directory of sovereign countries].
Area: 89 206 km² (*34 442 miles²*) – figure for East Bank only. See above.
Language: Arabic.
Religions: Islam (Sunni), Christian minority.
Capital city: 'Ammān, population 972 000 (1986 estimate).
Other principal towns (1986): As Zarqa (Zarka) 392 220; Irbid 271 000; Salt 134 100.
Highest point: Jaal Ramm, 1754 m (*5755 ft*).
Principal river: Jordan (321 km *200 miles*).
Head of State: HM King Husain ibn Talal, GCVO (b. 14 Nov 1935), succeeded upon the deposition through incapacitation by illness of his father King Talal 11 Aug 1952. Crown Prince: HRH Prince Hassan, younger brother of the King.
Prime Minister: Zaid bin Shaker.
Climate: Hot and dry, average temperatures 15°C (*60°F*) with wide diurnal variations. Cool winters, rainy season December to March. In Ammān, August hottest (average maximum 32°C *90°F*), January coolest (average minimum −1°C *39°F*). Absolute maximum temperatures 51°C (*124°F*), Dead Sea North, 22 June 1942; absolute minimum −7°C (*18°F*), Ammān, 28 Feb 1959.
All figures given are for the East Bank only.
Labour force: 535 440 in 1986: Agriculture 7%; Mining and manufacturing 9·8%; Construction 10·1%; Trade 9·2%; Services 43%.
Gross domestic product: 1241·2 million Jordanian dinar in 1986.
Exports: 225 615 000 Jordanian dinar in 1986: Phosphates 28·7%; Vegetables and fruit 18·6%.
Monetary unit: Jordanian dinar. 1 dinar = 1000 fils.

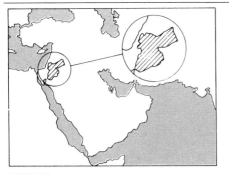

June 1967).
Length of roadways: 7663 km (*4759 miles*).
Length of railways: 618 km (*384 miles*).
Universities: 3.
Defence: Military service: selective conscription; total armed forces 80 300 (1987); defence expenditure: 276·6 million dinars in 1987.
Foreign tourists: 1 912 038 in 1986.

Kampuchea (reverted to Cambodia 1.5.1989)

JORDAN

Denominations:
Coins 1, 5, 10, 20, 25, 50, 100, 250 fils.
Notes 500 fils; 1, 5, 10, 20 dinars.
Political history and government: Formerly part of Turkey's Ottoman Empire, Turkish forces were expelled in 1918. Palestine and Transjordan were administered by Britain under League of Nations mandate, established in 1922. Transjordan became an independent monarchy, under an Amir, on 22 Mar 1946. The Amir became King, and the country's present name was adopted, on 25 May 1946. In the Arab-Israeli war of 1948 Jordanian forces occupied part of Palestine, annexed in December 1949 and fully incorporated on 24 Apr 1950. This territory was captured by Israel in the war of 5–10 June 1967.

Under the constitution, adopted on 7 Nov 1951, legislative power is vested in a bicameral National Assembly comprising a Chamber of Notables (30 members appointed by the King for 8 years, half retiring every 4 years) and a Chamber of Deputies formerly with 60 members (50 Muslims and 10 Christians) elected by universal adult suffrage for 4 years (subject to dissolution). In each Chamber there was equal representation for the East Bank and the (occupied) West Bank, but in 1988 the King dissolved all legal ties with the West Bank. The Kingdom now consists of only the East Bank and the composition of the National Assembly in future will reflect that fact. Executive power is vested in the King, who rules with the assistance of an appointed Council of Ministers, responsible to the Assembly. On 9 Nov 1974 both Chambers of the Assembly approved constitutional amendments which empowered the King to dissolve the Assembly and to postpone elections for up to 12 months. The Assembly was dissolved on 22 Nov 1974 and reconvened on 5–7 Feb 1976, when it approved a constitutional amendment giving the King power to postpone elections indefinitely and to convene the Assembly as required. A royal decree of 19 Apr 1978 provided for the creation of a National Consultative Council, with 60 members appointed by the King, on the Prime Minister's recommendation, to debate proposed legislation. The Council, whose members serve for two years (subject to dissolution by the King), first met on 24 Apr 1978 and was renewed on 20 Apr 1980. The Council was subsequently dissolved by the King and replaced by the bicameral National Assembly in 1984 (again, appointed by the King).

Jordan comprises 5 administrative districts, all on the East Bank. (The three districts on the West Bank have been under Israeli occupation since

Official name: Formerly Sathearanakrath Pracheachon Kampuchea (People's Republic of Kampuchea); since May 1989 State of Cambodia.
Population: 7 492 000 (1986 estimate).
Area: 181 035 km² (*69 898 miles²*).
Languages: Khmer (official), French.
Religion: Buddhist.
Capital city: Phnom-Penh, population 700 000 (1986 estimate).
Other principal towns: Battambang, Kompong Chhnang, Kompong Cham, Kompong Som (Sihanoukville).
Highest point: Mt Ka-Kup, 1774 m (*5722 ft*).
Principal mountain range: Chaîne des Cardamomes.
Principal river: Mekong (4184 km (*2600 miles*)).
Head of State: Heng Samrin (b. 1934), Chairman of the People's Revolutionary Council; also Secretary-General of the Kampuchean People's Revolutionary Party.
Prime Minister: Hun Sen.
Climate: Tropical and humid. Rainy season June–November. In Phnom-Penh, average maximum 30°C (*86°F*) (November, December) to 34°C (*94°F*) (April), minimum 21°C (*70°F*) (January) to 24°C (*76°F*) (April–October), September rainiest (19 days).
Labour force: 3 602 000 in 1985: Agriculture, forestry and fishing 72·3%.
Gross domestic product: No figures are published by the Government.
Exports: No figures are published by the Government.
Monetary unit: New riel. 1 riel = 100 sen.
Denominations:
Coins 5 sen.
Notes 10, 20, 50 sen; 1, 5, 10, 20, 50 riels.
Political history and government: As Cambodia, formerly a monarchy and part of French Indo-China. Norodom Sihanouk became King on 26 Apr 1941. On 6 May 1947 he promulgated a constitution providing for a bicameral Parliament, including an elected National Assembly. Cambodia became an Associate State of the French Union on 8 Nov 1949 and a fully independent kingdom on 9 Nov 1953. Sihanouk abdicated on 2 Mar 1955 in favour of his father, Norodom Suramarit. King Suramarit died on 3 Apr 1960 and Parliament elected Prince Sihanouk to become Head of State (without taking the title of King) on 20 June 1960.

On 18 Mar 1970 Prince Sihanouk was deposed by his Prime Minister, Lt-Gen. (later Marshal) Lon Nol, who proclaimed the Khmer Republic on 8 Oct 1970. Sihanouk went into exile and formed a Royal Government of National Union, supported by the pro-Communist *Khmers Rouges* ('Red Cambodians'). Sihanoukists and the *Khmers Rouges*

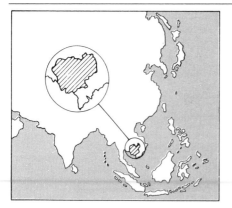

KAMPUCHEA

formed the National United Front of Cambodia (NUFC). Their combined forces defeated the republicans and Phnom-Penh surrendered on 17 Apr 1975, when the Royal Government took power. On 14 Dec 1975 a congress of the NUFC approved a new republican constitution, promulgated on 5 Jan 1976, when the name of the country was changed to Democratic Kampuchea. Elections were held on 20 March 1976 for the People's Representative Assembly (250 members). Prince Sihanouk resigned as Head of State on 4 Apr 1976. In his place the Assembly chose a three-man State Presidium on 11 Apr 1976. Pol Pot was appointed Prime Minister two days later. On 27 Sept 1977 it was officially revealed that the ruling organization was the Communist Party of Kampuchea, with Pol Pot as its Secretary. Rival Communists, opponents of Pol Pot, established the Kampuchean National United Front for National Salvation (KNUFNS), announced on 3 Dec 1978. After a year of border fighting, Vietnamese forces, supporting the KNUFNS, invaded Cambodia on 25 Dec 1978, capturing the capital on 7 Jan 1979. The next day the KNUFNS established the People's Revolutionary Council (8 members) and on 10 Jan 1979 the country's present name was adopted. The second Congress of the KNUFNS, held on 29–30 Sept 1979, elected a Central Committee of 35 members.

Elections were held on 1 May 1981 for 117 members of a new National Assembly. The Assembly began its first session on 24 June 1981 and ratified a new constitution on 27 June. The supreme organ of state power is the unicameral Assembly, elected by universal adult suffrage for a five-year term. The Assembly chooses seven of its members to form the Council of State, its permanent organ, which appoints the Council of Ministers. The new régime is based on the Kampuchean People's Revolutionary Party. The Government is supported by some 140 000 Vietnamese troops whose withdrawal began late in 1988. The Government does not control the whole country and border regions into Thailand are in the hands of various elements of the Khmer Rouge and their allies. Preliminary discussions for a Kampuchean settlement were (inconclusively) held in the autumn of 1988.
Length of roadways: *c.* 11 000 km (*c. 6835 miles*).
Length of railways: 260 km (*160 miles*).
Universities: 1.
Defence: Military service: conscription; total armed

forces about 50 000 (1987), also about 140 000 Vietnamese troops.

Kenya

Official name: Jamhuri ya Kenya (Republic of Kenya).
Population: 21 163 000 (1986 estimate).
Area: 580 367 km² (*224 081 miles²*).
Languages: Swahili (official), English, Kikuyu, Luo.
Religions: Christian 58% (1962), Islam (Sunni).
Capital city: Nairobi, population 1 103 554 (1985 estimate).
Other principal towns (1985 estimates): Mombasa 478 000; Nakuru 130 000; Kisumu 215 000; Machakos 117 000; Meru 98 000; Eldoret 71 000; Thika 57 000.
Highest point: Mount Kenya (5199 m (*17 058 ft*)).
Principal mountain range: Aberdare Mountains.
Principal rivers: Tana, Umba, Athi, Mathioya.
Head of State: Daniel Toroitich arap Moi (b. September 1924), President.
Climate: Varies with altitude. Hot and humid on coast, with average temperatures of 20°C to 32°C (*69°F to 90°F*), faling to 7°C to 27°C (*45°F to 80°F*) on land over 1524 m (*5000 ft*). Ample rainfall in the west and on highlands, but very dry in the north. In Nairobi, average maximum 20°C (*69°F*) (July) to 26°C (*79°F*) (February), minimum 10°C (*51°F*) (July) to 14°C (*58°F*) (April), May rainiest (17 days).
Labour force: 1 174 400 in 1985: Agriculture, forestry and fishing 20·5%; Manufacturing 13·5%; Trade 7·6%; Community, social and personal services 42·9%.
Gross domestic product: K£4832·8 million in 1986: Traditional economy 6·6%; Monetary economy: Agriculture, forestry and fishing 28%; Manufacturing 11·9%; Trade 13%; Financial services 7·2%; Government services 15·7%.
Exports: 16 046·8 million Kenyan shillings in 1985: Coffee 29·7%; Tea 24·7%; Petroleum products 13·9%.
Monetary unit: Kenya shilling. 1 shilling = 100 cents; 20 shillings = K£1.
Denominations:
Coins 5, 10, 50 cents; 1, 5 shillings.
Notes 10, 20, 100 shillings.
Political history and government: Formerly a British colony and protectorate. Became independent, within the Commonwealth, on 12 Dec 1963 and a republic on 12 Dec 1964. A one-party state since 30 Oct 1969. Legislative power is held by the unicameral National Assembly, with 172 members (158 elected by universal adult suffrage, the Attorney-General, the Speaker and 12 members nominated by the President) serving a term of five years (subject to dissolution). Executive power is held by the President, also directly elected for five years. He is assisted by an appointed Vice-President and Cabinet. Kenya has 40 districts, each with a District Development Committee responsible for all development projects.
Length of roadways: 97 512 km (*60 555 miles*) (1987).
Length of railways: 2733 km (*1697 miles*).
Universities: 2.
Adult illiteracy: 40·8% in 1985.
Defence: Military service voluntary; total armed forces 13 350 (1987); defence expenditure: 2546 million Kenya shillings in 1985–6.
Foreign tourists: 614 200 in 1986.

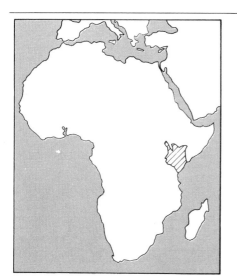

KENYA

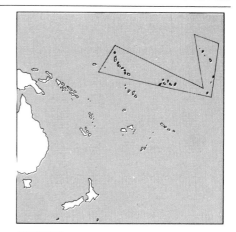

KIRIBATI

Kiribati

Population: 66 250 (1986 estimate).
Area: 717 km² (277 miles²).
Languages: Kiribati (Gilbertese), English.
Religion: Christian (Anglican, Methodist, Roman Catholic, Mormons, Seventh Day Adventists).
Capital city: Tarawa atoll, population 21 393 (1985 census).
Highest point: 81 m (265 ft), on Banaba (Ocean Island).
Head of State: Ieremia T. Tabai, GCMG (b. 16 Dec 1950), Beretitenti (President).
Climate: Warm and pleasant, with day temperatures between 27°C and 32°C (80°F and 90°F) and a minimum of about 23°C (77°F) at night. Average annual rainfall varies widely between atolls, ranging from 762 mm to 3810 mm (30 in to 150 in). Rainy season December to February, dry from August to October.
Labour force: 7869 in 1985: Government service and private enterprise 86%; Seamen 8·3%; Phosphate mining in Nauru 5·7%.
Gross domestic product: A$24 million: (in 1985) Agriculture 16·1%; Fishing 13·1%; Trade and tourism 13%; Services 52·4%.
Exports: A$13 006 000 in 1984: Copra 53·7%; Fish 17·6%.
Monetary unit: Australian currency (q.v.).
Political history and government: In 1892 a United Kingdom protectorate was established over the 16 atolls of the Gilbert Islands and the 9 Ellice Islands (now Tuvalu) the two groups being administered together. Ocean Island (now Banaba) was annexed on 28 Nov 1900. The Gilbert and Ellice Islands were annexed on 10 Nov 1915, effective from 12 Jan 1916, when the protectorate became a colony. Later in 1916 the new Gilbert and Ellice Islands Colony (GEIC) was extended to include Ocean Island and two of the Line Islands. Christmas Island (now Kiritimati), in the Line Islands, was annexed in 1919 and the 8 Phoenix Islands on 18 Mar 1937. Two of the Phoenix Islands, Canton (now Kanton)

and Enderbury, were also claimed by the USA and a joint British-US administration was agreed on 6 Apr 1939. The 5 uninhabited Central and Southern Line islands became part of the GEIC on 1 Jan 1972. The Ellice Islands were allowed to form a separate territory, named Tuvalu, on 1 Oct 1975. The remainder of the GEIC was renamed the Gilbert Islands and obtained self-government on 1 Jan 1977. Following a constitutional conference on 21 Nov–7 Dec 1978, this territory became an independent republic, within the Commonwealth, on 12 July 1979, taking the name Kiribati (pronounced 'Kiribass'). The USA has agreed to renounce its claim to Kanton and Enderbury Islands under a 1982 Treaty of Friendship.

Legislative power is vested in the Maneaba ni Maungatabu, a unicameral body. It has 36 members elected by universal adult suffrage for 4 years (subject to dissolution), one nominated representative of the Banaban community and, if he is not an elected member, the Attorney-General as an ex officio member. Executive power is vested in the Beretitenti (President), who is Head of State and Head of Government. The Beretitenti is elected. After each general election for the Maneaba, it will nominate, from among its members, three or four candidates from whom the Beretitenti will be elected by universal adult suffrage. The Maneaba is empowered to remove the Beretitenti from office.

The Beretitenti governs with the assistance of a Kauoman-ni-Beretitenti (Vice-President) and Cabinet, whom he appoints from among members of the Maneaba. The Cabinet is responsible to the Maneaba.

Length of roadways: 640 km (400 miles).
Foreign tourists: 3350 in 1986.

Korea (North)

Official name: Chosun Minchu-chui Inmin Konghwa-guk (Democratic People's Republic of Korea).
Population: 20 883 000 (1986 estimate).
Area: 120 538 km² (46 540 miles²) (excluding demilitarized zone).
Language: Korean.

Religions: Buddhist, Confucian, Taoist.
Capital city: Pyongyang, population 1 280 000 (1981 estimate).
Other principal towns (1981): Hungnam 77 500; Chongjin 490 000; Kimchaek (formerly Songjin) 490 000; Wonsan 398 000.
Highest point: Pektu San (Pait'ou Shan), 2744 m (*9003 ft*) (first climbed 1886).
Principal mountain range: Nangnim Sanmaek.
Principal rivers: Imjin, Ch'ongch'ŏn, Yalu (482 km *300 miles*) on frontier.
Head of State: Marshall Kim Il Sung (*né* Kim Sung Chu, b. 15 Apr 1912), President; also General Secretary of the Central Committee of the Korean Workers' Party.
Head of Government: Li Gun Mo, Premier of the Administration Council.
Climate: Continental; hot, humid, rainy summers (average temperature 25°C 77°F) and cold, dry winters (average −6°C 21°F).
Labour force: 9 346 000 in 1986: Agriculture, forestry and fishing 35·9%.
Gross national product: The Government does not publish any figures.
Exports: The Government does not publish any figures.
Monetary unit: Won. 1 won = 100 chon (jun).
Denominations:
Coins 1, 5, 10, 50 chon.
Notes 1, 5, 10, 50, 100 won.
Political history and government: Korea was formerly a kingdom, for long under Chinese suzerainty. Independence was established on 17 Apr 1895. Korea was occupied by Japanese forces in November 1905 and formerly annexed by Japan on 22 Aug 1910, when the monarch was deposed. After Japan's defeat in the Second World War, Korea was divided at the 38th parallel into military occupation zones, with Soviet forces in the North and US forces in the South. After the failure of negotiations in 1946 and 1947, the country remained divided. With Soviet backing, a Communist-dominated administration was established in the North. Elections were held on 25 Aug 1948 and the Democratic People's Republic of Korea was proclaimed on 9 Sept 1948. After the Korean War of 1950–53 a cease-fire line replaced the 38th parallel as the border between North and South.
In North Korea a new constitution was adopted on 27 Dec 1972. The highest organ of state power is the unicameral Supreme People's Assembly, with 655 members elected (unopposed) for four years by universal adult suffrage. The Assembly elects for its duration the President of the Republic and, on the latter's recommendation, other members of the Central People's Committee to direct the government. The Assembly appoints the Premier and the Committee appoints other Minsiters to form the Administration council, led by the President.
Political power is held by the (Communist) Korean Workers' Party (KWP), which dominates the Democratic Front for the Reunification of the Fatherland (including two other minor parties). The Front presents an approved list of candidates for elections to representative bodies. The KWP's highest authority is the Party Congress. The Congress elects a Central Committee to supervise Party work. To direct its policy, the Committee elects a Political Bureau (16 full and 10 alternate members were elected in March 1988). The three-member Presidium of the Political bureau is the Party's most powerful policy-making body.

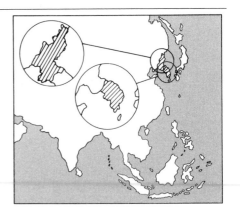

above: **KOREA (NORTH**
below: **KOREA (SOUTH)**

North Korea comprises nine provinces and two cities, each with an elected People's Assembly.
Length of roadways: 22 000 km (*13 662 miles*) (1984).
Length of railways: 4549 km (*2825 miles*) (1987).
Universities: 3.
Defence: Military service: Army, Navy 5 years, Air force 3–4 years; total armed forces 838 000 (1987); defence expenditure: 14% of total government expenditure in 1985.
Foreign tourists: 85 000 in 1986.

Korea (South)

Official name: Daehan-Minkuk (Republic of Korea).
Population: 41 568 640 (1986 estimate).
Area: 99 022 km² (*38 232 miles²*).
Language: Korean.
Religions: Buddhist, Christian, Confucian, Chundo Kyo.
Capital city: Sŏul (Seoul), population 9 645 824 (1985 census).
Other principal towns (1985): Pusan (Busan) 3 516 768; Taegu (Daegu) 2 030 649; Inchŏ'n (Incheon) 1 387 475.
Highest point: Halla-san, 1950 m (*6398 ft*).
Principal rivers: Han, Naktong (with Nam), Kum, Somjin, Yongsan.
Head of State: Roh Tae-Woo.
Prime Minister: Lee Hyun-jae.
Climate: Hot, humid summers (average temperature 25°C (*77°F*) and cold, dry winters (average −6°C 21°F). In Seoul, August hottest (22°C to 30°C 71°F to 87°F), January coldest (−9°C to 0°C 15°F to 32°F), July rainiest (16 days). Absolute maximum temperature 40°C (*104°F*), Taegu, 1 Aug 1942; absolute minimum −43·6°C (*−46·5°F*), Chungkangjin, 12 Jan 1933.
Labour force: 16 116 000 in 1986: Agriculture, forestry and fishing 22·7%; Manufacturing 23·7%; Services 16·7%.
Gross domestic product: 86 509 900 million won in 1986: Agriculture 12·3%; Manufacturing 30%; Trade 13·1%.
Exports: US$34·7 billion in 1986: Fish 1·7%; Textiles yarn/thread 1·8%; Textile fabrics 5·3%; Electrical machinery 8·2%; Transport equipment 11·5%; Footwear 5·9%.

Monetary unit: Won. 1 won = 100 chun (jeon).
Denominations:
Coins 1, 5, 10, 50, 100, 500 won.
Notes 500, 1000, 5000, 10 000 won.
Political history and government: (For events before partition, *see* North Korea, above). After UN-supervised elections for a National Assembly on 10 May 1948, South Korea adopted a constitution and became the independent Republic of Korea on 15 Aug 1948. North Korean forces invaded the South on 25 June 1950 and war ensued until 27 July 1953, when an armistice established a cease-fire line (roughly along the 38th parallel) between North and South. This has become effectively an international frontier.

On 16 May 1961 South Korea's government was overthrown by a military *coup*, led by Maj.-Gen. Pak chung Hi, who assumed power, dissolved the National Assembly, suspended the constitution and disbanded political parties. A new constitution was approved by referendum on 17 Dec 1962. Gen. Pak was elected President on 15 Oct 1963 and inaugurated on 17 Dec 1963, when a newly-elected National Assembly was convened. Martial law was imposed on 17 Oct 1972 and another constitution approved by referendum on 21 Nov 1972. This *Yushin* ('Revitalizing') Constitution provided for the President to be elected indirectly by a 'National Conference for Unification' (NCU), comprising delegates elected by popular vote. The National Assembly had two-thirds of its members directly elected and one-third nominated by the NCU. Emergency Decree No. 9, issued on 13 May 1975, banned virtually all opposition activities.

President Pak was assassinated on 26 Oct 1979. On the next day, martial law was introduced (with the Army Chief of Staff as martial law administrator), except on the island of Cheju, and the Prime Minister, Choi Kyu Ha, became Acting President. On 6 Dec 1979 he was elected President by the NCU and on the next day he rescinded Emergency Decree No. 9. In a virtual *coup* on 12–13 Dec 1979 the martial law administrator and other officers were arrested by troops under Lt.-Gen. (later Gen.) Chun Doo Hwan, head of the Army Security Command. President Choi was inaugurated on 21 Dec 1979 to complete his predecessor's last term (1978–84). Following a wave of strikes and demonstrations, martial law was extended throughout the country on 17 May 1980. All political activities were banned and the National Assembly was closed on 19 May. The Cabinet resigned on 20 May and a new Prime Minister was appointed the next day. On 31 May 1980 the government established a Special Committee for National Security Measures, an advisory body controlled by the armed forces, which assumed political power. Following a 'purification' campaign, involving mass arrests and purges, President Choi resigned on 16 Aug 1980. To succeed, him, Gen. Chun was endorsed by the armed services and (after retiring from the Army) was elected unopposed on 27 Aug. He was sworn in on 1 Sept and a new Cabinet was formed.

A new constitution was approved by referendum on 22 Oct 1980 and came into effect on 27 Oct, when the 'Fifth Republic' was inaugurated. The National Assembly and existing political parties were dissolved. Martial law was lifted on 24 Jan 1981. Under this constitution, the electoral college elected President Chun on 25 Feb and he was sworn in on 3 Mar, when the college was dissolved. A new constitution was approved by a national ref-erendum in October 1987 and came into force in February 1988. It provides for a President (directly elected for a single seven year term by an electoral college of 5271 members who are directly elected. There is a State Council of Ministers appointed and lead by the President and a National Assembly of 276 members directly elected for 4 years.
Length of roadways: 53 936 km (*33 521 miles*) (1984).
Length of railways: 6443 km (*4001 miles*) (1987).
Universities: 100 institutions of university level.
Defence: Military service: Army and Marines 2½ years, Navy and Air Force 3 years; total armed forces 629 000 (1987); defence expenditure: 4915·3 billion won in 1987.
Foreign tourists: 1 600 000 in 1986.

Kuwait

Official name: Daulat al-Kuwait (State of Kuwait). Kuwait means 'little fort'.
Population: 1 790 513 (1986 estimate).
Area: 17 818 km² (*6880 miles²*).
Language: Arabic.
Religions: Islam (Sunni); Christian minority.
Capital city: Kuwait City, population 1 112 000 (1985 census) (Kuwait City Governate had a population of 167 768 and the city proper 44 335; the above figure includes all of Hawalli Governate).
Other principal towns (1985): Salmiya 153 369; Farawaniva 68 701.
Highest point: 289 m (*951 ft*).
Head of State: HH Shaikh Jabir al-Ahmad al-Jabir as-Sabah (b. 1928), Amir. HH Shaikh Jabir, 13th Amir of Kuwait, succeeded to the throne on 31 Dec 1977. Crown Prince: HH Shaikh Saad al-Abdullah as Salim as-Sabah.
Prime Minister: HH Shaikh Saad al-Abdullah as Salim as-Sabah.
Climate: Humid, average temperature 24°C (*75°F*). In Kuwait City, maximum recorded temperature 51°C (*124°F*). July 1954; minimum (−2·6°C (*27·3°F*), January 1964.
Labour force: 662 588 in 1985: Agriculture, fishing 1·9%; Manufacturing industries 7·7%; Construction 18·7%; Trade 11·5%; Services 49·3%.
Gross domestic product: 4998 million Kuwaiti dinars in 1986: Mining (oil and natural gas) 36·9%; Manufacturing 11·1%; Trade 10·3%; Financial services 9·4%; Public administration 10·2%; Other services 23·9%.

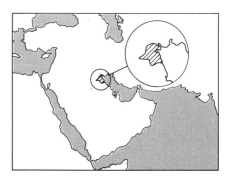

KUWAIT

Exports: 3632·4 million Kuwaiti dinars in 1986: Crude petroleum and petroleum products 89·7%; Machinery and transport equipment 3·5%.
Monetary unit: Kuwaiti dinar. 1 dinar = 1000 fils.
Denominations:
  Coins 1, 5, 10, 20, 50, 100 fils.
  Notes 250, 500 fils; 1, 5, 10 dinars.
Political history and government: A monarchy formerly ruled by a Shaikh. Under British protection from 23 Jan 1899 until achieving full independence, with the ruling Shaikh as Amir, on 19 June 1961. Present constitution adopted on 16 Dec 1962. Executive power is vested in the Amir (chosen by and from members of the ruling family) and is exercised through a Council of Ministers. The Amir appoints the Prime Minsiter and, on the latter's recommendation, other Ministers. Legislative power is vested in the unicameral National Assembly, whose members serve for four years (subject to dissolution) and are elected by literate civilian adult male Kuwaiti citizens. On 29 Aug 1976 the Amir dissolved the Assembly and suspended parts of the constitution, including provisions for fresh elections. In accordance with an Amiri decree of 24 Aug 1980, a new 50-seat National Assembly (two deputies from each of 25 constituencies) was elected on 23 Feb 1981. The Assembly's first session opened on 9 Mar 1981. Political parties are not legally permitted. Kuwait comprises four governates.
Length of roadways: 3590 km (2229 miles) (1985).
Universities: 1.
Adult illiteracy: 30% in 1985.
Defence: Military service 18 months; total armed forces 16 100 (1987); defence expenditure: KD390 million in 1987–8.

Laos

Official name: Saathiaranagrõat Prachhathippatay Prachhachhon Lao (Lao People's Democratic Republic).
Population: 3 584 803 (1985 census).
Area: 236 800 km² (91 400 miles²).
Languages: Lao (official), French.
Religions: Buddhist, tribal.
Capital city: Viengchane (Vientiane), population 377 409 (1985).
Other principal towns (1973): Savannakhet 50 690; Pakse 44 860; Luang Prabang 44 244.
Highest point: Phou Bia, 2820 m (9252 ft).
Principal mountain range: Annamitic Range.
Principal river: Mekong (4184 km 2600 miles).
Head of State: Phoumi Vongvichit, President.
Prime Minister: Kaysone Phomvihane (b. 13 Dec 1920), also General Secretary of the Lao People's Revolutionary Party.
Climate: Tropical (warm and humid). Rainy monsoon season May–October. In Vientiane, average maximum 28°C (83°F) (December, January) to 34°C (93°F) (April), minimum 14°C (57°F) (January) to 24°C (75°F) (June to September), July and August rainiest (each 18 days). Maximum recorded temperature 44·8°C (112·6°F), Luang Prabang, April 1960; minimum 0·8°C (33·4°F), Luang Prabang, January 1924.
Labour force: 2 057 000 in 1986: Agriculture, forestry and fishing 73·3%.

Gross domestic product: The Government does not publish any figures.
Exports: The Government does not publish any figures.
Monetary unit: New kip. 1 kip = 100 at.
Denominations:
  Notes 1, 5, 10, 20 kips.
Political history and government: Formerly the three principalities of Luang Prabang, Vientiane and Champassac. Became a French protectorate in 1893. The three principalities were merged in 1946 and an hereditary constitutional monarchy, under the Luang Prabang dynasty, was established on 11 May 1947. The Kingdom of Laos became independent, within the French Union, on 19 July 1949. Full sovereignty was recognized by France on 23 Oct 1953. After nearly 20 years of almost continuous civil war between the Royal Government and the Neo Lao Hak Sat (Lao Patriotic Front or LPF), a Communist-led insurgent movement whose armed forces were known as the Pathet Lao, a peace agreement was signed on 21 Feb 1973. A joint administration was established on 5 Apr 1974 but the LPF became increasingly dominant. The National Assembly was dissolved on 13 Apr 1975. The King abdicated on 29 Nov 1975 and on 1 Dec 1975 a National Congress of People's Representatives (264 delegates elected by local authorities) proclaimed the Lao People's Democratic Republic, with Prince Souphanouvong, Chairman of the LPF, as President. The Congress installed a Council of Ministers, led by a Prime Minister, and appointed a Supreme People's Council (SPC), chaired by the President, to draft a new constitution. The SPC held its first plenary session on 12–17 June 1976.
  Political power is held by the Lao People's Revolutionary Party (LPRP), formerly called the People's Party of Laos. The Communist LPRP has a Central Committee, headed by a seven-member Political Bureau.
Length of roadways: 12 983 km (8069 miles) (1985).
Universities: 8 university level institutions.
Adult illiteracy: 10% (1984).
Defence: Military service: 18 months; total armed forces 55 000 (1987), plus about 50 000 Vietnamese troops; defence expenditure: 12% of total government expenditure in 1981.

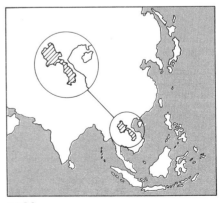

LAOS

Lebanon

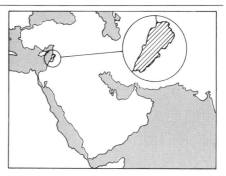

LEBANON

Official name: Al-Jumhuriya al-Lubnaniya (the Lebanese Republic), abbreviated to al-Lubnan.
Population: 2 707 000 (1986 estimate).
Area: 10 452 km² (*4036 miles²*).
Languages: Arabic (official), French, Armenian.
Religions: Christian (Roman Catholic, Orthodox), Islam (mainly Sunni), Druze.
Capital city: Beirut, population 1 500 000 (1988 estimate). (In 1980 Beirut had an estimated population of 702 000; since then large scale movements of population have occurred during the civil war. No reliable estimate is available.)
Other principal towns (1980): Tripoli 175 000; Zahlé 46 800; Saida (Sidon) 24 740; Tyre 14 000.
Highest point: Qurnat as-Sawdā, 3088 m (*10 131 ft*).
Principal mountain ranges: Lebanon, Jabal ash-Sharqī (Anti-Lebanon).
Principal river: Nahr al-Litāni (Leontes).
Head of State: Shaikh Amin Gemayel, Acting President. (Amin Gemayel's six year term of office came to an end in September 1988 – there has been no quorum to elect a new President owing to the breakdown of government.)
Prime Minister: Dr Selim Hoss formed a Cabinet in December 1987 but its authority is confined to certain parts of the country. General Michel Aoun has formed an administration in the Christian area of Beirut which is recognised by some authorities as a government, but effectively Lebanon has no central government.
Climate: Coastal lowlands are hot and humid in summer, mild (cool and damp) in winter. Mountains cool in summer, heavy snowfall in winter. Beirut, average maximum 16°C (*62°F*) (January) to 32°C (*89°F*) (August), minimum 10°C (*51°F*) (January, February) to 23°C (*74°F*) (August), January rainiest (15 days).
Labour force: 452 900 in 1985: Agriculture etc 22·8%; Trade 17·2% (Large areas of the country have ceased to exist because of the civil war.)
Gross domestic product: £L12 600 in 1982.
Exports: £L4973 million in 1985: Food products 2·3%; Clothing 5·2%; Pharmaceuticals 4·9%; Metal products 4·8%; Jewellery 10·2%.
Monetary unit: Lebanese pound (£L). 1 pound = 100 piastres.
Denominations:
Coins 1, 2½, 5, 10, 25, 50 piastres; 1 pound.
Notes 1, 5, 10, 25, 50, 100, 250 pounds.
Political history and government: Formerly part of Turkey's Ottoman Empire. Turkish forces were expelled in 1918 by British and French troops, with Arab help. Administered by France under League of Nations mandate from 1 Sept 1920. Independence declared on 26 Nov 1941. A republic was established in 1943 and French powers transferred on 1 Jan 1944. All foreign troops left by December 1946.
Legislative power was vested in the unicameral Chamber of Deputies, with 99 members elected by adult suffrage for 4 years (subject to dissolution), using proportional representation. Seats are allocated on a religious basis (53 Christian, 45 Muslim). Elections to the Chamber due in April 1976 were postponed because of civil disorder. On 15 Mar 1979 the Chamber renamed itself the National Assembly. On 15 Mar 1980 the term of the Assembly was extended, for a third time, until the end of 1981. Executive power is vested in the President, elected for 6 years by the Assembly. He appoints a

Prime Minister and other Ministers to form a Cabinet, responsible to the Assembly. By convention, the President is a Maronite Christian, the Prime Minister a Sunni Muslim, and the Speaker of Parliament a Shiite Muslim.
In the late 1970s and 1980s Lebanon has been torn apart by constant feuding between various militias, with the government holding little if any control over the country. By the autumn of 1988 effective government of the Lebanon had completely broken down. Israel controlled southern districts; the Syrians much of the east and most of Muslim Beirut; the Palestinians are an important influence in some Muslim areas; various groups of Christian militia control northern districts and the Christian areas of Beirut; the Druze militia has its own spheres of influence while the radical pro-Iranian *Hezbollah* Muslim militia controls parts of south Beirut, parts of southern Shia Lebanon and the Beka'a Valley. A United Nations Interim Force (UNIFIL) exercises partial control over a buffer zone in the south adjoining the Israeli-controlled district.
Length of roadways: 7400 km (*4598 miles*).
Length of railways: 222 km (*138 miles*) – from Beirut to the Syrian border. the rest of the railway network has been destroyed by the civil war.
Universities: 5.
Adult illiteracy: 23% in 1985.
Defence: Owing to the existence of several sectarian militia forces there is no longer a recognizable national army. The armed forces have divided along sectarian lines. The Lebanon also contains 30 000 Syrian troops, the Israeli-backed south Lebanese Army, Palestinian guerrillas and UN forces (5780 in 1987).

Lesotho

Official name: The Kingdom of Lesotho.
Population: 1 626 500 (1987 estimate).
Area: 30 355 km² (*11 720 miles²*).
Languages: Sesotho, English.
Religion: Christian.
Capital city: Maseru, population 109 400 (1986 estimate).
Other principal towns: Mafeteng, Leribe, Mohale's Hoek.
Highest point: Thabana Ntlenyana (Thadentsonyane), 3482 m (*11 425 ft*).
Principal mountain range: Drakensberg.

Principal rivers: Orange, Caledon (on northern frontier).
Head of State: HM King Motlotlehi Moshoeshoe II (b. 2 May 1938). HM King Motlotlehi Moshoeshoe II became king upon independence on 4 Oct 1966 – he had been Paramount Chief since 1940.
Head of Government: Maj.-Gen. Justin Lekhanya, Chairman of the Military Council.
Climate: In lowlands, maximum temperature in summer 32°C (*90°F*), winter minimum −6°C (*20°F*). Range wider in highlands. Average annual rainfall 736 mm (*29 in*). Rainy season October–April.
Labour force: 745 000 in 1986: Agriculture, forestry and fishing 82·4%. In 1981 23% of the total labour force worked in South Africa.
Gross domestic product: 480·1 million maloti in 1984/5.
Exports: 45 million maloti in 1985: (in 1979) Wool 8·9%; Mohair 11·4%; Diamonds 56%.
Monetary unit: Loti (plural: maloti). 1 loti = 100 lisente.
Denominations:
Coins 1, 2, 5, 10, 25, 50 lisente; 1 loti.
Notes 2, 5, 10 maloti.
Political history and government: An hereditary monarchy, formerly the British colony of Basutoland. Granted internal self-government on 30 Apr 1965. Became independent (under present name), within the Commonwealth, on 4 Oct 1966. Under the constitution, legislative power was vested in a bicameral Parliament, comprising a Senate of 33 members (22 Chiefs and 11 Senators nominated by the King for 5-year terms) and a National Assembly of 60 members elected by universal adult suffrage for 5 years (subject to dissolution). Executive power is exercised by the Cabinet, led by the Prime Minister, which is responsible to Parliament. The Assembly elections of 27 Jan 1970 were annulled three days later by the Prime Minister, who declared a state of emergency and suspended the constitution. The Cabinet assumed full power. No more elections have been held but an interim National Assembly of 93 members (the former Senate and 60 nominated members) was inaugurated on 27 Apr 1973. Elections were to have been held in 1985, but no opposition candidates offered themselves. In January 1986 the government was overthrown by the military. Lesotho comprises 10 administrative districts, each under an appointed District Administrator.
Length of roadways: 3085 km (*1916 miles*) (1986).
Length of railways: 1·5 km (*1 mile*).
Universities: 1.
Adult illiteracy: 26·4% (1985).
Defence: Defence force (established 1986) to replace paramilitary forces, numbering 1500 in 1986; defence expenditure: 29·8 million maloti 1985–6.
Foreign tourists: 35 000 in 1982.

Liberia

Official name: The Republic of Liberia.
Population: 2 221 000 (1986 estimate).
Area: 111 369 km² (*43 000 miles²*).
Languages: English (official), tribal languages.
Religions: Christian; Islam (Sunni) and Animist minorities.

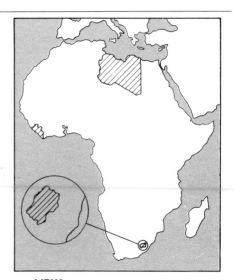

top: **LIBYA**
left: **LIBERIA**
encircled: **LESOTHO**

Capital city: Monrovia, population 425 000 (1984 estimate).
Other principal towns: Habel, Buchanan, Greenville (Sinoe), Harper (Cape Palmas).
Highest point: On Mt Nimba, 1372 m (*4500 ft*).
Principal mountain range: Guinea Highlands.
Principal rivers: St Paul, St John, Cess.
Head of State: Samuel Kanyon Doe (b. 6 May 1952), President.
Climate: Tropical (hot and humid), with temperatures from 13°C to 49°C (*55°F to 120°F*). Rainy season April to October. In Monrovia, average maximum 27°C (*80°F*) (July, August) to 30°C (*87°F*) (March, April), minimum 22°C to 23°C (*72°F to 74°F*) all year round, June and September rainiest (each 26 days).
Labour force: 548 615 in 1980: Agriculture, forestry and fishing 71·6%; Mining 5·1%; Trade 3·8%; Services 10%.
Gross domestic product: L$819 million in 1984: Agriculture, forestry and fishing 18·3%; Mining and quarrying 12·9%; Trade, restaurants and hotels 7·4%; Community, social and personal services (including all government services) 18·8%.
Exports: L$435·6 million in 1985: Iron ore and concentrates 64·1%; Rubber 17·7%; Timber 5·8%; Coffee 6·3%.
Monetary unit: Liberian dollar (L$). 1 dollar = 100 cents.
Denominations:
Coins 1, 2, 5, 10, 25, 50 cents; 1, 5 Liberian dollar. US coins are also in circulation.
Notes 1, 5, 10, 20 US dollars. (There are no Liberian banknotes).
Political history and government: Settled in 1822 by freed slaves from the USA. Became independent on 26 July 1847. The constitution was modelled on that of the USA. Legislative power was vested in a bicameral Congress, comprising a Senate and a House of Representatives, both chambers elected by universal adult suffrage. Executive power was vested in the President, also directly elected. On 26

Apr 1979, following anti-government riots, legislature granted the President emergency powers for one year. Leaders of an opposition party were arrested on 9 Mar 1980 and charged with attempting to overthrow the government. They were due to face trial on 14 Apr but on 12 Apr the President was deposed and killed in a military *coup*. Power was assumed by a People's Redemption Council (PRC), which released the former President's opponents. On 25 Apr 1980 the PRC suspended the constitution and imposed martial law. A new constitution came into force in January 1986. This provides for a National Assembly consisting of a Senate (of 26 members) and a House of Representatives (of 64 members). Following elections (October 1985) civilian rule was restored.

Length of roadways: 10 085 km (*6268 miles*) (1981).
Length of railways: 490 km (*304 miles*).
Universities: 2.
Adult illiteracy: 65% in 1985.
Defence: Total armed forces 5300 (1987); defence expenditure: 10% of total government expenditure in 1986/7.

Libya

Official name: Daulat Libiya al-'Arabiya al-Ishtrakiya al-Jumhuriya (Socialist People's Libyan Arab Jamahiriya – 'state of the masses').
Population: 3 955 000 (1986 estimate).
Area: 1 759 540 km² (*679 363 miles²*).
Language: Arabic.
Religion: Islam (Sunni).
Capital city: Tripoli (Tarābulus), population 990 697 (1984); in January 1987 Col. Qadhafi designated Hun, a small town 1045 km (*650 miles*) south east of Tripoli, as the future administrative capital of Libya – no moves have yet been taken to put this into effect.
Other principal towns (1984): Benghazi 485 386; Misrātah (Misurata) 178 295.
Highest point: Pico Bette, 2286 m (*7500 ft*).
Principal mountain ranges: Jabal as-Sawdā, Al Kufrah, Al Harūj al-Aswad, Jabal Nafūsah, Hamada de Tinrhert.
Principal river: Wādi al-Fārigh.
Head of State: Col. Mu'ammar Muhammad Abdulsalam Abu Miniar al-Qadhafi (b. September 1942), Revolutionary Leader – although he has no formal position under the constitution.
Head of Government: Umar Mustafa al-Muntasir, Secretary-General of the General People's Congress.
Climate: Very hot and dry, with average temperatures between 13°C and 38°C (*55°F and 100°F*). Coast cooler than inland. In Tripoli, August hottest (22°C to 30°C *72°F to 86°F*), January coolest (8°C to 16°C *47°F to 61°F*). Absolute maximum temperature 57·3°C (*135·1°F*), Al 'Aziziyah (El Azizia), 24 Aug 1923; absolute minimum −9°C (*15·8°F*), Hon, 10 Jan 1938.
Labour force: 800 000 in 1981.
Gross domestic product: 6473 million dinars in 1986: In 1982, mining and quarrying (oil and natural gas) accounted for 50%.
Exports: 3235·2 million dinars in 1985: Crude petroleum 99·9%.
Monetary unit: Libyan dinar. 1 dinar = 1000 dirhams.

Denominations:
Coins 1, 5, 10, 20, 50, 100 dirhams.
Notes 250, 500 dirhams; 1, 5, 10 dinars.
Political history and government: Formerly part of Turkey's Ottoman Empire. Became an Italian colony in September 1911. Italian forces were expelled in 1942–43 and the country was under British and French administration from 1943 until becoming an independent kingdom, under the Amir of Cyrenaica, on 24 Dec 1951. The monarchy was overthrown by an army *coup* on 1 Sept 1969, when a Revolutionary Command Council (RCC) took power and proclaimed the Libyan Arab Republic. The bicameral Parliament was abolished and political activity suspended. On 8 Sept 1969 the RCC elected Col. Mu'ammar al'Qadhafi as its Chairman. A provisional constitution, proclaimed in December 1969, vested supreme authority in the RCC, which appointed a Council of Ministers. On 11 June 1971 the Arab Socialist Union (ASU) was established as the sole political party. Under a decree of 13 Nov 1975 provision was made for the creation of a 618-member General National Congress of the ASU. This later became the General People's Congress (GPC), comprising members of the RCC, leaders of existing 'people's congresses' and 'popular committees', and trade unions and professional organizations. The Congress held its first session on 5–18 Jan 1976. On 2 Mar 1977 the GPC approved a new constitution, which adopted the country's present name. Under the constitution, the RCC and Council of Ministers were abolished and power passed to the GPC, assisted by a General Secretariat. The Council of Ministers was replaced by a General People's Committee. The first Secretary-General of the GPC was Col. Qadhafi. At a GPC meeting on 1–2 Mar 1979 he relinquished this post, although remaining Supreme Commander of the Armed Forces. Libya is divided into 24 municipalties which are grouped into 13 areas each governed by a Municipality People's Congress.
Length of roadways: 25 675 km (*15 944miles*) (1984).
Universities: 3.
Adult illiteracy: 33·1% in 1985.
Defence: Military service: conscription; total armed forces 76 500 (1987); defence expenditure: 380 million Libyan dinar in 1987.
Foreign tourists: 126 000 in 1980.

Liechtenstein

Official name: Fürstentum Liechtenstein (Principality of Liechtenstein).
Population: 27 399 (1986 estimate).
Area: 160·0 km² (*61·8 miles²*).
Language: German.
Religions: Roman Catholic; Protestant minority.
Capital city: Vaduz, population 4920 in 1986 (estimate).
Other principal towns (1986): Schaan 4757; Balzers 3477; Triesen 3180; Eschen 2844; Mauren 2713; Triesenberg 2277.
Highest point: Grauspitze, 2599 m (*8526 ft*).
Principal mountain range: Alps.
Principal rivers: Rhein (Rhine) (1319 km *820 miles*, 27 km *17 miles* in Liechtenstein), Samina.
Head of State: HSH Prince Franz Josef II (b. 16 Aug 1906). HSH Prince Franz Josef succeeded his great

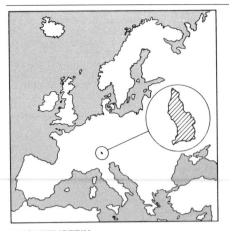

LIECHTENSTEIN

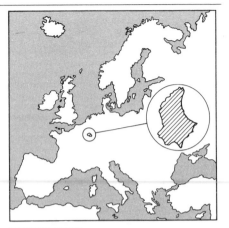

LUXEMBOURG

uncle on 26 July 1938. Crown Prince: HSH Prince Hans Adam (who has acted as Regent since 26 Aug 1984) (b. 14 Feb 1945), eldest son of the reigning Prince.
Head of Government: Hans Brunhart (b. 28 Mar 1945).
Climate: Alpine, with mild winters. Temperature extremes for Sargans, in Switzerland, a few miles from the Liechtenstein border: absolute maximum 38·0°C (*100·4°F*), 29 July 1947; absolute minimum −25·6°C (*−14·1°F*), 12 Feb 1929.
Labour force: 13 112 in 1986: Agriculture 2·8%; Industry, construction, commerce 43·8%; Services 53·4%.
Exports: 1291 million Swiss francs in 1986.
Monetary unit: Swiss currency (*q.v.*).
Political history and government: An hereditary principality, independent since 1866. Present constitution adopted on 5 Oct 1921. Legislative power is exercised jointly by the Sovereign and the unicameral Diet (*Landtag*), with 15 members elected (by men only) for 4 years, using proportional representation. A 5-man Government (*Regierung*) is elected by the Diet for its duration and confirmed by the Sovereign.
Length of roadways: 250 km (*155 miles*).
Length of railways: 18·5 km (*11·5 miles*).
Foreign tourists: 76 440 in 1986.

Luxembourg

Official name: Grand-Duché de Luxembourg (French), Grouscherzogdem Lezebuurg (Luxembourgois) or Grossherzogtum Luxemburg (German): Grand Duchy of Luxembourg.
Population: 369 500 (1986 estimate).
Area: 2586 km² (*999 miles²*).
Languages: Letzeburgesch (Luxembourgois), French, German.
Religion: Roman Catholic.
Capital city: Luxembourg-Ville, population 78 900 (1981 census).
Other principal towns (1981): Esch-sur-Alzette 25 500; Differdange 17 100; Dudelange 14 100; Petange 12 300.
Highest point: Bourgplatz, 559 m (*1833 ft*):

Principal mountain range: Ardennes.
Principal rivers: Mosel (Moselle), Sûre (172 km *107 miles*, 159 km *99 miles* in Luxembourg), Our, Alzette.
Head of State: HRH Jean (Benoît Guillaume Marie Robert Louis Antoine Adolphe Marc d'Aviano) (b. 5 Jan 1921), Grand Duke. HRH Grand Duke Jean succeeded to the throne upon the abdication of his mother Grand Duchess Charlotte 12 Nov 1964. Crown Prince: HRH Hereditary Grand Duke Prince Henri (b. 16 Apr 1955), eldest son of Grand Duke Jean.
Head of Government: Jacques Santer (b. 18 May 1937), President of the Government (Prime Minister).
Climate: Temperate (cool summers and mild winters). Absolute maximum temperature 37·0°C (*98·6°F*), Luxembourg-Ville, 28 July 1895, and Grevenmacher, 6 July 1957; absolute minimum −24·3°C (*−11·7°F*), Wiltz, 5 Feb 1917.
Labour force: 161 000 in 1985: Agriculture, forestry and fishing 4·3%; Mining and manufacturing 23·9%; Trade 34·2%; Community, social and personal services 14·8%.
Gross domestic product: 238 994 million Luxembourg francs in 1985: (in 1982) Mining and manufacturing 25·7%; Trade 29·8%.
Exports: 168 044 million Luxembourg francs in 1985: Base metals and manufactures 47·4%; Plastics, rubber etc 12·8%; Machinery (including electrical) 8·7%.
Monetary unit: Luxembourg franc. 1 franc = 100 centimes.
Denominations:
    Coins 25 centimes; 1, 5, 10, 20 Luxembourg francs.
    Notes 50, 100 Luxembourg francs; 50, 100, 500, 1000, 5000 Belgian francs.
Political history and government: An hereditary grand duchy, independent since 1867. Luxembourg is a constitutional monarchy. Legislative power is exercised by the unicameral Chamber of Deputies, with 64 members elected by universal adult suffrage for 5 years (subject to dissolution) on the basis of proportional representation. Some legislative functions are also entrusted to the advisory Council of State, with 21 members appointed for life by the Grand Duke, but the council can be overridden by the Chamber. Executive power is vested in the Grand Duke but is normally exercised by the

Council of Ministers, led by the President of the Government. The Grand Duke appoints Ministers but they are responsible to the Chamber. Luxembourg is divided into 12 cantons.
Length of roadways: 5220 km (*3242 miles*).
Length of railways: 274 km (*170 miles*).
Universities: 1.
Defence: Military service voluntary; total armed forces 630 (in 1987); defence expenditure: 1380 million Luxembourg francs in 1987.
Foreign tourists: 462 258 in 1986.

Madagascar

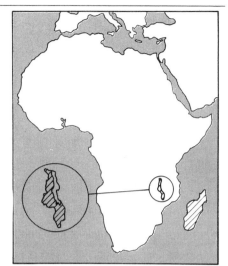

Official name: Repoblika Demokratika n'i Madagaskar (in Malagasy) or République démocratique de Madagascar (in French): Democratic Republic of Madagascar.
Population: 10 568 000 (1987 estimate).
Area: 587 041 km² (*226 658 miles²*).
Languages: Malagasy, French (both official).
Religions: Animist, Christian, Islam (Sunni).
Capital city: Antananarivo (Tananarive), population 662 585 (1985 estimate).
Other principal towns (1982): Toamasina 82 907; Mahajanga 80 881; Fianarantsoa 72 901; Antseranana 49 000; Toliary 48 929.
Highest point: Maromokotro, 2876 m (*9436 ft*).
Principal mountain ranges: Massif du Tsaratanan, Ankaratra.
Principal rivers: Ikopa, Mania, Mangoky.
Head of State: Lt.-Cdr. Didier Ratsiraka (b. 4 Nov 1936), President.
Prime Minister: Lt.-Col. Victor Ramahatra.
Climate: Hot on coast (average daily maximum 32°C (*90°F*)), but cooler inland. Fairly dry in south, but monsoon rains (December to April) in north. In Antananarivo, average maximum 20°C (*68°F*) (July) to 27°C (*81°F*) (November), minimum 8°C (*48°F*) (July, August) to 16°C (*61°F*) (January, February), January rainiest (21 days). Absolute maximum temperature 44·4°C (*111·9°F*), Behara, 20 Nov 1940; absolute minimum −6·3°C (*20·7°F*), Antsirabé, 18 June 1945.
Labour force: 4 605 000 in 1986: Agriculture, forestry and fishing 78·3%.
Gross domestic product: 1 806 900 million Malagasy francs in 1986: Agriculture, forestry and fishing 43%; Trade and services 39%.
Exports: 205 876 million Malagasy francs in 1986: Coffee 44·7%; Vanilla 14·5%.
Monetary unit: Franc malgache (Malagasy franc). 1 franc = 100 centimes.
Denominations:
Coins 1, 2, 5, 10, 50, 100 francs.
Notes 50, 100, 500, 1000, 5000 francs.
Political history and government: Formerly a French colony, Madagascar became the Malagasy Republic on achieving self-government, within the French community, on 14 Oct 1958. It became fully independent on 26 June 1960. Following disturbances, the President handed over full powers to the army commander on 18 May 1972, when Parliament was dissolved. A National Military Directorate was formed on 12 Feb 1975 and suspended all political parties. On 15 June 1975 the Directorate elected Lt.-Cdr. Didier Ratsiraka to be Head of State, as President of the Supreme Revolutionary Council (SRC). A referendum on 21 Dec 1975 approved a draft constitution and the appointment

encircled: **MALAWI**
right: **MADAGASCAR**

of Ratsiraka as Head of State for 7 years. The Democratic Republic of Madagascar was proclaimed on 30 Dec 1975 and Ratsiraka took office as President of the Republic on 4 Jan 1976 and was re-elected 7 Nov 1982.

Executive power is vested in the President, who rules with the assistance of the SRC and an appointed Council of Ministers. Legislative power is vested in the National People's Assembly, with 137 members elected by universal adult suffrage for 5 years. The Assembly was first elected on 30 June 1977, with a single list of candidates presented by the *Front national pour la défense de la révolution malgache*, a pro-government alliance of political parties. Elections were held in 1983 and 1988. The country is divided into 6 provinces.
Length of roadways: 17 300 km (*10 752 miles*).
Length of railways: 892 km (*554 miles*) (1986).
Universities: 1.
Adult illiteracy: 32·5% in 1985.
Defence: Military service 18 months; total armed forces 21 050 (1987); defence expenditure: US$58 million in 1987.
Foreign tourists: 26 913 in 1986.

Malawi

Official name: The Republic of Malawi.
Population: 7 278 925 (1986 estimate).
Area: 118 484 km² (*45 747 miles²*).
Languages: English (official), Chichewa.
Religions: Mainly traditional beliefs; Christians form 33% of population; Islam (Sunni).
Capital city: Lilongwe, population 158 500 (1983 estimate).
Other principal towns (1983 estimate): Blantyre 313 600; Zomba 46 000; Mzuzu 59 500.
Highest point: Mount Sapitwa, 3000 m (*9843 ft*).
Principal river: Shire.

Head of State: Dr Hastings Kamuzu Banda (b. 14 May 1906), President.
Climate: In the low-lying Shire valley temperatures can rise to 46°C (*115°F*) in October and November, but above 910 m (*3000 ft*) the climate is much more temperate and at the greatest heights the nights can be frosty. Dry season May to September, very wet season late December to March. Annual rainfall in the highlands is about 1270 mm (*50 in*) and in the lowlands 900 mm (*35 in*).
Labour force: 3 154 000 in 1986: Agriculture, forestry and fishing 78·6%.
Gross domestic product: 845·9 million kwacha in 1987: Agriculture, forestry and fishing 36·7%; Manufacturing 11·8%; Trade 12·4%; Financial services 6·4%; Government services 13·4%.
Exports: 445·9 million kwacha in 1986: Tobacco 54·8%; Tea 15·3%; Sugar 9%.
Monetary unit: Malawi kwacha. 1 kwacha = 100 tambala.
Denominations:
Coins 1, 2, 5, 10, 20 tambala.
Notes 50 tambala; 1, 5, 10, 20 kwacha.
Political history and government: Formerly the British protectorate of Nyasaland. Granted internal self-government on 1 Feb 1963 and became independent, within the Commonwealth, on 6 July 1964, taking the name Malawi. Became a republic, and a one-party state, on 6 July 1966, when Dr Hastings Banda (Prime Minister since 1963) became President. Under a constitutional amendment of November 1970, he became President for life on 6 July 1971. Legislative power is held by the unicameral National Assembly, with 102 members elected by universal adult suffrage for 5 years (subject to dissolution) and 5 additional members nominated by the President. All members must belong to the ruling Malawi Congress Party. All candidates were returned unopposed in 1964, 1971 and 1976 but on 29 June 1978 voting took place (for 47 seats) for the first time since 1961. A partial election took place in 1983.
Executive power is vested in the President, who rules with the assistance of an appointed Cabinet. Malawi has three administrative regions, each the responsibility of a Cabinet Minister.
Length of roadways: 12 215 km (*7586 miles*) (1985).
Length of railways: 800 km (*500 miles*).
Universities: 1 (with five constituent colleges).
Adult illiteracy: 58·8% in 1985.
Defence: Total armed forces 5250 (1987); defence expenditure: 35·5 million kwacha (1987).
Foreign tourists: 52 570 in 1986.

Malaysia

Official name: Persekutuan Tanah Melaysiu (Federation of Malaysia).
Population: 16 108 700 (1986 estimate).
Area: 330 433 km² (*127 581 miles²*).
Languages: Malay (official), Chinese, Tamil, Iban, English.
Religions (1970): Islam (Sunni) 50%; Buddhist 25·7%; Hindu; Christian.
Capital city: Kuala Lumpur, population 937 875 (1980 census).
Other principal towns (1980): Ipoh 300 727; Georgetown 250 578; Johore Bharu 249 880; Kuala

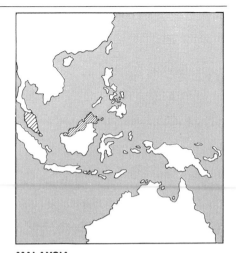

MALAYSIA

Trengganu 186 608; Kota Bharu 170 559; Kuantan 136 625; Seremban 136 252; Kuching 120 000.
Highest point: Mount Kinabalu, 4101 m (*13 455 ft*), in Sabah.
Principal mountain range: Trengganu Highlands.
Principal rivers: Pahang, Kelantan.
Head of State: HM Rajah Tun Sultan Azlan Muhibbuddim Shah, Sultan of Perak (the elected King of Malaysia) *Yang di-Pertuan Agong* (Supreme Head of State) succeeded 26 Apr 1989.
Prime Minister: Dato Seri Dr Mahathir bin Mohamad (b. 20 Dec 1925).
Climate: Peninsular Malaysia is hot and humid, with daytime temperatures around 29°C (*85°F*) and little variation throughout the year. The average daily range on the coast is 22°C to 33°C (*72°F to 92°F*). Rainfall is regular and often heavy. Maximum recorded temperature 39·4°C (*103·0°F*), Pulau Langkawi, 27 Mar 1931; minimum 2·2°C (*36·0°F*), Cameron Highlands, 6 Jan 1937.
Sabah is generally fairly humid but relatively cool. In Kota Kinabalu, average temperatures are 23°C to 31°C (*74°F to 87°F*), average annual rainfall 2640 mm (*104 in*). The north-east monsoon is from mid-October to March or April, the south-west monsoon from May to August.
Sarawak is humid, with temperatures generally 22°C to 31°C (*72°F to 88°F*), sometimes reaching 36°C (*96°F*). It has heavy rainfall (annual average 3050 mm to 4060 mm (*120 in to 160 in*), especially in the north-east monsoon season (October to March).
Labour force: 5 568 000 in 1986: Agriculture, forestry and fishing 32·1%; Manufacturing 14·7%; Government services 14·9%.
Gross domestic product: 71 731 million ringgit in 1986: Agriculture, forestry and fishing 21·2%; Mining 11·1%; Manufacturing 20·9%; Trade 11·6%; Financial services 8·2%; Government services 12·3%.
Exports: 35 801 million ringgit in 1986: Food and live animals 5·5%; Rubber, timber etc 22%; Petroleum 15·1%; Basic manufactures 7·2%; Machinery and transport equipment 25·1%.

Monetary unit: Ringgit (Malaysian dollar). 1 ringgit = 100 sen.
Denominations:
Coins 1, 5, 10, 20, 50 sen.
Notes 1, 5, 10, 50, 100, 1000 ringgit.
Political history and government: Peninsular (West) Malaysia comprises 11 states plus the Federal Capital Territory (nine with hereditary rulers, two with Governors) formerly under British protection. They were united as the Malayan Union on 1 Apr 1946 and became the Federation of Malaya on 1 Feb 1948. The Federation became independent, within the Commonwealth, on 31 Aug 1957. On 16 Sept 1963 the Federation (renamed the States of Malaya) was merged with Singapore (*q.v.*), Sarawak (a British colony) and Sabah (formerly the colony of British North Borneo) to form the independent Federation of Malaysia, still in the Commonwealth. On 9 Aug 1965 Singapore seceded from the Federation. On 5 Aug 1966 the States of Malaya were renamed West Malaysia, now known as Peninsular Malaysia.

Malaysia is an elective monarchy. The nine state rulers of Peninsular Malaysia (the Sultans of Johor, Kedah, Selangor, Kelantan, Trengganu and Pahang, the Rajas of Perlis and Perak and the Ruler of Negeri Sembilan) choose from their number a Supreme Head of State and a Deputy, to hold office for 5 years. Executive power is vested in the Head of State but is normally exercised on the advice of the Cabinet. Legislative power is held by the bicameral Parliament. The Senate (*Dewan Negara*), with limited powers, has 68 members, 32 appointed by the Head of State and elected by State Legislative Assemblies for 3 years. The House of Representatives (*Dewan Rakyat*) has 177 members elected by universal adult suffrage for 5 years (subject to dissolution). The Head of State appoints the Prime Minister and, on the latter's recommendation, other Ministers. The cabinet is responsible to Parliament.

Malaysia comprises 13 states and, since 1 Feb 1974, the Federal Territory of Kuala Lumpur. Each state has a unicameral Legislative Assembly, elected by universal adult suffrage.
Length of roadways: 41 344 km (*25 675 miles*).
Length of railways: 2267 km (*1408 miles*).
Universities: 7.
Defence: Military service voluntary; total armed forces 113 000 (1987); defence expenditure: 2150 million ringgit in 1987.
Foreign tourists: 3 200 000 in 1985.

Maldives

Official name: Dhivehi Jumhuriya (Republic of Maldives).
Population: 189 000 (1986 estimate).
Area: 298 km² (*115 miles²*).
Language: Dhivehi (Maldivian).
Religion: Islam (Sunni).
Capital city: Malé, population 46 334 (1985 census).
Head of State: Maumoon Abdul Gayoom (b. 29 Dec 1937), President.
Climate: Very warm and humid. Average temperature 27°C (*80°F*), with little daily variation. Annual rainfall 2540–3800 mm (*100–150 in*).
Labour force: 67 384 (December 1977).

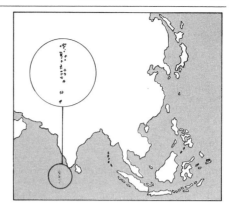

MALDIVES

Gross domestic product: 536 million rufiyaa in 1984: Agriculture, fishing 29·2%; Trade 9·9%; Government services 17·7%.
Exports: US$8 649 000 in 1981: Fish and fish products 81·6%; Fabricated mica 2·4%.
Monetary unit: Rufiyaa (Maldivian rupee). 1 rufiyaa = 100 laaris (larees).
Denominations:
Notes 2, 5, 10, 50, 100 rufiyaa.
Political history and government: Formerly an elective sultanate, called the Maldive Islands. Under British protection, with internal self-government, from December 1887 until achieving full independence, outside the Commonwealth, on 26 July 1965. Following a referendum in March 1968, the islands became a republic on 11 Nov 1968, with Ibrahim Nasir (Prime Minister since 1954) as President. Name changed to Maldives in April 1969. Legislative power is held by the unicameral Citizens' Council (*Majilis*), with 48 members, including eight appointed by the President and 40 (two from each of 20 districts) elected for five years by universal adult suffrage. Executive power is vested in the President, also directly elected for five years. He rules with the assistance of an appointed Cabinet, responsible to the *Majilis*. Near the end of his second term, President Nasir announced his wish to retire. the *Majilis* chose a single candidate who was approved by referendum on 28 July 1978 and sworn in on 11 Nov 1978. There are no political parties. The country has 20 administrative districts: the capital is centrally administered while each of the 19 atoll groups is governed by an appointed atoll chief (*verin*) who is appointed by the President and advised by an elected committee.
Adult illiteracy: 6·2% (the lowest in South Asia) in 1986.
Foreign tourists: 113 953 in 1986.

Mali

Official name: La République du Mali (the Republic of Mali).
Population: 7 620 225 (1987 census).
Area: 1 240 000 km² (*478 767 miles²*).
Languages: French (official language); Bambara 60%; Fulani.

Religions: Islam (Sunni) 65%; traditional beliefs 30%.

Capital city: Bamako, population 404 022 (including suburbs) at 1976 census.

Other principal towns (1976): Ségou 65 000; Mopti 54 000; Sikasso 47 000; Kayes 45 000.

Highest point: Hombori Tondo, 1155 m (*3789 ft*).

Principal mountain ranges: Mandinqué Plateau, Adrar des Iforas.

Principal rivers: Sénégal, Niger, Falémé.

Head of State: Gen. Moussa Traoré (b. 25 Sept 1936), President; also President of the Government (Prime Minister).

Climate: Hot. Very dry in the north, wetter in the south (rainy season June to October). Average temperatures in the south 24°C to 32°C (*75°F to 90°F*), higher in the Sahara. In Bamako, average maximum 30°C (*87°F*) (August) to 39°C (*103°F*) (April), minimum 16°C to 24°C (*61°F to 76°F*). In Timbuktu, average maximum 30°C (*87°F*) (August) to 43°C (*110°F*) (May), minimum 13°C (*55°F*) (January) to 26°C (*80°F*) (June), July and August rainiest (each 9 days).

Labour force: 4 127 000 in 1984: Agriculture, forestry and fishing 84·9%.

Gross domestic product: 127 100 million Mali francs in 1983: Cotton 40·8%; Groundnuts 1%.

Exports: 38 365 million francs CFA in 1982: Live animals 29·1%; Cotton 55·7%.

Monetary unit: Franc de la Communauté financière africaine (CFA) (=2 Mali francs). The Mali franc was abolished as a unit of currency in June 1984 and replaced by the franc CFA.

Denominations:

Coins 1, 2, 5, 10, 25, 50, 100 francs CFA.

Notes 100, 500, 1000, 5000, 10 000 francs CFA.

Political history and government: Formerly French Sudan, part of French West Africa. Joined Senegal to form the Federation of Mali on 4 Apr 1959. By agreement with France, signed on 4 Apr 1960, the Federation became independent on 20 June 1960. Senegal seceded on 20 Aug 1960 and the remnant of the Federation was proclaimed the Republic of Mali on 22 Sept 1960. The elected National Assembly was dissolved on 17 Jan 1968. The government was overthrown by an army *coup* on 19 Nov 1968, when a Military Committee for National Liberation (CMLN), led by Lt. (later Brig.-Gen. Moussa Traoré, was established. The constitution was abrogated and political parties banned. The CMLN ruled by decree with the assistance of an appointed Council of Ministers. The President of the CMLN assumed the functions of Head of State on 6 Dec 1968 and became also Prime Minister on 19 Sept 1969. The CMLN published a new constitution on 26 Apr 1974 and it was approved by referendum on 2 June 1974. This provides for a one-party state with an elected President and National Assembly, with the CMLN remaining in power for a transitional period of five years. The formation of the ruling party, the *Union démocratique du peuple malien* (UDPM), was announced on 22 Sept 1976. The UDPM was formally constituted on 30 Mar 1979 and nominated Traoré as presidential candidate on 18 May. Elections were held on 19 June 1979 for a National Assembly (82 members serving a three-year term) and for a President (with a five-year term) and again for both on 9 June 1985. Mali has eight administrative regions.

Length of roadways: 18 000 km (*11 200 miles*).

Length of railways: 642 km (*399 miles*).

Adult illiteracy: 83·2% in 1985.

Defence: Military service voluntary; total armed forces 7350 (1987); defence expenditure: 23·3% of total government expenditure in 1987.

Foreign tourists: 23 000 in 1983.

Malta

Official name: Repubblika ta Malta (Republic of Malta).

Population: 343 334 (1986 estimate).

Area: 316 km² (*122 miles²*), including Gozo (67 km² *25·9 miles²*) and Comino (2·77 km² *1·07 miles²*).

Languages: Maltese, English, Italian.

Religion: Roman Catholic.

Capital city: Valletta, population 14 013 (1984 estimate) but the conurbation around Valletta had a total population of 213 600 in 1985.

Other principal towns (1984): Sliema 20 071; Birkirkara 18 041; Qormi 17 130.

Highest point: 249 m (*816 ft*).

Head of State: Dr Vincent Tabone, President.

Prime Minister: Dr Eddie Fenech Adami.

Climate: Basically healthy without extremes. The temperature rarely drops below 4°C (*40°F*) and in most years does not rise above 38°C (*100°F*). The average annual rainfall in Valletta is 576 mm (*22·7 in*). In the summer the nights are cool except when the *Sirocco* desert wind blows from the south-east.

Labour force: 122 700 in 1986: Agriculture and fishing 4·4%; Manufacturing 27·6%; Trade 12·3%; Private services 34·4%.

Gross domestic product: 476 million Maltese liri in 1985.

Exports: 181 364 000 Maltese liri in 1984: Food and live animals 2·9%; Beverages and tobacco 3·4%; Mineral fuels and lubricants 3·5%; Basic manufactures 10·5%; Machinery and transport equipment 22·2%; Clothing 33·9%.

Monetary unit: Maltese lira (LM). 1 lira = 100 cents = 1000 mils.

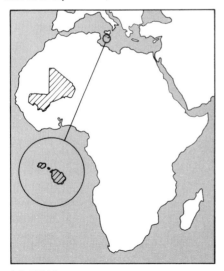

left : **MALI**

encircled : **MALTA**

Denominations:
Coins 2, 3, 5 mills; 1, 2, 5, 10, 25, 50 cents.
Notes 1, 5, 10 liri.
Political history and government: A former British colony. Became independent, within the Commonwealth, on 21 Sept 1964. A republic since 13 Dec 1974, when the Governor-General became President. Legislative power is held by the unicameral House of Representatives, with 69 members elected for 5 years (subject to dissolution) by universal adult suffrage, using proportional representation. The President is a constitutional Head of State, elected for 5 years by the House, and executive power is exercised by the Cabinet. The President appoints the Prime Minister and, on the latter's recommendation, other Ministers. The Cabinet is responsible to the House.
Length of roadways: 1289 km (*801 miles*) (1983).
Universities: 1.
Defence: Military service voluntary; total armed forces 910 (1987); defence expenditure 6·54 million Maltese liri in 1987.
Foreign tourists: 573 000 in 1986.

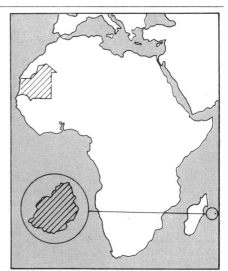

left: **MAURITANIA**
encircled: **MAURITIUS**

Mauritania

Official name: République Islamique de Mauritanie (French) or Jumhuriyat Muritaniya al-Islamiya (Arabic): Islamic Republic of Mauritania.
Population: 1 946 000 (1986 estimate).
Area: 1 030 700 km² (*397 955 miles²*).
Languages: Arabic, Hassaniya, French.
Religion: Islam (Sunni).
Capital city: Nouakchott, population 350 000 (including suburbs) (1984).
Other principal towns (1976): Nouadhibou (Port-Etienne) 21 961; Kaédi 20 848; Zouérate 17 474; Rosso 16 466; Atar 16 326.
Highest point: Kediet Ijill, 915 m (*3002 ft*).
Principal river: Sénégal.
Head of State: Lt.-Col. Maouya Ould Sidi Ahmed Taya (b. 1943), Chairman of the Military Committee for National Salvation and Prime Minister.
Climate: Hot and dry, with breezes on coast. In Nouakchott, average maximum 28°C to 34°C (*83°F to 93°F*). In interior, F'Derik has average July maximum of 43°C (*109°F*).
Labour force: 606 000 in 1986: Agriculture, forestry and fishing 66·7%.
Gross domestic product: 44 500 million ouguiya in 1984.
Exports: 25 950 million ouguiya in 1986: Iron ore 40·8%; Fish 59·1%.
Monetary unit: Ouguiya. 1 ouguiya = 5 khoums.
Denominations:
Coins 1 khoum; 1, 5, 10, 20 ouguiya.
Notes 100, 200, 1000 ouguiya.
Political history and government: Formerly part of French West Africa, Mauritania became a self-governing member of the French Community on 28 Nov 1958. Moktar Ould Daddah became Prime Minister on 23 June 1959. The country became fully independent on 28 Nov 1960, with Daddah as Head of State. Under the constitution of 20 May 1961, Daddah became President on 20 Aug 1961. A one-party state, under the Mauritanian People's Party (PPM), was introduced in 1964. On 28 Feb 1976 Spain ceded Spanish Sahara to Mauritania and

Morocco, to be apportioned between them. Mauritania occupied the southern part of this territory, which it named Tiris el-Gharbia.

President Daddah was deposed by the armed forces on 10 July 1978, when power was assumed by a Military Committee for National Recovery (CMRN), led by Lt.-Col. Moustapha Ould Mohamed Salek. The constitution was suspended and the National Assembly and ruling party dissolved. On 20 July 1978 the new regime published a Constitutional Charter, under which the Chairman of the CMRN would exercise executive authority. On 6 Apr 1979 the CMRN was replaced by a Military Committee for National Salvation (CMSN), also led by Salek, but he relinquished the post of Prime Minister to Lt.-Col. Ahmed Ould Bouceif (Bousseif). On 11 Apr 1979 the CMSN adopted a new Constitutional Charter, assuming legislative power for itself and separating the roles of Head of State and Head of Government. Bouceif was killed in an air crash on 27 May and the CMSN appointed a new Prime Minister, Lt.-Col. Mohamed Khouna Ould Haidalla, on 31 May. Salek, then only titular Head of State, resigned on 3 June 1979, being replaced by Lt.-Col. Mohamed Mahmoud Ould Ahmed Louly.

Following negotiations with the *Frente Popular para la Liberación de Sakiet el Hamra y Río de Oro* (the Polisario Front), a Saharan nationalist group, Mauritania signed an agreement on 5 Aug 1979 providing for its withdrawal from its portion of Western (formerly Spanish) Sahara. It formally withdrew on 15 Aug 1979, although Morocco had previously announced its annexation of the area (in addition to the northern part which it already held).

On 4 Jan 1980 Louly was deposed by Haidalla, who (despite the previous separation of powers) became Head of State while remaining Prime Minister. He relinquished the premiership on 15 Dec 1980, when an almost entirely civilian Cabinet was formed. This was replaced on 25 Apr 1982, when the Army Chief of Staff became Prime Minister.

In December 1984, Col. Taya assumed office as

President and Prime Minister. On 19 Dec 1980 the CMSN published a draft constitution, to be submitted to a referendum. The constitution envisages a National Assembly, elected for four years, and a President serving a single six-year term. Executive power would be held by the Prime Minister, to be designated by the President (from among the majority in the Assembly) and approved by the Assembly. Political parties would be permitted but the PPM would remain banned. However, all legislative and executive power remains in the hands of the 24-member CMSN.

Length of roadways: 8900 km (*5550 miles*).
Length of railways: 670 km (*416 miles*).
Adult illiteracy: 82·6% (population aged 6 and over) in 1977.
Defence: Total armed forces 14 870 (1987); military service is voluntary; in 1983, defence expenditure: 2640 million ouguiya.

Mauritius

Population: 1 029 000 (1986 estimate).
Area: 2045 km² (*789·5 miles²*).
Languages (1984): The official language is English. Arabic 7%; Bhojpuri 19%; Chinese 2%; Creole 29%; French 3%; Hindi 22%; Marathi 2%; Tamil 7%; Telegu 3%; Urdu 6%.
Religions (1962): Hindu 52%; Christian 30%; Islam (Sunni) 16%.
Capital city: Port Louis, population 136 323 (1985 estimate).
Other principal towns (1985): Beau Bassin-Rose Hill 91 786; Curepipe 63 181; Quatre Bornes 64 506; Vacoas-Phoenix 54 430.
Highest point: Piton de la Rivière Noire (Black River Mountain), 826 m (*2711 ft*).
Head of State: HM Queen Elizabeth II, represented by Sir Veerasamy Ringadoo, Governor-General.
Prime Minister: Aneerood Jugnauth.
Climate: Generally humid, with south-east trade winds. Average temperatures between 19°C (*66°F*) at 610 m (*2000 ft*) and 23°C (*75°F*) at sea-level. At Vacoas, 425 m (*1394 ft*), maximum 37°C (*98·6°F*), minimum 8°C (*46·4°F*). Average annual rainfall between 890 and 5080 mm (*35 and 200 in*) on highest parts. Wettest months are January to March. Tropical cyclones between September and May.
Labour force: 294 739 at 1983 census (island of Mauritius only): Agriculture, forestry and fishing 25·3%; Manufacturing 20·8%; Construction 7·5%; Trade 12%; Transport, storage and communications 6%; Community, social and personal services 24·4%. The island of Rodrigues had a labour force of 8206 in 1972.
Gross domestic product: 15 040 million rupees in 1986: Agriculture, forestry and fishing 14·3%; Manufacturing 22·1%; Trade 13·4%; Financial services 15·3%; Government services 10·6%.
Exports: 3971·8 million rupees in 1986: Sugar and molasses 91·3%; Tea 2·6%.
Monetary unit: Mauritian rupee. 1 rupee = 100 cents.
Denominations:
Coins 1, 2, 5, 10, 25, 50 cents; 1 rupee.
Notes 5, 10, 25, 50 rupees.
Political history and government: A former British colony. On 12 Mar 1964 the Chief Minister became

Premier. On 8 Nov 1965 the United Kingdom transferred the Chagos Archipelago, a Mauritian dependency, to the newly-created British Indian Ocean Territory. A new constitution was adopted, and Mauritius achieved self-government, on 12 Aug 1967, when the Premier became Prime Minister. Following communal riots, a state of emergency was declared on 21–22 Jan 1968. Mauritius became independent, within the Commonwealth, on 12 Mar 1968.

Executive power is vested in the British monarch and exercisable by the Governor-General, who is appointed on the recommendation of the Prime Minister and acts in almost all matters on the advice of the Council of Ministers. Legislative power is held by the unicameral Legislative Assembly, with 71 members: the Speaker, 62 members elected by universal adult suffrage for 5 years and 8 'additional' members (the most successful losing candidates of each community). The Governor-General appoints the Prime Minister and, on the latter's recommendation, other Ministers. The Council of Ministers is responsible to the Assembly.

By a constitutional amendment of 18 Nov 1969, the term of the Assembly (elected on 7 Aug 1967) was extended by four years and the election due in 1972 was not held until 20 Dec 1976. The state of emergency was lifted on 31 Dec 1970 but, after industrial unrest, it was reimposed on 16 Dec 1971.
Length of roadways: 1800 km (*1100 miles*)
Universities: 1.
Adult illiteracy: 17·2% in 1985.
Defence: No standing force.
Foreign tourists: 180 000 in 1988.

Mexico

Official name: Estados Unidos Mexicanos (United Mexican States).
Population: 81 163 256 (1987 estimate).
Area: 1 958 201 km² (*756 062 miles²*).
Languages: Spanish 90%, indigenous.
Religion: Roman Catholic 96%.
Capital city: Ciudad de México (Mexico City), population 17 321 800 (1985 census).
Other principal towns (1980): Guadalajara 2 244 715; Monterrey 1 916 472; Heróica Puebla de Zaragoza (Puebla) 835 759; Léon 655 809; Ciudad Juárez 567 365; Rosales 560 011; Mexicali 510 554; Tijuana 461 257; Mérida 424 529; Acapulco 409 335; Chihuahua 406 830; San Luis Potosí 406 630.
Highest point: Pico de Orizaba (Volcán Citlaltepetl), 5610 m (*18 405 ft*).
Principal mountain ranges: Sierra Madre Occidental, Sierra Madre Oriental, Sierra Madre del Sur, Sistema Volcánico Transversal.
Principal rivers: Río Bravo del Norte (Río Grande) (3033 km (*1885 miles*)), Balsas, Grijalva, Pánuco.
Head of State: Carlos Salinas de Gortari, President.
Climate: Tropical (hot and wet) on coastal lowlands and in south, with average temperature of 18°C (*64°F*). Temperature on highlands of central plateau. Arid in north and west. In Mexico City, average maximum 19°C (*66°F*) (December, January) to 25°C (*78°F*) (May), minimum 5°C (*42°F*) (January) to 13°C (*55°F*) (June). July and August rainiest (27

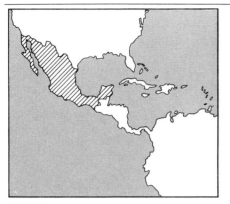

MEXICO

days each). Absolute maximum temperature 58°C (*136°F*), San Luis Potosí, 11 Aug 1933; absolute minimum −28°C (*−19°F*), Balerio, 30 Jan 1949.
Labour force: 26 908 000 (1986); and 21 941 693 (1980 census): Agriculture, forestry and fishing 24·9%; Mining 2%; Manufacturing 11·7%; Building industry 5·9%; Commerce, restaurants and hotels 7·8%; Transport and communications 3%; Personal, social and communal services 10·9%.
Gross domestic product: 28 748 889·1 million pesos in 1984: Agriculture, forestry and fishing 9·7%; Manufacturing 24·1%; Commerce, restaurants and hotels 23·3%; Finance, insurance and real estate 11%; Personal, social and communal services 15·6%.
Exports: US$21 820 million in 1985: Crude oil and natural gas 61%; Vehicles 5·6%; Coffee 2·2%.
Monetary unit: Mexican peso. 1 peso = 100 centavos.
Denominations:
Coins 1, 5, 10, 20, 50, 100, 200 pesos.
Notes 500, 1000, 5000, 10 000, 20 000, 50 000 pesos.
Political history and government: A federal republic of 31 states and Federal District (around the capital). Present constitution was proclaimed on 5 Feb 1917. Legislative power is vested in the bicameral National Congress. The Senate has 64 members – two from each state and the Federal District – elected by universal adult suffrage for 6 years. The Chamber of Deputies, directly elected for 3 years, has 400 seats, of which 300 are filled from single-member constituencies. The remaining 100 seats, allocated by proportional representation, are filled from minority parties' lists. Executive power is held by the President, elected for 6 years by universal adult suffrage at the same time as the Senate. He appoints and leads a Cabinet to assist him. Each state is administered by a Governor (elected for 6 years) and an elected Chamber of Deputies.
Length of roadways: 225 684 km (*140 150 miles*) (1986).
Length of railways: 20 038 km (*12 444 miles*) (1987).
Universities: 82.
Adult illiteracy: 9·7% in 1985.
Defence: Military service: voluntary, with part-time conscript militia; total regular armed forces 134 500 (1987); defence expenditure: 374 700 million pesos in 1986.
Foreign tourists: 5 400 000 in 1987.

Monaco

Official name: Principauté de Monaco (Principality of Monaco).
Population: 27 063 (1982 census).
Area: 1·95 km² (*0·75 mile²*).
Language: French.
Religion: Mainly Roman Catholic.
Capital city: Monaco-Ville, population 2422.
Other principal town: Monte Carlo, population 9948 (1968).
Highest point: On Chemin de Révoirés, 162 m (*533 ft*).
Principal river: Vésubie.
Head of State: HSH Prince Rainier III (b. 31 May 1923), succeeded on the death of his grandfather, Prince Louis II, on 9 May 1949. Crown Prince: HSH Prince Albert, Marquis des Baux (b. 14 March 1958), only son of Prince Rainer.
Minister of State: Jean Ausseil.
Climate: Mediterranean, with warm summers (average July maximum 28°C *83°F*) and very mild winters (average January minimum 3°C *37°F*), 62 rainy days a year (monthly average maximum seven days in winter). Absolute maximum temperature 34°C (*93°F*), 29 June 1945 and 3 Aug 1949; absolute minimum −2·3°C (*27·8°F*).
Labour force: 10 093 (excluding 232 unemployed) aged 15 and over (census of 1 Mar 1968): Industry 21·9% (manufacturing 14·8%); Services 77·9% (commerce 18·7%).
Monetary unit: French currency (*q.v.*).
Political history and government: An hereditary principality, in close association with France since 2 Feb 1861. Monaco became a constitutional monarchy on 5 Jan 1911. The present constitution was promulgated on 17 Dec 1962. Legislative power is held jointly by the Sovereign and the unicameral National Council, with 18 members elected by universal adult suffrage for 5 years. The electorate comprises only true-born Monégasque citizens aged 21 years or over. Executive power is vested in the Sovereign and exercised jointly with a 4-man Council of Government, headed by a Minister of State (a French civil servant chosen by the Sovereign). Monaco comprises 3 *quartiers*.
Length of roadways: 47 km (*29 miles*).
Length of railways: 1·7 km (*1·1 miles*).
Foreign tourists: 241 812 hotel arrivals in 1985.

MONACO

Mongolia

Official name: Bügd Nairamdakh Mongol Ard Uls (Mongolian People's Republic).
Population: 1 965 000 (1987 estimate).
Area: 1 565 000 km² (*604 250 miles²*).
Language: Khalkh Mongolian.
Religion: Buddhist.
Capital city: Ulan Bator (Ulaan Baatar), population 515 000 (1987 estimate).
Other principal towns (1986): Darhan 74 000; Erdenet 45 400.
Highest point: Mönh Hayrhan Uul, 4362 m (*14 311 ft*).
Principal mountain ranges: Altai Mts, Hangayn Nuruu.
Principal rivers: Selenge (Selenga) with Orhon, Hereleng (Kerulen).
Head of State: Jambyn Batmunkh (b. 10 Mar 1926), Chairman of the Praesidium of the Peoples' Great Hural.
Head of Government: Dumaagyn Sodnom (b. 14 July 1933), Chairman of the Council of Ministers.
Climate: Dry. Summers generally mild, winters very cold. In Ulan Bator, July warmest (10°C to 22°C *51°F to 71°F*) and rainiest (10 days), January coldest (−32°C to −18°C *−26°F to −2°F*).
Labour force: 919 000 (estimate for 1986): Agriculture and forestry 34·1%.
Gross national product: The Government does not publish any figures.
Exports: 1816 million tugriks in 1983: Fuels, minerals, metals 40·1%; Raw materials (including foodstuffs) 40·5%.
Monetary unit: Tugrik. 1 tugrik = 100 möngö.
Denominations:
Coins 1, 2, 5, 10, 15, 20, 50 möngö; 1 tugrik.
Notes 1, 3, 5, 10, 25, 50, 100 tugrik.
Political history and government: Formerly Outer Mongolia, a province of China. With backing from the USSR, the Mongolian People's (Communist) Party – called the Mongolian People's Revolutionary Party (MPRP) since 1921 – established a Provisional People's Government on 31 Mar 1921. After nationalist forces, with Soviet help, overthrew Chinese rule in the capital, independence was proclaimed on 11 July 1921. The USSR recognized the People's Government on 5 Nov 1921. The Mongolian People's Republic was proclaimed on 26 Nov 1924 but was not recognized by China. A plebiscite on 20 Oct 1945 voted 100% for independence, recognized by China on 5 Jan 1946. A new constitution was adopted on 6 July 1960.

The supreme organ of state power is the People's Great Hural (Assembly), with 370 members elected (unopposed) by universal adult suffrage for five years. The Assembly usually meets only twice a year but elects a Presidium (9 members) to be its permanent organ. The Chairman of the Presidium is Head of State. The highest executive body is the Council of Ministers, appointed by (and responsible to) the Assembly.

Political power is held by the MPRP, the only legal party. The MPRP presents a single list of approved candidates for elections to all representative bodies. The MPRP's highest authority is the Party Congress, which elects the Central Committee (91 full members and 71 candidate members were elected in May 1981) to supervise Party work. The Committee elects a Political bureau (6

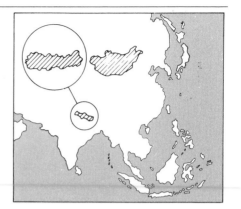

top: **MONGOLIA**   *below:* **NEPAL**

full members and 3 candidate members) to direct ts policy.

For local administration, Mongolia is divided into 18 provinces and 3 municipalities.
Length of roadways: c. 75 000 km (*c. 46 600 miles*).
Length of railways: 1775 km (*1102 miles*).
Universities: 1.
Defence: Military service: 2 years; total armed forces 33 500 (1987); defence expenditure: 13·5% of total government expenditure in 1988.
Foreign tourists: 250 000 in 1986.

Morocco

Official name: Al-Mamlaka al-Maghribiya (the Kingdom of Morocco).
***Population:** 22 312 000 (1986 census).
***Area:** 458 730 km² (*177 115 miles²*).
Languages: Arabic, Berber, French, Spanish.
Religions: Islam (Sunni); Christian minority.
Capital city: Rabat, population 1 020 001 (1982 census).
Other principal towns (1982): Casablanca 2 436 664; Marrakech 548 700; Fes 56 200; Meknes 48 600; Tanger 304 000; Oujda 470 500; Tetouan 371 700; Kenitra 449 700; Safi 255 700.
Highest point: Jebel Toubkal, 4165 m (*13 665 ft*) (first climbed in 1923).
Principal mountain ranges: Haut (Grand) Atlas, Moyen (Middle) Atlas, Anti Atlas.
Principal rivers: Oued Dra (539 km (*335 miles*), Oued Oum-er-Rbia, Oued Moulouya (515 km *320 miles*), Sebou (450 km (*280 miles*).
Head of State: HM King Hassan II (b. 9 July 1929), succeeded upon the death of his father King Mohammed V on 3 Mar 1961. Crown Prince: HRH Prince Sidi Mohammed (b. 21 Aug 1963), son of King Hassan II.
Prime Minister: N. Azzeddine Laraki.
Climate: Semi-tropical. Warm and sunny on coast, very hot inland. Rainy season November to March. Absolute maximum temperature 51·7°C (*125·0°F*), Agadir, 17 Aug 1940; absolute minimum −24°C (*−11·2°F*), Ifrane, 11 Feb 1935.

* Figures exclude Western (formerly Spanish) Sahara. See separate entry under Other Territories.

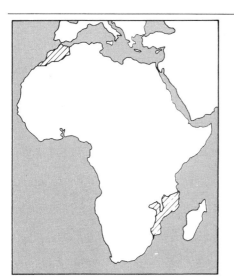

top left: **MOROCCO**
bottom right: **MOZAMBIQUE**

1 Mar 1972 and promulgated on 10 Mar 1972, provides for a modified constitutional monarchy. Legislative power is vested in a unicameral Chamber of Representatives, which has 306 members, of which 204 are elected directly and 102 chosen by an electoral college.

Executive power is vested in the King, who appoints (and may dismiss) the Prime Minister and other members of the Cabinet. The King can also dissolve the Chamber.

Length of roadways: 57 792 km *(35 918 miles).*
Length of railways: 1893 km *(1176 miles).*
Universities: 6.
Adult illiteracy: 66·9% in 1985.
Defence: Military service: 18 months; total armed forces 203 500 (1987); defence expenditure: 7190 million dirhams in 1987.
Foreign tourists: 2 186 444 in 1986.

Mozambique

Official name: A República Popular de Moçambique (the People's Republic of Mozambique).
Population: 14 174 000 in 1986.
Area: 799 380 km² *(308 774 miles²).*
Languages: Portuguese (official), many African languages.
Religions: Animist; Christian and Muslim minorities.
Capital city: Maputo (formerly Lourenço Marques), population 1 006 765 (1987).
Other principal towns (1986): Beira 269 700; Nampula 182 600.
Highest point: Monte Binga, 2436 m *(7992 ft).*
Principal mountain range: Lebombo Range.
Principal rivers: Limpopo, Zambezi, Rovuma, Shire.
Head of State: Joaquím Alberto Chissano, President.
Prime Minister: Mario da Graça Machungo.
Climate: Varies from tropical to sub-tropical except in a few upland areas. Rainfall is irregular but the rainy season is usually from November to March, with an average temperature of 28°C *(83°F)* in Maputo. In the dry season, average temperatures 18°C to 20°C *(65°F to 68°F).*
Labour force: 7 818 000 in 1986: Agriculture 82·8%.
Gross domestic product: 158·4 billion meticais in 1986.
Exports: 3198·4 million meticais in 1986: Fish 48·4%; Cashew nuts 21·1%; Sugar 10·2%.
Monetary unit: Metical (plural: meticais). 1 metical = 100 centavos.
Denominations:
   Coins 10, 20, 50 centavos; 1, 2½, 5, 10, 20 meticais.
   Notes 50, 100, 500, 1000 meticais.
Political history and government: Formerly a Portuguese colony, independent since 25 June 1975. The independence movement was dominated by the *Frente de Libertação de Moçambique* (Frelimo), the Mozambique Liberation Front. Before independence Frelimo was recognized by Portugal and its leader became the first President. The independence constitution proclaims that Frelimo is the directing power of the state and of society. At its third Congress, in February 1977, Frelimo was reconstituted as the Frelimo Party, a 'Marxist-Leninist vanguard party'. Legislative power is vested in the People's Assembly, with 250 members,

Labour force: 5 451 556 in 1982: Agriculture, fishing 43·1%; Manufacturing 17·1%; Trade 9·1%; Finance, business and personal services 18·5%.
Gross domestic product: 134 337 million dirhams in 1986: Agriculture, forestry and fishing 21·3%; Manufacturing 17·5%; Trade 17·4%; Public administration 11·8%.
Exports: 22 103·5 million dirhams in 1986: Food, beverages, tobacco 29·5% (Citrus fruit 7·8%); Phosphates 17%; Phosphoric acid 13·7%; Clothing 7·7%.
Monetary unit: Dirham. 1 dirham = 100 francs (centimes).
Denominations:
   Coins 1, 5, 10, 20, 50 francs; 1, 5 dirhams.
   Notes 5, 10, 50, 100 dirhams.
Political history and government: An hereditary monarchy, formerly ruled by a Sultan. Most of Morocco (excluding the former Spanish Sahara) became a French protectorate on 30 Mar 1912. A smaller part in the north became a Spanish protectorate on 27 Nov 1912. Tangier became an international zone on 18 Dec 1923. The French protectorate became independent on 2 Mar 1956 and was joined by the Spanish protectorate on 7 Apr 1956. The Tangier zone was abolished on 29 Oct 1956. The Sultan became King on 18 Aug 1957. The northern strip of Spanish Sahara was ceded to Morocco on 10 Apr 1958 and the Spanish enclave of Ifni was ceded on 30 June 1969. On 28 Feb 1976 the rest of Spanish Sahara was ceded to Morocco and Mauritania, to be apportioned between them. After Mauritania announced its intention to withdraw from Tiris el-Gharbia, its section of Western (formerly Spanish) Sahara, Morocco annexed that portion also (and renamed it Oued Eddaheb) on 14 Aug 1979. This inclusion of the Western Sahara within the boundaries of Morocco is not recognized by many members of the international community – see separate entry for Western Sahara under Other Territories following the directory of sovereign nations.

A new constitution, approved by referendum on

mainly Frelimo Party officials, elected December 1986. Executive power is held by the President, who appoints and leads a Council of Ministers. Mozambique has 11 provinces. Large areas of the country are controlled by opposition guerrilla groups.
Length of roadways: 27 000 km (*16 800 miles*) (1982).
Length of railways: 3843 km (*2386 miles*) (1987).
Universities: 1.
Adult illiteracy: 62% in 1985.
Defence: Military service: two years (including women); total armed forces 31 700 (1987); defence expenditure, 1987: $146·5 million.
Foreign tourists: 1000 in 1981.

Nauru

Official name: The Republic of Nauru (Naoero).
Population: 8042 (1983 census).
Area: 21 km² (*8·2 miles²*).
Languages: English, Nauruan.
Religions: Protestant; Roman Catholic.
Highest point: 68 m (*225 ft*).
Head of State: Hammer DeRoburt, OBE (b. 25 Sept 1922), President.
Climate: Tropical; day temperature 30°C (*85°F*); rainfall variable, averaging 2000 mm (*80 in*); wettest periods November to February.
Exports: $Australian 100 million in 1984–5: Phosphates 100%.
Monetary unit: Australian currency (*q.v.*).
Political history and government: Annexed by Germany in October 1888. Captured by Australian forces in November 1914. Administered by Australia under League of Nations mandate (17 Dec 1920) and later as UN Trust Territory. A new constitution was adopted on 31 Jan 1968. Hammer DeRoburt, Head Chief of Nauru since 1956, was elected the country's first President on 19 May 1968. Under an agreement announced on 29 Nov 1968, Nauru became a 'special member' of the Commonwealth. Legislative power is held by a unicameral Parliament, with 18 members elected by universal adult suffrage for three years (subject to dissolution). Executive power is held by the President, who is elected by Parliament for its duration and rules

NAURU

with the assistance of an appointed Cabinet, responsible to Parliament. Nauru's first political party was formed in 1976.
Length of roadways: 19 km (*12 miles*).
Length of railways: 5·2 km (*3·2 miles*).

Nepal

Official name: Nepal Adhirajya (Kingdom of Nepal).
Population: 17 632 900 (1987 estimate).
Area: 140 797 km² (*54 362 miles²*).
Languages (1971): Nepali (official) 52·4%; Maithir 11·5%; Bhojpuri 7·0%; Tamang 4·8%; Tharu 4·3%; Newari 3·9%; Abadhi 2·7%; Magar 2·5%; Raikirati 2·0%.
Religions (1971): Hindu 89·4%; Buddhist 7·5%; Islam (Sunni) 3·0%.
Capital city: Kathmandu, population 393 494 (1981 census).
Other principal towns (1981): Morang 93 544; Lalitpur 79 875; Bhaktapur 48 472.
Highest point: Mount Everest, 8848 m (*29 028 ft*) (on Chinese border). First climbed 29 May 1953.
Principal mountain range: Nepal Himalaya (Mahabharat Range).
Principal rivers: Karnali, Naryani, Kosi.
Head of State: HM King Birenda Bir Bikram Shah Dev (b. 28 Dec 1945) who succeeded his father King Mahendra on 31 Jan 1972. King Birenda was crowned on 24 Feb 1975. Crown Prince: HRH Prince Dipendra (b. 27 June 1971), son of the King.
Prime Minister: Lokendra Bahadur Chand.
Climate: Varies sharply with altitude, from Arctic in Himalaya to humid sub-tropical in the central Vale of Kathmandu (annual average 11°C *52°F*), which is warm and sunny in summer. Rainy season June to October. In Kathmandu, average maximum 18°C (*65°F*) (January) to 30°C (*86°F*) (May), minimum 2°C (*35°F*) (January) to 20°C (*68°F*) (July, August), July (21 days) and August (20 days) rainiest. Maximum temperature recorded in Kathmandu is 37°C (*99°F*) (2 May 1960) and minimum is −3°C (*26°F*) (20 Jan 1964).
Labour force: 6 850 886 in 1981: Agriculture, forestry and fishing 91·1%; Trade 1·6%; Community, social and personal services 4·6%.
Gross domestic product: 38 184 million Nepal rupees in 1983–4: Agriculture, forestry and fishing 57·8%; Manufacturing (including cottage industries) 4·3%; Construction 6·6%; Financial services 8·9%; Community, social and personal services 7·3%.
Exports: 1703·9 million Nepal rupees in 1983–4: Food and live animals 34·3%; Crude materials (except fuels) 21·8%; Basic manufactures 32·6%.
Monetary unit: Nepalese rupee. 1 rupee = 100 paisa.
Denominations:
Coins 1, 5, 10, 25, 50 paiesa; 1 rupee.
Notes 1, 5, 10, 100, 500, 1000 rupees.
Political history and government: An hereditary kingdom. A limited constitutional monarchy was proclaimed on 18 Feb 1951. In a royal *coup* on 15 Dec 1960 the King dismissed the Cabinet and dissolved Parliament. A royal proclamation of 5 Jan 1961 banned political parties. A new constitution, adopted on 16 Dec 1962, vested executive power in the King and established a National Assembly

(*Rashtriya Panchayat*) whose members (most of them indirectly elected, the remainder nominated by the King) had only consultative functions. A referendum held on 2 May 1980 approved the retention of the non-party system. Under a decree of 15 Dec 1980, the constitution was amended to provide for a National Assembly of 140 members (112 directly elected by universal adult suffrage for five years, 28 nominated by the King). The Prime Minister is elected by the Assembly, with other members of the Council of Ministers appointed by the King on the Prime Minister's recommendation. The Council is responsible to the Assembly.

Nepal comprises 14 zones, each administered by an appointed Commissioner.

Length of roadways: 6015 km (*3735 miles*) (1986).
Length of railways: 101 km (*63 miles*).
Universities: 1.
Adult illiteracy: 74·4% in 1985.
Defence: Military service voluntary; total armed forces 30 000 (1987); defence expenditure: 16·5% of total government expenditure in 1986–7.
Foreign tourists: 226 236 in 1986.

The Netherlands

Official name: Koninkrijk der Nederlanden (Kingdom of the Netherlands).
Population: 14 661 293 (1987 estimate).
Area: 41 785 km² (*16 140 miles²*).
Language: Dutch.
Religions: Roman Catholic 38%; Protestant 33%.
Capital city: Amsterdam, population 1 015 916 in 1987. Amsterdam is the capital in name only. The capital *de facto* – seat of the government, the Royal Family, the diplomatic corps, ministries, the Supreme Court etc is 's Gravenhage (Den Haag or The Hague), population 678 173 (1987).
Other principal towns (1987): Rotterdam 1 030 696; Utrecht 516 064; Eindhoven 378 247; Arnhem 295 380; Heerlen-Kerkrade 266 642; Enschede-Hengelo 248 832; Nijmegan 239 535; Tilburg 224 050; Haarlem 214 418; Groningen 206 910; Dordrecht 201 121; 's-Hertogenbosch 190 842. (All figures include suburbs.)
Highest point: Vaalserberg, 321 m (*1053 ft*).
Principal rivers: Maas (Meuse), Waal, Rhine, Ijssel.
Head of State: HM Queen Beatrix (Wilhelmina Armgard) (b. 31 Jan 1938), succeeded upon the abdication of her mother Queen Juliana on 1 May 1980. Crown Prince: HRH Prince Willem-Alexander, the Prince of Orange, (b. 27 Apr 1967), eldest son of Queen Beatrix.
Prime Minister: Ruud F. M. Lubbers.
Climate: Temperate, generally between −17°C and 21°C (*0°F and 70°F*). Often foggy and windy. In Amsterdam, average maximum 4°C (*40°F*) (January) to 20°C (*69°F*) (July), minimum 1°C (*34°F*) (January, February) to 15°C (*59°F*) (July, August). November, December, January rainiest (each 19 days). Absolute maximum temperature 38·6°C (*101·5°F*), Warnsveld, 23 Aug 1944; absolute minimum −27·4°C (*−17·3°F*), Winterswijk, 27 Jan 1942.
Labour force: 4 670 000 in 1986: Agriculture, fishing 5·8%; Manufacturing 19·5%; Construction 7·3%; Trade 17·9%; Public sector 15·8%.
Gross domestic product: 429·6 billion guilders in 1986: Agriculture and fisheries 4%; Industry 35%; Services 45%.

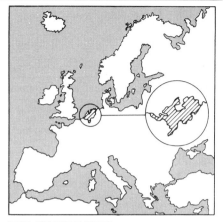

THE NETHERLANDS

Exports: 196 977 million guilders in 1986: Food, drink and live animals 17·7%; Fuel and gas 15·2%; Chemicals 17·2%; Basic manufactures 13·6%; Machinery and transport equipment 19·8%.
Monetary unit: Netherlands gulden (guilder) or florin. 1 guilder = 100 cents.
Denominations:
Coins 5, 10, 25 cents; 1, 2½ guilders.
Notes 5, 10, 25, 50, 100, 250, 1000 guilders.
Political history and government: A constitutional and hereditary monarchy. Legislative power is held by the bicameral States-General. The First Chamber has 75 members indirectly elected for 4 years by the 12 Provincial Councils. The Second Chamber has 150 members directly elected by universal suffrage for 4 years (subject to dissolution), using proportional representation. The Head of State has mainly formal prerogatives and executive power is exercised by the Council of Ministers, which is responsible to the States-General. The monarch appoints the Prime Minister and, on the latter's recommendation, other Ministers. Each of the 12 provinces is administered by an appointed Governor and an elected Council.
Length of roadways: 111 891 km (*69 484 miles*) (1985).
Length of railways: 2867 km (*1780 miles*) (1985).
Universities: 21 universities and institutions of university status.
Defence: Military service: Army 14 months, Navy and Air Force 14–17 months; total armed forces 108 700 (1987); defence expenditure: 7·9% of total government expenditure in 1987.
Foreign tourists: 3 126 900 in 1986.

Netherlands External Territories

Aruba

Population: 67 000 (1983 estimate).
Area: 193 km² (*74·5 miles²*).
Capital city: Oranjestad, population 17 000 in 1985.
Other principal town: Sint Nicolaas 17 000.
NB: Aruba was constitutionally separated from the

Netherlands Antilles on 1 Jan 1986. The island will
gain independence after 1 Jan 1996.

Netherlands Antilles

Population: 183 000 (1985 estimate).
Area: 800 km² (*309 miles²*).
(Curaçao 444 km² (*170 miles²*), Bonaire 288 km² (*110 miles²*), St Maarten 34 km² (*13 miles²*), St Eustatius 21 km² (*8 miles²*), Saba 13 km² (*5 miles²*)).
Capital city: Willemstad (on Curaçao), population 50 000 in 1985.
Other principal towns (1986): Philipsburg (on Sint Maarten) 6000, Kralendijk (on Bonaire) 1200, Oranjestad (on St Eustatius), Leverock (on Saba).

New Zealand

Official name: Dominion of New Zealand.
Population: 3 320 000 (1987 estimate).
Area: 268 676 km² (*103 736 miles²*).
Languages: English, Maori.
Religions: Church of England, Presbyterian, Roman Catholic.
Capital city: Wellington, population 351 400 (1987 estimate).
Other principal towns (1987): Auckland 889 200; Christchurch 333 200; Hamilton 169 000; Dunedin 113 200; Napier-Hastings 115 700; Palmerston North 93 700.
Highest point: Mt Cook, 3764 m (*12 349 ft*).
Principal mountain range: Southern Alps.
Principal rivers: Waikato, Clutha (338 km (*210 miles*), Waihou, Rangitaiki, Mokau, Wanganui, Rangitikei, Manawatu.
Head of State: HM Queen Elizabeth II, represented by the Most Rev. Sir Paul Reeves, Governor-General.
Prime Minister: The Rt Hon. David Russell Lange (b. 1942).
Climate: Temperate and moist. Moderate temperatures (annual averages 11°C (*52°F*) except in the hotter far north. Small seasonal variations. In Wellington, January and February warmest (13°C to 20°C *56°F to 69°F*), July coolest (5°C to 12°C *42°F to 53°F*) and rainiest (18 days), February driest (nine days). In Auckland, average maximum 13°C (*56°F*) (July) to 23°C (*73°F*) (January, February), minimum 8°C (*46°F*) (July, August) to 15°C (*60°F*) (January, February), July rainiest (21 days).
Labour force: 1 371 000 in 1984: Agriculture, forestry and fishing 10·4%; Manufacturing 22%; Construction 6·4%; Trade 16·1%; Transport, storage and communications 7·5%; Financial services 7·2%; Community, social and personal services 22%; Unemployed 5·7%.
Gross domestic product: NZ$44 869 million in 1985–6: Agriculture, forestry and fishing 9·3%; Manufacturing 22·4%; Trade 19%; Financial services 17·1%; Community, social and personal services 16%.
Exports: NZ$10 139 in 1985/6: Meat and meat products 17·1%; Dairy products 7·9%; Fruit and vegetables 6·4%; Wool 12·6%; Forest products 7·2%.
Monetary unit: New Zealand dollar (NZ$). 1 dollar = 100 cents.
Denominations:
Coins 1, 2, 5, 10, 20, 50 cents.
Notes 1, 2, 5, 10, 20, 50, 100 dollars.

NEW ZEALAND

Political history and government: A former British colony. Became a dominion, under the British crown, on 26 Sept 1907. Fully independent, within the Commonwealth, under the Statute of Westminster, promulgated in the United Kingdom on 11 Dec 1931 and accepted by New Zealand on 25 Nov 1947. Executive power is vested in the British monarch and exercisable by the Governor-General, who is appointed on the recommendation of the Prime Minister and acts in almost all matters on the advice of the Executive Council (Cabinet), led by the Prime Minister. Legislative power is held by the unicameral House of Representatives, with 97 members (including four Maoris) elected by universal adult suffrage for three years (subject to dissolution). The Governor-General appoints the Prime Minister and, on the latter's recommendation, other Ministers. The Cabinet is responsible to the House. New Zealand is divided into 22 regions – 2 of which (Wellington and Auckland) are governed by directly-elected councils; the other 20 have councils appointed by the smaller second-tier authorities into which they are divided.
Length of roadways: 92 971 km (*57 735 miles*) (1986).
Length of railways: 4273 km (*2654 miles*).
Universities: 6.
Defence: Military service: voluntary, supplemented by Territorial Army service of 12 weeks basic, 20 days per year; total armed forces 12 600 (1987); defence expenditure: NZ$1060 million in 1986/7.
Foreign tourists: 750 000 in 1986.

New Zealand Dependencies

Cook Islands

Location: In the southern Pacific Ocean, between about 2816 km (*1750 miles*) and 3782 km (*2350 miles*) north-east of New Zealand, between 8°S and 23°S, and 156°W and 167°W. Comprises 15 atolls or islands (Northern group 7, Lower group 8).
Area: 237 km² (*91·5 miles²*). Main islands are Rarotonga (6718 ha *16 602 acres*), Mangaia (5180 ha

12800 acres), Atiu (2693 ha *6654 acres),* Mitiaro (2226 ha *5500 acres),* Mauke (Parry Is.) (1842 ha *4552 acres),* Aitutaki (1805 ha *4461 acres)* and Penrhyn (Tongareva) (985 ha *2432 acres).*
Population: 17 185 (1986); approx. 24 500 Cook Islanders in New Zealand (1982).
Chief Town: Avarua, on Rarotonga Island.

Niue

Location: Niue Island is in the southern Pacific Ocean, 2161 km *(1343 miles)* north of Auckland, New Zealand, between Tonga and the Cook Islands.
Area: 64 028 acres (259 km² *(100·04 miles²).*
Population: 2531 (1986 census); approx. 10 000 Niueans in New Zealand (1982).
Capital: Alofi, population 986 in 1981.

Tokelau

Location: Tokelau (formerly known as Tokelau Islands) consist of three atolls in the central Pacific Ocean, about 483 km *(300 miles)* north of Western Samoa.
Area: Approximately 1010 ha *(2500 acres)* (Nukunonu 545 ha *(1350 acres),* Fakaofo 260 ha *(650 acres),* Atafu 200 ha *(500 acres)),* or about 10 km² *(4 miles²).*
Population: 1690 in 1986.

Nicaragua

Official name: República de Nicaragua.
Population: 3 272 000 (1985 estimate).
Area: 148 000 km² *(57 150 miles²).*
Language: Spanish; English/Miskito on the Atlantic Coast.
Religion: Roman Catholic; Protestant minority.
Capital city: Managua, population 682 111 (1985 estimate).
Other principal towns (1985): León 100 982; Granada 88 636; Masaya 74 946; Chinandega 67 792.
Highest point: Pico Mogotón, 2107 m *(6913 ft).*
Principal mountain ranges: Cordillera Isabelia, Cordillera de Darién.
Principal rivers: Coco (Segovia) (482 km *300 miles),* Rio Grande, Escondido, San Juan.
Head of State: Daniel Ortega Saavedra, President.
Climate: Tropical (hot and humid) with average annual temperature of 26°C *(78°F).* Rainy season May–December. Annual rainfall 2540 mm *(100 in)* on east coast. In Managua, annual average over 27°C *(80°F)* all year round.
Labour force: 813 000 (excluding unemployed) in 1980: Agriculture, forestry and fishing 42%; Manufacturing 16%; Trade, restaurants and hotels 13%; Community, social and personal services 18%.
Gross domestic product: 435 742·3 million cordobas in 1986: Agriculture, forestry and fishing 20·8%; Manufacturing 27·7%; Trade 23·9%; Services 17·5%.
Exports: US$242·5 million: Coffee 43·3%; Cotton 17·7%.
Monetary unit: Córdoba. 1 córdoba = 100 centavos. Owing to hyperinflation a new currency, the New Córdoba, has been introduced (1988).
Denominations:
Coins 5, 10, 25, 50 centavos; 1 córdoba.
Notes 10, 20, 50, 100, 500, 1000 córdobas.

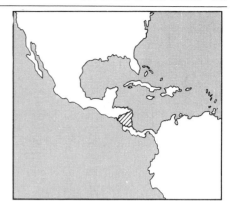

NICARAGUA

Political history and government: A republic comprising 16 departments and one territory. At the government's request, US forces intervened in Nicaragua in 1912 and established bases. They left in 1925 but returned in 1927, when a guerrilla group, led by Augusto César Sandino, was organized to oppose the US occupation. The US forces finally left in 1933, when their role was assumed by a newly-created National Guard, commanded by Gen. Anastasio Somoza García. Sandino was assassinated in 1934, apparently on Somoza's orders, but his followers ('Sandinistas') remained active in opposing the new régime. Somoza became President in 1936 and, either in person or through nominees, held power until his assassination by a 'Sandinista' in 1956. Political power, exercised within a constitutional framework, was retained by a member of the Somoza family, either directly as President or as Commander of the National Guard. From 1960 the régime was opposed by a guerrilla group which in 1962 formed the *Frente Sandinista de Liberación Nacional* (FSLN), the Sandinist National Liberation Front. General Anastasio Somoza Debayle, son of the former dictator, was President from 1967 to 1972 and again from 1 Dec 1974. The FSLN allied with other opponents of the régime in 1977. Armed clashes with the National Guard developed into civil war. After 6 months of heavy fighting, President Somoza resigned and left the country on 17 July 1979. The President of the National Congress was nominated as interim President but he left after two days, when the capital fell to the Sandinistas.

The guerrilla groups had formed a provisional Junta of National Reconstruction (initially five members) on 16 June 1979. The Junta named a Provisional Governing Council on 16 July and this Council took office as the Government of National Reconstruction on 20 July 1979. The 1974 constitution was abrogated and the bicameral National Congress (a Senate and a Chamber of Deputies) dissolved. The National Guard was also dissolved, being replaced by the 'Sandinista People's Army', officially established on 22 Aug 1979.

On taking office, the junta published a Basic Statute, providing for the creation of an appointed 33-member Council of State to act as an interim legislature and to draft a new constitution. On 21 Aug 1979 the junta issued a 'Statute on Rights and Guarantees for the Citizens of Nicaragua', promising a wide range of democratic reforms. Elections took place in March 1985, and a new constituion was approved in November 1986, and enacted from January 1987. This provides for a single Chamber National Assembly of 90 members directly elected by proportional representation and for a President and Vice-President directly elected for a 6-year term. This has not yet been put into force and civil liberties were suspended during the state of emergency. Anti-government forces, the Contras, continued to make incursions into Nicaragua and in November 1987 the Government agreed to engage in indirect talks with the Contra leaders. In January 1988 the state of emergency was lifted and in February 1988, following the cessation of military aid to the Contras, hostilities greatly decreased.

Length of roadways: 25 000 km (*15 500 miles*) (1984).
Length of railways: 321 km (*199 miles*) (1987).
Universities: 3.
Adult illiteracy: Approx. 12·5% after the 1980 literacy campaign.
Defence: Total armed forces 78 400 (1987); compulsory military service 2 years; defence expenditure: US$436 million in 1986 – the Government also receives military aid from Eastern bloc countries.
Foreign tourists: 100 000 in 1985.

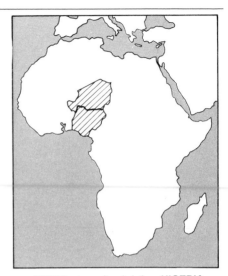

top: **NIGER** *immediately below:* **NIGERIA**

Niger

Official name: République du Niger.
Population: 6 608 000 (1987 estimate).
Area: 1 267 000 km² (*489 191 miles²*).
Languages: French (official), Hausa, Tuareg, Djerma, Fulani.
Religions: Islam (Sunni) 85%; Animist, Christian.
Capital city: Niamey, population 399 100 (1983 estimate).
Other principal towns (1983): Zinder 82 800; Maradi 65 100; Tahoua 41 900; Agadèz 27 000.
Highest point: Mont Gréboun, 2000 m (*6562 ft*).
Principal mountain ranges: Aïr (Azbine), Plateau du Djado.
Principal rivers: Niger (595 km *370 miles* in Niger), Dillia.
Head of State: Col. Ali Seybou, President of the Supreme Military Council and Chairman of the Council of Ministers.
Prime Minister: Hamid Algabid.
Climate: Hot and dry. Average temperature 29°C (*84°F*). In Niamey, average maximum 34°C (*93°F*) (January) to 42°C (*108°F*) (April).
Labour force: 3 282 000 in 1986: Agriculture, forestry and fishing 88·9%.
Gross domestic product: 653 400 million CFA francs in 1982: Agriculture, forestry and fishing 49%; Mining and quarrying 9·9%; Trade 11·7%; Public administration and defence 8%.
Exports: 119 495 million CFA francs in 1984: Live animals 9·2%; Uranium ore 77·8%.
Monetary unit: Franc de la Communauté financière africaine.
Denominations:
Coins 1, 2, 5, 10, 25, 50, 100 CFA francs.
Notes 50, 100, 500, 1000, 5000 CFA francs.
Political history and government: Formerly part of French West Africa, independent since 3 Aug 1960. Under military rule since 15 Apr 1974, when the constitution was suspended and the National

Assembly dissolved. Niger is ruled by a Supreme Military Council, composed of 12 army officers, which has appointed a provisional government. A 150-member Development Council is drawing up a new constitution. The country has 16 administrative districts.
Length of roadways: 19 000 km (*11 800 miles*) (1986).
Universities: 1.
Adult illiteracy: 80·6% in 1985.
Defence: Total armed forces 3150 (1987); defence expenditure: 5300 million CFA francs in 1985.
Foreign tourists: 50 453 in 1984.

Nigeria

Official name: The Federal Republic of Nigeria.
Population: 98 517 000 (1986 estimate).
Area: 923 768 km² (*356 669 miles²*).
Languages: English (official), Hausa, Ibo, Yoruba and other linguistic groups.
Religions: Islam (Sunni), Christian.
Capital city: Lagos, population 1 097 000 (in 1983). A new federal capital is currently under construction at Abuja, and is expected to be completed by 1990.
Other principal towns (1983): Ibadan 1 060 000; Ogbomosho 527 400; Kano 487 100; Oshogbo 344 500; Ilorin 343 900; Abeokuta 308 800; Port Harcourt 296 200; Zaria 274 000; Ilesha 273 400; Onitsha 268 700; Ado-Ekiti 265 800; Iwo 261 600; Kaduna 247 100.
Highest point: Dimlang, 2042 m (*6700 ft*).
Principal mountain range: Jos Plateau.
Principal rivers: Niger (4184 km *2600 miles* in total length), Benue, Cross.
Head of State: Maj.-Gen. Ibrahim Babangida, President.
Climate: On the coast it is hot (average daily maximum temperature at Lagos 32°C (*89°F*) and unpleasantly humid. In the north it is drier and semi-tropical. Annual rainfall ranges from 625 to 3800 mm (*25 to 150 in*).

Labour force: 33 708 000 (1984 estimate): Agriculture, forestry and fishing 50%.
Gross domestic product: 48 651 million naira in 1983–4: Agriculture, forestry and fishing 25%; Mining and quarrying 20·4%; Manufacturing 4·9%; Trade 21·6%.
Exports: 11 720·8 million naira in 1982: Petroleum 96·7%; Cocoa 2·1%.
Monetary unit: Naira. 1 naira = 100 kobo.
Denominations:
Coins ½, 1, 5, 10, 25 kobo.
Notes 50 kobo; 1, 5, 10, 20 naira.
Political history and government: In 1914 the British dependencies of Northern and Southern Nigeria were unified. In 1947 the United Kingdom introduced a new Nigerian constitution, establishing a federal system of government based on three regions. The Federation of Nigeria became independent, within the Commonwealth, on 1 Oct 1960. The northern part of the British-administered Trust Territory of Cameroon was incorporated into the Northern Region of Nigeria on 1 June 1961. A fourth region was created by dividing the Western Region under legislation approved on 8 Aug 1963. The country became a republic, under its present name, on 1 Oct 1963. The government was overthrown by a military *coup* on 15 Jan 1966 and power was assumed by a Supreme Military Council (SMC), ruling by decree. Political parties were banned on 24 May 1966. The four regions were replaced by 12 States on 1 Apr 1968. These were reorganized into 19 States on 17 Mar 1976.

The SMC published a draft constitution on 7 Oct 1976. Local government councils were elected (directly in some States, indirectly in others) in November–December 1976. A constituent assembly of 233 members (203 selected by the local councils on 31 Aug 1977, 22 nominated by the SMC and 8 from the constitutional drafting committee) was inaugurated on 6 Oct 1977 to finalize the constitution in preparation for a return to civilian rule. The assembly closed on 5 June 1978. A new constitution was issued on 21 Sept 1978, when the régime ended the ban on political parties and the state of emergency in force since 1966.

The constitution came into force on 1 Oct 1979, when military rule was ended and the civilian President sworn in. The National Assembly opened on 9 Oct 1979. Elections were held in August 1983, but in December 1983 the military took over control again, and in January 1984 an 18-member Supreme Military Council was sworn in. This was subsequently superseded by a 29-man Armed Forces Ruling Council, which includes the president. The AFRC appoints a National Council of Ministers, as well as the military governors for the 19 states and the Abuja Federal Territory; these latter appoint state executive councils. It is proposed that civilian rule be reintroduced in 1992.
Length of roadways: 107 990 km (*67 116 miles*) (1980).
Length of railways: 3505 km (*2178 miles*).
Universities: 24.
Adult illiteracy: 35% in 1984.
Defence: Military service voluntary; total armed forces 94 000 (1987); defence expenditure, 809·8 million naira in 1987.
Foreign tourists: 890 000 in 1986.

Norway

Official name: Kongeriket Norge (Kingdom of Norway).
Population: 4 174 005 (1987 estimate).
Area: 386 958 km² (*149 469 miles²*) (including Svalbard and Jan Mayen).
Languages: Norwegian; small Lapp minority.
Religion: Lutheran.
Capital city: Oslo, population 451 099 (1987 estimate).
Other principal towns (1987): Bergen 208 809; Trondheim 134 496; Stavanger 95 437; Kristiansand 63 293; Drammen 51 324.
Highest point: Galdhøpiggen 2469 m (*8098 ft*).
Principal mountain range: Langfjellene.
Principal rivers: Glomma (Glama) (598 km *372 miles*), Lågen (337 km *209 miles*), Tanaelv (360 km *224 miles*).
Head of State: HM King Olav V, KG, KT, GCB, GCVO (b. 2 July 1903), succeeded on the death of his father King Haakon VII on 21 Sept 1957. Crown Prince: HRH Prince Harald (b. 21 Feb 1937), only son of King Olav.
Prime Minister: Mrs Gro Harlem Brundtland (b. 20 Apr 1939).
Climate: Temperate on coast, but cooler inland. In Oslo, average maximum −1°C (*30°F*) (January) to 23°C (*73°F*) (July), minimum −7°C (*20°F*) (January, February) to 13°C (*56°F*) (July), August rainiest (11 days). Absolute maximum temperature 35°C (*95°F*), Oslo, 21 July 1901, and Trondheim, 22 July 1901; absolute minimum −51·4°C (*−60·5°F*), Karasjok, 1 Jan 1886.
Labour force: 2 086 000 in 1986: Agriculture, forestry and fishing 6·3%; Manufacturing 17·2%; Construction 7·4%; Commerce and finance 18%; Government and business services 34·1%.
Gross domestic product: 516 022 million kroner in 1986: Agriculture, forestry and fishing 3·7%; Crude petroleum and natural gas 10·1%; Manufacturing 15·4%; Wholesale and retail trade 12·9%; Services 35·1%.
Exports: 133 847·4 million kroner in 1986: Fish 6·1%; Petroleum and petroleum products 23·3%; Natural gas 18·9%; Basic manufactures 18·3%; Machinery and transport equipment 17·7%.

NORWAY

Monetary unit: Norwegian krone (plural: kroner). 1 krone = 100 øre.
Denominations:
Coins 50 øre; 1, 5, 10 kroner.
Notes 50, 100, 500, 1000 kroner.
Political history and government: Formerly linked with Sweden. Independence declared on 7 June 1905; union with Sweden ended on 26 Oct 1905. Norway is a constitutional monarchy, headed by an hereditary King. Legislative power is held by the unicameral Parliament (*Storting*), with 157 members elected for 4 years by universal adult suffrage, using proportional representation. For the consideration of legislative proposals, the *Storting* divides itself into two chambers by choosing one quarter of its members to form the *Lagting* (upper house), the remainder forming the *Odelsting* (lower house). Executive power is nominally held by the King but is exercised by the Council of Ministers (*Statsråd*), led by the Prime Minister, who are appointed by the King in accordance with the will of the *Storting*, to which the Council is responsible. Norway comprises 19 counties.
Length of roadways: 86 143 km (*53 495 miles*) (1986).
Length of railways: 4219 km (*2620 miles*) (1986).
Universities: 4 plus 10 colleges of equivalent status.
Defence: Military service: Army 12 months; Navy and Air Force 12–15 months; total armed forces 34 500 in 1987; defence expenditure: 18 460 million kroner in 1987.

Oman

Official name: Sultanat 'Uman (Sultanate of Oman).
Population: 1 242 000 (1985 estimate) but no census has ever been held.
Area: 212 457 km² (*82 030 miles²*).
Language: Arabic.
Religion: Islam (Sunni).
Capital city: Masqat (Muscat), population 50 000.
Other principal towns: Matrah; Salalah.
Highest point: Jabal ash Sham, 3170 m (*10 400 ft*).
Principal mountain ranges: Jabal Akhdas ('Green Mountains').
Head of State: HM Sultan Qabus ibn Sa'id (b. 18 Nov 1940), succeeded his father Sultan Said bin Taimur 23 July 1970 in a palace *coup*.
Climate: Extremely hot summers (temperatures rising to 55°C *130°F*) and mild winters. Cooler in the mountains. Average annual rainfall 75 to 150 mm (*3 to 6 in*).
Labour force: estimated at 150 000 in 1972.
Gross domestic product: 2831·9 million Omani rials in 1986: Crude petroleum 33·5%; Trade 13·5%; Financial services 10·1%; Government services 17·5%.
Exports: 1092·6 million Omani rials in 1986: Petroleum 89·8%.
Monetary unit: Rial Omani. 1 rial = 1000 baiza.
Denominations:
Coins 5, 10, 25, 50, 100, 250, 500 baiza.
Notes 100, 250, 500 baiza; 1, 5, 10, 20, 50 rials.
Political history and government: A sultanate, formerly called Muscat and Oman, under British influence since the 19th century. Full independence was recognized by the treaty of friendship with the UK on 20 Dec 1951. The port and peninsula of

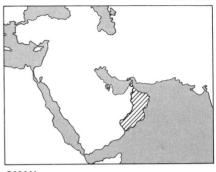

OMAN

Gwadur were ceded to Pakistan on 8 Sept 1958. Sultan Sa'id ibn Taimur was deposed by his son, Qabus, on 23 July 1970 and the country adopted its present name on 9 Aug 1970. The Sultan is an absolute ruler and legislates by decree. He is advised by an appointed Cabinet. On 20 Oct 1981 Sultan Qabus issued decrees creating a State Advisory Council, with 45 members nominated for 2 years. There are no political parties.
Length of roadways: 22 696 km (*14 094 miles*) (1986).
Universities: 1.
Defence: Military service voluntary; total armed forces 21 500 (1987); defence expenditure: 533 million rials in 1988.

Pakistan

Official name: Islami Jamhuria-e-Pakistan (Islamic Republic of Pakistan). 'Pakistan' means 'land of the pure' in the Urdu language.
Population: 99 163 000 (1986 estimate).
Area: 888 102 km² (*333 897 miles²*) – figure includes the Pakistani-held areas of Kashmir (known as Azad Kashmir) and Northern Areas.
Languages: Urdu (national), Punjabi, Pashto, Baluchi, Sindhi, English (official).
Religions: Islam (Sunni) 97·1%; Hindu 1·6%; Christian 1·3% (1961).
Capital city: Islamabad, population 201 000 (1981 census).
Other principal towns (1981): Kashmir 5 103 000; Lahore 2 922 000; Faisalabad 1 092 000; Rawalpindi 806 000; Hyderabad 795 000; Multan 730 000; Gujranwala 597 000; Peshawar 555 000.
Highest point: K2 (Mt Godwin Austen), 8611 m (*28 250 ft*) (first climbed 31 July 1954).
Principal mountain ranges: Hindu Kush, Pamirs, Karakoram.
Principal rivers: Indus and tributaries (Sutlej, Chenab, Ravi, Jhelum).
Head of State: Ghulam Ishaq Khan.
Prime Minister: Miss Benazir Bhutto.
Climate: Dry, and generally hot, with average temperature of 27°C (*80°F*) except in the mountains, which have very cold winters. Temperatures range from −1°C (*30°F*) in winter to 49°C (*120°F*) in summer. In Karachi, June warmest (averages 28°C to 34°C *82°F to 93°F*), January coolest (13°C to 25°C *55°F to 77°F*), rainfall negligible throughout the year. In Lahore, average maximum 21°C (*69°F*) (January) to 41°C (*106°F*) (June), minimum 5°C

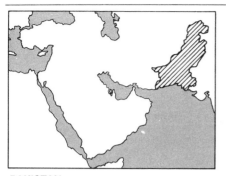

PAKISTAN

(*40°F*) (December, January) to 27°C (*80°F*) (July), July and August rainiest (each six days). Absolute maximum temperature 53°C (*127°F*), Jacobabad, 12 June 1919.

Labour force: 28 596 000 in 1985: Agriculture, forestry and fishing 50·7%; Manufacturing 12·9%; Trade 11·5%; Community, personal and social services 9·8%.

Gross domestic product: 537 275 million rupees in 1986–7: Agriculture and livestock 23%; Manufacturing 17·7%; Trade 16·6%; Public administration and defence 8·9%.

Exports: 50 815·8 million rupees in 1986–7: Raw cotton 15·1%; Cotton fabrics and cotton yarn and thread 28·9%; Carpets and rugs 6·7%.

Monetary unit: Pakistani rupee. 1 rupee = 100 paisa.

Denominations:

Coins 1, 2, 5, 10, 25, 50 paisa; 1 rupee.

Notes 1, 2, 5, 10, 50, 100, 500 rupees.

Political history and government: Pakistan was created as an independent dominion within the Commonwealth on 15 Aug 1947, when former British India was partitioned. Originally in two parts, East and West Pakistan, the country became a republic on 23 Mar 1956. The port and peninsula of Gwadur were ceded to Pakistan by Muscat and Oman (now Oman) on 8 Sept 1958. Military rule was imposed on 27 Oct 1958. Elections for a Constituent Assembly were held on 7 Dec 1970, giving a majority to the Awami League, which sought autonomy for East Pakistan. After negotiations on a coalition government failed, East Pakistan declared independence as Bangladesh on 26 Mar 1971. Following Indian intervention on behalf of the Bengalis, Pakistan's forces surrendered on 16 Dec 1971, when Bangladesh's independence became a reality. Pakistan was confined to the former western wing. Military rule ended on 20 Dec 1971. Zulfiqar Ali Bhutto became President and Prime Minister. Pakistan left the Commonwealth on 30 Jan 1972. A new constitution came into force on 14 Aug 1973. Under this constitution, Pakistan became a federal republic comprising four provinces (each under a Governor) plus the Federal Capital Territory and 'tribal areas' under federal administration. President Bhutto took office as executive Prime Minister, whose advice was binding on the constitutional President. On 5 July 1977 the government was deposed by a military *coup*. A martial law régime was established, with Gen. Mohammad Zia ul-Haq, the Army Chief of Staff, as Chief Martial Law Administrator. The constitution was suspended, although the President remained in office, and a 4-

man Military Council was formed to direct the government. The Federal legislature (a Senate and a National Assembly) and provincial Assemblies were dissolved. Gen. Zia appointed a mainly civilian Cabinet on 5 July 1978. The President resigned on 16 Sept 1978, when Gen. Zia assumed his office. He announced on 23 Mar 1979 that general elections would be held on 17 Nov. Bhutto, the former Prime Minister, was executed (following conviction on a murder charge) on 4 Apr 1979. Local elections, on a non-party basis, were held on 20–27 Sept 1979. The President announced on 16 Oct 1979 that general elections were postponed indefinitely, political parties dissolved and political activity banned. On 24 Mar 1981 he promulgated an interim constitution. This provided for an advisory Federal Council, to be nominated by the President. On 24 Oct 1981 President Zia announced that the Council would draft a new constitution. Martial law was lifted at the end of 1985. In 1988, President Zia was killed in an air crash the cause of which has still not been determined. The Chairman of The Senate, Ghulam Ishaq Khan, became Acting President under the terms of the Constitution. Elections were held and were won by the Pakistan People's Party led by Miss Benazir Bhutto, daughter of President Bhutto. Miss Bhutto was sworn in as Prime Minister. Ghulam Ishaq Khan became President.

Length of roadways: 103 428 km (*64 229 miles*) (1986).

Length of railways: 12 660 km (*7862 miles*) (1987).

Universities: 22.

Adult illiteracy: 70·4% (1985).

Defence: Military service voluntary; total armed forces 480 600 in 1987; defence expenditure: 44 252 million rupees in 1987/8.

Foreign tourists: 432 000 in 1986.

Panama

Official name: La República de Panamá.

Population: 2 274 448 (1987 estimate).

Area: 78 046 km² (*30 134 miles²*).

Language: Spanish.

Religions: Roman Catholic, Protestant minority.

Capital city: Panamá (City), population 542 754 at 1980 census.

Other principal towns (1980): Colón, population 59 043; David 50 621.

Highest point: Volcán de Chiriquí, 3475 m (*11 467 ft*).

Principal mountain ranges: Serrania de Tabasará, Cordillera de San Blas.

Principal rivers: Tuira (with Chucunaque), Bayano, Santa María.

Head of State: Manuel Solis Palma, President.

Climate: Warm, humid days with cool nights. Little seasonal temperature change. Absolute maximum temperature 36·7°C (*98°F*) at Madden Dam, in the former Canal Zone, 13 Apr 1920, and Panamá (City), 16 Apr 1958; absolute minimum 15°C (*59°F*) at Madden Dam, 4 Feb 1924.

Labour force: 681 100 in 1987: Agriculture, forestry and fishing 26·6%; Manufacturing 10·4%; Trade 16%; Community, social and personal services 28%.

Gross domestic product: 5288 million balboas in 1986: Agriculture, forestry and fishing 9·3%; Manufacturing 8·2%; Trade 13·7%; Transport, storage and communications 19·5%; Financial services 18·7%; Government services 14·8%.

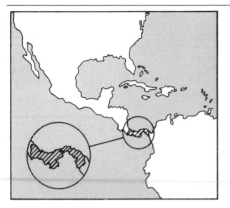

PANAMA

Exports: 326 864 million balboas in 1986: Sugar 6·1%; Bananas 21·4%; Coffee 9·3%; Shrimps 20·8%.
Monetary unit: Balboa. 1 balboa = 100 centésimos.
Denominations:
Coins 1, 5, 10, 25, 50 centésimos; 1, 100 balboas.
Notes US$1, 2, 5, 10, 20, 50, 100 (there are no Panamanian bank notes).
Political history and government: Formerly part of Colombia, independence declared on 3 Nov 1903. The elected President was deposed by a *coup* on 11–12 Oct 1968, when power was seized by the National Guard, led by Col. (later Brig.-Gen.) Omar Torrijos Herrera. A Provisional Junta was established, the National Assembly dissolved and political activity suspended. Political parties were abolished in February 1969. On 6 Aug 1972 elections were held for a National Assembly of Community Representatives (505 members to hold office for six years) to approve a new constitution. On 13 Sept 1972 the Assembly approved measures to legalize, for a transitional period of six years from 11 Oct 1972, the assumption of full executive authority by Gen. Torrijos as Chief of Government and Supreme Leader of the Panamanian Revolution. A new Assembly was elected on 6 Aug 1978, although political parties were still banned. On 11 Oct 1978 Torrijos resigned as Chief of Government (although remaining Commander of the National Guard until his death in an air crash on 31 July 1981) and the Assembly elected a new President, with full governing powers, for six eyars. Three political parties were legally registered in March–June 1979. The National Legislative Council, which performs the National Assembly's functions when the Assembly is not in session, was increased from 38 members (all appointed from the Assembly) when elections were held on 28 Sept 1980 for 19 additional seats, with political parties contesting for the first time since 1968. Full legislative elections and a direct presidential election took place in 1984. In February 1988 Gen. Noriega, the commander of the defence forces and the *de facto* ruler of Panama, deposed the elected President and replaced him with President Solis. Elections (May 1988) were declared null and void. Amid considerable public disorder, Gen. Noriego remains *de facto* ruler of Panama.
  Territorial jurisdiction over the Canal Zone was granted to the USA 'in perpetuity' by treaty of 18 Nov 1903. Treaties to restore Panamanian rule were signed on 7 Sept 1977 and approved by a referendum in Panama on 23 Oct 1977. Under these treaties, ratified on 16 June 1978, the Zone reverted to Panama on 1 Oct 1979. The Panama Canal itself is to be administrered by a joint US-Panamanian commission until 31 Dec 1999.
Length of roadways: 9694 km (*6020 miles*) (1986).
Length of railways: 578 km (*359 miles*) (1984).
Universities: 3.
Adult illiteracy: 11·8% in 1985.
Defence: Total armed forces (including a paramilitary National Guard) 14 000 (1987); defence expenditure: US$104·6 million in 1987.
Foreign tourists: 318 489 in 1986.

Papua New Guinea

Official name: The Independent State of Papua New Guinea.
Population: 3 479 400 (1987 estimate).
Area: 462 840 km² (*178 704 miles²*).
Languages: English (official), Pidgin, Moru.
Religion: Christian 92·8% (1966).
Capital city: Port Moresby, population 145 300 (1987 estimate).
Other principal towns (1980): Lae 61 617; Rabaul 14 954; Madang 21 335; Mt Hagen 13 441.
Highest point: Mt Wilhelm, 4694 m (*15 400 ft*).
Principal mountain range: Bismarck Range.
Principal rivers: Fly (with Strickland), Sepik (1110 km *690 miles*).
Head of State: HM Queen Elizabeth II, represented by Sir Kingsford Dibela, KGM, Governor-General.
Prime Minister: Rabbie Namaliu.
Climate: Generally hot and humid, cooler in highlands. Average annual rainfall between 1000 and 6350 mm (*40 and 250 in*). In Port Moresby, average maximum temperature 28°C (*82°F*) (August) to 32°C (*90°F*) (December), minimum 23°C (*73°F*) (July, August) to 25°C (*76°F*) (November to March), rainiest month is March (9 days).
Labour force: 732 800 in 1980: Agriculture, forestry and fishing 77%; Construction 2·9%; Trade 3·4%; Community, social and personal services 10·5%.
Gross domestic product: 2471·5 million kina in 1986.
Exports: 1 013 776 million kina in 1986: Cocoa beans 5·5%; Coffee 20·1%; Timber 6·2%; Palm oil 2·9%; Copper ore and concentrates 34·9%.
Monetary unit: Kina. 1 kina = 100 toea.
Denominations:
Coins 1, 2, 5, 10, 20 toea; 1 kina.
Notes 2, 5, 20 kina.
Political history and government: Formed by a merger of the Territory of Papua (under Australian rule from 1906) and the Trust Territory of New Guinea, administered by Australia from 1914, later under a trusteeship agreement with the United Nations. A joint administration for the two territories was established by Australia on 1 July 1949. The combined territory achieved self-government on 1 Dec 1973 and became independent, within the Commonwealth, on 16 Sept 1975. Executive authority is vested in the British monarch and exercisable by the Governor-General, who is appointed on the recommendation of the Prime Minister and acts in almost all matters on the advice of the National Executive Council (the Cabinet). Legislative power is vested in the unicameral National Parliament (109 members directly elected for four years by universal adult suffrage). The pre-independence House of Assembly became the first Parliament.

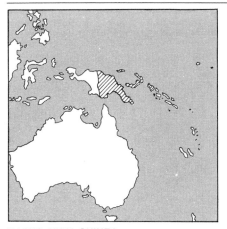

PAPUA NEW GUINEA

The Cabinet is responsible to Parliament, where the Prime Minister, appointed by the Governor-General on Parliament's proposal, must command majority support. Other Ministers are appointed on the Prime Minister's proposal. The country comprises 19 provinces plus the National Capital Territory.
Length of roadways: 19 736 km (*12 256 miles*).
Universities: 2.
Defence: Military service voluntary; total armed forces 3530 (1987); defence expenditure: 33·5 million kina in 1986.
Foreign tourists: 31 900 in 1986.

Paraguay

Official name: La República del Paraguay.
Population: 3 807 000 (1986 estimate).
Area: 406 752 km² (*157 048 miles²*).
Languages: Spanish (official), Guaraní.
Religion: Roman Catholic.
Capital city: Asunción, population 729 307 (1984) – includes suburbs.
Other principal towns (1984): Ciudad Oriental (formerly Puerto Presidente Stroessner) 110 000; Pedro Juan Caballero 80 000; Encarnación 31 400.
Highest point: Cerro Tatug, 700 m (*2297 ft*).
Principal mountain ranges: Cordillera Amambay, Sierra de Maracaju.
Principal rivers: Paraguay (2414 km *1500 miles*), Paraná (4023 km *2500 miles*), Pilcomayo (1609 km *1000 miles*).
Head of State: Gen. Andrés Rodríguez, Acting President.
Climate: Sub-tropical and humid, average temperatures 18°C to 29°C (*65°F to 85°F*). Hot December–March. Cool season May–September. Wet season March–May. In Asunción, average maximum 22°C (*72°F*) (June) to 35°C (*95°F*) (January), minimum 12°C (*53°F*) (June, July) to 22°C (*72°F*) (January, February), October, November and January rainiest (each 8 days).
Labour force: 1 055 650 in 1982: Agriculture, forestry and fishing 40·9%; Manufacturing 11·8%; Construction 6·4%; Trade 8·1%; Community, personal and social services 16%; Unemployed 4·3%.

Gross domestic product: 1 393 890 million guaraníes in 1985: Agriculture, forestry and fishing 29·3%; Manufacturing 16·2%; Trade, finance and insurance 25·9%; Other services 16·3%.
Exports: US$334·5 million in 1984: Cattle products 3·5%; Timber 6·7%; Tobacco 4·6%; Raw cotton 39·2%; Vegetable oils 5·7%; Seeds for industrial use 30·4%.
Monetary unit: Guaraní. 1 guaraní = 100 céntimos.
Denominations:
Coins (issued only for commemorative purposes).
Notes 1, 5, 10, 50, 100, 500, 1000, 5000, 10 000 guaraníes.
Political history and government: A republic comprising 16 departments. Gen. Alfredo Stroessner Mattiauda assumed power by a military *coup* on 5 May 1954. He was elected President on 11 July 1954 to complete his predecessor's term. President Stroessner was re-elected in 1958, 1963, 1968, 1973, 1978, 1983 and 1988. A new constitution was promulgated on 25 Aug 1967 and took effect in 1968. Legislative power is held by a bicameral National Congress, whose members serve for 5 years. The Senate has 30 members and the Chamber of Deputies 60 members. The party receiving the largest number of votes (since 1947 the National Republican Association, known as the Colorado Party) is allotted two-thirds of the seats in each chamber, the remaining seats being divided proportionately among the other contending parties. Executive power is held by the President, directly elected for 5 years at the same time as the Congress. He rules with the assistance of an appointed Council of State. The state of siege in force since 1947 was lifted in April 1987. President Stroessner was overthrown in a military *coup* in February 1989. Elections were scheduled for May 1989.
Length of roadways: 11 320 km (*7035 miles*) (1983).
Length of railways: 441 km (*274 miles*).
Universities: 2.

left: **PERU**   *centre:* **PARAGUAY**

Adult illiteracy: 12·5% in 1985.
Defence: Military service: 18 months (Navy 2 years); total armed forces 17 050 (1987); defence expenditure: 4·1% of total government expenditure in 1986.
Foreign tourists: 262 689 in 1985.

Peru

Official name: República del Perú.
Population: 20 207 100 (1986 estimate).
Area: 1 285 216 km² (496 225 miles²).
Languages: Spanish, Quéchua, Aymará.
Religion: Roman Catholic.
Capital city: Lima, population 5 008 400 (1985 estimate).
Other principal towns (1985): Arequipa 531 829; Callao 515 200; Trujillo 438 709; Chiclayo 347 702; Piura 256 150; Chimbote 253 289; Cuzco 225 683; Iquitos 215 275.
Highest point: Huascarán, 6768 m (22 205 ft).
Principal mountain ranges: Cordillera de los Andes (C. Oriental, C. Occidental, C. Blanca).
Principal rivers: Amazonas (Amazon), with Ucayali.
Head of State: Alan García Perez (b. 23 May 1949), President.
Prime Minister: Luis Alberto Sanchez.
Climate: Varies with altitude. Daily fluctuations greater than seasonal. Rainy season October–April. Heavy rains in tropical forests. In Lima, average maximum 19°C (66°F) (August) to 28°C (83°F) (February, March), minimum 13°C (56°F) (August) to 19°C (67°F) (February), August rainiest (two days). Absolute maximum temperature 38·5°C (101·3°F), Iquitos, 19 June 1948; absolute minimum −20·2°C (−4·4°F), Imata, 1 Aug 1947.
Labour force: 6 555 000 in 1985: Agriculture, forestry and fishing 36·4%; Manufacturing 10·6%; Trade 12%; Community, social and personal services 20·5%; Unemployed 3·1%.
Gross domestic product: 358 464 million inti in 1986: Agriculture and fishing 13·3%; Mining and petroleum 9·2%; Manufacturing 23·4%; Government 7·7%.
Exports: US$2509 million in 1986: Petroleum and derivatives 9·4%; Copper 17·5%; Zinc 9·8%; Fishmeal 8·2%; Coffee 10·9%.
Monetary unit: Inti. 1 inti = 100 céntimos.
Denominations:
Coins 50 céntimos; 1, 5, 10 inti.
Notes 10, 50, 100, 200, 500 inti.
Political history and government: A republic comprising 23 departments and one province. Following disputed presidential elections on 10 June 1962, a military junta took power in a *coup* on 18 July 1962 and annulled the election results. Congressional and presidential elections were held again on 9 June 1963. Fernando Belaúnde Terry, runner-up in 1956 and 1962, was elected President and took office for a six-year term on 28 July 1963, when military rule ended. On 3 Oct 1968 President Belaúnde was deposed by another military *coup*, led by the army commander, Gen. Juan Velasco Alvarado. The bicameral National Congress was abolished, political activity suspended and a revolutionary government of military officers took power, with

Gen. Velasco as President. Executive and legislative powers were exercised by the armed forces through the President, ruling by decree with the assistance of an appointed Council of Ministers. On 29 Aug 1975 President Velasco was deposed by the Prime Minister, Gen. Francisco Morales Bermúdez.

On 28 July 1977 President Morales announced plans for the restoration of civilian rule. On 18 June 1978 a Constituent Assembly of 100 members was elected by literate adults, using proportional representation. The Assembly was convened on 28 July 1978. It adopted a new constitution on 12 July 1979 and dissolved itself two days later. The constitution vests executive power in a President, elected for a five-year term by universal adult suffrage (including illiterates for the first time). Legislative power is vested in a bicameral National Congress, also directly elected for five years. The Congress comprises the Senate (60 members chosen on a regional basis plus ex-Presidents of constitutional governments) and the Chamber of Deputies (180 members chosen on the basis of proportional representation). Congressional and presidential elections were held on 18 May 1980, when ex-President Belaúnde was re-elected Head of State. Power was transferred to the new civilian authorities on 28 July 1980, when the new constitution came into force. Each of the 24 departments is administered by an appointed official.
Length of roadways: 69 942 km (43 434 miles) (1987).
Length of railways: 2399 km (1490 miles) (1987).
Universities: 35.
Adult illiteracy: 15·2% in 1985.
Defence: Military service: two years, selective; total armed forces 113 000 (including 69 000 conscripts); defence expenditure: 9800 million intis in 1986.
Foreign tourists: 303 601 in 1986.

The Philippines

Official name: República de Filipinas (in Spanish) or Repúblika ñg Pilipinas (in Tagalog): Republic of the Philippines.
Population: 56 004 000 (1986 estimate).
Area: 300 000 km² (115 831 miles²).
Languages: Cebuano; Tagalog; Ilocano; Panay-Hiligaynon; Bikol and about 70 other dialects belonging to the Malayo-Polynesian family of tongues. The national language, Pilipino, is based on Tagalog. English is widely understood and spoken.
Religions (1960): Roman Catholic 84%; Aglipayan 5%; Islam (Sunni) 5%; Protestant 3%.
Capital city: Manila, population 5 925 884 (1980 census).
Other principal towns (1980): (Quezon City 1 165 865 is part of the Manila conurbation); Davao 610 375; Cebu 490 281; Zamboanga 343 722; (Pasay 287 770 is part of the Manila conurbation); Bacolod 262 415; Iloilo 244 827; San Carlos (on Pangasinan) 101 243; San Carlos (on Negros Occidental) 91 627.
Highest point: Mt Apo (on Mindanao), 2953 m (9690 ft).
Principal mountain ranges: Cordillera Central (on Luzon), Diuata Range (on Mindanao).
Principal rivers: Cagayan (290 km 180 miles), Pampanga, Abra, Agusan, Magat, Laoang, Agno.

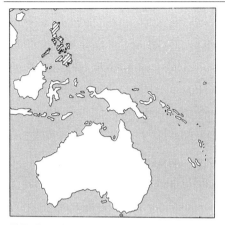

THE PHILIPPINES

Head of State: Mrs Corazon Cojuangco Aquino (b. 25 Jan 1933), President.
Climate: Tropical. Hot and humid, except in mountains. Heavy rainfall, frequent typhoons. In Manila, average maximum 30°C (86°F) (December, January) to 34°C (93°F) (April, May), minimum 21°C (69°F) (January, February) to 24°C (75°F) (May–August), July rainiest (24 days). Absolute maximum temperature 42·2°C (108·0°F), Tuguegarao, 29 Apr 1912; absolute minimum 7·3°C (45·1°F), Baguio City, 1 Feb 1930 and 11 Jan 1932.
Labour force: 20 926 000 in 1986: Agriculture, forestry and fishing 49·8%; Manufacturing 9·1%; Trade 13·6%; Community, social and personal services 17·4%.
Gross domestic product: 619 696 million pesos in 1986: Agriculture, forestry and fishing 26·4%; Manufacturing 24·8%; Trade 19·5%; Financial services 5·4%.
Exports: US$4841·8 million in 1986: Bananas 2·7%; Crude materials 10·7%; Coconut oil 6·9%; Machinery 9%.
Monetary unit: Philippine peso. 1 peso = 100 centavos.
Denominations:
Coins 1, 5, 10, 25, 50 centavos; 1, 5 pesos.
Notes 2, 5, 10, 20, 50, 100, 500 pesos.
Political history and government: Formerly a Spanish colony. After the Spanish-American War, Spain ceded the Philippines to the USA (10 Dec 1898). A constitution, ratified by plebiscite on 14 May 1935, gave the Philippines self-government and provided for independence after 10 years. The islands were occupied by Japanese forces in 1942–45. After the restoration of US rule, the Philippines became an independent republic on 4 July 1946.
The 1935 Constitution provided for a presidential system of government with an independent judiciary and legislature. The Philippines had a succession of six presidents until Ferdinand Edralin Marcos (1966–86) proclaimed martial law on 21 Sept 1972 and suspended the bicameral Congress. Opposition to his one-man rule and excesses in government power grew over the years. It culminated with the assassination of a prominent opposition figure, former Senator Benigno Aquino, on 21 Aug 1983. In November 1985 Marcos announced an early presidential election. Mrs Corazon C.

Aquino ran against Marcos in the 1986 elections where observers attributed large-scale fraud and intimidation to the ruling party. On 15 Feb 1986 the national assembly proclaimed Marcos as the winner of the election. The following day, Mrs Aquino announced her party's campaign for civil disobedience which eventually ended Marcos' rule and led to his exile in Hawaii. Mrs Aquino was inaugurated as the seventh President of the Philippine Republic on 25 Feb 1986. She proclaimed a revolutionary government and appointed a Constitutional Commission to draft a new Constitution. The new constitution restored the Philippine government to the presidential system with an independent judiciary, a bicameral congress (of an Upper House of 24 senators and a House of Representatives of 200 congressmen) and a presidential tenure limited to six years without re-election.
The country is divided into 13 regions and 73 provinces.
Length of roadways: 161 709 km (100 422 miles) (1986).
Length of railways: 1144 km (711 miles).
Universities: 66.
Adult illiteracy: 16·7% in 1980.
Defence: Military service: selective; total armed forces 105 000 (1987); defence expenditure: 10 500 million pesos in 1986.
Foreign tourists: 781 517 in 1986.

Poland

Official name: Polska Rzeczpospolita Ludowa (Polish People's Republic).
Population: 37 571 800 (1986 estimate).
Area: 312 683 km² (120 727 miles²).
Language: Polish.
Religion: Roman Catholic (over 70%).
Capital city: Warszawa (Warsaw), population 1 664 700 (1986).
Other principal towns (1986): Łódź 847 400; Kraków 744 000; Wrocław 640 000; Poznań 578 100; Gdańsk 468 400; Szczecin 395 000; Bydgoszcz 369 500; Katowice 367 300; Lublin 329 700.
Highest point: Rysy, 2499 m (8199 ft).
Principal mountain ranges: Carpathian Mountains (Tatra range), Beskids.
Principal rivers: Wisła (Vistula) with Narew, Odra (Oder).
Head of State: Gen. Wojciech Jaruzelski (b. 6 July 1923), Chairman of the Council of State.
Head of Government: Mieczysław Rakowski, Chairman of the Council of Ministers.
Climate: Temperate in west, continental in east. Short, rainy summers, but occasional dry spells; cold, snowy winters. In Warsaw, average maximum −0·4°C (31°F) (January) to 24°C (75°F) (July), minimum −6°C (21°F) (January) to 15°C (59°F) (July), June, July and August rainiest (each 6 days). Absolute maximum temperature 40·2°C (104·4°F), Prószków, 29 July 1921; absolute minimum −40·6°C (−41·1°F), Żywiec, 10 Feb 1929.
Labour force: 17 163 800 (1984): Agriculture and forestry 30·8%; Industry (Mining, quarrying, manufacturing, electricity, gas and water) 29·1%; Services 7·7%.
Net material product: 10 697·1 billion złotys in 1986: Agriculture and fishing 14·1%; Industry 47·3%; Trade 16%.

Exports: 2115·63 billion złotys in 1986: Hard coal 11·2%; Products of basic metal industries 7·6%; Products of electro-engineering industries 41·6%; Products of chemical industry 10·4%; Products of food industry 7·4%.
Monetary unit: Złoty. 1 złoty = 100 groszy.
Denominations:
Coins 1, 2, 5, 10, 20, 50 groszy; 1, 2, 5, 10, 20, 50 złotys.
Notes 50, 100, 200, 500, 1000, 2000, 5000, 10 000 złotys.
Political history and government: Formerly partitioned between Austria, Prussia and Russia. After the First World War an independent republic was declared on 11 Nov 1918. Parliamentary government was overthrown in May 1926 by military leaders who ruled until 1939, when invasions by Nazi Germany (1 Sept) and the USSR (17 Sept) led to another partition (29 Sept). After Germany declared war on the USSR (June 1941) its forces occupied the whole of Poland but they were driven out by Soviet forces in March 1945. With the end of the Second World War (May 1945) Poland's frontiers were redrawn. A provisional government was formed on 28 June 1945. A Communist régime took power after the elections of 19 Jan 1947 and a People's Republic was established on 19 Feb 1947. At a congress on 15–21 Dec 1948 the Polish Workers' (Communist) Party merged with the Polish Socialist Party to form the Polish United Workers' Party (PUWP). A new constitution was adopted on 22 July 1952.

The supreme organ of state power is the unicameral Parliament (*Sejm*), with 460 members elected by universal adult suffrage for four years (in the elections of 23 Mar 1980 there were 646 candidates). The *Sejm* elects a Council of State (17 members) to be its permanent organ. The highest executive and administrative body is the Council of Ministers, appointed by (and responsible to) the *Sejm*.

Political power is held by the Communist PUWP, which dominates the Front of National Unity (including some smaller parties). The Front presents an approved list of candidates for elections to representative bodies. The PUWP's highest authority is the Party Congress, normally convened every four years. The Congress elects a Central Committee (200 members) to supervise Party work. To direct its policy the Committee elects a Political Bureau (Politburo), with 15 full members (including the Committee's First Secretary) and five alternate members in 1988. In March 1989 discussions were held to form a new constitution. Poland is to have an executive President, an Upper House (or Senate) of 120 members elected on a multi-party basis by universal adult suffrage, and a Lower House (*Sejm*) of 460 members of whom 35% will be elected on a multi-party list, 55% elected from candidates chosen by the PUWP, 10% chosen by the PUWP. Poland has 49 voivodships (provinces).
Length of roadways: 154 000 km (*95 634 miles*) (1985).
Length of railways: 26 848 km (*16 673 miles*) (1986).
Universities: 11 (plus 18 technical universities).
Defence: Military service: Army, internal security forces and Air Force 2 years, Navy and special services 3 years; total regular forces 329 000 (1987); defence expenditure: 424 490 million złotys in 1987.
Foreign tourists: 4 800 000 in 1987.

Portugal

Official name: A República Portuguesa (the Portuguese Republic).
Population: 10 291 000 (1986 estimate) – including Madeira and the Azores.
Area: 92 082 km² (*35 553 miles²*) – including Madeira and the Azores.
Language: Portuguese.
Religion: Roman Catholic.
Capital city: Lisboa (Lisbon), population 1 612 000 (including suburbs) (1981 census).
Other principal towns (1981): Oporto 1 315 0000 (including suburbs); Coimbra 74 616; Setubal 77 885; Braga 63 033; Funchal (in Madeira) 44 111; Evora 34 851.
Highest point: 2351 m (*7713 ft*).
Principal mountain range: Serra da Estréla.
Principal river: Rio Tejo (Tagus).
Head of State: Dr Mário Alberto Nobre Lopes Soares (b. December 1924), President.
Prime Minister: Professor Aníbal Cavaco Silva.
Climate: Mild and temperate. Average annual temperature 16°C (*61°F*), drier and hotter inland. Hot summers, rainy winters in central areas, warm and very dry in south. In Lisbon, average maximum 13°C (*56°F*) (January) to 27°C (*80°F*) (August), minimum 8°C (*46°F*) (January) to 18°C (*64°F*) (August); March, November and December rainiest (each 10 days). Absolute maximum temperature 45·8°C (*114·4°F*), Coimbra, 31 July 1944; absolute minimum −11·0°C (*12·2°F*), Penhas Douradas, 25 Jan 1947.
Labour force: 4 030 000 in 1985: Agriculture, forestry and fishing 23·2%; Manufacturing 26%; Trade 13·7%; Community, social, personal and other services 20·8%.
Gross domestic product: 2826·7 billion escudos in 1984: Agriculture, forestry and fishing 8·5%; Mining and manufacturing industries 30%; Services 46·3%.
Exports: 967 400 million escudos in 1985: Food and live animals 4·5%; Crude materials (except fuels) 8·4%; Chemicals 7%; Textile manufactures 11·7%; Machinery and transport equipment 15·6%; Clothing 17·8%.
Monetary unit: Portuguese escudo. 1 escudo = 100 centavos.
Denominations:
Coins 50 centavos; 1, 2½, 5, 10, 20, 50, 100 escudos.
Notes 50, 100, 500, 1000, 5000, 10 000 escudos.
Political history and government: Formerly a kingdom. An anti-monarchist uprising deposed the King on 5 Oct 1910, when a republic was proclaimed. The parliamentary régime was overthrown by a military *coup* on 28 May 1926. Dr António Salazar became Prime Minister, with dictatorial powers, on 5 July 1932. A new constitution, establishing a corporate state, was adopted on 19 Mar 1933. Dr Salazar retained power until illness forced his retirement on 26 Sept 1968. His successor, Dr Marcello Caetano, was deposed on 25 Apr 1974 by a military *coup*, initiated by the Armed Forces Movement. Military leaders formed a Junta of National Salvation and appointed one of its members as President. He appointed a Prime Minister and, on the latter's recommendation, other Ministers to form a provisional government. The 1933 constitution was suspended and the bicameral Parliament dissolved.

On 14 Mar 1975 the Junta was dissolved and

left: **PORTUGAL** *right:* **POLAND**

three days later a Supreme Revolutionary Council (SRC) was established to exercise authority until a new constitution took effect. A Constitutional Assembly was elected on 25 Apr 1975 to formulate a new constitution. After approval by the SRC, the constitution, committing Portugal to make a transition to socialism, was promulgated on 2 Apr 1976. It provides for a unicameral legislature, the Assembly of the Republic, elected by universal adult suffrage for 4 years (subject to dissolution). The first Assembly, with 263 members, was elected on 25 Apr 1976, when the constitution entered into force. The SRC was renamed the Council of the Revolution, becoming a consultative body, headed by the President, with powers to delay legislation and the right of veto in military matters. Executive power is vested in the President, directly elected for 5 years. A new President was elected on 27 June and inaugurated on 14 July 1976. The President appoints a Prime Minister to lead a Council of Ministers, responsible to the Assembly. Legislation approved on 2 Oct 1978 reduced the Assembly to 250 members including four representing Portuguese abroad) at the next elections. The Assembly was dissolved by the President on 11 Sept 1979 and new elections held on 2 Dec 1979 to complete the Assembly's term, ending in October 1980. A new Assembly, with 243 members, was elected on 19 July 1987.

There are two autonomous regions in Portugal – Madeira and the Azores – and 18 districts.
Length of roadways: 51 929 km (*32 274 miles*) (1981).
Length of railways: 3588 km (*2229 miles*).
Universities: 13.
Defence: Military service: Army 12–15 months, Navy and Air Force 18–20 months; total armed forces 66 500 (38 850 conscripts) in 1987; defence expenditure: 133 760 million escudos in 1987.
Foreign tourists: 12 000 000 in 1986.

Portuguese Overseas Territory

Macau

Population: 426 400 (1986 estimate).
Area: 16·9 km² (*6·5 miles²*).

Capital: Macau (the territory is a single community).
NB: According to an agreement of 1987 Macau is to become a special administrative region of China (to be known as Macau, China) on 20 Dec 1999.

Qatar

Official name: Dawlat Qatar (State of Qatar).
Population: 369 079 (1986 census).
Area: 11 437 km² (*4416 miles²*).
Language: Arabic.
Religion: Islam (Sunni).
Capital city: Ad Dauhah (Doha), population 217 294 (1986).
Other principal towns: Dukhan, Umm Said.
Highest point: 73 m (*240 ft*).
Head of State: HH Shaikh Khalifa ibn Hamad al-Thani (b. 1932), Amir. HH the Amir succeeded to the Throne on 22 Feb 1972. Crown Prince: HH Shaikh Hamad bin Khalifa Al-Thani, who is the son of the Amir.
Head of Government: The Amir also holds the post of Prime Minister.
Climate: Very hot, with high humidity on the coast. Temperatures reach 49°C (*120°F*) in summer.
Labour force: 266 626 in 1986.
Gross domestic product: 27 836 million Qatar riyals in 1986: Mining and quarrying 45·8%; Manufacturing 6·3%; Trade, restaurants and hotels 4·2%; Finance, insurance, real estate and business services 6·5%; Petroleum 55·2%.
Exports: 12 895 million Qatar riyals in 1986: Crude petroleum oil 91%.
Monetary unit: Qatar riyal. 1 riyal = 100 dirhams.
Denominations:
Coins 5, 10, 25, 50 dirhams.
Notes 1, 5, 10, 50, 100, 500 riyals.
Political history and government: Became part of Turkey's Ottoman Empire in 1872. Turkish forces evacuated Qatar at the beginning of the First World War. The UK entered into treaty relations with the ruling Shaikh on 3 Nov 1916. A provisional constitution was adopted on 2 Apr 1970. Qatar remained under British protection until achieving full independence on 1 Sept 1971. On 22 Feb 1972 the ruler was deposed by his cousin and deputy, the Prime Minister.

Qatar is an absolute monarchy, with full powers vested in the ruler (called Amir since independence). It has no parliament or political parties. The ruler appoints and leads a Council of Ministers to exercise executive power. The Ministers are

QATAR

assisted by a nominated Consultative Council with 30 members.
Length of roadways: 1080 km (*671 miles*).
Universities: 1.
Defence: Total armed forces 7000 (1987); defence expenditure: 561·2 million Qatar riyals in 1987/8.

Romania

Official name: Republica Socialistă România (Socialist Republic of Romania).
Population: 22 823 479 (1986 estimate).
Area: 237 500 km² (*91 699 miles²*).
Languages (1966): Romanian 89·1%; Hungarian 7·7%; German 1·5%.
Religions: Romanian Orthodox (85% of believers), Roman Catholic, Reformed (Calvinist).
Capital city: Bucureşti (Bucharest), population 2 273 000 in 1986.
Other principal towns (1986): Brasov 351 493; Constanţa 327 676; Timişoara 325 272; Iaşi 313 060; Cluj-Napoca 310 017; Galaţi 295 372; Craiova 281 044; Brăila 235 620; Ploieşti 234 886; Oradea 213 846.
Highest point: Moldoveanu, 2544 m (*8346 ft*).
Principal mountain range: Carpathian Mountains.
Principal rivers: Dunărea (Danube) (2860 km *1777 miles*, 1075 km *668 miles* in Romania); Mureş (768 km *458 miles*); Prut (716 km *445 miles*).
Head of State: Nicolae Ceauşescu (b. 26 Jan 1918), President; also General Secretary of the Central Committee of the Romanian Communist Party.
Head of Government: Constantin Dăscălescu, Chairman of the Council of Ministers.
Climate: Hot and humid summers (average temperature 21°C *70°F*); cold, windy, snowy winters (average −2°C *28°F*). Moderate rainfall. Absolute maximum temperature 44·5°C (*112·1°F*), Ion Sion, 10 Aug 1951; minimum −38·5°C (*−37·3°F*), Bod, near Braşov, 25 Jan 1942.
Labour force: 10 586 100 in 1985: Agriculture and forestry 28·9%; Industry 37·1%; Services 12·5%.
Net material product: 750·8 billion lei in 1985.
Exports: 192 295 million lei in 1985: Industrial equipment 29·9%; Fuels and raw materials 28·3%; Foodstuffs 6·5%; Chemicals, fertilizers and rubber 10·7%.
Monetary unit: Leu (plural: lei). 1 leu = 100 bani.
Denominations:
Coins 5, 15, 25 bani; 1, 3, 5 lei.
Notes 10, 25, 50, 100 lei.
Political history and government: Formerly a monarchy. Under the Fascist 'Iron Guard' movement, Romania entered the Second World War as an ally of Nazi Germany. Soviet forces entered Romania in 1944. The Iron Guard régime was overthrown on 23 Aug 1944 and a predominantly Communist government took power on 6 Mar 1945. The Romanian Communist Party (RCP) merged with the Social Democratic Party, to form the Romanian Workers' Party (RWP), on 1 Oct 1947. The King was forced to abdicate on 30 Dec 1947, when the Romanian People's Republic was proclaimed. The RWP became the RCP again on 2 June 1965. A new constitution, introducing the country's present name, was adopted on 21 Aug 1965.

The supreme organ of state power is the unicameral Grand National Assembly, with 369 members elected by universal adult suffrage for five

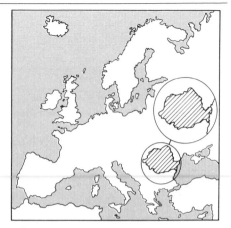

ROMANIA

years. The Assembly elects from its number the State Council (21 members) to be its permanent organ. The President of the Republic, elected by the Assembly for its duration, is also President of the State Council. The Council of Ministers, the highest organ of state administration, is elected by (and responsible to) the Assembly.

Political power is held by the RCP, the only legal party, which dominates the Socialist Democracy and Unity Front. The Front presents an approved list of candidates for elections to representative bodies. The Head of State is General Secretary of the RCP and Chairman of the Front. The RCP's highest authority is the Party Congress, convened every five years. The Congress elects a Central Committee (265 full members and 181 alternate members) to supervise Party work. The Central Committee elects from its members an Executive Political Committee (23 full members and 26 alternate members) to direct policy. The Executive Committee has an eight-member Permanent Bureau (including the President), which is the Party's most powerful policy-making body.

Romania comprises 40 administrative districts and the Municipality of Bucharest, each with a People's Council elected for five years.
Length of roadways: 72 799 km (*45 208 miles*) (in 1985).
Length of railways: 11 221 km (*6968 miles*) (in 1987).
Universities: 7 plus 5 technological universities.
Defence: Military service: Army and Air Force 16 months, Navy 18 months; total armed forces 179 500 in 1987; defence expenditure: 11 552 million lei in 1988.
Foreign tourists: 4 500 000 in 1986.

Rwanda

Official name: La République rwandaise (in French) or Republika y'u Rwanda (in Kinyarwanda).
Population: 5 757 000 (1983 estimate).
Area: 26 338 km² (*10 169 miles²*).
Languages: French, Kinyarwanda (both official), Kiswahili.

Religions: Roman Catholic, Animist; Protestant and Islam (Sunni) minorities.
Capital city: Kigali, population 156 650 in 1981.
Other principal towns (1978): Butare 21 691; Ruhengeri 16 025; Gisenyi 12 436.
Highest point: Mt Karisimbi, 4507 m (*14 787 ft*).
Principal mountain range: Chaîne des Mitumba.
Principal river: Luvironza (headwaters of the Nile).
Head of State: Maj.-Gen. Juvénal Habyarimana (b. 8 Mar 1937), President.
Climate: Tropical, tempered by altitude. Average temperature at 1463 m (*4800 ft*) is 23°C (*73°F*). Hot and humid in lowlands, cool in highlands. Average annual rainfall 785 mm (*31 in*). Main rainy season from February to May, dry season May to September.
Labour force: 3 150 000 in 1986: Agriculture, forestry and fishing 91·9%.
Gross domestic product: 141 930 million Rwanda francs in 1983: Agriculture, forestry and fishing 39·9%; Manufacturing 18·3%; Trade 14·3%; Services 4·4%; Public administration 12·1%.
Exports: 13 476 million Rwanda francs in 1984: Coffee 65·4%; Tea 17·6%; Tin ores and concentrates 9·5%.
Monetary unit: Franc rwandais (Rwanda franc). 1 franc = 100 centimes.
Denominations:
Coins 1, 2, 5, 10, 20, 50 francs.
Notes 100, 500, 1000, 5000 francs.
Political history and government: Formerly a monarchy, ruled by a *Mwami* (King). Part of German East Africa from 1899. Occupied in 1916 by Belgian forces from the Congo (now Zaire). From 1920 Rwanda was part of Ruanda-Urundi, administered by Belgium under League of Nations mandate and later as a UN Trust Territory. Following a referendum on 25 Sept 1961, the monarchy was abolished and the republic which had been proclaimed on 28 Jan 1961 was recognized by Belgium on 2 Oct 1961. Rwanda became independent on 1 July 1962. On 5 July 1973 the government was overthrown by a military *coup*, led by Maj.-Gen. Juvénal Habyarimana, who became President. The National Assembly was dissolved and political activity suspended. On 5 July 1975 President Habyarimana established a new ruling party, the *Mouvement révolutionnaire national pour le développement* (MRND), the National Revolutionary Movement for Development. A referendum on 17 Dec 1978 approved a new constitution legalizing Habyarimana's régime. Executive power is vested in the President, elected by universal adult suffrage for a five-year term. The constitution provides for a 50-member National Development Council (NDC), also to be directly elected for five years. The NDC is granted limited legislative powers but is unable to change government policy. The MRND became the sole political organization. Habyarimana was elected (unopposed) on 24 Dec 1978 and re-elected in December 1983 to continue as President. The President appoints and leads a Council of Ministers. Rwanda comprises 10 prefectures, each administered by an appointed official.
Length of roadways: 12 070 km (*7496 miles*) (1986).
Universities: 1.
Adult illiteracy: 54·3% in 1985.
Defence: Total armed forces 5150 (1987); defence expenditure is US$37·4 million in 1987.
Foreign tourists: 19 700 in 1984.

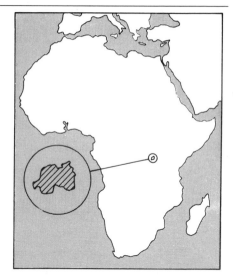

RWANDA

Saint Christopher and Nevis

(normally called St Kitts-Nevis)
Official name: The Federation of St Christopher and Nevis.
Population: 46 000 (1983 estimate).
Area: 261·6 km² (*162·5 miles²*) (St Kitts 168·4 km², Nevis 93·2 km²).
Language: English.
Religions: Anglican 36%; Methodist 32%; Roman Catholic 11% (in 1985).
Capital city: Basseterre (on St Kitts) 14 161 in 1980.
Other principal towns: Charlestown (on Nevis) 1243 in 1980.
Highest point: Nevis Peak 985 m (*3232 ft*).
Head of State: HM Queen Elizabeth II, represented by Sir Clement Athelston Arrindell, GCMG, GCVO.
Prime Minister: The Rt Hon. Dr Kennedy Alphonse Simmonds.
Climate: Warm and moist, with a mean annual temperature of 26°C (*78·8°F*). Average rainfall on St Kitts 1372 mm (*54 in*) and on Nevis 1219 mm (*48 in*) – rainfall increases inland on each island.
Labour force: 17 125 in 1980.
Gross domestic product: EC$148·9 million in 1984: Agriculture, fishing etc. 13·2%; Manufacturing 15·2%; Trade, restaurants and hotels 17·4%; Finance 13·1%; Government services 18·9%.
Exports: EC$18·8 million in 1982: Sugar and sugar preparations 61·7%; Machinery 14·9%.
Monetary unit: East Caribbean dollar (EC$). 1 dollar = 100 cents.
Denominations:
Coins 1, 2, 5, 10, 25, 50 cents.
Notes 1, 5, 20, 100 dollars.
Political history and government: A former British dependency, St Kitts-Nevis was administered by the Governor of the Leeward Islands until 1958. From 1960 the islands, then united with Anguilla, had a new constitution and their own Administrator. On 27 Feb 1967, St Christopher-Nevis-Anguilla became one of the West Indies Associated States, with full internal self-government. The Administrator became Governor and the Chief Minister

restyled Premier. In July 1967 Anguilla unilaterally declared independence and after British intervention that island came under direct British rule again, under the Anguilla Act of July 1971. In 1980 all links between Anguilla and St Kitts were severed.

After a constitutional conference, St Christopher and Nevis became a fully independent federal state on 19 Sept 1983. Nevis was given its own Island Assembly and has the right of secession from the federation. The Governor became Governor-General and the Premier took office as Prime Minister. St Kitts-Nevis is a constitutional monarchy. Executive power is vested in the British monarch and is exercisable by the Governor-General, who is appointed on the advice of the Prime Minister and acts in almost all matters on the advice of the Cabinet. Legislative power is vested in the unicameral Parliament or National Assembly consisting of 11 elected Representatives (eight from St Kitts and three from Nevis) and three appointed Senators. The 11 Representatives are elected from single-member constituencies by universal adult suffrage. The Governor-General appoints the Prime Minister, and, on the latter's recommendation, other ministers from the National Assembly. The Cabinet is responsible to the Assembly.
Length of roadways: 300 km (*186 miles*).
Foreign tourists: 82 094 in 1986.

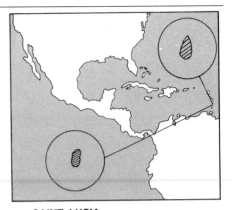

top: **SAINT LUCIA**
below: **SAINT VINCENT AND THE GRENADINES**

Saint Lucia

Population: 139 500 (1986 estimate).
Area: 616 km² (*238 miles²*).
Language: English.
Religion: Christian (mainly Roman Catholic, also Anglican and Methodist).
Capital city: Castries, population 52 868 (1986 estimate).
Other principal towns: Vieux Fort, Soufrière.
Highest point: Morne (Mt) Gimie, 959 m (*3145 ft*).
Head of State: HM Queen Elizabeth II, represented by Sir Vincent Floissac, CMG, QC.
Prime Minister: The Rt Hon. John Compton.
Climate: Warm and moist. Dry season January–April, rainy May–August. In Castries, average annual temperature 28°C (*82°F*), rainfall 2234 mm (*88 in*), rising to 3480 mm (*137 in*) inland.
Labour force: 48 012 (1981).
Gross domestic product: EC$426·6 million in 1986: Agriculture, forestry and fishing 16·6%; Manufacturing 8%; Construction 7·5%; Trade 22·1%; Financial services 10·6%; Government services 21·6%.
Exports: EC$213·2 million in 1986: Food and live animals 72·7%; Beverages and tobacco 3·1%; Basic manufactures 8%.
Monetary unit: East Caribbean dollar (EC$). 1 dollar = 100 cents.
Denominations:
Coins 1, 2, 5, 10, 25, 50 cents.
Notes 1, 5, 20, 100 dollars.
Political history and government: A former British dependency, St Lucia was administered by the Governor of the Windward Islands until 31 Dec 1959. From 1 Jan 1960 it had a new constitution, with its own Administrator. On 1 Mar 1967 St Lucia became one of the West Indies Associated States, with full internal self-government. The Administrator became Governor and the Chief Minister was

restyled Premier. After a constitutional conference on 24–27 July 1978, Saint Lucia (as it was restyled) became fully independent, within the Commonwealth, on 22 Feb 1979. The Governor became Governor-General and the Premier took office as Prime Minister.

Saint Lucia is a constitutional monarchy. Executive power is vested in the British monarch and is exercisable by the Governor-General, who is appointed on the advice of the Prime Minister and acts in almost all matters on the advice of the Cabinet. Legislative power is vested in a bicameral Parliament, comprising a Senate (11 members appointed by the Governor-General) and a House of Assembly (17 members) elected from single-member constituencies by universal adult suffrage for 5 years (subject to dissolution). The Governor-General appoints the Prime Minister and, on the latter's recommendation, other Ministers from among members of the Senate and the House. The Cabinet is responsible to the House.
Length of roadways: 970 km (*602 miles*).
Foreign tourists: 174 218 in 1986.

Saint Vincent and the Grenadines

Population: 138 000 (1985 estimate).
Area: 389 km² (*150·3 miles²*).
Language: English.
Religion: Christian (mainly Anglican).
Capital: Kingstown, population 18 830 (1986 estimate).
Other principal towns: Georgetown, Barrouaillie, Chateaubelair, Layou.
Highest point: Soufrière, 1234 m (*4048 ft*).
Head of State: HM Queen Elizabeth II, represented by Joseph Lambert Eustace, Governor-General.
Prime Minister: The Rt Hon. James Mitchell.
Climate: Warm and moist, with average temperatures between 19°C and 32°C (*67°F and 89°F*).
Labour force: 40 000 (1983).

Gross domestic product: EC$249·0 million in 1982: Agriculture, forestry and fishing 17·7%; Manufacturing 10·6%; Trade 11·5%; Financial services 10·4%; Government services 17·9%.

Exports: EC$169·7 million in 1986: Food and live animals 86·2% (which includes Bananas 30·9%; Tubers 18·6%).

Monetary unit: East Caribbean dollar (EC$). 1 dollar = 100 cents.

Denominations:
Coins 1, 2, 5, 10, 25, 50 cents.
Notes 1, 5, 20, 100 dollars.

Political history and government: A former British dependency. The islands, collectively known as St Vincent, were administered by the Governor of the Windward Islands until 31 Dec 1959. From 1 Jan 1960 St Vincent had a new constitution, with its own Administrator. On 27 Oct 1969 it became one of the West Indies Associated States, with full internal self-government. The Administrator became Governor and the Chief Minister was restyled Premier. After a constitutional conference on 18–21 Sept 1978, the islands, under their present name, became fully independent, as a 'special member' of the Commonwealth, on 27 Oct 1979. The Governor became Governor-General and the Premier took office as Prime Minister.

The country is a constitutional monarchy. Executive power is vested in the British monarch and is exercisable by the Governor-General, who is appointed on the advice of the Prime Minister and acts in almost all matters on the advice of the Cabinet. Legislative power is vested in the unicameral House of Assembly, with 19 members serving for 5 years (subject to dissolution). The House has 6 Senators (nominated by the Governor-General) and 13 members elected by universal adult suffrage from single-member constituencies. The 13 members of the pre-independence House took office as the elective members of the new House. The Governor-General appoints the Prime Minister and, on the latter's recommendation, other Ministers from among members of the House. The Cabinet is responsible to the House.

Length of roadways: 1050 km (*652 miles*).
Foreign tourists: 80 213 in 1986.

San Marino

Official name: Serenissima Repubblica di San Marino (Most Serene Republic of San Marino).
Population: 22 638 (1987 estimate).
Area: 60·5 km² (*23·4 miles²*).
Language: Italian.
Religion: Roman Catholic.
Capital city: San Marino, population 4179 (1986 estimate).
Highest point: Mt Titano, 739 m (*2424 ft*).
Head of State: There are two Captains-Regent (*Capitani reggentii*) appointed every six months.
Climate: Warm summers, average maximum 29°C (*85°F*); dry, cold winters.
Labour force: 12 118 in 1987: Manufacturing 34·6%; Commerce 18%; Services 5·6%; Government administration 15·3%.
Monetary unit: Italian currency (*q.v.*) and San Marino currency.
Political history and government: Founded as a city-state in AD 301. In customs union with Italy since

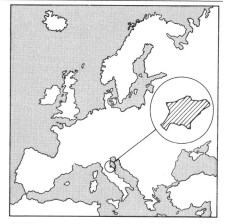

SAN MARINO

1862. Legislative power is vested in the unicameral Great and General Council, with 60 members elected by universal adult suffrage for 5 years (subject to dissolution). Women have had the right to vote since 1960 and to stand for election since 1973. The Council elects two of its members (one representing the capital, one the rest of the country) to act jointly as Captains-Regent, with the functions of Head of State and Government, for 6 months at a time. The first female Captain-Regent took office on 1 Apr 1981. Executive power is held by the Congress of State, with 10 members elected by the Council for the duration of its term. San Marino comprises nine administrative areas, called 'castles', each with an elected committee led by the 'Captain of the Castle', chosen for a 6-month term.
Length of roadways: 220 km (*137 miles*).
Foreign tourists: 2 561 221 in 1984.

São Tomé and Príncipe

Official name: A República Democrática de São Tomé e Príncipe (the Democratic Republic of São Tomé and Príncipe).
Population: 113 000 (1987 estimate).
Area: 964 km² (*372 miles²*).
Language: Portuguese (official).
Religion: Roman Catholic.
Capital city: São Tomé, population 25 000 (1984 estimate).
Other principal town: Santo António (on Príncipe).
Highest point: Pico Gago Coutinho (Pico de São Tomé), 2024 m (*6640 ft*).
Head of State: Dr Manuel Pinto da Costa (b. 1910), President.
Prime Minister: Celestino Rocha da Costa.
Climate: Warm and humid, with an average temperature of 27°C (*80°F*).
Labour force: 30 607 in 1981: Agriculture, forestry and fishing 53·9%; Mining and manufacturing 5·3%; Trade 6·5%; Community, social and personal services 19%; Unemployed 4·6%.
Gross domestic product: 1609 million dobra in 1984: Agriculture, forestry and fishing 23·6%; Manufacturing 8·8%; Trade 8·8%; Public administration 26%.
Exports: 539·6 million dobra in 1984.

Monetary unit: Dobra. 1 dobra = 100 centavos.
Denominations:
Coins 50 centavos; 1, 2, 5, 10, 20 dobra.
Notes 50, 100, 500, 1000 dobra.
Political history and government: A former Portuguese territory, independent since 12 July 1975. Before independence, Portugal recognized the islands' Liberation Movement (MLSTP), whose leader became first President. A Constitutional Assembly, elected on 6 July 1975, approved a new constitution on 12 Dec 1975. Under the constitution, the MLSTP is 'the leading political force of the nation'. The supreme organ of state is the People's Assembly, with 40 members (mostly MLSTP officials) serving a 4-year term. Executive power is vested in the President, elected for 4 years by the Assembly on the proposal of the MLSTP. He directs the government and appoints Ministers. The government is responsible to the Assembly. The post of Prime Minister, abolished in April 1979 was revived in 1988.
Length of roadways: 287 km (*178 miles*).
Adult illiteracy: 42·6% in 1981.
Defence: Total armed forces 1000 (1983); some 500 Angolan troops are stationed on the islands as well as Cuban and Soviet military advisers.
Foreign tourists: 500 in 1987.

Saudi Arabia

Official name: Al-Mamlaka al-'Arabiya as-Sa'udiya (the Kingdom of Saudi Arabia).
Population: 12 006 000 (1986 estimate).
Area: 2 149 690 km² (*830 000 miles²*).
Language: Arabic.
Religion: Islam (85% Sunni; 15% Shia).
Capital city: Ar Riyād (Riyadh), population 666 840 at 1974 census. Jeddah is the administrative capital.
Other principal towns (1974): Jidda (Jeddah) 561 194; Makkah (Mecca) 366 801; At Ta'if 204 857; Al Madinah (Medina) 198 186; Ad Dammam 127 844; Al Hufuf 101 271.
Highest point: Jebel Razikh, 3658 m (*12 002 ft*).
Principal mountain range: Tihā matash Shām.
Principal rivers: The flows are seasonal only.
Head of State and Prime Minister: HM King Fahd bin Abdulaziz, who succeeded to the Throne on 13 June 1982, on the death of his brother King Khalid. Crown Prince: HRH Prince Abdullah bin Abdulaziz, brother of King Fahd.
Climate: Very hot and dry. Mostly desert; frequent sandstorms. Average summer temperature 38°C to 49°C (*100°F to 120°F*) on coast, up to 54°C (*130°F*) inland. High humidity. Some places have droughts for years. In Riyadh, average maximum is 42°C (*107°F*) (June–August); January coldest (4°C to 21°C (*40°F to 70°F*). In Jeddah, average maximum 29°C (*84°F*) (January, February) to 37°C (*99°F*) (July, August), minimum 18°C (*65°F*) (February) to 27°C (*80°F*) (August), rainiest month is November (two days).
Labour force: 3 530 000 in 1986: Agriculture 42·8%.
Gross domestic product: 286 687 million riyals in 1985–6: Crude petroleum and natural gas 28·3%; Petroleum refining 5·4%; Construction 12·1%; Trade 8·4%; Financial services 8·1%.
Exports: 129 790 million riyals in 1985: Crude petroleum 88·2%.
Monetary unit: Saudi riyal. 1 riyal = 100 halalah.

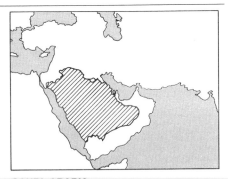

SAUDI ARABIA

Denominations:
Coins 1, 5, 10, 25, 50 halalah.
Notes 1, 5, 10, 50, 100 riyals.
Political history and government: Formerly part of Turkey's Ottoman Empire. In 1913 the Sultan of Nejd overthrew Turkish rule in central Arabia. Between 1919 and 1925 he gained control of the Hijaz and was proclaimed King there on 8 Jan 1926. On 23 Sept 1932 the Hijaz and Nejd were combined and named Saudi Arabia. The country is an absolute monarchy, with no parliament or political parties. The King rules in accordance with the *Sharia*, the sacred law of Islam. He appoints and leads a Council of Ministers, which serves as the instrument of royal authority in both legislative and executive matters. The King is also assisted by advisory councils, nominated or approved by him.
Length of roadways: 91 350 km (*56 728 miles*).
Length of railways: 893 km (*555 miles*).
Universities: 9.
Adult illiteracy: 75·4% in 1980.
Defence: Military service voluntary; total armed forces 73 500 (1987); defence expenditure: 60 752 million riyals in 1987.
Foreign tourists: about 1 600 000 in 1985.

Senegal

Official name: La République du Sénégal.
Population: 6 700 000 (1986 estimate).
Area: 196 722 km² (*75 954 miles²*).
Languages: French (official), Wolof, Fulani (Peulh), Serer, Toucouleur.
Religions: Islam (Sunni) 90%; Christian (mainly Roman Catholic) 5%.
Capital city: Dakar, population 978 553 (1979 estimate).
Other principal towns (1979): Thiès 126 886; Kaolack 115 679; Saint-Louis 96 594; Ziguinchor 79 464; Diourbel 55 307.
Highest point: Gounou Mt, 1515 m (*4970 ft*).
Principal mountain range: Fouta Djalon.
Principal rivers: Gambie (Gambia), Casamance, Sénégal.
Head of State: Abdou Diouf (b. 7 Sept 1935), President.
Climate: Tropical. Hot, with long dry season and short wet season. Average annual temperature about 29°C (*84°F*). Heavy rainfall on coast. Average maximum 32°C to 42°C (*90°F to 108°F*) in interior; average minimum about 15°C (*60°F*). In

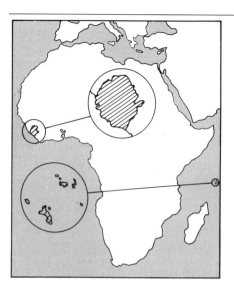

above: **SIERRA LEONE**
below: **SEYCHELLES**

Dakar, on coast, average maximum 26°C (*79°F*) (January) to 32°C (*89°F*) (September, October); minimum 17°C (*63°F*) (February) to 24°C (*76°F*) (July to October); rainiest month is August (13 days).
Labour force: 2953000 in 1986: Agriculture 79·3%.
Gross domestic product: 1186·9 billion CFA francs in 1985: Agriculture, forestry and fishing 18·4%; Industry (manufacturing, mining, utilities) 21·2%; Trade, transport and communications 38·1%.
Exports: 233974 million CFA francs in 1984: Fisheries 21·1%; Fuels 18·4%; Peanut oil 15·3%.
Monetary unit: Franc de la Communauté financière africaine.
Denominations:
Coins 1, 2, 5, 10, 25, 50, 100 CFA francs.
Notes 50, 100, 500, 1000, 5000 CFA francs.
Political history and government: Formerly part of French West Africa, Senegal joined French Sudan (now the Republic of Mali) to form the Federation of Mali on 4 Apr 1959. By agreementc with France, signed on 4 Apr 1960, the Federation became independent on 20 June 1960. Senegal seceded, and became a separate independent state, on 20 Aug 1960. The Republic of Senegal was proclaimed on 5 Sept 1960, with Léopold-Sédar Senghor as first President. A new constitution was promulgated on 7 Mar 1963. Senegal became a one-party state in 1966 but two legal opposition parties were subsequently formed (in July 1974 and February 1976). A constitutional amendment, approved by the government on 10 Mar 1976, fixed the maximum number of permitted parties at three. On 3 Apr 1978 the President announced that a fourth party would be permitted. Legislative power rests with the unicameral national Assembly, with 120 members elected for 5 years by universal adult suffrage (the elections of 26 Feb 1978 were contested by three parties). Executive power is held by the President, also directly elected for 5 years at the same time as the Assembly. He appoints and leads a Cabinet, including a Prime Minister. President Senghor retired on 31 D℮c 1980 and was succeeded by the

Prime Minister, Abdou Diouf. On 24 Apr 1981 the National Assembly adopted a constitutional amendment, effective from 6 May, lifting restrictions on political parties. By July a further 7 parties had registered. On 1 Feb 1982 Senegal and The Gambia formed a confederation named Senegambia, led by President Diouf.
Length of roadways: 15000 km (*9315 miles*) (1986).
Length of railways: 1034 m (*642 miles*).
Universities: 2.
Adult illiteracy: 71·9% in 1985.
Defence: Military service: two years, selective; total armed forces 9700 (1987); defence expenditure: 3240 million CFA francs in 1986/7.
Foreign tourists: 241017 in 1985.

Seychelles

Official name: The Republic of Seychelles.
Population: 65244 (1985 estimate).
Area: 453 km² (*174·9 miles²*).
Languages: Creole 94·4%; English 3·0%; French 1·9% (census of 5 May 1971).
Religions: Christian (mainly Roman Catholic) 98·2% (1971).
Capital city: Victoria (formerly Port Victoria), population 23334 (including suburbs) at 1977 census.
Other principal town: Takamaka.
Highest point: Morne Seychellois, 912 m (*2992 ft*).
Head of State: France Albert René (b. 16 Nov 1935), President.
Climate: Warm and pleasant, with temperatures generally between 24°C to 30°C (*75°F to 85°F*), cooler on high ground. Hottest during north-west monsoon, December to May. South-east monsoon is from June to November. Average annual rainfall on Mahé between 1780 and 3430 mm (*70 and 135 in*). In Victoria, average annual temperature 29°C (*84°F*), rainfall 2300 mm (*91 in*).
Labour force: 27700 in 1985.
Gross domestic product: 1074·3 million Seychelles rupees in 1984: Agriculture, forestry and fishing 6·9%; Mining, manufacturing and handicrafts 9·3%; Transport, distribution and communications 31·1%; Hotels and restaurants 8·2%; Financial services 10·3%; Government services 16·2%.
Exports: 21857 million Seychelles rupees in 1985: Food and live animals 63·2%.
Monetary unit: Seychelles rupee. 1 rupee = 100 cents.
Denominations:
Coins 1, 5, 25, 50 cents; 1, 5 rupees.
Notes 10, 25, 50, 100 rupees.
Political history and government: Formerly a British colony, with internal self-government from 1 Oct 1975. Following a constitutional conference on 19–22 Jan 1976, Seychelles became an independent republic, within the Commonwealth, on 29 June 1976. At the same time three islands which formed part of the British Indian Ocean territory (established on 8 Nov 1965) were returned to Seychelles. The pre-independence Prime Minister, James Mancham, became the first President, leading a coalition government comprising members of his own Seychelles Democratic Party and of the Seychelles People's United Party (SPUP), formerly in opposition. The SPUP leader, Albert René, became Prime Minister. President Mancham was

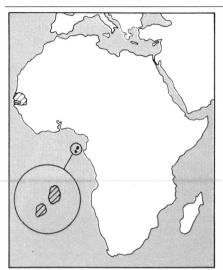

left: SENEGAL
encircled: SÃO TOMÉ AND PRÍNCIPE

deposed on 5 June 1977 in a *coup* by armed opponents of his rule. At the request of the *coup* leaders, René became President. The constitution was suspended and the elected National Assembly dissolved. President René assumed power to rule by decree. In May 1978 the SPUP was renamed the Seychelles People's Progressive Front (SPPF). A new constitution was proclaimed on 26 Mar 1979 and took effect from 5 June. It provides for a one-party state, with a unicameral People's Assembly of 25 members (two nominated to represent uninhabited islands and 23 elected by universal adult suffrage), serving a four-year term. Executive power is vested in the President, directly elected for five years. Elections for the President (with René as sole candidate) and the Assembly (all candidates being from the SPPF) were held in June 179. Similar elections were held for the Assembly in 1983 and 1988 and the President in 1984. There have been a number of *coup* attempts.

The President appoints and leads the Cabinet, his nominations being subject to ratification by the Assembly.

Length of roadways: 259 km (*161 miles*) (1985).
Adult illiteracy: 40% in 1983.
Defence: Total armed forces: 1300 in 1987; total defence expenditure: US$11·4 million in 1986.
Foreign tourists: 66 800 in 1986.

Sierra Leone

Official name: The Republic of Sierra Leone.
Population: 3 517 530 (1985 census).
Area: 71 740 km² (*27 699 miles²*).
Languages: English (official), Krio, Mende, Temne.
Religions: Animist; Islam (Sunni) and Christian minorities.
Capital city: Freetown, population 469 776 (1985 census).

Other principal towns (1985): Makeni 20 000; Kenema 13 000; Bo 26 000; Koidu 80 000.
Highest point: Bintimani and Kundukonko peaks, 1948 m (*6390 ft*).
Principal mountain range: Loma.
Principal rivers: Siwa, Jong, Rokel.
Head of State: Maj.-Gen. Joseph Saidu Momoh, President.
Climate: Generally hot with two main seasons: wet (May–October), when humidity is tryingly high, and dry (November–April). The average annual rainfall at Freetown is 3505 mm (*138 in*) and the average daily high temperature nearly 29°C (*85°F*).
Labour force: 1 369 000 in 1986: Agriculture, forestry and fishing 65·2%.
Gross domestic product: 2761·9 million leones in 1983–4: Agriculture, forestry and fishing 30·9%; Mining 9·4%; Manufacturing 7·3%; Trade 12·6%; Financial services 7·5%; Government services 2·5%.
Exports: 370·9 million leone in 1984: Coffee 9·2%; Cocoa beans 15·7%; Palm kernels 3·5%; Bauxite 12·8%; Diamonds 34·5%; Rutile 16·1%; Iron ore 2·9%.
Monetary unit: Leone. 1 leone = 100 cents.
Denominations:
Coins 1, 5, 10, 20, 50 cents; 1 leone.
Notes 2, 5, 10, 20 leones.
Political history and government: A former British dependency which became independent, within the Commonwealth, on 27 Apr 1961. At independence the Sierra Leone People's Party was in power, with the All-People's Congress (APC) in opposition. Following disputed elections, the army assumed power on 21 Mar 1967. Two days later, in a counter-*coup*, another group of officers established a National Reformation Council (NRC), which suspended the constitution. The NRC was overthrown on 17–18 Apr 1968 by junior officers who restored constitutional government and civilian rule on 26 Apr 1968, when Dr Siaka Stevens of the APC, appointed Prime Minister in 1967, was sworn in. A republic was established on 19 Apr 1971 and two days later Dr Stevens was elected President and took Office. Legislative power is held by the unicameral House of Representatives, with 124 members: 105 elected by universal adult suffrage for 5 years (subject to dissolution), 12 Paramount Chiefs (one from each District) and 7 members appointed by the President. A constitutional amendment bill, published on 13 May 1978, provided for the repeal of the 1971 constitution and for the introduction of one-party government under the APC; for an extension of the President's term of office from 5 to 7 years; and for the abolition of the office of Prime Minister. After approving the bill, the House was prorogued on 26 May 1978. A referendum on 5–12 June 1978 supported the proposed changes and President Stevens was sworn in on 14 June for a 7-year term. Under the new constitution, the President, formerly elected by the House, is elected by the National Delegates' Conference of the APC. He holds executive power and he appoints and leads the Cabinet.
Length of roadways: 7395 km (*4595 miles*) (31 Dec 1979).
Length of railways: 84 km (*52 miles*).
Universities: 1.
Adult illiteracy: 70·7% in 1985.
Defence: Total armed forces 3100 (1987); defence expenditure: 105 million leone in 1988.
Foreign tourists: 55 000 in 1983.

Singapore

Official name: Hsing-chia p'o Kung-ho Kuo (Chinese) or Republik Singapura (Malay): Republic of Singapore.
Population: 2 586 200 (1986).
Area: 620·5 km² (*384·2 miles²*).
Languages: Malay, Mandarin Chinese, Tamil, English.
Religions: Islam (Sunni), Buddhist, Hindu, Christian.
Capital city: Singapore City, (the republic has one conurbation which includes Singapore City).
Highest point: Bukit Timah (Hill of Tin), 177 m (*581 ft*).
Principal river: Sungei Seletar (14 km (*9 miles*).
Head of State: Wee Kim Wee, President.
Prime Minister: Lee Kuan Yew (b. 16 Sept 1923).
Climate: Hot and humid throughout the year, with average maximum of 30°C to 32°C (*86°F to 89°F*), minimum 23°C to 24°C (*73°F to 75°F*). Frequent rainfall (between 11 and 19 days each month).
Labour force: 1 148 900 (1986): Manufacturing 25·3%; Commerce 8·7%; Community, social and personal services 22·6%.
Gross domestic product: S$39 185·2 million in 1986: Manufacturing 27·2%; Trade 19·1%; Financial services 23·1%.
Exports: S$48·99 billion in 1986: Machinery and transport equipment 38·6%; Mineral fuels 20·7%.
Monetary unit: Singapore dollar (S$). 1 dollar = 100 cents.
Denominations:
Coins 1, 5, 10, 20, 50 cents; 1 dollar.
Notes 1, 5, 10, 20, 25, 50, 100, 500, 1000, 10 000 dollars.
Political history and government: A former British colony, with internal self-government from 3 June 1959. Singapore became a constituent state of the independent Federation of Malaysia, within the Commonwealth, on 16 Sept 1963 but seceded and became a separate independent country on 9 Aug 1965. The new state joined the Commonwealth on 16 Oct 1965 and became a republic on 22 Dec 1965. Legislative power rests with the unicameral Parliament, with 77 members elected by universal adult suffrage (voting being compulsory) from single-member constituencies for 5 years (subject to dissolution). The President is elected by Parliament for a 4-year term as constitutional Head of State. Effective executive authority rests with the Cabinet, led by the Prime Minister, which is appointed by the President and responsible to Parliament.
Length of roadways: 2686 km (*1668 miles*) (1986).
Length of railways: 26 km (*16 miles*) (1986).
Universities: 1.
Adult illiteracy: 13·6% in 1986.
Defence: Military service: 24–30 months; total armed forces 55 500 (1987); defence expenditure: S$2350 million in 1987–8.
Foreign tourists: 3 191 058 in 1986.

Solomon Islands

Population: 285 796 (1986 census).
Area: 28 446 km² (*10 983 miles²*).
Languages: English (official), Pidgin English (national) and 87 local (mainly Melanesian) languages.
Religion: mainly Christian (Anglican and Roman Catholic).
Capital city: Honiara, population 30 499 (1986 census).
Other principal towns: Gizo, Auki, Kirakira.
Highest point: Mt Makarakombou, 2447 m (*8028 ft*).
Head of State: HM Queen Elizabeth II, represented by Sir Baddeley Devisi, GCMG, GCVO (b. 16 Oct 1941), Governor-General. (His continuation in office was under discussion at the time of going to press.)
Prime Minister: Solomon Mamaloni.
Climate: Warm season during north-west trade winds, November–April; cooler during south-east season, April–November. In Honiara, average annual temperature is 27°C (*80°F*), average annual rainfall about 2160 mm (*85 in*).
Labour force: 24 796 in 1985: Agriculture, forestry and fishing 32·4%; Manufacturing 7%; Trade 10·3%; Transport and communications 8·7%; Services 28·7%.
Gross domestic product: SI$175 million in 1983.
Exports: SI$114 969 in 1986: Fish 46%; Copra 5·2%; Timber 31·1%; Cocoa 5·6%.
Monetary unit: Solomon Islands dollar (SI$). 1 dollar = 100 cents.
Denominations:
Coins 1, 2, 5, 10, 20 cents; 1 dollar.
Notes 2, 5, 10, 20, 50 dollars.
Political history and government: The Northern Solomon Islands became a German protectorate in 1885 and the Southern Solomons a British protectorate in 1893. Germany ceded most of the Northern Solomons to the United Kingdom between 1898 and 1900. The combined territory was named the British Solomon Islands Protectorate. The first Chief Minister was appointed on 28 Aug 1974. In June 1975 the territory was renamed the Solomon Islands, although retaining protectorate status. Full internal self-government was achieved on 2 Jan 1976. After a constitutional conference on 6–16 Sept 1977, Solomon Islands (as it was restyled) became independent, within the Commonwealth, on 7 July 1978, with the Chief Minister as the first Prime Minister.
Legislative power is vested in the unicameral National Parliament, with 38 members elected by universal adult suffrage for 4 years (subject to disso-

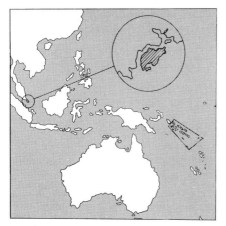

top encircled: **SINGAPORE**
below: **SOLOMON ISLANDS**

lution). The pre-independence Legislative Assembly became the first Parliament. Executive power is vested in the British monarch and is exercisable by the Governor-General, who is appointed for up to 5 years on the advice of Parliament and acts in almost all matters on the advice of the Cabinet. The Prime Minister is elected by and from members of Parliament. Other Ministers are appointed by the Governor-General, on the Prime Minister's recommendation, from members of Parliament. The Cabinet is responsible to Parliament. The country comprises seven provinces.
Length of roadways: 2300 km (*1425 miles*).
Universities: 1.
Foreign tourists: 12 555 in 1987.

Somalia

Official name: Jamhuuriyadda Dimuqraadiga Soomaaliya (Somali Democratic Republic).
Population: 6 110 000 (1987 estimate) including refugees.
Area: 637 657 km² (*246 201 miles²*).
Language: Somali, Arabic (both official); English, Italian.
Religions: Islam (Sunni); Christian minority.
Capital city: Muqdisho (Mogadishu or Mogadiscio), population 377 000 (1982 estimate).
Other principal towns (1982): Hargeisa 70 000; Kisimayu 70 000; Merca 60 000; Berbera 55 000.
Highest point: Surud Ad, 2406 m (*7894 ft*).
Principal mountain range: Guban.
Principal rivers: Juba (Giuba), Shebelle (Scebeli).
Head of State: Maj.-Gen. Muhammad Siyad Barre (b. 1919), President and Prime Minister.
Climate: Hot and dry. Average temperature of 27°C (*80°F*). Average maximum over 32°C (*90°F*) in interior and on Gulf of Aden. Average rainfall less than 430 mm (*17 in*). In Mogadishu, average maximum 28°C (*83°F*) (July, August) to 32°C (*90°F*) (April), minimum 23°C (*73°F*) (January, July, August) to 25°C (*78°F*) (April), rainiest month is July (20 days).
Labour force: 2 027 000 (1986 estimate): Agriculture, forestry and fishing 72·4%.
Gross domestic product: 16 061 million Somali shillings in 1981: Agriculture, hunting etc 43%; Trade 9·4%; Transport and communications 6·9%; Finance 6·4%; Government services 7·2%.
Exports: 1423 million Somali shillings in 1983: Livestock 78·9%; Bananas 7·3%; Myrrh 6·3%; Petroleum products 3%.
Monetary unit: Somali shilling. 1 shilling = 100 centesimi.
Denominations:
   Coins 1, 5, 10, 50 centesimi; 1 shilling.
   Notes 5, 10, 20, 100 shillings.
Political history and government: Formed on 1 July 1960 as an independent country, called the Somali Republic, by a merger of the Trust Territory of Somaliland, under Italian protection, with British Somaliland (a protectorate until 26 June 1960). Following the assassination of the President on 15 Oct 1969, the government was overthrown by a military *coup* on 21 Oct 1969, when the constitution and political parties were abolished and the National Assembly dissolved. A Supreme Revolutionary council (SRC) was established and the country's present name adopted on 22 Oct 1969. The President of the SRC, Maj.-Gen. Muhammad Siyad

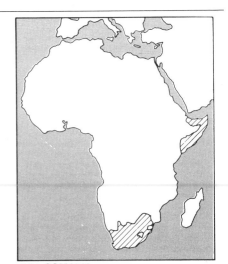

right: **SOMALIA**
below: **SOUTH AFRICA**

Barrah, became Head of State. On 1 July 1976 the SRC was dissolved and its power transferred to the newly-formed Somali Revolutionary Socialist Party (SRSP). All members of the SRC became members of the ruling party's central committee and the President is the party's secretary-general.
A meeting of the SRSP on 20–25 Jan 1979 produced a draft constitution, endorsed by the SRSP Central Committee on 20 May 1979. After approval by referendum on 25 Aug 1979, the constitution was promulgated on 29 Aug and came into force on 23 Sept 1979. It defines the SRSP as the sole political party and the country's 'supreme authority'. Legislative power is vested in the People's Assembly, with six members appointed by the President and 171 elected by universal adult suffrage for 5 years (subject to dissolution) and six further members appointed by the President. Elections to the Assembly were first held on 30 Dec 1979 and its first session opened on 24 Jan 1980. Executive power is vested in the President, nominated by the SRSP Central Committee and elected by the Assembly for 6 years. He appoints and leads the Council of Ministers. On 26 Jan 1980 Gen. Siyad Barrah was elected President. On 21 Oct 1980 he declared a state of emergency and reinstituted the SRC, with extensive powers. The SRC's 17 members are all officers in the armed forces. There is unrest in the northern part of Somalia and some 750 000 Ethiopian refugees are currently (1988) in the country.
Length of roadways: 21 297 km (*13 225 miles*) (1983).
Universities: 1.
Adult illiteracy: 88·4% in 1985.
Defence: Military service voluntary; total armed forces 65 000 (1987); defence expenditure: 5300 million Somali shillings in 1985.

South Africa

Official name: Republic of South Africa, or Republiek van Suid-Afrika.
Population: 35 200 000 (1987 estimate) – of which

South Africa minus Transkei, Bophuthatswana, Venda and Ciskei but including other 'homelands' (GazanKulu, KaNgwane, KwaNdebele, KwaZulu, Lebowa and Qwaqwa) 29 025 000 in 1987; Transkei, Bophuthatswana, Venda and Ciskei had a combined population in 1985 of 5 954 400; Walvis Bay had a population of 20 800 in 1981.

Area: 1 222 161 km² (*471 879 miles²*) (including all the 'homelands' and Walvis Bay); (South Africa excluding Transkei, Bophuthatswana, Venda and Ciskei has an area of 1 125 500 km² (*434 558 miles²*)); the area including all 'homelands' is 1 221 037 km² (*471 445 miles²*) excluding Walvis Bay.

Languages: Afrikaans, English, Xhosa, Zulu, Sesuto (Sesotho), Tswana (Setswana), Sepedi.

Religions: Christian; Islam (Sunni) and Hindu minorities.

Capital city: Administrative: Pretoria, population 822 925 (including suburbs) (1985 census). Legislative: Cape Town (Kaapstad), population 1 911 521 (including suburbs) (1985 census).

Other principal towns (1985): Johannesburg 1 609 408 (including suburbs); Port Elizabeth 651 993 (including suburbs); Vereeniging 540 142 (including conurbation); Bloemfontein 232 984 (including suburbs); East London 193 819 (including suburbs); Pietermaritzburg 192 417 (including suburbs); Kimberley 149 667 (including conurbation).

Highest point: Injasuti, 3408 m (*11 182 ft*).

Principal mountain range: Drakensberg.

Principal rivers: Orange (Oranje), 2092 km (*1300 mile*); Limpopo; Vaal.

Head of State: Pieter Willem Botha (b. 12 Jan 1916), State President.

Climate: Generally temperate (cool summers, mild winters). Average temperatures about 17°C (*63°F*). In Cape Town, average maximum 17°C (*63°F*) (July) to 26°C (*79°F*) (February), minimum 7°C (*45°F*) (July) to 15°C (*60°F*) (January, February), rainiest month is July (10 days). In Johannesburg, average maximum 17°C (*62°F*) (June) to 25°C (*78°F*) (December, January), minimum 4°C (*39°F*) (June, July) to 14°C (*58°F*) (January, February), rainiest month is January (12 days). Absolute maximum temperature 51·56°C (*124·8°F*), Main, 28 Jan 1903; absolute minimum −14·7°C (*5·5°F*), Carolina, 23 July 1926.

Labour force: 11 134 000 in 1986: (this figure includes all 'homelands').

Gross domestic product: (for South Africa including all 'homelands') 127 902 million rand in 1986: Agriculture, forestry and fishing 6·5%; Mining 18·7%; Manufacturing 24·8%; Trade 12·7%; Transport, storage and communications 10·1%; Finance 16·7%.

Exports: (South African Customs Union) 41 796·7 million rand in 1986: Gold 40%; Mineral products 11·7%; Base metals and articles of base metal 11·4%; Pearls, precious and semi-precious stones 7·3%.

Monetary unit: Rand. 1 rand = 100 cents.

Denominations:
Coins 1, 2, 5, 10, 20, 50 cents; 1 rand.
Notes 2, 5, 10, 20, 50 rand.

Political history and government: After the Boer War of 1899–1902 two former Boer republics, the Transvaal and the Orange Free State, became part of the British Empire. On 31 May 1910 they were merged with the British territories of Natal and Cape Colony (now Cape Province) to form the Union of South Africa, a dominion under the British crown. Under the Statute of Westminster, passed by the British Parliament in December 1931 and accepted by South Africa in June 1934, the Union was recognized as an independent country within the Commonwealth. Following a referendum among white voters on 5 Oct 1960, South Africa became a republic, outside the Commonwealth, on 31 May 1961. Under the initial republican constitution, legislative power was vested in a bicameral Parliament, made up exclusively of European (white) members holding office for 5 years (subject to dissolution). Under constitutional changes approved on 12 June 1980, the Senate was abolished from 1 Jan 1981, leaving the House of Assembly as the sole legislative chamber directly elected by Europeans only. Executive power is vested in the State President, elected by the three chambers of Parliament – by 50 members from the White House, 25 members from the Coloured House and 13 members from the Indian House – for a 7-year term as constitutional Head of State. He initiates legislation. The President is aided by a President's Council of 60 members: 20 from the White House; 10 from the Coloured House; 5 from the Indian House; 10 MPs chosen by the President and 10 MPs nominated by Opposition parties in Parliament. Each of the four provinces has an Adminstrator appointed by the President for 5 years and a provincial council elected by whites only for 5 years. The constitutional changes introduced on 4 Sept 1984, provides for a tri-cameral Parliament (elected for five years) consisting of: the House of Assembly with 178 members of whom 166 are directly elected and 8 indirectly elected by white voters; the House of Representatives of 85 members, 80 of whom are directly elected by coloured (mixed race) voters; and the House of Delegates with 45 members, 40 of whom are directly elected by Indian voters; Black voters have no Parliamentary vote and can only vote for the Executive Councils or Parliaments of their 'homelands' – these 10 territories consist of six with a degree of self-government (KwaZulu, GazanKulu, Lebowa, KaNgwane, KwaNdebele and Qwaqwa) and four to which South Africa has granted independence – the Transkei (26 Oct 1976), Bophuthatswana (6 Dec 1977), Venda (13 Sept 1979) and the Ciskei (4 Dec 1981), African 'homelands' established by the government, but not receiving international recognition.

Length of roadways: 185 133 km (*115 036 miles*) (1985, excluding Transkei, Ciskei, Venda and Bophuthatswana).

Length of railways: 23 607 km (*14 660 miles*) (1987).

Universities: 21 including those in 'homelands'.

Adult illiteracy: 50% in 1984 (including nearly 68% of blacks).

Defence: Military service: 24 months for whites; total armed forces 97 000 (1987); defence expenditure: 6683 million rand in 1987–8. This excludes details for Transkei, Ciskei, Bophuthatswana and Venda.

Foreign tourists: 644 502 in 1986.

Spain

Official name: The Kingdom of Spain.

Population: 38 668 319 (1986 estimate).

Area: 504 782 km² (*194 897 miles²*) including the Canary Islands and Balearic Islands.

Languages: Spanish (Castilian), Catalan, Basque, Galician.

Religion: Roman Catholic.

Capital city: Madrid, population 3 217 461 (1986 estimate).

Other principal towns (1986): Barcelona 1 756 905; Valencia 763 949; Sevilla 673 574; Zaragoza 592 666; Malaga 533 549; Bilbao 420 538; Las Palmas 379 693; Valladolid 335 374; Palma de Mallorca 313 376; Hospitalet 287 734; Cordoba 298 621.

Highest point: Mt Teide (Canary Is), 3716 m (*12 190 ft*).

Principal mountain ranges: Pyrenees, Cordillera Cantábrica.

Principal rivers: Ebro (895 km *556 miles*), Duero (Douro), Tajo (Tagus), Guadiana, Guadalquivir.

Head of State: HM King Juan Carlos I (b. 5 Jan 1938), who took the oath as King 22 Nov 1975.

Crown Prince: HRH Don Felipe, Prince of Asturias (b. 30 Jan 1968), only son of King Juan Carlos I.

Head of Government: Felipe Gonzalez (b. 5 Mar 1942), President of the Government (Prime Minister).

Climate: Cool summers and rainy winters on north coast; hot summers and cold winters in interior; hot summers and mild winters on south coast. In Madrid, average maximum 8°C (*47°F*) (January) to 30°C (*87°F*) (July), minimum 0·5°C (*33°F*) (January) to 17°C (*62°F*) (July, August), rainiest month is March (11 days). In Barcelona, average maximum 13°C (*56°F*) (January) to 28°C (*82°F*) (August), minimum 5°C (*42°F*) (January) to 20°C (*69°F*) (July, August), rainiest months are April, May, October (each 8 days). Absolute maximum temperature 46·2°C (*115·2°F*), Gualulcacin, 17 July 1943; absolute minimum −32·0°C (*−25·6°F*), Estangeno, 2 Feb 1956.

Labour force: 16 280 000 in 1986: Industry 21%; Construction 6·1%; Services 42·3%; Unemployed 18%.

Gross domestic product: 18 875·9 billion pesetas in 1985: Agriculture, forestry and fishing 6·5%; Mining, manufacturing, electricity, gas and water 27·9%; Construction 7·6%; Trade 18·5%.

Exports: 4 104 143 million pesetas in 1985: Metal products 15·4%; Cars 8·8%; Machinery 11·8%; Refined petroleum and related products 8·2%.

Monetary unit: Spanish peseta. 1 peseta = 100 céntimos.

Denominations:
Coins 1, 2, 5, 10, 25, 50, 100 pesetas.
Notes 100, 200, 500, 1000, 2000, 5000, 10 000 pesetas.

Political history and government: In the civil war of 1936–39 the forces of the republic (established on 14 Apr 1931) were defeated. Gen. Francisco Franco, leader of the successful insurgent forces, acted as Head of State until his death on 20 Nov 1975. The legislature, traditionally designated the *Cortes* (Courts), was revived in 1942 as a unicameral body, with strictly limited powers, named *Las Cortes Españolas*. In accordance with the 1947 Law of Succession, Prince Juan Carlos de Borbón, grandson of the last reigning monarch, became King on 22 Nov 1975. The government's Political Reform Bill, passed by the *Cortes* on 18 Nov 1976, was approved by a popular referendum on 15 Dec 1976. This provided for a new bicameral *Cortes*, comprising a Congress of Deputies (350 elected members) and a Senate of 248 members (207 elected, 41 nominated by the King). Elections for the new *Cortes* were held on 15 June 1977. The old *Cortes* expired on 30 June 1977; the new legislature was inaugurated on 13 July and formally opened on 23 July 1977.

In 1978 a new constitution was approved by both Houses of the *Cortes* on 31 Oct, endorsed by a referendum on 6 Dec and ratified by the King on 27 Dec. It entered into force on 29 Dec 1978 and the *Cortes* was dissolved on 2 Jan 1979. The constitution confirmed Spain as a parliamentary monarchy, with freedom for political parties, and it recognized and guaranteed the right of Spain's 'nationalities and regions' to autonomy. All the 'fundamental laws' of the Franco régime were repealed and the Roman Catholic Church was disestablished. The monarchy is hereditary, with the King having mainly formal prerogatives. Legislative power is vested in the bicameral *Cortes Generales*, comprising a Senate and a Congress of Deputies, both Houses elected by universal adult suffrage for 4 years (subject to dissolution). Members of the Congress are elected on the basis of proportional representation. For the elections of 1986 the Congress had 350 seats and the Senate 208: 188 for continental Spain (4 for each of the 47 provinces), 5 for the Balearic Islands, 11 for the Canary Islands (2 provinces) and 2 each for the African enclaves of Ceuta and Melilla. Executive power is held by the Council of Ministers, led by the President of the Government (Prime Minister), who is appointed by the King with the approval of the *Cortes*. Other Ministers are appointed on the Prime Minister's recommendation. The Government is responsible to the Congress. Spain comprises 17 autonomous communities in a semi-federal structure, each having its own Parliament elected by adult universal suffrage. Ceuta and Melilla, on the African coast, are municipalities not included in any of the 17 units.

Length of roadways: 318 991 km (*198 093 miles*) (1986).

Length of railways: 17 240 km (*10 706 miles*).

Universities: 20 state universities, 1 open, 4 polytechnics of university status, 4 independent or autonomous universities and 8 technical universities.

Defence: Military service: 12 months; total armed forces 325 500 (209 000 conscripts) in 1987; defence expenditure: 630 980 million pesetas in 1986.

Foreign tourists: 54 000 000 in 1988.

SPAIN

Sri Lanka

Official name: Sri Lanka Prajatantrika Samajawadi Janarajaya (Democratic Socialist Republic of Sri Lanka – 'Exalted Ceylon').
Population: 16 361 000 (1987 estimate).
Area: 65 610 km² (*25 332 miles²*).
Languages: Sinhala (Official) 69%; Tamil 23%; English.
Religions (1981): Buddhist 69·3%; Hindu 15·5%; Islam (Sunni) 7·6%; Christian 7·5%.
Capital city: Colombo, population 683 000 in 1986.
Other principal towns (1986): Dehiwala-Mount Lavinia 191 000; Jaffna 143 000 (which figure has been greatly changed owing to the unrest in the area); Moratuwa 138 000; Kandy 130 000; Galle 109 000; Kotte 104 000.
Highest point: Pidurutalagala, 2527 m (*8292 ft*).
Principal rivers: Mahaweli Ganga (327 km *203 miles*), Kelani Ganga.
Head of State: Ranasinghe Premadasa (b. 23 June 1924).
Prime Minister: D. B. Wijetunge.
Climate: Tropical, with average temperature of about 27°C (*80°F*). Monsoon strikes the south-west of the island. In Colombo, average maximum 29°C (*85°F*) (June to December) to 31°C (*88°F*) (March, April); minimum 22°C (*72°F*) (December, January, February) to 25°C (*78°F*) (May); May and October rainiest (each 19 days).
Labour force: 5 972 004 in 1985–6: Agriculture, forestry and fishing 42·4%; Manufacturing 10·9%; Trade 8·6%; Community, social and personal services 10·6%.
Gross domestic product: 172·4 billion rupees in 1986: Agriculture, forestry and fishing 22·9%; Manufacturing 15·6%; Transport, storage and communications 11·4%; Trade 19%; Public administration 6·5%.
Exports: 34 094 million rupees in 1986: Tea 27%; Rubber 7·7%; Desiccated coconut 2·5%.
Monetary unit: Sri Lanka rupee. 1 rupee = 100 cents.
Denominations:
Coins 1, 2, 5, 10, 25, 50 cents; 1, 2, 5, 10 rupees.
Notes 2, 5, 10, 20, 50, 100, 500, 1000 rupees.
Political history and government: Formerly, as Ceylon, a British dependency. It became independent, as a monarchy within the Commonwealth, on 4 Feb 1948. The country's name and status were changed on 22 May 1972, when it became the Republic of Sri Lanka. Under the first republican constitution, the President was a non-executive Head of State and direction of the government was vested in the Cabinet. Legislative power was vested in the unicameral National State Assembly (formerly the House of Representatives), with 168 members elected for 6 years by universal adult suffrage. On 4 Oct 1977 the Assembly adopted an amendment to the constitution to provide for a directly elected executive President. Under the amendment, signed into law on 20 Oct 1977, the Prime Minister in office (J. R. Jayawardene) became President. It provided for the President to be Head of Government but also to appoint a Prime Minister. Jayawardene was sworn in as President for a 6-year term on 4 Feb 1978 and was re-elected in 1982. In 1988, R. Premadasa was elected President.

A new constitution was adopted by the Assembly on 16 Aug 1978 and came into force on 7 Sept 1978.

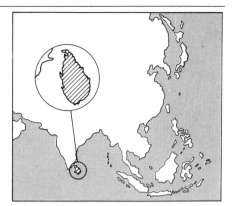

SRI LANKA

The country's present name was introduced and the Assembly renamed Parliament. Future elections to Parliament are to be on the basis of proportional representation and Parliament is to have 168 members elected for 6 years (subject to dissolution). The President appoints the Prime Minister and other Ministers from among the members of Parliament. The President is not responsible to Parliament and may dissolve it. Sri Lanka comprises 25 administrative districts, each with a development council, and these are grouped into eight provinces (in 1988). There is considerable unrest in the country with Tamil separatists conducting a guerrilla movement in the North and East and Marxist Guerrillas in the South. In 1988, the Northern and Eastern provinces were grouped together to form an autonomous Tamil region. The intercommunal violence which began in 1982 – and which led to a state of emergency being declared in May 1983 – continues.
Length of roadways: 152 423 km (*94 655 miles*).
Length of railways: 1944 km (*1207 miles*).
Universities: 8.
Adult illiteracy: 14% in 1981.
Defence: Military service voluntary; total armed forces 47 700 (1987); defence expenditure: 9200 million rupees in 1988; there is an Indian peace-keeping force in the North and East under an agreement between Sri Lanka and the Indian Government.
Foreign tourists: 230 106 in 1986.

Sudan

Official name: Al Jumhuriyat as-Sudan (the Republic of Sudan).
Population: 25 550 000 (1987 estimate).
Area: 2 505 813 km² (*967 500 miles²*).
Languages: Arabic, Nilotic, others.
Religions: Islam (Sunni) (in North), Animist (in South).
Capital city: El Khartum (Khartoum), population 1 343 651 at 1983 census – of which Khartoum 476 218, Umm Durman (Omdurman) 526 287 and El Khartum Bahri (Khartoum North) 341 146.
Other principal towns (1983): Bur Sudan (Port Sudan) 206 727; Wadi Medani 141 065; El Obeid 140 024.

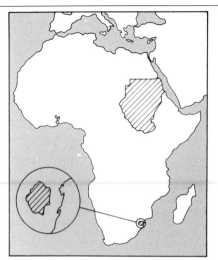

top: **SUDAN**
below: **SWAZILAND**

new definitive constitution was introduced on 8 May 1973. In March 1985 President Numairi was deposed while out of the country.

Legislative power is vested in the Legislative Assembly which was elected in May 1986. The assembly elected a Council of Five to head the state, led by the President. A Prime Minister is elected, according to the temporary constitution introduced by the assembly, for 4 years. At the end of this period a permanent constitution will be drawn up by the present elected assembly (of 301 members) for a permanent democratic system in Sudan.

A transitional council has been formed to take over the governing of Southern Sudan until the constitutional conference is held to decide the future of the area. Unrest continues in the South where the situation worsened in 1983. A state of emergency was declared in the Southern (non-Islamic) Region in April 1984 when the internal rebellion became more serious.

Length of roadways: *c.* 50 000 km (*c. 31 070 miles*).
Length of railways: 5500 km (*3418 miles*).
Universities: 4 (plus the Khartoum branch of Cairo University).
Adult illiteracy: 50% in 1985 (estimate).
Defence: Military service: conscription; total armed forces 58 500 (1987); defence expenditure: £S1100 million in 1986–7.

Highest point: Mt Kinyeti, 3187 m (*10 456 ft*).
Principal mountain ranges: Darfur Highlands, Nubian Mts.
Principal rivers: Nile (the Blue Nile and White Nile join at Khartoum), 6670 km (*4145 miles*).
President and Prime Minister: General Omar Hussan al-Bashir.
Climate: Hot and dry in desert areas of north (average maximum up to 44°C *111°F*); rainy and humid in tropical south. Average temperature about 21°C (*70°F*). In Khartoum, average maximum 32°C (*90°F*) (January) to 42°C (*107°F*) (May), minimum 15°C (*59°F*) (January) to 26°C (*79°F*) (June); rainiest month is August (6 days). Absolute maximum 49·0°C (*120·2°F*), Wadi Halfa, 7 and 8 June 1932, 9 and 13 June 1933, 19 June 1941; absolute minimum −0·8°C (*30·6°F*), Zalingei, 6 Feb 1957.
Labour force: 7 195 000 in 1986: Agriculture 64·7%.
Gross domestic product: £S14 097 million in 1985–6.
Exports: £S893·5 million in 1984: Cotton 50·1%; Livestock 10·2%; Sesame seed 9·8%; Gum arabic 9·4%.
Monetary unit: Sudanese pound (£S). 1 pound = 100 piastres.
Denominations:
Coins 1, 2, 5, 10 piastres.
Notes 25, 50 piastres; 1, 5, 10, 20 pounds.
Political history and government: An Anglo-Egyptian condominium from 19 Jan 1899 until becoming an independent parliamentary republic on 1 Jan 1956. On 25 May 1969 the civilian government was overthrown by army officers, under Col. (promoted Maj.-Gen.) Ga'afar an-Numairi, who established a Revolutionary Command Council (RCC). Gen. Numairi became Prime Minister on 28 Oct 1969. On 13 Aug 1971 the RCC promulgated a provisional constitution, proclaiming socialist principles. Gen. Numairi was elected President (unopposed) in September 1971 and inaugurated for a 6-year term on 12 Oct 1971. The RCC was dissolved and the Sudanese Socialist Union (SSU) established as the country's sole political party. A

Suriname

Official name: Republiek Suriname (Republic of Suriname).
Population: 393 748 (1985 estimate).
Area: 163 265 km² (*63 037 miles²*).
Languages: Dutch 37·1%; Hindustani 31·7%; Javanese 15·4%; Creole 13·8% (1964).
Religions: Christian 45·1%; Hindu 27·8%; Islam (Sunni) 20·2% (1964).
Capital city: Paramaribo, population 103 738 (1971 census).
Other principal towns: Nieuw Nickerie, Nieuw Amsterdam.
Highest point: Julianatop, 1286 m (*4218 ft*).
Principal mountain ranges: Wilhelmina Gebergte, Kayser Gebergte.
Principal rivers: Corantijn, Nickerie, Coppename, Saramacca, Suriname, Commewijne, Maroni (Marowijne).
Head of State: Ramsewak Shankar, President.
Prime Minister: Henck Arron.
Climate: Sub-tropical, with fairly heavy rainfall and average temperatures of 21°C to 30°C (*73°F to 88°F*).
Labour force: 99 240 in 1985: Agriculture, forestry and fishing 17·2%; Mining 4·6%; Manufacturing 11%; Trade 12·9%; Government services 40·5%.
Gross domestic product: 1741·3 million Suriname guilders in 1985.
Exports: 650·7 milion Suriname guilders in 1985: Alumina 54·6%; Aluminium 11·6%; Bauxite 12·9%; Rice 11·4%.
Monetary unit: Suriname gulden (guilder) or florin. 1 guilder = 100 cents.
Denominations:
Coins 1, 5, 10, 25 cents; 1, 2½ guilders
Notes 5, 10, 25, 100, 500 guilders.
Political history and government: Formerly a Dutch possession, with full internal autonomy from 29

SURINAME

Dec 1954. Suriname became an independent republic on 25 Nov 1975.

The government was overthrown in a *coup* on 25 Feb 1980, when a National Military Council (NMC), comprising eight army officers, took power. The Cabinet resigned on the next day but the President remained in office. On 15 Mar 1980 the NMC appointed a mainly civilian Cabinet, with Dr Henrik (Henk) Chin A Sen as Prime Minister. Elections to the *Staten*, planned for 27 Mar 1980, were postponed until October 1981, as originally due. On 15 Aug 1980 the NMC dismissed the President and Dr Chin A Sen assumed this office while remaining Prime Minister. At the same time a state of emergency was declared and the constitution suspended. The *Staten* was replaced by an advisory assembly. On 20 Nov 1980 Dr Chin A Sen became the country's first executive President and the office of Prime Minister was abolished. On 21 Dec 1980 general elections were further postponed for 'at least two years'. In 1982 Dr Chin A Sen was dismissed by the NMC and in 1984 the subsequent Prime Minister was dismissed.

Martial law was imposed in 1983 and although a civilian Cabinet was appointed, Lt-Col. Désiré Bouterse remained in control. In December 1984 plans for a National Assembly were announced – this was inaugurated in January 1985. A further new constitution was approved on 31 Mar 1987, against a background of guerrilla attacks and attempted *coups*. A general election for a 51 seat National Assembly was held on 25 Nov 1987. Under the new constitution there is provision for a President and Vice-President, elected by the National Assembly – the Vice-President is concurrently Prime Minister. A five man Military Council has been appointed (December 1987) to guarantee the constitution.

Suriname comprises nine districts.

Length of roadways: 8889 km (*5525 miles*).
Length of railways: 167 km (*104 miles*).
Universities: 1.
Adult illiteracy: 10% in 1985.
Defence: Total armed forces about 2690 (1987); defence expenditure: 41 million Suriname florins (1987).
Foreign tourists: 66 200 in 1985.

Swaziland

Official name: The Kingdom of Swaziland.
Population: 676 089 (1986 census).
Area: 17 363 km² (*6704 miles²*).
Languages: English, Siswati.
Religions: Christian 60%, Animist.
Capital city: Mbabane, population 38 636 (1982).
Other principal towns (1976): Manzini 18 818; Havelock 4838; Mhlume 3921; Pigg's Peak 2192; Big Bend 2083.
Highest point: Emlembe, 1863 m (*6113 ft*).
Principal mountain ranges: Lubombo.
Principal rivers: Usutu, Komati, Umbuluzi, Ingwavuma.
Head of State: HM King Mswati III (b. April 1968), succeeded 25 Apr 1986 upon the termination of the Regency of HM Queen Ntombi, Queen Regent, mother of the King.
Prime Minister: Sotsha Dlamini.
Climate: Rainy season October to March. Annual average at Mbabane, in high veld, 1395 mm (*55 in*), in low veld 635 mm (*25 in*). Average temperatures 11°C to 22°C (*52°F to 72°F*) at Mbabane, 13°C to 27°C (*56°F to 80°F*) at Manzini, warmer on low veld.
Labour force: 317 879 in 1982.
Gross domestic product: 957 million emalangeni in 1985/6.
Exports: 323·7 million emalangeni in 1983: Sugar 37·9%; Wood pulp 13·8%; Chemicals 13·2%.
Monetary unit: Lilangeni (plural: emalangeni). 1 lilangeni = 100 cents. (South African currency is also legal tender).
Denominations:
 Coins 1, 2, 5, 10, 20, 50 cents; 1 lilangeni.
 Notes 2, 5, 10, 20 emalangeni.
Political history and government: A former British protectorate, with internal self-government from 25 Apr 1967 and full independence, within the Commonwealth, from 6 Sept 1968. Swaziland is a monarchy, with executive authority vested in the King. He appoints a Cabinet, led by a Prime Minister. Under the independence constitution, legislative power was vested in a bicameral Parliament. On 12 Apr 1973, in response to a motion passed by both Houses, the King repealed the constitution, suspended political activity and assumed all legislative, executive and judicial powers. On 24 May 1977 the King announced the abolition of the parliamentary system and its replacement by traditional tribal communities called *tinkhundla*. On 28 Oct 1983 a general election took place to elect a college of 80 members, with 2 members elected from each traditional tribal community (Inkhundla). This college elects from its members, 40 members (deputies) to a House of Assembly, the remaining 10 deputies being chosen by the King. An Upper House, the Senate, has 20 members – 10 chosen by the House of Assembly and 10 by the King. Swaziland has 4 districts, each administered by an appointed District Commissioner.
Length of roadways: 2723 km (*1692 miles*) (1983).
Length of railways: 370 km (*230 miles*) (1987).
Universities: 1.
Adult illiteracy: 32·1% in 1985.
Defence: An army of 6250 (1986); compulsory military service; defence expenditure: 5·4% of total government expenditure in 1988.
Foreign tourists: 130 135 in 1984.

Sweden

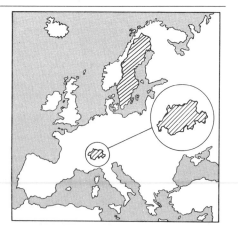

top: **SWEDEN**
encircled: **SWITZERLAND**

Official name: Konungariket Sverige (Kingdom of Sweden).
Population: 8 414 083 (1986 estimate).
Area: 449 793 km² (*173 654 miles²*).
Languages: Swedish; Finnish and Lapp in north.
Religion: Lutheran 95%.
Capital city: Stockholm ('log island'), population 1 420 198 in 1984.
Other principal towns (1984): Göteborg 669 151; Malmö 455 377; Uppsala 152 579; Norrköping 118 451; Västerås 117 658; Örebro 117 569; Linköping 115 600; Jönköping 107 031; Helsingborg 104 689.
Highest point: Kebnekaise, 2123 m (*6965 ft*).
Principal mountain ranges: Norrland Mountains, Smaland Highlands.
Principal rivers: Ume (499 km *310 miles*), Torne (569 km *354 miles*), Angerman (499 km *279 miles*), Klar (489 km *304 miles*), Dal (520 km *323 miles*).
Head of State: HM King Carl XVI Gustav (b. 30 Apr 1946), succeeded upon the death of his grandfather King Gustaf VI Adolf on 15 Sept 1973. Crown Princess: HRH Crown Princess Victoria (b. 14 July 1977), eldest child of King Carl Gustaf. (Since 1980 the first-born Royal child has the right of succession whether male or female).
Prime Minister: Ingvar Carlsson (b. 9 Jan 1934).
Climate: Summers mild and warm; winters long and cold in north, more mdoerate in south. In Stockholm, average maximum −0·5°C (*31°F*) (January, February) to 21°C (*70°F*) (July), minimum −5°C (*22°F*) (February) to 12°C (*55°F*) (July), rainiest month is August (10 days). Absolute maximum temperature 38·0°C (*100·4°F*), Ultuna, 9 July 1933; absolute minimum −53·3°C (*−63·9°F*), Laxbacken, 13 Dec 1941.
Labour force: 4 337 000 in 1987: Agriculture, forestry and fishing 3·9%; Mining and manufacturing 22·4%; Trade, restaurants and hotels 14%; Finance 7·6%; Public services 37·5%.
Gross domestic product: 861 billion kronor in 1985: Agriculture, forestry and fishing 3·7%; Mining and manufacturing 24·8%; Electricity, gas and water-works 3·4%; Construction 8·1%; Private services 35·4%; Public services 24·6%.
Exports: 265 040 million kronor in 1986: Cork and wood 3·6%; Pulp and waste paper 3·3%; Iron ore 1%; Paper, paperboard and manufactures 10·4%; Iron and steel 6·2%; Machinery and transport equipment 43·8%.
Monetary unit: Swedish krona (plural: kronor). 1 krona = 100 öre.
Denominations:
Coins 10, 50 öre; 1, 5 kronor.
Notes 5, 10, 50, 100, 500, 1000, 10 000 kronor.
Political history and government: Sweden has been a constitutional monarchy, traditionally neutral, since the constitution of 6 June 1809. Parliamentary government was adopted in 1917 and universal adult suffrage introduced in 1921. A revised constitution was introduced on 1 Jan 1975. The King is Head of State but has very limited formal prerogatives. Legislative power is held by the Parliament (*Riksdag*), which has been unicameral since 1 Jan 1971. It has 310 members elected by universal adult suffrage for 3 years from constituencies, plus 39 seats elected from a nationwide pool using pro-portional representation. Executive power is held by the Cabinet, led by the Prime Minister, which is responsible to the *Riksdag*. Under the 1975 constitu-tion, the Prime Minister is nominated by the Speaker of the *Riksdag* and later confirmed in office by the whole House. After approval, the Prime Min-ister appoints other members of the Cabinet. Swe-den is divided into 24 counties, each administered by a nominated governor.
Length of roadways: 174 291 km (*108 323 miles*) (1985).
Length of railways: 11 536 km (*7164 miles*) (1986).
Universities: 34 (including university colleges).
Defence: Military service: Army and Navy 7½ to 15 months; Air Force 8 to 12 months; total armed forces 67 000 (including 48 950 conscripts) (1987); defence expenditure: 26 368 million kronor 1986–7.
Foreign tourists: 3 363 000 in 1983.

Switzerland

Official name: Schweizerische Eidgenossenschaft (German), Confédération Suisse (French), Confederazione Svizzera (Italian): Swiss Confed-eration.
Population: 6 523 413 (1987 estimate).
Area: 41 293 km² (*15 943 miles²*).
Languages: German 65%; French 18%; Italian 10%; Romansch 1%; Others 6%.
Religions: Roman Catholic 48%; Protestant 44%.
Capital city: Bern (Berne), population 300 316 (1986 estimate).
Other principal towns (1986): Zürich 840 313; Basel (Bâle) 363 029; Genève (Genf, Geneva) 384 507; Lausanne 262 217; Winterthur 107 812; St Gallen (Saint Gall) 125 879; Luzern (Lucerne) 160 594.
Highest point: Dufourspitze (Monte Rosa), 4634 m (*15 203 ft*) (first climbed 1855).
Principal mountain range: Alps.
Principal rivers: Rhein (Rhine) and Aare, Rhône, Inn, Ticino.
Head of State: Jean-Pascal Delamuraz, President for 1989.
Climate: Generally temperate, with wide variations due to altitude. Cooler in north, warm on southern

slopes. In Zürich, average maximum 9°C (*48°F*) (January) to 30°C (*86°F*) (July), minimum −10°C (*14°F*) (January) to 10°C (*51°F*) (July), rainiest months are June and July (each 15 days). In Geneva, January coldest (−2°C to 4°C *29°F to 39°F*), July warmest (14°C to 25°C *58°F to 77°F*). Absolute maximum temperature 38·7°C (*101·7°F*), Basel, 29 July 1947; absolute minimum −35·8°C (*−34·4°F*), Jungfraujoch, 14 Feb 1940.
Labour force: 3170900 in 1985: Agriculture 6·6%; Industry 38%; Services 55·4%.
Gross domestic product: 254510 million Swiss francs in 1986.
Exports: 67004 million Swiss francs in 1986: Metal manufactures 52·3%; Chemicals 21·3%; Textiles and clothing 6·9%; Precious metal articles and jewellery 7%.
Monetary unit: Schweizer Franken (Swiss franc). 1 franc = 100 Rappen (centimes).
Denominations:
Coins 1, 2, 5, 10, 20, 50 centimes; 1, 2, 5 francs.
Notes 10, 20, 50, 100, 500, 1000 francs.
Political history and government: Since 1815 Switzerland has been a neutral confederation of autonomous cantons. The present constitution, establishing a republican form of government, was adopted on 29 May 1874. The cantons hold all powers not specifically delegated to the federal authorities. On 1 Jan 1979 a new canton, the first since 1815, was established when the Jura seceded from Bern. Switzerland now has 20 cantons and 6 half-cantons.

Legislative power is held by the bicameral Federal Assembly: a Council of States with 46 members representing the cantons (two for each canton and one for each half-canton), elected for 3 to 4 years; and the National Council with 200 members directly elected by universal adult suffrage for 4 years, using proportional representation. The two Houses have equal rights. A referendum on 7 Feb 1971 approved women's suffrage in federal elections. Executive power is held by the Federal Council, which has 7 members (not more than one from any canton) elected for 4 years by a joint session of the Federal Assembly. Each member of the Council, which is responsible to the Assembly, has ministerial responsibility as head of a Federal Department. The Assembly elects one Councillor to be President of the Confederation (also presiding over the Council) for one calendar year at a time. Each canton has a constitution, an elected unicameral legislature and an executive.
Length of roadways: 70578 km (*43829 miles*) (1985).
Length of railways: 5055 km (*3139 miles*) (1986).
Universities: 17 (plus 2 technical universities).
Defence: Military service: 17 weeks recruit training, followed by reservist refresher training of three weeks per year for 8 out of 12 years, two weeks for 3 of 10 years, and one week for 2 of 8 years; total armed forces on mobilization: 625000 in 1987; defence expenditure: 4810 million Swiss francs in 1987.
Foreign tourists: 35182000 overnight stays in 1985.

Syria

Official name: Al-Jumhuriya al-'Arabiya as-Suriya (the Syrian Arab Republic).
Population: 10612000 (1986 estimate).
Area: 185180 km² (*71498 miles²*).

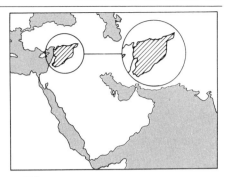

SYRIA

Languages: Arabic (official); Kurdish; Armenian; Turkish; Circassian.
Religion: Islam (90% Sunni); Christian minority.
Capital city: Dimash'q (Damascus), population 1112214 (1981 census).
Other principal towns (1981): Halab (Aleppo) 985413; Homs 346871; Al Ladhiqiyah (Latakia) 196791; Hama 177208.
Highest point: Jabal ash-Shaikh (Mt Hermon), 2814 m (*9232 ft*).
Principal mountain ranges: Ansariyah range, Jabal ar-Ruwā.
Principal rivers: Al Furat (Euphrates headwaters) (676 km *420 miles* out of 2253 km *1400 miles*), Asi (Orontes).
Head of State: Lt.-Gen. Hafiz al-Assad (b. 6 Oct 1930), President.
Prime Minister: Mahmoud Zubi.
Climate: Variable. Hot summers, mild winters and ample rainfall on coast. Inland it is arid with hot, dry summers and cold winters. In Damascus, average maximum 12°C (*53°F*) (January) to 37°C (*99°F*) (August), minimum 2°C (*36°F*) (January) to 18°C (*64°F*) (July, August), rainiest month is January (seven days).
Labour force: 2356000 in 1984: Agriculture, forestry and fishing 24·3%; Manufacturing 14·3%; Trade 10·7%; Community, social and personal services 22·8%.
Gross domestic product: S£79549 million in 1985: Agriculture, forestry and fishing 21·8%; Manufacturing 6·4%; Trade 21·7%; Services 23%.
Exports: S£6426·5 million in 1985: Raw cotton 8·5%; Textiles 8·3%; Crude petroleum and petroleum products 74·1%.
Monetary unit: Syrian pounds (S£). 1 pound = 100 piastres.
Denominations:
Coins 2½, 5, 10, 25, 50 piastres; 1 pound.
Notes 1, 5, 10, 25, 50, 100, 500 pounds.
Political history and government: Formerly part of Turkey's Ottoman Empire. Turkish forces were defeated in the First World War (1914–18). In 1920 Syria was occupied by French forces, in accordance with a League of Nations mandate. Nationalists proclaimed an independent republic on 16 Sept 1941. The first elected parliament met on 17 Aug 1943, French powers were transferred on 1 Jan 1944 and full independence achieved on 12 Apr 1946. Syria merged with Egypt to form the United Arab Republic, proclaimed on 1 Feb 1958 and established on 21 Feb 1958. Following a military *coup* in

Syria on 28 Sept 1961, the country resumed separate independence, under its present name, on 29 Sept 1961. Left-wing army officers overthrew the government on 8 Mar 1963 and formed the National Council of the Revolutionary Command (NCRC), which took over all executive and legislative authority. The NCRC installed a Cabinet dominated by the Arab Socialist Renaissance (Ba'ath) Party. This party has held power ever since. Lt.-Gen. Hafiz al-Assad became Prime Minister on 18 Nov 1970 and assumed Presidential powers on 22 Feb 1971. His position was approved by popular referendum on 12 Mar 1971 and he was sworn in for a 7-year term as President on 14 Mar 1971. Legislative power is held by the People's Council, originally appointed for two years on 16 Feb 1971 to draft a permanent constitution. The constitution, proclaiming socialist principles, was approved by referendum on 12 Mar 1973 and adopted two days later. It declares that the Ba'ath party is 'the leading party in the state and society'. The People's Council became a full legislature after election by universal adult suffrage on 25–26 Mar 1973. For the elections of 1–2 Aug 1977 the Council was increased to 195 members. Political power is held by the Progressive Front of National Unity, formed on 7 Mar 1972 by a merger of the Ba'ath Party and four others. The Head of State is leader of the Ba'ath Party and President of the Front. Syria has 14 administrative districts.

Length of roadways: 28 960 km (*17 984 miles*).
Length of railways: 1601 km (*995 miles*).
Universities: 4.
Adult illiteracy: 40% in 1985.
Defence: Military service: 30 months; total armed forces 407 500 (1987); defence expenditure: US$3950 million in 1987.
Foreign tourists: 985 514 in 1985.

Tanzania

Official name: United Republic of Tanzania (Jamhuri ya Muungano wa Tanzania).
Population: 22 462 000 (1986 estimate).
Area: 945 087 km² (*364 900 miles²*).
Languages: English, Swahili.
Religions: Traditional beliefs, Christian, Islam (Sunni).
Capital city: Dodoma, population 45 703 (1978 census).
Other principal towns (1978): Dar es Salaam (former capital) 757 346; Zanzibar Town 110 669; Mwanza 110 611; Tanga 103 409; Mbeya 76 606; Morogoro 61 890; Arusha 55 281.
Highest point: Mount Kilimanjaro, 5894 m (*19 340 ft*).
Principal mountain range: Southern Highlands.
Principal rivers: Pangani (Ruvu), Rufiji, Rovuma.
Head of State: Ndugu Ali Hassan Mwinyi, President.
Prime Minister: Joseph S. Warioba.
Climate: Varies with altitude. Tropical (hot and humid) on Zanzibar, and on the coast and plains. Cool and semi-temperate in the highlands. In Dar es Salaam, average maximum 28 °C to 31 °C (*83 °F to 88 °F*), minimum 19 °C to 25 °C (*66 °F to 77 °F*). In Zanzibar Town, average maximum 28 °C (*82 °F*) (July) to 33 °C (*91 °F*) (February, March), minimum 22 °C (*72 °F*) (July–September) to 25 °C (*77 °F*)

(March–April), average annual rainfall 1575 mm (*62 in*), April rainiest (16 days), July driest (four days).
Labour force: 9 508 000 (1980): Agriculture 85·6%; Industry 4·5%.
Gross domestic product: 26 258 million shillings in 1986: Agriculture, forestry and fishing 38·3%; Manufacturing 7·4%; Trade 10·2%; Financial services 11·7%; Community, social and personal services 20·5%.
Exports: 11 116 million shillings in 1986.
Monetary unit: Tanzanian shilling. 1 shilling = 100 cents.
Denominations:
Coins 5, 10, 20, 50 cents; 1, 5, 10 shillings.
Notes 5, 10, 20, 100, 200 shillings.
Political history and government: Tanganyika became a German protectorate in 1885. During the First World War (1914–18) the territory was occupied by British and Belgian forces. In 1919 United Kingdom was granted a League of Nations mandate over Tanganyika. On 13 Dec 1946 it became a United Nations Trust Territory under British administration. Tanganyika became an independent member of the Commonwealth on 9 Dec 1961 and a republic on 9 Dec 1962. Zanzibar, a sultanate under British protection since 1890, became an independent constitutional monarchy within the Commonwealth on 10 Dec 1963. The Sultan was overthrown by revolution on 12 Jan 1964 and the People's Republic of Zanzibar proclaimed. A new constitution was decreed on 24 Feb 1964. The two republics merged on 26 Apr 1964 to form the United Republic of Tanganyika and Zanzibar (renamed Tanzania on 29 Oct 1964) and remained in the Commonwealth.

An interim constitution, declaring Tanzania a one-party state, was approved by the legislature on 5 July 1965 and received the President's assent three days later. Legislative power was vested in the unicameral national Assembly, with a term of five years (subject to dissolution). Executive power lies with the President, elected by popular vote for five years. He appoints a First Vice-President (who is Chairman of the Zanzibar Revolutionary Council), a Prime Minister and a Cabinet.

At a joint conference the ruling parties of Tanganyika and Zanzibar decided on 21 Jan 1977 to merge into a single party, *Chama Cha Mapinduzi* (CCM or Revolutionary Party), formed on 5 Feb 1977. The Party's leading decision-making organ is the National Executive, elected by party members.

On 25 Apr 1977 the National Assembly approved a permanent constitution for Tanzania. There is a 244-member Assembly – of which 169 members are elected by universal suffrage from single member constituencies (119 from the mainland and 50 from Zanzibar); 15 National members elected by the National Assembly; 15 women members also elected by the National Assembly, (5 of them from Zanzibar); 5 members elected by the Zanzibar House of Representatives; 25 ex-officio members (20 Regional Commissioners from the mainland and 5 from Zanzibar); plus 15 members nominated by the President (5 of them from Zanzibar).

Nyerere stepped down as President at the end of his term in 1985, and was succeeded by Ali Hassan Mwinyi, the sole candidate of the CCM Congress.

In Zanzibar, comprising the islands of Zanzibar and Pemba, a Revolutionary Council is responsible for internal government. On 13 Oct 1979 this Council adopted a new constitution for the territory. A

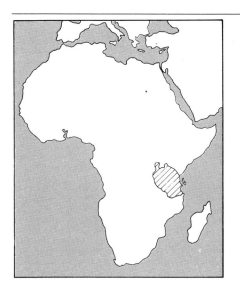

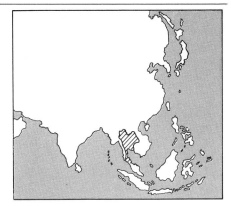

THAILAND

TANZANIA

special session of the CCM approved the new Zanzibar constitution on 28 Dec 1979 and legislation incorporating the necessary amendments to the Tanzanian constitution was approved on 2 Jan 1980 – although Zanzibar is currently ruled by decree.
Length of roadways: 81 895 km (*50 857 miles*) (1985).
Length of railways: 4460 km (*2770 miles*).
Universities: 2.
Adult illiteracy: 15% in 1983.
Defence: Military service voluntary; total armed forces 40 050 (1987); defence expenditure: 4170 million shillings in 1985/6.
Foreign tourists: 103 209 in 1987.

Thailand

Official name: Prathet Thai (Kingdom of Thailand), also called Prades Thai or Muang-Thai (Thai means free).
Population: 53 605 000 (1987 estimate).
Area: 514 000 km² (*198 457 miles²*).
Language: Thai.
Religions: Buddhist, Islamic (Sunni) minority.
Capital city: Krungt'ep (Bangkok), population 5 446 708 (1986).
Other principal towns (1980): Chiang Mai 101 595; Nakhon Ratchasima 78 246; Khon Kaen 85 863; Udon Thani 71 142; Pitsanulok 79 942; Hat Yai 93 519.
Highest point: Doi Inthanon, 2576 m (*8452 ft*).
Principal rivers: Mekong (4184 km (*2600 miles*)), Chao Pyha (247 km (*154 miles*)).
Head of State: HM King Bhumibol Adulyadej (b. 5 Dec 1927), succeeded upon the death of his brother King Ananda Mahidol, 9 June 1946. Crown Prince: HRH Prince Vagiralongkorn (b. 28 July 1952), son of King Bhumibol.
Prime Minister: Maj.-Gen. Chatichai Choonhaven.
Climate: Tropical monsoon climate (humid). Three

seasons – hot, rainy and cool. Average temperature 29°C (*85°F*). In Bangkok, average maximum 30°C (*87°F*) (November, December) to 35°C (*95°F*) (April), minimum 20°C (*68°F*) (December, January) to 25°C (*77°F*) (April, May), rainiest month is September (15 days). Absolute maximum temperature 44·1°C (*111·4°F*), Mae Sariang, 25 Apr 1958; absolute minimum 0·1°C (*32·2°F*), Loey, 13 Jan 1955.
Labour force: 37 733 500 in 1985: Agriculture, forestry and fishing 68·8%; Manufacturing 7·9%; Commerce 9·6%; Services 9·7%.
Gross domestic product: 1 098 362 million baht in 1986: Agriculture 16·7%; Manufacturing 20·6%; Trade 18·6%; Services 15·8%.
Exports: 231 224 million baht in 1986: Food and live animals 44%; Crude materials except fuel 8·9%; Basic manufactures 18·9%.
Monetary unit: Baht. 1 baht = 100 satangs.
Denominations:
 Coins 1, 2, 5 baht.
 Notes 5, 10, 20, 50, 100, 500 baht.
Political history and government: Thailand, called Siam before 1939, is a kingdom with an hereditary monarch as Head of State. The military régime established on 17 Nov 1971 was forced to resign, following popular demonstrations, on 14 Oct 1973. An interim government was formed and a new constitution, legalizing political parties, was promulgated on 7 Oct 1974. The constitutional government was overthrown on 7 Oct 1976 by a military junta, the National Administrative Reform Council (NARC), which declared martial law, annulled the 1974 constitution, dissolved the bicameral National Assembly and banned political parties. A new constitution, promulgated on 22 Oct 1976, provided for a National Administrative Reform Assembly (340 members appointed for 4 years by the King on 20 Nov 1976). A new Prime Minister was appointed and the NARC became the Prime Minister's Advisory Council. On 20 Oct 1977 a Revolutionary Council of military leaders (almost identical to the NARC) deposed the government, abrogated the 1976 constitution and abolished the Advisory Council. An interim constitution was promulgated on 9 Nov 1977. It provided that the Revolutionary Council would become the National Policy Council (NPC) and that the Prime Minister would be appointed by the King on the advice of the NPC's chairman. General Kriangsak Chamanan,

Supreme Commander of the Armed Forces and Secretary-General of the NPC, became Prime Minister on 11 Nov 1977. Other Ministers were appointed by the King on the Prime Minister's recommendation. On 16 Nov 1977 a National Legislative Assembly (NLA) of 360 members was nominated by the King on the advice of the NPC's chairman. On 23 Nov the NLA opened and on 1 Dec 1977 it appointed a 35-member committee to draft a new constitution.

A new constitution was approved by the NLA on 18 Dec 1978 and promulgated on 22 Dec 1978. Legislative power is vested in a bicameral National Assembly, comprising a House of Representatives (349 members elected for 4 years by universal adult suffrage) and a Senate (268 members appointed for 6 years by the King on the recommendation of the incumbent Prime Minister). The two chambers meet in joint session to appoint the Prime Minister and to debate motions of confidence. Elections to the House were held on 22 Apr 1979. The nominated Senators were almost all military officers. On 11 May 1979 the Assembly invited Gen. Kriangsak to continue as Prime Minister. After a new Cabinet was formed, the NPC was dissolved. Kriangsak resigned on 29 Feb 1980. Gen. Prem Tinsulanonda, Minister of Defence and Army Commander-in-Chief, was nominated by the Assembly to become Prime Minister, and was appointed by the King, on 3 Mar 1980. A general election was held on 27 July 1986 and on 24 July 1988.

Thailand comprises 73 provinces, each headed by an appointed governor.

Length of roadways: 76 315 km (*47 392 miles*) (1984).
Length of railways: 4440 km (*2757 miles*) (1987).
Universities: 16.
Adult illiteracy: 9% in 1985.
Defence: Military service: 2 years; total armed forces 256 000 (1987); defence expenditure: 42 985 million baht in 1987/8.
Foreign tourists: 2 818 192 in 1987.

Togo

Official name: La République togolaise (the Togolese Republic).
Population: 3 158 000 (1987 estimate).
Area: 56 785 km² (*21 933 miles²*).
Languages: French (official), Ewe, Kabiye.
Religions: Animist; Christian and Islamic (Sunni) minorities.
Capital city: Lomé, population 366 476 (1983 estimate).
Other principal towns (1981): Sokodé 48 098; Kpalimé 31 800; Atakpamé 27 100; Bassari 21 800.
Highest point: 919 m (*3018 ft*).
Principal rivers: Mono, Oti.
Head of State: Gen. Gnassingbe Eyadéma (b. 26 Dec 1937), President.
Climate: Equatorial (hot and humid). On coast, average temperatures 24°C to 28°C (*76°F to 82°F*), higher inland (average 36°C (*97°F*) in drier north).
Labour force: 901 543 in 1981: Agriculture etc 64·3%; Manufacturing 6%; Trade 11·6%; Community, social and personal services 7·1%.
Gross domestic product: 209·38 million CFA francs in 1981.

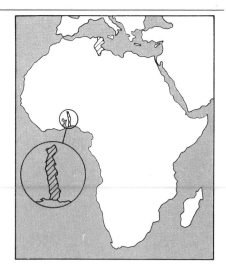

top: **TUNISIA**
encircled: **TOGO**

Exports: 85 380 million CFA francs in 1985: Coffee 13·9%; Phosphates 50·2%; Cocoa beans 8%; Cotton 13·6%.
Monetary unit: France de la Communauté financière africaine.
Denominations:
Coins 1, 2, 5, 10, 25, 50, 100, 500 CFA francs.
Notes 50, 100, 500, 1000, 5000 CFA francs.
Political history and government: Formerly a United Nations Trust Territory under French administration, an independent republic since 27 Apr 1960. An army *coup* on 13 Jan 1967 deposed the President and established military rule under Lt.-Col. (later Maj.-Gen.) Etienne Gnassingbe Eyadéma, who suspended the constitution and dissolved the National Assembly. Eyadéma proclaimed himself President on 14 Apr 1967. Political parties were banned and the President ruled by decree through an appointed Council of Ministers. On 29 Nov 1969 the President established a single ruling party, the *Rassemblement du peuple togolais* (RPT). A congress of the RPT on 27–29 Nov 1979 approved a new constitution for Togo. This provides for a one-party state, with legislative power vested in a 77-member National Assembly (elected for five years by universal adult suffrage) while executive power is held by the President, directly elected for seven years. The constitution was approved by referendum on 30 Dec 1979, when President Eyadéma was re-elected (unopposed) and the new Assembly elected (from a single list of RPT candidates). On 13 Jan 1980 the President proclaimed the 'Third Republic'. Togo is divided into five regions, each administered by an appointed Inspector. In December 1986, Gen. Eyadéma was again elected unopposed.
Length of roadways: 7850 km (*4879 miles*) (1981).
Length of railways: 525 km (*325 miles*).
Universities: 1.
Adult illiteracy: 40·7% in 1985.
Defence: Total armed forces 5910 (1987); defence expenditure: 8500 million CFA francs in 1986.
Foreign tourists: 114 600 in 1986.

Tonga

Official name: Pule'anga Fakatu'i 'o Tonga (Kingdom of Tonga).
Population: 94 535 (1986 census).
Area: 699 km² (270 miles²).
Languages: Tongan, English.
Religions: Christian, mainly Wesleyan.
Capital city: Nuku'alofa, population 28 899 (1986).
Highest point: Kao, 1030 m (3380 ft).
Head of State: HM King Taufa'ahau Tupou IV, GCMG, GCVO, KBE (b. 4 July 1918), succeeded his mother Queen Salote Tupou III on 16 Dec 1965. Crown Prince: HRH Prince Tupouto'a, son of King Taufa'ahau Tupou IV.
Prime Minister: HRH Prince Fatafehi Tu'ipelehake, KCMG, KBE (b. 7 Jan 1922), brother of the King.
Climate: Warm and pleasant. Average annual temperature is 23°C (73°F). Hot and humid from January to March (32°C 90°F). Average annual rainfall 1600 mm (63 in) on Tongatapu, 2080 mm (82 in) on Vava'u.
Labour force: 18 626 at 1976 census: Agriculture, forestry and fishing 56·1%; Community, social and personal services 24·0%.
Gross domestic product: 86·3 million pa'anga in 1982–3.
Exports: 8 186 800 pa'anga in 1986 (mainly coconut oil, water melons and vanilla).
Monetary unit: Pa'anga. 1 pa'anga = 100 seniti.
Denominations:
Coins 1, 2, 5, 10, 20, 50 seniti; 1, 2 pa'anga.
Notes 50 seniti; 1, 2, 5, 10, 20 pa'anga.
Political history and government: Tonga is a kingdom ruled by an hereditary monarch. It was under British protection from 18 May 1900 until becoming independent, within the Commonwealth, on 4 June 1970. The King is Head of State and Head of Government. He appoints, and presides over, a Privy Council which acts as the national Cabinet. Apart from the King, the Council includes six Ministers, led by the Prime Minister (currently the King's brother), and the Governors of two island groups. The unicameral Legislative Assembly comprises 29 members: the Privy Council (of 11 members), nine hereditary nobles elected by their peers

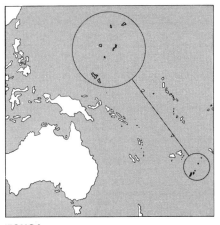

TONGA

and nine representatives elected by literate adults (male voters must be tax-payers). Elected members hold office for three years. There are no political parties.
Length of roadways: 433 km (269 miles).
Universities: 1 institute of university status.
Defence: No figure published for defence budget.
Foreign tourists: 44 677 in 1986.

Trinidad and Tobago

Official name: The Republic of Trinidad and Tobago.
Population: 1 199 200 (1986 estimate).
Area: 5130 km² (1981 miles²).
Languages: English (official), Hindi, French, Spanish.
Religions: Christian; Hindu and Islamic minorities.
Capital city: Port of Spain, population 58 400 (1985).
Other principal towns (1985): San Fernando 34 200; Arima 24 600.
Highest point: Cerro Aripo, 940 m (3085 ft).
Principal mountain ranges: Northern and Southern, Central.
Principal rivers: Caroni, Ortoire, Oropuche.
Head of State: Noor Hassanali, President.
Prime Minister: A. N. R. Robinson (b. 16 Dec 1926).
Climate: Tropical, with an annual average temperature of 29°C (84°F). The dry season is January to May.
Labour force: 465 800 in 1985: Petroleum, mining and quarrying 2·3%; Agriculture, forestry, fishing 6·4%; Manufacturing 10·6%; Construction 15·6%; Government services 16·8%; Unemployed 15·6%.
Gross domestic product: TT$18 971·9 million in 1985: Petroleum 24%; Manufacturing 6·7%; Agriculture 3·4%; Construction and quarrying 11%; Transportation 10·1%; Government services 15·3%.
Exports: TT$5301·2 million in 1984: Mineral fuel and lubricants 81·4%; Chemicals 10·9%; Manufactured goods 3·2%.
Monetary unit: Trinidad and Tobago dollar (TT$) 1 dollar = 100 cents.
Denominations:
Coins 1, 5, 10, 25, 50 cents; 1 dollar.
Notes 1, 5, 10, 20, 100 dollars.
Political history and government: Formerly a British dependency. The colony's first Chief Minister, Dr Eric Williams, took office on 28 Oct 1956. A new constitution was introduced, with Dr Williams as Premier, on 20 July 1959. Internal self-government was granted after elections on 4 Dec 1961. Following a constitutional conference on 28 May–8 June 1962, Trinidad and Tobago became an independent member of the Commonwealth, with the Premier as Prime Minister, on 31 Aug 1962. The country became a republic on 1 Aug 1976. Dr Williams, Prime Minister since independence, died on 29 Mar 1981.
Legislative power is vested in a bicameral Parliament, comprising a Senate with 31 members, appointed for up to five years by the President (16 on the advice of the Prime Minister, 6 on the advice of the Leader of the Opposition and 9 at the President's own discretion), and a House of Representatives (36 members elected by universal adult suffrage for five years). The President is a constitutional Head of State elected for five years by both Houses of Parliament. He appoints the Prime

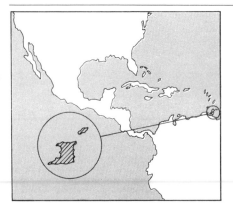

TRINIDAD AND TOBAGO

Minister to form a Cabinet from members of Parliament. The Cabinet has effective control of the government and is responsible to Parliament. Tobago has its own 15 member House of Assembly with limited powers.

Length of roadways: 5175 km (*3216 miles*) (1985).
Universities: 1 (shared with Jamaica, Barbados and other Caribbean territories).
Defence: Total armed forces: 2075 in 1987; defence expenditure: TT$180 million in 1985.
Foreign tourists: 187 090 in 1985.

Tunisia

Official name: Al-Jumhuriya at-Tunisiya (the Republic of Tunisia).
Population: 7 464 900 (1986 estimate).
Area: 164 150 km² (*63 400 miles²*).
Languages: Arabic, French.
Religions: Islam (Sunni); Jewish and Christian minorities.
Capital city: Tunis, population 556 654 (1984).
Other principal towns (1984): Sfax (Safaqis) 231 911; Bizerte 94 509; Djerba 92 269; Gabes 92 259; Sousse 83 509; Kairouan 72 254; Gafsa 60 970.
Highest point: Djebel Chambi, 1544 m (*5066 ft*).
Principal river: Medjerda (482 km *300 miles*).
Head of State: Zine El Abidine Ben Ali, President.
Prime Minister: Hedi Baccouche.
Climate: Temperate, with winter rain, on coast; hot and dry inland. In Tunis, August warmest (20°C to 33°C *69°F to 91°F*), January coolest (6°C to 14°C *43°F to 58°F*), December rainiest (14 days). Absolute maximum temperature 55·0°C (*131·0°F*), Kébili, 7 Dec 1931; absolute minimum −9·0°C (*15·8°F*), Fort-Saint, 22 Dec 1940.
Labour force: 2 137 100 in 1984: Agriculture etc 22·2%; Manufacturing 16·1%; Construction 11·1%; Trade, banking etc 6·6%; Other services 17·6%.
Gross domestic product: 7935 million dinars in 1987.
Exports: 1770·7 million dinars in 1987: Petroleum derivatives 23·6%; Fertilizers 12·3%; Clothing and accessories 20%; Olive oil 3·7%.
Monetary unit: Tunisian dinar. 1 dinar = 1000 millimes.

Denominations:
Coins 1, 2, 5, 10, 20, 50, 100, 500 millimes; 1, 5 dinars.
Notes 500 millimes; 1, 5, 10, 20 dinars.
Political history and government: Formerly a monarchy, ruled by the Bey of Tunis. A French protectorate from 1883 until independence on 20 Mar 1956. The campaign for independence was led by the Neo-Destour Party (founded by Habib Bourguiba), since October 1964 called the *Parti Socialiste Destourien* (PSD), the Destourian (Constitutional) Socialist Party. Elections were held on 25 Mar 1956 for a Constitutional Assembly, which met on 8 Apr 1956 and appointed Bourguiba as Prime Minister two days later. On 25 July 1957 the Assembly deposed the Bey, abolished the monarchy and established a republic, with Bourguiba as President. A new constitution was promulgated on 1 June 1959. Legislative power is vested in the unicameral national Assembly, first elected on 8 Nov 1959. The Assembly's members are elected by universal adult suffrage for five years. Executive power is held by the President, elected for five years by popular vote at the same time as the Assembly. On 3 Nov 1974 President Bourguiba was re-elected for a fourth term of office but on 18 Mar 1975 the Assembly proclaimed him 'President for life'. The President, who is Head of State and Head of Government, appoints a Council of Ministers, headed by a Prime Minister, which is responsible to him. From 1963 to 1981 the PSD was the only legal party. An 18-year ban on the Tunisian Communist Party was lifted on 18 July 1981. Elections were held on 2 Nov 1986 for a new National Assembly, when all 125 seats in the National Assembly were won by the *Front National*, an alliance of the PSD, renamed the RDC (*Rassemblement Democratique Constitutionelle*) and the *Union générale des travailleurs tunisiens*. In November 1987, President Bourguiba was declared incapable of continuing to rule and a new President was installed.
Length of roadways: 26 689 km (*16 574 miles*) (1986).
Length of railways: 2175 km (*1351 miles*) (1987).
Universities: 3.
Adult illiteracy: 45·8% in 1985.
Defence: Military service: 12 months, selective; total armed forces 42 100 (1987); defence expenditure: 434·1 million dinars in 1987.
Foreign tourists: 1 502 092 in 1986.

Turkey

Official name: Türkiye Cumhuriyeti (Republic of Turkey).
Population: 51 420 757 (1985 census).
Area: 779 452 km² (*301 076 miles²*).
Languages: Turkish 90·2%; Kurdish 6·9%; Arabic 1·2%; Zaza 0·5% (1965).
Religion: Islam (Sunni) 98%.
Capital city: Ankara (Angora), population 2 251 533 in 1985.
Other principal towns (1985): Istanbul 5 494 916; Izmir (Smyrna) 1 489 817; Adana 1 776 000; Bursa 614 133; Konya 438 859.
Highest point: Büyük Ağridaği (Mt Ararat), 5185 m (*17 011 ft*).
Principal mountain ranges: Armenian Plateau, Toros Dağlari (Taurus Mts), Kuzey Anadolu Dağlari.

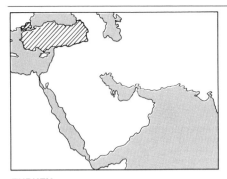

TURKEY

Principal rivers: Firat (Euphrates), Dicle (Tigris), Kizilirmak (Halys), Sakarya.
Head of State: Gen. Kenan Evren (b. 1918), President.
Prime Minister: Turgut Özal.
Climate: Hot, dry summers and cold, snowy winters in interior plateau; mild winters and warm summers on Mediterranean coast. In Ankara, average maximum 4°C (*30°F*) (January) to 30°C (*87°F*) (August), minimum −4°C (*24°F*) (January) to 15°C (*59°F*) (July, August), rainiest month is December (9 days). In Istanbul, average maximum 7°C (*45°F*) (January) to 27°C (*81°F*) (July, August), minimum 2°C (*36°F*) (January) to 19°C (*66°F*) (August), rainiest month is December (15 days). Absolute maximum temperature 46·2°C (*115·2°F*), Diyarbakir, 21 July 1937; absolute minimum −43·2°C (*−45·8°F*), Karaköse, 13 Jan 1940.
Labour force: 19 212 193 in 1980: Agriculture, forestry and fishing 57·8%; Manufacturing 10·3%; Trade 5·6%; Community, personal and social services 12·6%; Unemployed 3·4%.
Gross domestic product: 55 757·2 billion liras in 1987: Agriculture 15·3%; Manufacturing 23·2%; Trade 15·3%; Transport, storage and communications 9·1%; Government services 5·8%.
Exports: US$7457 million in 1986: Fruit 4·8%; Animal products 2·8%; Mining and quarrying products 2·3%; Processed agricultural products 6·1%; Food industry 5·2%; Textiles 17·9%.
Monetary unit: Turkish lira. 1 lira = 100 kuruş.
Denominations:
Coins 25, 50 kuruş; 1, 2½, 5, 10, 100 liras.
Notes 5, 10, 20, 50, 100, 500, 1000, 5000, 10 000 liras.
Political history and government: Formerly a monarchy, ruled by a Sultan. Following the disintegration of the Ottoman Empire after the First World War, power passed to the Grand National Assembly, which first met on 23 Apr 1920. The Assembly approved a new constitution on 20 Jan 1921, vesting executive and legislative authority in itself. It abolished the sultanate on 1 Nov 1922 and declared Turkey a republic on 29 Oct 1923. The armed forces overthrew the government on 27 May 1960, the Assembly was dissolved and political activities suspended until 12 Jan 1961. A new constitution was approved by referendum on 9 June 1961 and took effect on 25 Oct 1961. Legislative power was vested in the bicameral Grand National Assembly, comprising the Senate of the Republic (with, in 1980, 19 life senators plus 150 elected and 15 appointed members serving a six-year term) and the National Assembly (450 members elected by universal adult suffrage for four years). The Grand National Assembly elected one of its members to be President of the Republic for a single seven-year term. The President appointed the Prime Minister from among members of the legislature.

Following a period of severe political violence, martial law was proclaimed on 26 Dec 1978 in 13 of Turkey's 67 provinces. This was later extended to other provinces. The President's term of office ended on 6 Apr 1980 but, despite more than 100 ballots in the Grand National Assembly, no candidate gained enough support to succeed him. On 11–12 Sept 1980 a military *coup* deposed the civilian government. Power was assumed by a five-member National Security Council (NSC), led by the Chief of the General Staff, Gen. Kenan Evren. Martial law was extended to the whole country and the Grand National Assembly dissolved. General Evren became Head of State and the NSC was sworn in on 18 Sept. A mainly civilian council of Ministers was appointed on 21 Sept. The NSC adopted a provisional constitution, giving itself unlimited powers, on 27 Oct 1980. All political parties were dissolved on 16 Oct 1981. A Consultative Assembly of 160 members (40 nominated by the NSC and 120 selected from provincial governors' lists), appointed to draft a new constitution, opened on 23 Oct 1981. In 1982 Evren was elected as president. Under a new constitution – approved by a national referendum of 7 Nov 1982 – there is a single chamber Grand National Assembly of 450 members elected by universal adult suffrage for five years. Executive power is vested in a President elected for 7 years by the National Assembly. The President appoints the Prime Minister.
Length of roadways: 319 123 km (*198 175 miles*).
Length of railways: 10 328 km (*6414 miles*) (1987).
Universities: 22.
Adult illiteracy: 25·8% in 1984.
Defence: Military service: 18 months; total armed forces 654 400 (575 800 conscripts) in 1987; defence expenditure: 1 903 000 million lira in 1987.
Foreign tourists: 3 000 000 in 1987.

Tuvalu

Population: 8299 (1985 mini-census).
Area: 24·6 km² (*9·5 miles²*).
Languages: Tuvaluan, English.
Religion: Christian (Congregational 97%).
Capital city: Fongafale (in Funafuti atoll, population 2810 in 1985).
Other principal atolls: Nanumea, Niutau, Vaitupu.
Head of State: HM Queen Elizabeth II, represented by Tupua Leupena, GCVO, MBE, Governor-General.
Prime Minister: The Rt Hon. Dr Tomasi Puapua.
Climate: Warm and pleasant, with day temperatures between 27°C and 32°C (*80°F and 90°F*) and a minimum of about 21°C (*70°F*) at night. Average annual rainfall about 3050 mm (*120 in*). Rainy season December–February, dry August–October.
Labour force: 936 in 1979.
Exports: A$36 766 in 1982: Copra 72·5%.
Monetary unit: Tuvaluan dollar = 100 cents (on a par with the Australian dollar. Australian currency is also in circulation).

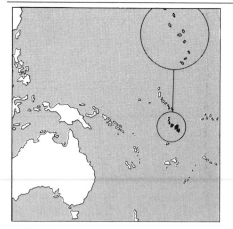

TUVALU

Denominations:
Coins 1, 2, 5, 10, 20, 50 cents.
Notes 1, 2, 5, 10, 20, 50 dollars.
Political history and government: Formerly known as the Ellice (Lagoon) Islands. In September 1892 the group became a United Kingdom protectorate and was linked administratively with the Gilbert Islands. The Gilbert and Ellice Islands were annexed by the UK on 10 Nov 1915, effective from 12 Jan 1916, when the protectorate became a colony. The Gilbert and Ellice Islands Colony (GEIC) was later expanded to include other groups. A referendum was held in the Ellice Islands in August–September 1974, when over 90% of the voters favoured separation from the GEIC. The Ellice Islands, under the old native name of Tuvalu ('eight standing together'), became a separate British dependency on 1 Oct 1975. The 8 Ellice representatives in the GEIC House of Assembly became the first elected members of the new Tuvalu House of Assembly. They elected one of their number to be Chief Minister. Tuvalu's first separate elections were held on 29 Aug 1977, when the number of elective seats in the House was increased from 8 to 12. Following a 4-day conference in London, a new constitution was finalized on 17 Feb 1978. After 5 months of internal self-government, Tuvalu became independent on 1 Oct 1978, with the Chief Minister as the first Prime Minister. Tuvalu is a 'special member' of the Commonwealth and is not represented at meetings of Heads of Government.
Tuvalu is a constitutional monarchy. Executive power is vested in the British monarch and is exercisable by the Governor-General, who is appointed on the recommendation of the Prime Minister and acts in almost all matters on the advice of the Cabinet. Legislative power is vested in the unicameral Parliament, with 12 members elected by universal adult suffrage for 4 years (subject to dissolution). The pre-independence House of Assembl;y became the first Parliament. The Cabinet is led by the Prime Minister, elected by and from members of Parliament. Other Ministers are appointed by the Governor-General, on the Prime Minister's recommendation, from members of Parliament. The Cabinet is responsible to Parliament. Each of the 8 inhabited atolls has an elected Island Council.
Universities: 1 university centre.

Uganda

Official name: The Republic of Uganda.
Population: 16 789 000 (1987 estimate).
Area: 236 036 km² (*91 134 miles²*).
Languages: English (official), Luganda, Ateso, Runyankore.
Religions: Christian, Islam (Sunni), traditional beliefs.
Capital city: Kampala, population 454 974 (1981 estimate).
Other principal towns (1981): Jinja-Njeru 45 060; Mbale 28 039; Entebbe 20 472.
Highest point: Mount Stanley, 5109 m (*16 763 ft*) (first climbed 1900), on the border with Zaire.
Principal mountain range: Ruwenzori.
Principal rivers: Nile, Semliki.
Head of State: Yoweri Museveni, President.
Prime Minister: Dr Samson Kisekka.
Climate: Tropical, with an average temperature of 22°C (*71°F*). There is a seasonal variation of only 11°C (*20°F*).
Labour force: 6 086 000 in 1984: Agriculture, forestry and fishing 78·5%.
Gross domestic product: 7375 million shillings in 1983: Agriculture 57·5%; Manufacturing 3·9%; Services 25·3%.
Exports: 138 753 million shillings in 1984: Coffee 91·8%.
Monetary unit: Uganda new shilling. 1 new shilling = 100 cents.
Denominations:
Coins 5, 10, 20, 50 cents; 1, 2, 5 new shillings.
Notes 10, 20, 50, 100 new shillings.
Political history and government: Formerly a British dependency. The first Council of Ministers took office on 13 Apr 1961 and the first Chief Minister was appointed on 2 July 1961. Uganda was granted internal self-government on 1 Mar 1962, when the Chief Minister became Prime Minister. The leader of the Uganda People's Congress (UPC), Dr Milton Obote, became Prime Minister on 30 Apr 1962. The country achieved independence, within the Commonwealth, on 9 Oct 1962. Uganda became a republic, with a nominal President and Dr Obote continuing as executive Prime Minister, on 9 Oct 1963. The constitution was suspended, and the President deposed, on 24 Feb 1966. A provisional constitution, effective from 15 Apr 1966, ended the former federal system and introduced an executive presidency, with Dr Obote as Head of State. A unitary republic was established on 8 Sept 1967. After an assassination attempt against President Obote on 19 Dec 1969, all parties other than the UPC were banned.
President Obote was deposed on 25 Jan 1971 by an army *coup*, led by Maj.-Gen. (later Field Marshal) Idi Amin Dada, who assumed full executive powers as Head of the Military Government and suspended political activity. The National Assembly was dissolved on 2 Feb 1971, when Amin declared himself Head of State, took over legislative powers and suspended parts of the 1967 constitution. He was proclaimed President on 21 Feb 1971 and ruled with the assistance of an appointed Council of Ministers. On 25 June 1976 the Defence Council appointed Amin 'President for Life'. No legislature was formed under Amin but a large advisory assembly, the National Consultative Forum, held its first meeting on 15–20 Jan 1978.

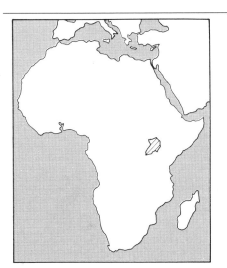

UGANDA

After border fighting with Tanzanian forces in 1978, Ugandan troops captured the northern part of Tanzania. Amin announced Uganda's annexation of this territory on 1 Nov 1978. Tanzania retaliated and its forces entered Uganda in January 1979. The Ugandan capital fell to combined Tanzanian and Uganda National Liberation Front forces on 10–11 Apr 1979 and Amin's rule was overthrown. On 11 Apr 1979 the UNLF formed a provisional government, the National Executive Committee (NEC), and on 13 Apr it was sworn in. Lule became Chairman of the NEC and Head of State. On 8 May 1979 the new régime announced a two-year ban on political parties. The UNLF, the sole authorized political organization, formed a 30-member National Consultative Council (NCC) as a provisional parliament. On 20 June the NCC replaced President Lule by Godfrey Binaisa. In September 1979 the UNLF nominated members of 33 district councils. On 3 Oct these councils elected 61 members of an expanded NCC. Additional members were appointed from the Uganda National Liberation Army (UNLA). The new NCC, with 127 members, was inaugurated on 6 Oct 1979.

On 12 May 1980 President Binaisa was relieved of his post when power was assumed by the UNLF's Military Commission, led by Paulo Muwanga. Muwanga stated that the new régime was an interim one and committed to general elections. On 22 May a three-man Presidential Commission was appointed. On 23 June it was reported that four political parties, including the UPC (led by ex-President Obote), would be allowed to contest the elections.

Voting took place on 10–11 Dec 1980 for the 126 elective seats in a new National Assembly. Deputies to the Assembly, representing single-member constituencies, were elected by universal adult suffrage. The UPC gained a majority and, as the party's presidential candidate, Dr Obote was declared Head of State. He was sworn in on 15 Dec when constitutional rule was restored.

In 1985 Obote was overthrown by an army *coup*, and Lt.-Gen. Tito Okello became president. He in turn was overthrown by Yoweri Museveni, whose National Resistance Army gained control of the country in 1986. A 24-member National Resistance Council was formed in January 1986.
Length of roadways: 28 332 km (*17 594 miles*) (1986).
Length of railways: 1286 km (*799 miles*).
Universities: 2.
Adult illiteracy: 52% (1983).
Defence: Total armed forces 20 000 (1987); defence expenditure: 15 280 million new shillings in 1986/7.
Foreign tourists: 12 786 in 1983.

The Union of Soviet Socialist Republics

Official name: Soyuz Sovyetskikh Sotsialisticheskikh Respublik (abbreviation in Cyrillic script is CCCP), sometimes shortened to Sovyetskiy Soyuz (Soviet Union).
Population: 284 500 000 (1988 estimate).
Area: 22 402 200 km² (*8 649 540 miles²*). This official total includes two areas of ocean, the White Sea (90 000 km² *34 750 miles²*) and the Sea of Azos (37 300 km² *14 400 miles²*).
Republics: Armenian SSR, population 3 369 000 (1986), area 29 800 km² (*11 500 miles²*), Capital Yerevan; **Azerbaidzhan SSR**, population 6 718 000 (1986), area 86 600 km² (*33 440 miles²*), Capital Baku; **Byelorussian SSR**, population 10 002 000 (1986), area 207 600 km² (*80 150 miles²*), Capital Minsk; **Estonian SSR**, population 1 541 000 (1986), area 45 100 km² (*17 400 miles²*), Capital Tallinn; **Georgian SSR**, population 5 239 000 (1986), area 69 700 km² (*26 900 miles²*), Capital Tbilisi; **Kazakh SSR**, population 16 036 000 (1986), area 2 717 300 km² (*1 049 150 miles²*), Capital Alma-Ata; **Kirghiz SSR**, population 4 055 000 (1986), area 198 500 km² (*76 600 miles²*), Capital Frunze; **Latvian SSR**, population 2 621 000 (1986), area 63 700 km² (*24 600 miles²*), Capital Riga; **Lithuanian SSR**, population 3 603 000 (1986), area 65 200 km² (*25 200 miles²*), Capital Vilnius; **Moldavian SSR**, population 4 142 000 (1986), area 33 700 km² (*13 000 miles²*), Capital Kishinev; **Russian SSR**, population 144 027 000 (1986), area 17 075 400 km² (*6 592 800 miles²*), Capital Moscow; **Tadzhik SSR**, population 4 643 000 (1986), area 143 100 km² (*55 250 miles²*), Capital Dushanbe; **Turkmen SSR**, population 327 000 (1986), area 488 100 km² (*188 400 miles²*), Capital Ashkhabad; **Ukrainian SSR**, population 50 973 000 (1986), area 603 700 km² (*233 000 miles²*), Capital Kiev; **Uzbek SSR**, population 18 479 000 (1986), area 447 400 km² (*172 400 miles²*), Capital Tashkent.
Languages (1970): Russian (official) 58·7%; Ukrainian 14·6%; Uzbek 3·8%; Byelorussian 3·2%; Tatar 2·4%; Kazakh 2·2%; over 130 languages in total.
Religions: No state religion. Christian with Jewish and Islamic minorities.
Capital city: Moskva (Moscow), population 8 703 000 (1986).
Other principal towns (1986): Leningrad 4 901 000; Kiyev (Kiev) 2 495 000; Tashkent 2 073 000; Baku 1 722 000; Kharkov 1 567 000; Minsk 1 510 000; Gorky 1 409 000; Novosibirsk 1 405 000; Sverdlovsk 1 316 000; Kuybyshev 1 267 000; Tbilisi 1 174 000; Dnepropetrovsk 1 166 000; Yerevan 1 148 000; Odessa 1 132 000; Omsk 1 124 000; Chelyabinsk

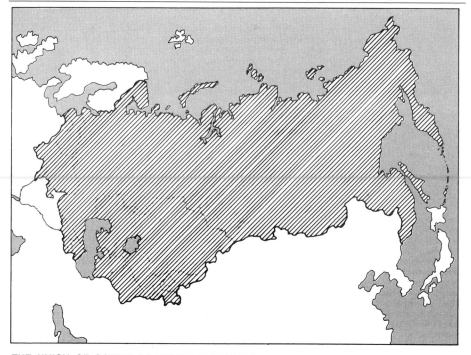

THE UNION OF SOVIET SOCIALIST REPUBLICS

1 107 000; Alma-Ata 1 088 000; Donetsk 1 081 000; Ufa 1 077 000; Perm 1 066 000; Kazan 1 057 000; Rostov-on-Don 993 000.

Highest point: Pik Kommunizma (Garmo, later Pik Stalin), 7494 m (24 589 ft) (first climbed 3 Sept 1933).

Principal mountain ranges: Caucasus, Urals, Pamirs, Tien Shan.

Principal rivers: 14 rivers over 1609 km (1000 miles) in length (see pages 17–21).

Head of State: Mikhail Gorbachev, President of the Presidium of the Supreme Soviet of the USSR, and General Secretary of the Communist Party of the Soviet Union.

Head of Government: Nikolai I. Ryzhkov, Chairman of the Council of Ministers.

Climate: Great variations. Summers generally short and hot, winters long and cold. Very hot in central Asia, extremely cold in north-east Siberia. Average maximum and minimum temperatures for selected places:

Moscow: Average maximum −6°C (21°F) (January) to 24°C (76°F) (July). Average minimum −13°C (9°F) (January) to 13°C (55°F) (July). Rainiest months July, August (each 12 days).

Archangel: Average maximum −13°C (9°F) (January) to 18°C (64°F) (July). Average minimum −18°C (0°F) (February) to 10°C (51°F) (July). Rainiest month October (12 days).

Odessa: Average maximum −2°C (28°F) (January) to 26°C (79°F) (July). Average minimum −5°C (22°F) (January) to 18°C (65°F) (July, August). Rainiest months January and June (each 7 days).

Yakutsk: Average maximum −43°C (−45°F) (January) to 23°C (73°F) (July). Average minimum

−47°C (−53°F) (January) to 12°C (54°F) (July). Rainiest months September, October, November (each 10 days).

Absolute maximum temperature 50·0°C (122·0°F), Termez (Uzbekistan), July 1912; absolute minimum −71·1°C (−96·0°F), Oymyakon, 1964.

Labour force: 129 474 000 in 'socialized' sector in 1984: Agriculture and forestry 19·5%; Industry 29·3%; Transport 8·4%; Construction 8·8%; Distribution, supplies and catering 7·7%; Education 7·5%.

Net material product: 575·5 billion roubles in 1985: (in 1984) Agriculture 19·8%; Industry 46%; Construction 10·7%; Transport and communications 6%; Distribution and supply 17·6%.

Exports: 68 347 million roubles in 1986: Petroleum and petroleum products 32·9%; Machines and equipment 15%.

Monetary unit: Rubl' (ruble or rouble). 1 rouble = 100 kopeks.

Denominations:
Coins 1, 2, 3, 5, 10, 20, 50 kopeks; 1 rouble.
Notes 1, 3, 5, 10, 25, 50, 100 roubles.

Political history and government: Formerly the Russian Empire, ruled by an hereditary Tsar (of the Romanov dynasty from 1613). Prompted by discontent with autocratic rule and the privation caused by the First World War, a revolution broke out on 27 Feb (12 March new Style) 1917, causing the abdication of the last Tsar three days later and the establishment of a provisional government. During the following months Soviets (councils) were elected by some groups of industrial workers and peasants. A republic was proclaimed on 1 Sept (14 Sept NS) 1917. A political struggle developed between government supporters and the Bolshevik Party (founded in 1903 and called the Communist Party from 1919), which advocated the assumption of power by the Soviets. On 25 Oct (7 Nov NS) 1917 the Bolsheviks led an insurrection, arrested the provisional government and transferred power to the All-Russian Congress of Soviets. The Bolsheviks won only 175 out of 707 seats in the elections of 25–27 Nov 1917 for the Constituent Assembly. The Assembly met on 18 Jan 1918 but was forcibly dissolved by the Bolsheviks, who proclaimed a 'dictatorship of the proletariat'. On 31 Jan 1918 Russia was proclaimed a Republic of Soviets. A constitution for the Russian Soviet Federative Socialist Republic (RSFSR) was adopted on 10 July 1918. Armed resistance to Communist rule developed into civil war (1917–22) but was eventually crushed. During the war other Soviet Republics were set up in the Ukraine, Byelorussia (White Russia) and Transcaucasia. These were merged with the RSFSR by a Treaty of Union, establishing the USSR, on 30 Dec 1922. The USSR's first constitution was adopted on 6 July 1923. By splitting the territory of the original four, two more Republics were added in 1925 and another in 1929. A new constitution was adopted on 5 Dec 1936, when the number of Soviet Socialist Republics (SSRs) was raised from seven to eleven. On 31 Mar 1940 territory ceded by Finland became part of the newly-formed Karelo-Finnish SSR. Territory ceded by Romania on 28 June 1940 became part of the new Moldavian SSR on 2 Aug 1940. The three Baltic republics of Lithuania, Latvia and Estonia were annexed on 3–6 Aug 1940, raising the number of Union Republics to 16. This was reduced to the present 15 on 16 July 1956, when the Karelo-Finnish SSR was merged with the RSFSR.

A new constitution took effect on 7 Oct 1977. According to the constitution, the Communist Party is 'the leading and guiding force of Soviet society'. Early in 1978 new constitutions, modelled on that for the USSR, came into force in all 15 Union Republics.

The Soviet Union is formally a federal state comprising 15 Union (constituent) Republics of equal status, voluntarily linked and having the right to secede. Some of the 15 Union Republics contain Autonomous Republics and Autonomous Regions. The RSFSR also includes 10 National Areas. The highest organ of state power was the bicameral legislature, the Supreme Soviet of the USSR, comprising the Soviet (Council) of the Union, with 750 members elected from constituencies, and the Soviet (Council) of Nationalities, with 750 members (32 from each of the 15 Union republics; 11 from each of the 20 Autonomous Republics; five from each of the eight Autonomous Regions; one from each of the 10 National Areas). Both houses had equal right and powers and their terms ran concurrently. Members were directly elected (from a single list of candidates) for five-year terms by universal adult suffrage. At a joint session the members elected the Presidium of the Supreme Soviet (39 members, including, as *ex officio* deputy chairmen, the 15 chairmen of the Supreme Soviets of the Union Republics) to be the legislature's permanent organ. The Chairman of the Presidium served as Head of State. The Supreme Soviet also appointed the Council of Ministers (called People's Commissars until 16 Mar 1946), headed by a Chairman, to form the executive and administrative branch of government, responsible to the Supreme Soviet.

Under *perestroika* (reconstruction), introduced by Mr Gorbachev, elections were held in March 1989 for a new supreme representative body to be known as the Congress of People's Deputies, of 1500 deputies elected on universal suffrage from constituencies (multi-candidate ballots being allowed) and a further 750 deputies elected by the Communist Party, the Leninist Young Communist League (*Komsomol*) and other organizations, e.g. unions and academies. The Congress is elected for 5 years and will convene annually to decide major political, social, economic and constitutional matters. The Congress elects from its own members 525 deputies to a Supreme Soviet, responsible for all legislative and administrative matters. Elections took place in May 1989 for the post of President of the Supreme Soviet – a post combining Head of State and leadership of the Communist Party. The President, Mikhail Gorbachev, was elected by the Congress and will preside over a Presidium of 2 First Vice-Presidents, 15 Vice-Presidents (one from each of the Union republics) plus the chairmen of the Supreme Soviet, its standing commissions and committees. The President nominates the Chairman of the Council of Ministers.

Each of the 15 Union Republics has a constitution and state structure on the same pattern as the central government, and these bodies in each republic are expected to reflect the changes in national administration which will be introduced in 1989. The Chairmen of the Councils of Ministers of the Union Republics are *ex officio* members of the USSR Council of Ministers. The Union Republics are entitled to maintain direct relations with foreign countries. Two of them, the Ukrainian and Byelorussian SSR's, are separately represented in the United Nations.

Throughout the whole country, real power is held by the highly centralized Communist Party of the Soviet Union (CPSU), the only legal party, which has an absolute monopoly of power in all political affairs and controls government at all levels. The Party had over 19·4 million members in 1987. Its highest authority is, in theory, the Party Congress, which should be convened at least every five years (the 27th Congress was held on 25 Feb–6 Mar 1986). The Congress elects the Central Committee (308 full members and 170 candidates, i.e. non-voting members, were chosen in 1986) which supervizes Party work and directs state policy. The Committee, which meets twice a year, elects a Political Bureau (Politburo), which is the Party's most powerful policy-making body. In 1988 the Politburo had 13 full members (including the General Secretary) and seven candidate members. Apart from the RSFSR, each Union Republic has its own Communist Party, with a Central Committee led by a First Secretary, but they are subsidiary to, and form an integral part of, the CPSU.

Length of roadways: 1 516 700 km (*942 635 miles*) (1984).

Length of railways: 148 000 km (*92 000 miles*) (1987).

Universities: 69.

Defence: Military service: Army and Air Force 2–3 years, Navy 5 years; total armed forces over 5 226 000 (Western estimate) in 1987; defence expenditure, 1988: official figure was 20 401 million roubles, but Western estimates put the figure at several times this amount.

Foreign tourists: 6 777 000 in 1983.

The United Arab Emirates

Official name: Al-Imarat Al'A'rabiya Al-Muttahida.
Population: 1 770 000 (1986 estimate).
Area: 92 100 km² (*35 575 miles²*).
Language: Arabic.
Religion: Islam (Sunni).
Capital city: Abu Dhabi, population 670 000 (1985 estimate).
Other principal towns (1985): Dubai 419 000; Sharjah 269 000; Ras al Kaimah 116 000.
Highest point: Western Al-Hajar, 1189 m (*3900 ft*).
Principal mountain range: Al-Hajar.
Head of State: HH Shaikh Zayed bin Sultan Al-Nahayan (b. 1918), President.
Prime Minister: HH Shaikh Rashid bin Sa'id Al-Maktoum (b. 1914).
Shaikhs: The hereditary rulers of the seven states are:
Abu Dhabi: HH Shaikh Zayed bin Sultan Al-Nahayan (President of the UAE).
Ajman: HH Shaikh Humaid bin Rashid Al-Nuaimi.
Dubai: HH Shaikh Rashid bin Sa'id Al-Maktoum (Prime Minister of the UAE).
Fujairah: HH Shaikh Hamad bin Mohammed Al-Sharqi.
Ras al-Khaimah: HH Shaikh Saqr bin Mohammed Al-Qasimi.
Sharjah: HH Shaikh Sultan bin Mohammed Al-Qasimi.
Umm al Qaiwain: HH Shaikh Rashid bin Ahmed Al-Mualla.
Climate: Very hot and humid, with summer temperatures of over 38°C (*100°F*); cooler in the eastern mountains.
Labour force: 600 000 (1985 estimate); Construction 30%; Trade, restaurants and hotels 15%; Community, social and personal services 30%.
Gross domestic product: 106 448 million dirhams in 1983: Agriculture, forestry and fishing 1·1%; Oil and natural gas 42·6%; Manufacturing 8·5%; Construction 10·3%; Trade 9·3%; Financial services 10·4%.
Exports: 48 180 million dirham in 1985: Oil 88·5%.
Monetary unit: UAE dirham. 1 dirham = 100 fils.
Denominations:
Coins 1, 5, 10, 25, 50 fils; 1 dirham.
Notes 1, 5, 10, 50, 100, 500, 1000 dirhams.
Political history and government: Formerly the seven shaikhdoms of Trucial Oman (the Trucial States), under British protection. An independent federation (originally of six states), under a provisional constitution, since 2 Dec 1971. The seventh, Ras al-Khaimah, joined the UAE on 11 Feb 1972. The highest federal authority is the Supreme Council of the Union, comprising the hereditary rulers of the seven emirates (the rulers of Abu Dhabi and Dubai have the power of veto). From its seven members the Council elects a President and a Vice-President, each with a 5-year term. The President appoints a Prime Minister and a Union (Federal) Council of Ministers, responsible to the Supreme Council, to hold executive authority. The legislature is the Federal National Council, a consultative assembly (comprising 40 members appointed for two years by the rulers of the constituent emirates) which considers laws proposed by the Council of Ministers. The provisional constitution, originally in force for 5 years, was extended to 1981 by a decree of 28 Nov 1976. There are no political parties. In local affairs each ruler has absolute power over his subjects.
Length of roadways: 2200 km (*1367 miles*) (1984).
Universities: 1.
Defence: Military service voluntary; total armed forces 43 000 (1987); defence expenditure: 5800 million dirhams in 1987.

The United Kingdom of Great Britain and Northern Ireland

Population: 56 763 300 (1986 estimate).
Area: 244 103 km² (*94 249 miles²*).
Language: English (Welsh speaking minority in Wales, Gaelic in the Western Isles).
Religions: Christian – Anglican, Presbyterian, Methodist, Roman Catholic, Baptist.
Capital city: London, population 6 775 200 (1986) (for the Greater London area).
Other principal towns: (local authority areas) (1986) Birmingham 1 004 100; Glasgow 725 100; Leeds 710 900; Sheffield 534 300; Liverpool 483 000; Bradford 463 100; Manchester 451 400; Edinburgh 438 200; Bristol 391 500; Kirklees (Huddersfield area) 376 600; Wirral (Birkenhead area) 334 800; Coventry 310 400; Wakefield 309 300; Wigan 306 600; Belfast 303 600; Sandwell (West Bromwich area) 301 100; Dudley 300 900; Sefton (Bootle-Crosby-Southport area) 298 000; Sunderland 297 700; Stockport 289 900; Doncaster 289 300; Newcastle-upon-Tyne 281 400; Leicester 281 100; Cardiff 279 500; Nottingham 277 800; Walsall 261 800; Bolton 261 600; Kingston-upon-Hull 258 000; Plymouth 256 000; Rotherham 252 100; Wolverhampton 251 900.

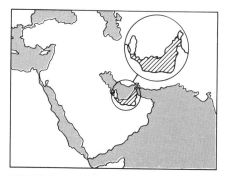

THE UNITED ARAB EMIRATES

Countries of the United Kingdom

England

population 47 254 500 in 1986, area 130 441 km² (*50 363 miles²*), Capital: London.

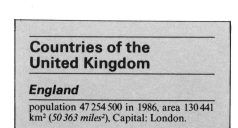

Scotland

population 5 121 000 in 1986, area 78 775 km² *(30 415 miles²)*, Capital: Edinburgh.

Wales

population 2 821 000 in 1986, area 20 768 km² *(8019 miles²)*, Capital: Cardiff.

Northern Ireland

population 1 566 800 in 1986, 14 120 km² *(5452 miles²)*, Capital: Belfast.

Crown Dependencies associated with but not part of the United Kingdom

GUERNSEY

(including Alderney and Sark): population 56 984 in 1986, area 76·3 km² *(29·4 miles²)*, Capital: St Peter Port.

JERSEY

population 80 212 in 1986, area 116·2 km² *(44·8 miles²)*, Capital: St Helier.

ISLE OF MAN

population 64 282 in 1986, area 572 km² *(221 miles²)*, Capital: Douglas.

Highest point: Ben Nevis, 1392 m *(4406 ft)*.
Principal mountain ranges: Grampians, North West Highlands, Pennines, Cambrian Mountains.
Principal rivers: Severn (354 km *220 miles)*, Thames, Trent, Aire, Wye.
Head of State: HM Queen Elizabeth II (Alexandra Mary, Queen, Head of the Commonwealth (b. 21 Apr 1926), succeeded her father King George VI on 6 Feb 1952. Heir: HRH Prince Charles, Prince of Wales (b. 14 Nov 1948), eldest son of the Queen.
Prime Minister: Rt Hon. Margaret Hilda Thatcher (b. 1925).
Climate: Temperate yet variable. Great regional and local diversity. Rainfall between 500 mm *(20 in)* in East Anglia to 5100 *(200 in)* in the Scottish Highlands – average rainfall 900 to 1000 mm *(35–40 in)* with rain fairly evenly distributed through the year although October, December and August are often the wettest months. Average temperature in summer 15°C *(59°F)*, in winter 5°C *(41°F)*, maximum recorded temperature 36·8°C *(98·2°F)*, minimum recorded temperature −27·2°C *(−17°F)*.
Labour force: 24 221 000 in 1986: Agriculture, forestry and fishing 2·5%; Manufacturing 22·5%; Construction 6·1%; Trade, restaurants and hotels 20·6%; Transport, storage and communications 6%; Finance etc 10·1%; Community, social and personal services 29·9%.
Gross domestic product: £374 895 million in 1986: Agriculture 1·6%; Manufacturing 21·1%; Construction 5·4%; Distribution, hotels and catering 12·2%;

Banking, finance, insurance etc 13·7%; Education and health services 7·9%.
Exports: £73 009 million in 1986: Food and live animals 5·1%; Petroleum and petroleum products 11·3%; Chemicals and related products 13·3%; Power generating machinery 4·5%; Office machines etc 4·9%; Road vehicles and parts 5·4%; Basic manufactures 15%.
Monetary unit: Pound sterling (£). 1 pound = 100 new pence (pennies).
Denominations:
Coins 1, 2, 5, 10, 20, 50 pence; £1.
Notes £5, £10, £20, £50. (Scottish banks also have the authority to issue notes).
Political history and government: By the Act of Union 1801 Great Britain (England, Scotland and Wales) and Ireland were legislatively united as the United Kingdom of Great Britain and Ireland. On the separation of Ireland in 1921, Northern Ireland remained within the Union which was renamed the United Kingdom of Great Britain and Northern Ireland. The United Kingdom does not include Guernsey (and its dependencies), Jersey and the Isle of Man, which are Crown Dependencies with their own systems of government, but which are associated with the United Kingdom for many purposes.

The United Kingdom is a constitutional monarchy without a written constitution – constitutional government is based upon established practice, precedent and tradition. Legislative power is vested in Parliament which has two Houses, the House of Lords and the House of Commons – a division which dates back to the 14th century.

The House of Lords consists of (1988): 789 hereditary peers and peeresses who take their seats by virtue of inheritance or creation; 21 Lords of Appeal (life peers); 359 life peers (whose creation dates from the Life Peerages Act of 1958); 2 archbishops and 24 bishops of the Church of England.

The House of Commons of 650 members (523 from England, 72 from Scotland, 38 from Wales, 17 from Northern Ireland) is elected for a maximum period of 5 years by adult (over 18) universal suffrage from single member constituencies.

Executive government is in name vested in the Crown but in practice in a Cabinet of Ministers which depends on the support of a majority of the members of the House of Commons. The leader of that majority is, in practice, appointed by the Crown to be Prime Minister. The Prime Minister recommends other members of that majority to be appointed as Ministers and members of the Cabinet by the Crown. Ministers may also be appointed from the House of Lords and Ministers may not necessarily be appointed as members of the Cabinet.

In local government in England and Wales there are 47 non-metropolitan counties whose members are elected by universal adult suffrage for a term of 4 years. In England there are 7 metropolitan councils, without county councils, in which the local government functions are exercised by 36 district councils. Greater London has since 1 Apr 1986 had no council but is administered by 32 elected councils in the London boroughs and the Corporation of the City of London.

In Scotland, since local government reform, there have been 9 regional councils and 3 island councils elected for 4 years by universal adult suffrage.

Northern Ireland, constitutionally a part of the

United Kingdom, had until 1972, its own legislature with limited internal self-government. The breakdown of law and order in 1968–69 through a series of major disturbances, originally associated with a civil rights movement, and the increase of terrorism, resulted in the assumption of direct rule of the province. In March 1973 a plebiscite returned a majority of nearly 60% of the electorate wishing to remain within the United Kingdom. A new constitution (of 1973), including provisions for power sharing between the various communities in the province, was suspended in 1974 and the province has since been under direct rule. Northern Ireland has 26 district councils.

Length of roadways: 374 338 km (*232 603 miles*).
Length of railways: 17 985 km (*11 169 miles*).
Universities: 43.
Defence: Military service voluntary; total armed forces 318 700 (1987); defence expenditure: £18 780 million in 1987/8.
Foreign tourists: 15 600 000 in 1987.

Territories administered by the United Kingdom

Anguilla

Location: Anguilla (with Scrub I. and other offshore islands) lies about 8 km (*5 miles*) north of St Martin, in the Leeward Islands, West Indies. Sombrero I. lies about 48 km (*30 miles*) north of Anguilla.
Area: 96 km² (*37 miles²*) (Anguilla 91 km² *35 miles²*, Sombrero 5 km² *2 miles²*).
Population: 7000 (1984 estimate).
Capital: The Valley.

Bermuda

Location: The Bermudas (or Somers Islands) are a group of islands in the western North Atlantic Ocean, about 917 km (*570 miles*) east of Cape Hatteras in North Carolina, USA.
Area: 53·3 km² (*20·59 miles²*).
Population: 57 145 (1985 estimate). 20 islands are inhabited.
Capital: Hamilton (population about 3000 in 1985), on Bermuda I.

British Antarctic Territory

See Other Territories Section at the end of the listing of Sovereign Countries.

British Indian Ocean Territory

Location: The territory is now confined to the Chagos Archipelago (or Oil Islands) which is 1899 km (*1180 miles*) north-east of (and formerly administered by) Mauritius. The islands of Aldabra, Farquhar and Desroches (originally parts of the territory) were restored to Seychelles when the latter became independent on 29 June 1976.
Area: c. 52 km² (*c. 20 miles²*).
Population: The territory has a 'floating' population of contract labourers, but no permanent population.

British Virgin Islands

Location and Composition: Comprises the eastern part of the Virgin Islands group (the western part is a US colony), and lies to the est of Puerto Rico, in the West Indies.
Area: c. 153 km² (*59 miles²*) (Tortola 54 km² *21 miles²*, Virgin Gorda 21 km² *8·25 miles²*, Anegada 39 km² *15 miles²*, Jost van Dyke 8 km² *3·25 miles²*).
Population: 12 034 in 1980 (Tortola 9322; Virgin Gorda 1443; Anegada 169; Jost van Dyke 136; other islands 82; marine population 220; institutional population 662).
Capital: Road Town (population 3976 in 1980); on Tortola.

Cayman Islands

Location: A group of three islands, in the Caribbean Sea, south of Cuba. The principal island, Grand Cayman, is 286 km (*178 miles*) west of Jamaica.
Area: c. 259 km² (*100 miles²*) (Grand Cayman 197 km² *76 miles²*, Cayman Brac 36 km² *14 miles²*, Little Cayman 26 km² *10 miles²*).
Population: 16 677 (Grand Cayman 15 000, Cayman brac 1607, Little Cayman 70) at census of 1 July 1979, 20 300 (1985 estimate).
Capital: George Town (population 8900 in 1985).

Falkland Islands

Location: A group of islands in the south-western Atlantic Ocean, about 772 km (*480 miles*) north-east of Cape Horn, South America.
Area: 12 173 km² (*4700 miles²*) (East Falkland and adjacent islands 6760 km² *2610 miles²*, West Falkland, etc., 5413 km² *2090 miles²*).
Population: 1919 (census of 1986).
Capital: Port Stanley (population 1100 in 1984), on East Falkland.

City of Gibraltar

Location: A narrow peninsula on the south coast of Spain, commanding the north side of the Atlantic entrance to the Mediterranean Sea.
Area: 5·5 km² (*2·1 miles²*) (4·4 km *2·75 miles* long, greatest breadth nearly 1·6 km *1 mile*).
Population: 29 166 (1986 estimate).
Chief (and only) Town: Gibraltar, at north-western corner of the Rock.

Hong Kong

Location: A peninsula in the central south coast of the Guangdong (Kwangtung) province of southern China, the island of Hong Kong and some 235 other islands, the largest of which is Lantao (150 km² *58 miles²*).
Area: 1059·8 km² (*409·2 miles²*) (Hong Kong Island 78·0 km² *30·1 miles²*, Kowloon peninsula 10·5 km² *4·1 miles²*, Stonecutters Island 0·6 km² *0·25 mile²*, New Territories (leased) 970·7 km² *374·8 miles²*). Including the ocean area within administrative boundaries, the total is 2916 km² (*1126 miles²*).
Population: 5 588 000 (1986 estimate). About 98% are Chinese, many being British subjects by virtue of birth in the Colony.

Languages: Mainly Chinese (Cantonese); English 8·5%.

Religion: Predominantly Buddhist.

Capital City and Other Principal Towns (population at Census, 1976): Victoria (501 680), on Hong Kong Island; Kowloon; New Kowloon; North Point; Tsuen Wan; Cheung Chau (an island).

Status and Government: A Crown Colony with the Governor assisted by an Executive Council (16 in 1980) and a Legislative Council (47, including 26 elected, in 1980).

Recent History: British colony, 1841. New Territories leased in 1898 for 99 years. Attacked by Japan, 8 Dec 1941. Surrendered, 25 Dec 1941. Recaptured by UK forces, 30 Aug 1945. UK military administration, 3 Sept 1945 to May 1946. Formal Japanese surrender, 16 Sept 1945. Many refugees during Chinese civil war 1948–50, and subsequently, notably on 1–25 May 1962. On 19 Dec 1984, the United Kingdom and China signed a declaration under the terms of which China would recover sovereignty over Hong Kong on 1 July 1997. The territory will become a Special Administrative Region – to be known as Hong Kong, China – and the existing social and economic systems will continue for 50 years.

Economic Situation: The principal occupations are manufacturing (notably cotton piece goods, shirts, electrical products, cameras, toys and games, footwear), services and commerce. Agriculture (poultry and pigs), fishing and mining (notably iron) are carried on.

Currency: 100 cents = 1 Hong Kong dollar.

Climate: The sub-tropical summer (28°C (82°F) July) is hot and humid with the winter cool and dry (15°C (59°F) February). The average annual rainfall is 2160 mm (85 in), three-quarters of which falls from June to August in the south-west monsoon season.

Montserrat

Location: An island about 56 km (35 miles) north of Basse Terre, Guadeloupe, in the Leeward Islands, West Indies.

Area: 98 km² (38 miles²).

Population: 11 852 (1985 estimate).

Capital: Plymouth (population 3500 in 1985), on south-west coast.

Pitcairn Islands Group

Location: Four islands in the south Pacific Ocean, about 4828 km (3000 miles) east of New Zealand and 5632 km (3500 miles) south-west of Panama: Pitcairn, Henderson, Ducie, Oeno.

Area: 48 km² (18·5 miles²), including Pitcairn 4·5 km² (1·75 miles²).

Population: Pitcairn 57 (1987 count).

Principal settlement: Adamstown.

St Helena and Dependencies

Location and Composition: An island in the South Atlantic Ocean, 1931 km (1200 miles) west of Africa. The dependencies are: (a) Ascension, an island 1126 km (700 miles) to the north-west; (b) the Tristan da Cunha group, comprising: Tristan da Cunha, 2124 km (1320 miles) south-west of St Helena; Inac-

cessible Island, 32 km (20 miles) west of Tristan; the three Nightingale Islands (Nightingale, Middle Island and Stoltenhoff Island), 32 km (20 miles) south of Tristan; Gough Island (Diego Alvarez), 354 km (220 miles) south of Tristan.

Area: 419 km² (162 miles²) (St Helena 122 km² (47·3 miles²), Ascension 88 km² (34 miles²), Tristan da Cunha 98 km² (38 miles²), Gough 90 km² (35 miles²), Inaccessible 10 km² (4 miles²), Nightingale 2 km² (0·75 mile²).

Population: St Helena 5895 (1985); Ascension 1708; Tristan da Cunha 325.

Capital: Jamestown (population 1862 at 31 Dec 1978).

Principal Settlements: Ascension – Georgetown (or Garrison); Tristan da Cunha – Edinburgh.

South Georgia and South Sandwich Islands

Location: South Georgia is an island 1287 km (800 miles) to the east of the Falkland Islands. South Sandwich Islands are 756 km (470 miles) south-east of South Georgia.

Area: South Georgia 3755 km² (1450 miles²); South Sandwich Islands 336 km² (130 miles²).

Population: South Georgia has a small population (22 in 1980) which is not permanent.

Settlement: Grytviken (on South Georgia).

Turks and Caicos Islands

Location: Two groups of islands at the south-eastern end of the Bahamas, 193 km (120 miles) north of Hispaniola (Haiti and Dominican Republic), in the West Indies. There are over 30 islands, including eight Turks Islands.

Area: 430 km² (166 miles²).

Population: 7436 (1980 census). There are six inhabited islands (two in the Turks Islands, four in the Caicos Islands).

Capital: Cockburn Town, on Grand Turk Island (population 2897 in 1978).

The United States of America

Population: 243 249 000 (1987 estimate).

Area: 9 363 123 km² (3 615 122 miles²).

Language: English.

Religions: Protestant, Roman Catholic, Jewish, Orthodox (see pp. 162–168).

Capital city: Washington, D.C., population 626 000 (city) in 1984, conurbation 3 061 000.

Other principal towns (conurbation figure 1980; city figure 1984): New York 16 121 000 (city 7 262 700); Los Angeles 11 498 000 (city 3 259 340); Chicago 7 870 000 (city 3 009 530); Philadelphia 5 548 000 (city 1 642 900); San Francisco 5 180 000 (city 749 000); Detroit 4 618 000 (city 1 086 220); Boston 3 448 000 (city 573 600); Houston 3 101 000 (city 1 728 910); Dallas 2 975 000 (city 1 003 520); Cleveland 2 834 000 (city 535 830); Miami 2 644 000 (city 373 940); St Louis 2 356 000 (city 426 300); Pittsburgh 2 264 000 (city 387 490); Baltimore 2 174 000 (city 752 800); Mineapolis-St Paul 2 114 000 (city of Minneapolis 356 840); Seattle 2 093 000 (city 486 200);

Atlanta 2 030 000 (city 421 910); San Diego 1 817 000 (city 1 015 190); Cincinnati 1 660 000 (city 369 750); Denver 1 621 000 (city 505 000); Milwaukee 1 570 000 (city 605 090); Tampa 1 569 000 (city 272 000 in 1980); Phoenix 1 509 000 (city 894 070); Kansas City 1 327 000 (city 441 070); Indianapolis 1 306 000 (city 719 820); Portland 1 243 000 (city 387 870); Buffalo 1 243 000 (city 324 820); New Orleans 1 187 000 (city 554 500); Providence 1 096 000 (city 157 000 in 1980); Columbus 1 093 000 (city 566 030); San Antonio 1 072 000 (city 914 350); Sacramento 1 014 000 (city 323 550); Dayton 1 014 000 (city 203 000 in 1980).

Head of State: George Herbert Walker Bush (b. 12 June 1924), President.

Climate: Its continental dimensions ensure extreme variety, ranging in temperature between the 56·7°C (*134°F*) recorded in Death Valley, California, on 10 July 1913, and the −60·0°C (*−76°F*) at Tanana, Alaska, in January 1886. Mean annual averages range between 24·7°C (*76·6°F*) at Key West, Florida, and −12·1°C (*10·1°F*) at Barrow, Alaska. Excluding Alaska and Hawaii, rainfall averages 736 mm (*29 in*) per year and ranges between 1412 mm (*55·6 in*) in Louisiana and 218 mm (*8·6 in*) in Nevada.

Climate in representative population centres are:
Anchorage, Alaska: Average daily high 18°C (*65°F*) July; −7°C (*19°F*) January. Average daily low −15°C (*5°F*) January; 9°C (*49°F*) July. Days with rain 15 in August; 4 in April.

San Francisco, Cal: Average daily high 20°C (*69°F*) September; 13°C (*55°F*) January. Average daily low 7°C (*45°F*) January; 13°C (*55°F*) September. Days with rain 11 in January–February; nil in July–August.

Washington, DC: Average daily high 30°C (*87°F*) July; 5°C (*42°F*) January. Average daily low −3°C (*27°F*) January; 20°C (*68°F*) July. Days with rain 12 in March, May; 8 in September–October.

Chicago, Illinois: Average daily high 27°C (*81°F*) July; 0°C (*32°F*) January. Average daily low −8°C (*18°F*) January; 19°C (*66°F*) July. Days with rain 12 in March, May; 9 in July–October.

Honolulu, Hawaii: Average daily high 28°C (*83°F*) August–September; 24°C (*76°F*) January–February. Average daily low 19°C (*67°F*) February–March; 23°C (*74°F*) September–October. Days with rain 15 in December; 11 in February, May.

New York, NY: Average daily high 28°C (*82°F*) July; 3°C (*37°F*) January. Average daily low −4°C (*24°F*) January–February; 19°C (*66°F*) July–August. Days with rain 12 in January, March, July; 9 in September–November.

Miami, Florida: Average daily high 31°C (*88°F*) July–August; 23°C (*74°F*) January. Average daily low 16°C (*61°F*) January–February; 24°C (*76°F*) July–August. Days with rain 18 in September; 6 in February.

Labour force: 121 602 000 in 1987: Agriculture, forestry and fishing 2·8%; Construction 6·1%; Manufacturing 17·2%; Wholesale and retail trade 19·2%; Finance, insurance and real estate 6·4%; Professional and related services 20·1%; Other services 29·5%.

Gross domestic product: $4185·5 billion in 1986: Agriculture, forestry and fishing 2·1%; Manufacturing 19·9%; Tade 17·4%; Financial services 23·9%; Community, social and personal services 9·2%.

Exports: $217 304 million in 1986: Food and live

animals 8%; Crude materials 7·9%; Machinery and transport equipment 43·9%; Chemicals 10·5%.

Monetary unit: US dollar ($). 1 dollar = 100 cents.
Denominations:
Coins 1, 5, 10, 25, 50 cents; 1 dollar.
Notes 1, 2, 5, 10, 20, 50, 100 dollars.
Length of roadways: 6 261 876 km (*3 891 781 miles*) (1984).
Length of railways: 236 602 km (*147 049 miles*).
Universities: over 3000 (including colleges) in 1978.
Defence: Military service voluntary; total armed forces 2 158 000 (1987); defence expenditure: $297 536 million in 1987/8.
Foreign tourists: 20 800 000 (including visits for study or transit) in 1984.

The United States of America ranks fourth in area (9 363 123 km² (*3 615 122 miles²*), fourth in population (an estimated 243 249 000 in 1987) and first in economic production of all the countries in the world.

The area of the 48 coterminous states comprises 7 827 617 km² (*3 022 260 miles²*). The principal mountain ranges are listed on p. 12. The highest point is Mount McKinley (6194 m *20 320 ft*) in Alaska.

There are eight US river systems involving rivers in excess of 1609 km (*1000 miles*) in length, of which by far the vastest is the Mississippi–Missouri (see page 16).

At the 1980 census the declared racial origins of the population were: White 83·2%; Black 11·7%; Indigenous 0·6%; Asian and Pacific Islander 1·5%; Other 3·0%. The population of foreign origin included at March 1972:

British (UK)	29 548 000
German	25 543 000
Irish (Republic)	16 408 000
Spanish and Spanish origin	9 178 000
Italian	8 764 000
Jewish	6 460 000
French	5 420 000
Polish	5 105 000
Russian	2 188 000

The principal religious denominations in 1984 were (in millions):

Roman Catholic	52·1
Baptist	25·8
Methodist	13·6
Lutheran	8·3
Jewish	5·7
Eastern Orthodox	3·9
Mormon	3·7
Presbyterian	3·2
Protestant Episcopal Church	2·8
United Church of Christ	1·7

The capital city is Washington, District of Columbia (DC). The District of Columbia (population 631 000, 1981 estimate city only) is the seat of the US Federal Government, comprising 179 km² (*69 miles²*) from west central Maryland on the Potomac River opposite Virginia. The site was chosen in October 1790 by President Washington and the Capitol corner stone laid by him on 18 Sept 1793. Washington became the capital (Philadelphia 1790–1800) on 10 June 1800.

Historical note: Evidence from the most recent radiometric dating has backdated human habitation of North America to *c.* 35 000 BC. This occupa-

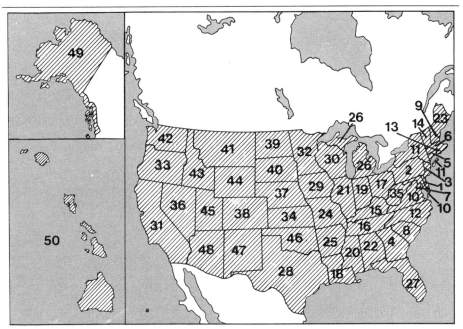

THE FIFTY STATES OF THE UNITED STATES OF AMERICA
(in order of admission)
1. Delaware. 2. Pennsylvania. 3. New Jersey. 4. Georgia. 5. Connecticut. 6. Massachusetts. 7. Maryland. 8. South
Carolina. 9. New Hampshire. 10. Virginia. 11. New York. 12. North Carolina. 13. Rhode Island. 14. Vermont. 15. Kentucky.
16. Tennessee. 17. Ohio. 18. Louisiana. 19. Indiana. 20. Mississippi. 21. Illinois. 22. Alabama. 23. Maine. 24. Missouri.
25. Arkansas. 26. Michigan. 27. Florida. 28. Texas. 29. Iowa. 30. Wisconsin. 31. California. 32. Minnesota. 33. Oregon.
34. Kansas. 35. West Virginia. 36. Nevada. 37. Nebraska. 38. Colorado. 39. North Dakota. 40. South Dakota.
41. Montana. 42. Washington. 43. Idaho. 44. Wyoming. 45. Utah. 46. Oklahoma. 47. New Mexico. 48. Arizona.
49. Alaska. 50 Hawaii (see note)

Note: The state of Hawaii consists of a chain of more than 100 islands (including 8 large ones) stretching for about 2575
km (*1600 miles*). The map shows the island of Hawaii (largest and easternmost of the group) but about 80% of the
population are on the island of Oahu, which contains Honolulu and Pearl Harbor.

tion was probably achieved via the Bering Bridge
(now the 88·5 km (*55 miles*) wide Bering Strait) from
north-east Asia.

The continent derived is name from the Italian
explorer Amerigo Vespucci (1454–1512), discoverer
of the north-east South American coastal regions in
1498. The German cartographer Martin Waldsee-
müller named the New World 'Terra America' in
his atlas published in St Dié, France, in April 1507.
The earliest European landing on present US territory was on 27 Mar 1513 by the Spaniard Juan
Ponce de León in Florida. The discovery of the US
Pacific coast was by Juan R. Cabrillo who landed
from Mexico on 28 Sept 1542, near San Diego, California. The oldest town of European origin is St
Augustine, Florida, founded on 8 Sept 1565 on the
site of Seloy by Pedro Menéndez de Avilés with
1500 Spanish colonists. The British exploration of
what is now US territory began with Philip Amadas
and Arthur Barlowe in Virginia in 1584. Henry
Hudson sailed into New York harbour in September 1609. The Plymouth Pilgrims reached Cape
Cod 54 days out from Plymouth, England, in the
Mayflower (101 passengers and 48 crew) on 9 Nov
1620. On 6 May 1626 Peter Minuit bought Manhat-
tan island for some trinkets valued at $39. In 1664

the area was seized by the British and granted to
Charles II's brother, the Duke of York, and the city
of New Amsterdam was renamed New York.

By the 18th century there were 13 British colonies
along the Atlantic seaboard of North America. The
American revolution and the War of Independence
(total battle deaths 4435) occupied the years 1763–
83. The incident of the Boston Tea Party occurred
on 16 Dec 1773 and the Battle of Bunker Hill on 17
June 1775. The Declaration of Independence was
made on 4 July 1776. This was recognized by Britain in March 1782. General George Washington
was chosen President in February 1789 and the first
US Congress was called on 4 Mar 1789, when the
US Constitution took effect. Washington took
office on 30 Apr 1789.

The War of 1812 between the US and Great Britain was declared by Congress on 18 June 1812,
because Britain seized US ships running her block-
ade of France, impressed 2800 seamen and armed
Indians who raided US territory. In 1814 Maj.-Gen.
Robert Ross burnt the Capitol and the White
House in Washington. The war which inspired
national unity cost only 2260 battle deaths. The
Monroe Doctrine (the isolationism of the Americans from Europe) was declared on 2 Dec 1823.

On 1 Nov 1835 Texas proclaimed independence from Mexico. In the Alamo in San Antonio a US garrison was massacred (including Sen. David Crockett) on 6 Mar 1836.

The secession of States over the question of slave labour on cotton plantations began with South Carolina on 20 Dec 1860. The Southern States of South Carolina, Georgia, Alabama, Mississippi, Louisiana and Florida formed the Confederate States of America on 8 Feb 1861. War broke out on 12 Apr 1861 with the bombardment of Fort Sumter in Charleston Harbor, South Carolina. The war culminated in the Battle of Gettysburg in July 1863 during which there was a total of 43 000 casualties. President Abraham Lincoln was assassinated on 14 Apr 1865. Slavery was abolished by the adoption of the 13th Amendment (to the Constitution) on 18 Dec 1865.

The total fatal casualties in the Civil War were c. 547 000 of which the Union forces (North) lost 140 400 in the field and the Confederates (South) 74 500 in battle and c. 28 500 in Union prisons. In 1867 the USA purchased Alaska from Russia. By 1890 the USA was in full possession of the continental territories which now comprise the 48 contiguous states (statehood being granted to all by 1912). Hawaii was annexed in 1898. The dates of the United States' entry into the World Wars of 1914–18 and 1939–45 respectively were 6 Apr 1917 and 8 Dec 1941. Alaska and Hawaii became the 49th and 50th states in 1959.

Government: The 1789 constitution established a federal republic in which extensive powers are reserved to the component states (originally 13, now 50).

At federal level, legislative power is held by the bicameral Congress of the United States. The upper house is the Senate, with 100 members (two from each state) elected by universal adult suffrage for six years (one-third retiring every two years). The second chamber is the House of Representatives, with 435 voting members directly elected from single-member constituencies for two years. The number of Representatives per state is determined periodically according to population but each state is entitled to at least one Representative. Since 1970 the District of Columbia has been represented by a non-voting delegate.

Federal executive power is vested in the President, who serves for a four-year term and (by a constitutional amendment ratified on 26 Feb 1951) limited to two terms in office. The President, with a Vice-President, is elected by an Electoral College composed of electors (themselves chosen by direct popular vote) from each state and the District of Columbia. Usually, the presidential candidate with a majority of popular votes in any state receives the whole of that state's Electoral College votes. The President appoints a Cabinet which must be approved by the Senate. A presidential veto on legislative proposals may be overridden by a separate two-thirds vote in each house of the Congress.

Each state has a constitution modelled on the federal pattern, with its own legislature (all but one bicameral) and executive power held by a popularly elected Governor.

20th century presidents

Name	Dates of Birth and Death	Party	Dates in Office
Theodore Roosevelt	27 Oct 1858 to 6 Jan 1919	Republican	1901–09
William Howard Taft	15 Sept 1857 to 8 Mar 1930	Republican	1909–13
Thomas Woodrow Wilson	28 Dec 1856 to 3 Feb 1924	Democratic	1913–21
Warren Gamaliel Harding	2 Nov 1865 to 2 Aug 1923	Republican	1921–23
John Calvin Coolidge	4 July 1872 to 5 Jan 1933	Republican	1923–29
Herbert Clark Hoover	10 Aug 1874 to 20 Oct 1964	Republican	1929–33
Franklin Delano Roosevelt	30 Jan 1882 to 12 Apr 1945	Democratic	1933–45
Harry S Truman	8 May 1884 to 26 Dec 1972	Democratic	1945–53
Dwight David Eisenhower	14 Oct 1890 to 28 Mar 1969	Republican	1953–61
John Fitzgerald Kennedy	29 May 1917 to 22 Nov 1963	Democratic	1961–63
Lyndon Baines Johnson	27 Aug 1908 to 22 Jan 1973	Democratic	1963–69
Richard Milhous Nixon	b. 9 Jan 1913	Republican	1969–74
Gerald Rudolph Ford	b. 14 July 1913	Republican	1974–77
James Earl Carter	b. 1 Oct 1924	Democratic	1977–81
Ronald Wilson Reagan	b. 6 Feb 1911	Republican	1981–88
George Herbert Walker Bush	b. 12 June 1924	Republican	1988–

The 50 states of the United States of America

Name, with date and order of (original) admission into the Union. Nicknames	Area (inc inland water). Population 1986 estimate (with rankings). State Capital. Admin. divisions	Major Cities (with population at 1 Apr 1980) – this figures excludes suburbs
Alabama (Ala) 14 Dec 1819 (22nd) 'Heart of Dixie' 'Cotton State' 'Yellowhammer State'	134 623 km² (51 988 miles²) (29th) 4 052 000 (22nd) Montgomery 67 counties	Birmingham (284 413) Mobile (200 452) Montgomery (178 157) Huntsville (142 513) Tuscaloosa (75 143) Dothan (48 750) Gadsden (47 565)

Name, with date and order of (original) admission into the Union. Nicknames	Area (inc inland water). Population 1986 estimate (with rankings). State Capital. Admin. divisions	Major Cities (with population at 1 Apr 1980) – this figures excludes suburbs
Alaska (Aleut, 'Great Land') 3 Jan 1959 (49th) 'The Last Frontier' 'Land of the Midnight Sun'	1 530 109 km² (591 004 miles²) (1st) 534 000 (50th) Juneau* 19 election districts	Anchorage (173 017) Kenai Peninsula borough (25 282) Fairbanks (22 645) Juneau (19 528)
Arizona (Ariz) 14 Feb 1912 (48th) 'Grand Canyon State' 'Apache State'	293 637 km² (113 417 miles²) (6th) 3 319 000 (25th) Phoenix 14 counties	Phoenix (764 911) Tucson (330 537) Mesa (152 453) Tempe (106 743) Glendale (96 988)
Arkansas (Ark) 15 June 1836 (25th) 'Land of Opportunity' 'Wonder State' 'Bear State'	137 701 km² (53 187 miles²) (27th) 2 372 000 (33rd) Little Rock 75 counties	Little Rock (158 461) Fort Smith (71 384) North Little Rock (64 419) Pine Bluff (56 576) Fayetteville (36 604) Hot Springs (35 166)
California (Cal) 9 Sept 1850 (31st) 'Golden State'	410 890 km² (158 706 miles²) (3rd) 26 981 000 (1st) Sacramento 58 counties	Los Angeles City (2 966 763) San Diego (875 504) San Francisco (678 974) San Jose (636 550) Long Beach (361 334) Oakland (339 288) Sacramento (275 741) Anaheim (221 847) Fresno (218 202) Santa Ana (203 713)

Sixteen other towns in California had a 1980 population of over 100 000: Riverside (170 876); Huntingdon Beach (170 505); Stockton (149 779); Glendale (139 060); Fremont (131 945); Torrance (131 497); Garden Grove (123 351); Pasadena (119 374); San Bernadino (118 057); Oxnard (108 195); Sunnyvale (106 618); Modesto (106 105); Bakersfield (105 611); Berkeley (103 328); Concord (103 251); Fullerton (102 034)

Colorado (Colo) 1 Aug 1876 (38th) 'Centennial State'	269 489 km² (104 090 miles²) (8th) 3 267 000 (27th) Denver 63 counties	Denver (491 396) Colorado Springs (215 150) Aurora (158 588) Lakewood (112 848) Pueblo (101 686) Arvada (84 576) Boulder (76 658) Fort Collins (64 632)
Connecticut (Conn) 9 Jan 1788 (5th) 'Constitution State' 'Nutmeg State'	12 992 km² (5018 miles²) (48th) 3 189 000 (28th) Hartford 8 counties	Bridgeport (142 546) Hartford (136 392) New Haven (126 109) Waterbury 103 266) Stamford (102 453) Norwalk (77 767) New Britain (73 840)
Delaware (Del) 7 Dec 1787 (1st) 'First State' 'Diamond State'	5292 km² (2044 miles²) (49th) 633 000 (47th) Dover 3 counties	Wilmington (70 195) Newark (25 247) Dover (23 512) Elsmere (6493) Milford (5358) Seaford (5256)
Florida (Fla) 3 Mar 1845 (27th) 'Sunshine State' 'Peninsula State'	151 881 km² (58 664 miles²) (22nd) 11 675 000 (5th) Tallahassee 67 counties	Jacksonville (540 898) Miami (346 931) Tampa (271 523) St Petersburg (236 898) Fort Lauderdale (153 256) Hialeah (145 254) Orlando (128 394) Hollywood (117 188)
Georgia (Ga) 2 Jan 1788 (4th) 'Empire State of the South' 'Peach State'	152 518 km² (58 910 miles²) (21st) 6 104 000 (11th) Atlanta 159 counties	Atlanta (425 022) Columbus (169 441) Savannah (141 634) Macon (116 860) Albany (73 934) Augusta (47 532)

* On 4 Nov. 1976 Alaskan voters approved a proposal to move the state capital to Willow South.

Name, with date and order of (original) admission into the Union. Nicknames	Area (inc inland water). Population 1986 estimate (with rankings). State Capital. Admin. divisions	Major Cities (with population at 1 Apr 1980) – this figures excludes suburbs
Hawaii 21 Aug 1959 (50th) 'Aloha State'	16 753 km² (*6471 miles²*) (47th) 1 062 000 (40th) Honolulu (on Oahu) 5 counties	Honolulu (365 048) Ewa (190 037) Koolaupoko (109 373) Wahiawa (41 562)
Idaho 3 July 1890 (43rd) 'Gem State' 'Gem of the Mountains'	216 347 km² (*83 564 miles²*) (13th) 1 002 000 (41st) Boise City 44 counties, plus small part of Yellowstone Park	Boise City (102 451) Pocatello (46 340) Idaho Falls (39 590) Lewiston (27 986) Twin Falls (26 209) Nampa (25 112)
Illinois (Ill) 3 Dec 1818 (21st) 'Prairie State'	146 020 km² (*56 400 miles²*) (24th) 11 552 000 (6th) Springfield 102 counties	Chicago (3 005 072) Rockford (139 712) Peoria (124 160) Springfield (99 637) Decatur (94 081) Joliet (77 956) Evanston (73 706)
Indiana (Ind) 11 Dec 1816 (19th) 'Hoosier State'	93 683 km² (*36 185 miles²*) (38th) 5 504 000 (14th) Indianapolis 92 counties	Indianapolis (700 807) Fort Wayne (172 196) Gary (151 953) Evansville (130 496) South Bend (109 727) Hammond (93 714) Muncie (77 216)
Iowa (Ia) 28 Dec 1846 (29th) 'Hawkeye State'	145 696 km² (*56 275 miles²*) (25th) 2 851 000 (29th) Des Moines 99 counties	Des Moines (191 003) Cedar Rapids (110 243) Davenport (103 264) Sioux City (82 003) Waterloo (75 985) Dubuque (62 321) Council Bluffs (56 449)
Kansas (Kan) 29 Jan 1861 (34th) 'Sunflower State' 'Jayhawk State'	213 015 km² (*82 277 miles²*) (14th) 2 460 000 (32nd) Topeka 105 counties	Wichita (279 272) Kansas City (161 087) Topeka (115 266) Overland Park (81 784) Lawrence (52 738) Salina (41 843)
Kentucky (Ky) (officially the Commonwealth of Kentucky) 1 June 1792 (15th) 'Bluegrass State'	104 619 km² (*40 409 miles²*) (37th) 3 729 000 (23rd) Frankfort 120 counties	Louisville (298 451) Lexington (204 165) Owensboro (54 450) Covington (49 013) Bowling Green (40 450) Paducah (29 315)
Louisiana (La) 30 Apr 1812 (18th) 'Pelican State' 'Creole State' 'Sugar State' 'Bayou State'	135 800 km² (*52 453 miles²*) (31st) 4 501 000 (18th) Baton Rouge 64 parishes (counties)	New Orleans (557 482) Shreveport (205 815) Baton Rouge (219 486) Lafayette (81 961) Lake Charles (75 051)
Maine (Me) 15 Mar 1820 (23rd) 'Pine Tree State'	86 123 km² (*33 265 miles²*) (39th) 1 173 000 (38th) Augusta 16 counties	Portland (61 572) Lewiston (40 481) Bangor (31 643) Auburn (23 128)
Maryland (Md) 28 Apr 1788 (7th) 'Old Line State' 'Free State'	27 081 km² (*10 460 miles²*) (42nd) 4 463 000 (19th) Annapolis 23 counties, plus the independent city of Baltimore	Baltimore (786 775)

Name, with date and order of (original) admission into the Union. Nicknames	Area (inc inland water). Population 1986 estimate (with rankings). State Capital. Admin. divisions	Major Cities (with population at 1 Apr 1980) – this figures excludes suburbs
Massachusetts (Mass) 6 Feb 1788 (6th) 'Bay State' 'Old Colony State'	21 447 km² (8284 miles²) (45th) 5 832 000 (12th) Boston 14 counties	Boston (562 994) Worcester (161 799) Springfield (152 319) New Bedford (98 478) Cambridge (95 322)
Michigan (Mich) 26 Jan 1837 (26th) 'Wolverine State'	151 526 km² (58 527 miles²) (23rd) 9 145 000 (8th) Lansing 83 counties	Detroit (1 203 339) Grand Rapids (181 843) Warren (161 134) Flint (159 611) Lansing (130 414)
Minnesota (Minn) 11 May 1858 (32nd) 'North Star State' 'Gopher State'	218 517 km² (84 402 miles²) (12th) 4 214 000 (21st) St Paul 87 counties	Minneapolis (370 951) St Paul (270 230) Duluth (92 811) Bloomington (81 831) Rochester (57 855)
Mississippi (Miss) 10 Dec 1817 (20th) 'Magnolia State'	123 467 km² (47 689 miles²) (32nd) 2 625 000 (31st) Jackson 82 counties	Jackson (202 895) Biloxi (49 311) Meridian (46 577) Hattiesburg (40 829) Greenville 40 613)
Missouri (Mo) 10 Aug 1821 (24th) 'Show Me State'	178 499 km² (68 945 miles²) (19th) 5 066 000 (15th) Jefferson City 114 counties, plus the independent city of St Louis	St Louis (453 085) Kansas City (448 159) Springfield (133 116) Independence (111 806) St Joseph (76 691) Columbia (62 061)
Montana (Mont) 8 Nov 1889 (41st) 'Treasure State'	380 940 km² (147 138 miles²) (4th) 819 000 (44th) Helena 56 counties, plus small part of Yellowstone National Park	Billings (66 798) Great Falls (56 725) Missoula (37 205) Butte (33 388) Helena (23 938)
Nebraska (Nebr) 1 Mar 1867 (37th) 'Cornhusker State' 'Beef State' 'Tree Planter's State'	200 272 km² (77 355 miles²) (15th) 1 598 000 (36th) Lincoln 93 counties	Omaha (311 681) Lincoln (171 932) Grand Island (33 180) North Platte (24 479) Fremont (23 979)
Nevada (Nev) 31 Oct 1864 (36th) 'Sagebrush State' 'Silver State' 'Battle Born State'	286 242 km² (110 561 miles²) (7th) 963 000 (43rd) Carson City 17 counties	Las Vegas (164 674) Reno (100 756) North Las Vegas (42 739) Sparks (40 780) Carson City (32 022)
New Hampshire (NH) 21 June 1788 (9th) 'Granite State'	24 023 km² (9279 miles²) (44th) 1 027 000 (39th) Concord 10 counties	Manchester (90 936) Nashua (67 865) Concord (30 400) Portsmouth (26 254)
New Jersey (NJ) 18 Dec 1787 (3rd) 'Garden State'	20 161 km² (7787 miles²) (46th) 7 619 000 (9th) Trenton 21 counties	Newark (329 248) Jersey City (223 532) Paterson (137 970) Elizabeth (106 201) Camden (102 551) Trenton (92 124) Woodbridge (90 074)
New Mexico (NM) 6 Jan 1912 (47th) 'Land of Enchantment' 'Sunshine State'	314 136 km² (121 335 miles²) (5th) 1 479 000 (37th) Santa Fe 32 counties	Albuquerque (331 767) Santa Fe (48 899) Las Cruces (45 086) Roswell (39 676) Clovis (31 194)

Name, with date and order of (original) admission into the Union. Nicknames	Area (inc inland water). Population 1986 estimate (with rankings). State Capital. Admin. divisions	Major Cities (with population at 1 Apr 1980) – this figures excludes suburbs
New York (NY) 26 July 1788 (11th) 'Empire State'	127 141 km² (*49 108 miles²*) (30th) 17 772 000 (2nd) Albany 62 counties	New York City (7 071 030) Buffalo (357 870) Rochester (241 741) Yonkers (195 351) Syracuse (170 105) Albany (101 727) Utica (75 632) Niagara Falls (71 384)
North Carolina (NC) 21 Nov 1789 (12th) 'Tar Heel State' 'Old North State'	136 360 km² (*52 669 miles²*) (28th) 6 333 000 (10th) Raleigh 100 counties	Charlotte (314 447) Greensboro (155 642) Raleigh (149 771) Winston-Salem (131 885) Durham (100 831) High Point (64 107) Fayetteville (59 507)
North Dakota (ND) 2 Nov 1889 (39th) 'Sioux State' 'Flickertail State'	182 952 km² (*70 665 miles²*) (17th) 679 000 (46th) Bismarck 53 counties	Fargo (61 308) Bismarck (44 485) Grand Forks (43 765) Minot (32 843) Jamestown (16 280)
Ohio 1 Mar 1803 (17th) 'Buckeye State'	107 003 km² (*41 330 miles²*) (35th) 10 752 000 (7th) Columbus 88 counties	Cleveland (573 822) Columbus (564 871) Cincinnati (385 457) Toledo (354 635) Akron (237 177) Dayton (203 588) Youngstown (115 436) Canton (94 730)
Oklahoma (Okla) 16 Nov 1907 (46th) 'Sooner State'	181 020 km² (*69 919 miles²*) (18th) 3 305 000 (26th) Oklahoma City 77 counties	Oklahoma City (403 213) Tulsa (360 919) Lawton (80 054) Norman (68 020) Enid (50 363) Midwest City (49 559)
Oregon (Ore) 14 Feb 1859 (33rd) 'Beaver State'	251 322 km² (*97 073 miles²*) (10th) 2 698 000 (30th) Salem 36 counties	Portland (366 383) Eugene (105 624) Salem (89 233) Springfield (41 621)
Pennsylvania (Pa) 12 Dec 1787 (2nd) 'Keystone State'	117 302 km² (*45 308 miles²*) (33rd) 11 888 000 (4th) Harrisburg 67 counties	Philadelphia (1 688 210) Pittsburgh (423 938) Erie (119 123) Allentown (103 758) Scranton (88 117) Reading (78 686) Bethlehem (70 419)
Rhode Island (RI) 29 May 1790 (13th) 'Little Rhody'	3143 km² (*1214 miles²*) (50th) 975 000 (42nd) Providence 5 counties	Providence (156 804) Warwick (87 123) Cranston (71 992) Pawtucket (71 204) East Providence (50 980) Woonsocket (45 914) Newport (29 259)
South Carolina (SC) 23 May 1788 (8th) 'Palmetto State'	80 552 km² (*31 113 miles²*) (40th) 3 377 000 (24th) Columbia 46 counties	Columbia (99 296) Charleston (69 510) North Charleston (65 630) Greenville (58 242) Spartanburg (43 968)

Name, with date and order of (original) admission into the Union. Nicknames	Area (inc inland water). Population 1986 estimate (with rankings). State Capital. Admin. divisions	Major Cities (with population at 1 Apr 1980) – this figures excludes suburbs
South Dakota (SD) 2 Nov 1889 (40th) 'Coyote State' 'Sunshine State'	199 653 km² (77 116 miles²) (16th) 708 000 (45th) Pierre 67 counties (64 county governments)	Sioux Falls (81 343) Rapid City (46 492) Aberdeen (25 956) Watertown (15 649) Brookings (14 951) Mitchell (13 916)
Tennessee (Tenn) 1 June 1796 (16th) 'Volunteer State'	109 111 km² (42 144 miles²) (34th) 4 803 000 (16th) Nashville 95 counties	Memphis (646 356) Nashville-Davidson (455 651) Knoxville (183 139) Chattanooga (169 565) Clarksville (54 777) Jackson (49 131)
Texas 29 Dec 1845 (28th) 'Lone Star State'	690 763 km² (266 807 miles²) (2nd) 16 685 000 (3rd) Austin 254 counties	Houston (1 594 086) Dallas (904 078) San Antonio (785 410) El Paso (425 259) Fort Worth (385 141) Austin (345 496) Corpus Christi (231 999) Lubbock (173 979) Arlington (160 123) Amarillo (149 230) Garland (138 857) Beaumont (118 102) Pasadena (112 560)
Utah 4 Jan 1896 (45th) 'Beehive State'	219 804 km² (84 899 miles²) (11th) 1 665 000 (35th) Salt Lake City 29 counties	Salt Lake City (163 033) Provo (73 907) Ogden (64 407) Orem (52 399) Sandy City (51 022) Bountiful (32 877) Logan (26 844)
Vermont (Vt) 4 Mar 1791 (14th) 'Green Mountain State'	24 891 km² (9614 miles²) (43rd) 541 000 (48th) Montpelier 14 counties	Burlington (37 712) Rutland (18 436) Bennington (15 815) Essex (14 392) Colchester (12 629)
Virginia (Va) (officially called the Commonwealth of Virginia) 26 June 1788 (10th) 'The Old Dominion' 'Cavalier State'	105 546 km² (40 767 miles²) (36th) 5 787 000 (13th) Richmond 98 counties, plus 32 independent cities	Norfolk (266 979) Virginia Beach (262 199) Richmond (219 214) Newport News (144 903) Hampton (122 617) Chesapeake (114 226) Portsmouth (104 577) Alexandria (103 217) Roanoke (100 427) Lynchburg (66 743)
Washington (Wash) 11 Nov 1889 (42nd) 'Evergreen State' 'Chinook State'	176 412 km² (68 139 miles²) (20th) 4 462 000 (20th) Olympia 39 counties	Seattle (493 846) Spokane (171 300) Tacoma (158 501) Bellevue (73 903) Everett (54 413) Yakima (49 826) Bellingham (45 794) Vancouver (42 834) Bremerton (36 208)

Name, with date and order of (original) admission into the Union. Nicknames	Area (inc inland water). Population 1986 estimate (with rankings). State Capital. Admin. divisions	Major Cities (with population at 1 Apr 1980) – this figures excludes suburbs
West Virginia (W Va) 20 June 1863 (35th) 'Mountain State' 'Panhandle State'	62 866 km² (24 282 miles²) (41st) 1 918 000 (34th) Charleston 55 counties	Charleston (63 968) Huntingdon (63 684) Wheeling (43 070) Parkersburg (39 967) Morgantown (27 605) Weirton (24 763) Fairmont (23 863)
Wisconsin (Wisc) 29 May 1848 (30th) 'Badger State'	145 380 km² (56 153 miles²) (26th) 4 785 000 (17th) Madison 72 counties	Milwaukee (636 212) Madison (170 616) Green Bay (87 899) Racine (85 725) Kenosha (77 685) West Allis (63 982) Appleton (59 032)
Wyoming (Wyo) 10 July 1890 (44th) 'Equality State'	253 228 km² (97 809 miles²) (9th) 507 000 (49th) Cheyenne 23 counties, plus most of Yellowstone National Park	Casper (51 016) Cheyenne (47 283) Laramie (24 410) Rock Springs (19 458) Sheridan (15 146) Green River (12 807)

Territories administed by the United States

AMERICAN SAMOA
Population: 36 000 (1986 estimate); Area: 197 km² (76 miles²); Capital: Pago Pago, population 3075 at 1980 census.

GUAM
Population: 129 546 (1986 estimate); Area: 549 km² (212 miles²); Capital: Agaña.

JOHNSTON AND SAND ISLANDS
Population: 327 (1980); Area: less than 1 km² (0·5 mile²).

MARSHALL ISLANDS
Population: 35 000 (1986 estimate); Area: 180 km² (70 miles²); Capital: Majuro, population 12 800 in 1986.

MICRONESIA, FEDERATED STATES OF
Population: 88 375 (1984 estimate); Area: 702 km² (271 miles²); Capital: Kolonia.

MIDWAY ISLANDS
Population: 453 (1980 census); Area: 5 km² (2 miles²).

NORTH MARIANA ISLANDS, THE COMMONWEALTH OF
Population: 19 635 (1985 estimate); Area: 471 km² (184 miles²); Capital: Saipan, population 17 182 in 1985.

PALAU
Population: 15 000 (1987 estimate); Area: 497 km² (192 miles²); Capital: Koror, population 8100 in 1987.

PUERTO RICO, THE COMMONWEALTH OF
Population: 3 282 504 (1985 estimate); Area: 8959 km² (3459 miles²); Capital city: San Juan, population in 1980 434 849. Other principal towns (1980 census): Bayamón 196 206; Ponce 189 046; Carolina 165 954.

VIRGIN ISLANDS OF THE UNITED STATES
Population: 110 800 (1985 estimate); Area: 344 km² (133 miles²); Capital city: Charlotte Amalie, population 11 842 (1980 census).

WAKE ISLAND
Population: 300 (1980 census); Area: 8 km² (3 miles²).

Uruguay

Official name: La República Oriental del Uruguay (the Eastern Republic of Uruguay).
Population: 2 983 000 (1986 estimate).
Area: 176 215 km² (68 037 miles²).
Language: Spanish.
Religion: Roman Catholic.
Capital city: Montevideo, population 1 246 500 (1985 census).
Other principal towns (1985): Salto 77 400; Paysandú 75 200; Las Piedras 61 300; Rivera 55 400; Melo 39 600; Tacuarembó 38 600; Minas 33 700.
Highest point: Cerro de las Animas, 500 m (1643 ft).
Principal mountain range: Sierra de las Animas.
Principal river: Uruguay (1609 km (1000 miles)).
Head of State: Julio Maria Sanguinetta, President.
Climate: Temperate (average 16°C (61°F)). Warm summers and mild winters. Moderate rain. In Montevideo, average maximum 14°C (58°F) (July) to 28°C (83°F) (January), minimum 6°C (43°F) (June,

URUGUAY

affairs. On 13 Feb President Bordaberry accepted the military programme. On 27 June the President dissolved both Houses of Congress. On 19 Dec 1973 he appointed a new legislature, a 25-member Council of State, headed by a President, to control the executive and draft plans for constitutional reform. On 12 June 1976 the President was deposed by the armed forces and replaced by the Vice-President. On 27 June the new régime established the Council of the Nation, with 46 members (the Council of State and 21 officers of the armed forces). On 14 July the Council of the Nation elected a new President, who took office for a five-year term on 1 Sept 1976. A proposed constitution, which would have institutionalized the role of the armed forces within a 'restricted democracy', was rejected in a referendum on 30 Nov 1980. A new President, appointed by the Council of State, took office on 1 Sept 1981 for a 3½-year term, to prepare for elections and the return of civilian rule, and in February 1985 the military régime stood down following the completion of the election in November 1984.

Length of roadways: 52 000 km (*32 300 miles*).
Length of railways: 2991 km (*1857 miles*).
Universities: 1.
Defence: Military service voluntary; total armed forces 26 200 (1987); defence expenditure: 16 430 million new pesos in 1986.
Foreign tourists: 1 120 000 in 1986.

July, August) to 17°C (*62°F*) (January), rainiest months are August and December (each 7 days). Maximum recorded temperature 44°C (*111·2°F*), Rivera, February 1953; minimum −7°C (*19·4°F*), Paysandú, June 1945.
Labour force: 1 153 300 at 1985 census: Agriculture, forestry and fishing 15·5%; Manufacturing 18·3%; Trade, restaurants and hotels 11·9%; Community, social and personal services 31·3%.
Gross domestic product: 31 689 million new pesos in 1986: Agriculture, forestry and fishing 10·3%; Manufacturing 18·4%; Commerce 12·7%; Services 33·7%.
Exports: US$1087·8 million in 1986: Live animals and animal products 27·1%; Vegetable products 12·3%; Skins and Hides 13·7%; Textiles and textile products 29·1%.
Monetary unit: New Uruguayan peso. 1 new peso = 100 centésimos.
Denominations:
Coins 1, 2, 5, 10 new pesos.
Notes 50, 100, 500, 1000, 5000 new pesos.
Political history and government: A republic comprising 19 departments. A new constitution approved by plebiscite on 27 Nov 1966 and taking effect on 1 Mar 1967, provided that elections by universal adult suffrage be held every five years for a President, a Vice-President and a bicameral legislature, the General Assembly (Congress), comprising a Senate (30 elected members plus the Vice-President) and a 99-member Chamber of Representatives. Elections to both Houses were on the basis of proportional representation.

Executive power is held by the President, who appoints and leads the Council of Ministers. Juan María Bordaberry Arocena was elected President on 28 Nov 1971 and took office on 1 Mar 1972. The armed forces intervened on 8 Feb 1973 to demand reforms and military participation in political

Vanuatu

Official name: The Republic of Vanuatu.
Population: 140 154 (1986 estimate).
Area: 14 763 km² (*5700 miles²*).
Languages: Bislama (ni-Vanuatu pidgin), English, French.
Religion: Christian.
Capital city: Port Vila, population 14 184 (1986 estimate).
Other principal town: Luganville (Santo).
Highest point: Mt Tabwebesana, 1888 m (*6195 ft*).
Head of State: Fred Timakata (b. 1937), President.
Prime Minister: Rev. Walter Hadye Lini, CBE (b. 1943).
Climate: Warm and generally pleasant. South-east trade winds, May–October. Average annual rainfall from 1140 mm (*45 in*) in south to 6350 mm (*250 in*) in north. In Port Vila, average temperatures from 16°C to 33°C (*60°F to 92°F*), average annual rainfall 2050 mm (*81 in*).
Labour force: 51 130 in 1979: Agriculture, forestry and fishing 76·8%; Manufacturing 1·9%; Construction 2·2%; Trade 4·3%; Transport, storage and communications 2·6%; Community and social services 10·7%.
Gross national product: No recent figure has been published.
Exports: 1841 million vatu in 1986: Copra 25%; Fish 20·3%; Cocoa 10·6%; Meat and meat products 8·1%.
Monetary unit: Vatu (formerly New Hebrides franc). 1 vatu = 100 centimes.
Denominations:
Coins 1, 2, 5, 10, 20, 50 vatu.
Notes 100, 500, 1000 vatu.
Political history and government: Formerly the Anglo-French Condominium of the New Hebrides. the United Kingdom and France established a joint administration on 20 Oct 1906, each power being

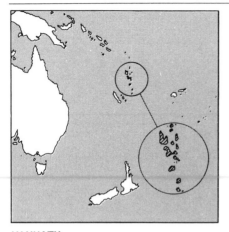

VANUATU

represented by a Resident Commissioner. The first elections under universal adult suffrage were held for two municipal councils on 16 Aug 1975. To increase the territory's autonomy, the administration's Advisory council, established in 1957, was replaced by a Representative Assembly of 42 members (including 29 popularly elected on 10 Nov 1975). The Assembly's first full working session was delayed until 29 Nov 1976. Later it was reduced to 39 members, all directly elected. The Assembly chose the territory's first Chief Minister on 5 Dec 1977 and he formed a Council of Ministers, with powers of internal self-government, on 13 Jan 1978. A conference ending on 19 Sept 1979 adopted a constitution providing for the islands to become an independent republic. The constitution was signed by the Resident Commissioners on 5 Oct and its terms were agreed on 23 Oct by an exchange of notes between the British and French governments. Elections were held on 14 Nov for a new Representative Assembly with increased powers. On 29 Nov 1979 the Assembly elected the Rev. Walter Lini to be Chief Minister. On 30 July 1980 the New Hebrides became independent, as Vanuatu ('our land'), and joined the Commonwealth. The Assembly was renamed Parliament and Lini became Prime Minister.

Legislative power is vested in the unicameral Parliament, elected for a four-year term by universal adult suffrage, partly on the basis of proportional representation. The President is a constitutional Head of State elected for five years by an electoral college consisting of Parliament and the presidents of regional councils. The first President was the former Deputy Chief Minister, George Kalkoa, who was elected on 4 July 1980 and adopted the surname Sokomanu ('leader of thousands'). Executive power is vested in the Prime Minister, elected by and from members of Parliament. Other ministers are appointed by the Prime Minister from among members of Parliament. The Council of Ministers is responsible to Parliament. The constitution also provides for a Council of Chiefs, composed of traditional tribal rulers, to safeguard Melanesian customs. Following a constitutional crisis in late 1988, the President was suspended and detained by the Prime Minister and replaced by Fred Timakata in February 1989.

Length of roadways: 1000 km (*620 miles*).
Universities: 1 university centre.
Foreign tourists: 17 500 in 1986.

The Vatican City

Official name: Stato della Città del Vaticano (State of the Vatican City).
Population: 1000 (1986 estimate).
Area: 44 hectares (*108·7 acres*).
Languages: Italian, Latin.
Religion: Roman Catholic.
Head of State: Pope John Paul II (b. Karol Wojtyla, 18 May 1920).
Head of Government: Cardinal Agostino Casaroli (b. 24 Nov 1914), Secretary of State.
Climate: See Italy for climate of Rome.
Monetary unit: Italian currency (*q.v.*).
Political history and government: An enclave in the city of Rome, established on 11 Feb 1929 by the Lateran Treaty with Italy. The Vatican City is under the temporal jurisdiction of the Pope, the Supreme Pontiff elected for life by a conclave comprising members of the Sacred College of Cardinals. He appoints a Pontifical Commission, headed by the Secretary of State, to conduct the administrative affairs of the Vatican, which serves as the international headquarters, and administrative centre, of the worldwide Roman Catholic Church.

The Holy See (a term designating Rome as the Pope's own bishopric) is a distinct, pre-existing entity. Both entities, although united in the person of the Pope, are subjects of international law. The Holy See has diplimatic relations with foreign states on the basis of its religious status.

The 'Apostolic Constitution' (*Regimini Ecclesiae Universae*) published on 15 Aug 1967, and effective from 1 Mar 1968, reformed the Roman Curia, the Papal Court which acts as the central administrative body of the Church. The Vatican City remains an absolute monarchy, with legislative, executive and judicial power vested in the Pope. The College of Cardinals, whose members are created by the Pope, serves as the chief advisory body (in 1987 there were 138 Cardinals). An Apostolic Letter of 21 Nov 1970 decreed that, from 1 Jan 1971, Cardinals

THE VATICAN CITY

reaching the age of 80 would lose the right to elect the Pope. On 5 Mar 1973 the Pope announced that the number of Cardinals permitted to participate in the conclave would be limited to 120. Rules governing the conclave, issued on 13 Nov 1975, included these limits and also stipulated that, to be successful, a candidate should normally have a two-thirds majority plus one vote.

Length of railways: 0·86 km (0·54 mile).
Universities: There are 5 pontifical universities in Rome.

Venezuela

Official name: La República de Venezuela ('Little Venice').
Population: 18 272 157 (1987 estimate).
Area: 1842 km² (1097 miles²).
Languages: Samoan, English.
Religion: Roman Catholic.
Capital city: (Santiago de León de los) Caracas, population 3 247 698 (1987 estimate).
Other principal towns (1987): Maracaibo 1 295 421; Valencia 1 134 623; Maracay 857 982; Barquisimeto 718 197; Ciudad Guyana 466 418; Barcelona/Puerto La Cruz 417 501; San Cristóbal 338 188.
Highest point: La Pico Columna (Pico Bolívar), 5007 m (16 427 ft).
Principal mountain ranges: Cordillera de Mérida, Sierra de Perijá, La Gran Sabana.
Principal river: Orinoco (2736 km (1700 miles)).
Head of State: Carlos Andrés Pérez, President.
Climate: Varies with altitude from tropical in steamy lowlands to cool in highlands. Maximum recorded temperature 38°C (100·4°F), minimum −6°C (21·2°F), average minimum temperature 20°C (69°F), average maximum 20°C (75°F) (January) to 27°C (81°F) (April), minimum 13°C (56°F) (January, February) to 17°C (62°F) (May, June), rainiest months are July and August (each 15 days).
Labour force: 6 142 000 in 1987: Agriculture, forestry and fishing 13·8%; Manufacturing 17·1%; Trade 19·3%; Financial services 5·3%; Community, social and personal services 26·3%.
Gross domestic product: 403 860 million bolívares in 1986.
Exports: US$10 052 million in 1986: Petroleum and iron ore 86·4%; Basic manufactures 8·4%.
Monetary unit: Bolívar. 1 bolívar = 100 céntimos.
Denominations:
Coins 5, 12½, 25, 50 céntimos; 1, 2, 5 bolívares.
Notes 10, 20, 50, 100, 500 bolívares.
Political history and government: A federal republic of 20 states, two Federal Territories and a Federal District (contining the capital), each under an appointed Governor. The last military dictatorship was overthrown by popular revolt on 21–22 Jan 1958, after which Venezuela returned to democratic rule. A new constitution was promulgated on 23 Jan 1961. Legislative power is held by the bicameral National Congress, comprising a Senate (44 elected members plus ex-Presidents of the Republic) and a Chamber of Deputies (200 members). Executive authority rests with the President. Senators, Deputies and the President are all elected for 5 years by universal adult suffrage. Members of both houses of Congress, whose terms run concurrently with that of the President, are chosen partly by direct election and partly on the basis of propor-

VENEZUELA

tional representation, with seats for minority parties. The President has wide powers and appoints a Council of Ministers to conduct the government. He may not have two consecutive terms of office.
Length of roadways: 100 571 km (62 455 miles) (1986).
Length of railways: 619 km (384 miles).
Universities: 11.
Adult illiteracy: 13·1% in 1985.
Defence: Military service: 2 years, selective; total armed forces 49 000 (1987); defence expenditure: 6610 million bolívares.
Foreign tourists: 653 000 in 1986.

Viet-Nam

Official name: Công hoa xã hôi chu nghia Viêt Nam (Socialist Republic of Viet-Nam).
Population: 60 919 000 (1986 estimate).
Area: 332 559 km² (128 402 miles²).
Language: Vietnamese.
Religions: Buddhist, Taoist, Confucian, Christian.
Capital city: Hà-nôi (Hanoi), population 2 674 400 (1983).
Other principal towns (1979): Ho Chi Minh City (formerly Saigon) 3 419 978 (including Cholon); Haiphong 1 279 067; Da-Nhang (Tourane) 492 194 (1973); Nha-trang 216 227 (1973); Qui-Nhon 213 757 (1973); Hué 209 043 (1973).
Highest point: Fan si Pan, 3142 m (10 308 ft).
Principal rivers: Mekong (4184 km 2600 miles), Songkoi (Red River), Songbo (Black River), Ma.
Head of State: Vo Chi Cong, Chairman of the Council of State.

Political Leader: Nguyen Van Linh, First Secretary of the Central Committee of the Communist Party of Viet-Nam.
Prime Minister: Do Muoi.
Climate: Hot and wet in the north, warm and humid in the south. The rainy monsoon season is from April or May to October. In Hanoi, average maximum temperature 20°C *(68°F)* (January) to 33°C *(92°F)* (June), minimum 13°C to 25°C *(56°F to 78°F)* (June, July, August); rainiest month August (16 days). In Ho Chi Minh City, average maximum 30°C *(87°F)* (November, December) to 35°C *(95°F)* (April), minimum 21°C *(70°F)* (January) to 24°C *(76°F)* (April, May); rainiest month July (23 days).
Labour force: 23 100 000 in 1984: Agriculture, forestry and fishing 68%.
Gross national product: No recent figures published.
Exports: US$595·8 million in 1986.
Monetary unit: Dông. 1 dông = 10 hào = 100 xu.
Denominations:
Coins 1, 2, 5 xu.
Notes 2, 5 xu; 1, 2, 5 hào; 1, 2, 5, 10, 20, 30, 50, 100 dông.
Political history and government: Formerly part of French Indo-China, Viet-Nam was occupied by Japanese forces, with French co-operation, in September 1940. On 6 June 1941 nationalist and revolutionary groups, including the Communist Party of Indo-China, formed the *Viet-Nam Doc-Lap Dong Minh Hoi* (Revolutionary League for the Independence of Viet-Nam), known as the *Viet-Minh*, to overthrow French rule. On 9 Mar 1945 French administrative control was ended by a Japanese *coup* against their nominal allies. After Japan's surrender in August 1945, *Viet-Minh* forces entered Hanoi and formed a provisional government under Ho Chi Minh, leader of the Communist Party. On 2 Sept 1945 the new régime proclaimed independence, as the Democratic Republic of Viet-Nam (DRV), with Ho as President. On 6 Mar 1946, after French forces re-entered Viet-Nam, an agreement between France and the DRV recognized Viet-Nam as a 'free' state within the French Union. The DRV government continued to press for complete independence but negotiations broke down and full-scale hostilities began on 19 Dec 1946. The war continued until cease-fire agreements were made on 20–21 July 1954. These provided that DRV forces should regroup north of latitude 17°N. Thus the DRV was confined to North Viet-Nam.

On 8 Mar 1949, during the first Indo-China war, the French government made an agreement with anti-Communist elements for the establishment of the State of Viet-Nam, under Bao Dai, Emperor of Annam. Originally within the French Union, the State made an independence agreement with France on 4 June 1954. After the cease-fire agreements of 20–21 July 1954 French forces withdrew, leaving the State's jurisdiction confined to the zone south of latitude 17°N. Complete sovereignty was transferred by France on 29 dec 1954. Following a referendum, Bao Dai was deposed and the Republic of Viet-Nam proclaimed on 26 Oct 1955. In 1959 an insurgent movement, supported by North Viet-Nam, launched guerrilla warfare to overthrow the Republic. On 20 Dec 1960 the insurgents formed the National Front for the Liberation of South Viet-Nam, known as the National Liberation Front (NLF). From 1961 the USA supported the Republic with troops, numbering over 500 000 by 1969. From 1964 regular forces from North Viet-Nam, number-

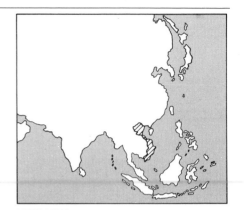

VIET-NAM

ing about 250 000 by 1975, moved south to support the NLF. On 10 June 1969 the NLF announced the formation of a Provisional Revolutionary Government (PRG) to administer 'liberated' areas. A 'peace' agreement on 27 Jan 1973 led to the withdrawal of US forces but fighting continued until the Republic surrendered to the PRG on 30 Apr 1975. The territory was renamed the Republic of South Viet-Nam.

Following the PRG victory, it was agreed to merge North and South Viet-Nam. Elections were held on 25 Apr 1976 for a single National Assembly (for both North and South) of 492 members. The new Assembly met on 24 June and the country was reunited as the Socialist Republic of Viet-Nam on 2 July 1976.

On 18 Dec 1980 the National Assembly adopted a new constitution. The highest state authority is the Assembly, a unicameral body elected by universal adult suffrage for five years. The Assembly elects from its members a Council of State to be its permanent organ, with a term of office corresponding to that of the Assembly. The Council's Chairman serves as Head of State. The highest administrative organ is the Council of Ministers, headed by a Prime Minister, which is elected by, and responsible to, the Assembly. A new National Assembly was elected on 26 Apr 1981, when 496 members were chosen from 93 constituencies. The first Chairman of the Council of State was elected on 4 July 1981.

Political power is held by the Communist Party of Viet-Nam, described by the constitution as 'the only force leading the state and society'. The Party was established on 20 Dec 1976 in succession to the *Dang Lao Dong Viet-Nam* (Viet-Nam Workers' Party), formed in 1951. The Party Congress of 1986 elected a Central Committee to supervise Party work. The Central Committee elected a Political Bureau (Politburo), with 12 full and one alternate member, to direct its policy.

On 6 July 1976 representatives of the former DRV's Communist-led National Fatherland Front, the NLF and other groups met to organize a united Viet-Nam Fatherland Front, formally launched during a congress on 31 Jan–4 Feb 1977. The Front presents an approved list of candidates for elections to all representative bodies.

Viet-Nam comprises 37 provinces and three cities.

Length of roadways: 347 243 km (*215 767 miles*) (1983).
Length of railways: 2600 km (*1616 miles*) (1983).
Universities: 3.
Adult illiteracy: 16% in 1979.
Defence: Military service: 2 years minimum; total armed forces 1 260 000 (1986).

Western Samoa

Official name: The Independent State of Western Samoa (Samoa i Sisifo).
Population: 158 940 (1986 census).
Area: 2842 km² (*1097 miles²*).
Languages: Samoan, English.
Religions: Congregational, Roman Catholic, Methodist, Mormon.
Capital city: Apia, population 33 170 (1981 census).
Highest point: Mauga Silisli, 1857 m (*6094 ft*).
Head of State: HH Malietoa Tanumafili II, CBE (b. 4 Jan 1913).
Prime Minister: Tofilau Eti Alesana.
Climate: Warm all the year round. Rainy season November to April. In Apia, average maximum 29°C to 30°C (*84°F to 86°F*), minimum 23°C to 24°C (*74°F to 76°F*); rainiest month is January (22 days).
Labour force: 41 506 in 1981: Agriculture, forestry and fishing 60·4%; Construction 5·5%; Trade 4·4%; Government services 19·8%.
Gross domestic product: No recent figures published.
Exports: 27·4 million tala in 1983: Copra 5·1%; Cocoa 16·8%; Taro and taamu 8·7%.
Monetary unit: Tala. 1 tala = 100 sene.
Denominations:
  Coins 1, 2, 5, 10, 20, 50 sene; 1 tala.
  Notes 2, 10, 20 tala.
Political history and government: The islands became a German protectorate in 1899. They were occupied by New Zealand forces during the First World War (1914–18). In 1919 New Zealand was granted a League of Nations mandate over the islands. In 1946 Western Samoa was made a United Nations Trust Territory, administered by New Zealand. An independence constitution, adopted by a Constitutional Convention on 28 Oct 1960, was approved by a UN-supervised plebiscite in May 1961. The islands duly became independent on 1 Jan 1962. The position of Head of State (*O le Ao o le Malo*) was held jointly by two tribal leaders, one of whom died on 5 Apr 1963. The other remains Head of State for life, performing the duties of a constitutional monarch. In the absence of the Head of State, his functions are performed by a Council of Deputies. Future Heads of State will be elected for five years by the Legislative Assembly. The Assembly is a unicameral body of 47 members, including 45 Samoans elected by about 11 000 *matai* (elected clan chiefs) in 41 constituencies and two members popuparly elected by voters (mainly Europeans) outside the *matai* system. Members hold office for three years (subject to dissolution). The country's first political party was formed by an anti-government group in March 1979.

In most cases, executive power is held by the Cabinet, comprising a Prime Minister and 8 other members of the Assembly. The Prime Minister, appointed by the Head of State, must have the support of a majority in the Assembly. Cabinet decisions may be reviewed by the Executive Council, comprising the Head of State, the Prime Minister and some other Ministers.

Western Samoa joined the Commonwealth on 28 Aug 1970.
Length of roadways: 2085 km (*1296 miles*).
Universities: A national university is planned.
Foreign tourists: 36 717 in 1983.

The Yemen Arab Republic

Official name: Al-Jamhuriya al-'Arabiya al-Yamaniya.
Population: 9 274 173 (1986 estimate).
Area: 195 000 km² (*75 290 miles²*).
Language: Arabic.
Religion: Islam (Sunni).
Capital city: Sana'a, population 427 185 (1986 estimate).
Other principal towns (1981): Hodeida 126 386; Ta'iz 119 572.
Highest point: Jebel Hadhar, 3760 m (*12 336 ft*).
Principal mountain range: Yemen Highlands.
Head of State: Col. 'Ali Abdullah Saleh (b. 1942), President.
Prime Minister: Maj. 'Abd ul Aziz Abdul Ghani.
Climate: Very hot (up to 54°C (*130°F*)) and extremely humid on semi-desert coastal strip. Cooler on highlands inland (average maximum of 22°C *71°F* in June) with heavy rainfall and winter frost. Desert in the east.
Labour force: 1 127 572 in 1975: Agriculture 73·6%; Manufacturing 3%; Construction 4·7%; Trade 6·1%; Social services 7·6%; Unemployed 6·2%.
Gross domestic product: 14 637 million riyals in 1982–3: Agriculture, forestry and fishing 28·3%; Trade 18·2%; Government services 18·3%; Finance 11·7%.
Exports: 122·6 million riyals in 1983: Biscuits 13·2%; Hides and skins 1%; Coffee 1% (1981).
Monetary unit: Yemeni riyal. 1 riyal = 100 rials.
Political history and government: Formerly a monarchy, ruled by an hereditary Imam. Army officers staged a *coup* on 26–27 Sept 1962, declared the

WESTERN SAMOA

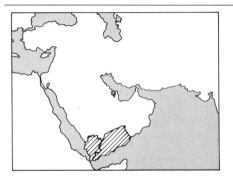

left: **THE YEMEN ARAB REPUBLIC**
right: **THE PEOPLE'S DEMOCRATIC REPUBLIC OF YEMEN**

Imam deposed and proclaimed a republic. Civil war broke out between royalist forces, supported by Saudi Arabia, and republicans, aided by Egyptian troops. The republicans gained the upper hand and Egyptian forces withdrew in 1967. A Republican Council, led by a Chairman, took power on 5 Nov 1967 and announced a new constitution (which did not permit political parties) on 28 Dec 1970. This provided for a unicameral legislature, the Consultative council of 179 membes (20 appointed by the Republican Council and 159 directly elected for 4 years by general franchise on 27 Feb–18 Mar 1971). On 13 June 1974 power was seized by army officers who suspended the constitution and established a Military Command Council. On 19 June 1974 the new régime published a provisional constitution which, for a transitional period, gave full legislative and executive authority to the Command Council, whose Chairman was granted the powers of Head of State. The Consultative council was dissolved after the *coup*, later reinstated but dissolved again on 22 Oct 1975. The first Chairman of the Command Council, Lt.-Col. Ibrahim al-Hamadi, was assassinated on 11 Oct 1977. The remaining three members of the Command Council formed a Presidential Council, under Lt.-Col. Ahmad Husain al-Ghashmi, and imposed martial law.

On 6 Feb 1978 the Command Council issued a decree providing for the formation of a Constituent People's Assembly, with 99 members appointed by the Council for 2 to 3 years. The new Assembly first met on 25 Feb 1978. On 22 Apr it elected Ghashmi to be President for a 5-year term. The Command Council was then dissolved. President Ghashmi was assassinated on 24 June 1978 and the Assembly formed a four-man provisional Presidential Council. On 17 July 1978 the Assembly elected a member of the Presidential Council to be President and he was sworn in on 18 July. On 8 May 1979 the President signed a constitutional declaration which provided that the Assembly would be expanded to 159 members, with a two-year term of office. On the same day 60 new members were selected. The President rules with the assistance of an appointed Cabinet, led by a Prime Minister. Yemen comprises five provinces and the city of Sana'a (the capital). There is also a national General People's Congress of 700 elected and 300 appointed representatives. The Congress meets every two years and is elected every four years and chooses from its members a Permanent Committee of 75 members divided into five sub-committees with responsibilities in economic,

political, administrative, cultural and other matters.
Length of roadways: 37 223 km (*23 129 miles*).
Universities: 1.
Adult illiteracy: 83·6% in 1985.
Defence: Military service: 3 years; total armed forces 36 800 (1987); defence expenditure: 3720 million riyals in 1987.
Foreign tourists: 42 235 in 1983.

The People's Democratic Republic of Yemen

Official name: Jumhuriyat al-Yaman al-Dimuqratiya ash-Sha'abiya.
Population: 2 365 000 (1986 estimate).
Area: 336 869 km² (*130 066 miles²*).
Language: Arabic.
Religion: Islam (Sunni).
Capital city: Aden, population 318 000 (1984).
Other principal towns: Al Mukalla, population 100 000 in 1984.
Highest point: Qaured Audilla, 2499 m (*8200 ft*).
Head of State: Heidar al-Attas, President.
Climate: Summer extremely hot (temperatures over 54°C *130°F*) and humid. Very low rainfall (average less than 76 mm *3 in* per year). Winter can be very cold in high areas.
Labour force: 452 600 in 1981: Agriculture and fishing 45·2%; Industry 10·6%; Construction 7·5%; Transport 6·4%; Commerce 9·2%; Services 21·2%.
Gross domestic product: 320 million dinars in 1982: Agriculture, forestry and fishing 19·4%; Manufacturing 25·2%; Trade, restaurants and hotels 12·7%.
Exports: 222·9 million dinar in 1984: Petroleum products 95·9%.
Monetary unit: Yemeni dinar. 1 dinar = 1000 fils.
Denominations:
Coins 5, 25, 50 fils.
Notes 250, 500 fils; 1, 5, 10 dinars.
Political history and government: Formerly the British colony of Aden and the Protectorate of South Arabia. Became independent, outside the Commonwealth, on 30 Nov 1967 as the People's Republic of Southern Yemen. Power was held by a revolutionary movement, the National Liberation front, renamed the National Front (NF). The interim legislative authority was the NF's Supreme General Command. On 22 June 1969 the country's first President was replaced by a Presidential Council. Salim Rubayyi 'Ali became Chairman of the Council on 24 June 1969. A new constitution, adopted on 30 Nov 1970, gave the country its present name and provided for the establishment of a unicameral legislature, the Supreme People's Council (SPC). A Provisional SPC, inaugurated on 14 May 1971, had 101 members, including 86 elected by the NF's General Command and 15 by trade unions. It was empowered to appoint members of the Presidential Council and the Cabinet. In October 1975 the ruling NF merged with two smaller parties to form the United Political Organization-National Front (UPO-NF).

On 26 June 1978 the Head of State, Rubayyi 'Ali, was ousted from power and executed by opponents within the UPO-NF. The Prime Minister, 'Ali Nasir Muhammad, became interim Head of State. It was announced on 28 June that the three parties within the UPO-NF had agreed to form a Marxist-Leninist 'vanguard' party. The constituent congress of the new party, the Yemen Socialist Party (YSP), was held on 11-14 Oct 1978. Constitutional amendments providing for a new form of legislature and the abolition of the Presidential Council were approved on 31 Oct 1978. A 111-member People's Supreme Assembly (PSA), replacing the SPC, was elected on 16-18 Dec. At its first session, on 27 Dec 1978, the PSA elected an 11-member Presidium (to replace the Presidential Council) and elected as Chairman of the Presidium (and thus as Head of State) 'Abd al-Fattah Isma'il, Secretary-General of the YSP, the sole legal party. On 21 Apr 1980 Isma'il relinquished his positions as Head of State and YSP leader, being replaced in both offices by the Prime Minister, previously Deputy Chairman of the PSA Presidium.

In January 1986 a *coup* attempt developed into civil war and the government of 'Ali Nasir Muhammad was overthrown.

The country, also called Democratic Yemen, is divided into six governates.

Length of roadways: 10 495 km (*6517 miles*).
Universities: 1.
Adult illiteracy: 58·6% in 1985.
Defence: Military service: 2 years; total armed forces 27 500 (1987); defence expenditure: 67 million dinar in 1984.

Yugoslavia

Official name: Socijalistička Federativna Republika Jugoslavija (Socialist Federal Republic of Yugoslavia).
Population: 23 270 000 (1986 estimate).
Area: 255 804 km² (*98 766 miles²*).
Languages: Serbo-Croatian/Croato-Serbian, Slovenian, Macedonian.
Religions: Serbian Orthodox, Roman Catholic, Islam (Sunni), Macedonian Orthodox and smaller Protestant groups.
Capital city: Beograd (Belgrade), population 1 470 075 at 1981 census.
Other principal towns (1981): Zagreb 855 568; Skopje 504 932; Sarajevo 448 519; Ljubljana

YUGOSLAVIA

305 211; Novi Sad 257 685; Priština 210 040; Titograd 132 290.
Republics: Bosnia and Herzegovina Population: 4 124 008 (1981); Area: 51 129 km² (*19 741 miles²*); Capital: Sarajevo. **Croatia:** Population: 4 601 469 (1981); Area: 56 538 km² (*21 829 miles²*); Capital: Zagreb. **Macedonia:** Population: 1 912 257 (1981); Area: 25 713 km² (*9928 miles²*); Capital: Skopje. **Montenegro:** Population: 584 310 (1981); Area: 13 812 km² (*5333 miles²*); Capital: Titograd. **Serbia** (including Kosovo and Vojvodina autonomous provinces): Population: 9 313 677 (1981); Area: 88 361 km² (*34 116 miles²*); Capital: Belgrade. **Slovenia:** Population: 1 891 864 (1981); Area: 20 251 km² (*7819 miles²*); Capital: Ljubljana.
Highest point: Triglav, 2864 m (*9396 ft*).
Principal mountain ranges: Slovene Alps, Dinaric Mts, Šar-Pindus and Rhodope ranges, Carpathian and Balkan Mts.
Principal rivers: Dunav (Danube) (2848 km *1700 miles* total length, in Yugoslavia 588 km *368 miles*) and tributaries (Drava, Sava (945 km *590 miles*), Morava), Vardar.
Head of State: Janez Drnovsek, President of the Presidency of the SFRY for 1989-90.
Head of Government: Ante Markovic, President of the Federal Executive Council.
President of the Central Committee of the League of Communists: Milan Pancěvski.
Climate: Mediterranean climate on Adriatic coast (dry, warm summers; mild, rainy winters). Continental climate (cold winters) in hilly interior. In Belgrade, average maximum 3°C (*37°F*) (January) to 29°C (*85°F*) (July), minimum −3°C (*27°F*) (January, February) to 16°C (*61°F*) (July). Rainiest months are April, May, June, December (each 9 days). In Split, average maximum 14°C (*57°F*) (January) to 30°C (*87°F*) (July, August), minimum 4°C (*39°F*) (January, February) to 20°C (*68°F*) (July), rainiest month is December (11 days). Absolute maximum temperature 46·2°C (*115·2°F*), Mostar, 31 July 1901; absolute minimum −37·8°C (*−36·0°F*), Sjenica, 26 Jan 1954.
Labour force: 9 358 671 in 1981: Agriculture, forestry and fishing 28·7%; Mining and manufacturing 23·6%; Trade 8·8%; Community, social and personal services 16·9%; Unemployed 6·2%.
Gross material product: 22 138 962 million dinar in 1986: Agriculture, forestry and fishing 12%; Manufacturing and mining 42·8%; Trade 18·2%; Transport and communications 7·3%.
Exports: 1 279 736 million dinar in 1984: Food and live animals 8·6%; Chemicals 9·7%; Basic manufactures 22·8%; Machinery and transport equipment 31%; Miscellaneous manufactures 17·9%.
Monetary unit: 1 dinar = 100 para.
Denominations:
Coins 1, 2, 5, 10, 20, 50, 100 dinars.
Notes 5, 10, 20, 50, 100, 500, 1000 dinars.
Political history and government: Yugoslavia was formed by a merger of Serbia, Croatia, Slovenia, Montenegro and Bosnia-Herzegovina. A pact between Serbia and other South Slavs was signed on 20 July 1917 to unite all the territories in a unitary state under the Serbian monarchy. The Kingdom of Serbs, Croats and Slovenes was proclaimed on 1 Dec 1918. It was renamed Yugoslavia on 3 Oct 1929. The Kingdom was invaded by German and Italian forces on 6 Apr 1941. Resistance was divided between royalists and Partisans, led by the Communist Party under Marshal Tito (*né* Josip Broz). Their rivalry led to civil war, won by the Partisans,

who proclaimed the Federal People's Republic of Yugoslavia, with Tito as Prime Minister, on 29 Nov 1945. A Soviet-type constitution, establishing a federation of 6 republics, was adopted on 31 Jan 1946. Yugoslav leaders followed independent policies and the country was expelled from the Soviet-dominated Cominform in June 1948. At its 6th Congress, on 2–7 Nov 1952, the Communist Part was renamed the League of Communists of Yugoslavia (LCY). A new constitution was adopted on 13 Jan 1953 and Tito sworn in as President the next day.

Another constitution, promulgated on 7 Apr 1963, introduced the country's present name. Since 29 July 1971 national leadership has been held by a Collective Presidency. Tito was elected 'President for life' on 16 May 1974. With his death, on 4 May 1980, the office of President was terminated.

The present constitution, which increased decentralization was adopted on 21 Feb 1974. Legislative power was vested in the bicameral Federal Assembly, comprising a Federal Chamber of 220 members (30 from each of the 6 republics and 20 each from the two autonomous provinces within Serbia) and a Chamber of Republics and Provinces, with 88 members (12 from each Republican Assembly and 8 from each Provincial Assembly). Members are elected for four years by communal assemblies which have been chosen by about 1 million delegates, themselves elected by universal adult suffrage, with voters grouped according to their place of work.

The Collective Presidency has nine members: the President of the Presidium of the LCY's Central Committee (*ex officio*) and eight others (one each from the republics and provinces) elected by the Federal Assembly for five years. The posts of President and Vice-President of the Collective Presidency rotate annually in a fixed sequence among the members. The Federal Assembly also elects the Federal Executive Council, led by a President and five Vice-Presidents (one from each of the six republics), for a four-year term as the administrative branch of government.

The only authorized political party is the LCY, which controls political life through the Socialist Alliance of the Working People of Yugoslavia. The LCY's highest authority is the Congress. The 13th Congress, held in 1986, elected a Central Committee of 163 members (equal number of members from each republic, and a corresponding number of members from the provinces and from the Army) to supervize the LCY's work. The Committee elected a Presidium of 23 members to direct its policy. Since the death of Tito, the President of the Presidium is chosen annually on a rotation basis among the republics and provinces. The Presidium had decided on 15 May 1979 that the post of Presidium Secretary (previously nominated by Tito) should be similarly filled by rotation, though for a two-year term.

Each constituent republic has its own government, with an indirectly elected assembly and an executive. There is currently unrest in Kosovo autonomous region between the Albanian majority and Serbian minority.

Length of roadways: 117 744 km (*73 119 miles*) (1985).
Length of railways: 9393 km (*5833 miles*).
Universities: 19.
Adult illiteracy: 8·8% in 1985.
Defence: Military service: 15 months (12 months for the sole supporter of the family); total armed forces 213 500 (123 000 conscripts) in 1987; defence

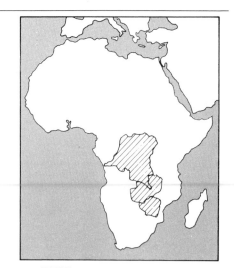

top: **ZAIRE**
centre: **ZAMBIA**
below: **ZIMBABWE**

expenditure: 1 320 000 million dinar in 1987.
Foreign tourists: 8 900 000 in 1987.

Zaire

Official name: La République du Zaïre (the Republic of Zaire).
Population: 30 850 000 (1986 estimate).
Area: 2 344 885 km² (*905 365 miles²*).
Languages: French (official), Lingala, Kiswahili, Tshiluba, Kikongo.
Religions: Animist, Roman Catholic, Protestant.
Capital city: Kinshasa (formerly Léopoldville), population 2 778 281 (1985).
Other principal towns (1976): Kananga (Luluabourg) 704 211; Lubumbashi (Elisabethville) 451 332; Mbuji-Mayi 382 632; Kisangani (Stanleyville) 339 210; Bukavu (Costermanville) 209 051.
Highest point: Ngaliema (Mt Stanley), 5109 m (*16 763 ft*) (first climbed 1900), on the border with Uganda.
Principal mountain ranges: Chaîne des Mitumba, Ruwenzori.
Principal rivers: Zaïre (Congo), Uganbi, Kasai.
Head of State: Lt.-Gen. Mobutu Sese Seko Kuku Ngbendu wa Za Banga (b. Joseph-Désiré Mobutu, 14 Oct 1930), President.
Prime Minister: Mabi Mulumba, First State Commissioner.
Climate: Tropical. Hot and humid in Congo basin, cool in highlands. In Kinshasa, March and April hottest (22°C to 32°C *71°F to 89°F*), July coolest (18°C to 27°C *64°F to 81°F*) and driest, April and November rainiest (16 days each). Absolute maximum temperature 41·0°C (*105·8°F*) at Yahila; absolute minimum −1·5°C (*29·3°F*), Sakania, 11 Jan 1949.
Labour force: 11 666 000 in 1985: Agriculture, forestry and fishing 67·1%.

Gross domestic product: 31 295·9 million zaires in 1982: Agriculture 35·7%; Construction and public works 6%; Mining and metallurgy 11·5%; Commerce 21·3%; Services 18·5%.

Exports: 9925 million zaires in 1982: Copper 42·4%; Cobalt 9·7%; Zinc 2·3%; Diamonds 4·4%; Crude petroleum 14·7%; Coffee 6·2%; Industrial products 15·5%.

Monetary unit: Zaire. 1 zaire = 100 makuta (singular: likuta) = 10 000 sengi.

Denominations:
Coins 10 sengi; 5, 10, 20 makuta.
Notes 50 makute; 1, 5, 10, 50 zaires.

Political history and government: Formerly the Belgian Congo, independent as the Republic of the Congo on 30 June 1960. Renamed the Democratic Republic of the Congo on 1 Aug 1964. Power was seized on 24 Nov 1965 by army officers, led by Maj.-Gen. (later Lt.-Gen.) Joseph-Désiré Mobutu (from January 1972 called Mobutu Sese Seko). The new régime, with Mobutu as President, was approved by Parliament on 28 Nov 1965. A new constitution approved by referendum, was adopted on 24 June 1967. Mobutu was elected President by popular vote on 31 Oct–1 Nov 1970 and inaugurated for a 7-year term on 5 Dec 1970. The country's present name was introduced on 27 Oct 1971. A unicameral National Legislative Council of 224 members, led by Mobutu was elected by acclamation for 5 years on 2 Nov 1975. The President appoints and leads the National Executive Council, a cabinet of State Commissioners with departmental responsibilities. On 6 July 1977 the President appointed a First State Commissioner, equivalent to a Prime Minister. Direct elections for a new Legislative Council were held on 15–16 Oct 1977, when 268 members were elected (from 2080 candidates) to serve a 5-year term. The National Legislative had, in 1987, 310 members. Mobutu was re-elected President (unopposed) and sworn in on 5 Dec 1977 and re-elected in July 1984.

Since 1970 the only authorized political party has been the *Mouvement populaire de la révolution* (MPR) or People's Revolutionary Movement. The highest policy-making body is the MPR's Political Bureau. In 1979 the Bureau had 38 members, including 20 appointed by the President and 18 elected (two from each region and two from Kinshasa). The Bureau has a 7-member Permanent Committee. On 14 Feb 1980 the Legislative Council approved constitutional changes, including the dissolution of the MPR's executive secretariat and the replacement of elected members of the MPR's Political Bureau, when their terms expired in 1982, by presidential nominees. A meeting of the Political Bureau on 31 July–4 Aug 1980 agreed on the establishment of a central committee (114 members appointed by the President on 2 Sept) and the creation of a new executive secretariat.

Zaire comprises eight regions, each headed by an appointed Commissioner, and the capital district of Kinshasa, under a Governor.

Length of roadways: 145 000 km (*90 100 miles*).
Length of railways: 4750 km (*2950 miles*) (1986).
Universities: 4.
Adult illiteracy: 38·8% in 1985.
Defence: Military service compulsory; total armed forces 26 000 (1987); defence expenditure: 5000 million zaires in 1987.
Foreign tourists: 25 000 in 1984.

Zambia

Official name: The Republic of Zambia.
Population: 7 267 500 (1987 estimate).
Area: 752 614 km² (*290 586 miles²*).
Languages: English (official), Nyanja, Bemba, Tonga, Lozi, Lunda, Luvale.
Religions: Roman Catholic, Protestant, Animist.
Capital city: Lusaka, population 818 994 (1987).
Other principal towns (1987 estimate): Kitwe 449 442; Ndola 418 142; Mufulira 192 323; Kabwe (Broken Hill) 190 752; Chingola 187 310; Luanshya 160 667; Livingstone 94 637.
Highest point: 1893 m (*6210 ft*).
Principal mountain range: Muchinga Mts.
Principal rivers: Zambezi and tributaries Kafue, Luangwa), Luapula.
Head of State: Dr Kenneth David Kaunda (b. 28 Apr 1924), President.
Prime Minister: Kebby S. K. Musokotwane.
Climate: Hot season September–November, rainy season November–April, winter May–September. Day temperatures 27°C to 38°C (*80°F to 100°F*) in hot season, sharp fall at night. Average annual rainfall from 635 mm (*25 in*) in south to 1270 mm (*50 in*) in north. In Lusaka, average annual minimum 18°C (*64°F*), maximum 31°C (*88°F*), average rainfall 8382 mm (*33 in*).
Labour force: 360 500 in 1986: Agriculture, forestry and fisheries 9·7%; Mining and quarrying 15·8%; Manufacturing 13·6%.
Gross domestic product: 18 080 million kwacha in 1987: Agriculture, forestry and fishing 11·7%; Mining and quarrying 15·3%; Manufacturing 22%; Trade 16·1%; Community and social services 8·2%.
Exports: 3074·4 million kwacha in 1986: Copper 86·3%; Zinc 1·7%.
Monetary unit: Zambian kwacha. 1 kwacha = 100 ngwee.
Denominations:
Coins 1, 2, 5, 10, 20, 50 ngwee.
Notes 1, 2, 5, 10, 20, 50 kwacha.
Political history and government: Formerly the British protectorate of Northern Rhodesia. On 24 Oct (UN Day) 1964 the territory became an independent republic, as Zambia (named from the Zambezi river), and a member of the Commonwealth. A one-party state was proclaimed on 13 Dec 1972 and inaugurated by a new constitution on 25 Aug 1973. Legislative power is held by the unicameral National Assembly, with 135 members (10 nominated by the President and 125 elected for five years by universal adult suffrage). There is also an advisory House of Chiefs (27 members) to represent traditional tribal authorities. Executive power is held by the President, elected by popular vote at the same time as the Assembly. He appoints a Cabinet, led by a Prime Minister, to conduct the administration. The sole authorized party is the United National Independence Party (UNIP), led by the President. The highest policy-making body is UNIP's Central committee (25 members), to which the Cabinet is subordinate. Zambia is divided into 9 provinces, each administered by a member of the Central Committee.
Length of roadways: 37 232 km (*23 121 miles*) (1986).
Length of railways: 2157 km (*1339 miles*) (1986).
Universities: 2.
Adult illiteracy: 24·3% in 1985.
Defence: Military service voluntary; total armed

forces 16 200 (1987); defence expenditure: not specified in current Budget.
Foreign tourists: 100 219 in 1986.

Zimbabwe

Population: 8 640 000 (1986 estimate).
Area: 390 580 km² (*150 804 miles²*).
Languages: English (official), Sindebele, Chishona.
Religions: Tribal beliefs, Christian minority.
Capital city: Harare (Salisbury), population 656 000 (1982 census).
Other principal towns (1982): Bulawayo 414 000; Chitungwize 175 000; Gweru (Gwelo) 79 000; Mutara (Umtali) 70 000; Kwekwe (Que Que) 48 000; Kadoome (Gatooma) 45 000; Hwange (Wankie) 39 000; Masvingo (Fort Victoria) 31 000.
Highest point: Mount Inyangani, 2592 m (*8503 ft*).
Principal mountain ranges: Enyanga, Melsetter.
Principal rivers: Zambezi and tributaries (Shangani, Umniati), Limpopo and tributaries (Umzingwani, Nuanetsi), Sabi and tributaries (Lundi, Odzi).
Head of State: Robert Gabriel Mugabe (b. 21 Feb 1924), President.
Climate: Tropical, modified by altitude. Average temperature 18°C to 24°C (*65°F to 75°F*). In Harare, average daily maximum 21°C (*70°F*) (June, July) to 28°C (*83°F*) (October), minimum 7°C (*44°F*) (June, July) to 15°C (*60°F*) (November–February), January rainiest (18 days).
Labour force: 3 506 000 in 1986: Agriculture 70·1%.
Gross domestic product: Z$8422 million in 1986: Agriculture and forestry 11·1%; Mining 6·8%; Manufacturing 29·6%; Finance and insurance 4·6%; Distribution, hotels and restaurants 12·7%; Public administration and education 12·2%.
Exports: Z$1703·8 million in 1986: Food and live animals 19·2%; Tobacco 24·7%; Cotton lint 7·7%; Asbestos 4·9%; Ferro-alloys 12·3%; Nickel metal 4·9%.
Monetary unit: Zimbabwe dollar (Z$). 1 dollar = 100 cents.
Denominations:
Coins ½, 1, 2½, 5, 10, 20, 25, 50 cents; 1 dollar.
Notes 1, 2, 5, 10 dollars.
Political history and government: The British South Africa Company was granted a Royal Charter over the territory on 29 Oct 1889. On 12 Sept 1923 Southern Rhodesia (as it was known) was transferred from the Company to the British Empire and became a colony. It was granted full self-government (except for African interests and some other matters) on 1 Oct 1923. The colony became part of the Federation of Rhodesia and Nyasaland (the Central African Federation), proclaimed on 1 Aug 1953. A new constitution, which removed most of the UK's legal controls (except for foreign affairs), was promulgated on 6 Dec 1961 and made fully operative on 1 Nov 1962. This constitution provided for a limited African franchise and could have led to ultimate majority rule. The Federation was dissolved on 31 Dec 1963.

On 17 Dec 1961 leaders of the banned National Democratic Party formed the Zimbabwe African People's Union (ZAPU), using the site of an ancient African ruin as the name of the whole country. The party split on 9 July 1963 and a breakaway group

formed the Zimbabwe African National Union (ZANU) on 8 Aug 1963.

Ian Smith became Prime Minister on 13 Apr 1964. After Northern Rhodesia achieved independence as Zambia on 24 Oct 1964, Southern Rhodesia became generally (although not officially) known as Rhodesia. A state of emergency was declared on 5 Nov 1965 and Ian Smith made a unilateral declaration of independence (UDI) on 11 Nov 1965. The Smith régime abrogated the 1961 constitution and proclaimed its own, naming the country Rhodesia. The British Government regarded UDI as unconstitutional and having no legal validity, and no other country formally recognized the territory's independence. A new constitution was approved by referendum on 20 June 1969, adopted on 29 Nov 1969 and took effect on 2 Mar 1970, when a republic was proclaimed.

Attempts to reach a constitutional settlement acceptable to all parties proved unsuccessful. ZAPU and ZANU had both taken up arms against the illegal régime and a full-scale guerrilla war was begun by African nationalists in Dec 1972. After a meeting with the US Secretary of State on 19 Sept 1976, Smith announced that his régime had agreed to proposals leading to majority rule within two years. On 9 Oct, in preparation for negotiations, ZAPU and the Mugabe faction of ZANU announced the formation of an alliance as the Patrotic Front (PF). In 1977 Smith began negotiations with three African parties within Rhodesia, although the main guerrilla groups (based in neighbouring countries) did not participate. An agreement was signed on 3 Mar 1978 for an 'internal settlement' (not internationally recognized), providing for a transition to majority rule by 31 Dec 1978. A transitional administration, comprising Europeans and Africans, was formed but the elections leading to majority rule were postponed.

A 'majority rule' constitution, changing the name of the country to Zimbabwe Rhodesia, was approved by the House of Assembly on 20 Jan 1979. It vested legislative authority in a bicameral Parliament, comprising a 100-member House of Assembly (in which 72 seats were reserved for Africans and 28, including 20 directly elected, were to be held by Europeans for at least 10 years) and a Senate of 30 members.

The constitution, which included entrenched provisions safeguarding the position of whites, was approved by European voters in a referendum on 30 Jan 1979. The new constitution was not accepted by the United Kingdom and the new régime did not gain international recognition.

At the meeting of Commonwealth heads of government in Lusaka, Zambia, on 1–7 Aug 1979, agreement was reached on proposals for a fresh attempt to secure legal independence for the country. As a result, a constitutional conference was held in London from 10 Sept to 15 Dec 1979 between the British government, the Muzorewa régime, elected under the new constitution, and the PF. It was announced on 19 Oct that all parties had agreed on the terms of a new constitution for an independent republic of Zimbabwe. On 15 Nov agreement was reached on transitional arrangements for the pre-independence period, including the restoration of British rule and elections for a new government. The final agreement (covering constitutional, transitional and cease-fire arrangements) was signed on 21 Dec 1979.

The independence constitution provided for the

establishment of a republic under the name of Zimbabwe. Legislative power was vested in a bicameral Parliament, comprising a Senate and a House of Assembly. Executive power was vested in the President, a constitutional Head of State elected by Parliament for a six-year term, but was exercised in almost all cases on the advice of the Executive Council (Cabinet), led by the Prime Minister.

On 2 Jan 1980 the two parties in the PF announced that they would contest the elections to the new House of Assembly separately: as ZANU (PF), led by Mugabe, and as the Patriotic Front (ZAPU). The elections were again held in two stages: on 14 Feb for non-African members and on 27–29 Feb for African members. ZANU (PF) won an overall majority and Mugabe was appointed Prime Minister by the Governor. The 34 elective seats in the Senate were filled on 19 Mar and the six nominated Senators appointed on 11 Apr. ZANU (PF)'s nominee for President was the sole candidate. Zimbabwe became legally independent, and a member of the Commonwealth, on 18 Apr 1980, when the constitution entered into force and the President and Prime Minister were sworn in. The Emergency Powers Act of 1965 remained in force. The Constitution – as amended in 1987 – provides for a bicameral Parliament with a Senate of 40 members elected by a common roll with additional members – 10 chiefs elected by all the country's tribal chiefs and 6 members nominated by the Head of State. The lower House is the 100-member House of Assembly elected for five years by universal adult suffrage. The executive is headed by a President, elected by Parliament for a six-year term.
Length of roadways: 170 400 km (*105 900 miles*).
Length of railways: 2745 km (*1705 miles*) (1986).
Universities: 1.
Defence: Military service selective; total armed forces 47 000 (1987); defence expenditure: Z$720·1 million in 1987/8.

Other territories

The following territories are of uncertain or disputed status.

Antarctica

Population: No permanent population but over 40 major scientific stations are maintained by those countries with territorial claims in Antarctica and by other nations including the United States of America and the Soviet Union.
Area: 13 900 000 km² (*5 367 000 miles²*).
Note: All territorial claims south of latitude 60°S are in abeyance for the 30-year duration of the Antarctic Treaty signed in 1959. Territorial claims have been made in the Antarctic continent by Argentina, Australia, Chile, France, New Zealand, Norway and the United Kingdom. Some of these claims – the Argentinian, British and Chilean – overlap, while part of the continent between 90°W and 150°W is not claimed by any power. None of these claims is recognized by either the United States of America or the Soviet Union, except for Norwegian claims to Bouvet Island.

ADÉLIE LAND
(French Antarctic Territory)
Official name: Terre Adélie.
Area: 432 000 km² (*166 800 miles²*).
Note: Adélie Land is part of the territory of Terres Australes et Antarctiques Françaises (created in 1955) with an administration based in Paris. Adélie Land is that part of Antarctica between 136° and 142°E longitude.

AUSTRALIAN ANTARCTIC TERRITORY
Area: 6 120 000 km² (*2 320 000 miles²*).
Note: The Australian Antarctic Territory is that part of Antarctica, other than Adélie Land, between 160° and 45°E longitude.

BRITISH ANTARCTIC TERRITORY
Area: 1 810 000 km² (*700 000 miles²*).
Note: The British Antarctic Territory is that part of Antarctica between 20°W and 80°W longitude.

ROSS DEPENDENCY
(New Zealand Antarctic Territory)
Area: 450 000 km² (*175 000 miles²*).
Note: The Ross Dependency is that part of Antarctica between 160°E longitude and 150°W longitude.

QUEEN MAUD LAND
(Norwegian Antarctic Territory)
Official name: Dronning Maud Land.
Area: As the inland limits of Queen Maud Land are undefined no estimate can be made of the territory's area.
Note: Queen Maud Land is that part of Antarctica between 20°W and 45°E. In 1957 Queen Maud Land became a Norwegian dependency.

ARGENTINIAN ANTARCTIC TERRITORY
Official name: Antárdida Argentina.
Note: Argentina claims that part of Antarctica between 74°W and 25°W.

CHILEAN ANTARCTIC TERRITORY
Official name: Antárdida Chilena.
Note: Chile claims that part of Antarctica between 90°W and 53°W.

BOUVET ISLAND
(Norwegian)
Area: 50 km² (*19 miles²*).
Note: An uninhabited island, 54° 25'S latitude and 3° 21'E longitude. Declared a Norwegian dependency in 1930. As Bouvet is north of 60°S latitude, the provisions of the Antarctic Treaty of 1959 do not apply and Norway's claim to the island is uncontested.

PETER ISLAND
(Norwegian)
Area: 180 km² (*69 miles²*).
Note: An uninhabited island, 68° 48'S latitude and 90° 35'W longitude. Placed under Norwegian sovereignty in 1931 and incorporated as a Norwegian dependency in 1933.

Gaza and West Bank

(Under Israeli occupation)
Population: Gaza 545000 (1986 estimate), West Bank 836000 (1986 estimate).
Area: Gaza 378 km² (*146 miles²*); West Bank 5879 km² (*2270 miles²*).
Principal towns: Gaza, Hebron.
Note: The Gaza Strip, formerly under Egyptian rule, was occupied by Israeli forces in June 1967. The West Bank, formerly under Jordanian administration, was occupied by Israeli forces from 6–11 June 1967. In 1988, Jordan severed all legal ties with the West Bank. Beginning in 1988, an uprising (*intifada*) by the Palestinians in Gaza and the West Bank has increased tension in these Israeli administered territories. On 15 Nov 1988, the Palestinian Liberation Organization issued a declaration of Palestinian independence with the objective of achieving an independent state in Gaza and the West Bank. This declaration has received recognition by over 30 countries.

Namibia

Population: 1 184000 (1986 estimate).
Area: 823 145 km² (*317 827 miles²*) – excluding Walvis Bay, an enclave administered by South Africa.
Capital city: Windhoek, population at 1981 census 110 644.
Note: Under South African administration since 1920; in 1966 the General Assembly of the United Nations terminated South Africa's mandate to administer this former German colony as a UN Trusteeship, but South Africa continued to administer the territory in defiance of the UN. Called South West Africa since 1884, the name of the territory was changed to Namibia by the UN in June 1968. Talks in 1988 have secured agreement for independence in November 1989. UN troops will oversee the transition to independence and the withdrawal of South African forces.

Sovereign Military Order of Malta, Territory of

Population: 30 Knights of Justice.
Area: 1·2 ha (*3 acres*).
Head of State: HEH (His Eminent Highness) Fra' Andrew Bertie, Prince and Grand Master of the Sovereign Military Order of Malta, elected on 8 April 1988 in succession to Prince and Grand Master Fra' Angelo De Mojana di Cologna. (The reigning Prince and Grand Master was born a Scot in 1930).
Note: The 'Knights of Malta' were rulers of Rhodes until expelled by the Turks, and then of Malta until expelled by Napoléon I. Since the 1830s their extraterritorial territory has been reduced to the Villa del Priorato di Malta on the Aventine Hill in Rome and 68 via Condotti in the same city. The Knights are a charitable, monastic Roman Catholic order whose Knights of Justice live as a religious community in Rome. They elect one of their number as Prince and Grand Master who is recognized as a sovereign in over 40 countries, excluding the United Kingdom. The military order, which issues its own passports, has many of the trappings of a state and is frequently stated to be the smallest 'country' in the world.

Western Sahara

Population: 180 000 (1986 estimate); another 165 000 Saharawis live in exile in refugee camps in Algeria.
Area: 266 769 km² (*102 680 miles²*).
Capital: El-Aaiun, population 96 784 (1982 census).
Note: A former Spanish province in North West Africa. In 1975, Spain, Morocco and mauritania reached an agreement to transfer and divide the Western Sahara between Morocco and Mauritania. The territory ceased to be Spanish on 31 Dec 1975 and was partitioned between Morocco and Mauritania on 28 Feb 1976. Morocco organized its sector into three provinces and upon the withdrawal of Mauritania from its sector in August 1979, organized that territory into a fourth province. A liberation movement (the *Polisario*) had been fighting Spanish rule since 1973. The *Polisario* have declared the territory (March 1976), the Saharawi Arab Democratic Republic (SADR), which is a member of the Organization of African Unity since 1982 and diplomatically recognized by nearly 30 states. The SADR controls part of the Western Sahara and continues guerrilla activity against the Moroccans. Talks in 1988 to secure a settlement were inconclusive.

SOURCES
Population: Primarily *de facto* but for some countries the figures cover *de jure* population. *Source:* mainly UN, *Population and Vital Statistics Report*.
Area, Capital city and Principal towns: *Source:* national data; also UN, *Demographic Yearbook*.
Labour force: Figures refer to the total economically active population. The categorization of the labour force is, in most cases, according to the International Standard Industrial Classification of all Economic Activities (ISIC). *Sources:* ILO, *Year Book of Labour Statistics* and *Labour Force Estimates and Projections, 1950–2000*.
Gross domestic product: Unless otherwise indicated, GDP is given in terms of purchasers' values (market prices), i.e. GDP at factor cost (producers' values) plus indirect taxes net of subsidies. Net domestic product is GDP less consumption (depreciation) of fixed capital. Gross National Product (GNP) is GDP plus net income from abroad. National income is net national product, i.e. GNP less capital consumption. Net material product (NMP) comprises the net value of goods and 'material' services produced, i.e. gross output (including turnover taxes) minus intermediate material (including capital) consumption. Gross material product (GMP) is NMP plus consumption of fixed capital. *Source:* UN, *Yearbook of National Accounts Statistics* and *Monthly Bulletin of Statistics*; International Bank for Reconstruction and Development, *World Bank Atlas*.
Exports: Total merchandise exports, valued f.o.b. (free on board). *Source:* mainly UN, *Yearbook of International Trade Statistics*.
Length of roads: *Source:* mainly International Road Federation, *World Road Statistics*.
Length of railways: *Source:* mainly *Railway Directory and Yearbook* (Railway Gazette International, IPC Transport Press).
Adult illiteracy: Unless otherwise stated, figures refer to persons aged 15 years and over. Literacy is defined as the ability to both read and write, so semi-literates are treated as illiterate. *Sources:* UNESCO, *Statistical Yearbook*; UN, *Demographic Yearbook*.
Defence: *Source:* International Institute for Strategic Studies, *The Military Balance*.
Foreign tourists: Unless otherwise indicated, figures refer to visits for leisure or business and cover persons staying at least 24 hours or making at least one overnight stay. *Source:* UN, *Statistical Yearbook* (quoting World Tourism Organization, Madrid).

UNITED KINGDOM

Physical and Political Geography

The various names used for the islands and parts of islands off the north-west coast of Europe geographically known as the British Isles are confusing. Geographical, political, legal and popular usages unfortunately differ, thus making definition necessary.

The British Isles is a convenient but purely *geographical* term to describe that group of islands lying off the north-west coast of Europe, comprising principally the island of Great Britain and the island of Ireland. There are four political units: the United Kingdom of Great Britain and Northern Ireland; the Republic of Ireland; the Crown dependencies of the Isle of Man and, for convenience, also the Channel Islands.
Area: 315 173 km² *(121 689 miles²).*

The United Kingdom (UK) (of Great Britain and Northern Ireland)
The political style of the island of Great Britain, with its offshore islands and, since the partition of Ireland (see below), the six counties of Northern Ireland. The term United Kingdom, referring to Great Britain and (the whole island of) Ireland, first came into use officially on 1 Jan 1801 on the Union of the two islands. With the coming into force of the Constitution of the Irish Free State as a Dominion on 6 Dec 1922, the term 'United Kingdom of Great Britain and Ireland' had obviously become inappropriate. It was dropped by Statute from the Royal style on 13 May 1927 in favour of 'King of Great Britain, Ireland and of, etc.'. On the same date Parliament at Westminster adopted as its style 'Parliament of the United Kingdom of Great Britain and Northern Ireland'. On 29 May 1953 by Proclamation the Royal style conformed to the Parliamentary style – Ireland having ceased to be a Dominion within the Commonwealth on 18 Apr 1949.
Area: 244 103 km² *(94 249 miles²).*
Population: 56 763 300 (1986 estimate).

Great Britain (GB) is the geographical and political name of the main or principal island of the solely geographically named British Isles group. In a strict geographical sense, off-shore islands, for example the Isle of Wight, Anglesey, or Shetland, are not part of Great Britain. In the political sense Great Britain was the political name used unofficially from 24 Mar 1603, when James VI of Scotland succeeded his third cousin twice removed upwards, Queen Elizabeth of England, so bringing about a Union of the Crowns, until on 1 May 1707 the style was formally adopted with the Union of the Parliaments of England and Scotland and was used until 1 Jan 1801. The government of Great Britain is unitary.
Area: 229 988 km² *(88 799 miles²).*
Population (1986): 55 196 500.

England is geographically the southern and greater part of the island of Great Britain. The islands off the English coast, such as the Isle of Wight and the Isles of Scilly, are administratively part of England. Politically and geographically England (historically a separate Kingdom until 1707) is that part of Great Britain governed by English law which also pertains in Wales and, since 1746, in Berwick-upon-Tweed.
The term 'England' is widely (but wrongly) used abroad to mean the United Kingdom or Great Britain.
Area: 130 441 km² *(50 363 miles²).*
Population: 47 254 500 (1986 estimate).

Isles of Scilly
Area: 1635 ha *(4041 acres)* (16·35 km² *(6·31 miles²).*
Population: 2006 (1981 estimate). There are five populated islands (1981 estimates) – Bryher (pop. 155), St Agnes (pop. 60), St Martin's (pop. 80), St Mary's (pop 1650) and Tresco (pop. 155). There are 19 other islands and numerous rocks and islets.
The islands are administered by 25 councillors, which is a unique type of local government unit set up by an Order made under the Local Government Act, 1974. For some purposes the Isles are administered in company with the Cornwall County Council. The islands form part of the St Ives electoral division.

Wales (The principality of) now comprises eight instead of twelve counties. The area was incorporated into England by Act of Parliament in 1536. The former county of Monmouthshire, though for all administrative intents and purposes part of Wales, only became an integral part of Wales on 1 Apr 1974. The other boundaries between England and Wales expressly could not be altered by the ordinary processes of local government reorganization.
Wales may not, by Statute, be represented by fewer than 35 MPs at Westminster.
Area: 20 768 km² *(8019 miles²).*
Population: 2 821 000 (1986 estimate).

Scotland consists of the northern and smaller part of the island of Great Britain. The Kingdom of Scotland effectively lost much of its independence on 24 Mar 1603 when King James VI of Scotland (ascended 1567) became also King James I of England – although Scotland remained (for part of the time only nominally) an independent nation. Both countries continued to have their separate Parliaments until the Union of the Parliaments at Westminster, London, on 1 May 1707. Scotland continues to have its own distinctive legal system. By Statute Scotland may not be represented by less than 71 MPs at Westminster. On 16 May 1975 the 33 traditional counties were reduced to 9 geographical regions and 3 island authorities.
Area: 78 775 km² *(30 415 miles²).*
Population: 5 121 000 (1986 estimate).

Ireland is the name of the second largest island in the geographical British Isles. Henry VIII assumed the style 'King of Ireland' in 1542, although Governors of Ireland (the exact title varied) ruled on behalf of the Kings of England from 1172. The viceroyalty did not disappear until 1937. The Union of the Parliaments of Great Britain and Ireland occurred on 1 Jan 1801.

Northern Ireland consists of six counties in the north-eastern corner of the island. County government has been replaced by 26 districts. They are all within the larger ancient province of Ulster which originally consisted of nine counties. The government's relationship to the Imperial Parliament in England was federal in nature. Certain major powers were reserved by the Imperial Parliament, the sovereignty of which was unimpaired. There is a provision in the Ireland Act of 1949 that Northern Ireland cannot cease to be part of the United King-

dom, or part of the Queen's Dominions without the express consent of her Parliament. This Parliament, known as Stormont and established in 1921, was however abolished by the Northern Ireland Constitution Act, 1973. Devolved government came into effect on 1 Jan 1974, but the Northern Ireland Assembly was prorogued on 29 May 1974 after the Executive collapsed. Arrangements for a Constitutional Convention, under the Northern Ireland Constitution Act 1974, which came into force in July 1974, collapsed in February 1976. Northern Ireland is represented by the fixed number of twelve Members of the Imperial Parliament at Westminster.
Area: 14 120 km² (*5452 miles²*).
Population: 1 566 800 (1986 estimate).

The Republic of Ireland
(See separate entry).

United Kingdom mountain and hill ranges

Range	Length (km)	Length (miles)	Culminating peak	Height (m)	Height (ft)
Scotland					
Grampian Mountains	250	155	Ben Macdhui, Grampian	1310	4300
North West Highlands	225	140	Càrn Eige, Highland	1181	3877
*Southern Uplands	200	125	Merrick, Dumfries & Galloway	842	2764
(Scottish Lowlands)					
Liath Mountains	55	35	Càrn Dearg, Highland	942	3093
England					
Pennines	195	120	Cross Fell, Cumbria	893	2930
North Downs	135	85	Leith Hill, Surrey	294	965
Cotswold Hills	95	60	Cleeve Hill, Gloucestershire	330	1083
South Downs	85	55	Butser Hill, Hampshire	271	888
Cheviot Hills	70	45	The Cheviot, Northumberland	815	2676
Chiltern Hills	70	45	Coombe Hill, Buckinghamshire	259	852
Berkshire Downs	55	35	Walbury Hill, Berkshire	296	974
(White Horse Hills)					
Cumbrian Mountains	50	30	Scafell Pike, Cumbria	978	3210
Exmoor	50	30	Dunkery Beacon, Somerset	519	1706
North Yorkshire Moors	50	30	Urra Moor, Bottom Head	454	1491
(Cleveland and Hambleton Hills)					
Hampshire Downs	40	25	Pilot Hill, Hampshire	285	938
Yorkshire Wolds	35	22	Garrowby Hill, Humberside	246	808
Wales					
Cambrian Mountains	175	110	Snowdon (Yr Wyddfa), Gwynedd	1085	3560
Berwyn Mountains	65	40	Aran Fawddwy, Gwynedd	905	2972
Northern Ireland					
Sperrin Mountains	65	40	Sawel Mt, Londonderry-Tyrone	682	2240
Mountains of Mourne	50	30	Slieve Donard, County Down	852	2796
Antrim Hills	40	25	Trostan, Antrim	553	1817

* Includes: Lammermuir Hills (Lammer Law, Lothian 528 m (*1733 ft*)); Lowther Hills (Green Lowther, Strathclyde, 732 m (*2403 ft*)); Pentland Hills (Scald Law, Lothian, 578 m (*1898 ft*) and the Tweedsmuir Hills (Broad Law, Borders, 839 m (*2754 ft*).

British Isles extremities

Island of Great Britain
Great Britain, the eighth largest island in the world, has extreme (mainland) dimensions thus:

Most Northerly Point	Easter Head, Dunnet Head, Highland	Lat	58°	40'	24" N
Most Westerly Point	Corrachadh Mor, Ardnamurchan, Highland	Long	6°	14'	12" W
Most Southerly Point	Lizard Point, Cornwall	Lat	49°	57'	33" N
Most Easterly Point	Lowestoft Ness, Lowestoft, Suffolk	Long	1°	46'	20" E

Other extreme points (mainland) in its 3 constituent countries are:

Most Southerly Point in Scotland	Gallie Craig, Mull of Galloway, Dumfries & Galloway	Lat	54°	38'	27" N

Most Easterly Point in Scotland	Keith Inch, Peterhead, Grampian	Long	1° 45' 49" W
Most Northerly Point in England	Meg's Dub, Northumberland	Lat	55° 48' 37" N
Most Westerly Point in England	Dr Syntax's Head, Land's End, Cornwall	Long	5° 42' 15" W
Most Northerly Point in Wales	Point of Air, Clwyd	Lat	53° 21' 08" N
Most Westerly Point in Wales	Porthtaflod, Dyfed	Long	5° 19' 43" W
Most Southerly Point in Wales	Rhoose Point, South Glamorgan	Lat	51° 22' 40" N
Most Easterly Point in Wales	Lady Park Wood, Gwent	Long	2° 38' 49" W

Island of Ireland (20th largest island in the world)

Most Northerly Point in Ireland	Malin Head, Donegal	Lat	55° 22' 30" N
Most Northerly Point in Northern Ireland	Benbane Head, Moyle, Antrim	Lat	55° 15' 0" N
Most Westerly Point in Ireland	Dunmore Head, Kerry	Long	10° 28' 55" W
Most Westerly Point in Northern Ireland	Cornaglah, Fermanagh	Long	8° 10' 30" W
Most Southerly Point in Ireland	Brow Head, Cork	Lat	51° 26' 30" N
Most Southerly Point in Northern Ireland	Cranfield Point, Newry and Mourne, Down	Lat	54° 01' 20" N
Most Easterly Point in Ireland (Northern)	Townhead, Ards Peninsula, Down	Long	5° 26' 52" W
Most Easterly Point in Republic of Ireland	Wicklow Head, Wicklow	Long	5° 59' 40" W

The Crown Dependencies

The Isle of Man

The Isle of Man (Manx-Gaelic, *Ellan Vannin*) is a Crown dependency.
Area: 57 200 ha (*141 440 acres*) (572 km² *221 miles²*).
Population: 64 282 (1986 census).
Administrative headquarters: Douglas 20 368. The ancient capital was Castletown (3019).
History: Habitation of the island has been traced to the Mesolithic period. The island was converted to Christianity in the 5th or 6th century probably by monks from Ireland. At this time the island's people spoke Gaelic. Norsemen from Scandinavia plundered the island towards the end of the 8th century but became settled around the middle of the 9th century. During the ensuing period of Norse rule, Tynwald was established as the national Parliament. In 1266 the island was sold by Norway to Scotland, but the island alternated between English and Scottish rule until 1333 when it came under England. The island was held by a succession of English noblemen until 1405, when Henry IV granted it to the Stanley family who ruled until 1736 apart from the period 1651 to 1660 when it was under the rule of the English Commonwealth. The Stanleys became the Earls of Derby in 1485 and adopted the title Lord of Mann and the Isles. The Stanleys were succeeded by the Dukes of Atholl who sold the Lordship of Mann to the British Crown in 1765, when the island became a Crown dependency, although it has never been part of the United Kingdom, A period of rule under English officialdom followed. In 1866 the House of Keys became a popularly elected legislature for the first time since the rule of the Norse and women in the Isle of Man got the right to vote in 1881. More recent times have seen the Isle of Man gaining increasing independence from the United Kingdom. Tynwald is the oldest continuous national Parliament in the world and celebrated its millenium in 1979.
Legislature: Her Majesty the Queen as Lord of Mann appoints the Lieutenant Governor who is the nominal head of the Isle of Man Government. The island's legislative assembly is the Court of Tynwald which comprises the Legislative Council and the House of Keys. The upper house, the Legis-

lative Council, consists of 8 members elected by the House of Keys and 2 ex-officio members, the Lord Bishop of Sodor and Man and the Attorney-General. The House of Keys is made up of 24 members who are elected from the island's 13 constituencies.
Highest point above sea-level: Snaefell (619 m *2034 ft*).
Leading Industries: Finance, agriculture, manufacturing, tourism.
Events and Attractions: Tynwald Hill, St John's; Peel Castle; Castle Rushen; Castletown; Laxey waterwheel; steam railway; electric railway; TT motor-cycle races.

THE CHANNEL ISLANDS

The Channel Islands (French: *Iles Anglo-Normandes*) are a Crown dependency. There is a Channel Isle department in the Home Office, Whitehall, London.
Area: 19 458 ha (*48 083 acres*) (194·6 km² *75·13 miles²*).
Guernsey (French: *Guernesey*) – 6334 ha (*15 654 acres*) (63·3 km² *24·46 miles²*).
Jersey – 11 621 ha (*28 717 acres*) (116·2 km² *44·87 miles²*).
Dependencies of Guernsey:
Alderney (French: *Aurigny*) – 794 ha (*1962 acres*) (7·9 km² *3·07 miles²*).
Sark (Sercq) – 515 ha (*1274 acres*) (5·1 km² *1·99 miles²*). (Great Sark, 419 ha (*1035 acres*) 4·2 km²; Little Sark, 96 ha (*239 acres*) 0·9 km²).
Herm – 129 ha (*320 acres*) 1·29 km².
Brechau (Brecqham) – 30 ha (*74 acres*) 0·3 km².
Jethou – 18 ha (*44 acres*).
Lihou (Libon) – 15 ha (*38 acres*).
Other islands include Ortach, Burhou, the Casquets, Les Minquiers (including Maîtresse Ile) and the Ecrehou Islands (including Marmaoutier, Blanche Ile, and Maître Ile).
Population: 137 200 (1986 estimate).
Jersey – 80 212   Alderney – 2000
Guernsey – 54 380   Sark – 604.
Administrative headquarters: Jersey – St Helier, Guernsey and dependencies – St Peter Port.
History: The islands are known to have been inhabited by Acheulian man (before the last Ice Age) and by Neanderthal man. Continuously inhabited since Iberian settlers, who used flint implements, arrived in the 2nd millennium BC. The islands were

later settled by the Gauls, and after them the Romans; Christian missionaries came from Cornwall and Brittany in the 6th century AD. The Vikings began raiding the islands in the 9th century. Rollo, the Viking nobleman, established the duchy of Normandy in AD 911. His son, the second duke, William I 'Longsword' annexed the Channel Islands in 933. Jethou was ceded to England in 1091. The other islands were annexed by the crown in 1106. Normandy was conquered by France, and the King (John) was declared to have forfeited all his titles to the duchy. The islanders, however, remained loyal to John. Administration has since been under the control of his successors, while maintaining a considerable degree of home rule and, until 1689, neutrality. Before the Reformation the islands formed part of the diocese of Coutances, but were later placed under the bishops of Winchester. From the 9th century everyone in the islands spoke Norman French, but English became dominant by the mid-19th century. The islands were occupied by Nazi Germany on 30 June–1 July 1940, and fortified for defence. They were relieved by British forces on 9 May 1945.

Administration: The islands are divided into two Bailiwicks, the States of Jersey and the States of Guernsey. The two Bailiwicks each have a Lieutenant-Governor and Commander-in-Chief, who is the personal representative of the Monarch and the channel of communication between HM Government and the Insular Governments. The Crown appoints Bailiffs, who are both Presidents of the Assembly of the States (the Legislature) and of the Royal Court. In Jersey the States consists of elected senators, *connétables* (constables) and deputies; in Guernsey, *conseillers* (councillors), elected by an intermediate body called the States of election, people's deputies, representatives of the *douzaines* (parish councils) and representatives of Alderney.

Highest points above sea-level:
Jersey – 138 m *(453 ft)*
Guernsey – 106 m *(349 ft)*
Alderney – 85·5 m *(281 ft)*
Sark – 114 m *(375 ft)*
Herm – 71·5 m *(235 ft)*
Jethou – 81 m *(267 ft)*
Lihou – 21 m *(68 ft)*

Leading Industries: Agriculture, chiefly cattle, potatoes, tomatoes, grapes and flowers; tourism; finance and industry.

Places of Interest: The Museum of the Société Jersiaise; the church of St Peter Port.

New Towns

There are 28 New Towns built by government-appointed Development Corporations in England (21), Wales (2) and Scotland (5). When development of a New Town in England and Wales is substantially completed it is transferred to the *Commission for the New Towns*. Between 1862 and February 1989 this stage was reached in 21 towns (*below). The Development Corporations for Telford and Milton Keynes will be wound up in 1991 and 1992 respectively.

Population (1986).
*Stevenage, Herts. (1946) – 73 800
*Crawley, Sussex. (January 1947) – 84 000
*Hemel Hemstead, Herts. (February 1947) – 77 100
*Harlow, Essex. (May 1947) – 72 900
*Aycliffe, Durham. (July 1947) – 25 500
East Kilbride, Strathclyde. (August 1947) – 69 400
*Peterlee, Durham. (March 1948) – 23 400
*Welwyn Garden City, Herts. (June 1948) – 40 500
*Hatfield, Herts. (June 1948) – 25 200
Glenrothes, Fife. (October 1948) – 38 000
*Basildon, Essex. (February 1949) – 101 700
*Bracknell, Berks. (October 1949) – 50 700
*Cwmbran, Gwent. (November 1949) – 48 000
*Corby, Northants. (1950) – 48 500
Cumbernauld, Stratclyde. (1956) – 49 200
*Skelmersdale, Lancashire. (1962) – 41 800
Livingston, Lothian. (1962) – 41 000
Telford, Shropshire. (1963) – 110 000
*Runcorn, Cheshire. (1964) – 68 600
*Redditch, Hereford & Worcester. (1964) – 76 600
*Washington, Tyne & Wear. (1964) – 55 000
Irvine, Strathclyde. (1966) – 57 000
Milton Keynes, Buckinghamshire. (1967) – 138 000
*Newtown, Powys. (1967) – 10 000
*Northampton. (1968) – 177 200
*Peterborough. (1968) – 151 200
*Warrington, Cheshire. (1968) – 148 500
*Central Lancashire New Town. (1970)
Stonehouse, Strathclyde was scheduled in 1973 but development plans were abandoned in 1976.

WATERFALLS
The principal waterfalls of the British Isles are:

Height (m)	Height (ft)	Name
200	658	Eas-Coul-Aulin, Highland
112	370	Falls of Glomach, Highland
106	350	Powerscourt Falls, County Wicklow
>90	>300	Pistyll-y-Llyn, Powys-Dyfed
73	240	Pistyll Rhaiadr, Clwyd
62	205	Foyers, Highland
62 (total)	204	Falls of Clyde, Strathclyde (comprises Bonnington Linn (9 m *30 ft*), Corra Linn (25 m *84 ft*), Dundaff Linn (3 m *10 ft*) and Stonebyres Linn (24 m *80 ft*) cataracts)
60	200	Falls of Bruar, Tayside (upper fall)
60	200	Cauldron (or Caldron) Snout, Cumbria
60	200	Grey Mare's Tail, Dumfries & Galloway

DEPRESSIONS
A very small area of Great Britain is below sea-level. The largest such area is in the Fenland of East Anglia, and even here a level of 2·7 m *(9 ft)* below sea-level is not exceeded in the Holme Fen near Ely, Cambridgeshire. The beds of three Lake District lakes are below sea-level with the deepest being part of the bed of Windermere, Cumbria at −27 m *(−90 ft)*. The bed of Loch Morar, Highland, Scotland reaches 301 m *(987 ft)* below sea-level.

CAVES
Large or deep caves are few in Great Britain. Great Britain's deepest cave is Ogof Ffynnon Ddu (308 m *(1010 ft)*) in Powys, Wales. The largest system is the Easegill system with 52·4 km *(32·5 miles)* of surveyed passages. England's deepest cave is Giant's Hole, Oxlow Caverns, Derbyshire at 214m *(702 ft)*. Scotland's deepest cave is Cnoc nan Uamh which is 76

UK lochs and lakes

Area (km²)	Area (miles²)	Name and Country	Max. Length (km)	Max. Length (miles)	Max. Breadth (km)	Max. Breadth (miles)	Max. Depth (m)	Max. Depth (ft)
Northern Ireland								
381·7	147·39	Lough Neagh, Antrim, Down, Armagh, Tyrone, Londonderry	28	18	17	11	31	102
105·0	40·57	Lower Lough Erne, Fermanagh	28	18	8·8	5·5	68	226
31·7	12·25	Upper Lough Erne, Fermanagh – Cavan	16	10	5·6	3·5	27	89

Scotland (Fresh-water (inland) lochs, in order of size of surface area)								
71·2	27·5	Loch Lomond, Strathclyde-Central	36·4	22·64	8	5	189	623
56·6	21·87	Loch Ness, Highland	36·6	22·75	3·2	2	228	751
38·7	14·95	Loch Awe, Strathclyde	41·0	25·5	3·2	2	93	307
28·4	11·0	Loch Maree, Highland	21·7	13·5	3·2	2	111	367
26·6	10·3	Loch Morar, Highland	18·5	11·5	2·4	1·5	309	1017
26·3	10·19	Loch Tay, Tayside	23·4	14·55	1·7	1·07	154	508
22·5	8·70	Loch Shin, Highland	27·7	17·35	1·6	1	49	162
19·5	7·56	Loch Shiel, Highland	28·1	17·5	1·4	0·9	128	420
19·0	7·34	Loch Rannoch, Tayside	15·6	9·75	1·7	1·1	134	440
18·5	7·18	Loch Ericht, Highland–Tayside	23·4	14·6	1·7	1·1	156	512
16·1	6·25	Loch Arkaig, Highland	19·3	12·0	1·4	0·9	109	359
15·2	5·9	Loch Lochy, Highland	15·9	9·9	2·0	1·25	161	531

England (Lake District lakes in order of size of surface area) (all in Cumbria)

						Max Breadth (yd)		
14·7	5·69	Windermere	16·8	10·50	1·47	1610	66	219
8·9	3·44	Ullswater	11·8	7·35	1·0	1100	62	205
5·3	2·06	Bassenthwaite Water	6·1	3·83	1·18	1300	21	70
5·3	2·06	Derwentwater	4·6	2·87	1·94	2130	21	72
4·8	1·89	Coniston Water	8·7	5·41	0·79	870	56	184
2·9	1·12	Ennerdale Water	3·8	2·40	0·9	1000	45	148
2·9	1·12	Wastwater	4·8	3·00	0·8	880	78	258
2·5	0·97	Crummock Water	4·0	2·50	0·9	1000	43	144
1·3	0·54	Haweswater	3·7	2·33	0·54	600	31	103
0·9	0·36	Buttermere	2·0	1·26	0·61	670	28	94

England (reservoir) Kielder Reservoir is Europe's largest man-made lake. It has a maximum length of 14·5 km (9 miles).

Wales

8·2	3·18	Lake Vyrnwy (dammed), Powys	7·5	4·7	0·06	1000	36	120
4·3	1·69	Bala Lake (Llyn Tegid), Gwynedd	6·1	3·8	0·53	850	38	125

m (249 ft) deep. The Republic of Ireland's deepest is Carrowmore Cavern, County Sligo being 150 m (459 ft) deep. Northern Ireland's deepest is Reyfad Pot, Fermanagh being 179 m (587 ft) deep.

Highest peaks in the British Isles

Though the eighth largest island in the world, Great Britain does not possess any mountains of great height.

In only two Scottish regions, those of Grampian and Highland, does the terrain surpass a height of 1219 m (4000 ft). In Great Britain there are seven mountains and five subsidiary points (tops) above 1219 m (4000 ft) all in Scotland, and a further 283 mountains and 271 tops between 914 m and 1219 m (3000–4000 ft) of which only 21 (see below) are in England or Wales. South of the border, 914 m (3000 ft) is only surpassed in Gwynedd and Cumbria, Scotland possesses 54 mountains higher than Snowdon and 165 higher than the Scafell Pike. Ben Nevis was probably first climbed about 1720 and

Ben Macdhui was thought to be Great Britain's highest mountain until as late as 1847.

Scotland's ten highest peaks	m	ft
1. Ben Nevis, Highland	1392	4406
2. Ben Macdhui, Grampian	1310	4300
3. Braeriach, Grampian-Highland border	1294	4248
North top (Ben Macdhui)	1293	4244
4. Cairn Toul, Grampian	1292	4241
South Plateau (Braeriach) (also c. 1268 m (4160 ft)	1264	4149
Sgor an Lochan Uaine (Cairn Toul)	1254	4116
Coire Sputan Dearg (Ben Macdhui)	1248	4095
5. Cairngorm, Grampian-Highland border	1244	4084
6. Aonach Beag, Highland	1237	4060
Coire an Lochain (Braeriach)	1230	4036
7. Càrn Mor Dearg, Highland	1222	4012
8. Aonach Mor, Highland	1218	3999
Carn Dearg (Ben Nevis)	1216	3990
Coire an t'Saighdeir (Cairn Toul)	1215	3989

9. Ben Lawers, Tayside	1214	*3984*
Cairn Lochan (Cairngorm)	*1214*	3983
10. Beinn a'Bhùird (North Top),	1196	*3924*
Grampian		

Wales' ten highest peaks
(all in Gwynedd)

	m	*ft*
1. Snowdon (Yr Wyddfa)	1085	*3560*
Garnedd Ugain or Crib Y Ddisg	*1065*	3493
(Yr Wyddfa)		
2. Carnedd Llewelyn	1062	*3484*
3. Carnedd Dafydd	1044	*3426*
4. Glyder Fawr	999	*3279*
5. Glyder Fâch	994	*3262*
Pen Yr Oleu-wen (Carnedd	978	*3210*
Dafydd)		
Foel Grach (Carnedd Llewelyn)	974	*3195*
Yr Elen (Carnedd Llewelyn)	960	*3151*
6. Y Garn	946	*3104*
7. Foel Fras	942	*3091*
8. Elidir Fawr	923	*3029*
Crib Goch (Yr Wyddfa)	921	3023
9. Tryfan	917	*3010*
10. Aran Fawddwy	905	*2970*

Ireland's ten highest peaks

	m	*ft*
1. Carrauntual (or Carrauntoohil),	1041	*3414*
Kerry		
2. Beenkeragh, Kerr7	1010	*3314*
3. Caher, Kerry	975	*3200*
4. Ridge of the Reeks (*two* other tops		
of the same height, a *third* of		
957 m (*3141 ft*), and a *fourth* of		
c. 930 m (*3050 ft*)), Kerry	*c.* 975	*c. 3200*
5. Brandon, Kerry	953	*3127*
Knocknapeasta (Ridge of the Reeks)	933	3062
6. Lugnaquillia, Wicklow	926	*3039*
7. Galtymore, Tipperary	920	*3018*
8. Slieve Donard, County Down	*852	2796
9. Baurtregaum, Kerry	852	*2796*
10. Mullaghcleevaun, Wicklow	849	*2788*

England's ten highest peaks
(all in Cumbria)

	m	*ft*
1. Scafell Pike	978	*3210*
2. Sca Fell	963	*3162*
3. Helvellyn	950	*3116*
Broad Crag (Scafell Pikes)	930	*3054*
4. Skiddaw	930	*3053*
Lower Man (Helvellyn)	922	3033
Ill Crags (Scafell Pikes)	*c.* 922	*c.* 3025
Great End (Scafell Pikes)	909	*2984*
5. Bow Fell	902	*2960*
6. Great Gable	898	*2949*
7. Cross Fell	893	*2930*
8. Pillar Fell	892	*2927*
Catstye Cam (Helvellyn)	889	2917
9. Esk Pike	884	*2903*
Raise (Helvellyn)	880	2889
10. Fairfield	872	*2863*

United Kingdom's largest islands

England (12 largest)

	km²	*miles²*
Isle of Wight	380·99	*147·09*
*Sheppey	94·04	*36·31*
*Hayling	26·84	*10·36*
*Foulness	26·14	*10·09*
*Portsea	24·25	*9·36*
*Canvey	18·45	*7·12*
*Mersea	18·04	*6·96*
*Walney	12·99	*5·01*
*Isle of Grain	12·85	*4·96*
*Wallasea	10·65	*4·11*
St Mary's, Isles of Scilly	6·29	*2·43*
*Thorney	4·96	*1·91*

Scotland (12 largest)

	km²	*miles²*
Lewis with Harris	2225·30	*859·19*
Skye	1666·08	*643·28*
Mainland, Shetland	967·00	*373·36*
Mull	899·25	*347·21*
Islay	614·52	*246·64*
Mainland, Orkney	536·10	*206·99*
Arran	435·32	*168·08*
Jura	370·35	*142·99*
North Uist	351·49	*135·71*
South Uist	332·45	*128·36*
Yell, Shetland	214·16	*82·69*
Hoy, Orkney	136·85	*52·84*

Wales (12 largest)

	km²	*miles²*
*Anglesey (Ynys Mon)	713·80	*275·60*
Holy I	39·44	*15·22*
Skomer	2·90	*1·12*
Ramsey	2·58	*0·99*
Caldey	2·79	*0·84*
Bardsey	1·99	*0·76*
Skokholm	1·06	*0·41*
Flat Holm	0·33	*0·13*
*Llanddwyn I	0·31	*0·12*
Puffin Island	0·28	*0·11*
The Skerries	0·15	*0·06*
Cardigan Island	0·15	*0·06*

Crown Dependencies:

	km²	*miles²*
Isle of Man	571·66	*220·72*
Calf of Man	2·49	*0·96*

The principal Channel Isles comprise

Jersey	116·21	*44·87*
Guernsey	63·34	*24·46*
Alderney	7·94	*3·07*
Sark	5·15	*1·99*
Herm	1·29	*0·50*

Northern Ireland's principal offshore island is Rathlin Island 14·41 km² (*5·56 miles²*)

---

* Highest peak in Northern Ireland

* Bridged or causewayed to the mainland

Longest rivers in the United Kingdom

Specially compiled maps issued by the Ordnance Survey in the second half of the last century are still the authority for the length of the rivers of the United Kingdom. It should, however, be noted that these measurements are strictly for the course of a river bearing the one name; thus for example where the principal head stream has a different name its additional length is ignored – unless otherwise indicated.

Length (km)	Length (miles)	Names	Remotest source	Mouth	Area of basin (km²)	Area of basin (miles²)*	Extreme Discharge (cusecs)†
354	220	Severn (for 254 km)	Lake on E side of Plinlimmon, Powys	Bristol Channel	11421	4409·7	23100 (1937)
346	215	Thames (for 178 km) – Isis (69 km) – Churn	Severn Springs, Gloucestershire	North Sea (The Nore)	9948	3841·6	27900 (1894)
297	185	Trent (236 km) – Humber (61 km)	Biddulph Moor, Staffs	North Sea (as Humber)	10436	4029·2	5510
259	161	Aire (126 km) – (Yorkshire) Ouse (72 km) and Humber (61 km)	NW of North Yorks	North Sea (as Humber)	11366	4388·4	4580 (Aire only)
230	143	Ouse (Great or Bedford)	nr Brackley, Northamptonshire	The Wash	8582	3313·6	11000
215	135	Wye (or Gwy)	Plinlimmon, Powys	Into Severn 4 km (2·5 miles) S of Chepstow, Gwent	4184	1615·3	32000
188	117	Tay (150 km) – Tummel	(Tay) Beinn Oss' Tayside	North Sea	5080	1961·6	49000
161	100	Nene (formerly Nen)	nr Naseby, Northants	The Wash	2369	914·5	13500
158	98·5	Clyde (inc. Daer Water)	nr Earncraig Hill, extreme S Strathclyde	Atlantic Ocean (measured to Port Glasgow)	3040	1173·8	20200
157·5	98·0	Spey	Loch Spey, Highland	North Sea	2988	1153·5	34200
155·3	96·5	Tweed	Tweed's Well, Borders	North Sea	5160	1992·3	21400
137·1	85·2	Dee (Aberdeenshire)	W of Cairn Toul, Grampian	North Sea	2116	817·2	40000
136·7	85	Avon (Warwickshire or Upper)	nr Naseby, Northants	Into Severn at Tewkesbury	(part of Severn Basin)		8560
129·5	80·5	Don (Aberdeenshire)	Carn Cuilchathaidh, Grampian	North Sea	1336	515·7	Not available
127	79	Tees	Cross Fell, Cumbria	North Sea	2237	863·6	13600
122	76	Bann (Upper Bann – Lough Neagh – Lower Bann)	Mountains of Mourne, SW Down	Atlantic Ocean	—	—	—
118·5	73	Tyne (55 km) – North Tyne (63 km)	Cheviots between Peel Fell and Carter Fell	North Sea	2917	1126·4	42000
112·5	70	Dee (Cheshire)	Bala Lake, Gwynedd	Irish Sea	2119	818·1	16000
111	69	Eden (Cumberland)	Pennines, SE of Kirby Stephen	Solway Firth, Irish Sea	2400	926·7	—
104·5	65	Usk	Talsarn Mt, Powys	Bristol Channel	1740	672·0	23700
104·5	65	Wear	W of Wearhead, Northumberland	North Sea	1198	462·6	6130
104·5	65	Wharfe	12 km (7·5 miles) S of Hawes, North Yorks	Into York Ouse, nr Cawood	(part of Yorks Ouse Basin)		15300
103·5	64·5	Forth	Duchray Water (21·7 km 13·5 miles), Ben Lomond	Firth of Forth, North Sea	1626	627·9	—

* This column gives the hydrometric area of the whole river system as per *The Surface Water Survey*.
† This column gives the highest recorded discharge in cubic feet per second (*note*: 1 cusec = 0·0283168 m³/sec 538170 gallons per day) taken at the lowest sited gauging on the name river.

The 58 cities of the United Kingdom

The term City as used in the United Kingdom is a title of dignity applied to 58 towns of varying local Government status by virtue of their importance as either archiepiscopal or episcopal sees or former sees, or as commercial or industrial centres. The right has been acquired in the past by (1) traditional usage – for example, the Domesday Book describes Coventry, Exeter and Norwich as *civitas*; by (2) statute; or by (3) royal prerogative, and in more recent times solely by royal charter and letters patent – the most recent examples are Lancaster (1937), Cambridge (1951). Southampton (1964), Swansea (1969), the extension of the City of Westminster to include the former Metropolitan Boroughs of Paddington and St Marylebone in 1965 and Derby (1977). St David's (Dyfed) is a city only by repute; the title is used ecclesiastically because it has a cathedral.

Name of City with Geographical County or Region	First Recorded Charter	Title of Civic Head
Aberdeen, Grampian, Scotland	1179	Lord Provost
Bangor, Gwynedd, Wales	1883	Mayor
Bath, Avon	1590	Mayor
Belfast, Antrim, Northern Ireland	1613	Lord Mayor*
Birmingham, West Midlands	1838	Lord Mayor
Bradford, West Yorkshire	1847	Lord Mayor
Bristol, Avon	1188	Lord Mayor
Cambridge, Cambridgeshire	1207	Mayor
Canterbury, Kent	1448	Mayor
Cardiff, South Glamorgan, Wales	1608	Lord Mayor
Carlisle, Cumbria	1158	Mayor
Chester, Cheshire	1506	Mayor
Chichester, West Sussex	1135–54	Mayor
Coventry, West Midlands	1345	Lord Mayor
Derby, Derbyshire	1154 (present charter 1977)	Mayor
Dundee, Tayside, Scotland	c. 1179	Lord Provost
Durham, Durham	1602	Mayor
Edinburgh, Lothian, Scotland	c.1124	Lord Provost
Elgin, Grampian, Scotland	1234	Lord Provost
Ely, Cambridgeshire	no charter	Mayor
Exeter, Devon	1156	Mayor
Glasgow, Strathclyde, Scotland	1690	Lord Provost*
Gloucester, Gloucestershire	1483	Mayor
Hereford, Hereford and Worcester	1189	Mayor
Kingston upon Hull, Humberside	1440	Lord Mayor
Lancaster, Lancashire	1193	Mayor
Leeds, West Yorkshire	1626	Lord Mayor
Leicester, Leicestershire	1589	Lord Mayor
Lichfield, Staffordshire	1549	Mayor
Lincoln, Lincolnshire	1154	Mayor
Liverpool, Merseyside	1207	Lord Mayor
London, Greater London	1066–87	Lord Mayor*
Londonderry, Londonderry, Northern Ireland	1604	Mayor
Manchester, Greater Manchester	1838	Lord Mayor
Newcastle upon Tyne, Tyne and Wear	1157	Lord Mayor
Norwich, Norfolk	1194	Lord Mayor
Nottingham, Nottinghamshire	1155	Lord Mayor
Oxford, Oxfordshire	1154–87	Lord Mayor
Perth, Tayside, Scotland	1210	Lord Provost
Peterborough, Cambridgeshire	1874	Mayor
Plymouth, Devon	1439	Lord Mayor
Portsmouth, Hampshire	1194	Lord Mayor
Ripon, North Yorkshire	886	Mayor
Rochester, Kent	1189	Mayor
St Albans, Hertfordshire	1553	Mayor
Salford, Greater Manchester	1835	Mayor
Salisbury, Wiltshire	1227	Mayor
Sheffield, South Yorkshire	1843	Lord Mayor
Southampton, Hampshire	1447	Mayor
Stoke-on-Trent, Staffordshire	1874 (present charter 1910)	Lord Mayor
Swansea, West Glamorgan, Wales	1169 (present charter 1969)	Mayor
Truro, Cornwall	1589	Mayor
Wakefield, West Yorkshire	1848	Mayor
Wells, Somerset	1201	Mayor
Westminster, Greater London	1256 (present charter 1965)	Lord Mayor
Winchester, Hampshire	1155	Mayor
Worcester, Hereford and Worcester	1189	Mayor
York, North Yorkshire	1396	Lord Mayor*

Cities, towns and districts in the United Kingdom with a population of over a quarter of a million

Since the recent reform of local government the definition of many towns has been difficult: a few new districts show an improved delineation of towns, but many new districts have Borough status, although the towns from which they take their nomenclature may represent but a fraction of their population. Also, some urban districts, usually with Borough status, do not bear the name of the principal town; e.g. the Borough in which West Bromwich is the main town is called Sandwell.

Estimated mid 1986:

1. London	Greater London	6 775 200
2. Birmingham	West Midlands	1 004 100
3. Glasgow City	Strathclyde	725 100
4. Leeds	West Yorkshire	710 900
5. Sheffield	South Yorkshire	534 300
6. Liverpool	Meseyside	483 000
7. Bradford	West Yorkshire	463 100
8. Manchester	Greater Manchester	451 400
9. Edinburgh City	Lothian	438 200
10. Bristol	Avon	391 500
11. Kirklees	West Yorkshire	376 600
12. Wirral	Merseyside	334 800

* Is styled 'Rt Hon..

13.	Coventry	West Midlands	310 400
14.	Wakefield	West Yorkshire	309 300
15.	Wigan	Greater Manchester	306 600
16.	Belfast City	N. Ireland	303 600
17.	Sandwell	West Midlands	301 000
18.	Dudley	West Midlands	300 900
19.	Sefton	Merseyside	298 000
20.	Sunderland	Tyne and Wear	297 700
21.	Stockport	Greater Manchester	289 900
22.	Doncaster	South Yorkshire	289 300
23.	Newcastle-upon-Tyne	Tyne and Wear	281 400
24.	Leicester	Leicestershire	281 100
25.	Cardiff	South Glamorgan	279 500
26.	Nottingham	Nottinghamshire	277 800
27.	Walsall	West Midlands	261 800
28.	Bolton	Greater Manchester	261 600
29.	Kingston-upon-Hull	Humberside	258 000
30.	Plymouth	Devon	256 000
31.	Rotherham	South Yorkshire	252 100
32.	Wolverhampton	West Midlands	251 900

URBAN AREAS
(population estimates at mid-1986)

Recognizing the difficulty of defining the population of towns, the Office of Population Censuses and Surveys has defined a number of conurbations and urban areas.

Many of the districts shown in the previous list – *Cities, towns and districts in the United Kingdom with a population of over a quarter of a million* – do not meet the ordinary concepts of a town, e.g. Kirklees, Wirral and Sefton. In some cases, e.g. Newcastle and Nottingham, the local government boundary has been drawn so close to the city centre that most of the suburbs have been excluded from the total. In yet other cases, the figures given in the list above include large areas of countryside, e.g. Doncaster. The existing local government boundaries in the majority of cases do not reflect the true extent of cities.

The urban areas listed here give a more accurate impression of the size of the major centres in the United Kingdom and have been defined in a manner similar to the urban areas whose population figures are recorded under the heading *Principal towns* in the vast majority of cases in the *Countries of the World* section of this publication.

1. **London** — 7 680 000
   Greater London Urban Area of which Greater London 6 775 200
2. **Birmingham** — 2 355 000
   West Midlands Urban Area of which Birmingham (City) 1 004 100
3. **Manchester** — 2 340 000
   Greater Manchester Urban Area of which Manchester (City) 451 400
4. **Glasgow** — 1 680 000
   Central Clydesdale Urban Area of which Glasgow (City) 725 100
5. **Leeds** — 1 480 000
   West Yorkshire Urban Area of which Leeds (City) 710 900, Bradford (City) 463 100
6. **Newcastle-upon-Tyne** — 780 000
   Tyneside Urban Area of which Newcastle-upon-Tyne (City) 281 400

7. **Liverpool** — 755 000
   Liverpool Urban Area of which Liverpool (City) 483 000
8. **Sheffield** — 645 000
   Sheffield Urban Area of which Sheffield (City) 534 400
9. **Nottingham** — 600 000
   Nottingham Urban Area of which Nottingham (City) 277 800
10. **Bristol** — 525 000
    Bristol Urban Area of which Bristol (City) 391 500
11. **Edinburgh** — 460 000
    Edinburgh Urban Area of which Edinburgh (City) 438 200
12. **Belfast** — 435 000
    Belfast Urban Area of which Belfast (City) 303 600
13. **Brighton** — 430 000
    Brighton-Worthing-Littlehampton of which Brighton (Borough) 141 900
14. **Portsmouth** — 415 000
    Portsmouth Urban Area of which Portsmouth (City) 186 900
15. **Leicester** — 410 000
    Leicester Urban Area of which Leicester (City) 281 100
16. **Middlesbrough** — 380 000
    Teesside Urban Area of which Middlesbrough (Borough) 144 300
17. **Stoke-on-Trent** — 375 000
    The Potteries Urban Area of which Stoke-on-Trent (City) 246 900
18. **Coventry** — 350 000
    Coventry-Bedworth Urban Area of which Coventry (City) 310 400
19. **Bournemouth** — 330 000
    Bournemouth Urban Area of which Bournemouth (Borough) 152 200
20. **Hull** — 325 000
    Kingston-upon-Hull Urban Area of which Kingston-upon-Hull (City) 258 000
21. **Swansea** — 285 000
    Swansea Urban Area of which Swansea (City) 187 000
22. = **Birkenhead** — 280 000
    Birkenhead Urban Area which is part of Wirral district of which Birkenhead (former Borough) 99 000
22. = **Cardiff** — 280 000
    Cardiff Urban Area coterminous with Cardiff (City) 279 500
24. **Southampton** — 275 000
    Southampton-Eastleigh Urban Area of which Southampton (City) 200 500
25. **Southend** — 270 000
    Southend Urban Area of which Southend-on-Sea (Borough) 159 900
26. **Blackpool** — 265 000
    Blackpool Urban Area of which Blackpool (Borough) 145 400
27. **Plymouth** — 256 000
    Plymouth Urban Area of which Plymouth (City) 256 000
28. **Preston** — 247 000
    Preston Urban Area of which Preston (Borough) 125 000
29. **Rochester** — 242 000
    The Medway Towns Urban Area of which Rochester-upon-Medway (City) 146 200

30.	**Aldershot**	230 000

Aldershot Urban Area of which
Aldershot (former Borough) 55 000

| 31. | =**Aberdeen** | 216 000 |

Aberdeen Urban Area coterminous with
Aberdeen (City) 216 000

| 31. | =**Derby** | 216 000 |

Derby Urban Area coterminous with
Derby (City) 216 000

| 33. | **Luton** | 215 000 |

Luton-Dunstable Urban Area of which
Luton (Borough) 166 300

| 34. | **Reading** | 210 000 |

Reading Urban Area of which Reading
(Borough) 135 000

| 35. | **Sunderland** | 200 000 |

Sunderland-Whitburn Urban Area
which is part of Sunderland
Metropolitan Borough

| 36. | **Norwich** | 190 000 |

Norwich Urban Area of which Norwich
(City) 121 600

The United Kindom counties, regions and island authorities

The United Kingdom of Great Britain and Northern Ireland's traditional 91 counties were, in 1974 and 1975, reduced to 66 in Great Britain and six in Northern Ireland.

England has 45 *administrative* counties plus Greater London
Scotland has 9 regions and 3 island authorities (formerly 33 counties)
Wales has 8 *administrative* counties (formerly 12)
Northern Ireland has 6 *geographical counties (divided into 26 districts)*

Population: A mid-1987 estimate is given.

County worthies by birth: The term 'worthy' is used in its sense of famous man or woman and in some cases fame includes notoriety.

Metropolitan Counties: The councils of the metropolitan counties were abolished on 31 March 1986. These names are marked by an asterisk.

Avon

First recorded name and derivation: 1973. From the river of that name. (Afon is Welsh for river.)
Area: 1345·39 km² (*519 miles²*)
Population: 951 200
Density: 707 per km² (*1833 per mile²*)
Administrative HQ: Avon House, The Haymarket, Bristol.
Highest point above sea-level: Nett Wood, East Harptree 251 m (*825 ft*).

Road lengths:

	km	*miles*
motorway and trunk	122·6	*76·1*
principal	400·0	*248·4*
other	4137·3	*2569·3*

Schools and colleges: Nursery 16; Primary 373; Secondary 61; Special 31; Colleges 10 including 1 Polytechnic.
Places of interest: Bath (Roman remains); Bath Abbey; Clevedon Court; Bristol Cathedral; Cabot Tower; Stanton Drew (standing stones); Clifton suspension Bidge; Clifton Cathedral.

County worthies by birth: John Locke (1632–1704); Thomas Chatterton (1752–70); Robert Southey (1774–1843); Samuel Plimsoll (1824–98); W. G. Grace (1848–1915).

Bedfordshire

First recorded use of name and derivation: 1011 (Bedanfordscir), Beda's ford, or river crossing.
Area: 1235 km² (*477 miles²*).
Population: 520 100.
Density: 421 per km² (*1090 per mile²*).
Administrative HQ: County Hall, Cauldwell St, Bedford.
Highest point above sea-level: Dunstable Downs 243 m (*798 ft*).

Road lengths:

	km	*miles*
motorway	25·7	*16·0*
trunk	112·6	*70·0*
principal	214·0	*133·0*
others	1850·7	*1150·0*

Schools and colleges: Nursery 12; Lower/primary 218; Middle 43; Upper/secondary 30; Sixth form college 1; Special 15; Colleges of higher education 2; Colleges 2.
Places of interest: Woburn Abbey; Whipsnade Park (Zoo); Luton Hoo; Elstow Moot Hall; Dunstable Priory Church; Wrest Park; Old Warden Shuttleworth Collection.
County worthies by birth: John Bunyan (1628–88); Thomas Tompion (1638–1713); John Howard (1726–90); Sir Joseph Paxton (1801–65).

Berkshire

First recorded use of name and derivation: AD 860, wooded hill district named after Bearuc hill.
Area: 1256 km² (*485 miles²*).
Population: 748 600.
Density: 596 per km² (*1543 per mile²*).
Administrative HQ: Shire Hall, Shinfield Park, Reading.
Highest point above sea-level: Walbury Hill 297 m (*974 ft*).

Road lengths:

	km	*miles*
motorway	111	*69·0*
trunk	51	*31·7*
principal	323	*200·7*
others	2729	*1695·8*

Schools and colleges: Nursery18; Primary 280; Special 12; Establishments of Further Education 13.
Places of interest: Windsor Castle; St George's Chapel; Royal Military Academy, Sandhurst; Basildon Park (National Trust); Cliveden (National Trust); Donnington Castle (ruin); Eton College.
County worthies by birth: Edward III (1312–77); Henry VI (1421–71); Archbishop William Laud (1628–88); Sir John Herschel (1792–1871).

Borders

First recorded use of name and derivation: 1975, from the district bordering on the boundary between England and Scotland from the Middle English word *bordure;* Term 'border' used in Act of the English Parliament, 1580.
Area: 4705 km² (*1817 miles²*).
Population: 102 141.
Density: 22 per km² (*56 per mile²*).
Administrative HQ: Regional Headquarters, Newtown St Boswells.
Highest point above sea-level: Broad Law (Southern summit) 840 m (*2756 ft*).

Melrose Abbey. (Borders Regional Council)

James Hogg, Ettrick shepherd inspired to write poetry by the natural beauty of the Ettrick Valley in which he was born. (Borders Regional Council)

Districts: Berwickshire 18 833: Ettrick and Lauderdale 33 441; Roxburgh 35 133; Tweeddale 14 734.

Road lengths:	km	*miles*
trunk	182·6	*113·5*
principal	434·6	*270·1*
classified	1348·4	*837·9*
unclassified	1030·4	*663·1*

Schools and colleges: Primary 77; Secondary 9; Colleges of further education 2.

Places of interest: Melrose Abbey; Jedburgh Abbey; Kelso Abbey; Dryburgh Abbey; Abbotsford House; Floors Castle, Traquair House, Priorwood Gardens.

County worthies by birth: Johannes Duns Scotus (*c.* 1266–1308); James Thomson (1700–48); Mungo Park (1711–1806); James Hogg (1770–1835); Dr John Leyden (1775–1811); Sir David Brewster (1781–1868); Henry Lyte (1793–1847); James Parish Lee (1831–1904); Sir James Murray (1837–1915).

Buckinghamshire

First recorded use of name and derivation: 1016 (Buccingahamscir) the hamm (watermeadow) of Bucca's people.

Area: 1883 per km² (*727 miles²*).

Population: 628 700.

Density: 334 per km² (*864 per mile²*).
Administrative HQ: County Hall, Aylesbury.
Highest point above sea-level: Nr. Aston Hill 267 m
(*876 ft*).

Road lengths:	km	miles
motorway	69	42·8
trunk	61	37·9
principal	409	254·0
others	3401	2113·0

Schools and colleges: Nursery 5; First 134; Middle
68; Combined 100; Secondary 49; Special 19; Colleges 4.
Places of interest: Claydon House; Cliveden House,
Hughenden Manor; Stowe House; Chequers; Hellfire Caves (West Wycombe); Chiltern Open Air
Museum; Milton's Cottage; Waddesdon Manor;
Ascott House.
County worthies by birth: Edmund Waller (1605–
87); Sir William Herschel (1792–1871); James
Brudenell, 7th Earl of Cardigan (1797–1868); Sir
(George) Gilbert Scott (1811–78); William Grenfell,
Baron Desborough (1855–1945); William Malcolm,
Baron Hailey (1872–1969).

Cambridgeshire

First recorded use of name and derivation: 1010
(Grantabricscir), a Norman corruption of
Grantabrice (bridge over River Granta).
Area: 3409 km² (*1316 miles²*).
Population: 641 700.
Density: 188 per km² (*487 per mile²*).
Administrative HQ: Shire Hall, Castle Hill, Cambridge.
Highest point above sea-level: 275 m (*300 yd*) south of
the Hall, Great Chishill, 145 m (*478 ft*).

Road lengths:	km	miles
motorway	70·8	44
trunk	291·2	181
principal	450·6	280
others	3889·7	2417

Schools and colleges: Nursery and Primary 28; Secondary 49; Special 18; Colleges 6.
Places of interest: Burghley House; Cambridge
University; The Backs, Cambridge; Ely Cathedral;
Peterborough Cathedral; Sawston Hall, near Cambridge; Peckover House and The Brinks, Wisbech;
Kimbolton Castle, near Huntingdon; Imperial War
Museum, Duxford; Cromwell Museum, Huntingdon; Wimpole Hall, near Cambridge; Fitzwilliam
Museum, Cambridge.
County worthies by birth: Orlando Gibbons (1583–
1625); Oliver Cromwell (1599–1658); Jeremy Taylor
(1613–67); Octavia Hill (1838–1912); Lord Keynes
(1883–1946).

Central Scotland

First recorded use of name and derivation: Self-explanatory, pertaining to the centre, the word 'central', first recorded in this sense, 1647.
Area: 2637 km² (*1018 miles²*).
Population: 272 077.
Density: 103 per km² (*267 per mile²*).
Administrative HQ: Central Regional Council,
Viewforth, Stirling.
Highest point above sea-level: Ben More 1174 m
(*3852 ft*).
Districts (with population): Clackmannan 47 412;
Falkirk 143 229; Stirling 81 436.

Road lengths:	km	miles
motorway	69·0	42·9

trunk	112·8	70·1
principal	336·6	209·2
classified	611·5	380·0
unclassified	942·2	585·5

Schools and colleges: Nursery 11; Primary 117; Secondary 19; Colleges 2.
Places of interest: Stirling Castle; Old Stirling
Bridge; Cambuskenneth Abbey; Field of
Bannockburn; Loch Lomond (east side); Doune
Castle; Castle Campbell; Dunblane Cathedral and
Wallace Monument.
County worthies by birth: George Buchanan (1506–
82); Rob Roy McGregor (1671–1734); Sir George
Harvey (1806–76); Marshal of the RAF Lord
Tedder (1890–1967).

Cheshire

First recorded use of name and derivation: AD 980
(Legaeceastersir), corrupted from the camp (*castra*)
of the legions (*legiones*).
Area: 2328 km² (*899 miles²*).
Population: 951 900.
Density: 409 per km² (*1059 per mile²*).
Administrative HQ: County Hall, Chester.
Highest point above sea-level: Shining Tor 559 m
(*1834 ft*).

Road lengths:	km	miles
motorway	207·5	129·7
trunk	215·5	134·7
principal	684·2	427·6
classified	1397·5	873·4
unclassified	3176·6	1985·4

Schools and colleges: Nursery 8; Primary 473; Secondary 75; Special 22; Colleges 8.
Places of interest: Roman remains within walled
city of Chester; Chester Cathedral; Gawsworth
Hall; Jodrell Bank; Tatton Hall; Styal Mill; Chester
Zoo; Stapeley Water Gardens.
County worthies by birth: John Bradshaw (1602–59);
Emma, Lady Hamilton (*c.* 1765–1815); Rev. Charles
Dodgson (Lewis Carroll) (1832–98).

Cleveland

First recorded use of name and derivation: 1110,
Clivelanda, 'the hilly district'.
Area: 583 km² (*225 miles²*).
Population: 554 500.
Density: 951 per km² (*2464 per mile²*).
Administrative HQ: Municipal Buildings, Middlesbrough.
Highest point above sea-level: Hob on the Hill 328 m
(*1078 ft*).

Road lengths:	km	miles
trunk	70	43·5
principal	277	172·0
others	1882	1169·0

Schools and colleges: Nursery 2; Primary 208; Secondary 46; Special 16; Colleges of further education
6; Polytechnic 1.
Places of interest: Church of St Hilda (Hartlepool);
Capt. James Cook Museum (Marton); Guisborough Priory; Preston Hall; Ormesby Hall.
County worthies by birth: Capt. James Cook (1728–
79); Thomas Sheraton (1751–1806); John Walker
(1781–1859); Sir Compton Mackenzie (1823–1972).

Bodelwyddan Castle, Clwyd. (Clwyd County Council)

Clwyd

First recorded use of name and derivation: 1973 from the river of that name.
Area: 2425 km² (*936 miles²*).
Population: 397 900.
Density: 163 per km² (*423 per mile²*).
Administrative HQ: Shire Hall, Mold.
Highest point above sea-level: Moel Sych 826 m (*2713 ft*).

Road lengths:	km	miles
trunk	191·5	*119·0*
principal	423·2	*263·0*
classified	1915·1	*1190·0*
unclassified	2019·7	*1255·0*

Schools and colleges: Nursery 5; Primary 218; Secondary 33; Special 13; Colleges 7.
Places of interest: Denbigh Castle; Valle Crucis (Cistercian Abbey); Rhuddlan Castle (ruins); Bodrhyddan Hall; Wrexham Church; Erddig Hall; Brenig Reservoir; St Asaph's Cathedral.
County worthies by birth: William Salisbury (c. 1520–84); Sir Hugh Myddleton (1560–1631); Judge George Jeffreys (1648–1689); Sir Henry M. Stanley (1841–1904).

Cornwall (and Isles of Scilly)

First recorded use of name and derivation: 884 (Cornubia) and 981 (Cornwalum), possibly the territory of the Welsh tribe Cornovii.
Area: 3564 km² (*1376 miles²*).
Population: 453 100.
Density: 127 per km² (*329 per mile²*).
Administrative HQ: County Hall, Truro.
Highest point above sea-level: Brown Willy 419 m (*1375 ft*).

Road lengths:	km	miles
trunk	236·5	*147*
principal	471·4	*293*
classified	3047·4	*1894*
unclassified	3559·1	*2212*

Schools and colleges: Nursery 2; Primary 264; Secondary 33; Special 4; Colleges of further education 4.
Places of interest: Chun Castle (ring-fort); Chysauster (Iron Age village); Cotehele House (Tudor house); Land's End; Lanhydrock House (17th century house); Lanyon Quoit; The Lizard; Rame Head; Restormel (moated castle); St Buryan (Bronze Age stone and 15th century church); St Michael's Mount; St Neot church (stained glass); Tintagel (ruins); Kynance Cove; Truro Cathedral.
County worthies by birth: Samuel Foote (1720–77); John Opie (1761–1807); Richard Trevithick (1771–1833); Sir Humphrey Davy (1778–1829); Richard (1804–34) and John (1807–39) Lander; Robert Fitzsimons (1862–1917); Sir Arthur Quiller-Couch (1863–1944).

The Isles of Scilly are included with Cornwall for many purposes but administratively they form a separate unit.

Cumbria

First recorded use of name and derivation: AD 935 Cumbra land, land of the Cumbrians from the Welsh *Cymry*.
Area: 6819 km² (*2633 miles²*).
Population: 487 700.
Density: 72 per km² (*186 per mile²*).
Administrative HQ: The Courts, Carlisle.
Highest point above sea-level: Scafell Pike 978 m (*3210 ft*).

Road lengths:	km	miles
motorway	97·0	60·2
trunk	349·0	217·4
principal	650·3	404·1
others	6268·0	3895·2

Schools and colleges: Nursery 8; Primary 328; Secondary 44; Special 11; Colleges 7.

Places of interest: Hadrian's Wall; Lake District; Grasmere (Wordsworth monuments – museum, cottage, grave); Levens Hall; Carlisle Cathedral.

County worthies by birth: Queen Catherine Parr (c. 1512–48); George Romney (1734–1802); John Dalton (1766–1844); William Wordsworth (1770–1850); John Peel (1776–1854); Sir William H. Bragg (1862–1942).

Derbyshire

First recorded use of name and derivation: 1049 (Deorbyscir), village with a deer park.
Area: 2631 km² (*1016 miles²*).
Population: 916 800.
Density: 348 per km² (*902 per mile²*).
Administrative HQ: County Offices, Matlock.
Highest point above sea-level: Kinder Scout 636 m (*2088 ft*).

Road lengths:	km	miles
motorway	34·3	21·3
trunk	257·0	159·7
principal	533·9	331·7
classified	1817·2	1129·2
unclassified	3014·2	1873·0

Schools and colleges: Nursery 18; Primary 450; Secondary 77; Special 27; Colleges of further education 6; Colleges of higher education 1.

Places of interest: Peak District; Chatsworth House; Repton School; Haddon Hall; Hardwick Hall; Melbourne Hall; Dove Dale.

County worthies by birth: Samuel Richardson (1689–1761); James Brindley (1716–72); Thomas Cook (1808–92); Marquess Curzon of Kedleston (1859–1925).

Devon

First recorded use of name and derivation: AD 851 (Defenascir), territory of the Dumonii (an aboriginal Celtic tribal name adopted by the Saxons).
Area: 6715 km² (*2592 miles²*).
Population: 1 010 000.
Density: 150 per km² (*390 per mile²*).
Administrative HQ: County Hall, Exeter.
Highest point above sea-level: High Willhays 621 m (*2038 ft*).

Road lengths:	km	miles
motorway	40·9	24·9
trunk	346·5	215·3
principal	931·4	578·8
classified	5218·3	3242·6
unclassified	7295·8	4533·5

Schools and colleges: Nursery 3; Primary 446; Secondary 75; Special 23; Establishments of further education 9; Polytechnic 1.

Places of interest: Exeter Castle (ruins); Exeter Cathedral; Devonport dockyard; Dartmoor; Buckfast Abbey; Clovelly; Powderham Castle; Dartmouth (port, castle and Royal Naval College); Exeter Maritime Museum; Exmoor National Park; Plymouth Hoe; Buckland Abbey.

County worthies by birth: St Boniface (c. 680–755); Sir John Hawkins (1532–95); Sir Francis Drake (c. 1540–96); Sir Walter Raleigh (?1552–1618); 1st Duke of Albermarle (George Monk) (1608–70); 1st Duke of Marlborough (1650–1722); Thomas Newcomen (1663–1729); Sir Joshua Reynolds (1723–92); Samual Taylor Coleridge (1772–1834); Sir Charles Kingsley (1819–75); William Temple (1881–1944); Dame Agatha Christie (1891–1976).

Dorset

First recorded use of name and derivation: AD 940 (Dorseteschire), (suggested meaning) dwellers (*saete*) of the place of fist-play (*Dorn-gweir*).
Area: 2654 km² (*1024 miles²*).
Population: 648 600.
Density: 244 per km² (*633 per mile²*).
Administrative HQ: County Hall, Dorchester.
Highest point above sea-level: Pilsdon Pen 277 m (*909 ft*).

Road lengths:	km	miles
trunk	93·0	58
principal	468·0	291
classified	1583·5	984
unclassified	2590·0	1609

Schools and colleges: Primary/First 192; Middle 26; Secondary/Upper 43; Special14; Colleges of further/higher education 5.

Places of interest: Corfe Castle; Sherborne Abbey; Wimborne Minster; Maiden Castle; Clouds Hill (National Trust); Cerne Giant; Forde Abbey; Milton Abbey; Poole Harbour; Christchurch Priory; Compton Acres Gardens.

County worthies by birth: John, Cardinal Morton (c. 1420–1500); 1st Earl of Shaftesbury (1621–83); Sir James Thornhill (1676–1734); Thomas Love Peacock (1785–1866); William Barnes (?1800–86); Thomas Hardy (1840–1928); Sir Frederick Treves (1853–1923).

Dumfries and Galloway

First recorded use of name and derivation: Dumfries c. 1183, Fort *Dum*, of the Welsh *prys* (copse). Galloway: c. 990, Gall-Gaidheal, the foreign Gael.
Area: 6475 km² (*2499 miles²*).
Population: 146 810.
Density: 23 per km² (*59 per mile²*).
Administrative HQ: Regional Council Offices, Dumfries.
Highest point above sea-level: Merrick 844 m (*2770 ft*).
Districts (with population): Annandale and Eskdale 35 680; Nithsdale 57 102; Stewartry 22 915; Wigtown 30 113.

Road lengths:	km	miles
trunk	346·8	215·5
principal	449·8	310·6
classified	1822·8	1132·1
unclassified	1660·7	1032·0

Schools and colleges: Primary 119; Secondary 16; Special 18; Establishments of further education 5.

Places of interest: Whithorn Priory; Dunskey Castle; St Ninian's Cave; Glenluce Abbey; Threave Castle (ruins); Glentrool National Park; The Ruthwell Cross; Caerlaverock Castle; Drumlanrig Castle, Burns' House and Mausoleum (Dumfries); Gretna Green; Dundrennan Abbey; Costume Museum, New Abbey; Logan Botanic Gardens; Castle Kennedy Gardens; Galloway Forest Park.

County worthies by birth: Robert the Bruce (1274–1329); John Dalrymple, 1st Earl of Stair (1646–95); William Paterson (1660–1719); Annie Laurie (1682–1764); John Paul Jones (1747–1792); Thomas Telford (1757–1834); Sir John Ross (1777–1856); Thomas Carlyle (1795–1881); Hugh MacDiarmid (1892–1978).

The picturesque village of Clovelly in North Devon, one of the county's many tourist attractions. (Devon County Council)

Durham

First recorded use of name and derivation: c. 1000 (Dunholme), the hill (old English, *dun*) crowning a holm or island.
Area: 2436 km² (*940 miles²*).
Population: 599 600
Density: 246 per km² (*638 per mile²*).
Administrative HQ: County Hall, Durham.
Highest point above sea-level: Mickle Fell 798 m (*2591 ft*).
Road lengths:

	km	miles
motorway	45·40	28·2
trunk	92·17	57·2
principal	377·66	234·5
classified	1568·83	974·2
unclassified	2173·29	1349·6

Schools and colleges: Nursery 27; Primary 301; Secondary 46; Special 17; Colleges of further education 5.
Places of interest: Durham Cathedral, Bowes Museum, Raby Castle.
County worthies by birth: Elizabeth Barrett Browning (1806–61); Earl of Avon (Anthony Eden) (1897–1977).

Dyfed

First recorded use of name and derivation: The name of an ancient 5th century kingdom.
Area: 5765 km² (*2225 miles²*).
Population: 343 200.
Density: 60 per km² (*154 per mile²*).
Administrative HQ: County Hall, Carmarthen.
Highest point above sea-level: Carmarthen Fan Foel 762+ m (*2500+ ft*).
Road lengths:

	km	miles
trunk	377·9	234·7
principal	554·5	344·3
classified	3918·0	2433·0
unclassified	3274·0	2033·0

Schools and colleges: Nursery 4; Primary 325; Secondary 33; Special 5; Colleges 5.
Places of interest: Cardigan Castle (ruins); Aberystwyth Castle (ruins); Strata Florida Abbey; Nanteos Mansion; Kidwelly Castle; Carreg-Cennen Castle; Talley Abbey; Pendine Sands; Laugharne; St David's Cathedral and Bishop's Palace; Pentre Ifan (burial chamber), near Newport; Pembroke Castle; Carew Castle; Bishop's Palace, Lamphey; Manorbier Castle; Cilgerran Castle; Pembrokeshire Coast National Park.
County worthies by birth: St David (d. 601?); Bishop Asser (d. 909 or 910); Giraldus Cambrensis (c. 1147–c. 1223); Dafydd ap Gwilym (c. 1340–1370); Robert Recorde (1510?–58); Griffith Jones of Llanddowror (1683–1761); John Dyer (1701–1757); Sir Lewis Morris (1833–1907); Sir John Rhys (1840–1915); Augustus John (1878–1961).

East Sussex

First recorded use of name and derivation: AD 722 (Suth Seaxe), the territory of the southern Saxons or suthseaxa.
Area: 1795 km² (*693 miles²*).
Population: 698 000.
Density: 389 per km² (*1007 per mile²*).
Administrative HQ: Pelham House, St Andrew's Lane, Lewes.
Highest point above sea-level: Ditchling Beacon, 248 m (*813 ft*).

Giraldus Cambrensis, also known as Gerald of Wales, (1147–1223) archdeacon of Brecknock, historian and vigorous opponent of Anglo-Norman authority over the Welsh church. (Dyfed County Council)

Road lengths:

	km	miles
trunk	100·1	62·2
principal	395·2	245·6
classified	1036·8	644·3
unclassified	2048·0	1273·1

Schools and colleges: Nursery 3; Primary and Junior/Middle 442; Secondary 35; Sixth form colleges 4; Special 20; Colleges of further educaiton 5; Polytechnic 1.
Places of interest: Pevensey Castle; Bodiam Castle; Brighton Pavilion; Lewes Castle; Herstmonceux (Royal Observatory); Bentley Wildfowl; Battle Abbey.
County worthies by birth: John Fletcher (1579–1625); Aubrey Beardsley (1872–98).

Essex

First recorded use of name and derivation: AD 604 (East Seaxe), territory of the eastern Saxons.
Area: 3674 km² (*1418 miles²*).
Population: 1 521 800.
Density: 414 per km² (*1441 per mile²*).
Administrative HQ: County Hall, Chelmsford.
Highest point above sea-level: In High Wood, Langley 146 m (*480 ft*).
Road lengths:

	km	miles
motorway/trunk	256·8	159·6
principal	664·4	412·9
classified	2408·4	1496·6
unclassified	4270·3	2653·5

Schools and colleges: Nursery 2; Primary 583; Secondary 116; Sixth form colleges 3; Special 38; Colleges of further education 4; College of education 1.
Places of interest: Waltham Abbey; Colchester

Audley End House, near Saffron Walden. (Essex Tourism)

Engraving of Adam Smith 1818 – economist and author of *Wealth of Nations*. (Fife Regional Council)

Castle; Epping Forest (part of); Thaxted Church and Guildhall; Hadleigh Castle; Castle Hedingham Keep; St Osyth Priory; Chelmsford Cathedral. **County worthies by birth:** William Gilbert (1540–1603); John Ray (1627–1705); Dick Turpin (1705–39); Samuel Courtauld (1799–1881); Lord Rayleigh (1842–1919); Lawrence Oates (1880–1912); Field Marshal Lord Wavell (1883–1950).

Fife

First recorded use of name and derivation: AD *c.* 590 from Fibh (disputed), possibly one of the seven sons of Cruithne, British patriot.
Area: 1308 km² (*505 miles²*).
Population: 344 590.
Density: 263 per km² (*682 per mile²*).
Administrative HQ: The Regional Council meets at Fife House, North Street, Glenrothes.
Highest point above sea-level: West Lomond 522 m (*1713 ft*).
Districts (with population): Dunfermline 129 049, Kirkcaldy 147 963, North East Fife 67 578.

Road lengths:	km	*miles*
motorway/trunk	160·8	*99·8*
principal	339·4	*210·9*
classified	575·0	*357·3*
unclassified	1206·4	*749·6*

Schools and colleges: Nursery 90; Primary 147; Secondary 19; Colleges of further education 4; Residential schools 4; Special schools 6.

Places of interest: St Andrews; Falkland; East Neuk Villages; Isle of May; Culross; Inchcolm; Dunfermline; Kellie Castle; Hill of Tarvit (Nr. Cupar); Earlshall Castle; Scottish Deer Centre (Nr. Cupar); Forth/Tay Bridges.

County worthies by birth: Sir David Lyndsay (c. 1486–1555); David, Cardinal Beaton (1494–1546); Charles I (1600–49); Alexander Selkirk (1676–1721); Adam Smith (1723–90); Robert (1728–92) and James (1730–94) Adams; Dr Thomas Chalmers (1780–1847); Sir David Wilkie (1785–1841); Sir Joseph Noel Paton (1821–1901); Andrew Carnegie (1835–1919).

Braemar (annual Highland games); Crathes Castle; Craigievar Castle; Pluscarden Abbey; Findlater Castle; Duff House (Banff); Maiden Stone; Haddo House; Leith Hall; Huntly Castle; Elgin Cathedral (ruins); Cairngorms (National Nature Reserve).

County worthies by birth: John Barbour (c. 1316–95); James Sharp (1618–79); Alexander Cruden (1701–1770); James Ferguson (1710–76); Sir James Clark (1788–1870); James Gordon Bennett (1795–1872); William Dyce (1806–64); Mary Slessor (1848–1915); James Ramsay Macdonald (1866–1937); John Charles Walsham Reith, 1st Baron (1889–1971).

Gloucestershire

First recorded use of name and derivation: AD 1016 (Gleawcestrescir), the shire around the fort (ceaster) at the splendid place (Old Welsh, gloiu).
Area: 2638 km² (1018 miles²).
Population: 517 100.
Density: 196 per km² (508 per mile²).
Administrative HQ: Shire Hall, Gloucester.
Highest point above sea-level: Cleeve Cloud 330 m (1083 ft).

Road lengths:	km	miles
motorway	49·0	30·4
trunk	163·2	101·4
principal	436·2	270·9
classified	1791·8	1112·9
unclassified	2318·2	1439·9

Schools and colleges: Primary 262; Secondary 43; Special 16; Colleges of further education 4.
Places of interest: Tewkesbury Abbey; Gloucester Cathedral; Roman remains at Chedworth and Cirencester; Berkeley Castle; Sudeley Castle; Forest of Dean; The Cotswolds; Prinknash Abbey; Slimbridge Wildfowl Trust.
County worthies by birth: Edward Jenner (1749–1823); Rev. John Keble (1792–1866); Ralph Vaughan Williams (1872–1958); Gustav Theodore Holst (1874–1934).

Grampian Region

First recorded use of name and derivation: 1526 derivation uncertain, perhaps from Gaelic greannich 'gloomy or rugged', or from the Celtic root grug 'curved, rounded' and related to the old Welsh crwb 'a haunch or hump'.
Area: 8550 km² (3300 miles²).
Population: 502 863.
Density: 59 per km² (152 per mile²).
Administrative HQ: Woodhill House, Westburn Road, Aberdeen.
Highest point above sea-level: Ben Macdhui 1310 m (4300 ft).
Districts (with population): Aberdeen (city) 213 228; Banff and Buchan 83 753; Gordon 71 986; Kincardine and Deeside 48 402; Moray 85 494.

Road lengths:	km	miles
trunk	342·7	213·0
principal	844·7	525·0
classified	3107·0	1931·0
unclassified	3317·8	2062·0

Schools and colleges: Nursery 19; Primary 274; Secondary 40; Special 20; Colleges of further education 5.
Places of interest: Balmoral Castle (near Crathie); Kildrummy Castle (ruins); Aberdeen University;

Greater London*

First recorded use of name and derivation: AD 115 (Londinium), possibly from the Old Irish Londo, a wild or bold man.
Area: 1580 km² (610 miles²).
Population: 6 775 200
Density: 4288 per km² (11 106 per mile²).
Administrative HQ: No central authority. Functions rest with individual Boroughs and the City of London.
Highest point above sea-level: 246 m (809 ft); 30 m (33 yd) South-east of Westerham Heights (a house) on the Kent–GLC boundary.

Population of London boroughs (1987 estimate)

Barking and Dagenham	147 800	Islington	168 700
Barnet	305 900	Kensington and Chelsea	133 100
Bexley	220 600	Kingston upon Thames	132 200
Brent	256 600		
Bromley	298 200	Lambeth	243 200
Camden	184 900	Lewisham	231 600
Croydon	319 200	Merton	164 000
Ealing	296 900	Newham	206 500
Enfield	261 500	Redbridge	230 100
Greenwich	216 600	Richmond-on-Thames	163 000
Hackney	187 400		
Hammersmith and Fulham	151 100	Southwark	216 800
		Sutton	168 600
Haringey	193 700	Tower Hamlets	159 000
Harrow	200 100	Waltham Forest	214 500
Havering	237 300	Wandsworth	258 100
Hillingdon	231 200	Westminster, City of	173 400
Hounslow	197 800		

The City of London, population 4700 (1987 estimate) is not a London borough.

Road lengths (1986):	km	miles
motorway	70·8	44·0
trunk	208·0	129·2
principal	1415·6	879·6
classified	1463·1	909·1
unclassified	9731·2	6046·7

Schools and colleges: (including ILEA). Nursery 129; Primary and Middle 2104; Secondary and Middle including Sixth form colleges 496; Special 187; Colleges 63; Polytechnics 8.
Places of interest: Buckingham Palace; Houses of Parliament; St Paul's Cathedral; Tower of London; Westminster Abbey; British Museum; National Gallery; Trafalgar Square; Port of London; Hampton Court Palace; Syon House, Isleworth; Chiswick House, W4; Osterley Park, Osterley; Harrow School; London Airport (Heathrow); Kew Gardens; Tower Bridge; Greenwich (Cutty Sark, Maritime Museum and Royal Observatory); South Kensington Museums; Westminster Cathedral; Telecom Tower.

County worthies by birth:
The following 18 Kings and Queens (see separate section for details): Mathilda, Edward I, Edward V, Henry VIII, Edward VI, Mary I, Elizabeth I, Charles II, James II, Mary II, Anne, George III, George IV, William IV, Victoria, Edward VII, George V, Elizabeth II.

The following 15 Prime Ministers (see separate section for details): Earl of Chatham, Duke of Grafton, Lord North, William Pitt, Henry Addington, Spencer Perceval, George Canning, Viscount Goderich, Viscount Melbourne, Lord John Russell, Benjamin Disraeli, Earl of Rosebery, Earl Attlee, Harold Macmillan, Lord Home of the Hirsel.

Thomas à Becket (1118–70); Geoffrey Chaucer (*c.* 1340–1400); Sir Thomas More (1478–1535); Thomas Cromwell, Earl of Essex (*c.* 1485–1540); Edmund Spenser (1552–99); Sir Francis Walsingham (*c.* 1530–90); Francis Bacon (1561–1626); Ben Jonson (1572–1637); Inigo Jones (1573–1652); Earl of Stafford, Thomas Wentworth (1593–1641); John Hampden (*c.* 1595–1643).

Sir Thomas Browne (1605–82); John Milton (1608–74); Samuel Pepys (1633–1703); William Penn (1644–1718); Edmond Halley (1656–1742); Henry Purcell (*c.* 1658–95); Daniel Defoe (1660–1731); Viscount Bolingbroke (1678–1751); Alexander Pope (1688–1744); Earl of Chesterfield (1694–1773).

Thomas Gray (1716–71); Horace Walpole (1717–97); Richard Howe (1726–99); Edward Gibbon (1737–94); Charles James Fox (1749–1806); John Nash (1752–1835); Joseph Turner (1775–1851); Sir Charles Napier (1782–1853); Viscount Palmerston (1784–1865); Viscount Stratford de Redcliffe (1786–1880); George Gordon, Lord Byron (1788–1824); Michael Faraday (1791–1867); John Keats (1795–1821); Thomas Hood 1799–1855).

John Stuart Mill (1806–73); Robert Browning (1812–89); Anthony Trollope (1815–82); George F. Watts (1817–1904); John Ruskin (1819–1900); Lord Lister (1827–1912); Dante Gabriel Rossetti (1828–82); William Morris (1834–96); Sir William Gilbert (1836–1911); Algernon Charles Swinburne (1837–1909); Sir Arthur Sullivan (1842–1900); Gerard Manley Hopkins (1844–89); Lord Baden-Powell (1857–1941); Marquess of Reading (1860–1935); H. G. Wells (1866–1946); John Galsworthy (1867–1933); Sir Max Beerbohm (1873–1956); G. K. Cheston (1874–1936); Virginia Woolf (1882–1941); Sir Charles Chaplin (1889–1978); Evelyn Waugh (1903–66).

Greater Manchester*

First recorded use of name and derivation: AD 923 *Mameceaster*, first element reduced from the Old British *Mamucion* to which was added the Old English *ceaster*, a camp.
Area: 1286 km² *(496 miles²)*.
Population: 2 579 500.
Density: 2006 per km² *(5201 per mile²)*.
Administrative HQ: No central authority. Functions rest with individual Boroughs.
Highest point above sea-level: Featherbed Moss 540 m *(1774 ft)*.

Road lengths: (1986)	km	miles
motorway	169·0	105·0
trunk	43·0	26·7
principal	815·0	506·4
classified	809·0	502·6
unclassified	6008·0	3733·1

Schools and colleges: Nursery 54; Primary 968;

Middle and Secondary 199; Sixth form colleges 15; Special 84; Establishments of further education 35; Polytechnic 1.
Places of interest: Castlefield (Britain's first urban heritage park); Foxdenton Hall; Haigh Hall; Peel Tower; Salford Art Gallery and Museum; Manchester: Chethams School and Library, Cathedral, Ship Canal, Bramhall Hall; Dunham Massey Hall; Heaton Hall; Lyme Hall and Park.
County worthies by birth: Samuel Crompton (1753–1827); Sir Robert Peel (1788–1850); William Harrison Ainsworth (1805–82); John Bright (1811–89); James Prescott Jowle (1818–89); Emmeline Pankhurst (1858–1928); 1st Earl Lloyd-George of Dwyfor (1863–1945); L. S. Lowry (1887–1976); John William Alcock (1892–1919); Gracie Fields (1898–1979); Sir William Walton (b. 1902).

Gwent

First recorded use of name and derivation: The name of an ancient kingdom dating from 5th century.
Area: 1376 km² *(531 miles²)*.
Population: 441 800.
Density: 321 per km² *(832 per mile²)*.
Administrative HQ: County Hall, Cwmbran.
Highest point above sea-level: Chwarel-y-Fan 679 m *(2228 ft)*.

Road lengths:	km	miles
motorway	52·1	32·3
trunk	134·1	83·3
principal	221·2	137·4
classified/unclassified	3053·1	1897·2

Schools and colleges: Nursery 15; Primary 233; Secondary 33; Special 7; Colleges of further education 7.
Places of interest: Tintern Abbey; Caldicot Castle; Caerleon (Roman remains); Chepstow Castle; Wye Valley; Raglan Castle; Big Pit; Blaenavon, Sirhowy Ironworks; Penhow Castle; Tredegar House; St Woolloo's Cathedral, Newport.
County worthies by birth: Henry V (1387–1422); Bertrand Russell (1872–1970); Charles S. Rolls (1877–1910); W. H. Davies (1877–1940); Aneurin Bevan (1897–1960); Neil Kinnock (b. 1942).

Gwynedd

First recorded use of name and derivation: The name of an ancient kingdom or principality dating from the 5th century.
Area: 3868 km² *(1493 miles²)*.
Population: 236 300.
Density: 61 per km² *(158 per mile²)*.
Administrative HQ: County Offices, Caernarfon (formerly Caernarvon).
Highest point above sea-level: Snowdon 1085 m *(3560 ft)*.

Road lengths:	km	miles
trunk	330	205
principal	433	269
classified	1824	1133
unclassified	2135	1327

Schools and colleges: Primary 198; Secondary 24; Special 7; Establishments of further education 4.
Places of interest: Castles: Harlech, Beaumaris, Caernarfon, Conwy (Conway), Criccieth, Dolbadarn (Llanberis), Dolwyddelan, Penrhyn, Gwydyr; Snowdonia National Park *(840 miles²)*; Bryn Celli Ddu; Portmeirion; Lloyd George Memorial and Museum, Llanystumdwy; Snowdon Mountain Railway; Ffestiniog Narrow Gauge Railway.

County worthies by birth: Edward II (1284–1327); Lewis Morris (1700–65); Goronwy Owen (1723–69); Sir Hugh Owen (1804–81); T. E. Lawrence (1888–1935).

Hampshire

First recorded use of name and derivation: AD 755 (Hamtunscir), the shire dependent on Hamtun (*hamm*, a meadow; *tun*, a homestead).
Area: 3781 km² (*1460 miles²*).
Population: 1 527 600.
Density: 404 per km² (*1046 per mile²*).
Administrative HQ: The Castle, Winchester.
Highest point above sea-level: Pilot Hill 285 m (*937 ft*).

Road lengths:

	km	miles
motorway	124	78
trunk	196	123
other	8936	5565

Schools and colleges: Primary 586; Secondary and Sixth form colleges 108; Special 47; Colleges of further education 14; Polytechnic 1.
Places of interest: Winchester Cathedral; Beaulieu Palace House and Motor Museum; New Forest; Art Gallery, Southampton; Portsmouth dockyard (with HMS Victory and Mary Rose); Romsey Abbey; Portsmouth Cathedrals; Great Hall, Winchester (Round Table).
County worthies by birth: Henry III (1207–72); William of Wykeham (1324–1404); Gilbert White (1720–93); Jane Austen (1775–1817); Isambard Kingdom Brunel (1806–59); Charles Dickens (1829–70); Sir John Everett Millais (1829–96); Admiral Lord Jellicoe (1859–1935); Lord Denning (b. 1899); James Callaghan (Baron Callaghan of Cardiff) (b. 1912).

Hereford and Worcester

First recorded use of name and derivation: AD c. 1038 Hereford, *herepaeth*, military road, meaning ford, a river crossing and AD 889 *Uuegorna ceastre*, the fort (Latin *caester*) of the Weogoran tribe, probably named from the Wyre Forest.
Area: 3927 km² (*1516 miles²*).
Population: 665 100.
Density: 169 per km² (*439 per mile²*).
Administrative HQ: County Hall, Worcester.
Highest point above sea-level: In Black Mountains 702 m (*2306 ft*).

Road lengths:

	km	miles
motorway	83·2	51·7
trunk	179·8	111·7
principal	762·6	473·6
other	6299·0	3911·0

Schools and colleges: Primary 284; Middle 42; Secondary 46; Special 15; Sixth form colleges 2; Colleges 11.
Places of interest: Offa's Dyke; Hereford Cathedral; Worcester Cathedral; Malvern Priory; Pershore Abbey; Dinmore Manor; Symond's Yat and Wye Valley; Brockhampton Court; Goodrich Castle; Bulmer Railway Centre; Hereford Museum of Cider; Hergest Croft Gardens; Eastnor Castle; Croft Castle; Severn Valley Railway; West Midlands Safari Park; Avoncroft Museum of Buildings; Hagley Hall; Hanbury Hall; Harvington Hall; Hartlebury Castle; County Museum; Elgar's Birthplace; National Needle Museum.
County worthies by birth: Richard Hakluyt (1553–1616); Robert Devereux, Earl of Essex (1567–1601); Samuel Butler (1612–80); David Garrick (1717–79);

Sir Rowland Hill (1795–1879); Sir Edward Elgar (1857–1934); A. E. Housman (1859–1936); Stanley Baldwin (1867–1947).

Hertfordshire

First recorded use of name and derivation: AD 866 (Heortfordscir), the river crossing (ford) of the stags (harts).
Area: 1634 km² (*631 miles²*).
Population: 986 800.
Density: 600 per km² (*1554 per mile²*).
Administrative HQ: County Hall, Hertford.
Highest point above sea-level: Hastoe 244 m (*802 ft*).

Road lengths:

	km	miles
motorway	151	94
trunk	117	73
principal	349	217
other	3726	2314

Schools and colleges: Primary and Nursery 466; Secondary and Middle 101; Special 30; Further education establishments 9; Polytechnic 1.
Places of interest: St Albans Cathedral, Roman remains of Verulamium (now at St Albans); Hatfield House; Knebworth House; Salisbury Hall.
County worthies by birth: Nicholas Breakspear (Pope Adrian IV) (1100–59); Sir Richard Fanshawe (1608–66); William Cowper (1731–1800); Henry Manning (1808–92); Sir Henry Bessemer (1813–98); Third Marquess of Salisbury (1830–1903); Cecil Rhodes (1853–1902); Queen Elizabeth, the Queen Mother (b. 1900).

Highland Region

First recorded use of name and derivation: c. 1425 (implied in *hielandman*) from adjective *high*, noun *land*.
Area: 26 136 km² (*10 088 miles²*).
Population: 200 608.
Density: 8 per km² (*20 per mile²*).
Administrative HQ: Regional Buildings, Glenurquhart Road, Inverness. Regional Council meets at County Buildings, Dingwall.
Highest point above sea-level: Ben Nevis 1342 m (*4406 ft*).
Districts (with population): Badenoch and Strathspey 10 765; Caithness 27 025; Inverness 61 077; Lochaber 19 117; Nairn 10 310; Ross and Cromarty 47 897; Skye and Lochalsh 11 332; Sutherland 13 085.

Road lengths:

	km	miles
trunk	748	465
principal	1681	1045
classified	2374	1475
other	2608	1621

Schools and colleges: Primary 210; Secondary 27; Special 7; Establishments of further education 3.
Places of interest: House of John O'Groat's House (Pentland Firth); Dunrobin Castle; Culloden Battlefield; Glenfinnan Monument (raising of Prince Charles Stewart's standard); Loch Ness; Eilean Donan Castle; Dunvegan Castle (Skye); Cawdor Castle (Nairn); Beauly Priory (Inverness); Clava Cairns (Inverness); Fortrose Cathedral; Glenelg Brochs; Highland Folk Museum; Camster Cairns; Inverewe Gardens; Urquhart Castle; Glencoe; Osprey Hide (Boat of Garten); The Cairngorms.
County worthies by birth: Hugh Mackay (?1640–92); Simon Fraser, Lord Lovat (?1667–1749); Duncan Forbes (1685–1746); Gen. Arthur St Clair (1734–1818); Sir John Sinclair (1754–1835); Sir Alexander

Mackenzie (1755-1820); Hugh Miller (1802-56); Alexander Bain (1810-77); Sir Hector MacDonald (1853-1903); William Smith (1854-1914).

Humberside

First recorded use of name and derivation: AD *c.* 730 *humbri*, the British river name, side.
Area: 3512 km² (*1356 miles²*).
Population: 846 500.
Density: 241 per km² (*624·3 per mile²*).
Administrative HQ: County Hall, Beverley, N. Humberside.
Highest point above sea-level: Cot Nab 246 m (*808 ft*).

Road lengths:	km	miles
motorway	109·0	67·7
trunk	128·0	79·5
principal	494·8	307·5
other	5019·2	3118·9

Schools and colleges: Nursery 9; Primary 361; Secondary 67; Special 16; Colleges 6.
Places of interest: Kingston upon Hull; Trinity House, Wilberforce House, Town Docks Museum; Beverley Minster; Thornton Abbey; St Mary's Church; Museum of Army Transport; Burton Agnes Hall; Burton Constable Hall; Elsham Hall; Old Rectory, Epworth; Danes Dyke, Flamborough; Humber Bridge; Sandtoft Transport Centre; Normanby Hall, Scunthorpe; Spurn Point.
County worthies by birth: John Fisher (*c.* 1469-1535); Andrew Marvell (1621-78); John (1703-91) and Charles (1707-88) Wesley; William Wilberforce (1759-1833); Sir Mark Sykes (1979-1919); Henry Frederick Lindley, 1st Earl of Halifax (1881-1959); Amy Johnson (1903-41).

Isle of Wight

First recorded use of name and derivation: The Celtic name Ynys-yr-Wyth, from which the Romans derived Vectis predates the Roman conquest.
Area: 381 km² (*147 miles²*).
Population: 126 900.
Density: 333 per km² (*863 per mile²*).
Administrative HQ: County Hall, Newport.
Highest point above sea-level: St Boniface Down 240 m (*787 ft*).

Road lengths:	km	miles
trunk	nil	nil
principal	122	76
classified	269	167
unclassified	351	218

Schools and colleges: Primary 46; Middle 16; Secondary 5; Special 2; College of further education 1.
Places of interest: Osborne House; Carisbrooke Castle; Brading and Newport (Roman villas); Blackgang Chine Fantasy Theme Park.
County worthies by birth: Sir Thomas Fleming (1544-1613); Dr Thomas James (1580-1629); Robert Hooke (1635-1703); Dr Thomas Arnold (1795-1842).

Kent

First recorded use of name and derivation: *c.* 308 BC Celtic *canto*, a rim or coastal area.
Area: 3732 km² (*1441 miles²*).
Population: 1 510 500.
Density: 405 per km² (*1048 per mile²*).
Administrative HQ: County Hall, Maidstone.
Highest point above sea-level: Betsom's Hill, Westerham 251 m (*824 ft*).

Road lengths:	km	miles
motorway	166	103
trunk	214	133
principal	767	476
non-principal	7546	4686

Schools and colleges: Nursery and primary 587; Middle 10; Secondary 139; Special 38; Colleges of further and higher education 10.
Places of interest: Canterbury Cathedral; Dover Cliffs; Pilgrim's Way; North Downs; Knowle; Penshurst Place; Deal Castle; Chartwell; Rochester Castle and Cathedral; Leeds Castle.
County worthies by birth: William Caxton (*c.* 1422-91); Christopher Marlow (1564-93); Sir William Harvey (1578-1657); General James Wolfe (1727-59); William Hazlitt (1778-1830); Sir William Jenner (1815-98); Robert Bridges (1844-1930); Edward Richard George Heath (b. 1916).

Lancashire

First recorded use of name and derivation: the shire around *Lancastre* AD 1087; camp, (*castrum*) on the River Lune.
Area: 3063 km² (*1183 miles²*).
Population: 1 380 700.
Density: 451 per km² (*1167 per mile²*).
Administrative HQ: County Hall, Preston.
Highest point above sea-level: Gragareth 627 m (*2058 ft*).

Road lengths:	km	miles
motorway	139	86·4
trunk	179	111·2
principal	623	387·1
classified	1798	1117·3
unclassified	4608	2863·4

Schools and colleges: Nursery 38; Primary 606; Secondary 114; Special 42; Establishments of further education 10; Polytechnic 1.
Places of interest: Blackpool Tower; Hoghton Tower; Leighton Hall; Lancaster Castle and Ashton Memorial; Helmshore Textile Museum; Wycoller Country Park.
County worthies by birth: Sir Richard Arkwright (1732-92); James Hargreaves (?1745-78); Sir Ambrose Fleming (1849-1945).

Leicestershire

First recorded use of name and derivation: 1086 (Domesday Book) Ledecestrescire. From the camp (*castra*) of the *Ligore*, dwellers on the River Legra (now the R. Soar).
Area: 2553 km² (*985 miles²*).
Population: 875 000.
Density: 343 per km² (*888 per mile²*).
Administrative HQ: County Hall, Glenfield, Leicester.
Highest point above sea-level: Bardon Hill 277 m (*912 ft*).

Road lengths:	km	miles
motorway	126	78
trunk	301	187
principal	687	427
classified	2745	1706
unclassified	4423	2749

Schools and colleges: Nursery 1; Primary 335; High 37; Upper 17; (11-16) 16; (11-18) 8; Special 22; Community colleges 3; Sixth form colleges 4; Colleges of further education 7; Other colleges 2; Polytechnic 1.
Places of interest: Belvoir Castle; Ashby-de-la-Zouch Castle; Kirby Muxloe Castle; Stanford Hall;

The Ashton Memorial, Williamson Park, Lancaster. (Lancashire County Council)

Battlefield of Bosworth; Oakham Castle; Rutland Water; Stapleford Park; Bradgate Park. **County worthies by birth:** Latimer (?*c.* 1485–1555); Queen Jane (1537–54); Robert Burton (1577–1640); Francis Beaumont (1584?–1616); George Villiers, Duke of Buckingham (1592–1628); George Fox (1624–91); Hugh Titus Oates (1649–1705); Robert Hall (1764–1831); Daniel Lambert (1770–1809); Thomas Babington Macaulay (1800–59); C. P. Snow (1905–1980).

Lincolnshire

First recorded use of name and derivation: 1016 (Lincolnescire), a colony (*colonia*) by the *lindum* (a widening in the river, i.e. River Witham).
Area: 5885 km² (*2272 miles²*).
Population: 566 200.
Density: 96 per km² (*249 per mile²*).
Administrative HQ: County Offices, Lincoln.
Highest point above sea-level: Normanby-le-Wold 167 m (*548 ft*).

Road lengths:	km	miles
motorway	nil	nil
trunk	355·3	221·4
principal	764·7	475·2
classified	3546·8	2204·0
unclassified	3878·4	2410·0

Schools and colleges: Nursery 3; Primary 296; Secondary 67; Special 19; Establishments of further education 7.
Places of interest: Lincoln: Cathedral, Castle, Art Gallery; Tattershall Castle; Boston Stump.
County worthies by birth: Henry IV (1367–1413); John Foxe (1516–87); William Cecil, Lord Burghley (1520–98); Sir Isaac Newton (1642–1727); Sir John Franklin (1786–1847); Alfred, Lord Tennyson (1809–92); Sir Malcolm Sargent (1895–1967); Margaret Thatcher (b. 1925).

Lothian

First recorded use of name and derivation: c. AD 970 from personal name, possibly a Welsh derivative of Laudinus.
Area: 1767 km² (*682 miles²*).
Population: 743 700.
Density: 421 per km² (*1090 per mile²*).
Administrative HQ: Regional Headquarters, George IV Bridge, Edinburgh.
Highest point above sea-level: Blackhope Scar 651 m (*2137 ft*).
Length of coastline: 101 km (*63 miles*).
Districts (with population): East Lothian 81 855; Edinburgh (city) 438 721; Midlothian 81 440; West Lothian 141 864.

Road lengths:	km	miles
motorway	48·7	30·3
trunk	107·6	66·9
principal	451·5	280·6
classified	945·9	587·8
unclassified	2052·8	1275·6

Schools and colleges: Primary 244; Secondary 51; Special 23; Colleges of further education 4; Colleges of agriculture 1.
Places of interest: Dunbar Castle; Tantallon Castle (ruins); Muirfield Golf Centre (Gullane); Aberlady (bird sanctuary); Rosslyn chapel; Borthwick Castle; Newbattle Abbey; Dalkeith Palace; Edinburgh Castle; St Giles Cathedral; Crichton Castle; Palace of Holyrood House; Craigmillar Castle; Linlithgow Palace; Dundas Castle; The Binns (near Queensferry); Torphichen Church; Hopetoun House; The Forth Bridges.
County worthies by birth: John Knox (c. 1505–72); Mary, Queen of Scots (1542–87); John Napier (1550–1617); James VI of Scotland and I of England (1566–1625); David Hume (1711–76); James Boswell (1740–95); Sir Walter Scott (1771–1832); George Gordon, 4th Earl of Aberdeen (1784–1860); James Nasmyth (1808–90); Alexander Melville Bell (1819–1905); Sir Herbert Maxwell (1845–1937);

Alexander Graham Bell (1847–1922); Arthur James Balfour (1848–1930); Robert Louis Stevenson (1850–94); Sir Arthur Conan Doyle (1859–1930); Field Marshal Douglas Haig (1861–1928).

Merseyside*

First recorded use of name and derivation: AD 1002 *Maerse* from Old English *Maeres-ea* boundary river (between Mercia and Northumbria).
Area: 652 km² (*252 miles²*).
Population: 1 467 600.
Density: 2251 per km² (*5824 per mile²*).
Administrative HQ: No central authority. Functions rest with individual Boroughs.
Highest point above sea-level: Billinge Hill 179 m (*588 ft*).

Road lengths (1986):	km	miles
motorway	48·7	30·3
trunk	66·6	41·4
principal	362·2	225·1
classified	484·7	301·2
unclassified	3573·3	2220·4

Schools and colleges: Nursery 14; Primary (inc. Middle) 530; Secondary 115; Special 63; Establishments of further and higher education 24; Polytechnic 1.
Places of interest: Liverpool: Roman Catholic Cathedral and Anglican Cathedral, Speke Hall, Croxteth Hall; Walker Art Gallery; Sudley Art Gallery; Merseyside: County Museum, Maritime Museum; Pilkington Glass Museum; Knowsley Safari Park; Ainsdale Nature Reserve; Albert Dock Village; Festival Gardens; Beatle City Museum.
County worthies by birth: George Stubbs (1724–1806); Edward Stanley, 14th Earl of Derby (1799–1869); William Ewart Gladstone (1809–98); 1st Earl of Birkenhead (1872–1930); Sir Thomas Beecham (1879–1961).

Mid-Glamorgan

First recorded use of name and derivation: 1242 (Gwlad Morgan) the terrain of Morgan, a 10th century Welsh Prince.
Area: 1019 km² (*393 miles²*).
Population: 530 800.
Density: 521 per km² (*1350 per mile²*).
Administrative HQ: County Hall, Cathays Park, Cardiff, South Glamorgan (i.e. outside the county).
Highest point above sea-level: Near Craig-y-Llyn 585 m (*1919 ft*).

Road lengths:	km	miles
motorway and trunk	144·0	89·5
principal	546·2	339·4
classified	756·5	470·1
unclassified	2955·6	1836·6

Schools and colleges: Nursery 24; Primary 146; Infants 99; Junior 73; Comprehensive 42; Special 10; Colleges of higher and further education 6; College of agriculture 1; Polytechnic 1.
Places of interest: Ewenny Priory; Caerphilly Castle; Brecon Mountain Railway; Dare Valley Country Park; Stuart Crystal Glassworks, Aberdare; Llanharan House; Ogmore Castle; Kenfig Nature Reserve; Glyncornel Environmental Centre.
County worthies by birth: Richard Price (1723–91); Dr William Price (1800–93); Joseph Parry (1841–1903); Sir Geraint Evans (b. 1922); Stuart Burrows (b. 1933).

Norfolk

First recorded use of name and derivation: AD 1043 (Norfolk), the territory of the *nor* (northern) *folk* (people) of East Anglia.
Area: 5355 km² (*2067 miles²*).
Population: 736 200.
Density: 138 per km² (*356 per mile²*).
Administrative HQ: County Hall, Martineau Lane, Norwich.
Highest point above sea-level: Sandy Lane, east of Sheringham 102 m (*335 ft*).

Road lengths:	km	miles
trunk	247	153
principal	674	419
classified	3860	2397
unclassified	4617	2867

Schools and colleges: Nursery 4; Primary and middle 408; Secondary 57; Colleges 6.
Places of interest: The Broads; Sandringham House; Blicking Hall; Holkham Hall; Breckland; Scolt Head; Norwich Cathedral; The Castle, Norwich; Maddermarket Theatre, Norwich; Castle Acre; Grimes Graves; Walsingham.
County worthies by birth: Sir Edward Coke (1552–1634); 2nd Viscount Townshend (1674–1738); Sir Robert Walpole (1676–1745); Thomas Paine (1737–1809); Fanny Burney (1752–1840); 1st Viscount Nelson (1758–1805); Elizabeth Fry (1780–1845); George Borrow (1803–81); 1st Earl of Cromer (1841–1917); H. Rider Haggard (1856–1925); Edith Cavell (1865–1915); George VI (1895–1952).

Northamptonshire

First recorded use of name and derivation: *c.* AD 1011 (Hamtunscir) [see Hampshire], the northern homestead.
Area: 2367 km² (*914 miles²*).
Population: 554 400
Density: 234 per km² (*606 per mile²*).
Administrative HQ: County Hall, Northampton.
Highest point above sea-level: Arbury Hill 223 m (*734 ft*).

Road lengths:	km	miles
motorway	45·1	28·0
trunk	208·1	129·3
principal	397·0	246·6
classified	1157·8	719·4
unclassified	1926·5	1197·0

Schools and colleges: Nursery 38; Primary 273; Middle and secondary 66; Special 18; Establishments of further education 5.
Places of interest: Earls Barton Church; Sulgrave Mnaor; Fotheringhay; Brixworth Church; Althorp House; Castle Ashby House; Rockingham Castle; Deene Hall; Boughton House; Queen Eleanor Crosses (Northampton & Geddington); Naseby.
County worthies by birth: Richard III (1452–85); Christopher Hatton (1540–91); John Dryden (1631–1700).

Northumberland

First recorded use of name and derivation: AD 895 (Norohymbraland), the land to the north of the Humber.
Area: 5033 km² (*1943 miles²*).
Population: 303 500.
Density: 60 per km² (*156 per mile²*).
Administrative HQ: County Hall, Morpeth.

Highest point above sea-level: The Cheviot 815 m (*2676 ft*).

Road lengths:	km	miles
trunk	275·5	171·1
primary	323·8	201·2
secondary	566·3	351·9
local district	363·0	225·6
access	3403·3	2176·9

Schools and colleges: First 143; Middle 45; Secondary (High) 16; Special 11; Establishments of further education 2.
Places of interest: Hadrian's Wall; Lindisfarne Priory; Alnwick Castle; Warkworth Castle; Hexham Abbey; Bamburgh Castle; Norham Castle; Chillingham Castle (wild cattle); Blanchland; Kielder Reservoir.
County worthies by birth: William Turner (1508–68); Lancelot ('Capability') Brown (1716–83); Thomas Bewick (1753–1828); 2nd Earl Grey (1764–1845); George Stephenson (1781–1848); Grace Darling (1815–42); Robert ('Bobby') Charlton (b. 1937).

North Yorkshire

First recorded use of name and derivation: *c.* AD 150 Ebórakon (Ptolemy); AD 1050 *Eoferwicscir*, land possessed by Eburos.
Area: 8312 km² (*3209 miles²*).
Population: 705 700.
Density: 85 per km² (*219 per mile²*).
Administrative HQ: County Hall, Northallerton.
Highest point above sea-level: Whernside 737 m (*2419 ft*).

Road lengths:	km	miles
motorway	21·7	13·5
trunk	394·4	245·1
principal	750·9	466·6
other	8228·0	5113·0

Schools and colleges: Nursery 5; Primary 402; Secondary (various) 61; Special 17; Establishments of further and higher education 10.
Places of interest: Richmond Castle; Scarborough Castle; City of York (the Minster and the Five Sisters Windows); Byland Abbey; Castle Howard; Rievaulx Abbey; Fountains Abbey; Bolton Priory (ruins); Ripon Cathedral; The Yorkshire Dales; The North York Moors; Selby Abbey.
County worthies by birth: Alcuin (735–804); Henry I (1068–1135); Miles Coverdale (1488–1568); Roger Ascham (1515–68); Guy Fawkes (1570–1606); Thomas Fairfax (1612–71); John Flaxman (1755–1826); Sir George Cayley (1773–1857); William Etty (1787–1849); William Powell Frith (1819–1909); William Stubbs (1825–1901); Sir William Harcourt (1827–1904); Frederick, Lord Leighton (1830–78); Edith Sitwell (1887–1964); Sir Herbert Read (1893–1968); Wystan Hugh Auden (1907–73).

Nottinghamshire

First recorded use of name and derivation: 1016 (Snotingahamscir), the shire around the dwelling (ham) of the followers of Snot, a Norseman.
Area: 2164 km² (*835 miles²*).
Population: 1 007 800.
Density: 466 per km² (*1206 per mile²*).
Administrative HQ: County Hall, West Bridgford, Nottingham.
Highest point above sea-level: Herrod's Hill 198 m (*652 ft*).

Road lengths:	km	miles
motorway	15·0	9·3

trunk	238·2	*148·0*
other	4425·6	*2750·0*

Schools and colleges: Nursery and primary 430; Secondary 88; Special 28; Further education establishments 10; Polytechnic 1.
Places of interest: Southwell Cathedral; Sherwood Forest; The Dukeries; Wollaton Hall; Newstead Abbey.
County worthies by birth: Thomas Cranmer (1489–1556); Edmund Cartwright (1743–1823); Richard Bonington (1801–28); Glen William Booth (1829–1912); Samuel Butler (1835–1902); D. H. Lawrence (1885–1930).

Orkney

First recorded use of name and derivation: *c.* 308 BC as Orcas (Pytheas) from Celtic Innse Orc, islands of the Boars, the Boars being a Pictish tribe; later altered to the Norse Orkneyjar, islands of the Young Seals.
Area: 974 km² (*376 miles²*). Consists of 54 islands.
Population: 19 338.
Density: 20 per km² (*51 per mile²*).
Administrative HQ: Council Offices, Kirkwall.
Highest point above sea-level: Ward Hill, Hoy 478 m (*1570 ft*).

Road lengths:	km	*miles*
principal	160·9	*100*
classified	362·0	*225*
unclassified	420·0	*261*

Schools and colleges: Primary 20; Secondary 6; Special 1; College of further education 1.
Places of interest: Noltland Castle (ruins); the prehistoric village of Skara Brae; the stone circle at Brogar; Old Man of Hoy; Kirkwall Cathedral; Scapa Flow.
County worthies by birth: Sir Robert Strange (1721–92); John Rae (1813–93).

Oxfordshire

First recorded use of name and derivation: AD 1010 (Oxnfordscir), the shire around Oxford (a river ford for oxen). The town (city) was first recorded (as Osnaforda) in AD 912.
Area: 2611 km² (*1008 miles²*).
Population: 583 200.
Density: 223 per km² (*579 per mile²*).
Administrative HQ: County Hall, New Road, Oxford.
Highest point above sea-level: White Horse Hill 260 m (*856 ft*).

Road lengths:	km	*miles*
motorway	13·6	*8·5*
trunk	272·0	*169·0*
principal	391·0	*242·9*
classified	1529·0	*950·0*
unclassified	1706·0	*1060·0*

Schools and colleges: Nursery 12; First/primary 238; Middle and secondary 46; Special 16; Establishments of further education 6; Polytechnic 1.
Places of interest: Oxford Univesity; Blenheim Palace, nr Woodstock; Rollright Stones; Broughton Castle; Radcliffe Camera; Bodleian Library, Oxford; Christ Church Cathedral, Oxford; White Horse of Uffington; Dorchester Abbey.
County worthies by birth: Alfred (849–99); St Edward the Confessor (*c.* 1004–66); Richard I (1157–99); John (1167–1216); Sir William D'Avenant (1606–68); Warren Hastings (1732–1818); Lord Randolph Churchill (1849–95); Sir

Winston Churchill (1874–1965); William Morris, 1st Viscount Nuffield (1877–1963).

Powys

First recorded use of name and derivation: The name of an ancient province probably dating from *c.* 5th century AD.
Area: 5077 km² (*1960 miles²*).
Population: 113 300.
Density: 22 per km² (*58 per mile²*).
Administrative HQ: County Hall, Llandrindod Wells.
Highest point above sea-level: Pen-y-Fan (Cadet Arthur) 886 m (*2906 ft*).

Road lengths:	km	*miles*
trunk	425	*264*
principal	238	*148*
classified	2613	*1624*
unclassified	2390	*1485*

Schools and colleges: Primary 114; Secondary 13; Special 4; Colleges of further education 3.
Places of interest: Brecon Beacons; Elan Valley Reservoirs; Brecon Cathedral; Powis Castle and gardens; Lake Vyrnwy; Montgomery Castle; Gregynog Hall; Dan-y-Ogof Caves.
County worthies by birth: Owain Glyndwr (*c.* 1354–*fl* 1416); George Herbert (1593–1633); Robert Owen (1771–1858).

Shetland

First recorded use of name and derivation: 1289, land of Hjalto (Old Norse personal name cf. Scots, Sholto) or hilt-shaped land.
Area: 1430 km² (*552 miles²*). Consists of 117 islands.
Population: 22 913.
Density: 16 per km² (*42 per mile²*).
Administrative HQ: Town Hall, Lerwick.
Highest point above sea-level: Ronas Hill, Mainland 450 m (*1477 ft*).

Road lengths:	km	*miles*
principal	224·8	*139·7*
classified	149·8	*93·1*
unclassified	512·7	*318·6*

Schools and colleges: Primary 35; Secondary 9; Further education centre 1.
Places of interest: Scalloway Castle; Jarlshof; Broch of Mousa; Broch of Clickimin; St Ninian's Isle; Lerwick Museum; Muckle Flugga lighthouse; Sullom Voe Terminal; Lerwick Town Hall.
County worthies by birth: Arthur Anderson (1792–1868); Sir Robert Stout (1844–1930).

Shropshire

First recorded use of name and derivation: AD 1006 Scrobbesbyrigscir from Scrobbesbyrig or Shrewsbury.
Area: 3490 km² (*1347 miles²*).
Population: 398 400.
Density: 114 per km² (*296 per mile²*).
Administrative HQ: Shirehall, Abbey Foregate, Shrewsbury.
Highest point above sea-level: Brown Clee Hill 545 m (*1790 ft*).

Road lengths:	km	*miles*
motorway	37·5	*23·3*
trunk	225·5	*140·1*
principal	430·5	*267·5*
classified	2525·0	*1569·0*
unclassified	2585·0	*1606·0*

Schools and colleges: Nursery 2; Primary 218; Secondary (various) 42; Special 10; Colleges of further and higher education 5.
Places of interest: Offa's Dyke;, Ludlow Castle; Stokesay Castle; Coalbrookdale and Ironbridge; The Wrekin; Hodnet Hall Gardens; Severn Valley Railway; Bridgnorth; Acton Scott Working Farm Museum; Buildwas Abbey; Wenlock Priory; Wroxeter; Boscobel House.
County worthies by birth: Lord Clive of Plassey (1725-74); Thomas Minton (1766-1836); Charles Darwin (1809-82); Capt. Matthew Webb (1848-83); Mary Webb (1881-1927); Wilfred Owen (1893-1918).

Somerset

First recorded use of name and derivation: AD 845 *Sumorsaete*, the people who looked to Somerton (Sumortun) as the tribal capital of the 'land of summer' (Welsh *gwlad yr haf*).
Area: 3458 km² (*1335 miles²*).
Population: 452 300.
Density: 131 per km² (*339 per mile²*).
Administrative HQ: County Hall, Taunton.
Highest point above sea-level: Dunkery Beacon 519 m (*170 ft*).

Road lengths:	km	miles
motorway	53·1	33·0
trunk	96·6	60·0
principal	630·5	391·8
classified	3557·3	2210·5
unclassified	3067·4	1906·0

Schools and colleges: Primary 233; Middle 9; Secondary 29; Special 8; Colleges of further and higher education 6.
Places of interest: Cheddar Gorge; Wookey Hole; Wells Cathedral; Exmoor National Park; Glastonbury Abbey (ruins).
County worthies by birth: St Dunstan (*c.* 909-88); Roger Bacon (1214-94); John Pym (1584-1643); Robert Blake (1598-1657); Henry Fielding (1707-54); Sir Henry Irving (1838-1905); John Hanning Speke (1827-64); Ernest Bevin (1881-1951).

South Glamorgan

First recorded use of name and derivation: 1242 (Gwlad Morgan) the terrain of Morgan, a 10th century Welsh Prince.
Area: 416 km² (*161 miles²*).
Population: 399 500.
Density: 960 per km² (*2481 per mile²*).
Administrative HQ: County Hall, Atlantic Wharf, Cardiff.
Highest point above sea-level: Near Lisvane 264 m (*866 ft*).

Road lengths:	km	miles
motorway and trunk	64	40
principal	103	64
other	1579	981

Schools and colleges: Nursery 10; Primary 156; Secondary 28; Special 15; Establishments of further and higher education 4.
Places of interest: Cardiff: Castle, National Museum of Wales, The Welsh Industrial and Maritime Museum; Llandaff Cathedral; St Fagan's Castle (Welsh Folk Museum); St Donat's Castle; Fonmon Castle; Llantwit Major.

South Yorkshire*

First recorded use of name and derivation: *c.* AD 150 Ebórakon (Ptolemy). 1050 (Eoferwicscir), land possessed by Eburos.
Area: 1560 km² (*602 miles²*).
Population: 1 297 900.
Density: 832 per km² (*2155 per mile²*).
Administrative HQ: No central authority. Functions rest with individual Boroughs.
Highest point above sea-level: Margery Hill 546 m (*1793 ft*).

Road lengths (1986):	km	miles
motorway	118·0	73·3
trunk	133·0	82·6
classified	1339·0	832·0
unclassified	3413·0	2120·7

Schools and colleges: Nursery 10; Primary 565; Secondary 89; Special 29; Establishments of further education 13; Polytechnic 1.
Places of interest: Sheffield: Cathedral Church of SS Peter and Paul, Cutler's Hall, Abbeydale Industrial Hamlet, Bishops House, Kelham Island Industrial Museum, Cusworth Hall; Conisbrough Castle, Doncaster; Roche Abbey, Rotherham (ruins); Barnsley: Cannon Hall, Cawthorne Victoria Jubilee, Monk Bretton Priory, Worsborough Mill.
County worthies by birth: Thomas Osborne, Earl of Danby (1631-1712); Gordon Banks (b. 1938).

Staffordshire

First recorded use of name and derivation: 1016 (Staeffordscir), the shire around a ford by a *staeth* or landing place.
Area: 2716 km² (*1048 miles²*).
Population: 1 022 900 (1988 estimate).
Density: 377 per km² (*976 per mile²*).
Administrative HQ: County Buildings, Stafford.
Highest point above sea-level: Oliver Hill, near Flash, 513 m (*1684 ft*).

Road lengths:	km	miles
motorway	71	44
trunk	234	145
principal 'A'	601	373
class II	367	228
class III	1375	854
unclassified	3576	2222

Schools and colleges: Nursery 27; Primary 423; Middle 14; Secondary 71; Special 30; Sixth form college 1; Establishments of further and higher education 12; Polytechnic.
Places of interest: Lichfield Cathedral; Croxden Abbey; Cannock Chase; Alton Towers; Tamworth Castle; Shugborough Hall and County Museum; Stafford Castle; Gladstone Pottery Museum; Drayton Manor Park and Zoo; Wedgwood Visitor Centre; City Museum and Art Gallery, Stafford; Chatterley Whitfield Mining Museum; Peak District National Park; Tutbury Castle; Weston Park.
County worthies by birth: Isaak Walton (1593-1683); Admiral George Anson (1697-1762); Dr Samuel Johnson (1709-84); Josiah Wedgwood (1730-95); Admiral Earl of St Vincent (1735-1823); Sir Robert Peel (1788-1850); Arnold Bennett (1867-1931); Havergal Brian (1876-1972); Sir Stanley Matthews (b. 1915).

Strathclyde

First recorded use of name and derivation: *c.* AD 85 Clota, the river (per Tacitus) AD 875 Straecled Wenla cyning.

Shugborough Hall. (Staffordshire County Council)

Area: 13 856 km² (*5348 miles²*).
Population: 2 332 537.
Density: 168 per km² (*436 per mile²*).
Administrative HQ: Strathclyde House, 20 India St, Glasgow G2 4PF.
Highest point above sea-level: Bidean nam Bian 1147 m (*3766 ft*).
Districts (with population): Argyll and Bute 65 737; Bearsden and Milngavie 40 365; Clydebank 48 573; Clydesdale 58 436; Cumbernauld and Kilsyth 62 547; Cumnock and Doon Valley 43 302; Cunninghame 137 265; Dumbarton 79 704; East Kilbride 81 718; Eastwood 57 185; Glasgow (city) 715 621; Hamilton 107 018; Inverclyde 96 382; Kilmarnock and Loudoun 81 186; Kyle and Carrick 112 999; Monklands 106 187; Motherwell 147 542; Renfrew 201 295; Strathkelvin 89 475.

Road lengths:	km	miles
regional motorway	46	28·5
trunk motorway	98	60·9
trunk	728	452·0
principal	1700	1056·0
non principal	3674	2283·0
unclassified	6809	4231·0

Schools and colleges: Nursery 269; Primary 903; Secondary 190; Special schools and centres 185; Establishments of further education 21.
Places of interest: Fingal's Cave (Isle of Staffa); Iona; Loch Lomond; Dumbarton Rock and Castle; Newark Castle; Glasgow Cathedral; Bothwell Castle (ruins); Culzean Castle (National Trust for Scotland); Burns' Cottage and Museum (Alloway); Inveraray Castle; Brodick Castle; Rothesay Castle (Isle of Bute); Paisley Abbey; Kelvingrove Art Galleries and Museum, Burrell Collection, Glasgow; Livingstone Memorial, Blantyre; Dean Castle, Kilmarnock; Summerlee Heritage Park, Coatbridge; Strathclyde Park.
County worthies by birth: Sir William Wallace (1274–1305); James Watt (1736–1819); James Boswell (1740–95); William Murdoch (1754–1839); Robert Burns (1759–96); David Livingstone (1813–73); Lord Kelvin (1824–1907); John Boyd Dunlop (1840–1921); James Keir Hardie (1856–1915); Sir Alexander Fleming (1881–1955); John Logie Baird (1888–1946).

Suffolk

First recorded use of name and derivation: AD 895 (Suthfolchi), the territory of the southern folk (of East Anglia).
Area: 3800 km² (*1467 miles²*).
Population: 635 000.
Density: 170 per km² (*433 per mile²*).
Administrative HQ: County Hall, Ipswich.
Highest point above sea-level: Rede 128 m (*420 ft*).

Road lengths:	km	miles
trunk	263·0	163·4
principal	486·0	302·0
classified	2510·5	1560·0
unclassified	3057·6	1900·0

Schools and colleges: Nursery 1; Primary 267; Middle 41; High 39; Special 10; Colleges of further and higher education 5.
Places of interest: Flatford Mill and Willy Lott's Cottage; Framlingham Castle; Kyson Hill; Saxtead Green Windmill; Gainsborough's House; Laven-

Abbots Bromley Horn Dance – an ancient spectacle that takes place every year and is said to be unique in Europe. The dance starts at dawn and makes a 30-km (20-mile) circuit of local farms where the dancers are welcomed as bearers of good fortune and fertility. (Staffordshire County Council)

ham (Guild Hall, Wool Hall); Long Melford Church; Newmarket; Bury St Edmunds (Abbey ruins) and Cathedral (nave); Ickworth Mansion; The Maltings, Snape.
County worthies by birth: Thomas Wolsey (c. 1475–1530); Thomas Gainsborough (1727–88); Robert Bloomfield (1766–1823); John Constable (1776–1837); Edward Fitzgerald (1809–83); Sir Joseph Hooker (1817–1911); Cardinal Benjamin Britten (1913–76).

Surrey

First recorded use of name and derivation: AD 722 (Suthrige), from the Old English, *suthergé* or southern district.
Area: 1679 km² (*648 miles²*).
Population: 1 000 400.
Density: 596 per km² (*1543 per mile²*).
Administrative HQ: County Hall, Kingston upon Thames (i.e. outside the county). The traditional county town is Guildford. (At the time of going to press, there was a proposal to transfer Kingston upon Thames back to Surrey.)
Highest point above sea-level: Leith Hill 294 m (*965 ft*).
Road lengths:

	km	miles
motorway	106·7	66·3
trunk	62·5	38·8
principal	584·2	362·9
classified	997·1	619·3
unclassified	2881·0	1789·0

Schools and colleges: Nursery 5; Primary and middle 378; Secondary 61; Special 31; Establishments of further and higher education 7.
Places of interest: Guildford Cathedral; Waverley Abbey; Royal Horticultural Society Gardens, Wisley; Box Hill; Polesden Lacey; Loseley House.
County worthies by birth: William of Ockham (d. 1349?); John Evelyn (1620–1706); William Cobbett (1762–1835); Thomas Malthus (1766–1834); Mathew Arnold (1822–88); Aldous Huxley (1894–1936); Sir Lawrence Olivier (b. 1907).

Tayside

First recorded use of name and derivation: c. AD 85 *Taus* or *Tanaus* (Tacitus).
Area: 7668 km² (*2960 miles²*).
Population: 392 346.
Density: 51 per km² (*133 per mile²*).
Administrative HQ: Tayside House, Dundee.
Highest point above sea-level: Ben Lawers 1214 m (*3984 ft*).
Length of coastline: 122 km (*76 miles*).
Districts (with population): Angus 94 407; Dundee 176 208; Perth and Kinross 122 988.

Road lengths:

	km	miles
motorway	55	34
trunk	230	143
principal	711	442
classified	1844	1146
unclassified	1994	1239

Schools and colleges: Nursey 27; Primary 191; Secondary 32; Special 28; Establishments of further education 3.

Places of interest: Glamis Castle; Arbroath Abbey (ruins); Brechin Cathedral and Round Tower; Scone Palace; Bridge of Dun (near Montrose); Guthrie Castle; Blair Castle; Edzell Castle; Loch Leven Castle; Queen's View, Loch Tummel; Pitlochry Ladder and Fish Dam.

County worthies by birth: Pontius Pilate *fl* AD 36; James Chalmers (1822–53); Sir James Barrie (1860–1937); John Buchan 1st Baron Tweedsmuir (1875–1940); HRH The Princess Margaret, Countess of Snowdon (b. 1930).

Tyne and Wear*

First recorded use of name and derivation: *c.* AD 150 Tina (river) (Ptolemy) and *c.* AD 720 Wirus (river) (Bede).

Area: 540 km² (*208 miles²*).

Population: 1 135 500.

Density: 2103 per km² (*5459 per mile²*).

Administrative HQ: No central authority. Functions rest with individual Boroughs.

Highest point above sea-level: Leadgate near Chopwell 259 m (*851 ft*).

Road lengths:

	km	miles
motorway	9·0	5·5
trunk	63·0	39·1
principal	320·0	198·8
classified	456·0	283·3
unclassified	3190·0	1982·1

Schools and colleges: (administered at District Council level) Nursery 31; Primary and Middle 443; Secondary 79; Special 39; Colleges of further education 7; Polytechnics 2.

Places of interest: Church of St Andrew's Byker; Monkwearmouth (ruins); Tynemouth Castle and Priory; Washington Old Hall Plummer Tower; South Shields Roman Fort.

County worthies by birth: The Venerable Bede (673–735); Admiral (1st) Lord Collingwood (1750–1810); Sir Joseph Swann (1828–1914); Owen Brannigan (1908–73); Cardinal Basil Hume, Archbishop of Westminster (b. 1923).

Warwickshire

First recorded use of name and derivation: the name was recorded in 1001 and means dwellings by the weir.

Area: 1981 km² (*765 miles²*).

Population: 484 200.

Density: 244 per km² (*633 per mile²*).

Administrative HQ: Shire Hall, Warwick.

Highest point above sea-level: Ilmington Downs 260 m (*854 ft*).

Road lengths:

	km	miles
motorway	79	49
trunk	236	147
principal	297	184
classified	1188	738
unclassified	1695	1053

Schools and colleges: Nursery 9; Primary 252; Secondary 40; Special 16; Establishments of further and higher education 5.

Places of interest: Warwick Castle; Kenilworth Castle; Stratford-upon-Avon (Shakespeare's birthplace); Compton Wynyates; Charlecote; Coughton Court; Ragley Hall; Arbury Hall.

County worthies by birth: Sir Fulke Greville, 1st Baron Brooke (1554–1628); Michael Drayton (1563–1631); William Shakespeare (1564–1616); Sir William Dugdale (1605–1686); Francis Willoughby (1613–1666); Walter Savage Landor (1775–1864); Marian Evans (George Eliot) (1819–80); Joseph Arch (1826–1919); Rupert Brooke (1887–1915).

West Glamorgan

First recorded use of name and derivation: 1242 (Gwlad Morgan) the terrain of Morgan, a 10th century Welsh Prince.

Area: 818 km² (*316 miles²*).

Population: 363 200.

Density: 444 per km² (*1149 per mile²*).

Administrative HQ: County Hall, Swansea.

Highest point above sea-level: Cefnffordd 600 m (*1969 ft*).

Road lengths:

	km	miles
motorway	35·0	21·8
trunk	37·0	23·0
principal	209·0	129·9
classified	320·0	198·9
unclassified	1104·3	686·2

Schools and colleges: Nursery 2; Primary 170; Secondary 27; Special 6; Colleges 4; Institute of higher education 1.

Places of interest: Neath Abbey (ruins); Penrice Castle; Gower Peninsula; Margam Park; Aberdulais Falls and Basin; Afan Argoed Forest Park; Cefn Coed Colliery Museum; Welsh Miners Museum; Penscynor Wildlife Park.

County worthies by birth: Wynford Vaughan Thomas (1908–87); Dylan Thomas (1914–53); Daniel Jones (b. 1912); Harry Secombe CBE (b. 1921); Richard Burton (1925–1984).

West Midlands*

First recorded use of name and derivation: 1555 mydlande, mid lands (applied to the middle counties of England).

Area: 899 km² (*347 miles²*).

Population: 2 632 300.

Density: 2928 per km² (*7586 per mile²*).

Administrative HQ: No central authority. Functions rest with individual Boroughs.

Highest point above sea-level: Turner's Hill 267 m (*876 ft*).

Road lengths (1986):

	km	miles
motorway	70·0	43·5
trunk	68·5	42·6
principal	596·9	370·9
classified	733·0	455·5
unclassified	5045·8	3135·4

Schools and colleges: Nursery 52; Primary (inc. Middle) 970; Secondary 201; Special 76; Establishments of further and higher education 20; Polytechnics 3.

Places of interest: Dudley Castle; Birmingham: Aston Hall, City Museum and Art Gallery, Museum of Science and Industry; Coventry Cathedral; Birmingham Cathedrals.

County worthies by birth: Sir Edward Burne-Jones

Statue of George Eliot at Nuneaton. (Warwickshire County Council)

Warwick Castle. (Warwickshire County Council)

(1833–98); George Cadbury (1839–1922); Sir Henry Newbolt (1862–1938); Neville Chamberlain (1869–1940); Sir Frank Whittle (b. 1907).

West Sussex

First recorded use of name and derivation: AD 722 (*Suth Seaxe*), the territory of the southern Saxons or *suthseaxa.*

Area: 2016 km² (*778 miles²*).

Population: 700 000.

Density: 347 per km² (*900 per mile²*).

Administrative HQ: County Hall, West St, Chichester.

Highest point above sea-level: Blackdown Hill 280 m (*919 ft*).

Road lengths:	km	miles
motorway	6·9	4·3
trunk	90·7	56·4
principal	490·8	305·0
classified	1248·8	776·0
unclassified	1907·0	1185·0

Schools and colleges: Nursery 4; Primary 218; Middle 23; Secondary 44; Sixth form colleges 3; Special 14; Colleges of further and higher education 5.

Places of interest: Chichester Cathedral; Arundel Castle; Goodwood House; Petworth House; Uppark; Fishbourne Roman Palace; Arundel Cathedral (RC); Nymans Gardens; Wakehurst Place; Bluebell Railway; South Downs.

County worthies by birth: John Selden (1584–1654); William Collins (1721–59); Percy Bysshe Shelley (1792–1822); Richard Cobden (1804–65).

West Yorkshire*

First recorded use of name and derivation: c. AD 150 Ebórakon (Ptolemy), 1050 (Eoferwicscir), land possessed by Eburos.

Area: 2039 km² (*787 miles²*).

Population: 2 053 100.

Density: 1007 per km² (*2608 per mile²*).

Administrative HQ: County Hall, Wakefield.

Highest point above sea-level: Black Hill 581 m (*1908 ft*).

Road lengths (1986):	km	miles
motorway	63·0	39·1
trunk	100·0	62·1

principal	499·0	*310·0*
classified	607·8	*377·7*
unclassified	3550·7	*2206·4*

Schools and colleges: Nursery 91; Primary and middle 883; Secondary (various) 141 (inc. Sixth form colleges); Special 70; Establishments of further and higher education 23; Polytechnics 2.

Places of interest: Brontë Museum (Haworth); Kirkstall Abbey; Ilkley Moor; Temple Newsam House; Harewood House; Wakefield Cathedral.

County worthies by birth: Sir Martin Frobisher (*c.* 1535–94); Thomas Fairfax (1612–71); Thomas Chippendale (1718–79); Joseph Priestley (1733–1804); Charlotte Brontë (1816–55); Emily Brontë (1818–48); Anne Brontë (1820–49); Henry Herbert, Lord Asquith (1852–1928); Frederick Delius (1862–1934); Wilfred Rhodes (1877–1973); John Boynton Priestley (1894–1984); Barbara Hepworth (1903–75); James Harold Wilson (Baron Wilson of Rievaulx) (b. 1916).

Western Isles

First recorded use of name and derivation: Possibly 14th century (during the reign of David II the style 'Lord of the Isles' appears, whereas in the Treaty of Perth, 1266, the Norse name *sudreys* is used).
Area: 2901 km² (*1120 miles²*).
Population: 31 048.
Density: 11 per km² (*28 per mile²*).
Administrative HQ: Council Offices, Stornoway, Isle of Lewis.
Highest point above sea-level: Clisham, Harris 799 m (*2622 ft*).
Main Islands: The largest islands in the Long Island archipelago.

	km²	*miles²*
Lewis with Harris	2225·3	*859·2*
North Uist	351·5	*135·7*
South Uist	332·5	*128·4*
Road lengths:	km	*miles*
classified	426	*265*
unclassified	299	*186*

Schools and colleges: Primary 43; Secondary 15; College of further education 1.
Places of interest: Kisimul Castle (Isle of Barra); Kilpheder (South Uist); Callanish – stone circle and cairn (Isle of Lewis); St Kilda; Rockall; St Clement's Church, Rodel (Isle of Harris).
Islands worthy by birth: Flora Macdonald (1722–90).

Wiltshire

First recorded use of name and derivation: AD 878 (Wiltunscire), the shire around *Wiltun* (tun, town) on the River Wylye.
Area: 3481 km² (*1344 miles²*).
Population: 555 000.
Density: 159 per km² (*413 per mile²*).
Administrative HQ: County Hall, Trowbridge.
Highest point above sea-level: Milk Hill and Tan Hill (or St Anne's Hill) 293 m (*964 ft*).

Road lengths:	km	*miles*
motorway	53·1	*33·0*
trunk	135·2	*84·0*
principal	631·0	*392·0*
classified	2043·0	*1269·0*
unclassified	2099·0	*1304·0*

Schools and colleges: Primary 284; Middle and Secondary 44; Special 13; Establishments of further education 7.

Places of interest: Salisbury Cathedral; Longleat; Stonehenge; Avebury Stone Circle; Wilton House; Stourhead; Windmill Hill.
County worthies by birth: 1st Duke of Somerset (*c.* 1500–52); Thomas Hobbes (1588–1679); Edward (Hyde) 1st Earl of Clarendon (1609–74); Sir Christopher Wren (1632–1723); Joseph Addison (1672–1719); William H. F. Talbot (1800–77); Sir Isaac Pitman (1813–97).

England's Regises

The use of the suffix 'Regis' – meaning 'of the King' – is used in the names of 12 places in England. In most cases the term has arisen from local usage to distinguish a Royal Manor, rather than from any exercise of prerogative by the sovereign.

	Earliest Mention
Bere Regis, Dorset	1244
Bognor Regis, West Sussex (1929)*	680
Grafton Regis, Northamptonshire	1204
Houghton Regis, Bedfordshire	1353
Kingsbury Regis, Somerset	1200
Letcombe Regis, Berkshire	1136
Lyme Regis, Dorset	1285
Lynn Regis, Norfolk (1537)*	1085
Melcombe Regis, Dorset	1280
Milton Regis, Kent	
Rowley Regis, West Midlands (1933)*	1173
Wyke Regis, Dorset	998

* By royal prerogative.

Northern Ireland

Area: 14 120 km² (*5450 miles²*).
Population: 1 566 800 (1986 estimate).
Density: 111 per km² (*287 per mile²*).
Administrative HQ: Belfast.
Districts: The province is now divided into 26 districts, whose councils have responsibility for a wide range of local services including leisure, environmental, regulatory etc. The six geographical counties no longer exist as administrative units. Northern Ireland is divided into nine areas: five education and library areas plus four health and social services areas (other functions such as police, planning, roads, water, housing, fire services, etc., are run centrally from Stormont. The area boards are not directed elected: about a third of their members are district councillors while the rest are persons appointed by the appropriate United Kingdom minister. The six traditional geographic counties of Northern Ireland in order of size are:

County Tyrone

First recorded use of name and derivation: from Tir Eoghan, land of Eoghan (Owen son of Niall).
Area: 3400 km² (*1313 miles²*).
Former capital: Omagh on the river Strule.
Highest point: Sawel (in Sperrin Mts) 683 m (*2240 ft*).
Coastline length: nil.

County Antrim

First recorded use of name and derivation: from the 5th century monastery of Aentrebh.
Area: 3046 km² (*1176 miles²*).
Former capital: City of Belfast on the river Lagan.
Highest point: Trostan 544 m (*1817 ft*).
Coastline length: 145 km (*90 miles*).

County Down

First recorded use of name and derivation: From Dun, Irish gaelic for fort (i.e. St Patrick's fort).
Area: 2466 km² (*952 miles²*).
Former capital: Downpatrick on the river Quoile.
Highest point: Slieve Donard 852 m (*2796 ft*).
Coastline length: 201 km (*125 miles*).

County Londonderry

First recorded use of name and derivation: From the charter granted by James I in 1613 to the City of London (England) livery companies. Known as Derry prior to charter. 'Derry' is a corruption of the celtic *doire*, an oak grove *c.* AD 500.
Area: 2075 km² (*801 miles²*).
Former capital: City of Londonderry on the river Foyle.
Highest point: Sawel 683 m (*2240 ft*).
Coastline length: 29 km (*18 miles*).

County Fermanagh

First recorded use of name and derivation: from Fir Mhanach, territory of the men of Managh.
Area: 1851 km² (*715 miles²*).
Former capital: Enniskillen.
Highest point: Cuilcagh 667 m (*2188 ft*).
Coastline length: nil.

County Armagh

First recorded use of name and derivation: from Queen Macha *c.* 3rd century BC.
Area: 1326 km² (*512 miles²*).
Former capital: Armagh on the Blackwater tributary Callan.
Highest point: Slieve Gullion 577 m (*1894 ft*).
Coastline length: 3·2 km (*2 miles*).

Britain's prehistory

Britain's recorded *history* begins with the earliest known references to the island by Himilco (*c.* 525 BC) who was writing in the North African city of Carthage. Events prior to this belong to prehistory (a term which was coined by Daniel Wilson in 1851).

The events of prehistory are continuously reassessed as new dating methods are advanced. A major tool of modern archaeology is radiocarbon dating, a technique invented by the American Dr Willard F. Libby in 1949. This is based upon the decay rate of the radioactive carbon isotope C14 whose half-life is 5730 years (it was formerly thought to be 5568 years, a difference which clearly has an impact on dating archaeological finds).

Other modern methods of dating include dendrochronology (which is calibration by the study of tree-rings, a technique developed by Professor C. W. Ferguson since 1969), luminescence, pollen analysis and amino-acid testing.

BC
c. 400 000
Disputed evidence for *Homo erectus*, predecessor of *H. sapiens* in paleolithic hand-axes found 1975 near Westbury-sub-Mendip, Somerset.

?285 000–240 000
Anglian glaciation possibly contemporary with the Alpine Mindel glaciation with ice sheets reaching the Thames valley. Human occupation (known as pre-Hoxnian) may have occurred during a warmer interstadial phase (that is a period of brief duration in between two glacial stages) between advances of this glaciation. The coarse hand-axe culture, evidence of which has been found at Fordwich in Kent and Kent's Cavern, near Torquay, in Devon belongs to this period.

?240 000–130 000
Hoxnian interglacial (so named after Hoxne site, Suffolk, discovered 1797). The earliest British human remains (discovered at Swanscombe in Kent by Marston, 1935–6) date from this period. The Swanscombe site also yielded flake assemblages and evidence of a hand-axe industry. Sea level was then 30–35 m (*98–114 ft*) above the present base.

130 000–105 000
Wolstonian glaciation (named from a site at Wolston in Warwickshire) probably contemporary with the Alpine Riss glaciation.

105 000–75 000
Ipswichian interglacial – sea level 8 m (*26 ft*) above present base.

75 000–19 000
Last or Devensian glaciation, contemporary with the Alpine Würm glaciation, reaching to the latitude of York. Britain was probably discontinuously unpopulated but populated during the warmer Chelford interstadial of 59 000 BC and during a further interstadial of 40 000 to 36 000 BC.

26 700±450
Earliest radiocarbon dating from the Upper Palaeolithic period – Kent's Cavern (see above).

18 000–14 000
Maximum extension of ice-sheets. Sea-level fall of 100–150 m (*328–492 ft*).

10 500–8000
Mesolithic Creswellian period and the close of the late Upper Palaeolithic era.

c. 9050
Irish Sea land-bridge breached.

8400
Start of the present Flandrian post-glacial period. Mesolithic man may have had herds by 4300 BC.

c. **6850**
The North Sea land-bridge between Humberside
and Holland breached by rising sea-level.

c. **6450**
The English Channel attained its current width
under the extension of the sea known as the
Flandrian transgression.

6100
Earliest dated habitation in Scotland – microlithic
industry at Morton in Fife.

4580
Earliest dated habitation in Ireland – Neolithic site
at Ballynagilly, Tyrone, two centuries earlier than
England's earliest Neolithic sites at Broome Heath,
Norfolk; Findon, West Sussex; and Lambourn,
Berkshire.

4210–3990
Earliest dated British farming site at Hembury,
Devon (first excavated 1934–5).

3795
Earliest dated pottery at Ballynagilly (see above).

3650–3400
Avebury Stone Circle building, Wiltshire.

2930–2560
Giant Silbury Hill round barrow, Wiltshire.

2760
Earliest Bronze Age dating with Beaker pottery
from Ballynagilly (see above), four centuries before
earliest English datings at Chippenham, Cambridge and Mildenhall, Suffolk.

2285–2075
Phase I at Stonehenge (ditch construction).

1260
Earliest dated hill-fort, Ivinghoe, Buckinghamshire.

c. **750**
Introduction of iron into Britain from Hallstatt by
the Celts. Hill-forts proliferate.

c. **308**
First circumnavigation of Great Britain by Pytheas
the Greek sea-captain from Massilia (Marseille).

c. **300**
Provisional date from palaeobotanical evidence
of 'Lindow Man', a victim of ritual sacrifice
whose remarkably preserved remains have been
found in the bog of Lindow Moss, near Wilmslow
in Cheshire.

c. **125**
Introduction of Gallo-Belgic gold coinage via Kent
from the Beauvais region of France.

c. **90**
Earliest British coinage – Westerham gold staters so
named after the hoard find in Kent in 1927.

55 (26 Aug.)
Julius Caesar's exploratory expedition with 7th and
10th legions and 98 ships from Boulogne and
Ambleteuse.

54 (18 or 21 July)
Second Roman invasion with five legions and 2000
cavalry.

AD
43
Third (Claudian) Roman invasion and the start of
the Roman Occupation.

Roman Era, 55 BC–AD 410

Caesar arrived off Dover from Boulogne with 98
transports and two legions in the early hours of 26
Aug 55 BC. He landed against opposition from
Cantii between Deal and Walmer. Repeated skir-
mishing prevented the reconnaisance being a success and Caesar withdrew. He returned in 54 BC (on
either 18 or 21 July) with five legions and 800 vessels, and encamped on the Kentish shore and
crossed the Thames near Brentford. He was much
harried by the British leader, Cassivellaunus, based
on the old Belgic capital of St Albans (*Verulamium*).
The attempt to conquer Britain was not successful.
It was nearly a century later in AD 43 when the
third Roman landing was made with some 20000
men in three waves under the command of
Plautius. This invasion is referred to as the
Claudian Invasion, after the Roman emperor of
that time. The British leader, Cunobelinus, was
aged but resistance remained bitter. Roman
cruelties against the king of the Iceni tribe and his
family in East Anglia fired a native 'death or liberty'
revolt under his widow, Queen Bodicca (Boadicea)
in AD 61. Colchester (*Camulodunum*), London
(*Londinium*) and St Albans were in turn sacked. The
total death roll was put at 70000 by Tacitus.
Boadicea's horde of some 80000 was met by
Suetonius' 14th and 20th Legions of 10000 men on
a battlefield perhaps near Hampstead Heath,
North London. For the loss of only about 400 of the
fully-armed Romans, 70000 Britons were claimed
to have been killed. Subjugation, however, was not
achieved until AD 83, when Agricola, the Roman
Governor, won the Battle of Mons Graupius, suggested by some to be the Pass of Killiecrankie,
Tayside.
For nearly 300 years the Roman régime brought
law, order, peace, food, and even unknown warmth
and cleanliness for the few who aspired to villas.
The legions recruited locally to maintain 40000
troops, garrisoned at Chester, Caerleon-on-Usk,
York, and Hadrian's Wall. Hadrian arrived in Britain in 122 after the annihilation of the 9th Legion
by the Picts. The 120 km (*74½ mile*) long wall across
the Tyne–Solway isthmus was built between AD 122
and 129. The 59·5 km (*37 mile*) long Forth–Clyde or
Antonine Wall was built *c.* 150, but was abandoned
within 40 years. Emperor Severus re-established
military order in the period 208–11, but by the time
of Carausius, who ruled in 287–93, raids by the Saxons (the name comes from the word *Seax* meaning a
short, one-handed sword) from the Schleswig-Holstein area were becoming increasingly trouble-
some. In 400 Theodosius in turn sent his general,

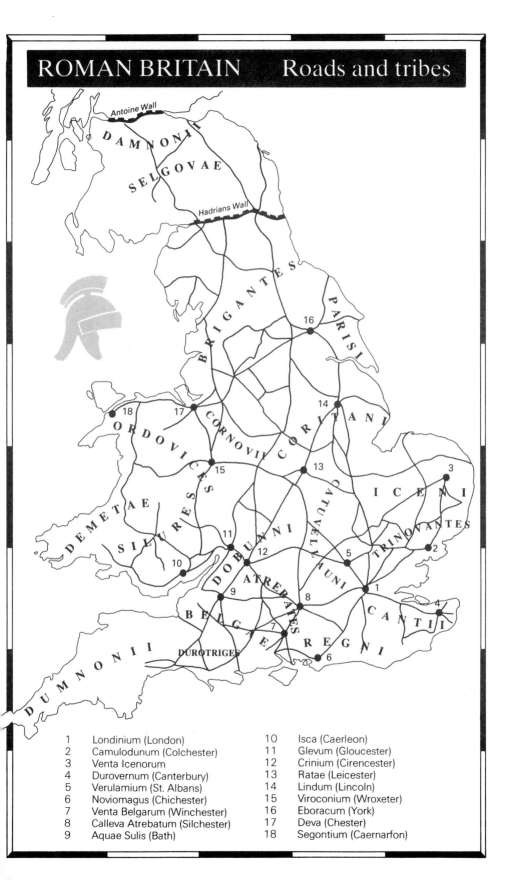

ROMAN BRITAIN   Roads and tribes

Antoine Wall

DAMNONII

SELGOVAE

Hadrians Wall

BRIGANTES

PARISI

ORDOVICES

CORNOVII

CORITANI

DEMETAE

SILURES

DOBUANI

CATUVELAUNI

ICENI

TRINOVANTES

ATREBATES

BELGAE

REGNI

CANTII

DUMNONII

DUROTRIGES

1	Londinium (London)	10	Isca (Caerleon)
2	Camulodunum (Colchester)	11	Glevum (Gloucester)
3	Venta Icenorum	12	Crinium (Cirencester)
4	Durovernum (Canterbury)	13	Ratae (Leicester)
5	Verulamium (St. Albans)	14	Lindum (Lincoln)
6	Noviomagus (Chichester)	15	Viroconium (Wroxeter)
7	Venta Belgarum (Winchester)	16	Eboracum (York)
8	Calleva Atrebatum (Silchester)	17	Deva (Chester)
9	Aquae Sulis (Bath)	18	Segontium (Caernarfon)

Stilicho, to deliver the Province from the ever-increasing pressure of the barbarians, but by 402 he was forced to recall the Roman garrison to help resist the incursions in Northern Italy of the Visigoths under Alaric. In 405 there was mutiny in the remaining garrison in Britain, who elected Gratianus, a Briton, as rival emperor. In 410 Emperor Honorius told the Britons from Rome that they must 'defend themselves' against the Saxons, Picts, and Scots.

AD 410-1066

British rulers between the end of the Roman occupation (AD 410) and the Norman conquest (1066).
By 449 a Jutish Kingdom had been set up in Kent by Hengist and Horsa. The 5th and 6th centuries were a period of utter confusion and misery with conflict between the English and the remaining Britons, whose last champion was reputedly King Arthur. Some time between 493 and 503 the Britons fought the Battle of Mountbadon against the Saxon invaders on an uncertain site, usually ascribed to Liddington Camp, Badbury, near Swindon, Wiltshire.

England (excluding Cumbria) did not again become a unified state before AD 954 when Athelstan united the country. Until then England was divided between a number of small kingdoms, traditionally said to be seven (the Heptarchy) but, in fact, more. Some earlier kings exercised direct rule over all England for intermittent periods during their reigns. Edward the Elder (899-924 or 925), son of Alfred (871-99) the most famous of the Kings of the West Saxons, had suzerainty over the whole of England though he did not directly rule the Danish kingdom of York, which was not finally extinguished until 954.

By the end of the 7th century most of southern Britain was divided between eight main kingdoms and a smaller number of 'sub-kingdoms', which were at times independent.
The map on p. 523 shows the situation as it existed in the early 8th century.

Kingdom	'Capital' Principal seat of King
[1] **Northumbria** Before 654 Northumbria was divided into	York
[1a] BERNICIA founded 547	Bamburgh
[1b] DEIRA founded 558	York

The kingdom of Northumbria was finally overthrown by the invading Danes in 878.

[2] **Lindsey**	Lincoln

Founded after 550; dependent on Mercia after c. 715; absorbed by Mercia between 790 and 795.

[3] **Mercia**	Tamworth

Founded c. 595; acknowledged overlordship of Wessex 829; divided between Wessex and the Danes from 880.

Two 'sub-kingdoms' briefly enjoyed independence but were more usually dependent upon the kings of Mercia.

[3a] **KINGDOM OF THE HWICCE**	Winchcombe

Founded 628; finally absorbed by Mercia 788.

[3b] **KINGDOM OF THE MAGONSAETAN**	Leominster

(Sometimes known as the Kingdom of the West Angles) founded c. 645; finally absorbed by Mercia 725.

[4] **East Anglia**	Elmham

Founded c. 600; dependent on Mercia c. 740-835; a Danish kingdom 876-917.

[5] **Essex**	London

(*London* until c. 730 when Middlesex and Hertfordshire were lost to Mercia; *Colchester* after c. 730.)
Founded before 604; dependent on Mercia after c. 730; absorbed by Wessex c. 825.

[6] **Kent**	Canterbury

Founded c. 455; dependent on Mercia from c. 786; absorbed by Wessex 825.

[7] **Sussex**	Chichester

Founded 477; absorbed by Mercia c. 774.

[8] **Wessex**	Winchester

Founded – as the principality of the Gewissae – 519; unified England 954.

In the late 9th and early 10th century much of England was occupied by the Danes. By the end of the 9th century the map of 'England' would have appeared like that on p. 524.

Kingdom	Principal seat of King
[1] **Saxon Earldom of Bamburgh**	Bamburgh

A remnant of the kingdom of Northumbria; absorbed by the Danish kingdom of York before 920.

[2] **Danish Kingdom of York**	York

Founded c. 875; overthrown by Wessex 954.

[3] **'The Five Boroughs'**	
[3a] Borough of Lincoln	
[3b] Borough of Nottingham	
[3c] Borough of Leicester	
[3d] Borough of Derby	
[3e] Borough of Stamford	

Five autonomous Danish communities, each based upon a stronghold.

[4] **Danish Kingdom in East Anglia**	Bury St Edmunds

Founded 876; overthrown by Wessex 916.

[5] **Saxon Kingdom of Wessex**	Winchester

See above.

[6] **Earldom of Mercia**	Tamworth

Taken from the Danes by Mercia 886; dependent on Wessex 886 onwards; fully absorbed by Wessex by 920.

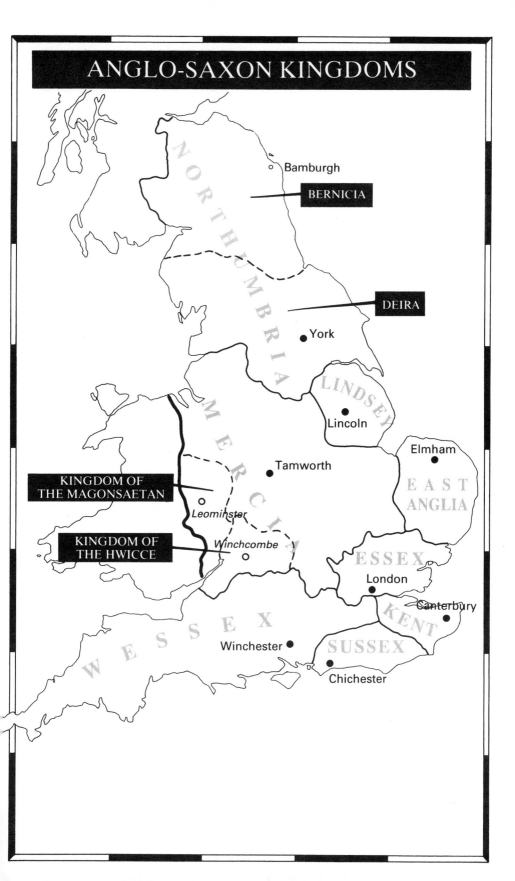

ANGLO-SAXON KINGDOMS

BERNICIA

DEIRA

KINGDOM OF
THE MAGONSAETAN

KINGDOM OF
THE HWICCE

NORTHUMBRIA

MERCIA

LINDSEY

EAST
ANGLIA

ESSEX

KENT

SUSSEX

WESSEX

Bamburgh

York

Lincoln

Elmham

Tamworth

Leominster

Winchcombe

London

Canterbury

Winchester

Chichester

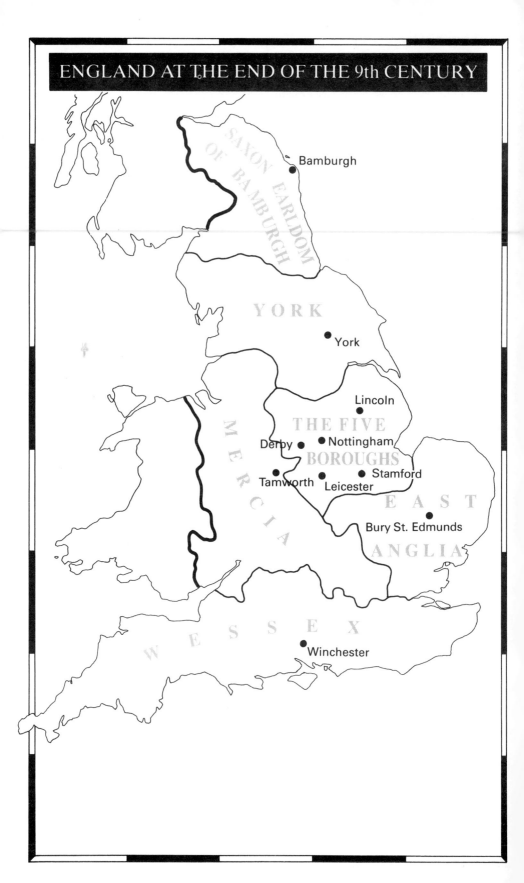

ENGLAND AT THE END OF THE 9th CENTURY

Bamburgh

SAXON EARLDOM OF BAMBURGH

YORK

York

Lincoln

THE FIVE

Derby • Nottingham

BOROUGHS

Tamworth • Leicester • Stamford

MERCIA

EAST

Bury St. Edmunds

ANGLIA

WESSEX

Winchester

The West Saxon King Egbert (802–39), grandfather of King Alfred, is often quoted as the first King of All England from AD 829, but in fact he never reduced the Kingdom of Northumbria ruled by Eanred (808 or 810 to 840 or 841).

Kings of All England

Athelstan, eldest son of the eldest son of King Alfred of the West Saxons, acceded 924 or 925. The first to establish rule over all England (excluding Cumbria) in 927; d. 27 Oct 939 aged over 40 years.

Edmund, younger half-brother of Athelstan; acceded 939 but did not regain control of all England until 944–45. Murdered, 26 May 946 by Leofa at Pucklechurch, near Bristol, Avon.

Edred, younger brother of Edmund; acceded May 946. Effectively King of All England 946–48, and from 954 to his death, on 23 Nov 955. Also intermittently during the intervening period.

Edwy, son of Edmund, b. *c.* 941; acceded November 955 (crowned at Kingston, Greater London); lost control of Mercians and Northumbrians in 957; d. 1 Oct 959 aged about 18.

Edgar, son of Edmund, b. 943; acceded October 959, as King of All England (crowned at Bath, 11 May 973); d. 8 July 975, aged *c.* 32.

Edward the Martyr, son of Edgar by Aethelflaed, b. *c.* 962; acceded 975; d. 18 Mar 978 or 979, aged 16 or 17.

Ethelred (*Unraed*, i.e. ill-counselled), second son of Edgar by Aelfthryth, b. ?968–69; acceded 978 or 979 (crowned at Kingston, 14 Apr 978 or 4 May 979); dispossessed by the Danish king, Swegn Forkbeard, 1013–14; d. 23 Apr 1016, aged *c.* 47 or 48.

Swegn Forkbeard, King of Denmark 987–1014, acknowledged King of All England from about September 1013 to his death, 3 Feb 1014.

Edmund Ironside, prob. 3rd son of Ethelred, b. *c.* 992; chosen King in London, April 1016. In summer of 1016 made agreement with Cnut whereby he retained dominion only over Wessex; d. 30 Nov 1016.

Cnut, younger son of King Swegn Forkbeard of Denmark, b. *c.* 995. Secured Mercia and Danelaw, summer 1016; assumed dominion over all England December 1016; King of Denmark 1019–35. King of Norway 1028–1035; overlord of the King of the Scots and probably ruler of the Norse-Irish kingdom of Dublin; d. 12 Nov 1035, aged *c.* 40 years.

Harold Harefoot, natural son of Cnut by Aelfgifu of Northampton, b. ?*c.* 1016–17; chosen regent for half-brother, Harthacnut, late 1035 or early 1036; sole King 1037; d. 17 Mar 1040, aged *c.* 23 or 24 years.

Harthacnut, son of Cnut by Emma, widow of King Ethelred (d. 1016) b. ?*c.* 1018; titular King of Denmark from 1028; effectively King of England from June 1040; d. 8 June 1042, aged *c.* 24 years.

Edward the Confessor, senior half-brother of Harthacnut and son of King Ethelred and Emma, b. 1002–5; resided with Harthacnut from 1041, acceded 1042, crowned 3 Apr 1043, d. 5 Jan 1066, aged between 60 and 64. Sanctified.

Harold Godwinson, brother-in-law of Edward the Confessor and brother of his Queen Edith, son of Godwin, Earl of Wessex, b. ?*c.* 1020; acceded 6 Jan 1066; d. or k. 14 Oct 1066.

Edgar Etheling, chosen by Londoners as king after the Battle of Hastings, October 1066; not apparently crowned, submitted to William I before 25 Dec 1066; believed still living *c.* 1125.

Rulers in Wales (547–1289)

Wales was divided into half a dozen small kingdoms and principalities, which by the start of the 8th century numbered:

Kingdom/ Principality:	Roughly corresponded to:
Gwynedd	North West Wales
Powys	North East and Central Wales
Ceredigion	Cardiganshire
Ystrad Towy	West Glamorgan/Carmarthenshire

(Ceredigion and Ystrad Towy were united as the Kingdom of **Seisyllwg** by the 9th century)

Buellt	North Brecknock/Radnorshire
Gwent	Gwent
Brycheiniog	South Brecknock
Glywising	Mid and South Glamorgan
Dyfed	Pembrokeshire

By *c.* 1170 these had been reduced to three kingdoms shown on the accompanying map, p. 526.

Kingdom	Principal seat of King
1 **Gwynedd**	*Deganwy*

Founded before 547 by Maelgwn Hir; in 1152 Owain Gwynedd submitted to Henry II as his overlord and changed his title to Prince of Gwynedd; Llywelyn II united all of North Wales and assumed the title Prince of Wales (1258) but Edward I of England overran all Gwynedd except Anglesey (1277) and Llywelyn was killed trying to retake his principality (1282); English rule began over all Gwynedd in 1283.

2 **Powys** – under the same King of Gwynedd 855–1063 ruled by Princes 1075–1160; divided into two lordships – South Powys (Powys Wenwynwyn) 1160–1208 when the area passed under English rule and North Powys (Powys Fadog) 1160–1269 when the area passed under English rule.

3 **Deheubarth**	*Dinefor*

Founded as personal union of the territories of Hywel Dda, King of Dyfed 904–950, King of Seisyllwg 909–50 – the other territories of South Wales were united from this time; the last King Rhys ap Tewdwr was murdered in 1093; a smaller principality of Deheubarth lasted from 1135 to 1201 during which time South Wales was gradually absorbed by the English.

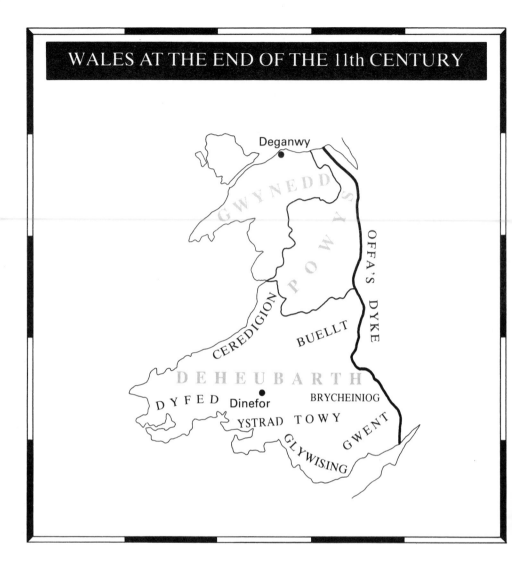

WALES AT THE END OF THE 11th CENTURY

Deganwy

GWYNEDD

POWYS

OFFA'S DYKE

CEREDIGION

BUELLT

DEHEUBARTH

DYFED   Dinefor   BRYCHEINIOG

YSTRAD   TOWY

GWENT

GLYWISING

Kings of Scotland

The formation of Scotland began in 843 when Kenneth I (MacAlpin), King of Dalriada (the kingdom of the Scots), became King of Caledonia (the kingdom of the Picts).

From the 6th to the 9th centuries, Scotland was divided into a number of smaller kingdoms whose names and boundaries were constantly changing. The map on p. 527 shows four of them.

	Kingdom	Principal seat of King
1	**Kingdom of the Isles** Covered the Western Isles, Orkney and Shetland – a Norse kingdom ruled from Scandinavia; reached its greatest extent in the middle of the 11th century.	

| 2 | **Strathclyde** | *Alclyde* (Dumbarton) |

2 Strathclyde   *Alclyde* (Dumbarton)
A British kingdom which included the sub-kingdom of Galloway; annexed by Scotland *c.* 1016.

3 Caledonia   *Scone*
The Pictish Kingdom; from 843 united with Dalriada as Alba.

4 Dalriada   *Dunstaffnage*
The Scottish kingdom; from 843 united with Caledonia as Alba.

Kings of Alba

Kenneth I (843–858/9), King of Dalriada from 841.

Donald I (858/9–862/3), brother of Kenneth I.

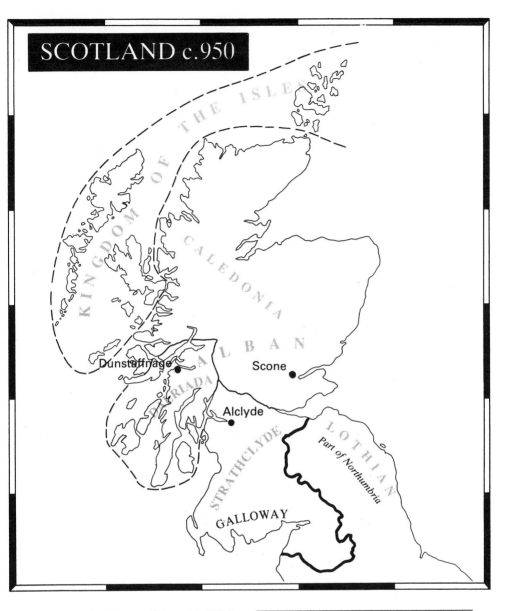

SCOTLAND c.950

Constantine I (862/3–877), son of Kenneth I. Killed in battle by the Danes.

Aedh (877–8), son of Kenneth I. Murdered by King Giric of Strathclyde.

Eochaid (878–89), nephew of Aedh. Deposed by Donald II.

Donald II (889–900), son of Constantine I.

Constantine II (900–42), son of Aedh. Abdicated to become Abbot of St Andrews; d. 952.

Malcolm I (942–54), son of Donald II. Murdered.

Indulf (954–62), son of Constantine II. Killed by the Vikings.

Dubh (962–966/7), son of Malcolm I. Murdered.

Culen (966/7–971), son of Indulf. Murdered.

Kings of Scots

Kenneth II (971–95), son of Malcolm I. Took the title King of Scots – Alba was from this time known as Scotland. Received Lothian from King Edgar of England.

Constantine III (995–7), son of Culen. Killed by Kenneth III.

Kenneth III (997–1005), son of Dubh. Killed by Malcolm II.

Malcolm II (1005–34), b. c. 954; d. 25 Nov 1034, aged c. 80 years. Formed the Kingdom of Scotland by annexing Strathclyde, c. 1016.

Duncan I (1034–40), son of Malcolm II's daughter, Bethoc.

Macbeth (1040–57), ?son of Malcolm II's daughter, Donada; d. aged c. 52 years.

Lulach (1057–8), stepson of Macbeth and son of his wife Gruoch; d. aged c. 26.

Malcolm III (Canmore) (1058–93), son of Duncan I; d. aged c. 62.

Donald Bane (1093–4 and 1094–7), son of Duncan I, twice deposed.

Duncan II (May–October 1094), son of Malcolm III; d. aged c. 34.

Edgar (1097–1107), son of Malcolm III, half-brother of Duncan II; d. aged c. 33.

Alexander I (1107–24), son of Malcolm III, brother of Edgar; d. aged c. 47.

David I (1124–53), son of Malcolm III and brother of Edgar; d. aged c. 68.

Malcolm IV (1153–65), son of Henry, Earl of Northumberland; d. aged c. 24.

William I (*The Lion*) (1165–1214), brother of Malcolm IV; d. aged c. 72 (from 1174 to 1189 King of England, acknowledged as overlord of Scotland).

Alexander II (1214–49), son of William I; d. aged 48.

Alexander III (1249–86), son of Alexander II; d. aged 44.

Margaret (Maid of Norway) (1286–90), daughter of Margaret (daughter of Alexander III) by King Eric II of Norway. Never visited her realm; d. aged 7.

First Interregnum 1290–2.

John (*Balliol*) (1292–6), son of Dervorguilla, a great-great-granddaughter of David I, awarded throne from 13 contestants by adjudication of Edward I who declared after four years that John would have to forfeit his throne for contumacy.

Second Interregnum 1296–1306.

Robert I (1306–29), son of Robert Bruce and grandson of a 1291 competitor; d. aged c. 55.

David II (1329–71), son of Robert I; d. aged 46. *Note:* Edward Balliol, son of John, was crowned King in 1332, acknowledged Edward III of England as overlord in 1333 and surrendered all claims to Scottish crown to him in 1356.

Robert II (1371–90), founder of the Stewart dynasty, son of Walter the Steward and Marjorie Bruce; d. aged 74.

Robert III (1390–1406), legitimated natural son of Robert II; d. aged c. 69.

James I (1406–37), son of Robert III, captured by English 13 days before accession and kept prisoner in England till March 1424; d. aged 42.

James II (1437–60), son of James I; d. aged 29.

James III (1460–88), son of James II; d. aged 36.

James IV (1488–1513), son of James III and Margaret of Denmark, married Margaret Tudor; d. aged 40.

James V (1513–42), son of James IV and Margaret Tudor; d. aged 30.

Mary (*Queen of Scots*) (1542–67), daughter of James V and Mary of Lorraine, acceded aged 6 or 7 days, abdicated 24 July 1567 and was succeeded by her son (James VI) (by her second husband, Henry Stuart, Lord Darnley). She was executed, 8 Feb 1587, aged 44.

James VI (1567–1625), son of Mary and Lord Darnley (see above), succeeded to the English throne as James I on 24 Mar 1603, so effecting a personal union of the two realms; d. aged 58.

The eleven royal houses of England since 1066

A royal dynasty normally takes its house name from the family's patronymic. It does not change by reason of a Queen Regnant's marriage – for example, Queen Victoria, a member of the House of Hanover and Brunswick, did not become a member of the House of Saxe-Coburg and Gotha (her husband's family) but her son, Edward VII, and her grandson, George V (until renamed in 1917), were members of the house of their respective fathers.

The House of Normandy (by right of conquest) (**69 years**)
The house name derives from the fact that William I was the 7th Duke of Normandy with the style William II. This was despite the fact that he was illegitimate because his father, Duke Robert II, had formally instituted as his legal heir.
William I (1066–87); William II (1087–1100); Henry I (1100–35) and Matilda.

The House of Blois (19 years)
The house name derives from the fact that the father of King Stephen was Stephen (sometimes called Henry), Count of Blois.
Stephen (1335–54).

The House of Anjou (331 years)
The house name derives from the fact that the father of King Henry II was Geoffrey V, 10th Count of Anjou and Maine. This family was alternatively referred to as the Angevins, the name deriving from Angers, the chief town of Anjou.
Henry II (1154–89) and the next 13 kings down to and including Richard III (1483–5).
Since the mid-15th century (and in fact less than 50 years before its male line became extinct) this house has been referred to as The House of Plantagenet. This name originates from Count Geoffrey's nickname 'Plantagenet', which in turn derived, it is said, from his habit of wearing a sprig of broom (*Planta genista*) in his cap during a crusade.
It is also usually sub-divided, after the deposing of Richard II in 1399, into The House of Lancaster with Henry IV (1399–1413); Henry V (1413–22); Henry VI (1422–61 and 1470–1), and The House of York with Edward IV (1461–83 – except 1470–1); Edward V (1483); Richard III (1483–5). The names Lancaster and York derived respectively from the titles of the 4th and 5th sons of Edward III; John of Gaunt (1340–99) was 1st Duke of Lancaster (of the second creation), and the father of Henry IV, and Edmund of Langley (1341–1402) was 1st Duke of York and a great-grandfather of Edward IV.

The House of Tudor (118 years)
This house name derives from the surname of Henry VII's father, Edmund Tudor, Earl of Richmond, and son of Sir Owen Tudor, by Catherine, widow of King Henry V.

Henry VII (1485–1509); Henry VIII (1509–47); Edward VI (1547–53); after the reign of Queen Jane, Mary I (1553–8); Elizabeth I (1558–1603).

The House of Grey or Suffolk (14 days)
This house name derives from the family and surname of the 3rd Marquess of Dorset, the father of Lady Guilford Dudley, who reigned as Queen Jane from 6 July 1553 for 14 days until 19 July when the House of Tudor regained the throne.

The House of Stuart and the House of Stuart and Orange (98 years and 5 years)
This house name is derived from the family and surname of Henry Stuart, Lord Darnley and Duke of Albany, the eldest son of Matthew, 4th Earl of Lennox. Lord Darnley was the second of three husbands and cousin of Mary Queen of Scots and the father of James VI of Scotland and I of England.

James I (1603–25); Charles I (1625–49); Charles II (de jure 1649 but de facto 1660–85); James II (1685–8).

The house name became The House of Stuart and Orange when in 1689 William III, son of William II, Prince of Orange, became the sovereign conjointly with his wife, Mary II, the 5th Stuart monarch.

The House of Stuart resumed from 1702 to 1714 during the reign of Queen Anne.

The House of Orange
William III reigned alone during his widowerhood from 1694 to 1702. William in fact possessed the sole regal power during his entire reign from 1689.

The House of Hanover and Brunswick-Lüneburg (187 years)
This house name derives from the fact that George I's father, Ernest Augustus, was the Elector of Hanover and a duke of the House of Brunswick-Lüneburg.

George I (1714–27); George II (1727–60); George III (1760–1820); George IV (1820–30); William IV (1830–7); Queen Victoria (1837–1901).

The House of Saxe-Coburg and Gotha (16 years)
This house name derives from the princely title of Queen Victoria's husband, Prince Albert, later Prince Consort.

Edward VII (1901–10); George V (1910–17); on 17 July 1917 King George V declared by Royal Proclamation that he had changed the name of the royal house to the House of Windsor.

The House of Windsor
George V (1917–36); Edward VIII (1936); George VI (1936–52); Elizabeth II (from 1952).

In the normal course of events Prince Charles, Prince of Wales, on inheriting the throne would become the first monarch of the House of Mountbatten, but by further Proclamations the Queen first declared in 1952 that her children and descendants would belong to the House of Windsor, and later in 1960 that this Declaration would only affect her descendants in the male line who will bear a royal style and title. Descendants outside this class will bear the surname 'Mountbatten-Windsor'.

Titles of the Royal House

Husbands of Queens Regnant
The husband of a queen regnant derives no title from his marriage. Philip II of Spain, husband of

Queen Mary I, was termed 'King Consort'. Prince George of Denmark, husband of Queen Anne, was created Duke of Cumberland. Prince Albert of Saxe-Coburg-Gotha, husband of Queen Victoria, was created 'Royal Highness' and 17 years after his marriage 'Prince Consort'. The Duke of Edinburgh, husband of Queen Elizabeth II, is HRH and a prince of the United Kingdom of Great Britain and Northern Ireland.

Queens Consort
A queen consort ranks with and shares the king's titles. In the event of her being widowed she cannot continue to use the title 'The Queen'. She must add to it her christian name and use the style additionally, or by itself, of 'Queen Mother' (if she has children), or, as in the case of the widow of King William IV, 'Queen Dowager'.

In the event of her re-marriage, which can only be with the consent of the Sovereign, she does not forfeit her royal status. The last such example was when Queen Catherine (Parr) married, as her fourth husband, Lord Seymour of Sudeley, KG, in 1547.

The Heir to the Throne
The Heir Apparent to the throne can only be the son or grandson (as in the case of the Prince of Wales from 1751 to 1760) of the reigning Sovereign. Should the first person in the order of succession bear any relationship other than in the direct male line, they are the Heir (or Heiress) Presumptive. The last Heiress Presumptive to the Throne was HRH the Princess Elizabeth (1936–52). A female could be an Heiress Apparent if she were the only or eldest daughter of a deceased Heir Apparent who had no male issue.

The eldest surviving son of a reigning Sovereign is born The Duke of Cornwall, The Duke of Rothesay, the Earl of Carrick and The Baron Renfrew, together with the styles of Lord of the Isles, Prince and Great Steward (or Seneschel) of Scotland. The titles Prince of Wales and Earl of Chester are a matter of creation and not of birthright. The Prince of Wales is a part of the establishment of The Order of the Garter. If, however, a Prince of Wales died, as in 1751, his eldest son would automatically succeed to that title and the Earldom of Chester but not to the Dukedom of Cornwall and the other honours because they are expressly reserved for the son (and not the grandson) of a Sovereign.

Princes, Princesses and Royal Highnesses
Since 1917 the style HRH Prince or Princess has been limited to the children of the Monarch and the children of the sons of the Monarch and their wives. Grandchildren of a Prince of Wales also would enjoy this style. In practice the sons of a Sovereign have a dukedom bestowed upon them after they become of age. Such 'Royal Dukedoms' only enjoy their special precedence (i.e. senior to the two Archbishops and other dukes) for the next generation. A third duke would take his seniority among the non-royal dukes according to the date of the original creation.

The title 'Princess Royal' is conferred (if vacant) for life on the eldest daughter of the Sovereign. HRH The Princess Anne was created Princess Royal in 1987.

The order of succession to the Crown

The order of succession is determined according to ancient Common Law rules but these may be upset by an enactment of the Crown in Parliament under powers taken in the Succession to the Crown Act of 1707, provided always (since 1931) that the parliaments of all the Members of the Commonwealth assent. At Common law the Crown descends lineally to the legitimate issue of the sovereign, males being preferred to females, in their respective orders of age. In the event of failure of such issue (e.g. King Edward VIII in 1936) the Crown passes to the nearest collateral being an heir at law. The common law of descent of the Crown specifically departs from the normal feudal rules of land descent at two points. First, in the event of two or more sisters being next in succession the eldest alone (e.g. The Princess Elizabeth from 1936 to 1952) shall be the heiress and shall not be merely a coparcener with her sister or sisters. Secondly, male issue by a second or subsequent marriage takes precedence over half sisters (e.g. King Edward VI, son of King Henry VIII's third wife, took precedence over Queen Mary I, daughter of his first marriage, and Queen Elizabeth I, daughter of his second marriage.

Below is set out the Order of Succession to the Crown.

1 The heir apparent is HRH The Prince CHARLES Philip Arthur George, KG, KT, The Prince of Wales, The Duke of Cornwall, The Duke of Rothesay, The Earl of Carrick, and the Baron Renfrew, Lord of the Isles and Great Steward of Scotland, b. 14 Nov 1948, then follows his son:

2 HRH Prince WILLIAM Arthur Philip Louis, b. 21 June 1982, then his brother:

3 HRH Prince HENRY Charles Albert David, b. 15 Sept 1984, then his uncle:

4 HRH The Prince ANDREW Albert Christian Edward, The Duke of York, The Earl of Inverness, and the Baron Killyleagh, b. 19 Feb 1960, then his daughter:

5 HRH Princess BEATRICE Elizabeth Mary of York, b. 8 Aug 1988, then her uncle:

6 HRH The Prince EDWARD Antony Richard Louis, b. 10 Mar 1964, then his sister:

7 HRH The Princess ANNE Elizabeth Alice Louise, The Princess Royal, Mrs Mark Phillips, b. 15 Aug 1950, then her son:

8 PETER Mark Andrew Phillips, b. 15 Nov 1977, then his sister:

9 Miss ZARA Anne Elizabeth Phillips, b. 15 May 1981, then her great-aunt:

10 HRH The Princess MARGARET Rose, CI, GCVO, The Countess of Snowdon, b. 21 Aug 1930, then her son:

11 DAVID Albert Charles Armstrong-Jones, Viscount Linley, b. 3 Nov 1961, then his sister:

12 The Lady SARAH Frances Elizabeth Armstrong-Jones, b. 1 May 1964, then her cousin, once removed:

13 HRH Prince RICHARD Alexander Walter George, Duke of Gloucester, b. 26 Aug 1944, then his son:

14 ALEXANDER Patrick George Richard, Earl of Ulster, b. 24 Oct 1974, then his sister:

15 The Lady DAVINA Elizabeth Alice Benedikte Windsor, b. 19 Nov 1977, then her sister:

16 The Lady ROSE Victoria Birgitte Louise Windsor, b. 1 Mar 1980, then her cousin once removed:

17 HRH Prince EDWARD George Nicholas Paul Patrick, GCVO, the (2nd) Duke of Kent, the Earl of St Andrews and the Baron Downpatrick, b. 9 Oct 1935, then his grandson:

18 EDWARD Edmund Maximilian George Windsor, Baron Downpatrick, b. 10 Dec 1988 (his father, Lord GEORGE Philip Nicholas Windsor, Earl of St Andrews, b. 26 June 1962, having forfeited his claim to the throne by his marriage (16 Jan 1988) to a Roman Catholic, Sylvana Tomaselli), then his uncle:

19 Lord NICHOLAS Charles Edward Jonathan Windsor, b. 25 July 1970, then his sister:

20 The Lady HELEN Marian Lucy Windsor, b. 28 Apr 1964, then her cousin:

21 Lord FREDERICK Michael George David Louis Windsor, b. 6 Apr 1979 (his father, HRH Prince MICHAEL George Charles Franklin of Kent, b. 4 July 1942, having forfeited his claim to the throne by his marriage (30 June 1978) to a Roman Catholic, Baroness Marie-Christine von Reibnitz), then his sister:

22 The Lady GABRIELA Marina Alexandra Ophelia Windsor, b. 23 Apr 1981, then her aunt:

23 HRH Princess ALEXANDRA Helen Elizabeth Olga Christabel of Kent, GCVO, the Lady Ogilvy, b. 25 Dec 1936, then her son:

24 JAMES Robert Bruce Ogilvy, Esq., b. 29 Feb 1964, then his sister:

25 Miss MARINA Victoria Alexandra Ogilvy, b. 31 July 1966, then her second cousin, once removed upwards, the Earl of Harewood.

Factors affecting the order

Two further factors should be borne in mind in determining the order of succession. First, no person may unilaterally renounce their right to succeed. Only an Act of Parliament can undo what another Act of Parliament (the Act of Settlement, 1701) has done. Secondly, some marriages among the descendants of George II are null and void and hence the descendants are not heirs at law, by failure to obtain the consent to marry as required by the Royal Marriage Act of 1772. In some cases this failure, prior to 1956, may have been inadvertent because it was only then confirmed by the House of Lords that every such descendant, born before 1948, is by a statute of 1705 deemed a British subject. So the escape from the requirements of the Royal Marriage Act accorded to all female descendants of George II who apparently married into *foreign* families is not so readily available as was once thought.

The Act of Settlement

On 6 Feb 1701 the Act of Settlement came into force. It laid down that failing issue from HRH The

Princess (later Queen Anne) George (of Denmark) and/or secondly from any subsequent marriage by her first cousin and brother-in-law, the widower King William III, the crown would vest in Princess Sophia, Dowager Electress of Hanover (1630–1714), the granddaughter of King James I, and the heirs of her body, with the proviso that all Roman Catholics, or persons marrying Roman Catholics, were for ever to be excluded, as if they 'were naturally dead'.

The Duke of Windsor

The only subsequent change in statute law was on 11 Dec 1936 by His Majesty's Declaration of Abdication Act, 1936, by which the late HRH The Prince Edward, MC (later HRH The Duke of Windsor), and any issue he might subsequently have had were expressly exluded from the succession.

Conditions of tenure

On succeeding to the Crown the Sovereign must (1) join in Communion with the established Church of England; (2) declare that he or she is a Protestant; (3) swear the oaths for the preservation of both the Established Church of England and the Presbyterian Church of Scotland, and (4), most importantly, take the coronation oath, which may be said to form the basis of the contract between Sovereign and subject, last considered to have been broken, on the Royal side, by King James II in 1688.

'The King never dies'

The Sovereign can never be legally a minor, but in fact a regency is provided until he or she attains the age of 18.

There is never an interregnum on the death of a Sovereign. In persuance of the common law maxim 'the King never dies' the new Sovereign succeeds to full prerogative rights instantly on the death of his or her predecessor.

Notes on the British peerage

There are five ranks in the British temporal peerage – in ascending order they are: 1. Barons or Baronesses; 2. Viscounts or Viscountesses; 3. Earls or Countesses; 4. Marquesses (less favoured, Marquises) or Marchionesses; 5. Dukes or Duchesses.

The British spiritual peerage is of two ranks, Archbishops (of Canterbury and of York) who rank between Royal Dukes and dukes, and twenty-four of the bishops (but always including the Bishops of London, Durham, and Winchester with the Bishop of Sodor and Man always excluded), based on their seniority, who rank between Viscounts and Barons.

A few women hold peerages in their own right and since The Peerage Act, 1963, have become peers of Parliament. The remaining category of membership of the House of Lords is life peers. These are of two sorts: (a) The Lords of Appeal in Ordinary, who are appointed by virtue of the Appellate Jurisdiction Act, 1876. Their number has been increased from the original four to six in 1913, to seven in 1929, and to nine since 1947; (b) by virtue of The Life Peerages Act, 1958, both men and women may be appointed for life membership of The House of Lords. Such creations so far have been confined to the rank of baron or baroness.

1. Peerages of England, i.e. those created prior to the union with Scotland on 1 May 1707.

2. Peerages of Scotland, i.e. those created before the union with England.
3. Peerages of Ireland (the last creation was in 1898 and no further ones are at present likely).
4. Peerages of Great Britain, i.e. those created between the union with Scotland (1707) and the union with Ireland (2 July 1800).
5. Peerages of the United Kingdom of Great Britain and (Northern) Ireland, i.e. those created since 2 July 1800.

All holders of peerages of England, Great Britain and the United Kingdom and (only since The Peerage Act, 1963) also of Scotland, are also peers of Parliament provided they are over 21 and are not unpardoned major felons, bankrupts, lunatics or of alien nationality. Peers who are civil servants may sit but neither speak nor vote.

The single exception to the rule concerning minors is that the Duke of Cornwall (HRH The Prince of Wales) has been technically entitled to a seat from the moment of his mother's accession, when he was only three years of age.

The peers (and peeresses in their own right) of Ireland are not peers of Parliament but they are entitled to stand for election to the House of Commons for any seat in the United Kingdom.

Only the holder of a peerage can be described as noble. In the eyes of the law the holder of a courtesy title is a commoner. For example, the Duke of Marlborough's son is known by courtesy as Marquess of Blandford. Note the omission of the definite article 'the'. The reason is that the Duke of Marlborough is also *the* Marquess of Blandford and his secondary peerage style is merely *lent* to this son.

Life Peers

The Crown in the past used on occasions to grant life peerages, both to men and women. The Wensleydale peerage case of 1856 acknowledged the Crown's right to do this but denied the consequent right of a seat in the House of Lords to such a peer. The two current categories of life peers are treated above. It should be noted that there is no provision for these non-hereditary peers or peeresses to disclaim their peerages.

Widows of Peers

The only correct style for the widow of a peer is 'The Dowager' prefixed to her peerage title of duchess, marchioness, countess, viscountess, or lady (*note:* 'baroness' is only normally used by a peeress in her own right). But in fact most widowed peeresses dislike this title because of its association with advanced age, so they prefix their Christian name to their title. In the event of a widow remarrying, she should forfeit her previous title but some, quite unjustifiably, retain it.

The Effect of Divorce

Some peeresses who divorce their husbands or have been divorced by them continue to bear their former husband's style though in strict English law they are probably no longer peeresses. If a new wife appears they adopt the practice of most widows and prefix their Christian name to their title. With Scottish peerages, however, the position of a divorced peeress is exactly the same as if her husband were dead and hence she takes her legal rights as a widow.

Courtesy Titles

According to the preamble of The Peerage Act, 1963, 'Courtesy titles are, by definition, not matters of law'. They are governed by custom and fall into two categories – those borne by all the children of a peer and those reserved for the heir. The children (except the eldest son) of a duke or marquess take the title 'Lord' or 'Lady' before their Christian name and the family name (e.g. Lord Charles Cavendish). The same applies to the daughters of an earl but not, oddly enough, to the younger sons who take the style 'Honourable' which is borne by *all* the children of a viscount, a baron and a temporal life peer. When male holders of this title marry, their wives also become 'The Honourable'. The heir to a dukedom is given the courtesy style 'Marquess', provided, of course, his father has a marquessate, which failing he takes the title 'Earl' but enjoys the precedence of a duke's eldest son. Likewise, the heir to a marquessate takes the courtesy style of 'Earl' (if available) and similarly the heir of an earldom takes the title of his father's viscountcy (if any) or barony.

In the Scottish peerage the term 'Master of' is used by the male heir to many peerages as of right. If he is married, his wife is styled 'The Hon. Mrs'.

Courtesy titles in the second generation extend only to the grandchildren who are the children of an elder son.

The Signature of Peers

A peer's signature, whether on a formal or informal document, is simply his title without any qualification of rank or the use of a Christian name. This also applies to peeresses in their own right. Members of the Royal Family who hold peerages, however, sign with their principal Christian name.

The Prefix 'Lady'

This title causes more confusion than any other, simply because of the wide range of its use. It can be used as a less formal alternative by marchionesses, countesses, viscountesses and the wives of barons. It is never used by duchesses. It is used, but only with the addition of their Christian names, by the daughters of dukes, marquesses and earls. It is also used by the wives of the younger sons of dukes and marquesses, e.g. Lady Charles Cavendish. It is used, but never with the definite article, by the wives of baronets and knights. There is one baronetess.

Special Remainders

The Crown has power to create what are termed 'special remainders' so that a peerage can, for example, pass to an elder brother or some other relative. An example is that the earldom of Mountbatten of Burma passed to the first earl's elder daughter and her male issue.

Dormant Peerages

A peerage is deemed dormant when there is no discoverable heir but there is a reasonable presumption that there may be an heir if he or she could be found. The Crown will not permit the use of a name of a peerage for a subsequent creation unless there is absolute certainty that the former creation is truly extinguished.

The Descent of Peerages

Usually a peerage descends in the male line. Illegitimate offspring are, of course, excluded. If the direct male line fails, then the succession may go back to the male line in an earlier cadet branch of the family.

Kings and Queens of England and Great Britain

The precise dates of all the main events in the lives of the earlier monarchs are not known, and probably now never will be. Where recognized authorities are in dispute, as quite frequently occurs in the first twenty or so reigns, we have adhered to the dates given by the Royal Historical Society's *Handbook of British Chronology* (second edition, 1961). This work includes the fruits of recent researches based on only acceptable evidence.

King or Queen Regnant Date of Accession and Final Year of Reign; Style	Date and Place of Birth and Parentage	Marriages and No. of Children	Date, Cause and Place of Death, and Place of Burial	Notes and Succession
1. **WILLIAM I** 25 Dec 1066–87 'The Conqueror' 'The Bastard' *Style:* 'Willielmus Rex Anglorum'	1027 or 1028 at Falaise, north France; illegitimate son of Robert I, 6th Duke of Normandy, and Herleva, dau. of Fulbert the Tanner	m. at Eu in 1050 or 1051 MATILDA (d. 1083), d of Baldwin V, Count of Flanders. 4s 5d.	d., aged 59 or 60, 9 Sept 1087 of an abdominal injury from his saddle pommel at the Priory of St Gervais, nr. Rouen. The Abbey of St Stephen at Caen (remains lost during French Revolution).	William I succeeded by right of conquest by winning the 'Battle of Hastings', 14 Oct 1066, from Harold II, the nominated heir of Edward III ('The Confessor'). Succeeded as King of England, by his third, but second surviving, son. William.
Events include 1086 onwards Domesday Book compiled				
2. **WILLIAM II** 26 Sept 1087–1100 'Rufus' *Style:* 'Dei Gratia Rex Anglorum'	between 1056 and 1060 in Normandy; third son of William I and Matilda	unmarried. Had illegitimate issue	d., aged between 40 and 44, 2 Aug 1100, (according to tradition) of impalement by a stray arrow while hunting in the New Forest nr. Brockenhurst, Hampshire. Winchester Cathedral	Succeeded by his younger brother, Henry
Events include 1096 First Crusade				
3. **HENRY I** 5 Aug 1100–35 'Beauclerc' *Style:* As No. 2 but also Duke of Normandy from 1106	in the latter half of 1068 at Selby, Yorks; fourth son of William I and Matilda	m. (1) at Westminster Abbey, 11 Nov 1100 EADGYTH (Edith), known as MATILDA (d. 1118), d of Malcolm III, King of the Scots, and Margaret (grand-d of Edmund 'Ironside') 1s, 1d and a child who died young. m. (2) 29 Jan 1121 ADELA (d. 1151), d of Godfrey VII, Count of Louvain. No issue	d., aged 67, 1 Dec 1135, from a feverish illness at St Denis-le-Ferment, nr. Grisors. Reading Abbey	Succeeded by his nephew, Stephen (the third, but second surviving, son of Adela, the fifth d of William I) who usurped the throne from Henry's only surviving legitimate child and d, Matilda (1102–67)
Events include 1106 Henry I acquires Normandy 1120 Loss of the *White Ship* and Henry's heir				

Kings and Queens of England and Great Britain *continued*

King or Queen Regnant Date of Accession and Final Year of Reign: Style	Date and Place of Birth and Parentage	Marriages and No. of Children	Date, Cause and Place of Death, and Place of Burial	Notes and Succession
4. **STEPHEN** 22 Dec 1135–54 *Style:* As No. 2	between 1096 and 1100 at Blois, France: third son of Stephen (sometimes called Henry), Count of Blois, and Adela	m. 1125. MATILDA (d. 1151), d of Eustace II, Count of Boulogne, and Mary, sister of Queen Matilda, wife of Henry I. 3s 2d	d., age between 54 and 58. 25 Oct 1154, from a heart attack at St Martin's Priory, Dover. Faversham Abbey	Succeeded by his first cousin once removed downwards, Henry. Between April and November 1141 he was not *de facto* King and was imprisoned in Bristol Castle
Events include 1139 Matilda lands in England 1141 Battle of Lincoln – Stephen captured 1146 Matilda returns to France				
5. **MATILDA** April–November 1141 'Empress Maud' *Style:* 'Imperatrix Henrici Regis filia et Anglorum domina'	Feb 1102 in London, only legitimate d of Henry I	m. (1) 1114 Henry V, Emperor of Germany (d. 1125). No issue. m. (2) 1130 GEOFFREY V, Count of Anjou (d. 1151). 3s	d., aged 65, 10 Sept 1167 of uncertain cause, nr. Rouen in Normandy. Fontevraud(?), France	Succeeded by her cousin, Stephen, whom she had deposed
Events include 1141 Matilda's flight from London				
6. **HENRY II** 19 Dec 1154–1189 *Style:* 'Rex Angliae, Dux Normaniae et Aquitaniae et Comes Andigaviae'	5 Mar 1133 at Le Mans, France; eldest son of Geoffrey V, Count of Anjou (surnamed Plantagenet), and Matilda (only d of Henry I)	m. at Bordeaux, 18 May 1152, ELEANOR (c. 1122–1204), d of William X, Duke of Aquitaine, and divorced wife of Louis, VII, King of France, 5s 3d	d., aged 56, 6 July 1189, of a fever at the Castle of Chinon, nr. Tours, France. Fontevraud abbey church in Anjou. Reburied Westminster Abbey	Succeeded by his third and elder surviving son, Richard. On 14 June 1170, Henry II's second and eldest surviving son Henry was crowned and three years later recrowned with his wife at Winchester as King of England. Contemporaneously he was called King Henry III. He predeceased his father, 11 June 1183
Events include 1169 Strongbow invades Ireland – start of English involvement in Ireland 1170 Murder of Becket 1174 King William of Scotland taken prisoner by English				

7. RICHARD I
3 Sept 1189–99
'Coeur de Lion'
Style: As No. 6

8 Sept 1157 at Oxford; third son of Henry II and Eleanor

Events include
1189 Third Crusade – Richard takes part
1190 Capture of Acre
1192 Richard, returning from Crusade, taken hostage in Austria
1194 Richard returns to England

m. at Limassol, Cyprus, 12 May 1191, BERENGARIA (d. soon after 1230), d of Sancho VI of Navarre. No issue

d., aged 41, 6 Apr 1199 from a mortal arrow wound while besieging the Castle of Chalus in Limousin, France. Fontevraud abbey church in Anjou. Reburied Westminster Abbey

Succeeded by his younger brother, John, who usurped the throne from his nephew Arthur, the only son of Geoffrey, Duke of Brittany (1158–86); and from his niece, Eleanor (1184–1241). Arthur (b. posthumously 1187) was murdered (unmarried) 3 Apr 1203 in his 17th year

8. JOHN
27 May 1199–1216
'Lackland'
Style: 'Joannes Rex Angliae et Dominus Hiberniae' etc.

24 Dec 1167 at Beaumont Palace, Oxford; fifth son of Henry II and Eleanor

Events include
1202 Murder of Prince Arthur
1209 John excommunicated
1215 Magna Carta signed at Runnymede

m. (1) at Marlborough, Wilts. 29 Aug 1189, ISABEL (d. 1217). No issue.
m. (2) at Angoulême, 24 Aug 1200, ISABELLA (d. 1246), d of Aimir, Count of Angoulême. 2s 3d

d., aged 48, 18–19 Oct 1216, of dysentery at Newark Castle, Nottinghamshire. Worcester Cathedral

In late 1215 the Crown was offered to Louis, son of Philip II of France but despite a visit in 1216 the claim was abandoned in September 1217. Succeeded by his elder son, Henry

9. HENRY III
28 Oct 1216–72
Style: 'Rex Angliae, Dominus Hiberniae et Dux Aquitaniae'

1 Oct 1207 at Winchester; elder son of John and Isabella

Events include
1258 Simon de Montfort forces reforms on Henry III
1264 Battle of Lewes – de Montfort defeats Henry III
1265 Battle of Evesham – de Montfort killed

m. at Canterbury, 20 Jan 1236, ELEANOR (d. 1291), d of Raymond Berengar IV, Count of Provence. 2s 3d at least 4 other children who died in infancy

d., aged 65, 16 Nov 1272, at Westminster. Westminster Abbey church

The style 'Dux Normaniae' and Count of Anjou was omitted from 1259. Succeeded by Edward, his first son to survive infancy (probably his third son)

Kings and Queens of England and Great Britain continued

King or Queen Regnant Date of Accession and Final Year of Reign; Style	Date and Place of Birth and Parentage	Marriages and No. of Children	Date, Cause and Place of Death, and Place of Burial	Notes and Succession
10. **EDWARD I** 20 Nov 1272–1307 'Longshanks' *Style:* As the final style of No. 8	17/18 June 1239 at Westminster; eldest son to survive infancy (probably third son) of Henry III and Eleanor	m. (1) at the monastery of Las Huelgas, Spain, 13–31 Oct 1254, ELEANOR (d. 1290), d of Ferdinand III, King of Castille. 4 s 7 d m. (2) at Canterbury, 10 Sept 1299, MARGARET (1282–1317), d of Philip III, King of France. 2 s 1 d	d., aged 68, 7 July 1307, at Burgh-upon-the-Sands, nr. Carlisle. Westminster Abbey	Succeeded by the fourth, and only surviving, son of his first marriage, Edward (created Prince of Wales, 7 Feb 1301)
Events include 1276 Edward I invades Wales 1282 Llewelyn, last Prince of Wales slain 1290 Queen Margaret of Scotland dies – throne disputed by 13 claimants 1295 The 'Model Parliament' 1296–8 Wallace leads Scottish war of independence 1306 Bruce becomes King of Scotland				
11. **EDWARD II** 8 July 1307 (deposed 20 Jan 1327) 'of Caernarfon' *Style:* As the final style of No. 8	25 Apr 1284 at Caernarfon Castle; fourth and only surviving son of Edward I and Eleanor	m. at Boulogne, c. 25 Jan 1308, ISABELLA (1292–1358), d of Philip IV, King of France. 2 s 2 d	murdered, aged 43, 21 Sept 1327 (traditionally by disembowelling with red-hot iron) at Berkeley Castle. The abbey of St Peter (now the cathedral), Gloucester	Succeeded by his elder son, Edward of Windsor. Edward II was deposed by Parliament on 20 Jan 1327, having been imprisoned on 16 Nov 1326
Events include 1314 Battle of Bannockburn				

12.
EDWARD III
25 Jan 1327–77
Style: As No. 10, until 13th
year when 'Dei Gratiá, Rex
Angliae, et Franciae et
Dominus Hiberniae'

Events include
1338 Start of Hundred Years War
1340 Battle of Sluys
1346 Battle of Crecy
1349 Black Death begins in
England
1350 Black Death reaches
Scotland
1356 Battle of Poitiers – great
victory of Black Prince
1362 English becomes official
language of courts and
Parliament

13 Nov 1312 at Windsor
Castle; elder son of
Edward II and Isabella

m. at York, 24 June 1328,
PHILIPPA (c. 1314–69), d of
William I, Count of Holland
and Hainault. 7s 5d

d. peacefully, aged 64, 21 June
1377 at Sheen (now in
Greater London).
Westminster Abbey

Succeeded by his grandson Richard, the
second and only surviving son of his
eldest son Edward, the Black Prince

13.
RICHARD II
22 June 1377–99
Style: As the final style of
No. 12

Events include
1381 Wat Tyler leads Peasants'
Revolt

6 Jan 1367 at Bordeaux;
second, but only surviving,
son of Edward, the Black
Prince, and Joane, commonly
called The Fair Maid of Kent
(grand-d of Edward I)

m. (1) at St Stephen's Chapel,
Westminster, 20 Jan 1382,
ANNE of Bohemia (1366–94),
d of Emperor Charles IV.
No issue.
m. (2) at St Nicholas' Church,
Calais, probably 4 Nov 1396,
ISABELLE (1389–1409), d of
Charles VI of France. No issue

d., aged 33, probably 14 Feb
1400, a sufferer from
neurasthenia, at Pontefract
Castle, Yorks.
Westminster Abbey

He was a prisoner of Henry, Duke of
Lancaster, later Henry IV, from 19 Aug
1399 until death. He was deposed 30
Sept 1399. Henry usurped the throne
from the prior claims of the issue of his
father John of Gaunt's deceased elder
brother, Lionel of Antwerp

14.
HENRY IV
30 Sept 1399–1413
Style: As No. 12

Events include
1400 Owen Glendower's revolt
begins in Wales

probably April 1366 at
Bolingbroke Castle, nr.
Spilsby, Lincolnshire; eldest
son of John of Gaunt, 4th son
of Edward III, and Blanche,
great-great-grand-d of
Henry III

m. (1) at Rochford, Essex,
between 1380 and March 1381,
Lady MARY de Bohun
(?1368/70–94), younger d of
Humphrey, Earl of Hereford.
5s 2d.
m. (2) at Winchester, 7 Feb
1403, JOAN (c. 1370–1437),
second d of Charles II, King of
Navarre. No issue

d., aged probably 46, 20 Mar
1413, of pustulated eczema
and gout in the Jerusalem
Chamber, Westminster.
Canterbury Cathedral

Succeeded by his second, but eldest
surviving, son, Henry of Monmouth

Kings and Queens of England and Great Britain continued

King or Queen Regnant Date of Accession and Final Year of Reign; Style	Date and Place of Birth and Parentage	Marriages and No. of Children	Date, Cause and Place of Death, and Place of Burial	Notes and Succession
15. HENRY V 21 Mar 1413–1422 *Style:* As No. 13, until 8th year when 'Rex Angliae, Haeres, et Regens Franciae, et Dominus Hiberniae'. **Events include** 1415 Battle of Agincourt 1420 English claim to throne of France recognized	probably 16 Sept 1387 at Monmouth; second and eldest surviving son of Henry IV and the Lady Mary de Bohun	m. at the church of St John, Troyes, 2 June 1420, CATHERINE of Valois (1401–37), youngest d of Charles VI of France. 1 s	d., aged probably 34, 31 Aug/ Sept 1422, of dysentery at Bois de Vincennes, France. Chapel of the Confessor, Westminster Abbey	Succeeded by his only child Henry
16. HENRY VI 1 Sept 1422–61 and 6 Oct 1470–1 *Style:* 'Dei Gratiá Rex Angliae et Franciae et Dominus Hiberniae' **Events include** 1431 Burning of Joan of Arc 1455 Battle of St Albans – start of Wars of the Roses 1461 Battle of Towton – Yorkist victory	6 Dec 1421 at Windsor; only son of Henry V and Catherine	m. at Tichfield Abbey, 23 Apr 1445, MARGARET (1430–82), d of René, Duke of Anjou. 1 s	murdered by stabbing, aged 49, 21 May 1471 at Tower of London. Windsor	Succeeded by the usurpation of his third cousin, Edward IV
17. EDWARD IV 4 Mar 1461–70 and 11 Apr 1471–83 *Style:* As No. 16 **Events include** 1470 Warwick the Kingmaker goes over to Lancastrian cause 1471 Battles of Barnet and Tewkesbury – Lancastrians defeated 1476 Caxton sets up printing press	28 Apr 1442 at Rouen; eldest son of Richard, 3rd Duke of York ('The Protector') and the Lady Cecily Nevill	m. at Grafton, Northamptonshire, 1 May 1464, ELIZABETH (c. 1437–92), eldest d of Sir Richard Woodville. 3 s 7 d	d., aged 40, 9 Apr 1483, of pneumonia at Westminster. Windsor	Edward IV was a prisoner of the Earl of Warwick in August and September of 1469; he fled to the Netherlands 3 Oct 1470; returned to England 14 Mar 1471, and was restored to kingship 11 Apr 1471. Succeeded by his eldest son, Edward

18.
EDWARD V
9 Apr–25 June 1483
Style: As No. 16

2 Nov 1470 in the Sanctuary at Westminster; eldest son of Edward IV and Elizabeth Woodville

unmarried

d. (traditionally murdered), possibly in 1483 or in 1486, at the Tower of London. A body with the stature and dentition of a 12-year-old male was discovered at the Tower on 6 July 1933

Edward V was deposed 25 June 1483, when the throne was usurped by his uncle, Richard III (the only surviving brother of his father)

19.
RICHARD III
26 June 1483–5
Style: As No. 16
Events include
1485 Battle of Bosworth Field

2 Oct 1452 at Fotheringay Northamptonshire; fourth and only surviving son of Richard, 3rd Duke of York ('The Protector'), and the Lady Cecily Nevill

m. 12 July 1472, the Lady ANNE (1456–85), younger d of Richard Nevill, Earl of Warwick ('The King Maker') and widow of Edward, Prince of Wales, only child of Henry VI. 1s

killed aged 32, 22 Aug 1485, at the battle of Bosworth Field. The Abbey of the Grey Friars, Leicester

Richard III was succeeded by his third cousin once removed downwards, Henry Tudor, 2nd Earl of Richmond

20.
HENRY VII
22 Aug 1485–1509
Style: As No. 16
Events include
1487 Revolt by Lambert Simnel
1497 Perkin Warbeck captured

27 Jan 1457 at Pembroke Castle; only child of Edmund Tudor, 1st Earl of Richmond, and Margaret Beaufort, great-great-grand-d of Edward III

m. at Westminster, 18 Jan 1486, ELIZABETH (1466–1503) d of Edward IV. 3s and 4d, of whom 2 died in infancy

d., aged 52, 21 Apr 1509, had rheumatoid arthritis and gout at Richmond. In his own chapel at Westminster

Succeeded by his second and only surviving son, Henry

21.
HENRY VIII
22 Apr 1509–47
Style: (from 35th year) 'Henry the eighth, by the Grace of God, King of England, France, and Ireland, Defender of the Faith and of the Church of England, and also of Ireland, on earth the Supreme Head'
Events include
1513 James IV of Scotland slain at Flodden Field
1515 Wolsey becomes Lord Chancellor
1534 Henry VIII claims supremacy over English Church
1535 More and Fisher executed
1536–9 Dissolution of the Monasteries

28 June 1491 at Greenwich; second and only surviving son of Henry VII and Elizabeth

m. (1) secretly at the chapel of the Observant Friars, 11 June 1509, CATHERINE of Aragon (1485–1536), d of Ferdinand II, King of Spain, and widow of Arthur, Prince of Wales. 2s 2d (one of whom died young)

Subsequent marriages of HENRY VIII:
m. (2) secretly 25 Jan 1533, ANNE Marchioness of Pembroke (b. 1507, beheaded 1536), d of Sir Thomas Boleyn, the Viscount Rochford. A daughter and possibly another child

Seymour. 1s
m. (4) at Greenwich, 6 Jan 1540, ANNE (1515–57), second d of John, Duke of Cleves. No issue
m. (5) at Oatlands, 28 July 1540, CATHERINE (beheaded 1542), d of Lord Edmund Howard. No issue
m. (6) at Hampton Court, 12 July 1543, CATHERINE (c. 1512–48), d of Sir Thomas Parr and widow of 1. Sir Edward Borough and 2. John Neville, 3rd Lord Latimer. No issue.

d., aged 55, 28 Jan 1547, had chronic sinusitis and periostitis of the leg at the Palace of Westminster. Windsor

Henry was the first King to be formally styled with a post nominal number in his own life time, i.e. VIII. Succeeded by his only surviving son, Edward

Kings and Queens of England and Great Britain *continued*

King or Queen Regnant Date of Accession and Final Year of Reign: Style	Date and Place of Birth and Parentage	Marriages and No. of Children	Date, Cause and Place of Death, and Place of Burial	Notes and Succession
22. **EDWARD VI** 28 Jan 1547–53 *Style:* As No. 21	12 Oct 1537 at Hampton Court; only surviving son of Henry VIII, by Jane Seymour	unmarried	d., aged 15, 6 July 1553, of pulmonary tuberculosis at Greenwich. Henry VII's Chapel, Westminster Abbey	Succeeded briefly by Lady Guilford Dudley (Lady Jane Grey), his first cousin once removed
Events include 1547 Somerset becomes Protector 1547 First English Book of Common Prayer 1550 Somerset deposed as Protector by Northumberland				
23. **JANE** 6 July (proclaimed 10 July) 1553 (deposed 19 July)	October 1537 at Bradgate Park, Leicestershire; eldest d of Henry Grey, 3rd Marquess of Dorset, and Frances (d of Mary Tudor, sister of Henry VIII)	m. at Durham House, London, 21 May 1553, Lord GUILFORD DUDLEY (beheaded 1554), 4th son of John Dudley, Duke of Northumberland. No issue	beheaded, aged 16, 12 Feb 1554, in the Tower of London. St Peter ad Vincula, within the Tower	Succeeded by her second cousin once removed upwards, Mary
24. **MARY I** 19 July 1553–8 *Style:* As No. 21 (but supremacy title was dropped) until marriage	18 Feb 1516 at Greenwich Palace; only surviving child of Henry VIII and Catherine of Aragon	m. at Winchester Cathedral, 25 July 1554, PHILIP (1527–98), King of Naples and Jerusalem, son of Emperor Charles V and widower of Maria, d of John III of Portugal. No issue	d., aged 42, 17 Nov 1558 of endemic influenza at London. Westminster Abbey	Philip was styled, but not crowned, king. Mary was succeeded by her half sister, Elizabeth, the only surviving child of Henry VIII
Events include 1555 Latimer and Ridley burned at stake 1556 Cranmer burned 1558 Loss of Calais, the last English possession in France				

25.
ELIZABETH I
17 Nov 1558–1603
Style: 'Queen of England, France and Ireland, Defender of the Faith' etc.

Events include
1561 Mary Queen of Scots returns to Scotland
1562 The Thirty-Nine Articles
1567 Mary Queen of Scots deposed and, 1568, imprisoned in England
1580 Drake returns from voyage round the world
1587 Mary Queen of Scots executed
1588 Spanish Armada

7 Sept 1533 at Greenwich; d of Henry VIII and Anne Boleyn

unmarried

d., aged 69, 24 Mar 1603, of sepsis from tonsillar abscess at Richmond. Westminster Abbey

Succeeded by her first cousin twice removed, James

26.
JAMES I
26 Mar 1603–25 and VI of Scotland from 24 July 1567
Style: 'King of England, Scotland, France and Ireland, Defender of the Faith' etc.

Events include
1603 Union of Crowns of England and Scotland
1605 Gunpowder Plot
1611 Plantation of Ulster
1616 Death of Shakespeare
1620 Pilgrim Fathers reach America

19 June 1566 at Edinburgh Castle; only son of Henry Stuart, Lord Darnley, and Mary, Queen of Scots (d of James V of Scotland, son of Margaret Tudor, sister of Henry VIII)

m. 20 Aug 1589 (by proxy) ANNE (1574–1619), d of Frederick II, King of Denmark and Norway. 3s 4d

d., aged 58, 27 Mar 1625, of Bright's disease at Theobalds Park, Hertfordshire. Westminster Abbey

Succeeded by his second and only surviving son, Charles

Kings and Queens of England and Great Britain *continued*

King or Queen Regnant / Date of Accession and / Final Year of Reign: Style	Date and Place of Birth and Parentage	Marriages and No. of Children	Date, Cause and Place of Death, and Place of Burial	Notes and Succession
27. **CHARLES I** 27 Mar 1625–49 *Style:* As No. 26	19 Nov 1600 at Dunfermline Palace, second and only surviving son of James I and Anne	m. in Paris, 1 May 1625 (by proxy) HENRIETTA MARIA (1609–69) d of Henry IV of France. 4s 5d	beheaded, aged 48, 30 Jan 1649, in Whitehall. Windsor	The Kingship was *de facto* declared abolished 17 Mar 1649
Events include 1628 Petition of Rights to Charles I 1629 Charles begins personal rule 1638 Covenant signed in Scotland 1640 Long Parliament begins 1642 Outbreak of Civil War – Battle of Edgehill 1644 Battle of Marston Moor 1645 New Model Army – Battle of Naseby 1646 Charles I surrenders to Scots and, 1647, handed over to Parliament				
28. **CHARLES II** 29 May 1660 (but *de jure* 30 Jan 1649) to 1685 *Style:* As No. 26	29 May 1630 at St James's Palace, London; eldest surviving son of Charles I and Henrietta Maria	m. at Portsmouth, 21 May 1662, CATHERINE (1638–1705), d of John, Duke of Braganza. No legitimate issue	d., aged 54, 6 Feb 1685, of uraemia and mercurial poisoning at Whitehall. Henry VII's Chapel, Westminster Abbey	Succeeded by his younger and only surviving brother, James
Events include 1649 Commonwealth established 1651 Battle of Worcester – Royalists defeated 1653 Cromwell becomes Protector 1658 Cromwell dies 1660 Royal Society founded 1665 Great Plague of London 1666 Great Fire of London 1673 Test Act 1678 Titus Oates' 'Popish Plot' 1683 Rye House Plot				

29.
JAMES II
6 Feb 1685-8
Style: As No. 26

14 Oct 1633 at St James's Palace, London; only surviving son of Charles I and Henrietta Maria

m. (1) at Worcester House, The Strand, London, 3 Sept 1660, ANNE (1637–71), eldest d of Edward Hyde. 4s 4d.
m. (2) at Modena (by proxy), 30 Sept 1673, MARY D'ESTE (1658–1718), only d of Alfonso IV, Duke of Modena. 2s 5d

d., aged 67, 6 Sept 1701, of a cerebral haemorrhage at St Germain, France. His remains were divided and interred at five different venues in France. All are now lost except for those at the parish church of St Germain

James II was deemed by legal fiction to have ended his reign 11 Dec 1688 by flight. A Convention Parliament offered the Crown of England and Ireland 13 Feb 1689 to Mary, his eldest surviving d, and her husband, his nephew, William Henry of Orange

Events include
1685 Battle of Sedgemoor – James II defeats Monmouth
1688 The 'Seven Bishops' protest against the King's religious tolerance – William of Orange lands

30.
WILLIAM III
13 Feb 1689–1702

4 Nov 1650 at The Hague; only son of William II, Prince of Orange, and Mary (Stuart), d of Charles I

They were married at St James's Palace, London, 4 Nov 1677. No issue

d., aged 51, 8 Mar 1702, of pleuro-pneumonia following fracture of right collarbone, in Kensington

The widower, King William III, was succeeded by his sister-in-law, Anne, who was also his first cousin

MARY II
13 Feb 1689–94

30 Apr 1662 at St James's Palace, London; elder surviving d of James II and Anne Hyde

d., aged 32, 28 Dec 1694, of confluent haemorrhagic smallpox with pneumonia, at Kensington. They were buried in Henry VII's Chapel, Westminster Abbey

Style: 'King and Queen of England, Scotland, France and Ireland, Defenders of the Faith' etc.

Events include
1690 Battle of the Boyne
1692 Massacre of Glencoe
1694 Bank of England founded
1701 Act of Settlement – Hanoverian succession regulated

Kings and Queens of England and Great Britain continued

King or Queen Regnant Date of Accession and Final Year of Reign; Style	Date and Place of Birth and Parentage	Marriages and No. of Children	Date, Cause and Place of Death, and Place of Burial	Notes and Succession
31. ANNE 8 Mar 1702–14 Style: Firstly as No. 25; secondly (after Union with Scotland 6 Mar 1707) 'Queen of Great Britain, France and Ireland, Defender of the Faith' etc.	6 Feb 1665 at St James's Palace, London; only surviving d of James II and Anne Hyde	m. at the Chapel Royal, St James's Palace, 28 July 1683, GEORGE (1653–1708), second son of Frederick III, King of Denmark. 2s 3d from 17 confinements	d., aged 49, 1 Aug 1714, of a cerebral haemorrhage and possibly chronic Bright's disease at Kensington. Henry VII's Chapel, Westminster Abbey	Succeeded in the terms of the Act of Settlement (which excluded all Roman Catholics and their spouses) by her second cousin, George Lewis, Elector of Hanover
Events include 1704 Gibraltar taken by British; Marlborough's victory at Blenheim 1706 Marlborough wins battle of Ramillies 1707 Union of England and Scotland 1708–9 Further victories by Marlborough's army 1711 Marlborough dismissed				
32. GEORGE I 1 Aug 1714–27 Style: 'King of Great Britain, France, Ireland, Duke of Brunswick-Lüneburg, etc., Defender of the Faith'	28 May 1660 at Osnabrück; eldest son of Ernest Augustus, Duke of Brunswick-Lüneburg and Elector of Hanover, and Princess Sophia, 5th and youngest d and 10th child of Elizabeth, Queen of Bohemia, eldest d of James I	m. 21 Nov 1682 (div. 1694), SOPHIA Dorothea (1666–1726), only d of George William, Duke of Lüneburg-Celle. 1s 1d	d., aged 67, 11 June 1727, of coronary thrombosis, at Ibbenbüren or Osnabrück. Hanover	The Kings of England were Electors of Hanover from 1714 to 1814. Succeeded by his only son, George Augustus
Events include 1715 Jacobite Rebellion 1720 South Sea Bubble 1721 Walpole becomes Britain's first Prime Minister				

33.
GEORGE II
11 June 1727–60
Style: As No. 32

Events include
1733 onwards Agricultural and industrial revolutions gain momentum
1743 George II leads his army at Battle of Dettingen, last British monarch to command own troops
1745 Jacobite Rebellion
1746 Charles Stuart defeated at Battle of Culloden
1752 New Style Calendar adopted in Britain
1756 Seven Years' War begins
1759 'Year of Victories' – Quebec, Minden etc.

30 Oct 1683 at Hanover; only son of George I and Sophia Dorothea

m. 22 Aug (O.S.), 2 Sept (N.S.), 1705, Wilhelmina Charlotte CAROLINE (1683–1737), d of John Frederick, Margrave of Brandenburg-Ansbach. 3s 5d

d., aged 76, 25 Oct 1760, of coronary thrombosis at the Palace of Westminster. Henry VII's Chapel, Westminster Abbey

Succeeded by his elder son's eldest son, George William Frederick

34.
GEORGE III
25 Oct 1760–1820
Style: As No. 31 (until Union of Great Britain and Ireland, 1 Jan 1801), whereafter 'By the Grace of God, of the United Kingdom of Great Britain and Ireland, King, Defender of the Faith'

1763 Peace of Paris: major expansion of British Empire
1774 First British Governor-General of India
1775 American War of Independence begins
1776 Declaration of American Independence
1789 French Revolution
1795–1815 Napoleonic Wars
1798 Battle of the Nile
1800 Union of GB and N. Ireland
1805 Battle of Trafalgar
1807 Slave trade abolished in British Empire
1815 Battle of Waterloo

24 May (O.S.) 1738 at Norfolk House, St James's Square, London; eldest son of Frederick Lewis, Prince of Wales (d. 20 Mar 1751) and Princess Augusta of Saxe-Gotha

m. at St James's Palace, London, 8 Sept 1761, CHARLOTTE Sophia (1744–1818), youngest d of Charles Louis Frederick, Duke of Mecklenburg-Strelitz. 9s 6d

d., aged 81 years 239 days, 29 Jan 1820, of senility at Windsor. St George's Chapel, Windsor

His eldest son became Regent owing to his insanity 5 Feb 1811. Hanover was made a kingdom in 1814. Succeeded by his eldest son, George Augustus Frederick

Kings and Queens of England and Great Britain continued

King or Queen Regnant Date of Accession and Final Year of Reign: Style	Date and Place of Birth and Parentage	Marriages and No. of Children	Date, Cause and Place of Death, and Place of Burial	Notes and Succession
35. **GEORGE IV** 29 Jan 1820–30 Style: As later style of No. 34	12 Aug 1762 at St James's Palace, London; eldest son of George III and Charlotte	m. (2)* at the Chapel Royal, St James's Palace, 8 Apr 1795, CAROLINE Amelia Elizabeth (1768–1821), his first cousin second d of Charles, Duke of Brunswick-Wolfenbüttel. 1d. *First married Maria FitzHerbert	d., aged 67, 26 June 1830, of rupture of the stomach blood vessels; alcoholic cirrhosis; and dropsy at Windsor. St George's Chapel, Windsor	Succeeded by his eldest surviving brother, William Henry (George's only child, Princess Charlotte, having died in childbirth 6 Nov 1817)
Events include 1825 First railway opened (Stockton–Darlington) 1829 Catholic Emancipation in Britain				
36. **WILLIAM IV** 26 June 1830–7 Style: As No. 34	21 Aug 1765 at Buckingham Palace; third and oldest surviving son of George III and Charlotte	m. at Kew, 11 July 1818, ADELAIDE Louisa Theresa Caroline Amelia (1792–1849), eldest d of George, Duke of Saxe-Meiningen. 2d	d., aged 71, 20 June 1837, of pleuro-pneumoia and alcoholic cirrhosis at Windsor. St George's Chapel, Windsor	On William's death the crown of Hanover passed by Salic law to his brother, Ernest, Duke of Cumberland. Succeeded by his niece, Alexandrina Victoria
Events include 1831–2 First Reform Bill (Parliamentary Reform) 1834 'Tolpuddle Martyrs' transported to Australia 1835 Tamworth Manifesto – defines Conservative Party aims 1836 People's Charter (the Chartists)				

37.
VICTORIA
20 June 1837–1901
Style: As (except for 'Queen')
No. 34 until 1 May 1876,
whereafter 'Empress of India'
was added

24 May 1819 at Kensington Palace, London; only child of Edward, Duke of Kent and Stratharn, 4th son of George III, and Victoria, widow of Emich Charles, Prince of Leiningen, and d of Francis, Duke of Saxe-Coburg-Saafeld

m. at St James's Palace, London, 10 Feb 1840, her first cousin Francis ALBERT Augustus Charles Emmanuel (1819–61), second son of Ernest I, Duke of Saxe-Coburg-Gotha. 4s 5d

d., aged 81 years 243 days, 22 Jan 1901 of senility at Osborne, I.o.W. Frogmore

Assumed title Empress of India 1 May 1876. Succeeded by her elder surviving son, Albert Edward

Events include
1840 Penny postage
1848 Chartist agitation
1851 Great Exhibition (Hyde Park)
1854–5 Crimean War
1857 Indian Mutiny
1867 Second Parliamentary Reform Bill
1870 Education Act – elementary education for all children in Britain
1871 Trade Unions legalized in Britain
1877 Victoria becomes Empress of India
1884 Third Parliamentary Reform – almost universal male suffrage
1885 Gordon slain at Khartoum
1886 Irish Home Rule Bill defeated
1893 Irish Home Rule Bill defeated
1896 Jameson Raid
1899 Boer War begins
1900 Relief of Ladysmith and Mafeking

Kings and Queens of England and Great Britain continued

King or Queen Regnant Date of Accession and Final Year of Reign; Style	Date and Place of Birth and Parentage	Marriages and No. of Children	Date, Cause and Place of Death, and Place of Burial	Notes and Succession
38. **EDWARD VII** 22 Jan 1901–10 Style: 'By the Grace of God, of the United Kingdom of Great Britain and Ireland and of the British Dominions beyond the Seas, King, Defender of the Faith, Emperor of India'	9 Nov 1841 at Buckingham Palace, London; elder surviving son of Victoria and Albert	m. at St George's Chapel, Windsor, 10 Mar 1863, ALEXANDRA Caroline Maria Charlotte Louisa Julia (1844–1925), d of Christian IX of Denmark. 3 s 3 d	d., aged 68, 6 May 1910, of bronchitis at Buckingham Palace. St George's Chapel, Windsor	Succeeded by his only surviving son, George Frederick Ernest Albert
Events include 1902 End of Boer War 1906 First Labour MPs in Parliament 1909 Old Age Pensions introduced in Britain				
39. **GEORGE V** 6 May 1910–36 Style: As for No. 37 until 12 May 1927, whereafter 'By the Grace of God, of Great Britain, Ireland, and of the British Dominions beyond the Seas, King, Defender of the Faith, Emperor of India'	3 June 1865 at Marlborough House, London; second and only surviving son of Edward VII and Alexandra	m. at St James's Palace, London, 6 July 1893, Victoria MARY Augusta Louise Olga Pauline Claudine Agnes (1867–1953), eldest d of Francis, Duke of Teck. 5 s 1 d	d., aged 70, 20 Jan 1936, of bronchitis at Sandringham House, Norfolk. St George's Chapel, Windsor	Succeeded by his eldest son, Edward Albert Christian George Andrew Patrick David
Events include 1911 Constitutional crisis – power of House of Lords reduced 1912 Sinking of the *Titanic* 1914–18 First World War 1915 Dardanelles campaign 1916 Sinn Fein rising in Ireland; Battle of Jutland; start of Battle of the Somme 1917 Vimy Ridge; Ypres; Passchendaele Ridge	1918 Naval raid on Zeebrugge and Ostend; major Allied advance (September); Armistice (11 Nov) 1919 German fleet scuttled at Scapa Flow 1921 Irish Free State 1924 Ramsey MacDonald leads first Labour Government 1926 General Strike 1928 Votes for women 1929 Wall Street crash			

40. **EDWARD VIII** 20 Jan–11 Dec 1936 *Style:* As for No. 39	23 June 1894 at the White Lodge, Richmond Park; eldest son of George V and Mary	m. at the Château de Candé, Monts, France, 3 June 1937, Bessie Wallis Warfield (b. 1896), previous wife of Lt. Earl Winfield Spencer, USN (div. 1927) and Ernest Simpson (div. 1936). No issue	d., aged 77, 28 May 1972, of cancer of the throat at 4, Route du Champ, D'Entrainement, Paris, XVIe, France	Edward VIII abdicated for himself and his heirs and was succeeded by his eldest brother, Albert Frederick Arthur George
41. **GEORGE VI** 11 Dec 1936–52 *Style:* As for No. 39 until the Indian title was dropped 22 June 1947	14 Dec 1895 at York Cottage, Sandringham; second son of George V and Mary	m. at Westminster Abbey, 26 Apr 1923, Lady ELIZABETH Angela Marguerite Bowes-Lyon (b. 1900), youngest d of 14th Earl of Strathmore and Kinghorne. 2d	d., aged 56, 6 Feb 1952, of lung cancer at Sandringham House, Norfolk. St George's Chapel, Windsor	Succeeded by his elder d, Elizabeth Alexandra Mary

Events include
1938 Munich Agreement
1939–45 Second World War
1939 War declared (3 Sept); British troops in France; Battle of River Plate
1940 British troops in Norway; National Government under Churchill; evacuation from Dunkirk; Channel Islands occupied; Air Battle of Britain begins
1941 Britain takes Abyssinia; evacuation of Greece; Hong Kong taken by Japanese
1942 Singapore falls; Battle of El Alamein
1943 Ruhr dams breached by RAF; invasion of Italy
1944 D-Day; Paris and Brussels liberated; Allies enter German territory
1945 War against Germany ends (8 May) and against Japan ends (14 Aug)
1947 Nationalization of coal; Indian independence
1948 Railways nationalized; Berlin airlift (Cold War)
1949 NATO founded
1950 Korean War begins

42. **ELIZABETH II** Since 6 Feb 1952 *Style:* (from 29 May 1953) 'By the Grace of God, of the United Kingdom of Great Britain and Northern Ireland and of Her other Realms and Territories, Queen, Head of the Commonwealth, Defender of the Faith'	21 Apr 1926 at 17 Bruton Street, London, W1; elder d of George VI and Elizabeth	m. at Westminster Abbey, 20 Nov 1947, her third cousin PHILIP (b. Corfu, Greece, 10 June 1921), only son of Prince Andrea (Andrew) of Greece and Princess Alice (great-grand-d of Queen Victoria). 3s 1d	—	The Heir Apparent is Charles Philip Arthur George, Prince of Wales, b. 14 Nov 1948

King George V, monarch from 6 May 1910–20 January 1936. (Hulton Picture Company)

UK Legislature

1983 by an Order in Council membership was increased by 15 to the present total of 650

The composition of the two Houses of Parliament

House of Lords

Peers of the Blood Royal	4
Archbishops of Canterbury and York	2
Dukes	25
Marquesses	28
Earls (including 5 Countesses in their own right)	157
Viscounts	103
Anglican Bishops (by seniority)	23
Barons and Scots Lords (hereditary)	
Baronesses in their own right (hereditary)	854
Life Peers (Barons)	
Life Peeresses (Baronesses)	
	1196

(as at February 1988)

House of Commons

The size of the House of Commons has frequently been altered:

1885 by a representation of the People Act (RPA) membership was increased by 12 to total 670

1918 by an RPA, membership was increased by 37 to an all-time high point of 707

1922 by two Acts of Parliament (the Partition of Ireland) membership was reduced by 92 to 615. (*Note:* Irish representation was reduced from 105 to 13 members representing Northern Ireland.)

1945 by an RPA, membership was increased by 25 to 640

1948 by an RPA, membership was decreased by 15 to 625. (*Note:* This took effect in 1950 and involved the abolition of the 12 university seats and 12 double-member constituencies.)

1955 by an Order in Council under the House of Commons (Redistribution of Seats) Act, membership was increased by 5 to a total of 630

1974 by an Order in Council membership was increased by 5 to a total of 635

The general elections of 1945 to 1987

1945 During the 10 years since the previous election the country underwent the traumatic total war of 1939–45. Baldwin resigned in 1937 and was succeeded by Neville Chamberlain who resigned in 1940 at the nadir of our wartime fortunes. For the remaining five years Winston Churchill gave dynamic leadership which secured victory over Nazi Germany in May 1945. In that month the wartime Coalition broke up and was replaced by a pre-determined Conservative administration. This Government, despite Churchill's premiership, was defeated by a Labour landslide. The new Government had Labour's first overall majority – 146 seats.

1950 Mr Attlee's administration launched the 'Welfare State' along the lines set out by various wartime White Papers, but his nationalization measures, especially as regards steel, met fierce resistance. A balance of payments crisis in the autumn of 1949 compelled the Government to devalue the pound against the dollar and make drastic economies. The result of the February election was a narrow Labour victory with an overall majority of only 5.

1951 After 20 months of precarious administration, during which time the Conservatives ceaselessly harried the Government ranks, especially over the nationalization of steel, Mr Attlee resigned. The last straw was another balance of payments crisis in September following the earlier resignation of Aneurin Bevan (Minister of Labour) and Harold Wilson (Pres., Board of Trade). The nation's reply to Mr Attlee's appeal over the radio for a larger majority was to elect the Conservatives with an overall majority of 17. Winston Churchill returned as Prime Minister.

The results of the general elections since 1945

			Result (and % share of Total Poll)			% Turn-out of
Election and Date	Total Seats	Conservatives	Liberals	Labour	Others	Electorate
1945 (5 July)	640	213 (39·8)	12 (9·0)	**393** (47·8)	22 (2·8)	72·7 of 33 240 391
1950 (23 Feb)	625	298 (43·5)	9 (9·1)	**315** (46·4)	3 (1·3)	84·0 of 33 269 770
1951 (25 Oct)	625	**321** (48·0)	6 (2·5)	295 (48·7)	3 (0·7)	82·5 of 34 465 573
1955 (25 May)	630	**344** (49·8)	6 (2·7)	277 (46·3)	3 (1·2)	76·7 of 34 858 263
1959 (8 Oct)	630	**365** (49·4)	6 (5·9)	258 (43·8)	1 (0·9)	78·8 of 35 397 080
1964 (15 Oct)	630	303 (43·4)	9 (11·1)	**317** (44·2)	1 (1·3)	77·1 of 35 894 307
1966 (31 Mar)	630	253 (41·9)	12 (8·5)	**363** (47·9)	2 (1·7)	75·9 of 35 965 127
1970 (18 June)	630	**330** (46·4)	6 (7·5)	288 (43·0)	6 (3·1)	72·0 of 39 247 683
1974 (28 Feb)	635	297 (38·2)	14 (19·3)	**301** (37·2)	23 (5·3)	78·8 of 39 752 317
1974 (10 Oct)	635	277 (35·8)	13 (18·3)	**319** (39·3)	26 (6·6)	72·8 of 40 083 286
1979 (3 May)	635	**339** (43·9)	11 (13·8)	268 (36·9)	17 (5·4)	75·9 of 41 093 262
1983 (9 June)	650	**397** (42·4)	17 (25·4) (Alliance)	209 (27·6)	21 (4·6)	72·7 of 42 197 344
1987 (11 June)	650	**375** (42·3)	17 (12·8)	229 (30·8)	24 (3·4)	75·4 of 43 181 321

1955 In April 1955, after 4½ years of government with a small majority, Sir Winston Churchill resigned as Prime Minister in favour of Sir Anthony Eden, who seven weeks later went to the country for a vote of confidence. The Conservatives had succeeded in restoring the nation's finances, had denationalized steel and road haulage, and twice reduced the standard rate of income tax by 6d. The Government's majority rose to 58 and the five years of near deadlock in the House was broken.

1959 In January 1957, following the strain of the Suez crisis, Eden resigned and Harold Macmillan became Prime Minister. The Government had been losing support, largely owing to some unpopularity over the Rent Act. The new Prime Minister, despite a number of difficulties, managed to repair Conservative fortunes. His 1959 visit to the USSR and the further reduction of income tax in April added to general contentment. The election was fought on the Conservative theme 'life is better with us' while Labour got into difficulties with Mr Gaitskell's promises of no higher taxes, yet very expensive projects. The result was that the Government again increased their overall majority to 100 seats.

1964 The Conservative Government, after 13 consecutive years of rule, went to the country in October, as required every five years by the Parliament Act of 1911. After the post-war high water mark of 1959 (majority 100) Conservative fortunes declined owing notably to the Profumo scandal and a public wrangle over the successorship to Mr Macmillan who resigned in October 1963 owing to ill health. The nation wanted a change: the Conservatives were however defeated by a rise in the Liberal vote from 5·9 per cent to 11·2 per cent rather than the Labour vote which was less than their 1959 total. Labour won by an overall majority of only 4.

1966 After 20 months in power, Mr Wilson became convinced (on the death of the Member for Falmouth in February) of the danger of continuing with his hairline majority. Labour fought the campaign on the slogan 'You Know Labour Government Works'. The Conservatives fought on a policy of entering the Common Market, reforming the 'over-mighty' Trade Unions and making the Welfare State less indiscriminate. Mr Wilson increased his overall majority from 3 to 97 and declared his intention to govern for five years to achieve 'a juster society'.

1970 Having completed four of the five years of his second term in power, Mr Wilson called the Labour Party to action in a bid for his hat-trick in May 1970. Remembered as the General Election most dominated by the pollsters, their findings consistently showed strong leads for Labour. Wages rates had risen in an unrestrained way in the five-month run-up but price levels were also just beginning to erode the reality of these monetary gains. Within six days of polling NOP showed a massive Labour lead of 12·4 per cent. In reality, however, the voters gave the Conservatives a 3·4 per cent lead, thus an overall majority of 30 seats.

1974 (Feb) This was the first 'crisis' election since 1931. It was called to settle 'Who governs Britain?' under the duress of the National Union of Mineworkers' coal strike against the restraints of Stage

III of the Incomes Policy. The situation was exacerbated by the Arab decision the previous November to raise the price of oil fourfold. A three-day week for most industries was decreed under Emergency Powers to start on 1 Jan. A ballot inviting the miners to give the NUM authority to call a strike was announced on 4 Feb, an election was called on 7 Feb, and a strike began on 10 Feb after 81 per cent of the miners had voted in favour of giving the NUM Executive the authority they sought. Mr Wilson spoke of conciliation in place of confrontation and the alternative possibilities under a 'Social Contract' agreed between the Labour Party and the TUC on 18 Feb 1973. The electorate, largely due to the impact of a successful Liberal campaign, spoke equivocally, giving Labour a majority of four over the Conservatives but 10 less than the combined Conservatives and Liberals. The Liberals rejected a coalition and appealed for a government of National Unity. Two hours after Mr Heath's resignation on 4 Mar, the Queen sent for Mr Wilson for a third time.

1974 (Oct) For the first time since 1910 there were two elections within the same year. On 11 Mar the miners returned to full working accepting a National Coal Board offer to raise their wage bill by 29 per cent. In June and July HM Opposition, with Liberal support, defeated Mr Wilson's precarious lobby strength 29 times, notably on the Trade Union and Labour Relation Bill. An election was called by Mr Wilson on 18 Sept. The campaign was fought mainly on the issue of inflation statistics, unemployment prospects and the promise by Labour to hold an EEC ballot. Though less than 29 out of each 100 persons eligible to vote cast votes for Labour candidates, only 27 such voters supported Conservative candidates. Thus Mr Wilson won his fourth General Election, with an overall majority of three seats, but with a secure working majority of 42 over the Conservatives, who were by far the largest party in a fragmented Opposition. Mr Wilson resigned and was replaced by Mr Callaghan, who had been elected leader of the Labour Party on 5 Apr 1976.

1979 (May) During the 1974–79 Parliament all three parties had changed their leaders: Callaghan for Wilson; Steel for Thorpe; and Mrs Thatcher for Heath. The period was one of falling living standards due in part to oil prices and inflation. The Conservatives fought the ensuing general election on trade union reform, cutting public expenditure, reducing taxation and Whitehall intervention. Mrs Thatcher gained 51 seats from Labour in a 5·2% swing mainly in the Midlands and South East to win a 44 overall majority. She became Britain's first and the world's 4th woman Prime Minister and had the largest margin of the popular vote since 1935.

1983 (June) Mrs Thatcher's success was only the second time a Conservative Prime Minister has ever been re-elected after a full term (Lord Salisbury in 1900 was the other). The Conservatives' increase of 58 seats over the 1979 result was also the largest ever by an incumbent government although allowance should be made for an estimated 21 seats gained through boundary changes. By contrast, Labour lost more than a quarter of its previous vote – the lowest ever share won by the principal party of opposition.

1987 (June) Mrs Thatcher's historic third successive electoral victory not only put her into the history books as the longest serving Prime Minister of the twentieth century, but also returned her with an unexpectedly healthy 105 overall majority. Despite attacks by Labour and the Alliance on the Conservatives' social policies, particularly education and the National Health Service, Mrs Thatcher won through primarily on economic performance and pro-nuclear defence. However, the voting pattern showed a nation divided North and South.

Prime Ministers of Great Britain and the United Kingdom

Below is a complete compilation of the 51 Prime Ministers of Great Britain and the United Kingdom. The data run in the following order: final style as Prime Minister (with earlier or later styles); date or dates as Prime Minister with party affiliation; date and place of birth and death and place of burial; marriage or marriages with number of children; education and membership of Parliament with constituency and dates.

1. The Rt Hon., Sir Robert **WALPOLE**, KG (1726) KB (1725, resigned 1726), (PC 1714), cr. 1st Earl of Orford (of the 2nd creation) in the week of his retirement; ministry, 3 Apr 1721 to 8 Feb 1742, (i) reappointed on the accession of George II on 11 June 1727, (ii) Walpole's absolute control of the Cabinet can only be said to have dated from 15 May 1730; Whig; b. 26 Aug 1676 at Houghton, Norfolk; d. 18 Mar 1745 at No. 5 Arlington St, Piccadilly, London; bur. Houghton, Norfolk; m. 1 (1700) Catherine Shorter (d. 1717), m. 2 (1738) Maria Skerrett (d. 1738); children, 1st, 3s and 2d; 2nd, 2d (born prior to the marriage); ed. Eton and King's, Camb. (scholar); MP (Whig) for Castle Rising (1701-2); King's Lynn (1702-42) (expelled from the House for a short period 1712-13).

2. The Rt Hon., the Hon. Sir Spencer Compton, 1st and last Earl of **WILMINGTON**, KG (1733), KB (1725, resigned 1733), (PC 1716), cr. Baron Wilmington 1728; cr. Earl 1730; ministry, 16 Feb 1742 to 2 July 1743; Whig; b. 1673 or 1674; d. 2 July 1743; bur. Compton Wynyates, Warwickshire; unmarried; no legitimate issue; ed. St Paul's School, London, and Trinity, Oxford; MP (originally Tory until about 1704) for Eye (1698-1710); East Grinstead (1713-15); Sussex (Whig) (1715-28); Speaker 1715-27.

3. The Rt Hon., the Hon. Henry **PELHAM** (PC 1725); prior to 1706 was Henry Pelham, Esq.; ministry 27 Aug 1743 to 6 Mar 1754 (with an interregnum 10-12 Feb 1746); Whig; b. c. 1695; d. 6 Mar 1754 at Arlington St, Piccadilly, London; bur. Laughton Church, nr. Lewes, E. Sussex; m. (1726) Lady Catherine Manners; children, 2s and 6d; ed. Westminster School and Hart Hall, Oxford; MP Seaford (1717-22); Sussex (1722-54).

4. The Rt Hon. Sir William Pulteney, 1st and last Earl of **BATH** (cr. 1742) PC (1716) (struck off 1731); kissed hands 10 Feb 1746 but unable to form a ministry; Whig; b. 22 Mar 1684 in London; d. 7 July 1764; bur. Westminster Abbey; m. Anna Maria

Gumley; ed. Westminster School and Christ Church, Oxford; MP Hedon (or Heydon) 1705-34; Middlesex 1734-42.

5. His Grace the 1st Duke of **NEWCASTLE** upon Tyne and 1st Duke of Newcastle-under-Lyme (The Rt Hon., the Hon. Sir Thomas Pelham-Holles), Bt, KG (1718). (PC 1717); added the surname Holles in July 1711; known as Lord Pelham of Laughton (1711-14); Earl of Claire (1714-15); cr. Duke of Newcastle upon Tyne 1715 and cr. Duke of Newcastle-under-Lyme 1756; ministry, (a) 16 Mar 1754 to 26 Oct 1756, (b) 2 July 1757 to 25 Oct 1760, (c) 25 Oct 1760 to 25 May 1762; Whig; b. 21 July 1693; d. 17 Nov 1768 at Lincoln's Inn Field, London; bur. Laughton Church, nr. Lewes, E. Sussex; m. (1717) Lady Henrietta Godolphin (d. 1776); no issue; ed. Westminster School and Claire Hall, Cambridge.

6. His Grace the 4th Duke of **DEVONSHIRE** (Sir William Cavendish), KG (1756), (PC 1751, but struck off roll 1762); known as Lord Cavendish of Hardwick until 1729 and Marquess of Hartington until 1755; ministry, 16 Nov 1756 to May 1757; Whig; b. 1720; d. 2 Oct 1764 at Spa, Belgium; bur. Derby Cathedral; m. (1748) Charlotte Elizabeth, Baroness Clifford (d. 1754); children, 3s and 1d; ed. privately; MP (Whig) for Co. Derby (1741-51). Summoned to Lords (1751) in father's Barony Cavendish of Hardwick.

7. The Rt Hon. James **WALDEGRAVE**, 2nd Earl of Waldegrave (pronounced Wallgrave) from 1741, PC (1752), KG (1757); kissed hands 8 June 1757 but returned seals 12 June being unable to form Ministry; b. 14 Mar 1715; d. 28 Apr 1763; m. Marion Walpole (niece of No. 1); children 3d; ed. Eton; took seat in House of Lords, 1741.

8. The 3rd Earl of **BUTE** (The Rt Hon., the Hon. Sir John Stuart, KG (1762), KT (1738, resigned 1762), (PC 1760)); until 1723 was The Hon. John Stuart; ministry, 26 May 1762 to 8 Apr 1763; Tory; b. 25 May 1713 at Parliament Square, Edinburgh; d. 10 Mar 1792 at South Audley St, Grosvenor Square, London; bur. Rothesay, Bute; m. (1736) Mary Wortley-Montagu later (1761) Baroness Mount Stuart (d. 1794); children, 4s and 4d (with other issue); ed. Eton.

9. The Rt Hon., the Hon. George **GRENVILLE** (PC 1754); prior to 1749 was G. Grenville Esq; ministry, 16 Apr 1763 to 10 July 1765; Whig; b. 14 Oct 1712 at ? Wotton, Bucks; d. 13 Nov 1770 at Bolton St, Piccadilly, London; bur. Wotton, Bucks; m. (1749) Elizabeth Wyndham (d. 1769); children, 4s and 5d; ed. Eton and Christ Church, Oxford; MP for Buckingham (1741-70).

10. The Most Hon. The 2nd Marquess of **ROCKINGHAM** (The Rt Hon. Lord Charles Watson-Wentworth), KG (1760), (PC 1765); known as Hon. Charles Watson-Wentworth until 1739; Viscount Higham (1739-46); Earl of Malton (1746-50); succeeded to Marquessate 14 Dec 1750; ministry, (a) 13 July 1765 to July 1766, (b) 27 March 1782 to his death on 1 July 1782; Whig; b. 13 May 1730; d. 1 July 1782; bur. York Minster; m. (1752) Mary Bright (her father was formerly called Liddell) (d. 1804); no issue; ed. Westminster School (and possibly St John's Camb.). Took his seat in House of Lords 21 May 1751.

11. The 1st Earl of **CHATHAM** (The Rt Hon. William Pitt (PC 1746)); cr. Earl 4 Aug 1766; ministry, 30 July 1766 to 14 Oct 1768; Whig; his health in 1767 prevented his being PM in other than name; b. 15 Nov 1708 at St James's, Westminster, London; d. 11 May 1788 at Hayes, Kent; bur. Westminster Abbey; m. (1754) Hon. Hester Grenville*, later (1761) cr. Baroness Chatham in her own right (d. 1803); children, 3s and 2d; ed. Eton, Trinity, Oxford (took no degree owing to gout), and Utrecht; MP (Whig) Old Sarum (1735–47); Seaford (1747–54); Aldborough (1754–6); Okehampton (1756–7) (also Buckingham (1756), Bath (1757–66)).

12. His Grace the 3rd Duke of **GRAFTON** (The Rt Hon. Sir Augustus Henry FitzRoy) KG (1769), (PC 1765); prior to 1747 known as the Hon. Augustus H. FitzRoy; 1747–57 as Earl of Euston; succeeded to dukedom in 1757; ministry, 14 Oct 1768 to 28 Jan 1770; Whig; he was virtually PM in 1767 when Lord Chatham's ministry broke down; b. 28 Sept 1735 at St Marylebone, London; d. 14 Mar 1811 at Euston Hall, Suffolk; bur. Euston, Suffolk; m. 1 (1765) Hon. Anne Liddell (sep. 1765, mar. dis. by Act of Parl. 1769) (d. 1804), m. 2 (1769) Elizabeth Wrottesley (d. 1822); children, 1st, 2s and 1d; 2nd, 6s and 6d (possibly also another d who died young); ed. private school at Hackney, Westminster School, and Peterhouse, Camb.; MP (Whig) Bury St Edmunds (1756–7).

13. Lord **NORTH** (The Rt Hon., the Hon. Sir Frederick North), KG (1772), (PC 1766); succ. (Aug 1790) as 2nd Earl of Guildford; ministry 28 Jan 1770 to 20 Mar 1782; Tory; b. 13 Apr 1732 at Albermarle St, Piccadilly, London; d. 5 Aug 1792 at Lower Grosvenor St, London; bur. All Saints' Church, Wroxton, Oxfordshire; m. (1756) Anne Speke (d. 1797); children, 4s and 3d; ed. Eton; Trinity, Oxford, and Leipzig; MP (Tory) for Banbury (1754–90) (can be regarded as a Whig from 1783). Took his seat in the House of Lords 25 Nov 1790.

14. The 2nd Earl of **SHELBURNE** (Rt Hon., the Hon. Sir William Petty, KG (1782) (PC 1763); formerly, until 1751, William Fitz-Maurice; Viscount Fitz-Maurice (1753–61); succeeded to Earldom 10 May 1761; cr. The 1st Marquess of Lansdowne (6 Dec 1784); Col. 1760; Maj. Gen. 1765; Lt. Gen. 1772, and Gen. 1783; ministry, 4 July 1782 to 24 Feb 1783; Whig; b. 20 May 1737 at Dublin, Ireland; d. 7 May 1805 at Berkeley Square, London; bur. High Wycombe, Bucks; m. 1 (1765) Lady Sophia Carerett (d. 1771), m. 2 (1779) Lady Louisa FitzPatrick (d. 1789); children, 1st, 2s; 2nd, 1s and 1d; ed. local school in S. Ireland, private tutor, and Christ Church, Oxford; MP Chipping Wycombe (1760–1). Took seat in House of Lords (as Baron Wycombe) 3 Nov 1761.

15. His Grace the 3rd Duke of **PORTLAND** (The Most Noble Sir William Henry Cavendish Bentinck, KG (1794) (PC 1765)); assumed additional name of Bentinck in 1775; assumed by Royal Licence surname of Cavendish-Bentinck in 1801; Marquess of Titchfield from birth until he succeeded to the dukedom on 1 May 1762; ministry (a)

2 Apr 1783 to Dec 1783, (b) 31 Mar 1807 to Oct 1809; (a) coalition and (b) Tory; b. 14th Apr 1738; d. 30 Oct 1809 at Bulstrode, Bucks; bur. St Marylebone, London; m. (1766) Lady Dorothy Cavendish (d. 1794); children, 4s and 1d; ed. Westminster or Eton and Christ Church, Oxford; MP (Whig) Weobley, Herefordshire (1761–2).

16. The Rt Hon., the Hon. William **PITT** (PC 1782) prior August 1766 was William Pitt, Esq.; ministry (a) 19 Dec 1783 to 14 Mar 1801, (b) 10 May 1804 to his death on 23 Jan 1806; Tory; b. 28 May 1759 at Hayes, nr. Bromley, Kent; d. 23 Jan 1806 at Bowling Green House, Putney, Surrey; bur. Westminster Abbey; unmarried; ed. privately and Pembroke Hall, Cambridge; MP (Tory) Appleby.

17. The Rt Hon. Henry **ADDINGTON** (PC 1789); cr. 1st Viscount Sidmouth 1805; ministry, 17 Mar 1801 to 30 April 1804; Tory; b. 30 May 1757 at Bedford Row, London; d. 15 Feb 1844 at White Lodge, Richmond Park, Surrey; bur. Mortlake; m. 1 (1781) Ursula Mary Hammond (d. 1811), m. 2 (1823) Hon. Mrs Marianne Townshend (*née* Scott) (d. 1842); children, 1st, 3s and 4d; 2nd, no issue; ed. Cheam, Winchester Col., Lincoln's Inn, and Brasenose, Oxford (Chancellor's Medal for English Essay); MP (Tory) Devizes (1783–1805). Speaker 1789–1801. As a peer he supported the Whigs in 1807 and 1812 administration.

18. The Rt Hon. the 1st Baron **GRENVILLE** of Wotton-under-Bernewood (William Wyndham Grenville (PC(I) 1782; PC 1783)); cr. Baron 25 Nov 1790; ministry, 10 Feb 1806 to Mar 1807; b. (the son of No. 9) 25 Oct 1759; d. 12 Jan 1834 at Dropmore Lodge, Bucks; bur. Burnham, Bucks; m. (1792) Hon. Anne Pitt (d. 1864 aged 91); no issue; ed. Eton, Christ Church, Oxford (Chancellor's prize for Latin Verse), and Lincoln's Inn; MP Buckingham (1782–4), Buckinghamshire (1784–90). Speaker January–June 1789.

19. The Rt Hon., the Hon. Spencer **PERCEVAL** (PC 1807), KC (1796); ministry, 4 Oct 1809 to 11 May 1812; b. 1 Nov 1762 at Audley Sq., London; murdered 11 May 1812 in lobby of the House; bur. Charlton; m. (1790) Jane Spencer-Wilson (later Lady Carr) (d. 1844); children, 6s and 6d; ed. Harrow, Trinity, Camb., and Lincoln's Inn; MP (Tory) Northampton (1796–7).

20. The Rt Hon. the 2nd Earl of **LIVERPOOL** (Sir Robert Banks Jenkinson, KG (1814) (PC 1799)); from birth to 1786 R. B. Jenkinson, Esq.; from 1786–96 The Hon. R. B. Jenkinson; from 1796–1808 (when he succeeded to the earldom) Lord Hawkesbury; ministry, (a) 8 June 1812 to 29 Jan 1820, (b) 29 Jan 1820 to 17 Feb 1827; Tory; b. 7 June 1770; d. 4 Dec 1828 at Coombe Wood, near Kingston-on-Thames; bur. at Hawkesbury; m. 1 (1795) Lady Louisa Theodosia Hervey (d. 1821), m. 2 (1822) Mary Chester (d. 1846); no issue; ed. Charterhouse and Christ Church, Oxford; summoned to House of Lords in his father's barony of Hawkesbury 15 Nov 1803 (elected MP (Tory) for Appleby (1790) but did not sit as he was under age); Rye (1796–1803).

21. The Rt Hon. George **CANNING** (PC 1800); ministry, 10 Apr 1827 to his death; Tory; b. 11 Apr 1770 in London; d. 8 Aug 1827 at Chiswick Villa, London; m. (1800) Joan Scott (later, 1828, cr. Vis-

---

* This lady had the extraordinary distinction of being the wife, the mother, the sister and the aunt of four British Prime Ministers. They were Nos. 11, 16, 9, and 18 respectively.

countess) (d. 1837); children, 3s and 1d; ed. in London; Hyde Abbey (nr. Winchester); Eton; Christ Church, Oxford (Chancellor's prize, Latin Verse), and Lincoln's Inn; MP (Tory) Newton, I.o.W. (1793–6); Wendover (1796–1802); Tralee (1802–6); Newton (1806–7); Hastings (1807–12); Liverpool (1812–23); Harwich (1823–6); Newport (1826–7), and Seaford (1827).

22. The Viscount **GODERICH** (Rt Hon., the Hon. Frederick John Robinson (PC 1812, PC (I) *c.* 1833); cr. Earl of Ripon 1833; ministry 31 Aug 1827 to 8 Jan 1828; Tory; b. 1 Nov 1782 in London; d. 28 Jan 1859 at Putney Heath, London; bur. Nocton, Lincolnshire; m. (1814) Lady Sarah Albinia Louisa Hobart (d. 1867); children, 2s and 1d; ed. Harrow; St John's Col., Cambridge, and Lincoln's Inn; MP Carlow (1806–7); Ripon (1807–27).

23. His Grace The 1st Duke of **WELLINGTON** (The Most Noble, The Hon. Sir Arthur Wellesley, KG (1813), GCB (1815), GCH (1816), (PC 1807, PC (I) 1807)); known as The Hon. Arthur Wesley until 1804; then as The Hon. Sir Arthur Wellesley, KB, until 1809 when cr. The Viscount Wellington; cr. Earl of Wellington February 1812; Marquess of Wellington October 1812 and Duke May 1814. Ensign (1787); Lieut. (1787); Capt. (1791); Major (1793); Lt.-Col. (1793); Col. (1796); Maj. Gen. (1802); Lt. Gen. (1808); Gen. (1811); Field Marshal (1813); ministry, (a) 22 Jan 1828 to 26 June 1830, (b) 26 June 1830 to 21 Nov 1830, (c) 17 Nov to 9 Dec 1834; Tory; b. 1 May 1769 at Mornington House, Upper Merrion St, Dublin; d. 14 Sept 1852 at Walmer Castle, Kent; bur. St Paul's Cathedral; m. (1806) the Hon. Catherine Sarah Dorothea Pakenham (d. 1831); children, 2s; ed. Browns Seminary, King's Rd, Chelsea, London; Eton; Brussels, and The Academy at Angiers; MP Rye (1806); St Michael (1807); Newport, Isle of Wight (1807–9). Took seat in House of Lords as Viscount, Earl, Marquess, and Duke 28 June 1814. Physical height: 1·76 m (*5 ft 9½ in*).

24. The 2nd Earl **GREY** (The Rt Hon., the Hon. Sir Charles Grey, Bt (1808), KG (1831), (PC 1806)); styled Viscount Howick 1806–7 and previously The Hon. Charles Grey; ministry, 22 Nov 1830 to July 1834; Whig; b. 13 Mar 1764 at Fallodon, Northumberland; d. 17 July 1845 and bur. at Howick House, Northumberland; m. (1794) Hon. Mary Elizabeth Ponsonby (d. 1861); children, 8s and 5d; ed. at a private school in Marylebone, London; Eton; Trinity, Camb., and Middle Temple; MP (Whig) Northumberland (1786–1807); Appleby (1807); Tavistock (1807).

25. The 3rd Viscount **MELBOURNE** (The Rt Hon., The Hon. Sir William Lamb, Bt (PC (UK & I) 1827)); ministry, (a) 17 July 1834 to November 1834, (b) 18 Apr 1835 to 20 June 1837, (c) 20 June 1837 to August 1841; Whig; b. (of disputed paternity) 15 Mar 1779 Melbourne House, Piccadilly, London; d. 24 Nov 1848 at Brocket; bur. Hatfield; m. (1805) Lady Caroline Ponsonby, separated 1824 (d. 1828); only 1s survived infancy; ed. Eton; Trinity, Cambridge; Glasgow University, and Lincoln's Inn; MP (Whig) Leominster (1806); Haddington Borough (1806–7); Portarlington (1807–12); Peterborough (1816–19); Hertfordshire (1819–26); Newport, Isle of Wight (1827); Bletchingley (1827–8). Took his seat in House of Lords 1 Feb 1829.

26. The Rt Hon. Sir Robert **PEEL**, Bt (PC 1812); prior to May 1830 he was Robert Peel, Esq., MP, when he succeeded as 2nd Baronet; ministry, (a) 10 Dec 1834 to 8 Apr 1835, (b) 30 Aug 1841 to 29 June 1846; Conservative; b. 5 Feb 1788 prob. at Chamber Hall, nr. Bury, Lancashire; d. 2 July 1850 after fall from horse; bur. Drayton Bassett; m. (1820) Julia Floyd (d. 1859); children, 5s and 2d; ed. Harrow; Christ Church, Oxford (Double First in Classics and Mathematics), and Lincoln's Inn; MP (Tory) Cashel (Tipperary) (1809–12); Chippenham (1812–17); Univ. of Oxford (1817–29); Westbury (1829–30); Tamworth (1830–50).

27. The Rt Hon. Lord John **RUSSELL** (PC 1830), and after 30 July 1861 1st Earl **RUSSELL**, KG (1862), GCMG (1869); ministry, (a) 30 June 1846 to February 1852, (b) 29 Oct 1865 to June 1866; (a) Whig and (b) Liberal; b. 18 Aug 1792 in Hertford St, Mayfair; d. 28 May 1878 at Pembroke Lodge, Richmond Park, Surrey; bur. Chenies, Bucks; m. 1 (1835) Adelaide (*née* Lister), Dowager Baroness Ribblesdale (d. 1838), m. 2 (1841) Lady Frances Anna Maria Elliot-Murray-Kynynmound (d. 1898); children, 1st, 2d; 2nd, 3s and 3d; ed. Westminster School and Edinburgh University; MP (Whig) Tavistock (1813–17, 1818–20 and 1830–1); Hunts (1820–6); Bandon (1826–30); Devon (1831–2); S. Devon (1832–5); Stroud (1835–41); City of London (1841–61). Took seat in the House of Lords on 30 July 1861.

28. The 14th Earl of **DERBY**, Rt Hon. Sir Edward Geoffrey Smith-Stanley, Bt, KG (1859), GCMG (1869), PC 1830, PC (I) (1831); prior to 1834 known as the Hon. E. G. Stanley; then known as Lord Stanley MP until 1844; ministry, (a) 23 Feb 1852 to 18 Dec 1852, (b) 20 Feb 1858 to 11 June 1859, (c) 28 June 1866 to 26 Feb 1868; Tory and Conservative; b. 19 Mar 1799 Knowsley, Lancs; d. 23 Oct 1869; bur. Knowsley, Lancs; m. (1825) Hon. Emma Caroline Wilbraham-Bootle (d. 1876); 2s, 1d; ed. Eton; Christ Church, Oxford (Chancellor's prize for Latin Verse); MP (Whig) Stockbridge (1822–6); Windsor (1831–2); North Lancs (1832–44). Summoned 1844 to House of Lords as Lord Stanley (of Bickerstaffe); succeeded to Earldom 1851; became a Tory in 1835.

29. The Rt Hon. Sir George Hamilton Gordon, Bt, 4th Earl of **ABERDEEN**, KG (1855), KT (1808), (PC 1814); prior to October 1791 known as the Hon. G. Gordon; from 1791 to August 1801 known as Lord Haddo; assumed additional name of Hamilton November 1818; ministry, 19 Dec 1852 to 5 Feb 1855; Peelite; b. 28 Jan 1784 in Edinburgh; d. 14 Dec 1860 at Argyll House, St James's, London; bur. at Stanmore, G. London; m. 1 (1805) Lady Catherine Elizabeth Hamilton (d. 1812), m. 2 (1815) her sister-in-law Harriet (*née* Douglas), Dowager Viscountess Hamilton (d. 1833); children, 1st, 1s and 3d; 2nd, 4s and 1d; ed. Harrow and St John's, Camb.; House of Lords 1814.

30. The Rt Hon. Sir Henry John Temple, 3rd and last Viscount **PALMERSTON** (a non-representative peer of Ireland), KG (1856), CGB (1832), (PC 1809); known (1784–1802) as the Hon. H. J. Temple; ministry, (a) 6 Feb 1855 to 19 Feb 1858, (b) 12 June 1859 to 18 Oct 1865; Liberal; b. 20 Oct 1784 at Broadlands, nr. Romsey, Hants (or possibly in Park St, London); d. 18 Oct 1865 at Brocket Hall, Hertfordshire; bur. Westminster Abbey; m. (1839)

Hon. Emily Mary (*née* Lamb), the Dowager Countess Cowper (d. 1869); no issue; ed. Harrow; Univ. of Edinburgh, and St John's, Cambridge; MP (Tory) Newport, Isle of Wight (18u7-11); Cambridge Univ. (1811-31); Bletchingley (1831-2); S. Hampshire (1832-4); Tiverton (1835-65); from 1829 a Whig and latterly a Liberal.

31. The Rt Hon. Benjamin **DISRAELI**, 1st and last Earl of **BEACONSFIELD**, KG (1878), (PC 1852); prior to 12 Aug 1876 Benjamin Disraeli (except that until 1838 he was known as Benjamin D'Israeli); ministry, (a) 27 Feb 1868 to Nov 1868, (b) 20 Feb 1874 to Apr 1880; Conservative; b. 21 Dec 1804 at either the Adelphi, Westminster, or at 22 Theobald's Rd, or St Mary Axe; d. 19 Apr 1881 at 19 Curzon St, Mayfair, London; bur. Hughenden Manor, Bucks (monument in Westminster Abbey); m. (1839) Mrs Mary Anne Lewis (*née* Evans) later (1868) Viscountess (in her own right) Beaconsfield; no issue; ed. Lincoln's Inn; MP (Con.) Maidstone (1837-41); Shrewsbury (1841-7); Buckinghamshire (1847-76), when he became a peer.

32. The Rt Hon. William Ewart **GLADSTONE** (PC 1841); ministry, (a) 3 Dec 1868 to February 1874, (b) 23 Apr 1880 to 12 June 1885, (c) 1 Feb 1886 to 20 July 1886, (d) 15 Aug 1892 to 3 Mar 1894; Liberal; b. 29 Dec 1809 at 62 Rodney St, Liverpool; d. 19 May 1898 (aged 88 yrs 142 days) at Hawarden Castle, Clwyd; bur. Westminster Abbey; m. (1839) Catherine Glynne (d. 1900); children, 4s and 4d; ed. Seaforth Vicarage; Eton and Christ Church, Oxford (Double First in Classics and Mathematics); MP Tory, Newark (1832-45); Univ. of Oxford (1847-65) (Peelite to 1859, thereafter a Liberal); S. Lancashire (1865-8); Greenwich (1868-80); Midlothian (1880-95).

33. The Rt Hon. Robert Arthur Talbot Gascoyne-Cecil, the 3rd Marquess of **SALISBURY**, KG (1878), GCVO (1902), (PC 1866); known as Lord Robert Cecil till 1865; and as Viscount Cranbourne, MP, from 1865 to 1868; ministry, (a) 23 June 1885 to 28 Jan 1886, (b) 25 July 1886 to August 1892, (c) 25 June 1895 to 22 Jan 1901, (d) 23 Jan 1901 to 11 July 1902; Conservative; b. 3 Feb 1830 at Hatfield House, Hertfordshire; d. 22 Aug 1903 at Hatfield House; bur. Hatfield; m. (1857) Georgiana Charlotte (*née* Alderson), Lady of the Royal Order of Victoria and Albert and C.I. (1899) (d. 1899); children, 4s and 3d; ed. Eton and Christ Church, Oxford (Hon. 4th Cl. Maths.); MP (Con.) for Stamford (1853-68).

34. The Rt Hon. Sir Archibald Philip Primrose, Bt, 5th Earl of **ROSEBERY**, KG (1892), KT (1895), VD (PC 1881); b. the Hon. A. P. Primrose; known as Lord Dalmeny (1851-68); Earl of Midlothian from 1911 but style not adopted by him; ministry, 5 Mar 1894 to 21 June 1895; Liberal; b. 7 May 1847 at Charles St, Berkeley Square, London; d. 21 May 1929 at 'The Durdans', Epsom, Surrey; bur. Dalmeny; m. (1878) Hannah de Rothschild (d. 1890); children, 2s and 2d; ed. Eton and Christ Church, Oxford.

35. The Rt Hon. Arthur James **BALFOUR** (PC 1885, PC (I) 1887); KG (1922), later (1922) the 1st Earl of Balfour, OM (1916); ministry, 12 July 1902 to 4 Dec 1905; Conservative; b. 25 July 1848 at Whittingehame, E. Lothian, Scotland; d. 19 Mar 1930 at Fisher's Hill, Woking, Surrey; bur. Whittingehame; unmarried; ed. Eton and Trinity, Camb.; MP (Con.)

Hertford (1874-85); E. Manchester (1885-1906); City of London (1906-22).

36. The Rt Hon. Sir Henry **CAMPBELL-BANNERMAN**, GCB (1895), (PC 1884); known as Henry Campbell until 1872; ministry, 5 Dec 1905 to 5 Apr 1908; Liberal; b. 7 Sept 1836 at Kelvinside House, Glasgow; d. 22 Apr 1908 at 10 Downing Street, London; bur. Meigle, Scotland; m. (1860) Sarah Charlotte Bruce (d. 1906); no issue; ed. Glasgow High School; Glasgow Univ. (Gold Medal for Greek); Trinity, Camb. (22nd Sen. Optime in Maths Tripos; 3rd Cl. in Classical Tripos); MP (Lib.) Stirling District (1868-1908).

37. The Rt Hon. Herbert Henry **ASQUITH** (PC 1892, PC (I) 1916); later (1925) 1st Earl of **OXFORD AND ASQUITH**, KG (1925); ministry, (a) 7 Apr 1908 to 7 May 1910, (b) 8 May 1910 to 5 Dec 1916 (coalition from 25 May 1915); Liberal; b. 12 Sept 1852 at Morley, W. Yorks; d. 15 Feb 1928 at 'The Wharf', Sutton Courtney, Berks; bur. Sutton Courtney Church; m. 1st (1877) Helen Kelsall Melland (d. 1891), 2ndly (1894) Emma Alice Margaret Tennant; children, 1st, 4s and 1d; 2nd, 1s and 1d; ed. City of London School; Balliol, Oxford (Scholar, 1st Class Lit. Hum.); MP (Lib.) East Fife (1886-1918); Paisley (1920-4).

38. The Rt Hon. (David) Lloyd **GEORGE**, OM (1919), (PC 1905); later (1945) 1st Earl **LLOYD-GEORGE** of Dwyfor; ministry, 7 Dec 1916 to 19 Oct 1922; Coalition; b. 17 Jan 1863 Manchester; d. 26 Mar 1945 Ty Newydd, nr. Llanystumdwy; bur. on the bank of the river Dwyfor; m. 1 (1888) Margaret Owen, GBE (1920) (d. 1941), m. 2 (1943) Frances Louise Stevenson, CBE; children, 1st, 2s and 3d; 2nd, no issue; ed. Llanystumdwy Church School and privately; MP Caernarvon Boroughs (1890-1945) (Lib. 1890-1931 and 1935-45; Ind. Lib. 1931-5). Physical height: 1·67 m (*5 ft 6 in*).

39. The Rt Hon. (Andrew) Bonar **LAW** (PC 1911); ministry, 23 Oct 1922 to 20 May 1923; Conservative; b. 16 Sept 1858 at Kingston, nr. Richibucto, New Brunswick, Canada; d. 30 Oct 1923 at 24 Onslow Gardens, London; bur. Westminster Abbey; m. (1891) Annie Pitcairn (d. 1909); children, 4s and 2d; ed. Gilbertfield School, Hamilton; Glasgow High School; MP (Con.) Blackfriars Div. of Glasgow (1900-6); Dulwich Div. of Camberwell (1906-10); MP Bootle Div. of Lancashire (1911-18); Central Div. of Glasgow (1918-23). Physical height: 1·83 m (*6 ft 0 in*).

40. The Rt Hon. Stanley **BALDWIN** (PC 1920, PC (Can.) 1927); later (1937) 1st Earl Baldwin of Bewdley, KG (1937); ministry, (a) 22 May 1923 to 22 Jan 1924 (Con.), (b) 4 Nov 1924 to 4 June 1929 (Con.), (c) 7 June 1935 to 20 Jan 1936 (Nat.), (d) 21 Jan 1936 to 11 Dec 1936 (Nat.), (e) 12 Dec 1936 to 28 May 1937 (Nat.); b. 3 Aug 1867 at Bewdley; d. Astley, 14 Dec 1947; bur. Worcester Cathedral; m. (1892) Lucy Ridsdale, GBE (1937) (d. 1945); children, 2s and 3d; ed. Harrow and Trinity, Camb.; MP (Con.) Bewdley Div. of Worcestershire (1908-37). Physical height: 1·74 m (*5 ft 8½ in*).

41. The Rt Hon. (James) Ramsay **MACDONALD** (PC 1924, PC (Can.) (1929); ministry, (a) 22 Jan 1924 to 4 Nov 1924 (Lab.), (b) 5 June 1929 to 7 June 1935 (Lab. and from 1931 National Coalition); b. 12 Oct

Neville Chamberlain exhibiting the 'Peace In Our Time' document after his historic visit to Munich. (Hulton Picture Company)

1866 at Lossiemouth, Grampian; d. 9 Nov 1937 at sea, mid-Atlantic; bur. Spynie Churchyard, nr. Lossiemouth, Scotland; m. (1896) Margaret Ethel Gladstone (d. 1911); children, 3s and 3d; ed. Drainie Parish Board School; MP (Lab.) Leicester (1906–18); (Lab.) Aberavon (1922–9); (Lab.) Seaham Div. Co. Durham (1929–31); (Nat. Lab.) (1931–5); MP for Scottish Univs. (1936–7). Physical height: 1·79 m (*5 ft 10½ in*).

42. The Rt Hon. (Arthur) Neville **CHAMBERLAIN** (PC 1922); ministry, 28 May 1937 to 10 May 1940; National; b. 18 Mar 1869 at Edgbaston, Birmingham; d. 9 Nov 1940 at High Field Park, Hickfield, nr. Reading; ashes interred Westminster Abbey; m. (1911) Annie Vere Cole (d. 12 Feb 1967); children, 1s and 1d; ed. Rugby School; Mason College (later Birmingham Univ.) (Metallurgy & Engineering Design); MP (Con.) Ladywood Div. of Birmingham (1918–29); Edgbaston Div. of Birmingham (1929–40). Physical height: 1·77 m (*5 ft 10 in*).

43. The Rt Hon. Sir Winston (Leonard **SPEN-CER-)CHURCHILL**, KG (1953), OM (1946), CH (1922), TD (PC 1907); ministry, (a) 10 May 1940 to 26

July 1945 (Coalition but from 23 May 1945 Con.), (b) 26 Oct 1951 to 6 Feb 1952 (Con.), (c) 7 Feb 1952 to 5 Apr 1955 (Con.); b. 30 Nov 1874 at Blenheim Palace, Woodstock, Oxfordshire; d. 24 Jan 1965 Hyde Park Gate, London; bur. Bladon, Oxfordshire; m. (1908) Clementine Ogilvy Hozier, GBE (1946), cr. 1965 (Life) Baroness Spencer-Churchill (d. 13 Dec 1977); children, 1s and 4d; ed. Harrow School and Royal Military College; MP (Con. until 1904, then Lib.) Oldham (1900–6); (Lib.) N.-W. Manchester (1906–8); (Lib.) Dundee (1908–18 and (Coalition Lib.) until 1922; Epping Div. of Essex (1924–45); Woodford Div. of Essex (1945–64). Physical height: 1·74 m (*5 ft 8½ in*).

44. The Rt Hon. Clement (Richard) **ATTLEE** CH (1945), (PC 1935); cr. 1955 1st Earl Attlee, KG (1956), OM (1951); ministry, 26 July 1945 to 26 Oct 1951; Labour; b. 3 Jan 1883 at Putney, London; d. Westminster Hospital, 8 Oct 1967; m. (1922) Violet Helen Millar; children, 1s and 3d; ed. Haileybury College and Univ. College, Oxford (2nd Cl. Hons. (Mod. Hist.)); MP Limehouse Div. of Stepney (1922–50); West Walthamstow (1950–5). Physical height: 1·73 m (*5 ft 8 in*).

45. The Rt Hon. Sir (Robert) Anthony **EDEN**, KG (1954), MC (1917), (PC 1934); cr. 1961 1st Earl of Avon; ministry, 6 Apr 1955 to 9 Jan 1957; Conservative; b. 12 June 1897, Windlestone, Durham; d. Alvediston, Wiltshire, 14 Jan 1977; m. 1 (1923) Beatrice Helen Beckett (m. dis. 1950) (d. 1957), m. 2 (1952) Anne Clarissa Spencer-Churchill; children, 1st, 2s; 2nd, no issue; ed. Eton and Christ Church, Oxford (1st Cl. Hons (Oriental Langs)); MP Warwick and Leamington (1923–57). Physical height; 1·83 m (6 ft 0 in).

46. The Rt Hon. (Maurice) Harold **MACMILLAN**, OM (1976) (PC 1942); cr. 1984 1st Earl of Stockton; ministry, 10 Jan 1957 to 18 Oct 1963; Conservative; b. 10 Feb 1894, 52 Cadogan Place, London; d. 29 Dec 1986; m. (1920) Lady Dorothy Evelyn Cavendish, GBE; children, 1s and 3d; ed. Eton (Scholar); Balliol, Oxford ((Exhibitioner) 1st Class Hon. Mods.); MP Stockton-on-Tees (1924–9 and 1931–45); Bromley (1945–64). Physical height: 1·83 m (6 ft 0 in).

47. The Rt Hon. Sir Alexander (Frederick) **DOUGLAS-HOME**, KT (1962) (PC 1951); known until 30 Apr 1918 as the Hon. A. F. Douglas-Home; thence until 11 July 1951 as Lord Dunglass; thence until his disclaimer of 23 Oct 1963 as the (14th) Earl of Home, Lord Home of the Hirsel; cr. 1974 Baron Home of the Hirsel (Life Peer); ministry, 19 Oct 1963 to 16 Oct 1964; Conservative; b. 2 July 1903, 28 South St, London; m. (1936) Elizabeth Hester Alington; children, 1s and 3d; ed. Eton; Christ Church, Oxford; MP South Lanark (1931–45); Lanark (1950–1); Kinross and West Perthshire (1963–74). Physical height: 1·80 m (5 ft 11 in).

48. The Rt Hon. Sir (James) Harold **WILSON**, KG (1976), OBE (civ.) (1945) (PC 1947); cr. 1983 Baron Wilson of Rievaulx (Life Peer); ministry, (a) 16 Oct 1964 to 30 Mar 1966, (b) 31 Mar 1966 to 17 June 1970, (c) 4 Mar 1974 to 10 Oct 1974, (d) 10 Oct 1974 to 5 Apr 1976; Labour; b. Linthwaite, W. Yorkshire, 11 Mar 1916; m. (1940) Gladys Mary Baldwin; children, 2s; ed. Milnsbridge C.S.; Royds Hall S.; Wirral G.S.; Jesus College, Oxford (1st Cl. Philosophy, Politics and Economics); MP Ormskirk (1945–50); Huyton (1950–83). Physical height: 1·74 m (5 ft 8½ in).

49. The Rt Hon. Edward Richard George **HEATH**, MBE (mil.) (1946), (PC 1955); ministry, 18 June 1970 to 3 Mar 1974; Conservative; b. 9 July 1916 at Broadstairs, Kent; unmarried; ed. Chatham House School, Ramsgate, and Balliol College, Oxford; MP Bexley (1950–74); Bexley-Sidcup from 1974. Physical height: 1·80 m (5 ft 11 in).

50. The Rt Hon. (Leonard) James **CALLAGHAN** (PC 1964); cr. 1987 Baron Callaghan of Cardiff (Life Peer); ministry 5 Apr 1976 to 4 May 1979; Labour; b. 27 Mar 1912 at 38 Funtingdon Rd, Portsmouth, Hampshire; m. (1938) Audrey Elizabeth Moulton; children 1s and 2d; ed. Portsmouth Northern Secondary Sch.; MP South Cardiff (1945–50); Southeast Cardiff (1950 to date). Physical height: 1·87 m (6 ft 1½ in).

51. The Rt Hon. Mrs Margaret (Hilda) **THATCHER** née Roberts (PC 1970); ministry (a) 4 May 1979 to 9 June 1983, (b) 10 June 1983 to 4 May 1987, (c) 12 June 1987 to date; Conservative; b. 13 Oct 1925, Grantham, Lincolnshire; m. (13 Dec 1951) Denis Thatcher MBE (b. 10 May 1915, he prev. m. Margaret D. Kempson, who in 1948 m. Sir Howard Hickman 3rd Bt.); 1s 1d (twins); ed. Kesteven & Grantham Girls' Sch.; Somerville Coll., Oxford (MA, BSc); MP Finchley (1959–74); Barnet, Finchley (1974 to date). Physical height: 1·65 m (5 ft 5 in).

Authorized post-nominal letters in their correct order

There are 72 Orders, Decorations, and Medals which have been bestowed by the Sovereign that carry the entitlement to a group of letters after the name. Of these, 54 are currently awardable. The order (vide London Gazette, supplement 27 Oct 1964) is as follows:

1	VC	Victoria Cross.
2	GC	George Cross.
3	KG	(but *not* for Ladies of the Order), Knight of the Most Noble Order of the Garter.
4	KT	(but *not* for Ladies of the Order), Knight of the Most Ancient and Most Noble Order of the Thistle.
5	GCB	Knight Grand Cross of the Most Honourable Order of the Bath.
6	OM	Member of the Order of Merit.
7*	GCSI	Knight Grand Commander of the Most Excellent Order of the Star of India.
8	GCMG	Knight (or Dame) Grand Cross of the Most Distinguished Order of St Michael and St George.
9*	GCIE	Knight Grand Commander of the Most Eminent Order of the Indian Empire.
10*	CI	Lady of The Imperial Order of the Crown of India.
11	GCVO	Knight (or Dame) Grand Cross of the Royal Victorian Order.
12	GBE	Knight (or Dame) Grand Cross of the Most Excellent Order of the British Empire.
13	CH	Member of the Order of Companions of Honour.
14	KCB	(but *not* if also a GCB) Knight Commander of the Most Honourable Order of the Bath.
15	DCB	(but *not* if also a GCB) Dame Commander of the Most Honourable Order of the Bath.
16*	KCSI	(but *not* if also a GCSI), Knight Commander of the Most Excellent Order of the Star of India.
17	KCMG	(but *not* if also a GCMG), Knight Commander of the Most Distinguished Order of St Michael and St George.
18	DCMG	(but *not* if also a GCMG) Dame Commander of the Most Distinguished Order of St Michael and St George.
19*	KCIE	(but *not* if also a GCIE), Knight Commander of the Most Eminent Order of the Indian Empire.

20	KCVO	(but *not* if also a GCVO), Knight Commander of the Royal Victorian Order.				decorations), Conspicuous Gallantry Medal.
21	DCVO	(but *not* if also a GCVO), Dame Commander of the Royal Victorian Order.	47	GM	George Medal.	
			48*	KPM		
			49*	KPFSM	King's or Queen's Police Medal	
			50	QPM	or Police & Fire Services Medal for	
22	KBE	(but *not* if also a GBE), Knight Commander of the Most Excellent Order of the British Empire.	51	QFSM	Gallantry.	
			*	DCM	(if for Royal West African Frontier Force), Distinguished Conduct Medal.	
23	DBE	(but *not* if also a GBE), Dame Commander of the Most Excellent Order of the British Empire.				
			*	DCM	(if for the King's African Rifles), Distinguished Conduct Medal.	
24	CB	(but *not* if also a GCB and/or a KCB), Companion of the Most Honourable Order of the Bath.	52*	IDSM	Indian Distinguished Service Medal.	
			53*	BGM	Burma Gallantry Medal.	
25*	CSI	(but *not* if also a GCSI and/or a KCSI), Companion of the Most Excellent Order of the Star of India.	54	DSM	Distinguished Service Medal.	
			55	MM	Military Medal.	
			56	DFM	Distinguished Flying Medal.	
			57	AFM	Air Force Medal.	
26	CMG	(but *not* if also a GCMG and/or a KCMG or DCMG), Companion of the Most Distinguished Order of St Michael and St George.	58	SGM	Medal for Saving Life at Sea (Sea Gallantry Medal).	
			*	IOM	(if in Civil Division), Indian Order of Merit.	
27*	CIE	(but *not* if also a GCIE and/or a KCIE), Companion of the Most Eminent Order of the Indian Empire.	59*	EGM	Empire Gallantry Medal (usable only in reference to pre-1940 honorary awards unexchangeable for the GC).	
28	CVO	(but *not* if also a GCVO and/or a KCVO or DCVO), Commander of the Royal Victorian Order.	60	CPM	Colonial Police Medal for Gallantry.	
			61	QGM	Queen's Gallantry Medal.	
29	CBE	(but *not* if also a GBE and/or a KBE or DBE), Commander of the Most Excellent Order of the British Empire.	62	QSM	Queen's Service Medal (NZ only).	
			63	BEM	British Empire Medal, for Gallantry, or the British Empire Medal.	
30	DSO	Companion of the Distinguished Service Order.	64*	CM	(or for French speakers M du C, Medaille du Canada), Canada Medal.	
31	MVO	(but *not* if also either a GCVO and/or a KCVO a DCVO, and/or a CVO), Lieutenant of the Royal Victorian Order.				
			*	KPM		
			*	KPFSM	See 48–51 above, but for distinguished or good service.	
32	OBE	(but *not* if also either a GBE and/or a KBE or DBE and/or a CBE), Officer of the Most Excellent Order of the British Empire.		QPM		
				QFSM		
			65*	MSM	(but only if awarded for Naval service prior to 20 July 1928), Medal for Meritorious Service.	
33	QSO	Queen's Service Order (NZ only).				
34	ISO	Companion of the Imperial Service Order.	66	ERD	Emergency Reserve Decoration (Army).	
	MVO	(but *not* if also either a GCVO and/or a KCVO or a DCVO, and/or a CVO and/or an LVO), Member of the Royal Victorian Order.	67*	VD	Volunteer Officers' Decoration (1892–1908); for India and the Colonies (1894–1930) and the Colonial Auxiliary Forces Officers' Decoration (1899–1930).	
35	MBE	(but *not* if also a GBE and/or a KBE or DBE and/or a CBE and/or an OBE), Member of the Most Excellent Order of the British Empire.	68	TD	(for either the obsolescent Territorial Decoration (1908–30) or for the current Efficiency Decoration (inst. 1930) when awarded to an officer of the (*Home*) Auxiliary Military Forces and the TAVR (inst. 1969)).	
36*	IOM	(if in Military Division), Indian Order of Merit.				
37*	OB	Order of Burma (when for gallantry).	69	ED	(if for the current Efficiency Decoration (inst. 1930) when awarded to an officer of *Commonwealth* or Colonial Auxiliary Military Forces).	
38	RRC	Member of the Royal Red Cross.				
39	DSC	Distinguished Service Cross.				
40	MC	Military Cross.				
41	DFC	Distinguished Flying Cross.	70	RD	Decoration for Officers of the Royal Naval Reserve.	
42	AFC	Air Force Cross.				
43	ARRC	(but *not* if also an RRC), Associate of the Royal Red Cross.	71*	VRD	Decoration for Officers of the Royal Naval Volunteer Reserve.	
44*	OBI	Order of British India.	72	CD	Canadian Forces Decoration.	
*	OB	Order of Burma (when for distinguished service).				
45	DCM	Distinguished Conduct Medal.				
46	CGM	(both the Naval and the Flying				

* This distinction is no longer awarded, but there are surviving recipients.

Any of the above post-nominal letters precede any others which may relate to academic honours or professional qualifications. The unique exception is that the abbreviation 'Bt.' (or less favoured 'Bart.'), indicating a Baronetcy, should be put before *all* other letters, e.g. The Rt Hon. Sir John Smyth, Bt., VC, MC.

The abbreviation PC (indicating membership of the Privy Council), which used to be placed after KG, is now not to be used, except possibly with peers, because in their case the style 'Rt Hon.' cannot be used to indicate membership of the Privy council, since Barons, Viscounts and Earls already enjoy this style *ipso facto* and Marquesses and Dukes have the superior styles 'Most Hon.' and 'Most Noble' respectively.

Obsolete post-nominal letters include: KP Knight of St Patrick; KB Knight of the Bath (prior to its division into 3 classes in 1815); GCH, KCH and KH Knight Grand Cross, Knight Commander or Knight of the Order of the Guelphs (1815–37); KSI Knight of the Star of India (1861–6); CSC Conspicuous Service Cross (1901–14); AM Albert Medal; EM Edward Medal; VD Volunteer Decoration.

National employment and unemployment

	Working Population (Thousands)	Unemployment Excluding School Leavers and Students	Percentage Rate
1965	25 504	338 200	1·4%
1970	25 293	602 000	2·6%
1971	25 124	775 800	3·4%
1972	25 234	855 000	3·7%
1973	25 578	611 000	2·6%
1974	25 515	600 100	2·6%
1975	25 665	929 000	3·6%
1976	25 886	1 273 500	4·9%
1977	26 310	1 378 200	5·2%
1978	26 433	1 375 700	5·2%
1979	26 443	1 307 300	4·9%
1980	26 324	1 667 600	6·3%
1981	26 079	2 464 300	9·4%
1982	23 373	2 687 900	11·5%
1983	24 013	3 025 700	12·6%
1984	24 108	3 013 600	12·5%
1985	24 204	3 146 600	13·0%
1986	24 221	3 055 000	12·6%

Distribution of work-force of the UK as at June 1986

Agriculture, forestry and fishing	603 000
Mining and quarrying	243 000
Manufacturing	5 455 000
Electricity, gas and water	293 000
Construction	1 487 000
Trade, restaurants and hotels	4 988 000
Transport, storage and communications	1 454 000
Financing, insurance, real estate and business services	2 456 000
Community, social and personal services	7 243 000
Total	˙24 221 000

The United Kingdom's National Debt

The National Debt is the nominal amount of outstanding debt chargeable on the Consolidated Fund of the United Kingdom Exchequer only, i.e. the debt created by the separate Northern Ireland Exchequer is excluded.

The National Debt became a permanent feature of the country's economy as early as 1692. The table below shows how the net total Debt has increased over the years (data being for 31 March of year shown):

Year	National Debt (£ million)	Year	National Debt (£ million)
1697	14	1945	21 365·9
1727	52	1946	23 636·5
1756	75	1947	25 630·6
1763	133	1948	25 620·8
1775	127	1949	25 167·6
1781	187	1950	25 802·3
1784	243	1951	25 921·6
1793	245	1952	25 890·5
1802	523	1953	26 051·2
1815	834	1954	26 538
1828	800	1955	26 933
1836	832	1956	27 038
1840	827	1957	27 007
1854	802	1958	27 232
1855	789	1959	27 376
1857	837	1960	27 732
1860	799	1961	28 251
1899	635	1962	28 674
1900	628·9	1963	29 847
1903	770·8	1964	30 226
1909	702·7	1965	30 440
1910	713·2	1966	31 340
1914	649·8	1967	31 985
1915	1 105·0	1968	34 193
1916	2 133·1	1969	33 984
1917	4 011·4	1970	33 079
1918	5 871·9	1971	33 441
1919	7 434·9	1972	35 839
1920[1]	7 828·8	1973	36 884
1921	7 574·4	1974	40 124
1923	7 742·2	1975	45 886
1931	7 413·3	1976	56 577
1934	7 822·3	1977	54 041
1935[2]	6 763·9	1978	79 000
1936	6 759·3	1979	82 597
1937	6 764·7	1980	91 245
1938	6 993·7	1981	112 780
1939	7 130·8	1982	117 959
1940	7 899·2	1983	127 072
1941	10 366·4	1984	142 545
1942	13 041·1	1985	158 101
1943	15 822·6	1986	162 191
1944	18 562·2	1987	186 000

[1] Beginning 1920, total excludes bonds tendered for death duties and held by the National Debt Commissioner.
[2] Beginning 1935, total excludes external debt, then £1036·5 million, arising out of the 1914–18 war.

Balance of payments £s million

	Visible Exports	Visible Imports	Visible Balance	Invisible Balance	Current Balance (−deficit +surplus)
1965	4 848	5 071	−223	+198	−27
1970	8 121	8 163	−42	+818	+776
1971	9 060	8 799	+261	+889	+1150
1972	9 450	10 172	−722	+930	+208
1973	12 115	14 498	−2383	+1508	−875
1974	16 538	21 773	−5235	+1928	−3307
1975	19 463	22 699	−3236	+1615	−1621
1976	25 441	29 012	−3601	+2759	−842
1977	32 148	33 892	−1744	+2037	+293
1978	35 432	36 607	−1175	+2207	+1032
1979	40 678	44 136	−3458	+2595	−863
1980	47 389	46 211	+1178	+2028	+3206
1981	50 977	47 325	+3652	+3620	+7272
1982	55 565	53 181	+2384	+3167	+5551
1983	60 658	61 158	−500	+2549	+2049
1984	70 367	74 751	−4384	+5858	+1474
1985	78 111	80 289	−2178	+5097	+2919
1986	72 843	81 306	−8463	+7483	−980

Sterling – US dollar exchange rates

$4·50–$5·00	Post War of Independence	1776
$12·00	All-time Peak (Civil War)	1864
$4·86 21/32	Fixed parity	1880–1914
$4·76 7/16	Pegged rate World War I	December 1916
$3·40	Low point after £ floated, 19 May 1919	February 1920
$4·86 21/32	Britain's return to Gold Standard	28 Apr 1925
$3·14½	Low point after Britain forced off Gold Standard (20 Sept 1931 [$3·43])	November 1932
$5·20	High point during floating period	March 1934
$4·03	Fixed rate World War II	4 Sept 1939
$2·80	First post-war devaluation	18 Sept 1949
$2·40	Second post-war devaluation	20 Nov 1967
$2·42	Convertibility of US dollar into gold was suspended on	15 Aug 1971
$2·58	£ refloated	22 June 1972
$1·99	£ broke $2 barrier	5 Mar 1976
$1·56	£ at new all-time low	28 Oct 1976
$1·76	Bank of England buying pounds	10 Oct 1977
$2·00	£ breaks back to $2 level (1978 av. $1·91)	15 Aug 1978
$2·26	Dollar weakens	June 1979
$2·19	Iranian crisis unresolved	8 Dec 1979
$1·99	£ again falls below $2	3 June 1981
$1·90	One year of 'Reaganomics'	20 Jan 1982
$1·04	Strength of dollar against all currencies	6 Mar 1985
$1·21	Recovery after Ohio Bank anxiety	11 Apr 1985
$1·47	1986 Budget	March 1986
$1·55	Pound strengthens	June 1986
$1·40	Dollar strong against other currencies – 'Big Bang'	October 1986
$1·60	Pound strong against other currencies	March 1987
$1·75	Beginning of Bush Presidency	February 1989

Imports

Principal Imports into the UK (1986) | *£ millions c.i.f.* *

Petroleum, petroleum products and related materials	4393·5
Road vehicles (including air cushion vehicles)	7939·7
Office machines and automatic data processing equipment	4545·1
Miscellaneous manufactured articles	11 391·0
Textile yarn, fabrics, made-up articles and related products	3162·6
Paper, paperboard and articles of paper pulp, of paper or of paperboard	2703·0
Non-metallic mineral manufactures	2661·7
General industrial machinery and equipment and machine parts	2755·4
Machinery specialized for particular industries	2362·2
Vegetables and fruit	2184·4
Organic chemicals	1830·9
Telecommunications and sound recording and reproducing apparatus and equipment	2402·3
Power generating machinery and equipment	1985·8
Iron and steel	1796·3
Other transport equipment	1434·4
Metalliferous ores and metal scrap	1139·8
Meat and meat preparations	1465·5

* Cost, insurance and freight.

Exports

Principal Exports from the UK
(1986)   *f.o.b.**

Petroleum, petroleum products and related materials	8221·2
Road vehicles (including air cushion vehicles)	3954·4
Office machines and automatic data processing equipment	3561·7
Miscellaneous manufactured articles	8575·5
Other transport equipment	3080·9
Power generating machinery and equipment	3248·6
Machinery specialized for particular industries	3101·5
General industrial machinery and equipment and machine parts	3035·2
Organic chemicals	2585·3
Non-metallic mineral manufactures	2549·2
Non-ferrous metals	1551·5
Iron and steel	1866·7
Textile yarn, fabrics, made-up articles and related products	1711·5
Manufactures of metal	1465·0
Medicinal and pharmaceutical products	1532·8
Artificial resins and plastic materials and cellulose esters and ethers	1401·4
Beverages	1331·7
Telecommunications and sound recording and reproducing apparatus and equipment	1402·3

* Free on board.

20 top nations – Imports into UK (1986)

	£ million	% of total UK imports
West Germany	14 139·1	16·4
USA	8468·2	9·8
France	7348·6	8·5
Netherlands	6615·9	7·7
Japan	4932·5	5·7
Italy	4658·0	5·4
Belgium & Luxembourg	4083·9	4·8
Norway	3265·2	3·8
Irish Republic	3053·8	3·5
Switzerland	2989·1	3·5
Sweden	2756·5	3·2
Spain	1777·3	2·1
Denmark	1752·2	2·0
Hong Kong	1530·8	1·8
Canada	1499·6	1·7
Finland	1346·1	1·6
South Africa	829·3	1·0
Portugal	768·5	0·9
Taiwan	705·8	0·8
Austria	705·7	0·8

20 top nations– Exports from UK (1986)

	£ million	% of total UK exports
USA	10 379·6	14·2
West Germany	8542·2	11·7
France	6210·2	8·5
Netherlands	5442·5	7·5
Belgium and Luxembourg	3832·6	5·3
Irish Republic	3558·4	4·9
Italy	3472·4	4·8
Sweden	2307·9	3·2
Spain	1905·5	2·6
Canada	1698·4	2·3
Switzerland	1575·2	2·2
Saudi Arabia	1507·1	2·1
Australia	1227·6	1·7
Denmark	1211·6	1·7
Japan	1193·9	1·6
Norway	1147·8	1·6
Hong Kong	961·0	1·3
India	941·2	1·3
South Africa	849·6	1·2
Finland	664·0	0·9

Gross national product

The economic power of a nation is reflected in its Gross National Product (GNP) and its National Income.

Gross National Product is derived from Gross Domestic Product at factor cost plus net property income from overseas. National Income is GNP less capital consumption.

Gross Domestic Product at factor cost can be determined in two ways, (A) by the expenditure generating it, or (B) the incomes, rent and profits which enable the expenditure. The components in any year are thus:

A	B
Consumers' expenditure	Income from employment
Public authority current spending	Income from self-employment
Gross fixed capital formation	Gross trading profits of companies
Value of work in progress	Gross profits and surpluses of public corporations
Value of physical increase in stocks	Rent *less* stock appreciation
Exports *less* imports	
Income from abroad *less* payments abroad	
Subsidies *less* taxes on expenditure	
= Gross Domestic Product	= Gross Domestic Product

Public expenditure
£s million

	1984	1985	1986
General public services	6 219	7 678	6 762
Defence	17 234	18 283	18 628
Public order and safety	5 913	6 191	6 692
Education	17 061	17 420	19 521
Health	16 756	17 878	19 446
Social security	42 406	46 389	50 195
Housing and community amenities	7 850	6 903	8 033
Recreational and cultural	2 098	2 189	2 247
Agriculture, forestry and fishing	2 194	2 725	2 397
Transport and communication	3 287	3 986	3 681
Total public expenditure	146 854	157 574	162 191

Cost of living

(General Index of Retail Prices, annual averages. Base: January 1987 = 100)

	1985	1986	1987
Food	94·9	98·1	101·1
Catering	90·9	96·6	102·8
Alcoholic drink	93·5	97·7	101·7
Tobacco	88·3	97·0	100·1
Housing	90·0	95·2	103·3
Fuel and light	98·7	100·0	99·1
Household goods	97·2	99·8	102·1
Household services	93·1	97·6	101·9
Clothing and footwear	96·6	99·3	101·1
Personal goods and services	92·7	97·5	101·9
Motoring expenditure	99·1	97·7	103·4
Fares and other travel costs	90·8	96·8	101·5
Leisure goods	98·3	100·1	101·6
Leisure services	94·4	98·9	101·6
All items	**94·6**	**97·8**	**101·9**

The judicial system

The supreme judicial court for the United Kingdom is the House of Lords as an ultimate court of appeal from all courts, except the Scottish criminal courts. Leave to appeal to it is not as of right and is usually reserved for important points of law. The work is executed by the Lord High Chancellor and nine Lords of Appeal in Ordinary. Only one case in 40 000 ever reaches them.

The Supreme Court of Judicature consists of the Court of Appeal under the Master of the Rolls and 27 Lord Justices of Appeal and The High Court of Justice with (a) the Chancery Division with 13 judges, (b) the Queen's Bench Division under the Lord Chief Justice of England and 51 judges, (c) the Court of Appeal (Criminal Division) with all the foregoing judges excepting the Chancery Division judges, (d) the Family Division with a President and currently 13 male and 2 female judges.

On 1 Jan 1972 the Crown Court replaced Assizes and Quarter Sessions. Under the Courts Service, First tier centres deal with both civil and criminal cases and Second tier centres with only criminal cases. Both are served by High Court (see above) and Circuit Judges. Third tier centres deal with criminal cases only but are served by Circuit Judges only. There are six circuits in England and Wales, viz.

Northern Circuit
North Eastern Circuit
Midland and Oxford
Wales and Chester
South Eastern Circuit
Western Circuit
and 300 county courts.

There are in addition over 430 Recorders.

Major urban areas have courts presided over by whole-time salaried magistrates known as Stipendiaries thus –
London
Bow Street (Chief Metropolitan Stipendiary and 4 Stipendiaries); Camberwell Green (4); Clerkenwell (3); Greenwich and Woolwich (3); Highbury Cor-

Income and expenditure *(£ million at current prices)*

	1984	1985	1986
INCOME			
Income from employment	180 053	194 434	209 445
Income from self-employment	27 716	30 481	34 340
Gross trading profits and surpluses	54 935	60 769	59 072
Gross domestic product at factor cost	**275 137**	**302 434**	**319 089**
Taxes on expenditure	52 538	56 735	62 273
Gross domestic product at market prices			
[GDP + Taxes on expenditure *less* subsidies]	**320 120**	**351 869**	**374 895**
Net property income from abroad	4 216	2 992	4 686
GROSS NATIONAL PRODUCT AT MARKET PRICES	*324 336*	*354 861*	*379 581*
EXPENDITURE			
Private consumers' expenditure	195 912	213 720	234 167
Government consumption expenditure	69 887	74 041	79 423
Gross domestic fixed capital formation [plus physical increase in stocks]	55 108	60 477	64 227
TOTAL DOMESTIC EXPENDITURE	*321 023*	*348 666*	*378 368*

Basic educational statistics

ENGLAND AND WALES

	1984	1985	1986
Number of schools	31 171	30 748	30 368
Teachers			
Maintained primary schools	177 288	175 828	176 602
Maintained secondary schools	238 943	232 575	226 245
Other schools	64 009	64 714	65 441
Total	*480 240*	*473 117*	*468 288*
Pupils			
(full time)			
Maintained nursery schools	13 754	13 356	13 105
Maintained primary schools	3 814 964	3 784 010	3 789 652
Maintained secondary schools	3 877 098	3 752 217	3 606 895
Special schools	123 005	112 046	116 112
Independent schools	512 252	512 435	513 719
Total	*8 341 073*	*8 174 064*	*8 039 483*
Further and higher education establishments (excluding universities)	546	543	537
Full time and sandwich students in further and higher education (excluding universities)	605 724	606 557	614 650

SCOTLAND

	1984	1985	1986
Schools			
Nursery	552	559	560
Primary	2481	2462	2426
Secondary	464	459	441
Special	330	328	339
Total	*3827*	*3808*	*3766*
Teachers	53 532	52 741	n/a
Pupils			
Nursery	36 883	38 120	n/a
Primary	454 156	443 604	435 916
Secondary	401 423	387 195	361 210
Special	10 316	10 053	9 892
Total	*902 778*	*878 972*	*n/a*
Further and higher education establishments (excluding universities)	78	66	66
Full time and sandwich students in further and higher education (excluding universities)	79 450	81 548	83 455

UNIVERSITIES (Great Britain)
(excluding Open University but including Cranfield Institute of Technology)

	1984	1985	1986
Full time teaching staff	42 058	42 500	43 967
Students			
Full-time/sandwich	291 722	290 611	295 481
Part-time	34 626	35 986	37 097

ner (4); Horseferry Road (3); Marlborough Street (2); Marylebone (4); Old Street (2); South Western (3); Thames (2); Tower Bridge (3); Wells Street (4); West London (2).

Other Stipendiaries operate in Kingston-upon-Hull, Leeds, Greater Manchester, Merseyside, Merthyr Tydfil, Mid Glamorgan, South Glamorgan, South Yorkshire and West Midlands.

In Scotland the Court of Session (established 1532) has an Inner House of 8 Judges (in which the Lord President presides over the First Division and the Lord Justice Clerk over the Second Division) and an Outer House of 12 Judges. The country is divided into 6 Sheriffdoms, each with a Sheriff Principal, Sheriffs and Procurators Fiscal: these are Grampian, Highland and Islands; Tayside, Central and Fife; Lothian and Borders; Glasgow and Strathkelvin; North Strathclyde; and South Strathclyde and Dumfries and Galloway.

Criminal statistics

ENGLAND AND WALES
Offences recorded by the Police – 1986

Offences	Number of Offences 1986
Violence against the person	125 500
Sexual offences	22 700
Burglary	931 600
Robbery	30 000
Theft and handling stolen goods	2 003 900
Fraud and forgery	133 400
Criminal damage	583 600
Other offences	16 700

SCOTLAND
Crimes and Offences recorded by the Police – 1986

TOTAL CRIMES	463 900
Non-sexual crimes of violence	15 700
Crimes of indecency	5 400
Crimes of dishonesty	342 500
Fire-raising, vandalism etc.	78 900
Other crimes	21 400
TOTAL OFFENCES	358 500
Miscellaneous offences	120 400
Motor vehicle offences	238 100

The 46 United Kingdom universities

There are 46 institutions of university or degree-giving status in the UK.

The list below is given in order of seniority of date of foundation, and the data run as follows: name, year of foundation, location, and population full-time as at 1989.

1. **The University of Oxford** 1249*
Oxford OX1 2JD
12 350
Colleges, Halls and Societies: University (1249), Balliol (1263), Merton (1264), Exeter (1314), Oriel (1326), Queen's (1340), New College (1379), Lincoln

(1427), All Souls (1438), Magdalen (1458), Brasenose (1509), Corpus Christi (1517), Christ Church (1546), Trinity (1554), St John's (1555), Jesus (1571), Wadham (1612), Pembroke (1624), Worcester (1714), Hertford (1874), St Edmund Hall (1270), Keble (1868), St Catherine's (1962), Campion Hall (1962), St Benet's Hall (1947), St Peter's (1929), St Antony's (1950), Nuffield (1937), Linacre House (1962), Mansfield (1886), Regent's Park (1810), Greyfriars Hall (1910), St Cross (1965). Lady Margaret Hall (1878), Somerville (1879), St Hugh's (1886), St Hilda's (1893), St Anne's (1952) [originally 1893].

2. **The University of Cambridge** 1284*
Cambridge
12 770
Peterhouse (1284), Clare (1326), Pembroke (1347), Gonville and Caius (1348), Trinity Hall (1350), Corpus Christi (1352), King's (1441), Queen's (1448), St Catherine's (1473), Jesus (1496), Christ's (1505), St John's (1511), Magdalene (1542), Trinity (1546), Emmanuel (1584), Sidney Sussex (1596), Downing (1800), Selwyn (1882), Churchill (1960), Fitzwilliam House (1896), Girton (1869), Newnham (1871), Hughes Hall (1885), Homerton (1894), St Edmund's (1896), New Hall (1954), Wolfson (1965), Lucy Cavendish (1965), Robinson (1977).

3. **The University of St Andrews** 1411
St Andrews KY16 9AJ
3680
Colleges: United College of St Salvator and St Leonard; College of St Mary.

4. **The University of Glasgow** 1451
Gilmorehill, Glasgow G12 8QQ
12 480

5. **The University of Aberdeen** 1495
Aberdeen AB9 1FX
5800

6. **The University of Edinburgh** 1583
Old College, South Bridge, Edinburgh EH8 9YL
9920

7. **The University of Durham** 1832
Old Shire Hall, Durham DH1 3HP
4704
Colleges: University, Hatfield, Grey, St Chad's, St John's, St Mary's, St Aidan's, Bede, St Hild's, Neville's Cross, St Cuthbert's Society, Van Mildert, Trevelyan, Collingwood, Ushaw, Graduate Society.

8. **The University of London** 1836
Greater London
40 600
Colleges and schools: Bedford College, Birkbeck College, Goldsmiths' College, Imperial College of Science and Technology, King's College, London School of Economics, Queen Mary College, Royal Holloway and Bedford New College, Royal Veterinary College, School of Oriental and African Studies, School of Pharmacy, School of Slavonic and East European Studies, University College, Westfield College, Wye College.
Medical Schools: Charing Cross and Westminster Medical School, King's Cross Hospital Medical and Dental Schools, London Hospital Medical College, Royal Free Hospital School of Medicine, St Bartholomew's Hospital Medical College, St

George's Hospital Medical School, St Mary's Hospital Medical School, United Medical Schools of Guy's and St Thomas's Hospitals, University College and Middlesex School of Medicine.

Institutes: Courtauld Institute of Art, Institute of Advanced Legal Studies, Institute of Archaeology, Institute of Classical Studies, Institute of Commonwealth Studies, Inter-collegiate Computer Science, Institute of Education, Institute of Germanic Studies, Institute of Historical Research, Institute of Latin American Studies, Institute of United States Studies, Warburg Institute, British Institute, Paris.

9. The University of Manchester[1] 1851
Oxford Road, Manchester M13 9PL
18 000

10. The University of Newcastle upon Tyne 1852
Newcastle upon Tyne NE1 7RU
7440

11. The University of Wales 1893
see colleges
18 700
Colleges: Abersystwyth, Bangor, Cardiff, Swansea, National School of Medicine (Cardiff), St David's College, Lampeter.

12. The University of Birmingham 1900
P.O. Box 363, Birmingham B15 2TT
8700

13. The University of Liverpool 1903
P.O. Box 147, Liverpool L69 3BX
7440

14. The University of Leeds 1904
Leeds LS2 9JT
10 410

15. The University of Sheffield 1905
Sheffield S10 2TN
7590

16. The Queen's University of Belfast 1908
Belfast BT7 1NN
6645

17. The University of Bristol 1909
Bristol BS8 1TH
7000

18. The University of Reading 1926
London Road, Reading RG6 2AH
5620

19. The University of Nottingham 1948
University Park, Nottingham NG7 2RD
6500

20. The University of Southampton 1952
Southampton SO9 5NH
6400

21. The University of Hull 1954
Kingston upon Hull HU6 7RX
4990

22. The University of Exeter 1955
Exeter EX4 4QJ
4770

23. The University of Leicester 1957
Leicester LE1 7RH
5270

24. The University of Sussex 1961
Brighton BN1 9RH
5400

25. The University of Keele 1962
Keele, Staffordshire ST5 5BG
2630

26. The University of Strathclyde† 1964
George Street, Glasgow G1 1XQ
6840

27. The University of East Anglia 1963
Norwich NR4 7TJ
4210

28. The University of York 1963
Heslington, York YO1 5DD
3420

29. The University of Lancaster 1964
Bailrigg, Lancaster LA1 4YW
4500

30. The University of Essex 1964
Wivenhoe Park, Colchester CO4 3SQ
3100

31. The University of Warwick 1965
Coventry CV4 7AL
5440

32. The University of Kent 1965
Canterbury CT2 7NZ
4070

33. New University of Ulster 1965
Coleraine, Co. Londonderry BT52 1SA, Northern Ireland
7600

34. Heriot-Watt University 1966
Riccarton, Edinburgh EH14 4AS
3310

35. Loughborough University of Technology 1966
Loughborough, Leicestershire LE11 3TU
6100

36. The University of Aston in Birmingham 1966
Gosta Green, Birmingham B4 7ET
4450

37. The City University 1966
London, EC1V 0NB
3970

38. Brunel University 1966
Uxbridge UB8 3PH
3250

39. University of Bath 1966
Claverton Down, Bath BA2 7AY
3600

40. University of Bradford 1966
Bradford BD7 1DP
4780

41. **University of Surrey** 1966
Guildford GU2 5XH
3750

42. **University of Salford** 1967
Salford M5 4WT
4030

43. **University of Dundee** 1967
Dundee DD1 4HN
3530

44. **University of Stirling** 1967
Stirling FK9 4LA
2650

45. **The Open University‡** 1969
Walton Hall, Milton Keynes MK7 6AA
77 000

46. **University of Buckingham §** 1976
Buckingham MK18 1EG
600

Cranfield Institute of Technology 1969
Bedford MK45 4DT
700
Includes: Silsoe College and Royal Military College
of Science at Shrivenham.

The 30 polytechnics of England and Wales

City of Birmingham Polytechnic 1971
Perry Barr, Birmingham B42 2SU

Brighton Polytechnic 1970
Moulsecoomb, Brighton BN2 4AT

Bristol Polytechnic 1969
Coldharbour Lane, Frenchay, Bristol BS16 1QY

Polytechnic of Central London 1970
309 Regent Street, London W1R 8AL

City of London Polytechnic 1970
Admissions Office, 31 Jewry Street, London
EC3N 2EY

Coventry Polytechnic 1970
Priory Street, Coventry CV11 5FB

East London Polytechnic 1970
(founded as North East London Polytechnic)
Romford Road, London E15 4LZ

Hatfield Polytechnic 1970
P.O. Box 109, Hatfield, Herts AL10 9AB

* Year of foundation of oldest constituent college.
† Formerly the Royal College of Science and Technology, founded 1796.
‡ Tuition mainly by correspondence.
§ Financed independently from the University Grants Committee and HM Treasury.
1 Includes Manchester Business School and Manchester Institute of Science and Technology.

Note: The Royal College of Art (1837) Kensington Gore, London (568 post graduates), grants degrees.

Huddersfield Polytechnic 1970
Queensgate, Huddersfield HD1 3DH

Kingston Polytechnic 1970
Penrhyn Road, Kingston upon Thames, Surrey
KT1 2EE

Lancashire Polytechnic 1972
Corporation Street, Preston PR1 2TQ

Leeds Polytechnic 1970
Calverley Street, Leeds LS1 3HE

Leicester Polytechnic 1969
P.O. Box 143, Leicester LE1 9BH

Liverpool Polytechnic 1970
Rodney House, 70 Mount Pleasant, Liverpool
L3 5UX

Manchester Polytechnic 1970
All Saints, Manchester M15 6BH

Middlesex Polytechnic 1973
114 Chase Side, London N14 5PN

Newcastle upon Tyne Polytechnic 1969
Ellison Building, Ellison Place, Newcastle upon
Tyne NE1 8ST

Nottingham Polytechnic 1971
(founded as Trent Polytechnic)
Burton Street, Nottingham NG1 4BU

Oxford Polytechnic 1970
Gypsy Lane, Headington, Oxford OX3 0BP

Polytechnic of North London 1971
Holloway Road, London N7 8DB

Polytechnic South West (founded as Plymouth
Polytechnic) 1970
Drake Circus, Plymouth PL4 8AA

Portsmouth Polytechnic 1969
Museum Road, Portsmouth PO1 2QQ

Sheffield City Polytechnic 1969
Pond Street, Sheffield S1 1WB

South Bank Polytechnic 1970
Borough Road, London SE1 0AA

Staffordshire Polytechnic 1970
College Road, Stoke on Trent, Staffordshire
ST4 2DE

Sunderland Polytechnic 1969
Langham Tower, Ryhope Road, Sunderland
SR2 7EE

Teesside Polytechnic 1970
Borough Road, Middlesbrough, Cleveland
TS1 3BA

Thames Polytechnic 1970
Wellington Street, Woolwich, London SE18 6PF

Wolverhampton Polytechnic 1969
The Polytechnic, Molineux Street, Wolverhampton
WV1 1SB

WALES
Polytechnic of Wales 1970
Llantwit Road, Treforest, Pontypridd, Mid-
Glamorgan CF37 1DL

INDEX

Persons listed but not discussed in the text are omitted from the index. Monarchs are indicated by *Q of E* etc. Prime ministers are separately indexed by surname and by title where relevant. Glossary entries are suffixed *g*; illustrations *i*; inventions *inv*.